W9-ADT-987

NAPOLEONIC MILITARY HISTORY

MILITARY HISTORY BIBLIOGRAPHIES
(General Editors: Robin Higham
                 Jacob Kipp)
Vol. 9

GARLAND REFERENCE LIBRARY
OF SOCIAL SCIENCE
Vol. 194

MILITARY HISTORY BIBLIOGRAPHIES

Advisory Editors:
Robin Higham
Jacob W. Kipp

NAPOLEONIC MILITARY HISTORY
A Bibliography

Edited by
Donald D. Horward

GARLAND PUBLISHING, INC. • NEW YORK & LONDON
1986

Library of Congress Cataloging-in-Publication Data

Horward, Donald D.
  Napoleonic military history.

  (Military history bibliographies ; vol. 9)
(Garland reference library of social science ; vol. 194)
    1. France—History, Military—1789–1815—Bibliography.
2. Napoleonic Wars, 1800–1814—Bibliography.
3. Napoleon I, Emperor of the French, 1769–1821—
Military leadership—Bibliography.   4. Europe—History,
Military—18th century—Bibliography.   5. Europe—
History, Military—19th century—Bibliography.
I. Title.   II. Series.   III. Series: Garland reference
library of social science ; v. 194.
Z2181.M5H67   1986   [DC151]   016.9402'7   83-48209
ISBN 0-8240-9058-6 (alk. paper)

Cover design by Renata Gomes

Printed on acid-free, 250-year-life paper
Manufactured in the United States of America

CONTENTS

v

THE GENERAL EDITORS' INTRODUCTION

Military history is a vast international field touching upon all aspects of society, yet guides to the immense literature it contains, essential for anyone writing in the field, have largely been conspicuous by their absence. Over fifteen years ago an international start was made by Robin Higham with *Official Histories* (1970), which for the first time enabled even official historians to check what other offices had produced. That work established a pattern of historical essays, some by the original authors, followed by a checklist of the works published. While this was in process, *A Guide to the Sources of British Military History* (1971) was commenced along slightly different lines. In this each author was asked to provide a bibliographic essay over a segment of the military, naval or air history of one country, with a numbered alphabetical list by authors of those cited following. A further feature of each chapter was a short concluding section suggesting what research remained to be undertaken as well as what could profitably be reviewed. So successful was this volume, published simultaneously in the United States and in Britain, that not only did it become a standard library reference work, but also the editor was asked to undertake a similar compilation for U.S. military history. This latter guide was completed in 1975 on a more far-seeing scheme in which quinquennial supplements were planned to keep the work up to date (the first of these was issued in 1981). It was on the basis of these three successful volumes that the editors were approached by Garland in May 1978 to undertake the present series.

By that time both editors were involved in the United States and in the International Commissions for Military History, Dr. Higham being on the Editorial Advisory Board and Dr. Kipp on the Bibliographical Committee. They agreed with Garland that they would undertake to produce an international series of some thirty-odd volumes to provide scholars access to the vast collections in all the countries of the world other than the United States and the United Kingdom. Those authors whose native language was not English should also produce a volume in their own tongue so that scholars of at least two major languages concerned with the military history of that country should benefit. No limits were set on length, though as with the two previous *Guides* it was not expected that these works would be either totally comprehensive or exhaustive, if for no other than the two very good reasons that in most cases there is a lot of repetitive material and that inevitably bibliographies are dated from the moment their sections are completed.

The very existence of the International Commission on Military History and the vigorous programs of the various national commissions that compose it confirm the vitality of the field of military history. Both editors believe that this bibliographic series can render a valuable service by facilitating the study of military history across national lines and in a comparative context. It is hoped that each volume will make explicit the general and particular historiographic approaches associated with an individual nation's military institutions. In such a manner researchers will be able to consult a single volume that will outline the historiographic developments for a particular nation's military experience or, in the case of major powers, of that of one of its principal armed services. Such a guide it is hoped will serve as a compass for further research, both enumerating what has been done and suggesting what still needs to be done.

Essentially the authors have been asked to provide readable essays that will guide the readers through the labyrinth of the most important sources as though walking through a library and archives, mentioning authors and titles, but leaving the details to be acquired by taking the works from the shelves, in this case the numbered lists at the back of each chapter. Both authors and Editors would be happy to have comments and suggestions from readers and users.

Robin Higham
Jacob Kipp
Department of History
Kansas State University
Manhattan, KS 66506, USA

PREFACE

When initially contacted by Professor Robin Higham about a military bibliography on Napoleon, I accepted his proposal confidently, without recognizing the enormity of the project. In 1973 I had spent a year compiling a 482-page bibliography of the French Revolution and Napoleon Collection at Florida State University so I assumed the task would be quite manageable. However, as I began to delve into the various aspects of Napoleon's military career and his impact upon Europe, it became obvious that such a task would be impossible for any one scholar. With perhaps 220,000 titles related to the Napoleonic period how could a one-volume bibliography do justice to the topic? A careful examination of the more useful bibliographies devoted to Napoleon made this quite evident. Very few bibliographies made any pretense at being comprehensive and usually they were woefully incomplete in the peripheral areas. There were guides to specific collections as well as a number of excellent national and topical bibliographies but they could not meet the needs of scholars for whom this volume is intended. It became increasingly clear why no one had attempted such a work during the past three-quarters of a century—no living scholar could have accumulated such a mass of knowledge in one lifetime.

Indeed, writing the chapter on the Peninsular War in my field of specialization was reassuring but the feeling of confidence was lost when working in other areas far removed from Iberia. It soon became obvious that if this bibliography was to be more than the general bibliography of Napoleonic materials, other specialists would have to be brought into the project to broaden the scope of the volume. Fortunately, as one of the directors of the Consortium on Revolutionary Europe for the past sixteen years, I have had an opportunity to become acquainted with the work of many prominent Napoleonic scholars in both the United States and Europe.

Consequently, I resolved to seek their expertise in the various specialties of the Napoleonic period. This decision assured a scope hitherto unavailable in any bibliographical guide, but raised problems of coordination, uniformity, duplication, style, etc.

Although this volume is in a military series and emphasizes a military theme, this does not preclude the inclusion of social, political, economic, and intellectual materials that are closely interrelated to the main theme. For example, Chapter XI, concerned with the Home Front, is not specifically military in nature but it helps to explain the basis of Napoleon's ability to make war; similarly, Chapter XIII on Germany analyzes the intellectual and administrative background for the rejuvenation of Prussia and its effort to make war. Each chapter is organized to concentrate on a specific theme and is an entity in itself, but the reader should also consult the first three chapters for useful basic material. Moreover, most of Napoleon's own published works can be found in Chapters I and III.

The contributors to this bibliography were given free rein in completing their chapters. Nevertheless, a general organization format was adopted so there are few organizational variations among the twenty-four chapters. Following a basic introduction to the field, most chapter-essays are organized with sections devoted to general works, bibliographies, published sources, specialized studies, periodicals, and suggestions for future research. There are some duplicate citations, but this has occurred only when more than one contributor regarded a particular volume as vital to their chapters. It should also be noted that Chapter I includes a general list of periodicals useful for the study of the Napoleonic field, but many chapters include specialized periodicals pertinent to a particular field; for example, there are specific journals relative to the study of Iberia, Russia, Poland, Germany, and the Caribbean.

Venturing into the vast areas influenced by the march of Napoleon's armies has made it necessary to face serious typographic variations. With the employment of fourteen languages in citing over 7,131 titles, diacritical marks became a nagging problem. When this project was begun, it was decided to prepare the manuscript on the recently acquired departmental

IBM Displaywriter rather than the suggested IBM Selectric type-writer. There were a few print wheels with diacritical marks available in the major European languages for use with the Displaywriter; however, this was not true of such languages as Danish, Finnish, Hungarian, Norwegian, Polish, Russian, Serbo-Croatian, Swedish, and Turkish. Although all titles were set in capital letters, circumventing this problem, and most of the lower-case diacritical marks could be made, there were instances where there were no letter-equivalents and the machine could not produce a particular character. Indeed, the contributors supplied the correct markings but it was beyond the capabilities of our equipment to reproduce some of the necessary typography, especially in Magyar, Polish, Serbo-Croatian, and the Scandinavian languages.

As this volume was brought to completion over a period of almost three years, each of the chapters was revised and corrected numerous times. The contributors have had several opportunities to proof their contributions and I have made every effort to incorporate their revisions into the text. Moreover, there has been a continuing effort to maintain continuity between the various chapters; nevertheless, with a volume of this size, diversity, and complexity, a few orthographic and organizational inconsistencies have escaped detection or been located only after alterations were no longer feasible. It should also be noted that many of the chapters were completed in 1983 and therefore will not include titles published thereafter. In several cases we have been able to add an addendum but in other instances time or space became a factor in updating chapters. We hope this will not impair the value of the bibliography for the users.

In the execution of such a complex project, I have incurred a debt to many who gave so freely of their effort and time. Without the collaborations of my colleagues in the field, a bibliography of this scope could not exist. They labored long hours to complete their chapters and fulfill my many requests for clarifications and detailed information on publication data and translations promptly from as far away as Paris, Munich, and Copenhagen. I must also express my gratitude to James P. Jones, Chairman of the History Department at Florida State University, for his encouragement and support in providing departmental equipment to set and print this book. At the same time, I would like to thank the dedicated office staff of the department for their efforts and perseverance in this long project. Celeste Plaisance began to set the first chapters on the departmental IBM Displaywriter in 1982 but the "job queue" extended preparation time. Once completed, each chapter was sent to the author for proofing before being dispatched to the general editors of the series. Jan Gadel continued work on the project after 1984 and she was followed in succession by Polly Edmiston, Dianne Weinstein, and Wanda Mitchell. During the fall of 1984 while I held the Conquest Chair in Humanities at Virginia Military Institute, Dean John Knapp and History Department Chairman Henry Bausum secured the services of Norma Stotz to set several chapters on the History Department's Fortune computer. Finally, this summer, when the text and bibliographies were ready for final duplication and pagination, Jan Gadel and Wanda Mitchell completed this arduous task. During this process, it has been necessary to shift chapters from my IBM-PC and VMI's Fortune computer first to an IBM 5520 and then to the IBM Displaywriter, a truly mind-boggling task; this was accomplished by Bob Graves, Systems Coordinator of Office Information Systems, and Tom James, Director of Administrative Information Systems at the University, who succeeded in programing the four machines to "talk to each other"— no mean feat since the basic systems, DOS and UNIX, were incompatible. Finally, at FSU, I must acknowledge the aid of Barbara Swanson and Joe Pettigrew of the Strozier Library who provided valuable bibliographical information for Chapter I.

I am indebted to Robin Higham and Jake Kipp, general editors of Garland's Military History Bibliographies, for their helpful suggestions and critical reading of each chapter. Julia Johnson of Garland Publishing Inc. has been most supportive and encouraging in the completion of this study. Finally, I would like to acknowledge my wife, Annabel. With her sharp eye for detail, she picked out many inconsistencies among the chapters that eluded me. Over a period of almost two years, she spent many long evenings proofing and confirming entries and for the last four months we have worked together evenings and weekends on the departmental Displaywriter to complete final revisions. I hope the value of this bibliography to Napoleonic scholars will justify the long hours devoted to its publication by all those involved. May it serve to encourage further research in the period and unlock the gates to aspiring historians of the Napoleonic period.

Donald D. Horward
Tallahassee, Florida

CHAPTER I

INTRODUCTION TO NAPOLEONIC RESEARCH

Donald D. Horward, Florida State University

More has been written about Napoleon Bonaparte and his era than any other figure who ever lived. In 1908 the renowned historian and Napoleonic bibliophile, Friedrich Kircheisen, estimated that over 200,000 books and articles had been devoted to the period, and this number has increased markedly with the renewed interest in the First Empire during the twentieth century. Books have been authored in every European language, reflecting the universality of the topic. Perhaps this phenomenon can be explained by the chain of events that shook Europe to its foundation, by the extraordinary personalities who appeared to harness the forces of history, by the clash of arms and the struggle for freedom, or by the rise of romanticism and nationalism. Above all, it must be attributed to the rise of a figure whose legacy was to have a dramatic impact upon western civilization--Napoleon Bonaparte.

Although Napoleon's personality and policies dominated this period, it was also the age of Wellington, Alexander I, vom Stein, Metternich, Castlereagh, Canning, Czartoriski, La Harpe, and Talleyrand to mention a few. It also marked the appearance of a unique number of brilliant military leaders, such as Masséna, Davout, Wellington, Lannes, Nelson, Archduke Charles, Soult, Suvorov, Bagration, Schwarzenburg, Wrend, and Poniatowski. Extraordinary leadership and achievement were not limited to politics and the battlefield. Such literary figures as Schiller, Goethe, de Staël, Chateaubriand, Byron, Scott, and a pantheon of other great writers were accompanied on the stage of history by such musical giants as Beethoven, Haydn, Schubert, Cherubini, Weber, as well as an array of brilliant artists led by David, Delacroix, Goya, and Lawrence. Thus, it is obvious why scholars and writers during the past 150 years have been attracted to this age of ferment and change.

Fortunately, many of those who lived during the Napoleonic period recognized the unique qualities of their age. Consequently, they carefully recorded and preserved details of events influencing their lives, thereby forming the foundation for future research in the period. Even before the end of the Empire, eyewitness accounts began to appear in print about events and personalities of the epoch. After Waterloo this stream of books became a flood that was to continue throughout the nineteenth century. The Napoleonic Legend, radiating across Europe from St. Helena, served as a catalyst for hundreds of publications about Napoleon. Those sympathetic to his cause wrote in defense of the fallen Emperor and his activities, while those opposed to what he represented attacked the basis of his success. This controversy continued at an increasing pace until thousands of writers had joined in the intellectual battle, publishing their letters, memoirs, journals, etc., to substantiate or attack the claims of the legions that supported Napoleon. Meanwhile, millions of documents were collected, catalogued, and preserved in the various public and private archives and libraries throughout Europe.

1

As these massive collections, both published and manuscript, were made available, scholars and writers concentrated on the First Empire. The goals and policies of Napoleon, as well as the other rulers of the European states, were reexamined and reinterpreted in light of this new material. Campaigns and battles were reexamined and refought repeatedly by those interested in determining the strengths and weaknesses of Napoleon's military system. Consequently, original research was encouraged and, as time passed, incisive and definitive studies began to appear. These efforts continued without respite throughout the nineteenth century. During the first decades of this century, thousands of volumes were published as the various European nations sought to commemorate the centennial of Napoleonic-related events that affected their countries. A vast number of studies appeared in the years following World War I, and during the past thirty years new emphasis seems to have been placed on the Napoleonic period, both in the United States and in Europe. As more original works have become available and research continues, it is now evident that there is much remaining to be done in the field. In fact, the evidence seems to indicate that there are literally thousands of available research topics in the period ready for exploitation by enthusiastic scholars.

GENERAL HISTORIES

Since the end of the Napoleonic period writers have attempted to capture the panorama of the entire epoch, but few have succeeded in this endeavor due to the massive scope of the undertaking. One of the first studies of the period, PRECIS DES EVENEMENTS MILITAIRES (67) was undertaken by Mathieu Dumas, but after completing twenty volumes, he had reached only 1807. A monumental twenty-eight-volume work, under the general editorship of Charles Beauvais, VICTOIRES, CONQUETES, DESASTRES, REVERS ET GUERRES CIVILES DES FRANCAIS, DE 1792 A 1815 (10) was begun in 1817. Many of Napoleon's former officers contributed to this sympathetic account of the wars; they attempted to trace the interrelationship between the various campaigns as well as details of each operation. Jean Capefigue completed a ten-volume study entitled L'EUROPE PENDANT LE CONSULAT ET L'EMPIRE DE NAPOLEON (38) that is dated but has useful information. One of the first officials of Napoleon to write about the period was Bignon, who had been left 100,000 francs in Napoleon's last will and testament to complete a study of French diplomacy during the Empire. Despite his sympathy for the Napoleonic cause, his work was surprisingly balanced and often critical of the Emperor. Armand Lefebvre was also sympathetic in his HISTOIRE DES CABINETS DE L'EUROPE (141), but unquestionably, the most comprehensive and apologetic contribution to the study of the Empire in the nineteenth century was Louis Adolphe Thiers's HISTORY OF THE CONSULATE AND THE EMPIRE (249). Jaurès's HISTOIRE SOCIALISTE (128) presented useful insights into the period; the more recent multivolume works by Louis Madelin (154) and the studies of Jean Thiry, found in appropriate chapters, present favorable histories of the period. Histories of diplomacy include the works of Sorel (241), Driault (65), and Bignon (20). Hubert Camon's five volumes (36) on Napoleon's campaigns provide an excellent introduction to operations during the period. A number of old works, including Alison's ten-volume HISTORY OF EUROPE (3), F.C.

Schlosser's seven-volume study (232), von Schulz's twenty-three volumes (235), and the fifteen-volume work of the Swiss tactician, Jomini (122), still include valuable details of the campaigns.

Turning to single volumes, Volume 9 of the 1906 edition of the CAMBRIDGE MODERN HISTORY (35) is probably the most comprehensive work available on the subject in English. Other important one-volume studies include Lachouque's NAPOLEON'S BATTLES (136) and ANATOMY OF GLORY(134), Villat's LA REVOLUTION ET L'EMPIRE (1789-1815) (257), Lefebvre's NAPOLEON (142) in the series PEUPLE ET CIVILIZATION, Pariset's NAPOLEON in the HISTOIRE GENERALE of the Lavisse series (140), and Quennevat's ATLAS DE LA GRANDE ARMEE (222). The standard accounts of Yorck von Wartenburg (261), Fournier (75), Rose (227), and Esposito and Elting (71) are valuable, and of the more recent scholarship, David Chandler's study (43) on Napoleon's campaigns has no peer.

BIBLIOGRAPHICAL GUIDES

There are a number of general bibliographical guides to the most extensive libraries in the world. The catalogues of the U.S. Library of Congress (147) in Washington, D.C., the Bibliothèque Nationale (97, 98) in Paris, and the British Library [Museum] (111) in London list well in excess of thirty million titles. In addition, the National Union Catalogue, published by Mansell (209), includes titles and locations of over twenty million volumes from various American libraries, and this list was updated continually ·through 1982. National lists do exist for works published in other countries, usually on the basis of language, geographic areas, or topics, but unfortunately, these lists are usually noncumulative and published annually. A very useful noncumulative bibliography begun during the Empire, BIBLIOGRAPHIE DE LA FRANCE, OU JOURNAL DE L'IMPRIMERIE ET DE LA LIBRAIRIE (101) was published from 1811 through the present. A more complete guide was published by Otto Lorenz; CATALOGUE GENERAL DE LA LIBRAIRE FRANCAISE (152) began to appear in 1840 and continued until 1925, when it was complemented first by the LIVRES DE L'ANNEE (150) in 1922, and by "BIBLIO" (13) in 1934. Finally in 1971, these volumes were merged to form the LIVRES DE L'ANNEE-BIBLIO (151), which appeared annually through 1979. Together with the Bibliothèque Nationale's CATALOGUE GENERAL DES LIVRES IMPRIMES (97) of some 270 volumes, these collections should include every author-title published in French since 1811. A more selective bibliography compiled prior to World War II by André Monglond, LA FRANCE REVOLUTIONNAIRE ET IMPERIALE (160), appeared listing various titles that were published during the Empire. Another useful guide is the BIBLIOGRAPHIE ANNUELLE DE L'HISTOIRE DE FRANCE (81) which lists, by topic, articles and periodicals published since 1954.

Of the other European states, Germany probably has the most complete national bibliographies of any other major state. Together the compilations of Kayser (130) and Heinsius (115), published in Gothic script, and HINRICH'S BUECHER-CATALOG in Fraktur (116), include a noncumulative list of all German works prior to 1910. A new publishing venture, the GESTAMTVERZEICHNIS DES DEUTSCHSPRACHIGEN SCHRIFTTMUS (105, 106), will give coverage of German and Austrian publishing in two broad cumulations, 1700-1910 and 1911-1965. The volumes for 1911-1965 are complete, those for 1700-1910 complete

through SCHEL as of April 1985. German publishing from 1966 to the
present can be found in the DEUTSCHES BUECHERVERZEICHNIS (61) for the
East German Government (DDR) and the DEUTSCHE BIBLIOGRAPHIE (60)
(BRD) for West Germany. Initially begun to supersede Kayser and
Hinrich, the former noncumulative publication has been continued to
the present. The West German equivalent, DEUTSCHE BIBLIOGRAPHIE, was
begun in 1945, but it is also is noncumulative and chronological.

There are rather complete cumulative bibliographies for Italian
(14, 15, 39, 213) and Spanish (40, 41, 117, 214) titles, but only
noncumulative catalogues exist for Belgium (17), Luxembourg (18),
Holland (1, 2, 28, 29), Switzerland (129, 236), Norway (210), Sweden
(148, 244, 245), and Denmark (32, 55).

Another useful bibliographical aid is SELECTED BIBLIOGRAPHY ON
MODERN FRANCE by John Bowditch and Raymond Grew (27), which lists
pertinent books and dissertations. Less reliable but quite valuable
was the LIST OF DOCTORAL DISSERTATIONS (6) published periodically
since 1905; first as a list in the AMERICAN HISTORICAL REVIEW and
after 1947 as a pamphlet or booklet. Although titles might be
altered or a dissertation might remain uncompleted, the list
indicated areas of current research. Unfortunately, this practice
was discontinued. Dissertations that were completed could be
obtained from University Microfilm in Ann Arbor, Michigan, or located
in the dissertation abstracts which have listed over 400,000
disserations. Taylor's bibliography of unpublished theses in
university libraries in the United Kingdom (247) should also prove
useful. Also of immense value is the list of military-oriented
dissertations published in MILITARY AFFAIRS (281) annually.

There are a large number of general biographical guides to the
Napoleonic period. The first major effort to organize and compile a
comprehensive guide to the literature of the period was by the noted
Italian historian, Alberto Lumbroso. After working for years on
Napoleonic topics, he began the publication of his monumental project
in 1894. Within two years he had published five volumes totaling 787
pages (153); he had reached the entry "Bernays" at the end of volume
five but his work was interrupted there, never to be resumed. In
1902 Friedrich Kircheisen published a relatively general
169-page-volume, BIBLIOGRAPHIE NAPOLEONIENNE (133), which included
topical listings as well as a section of memoirs, correspondence, and
biographies.   Six years later he began the publication of his
BIBLIOGRAPHIE DU TEMPS DE NAPOLEON (131).   Kircheisen attempted to
organize his first volume in chronological order within specialized
topics, but this form was less than ideal for users. His second
volume, dealing with the writings of Napoleon and his family, was
followed by the alphabetical listing of those who had written
memoirs, correspondence, and biographies. Although he planned a
nine-part bibliography, when he reached "G" in part five his work
was interrupted and never completed. However, Kircheisen did publish
two articles in the first issues of the REVUE DES ETUDES
NAPOLEONIENNES, entitled "Bibliographie Napoléonienne de l'année
1911" (132), which included all the books and articles published in
the banner year, 1911. This was the last attempt to publish a
comprehensive bibliography of Napoleon and his times. The project
seemed too massive for any one man to complete in a lifetime, so
today scholars have only a number of bibliographies limited to
specific geographical or topical works.

Before Kircheisen's publication was halted, Gustave Davois published his three-volume BIBLIOGRAPHIE NAPOLEONIENNE (56) which included a number of currently published works and a random selection of titles on the topic, but its use is limited. Between the wars, Napoleonic bibliographies appeared listing the holdings at Brown University in Providence, R.I. (31), and De Paul University in Chicago, Illinois (58), but it was not until John Hall Stewart's valuable volume, FRANCE 1715-1815; A GUIDE TO THE MATERIALS IN CLEVELAND (242), appeared in 1941 that scholars had an updated guide to Napoleonic history in the United States. By including the collections at Case-Western Reserve, Western Historical Society Library, and the excellent collection at Cleveland Public Library, Stewart not only listed some 2,996 titles on the Revolutionary period, but he also called attention to the fact that there was indeed a nucleus of research material available at Cleveland for anyone in the field. Seattle University's recent holdings, the Sonthagen Collection of Napoleonicia, was described in 1954 in a master's thesis written by Terence Curran (54). Meanwhile, John Cornelius at the U.S. Army Military History Institute at Carlisle Barracks completed a bibliography of the military forces of France (53), of which some fifty pages were devoted to the Napoleonic period.

Another important contribution to the study of Napoleonic history appeared in 1971 with the publication of Jean Tulard's (252) valuable bibliography. This volume provided an annotated entry for 794 titles of memoirs written or translated into French. Finally in 1973 the first volume of a projected multivolume bibliographical guide appeared on the French Revolution and Napoleon Collection at Florida State University. This volume contained some 5,000 items including over 500 books, originally part of the private library of King Ernest August of Hanover, and some 1,500 volumes from the library of Alfred and Marie Antoinette Pardée of Cannes. The second volume of this collection, scheduled for publication in the future, is expected to include more than 5,000 titles related primarily to Austria and the German states during the Napoleonic period. Many of these volumes are from the library of the late Professor Marcel Dunan, who devoted much of his life to amassing one of the world's finest private libraries on the subject.

A number of readily accessible volumes devoted to the period have rather extensive bibliographies on the period. Among these works are Louis Villat's LA REVOLUTION ET L'EMPIRE (257), volume nine of Cambridge Modern History (35), August Fournier's NAPOLEON THE FIRST (75), William Sloane's LIFE OF NAPOLEON BONAPARTE (240), Pieter Geyl's NAPOLEON FOR AND AGAINST (107), Georges Lefebvre's NAPOLEON (142-144), Owen Connelly's NAPOLEON'S SATELLITE KINGDOMS (52), Louis Madelin's multivolume HISTOIRE DU CONSULAT ET DE L'EMPIRE (154), and the textbooks of Leo Gershoy (104) and Louis Gottschalk (110). Other more specialized bibliographies can be found under the appropriate chapter headings in this volume.

Useful bibliographies may be found in several historical journals. Almost every issue of REVUE DES ETUDES NAPOLEONIENNES (297) included valuable bibliographical material. FRENCH HISTORICAL STUDIES (274) publishes a list of recent books in the field; the REVUE DE L'INSTITUT NAPOLEON (292) includes the publication of both books and articles; and MILITARY AFFAIRS (281) compiles a list of

articles and dissertations relative to military history. The WAR AND
SOCIETY NEWSLETTER (319), published by the Militärgeschtliches
Forschungsamt at Freiburg, monitors 399 periodicals and publishes an
annual list of articles on military topics. The International
Commission of Military History publishes the BIBLIOGRAPHIE
INTERNATIONAL D'HISTOIRE MILITAIRE (50), listing all military studies
in English, French, Italian, Russian, Spanish and German. The
AMERICAN HISTORICAL REVIEW (262) published an annual bibliography of
recent works in history, but it was unfortunately discontinued.

Other possible sources of bibliographical information can be
gleaned from the numerous catalogues published by the new and used
booksellers of Paris. For many decades the Libraire Historique of
Jean and Raymond Clavreuil has issued one of the finest catalogues
available on this subject. The old catalogues of other Paris
bookshops such as Cart, d'Argences, Picard, Roullet, or Petitot often
provide new titles that exist in no library catalogues.

Catalogues drawn up for the sale of Napoleonic libraries also
provide valuable information (73, 145). When the vast collection of
Emile Brouwet was sold between 1934 and 1936 at the Hotel Drouot and
Sotheby's, three volumes were prepared for the sale under the
direction of the distinguished Napoleonic scholar Jacques Arnna (31).
These volumes included a list of hundreds of original letters with
descriptive information on each item. Another highly prized
catalogue, published for the sale of the collection of William J.
Latta of Philadelphia in 1913 and 1914, was described by authorities
familiar with the great collections of France and other countries as
"the finest in the world." The 598-page book-catalogue (254),
listing thousands of book titles and hundreds of portraits, battle
scenes, caricatures, original manuscripts, and bronzes, included a
staggering total of 5,121 items. Moreover, many of the catalogues
issued by Sotheby, Drouot, and other auction companies often include
priceless manuscripts, books, and memorabilia.

Still another area that might prove useful to scholars of the
period are the catalogues published for various expositions.
Information on many of the expositions between 1911 and 1938 can be
found mentioned in various issues of the REVUE DES ETUDES
NAPOLEONIENNES (297). Additional information can be gleaned from
announcements in the SOUVENIR NAPOLEONIEN (313), and REVUE DE
L'INSTITUT NAPOLEON (292). In 1969, the bicentennial of Napoleon's
birth, there was a rash of expositions (see Chapter III) on the
Emperor and scores, if not hundreds, of catalogues were published
listing books, manuscripts, and memorabilia of the period.

ARCHIVAL SOURCES

One of the most valuable bibliographical guides to the specific
archives in France is the CATALOGUE GENERAL DES MANUSCRITS DES
BIBLIOTHEQUES PUBLIQUES DE FRANCE: ARCHIVES DE LA GUERRE by Louis
Tuetey (76). This three-volume guide to the manuscript collection at
the Archives de la Guerre, administered by the Service historique de
l'armee housed at the Château de Vincennes in Paris, lists most of
the specific items in the 943 cartons labeled "Mémoires Historiques"
and the 1,175 cartons categorized as "Mémoires Réconnaissance." The
great bulk of materials in these collections is concerned with the
Revolutionary period. A more recent catalogue, INVENTAIRE DES

ARCHIVES CONSERVEES AU SERVICE HISTORIQUE DE L'ETAT-MAJOR DE L'ARMEE completed under the direction of Marc André Fabre, Jean Claude Devos, and others (93), is a vital guide to the documents at Vincennes prior to 1900. Among this collection are some 2,610 cartons concerning military correspondence, situations of the various armies, registers, as well as documents relative to military justice, etc. In addition, 209 cartons are related to the period between 1792 and 1804. There is also a catalogue of dossiers of the officers who served during the period that is priceless in tracing particular officers of the period.

The catalogue of the Archives Nationales by Charles Schmidt, LES SOURCES DE L'HISTOIRE DE FRANCE DEPUIS 1789 AUX ARCHIVES NATIONALES (233), is most useful in describing the innumerable cartons related to the First Empire. Series B and B III deal with the elections and the Imperial constitutions; Series C with the procès verbaux of the Council of Ancients, the Council of Five Hundred, and the Tribune until 1804; and Series CC with the procès verbaux of the Conservative Senate (1800-1815). Series F is of major importance because of the nature and scope of the holdings. With some fifty sub-categories which include everything from dossiers of the departmental, commune, and arrondissement officials to information concerning conscription, roads, mines, industry, police, public works, hospitals, prisons, etc., the F Series is invaluable for the period. Series O includes papers of the Maison de l'Empereur and Series BB is devoted to justice and court correspondence, but probably the most important series for the study of the Directory and the Empire is AF--Secrétaire d'état impériale. Included in AF III are documents related to the Directory, while Series AF IV contains manuscripts dealing with the Consulat and the Empire (1800-1815). This collection includes consular and imperial decrees, plus reports of all the ministers of the government as well as the Procès verbal des séances des conseils are also in this collection. Consequently, there are hundreds of cartons which touch on military operations. Many private collections have also been acquired by the Archives Nationales during this century, such as those of Ney and Daru. The latest acquisitions are updated periodically by Madame Chantal de Tourtier-Bonazzi who prepares articles each year for the REVUE DE L'INSTITUT NAPOLEON (292).

The diplomatic archives of the Ministère des affairs étrangères is a vast reservoir for scholars of the Napoleonic period. The "Correspondance Politique" includes government instructions to the ambassadors, ministers, and other consular officials and their correspondence with Paris. Among these papers are the correspondence of Champagny, Talleyrand, Androssey, La Forest, Reinhard, Lauriston, Caulaincourt, and de Pradt, all of which have a direct bearing on military relations. This archive also contains the important collection entitled "Mémoires et Documents"; it includes manuscripts written by French officials to foreign governments on various questions concerning military, economic, or political matters. Other manuscript sources, both public and private, can be traced in the catalogue of Charles Langlois and Henri Stein, LES ARCHIVES DE L'HISTOIRE DE FRANCE (139).

Valuable manuscript collections can be found in the Bibliothèque Nationale by consulting the CATALOGUE GENERAL DES MANUSCRITS FRANCAIS, published by A. Vedier and P. Perrier (256). Manuscripts related to the engineers, sieges, and artillery can be located by consulting the general catalogues of the manuscripts in the public libraries of France related to the military collections (94) which itemizes the holdings of each of the Army's archives. Another source of primary material can be located in the bibliothèque of the Musée de l'Empéri in Salon-de-Provence where many valuable letters of Napoleon and his generals are housed. Now organized as a section of the Musée de l'armée at the Invalides, it has one of the most comprehensive museums of the Revolutionary and Napoleonic period in Europe. This is thanks to the extraordinary commitment and efforts of Jean and Raoul Brunon who spent their lives amassing one of the finest, if not the finest, private collection of Napoleonic artifacts in existence. Today scholars working in the collection have the added advantage of seeing one of the foremost military museums in the world.

It should also be noted that there are a significant number of private collections in the hands of the descendants of leading military figures of the First Empire. Access to these collections is often possible but never easy. For archival materials related to other nations during the period, see the appropriate chapters following.

PRIMARY PUBLISHED DOCUMENTS

Several collections of published documents are of immense value to scholars. Series 3e-9e of the BULLETIN DES LOIS DE LA REPUBLIQUE FRANCAISE (91); the COLLECTION DUVERGIER (68); the HISTOIRE PARLIAMENTAIRE (35) of Buchez and Roux; the ARCHIVES PARLEMENTAIRES (79) of Madival, Laurent, and others; the REGISTRE DES DELIBERATIONS DU CONSULAT PROVISIONNAIRE (9) compiled by Aulard in the collection published by the Société d'histoire de la Révolution; the CONSEIL D'ETAT, RECUEIL DE PROJECTS DE LOIS ET ARRETES ... AN VIII (82); the RECUEIL DES LETTRES, CIRCULAIRES, INSTRUCTIONS, PROGRAMMES, DISCOURS ET AUTRES ACTES PUBLICS EMANES DU MINISTERE DE L'INTERIEUR (96); and Martens's RECUEIL DE TRAITES D'ALLIANCES (55) contains thousands of documents pertinent to Napoleon and the Revolutionary wars. The collection of the acts of the Directory published by A. Debidour (90) and the collection of French treaties published under the auspices of the Foreign Ministery by J. de Clercq (99) should also prove useful for scholars working on foreign policy and coalition warfare. There are also a number of newspapers published during the period that include government documents as well as the "official" view of events. Among these publications the MONITEUR UNIVERSEL (161), the JOURNAL DE L'EMPIRE (124), the JOURNAL DES DEBATES ET DES DECRETS (126), the ALMANACH NATIONAL and the ALMANACH IMPERIAL (5), the JOURNAL DES HOMMES LIBRE (127), the CITOYEN FRANCAIS (46), the JOURNAL DE PARIS (125), the PUBLICISTE (221), and the BIEN INFORME (19) are all of major importance in studying the Empire.

In addition to the publication of these documents, there are thousands of volumes of correspondence of those who served under Napoleon. Similarly thousands of volumes of documents have been published in the European nations that resisted Napoleon. These titles can be located in the appropriate chapters in this volume. Although all of the volumes and government publications listed above are valuable, the monumental 32-volume collection of letters published in the CORRESPONDANCE DE NAPOLEON Ier (175) is without

question the most important single work on the period. Although some
of the letters were edited or simply eliminated on Napoleon III's
orders if they reflected unfavorably upon his great uncle or upon the
family, most of these and other letters that have been discovered
over the past 170 years have been published in a series of volumes
which serve as supplements to this work. In addition to the numerous
titles listed in this chapter under "Napoleon," a complementary
listing is included in Chapter III, thereby providing most of
Napoleon's writings. Thousands of other unpublished letters have
also been published in various historical journals throughout the
world, thus increasing the number of available original
correspondence to almost 60,000 items. Many of these letters have
been translated into English as exemplified by Lloyd (194), Bingham
(203), Thompson (182), Howard (180), Houghton (206), Herold (188),
and Kerry (178). Moreover, the correspondence of Napoleon's
family--Joseph, Louis, Jérôme, Lucien, and Eugène de
Beauharnais--can be used to supplement Napoleon's own correspondence.
See Chapter III for these entries.

MEMOIRS, JOURNALS, AND EYEWITNESS ACCOUNTS

There are an extraordinary number of memoirs, journals, and
eyewitness accounts available for the period. They can be found in
the appropriate chapters of this volume.

PERIODICALS

In general, many of the historical journals published in Europe
and North America periodically include articles of the Napoleonic
epoch. However, in France, journal editors attuned to the Napoleonic
period enthusiastically published topics on the First Empire. Among
the first periodicals devoted primarily to this field was the
now-rare SPECTATEUR MILITAIRE (315), published between 1826 and 1899.
Founded by a number of former Napoleonic officers, namely, Pelet,
Marbot, Fririon, Lamarque, Haxo, and d'Houdelot, this publication
emphasized the Napoleonic period and sought to defend the events of
the Empire against its enemies. Before the SPECTATEUR expired, two
journals of equal importance to the study of the Empire were
established. The CARNET DE LA SABRETACHE (273) was founded in 1893
and is still published today, although with a shift in emphasis. It
published an extraordinary number of articles on the Empire during
the first decades of this century. Similarly, the REVUE D'HISTOIRE
(287), produced by the Historical Section of the Etat-major of the
French army, published under various names until the outbreak of
World War II, concentrated much of its attention on this period.
Unquestionably, the most significant journal published on the
Napoleonic period was the REVUE DES ETUDES NAPOLEONIENNES (297),
founded by Edouard Driault in 1912. As the table of contents of each
volume clearly indicates, all facets of the Napoleonic period were
carefully scrutinized by a long series of distinguished scholars who
published their findings in the journal. Publication of the REVUE
DES ETUDES NAPLEONIENNES ended in 1939. The BULLETIN DE L'INSTITUT
NAPOLEON (268) began publication in 1934. The same year the REVUE DE
L'INSTITUT NAPOLEON (292) began its renowned career. Under the
leadership of such distinguished scholars as Marcel Dunan

and Jean Tulard, the REVUE continues to flourish. Another important
publication, the REVUE DE LA SOCIETE DES AMIS DU MUSEE DE L'ARMEE
(294), quartered at the Hôtel des Invalides, has appeared annually
since 1905, usually with articles devoted to the Empire. The ANNALES
HISTORIQUES DE LA REVOLUTION FRANCAISE (264), published since 1924
under the leadership of a series of eminent scholars such as Mathiez,
Lefebvre, Soboul, and Godechot, has included numerous articles on the
Napoleonic period. The ANNALES REVOLUTIONNAIRES (265) also contains
material on the First Empire in many of its issues.

The BULLETIN HISTORIQUE DE LA SOCIETE DE SAUVEGARDE DU CHATEAU
IMPERIAL DE PONT-DE-BRIQUES (271), published under the direction of
Fernand Beaucour since 1969, and the BULLETIN DU MUSEE BERNADOTTE
(270), published by the Musée Bernadotte at Pau, are devoted
primarily to the First Empire. SOUVENIR NAPOLEONIEN (313),
published since 1937, is a popular journal devoted to the Empire in
general, but more particularly to those of the Bonaparte family--past
and present.

There are several foreign periodicals devoted specifically to
the study of the First Empire that should be noted. Alberto
Lumbroso's REVUE NAPOLEONIENNE (309) produced several significant
issues, but it only survived twelve years. The BULLETIN DE LA
SOCIETE BELGE D'ETUDES NAPOLEONIENNES (272), published by the
distinguished Belgian historian Théo Fleischman, included an index
of many important articles, but in 1975, after twenty-five years of
production, it succumbed to financial exigencies. The RIVISTA
ITALIANA DI STUDI NAPOLEONICI (310), published in Florence since
1965, replaced the BOLLETANO (266) of the Centro di Studi Napoleonici
e di Storia dell'Elba which was published for only three years. The
SOUVENIR NAPOLEONIEN (SECTION CANADIENNE) (314), produced under the
direction of Ben Weider in Montreal, includes numerous articles on
the period. A recent entry, the PROCEEDINGS OF THE CONSORTIUM ON
REVOLUTIONARY EUROPE (285), published following its annual meeting by
the University of Georgia Press, usually contains a large number of
original articles on Napoleon and the Revolutionary period,
demonstrating the vitality of the field. The French Society for
French Historical Studies also publishes its PROCEEDINGS (286); it
often includes articles on the Napoleonic period.

Of the journals devoted to the broad sweep of history, several
publish a number of Napoleonic articles each year. The REVUE
HISTORIQUE DE L'ARMEE (303), published by the Historical Service of
the French Army, produces four superb issues each year with numerous
articles devoted to the Empire. Other French military-oriented
periodicals, both those that have ceased to exist and those still
published, provide a wealth of articles on the Napoleonic period.
The most valuable among these periodicals are the JOURNAL DES SCIENCE
MILITAIRE DES ARMEES DE TERRE ET DE MER (278), ILLUSTRATION MILITAIRE
(276), MONITEUR DE L'ARMEE (283), LE VETERAN, JOURNAL DU TEMPS PASSE
(317), REVUE MILITAIRE FRANCAISE (305), REVUE DE CAVALERIE (293),
REVUE D'INFANTRIE (291), REVUE MILITIARE DES ARMEES ETRANGERES (308),
REVUE MILITAIRE DE L'ETRANGERES (307), REVUE MILITAIRE (306), REVUE
MARITIME (304), and the REVUE DU GENIE MILITAIRE (300). Pertinent
articles appear in other periodicals such as the REVUE HISTORIQUE
(302), REVUE DES DEUX MONDES (295, 296), REVUE HISTOIRE MODERNE ET
CONTEMPORAINE (290), MIRROR DE L'HISTOIRE (282), REVUE D'HISTOIRE
DIPLOMATIQUE (288), and the REVUE DES QUESTIONS HISTORIQUES (298).

In the English language there are several journals that publish articles on the Empire. Among them are the ROYAL UNITED SERVICE INSTITUTION MAGAZINE (311), Journal of the SOCIETY FOR ARMY HISTORICAL RESEARCH (312), MILITARY AFFAIRS (281), U.S. NAVAL WAR COLLEGE REVIEW (284), IRISH SWORD (277), FRENCH HISTORICAL STUDIES (274), and HISTORY TODAY (275). Articles of the period also appear in the hundreds of national and regional journals in Europe and the Americas but they are too numerous to mention here. They are listed in the appropriate chapters in this volume.

RESEARCH TOOLS

There are a number of volumes that will prove valuable to anyone working in the Napoleonic period. For biographical information on the French generals and admirals, Six's DICTIONNAIRE (237), based upon their service dossiers, is invaluable. Robinet's DICTIONNAIRE HISTORIQUE (226) or Mullié's BIOGRAPHIE DE CELEBRITES (164) could also be of value, although they are not as reliable as Six. However, to secure information on the thousands of individuals who played a significant role in the period is a much more difficult task. The eighty-five-volume BIOGRAPHIE UNIVERSELLE (22), edited by Michaud in Paris, the forty-six-volume NOUVELLE BIOGRAPHIE GENERALE (212), edited by Hoefer, and the twenty-volume BIOGRAPHIE UNIVERSELLE (21), published in Brussels, are most helpful in locating personalities of the period despite their nationality. If unlisted in these works, it would be wise to consult the DICTIONARY OF NATIONAL BIOGRAPHY (62), the sixty-volume BIOGRAPHISCHES LEXIKON DER KAISERTHUMS OESTERREICH (23), published under the direction of Würtzbach, or the twenty-five-volume ALLGEMEINE DEUTSCH BIOGRAPHIE (4), as well as the twenty-nine-volume Italian DIZIONARIO BIOGRAFICO DEGLI ITALIANI (63), and the various national biographic collections. There are many contemporary biographic encyclopedias available, but those mentioned are old enough to include individuals of limited importance.

A unique research tool is Martinien's massive volume (157) of losses suffered by the French armies during the Napoleonic period. The regimental bibliographies of Hanoteau and Bonnot (113) and White (260) also make a researcher's task easier. A number of Napoleonic dictionaries have appeared over the years including those by Richardson (225), Melchoir-Bonnet (158), Damas-Hinard (191), Sjostrom (239), and more recently the very useful volume of David Chandler (44). Alan Palmer's encyclopedia (215) appeared in 1984 and Owen Connelly's massive dictionary will soon be available.

Also of considerable value are the various itineraries that locate Napoleon on a particular day in any given year. The volumes of Perrot (216), Fabry (72), Schuermans (234), Denniée (57), and Garros (103) serve this need.

Another volume indispensable for any scholar working in the field is the GUIDE TO THE DIPLOMATIC ARCHIVES OF WESTERN EUROPE, edited by Daniel Thomas and Lynn Case (250). This work provides detailed information on the archives of the various countries of Western Europe and the procedure to be followed in gaining access to them.

BIBLIOGRAPHY: INTRODUCTION

1. Abkoude, Johannes van. ALPHABETISCHE NAAMLIJST VAN BOEKEN ...
    1790-1831. Amsterdam: Van Cleef, 1832-35.

2. Abkoude, Johannes van. NAMENREGISTER VAN BEKENDSTE EN MEEST IN
    GEBRUIK ZYNDE NEDERDUITSCHE BOEKEN ... 1600-1761. Rotterdam:
    Arrenberg, 1788-.

3. Alison, Archibald, bart. HISTORY OF EUROPE, FROM THE
    COMMENCEMENT OF THE FRENCH REVOLUTION TO THE RESTORATION OF THE
    BOURBONS IN 1815. Edinburgh: Blackwood, 1849. 14 vols.

4. ALLGEMEINE DEUTSCH BIOGRAPHIE. Leipzig: Duncker and Humblot,
    1875-1912. 56 vols.

5. ALMANACH NATIONAL DE FRANCE 1794-1804. [ALMANACH ROYALE 1805;
    ALMANACH IMPERIAL 1806-14]. Paris, 1793-1814.

6. American Historical Association. LIST OF DOCTORAL
    DISSERTATIONS IN HISTORY IN PROGRESS OF COMPLETED AT COLLEGES
    AND UNIVERSITIES IN THE UNITED STATES. Washington, D.C.:
    American Historical Association, 1937-74.

7. Arnault, Antoine Vincent. LIFE AND CAMPAIGNS OF NAPOLEON
    BONAPARTE: GIVING AN ACCOUNT OF ALL HIS ENGAGEMENTS, FROM THE
    SIEGE OF TOULON TO THE BATTLE OF WATERLOO. Translated from the
    French of A. Arnault and C.L.F. Panckoucke. Boston: Phillips,
    Sampson, 1850. 2 vols.

8. Aulard, Alphonse. REGISTER DES DELIBERATIONS DU CONSULAT
    PROVISOIRE. Paris: Au siège de la société, 1894.

9. Barante, Amable Guillaume Prosper Brugière de. HISTOIRE DU
    DIRECTOIRE DE LA REPUBLIQUE FRANCAISE. Paris: Didier, 1855.
    3 vols.

10. Beauvais de Préau, Charles Théodore, comp. VICTOIRES,
    CONQUETES, DESASTRES, REVERS ET GUERRES CIVILES DES FRANCAIS,
    DE 1792 A 1815, PAR UNE SOCIETE DE MILITAIRES ET GENS DE
    LETTRES. Paris: Panckoucke, 1818-1822. 27 vols.

11. Béchu, Marcel Ernest [Marcel Dupont]. NAPOLEON EN CAMPAGNE.
    Paris: Hachette, 1950-55. 3 vols.

12. Bertin, Ernest. LA SOCIETE DU CONSULAT ET DE L'EMPIRE. Paris:
    Hachette, 1890.

13. "BIBLIO". CATALOGUE DES OUVRAGES PARUS EN LANGUE FRANCAISE
    DANS LE MONDE ENTIER. Paris: Hachette, 1933-71.

14. BIBLIOGRAFIA ITALIANA. Florence: Bibliotecha Nazionale
    Centrale, 1886-1957.

15. BIBLIOGRAFIA NAZIONALE ITALIANA. Florence: Centro Nazionale per il Catalogue Unico delle Biblioteche Italiane e per le informazioni bibliografiche, 1961-85.

16. BIBLIOGRAPHIE ANNUELLE DE HISTORIE DE FRANCE DU CINQUIEME SIECLE A 1939. Paris: Center National de la researche scientifique, 1964.

17. BIBLIOGRAPHIE DE BELGIQUE. Valduz, Liechtenstein: Kraus, 1875-1944 and 1945 to present.

18. BIBLIOGRAPHIE LUXEMBOURGEOISE. Nendeln, Liechtenstein: Kraus, 1902 to present.

19. BIEN INFORME.

20. Bignon, Louis Pierre Edouard, baron. HISTOIRE DE FRANCE, DEPUIS LE 18 BRUMAIRE (NOVEMBRE 1799), JUSQU'A LA PAIX DE TILSITT (JUILLET 1807). Paris: Bechet, Firmin-Didot, 1829-50. 14 vols.

21. BIOGRAPHIE UNIVERSELLE, ANCIENNE ET MODERNE, OU DICTIONNAIRE DE TOUS LES HOMMES ... DEPUIS LE COMMENCEMENT DU MONDE JUSQU'A CE JOUR. Nouvelle édition, revue, corrigée et considérablement augmentée d'articles omis, nouveaux et de célébrités belges. Brussels: Meline, Cans, 1851. 20 vols.

22. BIOGRAPHIE UNIVERSELLE, ANCIENNE ET MODERNE, OU, HISTOIRE, PAR ORDRE ALPHABETIQUE, DE LA VIE PUBLIQUE ET PRIVEE DE TOUS LES HOMMES QUI SE SONT FAIT REMARQUER PAR LEURS ECRITS, LEURS ACTIONS, LEUR TALENTS, LEURS VERTUS OU LEURS CRIMES. Ouvrage entièrement neuf, rédigé par une Société de gens de lettres et de savants. Paris: Michaud, 1811-62. 85 vols.

23. BIOGRAPHISCHES LEXIKON DER KAISHERTHUMS OESTERREICH. [Under the direction of Constantin Würtzbach, ritter von Tannenberg]. Vienna: Hof-und Staatsdruckerei, 1856-91. 60 vols.

24. Blanchard, Pierre, ed. HISTOIRE DES BATAILLES, SIEGES ET COMBATS DES FRANCAIS, DEPUIS 1792 JUSQU'EN 1815. Par une société de militaires et de gens de letters. Paris: Blanchard, 1818.

25. Blond, Georges. LA GRANDE ARMEE, 1804-15. Paris: Laffont, 1979. 2 vols.

26. Bourgeois, Emile. MANUEL DE POLITIQUE ETRANGERE. Paris: Belin, 1897-98. 2 vols.

27. Bowditch, John, and Raymond Grew, comps. A SELECTED BIBLIOGRAPHY ON MODERN FRENCH HISTORY, 1600 TO THE PRESENT. Ann Arbor, Michigan: Xerox University Microfilm, 1974.

28. Brinkman, Carel Leonhard. ALPHABETISCHE NAAMLIJST VAN BOEKEN, PLAAT- EN KAARTWERKEN ... 1833-1849. Amsterdam: Brinkman, 1850-62.

29. BRINKMAN'S CATALOGUS VAN BOEKEN. Alphen aan den Rijn, Netherlands: Sijthoff, 1846 to present.

30. Brouwet, Emile. NAPOLEON ET SON TEMPS. CATALOGUE DE LA COLLECTIONS DE M. EMILE BROUWET, DONT LA VENTE AURA LIEU [1934-1936]. Hotel des commissaires-priseurs [et chez MM. Sotheby]. Paris and London: n.p., 1934-36. 3 vols.

31. Brown University Library. A CATALOGUE OF THE NAPOLEON COLLECTION FORMED BY WILLIAM HENRY HOFFMAN, 1867-1916. Given to Brown University in 1921 by Mira H. Hoffman. Providence, R.I.: The University, 1922.

32. Brunn, Christian Walther. BIBLIOTHECA DANICA ... FRA 1482 TIL 1830. Copenhagen: Rosenkilde, 1961.

33. Brunn, Geoffrey. EUROPE AND THE FRENCH IMPERIUM, 1799-1814. New York: Harper, 1938.

34. Buchez, Philippe Joseph, and Pierre Célestin Roux-Laverge. HISTOIRE DE LA REVOLUTION FRANCAISE, OU JOURNAL DES ASSEMBLEES NATIONALES, DEPUIS 1789 JUSQU'EN 1815. Paris: Paulin, 1834-38. 40 vols.

35. THE CAMBRIDGE MODERN HISTORY. Planned by Lord Acton, edited by Sir A.W. Ward, Sir G.W. Prothero, and Sir Stanley Leathes, K.G.B.... New York: Macmillan; Cambridge: The University Press, 1903-13. Vol. 9.

36. Camon, Hubert. LA GUERRE NAPOLEONIENNE. Paris: Chapelot, 1903-10. 5 vols.

37. Campardon, Emile. LISTE DES MEMBRES DE LA NOBLESSE IMPERIALE, DRESSEE D'APRES LES REGISTRES DE LETTERS PATENTS CONSERVES AUX ARCHIVES NATIONALES. Paris: Au siège de la société, 1889.

38. Capefigue, Jean Baptiste Honoré. L'EUROPE PENDANT LE CONSULAT ET L'EMPIRE DE NAPOLEON. Paris: Pitois-Levrault, 1840. 10 vols.

39. CATALOGO CUMULATIVO 1886-1957 DEL BOLLETTION DELLE PUBBLICAZIONI ITALIANE. Nendeln, Liechtenstein: Kraus, 1968-69. 41 vols.

40. CATALOGO GENERAL DE LA LIBRERIA ESPANOLA, 1931-1950. Madrid: Instituto Nacional del Libro Espanol, 1931-50.

41. CATALOGO GENERAL DE LA LIBERIA ESPANOLA E HISPANOAMERICANA, ANOS 1901-1930. Madrid and Barcelona: Camaras Oficiales del Libro, 1901-30.

42. Chalamet, Antoine, ed. GUERRES DE NAPOLEON (1800-1808). RACONTEES PAR DES TEMOINS OCULAIRES: GENERAL BIGARRE [et al.]. Paris: Firmin-Didot, 1895.

43. Chandler, David G. THE CAMPAIGNS OF NAPOLEON. New York: Macmillan, 1966.

44. Chandler, David G. DICTIONARY OF THE NAPOLEONIC WARS. London: Arms and Armour, 1979.

45. Chichester, Henry Manners, and George Burges-Short. THE RECORDS AND BADGES OF EVERY REGIMENT AND CORPS OF THE BRITISH ARMY. London: Gale and Polden, 1900.

46. CITOYEN FRANCAIS.

47. Clausewitz, Karl von. HINTERLASSENE WERKE DES GENERALS CARL VON CLAUSEWITZ UEBER KRIEG UND KRIEGFUEHRUNG. Berlin: Dümmler, 1832-1937. 10 vols.

48. Clausewitz, Karl von. ON WAR. Translated by Colonel J.J.Graham. London: Routledge & Kegan Paul, 1908. 3 vols.

49. Collection Baudouin. COLLECTION GENERAL DES LOIS ET DES ACTS DU CORPS LEGISLATIF ET DU DIRECTOIRE EXECUTIF. Paris: Baudouin, n.d. 18 vols.

50. Comité International des Sciences Historiques. Commission Internationale d'Histoire Militaire comparée. Committee de bibliographie. BIBLIOGRAPHIE INTERNATIONALE D'HISTOIRE MILITAIRE. Edited by Daniel Reichel. Berne: Imprimeries Réunies S.A., 1977 to present.

51. Connelly, Owen. FRENCH REVOLUTION-NAPOLEONIC ERA. New York: Holt, Rinehart and Winston, 1979.

52. Connelly, Owen. NAPOLEON'S SATELLITE KINGDOMS. New York: Free Press, 1965.

53. Cornelius, John C. SPECIAL BIBLIOGRAPHY 13: THE MILITARY FORCES OF FRANCE. Carlisle Barracks, Pa.: U.S. Army Military History Institute, 1977.

54. Curran, Terence John. THE NAPOLEON COLLECTION IN THE SEATTLE UNIVERSITY LIBRARY. M.A. thesis, Seattle University, 1954.

55. DANSK BOGFORTEGNELSE. Copenhagen: G.E.C. Gads, 1841-.

56. Davois, Gustave. BIBLIOGRAPHIE NAPOLEONIENNE FRANCAISE JUSQU'EN 1980. Paris: Edition bibliographique, 1909-11. 3 vols.

57. Denniée, Pierre Paul, baron. ITINERAIRE DE L'EMPEREUR NAPOLEON PENDANT LA CAMPAGNE DE 1812. Paris: Paulin, 1842.

58. De Paul University, Chicago. A CATALOGUE OF THE NAPOLEON LIBRARY OF DE PAUL UNIVERSITY. Complied by Virginia Boyd Goult with a perface by the Very Rev. Father Michael J. O'Connell, and an introduction by Stanley E. Read. Chicago: De Paul University, 1941.

59. Deutsch, Harold Charles. THE GENESIS OF NAPOLEONIC IMPERIALISM. Cambridge: Harvard University Press; London: H. Milford, Oxford University Press, 1938.

60. DEUTSCHE BIBLIOGRAPHIE. Frankfort: Buchhändler Vereinigung GMBH, 1945 to present.

61. DEUTSCHES BUECHERVERZEICHNIS. Leipzig: Deutschen Borsenvereins, 1916 to present.

62. DICTIONARY OF NATIONAL BIOGRAPHY. Oxford: Oxford University Press, 1917-.

63. DIZIONARIO BIOGRAFICO DEGLI ITALIANI. Rome: Enciclopedia a Italiana, 1960. 29 vols.

64. Dodge, Theodore Ayrault. NAPOLEON, A HISTORY OF THE ART OF WAR, FROM THE BEGINNING OF THE FRENCH REVOLUTION TO THE END OF THE EIGHTEENTH CENTURY, WITH A DETALIED ACCOUNT OF THE WARS OF THE FRENCH REVOLUTION. London: Gay and Bird, 1904-7. 4 vols.

65. Driault, Edouard. NAPOLEON ET L'EUROPE. Paris: Alcan, 1910-27. 5 vols.

66. Dufraisse, Marc Etienne Gustave. HISTOIRE DU DROIT DE GUERRE ET DE APIX DE 1789 A 1815. Paris: Le Chevalier, 1867.

67. Dumas, Mathieu, comte. PRECIS DES EVENEMENTS MILITAIRES, OU ESSAIS HISTORIQUES SUR LES COMPAGNES DE 1799 A 1814. Paris, Strasbourg, and London: Treuttel-Würtz, 1816-26. 19 vols.

68. Duvergier Collection. COLLECTION COMPLETE [sic] DES LOIS DECRETS, ORDONNANCES REGLEMENTS ET AVIS DU CONSEIL D'ETAT, PUBLIEE SUR LES EDITIONS OFFICIELLES DU LOUVRE, DE L'IMPRIMERIE, PAR BAUDOUIN, ET DU BULLETIN DES LOIS DE 1788 A 1824.... Paris, 1824-28. Vols. 12-19.

69. Elmer, Alexander. L'AGENT SECRET DE NAPOLEON, CHARLES-LOUIS SCHULMEISTER. D'APRES LES ARCHIVES SECRETES DE LA MAISON D'ARTICHE. Traduit de l'allemand par Lucien Thomas. Paris: Payot, 1932.

70. ENCYCLOPEDIE MODERN. DICTIONNAERIE ABRIDGE DES SCIENCE, DES LETTRES, DES ARTS, DE L'INDUSTRIE, DE L'AGRICULTURE ET DU COMMERCE. Sous la direction de Léon Renier. Paris: Didot: 1846-53. 27 vols.

71. Esposito, Vincent J., and John R. Elting. A MILITARY HISTORY AND ATLAS OF THE NAPOLEONIC WARS. New York: Praeger, 1965.

72. Fabry, Jean Baptiste. ITINERAIRE DE BOUNAPARTE DE L'ISLE D'ELBE A L'ILE SAINT HELENE. Paris: Le Normant, 1817. 2 vols.

73. Felissent, Jean Jacques Gayet de. CATALOGUE DE LA COLLECTION J.J DE FELISSENT EN VENTE AUX ENCHERES SOUS LA DIRECTION DES EXPERTS CARLO CLERICI [ET] CESARE CLERICI. A MILAN LE JOUR 27 AVRIL ET JOURS SUIVANTS A 14 HEURES PRECISES. Milan, 1914.

74. Fleischman, Théo. NAPOLEON AU BIVOUAC; LA VIE DE L'EMPEREUR EN CAMPAGNE. Brussels: Brepols, 1957.

75. Fournier, August. NAPOLEON THE FIRST, A BIOGRAPHY. Translated by Margaret Bacon Corwin and Arthur Dart Bissell; edited by Edward Gaylord Bouren. New York: Holt, 1904.

76. France. Archives de la guerre. CATALOGUE GENERAL DES MANUSCRITS DES BIBLIOTHEQUES PUBLIQUES DE FRANCE: ARCHIVES DE LA GUERRE. Par Louis Tuetey. Paris: Plon-Nouritt, 1912-20. 3 vols.

77. France. Archives Nationales. LES ARCHIVES DARU. Inventaire par Suzanne d'Huart, conservateur aux Archives Nationales. Paris: Imprimerie nationale, 1962.

78. France. Archives Nationales. LES ARCHIVES DU MARECHAL NEY ET DE SA FAMILLE CONSERVEES AUX ARCHIVES NATIONALES. Inventaire par Simone de Saint-Exupéry et Chantal de Tourtier. Paris: Imprimerie nationale, 1962.

79. France. Archives Parlementaires. ARCHIVES PARLEMENTAIRES DE 1787 A 1860; RECUEIL COMPLET DES DEBUTS LEGISLATIFS ET POLITIQUES DES CHAMBRES FRANCAISES IMPRIME PAR ORDRE DU SENAT ET DE LA CHAMBRE DES DEPUTES. Compiled by Jérôme Madival, Emile Laurent, et al. Paris: Librairie administrative de P. Dupont, 1862-.

80. France. Chambre des députés, 1814-1848. PROCES-VERBAL DES SEANCES DE LA CHAMBRE DES DEPUTES DES DEPARTEMENS; 1814. Paris: Hacquart, 1814. 6 vols.

81. France. Comité Français des Sciences Historiques. BIBLIOGRAPHIE ANNUELLE DE L'HISTOIRE DE FRANCE. Paris: Centre national de la recherche scientifique, 1964.

82. France. Conseil d'Etat. CONSEIL D'ETAT, RECUEIL DE PROJECTS DE LOIS ARRETES ... AN VIII, 1814. Paris, 38 vols.

83. France. Corps législatif. JOURNAL DES DEBATS ET DES DECRETS... (1795-99). Paris: Imprimerie du Journal des debats, 1795-1800. 51 vols.

84. France. Corps législatif, Conseil des anciens. PROCESS VERBAL DES SEANCES DU CONSEIL DES ANCIENS. Paris, an 4-an 8 [1796-1800]. 49 vols.

85. France. Corps législatif, Conseil de cinq-cent. PROCES VERBAL
    DES SEANCES PERMANENTS DU CONSEIL DES CINQ-CENT. Paris, an
    4-an 8 [1796-1800]. 50 vols.

86. France. Corps législatif, 1800-1814. [DOCUMENTS DIVERS,
    SESSION DE 1811: FEUILLETONS, DISCOURS, EXTRAITS DES MINUTES
    DE LA SECRETAIRERIE D'ETAT, PROCES-VERBAL DES SEANCES DE JUIN
    DE JUILLET. SESSION DE 1808. TABLE DES MATIERES DES NOMS DE
    NOMS DE LIEUX ET DES NOMS DES PERSONNES CONTENUS DANS LES
    PROCES-VERBAUX]. Paris: Hacquart, 1811. 1 vol. (various
    pagings).

87. France. Dépôt de la guerre. HISTOIRE DES CAMPAGNES DE
    L'EMPEREUR NAPOLEON. Directed by Jean Jacques Pelet. Paris:
    Maulde et Renou, 1843.

88. France. Dépôt de la guerre. MEMORIAL DU DEPOT DE LA GUERRE.
    Paris: Pinard, 1829. Vol 5.

89. France. Dépôt de la guerre. MEMORIAL TOPOGRAPHIQUE ET
    MILITAIRE, REDIGE AU DEPOT GENERAL DE LA GUERRE. Imprime par
    ordre du ministre. Paris: Imprimerie de la République an XI
    [1802]. 5 vols.

90. France. Directoire executif, 1795-1799. RECUEIL DES ACTES DU
    DIRECTOIRE EXECUTIF (PROCES-VERBAUX, ARRETES, INSTRUCTIONS,
    LETTRES ET ACTES DIVERS). Publiés et annotés par A. Debidour.
    Paris: Imprimerie nationale, 1910-17. 4 vols.

91. France. Laws, statutes, etc. BULLETIN DES LOIS DE LA
    REPUBLIQUE FRANCAISE. [Series 1, Vols. 1-3, 1794-96; Series 2,
    Vols. 1-9, 1796-1800; Series 3, Vols. 1-9, 1800-Apr. 1804;
    Series 4, Vols. 1-20, Apr. 1804-Mar. 1814; Series 5, Vols. 1-3,
    Mar. 1814-Mar. 1915; Series 6, June 1815]. Paris: Imprimerie
    nationale, 1794-1815. 45 vols.

92. France. Laws, statutes, etc. RECUEIL GENERAL ANNOTE DES LOIS,
    DECRETS, ORDONNANCES, etc., DEPUIS LE MOIS DE JUIN 1789
    JUSQU'AU MOIS D'AOUT 1830. Avec des notices par MM. Odilon
    Barrot, Vatimesnil, Ymbert; publié par les redacteurs du
    Journal des Notaires et des Avocats.... Paris:
    L'Administration du Journal des Notaires et des Avocats,
    1835-40. 20 vols.

93. France. Ministère de la guerre. INVENTAIRE DES ARCHIVES
    CONSERVEES AU SERVICE HISTORIQUE DE L'ETAT-MAJOR DE L'ARMEE
    (CHATEAU DE VINCENNES) (ARCHIVES MODERNES). Deuxième édition
    revue et completée par Marc André Fabre [et al.]. Paris:
    Ateliers d'impressions de l'armée, 1954.

94. France. Ministère de la guerre. Bibliothèque. CATALOGUE
    GENERAL DES MANUSCRITS DES BIBLIOTHEQUES PUBLIQUES DE FRANCE.
    BIBLIOTHEQUES DE LA GUERRE. Par F. Lemoine et F. Gebelin.
    Paris: Plon-Nourrit, 1911.

95. France. Ministère de l'instruction publique. CATALOGUE DES MANUSCRITS CONSERVES DANS LES DEPOTS D'ARCHIVES DEPARTEMENTALES, COMMUNALES ET HOSPITALIERES. Paris, 1886.

96. France. Ministère de l'intérieur. RECUEIL DES LETTRES, CIRCULAIRES, INSTRUCTIONS, PROGRAMMES, DISCOURS ET AUTRES ACTES PUBLICS EMANES DU MINISTERE DE L'INTERIEUR. Paris, an VII-1821. 20 vols.

97. France. Paris. Bibliothèque Nationale. CATALOGUE GENERAL DES LIVRES IMPRIMES. AUTEURS. Paris: Imprimerie nationale, 1900-. Vol. 1-270 (in progress).

98. France. Paris. Bibliothèque Nationale. CATALOGUE GENERAL DES MANUSCRITS FRANCAIS DE LA BIBLIOTHEQUE NATIONALE. Published by H. Omont. Paris, 1895.

99. France. Treaties, etc. RECUEIL DES TRAITES DE LA FRANCE, PUBLIE SOUS LES AUSPICES DU MINISTERE DES AFFAIRES ETRANGERES. Sous la direction de J. de Clercq. Paris: Amyot, 1864-1917. Vols. 1 and 2 [1713-1815].

100. France. Treaties, etc. TRAITE DE PAIX SIGNE A PARIS LE 30 MAI 1814, ET TRAITES ET CONVENTIONS SIGNES DANS LA MEME VILLE LE 20 NOVEMBRE 1815. Paris: Librairie Grecque-Latine-Allemande, 1815.

101. France. BIBLIOGRAPHIE DE LA FRANCE, OU JOURNAL GENERAL DE L'IMPRIMERIE ET DE LA LIBRAIRIE,... Nendeln, Liechtenstein: Kraus, 1970. (1811-1854. 45 vols.)

102. Gallois, Léonard. HISTOIRE DE NAPOLEON D'APRES LUI-MEME. Paris: Béchet, 1827.

103. Garros, Louis. ITINERAIRE DE NAPOLEON BONAPARTE, 1769-1821. Paris: Editions de l'Encyclopédie française, 1947.

104. Gershoy, Leo. THE FRENCH REVOLUTION AND NAPOLEON. New York: Appleton-Century-Crofts, 1964.

105. GESAMTVERZEICHNIS DES DEUTSCHSPRACHIGEN SCHRIFTTUMS (GV) 1700-1910. Munich, New York, and London: K.G. Saur, 1979-.

106. GESAMTVERZEICHNIS DES DEUTSCHSPRACHIGEN SCHRIFTTUMS (GV) 1911-1965. 150 vols.

107. Geyl, Pieter. NAPOLEON FOR AND AGAINST. Translated by Olive Renier. New Haven: Yale University Press, 1949.

108. Girod de l'Ain, Maurice. GRANDS ARTILLEURS: DROUOT, SENARMONT, EBLE. Paris: Berger-Levrault, 1911.

109. Godechot, Jacques Léon. L'EUROPE ET L'AMERIQUE A L'EPOQUE NAPOLEONIENNE (1800-1815). Paris: Presses Universitaires de France, 1967.

110. Gottschalk, Louis Reichenthal. THE ERA OF THE FRENCH REVOLUTION (1715-1815). Boston: Houghton, 1929.

111. Great Britain. British Museum, Department of Printed Books. BRITISH MUSEUM CATALOGUE OF PRINTED BOOKS. (holdings through 1955). London: 1965-79. 263 vols. with supplements 1956-65 (50 vols.); 1966-70 (26 vols.); 1971-1975 (13 vols.).

112. Guileet. ETAT ACTUEL DE LA LEGISLATION SUR LA ADMINISTRATION DES TROUPES. 1811. 3 vols.

113. Hanoteau, Jean, and Emile Bonnot. BIBLIOGRAPHIE DES HISTORIQUES DES REGIMENTS FRANCAIS. Paris: Champion, 1913.

114. Headley, Joel Tyler. NAPOLEON AND HIS MARSHALS. New York: Scribner, 1855.

115. Heinsius, Wilhelm. ALLGEMEINES BUECHER-LEXIKON. Leipzig: Glebisch, 1790-1892.

116. HINRICHS' BUECHER-CATALOG. Leipzig: Hinrichs'sche, 1851-1912.

117. Hispanic Society of America. CATALOGUE OF THE LIBRARY. Boston: G.K. Hall, 1962; 1970.

118. Holtman, Robert B. THE NAPOLEONIC REVOLUTION. Philadelphia: Lippencott, 1967.

119. Horward, Donald D. THE FRENCH REVOLUTION AND NAPOLEON COLLECTION AT FLORIDA STATE UNIVERSITY: A BIBLIOGRAPHICAL GUIDE. Tallahassee: Friends of the Florida State University Library, 1973.

120. Horward, Donald D. "Napoleon in Review: A Bibliographical Essay." MILITARY AFFAIRS 43 (1979): 144-50.

121. Iung, Théodore. BONAPARTE ET SON TEMPS, 1769-1799, D'APRES DES DOCUMENTS INEDITS. Paris: Charpentier, 1880-81. 3 vols.

122. Jomini, Antoine Henri, comte. HISTOIRE CRITIQUE ET MILITAIRE DES GUERRES DE LA REVOLUTION. Paris: Anselin et Pochard, 1820-24. 15 vols.

123. Jomini, Antoine Henri, comte. VIE POLITIQUE ET MILITAIRE DE NAPOLEON.... Paris: Anselin, 1827. 4 vols.

124. JOURNAL DE L'EMPIRE.

125. JOURNAL DE PARIS.

126. JOURNAL DES DEBATES ET DES DECRETS.

127. JOURNAL DES HOMMES LIBRE.

128. Juarès, Jean, directeur. HISTOIRE SOCIALISTE, 1789-1900. Paris: J. Rouff, 1901-8. 12 vols.

129. KATALOG DER SCHWEIZERISCHEN LANDESBIBLIOTHEK. Berne: Hans Huber, 1901-47.

130. Kayser, Christian Gottlob. VOLLSTAEDIGES BUECHER-LEXIKON. Leipzig: Tauchnitz, 1750-1910.

131. Kircheisen, Friedrich Max. BIBLIOGRAPHIE DU TEMPS DE NAPOLEON, COMPRENANT L'HISTOIRE DES ETATS-UNIS. New York: Burt Franklin, 1968. 2 vols.

132. Kircheisen, Friedrich Max. "Bibliographie napoléonienne de l'année 1911." REVUE DES ETUDES NAPOLEONIENNES 2 (1912): 303-20; 458-74.

133. Kircheisen, Friedrich Max. BIBLIOGRAPHIE NAPOLEONIENNE COLLECTIONS DE SOURCES CLASSEES PAR ORDRE DE MATIERES: Paris: Chapelot, 1902.

134. Lachouque, Henry. THE ANATOMY OF GLORY; NAPOLEON AND HIS GUARD, A STUDY IN LEADERSHIP. Adapted from the French by Anne S.K. Brown. Providence, R. I.: Brown University Press, 1961.

135. Lachouque, Henry. NAPOLEON: 20 [i.e. vingt] ANS DE CAMPAGNES. Paris: Arthaud, 1964.

136. Lachouque, Henry. NAPOLEON'S BATTLES: A HISTORY OF HIS CAMPAIGNS. Translated from the French by Roy Monkcom. New York: Dutton, 1967.

137. Lacroix, Désiré. LES MARECHAUX DE NAPOLEON. Paris: Garnier, 1896.

138. Lallement, Guillaume N. CHOIX DE RAPPORTS, OPINIONS ET DISCOURS PRONONCES A LA TRIBUNE NATIONALE DEPUIS 1789 JUSQU'A CE JOUR; RECUEILLIS DANS UN ORDRE CHRONOLOGIQUE ET HISTORIQUE. Paris: Eymery, 1818-25. 20 vols.

139. Langlois, Charles V., and Henri Stein. LES ARCHIVES DE L'HISTORIE DE FRANCE. Paris: Picard, 1891.

140. Lavisse, Ernest, and Alfred Rambaud, eds. HISTOIRE GENERALE DU IVe SIECLE A NOS JOURS. Vol. 8. LA REVOLUTION FRANCAISE, 1789-1800. Vol. 9. NAPOLEON, 1800-1815 [par Georges Pariset]. Paris: Colin, 1893-1905.

141. Lefebvre, Armand. HISTOIRE DES CABINETS DE L'EUROPE PENDANT LA CONSULAT ET EMPIRE. Paris: Gosselin, 1845-47. 3 vols.

142. Lefebvre, Georges. NAPOLEON. Paris: Presses Universitaires de France, 1941, 1953.

143. Lefebvre, Georges. NAPOLEON, FROM 18 BRUMAIRE TO TILSIT, 1799-1807. Translated from the French by Henry F. Stockhold. New York: Columbia University Press, 1969.

144. Lefebvre, Georges. NAPOLEON, FROM TILSIT TO WATERLOO. Translated by J.E. Anderson. New York: Columbia University Press, 1969.

145. Lêvi, Andrê. COLLECTION ANDRE LEVI. ARMES ET SOUVENIRS HISTORIQUES. Sabretache portêe au sacre de l'Empereur. Souvenirs du marêchal MacDonald, duc de Tarente. Dont la vente aux enchêres publiques aura lieu Hotel Drouot. 19 juin 1936. Paris: Lahure, 1936.

146. LIBRAIRIE FRANCAISE CATALOGUE GENERAL DES OUVRAGES EN LINGUE FRANCAISE ENTRE LE Ier JANVIER 1930 ET LE Ier JANVIER 1965. Paris: Cercle de la Librairie, 1930-65.

147. LIBRARY OF CONGRESS/NATIONAL UNION CATALOGUE. (various publishers). 1941-82.

148. Linnstrom, Hjalmar. SVENSKT BOKLEXIKON. AAREN 1830-1865. Stockholm: Linnstroms, 1883.

149. LISTE DE 16,000 MILITAIRES AU SERVICE DE LA FRANCE, FAITS RISONNIERS DE GUERRE DE 1810 A 1914, ET QUI SONT MORTS EN RUSSIE, EN POLOGNE ET EN ALLEMAGNE. Paris: n.p., 1825.

150. LES LIVRES DE L'ANNEE. Paris: Cercle de la Librairie, 1922-71.

151. LES LIVRES DE L'ANNEE-BIBLIO. BIBLIOGRAPHIE GENERALE DES OUVRAGES DE LANGUE GRANCAISE. Paris: Cercle de la Librairie, 1971-80.

152. Lorenz, Otto Henri. CATALOGUE GENERAL DE LA LIBRAIRIE FRANCAISE. Paris: various publishers, 1867.

153. Lumbroso, Alberto, barone. SAGGIO DI UNA BIBLIOGRAFICA RAGIONATA PER SERVICE ALLA STORIA DELL'EPOCHA NAPOLEONICA. Modena: Azuni and others, 1894-96. 5 vols.

154. Macdonell, Archibald Gordon. NAPOLEON AND HIS MARSHALS. New York: Macmillan, 1934.

155. Madelin, Louis. HISTOIRE DU CONSULAT ET DE L'EMPIRE. Paris: Hachette, 1937-51. 14 vols.

156. Martens, Georg Friedrich von, ed. RECUEIL DE TRAITES D'ALLIANCE ET D'AUTRES ACTES REMARQUABLES ... DEPUIS 1761 JUSQU'A PRESENT. Goettingue: Dieterich, 1817-39. Part 1, Vols. 4-8; Part 2, Vols. 1-3. [10 vols., 1761-1829].

157. Martinien, Aristide. TABLEAUX PAR CORPS ET PAR BATAILLES DES OFFICIERS TUES ET BLESSES PENDANT LES GUERRES DE L'EMPIRE (1805-1815). Paris: Charles-Lavauzelle, 1899.

158. Melchior-Bonnet, Bernardine. DICTIONNAIRE DE LA REVOLUTION ET DE L'EMPIRE. Paris: Larousse, 1965.

159. Montgaillard, Jean Gabriel Maurice, comte de. MEMOIRES DIPLOMATIQUES 1805-1819. Extraits du ministère de l'intérieur et publiés, avec une introduction et des notes, par Clément de Lacroise. Paris, 1896.

160. Monglond, André. LA FRANCE REVOLUTIONNAIRE ET IMPERIALE: ANNALES DE BIBLIOGRAPHIE METHODIQUE ET DESCRIPTION DES LIVRES ILLUSTRES. Grenoble: Arthaud, 1929-78. 10 vols.

161. MONITEUR UNIVERSEL.

162. [Morvan, Jean] Capitaine M. Tixier. LE SOLDAT IMPERIAL (1800-1814). Paris: Plon-Nourit, 1904. 2 vols.

163. Müller, P. L'ESPIONNAGE MILITAIRE SOUS NAPOLEON Ier. C. SCHULMEISTER. Paris: Berger-Levrault, 1896.

164. Mullié, C. BIOGRAPHIE DE CELEBRITES MILITAIRES DES ARMEES DE TERRE DE DE MER DE 1789 A 1850. Paris: Poignavant, 1851. 2 vols.

165. Napoleon I, Emperor of the French. ALLOCUTIONS ET PROCLAMATIONS MILITAIRE DE NAPOLEON Ier. Publiée pour la première fois d'après les textes authentiques par George Barral. Paris: Flammarion, 1896.

166. Napoleon I, Emperor of the French. LES BULLETINS DE LA GRANDE ARMEE PRECEDES ET ACCOMPAGNES DES RAPPORT SUR LES ARMEE FRANCAISE DE 1792 A 1815.... Par Adrien Pascal. Paris: Dumaine, 1843-44. 6 vols.

167. Napoleon I, Emperor of the French. BULLETINS OFFICIELS DU GRANDE ARMEE PAR L'EMPEREUR NAPOLEON. Collected by Alexandre Gonjon. Paris: Corréard, 1824. 2 vols.

168. Napoleon I, Emperor of the French. COLLECTION GENERAL ET COMPLETE DE LETTRES; PROCLAMATIONS; DISCOURS; MESSAGES, etc. DE NAPOLEON LE GRAND, EMPEREUR DES FRANCAIS. Publiée par Charles Fischer. Leipzig: n.p., 1808-13. 2 vols.

169. Napoleon I, Emperor of the French. CONFIDENTIAL CORRESPONDENCE OF THE EMPEROR NAPOLEON AND THE EMPRESS JOSEPHINE: INCLUDING LETTERS FROM THE TIME OF THEIR MARRIAGE UNTIL THE DEATH OF JOSEPHINE, AND ALSO SEVERAL PRIVATE LETTERS FROM THE EMPEROR TO HIS BROTHER JOSEPH, AND OTHER IMPORTANT PERSONAGES. By John S.C. Abbot, New York: Mason: 1856.

170. Napoleon I, Emperor of the French. CORRESPONDANCE AVEC LE MINISTRE DE LA MARINE DEPUIS 1804 JUSQU EN AVRIL 1815. Paris: Delloye et Lecou, 1837. 2 vols.

171. Napoleon I, Emperor of the French. CORRESPONDANCE, BULLETINS ET ORDRES DU JOUR DE NAPOLEON. Edited by Alexandre Keller. Paris: Mericant, 1905. 5 vols.

172. Napoleon I, Emperor of the French. CORRESPONDANCE INEDITE DE NAPOLEON AVEC LE COMMANDANT EN CHEF DE LA GRANDE ARMEE (Général Comte de la Riboissière). Par Adrien Pascal. Paris: Dumaine, 1843.

173. Napoleon I, Emperor of the French. CORRESPONDANCE MILITAIRE DE NAPOLEON Ier. EXTRAITE DE LA CORRESPONDANCE GENERALE ET PUBLIEE PAR ORDRE DU MINISTRE DE LA GUERRE. Paris: Plon-Nourrit, 1876-97. 10 vols.

174. Napoleon I, Emperor of the French. CORRESPONDANCE INEDIT, OFFICIELLE ET CONFIDENTIELLE DE NAPOLEON BONAPARTE AVEC LES COURS ETRANGERES, LES PRINCES, LES MINISTRES ET LES GENERALS FRANCAIS ET ETRANGERES. Publiée par le général Charles Beauvais. Paris: Panckoucke, 1819-10. 7 vols.

175. Napoleon I, Emperor of the French. CORRESPONDANCE DE NAPOLEON Ier; PUBLIEE PAR ORDER DE L'EMPEREUR NAPOLEON III. Paris: Imprimerie impériale, 1858-69. 32 vols.

176. Napoleon I, Emperor of the French. THE CORSICAN; A DIARY OF NAPOLEON'S LIFE IN HIS OWN WORDS. Compiled by R.M. Johnson. Boston: Houghton Mufflin, 1930.

177. Napoleon I, Emperor of the French. DICTIONNAIRE DE L'EMPEREUR. Compiled by André Palluel. Paris: Plon, 1969.

178. Napoleon I, Emperor of the French. THE FIRST NAPOLEON: SOME UNPUBLISHED DOCUMENTS FROM THE BOWOOD PAPERS. Edited by the Earl of Kerry [Henry William Edmund Petty FitzMaurice, 6th marquis of Lansdowne]. Boston and New York: Houghton Mifflin, 1925.

179. Napoleon I, Emperor of the French. IN THE WORDS OF NAPOLEON. Compiled and translated by Daniel S. Gray. Troy, Alabama: Troy State Universtiy, 1977.

180. Napoleon I, Emperor of the French. LETTERS AND DOCUMENTS. Selected and translated by John Eldred Howard. New York: Oxford University Press, 1961.

181. Napoleon I, Emperor of the French. LETTERS OF NAPOLEON TO JOSEPHINE. Complete collection, with preface by Dr. Leon Cerf. Translated by Henry W. Bunn. New York: Brentanto, 1931.

182. Napoleon I, Emperor of the French. LETTERS. Selected, translated, and edited by J.M. Thompson. London: Dent; New York: Dutton, 1954.

183. Napoleon I, Emperor of the French. LETTRES DE NAPOLEON A JOSEPHINE PENDANT LA PREMIERE CAMPAGNE D'ITALIE, LE CONSULAT ET L'EMPIRE; ET LETTRES DE JOSEPHINE A NAPOLEON ET A SA FILLE. Publiées par Mme. Salvage de Fayerolles. Paris: Firmin-Didot, 1833. 2 vols.

184. Napoleon I, Emperor of the French. "Lettres, ordres, et décrets de Napoléon Ier en 1812-1813-1814, non insérés dans la CORRESPONDANCE." Recueillis et publiés par M. le Vicomte de Grouchy. CARNET DE LA SABRETACHE 5 (1897): 4-19, 71-104, 219-34, 259-80.

185. Napoleon I, Emperor of the French. MEMOIRES ET OEUVRES DE NAPOLEON. ILLUSTRES D'APRES LES ESTAMPES ET LES TABLEAUX DU TEMPS PRECEDES D'UNE ETUDE LITTERAIRE. Paris: Librairie Nationale des beaux-arts, 1926.   .

186. Napoleon I, Emperor of the French. MEMOIRES ET OEUVRES DE NAPOLEON. Annotés par Tancrède Martel. Paris: A. Michel, 1910.

187. Napoleon I, Emperor of the French. MEMOIRES POUR SERVIR DE L'HISTOIRE DE LA CAMPAGNE DE 1812 EN RUSSIE; SUIVIS DES LETTRES DE NAPOLEON AU ROI WESTPHALIA PENDANT LA CAMPAGNE DE 1813. Par Albert Du Casse: Dumaine et Corréard, 1852.

188. Napoleon I, Emperor of the French. THE MIND OF NAPOLEON; A SELECTION FROM HIS WRITTEN AND SPOKEN WORDS. Edited and translated by J. Christopher Herold. New York: Columbia University Press, 1955.

189. Napoleon I, Emperor of the French. NAPOLEON AND MODERN WAR, HIS MILITARY MAXIMS. Revised and annotated by Conrad H. Lanza. Harrisburg, Pa.: Military Service Publishing Co., 1943.

190. Napoleon I, Emperor of the French. NAPOLEON PAR LUI-MEME. Textes choisis avec introduction et commentaires par Jules Romains. Paris: Perrin, 1936.

191. Napoleon I, Emperor of the French. NAPOLEON. SES OPINIONS ET JUGEMENS SUR LES HOMMES ET SUR LES CHOSES. Recueillis par ordre alphabetique, avec une introduction et des notes, par M. Damas-Hinard. Paris: Dufey, 1838. 2 vols.

192. Napoleon I, Emperor of the French. NAPOLEON'S MAXIMS OF WAR. With notes by General Burnod. Translated from the French by Lieutenant-General Sir G.C. D'Aguilar. Kansas City, Mo.: Hudson-Kimberly, n.d.

193. Napoleon I, Emperor of the French. NAPOLEON. TEXTES INEDITS
     ET VARIANTES. Publiés par Nada Tomiche Dagher. Geneva: Droz,
     1955.

194. Napoleon I, Emperor of the French. NEW LETTERS OF NAPOLEON I,
     OMITTED FROM THE EDITION PUBLISHED UNDER THE AUSPICES OF
     NAPOLEON III. From the French by Lady Mary Loyd. London:
     Heinemann, 1898.

195. Napoleon I, Emperor of the French. OEUVRES AMOUREUSES DE
     NAPOLEON D'APRES SES LETTERS D'AMOUR A JOSEPHINE. Avec une
     introduction et des notes du bibliophile Pol André. Paris: A.
     Michel, 1912.

196. Napoleon I, Emperor of the French. OEUVRES CHOISIES DE
     NAPOLEON. Mises en ordre et précédées d'une étude littéraire,
     par A. Pujol. Paris: Belin-Le Prieur, 1845.

197. Napoleon I, Emperor of the French. OEUVRES DE NAPOLEON.
     Paris: Panckoucke, 1821-22. 6 vols in 5.

198. Napoleon I, Emperor of the French. OUEVRES LITTERAIRES DE
     NAPOLEON BONAPARTE. Publiées d'après les originaux et les
     meilleurs textes, avec une introduction par Tancrède Martel.
     Paris: Savine, 1887-88. 4 vols.

199. Napoleon I, Emperor of the French. OEUVRES LITTERAIRES ET
     POLITIQUES DE NAPOLEON. Nouvelle édition. Paris: H.L.
     Delloye, 1840.

200. Napoleon I, Emperor of the French. THE OPINIONS AND
     REFLECTIONS OF NAPOLEON. Edited by Lewis Claflin Breed.
     Boston: Four Seas, 1926.

201. Napoleon I, Emperor of the French. PENSEES ET MAXIMES DE
     L'EMPEREUR, RECUEILLES DAN SES MEMOIRES ET SA CORRESPONDANCE
     PAR UNE OFFICIER GENERAL [Eugéne Alexandre Husson]. Paris:
     Dumain, 1852.

202. Napoleon I, Emperor of the French. LE REGISTRE DE L'ILE
     D'ELBE. LETTRES ET ORDRES INEDITS DE NAPOLEON Ier, 28 MAI
     1814-22 FEVRIER 1815. Publiés par Léon G. Pelissier. Paris:
     Fontemoing, 1897.

203. Napoleon I, Emperor of the French. A SELECTION FROM THE
     LETTERS AND DESPATCHES FROM THE FIRST NAPOLEON. With
     explanatory notes by D.A. Bingham. London: Chapman, 1884.

204. Napoleon I, Emperor of the French. THE TABLE TALK AND OPINIONS
     OF NAPOLEON BUONAPARTE. Philadelphia: Porter and Coates,
     1889.

205. Napoleon I, Emperor of the French. TEXTES CHOISIS ET COMMENTS
     PAR E. GUILLON. Paris, Plon-Nouritt, 1912.

206. Napoleon I, Emperor of the French. UNPUBLISHED CORRESPONDENCE OF NAPOLEON I, PRESERVED IN THE WAR ARCHIVES. Published by Ernest Picard ... and Louis Tuetey. Translated by Louis Seymour Houghton. New York: Duffield, 1913. 3 vols.

207. Napoleon I, Emperor of the French. VIRILITES: MAXIMES ET PENSEES. Avec une introduction par Jules Bertaut. Paris: Sansot, 1912.

208. NAPOLEON ET SON TEMPS. EXPOSITION ORGANISEE PAR L'AIDE AUX FAMILLES NOMBREUSES ... MUSEE DE PEINTURE DE ROUEN DE 19 MAI AU 15 JUILLET 1934. Catalogue. Rouen: Lecerf, 1934.

209. THE NATIONAL UNION CATALOGUE. New York: Mansell, 1968-82. 754 vols. (in progress).

210. NORSK BOK-FOTEGNELSE, 1814-1847. Christiania: Feilberg and Landmarks, 1814-.

211. Norvins, Jacques Marquet de, baron de Montbreton. HISTOIRE DE NAPOLEON. Paris: Furne, 1833. 4 vols.

212. NOUVELLE BIOGRAPHIE GENERALE DEPUIS LES TEMPS LES PLUS RECULES JUSQU'A NOS JOURS, AVEC LES RENSEIGNEMENTS BIBLIOGRAPHIQUES ET L'INDICATION DES SOURCES CONSULTER. Publiée par MM. Firmin-Didot frères, sous le direction de M. le Dr. Hoefer. Paris: Firmin-Didot, 1855-66. 46 vols.

213. Pagliaini, Attilio. CATALOGO GENERALE DELLA LIBRERIA ITALIANA 1847-99; and SUPPLEMENTOS 1900-1940. Milan: Tipografico Libraira Italiana, 1901-40.

214. Palau y Dulcet, Antonio. MANUAL DE LIBRERO HISPANO-AMERICANO. Barcelona: Palu, 1948.

215. Palmer, Alan. AN ENCYLOPEDIA OF NAPOLEON'S EUROPE. London: Weidenfeld and Nicholson, 1984.

216. Perrot, Aristide Michel. ITINERAIRE GENERAL DE NAPOLEON, CHRONOLOGIE DU CONSULAT ET DE L'EMPIRE, INDIQUANT JOUR PAR JOUR, PENDANT TOUTE SA VIE, LE LIEU OU ETAIT NAPOLEON, CE QU'IL A FAIT, ET LES EVENEMENTS LES PLUS REMARQUABLES QUI SE RATTACHENT A SON HISTOIRE, etc. Paris: Bistor, 1845.

217. Phipps, Ramsey. THE ARMIES OF THE FIRST FRENCH REPUBLIC AND THE RISE OF THE MARSHALS OF THE MARSHALS OF NAPOLEON I. London: Oxford University Press, 1926-39. 5 vols.

218. Picard, Louis. LA CAVALERIE DANS LES GUERRES DE LA REVOLUTION ET DE L'EMPIRE. Saumur: Milon, 1895-96. 2 vols.

219. Picard, Ernset, ed. PRECEPTES ET JUGEMENTS DE NAPOLEON. Paris and Nancy: Berger-Levrault, 1913.

220. Pingaud, Leonce. UN AGENT SECRET SOUS LA REVOLUTION ET
     L'EMPIRE: LE COMTE D'ANTRAGIGUES. Paris: Plon, Nourrit,
     1893.

221. PUBLICISTE.

222. Quennevat, Jean Claude. ATLAS DE LA GRANDE ARMEE, NAPOLEON ET
     SES CAMPAGNES, 1803-1815. Paris and Brussels: Sequoia, 1966.

223. Régnault, Jean Charles Louis. LES AIGLES IMPERIALES ET LE
     DRAPEAU TRICOLORE, 1804-1815. Preface par André Masséna.
     Paris: Peyronnet, 1967.

224. REIMPRESSION DE L'ANCIENNE MONITEUR SEULE HISTOIRE AUTHENTIQUE
     ET INALTEREE (1789-1799). Paris: Plon, 1858-63. 32 vols.

225. Richardson, Hubert N.B. A DICTONARY OF NAPOLEON AND HIS TIMES.
     London and New York: Cassell, 1920.

226. Robinet, Jean François Eugène. DICTIONNAIRE, HISTORIQUE ET
     BIOGRAPHIQUE, DE LA REVOLUTION ET DE L'EMPIRE, 1789-1815.
     Paris: Librairie historique de la Révolution et de l'Empire,
     1899. 2 vols.

227. Rose, John Holland. THE LIFE OF NAPOLEON I, INCLUDING NEW
     MATERIALS FROM THE BRITISH OFFICIAL RECORDS. New York:
     Macmillan, 1907. 2 vols.

228. Ross, Steven T. EUROPEAN DIPLOMATIC HISTORY 1789-1815; FRANCE
     AGAINST EUROPE. Garden City, N.Y.: Doubleday, 1969.

229. Sauzey, Camile. LES ALLEMAGNES SOUS LES AIGLES FRANCAISE.
     Paris: Chapelot, 1902-12. 6 vols.

230. Sauzey. ICONOGRAPHIE DU COSTUME MILITAIRE DE LA REVOLUTION ET
     DE L'EMPIRE. Paris: Dubois, 1901. Vol. 1.

231. Savant, Jean, ed. NAPOLEON IN HIS TIME. Translated from the
     French by Katherine John. New York: Nelson, 1958.

232. Schlosser, F.C. GESCHICHTE DES 18. JAHRHUNDERTS UND 19. BIS
     ZUM STURZ DES FRANZOESISCHEN KAISERREICH. Heidelberg: Mohr,
     1846-49. 7 vols.

233. Schmidt, Charles. LES SOURCES DE L'HISTOIRE DE FRANCE DEPUIS
     1789 AUX ARCHIVES NATIONALES. Paris: Champion, 1907.

234. Schuermans, Albert. ITINERAIRE GENERAL DE NAPOLEON Ier.
     Preface par Henry Houssaye. Paris: A. Picard, 1908.

235. Schulz, Oberst Gustav von. GESCHICHTE DER KRIEGE IN EUROPA
     SEIT DEM JAHRE DE 1792.... Leipzig and Berlin: Brockhaus,
     1827-53. 15 vols. in 23.

236. SCHWEIZER   BUECHERVERZEICHNIS.   Zurich: Verlag   des
     Schweizerischen buchhandler, 1951-.

237. Six, Georges.   DICTIONNAIRE BIOGRAPHIQUE DES GENERAUX ET
     AMIRAUX FRANCAIS DE LA REVOLUTION ET DE L'EMPIRE (1792-1814).
     Préface par le commandant André Lasseray. Paris: G. Saffroy,
     1934. 2 vols.

238. Six, Georges. LES GENERAUX DE LA REVOLUTION ET DE L'EMPIRE.
     Paris: Bordas, 1948.

239. Sjostrom, Ivar L.   HANDBOOK   OF   NAPOLEON   BONAPARTE.
     Philadelphia: Dorrance, 1928.

240. Sloane, William Milligan. LIFE OF NAPOLEON BONAPARTE. New
     York: Century, 1896. 4 vols.

241. Sorel, Albert Emile Edouard.   L'EUROPE ET LA REVOLUTION
     FRANCAISE. Paris: Plon-Nourrit, 1907-18. 8 vols.

242. Stewart, John Hall. FRANCE, 1715-1815; A GUIDE TO MATERIALS IN
     CLEVELAND, BEING A REPRESENTATIVE SELECTION FROM THE PRINCIPAL
     HOLDINGS OF THE LIBRARIES OF WESTERN RESERVE UNIVERSITY.   THE
     CLEVELAND PUBLIC LIBRARY, AND THE WESTERN RESERVE HISTORICAL
     SOCIETY. Cleveland: Western Reserve University Press, 1942.

243. Susane, Louis Auguste. HISTOIRE DE LA CAVALERIE FRANCAISE.
     Paris: Hetzel, 1874. 3 vols.

244. SVENSK   BOKFOERTECKNING.   Stockholm: Titningsaktiebolaget,
     1953-.

245. SVENSK BOKKATAGLO FOER AAREN 1866-1875. Stockholm: Samson and
     Wallin, 1866-1965.

246. Sybel, Heinrich Karl von. GESCHICHTE DER REVOLUTIONSZEIT VON
     1789-1800. Stuttgart: Ebner and Seubert, 1874-89. 3 vols.

247. Taylor, Alan Carey. BIBLIOGRAPHY OF UNPUBLISHED THESES ON
     FRENCH SUBJECTS DEPOSITED IN UNIVERSITY LIBRARIES OF THE UNITED
     KINGDOM (1905-1950). Oxford: Blackwell, 1964.

248. Thibaudeau, Antoine Claire, comte. LE CONSULAT ET L'EMPIRE OU
     HISTOIRE DE LA FRANCE ET DE NAPOLEON BONAPARTE DE 1799 A 1815.
     Paris: J. Renouard, 1834-35. 10 vols.

249. Thiers, Louis Adolphe. HISTORY OF THE CONSULATE AND THE EMPIRE
     OF FRANCE UNDER NAPOLEON. Translarted by D. Forbes Campbell
     and John Stebbing. London: Chatto and Windus, 1893-94.   12
     vols.

250. Thomas, Daniel H., and Lynn M. Case, eds.   GUIDE TO THE
     DIPLOMATIC   ARCHIVES   OF   WESTERN   EUROPE.   Philadelphia:
     University of Pennsylvania Press, 1959.

251. Titeux, Eugéne. SAINT-CYR ET L'ECOLE SPECIALE MILITAIRE EN FRANCE: FONTAINEBLEAU, SAINT-GERMAIN. Paris: Didot, 1898.

252. Tulard, Jean. BIBLIOGRAPHIE CRITIQUE DES MEMOIRES SUR LE CONSULAT ET L'EMPIRE, ECRITS OU TRADUITS EN FRANCAIS. Geneva: Droz, 1971.

253. Tulard, Jean. LA VIE QUOTIDIENNE DES FRANCAIS SOUS NAPOLEON. Paris: Hachette, 1978.

254. THE UNEQUALLED COLLECTION RELATIVE TO NAPOLEON AND THE FRENCH REVOLUTION OF WILLIAM LATTA OF PHILADELPHIA, PA. New York: Metropolitan Art Association, 1913. 4 parts.

255. Valynseele, Joseph. LES PRINCES ET DUCS DU PREMIER EMPIRE, NON MARECHAUX; LEUR FAMILLE ET LEUR DESCENDANCE. Avec une préface de Marcel Dunan. Paris: n.p., 1959.

256. Vidier, A., and Paul B. Perrier. Bibliothéque Nationale. Departement des manuscrits. CATALOGUE GENERAL DES MANUSCRITS FRANCAIS. Paris: Leroux, 1931. 6 vols.

257. Villat, Louis. LA REVOLUTION ET L'EMPIRE (1789-1815). Paris: Presses Universitaires de France, 1936, 1942. 2 vols.

258. Villemain, Abel François. NAPOLEON ET L'EUROPE EXPLIQUE PAR LUI-MEME, 1812-13. Paris: Stock, Delamain et Boutelleau, 1947.

259. Whitcomb, Edward. NAPOLEON'S DIPLOMATIC SERVICE. Durham, N.C.: Duke University Press, 1979.

260. White, Arthur S. A BIBLIOGRAPHY OF REGIMENTAL HISTORIES OF THE BRITISH ARMY. London: Society for Army Historical Research, 1965.

261. Yorck von Wartenburg, Maximilian, graf. NAPOLEON AS A GENERAL. London: Gilbert and Rivington, 1902. 2 vols.

PERIODICALS

262. AMERICAN HISTORICAL REVIEW. 1895 to present.

263. LES ANNALES NAPOLEONIENNE. [Puis REVUE D'ETUDES HISTORIQUES ET POLITIQUES]. 1905-29.

264. ANNALES HISTORIQUES DE LA REVOLUTION FRANCAISE. 1924 to present.

265. ANNALES REVOLUTIONNAIRES. 1908-1923.

266. BOLLETANO DI CENTRO DI STUDI NAPOLEONICI DE DI STORIA DELL'ELBA. 1962-64.

267. LE BRIQUET. 1959 to present.

268. BULLETIN DE L'INSTITUT NAPOLEON. 1934-37.

269. BULLETIN DE LA SOCIETE LITTERAIRE ET HISTORIQUE DE LA BRIE. 1897 to present.

270. BULLETIN DU MUSEE BERNADOTTE.

271. BULLETIN HISTORIQUE DE LA SOCIETE DE SAUVEGARDE DU CHATEAU IMPERIAL DE PONT-DE-BRIQUES. 1969 to present.

272. BULLETIN, SOCIETE BELGE D'ETUDES NAPOLEONIENNES. 1950-75.

273. LA CARNET DE LA SABRETACHE. 1893 to present.

274. FRENCH HISTORICAL STUDIES. 1958 to present.

275. HISTORY TODAY. 1951 to present.

276. ILLUSTRATION MILITAIRE. 1862-70.

277. IRISH SWORD. 1949 to present.

278. JOURNAL DES SCIENCE MILITAIRE DES ARMEES DE TERRE ET DE MER. 1825-1914.

279. THE JOURNAL OF THE ROYAL ARTILLERY. 1858 to present.

280. MARINER'S MIRROR. 1861 to present.

281. MILITARY AFFAIRS. THE JOURNAL OF MILITARY HISTORY INCLUDING THEORY AND TECHNOLOGY. 1933 to present.

282. MIRROR DE L'HISTOIRE. 1950 to present.

283. MONITEUR DE L'ARMEE. 1840-93.

284. NAVAL WAR COLLEGE REVIEW. 1948 to present.

285. PROCEEDINGS OF THE CONSORTIUM ON REVOLUTIONARY EUROPE 1750-1850. 1972 to present.

286. PROCEEDINGS OF THE WESTERN SOCIETY FOR FRENCH HISTORY. 1973 to present.

287. REVUE D'HISTOIRE. REDIGEE A L'ETAT-MAJOR DE L'ARMEE. SECTION HISTORIQUE. 1901-14.

288. REVUE D'HISTOIRE DIPLOMATIQUE. 1887 to present.

289. REVUE D'HISTOIRE MODERNE. 1926-51.

290. REVUE D'HISTOIRE MODERNE ET CONTEMPORAINE. 1954 to present.

291. REVUE D'INFANTRIE. 1887-1939.

292. REVUE DE L'INSTITUT NAPOLEON. 1938-40; 1948 to present.

293. REVUE DE CAVALERIE. 1885-1939.

294. REVUE DE LA SOCIETE DES AMIS DU MUSEE DE L'ARMEE. 1905 to present.

295. REVUE DES DEUX MONDES. 1819-1830.

296. LA REVUE [DES DEUX MONDES]. 1831 to present.

297. REVUE DES ETUDES NAPOLEONIENNES. 1912-40.

298. REVUE DES QUESTIONS HISTORIQUES. 1866-1939.

299. REVUE DES SOCIETES DES AMIS DE VERSAILLES.

300. REVUE DU GENIE MILITAIRE.

301. REVUE DU NORD. 1910-50.

302. REVUE HISTORIQUE. 1876-1950.

303. REVUE HISTORIQUE DE L'ARMEE. 1945 to present.

304. REVUE MARITIME. 1861 to present.

305. REVUE MILITAIRE FRANCAISE. 1921-36.

306. REVUE MILITAIRE. 1899-1900.

307. REVUE MILITAIRE DE L'ETRANGERES. 1872-98.

308. REVUE MILITAIRE DES ARMEES ETRANGERES. 1901-14.

309. REVUE NAPOLEONIENNE. 1901-12.

310. RIVISTA ITALIANA DI STUDI NAPOLEONICI. 1965 to present.

311. THE ROYAL UNITED SERVICE INSTITUTION MAGAZINE. 1888 to present.

312. SOCIETY FOR ARMY HISTORICAL RESEARCH. 1921 to present.

313. SOUVENIR NAPOLEONIEN. 1937 to present.

314. SOUVENIR NAPOLEONIEN (SECTION CANADIENNE). 1974 to present.

315. LE SPECTATEUR MILITAIRE. 1826-99.

316. UNITED STATES NAVAL INSTITUTE PROCEEDINGS. 1874 to present.

317. LE VETERAN, JOURNAL DU TEMPS PASSE. 1939-[?].

318. VIVAT HUSSAR. 1966 to present.

319. WAR AND SOCIETY NEWSLETTER. Edited by Geoffrey Best et al. Freiburg: Militärgeschichtliches   Forschungsamt.   1973   to present.

CHAPTER II

ARMIES OF THE NAPOLEONIC PERIOD

Steven T. Ross, U.S. Naval War College

Carl von Clausewitz in ON WAR wrote about war's grammar and logic. The logic, he asserted, was a function of the state's policy. Rulers and statesmen set war's scope, intensity, and political objectives. War then was an instrument, a means rather than an end in itself. The grammar of war included such factors as military structure and organization, combat doctrine, battle tactics, and strategy. War's means, of course, had a significant relationship to the ends of statecraft. Defeat, for example, might compel the state to abandon its objectives and seek peace. Defeat might, on the other hand, force the state to devote greater resources to the conflict and expand the objectives. Victory on the battlefield had a similar impact. A nation's leaders might seek to terminate a conflict immediately or triumphs might encourage them to demand greater sacrifices from the enemy. The means-ends relationship was, therefore, not static or constant, rather the relationship was dynamic, and statecraft and strategy were factors that constantly influenced each other.

Clausewitz also noted that the way armies organized, trained, and fought was a political and social phenomenon. Armies resembled and reflected the societies that created them. ·An Old Regime government, for example, could not seriously contemplate creating a levée en masse because its population was composed of subjects not citizens who felt that they had a personal stake in the regime's survival. The Revolution could unleash the energies of its entire populace precisely because it altered the political and social basis of the state. Military evolution thus reflects broader patterns of social development.

GENERAL WORKS

Within the framework of larger social, economic, and political evolution, statesmen and generals seek to organize and direct their armed forces. A number of historians have sought to examine military organizations within the larger context and have recognized the Revolutionary and Napoleonic era as a major watershed.

Hans Delbrück's (62) study, though somewhat dated, remains an essential work for any scholar who seeks to understand how and why warfare evolved. Delbrück, in a sense, established the study of warfare as a discipline that involved more than a description of battles. More recently, Theodore K. Ropp's book (170) has become an essential work. He describes the evolution of warfare since the Renaissance and notes the impact of both technology and social change on the nature of both tactics and strategy. Edward M. Earle (70) edited a study that takes a slightly different approach. It traces the evolution of war by examining important individuals and their particular impact. Robert R. Palmer's essay vividly illustrates the change from dynastic to national warfare by examining the life and work of Guibert and Bulow. Earle's book also contains excellent though dated essays on Jomini and Clausewitz, the chief interpreters

of Napoleon's impact on war's nature and conduct. Michael Howard
(112) and David Chandler (53) have also written excellent studies of
the evolution of warfare. Howard's approach is more thematic than
Chandler's. Chandler's work is oriented toward changes in
operational and strategic concepts, but both works are valuable for
an understanding of how and why war evolved as it did and for the
role played by the French Revolution and Napoleon. Other studies of
this nature include works by Alfred Vagts (202), Gordon B. Turner
(200), Quincy Wright (215), and Hoffman L. Nickerson (148).

Weapons systems and tactical doctrine play a crucial role in
battle. Furthermore, the two are inexorably linked. The range,
accuracy, and lethality of weapons of necessity influences the nature
of military formations and tactics. The introduction of artillery,
for example, put an end to the medieval system of fortifications, and
the musket ended the useful role of the pike on the field of battle.
Old Regime armies devised a linear style battle formation in order to
achieve massed firepower. Reformers tried to devise ways to attain
increased flexibility, and some of their ideas were then adopted by
the Revolutionary and Napoleonic armies. Coupled with particular
revolutionary innovations, the French armies became the most
effective in Europe and other states had to initiate reforms in order
to meet them on even terms.

SPECIALIZED WORKS: TACTICS

Jean Colin's (58) study of the transformation of war is one of
the first to examine the development of tactical doctrine. Colin
tends to emphasize the continuity between the tactics of the Old
Regime and the Revolution, clearly demonstrating the evolutionary
links between the two styles of warfare. Robert Quimby's (163) study
of pre-revolutionary military thinkers closely follows Colin's
original argument. Spencer Wilkinson's (211, 212) two studies on the
French army also seeks to establish links between the Old Regime
method of operations and Napoleonic tactics. G.F.R. Henderson's
(105) older study also emphasizes the evolution of weaponry and
tactical doctrine. Robert Home's (111) study of tactics is another
older work that still retains its usefulness.

There are also a number of studies that examine the tactics of
the individual service armies. A.L. Wagner's (209) book deals
effectively with the development of infantry tactics. Steven T. Ross
(171) and John Lynn (135) have also explored the changes in infantry
tactical doctrine produced by the Revolution. In varying degrees,
all three authors also attempt to distinguish the unique contribution
of the Revolution to infantry methods. T. Denison's (63) history of
cavalry, though dated, is still useful, as is Gaston Andlau's (4)
study of the mounted armies. B.P. Hughes's (113) study of firepower
lethality provides valuable data on weaponry, especially artillery.
Matti Laverma's (128) history of Revolutionary and Napoleonic
artillery also provides excellent background on the development of
artillery during the Old Regime. Claude Blair (25), Louis Napoléon
(30) and Ildephonse Favé (71, 72), and O.F.G. Hogg (110) have also
written useful studies on the development of artillery. Hermann von
Müller's work on siege warfare (146) and Albert C. Manucy's (136)
history of artillery are also valuable. Q. Hughes's (114) history
of military fortifications is well illustrated and useful. Siege

warfare was still important during the Revolutionary and Napoleonic wars; Bonaparte's Italian Campaign, for example, hinged on the siege of Mantua. Christopher Duffy's (66) study of fortress warfare provides useful insights into the complexities of this variety of combat.

SPECIALIZED STUDIES: THE NATIONAL ARMIES

Histories of particular national armies provide details about organization tactics and strategy, and allow scholars to examine the broader questions of military development within specific contexts.

J. Revol (165) and Marshal Maxine Weygand (210) have each written general histories of the French army. Patriotism and respect for the professional officer class influence both works, but the two books do provide a good general overview of the French army's history. David Chandler's (54) study of Napoleon's campaigns is more than a battle narrative. Chandler's book contains a wealth of information on the organization, administration, and tactical doctrine of the Republican and Napoleonic forces. R.W. Phipps's (157) five-volume study of the armies of the First Republic also provides useful insights into the questions of organization and administration. Phipps rationally covers the activities of the Army of Italy, Bonaparte's first major command. Otto von Pivka (160) and H.C.B. Rogers (168) have each written useful books on the Napoleonic era. Both books provide detailed order of battle data on the French and other armies. Louis Susane wrote a five-volume history of the artillery (193). All of his works (193-195) are replete with administrative and organizational detail. Emile Bourdeau's (34) three-volume work on campaigns has much valuable detail on tactics, and Belhomme's (17) history of the infantry contains valuable order of battle data. Edouard Desbrière and Maurice Sautai (65) wrote a four-volume study on French cavalry up to 1799; Louis Picard's (158) two-volume history of cavalry is excellent, and David Johnson (119) did a popular but sound study on Napoleon's cavalry. Colonel Augoyat (10) and Henri M.A. Berthaud (21) have each written a detailed multivolume on the engineers and Xavier Audouin's (9) old book on administration is still useful. L.J. Bégin (16), L.R.M. Brice (36), and Maurice Bottet (32, 36) have written studies on the medical corps.

There are a number of useful studies on the French army's personnel. Georges Six (189) has done an excellent book on French officers in which he examines their social origins and military backgrounds. Marcel Baldet (11) has written about the rank and file, but more work remains to be done in this area. There are some useful studies on recruiting. Guy d'Agauche (1) did a sound general study on recruiting, and the Historical Section of the French General Staff has done one on the development of conscription laws (75). The French General Staff also did a volume on army organization (77) which has data on personnel and recruiting. Joseph Vidal's (206) study of desertion is useful. There are as well numerous studies of recruiting in specific areas. Among the more useful are Gustave Vallée (203) on the Charênte and Roger Darquenne (61) on the department of Jemappes. Isser Woloch (213) has a first-rate work on French veterans and Fred and Liliane Funcken (84) have an excellent two-volume book on military uniforms. Hippolyte Bellange (18), L. de

Bouillé (33), and Alex Cart (51) have also produced studies of French uniforms and banners. Pierre Chalmin (52) has a good summary article on military education in France, while Eugène Fieffé (73) has written a two-volume work on foreign troops in French service.

John Fortescue's (74) massive nineteen-volume study is the standard history of the British army, largely a history of campaigns and battles. Fortescue's work also includes much detail on administration, organization, and tactics. Correlli Barnett (14) and Peter Young (216) have each done single-volume histories that give greater emphasis to social and political factors.

Charles W. Oman's older book (149) on Wellington's army provides an excellent picture of the structure and organization of British forces in Iberia. They were at least in part the product of several years of intensive reform efforts. J.F.C. Fuller (81, 83) has written two studies, perhaps his best works, on aspects of the reform of the British army, one dealing with the evolution of light infantry up to the Napoleonic era and the other with the work of Sir John Moore. Fuller emphasizes the requirement for more flexible doctrine needed to meet the French innovations in warfare. Richard Glover (94) has also done an excellent book on British military reforms. He demonstrates that when Wellington took command in Spain, the British army had already begun to accommodate itself to French tactics and was a very different force from the regiments that had been defeated in earlier campaigns in the Low Countries.

The Hapsburg army also had to devise methods to cope with French armies. Given the nature of the regime, it could not undertake drastic reforms to provide a new basis for raising and training land forces. The Austrians, therefore, undertook marginal adjustments in tactical methods and organization. Alphons von Wrede's (214) five-volume history of the Austrian army is a basic work. Like Fortescue, the primary interest is battles, leaders, and campaigns, but Wrede also supplies information on the army's structural evolution. J.B. Schels (179), Hermann Meynert (141), and Oscar Teuber (196) have also done sound histories of the Austrian army. Gunther Rothenberg (172-174) has written a number of studies on the Hapsburg armed forces in which he emphasizes Vienna's efforts to adjust to the changes in warfare wrought by the Revolution and Napoleon. Oskar Regele (164) has written ably about Austria's efforts to provide strategic direction of its field commanders.

Curt Jany's (117) four-volume history is the standard work on the Prussian army. Although he has almost unbounded admiration for the officer corps, his work is replete with data on the army's evolution. C.F. Gumtau's (97) three-volume study of Prussian light infantry is also very useful. The Historical Section of the General Staff produced several volumes on the Prussian army's operational history (89). Accurate and detailed, the volumes also provide a wealth of information on organizational and tactical evolution. W.O. Shanahan (183) and W. Hahlweg (98) have each written useful studies of the Prussian reform effort. Both authors indicate that military changes indeed stemmed from a broader effort and political and social reform, and that Prussia, in fact, succeeded in creating a genuine mass-conscript army. Peter Paret's (151) biography of Yorck is more than that. It is also a fine study of the evolution of light infantry in Prussia. Paret points out that by 1813, the Prussian's had a larger percentage of light infantrymen in their forces than

Napoleon had in his. Reinhard Sautermeister (176) has also written a useful study of Prussian tactical reform.

There are a number of sound studies of the armies of other German states. Sichart (187) has worked on the Hanovarian army, Muller and Braun (147) on the Bavarian army, and O. Schuster and F.A. Franke (181) on the Saxon forces. Though basically sound, all of these studies are old and scholars should find it rewarding to study the armed forces of the lesser German states incorporating the latest research and concepts into their work.

FUTURE RESEARCH

The Napoleonic era indeed marked significant changes in the art and organization of war. French military reforms forced other powers to respond. Although the literature of the era is large, there is still room for additional contributions. Despite the tremendous number of volumes dealing with Napoleonic armies there remain a number of areas for important research efforts. Studies of junior officers and NCO's could make a vital contribution to a greater understanding of the Imperial army. Studies of how small units operated would provide a basis upon which to construct a broader view of the internal mechanisms of the army. Studies of morale in Napoleon's forces would enable scholars to determine how motivation in the Republican armies resembled or differed from factors that contributed to the animating spirit of Imperial formations. An examination of French logistics would enable historians to go beyond common generalizations in their explanation of the Imperial supply system. Similar approaches could be usefully done on the forces of the Rhine Confederation, the Kingdoms of Italy and Naples, and the Grand Duchy of Warsaw. Thus much work remains to be done and scholars can find topics that are both interesting and useful.

BIBLIOGRAPHY: ARMIES OF THE PERIOD

1. Agauche, Guy d'. LE RECRUTEMENT DE L'ARMEE FRANCAISE. Mayenne, 1894.

2. Allix, Jacques Alexandre. SYSTEME D'ARTILLERIE DE CAMPAGNE. Paris: Anselin et Pochard, 1827.

3. Ambert, Joachim. ESQUISSES HISTORIQUES DES DIFFERNS CORPS QUI COMPOSENT L'ARMEE FRANCAISE. Samur: A. Degouy, 1835.

4. Andlau, Gaston, comte d'. DE LA CAVALERIE DANS LE PASSE ET DANS L'AVENIR. Paris: Bureau de la revue militaire français, 1869.

5. Andlau, Gaston, comte d'. ORGANISATION ET TACTIQUE DE L'INFANTERIE FRANCAISE DEPUIS SON ORIGINE JUSQU'A L'EPOQUE ACTUELLE. Paris: Dumaine, 1872.

6. Andolenko, Serge. HISTOIRE DE L'ARMEE RUSSE. Paris: Flammarion, 1967.

7. Andolenko, Serge. RECUEIL D'HISTORIQUES DE L'INFANTERIE FRANCAISE. Paris: Eurimprim, 1969.

8. Apffell, Général. "L'artillerie lourde de campagne au XVIIIe siècle (de Vallière à Bonaparte)." REVUE D'ARTILLERIE 115 (1935): 485-91.

9. Audouin, Xavier. HISTOIRE DE L'ADMINISTRATION DE LA GUERRE. Paris: Didot, 1811. 4 vols.

10. Augoyat, Antoine Marie. APERCU HISTORIQUE SUR LES FORTIFICATIONS, LES INGENIEURS ET SUR LE CORPS DU GENIE EN FRANCE. Paris: Dumaine, 1860-64. 3 vols.

11. Baldet, Marcel. LA VIE QUOTIDIENNE DANS LES ARMEES DE NAPOLEON. Paris: Hachette, 1964.

12. Bardin, [Etienne Alexandre], baron. DICTIONNAIRE DE L'ARMEE DE TERRE; OU, RECHERCHES HISTORIQUES SUR L'ART ET LES USAGES MILITAIRES DES ANCIENS ET DES MODERNES. Paris: Corréard, 1841. 8 vols.

13. Barnes, Robert Money. A HISTORY OF THE REGIMENTS AND UNIFORMS OF THE BRITISH ARMY. London: Seeley, 1950.

14. Barnett, Correlli. BRITAIN AND HER ARMY, 1509-1970. New York: Morrow, 1970.

15. Basset, M.A. "Essais sur l'historique des fabrications d'armement en France jusqu'au milieu du XVIIIe siècle." MEMOIRAL DE L'ARTILLERIE 14 (1935): 880-1280.

16. Bégin, Louis Jacques. ETUDES SUR LE SERVICE DE SANTE MILITAIRE EN FRANCE, SON PASSE, SON PRESENT, SON AVENIR. Paris: Ballière, 1849.

17. Belhomme, Victor Louis Jean. HISTOIRE DE L'INFANTERIE EN FRANCE. Paris: Charles-Lavauzelle, 1893-1902. 5 vols.

18. Bellange, Hippolyte. DIE SOLDATEN DER FRANZOESISCHEN REPUBLIK UND DES KAISERREICHS. Leipzig: Weber, 1842.

19. Bernard, Henri. DE MARATHON A HIROSHIMA: VINGT-CINQ SIECLES DE L'ART ET DE PENSEE MILITAIRES. Brussels: Imprimerie médicale et scientifique, 1948-49. 3 vols.

20. Bernard, Henri. LA GUERRE ET SON EVOLUTION A TRAVERS LES SIECLES. Brussels: Imprimerie médicale et scientifique, 1955-57. 2 vols.

21. Berthaud, Henri Marie Auguste. LES INGENIEURS GEOGRAPHES MILITAIRES 1624-1831, ETUDES HISTORIQUE. Paris: Imprimerie service géographie, 1902. 2 vols.

22. Beskrovnyi, L.G. OCHERKI PO ISTOCHNIKOVEDENIYU ISTORII ROSSI. Moscow: Akad. nauk SSSR, 1957.

23. Beskrovnyi, L.G. RUSSKAYA ARMIYA I FLOT V XVIII VEKE. Moscow: Akad. nauk SSSR, 1958.

24. Bezzel, Oskar. DIE GESCHICHTE DES KURPFAELZBAYERISCHEN HEERES. Munich: Schick, 1930. 8 vols.

25. Blair, Claude. EUROPEAN AND AMERICAN ARMS. London: Batsford, 1962.

26. Bleckwenn, Hans. DAS ALTPREUSSISCHE HEER; ERSCHEINUNGSBILD UND WESEN, 1713-1807. Osnabrück: Biblio Verlag, 1969.

27. Blin, E.C.H. HISTOIRE DE L'ORGANISATION ET DE LA TACTIQUE DES DIFFERENTES ARMES DE 1610 A NOS JOURS. Paris: Charles Lavauzelle, 1931.

28. Blumental, Maximilian. DER PREUSSISCHE LANDSTURM VON 1813. Berlin: Schröder, 1900.

29. Bodart, Gaston. MITITAER-HISTORISCHES KRIEGS-LEXIKON (1618-1905). Vienna and Leipzig: C.W. Stern, 1908.

30. Bonaparte, Louis N., and Ildephonse Favé. ETUDES SUR LE PASSE ET L'AVENIR DE L'ARTILLERIE. Paris: Dumaine, 1846-71. 6 vols.

31. Bonnal, Henri. L'ESPRIT DE LA GUERRE MODERNE; DE ROSBACH A ULM. Paris: Chapelot, 1903.

32. Bottet, Maurice. MONOGRAPHIE DE L'ARME A FEU PORTATIVE DES ARMEES FRANCAISES DE TERRE ET DE MER, DE 1718 A NOS JOURS. Paris: Flammarion, 1905.

33. Bouillé, L. de. LES DRAPEAUX FRANCAIS, ETUDE HISTORIQUE. Paris: Dumiane, 1875.

34. Bourdeau, Emile. CAMPAGNES MODERNES. Paris: Charles-Lavauzelle, 1912-1921. 3 vols.

35. Boutmy de Bavelaer, Henry de. L'UNIFORME FRANCAIS DE LOUVOIS A NOS JOURS. Paris: Chez l'auteur, 1937.

36. Brice, Léon Raoul Marie, and Maurice Bottet. LE CORPS DE SANTE MILITAIRE EN FRANCE, SON EVOLUTION--SON CAMPAGNES, 1708-1882. Paris and Nancy: Berger-Levrault, 1907.

37. Brunet, Jean Baptiste. HISTOIRE GENERALE DE L'ARTILLERIE. Paris: Angelin, 1842. 2 vols.

38. Buat, Edmond. L'ARTILLERIE DE CAMPAGNE; SON HISTOIRE--SON EVOLUTION--SON ETAT ACTUEL. Paris: Alcan, 1911.

39. Büsch, Otto. MILITAERSYSTEM UND SOZIALLEBEN IM ALTEN PREUSSEN, 1713-1807. Berlin: De Gruyter, 1962.

40. Buturlin, Dimitrii. HISTOIRE DES CAMPAGNES DES RUSSES AU 18ème SIECLE. St. Petersburg, 1819-21.

41. Cabanès, Augustin. CHIRURGIENS ET BLESSES A TRAVER L'HISTOIRE DES ORIGINES A LA CROIX-ROUGE. Paris: A. Michel, 1918.

42. Camon, Hubert. LA GUERRE NAPOLEONIENNE. Paris: Chapelot, 1903-10. 5 vols.

43. Camon, Hubert. QUAND ET COMMENT NAPOLEON A CONCU SON SYSTEME DE BATAILLE. Paris: Berger-Levrault, 1935.

44. Camon, Hubert. LA SYSTEME DE GUERRE DE NAPOLEON. Paris: Berger-Levrault, 1923.

45. Campana, Ignace Raphaël. L'ARTILLERIE DE CAMPAGNE, 1792-1901. Paris: Berger-Levrault, 1901.

46. Canby, Courtlandt. HISTOIRE DE L'ARMEMENT. Lausanne: Rencontre, 1963.

47. Canski, Josef. TABLEAU STATISTIQUE, POLITIQUE, ET MORAL DU SYSTEME MILITAIRE DE LA RUSSIE. Paris: Heidloeff et Campé, 1833.

48. Carman, W.Y. A HISTORY OF FIREARMS FROM EARLIEST TIMES TO 1914. London: Routledge and Paul, 1955.

49. Carrias, Eugène. L'ARMEE ALLEMANDE, SON HISTOIRE, SON ORGANISATION, SA TACTIQUE. Paris: Presses Universitaires de France, 1938.

50. Carrion-Nisas, Marie Henri, marquis de. ESSAI SUR L'HISTOIRE GENERAL DE L'ART MILITAIRE, DE SON ORIGINE, DE SES PROGRES ET DE SES REVOLUTIONS. Paris: Delaunay, 1824. 2 vols.

51. Cart, Alex. UNIFORMES DES REGIMENTS FRANCAIS DE LOUIS XV A NOS JOURS. Paris: Editions militaires, 1945.

52. Chalmin, Pierre. "Les Ecoles militaires françaises jusqu'en 1914." REVUE HISTORIQUE DE L'ARMEE 2 (1954): 129-66.

53. Chandler, David G. THE ART OF WARFARE ON LAND. London and New York: Hamlyn Publishing Group, 1974.

54. Chandler, David G. THE CAMPAIGNS OF NAPOLEON. New York: Macmillan, 1966.

55. Chelminski, Jan V., and A. Malibran. L'ARMEE DU DUCHE DE VARSOVIE. Paris: Leroy, 1913.

56. Choppin, Jean. LA CAVALERIE FRANCAISE. Paris: Garnier, 1893.

57. Colin, Jean Lambert. L'INFANTERIE AU XVIIIe SIECLE: LA TACTIQUE. Paris: Berger-Levrault, 1907.

58. Colin, Jean Lambert. LES TRANSFORMATIONS DE LA GUERRE. Paris: Flammarion, 1911.

59. Craig, Gordon A. THE POLITICS OF THE PRUSSIAN ARMY, 1640-1945. London and New York: Oxford University Press, 1955.

60. Creveld, Martin Levi van. SUPPLYING WAR: LOGISTICS FROM WALLENSTEIN TO PATTON. Cambridge: Cambridge University Press, 1977.

61. Darquenne, Roger. LA CONSCRIPTION DANS LE DEPARTEMENT DE JEMAPPES (1798-1813). Mons: Secretariat du cercle, 1970.

62. Delbrück, Hans. GESCHICHTE DER KRIEGSKUNST IM RAHMEN DER POLITISCHEN GESCHICHTE. Berlin: De Gruyter, 1964. 4 vols.

63. Denison, T. A HISTORY OF CAVALRY FROM THE EARLIEST TIMES WITH LESSONS FOR THE FUTURE. London: Macmillan, 1877.

64. Desbrière, Edouard. LA CAVALERIE SOUS LE DIRECTOIRE. Paris and Nancy: Berger-Levrault, 1910. 2 vols.

65. Desbrière, Edouard, and Maurice Sautai. LA CAVALERIE PENDANT LA REVOLUTION. Paris: Berger-Levrault, 1907-1908. 4 vols.

66. Duffy, Christopher. FIRE AND STONE, THE SCIENCE OF FORTRESS
    WARFARE, 1660-1860. London: Trinity Press, 1975.

67. Duffy, Christopher. RUSSIA'S MILITARY WAY TO THE WEST, ORIGINS
    AND NATURE OF RUSSIAN MILITARY POWER, 1700-1800. London:
    Routledge, 1981.

68. Dupuy, Trevor. THE EVOLUTION OF WEAPONS AND WARFARE.
    Indianapolis and New York: Bobbs-Merrill, 1980.

69. Dussieux, Louis Etienne. L'ARMEE EN FRANCE. HISTOIRE ET
    ORGANIZATION. Versailles: L. Bernard, 1884. 3 vols.

70. Earle, Edward M., ed. MAKERS OF MODERN STRATEGY. Princeton:
    Princeton University Press, 1943.

71. Favé, Ildephonse. HISTOIRE ET TACTIQUE DES TROIS ARMES ET PLUS
    PARTICULIEREMENT DE L'ARTILLERIE DE CAMPAGNE. Paris: Dumaine,
    1845.

72. Favé, Ildephonse, and Joseph T. Reinaud. HISTOIRE DE
    L'ARTILLERIE. Paris: Dumaine, 1845-47.

73. Fieffé, Eugène. HISTOIRE DES TROUPES ETRANGERES AU SERVICE DE
    FRANCE DEPUIS LEUR ORIGINE JUSQU'A NOS JOURS, ET DE TOUS LES
    REGIMENTS LEVES DANS LES PAYS CONQUIS SOUS LA PREMIERE
    REPUBLIQUE ET L'EMPIRE. Paris: Dumaine, 1854.

74. Fortescue, John W. A HISTORY OF THE BRITISH ARMY. London:
    Macmillan, 1910-30. 19 vols.

75. France. Etat-major de l'armée. HISTORIQUE DES DIVERSES LOIS
    SUR LE RECRUTEMENT DE L'ARMEE DEPUIS LA REVOLUTION JUSQU'A NOS
    JOURS. Paris: Imprimerie nationale, 1902.

76. France. Etat-major de l'armée. NOTICE HISTORIQUE SUR
    L'AVANCEMENT DANS L'ARMEE DEPUIS LA REVOLUTION JUSQU'A NOS
    JOURS. Paris: Imprimerie nationale, 1903.

77. France. Etat-major de l'armée. SECTION HISTORIQUE. NOTICE
    HISTORIQUE SUR L'ORGANISATION DE L'ARMEE DEPUIS LA REVOLUTION
    JUSQU'A NOS JOURS. Paris: Imprimerie nationale, 1902.

78. France. Ministère de la défense nationale et de la guerre. LE
    SERVICE GEOGRAPHIQUE DE L'ARMEE. SON HISTOIRE, SON
    ORGANISATION, SES TRAVAUX. Paris: Imprimerie Service
    géographique, 1934.

79. France. Ministère de la guerre. HISTORIQUES DES CORPS DE
    TROUPE DE L'ARMEE FRANCAISE (1569-1900). Paris:
    Berger-Levrault, 1900.

80. Fuller, John Frederick C. ARMAMENT AND HISTORY: A SURVEY OF
    THE INFLUENCE OF ARMAMENT ON HISTORY FROM THE DAWN OF CLASSICAL
    WARFARE TO THE SECOND WORLD WAR. New York: Scribner, 1945.

81. Fuller, John Frederick C. BRITISH LIGHT INFANTRY IN THE EIGHTEENTH CENTURY. London: Hutchinson, 1925.

82. Fuller, John Frederick C. THE CONDUCT OF WAR, 1789-1961. New Brunswick, N.J.: Rutgers University Press, 1961.

83. Fuller, John Frederick C. SIR JOHN MOORE'S SYSTEM OF TRAINING. London: Hutchinson, 1925.

84. Funcken, Fred, and Liliane Funcken. ARMS AND UNIFORMS: THE NAPOLEONIC WARS. London: Ward Lock, 1968. 2 vols.

85. Gallois, Pierre Marie. L'ART DE GUERRE DE NAPOLEON Ier. Paris: Hachette, 1965. 3 vols.

86. Garrison, Fielding. NOTES ON THE HISTORY OF MILITARY MEDICINE. Washington, D.C.: Association of Military Surgeons, 1922.

87. Gaudin, M. "Histoire de la fabrication des armes légère." REVUE HISTORIQUE DE L'ARMEE 4 (1956): 115-16.

88. Gayda, Marcel, and A. Krijitsky. L'ARMEE RUSSE SOUS LE TSAR ALEXANDRE I DE 1805 A 1815. Paris: La Sabretache, 1955.

89. German General Staff, Kriegsgeschichtliche Abteilung II. DAS PREUSSISCHE HEER DER BEFREIUNGSKRIEGE. Berlin: Mitter, 1912-14. 3 vols.

90. Gérôme, Auguste Clément. ESSAI HISTORIQUE SUR LA TACTIQUE DE L'INFANTERIE DEPUIS L'ORGANISATION DES ARMEES PERMANENTES JUSQU'A NOS JOURS. Paris: Charles-Lavauzelle, 1895.

91. Gérôme, Auguste Clément. ESSAI HISTORIQUE SUR LA TACTIQUE DE LA CAVALERIE. Paris: Charles-Lavauzelle, 1900.

92. Gieraths, Günther. DIE KAMPFHANDLUNGEN DER BRANDENBURGISCH-PREUSSISCHEN ARMEE, 1626-1807; EIN QUELLENHANDBUCH. Berlin: De Gruyter, 1964.

93. Gilbert, Gerald. THE EVOLUTION OF TACTICS. London: Hugh Rees, 1907.

94. Glover, Richard. PENINSULAR PREPARATION: THE REFORM OF THE BRITISH ARMY, 1795-1809. Cambridge: Cambridge University Press, 1963.

95. Godechot, Jacques. LES INSTITUTIONS DE LA FRANCE SOUS LA REVOLUTION ET L'EMPIRE. Paris: Presses Universitaires de France, 1951, 1968.

96. Grimoard, Philippe Henri. RECHERCHES SUR LA FORCE DE L'ARMEE FRANCAISE ET LES SECRETAIRES D'ETAT AU MINISTRES DE LA GUERRE DEPUIS HENRI IV JUSQU'A 1806. Paris: Treuttel et Würtz, 1806.

97. Gumtau, Carl Friedrich. DIE JAEGER UND SCHUETZEN DES PREUSSISCHEN HEERS. Berlin: Mittler, 1834. 3 vols.

98. Hahlweg, W. PREUSSISCHE REFORMZEIT UND REVOLUTIONAERER KRIEG. WEHRWISSENSCHAFTLICHE RUNDSCHAU. Beiheft 18 (1962).

99. Hamley, Edward Bruce. THE OPERATIONS OF WAR EXPLAINED AND ILLUSTRATED. London: Blackwood, 1907.

100. HANDBUCH DER NEUZEITLICHEN WEHRWISSENSCHAFTEN. Berlin: De Gruyter, 1937.

101. HANDBUCH ZUR DEUTSCHEN MILITAERGESCHICHTE, 1648-1939. Militaergeschichtlichtes Forschungsamt. Frankfurt a.M.: Graefe, 1964.

102. Haswell, Chetwynd John Drake. THE BRITISH ARMY: A CONCISE HISTORY. By Jock Haswell. London: Thames and Hudson, 1975.

103. Held, Robert. THE AGE OF FIREARMS, A PICTORIAL HISTORY. New York: Harper, 1957.

104. Hellie, Richard. ENSERFMENT AND MILITARY CHANGE IN MUSCOVY. Chicago: University of Chicago Press, 1971.

105. Henderson, G.F.R. THE SCIENCE OF WAR. London: Longmans, Green, 1912.

106. Herr, F.G. L'ARTILLERIE, CE QU'ELLE A ETE, CE QU'ELLE EST, CE QU'ELLE DOIT ETRE. Paris: Berger-Levrault, 1923.

107. Hicks, James E. FRENCH MILITARY WEAPONS, 1717 TO 1938. New Milford, Connecticut: Flayderman, 1964.

108. Hicks, James E., and André Jandot. NOTES ON FRENCH ORDNANCE, 1717 TO 1936. New York: Orans, 1937.

109. HISTORIQUE DES DIVERSES LOIS SUR LE RECRUTEMENT DEPUIS LA REVOLUTION JUSQU'A NOS JOURS. Paris: Imprimerie Nationale, 1902.

110. Hogg, O.F.G. ARTILLERY: ITS ORIGIN, HEYDAY AND DECLINE. Hamden, Connecticut: Archon Books, 1970.

111. Home, Robert. A PRECIS OF MODERN TACTICS. London: Clowes, 1873.

112. Howard, Michael. WAR IN EUROPEAN HISTORY. Oxford: Oxford University Press, 1976.

113. Hughes, Basil Perronet. FIREPOWER: WEAPONS EFFECTIVENESS ON THE BATTLEFIELD, 1630-1850. New York: Scribner, 1974.

114. Hughes, Q. MILITARY ARCHITECTURE. New York: St. Martin's Press, 1974.

115. Jablonski, Ludovic. L'ARMEE FRANCAISE A TRAVERS LES AGES. Paris: Charles-Lavauzelle, 1890-1894. 5 vols.

116. Jähns, M. GESCHICHTE DER KRIEGSWISSENSCHAFTEN, VORNEHMLICH IN DEUTSCHLAND. Munich and Leipzig: R. Oldenbourg, 1889-91.

117. Jany, Curt. GESCHICHTE DER KOENIGLICH-PREUSSISCHEN ARMEE. Berlin: K. Sigismund, 1928-33. 4 vols.

118. Jedlicka, L., ed. UNSER HEER. 300 JAHRE OESTERREICHISCHES SOLDATENTUM IN KRIEG UND FRIEDEN. Vienna: Furlinger, 1963.

119. Johnson, David. NAPOLEON'S CAVALRY AND ITS LEADERS. New York: Holmes & Meier, 1978.

120. Johnstone, Henry Melville. A HISTORY OF TACTICS. London: Hugh Rees, 1906.

121. Kannik, Preben. MILITARY UNIFORMS. London: Blandford, 1968.

122. Kitchen, Martin. A MILITARY HISTORY OF GERMANY FROM THE EIGHTEENTH CENTURY TO THE PRESENT DAY. Bloomington and London: Indiana University Press, 1975.

123. Kling, C. GESCHICHTE DER BEKLEIDUNG, BEWAFFNUNG UND AUSRUESTUNG DES KOENIGLICH PREUSSISCHEN HEERES. Weimar; 1912. 3 vols.

124. Knötel, Richard. UNIFORMENKUNDE. Rathenow: Babenzien, 1890-1921. 17 vols.

125. Knötel, Richard. UNIFORMS OF THE WORLD. Revised by Herbert Knötel, Jr. and Herbert Sieg. New York: Scribner, 1980.

126. La Barre-Duparcq, Edouard. ELEMENTS D'ART ET D'HISTOIRE MILITAIRES, COMPRENANT LE PRECIS DES INSTITUTIONS MILITAIRES DE LA FRANCE, L'HISTORIE DE LA TACTIQUE DES ARMES ISOLEES LA COMBINAISON DES ARMES ET LES PETITES OPERATIONS DE GUERRE. Paris: Tanera, 1858.

127. Laffont, Robert. HISTOIRE UNIVERSELLE DES ARMEES. Paris: Laffont, 1965. 4 vols.

128. Laverma, Matti. L'ARTILLERIE DE CAMPAGNE FRANCAISE PENDANT LES GUERRES DE LA REVOLUTION. Helsinki: Suomalainen Tiedeakatemia, 1956.

129. Lechartier, Georges. LES SOLDATS DE LA REVOLUTION ET DE L'EMPIRE. Paris: Charles-Lavauzelle, 1902.

130. Legrand, Robert. LE RECRUTEMENT DES ARMEES ET LES DESERTIONS (1791-1815): ASPECTS DE LA REVOLUTION EN PACARDIE. Abbeville: Société d'emulation et d'histoire d'Abbeville, 1957.

131. Legues, L. LES ADMINISTRATIONS MILITAIRES DEPUIS LES TEMPS
     ANCIENS JUSQU'A NOS JOURS. Tours: Ribaudeau et Chevallier,
     1875.

132. LES ARMES, DU MOYEN AGE AU XIXe SIECLE. Paris: Colin, 1905.

133. Lesquen, Colonel de. "Le Genie jusqu'en 1940." REVUE
     HISTORIQUE DE L'ARMEE 3 (1955): 67-88.

134. Lünsmann, Fritz. DIE ARMEE DES KOENIGREICHS WESTFALEN,
     1807-1813. Berlin: Leddihn, 1935.

135. Lynn, John. "Esquisse sur la tactique de l'infanterie."
     ANNALES HISTORIQUES DE LA REVOLUTION FRANCAISE 44 (1972):
     539-58.

136. Manucy, Albert C. ARTILLERY THROUGH THE AGES. Washington,
     D.C.: Government Printing Office, 1949.

137. Margerand, J. ARMEMENT ET EQUIPEMENT DE L'INFANTERIE FRANCAISE
     DU XVIe AU XXe SIECLE. Paris: Editions militaires illustrées,
     1956.

138. Martin, Paul, and Hans Joachim Ullrich. LE COSTUME MILITAIRE.
     Stuttgart: Franck, 1963.

139. Mauny, F. Reviers de. "Etude historique sur le corps de
     l'artillerie de France." REVUE D'ARTILLERIE 45, 46, 47
     (1895-1896).

140. Meyer, Mortiz. MANUEL HISTORIQUE DE LA TECHNOLOGIE DES ARMES A
     FEU. Tranlated by Rieffel. Paris: Corréard, 1893. 2 vols.

141. Meynert, Hermann. GESCHICHTE DER KK OESTERREICHISCHEN ARMEE.
     Vienna: C. Gerold, 1852-54. 4 vols.

142. Mollo, Boris. UNIFORMS OF THE IMPERIAL RUSSIAN ARMY. Poole,
     Eng.: Blandford, 1979.

143. Moltzheim, Auguste. L'ARTILLERIE FRANCAISE; COSTUMES,
     UNIFORMES, MATERIEL DEPUIS LE MOYEN AGE JUSQU'A NOS JOURS.
     Paris: Rothschild, 1870.

144. Montgomery of Alamein, Bernard Law, 1st viscount. A HISTORY OF
     WARFARE. Cleveland: World Publishing, 1968.

145. [Morvan, Jean] Capitaine M. Tixier. LE SOLDAT IMPERIAL
     (1800-1814). Paris: Plon, 1904. 2 vols.

146. Müller, Hermann von. GESCHICHTE DES FESTUNGSKRIEGES SEIT
     ALLGEMEINER EINFUEHRUNG DER FEUERWERWAFFEN. Berlin: Mittler,
     1892.

147. Muller and Braun. ORGANISATION DER KOENIGLICH-BAYERISCHEN
     ARMEE, 1806-1906. Berlin: Mittler, 1906.

148. Nickerson, Hoffman L. THE ARMED HORDE, 1793-1939; A STUDY OF THE RISE, SURVIVAL AND DECLINE OF THE MASS ARMY. New York: Putnam, 1940.

149. Oman, Charles W. WELLINGTON'S ARMY, 1809-1814. London: Edward Arnold, 1913.

150. Paret, Peter. "Colonial Experience and European Military Reform at the End of the Eighteenth Century." BULLETIN OF THE INSTITUTE OF HISTORICAL RESEARCH 37 (1964).

151. Paret, Peter. YORCK AND THE ERA OF PRUSSIAN REFORM, 1807-1815. Princeton N.J.: Princeton University Press, 1966.

152. Pascal, Adrien. HISTOIRE DE L'ARMEE ET DE TOUS LES REGIMENTS DEPUIS LES PREMIERS TEMPS DE LA MONARCHIE FRANCAISE JUSQU'A NOS JOURS.... Paris: Barbier, 1847-50. 5 vols.

153. Pernot, François Arthur. APERCU HISTORIQUE SUR LES SERVICE DES TRANSPORTS MILITAIRES. Paris: Charles-Lavauzelle, 1894.

154. Perré, Jean. LA GUERRE ET SES MUTATIONS DES ORIGINES A 1792. Paris: Payot, 1961.

155. Peterson, Harold Leslie, ed. ENCYCLOPEDIA OF FIREARMS. New York: Dutton, 1964.

156. Peterson, Harold Leslie. ROUND SHOT AND RAMMERS. Harrisburg, Pa.: Stackpole, 1969.

157. Phipps, Ramsey W. THE ARMIES OF THE FIRST FRENCH REPUBLIC AND THE RISE OF THE MARSHALS OF NAPOLEON I. London: Oxford University Press, 1926-29. 5 vols.

158. Picard, Louis. LA CAVALERIE DANS LES GUERRES DE LA REVOLUTION ET DE L'EMPIRE. Saumur: Milon, 1895-96. 2 vols.

159. Pichené, René. HISTOIRE DE LA TACTIQUE ET DE LA STRATEGIE JUSQU'A LA GUERRE MONDIALE. Paris: Editions de la Pensée moderne, 1957.

160. Pivka, Otto von. ARMIES OF THE NAPOLEONIC ERA. New York: Taplinger, 1979.

161. Pope, Dudley. GUNS; FROM THE INVENTION OF GUNPOWDER TO THE TWENTIETH CENTURY. London: Weidenfeld and Nicolson, 1965.

162. Preston, Richard; Sidney F. Wise; and Herman O. Werner. MEN IN ARMS: A HISTORY OF WARFARE AND ITS INTERRELATIONSHIPS WITH WESTERN SOCIETY. New York: Praeger, 1956.

163. Quimby, Robert S. THE BACKGROUND OF NAPOLEONIC WARFARE. New York: Columbia University Press, 1957.

164. Regele, Oskar. DER OESTERREICHISCHE HOFKRIEGSRAT. Vienna: Oesterreichische Staatsdruckerei, 1949.

165. Revol, Joseph Fortuné. HISTOIRE DE L'ARMEE FRANCAISE. Paris: Larousée, 1929.

166. Riencourt, Anne Honore, comte de. LES MILITAIRES BLESSES ET INVALIDES: LEUR HISTOIRE, LEUR SITUATION EN FRANCE ET A L'ETRANGER. Paris: Dumaine, 1875. 2 vols.

167. Rogers, Hugh C.B. ARTILLERY THROUGH THE AGES. London: Seeley, 1971.

168. Rogers, Hugh C.B. NAPOLEON'S ARMY. New York: Hippocrene, 1974.

169. Romagny, Charles. HISTOIRE GENERALE DE L'ARMEE NATIONALE DEPUIS BOUVINES JUSQU'A NOS JOURS (1214-1892). Paris: Charles-Lavauzelle, 1893.

170. Ropp, Theodore K. WAR IN THE MODERN WORLD. Durham, N.C.: Duke University Press, 1959.

171. Ross, Steven T. FROM FLINTLOCK TO RIFLE, INFANTRY TACTICS, 1740-1866. Rutherford, N.J.: Farleigh Dickinson University Press; London: Associated University Presses, 1979.

172. Rothenberg, Gunther. THE ART OF WARFARE IN THE AGE OF NAPOLEON. Bloomington and London: Indiana University Press, 1978.

173. Rothenberg, Gunther. "The Hapsburg Army in the Napoleonic Wars." MILITARY AFFAIRS 32 (1973): 1-5.

174. Rothenberg, Gunther. THE MILITARY BORDER IN CROATIA, 1740-1881. Chicago: University of Chicago Press, 1966.

175. Rustow, Wilhelm. GESCHICHTE DER INFANTERIE. Gotha: H. Scheube, 1857-58. 2 vols.

176. Sautermeister, Reinhard. DIE TAKTISCHE REFORM DER PREUSSISCHEN ARMEE NACH 1806. Tübingen: Becht, 1935.

177. Sauzey, Camille. ICONOGRAPHIE DES COSTUMES MILITAIRES (REVOLUTION Ier EMPIRE, IIe REPUBLIQUE, SECOND EMPIRE). Paris: Dubois and Chapelot, 1901-8. 3 vols.

178. Sauzey, Camille. ICONOGRAPHIE DU COSTUME MILITAIRE REVOLUTION-NAPOLEON. Paris: Dubois, 1901-03. 3 vols.

179. Schels, Johann Baptist. KRIEGSGESCHICHTE DER OESTERREICHER. Vienna: J.G. Heubner, 1844.

180. Schuller, R.E. THE ARMIES OF QUEEN ANNE. Oxford: Clarendon Press, 1966.

181. Schuster, O., and F.A. Franke. GESCHICHTE DER SAECHSISCHEN ARMEE.... Leipzig: Ducker and Humblot, 1885.

182. Serrant, H. LE SERVICE DU RECRUTEMENT DE 1789 A NOS JOURS. Paris: Charles-Lavauzelle, 1935.

183. Shanahan, William Oswald. PRUSSIAN MILITARY REFORMS, 1786-1813. New York: Columbia University Press, 1945.

184. Sheppard, Eric William. A SHORT HISTORY OF THE BRITISH ARMY. London: Constable, 1959.

185. Shields, Joseph W. FROM FLINTLOCK TO M 1. New York: Coward-McCann, 1954.

186. Sicard, François. HISTOIRE DES INSTITUTIONS MILITAIRES DES FRANCAIS. Paris: Corréard, 1834.

187. Sichart, Louis Heinrich. GESCHICHTE DER KOENIGLICH-HANNOVERSCHEN ARMEE. Hanover: Hahn, 1866-71. 4 vols.

188. Simond, H. HISTOIRE MILITAIRE DE LA FRANCE (1643-1871). 1895. 2 vols.

189. Six, Georges. LES GENERAUX DE LA REVOLUTION ET DE L'EMPIRE. Paris: Bordas, 1947.

190. Spaulding, O.; H. Nickerson; and J.W. Wright. WARFARE: A STUDY OF MILITARY METHODS FROM THE EARLIEST TIMES. Washington, D.C.: Infantry Journal Press, 1939.

191. Stein, F. von. GESCHICHTE DES RUSSISCHEN HEERES. Hanover: Helwing, 1885.

192. Stevens, Phillip. ARTILLERY THROUGH THE AGES. New York: F. Watts, 1965.

193. Susane, Louis Auguste. HISTOIRE DE L'ARTILLERIE FRANCAISE. Paris: Hetzel, 1874. 5 vols.

194. Susane, Louis Auguste. HISTOIRE DE L'INFANTERIE FRANCAISE. Paris: Dumaine, 1876. 5 vols.

195. Susane, Louis Auguste. HISTOIRE DE LA CAVALERIE FRANCAISE. Paris: Hetzel, 1874.

196. Teuber, Oscar. DIE OESTERREICHISCHE ARMEE VON 1700 BIS 1867. Vienna: Berté und Czeiger, 1895.

197. Thorburn, William Alexander. FRENCH ARMY REGIMENTS AND UNIFORMS FROM THE REVOLUTION TO 1870. Harrisburg, Pa.: Stackpole, 1969.

198. Thoumas, Charles A. LES TRANSFORMATIONS DE L'ARMEE FRANCAISE.
     Paris: Berger-Levrault, 1887. 2 vols.

199. Thouvenin, Théophile Edmond. HISTORIQUE GENERAL DU TRAIN DES
     EQUIPAGES MILITAIRES. Paris: Berger-Levrault, 1900.

200. Turner, Gordon B., ed. A HISTORY OF MILITARY AFFAIRS IN WESTERN
     SOCIETY SINCE THE EIGHTEENTH CENTURY. New York: Harcourt,
     Brace, 1953.

201. Unger, L.A. HISTOIRE CRITIQUE DES EXPLOITS ET VICISSITUDES DE
     CAVALERIE PENDANT LES GUERRES DE LA REVOLUTION ET DE L'EMPIRE.
     Paris: Corréard, 1848-49.

202. Vagts, Alfred. HISTORY OF MILITARISM. New York: Meridian,
     1959.

203. Vallée, Gustave. LA CONSCRIPTION DANS LE DEPARTEMENT DE LA
     CHARENTE (1798-1807). Paris: Librairie du Recueil Sirey, 1937.

204. Vernet, Horace. COLLECTION DES UNIFORMES DES ARMEES FRANCAISES
     DE 1791 A 1824. Paris: Gide, 1822-25. 2 vols.

205. Vernet, Horace, and E. Lami. COLLECTION DES UNIFORMES DES
     ARMEES FRANCAISES DE 1791 A 1814. Paris: Gide, 1882.

206. Vidal, Joseph. HISTOIRE ET STATISTIQUE DE L'INSOUMISSION.
     Paris: M. Giard et Brière, 1913.

207. Vidal de la Blanche, Joseph. LA REGENERATION DE LA PRUSSE.
     Paris: Berger-Levrault, 1910.

208. Voprosy, Voennoi. ISTORII ROSSII XVIII I PERVAYA POLOVINA XIX
     VEKOV. Moscow, 1969. (Military Historical Articles)

209. Wagner, Arthur Lockwood. ORGANIZATION AND TACTICS. Kansas
     City, Missouri: Franklin Hudson, 1912.

210. Weygand, Maxine. HISTOIRE DE L'ARMEE FRANCAISE. Paris:
     Flammarion, 1961.

211. Wilkinson, Spenser. THE FRENCH ARMY BEFORE NAPOLEON. Oxford:
     Clarendon Press, 1915.

212. Wilkinson, Spenser. THE RISE OF GENERAL BONAPARTE. Oxford:
     Clarendon Press, 1930.

213. Woloch, Isser. THE FRENCH VETERAN FROM THE REVOLUTION TO THE
     RESTORATION. Chapel Hill: University of North Carolina Press,
     1979.

214. Wrede, Alphons, freiherr von. GESCHICHTE DER K. UND K.
     WEHRMACHT. Vienna: Seidel, 1898-1903. 5 vols.

215. Wright, Quincy. A STUDY OF WAR. Chicago: University of Chicago Press, 1942.

216. Young, Peter. THE BRITISH ARMY. London: William Kimber, 1967.

217. Young, Peter, and J.P. Lawford. HISTORY OF THE BRITISH ARMY. London: Arthur Barker, 1970.

218. Zook, David H., and Robin Higham. A SHORT HISTORY OF WARFARE. New York: Twayne, 1965.

219. Zweguintzow, W. L'ARMEE RUSSE. Paris, 1967. 2 vols.

CHAPTER III

NAPOLEON AND HIS FAMILY--LIVES AND CAREERS

Owen Connelly, University of South Carolina*

Much literary garbage has been written about Napoleon and his
family. Little of it will be found herein. For Napoleon, I have
tried to offer what reveals the man, and only generally his various
careers (covered in other chapters). For the family, the
concentration is also on individuals, but more has been included on
the civil careers of such as the brothers-kings, Eugène de
Beauharnais (Napoleon's adopted son), and Murat (his brother-in-law).

GENERAL WORKS

The best of the new French biographies on the life-and-times of
Napoleon is Tulard (521). It shows the influence of the Annales
School, and is moderately leftist. This puts it in contrast to the
longtime French standard, Bainville (22), which is conservative.
Among scholarly biographies in English, Markham (352), Thompson
(510), and Chandler (109) are recommended, though the older ones,
such as Fisher (191) and Rose (463) should not be ignored. Among
popular works, probably Cronin (135) and Castelot (96) are the
leaders. Some books are listed for historiographic reasons; Lanfrey
(299) wrote the first scholarly anti-Napoleonic history (as opposed
to memoirs, of which many appeared earlier); Kircheisen (288) is the
all-time German expert on Napoleon; his biography distilled from his
nine-volume NAPOLEON: SEIN LEBEN UND SEIN ZEIT (289) is almost
saccharine in tone. Tarle (502) is a Soviet classic.
The histories of Stendhal [Beyle] (54) and Sir Walter Scott
(483) are curiosities, but Scott's biography brought screams of pain
from Bonapartists when it appeared. The study of Lefebvre (309, 310)
is surely the most famous study of Napoleon, though now superseded by
the volumes of Bergeron (41), and Lovie and Palleul (41), of which
R.R. Palmer has translated the first volume (42). The old popular
standard (in French and English) is the very pro-Napoleon, Madelin
(335, 336). The scholarly counterpart (also Napoleonist) is Driault
(157). The most readable, but wildly unreliable, except in cultural
matter, is the Durants' book, THE AGE OF NAPOLEON (172). Bignon (56)
produced the first extended history of the Napoleonic period on
commission from the exiled Emperor himself. Bourgeois (68) set forth
the still intriguing thesis that Napoleon had a fixation upon the
East and dreamed of being a new Alexander the Great. Alison's
multivolume study (8) was the standard English text from
mid-nineteenth century until c. 1914. Politically, the titles range
from the royalist of Taine (499) to the Communist of Soboul (490), of
which the latter is more friendly to Napoleon (seen as promoting the
dominance of the bourgeoisie, a necessary stage in the evolution of
the Utopian state). Mistler (387) brought together in 1969 the work

* I am indebted to Ms. Vicki Arnold who did much of the tedious work
of checking the final draft and searching out information to make all
citations complete.

of top French historians of the period--Bertier de Sauvigny, François
Crouzet, André Fugier, Jacques Godechot, Jean Tulard, and others--in
a book that is also a visual gem. The works of Zaghi (554) and
Göhring (232) serve to illustrate the continuing international
interest in Napoleon and his era. Connelly (124, 125) emphasizes
Napoleon's civil accomplishments, but the latter also follows the
military campaigns.

BIBLIOGRAPHIES

In addition to the bibliographies listed in Chapter I, the most
useful are Villat (536) and Godechot (224) in the CLIO and NOUVELLE
CLIO series, respectively. More recent titles may be gleaned from,
Godechot's review articles in the REVUE HISTORIQUE (229), which cover
the publications from 1966-1978. For new works, of course, there are
the review and bibliography sections of the journals.

ARCHIVAL SOURCES

The holdings of the Archives Nationales, Section Moderne:
Series F, especially F7, F9, and F70; Series O, especially O2; Series
AA and AB; and Series AF, especially AF IV--are the most important in
France for general Napoleonic history. These are followed by the
Archives du ministère des Affaires Etrangères, Series "Correspondance
politique" and "Mémoires et Documents", and Archives du ministère de
la Guerre at Vincennes. Other valuable collections can be found in
Paris at the archives of the Académie des Sciences, the Bibliothèque
de l'Institut de France, the Centre de Documentation de l'Institut
Français d'Histoire Sociale, the Bibliothèque de la Chambre de
Commerce et l'Industrie, the Archives de la Préfecture de Police, the
Bibliothèque de l'Arsenal, the Bibliothèque Nationale (Manuscripts),
and the Bibliothèque Thiers.

The various German archives which contain the most material on
Westphalia and Jérôme include Deutsches Zentralarchiv II at
Merseburg, the Hessisches Staatsarchiv at Marburg, the
Niedersächsisches Staatsarchiv at Wolfenbüttel, and the Staatsarchiv
at Münster, all of which deal with the Kindgom of Westphalia. The
Niedersächsisches Haupt-Staatsarchiv at Hanover, concentrates on
Hannoverian material. Manuscripts related to the Habsburgs can be
found in the Haus-, Hof-, und Staatsarchiv in Vienna.

For Italy the most useful collections can be found at the
Archivi Departimentali di Bologna, Modena, Brescia, Bergamo, and
Ravenna. The Archivio Centrale dello Stato (Rome), as well as the
Archivio di Stato di Firenze, Genova, Lucca, Mantua, Milano, Modena,
Napoli (Central Archives), Parma, Siena, Torino, and Venezia, and the
Museu del Risorgimento di Milano house valuable collections. The
Archivo di Segreteria di Stado at the Vatican contains the "Epoca
Napoleonica," and other useful fondi. These cover the various
Napoleonic states and areas annexed to France or ruled by Eugène,
Joseph, or Murat.

In Spain, the most valuable material dealing with the Napoleonic
period is located in the Archivo Histórico Nacional, Section Estado,
especially cartons in the 2000 and 3000 series. Other pertinent
material can be found at the Archivo de la Corona de Aragon (Section
9: Guerra de Independencia), the Archivo General de Navarra, the

Archivo General de Simancas (especially Negocios 3), the Biblioteca y Archivo de Palacio Real (Madrid), the Biblioteca Central Militar (Servicio Histórico Militar, Madrid), the Biblioteca Nacional, and the Real Biblioteca de El Escorial.

For studying the Netherlands, most of the material on the Kindgom of Holland and Louis Bonaparte can be found at the Algemeen Rijksarchief (The Hague), the Gemeente Archief Amsterdam, the Gemeente Archief Utrecht, the Rijksarchief in Gelderland (Arnhem), and the Rijksarchief in Utrecht.

PUBLISHED DOCUMENTS

Of primary importance are the letters and other writings of Napoleon, beginning with the basic CORRESPONDANCE (405), published under the Second Empire, with the supplements issued later. Though the original set of thirty-two volumes omitted some letters thought embarrassing to the imperial family, the items are honestly reproduced, and all possibly spurious letters are marked, and even discussed in footnotes. Moreover, later supplements contain no very startling revelations. The one exception is the volume of Picard and Tuetey (406) devoted largely to military matters. Of course Napoleon left no memoirs; those listed (422-425) are the work of Generals Montholon and Gourgaud, who were in exile with the Emperor on St. Helena. Napoleon's journals (85, 411) are apocryphal. The most valuable published documents related to the family are those of Eugène de Beauharnais (35), Jérôme Bonaparte (272), Joseph Bonaparte (277), Lucien Bonaparte as interpreted by Iung (271) and the Weil volumes on Murat in 1815 (541) and Eugène and Murat in 1814 (542).

MEMOIRS, JOURNALS, AND EYEWITNESS ACCOUNTS

Excluding military personnel (covered elsewhere), the most revealing view of Napoleon, personally, are the memoirs of his valets, Constant Wairy (130) and Marchand (347), the latter, not published until 1952, together with the mass of St. Helena documents. Of the latter, the CAHIERS of Bertrand (51) and Gorrequer's DIARY (285) are "new." Bertrand kept his CAHIERS in a personal cipher, finally broken in 1949 by Paul Fleuriot de Langle, who decoded and published them. Similarly, in 1969, Dr. James Kemble uncovered and published the diary of Gorrequer, secretary to Sir Hudson Lowe (Napoleon's "jailor" on St. Helena). The official Napoleon is best seen in the memoirs and letters of his ministers and high officials, such as Cambacérès (86) (for whose letters we are indebted to Jean Tulard), Caulaincourt (103), Champagny (108), Gaudin (215), Pasquier (441), Roederer (459), and others. Something of both Napoleon's private and public lives is shown in the memoirs of Ménéval (378). The memoirs of Fouché (197, 198) are of dubious authenticity, which is unfortunate, since the famous Minister of Police had "eyes and ears" everywhere. Those of his successor, as of 1810, Savary (480), are a valuable source on Napoleon, and on police, domestic, foreign, diplomatic, and military matters. The LETTERS FROM THE CAPE (314) is generally attributed to Napoleon.

SPECIALIZED WORKS

It is necessary to include books and articles on Napoleon's
early life, as exemplified by Armoises (10), Parker (440), and
Chuquet (115), as well as the plethora of St. Helena books, such as
Ganière (211) and Martineau (358-360), and those on the Hundred
Days--Lachouque (296, 297), Hubert (266), and MacKenzie (334).
Moreover, partial biographies reveal Napoleon's personality or
character in some way. Some treat his reaction to crisis, such as
his arrest in 1794, while still a fledgling general, when Jacobins
suddenly became suspect (473); his attempted suicide in 1814 (256);
his love life by Merezhkovskii (383), Saunders (478), and Savant
(479); his medical history from clinical in Kemble (284) and
Hillemand (257) to sensational in Weider and Hapgood (540); and his
relations with people (except military officers) as described by
Baelen (21), Boromé (65), Cassagne (94), Dard (137), Gromaire (240),
Horward (262), Lanzac de Laborie (300), and others. There are also
studies of particular aspects of his life: for example, at court by
Zieseniss (556), as a propagandist by Tulard (520), etc.; and there
are studies which reveal his idiosyncrasies, pragmatism and/or
beliefs and principles, such as his fussy attention to detail in
Cabanis (84), his attitude toward history and historians in Burton
(80), his policies on the Jews in Delpech (143), Napoleon as novelist
in Frayling (206), his attitude on religion when he lay dying (245),
his private routines in Lévy (317), and much else.

There are numerous genealogies on Napoleon, but the most
authoritative are by Sirjean (489) and Valynseele (529, 530). Of
books dealing with the Bonaparte family, it needs to be said only
that the exhaustive Masson (362) is the basis of most such works, and
that Geer (218) is an English condensation. Both are flawed because
Masson took Napoleon's opinions, expressed at St. Helena, as
"gospel." Thus, the Emperor's relatives--especially his brothers and
sisters--come off as unintelligent, bothersome, spoiled, and
ungrateful. This line persists, for example, in Delderfield's GOLDEN
MILLSTONES (142), despite the efforts of biographers, such as
Connelly (126), to rehabilitate the brothers-kings and others.

Volumes related to specific members of the Bonaparte family are
in abundance. Among the works on Napoleon's parents, Martineau (356,
357), in French or English, is a good place to start. On Joseph,
king of Naples and later Spain, the views of Connelly (126) and Girod
de l'Ain (222) should be balanced against the Spanish views of
Villa-Urrutia (535) and Mercader Riba (381). Rambaud (448) is
unsurpassed on Joseph's reign in Naples. On Louis, king of Holland,
the Dutch work of Colenbrander (120) is more favorable than the
French of Labarre de Raillicourt (295); Dutch historians have
generally given Louis good press. Lucien still lacks a good
biography, oddly enough. That of Piétri (443) is still standard.
Jérôme, for the Germans, is inseparable from the Kingdom of
Westphalia, though their view of him, personally, is not harsh.
Kircheisen (287) has written in German a light-hearted biography, and
Kleinschmidt (290) gives much attention to the youngest Bonaparte.
The French have viewed him as a playboy, and Melchior-Bonnet (375)
treats him as evil visited on the Germans by Napoleon. Americans
remember him for his marriage to Elizabeth Patterson of Baltimore,
which Napoleon had annulled so that he could marry his brother to a
royal princess, Catherine of Württemberg. "Betsy" has usually had
literary biographies, of which Desmond (146) is the most recent. The

story of her lifelong (and finally successful) battle to get her son recognized as legitimate is told by Didier (147), and the story of the American Bonapartes, politically prominent until c. 1919, is told by Macartney and Dorrance (331). The English view of Jérôme is well expressed by Sergeant (487)--THE BURLESQUE NAPOLEON. For a brief treatment of Jérôme's admirable governmental efforts in Westphalia, and his unjust dismissal during the Russian campaign, see Connelly (128), and on his valor at Waterloo, almost any book on the battle.

Among the sisters, Caroline, the most Machiavellian politician, was married to Marshal Joachim Murat, and in 1808 the two became king and queen of Naples. Usually, she is blamed for their betrayal of Napoleon in 1814--as detailed by Cole (118) and Fiore (189). The popular work of Turquan (527) on Caroline is still recommended, though originally published in 1899. The MURAT of Garnier (213) is readable and scholarly. The Italians, represented by Doria (149) and Valente (528), give Murat a generally good report as a reformer and would-be unifier of Italy. Elisa, princess of Pombino and Lucca, ruler of the Grand Duchy of Tuscany, is uniformly treated as a formidable personality, a good ruler, and a reformer; Fleuriot de Langle (193) is typical. Pauline, princess of Gustalla and wife of Prince Borghèse, has never escaped the stereotype of the scandalous beauty. Dixon (148) and Ortzen (439) give attention to the tragedy of her first marriage (her husband, General Leclerc, died in Haiti and their son died young) and her loyalty to family and friends.

Turning to the Beauharnais family, the Empress Josephine has many biographies and supporting studies (usually revealing some alleged scandal), of which a scattering are given here. Knapton (292), Cartland (93), and Castelot (98) are reasonably well balanced accounts. Her son (and Napoleon's adopted son) Eugène has generally been considered the most sterling character of the period--loyal to Napoleon to the end despite offers from the allies of a crown--competent viceroy of Italy--superb solder. Of the German biographies, that of Adalbert of Bavaria (5) is recommended; of the French, Bernardy (43); and in English, the work of Carola Oman (Lenanton) (313). On Hortense, who married Louis Bonaparte and became queen of Holland, there is much mention in the books on Louis and the Kingdom, mostly unfavorable. It is the scandals (real or otherwise) of her life after separating from Louis that have drawn a rash of biographers. Perhaps the old Turquan (526), published in 1896, has yet to be improved on. Bernardy (44) and Wright (552, 553) are more sympathetic.

Regarding the Empress Marie Louise, Bertaut (47) is reasonably scholarly, and the same can be said of Castelot's works on the King of Rome, Napoleon II, (95, 99). Driault (159) is more erudite, if equally sympathetic. Bernadotte and Désirée Clary are included among the family, since the latter's sister, Julie Clary, married Joseph Bonaparte. Bernadotte became crown prince of Sweden in 1810, and later king; the present royal family are their descendents. The most scholarly biography of Bernadotte is Barton (32). Désirée's biographies tend to be romances; Bearne (33) and Girod de l'Ain (221) are as good as any. Among others listed, Laure Junot, duchesse d'Abrantès [Bertaut (46)], wife of the general and close to the Bonapartes, was treated as family. She became a famous memoirist in the nineteenth century. On Madame Walewska, both the Comte d'Ornano (438) and Sutherland (498) are popular, but not overly inventive.

In the area of historiography, Bonapartism, and the Napoleonic legend, the works of Christophe (112), Driault (150, 151), Geyl (219), Godechot (228), Mayer (371), and Rosebery (466) are most concerns with historiography. The refutations of Sir Walter Scott's NAPOLEON (402, 450-452) are sources of historiography. They are included because they, together with Scott's history, expressed the basic "for and against" arguments used for the next 150 years. Bluche (60), Fisher (190), and Rothney (467) clearly deal with Bonapartism. Dechamps (140), Driault (150, 151) and Tulard (515, 518) deal with the myth or legend. Many items overlap.

FUTURE RESEARCH

We may safely predict that in the future, as always, popular historians and fiction writers will dominate in the field of petit histoire of the Bonapartes. Military historians could benefit, however, from scholarly evaluations of the campaigns (or any one of them) of Jérôme Bonaparte and the role of Joseph Bonaparte in the Peninsular War. In both cases, personalities should be given short shrift in favor of a detailed analysis of Napoleon's orders to the brothers and their performance, under those orders, as military commanders.

BIBLIOGRAPHY: NAPOLEON AND FAMILY

1. Abell, Lucia Elizabeth (Balcomb). NAPOLEON A SAINTE-HELENE: SOUVENIRS DE BETZY BALCOMBE. London: J. Murray, 1844.

2. Abell, Lucia Elizabeth (Balcomb). RECOLLECTIONS OF THE EMPEROR NAPOLEON. London: J. Murray, 1844.

3. Abrantès, Laure Saint-Martin Permon Junot, duchesse d'. THE HOME AND COURT LIFE OF THE EMPEROR NAPOLEON AND HIS FAMILY. London: Bentley, 1893.

4. Abrantès Laure Saint-Martin Permon Juont, duchesse d'. MEMOIRES DE MADAME FA DUCHESSE D'ABRANTES, [OU] SOUVENIRS HISTORIQUES SUR NAPOLEON. Paris: Garnier, 1893. 10 vols.

5. Adalbert, prince of Bavaria. EUGENE DE BEAUHARNAIS, BEAU-FILS DE NAPOLEON, PORTRAIT BIOGRAPHIQUE. Paris: Alsatia, 1944.

6. Albert-Samuel, C. "Napoléon Ier à Sainte Hélène. Bibliographie 1955-1971." REVUE DE L'INSTITUT NAPOLEON 120 (1971): 151-58.

7. ALBUM DE LA FAMILLE BONAPARTE. Nice: n.p., 1866.

8. Alison, Archibald. HISTORY OF EUROPE FROM THE COMMENCEMENT OF THE FRENCH REVOLUTION TO THE RESTORATION. Edinburgh: Blackwood, 1849. 14 vols.

9. Antommarchi, Francesco A. MEMOIRES DU DOCTEUR ANTOMMARCHI, OU DES DERNIERS MOMENTS DE NAPOLEON. Paris: Barrois, 1825. 2 vols.

10. Armoises, Olivier des. AVANT LA GLORIE: NAPOLEON ENFANT, NAPOLEON ET SES COMPATRIOTES. Paris: Montgredien, 1898.

11. Arnna, J. NAPOLEON Ier, LETTRES AU COMTE MOLLIEN, MINISTRE DU TRESOR PUBLIC (DU 16 MARS 1803 AU 9 JUIN 1815). [Rochecorbon:] C. Gay, [1959].

12. Aronson, Theo. THE GOLDEN BEES: THE STORY OF THE BONAPARTES. Greenwich, Conn.: New York Graphic Society, 1964.

13. Artom, Guido. NAPOLEON IS DEAD IN RUSSIA: THE EXTRAORDINARY STORY OF ONE OF HISTORY'S STRANGEST CONSPIRACIES. New York: Atheneum, 1970.

14. Ashton, John. ENGLISH CARICATURE AND SATIRE ON NAPOLEON I. With a new introduction by Leslie Shepard. London: Chatto and Windus, 1888. (Reissued, Detroit: Singing Tree Press, 1968.)

15. Askenazy, Szymon. MANUSCRITS DE NAPOLEON (1973-1795) EN POLOGNE. Varsovie: Librarire ancienne scientifique polonaise, 1929.

16. Atteridge, Andrew Hilliard. JOACHIM MURAT. New York: Brentano, 1911.

17. Aubry, Octave. L'AIGLON; DES TUILERIES AUX INVALIDES. Paris: Flammarion, 1941.

18. Aubry, Octave. THE KING OF ROME, NAPOLEON II, "L'AIGLON". Authorized translation by Elizabeth H. Abbott. Philadelphia and London: Lippincott, 1932.

19. Aubry, Octave. NAPOLEON, SOLDIER AND EMPEROR. Authorized translation by Arthur Livingston. Philadelphia and New York: Lippincott, 1938.

20. Aubry, Octave. VIE PRIVEE DE NAPOLEON. Paris: Flammarion, 1939.

21. Baelen, Jean. BENJAMIN CONSTANT ET NAPOLEON. Paris: Peyronnet, 1965.

22. Bainville, Jacques. NAPOLEON. Paris: Fayard, 1931. (New ed. with Jean Tulard. Paris, 1976.)

23. Baldensperger, F. "La France napoléonienne et la littérature étrangère." REVUE DES ETUDES NAPOLEONIENNES 5 (1914): 107-110.

24. Barbier, Antoine Alexandre. NAPOLEON ET LES PARTHES. Paris: n.p., 1842.

25. Barbier, Antoine Alexandre. NAPOLEON ET SES BIBLIOTHEQUES PORTATIVES. Paris: n.p., 1842.

26. Barbier, Antoine Alexandre. SOUVENIRS LITTERAIRES DE L'EMPIRE. Paris: Martinet, 1952.

27. Barbier, Pierre, and F. Vernillat. HISTOIRE DE FRANCE PAR LES CHANSONS; NAPOLEON ET SA LEGENDE. Paris: n.p., 1959.

28. Barnett, Correlli. BONAPARTE. New York: Hill and Wang, 1978.

29. Barras, Paul François Jean Nicolas, vicomte de. MEMOIRES DE BARRAS. Paris: Guy Le Prat, 1946.

30. Barraud, Charles. "Murat en Corse (1815)." REVUE DES ETUDES NAPOLEONIENNES 15 (1925): 217-44.

31. Bartel, Paul. LA JEUNESSE INEDITE DE NAPOLEON, D'APRES DE NOMBREUX DOCUMENTS. Paris: Amiot-Dumont, 1954.

32. Barton, Dunbar Plunket. BERNADOTTE, PRINCE AND KING, 1810-1844. London: J. Murray 1925.

33. Bearne, Catherine Mary (Charlton). A QUEEN OF NAPOLEON'S COURT: THE LIFE-STORY OF DESIREE BERNADOTTE. New York: Dutton, 1905.

34. Beaucour, Fernand. "La Famille maternelle de Napoléon."
    BULLETIN DE LA SOCIETE DE PONT DE BRIQUES 1 (1973): 8-13; 2
    (1974): 263-340.

35. Beauharnais, Eugène de, prince d'Eichstätt. MEMOIRES ET
    CORRESPONDANCE POLITIQUE ET MILITAIRE DU PRINCE EUGENE. Edited
    by Albert du Casse. Paris: Michel Lévy, 1858-60. 10 vols.

36. Beauharnais, Stéphanie de. "Souvenirs de Stéphanie de
    Beauharnais, Grande-Duchesse de Bade." REVUE DES DEUX MONDES
    (1932): 61-104.

37. Béchu, Marcel Ernest [Marcel Dupont]. MURAT; CAVALIER, MARECHAL
    DE FRANCE, PRINCE ET ROI. Paris: Hachette, 1934. (Reprint,
    1980).

38. Béchu, Marcel Ernest [Marcel Dupont]. NAPOLEON ET LA TRAHISON
    DES MARECHAUX, 1814. Paris: Hachette, 1939.

39. Belmontet, Louis. BIOGRAPHIE DE JOSEPH-NAPOLEON BONAPARTE.
    Paris: Levavasseur, 1833.

40. Belmontet, Louis. JOSEPH NAPOLEON JUGE PAR SES CONTEMPORAINS.
    Paris: Levavasseur, 1833.

41. Bergeron, Louis. L'EPISODE NAPOLEONIEN; ASPECTS INTERIEURS.
    Paris: Editions du seuil, 1972; Jacques Lovie and André
    Palluel. L'EPISODE NAPOLEON: ASPECTS EXTERIEURS. Paris:
    Editions du seuil, 1972. Vols. 4, 5 (Seuil NOUVELLE HISTOIRE DE
    FRANCE).

42. Bergeron, Louis. FRANCE UNDER NAPOLEON. Translated by R.R.
    Palmer. Princeton, N.J.: Princeton University Press, 1981.

43. Bernardy, Françoise de. EUGENE DE BEAUHARNAIS, 1781-1824.
    Paris: Perrin, 1973.

44. Bernardy, Françoise de. LA REINE HORTENSE (1783-1837). Paris:
    Perrin, 1968.

45. Bertaud, Jean Paul. LE PREMIER EMPIRE, LEGS DE LA REVOLUTION.
    Paris: Presses universitaires de France, 1973.

46. Bertaut, Jules. LA DUCHESSE D'ABRANTES. Paris: Flammarion,
    1949.

47. Bertaut, Jules. MARIE-LOUISE, FEMME DE NAPOLEON Ier, 1791-1847.
    Paris: Amiot-Dumont, 1940.

48. Bertaut, Jules. LE MENAGE MURAT. Paris: Le Livre
    contemporain, 1958.

49. Bertaut, Jules. LE ROI JEROME. Paris: Flammarion, 1954.

50. Bertin, Georges. JOSEPH BONAPARTE EN AMERIQUE. Paris: Librairie de la Nouvelle-Revue, 1893.

51. Bertrand, Henri Gratien, comte. CAHIERS DE SAINTE-HELENE. Paris: Sulliver, 1949-59. 3 vols.

52. Bertrand, Henri Gratien, comte. NAPOLEON AT SAINT HELENA. Extracts in translation from CAHIERS. Garden City, N.Y.: Doubleday, 1952.

53. Beugnot, Jacques Claude, comte. MEMOIRES DU COMTE BEUGNOT, 1779-1815. Paris: Dentu, 1866. 2 vols. (3d ed., 1889, 1 vol.)

54. Beyle, Maire Henri [Stendhal]. VIE DE NAPOLEON. Paris: Librairie Gründ, 1939.

55. "Bibliographie napoléonienne." REVUE DE L'INSTITUT NAPOLEON (1948-1983).

56. Bignon, Louis Pierre Edouard, baron. HISTOIRE DE FRANCE SOUS NAPOLÉON. Paris: Firmin-Didot, 1838-50. 14 vols.

57. Bignon, Louis Pierre Edouard, baron. HISTOIRE DE FRANCE DEPUIS LE 18 BRUMAIRE. Paris: C. Bechet, Firmin-Didot, 1825-50. 14 vols.

58. Billy, André. HORTENSE ET SES AMANTS, CHATEAUBRIAND, SAINTE-BEAUCE. Paris: Flammarion, 1961.

59. Binet-Valmer, Gustav. LA VIE AMOUREUSE DE MARIE WALEWSKA, L'EPOUSE POLONAISE DE NAPOLEON. PARIS: Flammarion, 1928.

60. Bluche, Frédéric. BONAPARTISME, AUX ORIGINES DE LA DROITE AUTORITAIRE. Paris: Nouvelles Editions Latines, 1980.

61. Bonaparte, Maria Letizia (Romolino). LETTERE DI LETIZIA BUONAPARTE, A CURA DI PIERO MISCIATTELLI. Milan: Hoepli, 1936.

62. Bond, Gordon Crews. "Louis Bonaparte and the Collapse of the Kingdom of Holland." PROCEEDINGS OF THE CONSORTIUM ON REVOLUTIONARY EUROPE 3 (1974): 141-53.

63. Bonnel, Ulane. "Etudes napoléoniennes de langue anglaise." REVUE DE L'INSTITUT NAPOLEON 127 (1973): 67-72.

64. Bordonove, Georges. NAPOLEON. Paris: Editions Pygmalion, 1978.

65. Boromé, J. "Louanges de Bonaparte par un fils de Toussaint-Louverture." REVUE DE L'INSTITUT NAPOLEON 133 (1977): 167-71.

66. Boulind, Richard. CAMBACERES AND THE BONAPARTES: UNPUBLISHED PAPERS OF JEAN-JACQUES-REGIS CAMBACERES. New York: Kraus, 1976.

67. Bourdon, Jean. NAPOLEON AU CONSEIL D'ETAT; NOTES ET PROCES-VERBZUX INEDITS DE JEAN-GUILLAUME LOCRE. Paris: Berger-Levrault, 1963.

68. Bourgeois, Emile. MANUEL HISTORIQUE DE POLITIQUE ETRANGERE. Paris: Belin, 1892-1926. 4 vols.

69. Bourgin, Georges. "Les Journaux de Bonaparte en Italie: le Courrier de l'Armée d'Italie." REVUE DES ETUDES NAPOLEONIENNES 17 (1922): 225-31.

70. Bourgin, Georges. "Note sur la Correspondance de Napoléon Ier et les documents napoléoniens conservés aux Archives de la Marine." REVUE DES ETUDES NAPOLEONIENNES 15(1919): 184-94.

71. Bourgoing, Jean de. MARIE-LOUISE VON OESTERREICH, KAISHERIN DER FRANZOSEN, HERZOGIN VON PARMA. Vienna: Europa Verlag, 1949.

72. Bourrienne, Louis Antoine Fauvelet de. MEMOIRES DE M. DE BOURRIENNE SUR NAPOLEON, LE DIRECTOIRE, LE CONSULAT, L'EMPIRE, ET LA RESTAURATION. Paris: Ladvocat, 1829. 10 vols.

73. Boyer, Ferdinand. "Les Etudes napoléoniennes en Italie." REVUE DE L'INSTITUT NAPOLEON 125 (1972): 179-82.

74. Boyer, Ferdinand. "Stendhal et les historiens de Napoleon." REVUE DE L'INSTITUT NAPOLEON 19 (1926): 68-71.

75. Brotonne, Léonce de. LES BONAPARTE ET LEURS ALLIANCES. Paris: Champion, 1901.

76. Browning, Oscar. THE FALL OF NAPOLEON. London: J. Lane, 1907.

77. Browning, Oscar. NAPOLEON, THE FIRST PHASE: SOME CHAPTERS ON THE BOYHOOD AND YOUTH OF BONAPARTE, 1769-1793. London and New York: J. Lane, 1905.

78. Bruhat, Jean. NAPOLEON, LES MYTHES ET LA REALITE. Paris: Cercle parisien de la Lique française de l'enseignment, 1969.

79. Bruun, Geoffrey. EUROPE AND THE FRENCH IMPERIUM, 1799-1814. New York: Harper, 1938.

80. Burton, June K. NAPOLEON AND CLIO: HISTORICAL WRITINGS, TEACHING, AND THINKING DURING THE FIRST EMPIRE. Durham: Carolina Academic Press, 1979.

81. Burton, June K. "Napoleon et l'Histoire." REVUE DE L'INSTITUT NAPOLEON 126 (1973): 1-5.

82. Burton, June K. "Napoleon, Patron of Historians." REVUE DE L'INSTITUT NAPOLEON 132 (176): 195-200.

83. Bush, R.D. "Guides des Archives et Collections privées de la Nouvelle-Orléans." REVUE DE L'INSTITUT NAPOLEON 135 (1979): 87-91.

84. Cabanis, J. LE SACRE DE NAPOLEON. Paris, 1975.

85. Caillet, Gérard. LE JOURNAL DE NAPOLEON. Paris: Denöul, 1978.

86. Cambacérès, Jean Jacques Regis de. LETTRES INEDITES A NAPOLEON, 1802-1814. Edited by Jean Tulard. Paris: Editions Klincksieck, 1973. 2 vols.

87. Cambronero y Martínez, Carlos. EL REY INTRUSO: APUNTES HISTORICOS REFERENTES A JOSE BONAPARTE. Madrid: Bibliofilos Españoles, 1909.

88. Canova, Antonio. ENTRETIEN DE NAPOLEON AVEC CANOVA EN 1810. Paris: Boucher, 1824.

89. Carlton, William Newnham Chattin. PAULINE: FAVORITE SISTER OF NAPOLEON. New York: Harper, 1930.

90. Carnot, Lazare Nicolas Marguerite, comte. MEMOIRES HISTORIQUES ET MILITAIRES SUR CARNOT REDIGES D'APRES SES MANUSCRITS, SA CORRESPONDANCE INEDITE ET SES ECRITS. Paris: Baudouin, 1824.

91. Carnot, Lazare Nicolas Marguerite, comte. MEMOIRES SUR CARNOT, PAR SON FILS. Paris: Pagnerre, 1861-1864. 2 vols.

92. Carrington, Dorothy. "Les Parents de Napoléon d'après des documents inédits." ANNALES HISTORIQUE DE LA REVOLUTION FRANCAISE 242 (1980): 585-607.

93. Cartland, Barbara. JOSEPHINE, EMPRESS OF FRANCE. London: Arrow Books, 1973.

94. Cassagne, A. "Chateaubriand et Napoleon." REVUE DES ETUDES NAPOLEONIENNES 2 (1912): 161-81.

95. Castelot, André. L'AIGLON: NAPOLEON DEUX. Paris: Livre contemporain, 1959.

96. Castelot, André. BONAPARTE. Paris: Perrin, 1967. 2 vols.

97. Castelot, André. HISTOIRE DE NAPOLEON BONAPARTE. Paris: Tallandier, 1969. 10 vols.

98. Castelot, André. JOSEPHINE. Paris: Rombaldi, 1974. 2 vols.

99. Castelot, André. KING OF ROME. Translated by Robert Baldick. New York: Harper, 1960; Westport, Conn.: Greenwood Press, 1974.

100. Castelot, André. LE LIVRE DE LA FAMILLE IMPERIALE. Paris: Perrin, 1969.

101. Catherine, queen consort of Jérôme, king of Wesphalia. BRIEFWECHSEL DER KOENIGHIN KATHARINA UND DES KOENIGS JEROME VON WESTFALEN, SOWIE DES KAISERS NAPOLEON I MIT DEM KOENIG FRIEDRICH VON WURTTEMBERG. Stuttgart: Kohlhammer, 1886-97. 3 vols.

102. Catherine, queen consort of Jérôme, king of Westphalia. CORRESPONDANCE INEDITE AVEC SA FAMILLE ET CELLE DU ROI JEROME. Paris: Bouillon, 1893.

103. Caulaincourt, Armand Augustin, marquis de, duc de Vicence. MEMOIRES DU GENERAL DE CAULAINCOURT. Paris: Plon, 1933. 3 vols.

104. Caulaincourt, Armand Augustin, marquis de, duc de Vicence. NO PEACE WITH NAPOLEON! CONCLUDING THE MEMOIRS OF ... CAULAINCOURT. Translated by George Libaire. New York: Morrow, 1936.

105. Caulaincourt, Armand Augustin, marquis de, duc de Vicence. WITH NAPOLEON IN RUSSIA: THE MEMOIRS OF ... CAULAINCOURT. Translated by George Libaire. New York: Grosset & Dunlap, 1935.

106. Challois, Léonard. HISTOIRE DU PRINCE EUGENE DE BEAUHARNAIS. Paris: n.p., 1821.

107. Chambrun, Marie de. LE ROI DE ROME. Paris: Plon, 1941.

108. Champagny, Jean Baptiste Nompère, comte de. SOUVENIRS DE M. DE CHAMPAGNY, DUC DE CADORE. Paris: Renouard, 1846. (Slatkine-Megariotis Reprint, 1976.)

109. Chandler, David G. NAPOLEON. New York: Saturday Review Press, 1973.

110. Chaptal de Chanteloup, Jean Antoine Claude, comte. MES SOUVENIRS SUR NAPOLEON, PAR LE COMTE CHAPTAL. Paris: Plon-Nourrit, 1893.

111. Chateaubriand, François Auguste René, vicomte de. MEMOIRES D'OUTRE-TOMBE. Paris: Penaud, 1849-50. 12 vols. (Many later editions.)

112. Christophe, Robert. NAPOLEON CONTROVERSE. Paris: Fayard, 1975.

113. Christophe, Robert. NAPOLEON, EMPEREUR DE L'ILE D'ELBE. Paris: Fayard, 1959.

114. Christophe, Robert. NAPOLEON ON ELBA. Translated from French by Len Ortzen. London: MacDonald, 1964.

115. Chuquet, Arthur Maxime. LA JEUNESSE DE NAPOLEON. Paris: Colin, 1897-99. 3 vols.

116. Ciana, Albert. LES BONAPARTES; AUTOGRAPHES, MANUSCRITS, SIGNATURES. Geneva: Editions Helvetia, 1941.

117. Clary et Aldringen, Carl von, prince. TROIS MOIS A PARIS LORS DU MARIAGE DE L'EMPEREUR NAPOLEON Ier ET DE L'ARCHDUCHESSE MARIE-LOUISE. Publié par le baron de Mitis et le comte de Pimodan. Paris: Plon-Nourrit, 1914.

118. Cole, Hubert. THE BETRAYERS: JOACHIM AND CAROLINE MURAT. London and New York: Saturday Review Press, 1972.

119. Cole, Hubert. JOSEPHINE. London: Heineman, 1962; New York: Viking Press, 1963.

120. Colenbrander, H.T. KONING LODEWIJK 1806-1810. 2 parts. 1909-10. Vol. 5 of GEDENKSTUKKEN DER ALGEMEENE GESCHIEDENIS VAN NEDERLAND 1795-1840. 10 vols. The Hague: Nijhoff, 1905-22.

121. Colletta, Pietro. HISTOIRE DE JOACHIM MURAT. Paris: Baudouin, 1843.

122. Colletta, Pietro. SUR LA CATASTROPHE DE L'EX-ROI DE NAPLES, JOACHIM MURAT. Paris: Ponthieu, 1823.

123. Columba, Hélène. MADAME WALEWSKA; LA PLUS BELLE HISTOIRE D'AMOUR SOUS L'EMPIRE. Paris: Editions du Scorpion, 1964.

124. Connelly, Owen. THE EPOCH OF NAPOLEON. New York: Holt, Rinehart and Winston, 1972, 1978.

125. Connelly, Owen. FRENCH REVOLUTION-NAPOLEONIC ERA. New York: Holt, Rinehart and Winston, 1979.

126. Connelly, Owen. THE GENTLE BONAPARTE. New York: Macmillan, 1968.

127. Connelly, Owen. "Napoléon européen." REVUE DE L'INSTITUT NAPOLEON (1970).

128. Connelly, Owen. NAPOLEON'S SATELLITE KINGDOMS. New York: Free Press, 1965.

129. Connelly, Owen; Felix Markham; Harold Parker; and Robert Holtman. Symposium. "Napoleon: Civil Executive and Revolutionary." PROCEEDINGS OF THE CONSORTIUM ON REVOLUTIONARY EUROPE 1 (1972): 18-49.

130. Constant, Louis Constant Wairy. MEMOIRES DE CONSTANT. Paris: 1830-31. 6 vols.; Paris: J. de Bonnot, 1969-70.

131. Constant de Rebecque, Henri Benjamin. JOURNAL INTIME, LETTER A SA FAMILLE ET A SES AMIS. Ed. by D. Melegari. Paris: Ollendorff, 1895. (New editions, J. Mistler, 1945, and A. Roulin and C. Roth, 1952.)

132. Constant de Rebecque, Henri Benjamin. MEMOIRES SUR LES CENT JOURS. Paris: Bechet, 1820-22.

133. Constant de Rebecque, Henri Benjamin. OEUVRES POLITIQUES DE BENJAMIN CONSTANT. Paris: Charpentier, 1874.

134. Corsing, Fritz. JEAN BAPTISTE BERNADOTTE: BIOGRAPHIE. Vienna: P. Neff, 1960.

135. Cronin, Vincent. NAPOLEON. London: Collins, 1971.

136. Dard, Emile. DANS L'ENTOURAGE DE L'EMPEREUR: NAPOLEON ROMANCIER. Paris: Plon, 1940.

137. Dard, Emile. NAPOLEON AND TALLEYRAND. Translated by Christopher R. Turner. New York: Appleton Century, 1937.

138. Decaux, Alain. LAETIZIA, MERE DE L'EMPEREUR. Paris: Bonne, 1949, 1959.

139. Decaux, Alain. LETIZIA; NAPOLEON ET SA MERE. Paris: Perrin, 1974.

140. Dechamps, Jules. "La Légende de Napoléon à travers le monde." REVUE DES ETUDES NAPOLEONIENNES 27 (1926): 30-45.

141. Defranceschi, J. "Le Role du Lieutenant Bonaparte au début de la Révolution française en Corse." REVUE DE L'INSTITUT NAPOLEON 134 (1978): 3-20.

142. Delderfield, Ronald Frederick. THE GOLDEN MILLSTONES: NAPOLEON'S BROTHERS AND SISTERS. London: Weidenfeld and Nicolson, 1964.

143. Delpech, F. "Les Juifs en France et dans l'Empire et la genèse du Grand Sanhedrin." REVUE HISTORIQUE DE LA REVOLUTION FRANCAISE 51 (1979): 1-26.

144. Derolin, Pierre. "Après Waterloo le Havre, porte de l'Amérique." REVUE DE L'INSTITUT NAPOLEON 134 (1978): 21-23.

145. Descotes, Maurice. LA LEGENDE DE NAPOLEON ET LES ECRIVAINS FRANCAIS DU XIXième SIECLE. Paris: Minard, 1967.

146. Desmond, Alice. BEWITCHING BETSY BONAPARTE. New York: Dodd, Mead, 1958.

147. Didier, Eugene Lemoine. THE LIFE AND LETTERS OF MADAME BONAPARTE. New York: Scribner, 1879.

148. Dixon, Pierson. PAULINE: NAPOLEON'S FAVORITE SISTER. New
     York: D. McKay, 1966.

149. Doria, Gino. MURAT RE DI NAPOLI. [Cava dei Tirreni:] Di
     Mauro, 1966.

150. Driault, Edouard. "Aprés un siècle de légende et d'histoire,
     conclusion   de   Napoléon-le-Grand."   REVUE   DES   ETUDES
     NAPOLEONIENNES 31 (1930): 87-100.

151. Driault, Edouard. "Au Centenaire de la Grand Légende." REVUE
     DES ETUDES NAPOLEONIENNES 42 (1936): 5-41.

152. Driault, Edouard. "Chronique de la cour de Cassel, sous le roi
     Jérôme (1809)." REVUE DES ETUDES NAPOLEONIENNES 1 (1912):
     414-21.

153. Driault, Edouard. "Le XIXième Siècle et Napoléon." REVUE DES
     ETUDES NAPOLEONIENNES 31 (1926): 87-100.

154. Driault, Edouard. "Les Historiens de Napoléon: Albert Sorel."
     REVUE DES ETUDES NAPOLEONIENNES 22 (1924): 5-26.

155. Driault, Edouard.   "Madame   Mère."   REVUE   DES   ETUDES
     NAPOLEONIENNES 42 (1936): 65-80.

156. Driault, Edouard. "Napoléon au Centenaire de sa mort (1921),
     étude bibliographique d'après Chassé, d'Auriac, Guyot,
     Lacout-Gayet." REVUE DES ETUDES NAPOLEONIENNES 27 (1922):
     49-76, 81-90.

157. Driault, Edouard.   NAPOLEON ET L'EUROPE.   Paris: Alcan,
     1910-27. 5 vols.

158. Driault, Edouard. "Napoleon-le-Grand (1769-1821." REVUE DES
     ETUDES NAPOLEONIENNES 31 (1930): 5-18.

159. Driault, Edouard. LE ROI DE ROME. Paris: Albert Morance,
     1928.

160. Driault, Edouard. "Les Sources napoléoniennes aux Archives des
     Affaires étrangères." REVUE DES ETUDES NAPOLEONIENNES 1 (1913):
     161-86.

161. Duboscq, André. LOUIS BONAPARTE EN HOLLANDE, D'APRES SES
     LETTRES. Paris: Emile-Paul, 1911.

162. Du Casse, Albert, baron, ed. LES ROIS FRERES DE NAPOLEON Ier.
     Paris: Germer, Baillière, 1883.

163. Ducrest, Georgette. MEMOIRES SUR L'IMPERATRICE JOSEPHINE.
     Paris: Fayard, 1828. 3 vols.

164. Duhamel, Jean. LES CINQUANTE JOURS DE WATERLOO A PLYMOUTH.
     Paris: Plon, 1963.

165. Duhamel, Jean. THE FIFTY DAYS: NAPOLEON IN ENGLAND. Translated by R. A. Hall. Coral Gables, Fla.: University of Miami Press, 1970.

166. Duman, Alexandre. MES MEMOIRES. Paris: Cadot, 1852-54. 22 vols.; Paris: Lévy, 1863. 10 vols.

167. Dumas, Mathieu. MEMOIRS OF HIS OWN TIME: INCLUDING THE EVOLUTION, THE EMPIRE AND THE RESTORATION. Philadelphia: Lea and Blanchard, 1839. 2 vols.

168. Dunan, Marcel. "La Génie littéraire de Napoléon." REVUE DE L'INSTITUT NAPOLEON 107 (1968): 49-52.

169. Dunan, Marcel. "Napoléon dans la littérature allemande contemporaine." REVUE DES ETUDES NAPOLEONIENNES 27 (1926): 176-88.

170. Dunan, Marcel. "Napoléon epistolier." REVUE DE L'INSTITUT NAPOLEON 118 (1971): 1-4.

171. Durand, Mme. Sophie (Cohondet). MEMOIRES SUR NAPOLEON, L'IMPERATRICE MARIE LOUISE ET LA COUR DES TUILERIES. Paris: Calmann-Lévy, 1886.

172. Durant, Will, and Ariel Durant. THE AGE OF NAPOLEON. New York: Simon and Schuster, 1976.

173. Elek, Oszkar. "Napoléon dans la littérature hongroise." REVUE DES ETUDES NAPOLEONIENNES 34 (1932): 143-56.

174. Epton, Nina C. JOSEPHINE: THE EMPRESS AND HER CHILDREN. London: Weidenfeld and Nicolson, 1975; New York: Norton, 1976.

175. Ettori, F. "Paoli, modele du jeune Bonaparte." REVUE HISTORIQUE DE LA REVOLUTION FRANCAISE 43 (1971): 45-55.

176. Exposition Napoléon Ier. AJACCIO: NAPOLEON ET LA FAMILLE IMPERIALE. Catalogue par David Yvan. Paris: Musées nationaux, 1969.

177. Exposition Napoléon Ier. NAPOLEON AU PAYS DE CAMBRONNE ET DE FOUCHE. Catalogue par Luce Courville. Nantes: Bibliothèque municipal, 1969.

178. Exposition Napoléon Ier. NAPOLEON BONAPARTE: SOUVENIRS PERSONNELS PRESENTES POUR LA PREMIERE FOIS A PARIS PAR LA SOCIETE DES AMIS DU MUSEE DE L'ARMEE A L'HOTEL DES INVALIDES. [Paris]: Exposition historique, 1949.

179. Exposition Napoléon Ier. NAPOLEON ET LES FRANCAIS DE SON TEMPS. Catalogue par Albert Ronsin. Saint-Die: Bibliotheque municipal, 1969.

180. Exposition Napoléon Ier. NAPOLEON ET SON TEMPS. EXPOSITION
     ORGANISEE PAR L'AIDE AUX FAMILLES NOMBREUSES ... MUSEE DE
     PEINTURE DE ROUEN DU 19 MAI AU 15 JUILLET 1934. Catalogue.
     Rouen: Lecerf, 1934.

181. Exposition Napoléon Ier. NAPOLEON TEL QU'EN LUI-MEME. Archives
     Nationales. Paris: Archives Nationales, 1969.

182. Exposition Napoléon Ier. PARIS, GRAND PALAIS: NAPOLEON.
     Paris: Musées nationaux, 1969.

183. Exposition Napoléon Ier. RUEIL-MALMAISON. AUTOUR DE NAPOLEON,
     HISTOIRE ET LEGEND. Paris: Réunion des musées nationaux, 1970.

184. Exposition Napoléon Ier. STRASBOURG: EXPOSITION NAPOLEON ET
     ALSACE. Strasbourg: La Municipalité, 1969.

185. Exposition Sélestat. SELESTAT SOUS LE CONSULAT ET L'EMPIRE.
     Sélestat: Bibliothèque Humaniste de Sélestat, 1969.

186. Fabre, Marc André. JEROME BONAPARTE: ROI DE WESTPHALIA.
     Paris: Hachette, 1952.

187. Fain, Agathon Jean François, baron. MEMOIRES DU BARON FAIN,
     PREMIER SECRETAIRE DU CABINET DE L'EMPEREUR. Paris:
     Plon-Nourrit, 1980.

188. Fesch, Joseph. CARDINAL FESCH PAR LUI-MEME. Lyon: E. Vitte,
     1970.

189. Fiore, Enzo. UN RE AL BIVIO. IL TANDIMENTO DI MURAT. Rome:
     Benincasa, 1972.

190. Fisher, Herbert Albert Laurens. BONAPARTISM. Oxford: Clarendon
     Press, 1980.

191. Fisher, Herbert Albert Laurens. NAPOLEON. London: Oxford
     University Press, 1950.

192. Fleischmann, Hector. LES NAPOLEONIDES: PAULINE BONAPARTE ET
     SES AMOURS. Paris: Librairie universelle, 1910.

193. Fleuriot de Langle, Paul. ELISA, SOEUR DE NAPOLEON. Paris:
     Denoël, 1947.

194. Fleuriot de Langle, Paul. LA PAOLINA, SOEUR DE NAPOLEON.
     Paris: Colbert, 1944.

195. Fleury de Chaboulon, Pierre Alexandre Edouard, baron. MEMOIRES
     DE FLEURY DE CHABOULON ... AVEC ANNOTATIONS MANUSCRITES DE
     NAPOLEON Ier. Edited by Lucien Cornet. Paris: Rouveyre, 1901.
     3 vols.

196. Forshufvud, Sten. NAPOLEON A-T-IL ETE EMPOISONNE? Translated
     from Swedish by Edy Maupois. Paris: Plon, 1961.

197. Fouché, Joseph, duc d'Otrante. MEMOIRES DE JOSEPH FOUCHE, DUC D'OTRANTE. Paris: Société des Bibliophiles, 1824. 2 vols.

198. Fouché, Joseph, duc d'Otrante. MEMOIRS OF JOSEPH FOUCHE. Boston and New York: Merrill & Baker, 1903. 2 vols.

199. Foulon, Brigitte. "Les Souvenirs de l'épopée impériale à Léningrad et Moscou." REVUE DE L'INSTITUT NAPOLEON 131 (1975): 183-84.

200. Fourmestraux, Eugène. LE PRINCE EUGENE. 2d ed. Paris: P. Dupont, 1867.

201. Francastel, Albert. "Ingres et Napoléon." REVUE DES ETUDES NAPOLEONIENNES 18 (1922): 204-11.

202. "La France à l'époque napoléonienne." Numéro Spécial. REVUE D'HISTOIRE MODERNE ET CONTEMPORANIE 17 (1970): 329-920.

203. Francechetti, Dominique Cesar. MEMOIRES SUR LES EVENEMENTS QUI ONT PRECEDE LA MORT DE JOACHIM Ier ROI DES DEUX SICILES. Paris: Beaudouin, 1826.

204. Francechetti, Dominique Cesar. SUPPLEMENT AUX MEMOIRES SUR LES EVENEMENTS. Paris: Beaudouin 1829.

205. Franceschini, Emile. "Saliceti et Napoléon." REVUE DES ETUDES NAPOLEONIENNES 31 (1930): 131-55.

206. Frayling, Christopher. NAPOLEON WROTE FICTION. New York: St. Martin's Press, 1972.

207. Gaffarel, Paul. LES BONAPARTE A MARSEILLE, 1793-1797. Paris: Plon, 1905.

208. Gallo, E. le. "Carnot et Napoléon pendant les Cent-Jours." REVUE DES ETUDES NAPOLEONIENNES 31 (1934): 65-83.

209. Galvani, Charles. MEMOIRES SUR LES EVENEMENTS QUI ONT PRECEDE LA MORT DE JOACHIM-NAPOLEON. Paris, 1843.

210. Gambiez, Fernand Charles Louis. "Napoléon Bonaparte, cadet-gentilhomme à l'Ecole royale militaire de Paris." REVUE DE L'INSTITUT NAPOLEON 123 (1972): 49-56.

211. Ganière, Paul. NAPOLEON A SAINTE HELENE. Paris: Amiot-Dumont, 1957-62. 3 vols.

212. Garnier, Athanase. MEMOIRES SUR LA COUR DE LOUIS NAPOLEON ET SUR LA HOLLANDE. Paris: Ladvocat, 1828.

213. Garnier, Jean Paul. MURAT, ROI DE NAPLES. Paris: Le Club du Meilleur Livre, 1959.

214. Garros, Louis. NAPOLEON, CET INCONNU. Paris: Beaudart, 1950.

215. Gaudin, Michel Martin Charles, duc de Gaëte. MEMOIRES, Souvenires, OPINIONS ET ECRITS DU DUC DE GAETE. Paris: Baudouin, 1826. 2 vols.

216. Gaudin, Michel Martin Charles, duc de Gaëte. SUPPLEMENT AUX MEMOIRES ET SOUVENIRS DE M. GAUDIN, DUC DE GAETE. Paris: Goetschy, 1834.

217. Gavoty, André. LES AMOUREUX DE L'IMPERATRICE JOSEPHINE. Paris: Fayard, 1961.

218. Geer, Walter. NAPOLEON AND HIS FAMILY. New York: Brentano, 1927-29. 3 vols.

219. Geyl, Pieter. NAPOLEON, FOR AND AGAINST. Translated by Olive Renier. New Haven: Yale University Press, 1949. (New ed., London, 1976.)

220. Girod de l'Ain, Gabriel. BERNADOTTE, CHEF DE GUERRE ET CHEF D'ETAT. Paris: Perrin, 1968.

221. Girod de l'Ain, Gabriel. DESIREE CLARY. Paris: Hachette, 1959.

222. Girod de l'Ain, Gabriel. JOSEPH BONAPRATE. Paris: Perrin, 1970.

223. Gobineau, Marcel. PAULINE BORGHESE: SOEUR FIDELE. Paris: Amiot, 1958.

224. Godechot, Jacques Léon. L'EUROPE ET L'AMERIQUE A L'EPOQUE NAPOLEONIENNE (1800-1815). Paris: Presses Universitaires de France, 1967.

225. Godechot, Jacques Léon. "Lettres inédites de Napoléon Bonaparte." REVUE HISTORIQUE DE LA REVOLUTION FRANCAISE (1932): 60-61.

226. Godechot, Jacques Léon. NAPOLEON. Paris: A. Michel, 1969.

227. Godechot, Jacques Léon. NAPOLEON: LE MEMORIAL DES SIECLES. Paris, 1969.

228. Godechot, Jacques Léon. "Napoléon: Pour ou Contre?" in L'EUROPE ET L'AMERIQUE A L'EPOQUE NAPOLEONIENNE. Paris: Presses Universitaires de France, 1968.

229. Godechot, Jacques Léon. "La Period révolutionnaire et impériale." REVUE HISTORIQUE 504 (1972): 445-494; 507 (1973): 149-208; 516 (1975): 399-466; 533 (1980): 101-147; 536 (1980): 399-469.

230. Godechot, Jacques Léon; Beatrice Hyslop; and David Dowd. THE NAPOLEONIC ERA IN EUROPE. New York: Holt, Rinehart and Winston, 1970, 1971.

231. Godlewski, Guy. TROIS CENTS JOURS D'EXIL: NAPOLEON A L'ILE D'ELBE. Paris: Hachette, 1961.

232. Göhring, Martin. NAPOLEON; VON ALTEN ZUM NEUEN EUROPA. Göttingen: Musterschmidt, 1959. (2d ed., Göttingen, 1965.)

233. Gonnard, Philippe. "Sainte-Hélène [documents]." REVUE DES ETUDES NAPOLEONIENNES 2 (1912): 132-51.

234. Gonnard, Philippe. "La Légende napoléonienne et la presse libérale (1817-1829)." REVUE DES ETUDES NAPOLEONIENNES 1 (1912): 235-58.

235. Gonnard, Philippe. "La Légende napoléonienne et la presse libérale: la 'Minerve.'" REVUE DES ETUDES NAPOLEONIENNES 1 (1914): 28-49.

236. Gonnard, Philippe. LES ORIGINES DE LA LEGENDE NAPOLEONIENNE. L'OEUVRE HISTORIQUE DE NAPOLEON A SAINTE-HELENE. Geneva: Slatkine-Megariotis Reprints, 1976.

237. Gosselin, Louis Leon Theodore [Georges Lenôtre]. NAPOLEON. Paris: Gautier-Languereau, 1962.

238. Gourgaud, Gaspard, baron. SAINTE-HELENE, JOURNAL INEDIT DE 1815 A 1818. Edited by Vicomte de Grouchy et Antoine Guillois. Paris: Flammarion, 1899. 2 vols.

239. Grand-Carteret, John. "La Légende napoléonienne par l'image, vue sous un jour nouveau." REVUE DES ETUDES NAPOLEONIENNES 20 (1923): 28-46.

240. Gromaire, G. "Arndt et Napoleon." REVUE DES ETUDES NAPOLEONIENNES 2 (1913): 372-401.

241. Grouard, A. "Les Dernier Historiens de 1815. Ligny." REVUE DES ETUDES NAPOLEONIENNES 1 (1913): 235-58, 367-90.

242. Grunwald, C. de. "Le Mariage de Napoléon et de Marie-Louise." (Letters of Comtesse Metternich). REVUE DES DEUX MONDES 38, 41 (1937).

243. Gruyer, Paul. NAPOLEON: ROI DE L'ILE D'ELBE. Paris: Hachette, 1906.

244. Guérard, Albert Léon. REFLECTIONS ON THE NAPOLEONIC LEGEND. New York: Scribner, 1924.

245. Guerrini, Maurice. NAPOLEON DEVANT DIEU. Introduction by Prince Napoleon. Paris: Peyronnet, 1960.

246. Guerrini, Maurice. NAPOLEON ET PARIS, TRENTE AND D'HISTOIRE. Paris: Tequi, 1967.

247. Hachette, Alfred. LA JOURNEE DU RETOUR DES CENDRES. Paris: F. Michel, 185?

248. Hachette, Alfred. "La Retour des Cendres et l'Image." REVUE DES ETUDES NAPOLEONIENNES 37 (1933): 329-46.

249. Handelman, Marcell. "Bulletin des ouvrages Napoléoniens parus en Pologne de 1901 à 1918." REVUE DES ETUDES NAPOLEONIENNES 18 (1922): 137-50.

250. Hanna, Alfred Jackson. A PRINCE IN THEIR MIDST: THE ADVENTUROUS LIFE OF ACHILLE MURAT ON THE AMERICAN FRONTIER. Norman, Okla.: University of Oklahoma Press, 1946.

251. Hanoteau, Jean Adolphe. JOSEPHINE AVANT NAPOLEON, LE MENAGE BEAUHARNAIS. Paris: Plon, 1935.

252. Hastier, Louis. LE GRAND AMOUR DE JOSEPHINE. Paris: Correa, 1955.

253. Hauterive, E. d'. "Lettres de jeunesse de Bonaparte (1789-1792)." LA REVUE DES DEUX MONDES (1934).

254. Helaey, F.G. THE LITERARY CULTURE OF NAPOLEON. Geneva: Droz, 1959.

255. Herold, J. Christopher. THE AGE OF NAPOLEON. New York: American Heritage, 1963.

256. Hillemand, Pierre. "Napoléon a-t-il tenté de se suicider à Fontainebleau?" REVUE DE L'INSTITUT NAPOLEON 119 (1971): 71-78.

257. Hillemand, Pierre. PATHOLOGIE DE NAPOLEON. Paris: La Palatine, 1970.

258. Hilt, Douglas, "Mr. Bonaparte of Bordentown, New Jersey." MANKIND (1972).

259. Hochschild, Karl Fredrik Lotarius, freiherr. DESIREE, REINE DE SUEDE ET DE NORVEGE. Paris: Plon-Nourrit, 1888.

260. Hortense, queen consort of Louis, king of Holland. "Lettres de la reine Hortense." Edited by J. Hugentobler. REVUE DES ETUDES NAPOLEONIENNES 37 (1933): 262-91.

261. Hortense, queen consort of Louis, king of Holland. MEMOIRES. 12th ed. Paris: Plon, 1927. 3 vols.

262. Horward, Donald D. "Napoleon and Beethoven." PROCEEDINGS OF THE CONSORTIUM ON REVOLUTIONARY EUROPE 9 (2) (1980): 3-13.

263. Houssaye, Henry. 1814. Paris: Perrin, 1888.

264. Houssaye, Henry. 1815. Paris: Perrin, 1889-1905. 3 vols.

265. Huart, S. d'. "Un Jugement récent à propos des papiers de famille. Les archives Méneval." REVUE DE L'INSTITUT NAPOLEON 122 (1972): 1-5.

266. Hubert, Emmanuelle. LES CENT JOURS. Paris: Julliard, 1966.

267. Humières, L., comtesse d'. "Une Femme. La Mère de Napoléon." REVUE DES ETUDES NAPOLEONIENNES 45 (1939): 98-112.

268. Imbert de Saint-Amand, Arthur Léon, baron. MARIE LOUISE L'ISLE D'ELBE ET LES CENT JOURS. Paris: Dentu, 1885.

269. Isola, Maria dell'. "La Mort de Napoléon." REVUE DES ETUDES NAPOLEONIENNES 22 (1933): 280-84.

270. "L'Italie Jacobin et napoléonienne." REVUE DES HISTORIQUE DE LA REVOLUTION FRANCAISE. Special Issue 230 (1977).

271. Iung, Théodore. LUCIEN BONAPARTE ET SES MEMOIRES, 1775-1840. Paris: Charpentier, 1882-83. 3 vols.

272. Jérôme Bonaparte, king of Westphalia. MEMOIRES ET CORRESPONDANCE DU ROI JEROME ET DE LA REINE CATHERINE. Paris: Dentu, 1861-66. 7 vols.

273. Jérôme Bonaparte, king of Westphalia, and Catherine de Westphalie. BRIEFWECHSEL. Stuttgart: W. Kohlhammer, 1886-87. 3 vols.

274. Johnston, Otto W. "Napoleon and the Germans: An Attempt at a Critical Dialogue." Commentary. PROCEEDINGS OF THE CONSORTIUM ON REVOLUTIONARY EUROPE 9 (1) (1980): 212-20.

275. Jones, R. Ben. NAPOLEON, MAN AND MYTH. New York: Holmes and Meier, 1979.

276. Joseph Bonaparte, king of Spain. LETTRES INEDITES OU EPARSES DE JOSEPH BONAPARTE A NAPLES 1806-08. Edited by Jacques Rambaud. Paris: Plon-Nourrit, 1911.

277. Joseph Bonaparte, king of Spain. MEMOIRES ET CORRESPONDANCE DU ROI JOSEPH. Edited by Albert Du Casse. 2d ed. Paris: Perrotin, 1854. 10 vols.

278. Joseph Bonaparte, king of Spain. LE ROI JOSEPH BONAPARTE. LETTRES D'EXIL INEDITES (AMERIQUE--ANGLETERRE--ITALIE). Paris: Charpentier et Fasquelle, 1912.

279. Joseph Bonaparte, king of Spain. SUITE AUX MEMOIRES DE ROI JOSEPH. Edited by Albert Du Casse. Paris: Perrotin, 1855.

280. Josephine, empress consort of Napoléon I. LES BEAUHARNAIS ET L'EMPEREUR, LETTERS DE L'IMPERATRICE JOSEPHINE ET DE LA REINE HORTENSE AU PRINCE EUGENE. Edited by Jean Adolphe Hanoteau. Paris: Librairie Plon, les petits-fils de Plon et Nourrit, 1936.

281. Josephine, empress consort of Napoléon I. MEMOIRES ET
     CORRESPONDANCE DE L'IMPERATRICE JOSEPHINE. Paris: Plancher,
     1820; and MEMOIRES HISTORIQUES ET SECRETS DE JOSEPHINE M.R.
     TASCHER DE LA PAGERIE, by A. le Normand. Paris, 1820. (Both
     apochryphal).

282. Kaisenberg, Moritz Leopold Ludolf von. KONIG JEROME NAPOLEON,
     EIN ZEIT UN LEBENSBILD. Leipzig: H. Schmidt & C. Gunther,
     1899.

283. Karmin, Otto. "Le Courage de Napoléon." REVUE HISTORIQUE DE LA
     REVOLUTION FRANCAISE 1 (1924): 79-79.

284. Kemble, James. NAPOLEON IMMORTAL: THE MEDICAL HISTORY AND
     PRIVATE LIFE OF NAPOLEON BONAPARTE. London: J. Murray, 1959.

285. Kemble, James. ST. HELENA DURING NAPOLEON'S EXILE: GORREQUER'S
     DIARY. London: Heinemann, 1969.

286. Kircheisen, Friedrich Max. BIBLIOGRAPHIE NAPOLEONS. Berlin:
     Mittler, 1902.

287. Kircheisen, Friedrich Max. JOVIAL KING, NAPOLEON'S YOUNGEST
     BROTHER. London: E. Mathews & Marrot, 1932.

288. Kircheisen, Friedrich Max. NAPOLEON. Stuttgart and Berlin:
     Cotta, 1927, 1929. 2 vols. (1 vol. English translation.
     London: G. Howe, 1931).

289. Kircheisen, Friedrich Max. NAPOLEON: SEIN LEBEN UND SEIN ZEIT.
     Munich and Leipzig: G. Muller, 1911-34. 9 vols.

290. Kleinschmidt, Arthur. GESCHICHTE DES KONIGREICHS WESTPHALEN.
     Gotha: F.A. Perthes, 1893.

291. Knapton, Ernest J. "A Contemporary Impression of Napoleon
     Bonaparte in 1797." FRENCH HISTORICAL STUDIES 1 (1960): 476-81.

292. Knapton, Ernest J. EMPRESS JOSEPHINE. Cambridge, Mass.:
     Harvard University Press, 1963.

293. Korngold, Ralph. THE LAST YEARS OF NAPOLEON: HIS CAPTIVITY ON
     ST. HELENA. New York: Harcourt, Brace, 1959.

294. Kuhn, Joachim. PAULINE BONAPARTE. Paris: Plon-Nourrit, 1937.

295. Labarre de Raillicourt, Dominique. LOUIS BONAPARTE, ROI DE
     HOLLANDE. Paris: J. Peyronnet, 1963.

296. Lachouque Henry. LES DERNIERS JOURS DE L'EMPIRE. Paris: B.
     Arthaud, 1965.

297. Lachouque, Henry. THE LAST DAYS OF NAPOLEON'S EMPIRE: FROM WATERLOO TO ST. HELENA. London: Allen & Unwin, 1966.

298. Lacretelle, Pierre de. SECRETS ET MALHEURS DE LA REINE HORTENSE. Paris: Hachette, 1936.

299. Lanfrey, Pierre. HISTOIRE DE NAPOLEON Ier. Paris: Charpentier, 1867-75. 5 vols.

300. Lanzac de Laborie, Léon de. "Napoléon et David." REVUE DES ETUDES NAPOLEONIENNES 1 (1913): 21-37.

301. Laplace, Marie Anne Charlotte de. LETTRES DE MADAME DE LAPLACE A ELISA NAPOLEON, PRINCESSE DE LUCQUES ET DE PIOMBINO. Réunies et annotées par Paul Marmottan. Paris: A. Charles, 1897.

302. Larrey, Felix Hippolyte, baron. MADAME MERE: NAPOLEONIS MATER. Paris: E. Dentu, 1892.

303. Las Cases, Marie Joseph Emmanuel Auguste Dieudonné, comte de. MEMOIRES D'EMMANUEL DIEUDONNE COMTE DE LAS CASES. Brussels: Maubach, 1818.

304. Las Cases, Marie Joseph Emmanuel Auguste Dieudonné, comte de. MEMOIRES OF THE EMPEROR NAPOLEON. London: Bentley, 1836.

305. Las Cases, Marie Joseph Emmanuel Auguste Dieudonné, comte de. MEMOIRES DE SAINTE-HELENE, OU JOURNAL. Paris: L'Auteur, 1823. vols. (New editions. 1824, 1830, 1835, 1840, 1841-42, 1951 [Marcel Dunan], 1957 [G. Walter], 1961 [A. Fugier], and 1968 [Joël Schmidt].)

306. Latreille, André. L'ERE NAPOLEONIENNE. Paris: A. Colin, 1975.

307. Laurent, Gustave. "Une Letter de Lucien Bonaparte à Barras à l'occasion du 9 thermidor." REVUE HISTORIQUE DE LA REVOLUTION FRANCAISE 2 (1925): 175-176.

308. Lazzareschi, E. LE SORELLE DI NAPOLEONE, PAOLINA. Florence: Rinascimento del libro, 1932.

309. Lefebvre, Georges. NAPOLEON. 4th ed. Paris: Presses Universitaires de France, 1953.

310. Lefebvre, Georges. NAPOLEON. Translated by Henry Stockhold. London: Routledge & K. Paul, 1969. 2 vols.

311. Le Gallo, Emile. "Murat et sa famille." REVUE DES ETUDES NAPOLEONIENNES 19 (1930): 295-98.

312. LA LEGENDE NAPOLEONIENNE, 1796-1900. Paris: Bibliothèque Nationale, 1969.

313. Lenanton, Carola (Oman). NAPOLEON'S VICEROY: EUGENE DE BEAUHARNAIS. London: Hodder & Stoughton, 1966.

314. LETTERS FROM THE CAPE OF GOOD HOPE, IN REPLY TO MR. WARDEN.
     London: n.p., 1817.

315. Lévy, Arthur. LES DISSENTIMENTS DE LA FAMILLE IMPERIALE.
     Paris: Villat, 1931.

316. Lévy, Arthur. NAPOLEON ET EUGENE DE BEAUHARNAIS. Paris:
     Calmann-Lévy, 1926.

317. Lévy, Arthur. NAPOLEON INTIME. Paris: Nelson, 1893.

318. Leynadier, C. HISTOIRE DE LA FAMILLE BONAPARTE DE L'AN 1050 A
     1848. Paris: Librairie historique et scientifique, 1866.

319. Lichtenaure, W.F. "La Visite de Napoléon à Rotterdam an 1811."
     REVUE DE L'INSTITUT NAPOLEON 128-129 (1973): 93-100.

320. Locre, Jean Guillaume. NAPOLEON AU CONSEIL D'ETAT. NOTES ET
     PROCES VERBAUX INEDITS DE JEAN-GUILLAUME LOCRE. Paris:
     Berger-Levrault, 1963.

321. Lote, Georges. "La Contre-légende napoléonienne et la mort de
     Napoléon." REVUE DES ETUDES NAPOLEONIENNES 30 (1930): 324-49.

322. Lote, Georges. "La Mort de Napoléon et l'opinion bonapartiste
     en 1821." REVUE DES ETUDES NAPOLEONIENNES 31 (1930): 19-58.

323. Louis Bonaparte, king of Holland. DOCUMENS HISTORIQUES ET
     REFLEXIONS SUR LE GOUVERNMENT DE LA HOLLANDE. Amsterdam: Samuel
     Delachaux, 1820.

324. LOUIS-NAPOLEON ET LA HOLLAND DE SON EPOQUE. [Catalogue
     d'exposition de l'Institut Néerlandais à Paris]. Paris, 1959.

325. Lucas-Dubreton, Jean. LE CULTE DE NAPOLEON, 1814-1848. Paris:
     A. Michel, 1960.

326. Lucas-Dubreton, Jean. NAPOLEON. Paris: Fayard, 1942.

327. Lucien Bonaparte, prince of Canino. "Lucien Bonaparte et sa
     soeur Elisa, lettres intimes inédites." Edited by Paul
     Marmottan. REVUE DES ETUDES NAPOLEONIENNES 22 (1931): 166-86.

328. Lucien Bonaparte, prince of Canino. MEMOIRES SECRETS SUR LA VIE
     PRIVEE, PUBLIQUE ET LITTERAIRE DE LUCIEN BONAPARTE. Paris:
     Delaunay, 1816.

329. Lucien Bonaparte, prince of Canino. MEMOIRES DE LUCIEN
     BONAPARTE, PRINCE DE CANINO. Paris: Gosselin, 1836.

330. Luzzato-Guerrini, Teresa. PAOLINA. Florence: "Nemi", 1932.

331. Macartney, Clarence Edward Noble, and Gordon Dorrance. THE
     BONAPARTES IN AMERICA. Philadelphia: Dorrance, 1939.

332. McErlean, J.M.P. "L'Indicible Secret de Napoléon Bonaparte et de Charles-André Pozzo di Borgo." REVUE HISTORIQUE DE LA REVOLUTION FRANCAISE 46 (1974): 672-91.

333. MacIntyre, Duncan. NAPOLEON. THE LEGEND AND THE REALITY. Glasgow: Blackie, 1976.

334. MacKenzie, Norma. THE ESCAPE FROM ELBA: THE FALL AND FLIGHT OF NAPOLEON, 1814-1815. New York: Oxford University Press, 1982.

335. Madelin, Louis. HISTOIRE DU CONSULAT ET DE L'EMPIRE. Paris: Hachette, 1937-54. 16 vols.

336. Madelin, Louis. HISTORY OF THE CONSULATE AND EMPIRE. London, 1932. 2 vols.; New York: Putnam, 1934-36.

337. Maitland, Frederick Lewis. NAPOLEON A BORD DU "BELLEROPHON". Paris: Plon, 1933.

338. Maitland, Frederick Lewis. NARRATIVE OF THE SURRENDER OF BUONAPARTE. London: H. Colburn, 1825.

339. Maitland, Frederick Lewis. RELATIONS DU CAPITAINE MAITLAND, EX-COMMANDANT DU BELLEROPHON CONCERNANT L'EMBARQUEMENT ET LE SEJOUR DE L'EMPEREUR NAPOLEON A BORD DE CE BAISSEAU. Translated from English by J.T. Pariset. Paris: Baudoin, 1826.

340. Malcolm, Clementina Elphinstone, lady. DIARY OF ST. HELENA. London: Allen & Unwin, 1899.

341. Malcolm, Clementina Elphinstone, lady. "Le Journal de Sainte-Hélène, trade. de Mme. Léon-Raynal." REVUE DES ETUDES NAPOLEONIENNES 33 (1931): 283-307.

342. Malo, Henri. "Le Fonds Frédéric-Masson à la Bibliothèque Thiers: discours prononcé à cérémonie d'inauguration." REVUE DES ETUDES NAPOLEONIENNES 26 (1926): 189-192.

343. Manceron, Claude. LE CITOYEN BONAPARTE: LA JEUNESSE DE NAPOLEON, 1769-1769. Paris: Gallimark, 1980.

344. Manceron, Claude. L'EPOPEE DE NAPOLEON. Paris: Pont Royal, 1965.

345. Manfred, Albert Zakharovich. NAPOLEON BONAPARTE. Translation from Russian to French. Moscow: Editions du Progrès, 1980.

346. Marcel-Paon, Anie. "Le Mariage de Jérôme Bonaparte et d'Elizabeth Patterson." REVUE DES ETUDES NAPOLEONIENNES 35 (1933): 65-87.

347. Marchand, Louis Joseph Narcisse, comte. MEMOIRES DE MARCHAND, PREMIER VALET DE CHAMBRE DE L'EMPEREUR. Edited by Jean Bourguignon and Henry Lachouque. Paris: Plon, 1952-55. 2 vols.

348. Maret, Hugues Bernard, duc de Bassano. SOUVENIRS INTIMES DE LA
     REVOLUTION ET DE L'EMPIRE. Brussels: de Potter, 1843. 2 vols.

349. Marie Louise, empress consort of Napoleon I. LETTRES A LA
     COMTESSE DE COLLEREDO ET A MLLE. DE POUTET. Paris: Plon, 1887.

350. Marie Louise, empress consort of Napoleon I. THE PRIVATE
     DIARIES OF THE EMPRESS MARIE LOUSIE, WIFE OF NAPOLEON I. Edited
     by Frédéric Masson. London: J. Murray, 1922.

351. Markham, Felix Maurice Hippisley. THE BONAPARTES. New York:
     Taplinger, 1975.

352. Markham, Felix Maurice Hippisley. NAPOLEON. New York: New
     American Library, 1963.

353. Markham, Felix Maurice Hippisley. NAPOLEON AND THE AWAKENING OF
     EUROPE. London: English Universities Press, 1954.

354. Marmottan, Paul. "Lucien Bonaparte, Ministre de l'Intérieur et
     des Arts." REVUE DES ETUDES NAPOLEONIENNES 25 (1925): 5-42.

355. Martin, Clude. JOSE NAPOLEON I, 'REY INTRUSO' DE ESPANA.
     Madrid: Editora Nacional, 1969.

356. Martineau, Gilbert. MADAME MERE. Paris: Editions
     France-Empire, 1980.

357. Martineau, Gilbert. MADAME MERE: NAPOLEON'S MOTHER.
     Translated by Frances Partridge. London: J. Murray, 1978.

358. Martineau, Gilbert. NAPOLEON'S LAST JOURNEY. London: J.
     Murray, 1976.

359. Martineau, Gilbert. NAPOLEON'S SAINT HELENA. Chicago: Rand
     McNally, 1969.

360. Martineau, Gilbert. NAPOLEON'S SURRENDERS. London: J. Murray,
     1971.

361. Masson, Frédéric. NAPOLEON A SAINTE-HELENE. Paris: Ollendorff,
     1912. (Translated by L.B. Frewen. NAPOLEON AT ST. HELENA.
     Oxford: Pen-in-Hand, 1949.)

362. Masson, Frédéric. NAPOLEON ET SA FAMILLE. Paris: Ollendorff,
     1900-19. 13 vols.

363. Masson, Frédéric. NAPOLEON, MANUSCRITS INEDITS. New ed. Paris:
     Ollendorff, 1908.

364. Masson, Frédéric, and Guido Biagi, eds. NAPOLEON INCONNU,
     PAPIERS INEDITS, 1769-1793. Paris: Ollendorff, 1895. 2 vols.

365. Mathiez, A. "Une Epigramme contre Bonaparte." REVUE HISTORIQUE
     DE LA REVOLUTION FRANCAISE 6 (1929): 88.

366. Mathiez, A. "Les Trafics de Joséphine avec les fournisseurs." REVUE HISTORIQUE DE LA REVOLUTION FRANCAISE 6 (1929): 289-90.

367. Maudre, Jacques. BONAPARTE. Paris: Gautier-Languereau, 1975.

368. Maurois, André. NAPOLEON: A PICTORIAL BIOGRAPHY. New York: Viking Press, 1964.

369. Maurois, André; J. Chastenet; R. Huyghe; and Marcel Dunan. NAPOLEON ET L'EMPIRE. Paris: Hachette, 1968.

370. "Maximes de Napoleon." REVUE DES ETUDES NAPOLEONIENNES 22 (1923): 131-32.

371. Mayer, Emile. "Les Historiens de Napoléon: le général Jean Colin." REVUE DES ETUDES NAPOLEONIENNES 14 (1918): 5-28.

372. Mazé, Jules. "Madame Mère à l'Hotel de Brienne." REVUE DES ETUDES NAPOLEONIENNES 42 (1936): 81-84.

373. Mazis, Alexandre Jean des. "Cahiers". In Paul Bartel's LA JEUNESSE INEDITE DE NAPOLEON. Paris: Amiot-Dumont, 1954.

374. Melchior-Bonnet, Bernardine. "Jérôme Bonaparte et 'La Belle de Baltimore'." NOUVELLE REVUE DES DEUX MONDES (1979).

375. Melchior-Bonnet, Bernardine. JEROME BONAPARTE: OU L'ENVERS DE LA CONQUETE. Paris: Perrin, 1979.

376. Melzi d'Eril, Duca di Lodi. MEMORIE, DOCUMENTI E LETTERE INEDITE DI NAPOLEONE Io E BEAUHARNAIS. Milan, 1865. 2 vols.

377. Melzi d'Eril, Francesco. EUGENIO BEAUHARNAIS E AUGUSTA DI BAVIERA, DOCUMENTI INEDITI. Munich, 1897.

378. Méneval, Claude François, baron de. MEMOIRES POUR SERVIR A L'HISTOIRE DE NAPOLEON Ier DUPUIS 1802 JUSQU'A 1815. New York: D. Appleton, 1894. 3 vols.

379. Méneval, Claude François, baron de. NAPOLEON ET MARIE-LOUISE. SOUVENIRS HISTORIQUES DE M. LE BARON DE MENEVAL. Paris: Amyot, 1844-45. 3 vols.

380. Méneval, Napoleon Joseph Ernest, baron de. THE EMPRESS JOSEPHINE. London: S. Low, Marston, 1912.

381. Mercader Riba, Juan. JOSE BONAPARTE, REY DE ESPANA, 1808-1813. Madrid: Consejo Superior de Investigaciones Cientificas, 1971.

382. Mercy-Argenteau, François Joseph Charles Marie, comte de. MEMOIRS OF THE Cte DE MERCY ARGENTEAU, NAPOLEON'S CHAMBERLAIN AND HIS MINISTER PLENIPOTENTIARY TO THE KING OF BAVARIA. New York: Putnam, 1917. 2 vols.

383. Merezhkovskii, Dmitrii Sergieevich. THE LIFE OF NAPOLEON.
     Translated from the Russian by Catherine Zvegintzov. New York:
     Dutton, 1929.

384. MERKWUERDIGE LEBENSGESCHICHTE DES PRINZEN EUGEN. Leipzig, 1824.

385. Meynier, Albert. "Pour et Contre Napoléon. Le procès
     historique de l'Empereur." REVUE DES ETUDES NAPOLEONIENNES 37
     (1933): 5-76.

386. Miot de Melito, André François, comte. MEMOIRES DU COMTE MIOT
     DE MELITO, ANCIEN MINISTRE, AMBASSADEUR, CONSEILLER D'ETAT ET
     MEMBRE DE L'INSTITUT (1788-1815). Paris: Michel Lévy, 1858. 3
     vols.

387. Mistler, Jean, ed. NAPOLEON ET L'EMPIRE. Paris: Hachette,
     1968. 2 vols. (2d ed. Paris, 1979.)

388. Mollien, François Nicolas, comte. MEMOIRES D'UN ANCIEN MINISTRE
     DU TRESOR PUBLIC DE 1800 A 1814. Paris, 1837. 4 vols. Paris:
     Guillaumin, 1898. 3 vols.

389. Monglond, André. LA FRANCE REVOLUTIONNAIRE ET IMPERIALE:
     ANNALES DE BIBLIOGRAPHIE METHODIQUE ET DESCRIPTION DES LIVRES
     ILLUSTRES. Grenoble: Arthaud, 1930-78. 10 vols.

390. Montagu, Violette M. EUGENE DE BEAUHARNAIS, ADOPTED SON OF
     NAPOLEON. London: J. Long, 1913.

391. Montesquiou-Fezensac, Raymond Aymery Philippe Joseph, duc de.
     THE RUSSIAN CAMPAIGN. Translated by Lee Kennett. Athens, Ga.:
     Univeristy of Georgia Press, 1970.

392. Montholon, Albine Hélène de Vassal, comtesse de. SOUVENIRS DE
     SAINTE-HELENE PAR LA COMTESSE DE MONTHOLON, 1815-1816. Paris:
     Emile-Paul, 1901.

393. Montholon, Charles François Tristan de. RECITS DE LA CAPTIVITE
     DE L'EMPEREUR NAPOLEON A SAINTE-HELENE. Paris: Didot, 1847. 2
     vols. (English trans. HISTORY OF THE CAPTIVITY OF NAPOLEON AT
     ST. HELENA. London: Colburn, 1846.)

394. Montholon, Charles Jean Tristan de, marquis de. LETTRES DU
     COMTE ET COMTESSE MONTHOLON. Edited by P. Gonnard. Paris:
     Picard, 1906.

395. Montholon, Charles Jean Tristan de, marquis de. MEMOIRS OF THE
     HISTORY OF FRANCE DURING THE REIGN OF NAPOLEON. London:
     Colburn, 1823-24. 7 vols.

396. Morgulis, G., ed. "Murat à Naples. Lettres inédites." REVUE
     DES ETUDES NAPOLEONIENNES 43 (1936): 206-12.

397. Mougins-Roquefort, Joseph de. NAPOLEON PRISONNIER VU PAR LES ANGLAIS: AVEC DE NOMBREUX TEMOIGANGES INEDITS EN FRANCAIS. Paris: J. Tallandier, 1978.

398. Murat, Inès. NAPOLEON AND THE AMERICAN DREAM. Translated by Frances Frenaye. Baton Rouge, La.: Louisiana State University Press, 1981.

399. Nabonne, Bernard. BERNADOTTE. Paris: A. Michel, 1940. Paris: La Nouvelle Edition, 1946.

400. Nabonne, Bernard. JOSEPH BONAPARTE, LE ROI PHILOSOPHE. Paris: Hachette, 1949.

401. Nabonne, Bernard. PAULINE BONAPARTE, LA VENUS IMPERIALE. Paris: Hachette, 1963.

402. Napoleon, Charles Louis, comte de Saint-Leu. REPONSE A SIR WALTER SCOTT SUR LA HISTOIRE DE NAPOLEON. Florence, 1831.

403. Napoleon I, Emperor of the French. "Clisson et Eugenie." OEUVRES LITTERAIRES ET ECRITS MILITAIRES. Edited by Jean Tulard. Paris: Société encyclopedique francaise, 1967-69. 3 vols.

404. Napoleon I, Emperor of the French. CONFIDENTIAL CORRESPONDANCE OF NAPOLEON BONAPARTE WITH HIS BROTHER JOSEPH. New York: Mason, 1856. 2 vols.

405. Napoleon I, Emperor of the French. CORRESPONDANCE DE NAPOLEON Ier; PUBLIEE PAR ORDRE DE L'EMPEREUR NAPOLEON III. Paris: Imprimerie impériale, 1858-70. 32 vols.

406. Napoleon I, Emperor of the French. CORRESPONDANCE INEDITE DE NAPOLEON, CONSERVEE AUX ARCHIVES DE LA GUERRE. Edited by E. Picard and L. Tuetey. Paris: Charles-Lavauzelle, 1911-13. 3 vols.

407. Napoleon I, Emperor of the French. CORRESPONDANCE (LETTRES INTIMES). Edited by Philippe Lebaud. Paris: Club de Livre, 1970. 2 vols.

408. Napoleon I, Emperor of the French. CORRESPONDANCE, SIX CENTS LETTRES DE TRAVAIL (1806-1810). Présentée par Maximilien Vox. Paris: Gallimard, 1943.

409. Napoleon I, Emperor of the French. DERNIERES LETTRES INEDITES DE NAPOLEON Ier. Edited by Léonce Brotonne. Paris: H. Champion, 1903.

410. Napoleon I, Emperor of the French. INEDITS NAPOLEONIENS. Edited by Arthur Chuquet. Paris: Fontemoing, 1913-19. 2 vols.

411. Napoleon I, Emperor of the French. JOURNAL SECRET DE NAPOLEON BONAPARTE. Edited by Giuseppe J.M. Lo Duca. Paris: J.J. Pauvert, 1962. (Apocryphal).

412. Napoleon I, Emperor of the French. "La Lettre de Bonaparte à
     Josephine, du 3 thermidor an IV." Edited by Emile-P. Brouwet.
     REVUE DES ETUDES NAPOLEONIENNES 27 (1929): 193-95.

413. Napoleon I, Emperor of the French. LETTRES A JOSEPHINE.
     Recueillies par Jacques Bourgeat. Paris: Guy Le Prat, 1941.

414. Napoleon I, Emperor of the French. LETTRES D'AMOUR A JOSEPHINE.
     Edited by Jean Tulard. Paris: Fayard, 1981.

415. Napoleon I, Emperor of the French. LETTRES DE NAPOLEON A
     JOSEPHINE ET LETTRES DE JOSEPHINE A NAPOLEON. Paris: Livre
     club de libraire, 1959.

416. Napoleon I, Emperor of the French. LETTRES, DECISIONS ET ACTES
     DE NAPOLEON A PONT-DE-BRIQUES ET AU CAMPE DE BOULOGNE (AN
     VI-1798--AN XII-1804). Edited by Fernand Emile Beaucour.
     Levallois: F.E. Beaucour, 1979.

417. Napoleon I, Emperor of the French. LETTRES INEDITES DE NAPOLEON
     Ier A MARIE-LOUISE ECRITES DE 1810 A 1814. Edited by Louis
     Madelin. Paris: Editions des Bibliotheques nationales de
     France, 1935.

418. Napoleon I, Emperor of the French. LETTRES INEDITES DE NAPOLEON
     Ier. Edited by Léonce de Brotonne. Paris: H. Champion, 1898.

419. Napoleon I, Emperor of the French. LETTRES INEDITES DE NAPOLEON
     Ier (AN VIII-1815). Edited by Léon Lecestre. Paris:
     Plon-Nourrit, 1897. 2 vols.

420. Napoleon I, Emperor of the French. LETTRES, ORDRES ET
     APOSTILLES DE NAPOLEON, EXTRAITS DES ARCHIVES DARU. Edited by
     Suzanne d'Huart. Paris: S.E.V.P.E.N., 1965.

421. Napoleon I, Emperor of the French. LETTRES PERSONNELLES DES
     SOUVERAINS A L'EMPEREUR NAPOLEON Ier. Paris: Plon, 1939.

422. Napoleon I, Emperor of the French. MEMOIRES DE NAPOLEON.
     Paris: Club de livre, 1969. 3 vols. [Condensed ed. of 423.]

423. Napoleon I, Emperor of the French. MEMOIRES POUR SERVIR A
     L'HISTOIRE DE FRANCE SOUS NAPOLEON Ier. Paris: Didot, 1823-25.
     8 vols. [Written by generals with Napoleon at St. Helena.]

424. Napoleon I, Emperor of the French. MEMOIRES. Paris: Granier,
     1904. 5 vols. [Condensed ed. of 423.]

425. Napoleon I, Emperor of the French. MEMOIRS OF THE HISTORY OF
     FRANCE UNDER NAPOLEON. London: Colburn, 1823-24. 7 vols.

426. Napoleon I, Emperor of the French. MY DEAREST LOUISE:
     MARIE-LOUISE AND NAPOLEON, 1813-1814. Collected and annotated
     by C.F. Palmstierna. Translated by E.M. Wilkinson. London:
     Methuen, 1958.

427. Napoleon I, Emperor of the French. NAPOLEON SELF REVEALED, IN THREE HUNDRED SELECTED LETTERS. Translated and edited by J.M. Thompson. Boston and New York: Houghton, Mifflin, 1934.

428. Napoleon I, Emperor of the French. NAPOLEON'S LAST WILL AND TESTAMENT. Edited by Jean Pierre Babelon and Suzanne d'Huart. Translated by Alex de Jonge. New York: Paddington Press; distributed by Grosset & Dunlap, 1977.

429. Napoleon I, Emperor of the French. OEUVRE ET L'HISTOIRE. Paris: Le Club français du livre, 1969-71. 12 vols.

430. Napoleon I, Emperor of the French. ORDRES ET APOSTILLES DE NAPOLEON, 1799-1815. Edited by Arthur Chuquet. Paris: H. Champion, 1911-12. 4 vols.

431. Napoleon I, Emperor of the French. PROCLAMATIONS, ORDRES DU JOUR ET BULLETINS DE LA GRANDE ARMEE. Edited by Jean Tulard. Paris: Union générale d'éditions, 1964.

432. Napoleon I, Emperor of the French. SUPPLEMENT A LA CORRESPONDANCE DE NAPOLEON, LETTRES CURIEUSES OMISES PAR LE COMITE DE PUBLICATION, RECTIFICATIONS. Edited by Albert Du Casse. Paris: E. Dentu, 1887.

433. NEW CAMBRIDGE MODERN HISTORY. Edited by C.W. Crawley. London: Cambridge Unversity Press, 1965. Vol. 9.

434. Ney, Michel Louis Félex, duc d'Elchingen, prince de la Moskowa. MEMORIES OF MARSHAL NEY. Edited by A. Bulos. Philadelphia: Carey, 1834. 2 vols.

435. Nobel, Alphons. KOENIGIN HORTENSE, DIE ERBIN NAPOLEONS. Frankfurt: Societats-verlag, 1938.

436. Normand, Suzanne. ...TELLE FUT JOSEPHINE. Paris: Editions du Sud, 1962.

437. O'Meara, Barry Edward. NAPOLEON EN EXIL. Paris: Chez tous les marchands de nouveautés, de l'imprimerie de Constant-Chantpie, 1822. 2 vols. (NAPOLEON IN EXILE. London: W. Simpkin and R. Marshall, 1822).

438. Ornano, Philippe Antoine, comte d'. MARIE WALEWSKA "L'EPOUSE POLONAISE" DE NAPOLEON. Paris: Hachette, 1938.

439. Ortzen, Len. IMPERIAL VENUS: THE STORY OF PAULINE BONAPARTE-BORGHESE. New York: Stein and Day, 1974.

440. Parker, Harold T. "The Formation of Napoleon's Personality: An Exploratory Essay." FRENCH HISTORICAL STUDIES 7 (1971): 6-26.

441. Pasquier, Etienne Denis, duc. SOUVENIRS DU CHANCELIER PASQUIER, 1767-1815. Edited by Robert Lacour-Gayet. Paris: Hachette, 1964.

442. Picard, Ernest, ed. PRECEPTES ET JUGMENTS DE NAPOLEON. Nancy: Berger-Levrault, 1913.

443. Piétri, François. LUCIEN BONAPARTE. Paris: Plon, 1939.

444. Piétri, François. LUCIEN BONAPARTE A MADRID. Paris: Grasset, 1951.

445. Pignatelli-Strongoli, Francesco. MEMORIE INTORNO ALLA STORIA DEL REGNO DI NAPOLI DELL'ANNO 1805 AL 1815. Naples, 1820.

446. Pinkney, David H., ed. NAPOLEON: HISTORICAL ENIGMA. Lexington, Mass.: Heath, 1969.

447. Pratt, Stephen. NAPOLEON. Hove: Weyland, 1976.

448. Rambaud, Jacques. NAPLES SOUS JOSEPH BONAPARTE, 1806-1808. Paris: Plon-Nourrit, 1911.

449. Ratcliffe, Bertram. PRELUDE TO FAME: AN ACCOUNT OF THE EARLY LIFE OF NAPOLEON UP TO THE BATTLE OF MONTENOTTE. London: Warne, 1981.

450. REFUTATION A SIR WALTER SCOTT SUR SON HISTOIRE DE NAPOLEON. Paris: Baudoin, 1828.

451. REFUTATION DE LA VIE DE NAPOLEON DE SIR WALTER SCOTT PAR M*** (J.F. Caze, d'après Barbier). Paris: Baudoin, 1827. 2 vols.

452. REFUTATION DE LA VIE DE NAPOLEON PAR LE GENERAL G[OURGAUD]. 2 parts. Paris: Dupont, 1827.

453. Reinhard, Christine Reimarus. UNE FEMME DE DIPOLMATE: LETTERS DE MADAME REINHARD A SA MERE, 1798-1815. Paris: Picard, 1900.

454. Rémusat, Claire Elizabeth Jeanne Gravier de Vergennes, comtesse de. MEMOIRES, 1802-1808. Edited by Paul L.E. de Rémusat. Paris: Calmann-Lévy, 1880. 3 vols.

455. Richard, A. "Un Succès peu connu de Bonaparte." REVUE HISTORIQUE DE LA REVOLUTION FRANCAISE 2 (1925): 393-94.

456. Richardson, Norval. MOTHER OF KINGS. New York and London: C. Scribner, 1928.

457. Rocquain, Félix. NAPOLEON Ier ET LE ROI LOUIS. Paris: Firmin-Didot, 1875.

458. Rodocanachi, Emmanuel Pierro. ELISA NAPOLEON (BACCIOCHI) EN ITALIE. Paris: Flammarion, 1900.

459. Roederer, Pierre Louis, comte. JOURNAL DU COMTE P.-L. ROEDERER, MINISTERE ET CONSEILLER D'ETAT. Edited by Maurice Vitrac. Paris: Daragon, 1909.

460. Roederer, Pierre Louis, comte. MEMOIRES SUR LA REVOLUTION, LE CONSULAT ET L'EMPIRE. Edited by Octave Aubry. Paris: Plon, 1942.

461. Roederer, Pierre Louis, comte. OEUVRES DU COMTE PIERRE LOUIS ROEDERER. Paris: Firmin-Didot, 1853-59. 8 vols.

462. Rollin, H. "L'Amiral Villeneuve et Napoléon." REVUE DES ETUDES NAPOLEONIENNE 1 (1913): 200-340.

463. Rose, John Holland. THE LIFE OF NAPOLEON I. 11th ed. London: G. Bell, 1934.

464. Rose, John Holland. NAPOLEONIC STUDIES. London: G. Bell, 1914.

465. Rose, John Holland. THE PERSONALITY OF NAPOLEON. New York and London: Putnam, 1912.

466. Rosebery, Archibald Philip Primrose, 5th earl of. NAPOLEON, THE LAST PHASE. New York and London: Harper, 1900.

467. Rothney, John. BONAPARTISM AFTER SEDAN. Ithaca, N.Y.: Cornell University Press, 1969.

468. Roux, Georges. MONSIEUR DE BUONAPARTE. Paris: Fayard, 1964.

469. Roy, Claude, ed. LA VIE DE NAPOLEON RACONTEE PAR NAPOLEON. Paris: R. Julliard, 1952.

470. Rufer, A. "Epitre à Buonaparte." REVUE HISTORIQUE DE LA REVOLUTION FRANCAISE 15 (1938): 554-56.

471. Ruffet, J. "L'Affaire Kleist." REVUE DE L'INSTITUT NAPOLEON 133 (1977): 173-80.

472. Rustam, mamluk de Napoleon I. SOUVENIRS DE ROUSTAM, MAMELUCK DE NAPOLEON Ier. Edited by Paul Cottin. Paris: Ollendorff, 1911.

473. "Saliceti et l'Arrestation de Bonaparte à Nice." REVUE DES ETUDES NAPOLEONIENNES 39 (1934): 261-63.

474. Salvatorelli, Luigi. LEGGENDA E REALTE DI NAPOLEONE. Turin: G. Einaudi, 1960.

475. Santini, Jean Noël. AN APPEAL TO THE BRITISH NATION. London: W. Hone, 1817.

476. Santini, Jean Noël. DE SAINTE-HELENE AUX INVALIDES. SOUVENIRS DE SANTINI, GARDIEN DU TOMBEAU DE L'EMPEREUR NAPOLEON Ier. Paris: Ledoyen, 1853.

477. Saunders, Edith. THE HUNDRED DAYS. London: Longmans, 1964.

478. Saunders, Edith. NAPOLEON AND MADEMOISELLE GEORGE. London: Longmans, 1958.

479. Savant, Jean. NAPOLEON ET JOSEPHINE. Paris: Fayard, 1960.

480. Savary, Anne Jean Marie René, duc de Rovigo. MEMOIRES DU DUC DE ROVIGO ECRITS DE SA MAIN POUR SERVIR A L'HISTORIE DE L'EMPEREUR NAPOLEON. Paris: Bossange, 1828; London: H. Colburn, 1828. 8 vols. (New ed. Paris: Garnier, 1900-01. 5 vols.)

481. Schlossberger, August, freiherr von, ed. POLITISCHE UND MILITARISCHE KORRESPONDENZ KOENIG FRIEDRICHS VON WUERTTEMBERG MIT KAISER NAPOLEON I, 1805-1813. Stuttgart: Kohlhammer, 1889.

482. Schneidawind, Franz Joseph Adolf. PRINZ EUGEN. Stockholm: P. Maatz, 1857.

483. Scott, Walter. THE LIFE OF NAPOLEON. London: Longman, Rees, Orme, Brown, & Green, 1827. 9 vols.

484. Seel, Heinrich. ERINNERUNGEN AUS DEN ZEITEN UND DEM LEBEN EUGENS HERZOG VON LEUCHTENBERG NACH AUTHENTISCHEN QUELLEN. Sulzbach: J.E. v. Seidel, 1827.

485. Seeley, John Robert. NAPOLEON. London: Colin, 1887.

486. Ségur, Philippe Paul, comte de. HISTOIRE DE NAPOLEON ET DE LA GRANDE ARMEE PENDANT L'ANNEE 1812, PAR LE GENERAL COMTE DE SEGUR. 14th ed. Paris: C. Gosselin, 1863.

487. Sergeant, Philip Walsingham. THE BURLESQUE NAPOLEON ... JEROME NAPOLEON BONAPARTE. London: T.W. Laurie, 1905.

488. Sieburg, Heinz Otto, ed. NAPOLEON UND EUROPA. Cologne and Berlin: Kiepenheuer u. Witsch, 1971.

489. Sirjean, Gaston. ENCYCLOPEDIE GENEALOGIQUE DES MAISONS SOUVERAINES. Vol. 7. LES BONAPARTE. Paris: n.p., 1961.

490. Soboul, Albert. PREMIER EMPIRE. Paris: Presses universitaires de France, 1973.

491. Soreau, Edomond. "Napoléon cavalier." REVUE DE L'INSTITUT NAPOLEON 116 (1970): 113-16.

492. Sorel, Albert Emile Edouard. L'EUROPE ET LA REVOLUTION FRANCAISE. Paris: Plon-Nourrit, 1885-1904. 8 vols.

493. Sorokine, Dimitri. LA JEUNESSE DE BONAPARTE. Paris: F. Nathan, 1967.

494. Stefani, Federico de. LE ANTICHITA DEI BUONAPARTE. Milan, 1854.

495. Stirling, Monica. MADAME LETIZIA. New York: Harper, 1961.

496. Stirling, Monica. A PRIDE OF LIONS: A PORTRAIT OF NAPOLEON'S MOTHER. London: Collins, 1961.

497. Stoeckl, Agnes. FOUR YEARS AN EMPRESS: MARIE-LOUISE, SECOND WIFE OF NAPOLEON. London: J. Murray, 1962.

498. Sutherland, Christine. MARIE WALEWSKA: NAPOLEON'S GREAT LOVE. New York: Vendome Press, 1979.

499. Taine, Hippolyte Adolphe. LES ORIGINES DE LA FRANCE CONTEMPORAINE. Paris: Hachette, 1875-94. 6 vols.

500. Talleyrand-Périgord, Charles Maurice de, prince de Bénévent. LETTRES INEDITES DE TALLEYRAND A NAPOLEON, 1800-1809. Paris: Perrin, 1889.

501. Talleyrand-Périgord, Charles Maurice de, prince de Bénévent. MEMOIRES. Edited by the duc de Broglie. Paris: Calmann-Lévy, 1891-92. 5 vols.

502. Tarle, Evgenii Viktorovich. NAPOLEON. Moscow: Editions en Langues Etrangéres, n. d. (German translation by E. Woog and H. Koplenig, Berlin: VEB Deutscher Verlag der Wissenschaften, 1968.)

503. Tartary, Madeleine. "Madame Mère au château de Pont-sur-Seine." REVUE DES ETUDES NAPOLEONIENNES 42 (1936): 85-132.

504. Tascher de la Pagerie, Pierre Claude Louis Robert, comte. LE PRINCE EUGENE. REFUTATION DES MEMOIRES DU DUC DE RAGUSE EN CE QUI CONCERNE LE PRINCE EUGENE. Extrait du Moniteur universel du 5 mars 1857. Paris: Panckoucke, 1857.

505. Tersen, Emile. NAPOLEON. Paris: Le Club français du livre, 1968.

506. Thiers, Louis Adolphe. HISTOIRE DU CONSULAT ET DE L'EMPIRE. Paris: Paulin, 1845-74. 21 vols.

507. Thiry, Jean. ANNEES DE JEUNESSE DE NAPOLEON BONAPARTE: 1769-1796. Paris: Berger-Levrault, 1975.

508. Thiry, Jean. LE COUP D'ETAT DU 18 BRUMAIRE. Paris: Berger-Levrault, 1947.

509. Thiry, Jean. LE ROI DE ROME. Paris: Berger-Levrault, 1968.

510. Thompson, James Matthew. NAPOLEON BONAPARTE, HIS RISE AND FALL. Oxford: Blackwell, 1952, 1963.

511. Thornton, Michael John. NAPOLEON AFTER WATERLOO, ENGLAND AND THE ST. HELENA DECISION. Stanford, Calif.: Stanford University Press, 1968.

512. Tourtier-Bonazzi, Chantal de. "Napoléon. Lettres d'amour à Joséphine: errata et addenda." REVUE DE L'INSTITUT NAPOLEON 138 (1982): 39-46.

513. Tourtier-Bonazzi, Chantal de, ed. OEUVRES LITTERAIRES ET ECRITS MILITAIRES. Paris, 1967-69. 3 vols.

514. Tourtier-Bonazzi, Chantal de. "Les Papiers de Joseph Bonaparte." HISTOIRE (1972).

515. Tulard, Jean. L'ANTI-NAPOLEON, LA LEGENDE NOIRE DE L'EMPEREUR. Paris: R. Julliard, 1965.

516. Tulard, Jean. BIBLIOGRAPHIE CRITIQUE DES MEMOIRES SUR LE CONSULAT ET L'EMPIRE, ECRITS OU TRADUITS EN FRANCAIS. Geneva: Droz, 1971.

517. Tulard, Jean. "L'Ere napoléonienne: Problèmes et Perspectives de Recherche." PROCEEDINGS OF THE CONSORTIUM ON REVOLUTIONARY EUROPE 11 (1976): 1-6.

518. Tulard, Jean. MYTHE DE NAPOLEON. Paris: Colin, 1971.

519. Tulard, Jean, ed. NAPOLEON A SAINTE-HELENE. Paris: Laffont, 1981.

520. Tulard, Jean. "Napoléon et la publicite." REVUE DE L'INSTITUT NAPOLEON 116 (1970): 117-18.

521. Tulard, Jean. NAPOLEON: OU LE MYTHE DU SAUVEUR. Paris: Fayard, 1977.

522. Turnbull, Patrick. NAPOLEON'S SECOND EMPRESS: A LIFE OF PASSION. New York: Walker, 1972.

523. Turquan, Joseph. CAROLINE, SOEUR DE NAPOLEON. Paris: J. Tallandier, 1954. (Reprint.)

524. Turquan, Joseph. ELISA ET PAULINE, SOEURS DE NAPOLEON. Paris: J. Tallandier, 1954. (Reprint.)

525. Turquan, Joseph. NAPOLEON AMOUREUX. Paris: Montgredien, 1897; (THE LOVE AFFAIRS OF NAPOLEON. London and New York: J. Lane, 1909.)

526. Turquan, Joseph. LA REINE HORTENSE (1783-1837) D'APRES LES TEMOIGNAGES DES CONTEMPORAINS. Utrecht and Paris: La Librairie illustrée, 1896.

527. Turquan, Joseph. LES SOEURS DE NAPOLEON. Paris: La Librairie illustrée, 1896; Paris: J. Tallandier, 1927.

528. Valente, Angela. GIOACCHINO MURAT E L'ITALIA MERIDIONALE. Turin: G. Einaudi, 1941, 1965.

529. Valynselle, Joseph. LA DESCENDANCE NATURELLE DE NAPOLEON Ier: LE COMPTE LEON, LE COMTE WALEWSKY. Paris: Chez l'Auteur, 1964.

530. Valynselle, Joseph. LE SANG DES BONAPARTE. Paris: Chez l'Auteur, 1954.

531. Vanel, Jean. LA MERE DE JOACHIM MURAT. Rabastens: J. Muray, 1971.

532. Vanel, Jean. LES ORIGINES DE LA FAMILLE MURAT. Rabastens: J. Muray, 1970.

533. Vaudoncourt, Frédéric François Guillaume, baron de. HISTOIRE POLITIQUE ET MILITAIRE DU PRINCE EUGENE NAPOLEON, VICE-ROI D'ITALIE. Paris: Mongie, 1828. 2 vols.

534. Versini, Xavier. MONSIEUR DE BUONAPARTE OU LE LIVRE INACHEVE. Paris: Albatros, 1977.

535. Villa-Urrutia, Marqués de. EL REY JOSE NAPOLEON. Madrid: F. Beltran, 1927.

536. Villat, Louis. LA REVOLUTION ET L'EMPIRE. Vol. 2. NAPOLEON (1799-1815). 3d ed. Paris: Presses universitaires de France, 1947. 2 vols.

537. Villeneuve, Germaine. "'Madame Mère.'" REVUE DES ETUDES NAPOLEONIENNES 34 (1934): 81-91.

538. Walsh, Robert. BIOGRAPHICAL SKETCH OF JOSPEH NAPOLEON BONAPARTE. London: J. Ridgway, 1833.

539. Warden, William. LETTERS WRITTEN ON BOARD THE "NORTHUMBERLAND" AND AT ST. HELENA. London: R. Ackerman, 1816.

540. Weider, Ben, and David Hapgood. THE MURDER OF NAPOLEON. New York: Congdon and Lattès, 1982. (French trans. QUI A TUE NAPOLEON? Paris, 1982.)

541. Weil, Maurice Henri. JOACHIM MURAT, ROI DE NAPLES. Paris: Fontemoing, 1909-10. 5 vols.

542. Weil, Maurice Henri. LE PRINCE EUGENE ET MURAT. Paris: Fontemoing, 1902. 5 vols.

543. Weiner, Margery. THE PARVENU PRINCESSES: THE LIVES AND LOVES OF NAPOLEON'S SISTERS. New York: Morrow, 1964.

544. Welschinger, Henri. LE DIVORCE DE NAPOLEON. Paris: Plon-Nourrit, 1889.

545. Welschinger, Henri. LE ROI DE ROME, 1811-1832. Paris: Plon-Nourrit, 1897.

546. Wertheimer, Eduard von. THE DUKE OF REICHSTADT. London: J. Lane, 1905.

547. Wheeler, Thomas. WHO LIES HERE? A NEW INQUIRY INTO NAPOLEON'S LAST YEARS. New York: Putnam, 1974.

548. Willm, Mme. Albert. "La Gênie de Napoléon." REVUE DES ETUDES NAPOLEONIENNES 35 (1932): 386-404.

549. Wilson, Robert McNair. THE EMPRESS JOSEPHINE: THE PORTRAIT OF A WOMAN. London: Eyre & Spottiswoode, 1952.

550. Wilson, Robert McNair. LETIZIA: DIE MUTTER NAPOLEONS. Frankfurt: Societats-verlag, 1934.

551. Wouters, Félix. HISTOIRE DE LA FAMILLE BONAPARTE DEPUIS MIL HUIT CENT QUINZE JUSQU'A CE JOUR. Paris: Librairie ethnographique, 1849.

552. Wright, Constance. DAUGHTER TO NAPOLEON [HORTENSE DE BEAUHARNAIS]. New York: Holt, Rinehart and Winston, 1961.

553. Wright, Constance. HORTENSE, REINE DE L'EMPIRE. Paris: Arthaud, 1964.

554. Zaghi, Carlo. NAPOLEONE E L'EUROPA. Naples: Cymba, 1969.

555. Zahorski, A. "La Légende napoléonienne en Pologne." REVUE HISTORIQUE DE LA REVOLUTION FRANCAISE 53 (1981): 572-607.

556. Zieseniss, Charles Otto. NAPOLEON ET LA COUR IMPERIALE. Paris: Tallandier, 1980.

CHAPTER IV

ITALY DURING THE NAPOLEONIC WARS (1792-1815)

Robert Epstein, School of Advanced Military Studies,
U.S. Army and Command and General Staff College, Fort Leavenworth

Europe entered a twenty-three year period of almost constant warfare in 1792. The years 1792 to 1815 are rich in military history with numerous campaigns and battles fought on every part of the continent. Although Napoleon Bonaparte did not initiate the conflict, his personality eventually overshadowed the history of the time and dominated military operations from 1805 to 1815. The Napoleonic Wars of 1803 to 1815 were a matter of personality as much as ideology. The character of Napoleon dominates the period to such an extent that contemporary and later historians have concentrated, for the most part, on Napoleon and on his conduct of military operations at the expense of other areas of military activity. The only secondary theater that has received as much attention as Napoleon's own campaigns has been the Duke of Wellington's campaigns in the Iberian peninsula. There are still great gaps in the military history of operations conducted prior to the emergence of the great Bonaparte or in the secondary theaters during the Napoleonic Wars. Work is needed to examine the campaigns of the revolutionary armies prior to 1796 in all theaters; in the Low Countries and Germany from 1799 to 1800; and in Italy, Naples, Istria, Dalmatia, the Grand Duchy of Warsaw, and the Low Countries during the period from 1805 to 1815.

Historians' treatment of the Italian peninsula is most peculiar. They have devoted great detail to Napoleon's 1796-1797 campaign there as well as his 1800 Marengo campaign. But the interest of military historians in operations in the peninsula declines after Napoleon himself left the area. This lack of military scholarship is inexcusable. Although it usually was not the primary theater of operations, Italy was an important secondary theater and the site of large battles. Forces of the French republic campaigned in Italy from 1793 to 1796 (prior to Napoleon's appointment as commander in chief of the Army of Italy), and the area witnessed major fighting prior to the Marengo campaign. The 1805 Italian conflict featured a major campaign between the Napoleonic Army of Italy under Marshal André Masséna and a larger Austrian force under Archduke Charles that climaxed in a battle in November at Caldiero. A combined Anglo-Russian force landed in Naples that year and threatened northern Italy. This invasion force withdrew only after the allied debacle at Austerlitz.

During 1805-1806 the French besieged Venice. General Gouvion Saint-Cyr commanded the besieging forces. A French army nominally under the command of Joseph Bonaparte, consisting of three corps commanded by Masséna, Saint-Cyr, and Reynier, invaded Naples in 1806. The Neapolitan campaign witnessed the long siege of Gaeta and the defeat of a French division at Maida in which the British, using linear tactics, defeated the columnar tactics of the French. This battle presaged future combats in the Iberian peninsula.

In 1808, Marshal Joachim Murat and his wife, Caroline, Napoleon's sister, became sovereigns of Naples replacing Joseph Bonaparte, who was transferred to Spain. Murat, anxious to win some martial glory independent of Napoleon, mounted a successful amphibious operation against Capri in October 1808. In 1809 Murat mobilized his forces to defend Naples against an attempted British invasion from Sicily. The British seized the island of Ischia but evacuated it after news of Wagram. The only other military action in Naples from 1808 to 1811 was against local guerrilla groups that were largely suppressed by 1811.

In 1809 northern Italy was once again the location of major military operations. The Kingdom of Italy was invaded by 65,000 Austrian troops under the command of Archduke John. Opposing him was a Franco-Italian army with a front line strength of 70,000 troops command by Eugène de Beauharnais, the viceroy of Italy. The Austrians won an inconclusive victory over the French at Sacile in April and drove the French back behind the Adige River. Later in May, the Austrians withdrew from the Adige front and were pursued by a numerically superior French army. Eugène intercepted the retreating Austrians on the banks of the Piave River near Conegliano and inflicted on them a decisive defeat. He then pursued his beaten foes into Austria and joined Napoleon's army for the climactic battle of the war at Wagram.

For the Italian kingdom the years of 1810 to 1813 were years of peace although large drafts of troops were sent to campaign in Spain and Russia. In the summer of 1813 Austria entered the coalition against Napoleon and Eugène once again had to wage a defensive campaign in northeastern Italy. Eugène defended Italy along the Adige River against a superior Austrian army from August 1813 until February 1814. During the winter of 1813-1814 Murat, hoping to keep his Neapolitan kingdom, defected to the allies and led his army of Neapolitan troops north towards Rome. His southern flank threatened, Eugène evacuated the Adige and withdrew to the Mincio where on February 8 he inflicted a severe defeat on Bellegarde's Austrian army. Murat, suffering from a crisis of conscience, merely demonstrated south of the Po River. Eugène held his position until Napoleon abdicated in March 1814. Napoleon's abdication ended the Kingdom of Italy as well as the French Empire.

Murat retained his throne for only a few months longer. Rallying to Napoleon's side after the return from Elba in March 1815, Murat attempted the conquest of the entire Italian peninsula. Murat's army moved north in mid-March and crossed the Po. Austrian forces under Frimont defeated Murat at Occhiobello. The Neapolitan army retreated to Tolentio where they suffered another defeat at the hands of the Austrians on May 3. The Neapolitan army then disintegrated and Murat lost his throne.

The purpose of this essay is to examine the various conflicts in the Italian peninsula during the period 1793 to 1815 with an eye to discussing the more important works in the field and to serve as a guide for further research.

GENERAL HISTORIES

Military operations throughout the Italian peninsula often are covered in broader military histories, biographies, etc. For background material regarding diplomacy and general military history there is Stephen Ross's EUROPEAN DIPLOMATIC HISTORY (191) and Owen Connelly's NAPOLEON'S SATELLITE KINGDOMS (53). Ross's work provides

an excellent survey of the diplomacy of the period and the war aims
of the various European powers. Owen Connelly's book provides an
overview of military operations in the Italian peninsula and should
serve as a starting point for any study of the area.

David Chandler's CAMPAIGNS OF NAPOLEON (42) is among the finest
histories ever written on Napoleon's campaigns. The chapters on
Bonaparte's 1796-1797 Italian campaigns as well as the Marengo
campaign of 1800 deserve study. A further guide to Napoleon's
operations in Italy is Esposito and Elting's military atlas (76).
Classic nineteenth-century accounts of Napoleon's Italian campaigns
are to be found in the studies by Jomini (124), Marmont (158), and
Thiers (207-209).

The biographies of many of Napoleon's commanders provide
important information on many of the operations in Italy in which
Napoleon was not present. Both Marshal Masséna and Saint-Cyr spent
considerable time campaigning in Italy.   Marshall-Cornwall's
biography of Masséna (159) offers one of the best accounts in English
of the operation of the Army of Italy prior to Napoleon's arrival and
also covers Masséna's operations in Italy from 1799 to 1806.
However, Marshall-Cornwall's work is only one volume in length and so
is limited in depth. A more detailed study of Masséna's operations
in Italy and Naples can be found in Gachot's books (91-94) and in
Masséna's own memoirs edited by Koch (163). Both works provide
orders of battle and in Koch's edition one can find a superb
collection of maps of Italy and Naples vital to any thorough military
history. As for Marshal Saint-Cyr, one should look at Gay de
Vernon's biography (99) as well as Saint-Cyr's own published memoirs
(106). The work on Saint-Cyr is dated and a fresh biography of this
marshal, who often served as an independent commander, is needed.
Some historians have considered Saint-Cyr to be among Napoleon's best
commanders and a detailed study of Saint-Cyr as an independent
commander should be made to address this view. Historians have
covered effectively the story of Marshal Murat both as a military
commander and as King of Naples. Garnier's biography (98) is among
the most recent.

Besides studying the lives of the marshals, much can be learned
from the biographies of the generals who fought in Italy. George
Six's two-volume work (201) is invaluable since it provides
biographical sketches of all the French general officers who served
in the French armies from 1789 to 1815. Two generals who fought in
Italy and later wrote their memoirs were Lecourbe (138) and Lamarque
(134). Milton Finley's dissertation (84) on General Reynier who
served as both a divisional and a corps commander during the
Napoleonic Wars should also be examined.

The serious student should endeavor to examine military
operations from the point of view of both belligerents. Gunther
Rothenberg's biography of Archduke Charles (193) is refreshingly new
and relies on Austrian rather than purely French sources, a rarity
among English language accounts. A particular problem for military
historians revolves around the question of numbers. How many troops
were engaged on each side? What were the casualties? Discrepancies,
whether intentional or not, do exist. Gaston Bodart's KREIGS-LEXIKON
(25) provides a clearer picture and is easy to follow even if one
does not read German. The KREIGS-LEXIKON provides the numbers of
troops engaged and casualties sustained by Austria and her enemies.

Since Austria served as the chief belligerent in Italy, this book is of great help. An important aid to further research is Alfoldi's bibliographical guide (5) published by the U.S. Army Military History Research Collection (now the Military History Institute) at Carlisle Barracks, Pennsylvania, and, of course, the documents indexed for Austria's war archives (13). The Military History Institute provides a trove of information on the Austrian Army.

ARCHIVAL SOURCES

For archival sources, the serious researcher must go to the Service historique de l'armée at the Château de Vincennes in Paris. Located here are manuscripts dealing with the Armies of Italy and Naples from 1792 to 1814. There are 418 cartons (B3) labeled "Sud-est, (1792-1803)" containing thousands of documents related to French operations in Italy. Seven cartons of documents concern Eugène de Beauharnais and 127 cartons (C4) of primary material are connected with the Army of Italy from 1804 to 1815. Information related to the Kingdom of Naples is held in 56 additional cartons. Princeton University also has a special collection of documents and letters of Prince Eugène de Beauharhais.

SPECIALIZED STUDIES

The period between 1792 and 1796 is among the least known regarding operations in Italy prior to Bonaparte's appointment as commander-in-chief of the Army of Italy. The standard work in English is Phipps's (176) voluminous work on the armies of the First French Republic. This work, however, is extremely dated and indicates how much more research is needed to fill out the story of military operations from 1792 to 1796. Marshall-Cornwall's biography of Masséna (159) makes some allusion to operations in Italy, particularly in respect to Napoleon's service in Italy as a general of brigade commanding the artillery of the Army of Italy. Other French works that are helpful are Fabry's account of the 1794 Italian campaign (79) and Saintine's (195) book on the Italian wars of 1792 to 1796.

Specific studies of Napoleon's first Italian campaign 1796 to 1797 are extensive. Two classics are the works by Clausewitz (51) and Jomini (123). An excellent and more recent account is Jackson's ATTACK IN THE WEST (120). Jackson's book analyzes Napoleon's first campaign and describes how it served as a basis for his later campaigns. The extensive works by Fabry (78-81) are also worthy of study. Fabry includes a detailed order of battle for the forces employed in the campaign. Pommereul (180) provides an interesting contemporary account of the campaign. Finally there is Tuetey's biography of one of the major but infrequently studied commanders, Sérurier (211).

For works on the period between 1799 and 1800, Rodger's WAR OF THE SECOND COALITION (189) is a good starting point for a diplomatic background to the period as is Saul's RUSSIA AND THE MEDITERRANEAN (199). Anthing's (10) story of Suvorov's Italian campaign provides an interesting contemporary account of the operations in Italy in 1799. Gachot's history of Suvorov in Italy (94) is more recent. The

best accounts of Masséna's defense of Genoa can be found in Gachot's
writings (91-93) and in Masséna's edited memoirs (163).

On the battle of Marengo in 1800, De Cugnac's account of this
campaign (57) is important. De Cugnac attempted to break some of the
myths concerning that campaign and provides a collection of official
reports. Sargent's book (197) is a bit brief but includes an account
of Moreau's operations in Germany. Furse's 1800 (90) is a first-
class campaign history. Lanza's source book on Marengo (135)
includes an English translation of Clericetti's description of the
siege of Fort Bard. Included in this book is a compendium of
Austrian accounts, after-action reports, and correspondence regarding
the campaign. This book is of some help to the serious student but
should not be used exclusively for primary material. Two fine
biographical studies are Martha-Beker's work on General Desaix (161)
and Rousseau's book on Suchet (194). A contemporary account of the
siege of Genoa by Thiébault (205) is also useful.

The Italian Campaign of 1805 and the Neapolitan Campaign of 1806
have been given less attention by historians than the events in Italy
from 1796 to 1800. Studies of Marshal André Masséna are the best
starting point since he commanded the Armies of Italy and Naples
during most of this period. Koch's edition of Masséna's memoirs
(163) which covers the operations of 1806 and 1806 is important and
so are the appropriate sections in the English language biography of
Masséna by Marshall-Cornwall (159). Gachot (92) provides the best
account of Masséna's operations in French, particularly in respect to
the Battle of Caldiero. Those who wish to read a recent account of
the Battle of Caldiero based on Austrian sources should consult
Rothenberg's biography of Archduke Charles (193) who was Masséna's
rival in 1805. Marshal Gouvion Saint-Cyr rose to prominence waging
war in Italy. Gay de Vernon's biography (99) should be read as well
as Saint-Cyr's own memoirs (106). Owen Connelly's NAPOLEON'S
SATELLITE KINGDOMS (53) provides a good overview of the diplomatic
and military history of the period. Joseph Bonaparte's tenure as the
king of Naples is well treated in Connelly's biography (52).

The 1805 campaign in Italy also marks the emergence of one
personality who played a major role in the military affairs of the
Kingdom of Italy from 1805 to 1814, Prince Eugène de Beauharnais.
Eugène briefly commanded a corps made up of second line units
organized to block an Anglo-Russian invasion from the Kingdom of
Naples. The best accounts of this minor role, as well as later
military operations conducted by Eugène in 1805 and 1806, are
Vaudoncourt's biography of Eugène (214) and Eugène's published
correspondence (18). A fine account of the Battle of Maida fought in
Naples between the French and British can be found in Milton Finley's
work on General Reynier (84).

In 1809 the war in the Italian theater marked the mid-point of
the Napoleonic Empire yet historians primarily have ignored it. The
most recent and detailed military history is Robert M. Epstein's
PRINCE EUGENE AT WAR: 1809 (74). Vaudoncourt (214) and Pelet (172)
wrote contemporary accounts. Two men who won their marshal's batons
at the end of this war, Macdonald (148) and Marmont (158), wrote of
their experiences in this campaign. There has been considerable
discussion of Eugène's conduct as a military commander in 1809.
Vaudoncourt and Albert Du Casse, the editor of Eugène's
correspondence (18), argue that Eugène was an excellent commander.

Macdonald, on the other hand, gives a totally different picture of the campaign stating that Eugène was totally incompetent and that it was he, not Eugène, who rallied the Army of Italy after its defeat at Sacile and was responsible for its later victories. Pelet's work (172) is good, but it is somewhat critical of Eugène's operations. This may be due to the fact that Pelet had been on Masséna's staff in 1805 and that there had been friction between Masséna and Eugène. Eugène's own correspondence (18) is most helpful and provides the best information concerning what went on at viceregal headquarters. Surprisingly most historians have relied on Macdonald's treatment of the campaign, in particular Thiers (209) and Petre (175). Most of the other biographies on Eugène, such as those written in this century by Bernardy (23), Lévy (142), and Oman (170) contain little about operational military history. Lamarque's memoirs (134) give a divisional commander's view of operations. Finally, there is an interesting section on Napoleon's plans for waging a strategic defense in Italy in 1809 in Haig's CAVALRY STUDIES (109).

For the campaigns of 1813-1815, Vaudoncourt's biography of Eugène (214), although dated, ranks among the best accounts of the military operations in Italy 1813 to 1814, especially his detailed rendition of the Battle of the Mincio in 1814. The history of this period centers on Eugène's refusal to withdraw his army from Italy in response to Napoleon's orders. Eugène argued that the army would disintegrate if he did so. Marmont criticizes Eugène for this (158) but Marmont is suspect because he himself betrayed the Emperor. A careful reading of the correspondence between Napoleon and Eugène (18, 168) reveals that Napoleon eventually believed Eugène to be right and approved his stepson's conduct. Albert Du Casse, in the biographical section of Eugène's published correspondence (18) defends Eugène on this point. More recent historians Bernardy (23), Lévy (142) and Oman (170) support this view as well saying that Eugène made the right decision and did not deliberately sabotage Napoleon's plans for a concentration of all his armies as Marmont implies.

There is an abundance of material concerning Murat and his kingdom in 1814 and 1815. Murat's correspondence is basic, especially that which relates to his defections in 1814 and 1815 (122). There are also the writings of Béchu concerning Murat, his wife Caroline, and their treason (20-22). Chavanon's biography (46) of Murat covers the years 1814 to 1815 quite well. Finally there is Derrécagaix's biography of General Belliard (63) who served as Murat's chief of staff.

FUTURE RESEARCH

As stated in the introduction of this chapter, studies of Bonaparte's campaigns in Italy are for the most part complete. A comprehensive study on the military career of Eugène is already under way. Other subjects, however, are in need of research. Fresh analysis of the Italian campaigns of Masséna, Saint-Cyr, Macdonald, Grenier, and Joubert are needed for the French commanding generals, as well as studies about Austrian commanders such as Archduke Charles, Archduke John, Fremont, and Bellegarde.

Other elements with broader implications need study as well. The problems of conducting successful coalition warfare has existed since ancient times. In our own day, the strains within NATO have raised serious questions as to its military effectiveness. Consequently, any study that would highlight the problems of conducting inter-allied operations would have a distinct contemporary relevance. There are numerous examples of combined operations in Italy, 1792-1815, that would serve as a basis of analysis for coalition warfare from tactical through strategic levels. A balanced study of Suvorov's 1799 campaign, for example, with a full examination of Austrian and Russian goals and actions would serve as an effective topic.

Another area for research could be the combat abilities of Italian-speaking units in the Napoleonic armies of Italy. The martial abilities of the Italian armed forces has been much maligned due to Italy's combat record in the twentieth century. However, the Italian regiments in Napoleon's army fought very well. A detailed combat history of the Italian regiments in the French army should help dispose of the myth of Italian military ineptitude.

Finally, an in-depth study of the Habsburg army in Italy is needed. Except for Archduke Charles, little is known about the other Austrian commanders from brigade through field army level. A social and ethnic study of the Austrian forces in Italy is needed. Did the Austrian army serving in Italy develop a character different from the field forces beyond the Alps? Were the same regiments who fought General Bonaparte in the 1790's still fighting in Italy in the first and second decades of the nineteenth century?

In short, vast treasures concerning the Italian peninsula remain waiting to be unearthed by a careful historian. One only needs patience and the will.

1. Abbott, John Stevens Cabot. HISTORY OF JOSEPH BONAPARTE, KING OF NAPLES AND OF ITALY. New York: Harper, 1869.

2. Acton, Harold Mario Mitchell. THE BOURBONS OF NAPLES, 1734-1825. New York: St. Martin, 1956.

3. Adalbert, prince of Bavaria. EUGENE DE BEAUHARNAIS, BEAU-FILS DE NAPOLEON: PORTRAIT BIOGRAPHIQUE. Ouvrage traduit de l'allemand par Marguerite Vabre, adapté par A. de Gouyon. Paris: Alsatia, 1938.

4. Adlow, Elijah. NAPOLEON IN ITALY, 1796-1797. Boston: William J. Rochfort, 1948.

5. Alfoldi, Laszlo M. THE ARMIES OF AUSTRIA-HUNGARY AND GERMANY, 1740-1914. Special Bibliography Series no. 12. Carlisle Barracks, Pa.: U.S. Army Military History Research Collection, 1975.

6. Ancemont, R. d'. MEMOIRES HISTORIQUES ET INEDITS SUR LA VIE POLITIQUE ET PRIVEE DE L'EMPEREUR NAPOLEON, DEPUIS SON ENTREE A L'ECOLE DE BRIENNE JUSQU'A SON DEPART POUR L'EGYPTE. Par le comte Charles d'Og.... Paris: Corréard, 1822.

7. Andolenko, Serge. AIGLES DE NAPOLEON CONTRE DRAPEAUX DU TSAR: 1799, 1805-1807, 1812-14: DRAPEAUX RUSSES CONQUIS PAR LES FRANCAIS, EMBLEMES FRANCAIS PRIS PAR LES RUSSES. Paris: Eurimprim, 1969.

8. Andreossy, Antoine, comte. OPERATIONS DES PONTONNIERS FRANCAIS EN ITALIE PENDANT LES CAMPAIGNS DE 1795 A 1797. Paris: Corréard, 1843.

9. Angeli, Moriz von. ERZHERZOG CARL ALS FELDHERR UND HERRESORGANISATOR. Vienna and Leipzig: Braumüller, 1896-98. 5 vols.

10. Anthing, Johann Friedrich. HISTORY OF THE CAMPAIGNS OF COUNT ALEXANDER SUWOROW RYMNIKSKI, FIELD-MARSHAL-GENERAL IN THE SERVICE OF HIS IMPERIAL MAJESTY, THE EMPEROR OF ALL THE RUSSIAS: WITH A PRELIMINARY SKETCH OF HIS PRIVATE LIFE AND CHARACTER. Translated from the German of Frederick Anthing. London: J. Wright, 1799. 2 vols.

11. Aronson, Theo. THE GOLDEN BEES; THE STORY OF THE BONAPARTES. Greenwich, Conn.: New York Graphics Society, 1964.

12. Atteridge, Andrew Hilliard. NAPOLEON'S BROTHERS. London: Methuen; New York: Brentano, 1909.

13. Austria. Direktion des Kriegsarchiv Wien. INVENTARE OESTERREICHISCHER ARCHIVE. Vol. 8. INVENTAR DES KREIGSARCHIVS WIEN. Vienna: Staatsarchiv, 1953. 2 vols.

14. Austria-Hungary. Kreigsarchiv. BIOGRAPHIEN K.K. HEERFUEHRER
UND GENERAELE. Vienna: K.K. Kreigsarchiv, 1888. 2 vols.

15. Azara y Perera, José Nicolás de, marqués de Nibbiano.
REVOLUCIONES DE ROMA QUE CAUSARON LA DESTITUCION DEL PAPA PIO VI
COMO SOBERANO TEMPORAL, Y EL ESTABLECIMIENTO DE LA ULTIMA
REPUBLICA ROMANA, ASI COMO LA CONQUISTA DE AQUELLA PARTE DE
ITALIA POR LOS FRANCESES MANDADOS POR NAPOLEON; Y RELACION DE LA
POLITICA DE ESPANA Y DE LOS SUCESOS DE FRANCIA POSTERIORES A
ESTOS ACONTECIMIENTOS. MEMORIAS ORIGINALES DE CELEBRE. Madrid:
Sánchez, 1847.

16. Beauchamp, Alphonse de. HISTOIRE DE LA CAMPAGNE DE 1814, ET DE
LA RESTAURATION DE LA MONARCHIE FRANCAISE. Paris: Le Normant,
1815. 2 vols.

17. Beauharnais, Eugène de, prince d'Eichstätt. BIBLIOTHEQUE
D'EUGENE DE BEAUHARNAIS ET DES DUCS DE LEUCHTENBERG PROVENANT DU
CHATEAU DE SEEON EN BAVIERE. Basel: Braus-Riggenbach, 1935.

18. Beauharnais, Eugène de, prince d'Eichstätt. MEMOIRES ET
CORRESPONDANCE POLITIQUE ET MILITAIRE DU PRINCE EUGENE.
Publiés, annotés et mis en ordre par baron Albert Du Casse.
Paris: Michel Lévy, 1858-60. 10 vols.

19. Beauregard, Louis Charles Octave Durand de, comte. LE MARECHAL
MASSENA, DUC DE RIVOLI, PRINCE D'ESSLING, ENFANT DE NICE. Nice:
Gauthier, 1902.

20. Béchu, Marcel Ernest [Marcel Dupont]. CAROLINE BONAPARTE, LA
SOEUR PREFEREE DE NAPOLEON. Paris: Hachette, 1937.

21. Béchu, Marcel Ernest [Marcel Dupont]. MURAT; CAVALIER,
MARECHAL DE FRANCE, PRINCE ET ROI. Paris: Hachette, 1934.

22. Béchu, Marcel Ernest [Marcel Dupont]. NAPOLEON ET LA TRAHISON
DES MARECHAUX, 1814. Paris: Hachette, 1939.

23. Bernardy, Françoise de. EUGENE DE BEAUHARNAIS. Paris: Perrin,
1973.

24. Berthier, Louis Alexandre. REGISTRE D'ORDRES DU MARECHAL
BERTHIER PENDANT LA CAMPAGNE DE 1813. Paris: Chapelot, 1909.
2 vols.

25. Bodart, Gaston. MILITAER-HISTORISCHES KRIEGS-LEXIKON (1618-
1905). Vienna and Leipzig: Stern, 1908.

26. Bohain, Capitaine. HISTOIRE DU 9e REGIMENT D'INFANTRIE DE LIGNE
(1615-1889). Commencée par le capitaine Bohain, continuée et
terminée par M. Puig, chef de bataillon au régiment. n.p.,
1890.

27. Bonaparte, Hortense de Beauharnais, queen consort of Louis, king of Holland. THE MEMOIRS OF QUEEN HORTENSE. Edited by Jean Hanoteau. New York: Cosmopolitan, 1927. 2 vols.

28. BONAPARTE A NICE. CAMPAGNE DES ALPES. LA PREMIERE CAMPAGNE D'ITALIE. Nice: Musée Masséna, 1938.

29. Bonnal, Henri. L'ESPRIT DE LA GUERRE MODERNE: DE ROSBACH A ULM. Paris: Chapelot, 1903.

30. Bonnechose, François Paul Emile Boisnormand de. LAZARE HOCHE, GENERAL EN CHEF DES ARMEES DE LA MOSELLE, D'ITALIE, DES COTES DE CHERBOURG, DE BREST, ET DE L'OCEAN, DE SAMBRE-ET-MEUSE ET DU RHIN, SOUS LA CONVENTION ET LE DIRECTOIRE, 1793-1797. Huitième ed. Paris: Hachette, 1880.

31. Botta, Carola Guiseppe Guglielmo. STORIA D'ITALIA DAL 1789 AL 1814. Italia: n.p., 1824.

32. Bouvier, Félix. BONAPARTE EN ITALIE, 1798. Paris: L. Cerf, 1899.

33. Brunn, Geoffrey. EUROPE AND THE FRENCH IMPERIUM, 1799-1814. New York: Harper, 1938.

34. Bukhari, Emil. FRENCH NAPOLEON LINE INFANTRY, 1796-1815. London: Almark, 1973.

35. Burton, Reginald George. NAPOLEON'S CAMPAIGNS IN ITALY, 1796-1797 AND 1800. London: Allen; New York: Macmillan, 1912.

36. Cahu, Théodore. HOCHE, MARCEAU, DESAIX. Paris: Boutigny, 1899.

37. CAMPAGNE DES AUSTRICHIENS CONTRE MURAT EN 1815. PRECEDEE D'UN COUP D'OEIL SUR LES NEGOCIATIONS SECRETES QUI EURENT LIEU A NAPLES DEPUIS LA PAIX DE PARIS. Brussels: Wahlen, 1821. 2 vols.

38. CAMPAGNES DES FRANCAIS EN ITALIE, EN EGYPTE, EN HOLLANDE, EN ALLEMAGNE, EN PRUSSE, EN POLOGNE, EN ESPAGNE, EN RUSSIE, EN SAXE. HISTOIRE COMPLETE DES GUERRES DE LA FRANCE PENDANT LA REVOLUTION ET L'EMPIRE DE 1792 A 1815. Lyon: Vitte et Perrussel, n.d.

39. Carolina Maria, queen consort of Ferdinand I, king of the Two Sicilies. CORRESPONDANCE INEDITE DE MARIA-CAROLINE, REINE DE NAPLES ET DE SICILE, AVEC LE MARQUIS DE GALLO. Publiée et annotée par le commandant M.-H. Weil et le marquis C. di Somma Circello. Préface de M.H. Welschinger. Paris: Emile-Paul, 1911. 2 vols.

40. Carolina Maria, queen consort of Ferdinand I, king of the Two Sicilies. MEMOIRE DE MARIE-CAROLINE, REINE DE NAPLES, INTITULE "DE LA REVOLUTION DE ROYAUME DE SICILE" ... PAR UN TEMOIN OCULAIRE. Publié pour la première fois, avec introduction, notes critiques, et deux facsimilés par R.M. Johnston. Cambridge, Mass.: Harvard University Press, 1912.

41. Chalamet, Antoine, ed. GUERRES DE NAPOLEON (1800-1807). RACONTEES PAR DES TEMOINS OCULAIRES: GENERAL BIGARRE et al. Paris: Firmin-Didot, 1895.

42. Chandler, David G. THE CAMPAIGNS OF NAPOLEON. New York: Macmillan, 1966.

43. Charavay, Jacques. LES GENERAUX MORTS POUR LA PATRIE, 1792-1871. Première série, 1792-1804. Paris: Au siège de la Société, 1893.

44. Chardigny, Louis. LES MARECHAUX DE NAPOLEON. Paris: Flammarion, 1946.

45. Chas, Jean. TABLEAU HISTORIQUE ET POLITIQUE DES OPERATIONS MILITAIRES ET CIVILES DE BONAPARTE. Paris: Bertrand, an X, 1801. 3

46. Chavanon, Jules Joseph, and Georges Saint-Yves. JOACHIM MURAT (1767-1815). Paris: Hachette, 1905.

47. Chevalier, Jean Michel. SOUVENIRS DES GUERRES NAPOLEONIENNES. Paris: Hachette, 1970.

48. Chodźko, Léonard Jakób Borjko. HISTOIRE DES LEGIONS POLANAISES EN ITALIE SOUS LE COMMANDEMENT DU GENERAL DOMBROWSKI. Paris: Barbezat, 1829.

49. Choury, Maurice. LES GROGNARDS ET NAPOLEON. Paris: Perrin, 1968.

50. Christophe, Robert. LES AMOURS ET LES GUERRES DU MARECHAL MARMONT, DUC DE RAGUSE. Paris: Hachette, 1955.

51. Clausewitz, Karl von. LA CAMPAGNE DE 1796 EN ITALIE. Translated into French by J. Colin. Paris: Boudoin, 1899.

52. Connelly, Owen. THE GENTLE BONAPARTE; A BIOGRAPHY OF JOSEPH, NAPOLEON'S ELDER BROTHER. New York: Macmillan, 1968.

53. Connelly, Owen. NAPOLEON'S SATELLITE KINGDOMS. New York: Free Press, 1966.

54. Courier de Méré, Paul Louis. PAMPHLETS POLITIQUES; ET, LETTRES D'ITALIE. Paris: La Renaissance du livre, 1912.

55. Currie, Laurence. THE BATON IN THE KNAPSACK: NEW LIGHT ON NAPOLEON AND HIS MARSHALS. London: J. Murray, 1934.

56. Darnay, Baron. NOTICES HISTORIQUES SUR S.A.R. LE PRINCE EUGENE, VICE-ROI D'ITALIE. Paris: David, 1830.

57. De Cugnac, Caspar J.M.R. CAMPAGNE DE L'ARMEE DE RESERVE EN 1800. Paris: Section Historique de l'Etat-major, 1900.

58. De Cugnac, Caspar J.M.R. CAMPAGNE DE MARENGO. Paris: Chapelot, 1904.

59. Delderfield, Ronald Frederick. THE GOLDEN MILLSTONES: NAPOLEON'S BROTHERS AND SISTERS. New York: Harper & Row, 1965.

60. Delderfield, Ronald Frederick. NAPOLEON'S MARSHALS. Philadelphia: Chilton Books, 1966.

61. De Paul University, Chicago. A CATALOG OF THE NAPOLEON LIBRARY OF DE PAUL UNIVERSITY. Compiled by Virginia Boyd Goult, with a preface by the Very Rev. Father Michael J. O'Connell, and an introduction by Stanley E. Read. Chicago: De Paul University, 1941.

62. DERNIERE CAMPAGNE DE L'ARMEE FRANCO-ITALIENNE, SOUS LES ORDRES D'EUGENE BEAUHARNAIS EN 1813 ET 1814, SUIVIE DE MEMOIRES SECRETS SUR LA REVOLUTION DE MILAN, DU 20 AVRIL 1814, ET LES DEUX CONJURATIONS DU 25 AVRIL 1815; LA CAMPAGNE DES AUTRICHIENS CONTRE MURAT; SA MORT TRAGIQUE, ET LA SITUATION POLITIQUE ACTUELLE DES DIVERS ETATS D'ITALIE. Par le chevalier S.J***. Paris: Dentu, 1817.

63. Derrécagaix, Victor Bernard. LE LIEUTENANT-GENERAL COMTE BELLIARD, CHEF D'ETAT-MAJOR DE MURAT. Paris: Chapelot, 1908.

64. Deutsch, Harold Charles. THE GENESIS OF NAPOLEONIC IMPERIALISM. Cambridge, Mass.: Harvard University Press; London: H. Milford, Oxford University Press, 1938.

65. Dixon, Pierson. PAULINE BONAPARTE. Traduit de l'anglais par Denise Van Moppès. Paris: Fayard, 1965.

66. Dodge, Theodore Ayrault. GREAT CAPTAINS, SHOWING THE INFLUENCE ON THE ART OF WAR OF THE CAMPAIGNS OF ALEXANDER, HANNIBAL, CAESAR, GUSTAVUS ADOLPHUS, FREDERICK AND NAPOLEON. Boston: Houghton, 1889.

67. Dodge, Theodore Ayrault. NAPOLEON, A HISTORY OF THE ART OF WAR, FROM THE BEGINNING OF THE FRENCH REVOLUTION TO THE END OF THE EIGHTEENTH CENTURY, WITH A DETAILED ACCOUNT OF THE WARS OF THE FRENCH REVOLUTION. London: Gay and Bird, 1904-7. 4 vols.

68. Du Casse, Albert, baron. LE GENERAL VANDAMME ET SA CORRESPONDANCE. Paris: Didier, 1870. 2 vols.

69. Du Casse, Albert, baron, comp. HISTOIRE DES NEGOCIATIONS DIPLOMATIQUES RELATIVES AUX TRAITES DE MORTFONTAINE, DE LUNEVILLE ET D'AMIENS, POUR FAIRE SUITE AUX MEMOIRES DU ROI JOSEPH; PRECEDEE DE LA CORRESPONDANCE INEDITE DE L'EMPEREUR NAPOLEON Ier AVEC LE CARDINAL FESCH. Paris: Dentu, 1855-57. 3 vols.

70. Du Casse, Albert, baron, ed. LES ROIS FRERES DE NAPOLEON Ier, DOCUMENTS INEDITS RELATIFS AU PREMIER EMPIRE. Paris: Germer, Baillière, 1883.

71. Dufourcq, Albert. LE REGIME JACOBIN EN ITALIE; ETUDE SUR LA REPUBLIQUE ROMAINE, 1798-1799. Paris: Perrin, 1900.

72. Du Teil, Joseph. ROME, NAPLES ET LE DIRECTOIRE, ARMISTICES ET TRAITES, 1796-1797. Paris: Plon-Nourrit, 1902.

73. Elmer, Alexander. L'AGENT SECRET DE NAPOLEON, CHARLES-LOUIS SCHULMEISTER. D'APRES LES ARCHIVES SECRETES DE LA MAISON D'AUTRICHE. Traduit de l'allemand par Lucien Thomas. Paris: Payot, 1932.

74. Epstein, Robert M. PRINCE EUGENE AT WAR: 1809. Arlington, Texas: Empire Games Press, 1984.

75. Espitalier, Albert. NAPOLEON AND KING MURAT, A BIOGRAPHY COMPILED FROM HITHERTO UNKNOWN AND UNPUBLISHED DOCUMENTS. Translated from the French by J. Lewis May. London: J. Lane, 1912.

76. Esposito, Victor J., and John R. Elting. A MILITARY ATLAS OF THE NAPOLEONIC WARS. New York: Praeger, 1964.

77. Esquieu, Louis. LE ROI JOACHIM MURAT ET SA COUR (1808). D'APRES LA CORRESPONDANCE INEDITE DU ROI AVEC NAPOLEON Ier. Traduit de l'italien du Baron Alberto Lumbroso. Cahors: J. Girma, 1899. 2 vols.

78. Fabry, Gabriel Joseph. HISTOIRE DE L'ARMEE D'ITALIE, 1796-1797. Paris: Champion, 1900-1901. 3 vols.

79. Fabry, Gabriel Joseph. HISTOIRE DE LA CAMPAGNE DE 1794 EN ITALIE. Paris: Chapelot, 1905. 2 vols. and atlas.

80. Fabry, Gabriel Joseph. MEMOIRE SUR LA CAMPAGNE DE 1796 EN ITALIE. Paris: Chapelot, 1905.

81. Fabry, Gabriel Joseph, ed. RAPPORTS HISTORIQUES DES REGIMENTS DE L'ARMEE D'ITALIE PENDANT LA CAMPAGNE DE 1796-1797. Paris: Chapelot, 1905.

82. Fazi du Bayet, Comte de. LES GENERAUX AUBERT DU BAYET, CARRA SAINT-CYR, ET CHARPENTIER; CORRESPONDANCES ET NOTICES BIOGRAPHIQUES, 1757-1834. Paris: Champion, 1902.

83. Ferrero, Guglielmo. THE GAMBLE: BONAPARTE IN ITALIE
    (1796-1797). Translated by Pritchard and Freeman. London: G.
    Bell, 1961.

84. Finley, Milton C. "The Career of General Count Jean Reynier,
    1792-1814." Ph.D. dissertation, Florida State University, 1972.

85. Foch, Ferdinand. THE PRINCIPLES OF WAR. Translated by J. de
    Morini. New York: H.K. Fly Co., 1918.

86. France. Archives de la guerre. CATALOGUE GENERAL DES
    MANUSCRITS DES BIBLIOTHEQUES PUBLIQUES DE FRANCE: ARCHIVES DE
    LA GUERRE. Par Louis Tuetey. Paris: Plon-Nourrit, 1912-20. 3
    vols.

87. France. Dépôt de la guerre. MEMORIAL TOPOGRAPHIQUE ET
    MILITAIRE, REDIGE AU DEPOT GENERAL DE LA GUERRE. Imprimé par
    ordre du ministre. Paris: Imprimerie de la République, an XI,
    1802. 5 vols.

88. France. Ministère de la guerre. CATALOGUE GENERAL DES
    MANUSCRITS DES BIBLIOTHEQUES PUBLIQUES DE FRANCE: BIBLIOTHEQUES
    DE LA GUERRE. Paris: Plon-Nourrit, 1911.

89. Fugier, André. NAPOLEON ET L'ITALIE. Paris: Janin, 1947.

90. Furse, George Armand. 1800: MARENGO AND HOHENLINDEN. London:
    William Clowers, 1903.

91. Gachot, Edouard. LA DEUXIEME CAMPAGNE D'ITALIE (1800). Paris:
    Perrin, 1899.

92. Gachot, Edouard. HISTOIRE MILITAIRE DE MASSENA. LA TROISIEME
    CAMPAGNE D'ITALIE (1805-1806) GUERRE DE L'AN XIV--EXPEDITION DE
    NAPLES--LE VRAI FRA DIAVOLO--LETTRES INEDITES DES PRINCES EUGENE
    ET JOSEPH NAPOLEON. Paris: Plon-Nourrit, 1911.

93. Gachot, Edouard. HISTOIRE MILITAIRE DE MASSENA. LE SIEGE DE
    GENES (1800). Paris: Plon-Nourrit, 1908.

94. Gachot, Edouard. SOUVAROW EN ITALIE. Paris: Perrin, 1903.

95. Gagnière, Albert. LA REINE MARIE-CAROLINE DE NAPLES, D'APRES
    DES DOCUMENTS NOUVEAUX. Paris: Ollendorff, 1886.

96. Gaillard, Capitaine, and Lieutenant Fleuriot. HISTORIQUE DU 62e
    REGIMENT D'INFANTERIE. Paris: Berger-Levrault, 1899.

97. Gallois, N. ARMEES FRANCAISES EN ITALIE, 1494-1849. Paris:
    Bourdillait, 1859.

98. Garnier, Jean Paul. MURAT, ROI DE NAPLES. Paris: Le Club du
    Meilleur Livre, 1959.

99. Gay de Vernon, Jean Louis Camille, baron. VIE DU MARECHAL
    GOUVION SAINT-CYR. Paris: Firmin-Didot, 1856.

100. Gerbaud, Capitaine. LE CAPITAINE GERBAUD, 1773-1799. Paris: Plon-Nourrit, 1910.

101. Gibbs, Montgomery B. MILITARY CAREER OF NAPOLEON THE GREAT. Chicago: Werner, 1895.

102. Giglioli, Constance H.D. (Stocker). NAPLES IN 1799. London: J. Murray, 1903.

103. Giorgetti, Niccolò, comp. LE ARMI TOSCANE E LE OCCUPAZIONI STRANIERE IN TOSCANA (1537-1860). Saggio di cronaca militare Toscana: Città di Castello, 1916. 3 vols.

104. Girod de l'Ain, Gabriel. JOSEPH BONAPARTE; LE ROI MALGRE LUI. Paris: Perrin, 1970.

105. Godeau, Camille. MASSENA. Paris: A. Méricant, 1910.

106. Gouvion Saint-Cyr, Laurent, marquis de. MEMOIRES POUR SERVIR A L'HISTOIRE MILITARIE SOUS LE DIRECTOIRE, LE CONSULAT ET L'EMPIRE. Paris: Anselin, 1834. 4 vols.

107. Grouchy, Emmanuel, marquis de. MEMOIRES DU MARECHAL DE GROUCHY. Paris: Dentu, 1873-74. 5 vols.

108. Guesdon, Alexandre Fursy. HISTOIRE MILITAIRE DES FRANCAIS, PAR CAMPAGNES, DEPUIS LE COMMENCEMENT DE LA REVOLUTION JUSQU'A LA FIN DU REGNE DE NAPOLEON. Revue, pour les détails stratégiques, par M. le général Beauvais. Paris: A. Dupont, 1826.

109. Haig, Douglas. CAVALRY STUDIES--STRATEGICAL AND TACTICAL. London: Hugh Rees, 1907.

110. Haig, Douglas. NAPOLEON AND HIS MARSHALS. New York: Burt, 1847. 2 vols.

111. Heim, Maurice. LE NESTOR DES ARMEES FRANCAISES, KELLERMANN, DUC DE VALMY. Paris: Nouvelle Edition, 1949.

112. Hénin de Cuvillers, Etienne Félix, baron d'. JOURNAL HISTORIQUE DES OPERATIONS MILITAIRES DU SIEGE DE PESCHIERA ET DE L'ATTAQUE DES RETRANCHEMENS DE SERMIONE COMMANDES PAR LE GENERAL DE DIVISION CHASSELOUP LAUBAT, INSPECTEUR GENERAL COMMANDANT EN CHEF DU GENIE A L'ARMEE D'ITALIE ... SUIVI D'UNE NOTE SUR LA MAISON DE CAMPAGNE DE CATULLE SITUEE A L'EXTREMITE DE LA PRESQU'ILE DE SERMIONE. Genoa: n.p., an IX (1801).

113. Heriot, Angus. THE FRENCH IN ITALY, 1796-1799. London: Chatto and Windus, 1957.

114. Heweston, W.B. HISTORY OF NAPOLEON BONAPARTE, AND WARS OF EUROPE. London: T. Kelly, 1834. 3 vols.

115. HISTOIRE DE NAPOLEON LE GRAND. Paris: Madame Veuve Desbleds, 1849.

116. Höjer, Torwald Torwaldson. BERNADOTTE, MARECHAL DE FRANCE. Traduit du suédois par Lucien Maury. Paris: Plon, 1943.

117. Holtman, Robert B. THE NAPOLEONIC REVOLUTION. Philadelphia: Lippincott, 1967.

118. Horoy, Adolphe. HISTORIQUE DES VOLONTAIRES DE L'OISE.... Paris: F. Henry, 1863.

119. Hunter, Thomas Marshall. NAPOLEON IN VICTORY AND DEFEAT. [Ottawa]: Directorate of Military Training, Army Headquarters, 1964.

120. Jackson, William Godfrey Fothergill. ATTACK IN THE WEST: NAPOLEON'S FIRST CAMPAIGN RE-READ TODAY. London: Eyre & Spottiswoode, 1953.

121. Joachim Murat, king of Naples. CORRESPONDANCE DE JOACHIM MURAT ... (JUILLET 1791-JUILLET 1808). Preface de M. Henry Houssaye. Turin: Roux Frassati, 1899.

122. Joachim Murat, king of Naples. LETTRES ET DOCUMENTS POUR SERVIR A L'HISTOIRE DE JOACHIM MURAT, 1767-1815. Publiés par S.A. le Prince Murat. Deuxième édition. Paris: Plon-Nourrit, 1908-14. 8 vols.

123. Jomini, Antoine de, baron. HISTOIRE CRITIQUE ET MILITAIRE DES GUERRES DE LA REVOLUTION. Paris: Magimel, Anselin et Pochard, 1819-24. 15 vols.

124. Jomini, Antoine de, baron. TRAITE DES GRANDES OPERATIONS MILITAIRES.... Paris: Magimel, 1816.

125. Jomini, Antoine de, baron. VIE POLITIQUE ET MILITAIRE DE NAPOLEON.... Paris: Anselin, 1827. 4 vols. and atlas.

126. Juin, Alphonse Pierre. LA CAMPAGNE D'ITALIE. Paris: G. Victor, 1962.

127. Kircheisen, Friedrich Max. BIBLIOGRAPHIE NAPOLEONIENNE. COLLECTION DE SOURCES CLASSEES PAR ORDRE DE MATIERES. Paris: Chapelot, 1902.

128. La Barre de Nanteuil, Hugues de. LE COMTE DARU OU L'ADMINISTRATION MILITAIRE SOUS LA REVOLUTION ET L'EMPIRE. Paris: J. Peyronnet, 1966.

129. Lachouque, Henry. THE ANATOMY OF GLORY; NAPOLEON AND HIS GUARD, A STUDY IN LEADERSHIP. Adapted from the French by Anne S.K. Brown. Providence, R. I.: Brown University Press, 1961.

130. Lachouque, Henry. NAPOLEON: 20 ANS DE CAMPAGNES. Paris: B. Arthaud, 1944.

131. Lachouque, Henry. NAPOLEON'S BATTLES: A HISTORY OF HIS CAMPAIGNS. Translated from the French by Roy Monkcom. New York: Dutton, 1967.

132. Lacroix, Désiré. LES MARECHAUX DE NAPOLEON. Paris: Garnier, 1896.

133. Lafolie, Charles Jean [Frédéric Coraccini]. HISTOIRE DE L'ADMINISTRATION DU ROYAUME D'ITALIE PENDANT LA DOMINATION FRANCAISE.... Traduite de l'italien. Paris: Audin, 1823.

134. Lamarque, Jean Maximilien. MEMOIRES ET SOUVENIRS DU GENERAL MAXIMILIEN LAMARQUE, PUBLIES PAR SA FAMILLE. Paris: H. Fournier, 1835-36. 3 vols.

135. Lanza, Conrad H., ed. MARENGO CAMPAIGN, 1800 SOURCE BOOK. Ft. Leavenworth, Kans.: General Service School Press, 1922.

136. La Tour, Jean Jacques de. DUROC, DUC DE FRIOUL, GRAND MARECHAL DU PALAIS IMPERIAL (1772-1813). Paris: Chapelot, 1913.

137. Lauerma, Matti. L'ARTILLERIE DE CAMPAGNE FRANCAISE PENDANT LES GUERRES DE LA REVOLUTION; EVOLUTION DE L'ORGANISATION ET DE LA TACTIQUE. Helsinki: Annales Academiae Scientiarum Fennicae, 1956.

138. Lecourbe, Claude Jacques. LE GENERAL LECOURBE D'APRES SES ARCHIVES, SA CORRESPONDANCE ET AUTRES DOCUMENTS. Paris: Charles-Lavauzelle, 1895.

139. Lefebvre, Georges. THE FRENCH REVOLUTION. Vol. 1. Translated by Elizabeth Moss Evanson. Vol. 2. Translated by John Hall Stewart and James Friguglietti. New York: Columbia University Press, 1962. 2 vols.

140. Lefebvre, Georges. NAPOLEON. Vol. 1. Translated by Henry F. Stoumbold. Vol. 2. Translated by J. E. Anderson. New York: Columbia University Press, 1967. 2 vols.

141. Lévi, André. COLLECTION ANDRE LEVI. ARMES ET SOUVENIRS HISTORIQUES. Paris: Lahure, 1936.

142. Lévy, Arthur. NAPOLEON ET EUGENE DE BEAUHARNAIS. Paris: Calmann-Lévy, 1926.

143. Long, Gabrielle Margaret Vere (Campbell) [Joseph Shearing, Marjorie Bowen]. PATRIOTIC LADY: EMMA, LADY HAMILTON, THE NEAPOLITAN REVOLUTION OF 1799, AND HORATIO, LORD NELSON. New York: Appleton-Century, 1936.

144. Long, Richard Melville. "The Relations of the Grand Duchy of Tuscany with Revolutionary France, 1790-1799." Ph.D. dissertation, Florida State University, 1972.

145. Lucas-Dubreton, Jean. MURAT. Paris: Fayard, 1944.

146. Ludwig, Emil. NAPOLEON. Translated by Eden and Cedar Paul. New York: Boni & Liveright, 1926.

147. Lumbroso, Alberto, barone. MELANGES MARENGO, PUBLIES PAR LE COMITIE INTERNATIONAL POUR LE CENTENAIRE DE LA BATAILLE DU 14 JUIN 1800. Paris: 1900-1902.

148. Macdonald, Jacques Etienne Joseph Alexandre, duc de Tarente. RECOLLECTIONS OF MARSHAL MACDONALD, DUKE OF TARENTUM. Edited by Camille Rousset. Translated by Stephen Louis Simeon. London: Bentley, 1892. 2 vols.

149. Macdonell, Archibald Gordon. NAPOLEON AND HIS MARSHALS. New York: Macmillan, 1934.

150. Macirone, Francis. INTERESTING FACTS RELATING TO THE FALL AND DEATH OF JOACHIM MURAT, KING OF NAPLES.... London: Ridgway, 1817.

151. Mackesy, Piers. THE WAR IN THE MEDITERRANEAN, 1803-1810. London and New York: Longmans, Green, 1957.

152. Macready, Edward Nevil. A SKETCH OF SUWAROW, AND HIS LAST CAMPAIGN. London: Smith, Elder, 1851.

153. Madelin, Louis. LA ROME DE NAPOLEON; LA DOMINATION FRANCAISE A ROME DE 1809 A 1814. Paris: Plon-Nourrit, 1906.

154. Mahon, Patrice. ETUDES SUR LES ARMEES DU DIRECTOIRE. JOUBERT A L'ARMEE D'ITALIE, CHAMPIONNET A L'ARMEE DE ROME, OCTOBRE 1798-JANVIER 1799. Paris: Chapelot, 1905. 3 vols.

155. Maingarnauld, Victor. CAMPAGNES DE NAPOLEON TELLES QU'IL LES CONCUT ET EXECUTA.... Paris: Everat, 1827. 2 vols.

156. Mangourit, Michel-Ange Bernard de. DEFENSE D'ANCONE, ET DES DEPARTEMENS ROMAINS, LE TRONTO, LE MUSONE ET LE METAURO, PAR LE GENERAL MONNIER, AUX ANNEES VII ET VIII. OUVRAGE MELE D'EPISODES SUR L'ETAT DE LA POLITIQUE, DE LA MORALE ET DES ARTS A RUGUSE, ET DANS LES VILLES PRINCIPALES DE L'ITALIE A CETTE EPOQUE. Paris: Pougens, an X, 1802. 2 vols.

157. Markham, Felix. NAPOLEON AND THE AWAKENING OF EUROPE. London: English Universities Press, 1954.

158. Marmont, Auguste Frédéric Louis Viesse de, duc de Raguse. MEMOIRES DU MARECHAL MARMONT, DUC DE RAGUSE.... Deuxième édition. Paris: Perrotin, 1857. 9 vols.

159. Marshall-Cornwall, James Handyside. MARSHAL MASSENA. London and New York: Oxford University Press, 1965.

160. Marshall-Cornwall, James Handyside. NAPOLEON AS MILITARY COMMANDER. London: Batsford, 1967.

161. Martha-Beker, Félix, comte de Mons. LE GENERAL DESAIX. Paris: Didier, 1852.

162. Martinien, Aristide. TABLEAUX PAR CORPS ET PAR BATAILLES DES OFFICIERS TUES ET BLESSES PENDANT LES GUERRES DE L'EMPIRE (1805-1815). Paris: Charles-Lavauzelle, 1899.

163. Masséna, André, prince d'Essling. MEMOIRES DE MASSENA.... Edited by General J.B.F. Koch. Paris: Paulin and Lechevalier, 1848-50. 7 vols.

164. Masson, Frédéric. NAPOLEON ET SA FAMILLE. Paris: Ollendorff, 1900-20. 13 vols.

165. Montagu, V.M. NAPOLEON AND HIS ADOPTED SON. New York: McBride, Nast, 1914.

166. Naples. Archivio di Stato. ARCHIVIO BORBONE. INVENTARIO SOMMARIO. Rome, 1961-72. 2 vols.

167. Napoleon I, Emperor of the French. CAMPAGNES D'ITALIE D'EGYPTE ET DE SYRIE. Paris: Hachette, 1872. 3 vols.

168. Napoleon I, Emperor of the French. LA CORRESPONDANCE DE NAPOLEON Ier. Paris: H. Plon and J. Dumaine, 1867. 36 vols.

169. Napoleon I, Emperor of the French. PIECES DIVERSES RELATIVES AUX OPERATIONS MILITAIRES ET POLITIQUES DU GENERAL BONAPARTE. Paris: Didot, 1800. 3 vols.

170. Oman, Carola (Lenanton). NAPOLEON'S VICEROY. London: Hodder and Stoughton, 1966.

171. Oman, Charles W. C. STUDIES IN THE NAPOLEONIC WARS. New York: Scribner, 1930.

172. Pelet, Jean Jacques Germain, baron. MEMOIRES SUR LA GUERRE DE 1809. Paris: Roret, 1824-26. 4 vols.

173. Pelevoi, Nikolai Alekseevich. GESCHICHTE DES FURSTEN ITALIISMI GRAFEN SUWOROFF-RIMNIKSKII. In freier deutscher herbertragung herausgegeben von J. de la Croix. Mitan: G.A. Reyher, 1851.

174. Pennsylvania. University. Library. FRENCH REVOLUTIONARY MATERIALS; MACLURE COLLECTION, University of Pennsylvania. New Haven, Conn.: Research Publications, 1970-71. Microfilm.

175. Petre, Francis Loraine. NAPOLEON AND THE ARCHDUKE CHARLES. New York: J. Lane, 1909.

176. Phipps, Ramsey Weston. THE ARMIES OF THE FIRST FRENCH REPUBLIC. London: Oxford University Press, 1926-39. 5 vols.

177. Picard, Louis Auguste. LA CAVALERIE DANS LES GUERRES DE LA REVOLUTION ET DE L'EMPIRE. Saumur: Milon, 1895-96. 2 vols.

178. Pingaud, A. "Le Premier Royaume d'Italie; Le developement du system Napoléonien." REVUE DES ETUDES NAPOLEONIENNES 21 (1923): 34-50, 100-110.

179. Piuma [pseud.] RECIT HISTORIQUE DE LA CAMPAGNE DE BUONAPARTE EN ITALIE, DAN LES ANNEES 1796 ET 1797. Par un temoin oculaire. London: T. Harper, 1808.

180. Pommereul, François René Jean, baron de. CAMPAGNE DU GENERAL BUONAPARTE EN ITALIE, PENDANT LE ANNEES IVe ET Ve DE LA REPUBLIQUE FRANCAISE. Paris: Plassan, 1797.

181. Pratt, Fletcher. THE EMPIRE AND THE GLORY: NAPOLEON BONAPARTE, 1800-1806. New York: W. Sloane, 1949.

182. Pulitzer, Albert. THE ROMANCE OF PRINCE EUGENE. Translated by B.M. Sherman. New York: Dodd, 1895. 2 vols.

183. Rabel, André. LE MARECHAL BESSIERES. Paris: Calmann-Lévy, 1903.

184. Rambaud, Jacques. NAPLES SOUS JOSEPH BONAPARTE, 1806-1808. Paris: Plon-Nourrit, 1911.

185. Rath, Reuben John. THE PROVISIONAL AUSTRIAN REGIME IN LOMBARDY-VENETIA, 1814-1815. Austin: University of Texas Press, 1969.

186. Reid, William Hamilton, comp. LIFE AND CAMPAIGNS OF NAPOLEON BONAPARTE. Translated from the French of M.A. Arnault and C.L.F. Panckoucke. New ed. Boston: Phillips, Sampson, 1855. 2 vols.

187. Reinhard, Marcel R. AVEC BONAPARTE EN ITALIE.... Paris: Hachette, 1946.

188. Reinhard, Marcel R. LE GRAND CARNOT. Paris: Hachette, 1950-1952. 2 vols.

189. Rodger, Alexander Bankier. THE WAR OF THE SECOND COALITION, 1798-1801. Oxford: Clarendon Press, 1964.

190. Ronco, Antonino. L'ASSEDIO DI GENOVA, 1800. Genoa: Sagep, 1976.

191. Ross, Stephen T. EUROPEAN DIPLOMATIC HISTORY, 1789-1815. Garden City, N. Y.: Doubleday, 1969.

192. Rothenberg, Gunther E. THE MILITARY BORDER IN CROATIA, 1740-1881. Chicago: University of Chicago Press, 1966.

193. Rothenberg, Gunther E. NAPOLEON'S GREAT ADVERSARIES: THE ARCHDUKE CHARLES AND THE AUSTRIAN ARMY, 1792-1814. Bloomington: Indiana University Press, 1982.

194. Rousseau, François. LA CARRIERE DU MARECHAL SUCHET.... Paris: Firmin-Didot, 1898.

195. Saintine, Joseph Xavier Boniface. HISTOIRE DES GUERRES D'ITALIE; PRECEDEE D'UNE INTRODUCTION. CONTENANT LES CAMPAGNES DES ALPES DEPUIS 1792 JUSQU'EN 1796. Paris: Dupont, 1827. 2 vols.

196. Saint-Marc, Pierre. LE MARECHAL MARMONT. Paris: Fayard, 1957.

197. Sargent, Herbert Howland. THE CAMPAIGN OF MARENGO. Chicago: A.C. McClurg, 1897.

198. Sargent, Herbert Howland. NAPOLEON BONAPARTE'S FIRST CAMPAIGN. Chicago: A.C. McClurg, 1917.

199. Saul, Norman E. RUSSIA AND THE MEDITERRANEAN, 1797-1807. Chicago: University of Chicago Press, 1970.

200. Schneidawind, Fraz Joseph Adolph. PRINZ EUGEN. Stockholm: P. Maatz, 1857.

201. Six, Georges. DICTIONNAIRE BIOGRAPHIQUE DES GENERAUX ET AMIRAUX FRANCAIS DE LA REVOLUTION ET DE L'EMPIRE (1792-1814). Paris: G. Saffroy, 1934. 2 vols.

202. Six, Georges. LES GENERAUX DE LA REVOLUTION ET DE L'EMPIRE. Paris: Bordas, 1948.

203. Stewart, John Hall. FRANCE, 1715-1815: A GUIDE TO MATERIALS IN CLEVELAND, BEING A REPRESENTATIVE SELECTION FROM THE PRINCIPAL HOLDINGS OF THE LIBRARIES OF WESTERN RESERVE UNIVERSITY, THE CLEVELAND PUBLIC LIBRARY, AND THE WESTERN RESERVE HISTORICAL SOCIETY. Cleveland, Ohio: Western Reserve University Press, 1942.

204. Taylor, Alan Carey. BIBLIOGRAPHY OF UNPUBLISHED THESES ON FRENCH SUBJECTS DEPOSITED IN UNIVERSITY LIBRARIES OF THE UNITED KINGDOM (1905-1950). Oxford: Blackwell, 1964.

205. Thiébault, Paul Charles François Adrien Henri Dieudonné, baron. JOURNAL DES OPERATIONS MILITAIRES ET ADMINISTRATIVES DU SIEGE ET BLOCUS DE GENES. Paris: Corréard, 1846-47. 2 vols.

206. Thierry, Augustin. MASSENA, L'ENFANT GATE DE LA VICTOIRE. Paris: A. Michel, 1947.

207. Thiers, Adolphe. ATLAS DES CAMPAGNES DE LA REVOLUTION FRANCAISE. Paris: Furne, Jovet, [1880].

208. Thiers, Adolphe. HISTOIRE DE LA REVOLUTION FRANCAISE. Paris: Lecointe, 1834. 10 vols.

209. Thiers, Adolphe. HISTORY OF THE CONSULATE AND THE EMPIRE OF FRANCE UNDER NAPOLEON. Translated by D. Forbes Campbell and

John Stebbing. London: Chatto and Windus; Philadelphia:
Lippincott, 1893-94. 12 vols.

210. Thiry, Jean. MARENGO. Paris: Berger-Levrault, 1949.

211. Tuetey, Louis. UN GENERAL DE L'ARMEE DE L'ITALIE: SERURIER,
1742-1819. Paris: Berger-Levrault, 1899.

212. Valente, Angela. GIOACCHINO MURAT E L'ITALIA MERIDIONALE.
Turin: Einaudi, 1976.

213. Valentin, René. LE MARECHAL MASSENA (1758-1817). Paris:
Charles-Lavauzelle, 1960.

214. Vaudoncourt, Frédéric François Guillaume, baron de. HISTOIRE
POLITIQUE ET MILITAIRE DU PRINCE EUGENE NAPOLEON, VICE-ROI
D'ITALIE. Paris: Mongie, 1828. 2 vols.

215. Weil, Maurice Henri. JOACHIM MURAT, ROI DE NAPLES; LA DERNIERE
ANNEE DE REGNE (MAI 1814-MAI 1815). Paris: Fontemoing,
1909-10. 5 vols.

216. Weil, Maurice Henri. LE PRINCE EUGENE ET MURAT, 1813-1814:
OPERATIONS MILITAIRES, NEGOCIATIONS DIPLOMATIQUES. Paris:
Fontemoing, 1902. 5 vols.

217. Wilkinson, Spencer. THE RISE OF GENERAL BONAPARTE. Oxford:
Clarendon Press, 1930.

218. Yorck von Wartenburg, Maximilian, graf. ATLAS TO ACCOMPANY
"NAPOLEON AS A GENERAL" BY COUNT VON WARTENBURG. Prepared by
the Department of Military Art and Engineering, United States
Military Academy, for the course on military history. West
Point, N. Y., [1942].

219. Yorck von Wartenburg, Maximilian, graf. NAPOLEON AS A GENERAL.
[London: Gilbert and Rivington, 1902]. 2 vols.

220. Zurlinden, Emile Auguste François Thomas. NAPOLEON ET SES
MARECHAUX. Paris: Hachette, 1910. 2 vols.

CHAPTER V

THE EGYPTIAN CAMPAIGN (1798-1801)

Jeanne A. Ojala, University of Utah

The importance of the French expedition in 1798 probably was not fully appreciated by the 38,000 officers and soldiers or by the 165 savants who accompanied the Armée d'Orient to Egypt. It is doubtful too that the Directory had considered the broad ramifications of their decision to establish a colony in Egypt, a proposal strongly supported by Talleyrand and Bonaparte. When the venture was authorized by the Directory in April 1798, it was thought that six months would suffice to accomplish the goals set out by its supporters. Moreover, Consul-general Magallon in Egypt had reported that the French could be confident of success there. As early as 1797 Talleyrand had recommended the resumption of colonial expansion. Egypt might replace the loss by France of her West Indian colonies and the untapped wealth of the country could be exploited for the benefit of the financially embarrassed government in France. If the Suez Canal could be opened, as the French planned, the lucrative trade routes to the East would boost the French economy and threaten British interests in India. Invading Egypt was less costly than an invasion of England, a fact which did not escape the attention of the Directory. Article 2 of the Directory's decrees on the expedition to Egypt specifically stated that it was their intention to improve the lot of the exploited peasantry. The French were undertaking a civilizing mission, in fact putting into practice the ideals of the French Revolution.

The Egyptian and Syrian campaigns are often viewed as a failure, for Bonaparte and for France. Through luck and obstinate perseverance Bonaparte transported his men and scholars to the fabled land of the Pharaohs. Despite constant grumblings from officers and men and open threats to himself, Bonaparte conquered Egypt, established order and began to transform the area into a well-run colony. However, the suffering of the French under harsh conditions in a hostile land could not be assuaged; the promise of six acres of land did not lessen their grievances or calm their disquiet. The most hardy and seasoned veterans complained of their condition. Disease, the cruel environment, and boredom took their toll. If the military exploits of the time were disappointing, the same cannot be said for the brilliant accomplishments of the enlightened French scientists, scholars, artists, and engineers who scoured the countryside and recorded their findings in words and drawings. Gaspar Monge, Claude Berthollet, Joseph Fourier, and Vivant-Denon are among the best known of these pioneers in Egyptology. On 22 August 1798, the French established the Institut d'Egypte. Monge presided over the Institut which was organized into four sections (Mathematics, Physics, Political Economy, and Literature and Arts). This proved to be one of the only lasting achievements of the expedition. It impressed the sheikhs as did some of the domestic reforms and changes carried out by the French conquerors.

The Egyptian expedition proved to be a testing ground for many who accompanied Bonaparte to this alien land; the soldiers' lament is seen in the words of a song they sang, "L'eau du Nil/n'est pas du

champagne: Pourquoi vouloir faire campagne/Dans un pays sans
cabarets?" Murat, Desaix, Kléber, and many others cursed Bonaparte
and their fate.   They hurled threats and accusations and fought
bravely, winning the admiration of their commander and their foes.
It has been said that Bonaparte already realized after the British
destroyed the French fleet that his colonizing mission was doomed to
failure. This is too simple. Success in the Syrian campaign might
have brought about negotiations with the Turks, and ultimately peace
with England.   Despite French losses and defeats, England was
genuinely concerned about French successes in Egypt. French military
achievements were not unimportant.   More has been written on the
military exploits of Bonaparte in Egypt than on the lasting influence
of the French in this region. But when Bonaparte departed for
France, leaving his army stranded in Egypt, he did not view the
undertaking as a failure. There is documented evidence to support
this.   Rather than the six months thought necessary to conquer and
pacify Egypt, Bonaparte had spent thirteen months and twenty days
without fully accomplishing his goals. Yet in spite of the inability
of the French to secure Egypt as a colony at this time, there were
lasting results of this expedition.
     It was obvious that the training and discipline of the French
troops gave them superiority over their formidable, though
ill-prepared foes. The importance of sea power was obvious; British
naval success in the battle of the Nile and at Acre doomed the French
army to failure and frustrated their colonial venture. There is no
doubt either that the expedition had raised the concern of the
British about threats to their trade and colonies and created
additional burdens for them. One cannot ignore the influence of this
adventure on Napoleon Bonaparte. He won some great victories in this
strange, new land. But his personal life suffered a blow at the
hands of his unfaithful wife Josephine. More than one study of
Bonaparte in Egypt explains his increasingly autocratic tendencies
and his ruthless and selfish behavior as being due to this
disappointment. The unreasonable demands made on his men, and the
massacres at Jaffa and Cairo are similarly blamed on Napoleon's
reaction to Josephine's conduct. Bonaparte was a changed man, which
had far-reaching consequences.   Finally, none of the objectives
stated in the Directory's decree had been achieved.   Only the
Institut d'Egypte proved to be long-lasting. And in the end, it has
been argued that the expedition led to the formation of the Second
Coalition. Despite these negative results writers since that time
have displayed an interest in this seemingly romantic, exotic
adventure; most have forgiven Bonaparte for not succeeding.
Unwittingly the French colonial project would serve later as a model
for future attempts at reform in Egypt and as an example to other
Western states attempting to colonize in Moslem areas of Africa and
the Middle East.

GENERAL HISTORIES

     The most authoritative and oft-quoted study of Bonaparte's
eastern venture is by La Jonquière (202); it is thorough and
objective, covering aspects other than the military operations of the
French. Most of the general histories have been written by the
French who retained a lively interest in the Near East. Bainville

(18, 19), Barthélemy (22, 24), Benoist-Méchin (32), Pastre (282), Bayon (25), and Martin (230) are illustrative of good general surveys on the subject. Both Thiers (348) and Thiry (349) published general works on the expedition of 1798 to 1801. Many studies are devoted mainly to the military aspects of the campaigns as one might expect; such as Guitry (165), Richardot (317), and Belliard (31), though Richardot includes statistics on Egypt, customs and manners of the people, and a map of the coast from Aboukir to Alexandria. Belliard's history covers military and scientific aspects of the conquest of Egypt. His memoirs (30) add details not found in his other work. Several titles deal with the subject of Egypt itself during the period 1798-1801. Among the best known are Brehier's history of Egypt, 1789-1900 (47), Galland's description of Egypt during the expedition (142), as well as Nikulā ibn Yūsuf's chronicle of Egypt, 1798-1804 (270), Redouté's article describing Egypt in 1798 (298), and Ryme study on Egypt (326). Berthier's three works on the campaigns in Egypt and Syria (36-38) also are worth reading, though unreliable and weak in areas outside of the military sphere. In English, perhaps the best known recent work is that by Herold (170) which is well-researched and thorough with a good bibliography. Elgood (119) covers similar ground, but his is not as concerned with reasons behind the Egyptian venture nor the results of it, other than military affairs. A good general history of the British expedition to Egypt is that of Sir Robert Thomas Wilson (371). Finally, Chandler has an excellent chapter in his book on Napoleon's campaigns (71). There had been less interest in this period of Napoleon's career recently. Few general works have appeared which concern all aspects of this French adventure or fit it into the context of the actively aggressive foreign policy of the Directory.

ARCHIVAL SOURCES

The most valuable and complete sources on the Army of the Orient are found in the Service historique de l'armée at the Château de Vincennes in a suburb of Paris (4). In the B6 series are included 195 cartons of correspondence relating to the expedition to Malta, Egypt, and Syria; registers, orders of the day, correspondence between various generals; and reports on assorted subjects. The numerous documents provide a broad picture of the French situation and condition in Egypt. The "Mémories Historiques" at Vincennes are essential to research on the Armée d'Orient, both on the military and civilian participants in this venture. Dossiers on individual personnel enable one to trace the activities and careers of the officers. The three sources--the B6 series, the "Mémories Historiques" and the dossiers--are readily available and have been used extensively by historians, past and present. The Bibliothèque Nationale contains numerous memoires, journals, and accounts which supply valuable eyewitness reportage on events from 1798 to 1801 in Egypt. The "Manuscrits Français" collection (224) at the Bibliothèque Nationale contains correspondence and notes relating to the publication of the twenty-four-volume DESCRIPTION DE L'EGYPTE (104). These documents illuminate the work and interests of the 165 savants, engineers, and technicians who contributed to the great study of Egypt in the last years of the eighteenth century. Documents in the Archives Nationales, Series AF III, include correspondence, decrees, and proposals made by members of the Directory regarding their colonial goals in Egypt, and instructions on how the expedition was to proceed.

In England the materials found at the British Library (British Museum) are not adequate for a study of the Egyptian expedition; it does contain both primary and secondary sources but not in great numbers. The Public Record Office has important collections of documents relating to the subject of the French and Egypt during the Directory period from 1797 through 1801; the numerous collections from the Foreign Office, the Admiralty, and the War Office reflect the British concern with the Egyptian venture and possible future incursions of the French into the Middle and Far East.

PUBLISHED DOCUMENTS

There are numerous published collections of documents relating to the expedition in Egypt other than those found in the thirty-two volumes of Napoleon's CORRESPONDANCE (257). Especially valuable are the CORRESPONDANCE OFFICIELLE DE L'ARMEE D'EGYPTE (93) and the CORRESPONDANCE INEDITE, OFFICIELLE ET CONFIDENTIELLE DE NAPOLEON BONAPARTE (258). Additional materials can be found in titles published under Napoleon's name such as CORRESPONDANCE, BULLETINS ET ORDRES, vol. 4, EGYPTE (256), PIECES DIVERSES RELATIVES AUX OPERA-TIONS MILITAIRES ET POLITIQUES DU GENERAL BONAPARTE, two vols. (265), and OEUVRES CHOISIES DE NAPOLEON BONAPARTE, vol. 1 and 2 (275). Volume 1 contains reports to the Directory on the French campaigns in Egypt and Syria, and volume 2 includes proclamations, dispatches, and official messages sent to the Directory. In volume 2 of the OEUVRES DE NAPOLEON BONAPARTE (276) are materials similar to those in OEUVRES CHOISIES (275) but fewer of them. Two collections of letters intercepted by Lord Nelson (90, 91) were published in 1799 in London, undoubtedly to serve as ammunition against French foreign policy and to reveal the actual condition of Bonaparte's army. The letters do not reflect the "gloire" achieved by French arms as stated in the official bulletins sent by Bonaparte to the Directory. The HISTOIRE SCIENTIFIQUE ET MILITAIRE DE L'EXPEDITION FRANCAISE EN EGYPTE in ten volumes (171) emphasizes the work of the savants as well as the military aspects of the time. The fourth volume of Keller's CORRESPONDANCE, BULLETINS, ET ORDRES DU JOUR DE NAPOLEON (192) pre-sents documents in an orderly, chronological format. A valuable source of information on Egypt is found in MEMOIRES SUR D'EGYPTE PUBLIES PENDANT LES CAMPAGNES DU GENERAL BONAPARTE, four volumes, published in Paris, ans VIII to XI (239). Examples of published documents that are not included in collections are Berenger's motion made in the Council of 500 or concerning Bonaparte (33), CONVENTION POUR L'EVACUATION DE L'EGYPTE (89), and FUITE DE BONAPARTE DE L'EGYPTE (138). Orders of the day, dispatches and other relative materials may be found in the B6 series at Vincennes, in the Bibliothèque Nationale, and in the British Library.

For an understanding of what the French attempted to do in Egypt and how they viewed their presence in the country one must consult LE COURRIER DE L'EGYPTE (94), a newspaper published in Cairo during the French occupation, and LA DECADE EGYPTIENNE (99), a review published in Cairo by the French.

MEMOIRS, JOURNALS, AND EYEWITNESS ACCOUNTS

Memoirs, souvenirs, letters, and eyewitness accounts of participants in the Egyptian expedition are numerous and wide-ranging in interests. This is not extraordinary since this is the only campaign of the revolutionary and Napoleonic periods in which the lasting contribution was made by civilians. One cannot discuss the venture without considering the role of the artists, engineers, orientalists and technicians who left accounts of their activities. From the first suggestions made to create a French colony, and for years after the French were driven from the East, the savants played an important part. Denon, a painter and engraver, made extensive and detailed sketches in Egypt and recounted his experiences in his valuable volume on both Upper and Lower Egypt (103). He later became the first Director of the Louvre where he founded the Egyptian collection. Gauthier's work on him is worth study also (145). Marcel (225) supervised the printing services in Egypt, Jollois (184) was an engineer, Villiers du Terrage (362) labored as a technician, and Arnault (6) was a savant; they all left accounts of their activities. Many others have been the subjects of biographers; Monge, the mathematician was undoubtedly one of the most important of the savants (8, 185). He cooperated with Bonaparte in recruiting the scholars and technical assistants; he gathered information and a small library which was transported to Egypt along with the Army. Fourier, a mathematician and physician, was praised in a book by Champollion-Figeac (70). Works on Dolomieu (199, 200), Champollion (117, 181), and Caffarelli (212) point up the successes of the civilians in Egypt. Laus de Boissy left an interesting account of Bonaparte in Egypt and of the country itself (40). Saint-Hilaire's published letters are also a good source of information on aspects of the expedition (327).

The medical aspects of this period are well covered, especially by Desgenettes who was physician in chief with the Armée d'Orient. His medical history of the Army (105) is indispensable to an understanding of the condition of Bonaparte's troops and the role played by disease and the environment on the effectiveness of these men. La Jonquière relies heavily on Desgenettes. His SOUVENIRS (106) are difficult to find, but essential in researching the medical problems encountered in Egypt. Works on Larrey (34, 173), the surgeon in chief of the army whom Napoleon called "the most virtuous man I have ever known," complement and supplement the writings of Desgenettes.

Memoirs and souvenirs of a military character are plentiful: Berthier (36-38), Bertrand (39), François (137) (he was called "le Dromadaire d'Egypte"), Lacorre (197) who was a ship's steward during the expedition, Rapp (297), Vertray (358, 359), and Richardot (315-317) provide insights into the performance of the Armée d'Orient in Egypt and Syria. Recently nineteen unedited letters of an eyewitness, Bernoyer (35), have been published. Murat's letters and personal papers (182, 183) are interesting, but self-serving. The memoirs of Bourrienne (46) who served as secretary to both Bonaparte and Monge, are partial and not always truthful. For another view of Bourrienne see Boulay de la Meurthe's book (45). The two volumes of memoirs of Lavalette (206) who married Josephine de Beauharnais's niece are not unbiased but add further details to an exciting time.

Letters, dispatches, and documents of Kléber, Menou, Desaix, Reynier, Davout, Dumas, Beauharnais, and others are available. Miot's memoirs (249) give a good picture of the French in Egypt and of Bonaparte's efforts to achieve his goals, but unfortunately they are not always reliable. Napoleon's Mameluke, Roustam, wrote his memoirs (325) which were published in 1911.

In addition to French recollections and accounts, there are important contributions made by the English concerning the expedition in Egypt. The letters and collected documents of Sir Sidney Smith (339), George Elphinstone Keith (191), and volume 3 of Lord Nelson's DISPATCHES AND LETTERS (268) are of particular interest. A FAITHFUL JOURNAL (128) by a private on board the British ship Dictator is picturesque but biased and narrowly drawn. It was published in 1802 and like Walsh's recounting of the campaign in Egypt (364) published in 1803, they are first-hand accounts which mitigate against a romanticized recall of events from the healing distance of time. This can be said too for Morier's memoir of a campaign with the Ottoman Army in Egypt (253). Another point of view is available in Gabarti's journal (139) written during the French occupation and published in 1838.

SPECIALIZED WORKS

The reasons for the Egyptian expedition in 1798, the plans laid for a new colony, preparations made by the Directory, and the aims and goals they hoped to achieve are subjects of Boulay de la Meurthe's book (44) on the Directory and the expedition. As background to this venture, a valuable source is Talleyrand's proposal for securing Egypt as a colony (345). Lokke (215) considers France and the colonial question, 1793-1801, in his book which incorporates the Egyptian expedition into the larger picture.

Outside of the military sphere of the Egyptian expedition the French have concentrated their interest on the formation and influence of the Institut d'Egypte. Auriant's article (16) on the origins of the Institut is informative; the same may be said of Guémard's works on the Institut (158-161, 163) and the role of the orientalists in Egypt (162). To understand fully the range and depth of the savants' accumulation of data and knowledge, one must become acquainted with the twenty-four volumes of their DESCRIPTION DE L'EGYPTE (104). Books and articles on specific areas of interest to French scholars include some excellent studies: Canivet on the library of the expedition (57), on the commission of the sciences and arts (58), and the printing service (59); Daressy's article on the engineer Girard and the Institut d'Egypte (97); and Dehérain's book on the exploration of Upper Egypt by the commission of the sciences and arts (101). Special studies have been done on the printing services: for example, Geiss (147), and Wassef's article (366) on the official press during the expedition. Hautecoeur has an informative article (168) on the Egyptian influence on French art during the Empire. Of interest too is Legrain's article (211) on Villoteau, a musicologist who accompanied the army to Egypt.

Works on Egypt contribute to an understanding of the French interest in the country and of the problems encountered by the French. Norry's book on the expedition includes a description of several monuments found there in 1798 (272). Redouté (298) describes

Egypt in 1798 and Ryme (326) considers Egypt during the time of French domination. Carré's book (62) on travelers and French writers in Egypt reveals the deep interest of the French in that country. Norden's two-volume study (271) on travels in Egypt and Nubia is a detailed analysis of the countries and their people. Cherfils (78), Spillman (342), and Ferry (131) look at Bonaparte and Islam, a subject which has fascinated critics and admirers of Bonaparte's attempts to win over the Egyptian population. A non-Western view of Egypt under French occupation is found in Nikulā's chronicle of Egypt, 1798-1804 (270). For an assessment of Bonaparte's governance of Egypt, Charles-Roux's book (74) covers a wide range of topics from the aims of the expedition, Bonaparte's campaigns and relations with the ruling elite in Egypt, to the preparations for the Syrian campaign and the work of the savants. Volume 5 of Dehérain's work on the history of Egypt (100) deals with Turkish Egypt, the role of the pashas and mamelukes from the sixteenth to the eighteenth centuries, and the French expedition to Egypt in 1798.

In the area of military history of the period both Phipps (287) and Dumolin (116) provide thorough and detailed analyses; Phipps covers all campaigns through 1799, Dumolin until 1809. Aubry (7) concentrates on the replenishment of stores for the army. A good source of information on the beginning of the Syrian campaign to the taking of Jaffa (124) was published by the French in Cairo, an VII. The atlas of Esposito and Elting (122) is a well-known work and is widely used. The importance of naval operations has interested many historians. Douin's work on the French fleet (110) is very good, but does not adequately explain Bonaparte's neglect of the safety of the fleet. The frustrating end to the French venture in Egypt is found in Inglis's article (174) on the English operations on the coast of Egypt in 1801. The most thorough and authoritative work on the subject of naval powers and its uses is Mahan's book on the influence of sea power during the Revolution and Empire (219).

The British response to the French enterprise in Egypt is an area which has been of interest to English historians. Rose wrote an article on the political reaction to the expedition (323), and Ingram (175, 176) and Jones (186) were concerned with the French threat to India. An early examination of the significance of the French incursion into the Near East by Tooke (353) was published in 1798. Reactions of Sir Sidney Smith (339), Keith (191), and others may be found among the collections of their correspondence and dispatches.

PERIODICALS

There are a number of French journals that indicate a continuing interest in Egypt on the part of the French. These include the REVUE INTERNATIONALE D'EGYPTE (310), BULLETIN DE L'INSTITUT D'EGYPTIENE (53), SOCIETE ROYALE DE GEOGRAPHIE D'EGYPTE (341), publications of the INSTITUT FRANCAIS D'ARCHEOLOGIE ORIENTALE (178) and the SOCIETE D'EDITIONS GEOGRAPHIQUES, MARITIMES, ET COLONIALES (340). Articles on the military are found in the CARNET DE LA SABRETACHE (61) which include valuable information on all aspects of the wars during the Revolution and Napoleonic period including memoirs and official documents. The REVUE DE LA SOCIETE DES AMIS DU MUSEE DE L'ARMEE (305) and the REVUE HISTORIQUE DE L'ARMEE (309) have published numerous articles of varying quality on the Egyptian and Syrian

campaigns. Several journals are dedicated to Napoleonic studies:
the BULLETIN DE LA SOCIETE BELGE D'ETUDES NAPOLEONIENNES (52) in
Belgium and the REVUE DES ETUDES NAPOLEONIENNES (307) have published
numerous articles on Napoleon in Egypt and Syria. The JOURNAL OF THE
SOCIETY FOR ARMY HISTORICAL RESEARCH (189) is an excellent reference
work covering the British armies at all times, in all places. In
addition, journals of more general historical interest should be
explored such as ETUDES D'HISTOIRE (123), REVUE HISTORIQUE (308),
REVUE RETROSPECTIVE (311), and the REVUE DE PARIS (306).

FUTURE RESEARCH

There has not been much written on the Egyptian and Syrian
campaigns by French or English historians in recent years. However,
the achievements of the scholars with the expedition still command
attention of historians of art and Egyptian culture. Areas of
further investigation could include the French and English views on
the possible threat to the English in India. Was the threat as
serious as Wellesley imagined and as the French intimated? A broader
examination of English records and dispatches and of French proposals
from the Directory, Talleyrand, and Bonaparte for establishing a
colony in Egypt should be made. How concerned were the English about
the diversionary tactic of invading Ireland by the French?
Much attention has been given to the military aspects of the
Egyptian expedition. For example, at least six works are available
on the creation and role of a French dromedary corps. Further
research could be done on the adaptation of Napoleon's military
tactics to operations in the Near East; was the artillery a major
factor in battle, and how did the Egyptian terrain affect the use of
cavalry? The consequences of a change of diet need to be studied.
How and why did the French modify their dress in Egypt? From the
numerous memoirs available, both of officers and savants, one could
assess how the French accommodated themselves to campaigning in an
alien environment. What diseases were prevalent? How did they
affect the fighting ability of Napoleon's army? Other than plague,
not much is known about the occurrence of diseases, vaguely labelled
"fevers," or their treatment. Since the French were cut off from
Europe, obviously they had to survive on local supplies. Was
Egyptian industry adequate to provide for the many needs of the army?
And how did campaigning in Egypt and Syria affect Napoleon's
logistical arrangements? Finally, what if any legacy remained from
the French military venture? Many studies have been done on the
Egyptian influence on French art, music, archeology, etc. In what
areas was the French presence on Egypt lasting? What reforms and
changes that occurred in Egypt in the nineteenth century were
modelled after those initiated by Bonaparte? And further, what
influence did the French experience in Egypt have on future
colonizing efforts by Western powers in Moslem areas of Africa and
elsewhere? Much can yet be said about the effects of the French
expedition by all of those involved in this dramatic, exciting
adventure.

1. Ader, Jean Joseph. HISTOIRE DE L'EXPEDITION D'EGYPTE ET DE SYRIE. REVUE POUR LES DETAILS STRATEGIQUES, PAR M. LE GENERAL BEAUVAIS. Paris: A. Dupont, 1826.

2. Amato, Attilio. ABUKIR. NAPOLEONE E L'INGHILTERRA IN LOTTA NELLA SPEDIZIONE D'AFRICA. Milan: LaProra, 1936.

3. Ancel, Jacques. MANUEL HISTORIQUE DE LA QUESTION D'ORIENT (1792-1923). Paris: n.p., 1923.

4. ARCHIVES DU SERVICE HISTORIQUE DE L'ARMEE, MINISTERE DE LA DEFENSE, CHATEAU DE VINCENNES, L'ARMEE D'ORIENT. Cartons B6, nos. 1-195.

5. "L'Armée d'Orient sous Kléber." REVUE D'HISTOIRE (1911-12): 127-36.

6. Arnault, A.V. SOUVENIRS D'UN SEXAGENAIRE. Paris: Duféy, 1834. Vol. 4.

7. Aubry, Charles. LA RAVITAILLEMENT DES ARMEES DE FREDERIC LE GRAND ET DE NAPOLEON. Paris: Charles-Lavauzelle, 1894.

8. Aubry, Paul V. MONGE: LE SAVANT AMI DE NAPOLEON BONAPARTE, 1746-1818. Paris: Gartheir-Villars, 1954.

9. AU QUARTIER-GENERAL A ALEXANDRIE, LE 18 MESSIDOR AN VI. TARIF DES MONIES. Alexandria: Imprimerie nationale, 1798.

10. AU QUARTIER-GENERAL DU KAIRE, LE 18 FLOREAL, AN 8 ... KLEBER, GENERAL EN CHEF, A L'ARMEE, ETC. (A general order relative to the proclamation of the new Constitution.) Cairo: Imprimerie nationale, 1800.

11. AU QUARTIER-GENERAL DU KAIRE, LE 17 BRUMAIRE AN 9 ... ORDRE DU JOUR. (Relative to the proposed monument to Generals Kléber and Desaix.) Cairo: Imprimerie nationale, 1800.

12. AU QUARTIER-GENERAL DU KAIRE, LE 8 BRUMAIRE AN 9. ORDRE DU JOUR, ETC. (Relating to the widows of soldiers belonging to the Army in Egypt.) Cairo: Imprimerie nationale, 1800.

13. AU QUARTIER-GENERAL DU KAIRE, LE 1er VENDEMIAIRE, AN 7 DE LA REPUBLIQUE FRANCAISE. ORDRE DU JOUR ... SIGNE A. BERTHIER. Cairo: Imprimerie nationale, 1798.

14. AU QUARTIER-GENERAL DU KAIRE, LE 4 VENDEMIAIRE AN 9 ... ORDRE DU JOUR, DU 4 VENDEMIAIRE AN 9. MENOU, GENERAL EN CHEF A L'ARMEE, ETC. (Giving the details of the successes of the French Armies in Europe.) Cairo: Imprimerie nationale, 1800.

15. AU QUARTIER-GENERAL DU KAIRE, LE 30 BRUMAIRE AN 9 ... ORDRE DU JOUR ... SIGNE MENOU. Cairo: Imprimerie nationale, 1800.

16. Auriant. "Les Origines de l'Institut Egyptien." JOURNAL DES SAVANTS 24 (1926): 217-27.

17. Baines, John, and Jaromir Malek. ATLAS OF ANCIENT EGYPT. New York: Facts on File Publications, 1980.

18. Bainville, Jacques. BONAPARTE EN EGYPTE. Geneva: Slatkine, 1936.

19. Bainville, Jacques. PRECIS DE L'HISTOIRE DE L'EGYPTE. Vol. 3. L'EXPEDITION FRANCAISE. Cairo: Imprimerie de l'Institut français d'archeologie orientale du Caire, 1934.

20. Barras, Paul Jean François Nicolas, vicomte de. MEMOIRES DE BARRAS, MEMBRE DU DIRECTOIRE. Paris: Hachette, 1895-96. 4 vols.

21. Barrow, John. THE LIFE AND CORRESPONDENCE OF ADMIRAL SIR WILLIAM SIDNEY SMITH. London: Bentley, 1848. 2 vols.

22. Barthélemy, Auguste Marseille. NAPOLEON EN EGYPTE. Paris: E. Bourdin, 1850.

23. Barthélemy, Auguste Marseille (et Méry). NAPOLEON EN EGYPTE, POEME EN HUIT CHANTS. Paris: A. Dupont, 1828.

24. Barthélemy, Auguste Marseille (et Méry). OEUVRES. Vol. 1. NAPOLEON EN EGYPTE. Geneva: Slatkine, 1838.

25. Bayon, Henry P. NAPOLEON'S EGYPTIAN EXPEDITION: BRILLIANT MILITARY VICTORIES--AND ULTIMATE DISASTER THROUGH DISEASE. Shrewsburg: Wilding, 1943.

26. Beauharnais, Eugène de, prince d'Eichstätt. MEMOIRES ET CORRESPONDENCE POLITIQUES ET MILITAIRES. Paris: Lévy, 1858-60. 10 vols.

27. Beauvais de Préau, Charles Théodore, comp. VICTOIRES, CONQUETES, DESASTRES, REVERS ET GUERRES CIVILES DES FRANCAIS DE 1792 A 1815. Paris: Panckoucke, 1818-19. Vols. 8-14.

28. Béchu, Marcel Ernest [Marcel Dupont]. GUIDES DE BONAPARTE ET CHASSEURS A CHEVAL DE LA GARDE. Paris: Les Editions Militaires Illustrées, 1946.

29. Béchu, Marcel Ernest [Marcel Dupont]. MURAT; CAVALIER, MARECHAL DE FRANCE, PRINCE ET ROI. Paris: Hachette, 1934.

30. Belliard, Augustin Daniel, comte de. MEMOIRES DU COMTE BELLIARD. Paris: Berquet et Pétion, 1842. 3 vols.

31. Belliard, Augustin Daniel, comte de, et al. HISTOIRE SCIENTIFIQUE ET MILITAIRE DE L'EXPEDITION FRANCAISE EN EGYPTE. Paris: A.J. Dénain, 1830-36. 10 vols.

32. Benoist-Méchin, Jacques Gabriel Paul Michel, baron. BONAPARTE
    EN EGYPTE: OU LE REVE INASSOUVI. Lausanne: Clairefontaine,
    1966.

33. Berenger, Jean. CORPS LEGISLATIFF. CONSEIL DES CINQ-CENTS:
    MOTION D'ORDRE FAITE PAR BERENGER. 10 NOV. 1799. CONCERNANT
    LE GENERAL BONAPARTE, etc. St. Cloud: Imprimerie nationale,
    1800.

34. Bergell, P., and K. Klitscher. LARREY, DER CHEFCHIRURG
    NAPOLEONS I. Berlin: Marschner, 1913.

35. Bernoyer, François Martin Noel. AVEC BONAPARTE EN EGYPTE ET EN
    SYRIE, 1798-1800: DIX-NEUF LETTRES INEDITES FRANCOIS BERNOYER,
    RETROUVEES, TRANSCRITES ET PRESENTEES PAR CHRISTIAN TORTEL.
    Abbeville: Les Presses françaises, 1976.

36. Berthier, Louis Alexandre. CAMPAGNE D'EGYPTE. Paris:
    Baudouin, 1827.

37. Berthier, Louis Alexandre. RELATION DES CAMPAGNES DU GENERAL
    BONAPARTE EN EGYPTE ET EN SYRIE. Paris: Didot, an IX.

38. Berthier, Louis Alexandre. RELATIONS DE L'EXPEDITION DE SYRIE,
    DE LA BATAILLE D'ABOUKIR ET DE LA REPRISE DU FORT DE CE NOM.
    IMPRIMEES SUR LES PIECES ORIGINALES ET OFFICIELLES. Paris:
    Gratiot, [1800?].

39. Bertrand, Henri Gratien, comte. CAHIERS DE SAINTE-HELENE.
    Edited by Paul Fleuriot de Langle. Paris: Michel, 1949-59. 3
    vols.

40. BONAPARTE AU CAIRE; OU, MEMOIRES SUR L'EXPEDITION DE CE GENERAL
    EN EGYPTE ... PAR UN DES SAVANS EMBARQUES SUR LA FLOTTE
    FRANCAISE. L. LAUS DE BOISSY. Paris: Prault, 1799.

41. Bonnal de Ganges, Edmond. HISTOIRE DE DESAIX: ARMEES DU RHIN,
    EXPEDITION D'ORIENT, MARENGO, D'APRES LES ARCHIVES DU DEPOT DE
    LA GUERRE. Paris: Dentu, 1881.

42. Borelli, Octave. NOTES A PROPOS DE DOCUMENTS RELATIFS A
    L'EXPEDITION FRANCAISE D'EGYPTE. Cairo: Barbier, 1888.

43. Boselli, Count. "La Prise de Malte en 1798 racontée par un
    témoin oculaire." REVISTA DEL COLLEGIO ARALDICO. Rome: n.p.,
    1909.

44. Boulay de la Meurthe, Alfred, comte de. LE DIRECTOIRE ET
    L'EXPEDITION D'EGYPTE. Paris: Hachette, 1885.

45. Boulay de la Meurthe, Alfred, comte de, et al. BOURRIENNE ET
    SES ERREURS. Paris: Herdelhof et Cassel, 1830. 2 vols.

46. Bourrienne, Louis Antoine Fauvelet de. MEMOIRES. Paris:
    Ladorcet, 1829. 5 vols.

47. Brehier, Louis. L'EGYPTE DE 1789 A 1900. Paris: Combet, 1903.

48. Browne, Haja A. BONAPARTE IN EGYPT AND THE EGYPTIANS OF TO-DAY. London: Unwin, 1907.

49. Brun, Vincent Félix. GUERRES MARITIMES DE LA FRANCE: PORT DE TOULON. Paris: Plon, 1861. Vol. 2.

50. Bryant, Arthur. THE YEARS OF ENDURANCE, 1793-1802. London: Collins, 1942.

51. Bull, John [pseud.] ANOTHER CONFIRMATION OF THE TENDER MERCIES OF BONAPARTE IN EGYPT! SELECTED BY HIS OLD FRIEND JOHN BULL. London: J. Asperne, 1803.

52. BULLETIN DE LA SOCIETE BELGE D'ETUDES NAPOLEONIENNES. 1950-75.

53. BULLETIN DE L'INSTITUT D'EGYPTIEN. 1859-1914.

54. CAMPAGNE DE BONAPARTE EN EGYPTE ET EN SYRIE, ECRITE SOUS LA DICTEE D'UN OFFICIER DE LA 32e DEMI-BRIGADE, PAR CHANUT or rather, composed by him. Troisième ed. Paris: Larrey, 1834.

55. CAMPAGNE D'EGYPTE. Vol 1. MEMOIRS DU MARECHAL BERTHIER, PRINCE DE NEUCHATEL ET DE WAGRAM, MAJOR GENERAL DES ARMEES FRANCAISES. Vol. 2. MEMOIRES DU COMTE REYNIER, GENERAL DE DIVISION. Geneva: Slatkine, 1927.

56. CAMPAGNES D'EGYPTE ET DE SYRIE. MEMOIRES POUR SERVIR A L'HISTOIRE DE NAPOLEON, DICTES PAR LUI-MEME A SAINTE-HELENE ET PUBLIES PAR LE GENERAL BERTRAND. Paris: Comon, 1847. 2 vols. and an atlas.

57. Canivet, R. "La Bibliothèque de l'expédition." REVUE INTERNATIONALE D'EGYPTE. n.p., 1906.

58. Canivet, R. "L'Expédition d'Egypte; La Commission des Sciences et des arts." REVUE INTERNATIONALE D'EGYPTE (1906).

59. Canivet, R. "L'Imprimerie de l'expédition d'Egypte: les journaux et les Procés-Verbaux de l'Institut, 1798-1801." BULLETIN DE L'INSTITUT EGYPTIEN, Series 5, 3 (1909): 1-22.

60. Carbuccia, Jean Luc. LA REGIMENT DES DROMADAIRES A L'ARMEE D'ORIENT, 1798-1801. Paris: Dumaine, 1853.

61. CARNET DE LA SABRETACHE: REVUE MILITAIRE RETROSPECTIVE. Paris: Société de La Sabretache, 1893 to present.

62. Carré, Jean Marie. VOYAGEURS ET ECRIVAINS FRANCAIS EN EGYPTE. Cairo: Imprimerie de l'Institut français d'archéologie orientale, 1932. 2 vols.

63. Caulaincourt, Armand Augustin Louis, marquis de, duc de Vicence. MEMOIRES. Paris: Plon, 1933. 3 vols.

64. "La Cavalerie en Egypte." REVUE D'HISTOIRE 63 (1907).

65. Cavaliero, Roderick. THE LAST OF THE CRUSADERS: THE KNIGHTS ST. JOHN AND OF MALTA IN THE EIGHTEENTH CENTURY. London: Hollis and Carter, 1960.

66. Ceram. DES DIEUX, DES TOMBEAUX, DES SAVANTS. Paris: Perrin, 1975.

67. Chabanier, Colonel J. SECRET D'UNE EPOPEE. La Roche-sur-Yon: Imprimerie Centrale de l'Ouest, 1974 (unpublished).

68. Chadrin, L. ODES AU PREMIER CONSUL, BONAPARTE, SUR SON RETOUR D'EGYPTE, ET SUR SES NOUVELLES VICTOIRES. Paris: Le Petite Jeune, 1800.

69. Chair, Somerset de, ed. NAPOLEON'S MEMOIRES. New York: Harper, 1949.

70. Champollion-Figeac. FOURIER ET NAPOLEON: L'EGYPTE ET LES CENT-JOURS. Paris: Firmin-Didot, 1844.

71. Chandler, David G. THE CAMPAIGNS OF NAPOLEON. New York: Macmillan, 1966.

72. Charles-Roux, François. L'ANGLETERRE ET L'EXPEDITION FRANCAISE EN EGYPTE. Cairo: Société royale de géographie d'Egypte, 1925. 2 vols.

73. Charles-Roux, François. BONAPARTE ET LA TRIPOLITAINE. Paris: Société d'éditions géographiques, maritimes et coloniales, 1929.

74. Charles-Roux, François. BONAPARTE, GOUVERNEUR D'EGYPTE. Geneva: Slatkine, 1935.

75. Charles-Roux, François. LES ORIGINES DE L'EXPEDITION D'EGYPTE. Paris: Plon-Nourrit, 1910.

76. Chauvin, Victor. LE LEGENDE EGYPTIENNE DE BONAPARTE. Mons: Desquesne-Marquillier, 1902.

77. Chavanon, Jules, and Georges Saint-Yves. JOACHIM MURAT, 1767-1815. Paris: Hachette, 1905.

78. Cherfils, Christian. BONAPARTE ET L'ISLAM. Paris: Pedone, 1914.

79. Chuquet, Arthur. "Comment Bonaparte quitta l'Egypte." ETUDES D'HISTOIRE. Geneva: Slatkine, n.d.

80. Chuquet, Arthur. "Comment Kléber remplaca Bonaparte." ETUDES
    D'HISTOIRE. Geneva: Slatkine, n.d.

81. Chuquet, Arthur. LETTRES ET NOTES INEDITES SUIVIES D'ANNEXES
    HISTORIQUES ET BIOGRAPHIQUES. Geneva: Slatkine, 1911.

82. CIRCULAIRES DU PAYEUR GENERAL DE L'ARMEE DE L'EGYPTE. Cairo:
    Imprimerie nationale, ans VII, VIII, and IX.

83. Colbert-Chabanais, Auguste Napoléon Joseph, marquis de.
    TRADITIONS ET SOUVENIRS, OU MEMOIRES TOUCHANT LE TEMPS ET LA
    VIE DU GENERAL AUGUSTE COLBERT, 1793-1809. Paris:
    Firmin-Didot, 1863-73. 5 vols.

84. Colrat, Jean Claude. "Les Dragons en Egypte." LE BRIQUET, 4
    (1982).

85. LA CONQUETE DE MALTE PAR BONAPARTE GENERAL EN CHEF DE L'ARMEE
    D'EGYPTE, DESCRIPTION DE CETTE FORTERESSE. APPERCU SUR SON
    IMPORTANCE: OBSERVATIONS HISTORIQUES ET POLITIQUES SUR L'ORDRE
    DE MALTE ET SON EXTINCTION. Parma: n.p., 1798.

86. Constanti, Pierre Dominique. BONAPARTE EN PALESTINE, AU MONT
    CARMEL, SIEGE D'ACRE, LA QUESTION D'ISRAEL, L'EUROPE UNIE.
    Paris: D'Halluin, 1967.

87. Constantini, Pierre Dominique. LE GRANDE PENSEE DE BONAPARTE,
    DE SAINT-JEAN-D'ACRE AU 18 BRUMAIRE. Paris: Baudinière, 1940.

88. Conté, N.J. "Un Inventeur oublie: N.J. Conté." Edited by
    Maurice d'Octagne. REVUE DES DEUX MONDES, 22 (1934): 912-24.

89. CONVENTION POUR L'EVACUATION DE L'EGYPTE PAR LE CORPS DE
    TROUPES DE L'ARMEE FRANCAISE ET AUXILIARES AUX ORDRES DU
    GENERAL DE DIVISION BELLIARD, etc., 27 juin 1801. Cairo:
    Imprimerie nationale, 1801.

90. COPIES DES LETTRES ORIGINALES DE L'ARMEE DU GENERAL BONAPARTE
    EN EGYPTE, INTERCEPTEES PAR LA FLOTTE SOUS LE COMMANDEMENT DE
    L'AMIRAL LORD NELSON. London: printed for J. Wright, 1799.

91. CORRESPONDANCE DE L'ARMEE FRANCAISE EN EGYPTE, INTERCEPTEE PAR
    L'ESCADRE DE NELSON. Publiée à Londres avec une introduction
    et des notes de la chancellerie anglaise, traduites en
    français; suivies d'observations, par E.T. Simon. Paris:
    Garnery, an VII (1799).

92. CORRESPONDANCE INEDITE OFFICIELLE ET CONFIDENTIELLE DE NAPOLEON
    BONAPARTE AVEC LES COURS ETRANGERES, LES PRINCES, LES MINISTRES
    ET LES GENERAUX FRANCAIS ET ETRANGERS, EN ITALIE, EN ALLEMAGNE,
    ET EN EGYPTE. Edited by C.T. Beauvais. Paris: Panckoucke,
    1819-20. 7 vols.

93. CORRESPONDANCE OFFICIELLE DE L'ARMEE D'EGYPTE, CONTENANT LES
    DERNIERES DEPECHES APPORTEES PAR LE GEN. VIAL, ET PAR

L'AIDE-DE-CAMP DU GENERAL MENOU, NETHERWOOD ... AVEC UN RECUIEL
DE PIECES DE LA PROCEDURE ET DU JUGEMENT DE L'ASSASIN DU
GENERAL KLEBER. PAR UN OFFICIER SUPERIEUR DE L'ARMEE D'EGYPTE.
Paris: Panckoucke, 1809.

94. LE COURRIER DE L'EGYPTE.

95. Damas, Hinard, ed. DICTIONNAIRE NAPOLEON. Paris: Plon, 1854.

96. Dard, Emile. NAPOLEON ET TALLEYRAND. Paris: Plon, 1935.

97. Daressy, G. "L'Ingenieur Girard et l'Institut d'Egypt."
BULLETIN DE L'INSTITUT EGYPTIEN, Series 5, 12 (1918): 13-32.

98. Debray, André. "La Pendule historique du docteur Antoine
Dubois à Luynes." BULLETIN DE LA SOCIETE BELGE D'ETUDES
NAPOLEONIENNES 89 (1975): 9-13.

99. LA DECADE EGYPTIENNE. Cairo: Institut d'Egypte, 1799-1800. 3
vols.

100. Dehérain, H. L'EGYPTE TURQUE; PACHAS ET MAMELUKS DU SEIZIEME
AU DIX-HUITIEME SIECLES; L'EXPEDITION DU GENERAL BONAPARTE.
Vol. 5.   HISTOIRE DE LA NATION EGYPTIENNE.   Edited by M.G.
Hanotaux. Paris: Société de l'histoire nationale, 1934.

101. Dehérain, H. "L'Exploration de la Haute-Egypte par la
Commission des Sciences et des Arts de l'armée d'Orient en
1799." REVUE HISTORIQUE 166 (1931): 256-65.

102. Denis, Commandant. "L'Emploi des camelins pendant la campagne
d'Egypte." REVUE HISTORIQUE DE L'ARMEE 19 (1963): 39-54.

103. Denon, Dominique Vivant. VOYAGE DANS LA BASSE ET LA HAUTE
EGYPTE, PENDANT LES CAMPAGNES DU GENERAL BONAPARTE. Paris:
Didot, 1803. 3 vols.

104. DESCRIPTION DE L'EGYPTE OU RECUEIL DES OBSERVATIONS ET DES
RECHERCHES QUI ONT ETE FAITES EN EGYPTE PENDANT L'EXPEDITION DE
L'ARMEE FRANCAISE. Edited by E.F. Jomard. Paris: Imprimerie
impériale, 1809-28. 24 vols. (10 vols. of text and 14 of
plates).

105. Desgenettes, René Nicolas. HISTOIRE MEDICALE DE L'ARMEE
D'ORIENT. Paris: Croullebois, Cossange, Masson, et Besson, an
X.

106. Desgenettes, René Nicolas. SOUVENIRS D'UN MEDECIN DE
L'EXPEDITION D'EGYPTE. Paris: Calmann-Lévy, 1892.

107. Desvernois, Nicolas Philibert, baron. MEMOIRES DU GENERAL
BARON DESVERNOIS. Paris: Plon-Nourrit, 1898.

108. Doguereau, Jean Pierre. JOURNAL DE L'EXPEDITION D'EGYPTE.
Paris: Perrin, 1904.

109. Doublet, Pierre Jean Louis Ovid. MEMOIRES HISTORIQUES SUR
     L'INVASION ET L'OCCUPATION DE MALTE PAR UNE ARMEE FRANCAISE, EN
     1798. Paris: Firmin-Didot, 1883.

110. Douin, Georges. LA FLOTTE DE BONAPARTE SUR LES COTES D'EGYPTE.
     Cairo: Imprimerie de l'Institut français d'archéologie
     orientale, pour la Société royale de géographie d'Egypte, 1922.

111. Driault, Edouard. MOHAMED ALY ET NAPOLEON. Cairo: Imprimerie
     de l'Institut français d'archéologie orientale, 1925.

112. Driault, Edouard, "Le Musée Bonaparte, au Cairo." REVUE DES
     ETUDES NAPOLEONIENNES 37 (1933): 188-202.

113. Driault, Edouard, and E. Houth. "Edme Jomard 'Egyptien'."
     BULLETIN DE L'INSTITUT D'EGYPTE 15 (1933): 259-269.

114. Dubois, Antoine. "Une Lettre d'Egypte." BULLETIN DE LA SOCIETE
     BELGE D'ETUDES NAPOLEONIENNES 89 (1975): 15-16.

115. Du Casse, Albert. LES ROIS FRERES DE NAPOLEON Ier. Paris:
     Germer, Baillière, 1883.

116. Dumolin, Maurice. PRECIS D'HISTOIRE MILITAIRE, REVOLUTION ET
     EMPIRE. Paris: Maison Andriveau-Goujon, 1906. 3 vols.

117. Dupont-Sommer, André. "Champollion et Napoléon." REVUE DE
     L'INSTITUT NAPOLEON 126 (1973): 5-10.

118. El-Djabarti, abd el-Rahman. MERVEILLES BIOGRAPHIQUES ET
     HISTORIQUES, OU CHRONIQUES. Trans. from the Arabic. Cairo:
     Imprimerie nationale, 1888-96. 9 vols.

119. Elgood, Percival George. BONAPARTE'S ADVENTURE IN EGYPT.
     London: Oxford University Press, 1931.

120. EMPLACEMENT DES TROUPES QUI COMPOSENT LES ARMEES DE LA
     REPUBLIQUE FRANCAISE, A L'EPOQUE DU 15 MESSIDOR AN 8. Paris:
     n.p., 1800.

121. Ernouf, Alfred Auguste, baron. LE GENERAL KLEBER ...
     EXPEDITION D'EGYPTE. Paris: Didier, 1870.

122. Esposito, Vincent J., and John R. Elting. A MILITARY HISTORY
     AND ATLAS OF THE NAPOLEONIC WARS. New York: Praeger, 1964.

123. ETUDES D'HISTOIRE.

124. EXPEDITION DE SYRIE JUSQU'A LA PRISE DE JAFFA. Cairo:
     Imprimerie nationale, an VII.

125. "L'Expédition française en Egypte, par un chretien du pay, Mou'
     Allem-Nicolas El-Turki, secretaire de prince des druses." REVUE
     RETROSPECTIVE 19 (n.d.).

126. "Les Extraordinaires tenues de l'armée d'Orient." LA GAZETTE DES UNIFORMES [Armes et Uniformes de l'Histoire, 1972] 21 (1974).

127. Fahmy-Bey, Mme Jeanne [Jehan d'Ivray]. BONAPARTE ET L'EGYPTE. Paris: Lemerre, 1914.

128. A FAITHFUL JOURNAL OF THE LATE EXPEDITION TO EGYPT. INCLUDING A CIRCUMSTANTIAL ACCOUNT OF THE VOYAGE, ... BATTLE OF ABOUKIR, SURRENDER OF ALEXANDRIA, DEATH OF ABERCROMBIE AND OTHER INTERESTING PARTICULARS. By a private on board the Dictator. London: L. Lee, 1802.

129. Farhi, David. "Nizam-I Jedid: Military Reforms in Egypt under Mehemet Ali." HAMIZRAH HEHADASH 20 (1970): 325-348.

130. Faulcon, F. COUPLETS DISTRIBUES AU BANQUET DONNE ... AUX GENERAUX BONAPARTE ET MOREAU, LE 15 BRUMAIRE, (6 NOV. 1799), DANS LE TEMPLE DE LA VICTOIRE. Paris: Baudouin, 1799.

131. Ferry, Commandant, ed. LA FRANCE EN AFRIQUE. (first part of the work entitled BONAPARTE ET LE MONDE MUSSULMAN). Paris: Colin, 1905.

132. Firer, John B. "Bonaparte in Egypt." CONFLICT 2 (1972): 16-20.

133. FIRMAN, EMANE DU GENERAL EN CHEF ... MENOU. (Formula of an appointment as sheikh of a village). In Fr. and Arab. Cairo: Imprimerie nationale, 1801.

134. Fleischmann, Hector. ROUSTAM: MAMELUCK DE NAPOLEON. D'APRES DES MEMOIRES ET DES NOMBREUX DOCUMENTS INEDITS TIRES DES ARCHIVES NATIONALES ET DES ARCHIVES DU MINISTERE DE LA GUERRE. Paris: Méricant, 1911.

135. Fouché, Joseph, duc d'Otrante. MEMOIRES. Paris: Le Rouge, 1824. 2 vols.

136. Francastel, A. "Les Dessins de Duterre au Musée de Versailles." REVUE DES ETUDES NAPOLEONIENNES. n.p., 1925.

137. François, Charles. JOURNAL DU CAPTAINE FRANCOIS, DIT LE DROMEDAIRE D 'EGYPTE, 1792-1830. Paris: Charles Carrington, 1903. 2 vols.

138. FUITE DE BONAPARTE DE L'EGYPTE. PIECES AUTHENTIQUES SUR SA DESERTION ... SUIVIES DE PLUSIEURS LETTRES QU'IL A ADRESSEES AU GRAND-VIZIR, etc. Paris: Le Rouge, 1814.

139. Gabarti, Abd al-Rahman al. JOURNAL D'ABDURRAHMAN GABARTI PENDANT L'OCCUPATION FRANCAISE EN EGYPTE. Paris: n.p., 1838.

140. Galea, Joseph. L'OCCUPATION DE MALTE PAR LES FRANCAIS: ETUDE BIBLIOGRAPHIQUE. Geneva: Comité de l'exposition permanente sur l'Ordre de Malte à Compesières, 1959.

141. Gallaher, John G. THE IRON MARSHALL: A BIOGRAPHY OF LOUIS N. DAVOUT. Carbondale: Southern Illinois University Press, 1976.

142. Galland, A. TABLEAU DE L'EGYPTE PENDANT LE SEJOUR DE L'ARMEE FRANCAISE. Paris: Cérioux, an XI. 2 vols.

143. Gallois, Léonard. HISTOIRE DE JOACHIM MURAT. Paris: Schubat et Heldcloff, 1828.

144. GARDE DES CONSULS. Patrouilles et rondes sorties du poste. (Blank returns). Paris: n.p., 1800.

145. Gauthier, Henri. "Vivant-Denon en Egypte, (juillet 1798-août 1799)." BULLETIN DE L'INSTITUT D'EGYPTE 5 (1923): 163-93.

146. G ... D A. TABLEAU DE L'EGYPTE PENDANT LE SEJOUR DE L'ARMEE FRANCAISE. Paris: Cerioux, an (1803).

147. Geiss, Albert. HISTOIRE DE L'IMPRIMERIE EN EGYPTE. Cairo: L'Institut français d'archéologie orientale, 1907.

148. LE GENERAL DE DIVISION KLEBER ... ORDONNE CE QUI SUIT. (Orders for precautions against the plague.) Dated, 24 messidor, an VI. In Fr. and Arab. Alexandria: Imprimerie nationale, 1798.

149. Ghorbal, Shafik. THE BEGINNINGS OF THE EGYPTIAN QUESTION AND THE RISE OF MEHEMET ALI. n.p.: Routledge, 1928.

150. Girgus, Samir. THE PREDOMINANCE OF THE ISLAMIC TRADITION OF LEADERSHIP IN EGYPT DURING BONAPARTE'S EXPEDITION. Bern: Herbert Lang, 1975.

151. Godechot, Jacques. "Le Rêve oriental de Bonaparte." REVUE DE DEFENSE NATIONALE 25 (1969): 1622-1634.

152. Gohier, Louis Jérôme. MEMOIRES. Paris: Bossange, 1824. 2 vols.

153. Gourgaud, Gaspard, baron. SAINTE-HELENE; JOURNAL INEDIT DE 1815 A 1818. Paris: Flammarion, 1899. 2 vols.

154. Granger, Alexis. UNE VISITE AU PANORAMA DE LA BATAILLE DES PYRAMIDES, POEME EN SIX CHANTS. Paris: Garnier, 1853.

155. Greverie, Capitaine P. de la. LE REGIMENT DES DROMADAIRES. Paris: Berger-Levrault, 1910.

156. Guedalla, Philip. NAPOLEON AND PALESTINE, etc. London: Allen & Unwin, 1925.

157. Guémard, Gabriel. AVENTURIERS MAMELUKS D'EGYPTE. Alexandria: Société royale d'archéologie d'Alexandrie, n.d.

158. Guémard, Gabriel. "Essai de Bibliographie critique de l'Institut d'Egypte et de la Commission des Sciences et des Arts." BULLETIN D'INSTITUT D'EGYPTE 4 (1924): 135-57.

159. Guémard, Gabriel. "Essai d'histoire de l'Institut d'Egypte et de la Commission des Sciences et Arts." BULLETIN DE L'INSTITUT D'EGYPTE 6 (1924): 41-84.

160. Guémard, Gabriel. HISTOIRE DE BIBLIOGRAPHIE CRITIQUE DE LA COMMISSION DES SCIENCES ET ARTS DE L'INSTITUT D'EGYPTE. Cairo: Chez de L'Auteur, 1936.

161. Guémard, Gabriel. "Nouvelle contribution a l'histoire de l'Institut d'Egypte et de la Commission des Sciences et Arts." BULLETIN DE L'INSTITUT D'EGYPTE 7 (1925): 71-93.

162. Guémard, Gabriel. "Les Orientalistes de l'armée d'Orient." REVUE DE L'HISTOIRE DES COLONIES FRANCAISES (1928).

163. Guémard, Gabriel. "Supplement à la bibliographie critique de l'Institut d'Egypte (1798-1801)." BULLETIN DE L'INSTITUT D'EGYPTE 7 (1926): 221-49.

164. Guerrini, Domenico. LA SPEDIZIONE FRANCESE IN EGITTO. Turin: Vaccarino, 1904.

165. Guitry, Paul Georges Marcel. L'ARMEE DE BONAPARTE EN EGYPTE; 1798-1799. Paris: Flammarion, 1898.

166. Guth, Rolf. "Betrachtungen über den unbedannten Gneisenau." ZEITSCHRIFT FUER RELIGIONS-UND GEISTESGESCHICHTE 27 (1975): 222-39.

167. Hallberg, Charles Williams. THE SUEZ CANAL: ITS HISTORY AND DIPLOMATIC IMPORTANCE. New York: Columbia University Press, 1931.

168. Hautecoeur, Louis. "L'Expédition d'Egypte et l'art français du Premier Empire." REVUE DES ETUDES NAPOLEONIENNES 24 (1925): 81-87.

169. Hauterive, Ernest d'. UN SOLDAT DE LA REVOLUTION: LE GENERAL ALEXANDRE DUMAS, 1793-1806. Paris: Ollendorff, 1897.

170. Herold, J. Christopher. BONAPARTE IN EGYPT. New York: Harper & Row, 1963.

171. HISTOIRE SCIENTIFIQUE ET MILITAIRE DE L'EXPEDITION FRANCAISE EN EGYPTE. Paris: Dénain, 1830-1836. 10 vols.

172. Homsy, Garton. LE GENERAL JACOB ET L'EXPEDITION DE BONAPARTE EN EGYPTE. Marseilles: Les Editions Indépendantes, 1921.

173. Horndasch, Max. DER CHIRURG NAPOLEONS: DAS LEBEN DES
     JEAN-DOMINIQUE LARREY. Bonn: Karl Glöckner, 1948.

174. Inglis, Charles. OPERATION ON THE COAST OF EGYPT, 1801.
     London: Navy Records Society, 1912.

175. Ingram, Edward. "The Defence of British India: The Invasion
     Scare of 1798." JOURNAL OF INDIAN HISTORY 48 (1970): 565-84.

176. Ingram, Edward. "The Defence of British India-III:
     Wellesley's Provocation of the Fourth Mysore War." JOURNAL OF
     INDIAN HISTORY: GOLDEN JUBILEE VOLUME (Trivandrum: University
     of Kerala, 1973), 595-622.

177. INSTITUT D'EGYPTE. MEMOIRES SUR L'EGYPTE. Paris: Didot, ans
     VIII-XI. 4 vols.

178. INSTITUT FRANCAIS D'ARCHEOLOGIE ORIENTALE.

179. Irwin, Eyles. AN ENQUIRY INTO THE FEASIBILITY OF THE SUPPOSED
     EXPEDITION OF BUONAPARTE TO THE EAST. London: Nicol, 1798.

180. Iung, Théodore. LUCIEN BONAPARTE ET SES MEMOIRES. Paris:
     Charpentier, 1882-83. 3 vols.

181. Janssen, Jacques J. "Jean François Champollion." SPIEGEL
     HISTORIAEL 7 (1972): 452-460.

182. Joachim Murat, king of Naples. CORRESPONDANCE DE JOACHIM
     MURAT, CHASSEUR A CHEVAL, GENERAL, MARECHAL D'EMPIRE, GRAND-DUC
     DE CLEVES ET DE BERG (JUILLET 1791-JUILLET 1808). Préface de
     Henry Houssaye. Turin: Roux Frassati, 1899.

183. Joachim Murat, king of Naples. LETTRES ET DOCUMENTS POUR
     SERVIR A L'HISTOIRE DE JOACHIM MURAT. Paris: Plon-Nourrit,
     1909-14. 8 vols.

184. Jollois, Prosper. JOURNAL D'UN INGENIEUR ATTACHE A
     L'EXPEDITION D'EGYPTE. Paris: P. Lefèvre-Pontalis, 1904.

185. Jomard, Edme François. SOUVENIRS SUR GASPARD MONGE ET SES
     RAPPORTS AVEC NAPOLEON. Paris: Thunot, 1853.

186. Jones, Edward B. "Henry Dundas, India, and British Reactions
     to Napoleon's Invasion of Egypt, 1798-1801." PROCEEDINGS OF
     THE SOUTH CAROLINA HISTORICAL ASSOCIATION 42 (1973): 41-57.

187. Joseph Bonaparte, king of Spain. MEMOIRES ET CORRESPONDANCE
     POLITIQUE ET MILITAIRE DU ROI JOSEPH. Edited by Albert Du
     Casse. 2d ed. Paris: Perrotin, 1854-55. 10 vols.

188. JOURNAL D'ABDURRAHMAN GABARTI, PENDANT L'OCCUPATION FRANCAISE
     EN EGYPTE, SUIVI D'UN PRECIS DE LA MEME CAMPAGNE PAR MOALLEM
     NICOLAS EL TURKI, SECRETAIRE DU PRINCE DES DRUSES. Translated
     by Alexandre Cardin. Paris: Rue Jacob #19, 1838.

189. JOURNAL OF THE SOCIETY FOR ARMY HISTORICAL RESEARCH. 1921 to present.

190. JUGEMENT RENDU PAR LE CONSEIL DE GUERRE PERMANENT DE LA PREMIERE DIVISION MILITAIRE DE L'ARMEE D'EGYPTE ... LE JOURD'HUR QUINZE PRAIRIAL AN HUIT, etc. Cairo: Imprimerie nationale, 1800.

191. Keith, George Elphinstone, viscount. THE KEITH PAPERS. London: Navy Records Society, 1927-55.

192. Keller, Alexander. CORRESPONDANCE, BULLETINS, ET ORDRES DU JOUR DE NAPOLEON. Vol. 4. EXPEDITION D'EGYPTE. Paris: Méricant, 1909-10. 5 vols.

193. Kircheisen, Friedrich Max. NAPOLEON IM LANDE DER PYRAMIDEN UND SEINE NACHFOLGER, 1798-1801. Munich: Georg Müller, 1918.

194. Kircheisen, Friedrich Max. NAPOLEON I. Munich and Leipzig: Georg Müller, 1914. Vol. 3.

195. Kircheisen, Gertrude. DIE FRAUEN UM NAPOLEON. Munich and Leipzig: Georg Müller, 1912.

196. Kirchenhoffer, Herman. THE BOOK OF FATE, FORMERLY IN THE POSSESSION OF NAPOLEON, LATE EMPEROR OF FRANCE; AND NOW FIRST RENDERED INTO ENGLISH, FROM A GERMAN TRANSLATION, OF AN ANCIENT EGYPTIAN MANUSCRIPT, FOUND IN THE YEAR 1801, BY M. SONINI, IN ONE OF THE ROYAL TOMBS, NEAR MOUNT LIBYCUS, IN UPPER EGYPT. London and New York: Anglo-American Authors' Association, 1822.

197. Lacorre, A. JOURNAL INEDIT D'UN COMMIS DE VIVRES PENDANT L'EXPEDITION D'EGYPTE. Bordeaux: Emile Crugy, 1852.

198. Lacour-Gayet, Georges. TALLEYRAND ET L'EXPEDITION D'EGYPTE. Paris: Picard, 1917.

199. Lacroix, Alfred. DEODAT DOLOMIEU. Paris: Perrin, 1921. 2 vols.

200. Lacroix, Alfred, and G. Daressy. "Dolomieu en Egypte (30 juin 1798-10 mars 1799)." MEMOIRES PRESENTE A L'INSTITUT D'EGYPTE. Cairo: Imprimerie de l'Institut français d'archéologie orientale, 1922.

201. Lacroix, Désiré. BONAPARTE EN EGYPTE. Paris: Garnier, 1899.

202. La Jonquière, Clément Etienne, marquis de. L'EXPEDITION D'EGYPTE, 1798-1801. Paris: Charles-Lavauzelle, 1899-1907. 5 vols.

203. La Revellière-Lépeaux, Louis Marie de. MEMOIRES. Paris: Plon-Nourrit, 1895. 3 vols.

204. Larrey, Dominique Jean. MEMOIRES DE CHIRURGIE MILITAIRE ET
      CAMPAGNES. Paris: J. Smith, 1812-17. 4 vols.

205. Las Cases, Marie Joseph, comte de. MEMORIAL DE SAINTE-HELENE.
      Paris: Dépôt du Mémorial, 1823. 8 vols.

206. Lavalette, Antoine Marie Chamant, comte de. MEMOIRES ET
      SOUVENIRS. Paris: Fournier, 1831. 2 vols.

207. Lee, John Theophilus. MEMOIRES OF THE LIFE AND SERVICES OF SIR
      J. THEOPHILUS LEE, OF THE ELMS, HAMPSHIRE. London: Published
      for the author, 1836.

208. Lefebvre, Georges. LE DIRECTOIRE. Paris: Colin, 1946.

209. Legrain, Georges. AUX PAYS DE NAPOLEON: L'EGYPTE. Grenoble:
      J. Rey, 1913.

210. Legrain, Georges. L'EXPEDITION D'EGYPTE, 1798-1799. LA
      COMMISSION D'EGYPTE. Grenoble: J. Rey, 1913.

211. Legrain, Georges. "Guillaume André Villoteau, musicographe de
      l'expédition Française d'Egypte, 1759-1839." BULLETIN DE
      L'INSTITUT D'EGYPTE 11 (1917): 1-30.

212. Lichtenberger, André. "Le général Caffarelli de Falga." LE
      SOCIALISME UTOPIQUE. Paris: Alcan, 1898.

213. LIVRE D'OR DE L'INSTITUT EGYPTIEN. Cairo: Imprimerie de
      l'Institut de bibliographie, 1899.

214. Lloyd, Christopher. THE NILE CAMPAIGN: NELSON AND NAPOLEON IN
      EGYPT. New York: Barnes and Noble, 1973.

215. Lokke, C.L. FRANCE AND THE COLONIAL QUESTION, 1763-1801. New
      York: Columbia Press, 1932.

216. Lucas-Dubreton, Jean. MURAT. Paris: Fayard, 1944.

217. McKenny, Ruth. MIRAGE. New York: Farrer, Straus and Cudahy,
      1956.

218. Madelin, Louis. L'ASCENSION DE BONAPARTE. Paris: Hachette,
      1937.

219. Mahan, Alfred T. THE INFLUENCE OF SEA POWER UPON THE FRENCH
      REVOLUTION AND EMPIRE. Boston: Little, Brown, 1894. 2 vols.

220. Mahan, Alfred T. THE LIFE OF NELSON. London: Sampson, Low,
      Marston, 1897. 2 vols.

221. Mahan, Alfred. THE LIFE OF NELSON, THE EMBODIMENT OF THE SEA
      POWER OF GREAT BRITAIN. Boston: Little, Brown, 1897. 2 vols.

222. Malus, Etienne Louis. L'AGENDA DE MALUS: SOUVENIRS DE L'EXPEDITION D'EGYPTE, 1798-1801. Publié et annoté par le général Thoumas. Paris: Champion, 1892.

223. Mandar, Michel Philippe. CHANT D'UN BARDE SUR LA CONQUETE DE L'ILE DE MALTHE PAR LES FRANCAIS LE 24 PRAIRIAL AN VI ... SOUS LES ORDRES DU GENERAL BUONAPARTE, etc. Paris: Imprimerie de "Journal des Campagnes et des armées," 1800.

224. MANUSCRITS FRANCAIS. Bibliothèque Nationale, département des manuscrits. Paris.

225. Marcel, Jean Joseph. "Souvenirs de quelques amis d'Egypte." SUPPLEMENT A TOUTES LES BIOGRAPHIES. Paris: Duduy, 1834.

226. Marmont, Auguste Frédéric Louis Viesse de, duc de Raguse. MEMOIRES DU MARECHAL MARMONT, DUC DE RAGUSE, DE 1792 A 1841. Paris: Perrotin, 1857. 9 vols.

227. Marquiset, Alfred. NAPOLEON STENOGRAPHIE AU CONSEIL D'ETAT. Paris: Champion, 1913.

228. Martel, Tancrède. MEMOIRES ET OEUVRES DE NAPOLEON ... PRECEDES D'UNE ETUDE LITTERAIRE. Paris: A. Michel, 1910.

229. Martha-Beker, Félix Victor, comte de Mons. ETUDES SUR DESAIX. Paris: Didier, 1852.

230. Martin, P.D. HISTOIRE DE L'EXPEDITION FRANCAISE EN EGYPTE. Paris: J.M. Eberhart 1815. 2 vols.

231. Masson, Frédéric. CAVALIERS DE NAPOLEON. Paris: Ollendorff, 1896.

232. Masson, Frédéric, and Guido Biagi, eds. NAPOLEON INCONNU: PAPIERS INEDITS (1786-1793). Paris: Michel, 1895. 2 vols.

233. Mathiez, Albert. LE DIRECTOIRE. Paris: Colin, 1934.

234. Maurel, André. LES TROIS DUMAS. Paris: Hachette, 1896.

235. Maurois, André. LES TROIS DUMAS. Paris: Hachette, 1957.

236. MEMOIRES DE BOURIENNE SUR NAPOLEON. Paris: Ladvocat, 1829. Vol. 2.

237. MEMOIRES POUR SERVIR A L'HISTOIRE DE FRANCE SOUS NAPOLEON. Paris: Firmin-Didot, 1823-24. 7 vols.

238. MEMOIRES SUR D'EGYPTE PUBLIES PENDANT LES CAMPAGNES DU GENERAL BONAPARTE, DANS DES ANNEES VI ET VII. Paris: Didot, 1800.

239. MEMOIRES SUR D'EGYPTE PUBLIES PENDANT LES CAMPAGNES DU GENERAL BONAPARTE DANS LES ANNEES VI ET VII. Vol. 1. PENDANT LES

ANNEES VII, VIII, ET IX. Paris: Didot, ans VIII to XI. 4 vols.

240. Méneval, Claude François, baron de. MEMOIRES POUR SERVIR A L'HISTOIRE DE NAPOLEON Ier DEPUIS 1802 JUSQU'A 1815. Paris: Dentu, 1894. 3 vols.

241. Méneval, Claude François, baron de. SUR LE RETOUR DU GENERAL BONAPARTE DE L'EGYPTE, etc. Paris: Bourgogne et Martinet, 1840.

242. Mengin. HISTOIRE D'EGYPTE SOUS LE GOUVERNEMENT DE MEHEMET-ALI. Paris: Bertrand, 1823. 2 vols.

243. MENOU, GENERAL EN CHEF, A TOUS LES HABITANS DE L'EGYPTE, ETC. (Announcement of several executions for robbery and instigation to revolt.) 29 brumaire, an IX. In Fr. and Arab. Cairo: Imprimerie nationale, 1800.

244. MENOU, GENERAL EN CHEF, AUX HABITANS DU KAIRE ET DE TOUTE L'EGYPTE. (A pacificatory proclamation.) 15 frimaire, an IX. In Fr. and Arab. Cairo: Imprimerie nationale, 1800.

245. Metz, Jean de. AUX PAYS DE NAPOLEON. L'EGYPTE, etc. La Commission d'Egypte. Grenoble: Rey, 1913.

246. Michalon, Roger, and Jacques Vernet. L'ADAPTATION D'UNE ARMEE FRANCAISE DE LA FIN DU XVIIIe SIECLE A UN THEATRE D'OPERATIONS PROCHE-ORIENTAL. Teheran: Colloque international d'histoire militaire, 1976.

247. Michelet, Jules. LES SOLDATS DE LA REVOLUTION. Paris: Calmann-Lévy, 1878.

248. Millet, P.J.S. LE CHASSEUR P. MILLET: SOUVENIRS DE LA CAMPAGNE, 1898-1901 [sic]. Paris: Emile-Paul, 1903.

249. Miot, Jacques François. MEMOIRES POUR SERVIR A L'HISTOIRE DES EXPEDITIONS EN EGYPTE ET EN SYRIE. Paris: Le Normant, 1804 and 1814.

250. Miot de Melito, André François, comte de. MEMOIRES. Paris: Calmann-Lévy, 1880.

251. Moore, John. DIARY OF SIR JOHN MOORE. London: Arnold, 1904. 2 vols.

252. Moorehead, Alan. THE BLUE NILE. New York: Harper & Row, 1962.

253. Morier, John Philip. MEMOIR OF A CAMPAIGN WITH THE OTTOMAN ARMY IN EGYPT. London: Debrett, 1801.

254. Napoléon I, Emperor of the French. AN ACCOUNT OF THE FRENCH EXPEDITION IN EGYPT; WRITTEN BY BUONAPARTE AND BERTHIER; WITH

SIR W. SIDNEY SMITH'S LETTERS. TO WHICH IS ADDED AN APPENDIX CONTAINING THE LIFE OF BUONAPARTE, DOWN TO NOV. 1799: AND ANECDOTES OF SIEYES, IN WHCIH IS GIVEN A SKETCH OF THE REVOLUTION. Leeds: printed by E. Baines, [1800].

255. Napoléon I, Emperor of the French. CAMPAGNES D'ITALIE, D'EGYPTE ET DE SYRIE. Paris: Hachette, 1872.

256. Napoléon I, Emperor of the French. CORRESPONDANCE, BULLETINS ET ORDRES DU JOUR DE NAPOLEON. Vol. 4. EXPEDITION D'EGYPTE. Paris: Méricant, 1909-10. 5 vols.

257. Napoléon I, Emperor of the French. CORRESPONDANCE DE NAPOLEON Ier, PUBLIEE PAR ORDRE DE L'EMPEREUR NAPOLEON III. Paris: Imprimerie impériale, 1858-69. 32 vols.

258. Napoléon I, Emperor of the French. CORRESPONDANCE INEDITE, OFFICIELLE ET CONFIDENTIELLE DE NAPOLEON BONAPARTE. Paris: Panckoucke, 1819-20. 7 vols.

259. Napoléon I, Emperor of the French. DERNIERS LETTRES INEDTIES DE NAPOLEON Ier. Edited by Léonce de Brotonne. Paris: H. Champion, 1903. 2 vols.

260. Napoléon I, Emperor of the French. GUERRE D'ORIENT. CAMPAGNES D'EGYPTE ET DE SYRIE, 1798-1799. MEMOIRES POUR SERVIR A L'HISTOIRE DE NAPOLEON, DICTES PAR LUI-MEME, ET PUBLIES PAR LE GENERAL BERTRAND. Paris: Comon, 1847. 2 vols.

261. Napoléon I, Emperor of the French. LETTRES DE NAPOLEON A JOSEPHINE. Edited by Léon Cerf. Paris: Ducharte & Van Buggenhoudt, 1929.

262. Napoléon I, Emperor of the French. LETTRES INEDITES DE NAPOLEON Ier. Edited by Léonce de Brotonne. Paris: Champion, 1898.

263. Napoléon I, Emperor of the French. LETTRES INEDITES DE NAPOLEON Ier. Edited by Léon Lecestre. 2d ed. Paris: Plon-Nourrit, 1897. 2 vols.

264. Napoléon I, Emperor of the French. MEMOIRES POUR SERVIR L'HISTOIRE DE FRANCE SOUS LE REGNE DE NAPOLEON I, ECRITS A SAINTE-HELENE, SOUS SA DICTEE, PAR LES GENERAUX QUI ONT PARTAGE SA CAPTIVITE. Edition nouvelle, avec introduction, notes et appendices, par Désiré Lacroix. Paris: Garnier, 1904. Vol. 2.

265. Napoléon I, Emperor of the French. PIECES DIVERSES RELATIVES AUX OPERATIONS MILITAIRES ET POLITIQUES DU GENERAL BONAPARTE EN EGYPTE. Paris: Didot, an VIII (1800). 2 vols.

266. Napoléon I, Emperor of the French. SUPPLEMENT A LA CORRESPONDANCE DE NAPOLEON Ier: LETTRES CURIEUSES OMISES PAR LE COMITEE DE PUBLICATION. Paris: Dentu, 1887.

267. NAPOLEON EN ITALIA; EGIPTE Y SYRIA, CELEBRES Y MEMORABLES
      CAMPANAS DE 1796-1800, CONOCIDAS HAJO EL TITULO DE La Y 2a DE
      ITALIA, Y DE ORIENTE, SACADAS DE SU CORRESPONDENCIA MILITAR.
      Traducidas del frances por F.M. Noriega. Paris: Librairie
      americana, 1837. 2 vols.

268. Nelson, Horatio, viscount. DISPATCHES AND LETTERS. Edited by
      Sir Nicholas Harris Nicolas.   London: Colburn, 1845. Vol.
      3.

269. Nicol, John. THE LIFE AND ADVENTURES OF JOHN NICOL, MARINER.
      Edinburgh: Blackwood, 1822.

270. Nikulā ibn Yūsuf, al-Turki. CHRONIQUE D'EGYPTE, 1798-1804.
      Edited and translated by Gaston Wiet. Cairo: Imprimerie de
      l'Institut français d'archéologie orientale, 1950.

271. Norden, Friedrich Lewis. TRAVELS IN EGYPT AND NUBIA. London:
      L. Davis & C. Reymers, 1757. 2 vols.

272. Norry, Ch. RELATION DE L'EXPEDITION D'EGYPTE, SUIVIE DE LA
      DESCRIPTION DE PLUSIEURS MONUMENTS DE CETTE CONTREE. Paris:
      Pougens, an VII.

273. Nuñez Iglisias, Indalecio. EL COLOQUIO DE BRION. Madrid:
      Museo Naval, 1977.

274. OBSERVATIONS SUR L'EXPEDITION DU GENERAL BUONAPARTE DANS LE
      LEVANT ... Traduit de l'Anglais par J.F. Andrē. Paris: Bureau
      de la Librairie, an VII, 1799.

275. OEUVRES CHOISIES DE NAPOLEON BONAPARTE, NOUVELLE EDITION, REVUE
      ET AUGMENTEE PAR M.B., GENERAL DE DIVISION DE L'EX-VIELLE
      GARDE. Vol. 1. RAPPORTS AU DIRECTOIRE (CAMPAGNE D'EGYPTE ET DE
      SYRIE). Vol. 2.   RAPPORTS AU DIRECTOIRE, 1799 in (CAMPAGNE
      D'EGYPTE DE SYRIE), PROCLAMATIONS, DISCOURS, DEPECHES ET
      MESSAGES OFFICIELS. Paris: Philippe, 1829.

276. OEUVRES DE NAPOLEON BONAPARTE. Vol. 2. CAMPAGNE D'ITALIE.
      EXPEDITION D'EGYPTE.   CONSULATE.   EMPIRE, 1804.   Paris:
      Panckoucke, 1821.

277. Ojala, Jeanne A. AUGUSTE DE COLBERT: ARISTOCRATIC SURVIVAL IN
      AN ERA OF UPHEAVAL, 1793-1809. Salt Lake City: University of
      Utah Press, 1979.

278. Ollivier, Albert. LE DIX-HUIT BRUMAIRE. Paris: Gallimard,
      1959.

279. O'Meara, Barry Edward. NAPOLEON IN EXILE; OR, A VOICE FROM ST.
      HELENA. Philadelphia: H.C. Carey and I. Lee, 1822. 2 vols.

280. ORDRE DU JOUR, DU 1er MESSIDOR. 1er complementaire, 7-29
      messidor, 28 thermidor, 30 fructidor an 8. Cairo: Imprimerie
      nationale, 1800.

281. Pallary, P. "Marie Jules César Savigny, sa vie et son oeuvre."
      MEMOIRES DE L'INSTITUT D'EGYPTE 17 (1931).

282. Pastre, Jean Louis Gaston.   BONAPARTE EN EGYPTE.   Paris:
      Editions des Portiques, 1932.

283. Pelet [de la Lozère], baron, ed.   OPINIONS DE NAPOLEON SUR
      DIVERS SUJETS DE POLITIQUE ET D'ADMINISTRATION.   Paris:
      Firmin-Didot, 1833.

284. Pelleport, Pierre, vicomte de. SOUVENIRS MILITAIRES ET INTIMES
      DE 1793 A 1853. Paris: Didier, 1857. 2 vols.

285. Peyre, R. L'EXPEDITION D'EGYPTE. Paris: Firmin-Didot, 1890.

286. Peyrusse, André.   EXPEDITION DE MALTE, D'EGYPTE, ET DE SYRIE.
      Paris: Service historique de l'armée "Terre", manuscript.

287. Phipps, Ramsey Weston. THE ARMIES OF THE FIRST FRENCH REPUBLIC
      AND THE RISE OF THE MARSHALS OF NAPOLEON I: THE ARMIES ON THE
      RHINE, IN SWITZERLAND, HOLLAND, ITALY, EGYPT, AND THE COUP
      D'ETAT OF BRUMAIRE, 1797 TO 1799. London: Oxford University
      Press, 1926-39. 5 vols.

288. Pietro, Dominique di. VOYAGE HISTORIQUE EN EGYPTE PENDANT LES
      CAMPAGNES DES GENERAUX BONAPARTE, KLEBER, ET MENOU. Paris:
      L'Huillier, 1818.

289. Pratt, Fletcher.   EMPIRE AND THE SEA. New York: Henry Holt,
      1946.

290. Pratt, Fletcher.   ROAD TO EMPIRE: THE LIFE AND TIMES OF
      BONAPARTE THE GENERAL. New York: Doubleday, Doran, 1939.

291. Prétot, P.L.   RECONNAISSANCE DE L'ISTHME ET DU CANAL DU SUEZ
      PAR LE GENERAL EN CHEF BONAPARTE ET ETABLISSEMENT DES FRANCAIS
      SOUS SA CONDUITS SUR DIVERS POINTS DE CETTE CONTREE EN 1798 TO
      1799. Paris: Bourdilliat, 1860.

292. PROCLAMATION AUX HABITANS DE L'EGYPTE ... MENOU, GENERAL EN
      CHEF ... AUX HABITANS DE L'EGYPTE. In Fr. and Arab. Cairo:
      Imprimerie nationale, 1800.

293. PROCLAMATION DE BONAPARTE A SON ARMEE ET AU PEUPLE D'EGYTPE.
      Paris: Archives Nationales, AF III 78.

294. Rabel, André.   LE MARECHAL BESSIERES, DUC D'ISTRIE.   Paris:
      Calmann-Lévy, 1903.

295. Raimes, Gaston de.   SOLDATS DE FRANCE; ACTIONS HEROIQUES.
      Paris: Lemerre, 1892-95. Vol. 2.

296. Rapp, Jean, comte. MEMOIRES DES CONTEMPORAINS, POUR SERVIR A
      L'HISTOIRE DE FRANCE, ET PRINCIPALEMENT A CELLE DE LA
      REPUBLIQUE ET DE L'EMPIRE. Paris: Bossange, 1823.

297. Rapp, Jean, comte. MEMOIRES DU GENERAL RAPP, AIDE-DE-CAMP DE NAPOLEON. Paris: Bossange, 1823.

298. Redouté, H.J.D. "L'Egypte en 1798, d'après le journal inedit d'un membre de l'Institut d'Egypte." REVUE POLITIQUE ET LITTERAIRE (1894-96).

299. "Le Régiment des dromadaires." LA GAZETTE DES UNIFORMES, [Armes et Uniformes de l'Histoire] 21 (1972).

300. "Le Régiment des dromadaires." REVUE D'HISTOIRE, 106-8 (1909).

301. Régis, Roger. PAULINE FOURES, DITE "BELLILOTE", MAITRESSE DE BONAPARTE EN EGYPTE. Paris: Editions de Paris, 1946.

302. REGLEMENT CONCERNANT L'EXERCISE ET LES MANOEUVRES DES REGIMENS D'INFANTERIE FRANCOISE CREES DEPUIS 1794. n.p., 1800.

303. Rémusat, Claire de Vergennes, comtesse de. MEMOIRES. 24th ed. Paris: Lévy, 1893. 3 vols.

304. REVUE DE L'INSTITUT NAPOLEON. 1938-1953.

305. REVUE DE LA SOCIETE DES AMIS DU MUSEE DE L'ARMEE. 1905 to present.

306. REVUE DE PARIS. 1894-1940.

307. REVUE DES ETUDES NAPOLEONIENNES. 1912-40.

308. REVUE HISTORIQUE. 1876 to present.

309. REVUE HISTORIQUE DE L'ARMEE. 1945 to present.

310. REVUE INTERNATIONALE D'EGYPTE. 1905 to present.

311. REVUE RETROSPECTIVE. 1884-1889.

312. Reynier, Jean Louis Ebénézer. DE L'EGYPTE APRES LA BATAILLE D'HELIOPOLIS, ET CONSIDERATIONS GENERALES SUR L'ORGANISATION PHYSIQUE ET POLITIQUE DE CE PAYS. Paris: Pougens, 1802.

313. Reynier, Jean Louis Ebénézer. MEMOIRES DU COMTE REYNIER, GENERAL DE DIVISION. CAMPAGNE D'EGYPTE. Paris: Baudouin, 1827.

314. Rhôné, Arthur. L'EGYPTE A PETITES JOURNEES. Paris: Société général d'editions, 1910.

315. Richardot, Charles. NOUVEAUX MEMOIRES SUR L'ARMEE FRANCAISE EN EGYPTE ET EN SYRIE, OU LA VERITE MISE AU JOUR SUR LE PRINCIPAUX FAITS ET EVENEMENTS DE CETTE ARMEE, LA STATISTIQUE DU PAYS, LES USAGES ET LES MOEURS DES HABITANTS, AVEC LE PLAN DE LA COTE D'ABOUKIR A ALEXANDRIE, etc. Paris: Corréard, 1848.

316. Richardot, Charles. REFUTATION DE QUELQUES ... ARTICLES DES MEMOIRES D'OUTRE-TOMBE ... EN CE QUI CONCERNE L'ARMEE D'ORIENT SOUS LES ORDRES DU GENERAL BONAPARTE. Paris: Corréard, 1849.

317. Richardot, Charles. RELATION DE LA CAMPAGNE DE SYRIE ... PAR UN OFFICER D'ARTILLERIE DE L'ARMEE D'ORIENT. [Paris]: Corréard, 1839.

318. Rigault, Georges. LE GENERAL ABDALLAH MENOU ET LA DERNIERE PHASE DE D'EXPEDITION D'EGYPTE. Paris: Plon-Nourrit, 1911.

319. LE RIVELAZIONI DEL GENERALE BONAPARTE AGLI AVANZI DELLA SUA ARMATA IN EGITTO, OPERETTA GENUINA E NECESSARIA PER CONOSCERE TUTTE LE TRAME DEI TRE MEMBRI DEL DIRETTORIO PER ASSOGGETTARSI LA FRANCIA E L'EUROPA CON I FALSI ALLARMI DI LIBERTA E DI EGUAGLIANZA. Florence: Puccinelli, 1799.

320. Roederer, Pierre Louis, comte. AUTOUR DE BONAPARTE: JOURNAL DU COMTE P.L. ROEDERER. Paris: Daragon, 1909.

321. Roloff, Gustav. NAPOLEONS AEGYPTISCHE EXPEDITION IM JAHRE 1798 ALS KAMPFMITTEL GEGEN ENGLAND. Berlin: Meereskunde. Jahrang 9, Heft 12, 1915.

322. Roloff, Gustav. DIE ORIENTPOLITIK NAPOLEONS I. Weimar: Kiepenheuer, 1916.

323. Rose, J.H. "The Political Reactions of Bonaparte's Eastern Expedition." ENGLISH HISTORICAL REVIEW 46 (1929): 48-58.

324. Rousseau, François. KLEBER ET MENOU EN EGYPTE, DEPUIS LE DEPART DE BONAPARTE, AOUT 1799-SEPTEMBRE 1801. Paris: Picard, 1900.

325. Roustam, Raza. SOUVENIRS DE ROUSTAM, MAMELOUCK DE NAPOLEON Ier. Paris: Ollendorff, 1911.

326. Ryme, Amédée. L'EGYPTE SOUS LA DOMINATION FRANCAISE. COLLECTION DE L'UNIVERS PITTORESQUE. Paris: Firmin-Didot, 1848.

327. Saint-Hiliare, E. Geoffroy. LETTRES ECRITES D'EGYPTE. Edited by E.T. Hamy. Paris: Hachette, 1901.

328. Sauzet, Armand. DESAIX, LE "SULTAN JUSTE". Paris: Hachette, 1954.

329. Savant, Jean. LES MAMELOUKS DE NAPOLEON. Paris: Calmann-Lévy, 1949.

330. Savary, Anne Jean Marie René, duc de Rovigo. MEMOIRES DU DUC DE ROVIGO, POUR SERVIR A L'HISTOIRE DE L'EMPEREUR NAPOLEON. Paris: Bossange, 1828. 8 vols.

331. Savary, Claude. LETTRES SUR L'EGYPTE. 2d ed. Paris: Onfroi, Librarie quai des Augustins, 1786. 3 vols.

332. al-Sāwī, Ahmad Husayn. FAJR AL-SIHAFAH FI MISR. Cairo: al-Hay'ah al-Misriyah al-'Amah Lil-Kitab, 1975.

333. Schulz, Edward. QUELLENKUNDE ZUR GESCHICHTE DE EROBERUNG MALTAS DURCH DIE FRANZOSEN 1798. Breslau: Schlesische, 1903.

334. Ségur, Philippe Paul, comte de. MEMOIRES. Paris: 1894-95. 3 vols.

335. Shaw, Stanford J. OTTOMAN EGYPT IN THE AGE OF THE FRENCH REVOLUTION. Cambridge: Harvard University Press, 1966.

336. THE SIEGE OF ACRE: OR DESCRIPTIVE COLLECTIONS RELATIVE TO THE LATE SCENE OF CONTEST IN SYRIA, BETWEEN THE BRITISH AND TURKISH FORCE, UNDER THE ORDERS OF SIR W.S. SMITH, AND THE REPUBLICAN FRENCH, COMMANDED BY GENERAL BUONAPARTE, etc. London: Glendinning, 1801.

337. Six, Georges. DICTIONNAIRE BIOGRAPHIQUE DES GENERAUX ET ADMIRAUX FRANCAIS DE LA REVOLUTION ET DE L'EMPIRE. Paris: Saffroy, 1934. 2 vols.

338. Skalkowski, Adam. LES POLONAIS EN EGYPTE, 1798-1801. Cracow: Gebethner, 1910.

339. Smith, William Sidney. NARRATIVE OF THE TREACHERY AND ... INHUMANITY OF THAT RENEGADE BUONAPARTE, AND THE DEFEAT OF HIS ARMY AT ACRE. Bristol: [1800]. (British Museum, Vol. 224, p. 868)

340. SOCIETE D'EDITIONS GEOGRAPHIQUES, MARITIMES, ET COLONIALES.

341. SOCIETE ROYALE DE GEOGRAPHIE D'EGYPTE.

342. Spillman, Georges. NAPOLEON ET L'ISLAM. Paris: Perrin, 1969.

343. Staël-Holstein, Anne Louise Germaine (Necker), baronne de. CONSIDERATIONS SUR LES PRINCIPAUX EVENEMENTS DE LA REVOLUTION FRANCAISE. Paris: Charpentier, 1843.

344. SUPPLEMENT A L'ORDRE DU JOUR DE 23 PLUVIOSE AN 9. MENOU, GENERAL EN CHEF ORDONNE L'INSERSION A L'ORDRE DU JOUR DE LA LETTRE QU'IL A ECRITE AU GRAND DIVAN AU KAIRE, etc. (Announcement of the armistice between France and Germany) In Fr. and Arab. Cairo: Imprimerie nationale, 1801.

345. Talleyrand-Périgord, Charles Maurice de, prince de Bénévent. ESSAI SUR LES AVANTAGES A TIRER DE COLONIES NOUVELLES DANS LES CIRCONSTANCES PRESENTEES. Edited by M. d'Hauterive. Paris: Baudouin, 1799.

346. Talleyrand-Périgord, Charles Maurice de, prince de Bénévent. MEMOIRES. 5 vols. Paris, 1891-92.

347. Thibaudeau, Antoine Claire, comte. HISTOIRE DE LA CAMPAGNE D'EGYPTE SOUS LE REGNE DE NAPOLEON-LE-GRAND. Paris: Huzard, 1839. 2 vols.

348. Thiers, Adolphe. L'EXPEDITION DE BONAPARTE EN EGYPTE. Edited with notes and vocabulary by C. Fabregou. Boston: D.C. Heath, 1900.

349. Thiry, Jean, baron. BONAPARTE EN EGYPTE: DECEMBRE 1797--24 AOUT 1799. Paris: Berger-Levrault, 1973.

350. Thiry, Jean, baron. "Les Motifs qui déterminerent Napoléon Bonaparte à entrependre l'expédition d'Egypte." REVUE DES TRAVAUS DE L'ACADEMIE DES SCIENCE MORALES ET POLITIQUE ET COMTPES RENDUS DE SES SEANCES 124 (1971): 223-36.

351. Thoumas, Charles Antoine. AGENDA DE MALUS, SOUVENIRS DE L'EXPEDITION D'EGYPTE, 1798-1801. Paris: H. Champion, 1892.

352. Thurman, Louis. BONAPARTE EN EGYPTE. Paris: Paul, 1902.

353. Tooke, William. OBSERVATIONS ON THE EXPEDITION OF GENERAL BUONAPARTE TO THE EAST. London: Cawthorne, 1798.

354. Tott, François, baron de. MEMOIRS OF THE TURKS AND TARTARS. English trans. Dublin: L. White, J. Cash, R. Marchbank, 1785. 2 vols.

355. Vandal, Albert. L'AVENEMENT DE BONAPARTE. Paris: Plon, 1907. 2 vols.

356. Vendreyes, Pierre. DE LA PROBABALITE EN HISTOIRE; L'EXAMPLE DE L'EXPEDITION D'EGYPTE. Paris: Michel, 1952.

357. Vertray, Captain. JOURNAL D'UN OFFICER DE L'ARMEE D'EGYPTE. Paris: Charpentier, 1883.

358. Vertray, M. L'ARMEE FRANCAISE EN EGYPTE. Manuscrit mis en ordre et publié par H. Galli. Paris: Charpentier, 1883.

359. Vertray, M. THE FRENCH ARMY IN EGYPT, 1798-1801. Translated by G.L.B. Killick. THE ENGLISH ARMY IN EGYPT, 1882. By G.L.B. Killick. London: Kennett, 1969.

360. Vigier, Henri, comte. DAVOUT: MARECHAL D'EMPIRE, DUC D'AUERSTAEDT, PRINCE D'ECKMUHL. Paris: Ollendorff, 1898. 2 vols.

361. Vigo-Roussillon, P. "Mémoires militaires." REVUE DES DEUX MONDES 1, 15 (1890): 576-607; 721-50.

362. Villiers du Terrage, René Edouard de. JOURNAL ET SOUVENIRS SUR L'EXPEDITION D'EGYPTE, 1798-1801. Paris: Plon-Nourrit, 1899.

363. Volney, Constantin François, comte de. VOYAGE EN EGYPTE ET EN SYRIE. Paris: Volland et Desenne, 1787. 2 vols.

364. Walsh, Thomas. JOURNAL OF THE LATE CAMPAIGN IN EGYPT. London: T. Cadell and W. Davies, 1803.

365. Warner, Oliver. THE BATTLE OF THE NILE. London: Batsford, 1960.

366. Wassef, Amin Sami. L'INFORMATION ET LA PRESSE OFFICIELLE EN EGYPTE JUSQU'A LA FIN DE L'OCCUPATION FRANCAISE. Cairo: Institut français d'archéologie orientale du Caire, 1975.

367. Watson, S.J. BY COMMAND OF THE EMPEROR. London: Bodley Head, 1957.

368. West, Theodor. GESCHICHTE DER FELDZUGE NAPOLEONS IN AEGYPTEN UND AUF DER PYRENAISCHEN HALBINSEL. Berlin: Tho. Bade, 1843.

369. Wheeler, Harold Felix Baker, and A.M. Broadley. NAPOLEON AND THE INVASION OF ENGLAND. London and New York: J. Lane, 1908. Vol. 1.

370. Wiet, Gaston. DEUX MEMOIRES INEDITS SUR L'EXPEDITION D'EGYPTE. Cairo: Société royale de géographie d'Egypte, 1941.

371. Wilson, Robert Thomas. HISTORY OF THE BRITISH EXPEDITION TO EGYPT. London: C. Rowarth, sold by T. Egerton, 1803. 2 vols.

372. Yorck von Wartenburg, Maximilian, graf. NAPOLEON AS A GENERAL. Edited by Walter H. James. London: Wolesby Series, n.d. 2 vols.

CHAPTER VI

THE WARS OF THE THIRD AND FOURTH COALITION (1803-07)

John G. Gallaher, University of Southern Illinois

The campaigns of 1805 and 1806 present the French army at its high point of efficiency, effectiveness, morale, and achievement. These years also witnessed the greatest accomplishments of the Emperor Napoleon I. His ability to organize and direct the numerous army corps on the long march from the English Channel to Vienna is considered to be one of the best examples of his strategic genius. His maneuvers against the Prussians in 1806 were masterful. The pursuit of the defeated Prussian army that followed the battles of Jena and Auerstädt was a textbook example of how a pursuit should be carried out. Napoleon's faculties were perhaps at their keenest in those years. He was able to assimilate the vast amounts of information that flowed into headquarters and to make quick decisions on the basis of that knowledge. He could grasp the significance of the terrain and the enemy's movements, the ability of his own officers and men, the importance of his lines of communication and supply, and the strengths and weaknesses of his adversaries. He could formulate plans in the face of the enemy, or, if need be, alter plans in accordance with mistakes of his foe. His first Italian campaign (1796-97) and the 1814 campaign of France are considered to be examples of Napoleon at his best, but in 1805 and 1806 his strategic and tactical genius reached their heights.

The French army is also seen at its height of accomplishments in those years. It was well organized and equipped. Its morale was excellent. Both officers and men were eager to prove themselves in combat under the eyes of the Emperor. There was honor, promotion, fame, and wealth to be found on the field of battle, and the men of France marched eagerly to gain all. The quality of the marshals and generals who commanded the army corps and divisions of the Grande Armée was superior to that of their counterparts in the Austrian, Prussian, and Russian armies. The French infantry was able to outmarch and outfight the forces of any European nation.

In the opening phase of the campaign of 1805, Napoleon proved himself a master of logistics. The movement of the entire French army from its camps on the English Channel and the North Sea on to the Danube was superb. At Austerlitz his tactical genius was unquestionable. He was always present with the army and personally directed the battles as well as the campaigns. His newly created marshals and his generals served directly under his orders as corps and division commanders, with little opportunity to display, or to develop, the necessary attributes needed for independent command. In fact, Marshal Davout was the only one among them who had the opportunity to command independently in battle (Auerstädt) during the campaigns of 1805-07. The Army of Italy, commanded by Marshal Masséna, was independent, but it only had a strategic impact on the course of the wars since almost all of the serious fighting took place in central and northern Europe. Finally, rivalries and jealousies were reduced to a minimum, although not completely eliminated, in the presence of the Emperor-general. This unity of

command and centralization of authority gave the French a notable
advantage over the coalition that opposed them.

GENERAL HISTORIES

Historians have tended either to write a general history of
Napoleon's campaigns or a history of a particular campaign. Thus one
finds numerous volumes on the Austerlitz campaign, the Jena-Auerstädt
campaign, and the Polish (1807) campaign. However, because the first
of these was fought between the French and the Austrian and Russian
armies, and the second between the French and Russians, few studies
deal with all three campaigns in question. Furthermore, while French
historians have written on all three campaigns, the Prussians have
tended to concentrate on 1806 while ignoring the 1805 campaign, and
the Austrians have written on 1805, but have shown little interest in
the campaigns of 1806 or 1807. Thus one must go either to histories
of the Napoleonic wars, such as David Chandler's fine one-volume, THE
CAMPAIGNS OF NAPOLEON (35), or to several volumes by the same author,
or different authors, as Jean Thiry's ULM, TRAFALGAR, AUSTERLITZ
(227), IENA (226), and EYLAU, FRIEDLAND, TILSIT (225). Therefore,
under each of the subheadings it is necessary to deal first with the
Third Coalition (the campaign of 1805) and then with the Fourth
Coalition (the campaigns of 1806-07).

The principal study of the campaign of the Third Coalition is by
Alambert and Colin, LA CAMPAGNE DE 1805 EN ALLEMAGNE (2). Written
between 1902 and 1908, this six-volume work was published by the
Section historique de l'état major de l'armée, and is the most
detailed account of the marches and battles of the campaign. Jean
Thiry's ULM, TRAFALGAR, AUSTERLITZ (227) is the best single volume by
a Frenchman. English historians have produced several good accounts
of the campaign: John H. Anderson, THE NAPOLEONIC CAMPAIGN OF 1805
(7), and the more recent THE EMPIRE AND THE GLORY: NAPOLEON
BONAPARTE: 1800-1806, by Fletcher Pratt (188). The Germans and the
Austrians have also written histories of the campaign. Heinrich D.
von Bülow's DER FELDZUG VON 1805, MILITAERISCH-POLITISCH BETRACHTET
(28) was published the year after the campaign and represents a
contemporary German's view which is long outdated. Carl Ritter von
Schönhals has presented a contemporary Austrian view in his DER
KRIEG, 1805 IN DEUTSCHLAND (207). Another Austrian, writing in 1877,
also gives a full account of the campaign: Elder von Angeli, ULM UND
AUSTERLITZ. STUDIE AUF GRUND ARCHIVALISCHE QUELLEN UEBER DE FELDZUG
1805 IN DEUTSCHLAND (61).

The most extensive study of the Fourth Coalition is Oscar von
Lettow-Vorbeck's four-volume DER KRIEG VON 1806 UND 1807 (133). It
is not surprising that the Germans have taken an interest in these
campaigns as it seemed necessary to explain what went wrong in the
Prussian system that led to the disaster. Furthermore, it was much
easier for the Germans to write on the Jena-Auerstädt Campaign after
their victories in the wars of unification. The pre-1870 two-volume
work of Friedrich E.A. von Hopfner, DER KRIEG VON 1806 UND 1807
(102), is also a good general study of the campaigns, but in less
detail and somewhat outdated. There are a number of good single
volumes on 1806 by German scholars that should be mentioned: Gerhard
Gieren, DER FREIMANERISCHE KRIEGSVERRAT VON 1806 (81); Colmar von der
Goltz, VON IENA BIS PR. EYLAU (84); August Ludwig Lefebur, ERLEBNISSE

AUS DEN KRIEGES JAHREN 1806 UND 1807 (125); Friedrich A.L. von der Marwitz, IENA, 1806 (156); and Carl von Plotho, TAGEBUCH WAEHREND DES KRIEGES ZWISCHEN RUSSLAND UND PREUSSEN EINERSEITS UND FRANKREICH ANDERSEITS IN DEN JAHREN 1806 UND 1807 (187). The earliest, and most detailed, French account of the campaigns is Jacques Peuchet's four-volume CAMPAGNE DES ARMEES FRANCAISES EN PREUSSE, EN SAXE, ET EN POLOGNE (184) which were published immediately following the Tilsit peace in 1807. However, the two volumes by Jean Thiry, IENA (226) and EYLAU, FRIEDLAND, TILSIT (225), provide the best French account of the Fourth Coalition. Another excellent one-volume study by a French historian is Henry Houssaye's IENA ET LA CAMPAGNE DE 1806 (104). A fine English study of the campaign was written by Francis Loraine Petre, NAPOLEON'S CONQUEST OF PRUSSIA--1806 (183). Paul Jean Foucart's two volumes entitled CAMPAGNE DE POLOGNE (68) is a detailed account of the Eylau and Friedland campaigns. There are two good accounts of the Polish campaign of 1806-1807. The first by Francis Loraine Petre, NAPOLEON'S CAMPAIGN IN POLAND, 1806-1807 (182), is excellent and the second by Pierre Grenier, ETUDE SUR 1807: MANOEUVRES D'EYLAU ET FRIEDLAND (89), is quite adequate.

ARCHIVAL SOURCES

The archives of the Service historique de l'armée, which are housed at the Château de Vincennes in an eastern suburb of Paris, contain a wealth of information on all aspects of the wars of the Third and Fourth Coalitions. The C2 series, entitled "Grande Armée (1805-1807)," contains 17 cartons, numbered 1 through 17, of correspondence and memoirs. In the same series (C2), under the title "Grande Armée, Armée du Rhin, Armées d'Allemagne, du Nord, etc.," the remaining 721 cartons contain literally hundreds of documents dealing with the two coalitions. These are made up of sections entitled: "Correspondance" (18-190); "Registres" (191-448); "Situations" (449-738). This is by far the most extensive collection of documents relating to every aspect of French armies during the campaigns of 1805, 1806, and 1807. In addition to this massive amount of material, there are also the personal papers and correspondence of individuals. The most extensive of these is the K1 series, "Donation Davout," which consists of one hundred cartons of letters and documents pertaining to the career of Marshal Davout. Others of note are the correspondence of Prince Eugène, C3 (6 cartons); the papers of General Gudin, D2 (9 cartons); and "Papiers du maréchal Oudinot," no. 2138 (1 carton).

Other collections that contain material on the coalitions are C11 "Livrets de situations des divisions militaires" (136 cartons) and C13 "Situations des Places à l'étranger sous le premier Empire" (22 cartons). The Xab series entitled "Garde Impériale" also contains material on the Guard during the years from its creation through 1807.

PUBLISHED DOCUMENTS

There are numerous volumes of published documents on the Third and Fourth Coalition. The vast majority of them are from French sources. The CORRESPONDANCE DE NAPOLEON Ier (170) and the various supplements (listed in Chapters I and III) contain several thousand

letters that deal with virtually every aspect of the campaigns from
orders and advice to his corps and division commanders to troop
movements and diplomatic instructions. The correspondence of other
principal participants has also been published. Charles de Mazade
published four volumes of Marshal Davout's letters in CORRESPONDANCE
DU MARECHAL DAVOUT (44). The families of Marshals Murat and Ney have
also published their respective correspondence and documents in
LETTRES ET DOCUMENTS POUR SERVIR A L'HISTOIRE DE JOACHIM MURAT,
1767-1815 (107) and MEMOIRS OF MARSHAL NEY, PUBLISHED BY HIS FAMILY
(172). Two other memoirs have included extensive letters and
documents: MEMOIRES DU MARECHAL MARMONT (150) and MEMOIRES D'ANDRE
MASSENA (157). Collectively these works provide the principal source
of published documents.
        THE JENA CAMPAIGN SOURCE BOOK (78), published by the General
Service Schools of the General Staff School (Fort Leavenworth),
provides a collection of documents and letters from 1806. However,
much of this material is taken from the memoirs of Marshals Davout,
Ney, and Murat; the correspondence of Napoleon; and Bonnal's work on
Jena. Other collections of documents deal with particular aspects of
the coalitions. On Anglo-French diplomacy in 1803, dealing with the
resumption of hostilities that led to the formation of the Third
Coalition, there is Charles W. Whitworth's work of 1887, ENGLAND AND
NAPOLEON IN 1803 (238); on the Third Coalition there is John Holland
Rose's SELECT DESPATCHES ... RELATING TO THE FORMATION OF THE THIRD
COALITION (195); Alves Slovak's LA BATAILLE D'AUSTERLITZ, DOCUMENTS
INEDITS (210); and on the Austerlitz campaign, PRECIS DE LA CAMPAGNE
DE 1805 EN ALLEMAGNE ET EN ITALIE (189), published in 1886 at
Brussels by the Bibliotheque Internationale d'histoire militaire.

MEMOIRS, JOURNALS, AND EYEWITNESS ACCOUNTS

        Virtually all of the principal military figures of the
Napoleonic wars took part in the campaigns of the Third and Fourth
Coalitions, with the exception of the English and Spanish. Their
memoirs and journals usually include one or more chapters on the
campaigns in which they took part. In particular, the French
marshals and generals are informative because of their willingness to
share with the world their role and that of their corps or divisions
in the outstanding victories of the French army. One of the best
accounts is by Marshal Davout, who commanded the French army corps at
Auerstädt. His OPERATION DU 3e CORPS, 1806-1807. RAPPORT DU MARECHAL
DAVOUT, DUC D'AUERSTAEDT (45) is the most thorough account of the
battle and of the movements of a French army corps following the
Prussian defeat. Volumes 4 (CAMPAGNE DE 1805) and 5 (CAMPAGNE DE
1806-7) of Mathieu Dumas's multivolume PRECIS DES EVENEMENTS
MILITAIRES, OU ESSAIS HISTORIQUES SUR LES CAMPAGNES DE 1799 A 1814
(58) are also excellent. Other good French accounts of various
aspects of the campaigns are: MEMOIRES DU MARECHAL DE GROUCHY (91)
by General Grouchy, who commanded a division under Murat; MEMOIRS OF
MARSHAL NEY: PUBLISHED BY HIS FAMILY (172) by Michel Ney, who
commanded the 6th Corps; MEMOIRES DU MARECHAL MARMONT (150) by
Marshal Marmont, who commanded the 2d Corps in 1805 and the army of
Dalmatia in 1806; MEMOIRES DU GENERAL BARON THIEBAULT (222) by
General Thiébault; and MEMOIRES DU GENERAL A.C. THIBAUDEAU (221) by
General Thibaudeau. Marshal Masséna commanded the French Army of

Italy and provides the only good personal account of the war south of
the Alps in his multivolume MEMOIRES D'ANDRE MASSENA (157).
Napoleon's valet de chambre, Louis Constant, has written of these
campaigns from the point of view of the Emperor's household in his
RECOLLECTIONS OF THE PRIVATE LIFE OF NAPOLEON (42). Other accounts
worthy of mention are by generals Bourrienne, MEMOIRS OF NAPOLEON
BONAPARTE (26); Rapp, MEMOIRES DU GENERAL RAPP, AIDE-DE-CAMP DE
NAPOLEON (193); Marbot, THE MEMOIRS OF BARON DE MARBOT (148);
Lejeune, MEMOIRS OF BARON LEJEUNE, AIDE-DE-CAMP TO MARSHALS BERTHIER,
DAVOUT, AND OUDINOT (128).

The best German account and explanation by an eyewitness of the
1806 "catastrophe" is by the Baron von Clausewitz, NOTES SUR LA
PRUSSE DAN SA GRANDE CATASTROPHE: 1806 (37). Colonel von Suckow
also provides a German perspective of 1806-7 in his FRAGMENTS DE MA
VIE; D'IENA A MOSCOU, PAR LE COLONEL DE SUCKOW (216). The English
general Sir Robert T. Wilson, who was with the Russian army in
1806-7, has also written a good account from his perspective in his
BRIEF REMARKS ON THE CHARACTER AND COMPOSITION OF THE RUSSIAN ARMY
AND A SKETCH OF THE CAMPAIGNS IN POLAND IN THE YEARS 1806 AND 1807
(239).

SPECIALIZED WORKS

Specialized works on the Third Coalition tend to center on the
battle of Austerlitz. The French have considered it to be the
classic Napoleonic battle, and because of its decisiveness,
historians, in general, have focused upon this one-sided struggle.
Henry Lachouque has written the best accounts of Austerlitz in his
NAPOLEON A AUSTERLITZ (118) and 2 DECEMBRE 1805 (116). AUSTERLITZ, 2
DECEMBRE 1805 (146) by Claude Manceron is also respectable, but Paul
de Clermont's LE SOLEIL D'AUSTERLITZ, 1800-1805 (38) is a
romanticized account of Napoleon and the French army. Karl von
Stutterheim's DIE SCHLACHT BEI AUSTERLITZ (215), although outdated,
presents the battle from a German point of view. The Ulm phase of
the campaign is well detailed in Frederic Natusch Maude's 1912
publication THE ULM CAMPAIGN, 1805 (159).

There are various other special studies of different aspects of
the campaign of 1805. Edouard Desbrière has written an excellent
five-volume work on the French plans and preparations for the
invasion of England. His PROJETS ET TENTATIVES DE DEBARQUEMENT AUX
ILES BRITANNIQUES (49) is the most detailed account of the French
army encamped along the English Channel in the years preceding the
march onto the Danube in the fall of 1805. Paul Azam's DU RHIN A ULM
(11) deals with the problems of the French army in the opening months
of the campaign and how they were solved. There are also several
studies of the war in the Tyrol in 1805; one by a Frenchman, Victor
Bernard Derrécagaix, NOS CAMPAGNES AU TYROL (48), and the very
detailed three-volume study by Alois Moriggl, published in Innsbruck,
DER FELDZUG DES JAHRES 1805 UND SEINE FOLGEN FUER OESTERREICH
UEBERHAUPT UND FUER TYROL INSBESONDERS MIT KARTEN (167). On the
fighting in Italy in 1805, the best single work is by the German
Alexander August von Einsiedel, DIE FELDZUGE DER OESTERREICHER IN
ITALIEN IM JAHRE 1805 (62).

The battles of Jena and Auerstädt tend to dominate the more
specialized studies of the Fourth Coalition. The excellent French

accounts of the combined battles written in recent years are Jean Thiry's IENA (226) and Henry Lachouque's IENA (117). A study that concentrates on Napoleonic strategy is Jules Louis Lewal's LA VEILLEE D'IENA: ETUDE DE STRATEGIE DE COMBAT (134). By far the best account of the battle of Auerstädt has been written by Marshal Louis N. Davout, Duke of Auerstädt, who commanded the French army that defeated the Prussians eleven miles north of Jena: OPERATIONS DU 3e CORPS, 1806-1807. RAPPORT DU MARECHAL DAVOUT, DUC D'AUERSTAEDT (45). German historians have not neglected this campaign despite the fact that it represents one of the least glorious chapters of Prussian arms. A study that presents the battle from the German point of view is C.J.F. Altrock's JENA UND AUERSTEDT (4), which contains an adequate German bibliography.

The battle of Eylau has attracted few scholars, but there exist two old works on this indecisive clash between the French and Russians. The German account by Ferdinand V. Schachtmeyer in 1857 is DIE SCHLACHT BEI PREUSSISCH-EYLAU UND DAS GEFECHT BEI WALTERSDORF IM JAHRE 1807 (203) and in French there is the contemporary BATAILLE D'EYLAU GAGNEE PAR LA GRANDE ARMEE, COMMANDEE EN PERSONNE PAR NAPOLEON, EMPEREUR DES FRANCAIS, ROI D'ITALIE, SUR LES ARMEES COMBINEES DE RUSSIE ET DE PRUSSE, LE 8 FEVRIER 1807 (15). On the battle of Friedland there are two notable French accounts: Y. Amiot's LA VICTOIRE, JUIN 1807 (5) and the earlier work by Victor Derode, NOUVELLE RELATION DE LA BATAILLE DE FRIEDLAND (14 JUIN 1807) COMPOSEE D'APRES LES PIECES DE DEPOT DE LA GUERRE, LES COMMUNICATIONS DES GENERAUX FRANCAIS, ET LES ECRITS LES PLUS ESTIMES (47).

There are a variety of studies of particular aspects of the campaigns of the Fourth Coalition. Louis A. Picard has written the history of the siege of Danzig, LE SIEGE DE DANTZIG EN 1807 (185), and Germain Lechartier has produced two volumes entitled LES SERVICES DE L'ARRIERE EN 1806-1807 ET LA MANOEUVRE DE PULTUSK (123). Baron Du Casse has studied in depth the operations of the 9th Corps: OPERATIONS DU NEUVIEME CORPS DE LA GRANDE ARMEE EN SILESIE, SOUS LE COMMANDEMENT DE S.A.I. LE PRINCE JEROME NAPOLEON, 1806-1807 (55), while Field Marshal Müffling concentrated his writings on the Prussian army in 1806 in his OPERATIONSPLAN DER PREUSSISCH-SAECHSISCHEN ARMEE IM JAHR 1806 (168). A good study of the use of cavalry in 1806, in particular the French pursuit following Jena-Auerstädt, is Paul J. Foucart's LA CAVALERIE PENDANT LA CAMPAGNE DE PRUSSE (70).

FUTURE RESEARCH

Although the campaigns of the Third and Fourth Coalitions have been adequately covered from the point of view of tactics, strategy, and the principal individuals who played a significant role, there is still room for additional study. The work of Marshal Alexandre Berthier and his staff is generally mentioned as a contributing factor to the Napoleonic victories in these years, but a good comprehensive study of the Imperial Staff has yet to be written. Furthermore, the problems of command could be studied in greater depth in the French army for the years 1805 and 1806, and in the Prussian army in 1806.

BIBLIOGRAPHY: THE THIRD AND FOURTH COALITIONS

1. Alambert-Goget, Paul Claude. CAMPAGNE DE L'AN 14 (1805) LE CORPS D'ARMEE AUX ORDRES DU MARECHAL MORTIER, COMBAT DE DURRENSTEIN. Paris: Berger-Levrault, 1897.

2. Alambert-Goget, Paul Claude, et Jean Lambert Alphonse Colin. LA CAMPAGNE DE 1805 EN ALLEMAGNE. Paris: Section historique de l'état-major de l'armée, 1902-8. 6 vols.

3. Almedingen, Martha Edith. THE EMPEROR ALEXANDER I. London: Bodley Head, 1964.

4. Altrock, Constantin von. JENA UND AUERSTEDT. Berlin: n.p., 1907.

5. Amiot, Y. LA VICTOIRE, JUIN 1807. Paris: n.p., 1880.

6. Anderson, John Henry. THE CAMPAIGN OF JENA, 1806. London: Rees, 1913.

7. Anderson, John Henry. THE NAPOLEONIC CAMPAIGN OF 1805. London: Rees, 1912.

8. Andolenko, Serge. AIGLES DE NAPOLEON CONTRE DRAPEAUX DU TSAR: 1799, 1805-7, 1812-1814: DRAPEAUX RUSSES CONQUIS PAR LES FRANCAIS, EMBLEMES FRANCAIS PRIS PAR LES RUSSES. Paris: Eurimprim, 1969.

9. ANFRECKTE MAENNER IM UNGLUECK, 1806-1807. Berlin: Kameradschaft, 1913.

10. Askenazy, Szymon. LES PRINCE JOSEPH PONIATOWSKI, MARECHAL DE FRANCE (1763-1813). Translated by B. Kozakiewicz and Paul Cazin. Paris: Plon-Nourrit, 1921.

11. Azan, Paul. DU RHIN A ULM. Paris: Section historique de l'état-major de l'armée, 1909.

12. Bailleu, Paul. "Die Schalcht von Auerstedt. Eigenhändige Relation König Freidrich Wilhelm III." DEUTSCHE RUNDSCHAU. 101 (1899): 382-399.

13. Baillot, Denis. FREDERIC A IENA. Paris: Ballard, 1807.

14. Barone, Enrico. STUDI SULLA CONDOTTA DELLA GUERRA. 1806 IN GERMANIA. Turin: Roux e Viarengo, 1900.

15. BATAILLE D'EYLAU GAGNEE PAR LA GRANDE ARMEE, COMMANDEE EN PERSONNE PAR NAPOLEON, EMPEREUR DES FRANCAIS, ROI D'ITALIE, SUR LES ARMEES COMBINEES DE RUSSIE ET DE PRUSSE, LE 8 FEVRIER 1807. n.p., 1808.

16. Beaumont, René, comte de. MEMOIRES D'UN DOLMAN DE CHASSEURS A CHEVAL SOUS LE PREMIER EMPIRE (1805-1806). Lille and Paris: Taffin-Lefort, 1898.

17. Below, H. von. ZUR GESCHICHTE DES JAHRES 1806. Berlin: K. Siegismund, 1893.

18. Benningsen, Levin August Gottlieb von. MEMOIRES, AVEC INTRODUCTION, ANNEXES ET NOTES PAR G. CAZALAS. Paris: Lavauzelle, 1907-08. 3 vols.

19. Björlin, Gustav. SVERIGS KRIG I TYSKLAND, AREN 1805-1807. Stockholm: Militärlitteratur-föreningens, 1882.

20. Blocqueville, Adélaïde Louis de. LE MARECHAL DAVOUT, PRINCE D'ECKMUHL: RACONTE PAR LES SIENS ET PAR LUI-MEME. Paris: Didier, 1879-80. 4 vols.

21. Bogdanovitch, Ivanovitch. HISTORIE DE LA RUSSIE SOUS ALEXANDRE Ier. Saint Petersburg, 1869-71. 6 vols.

22. Boguslawski, Albert von. ARMEE UND VOLK IM JAHRE 1806. Berlin: R. Eisenchmidt, 1900.

23. Bonnal, Henri. L'ESPRIT DE LA GUERRE MODERNE, DE ROSBACH A ULM ET LA MANOEUVRE D'IENA. Paris: Chapelot, 1903-4. 2 vols.

24. Bonnal, Henri. LA VIE MILITAIRE DU MARECHAL NEY, DUC D'ELCHINGEN, PRINCE DE LA MOSKOWA. Paris: Chapelot, 1910-14. 3 vols.

25. Bonnal de Ganges, Edmond. CAPITULATIONS MILITAIRES DE LA PRUSSE; ETUDE SUR LES DESASTRES DES ARMEES DE FREDERIC II D'IENA A TILSITT, D'APRES LES ARCHIVES DU DEPOT DE LA GUERRE. Paris: Dentu, 1879.

26. Bourrienne, Louis Antoine Fauvelet de. MEMOIRS OF NAPOLEON BONAPARTE. New York: Thomas Y. Crowell, 1885. 4 vols.

27. Bressonnet, Pascal. ETUDES TACTIQUES SUR LA CAMPAGNE DE 1806 (SAALFELD, IENA, AUERSTAEDT). Paris: Section historique de l'état-major de l'armée, 1909.

28. Bülow, Heinrich Dietrich, freiherr von. DER FELDZUG VON 1805, MILITAERISCH-POLITISCH BETRACHTET. Leipzig: Kosten des Verfassers, 1806. 2 vols.

29. Butterfield, Herbert. THE PEACE TACTICS OF NAPOLEON Ier, 1806-1808. Cambridge: Cambridge University Press, 1929.

30. Cambacérès, Jean Jacques de. CAMBACERES LETTRES INEDITES A NAPOLEON. Vol. 1. 1802-07. Paris: Klinsksieck, 1973.

31. CAMPAIGNS OF THE ARMIES OF FRANCE, IN PRUSSIA, SAXONY, AND POLAND, UNDER THE COMMAND OF HIS MAJESTY THE EMPEROR AND KING,

IN MDCCCVI AND VII. Translated from the French by Samuel MacKay. Boston: Farrand, Mallory, 1808. 4 vols.

32. Cartellieri, Alexander. WEIMAR UND IENA IN DER ZEIT DER DEUTSCHEN NOT UND ERHEBUNG 1806-1813. Iena: Fischer, 1913.

33. Castellane, Esprit Victor Elisabeth Boniface, comte de. JOURNAL DU MARECHAL DE CASTELLANE, 1804-1862. Paris: Plon, 1896-97. 5 vols.

34. Chalamet, Antoine, ed. GUERRES DE NAPOLEON (1800-1807) RACONTEES PAR DES TEMOINS OCULAIRES: GENERAL BIGARRE [et al]. Paris: Firmin-Didot, 1895.

35. Chandler, David G. THE CAMPAIGNS OF NAPOLEON. New York: Macmillan, 1966.

36. Chenier, L.J. Gabriel de. HISTOIRE DE LA VIEW POLITIQUE, MILITAIRE, ET ADMINISTRATIVE DU MARECHAL DAVOUT. Paris: Cosse, 1866.

37. Clausewitz, Karl von. NOTES SUR LA PRUSSE DANS SA GRANDE CATASTROPHE: 1806. Translated by A. Niessel. Paris: Chapelot, 1903.

38. Clermont, Paul de. LE SOLEIL D'AUSTERLITZ, 1800-1805. Paris: A. Michel, 1934.

39. Coelln, Freiherr von. BEITRAG SUR BESCHICHTE DER KRIEGER IN PRUESSEN, SCHLESIEN UND POLEN IN DEN JAHREN 1806 UND 1807-8. n.p., n.d.

40. Colin, Jean Lambert Alphonse. CAMPAGNE DE 1805 EN ALLEMAGNE. Paris: Chapelot, 1902-4. 5 vols.

41. Colin, Jean Lambert Alphonse. "La surprise des ponts de Vienne en 1805, Austerlitz, et la question des étangs d'Austerlitz." REVUE D'HISTOIRE (1905, 1907, 1908).

42. [Constant], Louis Constant Wairy. RECOLLECTIONS OF THE PRIVATE LIFE OF NAPOLEON BY CONSTANT, PREMIER VALET DE CHAMBRE. Translated by Walter Clark. Akron, Ohio: Saalfield, 1910. 3 vols.

43. Dallmann, Siegfried. VON IENA UND AUERSTAEDT BIS LEIPZIG (1806-1813). Berlin: Aufbare Verlags, 1954.

44. Davout, Louis Nicolas, duc d'Auerstädt et prince d'Eckmühl. CORRESPONDANCE DU MARECHAL DAVOUT, PRINCE D'ECKMUHL: SES COMMANDEMENTS, SON MINISTERE, 1801-15. Edited by Charles de Mazade. Paris: Plon, 1885. 4 vols.

45. Davout, Louis Nicolas, duc d'Auerstädt et prince d'Eckmühl. OPERATIONS DU 3e CORPS, 1806-1807. RAPPORT DU MARECHAL DAVOUT,

DUC D'AUERSTAEDT. Edited by General Léopold Davout. Paris:
Calmann-Lévy, 1896.

46. Delderfield, Ronald Frederick. NAPOLEON'S MARSHALS.
    Philadelphia: Chilton Books, 1966.

47. Derode, Victor. NOUVELLE RELATION DE LA BATAILLE DE FRIEDLAND
    (14 JUIN 1807) COMPOSEE D'APRES LES PIECES DE DEPOT DE LA
    GUERRE, LES COMMUNICATIONS DES GENERAUX FRANCAIS, ET LES ECRITS
    LES PLUS ESTIMES. Paris: Anselin et G. Laguionie, 1939.

48. Derrécagaix, Victor Bernard. NOS CAMPAGNES AU TYROL. Paris:
    Chapelot, 1910.

49. Desbrière, Edouard. PROJETS ET TENTATIVES DE DEBARQUEMENT AUX
    ILES BRITANNIQUES. Paris: Chapelot, 1900-1902. 5 vols.

50. Dodge, Theodore Ayrault. NAPOLEON: A HISTORY OF THE ART OF
    WAR FROM THE BEGINNING OF THE FRENCH REVOLUTION TO THE END OF
    THE EIGHTEENTH CENTURY, WITH A DETAILED ACCOUNT OF THE WARS OF
    THE FRENCH REVOLUTION. London: Gay and Bird, 1904-7. 4 vols.

51. Dokna. NAPOLEON IM FRUEHJAHR 1807. Leipzig: n.p., 1907.

52. Driault, Edouard. NAPOLEON ET L'EUROPE. AUSTERLITZ, LA FIN DU
    SAINT-EMPIRE (1804-1806). Paris: Alcan, 1912.

53. Driault, T. "Napoléon à Finkenstein (Avril-Mai 1807)." REVUE
    DIPLOMATIQUE 13 (1899).

54. Du Casse, Albert, baron. LE GENERAL VANDAMME ET SA
    CORRESPONDANCE. Paris: Didier, 1870. 2 vols.

55. Du Casse, Albert, baron. OPERATIONS DU NEUVIEME CORPS DE LA
    GRANDE ARMEE EN SILESIE, SOUS LE COMMANDEMENT DE S.A.I. LE
    PRINCE JEROME NAPOLEON, 1806-1807. Paris: J. Corréard, 1951.
    2 vols.

56. Dumas, Alexandre. MES MEMOIRS. Paris: Cadot, 1952-54. 22
    vols.

57. Dumas, Mathieu, comte. MEMOIRS OF HIS OWN TIMES; INCLUDING THE
    REVOLUTION, THE EMPIRE, AND THE RESTORATION. Philadelphia:
    Lea and Blanchard, 1839. 2 vols.

58. Dumas, Mathieu, comte. PRECIS DES EVENEMENTS MILITAIRES, OU
    ESSAIS HISTORIQUES SUR LES CAMPAGNES DE 1799 A 1814. Vol. 4.
    CAMPAGNE DE 1805; Vol. 5. CAMPAGNE DE 1806-7. Paris:
    Treuttel et Würtz, 1818-26.

59. Dunan, Marcel. NAPOLEON ET L'ALLEMAGNE: LE SYSTEME
    CONTINENTAL ET LES DEBUTS DE ROYAUME DE BAVIERE, 1806-1810.
    Paris: Plon, 1942.

60. [Dupont, Marcel] Marcel Ernest Béchu. NAPOLEON EN CAMPAGNE. Vol. 2. DE MARENGO A ESSLING. Paris: Hachette, 1952.

61. Edler von Angeli. ULM UND AUSTERLITZ. STUDIE AUF GRUND ARCHIVALISCHE QUELLEN UEBER DEN FELDZUG 1805 IN DEUTSCHLAND. Vienna: n.p., 1877.

62. Einsiedel, Alexander August von. DIE FELDZUEGE DER OESTERREICHER IN ITALIEN IM JAHRE 1805. Weimar: n.p., 1812.

63. Ernouf, Alfred Auguste, baron. LES FRANCAIS EN PRUSSE (1807-1808), D'APRES LES DOCUMENTS CONTEMPORAINS RECUEILLIS EN ALLEMAGNE. Paris: Didier, 1872.

64. Ernstberger, Anton. EINE DEUTSCHE UNTERGRUNDBEWEGUNG GEGEN NAPOLEON, 1806-1807. Munich: Beck, 1955.

65. Fezensac, Raymond Aymery Philippe Joseph, duc de. (See Montesquiou-Fezensac).

66. Fisher, Herbert Albert Laurens. STUDIES IN NAPOLEONIC STATESMANSHIP: GERMANY. Oxford: Clarendon Press, 1903.

67. Fleishman, Théo. NAPOLEON AU BIVOUAC: LA VIE DE L'EMPEREUR EN CAMPAGNE. Brussels: Brepols, 1957.

68. Foucart, Paul Jean. CAMPAGNE DE POLOGNE. Paris: Berger-Levrault, 1882. 2 vols.

69. Foucart, Paul Jean. CAMPAGNE DE PRUSSE (1806), IENA. Paris: Berger-Levrault, 1887.

70. Foucart, Paul Jean. LA CAVALERIE PENDANT LA CAMPAGNE DE PRUSSE. Paris: Berger-Levrault, 1880.

71. Funck, Karl Wilhelm Ferdinand von. IN THE WAKE OF NAPOLEON, BEING THE MEMOIRS (1807-1809) OF FERDINAND VON FUNCK, LIEUTENANT GENERAL IN THE SAXON ARMY AND ADJUTANT-GENERAL TO THE KING OF SAXONY. FROM THE HITHERTO UNPUBLISHED MANUSCRIPTS IN THE SAXON ARCHIVES. Edited by Oakley Williams. London: J. Lane, 1931.

72. Furse, George Armand. A HUNDRED YEARS AGO. BATTLES BY LAND AND BY SEA: ULM, TRAFALGAR, AUSTERLITZ. London: W. Clowes, 1905.

73. Gachot, Edouard. HISTOIRE MILITAIRE DE MASSENA. LA TROISIEME CAMPAGNE D'ITALIE (1805-1806) GUERRE DE L'AN XIV--EXPEDITION DE NAPLES--LE VRAI FRA DIAVOLO--LETTRES INEDITES DES PRINCES EUGENE ET JOSEPH NAPOLEON. Paris: Plon-Nourrit, 1911.

74. Gaffarel, Paul. CAMPAGNES DU CONSULTAT ET DE L'EMPIRE. PERIODE DES SUCCES (1800-1807). Paris: Hachette, 1888.

75. Gallaher, John G. THE IRON MARSHAL: A BIOGRAPHY OF LOUIS N. DAVOUT. Carbondale: Southern Illinois University Press, 1976.

76. Gallichet, Henri [H. Galli]. L'ARMEE FRANCAISE EN ALLEMAGNE (1806). Paris: Garnier, 1888.

77. Garros, Louis. NEY, LE BRAVE DES BRAVES. Paris: Amiot-Dumont, 1955.

78. General Service School, General Staff School. THE JENA CAMPAIGN SOURCE BOOK. Fort Leavenworth: General Service Schools Press, 1922.

79. Gentz, Friedrich von. D'ULM A IENA. CORRESPONDANCE INEDITE DU CHEVALIER DE GENTZ AVEC FRANCIS JAMES JACKSON, MINISTRE DE LA GRANDE-BRETAGNE A BERLIN (1804-1806). Paris: Payot, 1921.

80. Gibbs, Montgomery B. MILITARY CAREER OF NAPOLEON THE GREAT. Akron, Ohio: Saalfield, 1909.

81. Gieren, Gerhard. DER FREIMANERISCHE KRIEGSVERRAT VON 1806. Munich: Ludendorffs Verlags, 1939.

82. Gläser, W. von. LUEBECK UND RATEKAU IM NOVEMBER 1806. Lübeck: W. Gläser, 1884.

83. Goltz, Colmar, freiherr von der. JENA TO EYLAU, THE DISGRACE AND THE REDEMPTION OF THE OLD-PRUSSIAN ARMY; A STUDY IN MILITARY HISTORY. Translated by C.F. Atkinson. London: Kegan Paul, Trench Trübner, 1913.

84. Goltz, Colmar, freiherr von der. VON IENA BIS PR. EYLAU. Berlin: Mittler, 1907.

85. Goltz, Colmar, freiherr von der. VON ROSSBACH BIS IENA. Berlin: Mittler, 1883.

86. Gorlman, Ludwig von. TAGEBUCH UEBER DEN FELDZUG DES ERBGROSSHERZOGS KARL VON BADEN, 1806-1807. Freiburg: Herder, 1887.

87. Gouvin Saint-Cyr, Laurent, marquis de. MEMOIRES POUR SERVIR A L'HISTOIRE MILITAIRE SOUS LE DIRECTOIRE, LE CONSULAT, ET L'EMPIRE. Paris: Anselin, 1834. 4 vols.

88. Grade, Anders. SVERIGE OCH TILSIT ALLIANSES. Lund: Gleerupska, 1913.

89. Grenier, Pierre. ETUDE SUR 1807: MANOEUVRES D'EYLAU ET FRIEDLAND. Paris: Charles-Lavauzelle, 1901.

90. Gritti, Luigi. STUDI SUI SERVIZI LOGISTICI. 1806 IN GERMANIA. Rome: Unione cooperativa editrice, 1902.

91. Grouchy, Emmanuel, marquis de. MEMOIRES DU MARECHAL DE GROUCHY. Paris: Dentu, 1873-74. 5 vols.

92. Handelsman, Marceli. INSTRUCTIONS ET DEPECHES DES RESIDENTS DE FRANCE A VARSOVIE, 1807-1813. Cracow: Acad. des sciences, 1914. 2 vols.

93. Handelsman, Marceli. NAPOLEON ET LA POLOGNE, 1806-1807. Paris: Alcan, 1909.

94. Haussherr, Hans. ERFUELLUNG UND BEFREIUNG; DER KAMPF UM DIE DURCHFUEHRUNG DES TILSITER FRIEDENS, 1807-1808. Hamburg: Hanseatische, 1935.

95. Headley, Joel Tyler. THE IMPERIAL GUARD OF NAPOLEON: FROM MARENGO TO WATERLOO. New York: Scribner, 1851.

96. Heckscher, Eli Filip. THE CONTINENTAL SYSTEM. AN ECONOMIC INTERPRETATION. New York: H. Milford, 1922.

97. Heilmann, Johann. "Der Feldzug von 1805 in Bayern, Tirol, und Mahren." JAHRBUCHER FUER DIE DEUTSCHE ARMEE UND MARINE 62 (1887): 1-18, 124-146, 237-251; 63 (1887): 1-26.

98. Henderson, Ernest Flagg. BLUECHER AND THE UPRISING OF PRUSSIA AGAINST NAPOLEON, 1806-1815. New York: Putnam, 1911.

99. HISTOIRE DES CAMPAGNES DE L'EMPEREUR NAPOLEON DANS LA BAVIERE ET L'AUSTRICHE EN 1805, DANS LA PRUSSE ET LA POLOGNE EN 1806 ET 1807, DANS LA BAVIERE ET L'AUSTRICHE EN 1809. (Preface signed: G.P. presumed Gen. G. Petit). Paris: Picquet, 1843.

100. Höjer, Torwald Torwaldson. BERNADOTTE, MARECHAL DE FRANCE. Traduit du suédois par Lucien Maury. Paris: Plon, 1943.

101. Holl, Hermann. IENA UND UMGEBUNG. Neuenhan: n.p., 1931.

102. Hopfner, Friedrich Eduard Alexander von. DER KRIEG VON 1806 UND 1807. EIN BEITRAG ZUR GESCHICHTE DES PREUSSISCHEN ARMEE NACH DEN QUELLEN DES KRIEGSARCHIVS BEARBEITET. Berlin: S. Schropp, 1850-51. 2 vols.

103. Hourtoulle, Henry François Gabriel Léon. LE GENERAL COMTE CHARLES LASALLE, 1775-1809. Paris: Copernic, 1979.

104. Houssaye, Henry. IENA ET LA CAMPAGNE DE 1806. Paris: Perrin, 1912.

105. Hugo, Joseph Léopold Sigebert, comte. MEMOIRES DU GENERAL HUGO. Paris: Ladvocat, 1823. 3 vols.

106. Joachim Murat, king of Naples. CORRESPONDANCE DE JOACHIM MURAT, CHASSEUR A CHEVAL, GENERAL, MARECHAL D'EMPIRE, GRAND-DUC DE CLEVES ET DE BERG (JUILLET 1791-JUILLET 1808). Turin: Roux Frassati, 1899.

107. Joachim Murat, king of Naples. LETTRES ET DOCUMENTS POUR
      SERVIR A L'HISTOIRE DE JOACHIM MURAT, 1767-1815. Paris:
      Plon-Nourrit, 1908-14. 8 vols.

108. Jomini, Antoine Henri de, baron. VIE POLITIQUE ET MILITAIRE DE
      NAPOLEON, RACONTEE PAR LUI-MEME; AU TRIBUNAL DE CESAR,
      D'ALEXANDRE, ET DE FREDERIC. Paris: Anselin, 1927. 4 vols.
      and atlas.

109. Kállay, Béni. DIE GESCHICHTE DES SERBISCHEN AUFSTANDES,
      1807-1808. Vienna: Holzhausen, 1910.

110. Kieseritzky, Ernst Johann Otto. DIE SENDUNG VON HAUGWITZ NACH
      WIEN, NOVEMBER UND DEZEMBER 1805. Göttingen: Dieterich, 1895.

111. Kohl, Horst. DER UNTERGANG DES ALTEN PREUSSEN, IENA UND
      AUERSTEDT QUELLENBERICHTE ZSGEST. Leipzig: Voigtländer, 1913.

112. König, Bruno Emil. VOR 90 JAHREN. DIE SCHRECKENSTAGE VON
      SAALFELD A. S. UND DER HELDENTOD DES PRINZEN LUDWIG FERDINAND
      VON PREUSSEN. (10 Oktober 1806). Meiningen: Junghanss &
      Koritzer, 1896.

113. Kopfleisch, Charles. DIE SCLACHT BIE IENA NACH DEN BESTEN
      QUELLEN UND SCHRIFTEN. Jena: n.p., 1862.

114. Krauss, Alfred. DER FELDZUG UM ULM. Vienna: Seidel, 1912.

115. La Bédoyère, Georges Jean Louis Marie, comte de. LE MARECHAL
      NEY. Paris: Calmann-Lévy, 1902.

116. Lachouque, Henry. 2 DECEMBRE 1805. Paris: A. Dumur, 1968.

117. Lachouque, Henry. IENA. Besançon: Guy Victor, 1961.

118. Lachouque, Henry. NAPOLEON A AUSTERLITZ. Paris: Guy Victor,
      1961.

119. Lacour-Gayet, Georges. "Napoléon à Berlin en 1806." REVUE DES
      ETUDES NAPOLEONIENNES 52 (19--).

120. Langlois, Charles. RELATION DE LA BATAILLE D'EYLAU. Paris:
      Dupont, 1844.

121. Langsam, Walter Consuelo. THE NAPOLEONIC WARS AND GERMAN
      NATIONALISM IN AUSTRIA. New York: Columbia University Press,
      1930.

122. Lannes, Charles Louis Maurice, duc de Montebello. LE MARECHAL
      LANNES, DUC DE MONTEBELLO, PRINCE, SOUVERAIN DE SIEVERS, EN
      POLOGNE. RESUME DE SA VIE. Tours: A. Mame, 1900.

123. Lechartier, Germain Georges Félix. LES SERVICES DE L'ARRIERE
      EN 1806-1807 ET LA MANOEUVRE DE PULTUSK. Paris: Section
      historique de l'état-major de l'armée, 1910-11. 2 vols.

124. Ledermann, Richard. DER ANSCHLUSS BAYERNS AN FRANKREICH IM JAHRE 1805. Munich: F.P. Datterer, 1901.

125. Lefebur, August Ludwig. ERLEBNISSE AUS DEN KRIEGES JAHREN 1806 UND 1807. Berlin: n.p., 1855.

126. Lehmann, Max. DER FRIEDE VON TILSIT. Leipzig: n.p., 1911.

127. Leidolph, Eduard. DIE SCHLACHT BEI JENA. Jena: Frommann, 1896.

128. Lejeune, Louis François, baron. MEMOIRS OF BARON LEJEUNE, AIDE-DE-CAMP TO MARSHALS BERTHIER, DAVOUT, AND OUDINOT. Translated and edited by Mrs. Arthur Bell. London: Longmans, Green, 1897. 2 vols.

129. Lenin, W.I. DER TILSITER FRIEDEN. Berlin: n.p., 1954.

130. Lenz, Max. NAPOLEON UND PREUSSEN. Munich and Berlin: n.p., 1913.

131. Lenz, Max. TILSIT. Berlin: n.p., 1893.

132. Lesage, Charles. NAPOLEON Ier, CREANCIER DE LA PRUSSE (1807-1814). Paris: Hachette, 1924.

133. Lettow-Vorbeck, Oscar von. DER KRIEG VON 1806 UND 1807. Berlin: Mittler, 1892-99. 4 vols.

134. Lewal, Jules Louis. LA VEILLEE D'IENA: ETUDE DE STRATEGIE DE COMBAT. Paris: Chapelot, 1899.

135. L'Huillier, Fernand. ETUDES SUR LE BLOCUS CONTINENTAL. Paris, 1952.

136. Lilienstern, Otto August Johann Jakob Rühle, freiherr von. BERICHT EINES AUGENZEUGEN VON DEM FELDZUGE DER WAEHREND DEN MONATEN SEPTEMBER UND OKTOBER 1806 UNDER DEM KOMMANDO DES FUERSTEN FRIEDRICH LUDWIG ZU HOHENLOHE-INGELFINGEN GESTANDENEN KOENIGLICH PREUSSISCHEN UND CHURFUERSTLICH SAECHSISCHEN TRUPPEN. Tübingen: G. Cotta, 1807.

137. Lionnet, Albert. DIE INSURRECTIONS PLANE PREUSSISCHER PATRIOTEN. ENDE 1806 UND FRUEHJAHR 1807. Berlin: Ebering, 1913.

138. Loeffler, E. von. DAS TREFFEN DEI ELCHINGEN UND DIE KATASTROPHE VON ULM IM JAHRE 1805. Ulm: L. Frey, 1904.

139. Loret. ENTRE IENA ET TILSIT. Warsaw: n.p., 1962.

140. Lucas-Dubreton, Jean. LE MARECHAL NEY, 1769-1815. Paris: Fayard, 1941.

141. Lucas-Dubreton, Jean. MURAT. Paris: Fayard, 1944.

142. Lucas-Dubreton, Jean. SOLDATS DE NAPOLEON. Paris: Flammarion, 1948.

143. Madelin, Louis. HISTOIRE DU CONSULAT ET DE L'EMPIRE. Vol. 5. L'AVENEMENT DE L'EMPIRE; Vol. 6. VERS L'EMPIRE D'OCCIDENT 1806-1807. Paris: Hachette, 1939-40.

144. Maingarnauld, Victor. CAMPAGNES DE NAPOLEON TELLES QU'IL LES CONCUT ET EXECUTA; SUIVIES DE DOCUMENS QUI JUSTIFIENT SA CONDUITE MILITAIRE ET POLITIQUE. Paris: Everat, 1827. 2 vols.

145. Malo, Charles Albert [?]. PRECIS DE LA CAMPAGNE DE 1805 EN ALLEMAGNE ET EN ITALIE. Brussels and Leipzig: C. Muquardt, 1886.

146. Manceron, Claude. AUSTERLITZ, 2 DECEMBRE 1805. Paris: R. Laffont, 1960.

147. [Manson, Johann Kaspat Friedrich.] HISTORIE DES GUERRES DE PRUSSE ET D'ALLEMAGNE, DEPUIS FREDERIC-LE-GRAND JUSQU'A LA FIN DU REGNE DE NAPOLEON. Paris: Philippe, 1831. 3 vols.

148. Marbot, Jean Baptiste Antoine Marcelin, baron de. THE MEMOIRS OF BARON DE MARBOT, LATE LIEUTENANT-GENERAL IN THE FRENCH ARMY. Translated by Arthur John Butler. London: Longmans, Green, 1892. 2 vols.

149. Marin, Ibáñez. LA GUERRA MODERNA. CAMPANA DE PRUSIA EN 1806. Madrid: El Trabajo, 1906.

150. Marmont, August Frédéric Louis Viesse de, duc de Raguse. MEMOIRES DU MARECHAL MARMONT, DUC DE RAGUSE, DE 1792 A 1841, IMPRIMES SUR LE MANUSCRIT ORIGINAL DE L'AUTEUR. Paris: Perrotin, 1857. 9 vols.

151. Marmottan, Paul. LE PONT D'IENA. Paris: P. Cheronnet, 1917.

152. Marquessac, Urbain, vicomte de. NAPOLEON ET L'ANGLETERRE, CAMPAGNE DE POLOGNE (1806-1807). Paris: W. Coquebert, 1842.

153. Marshall-Cornwall, James Handyside. MARSHAL MASSENA. London: Oxford University Press, 1965.

154. Marshall-Cornwall, James Handyside. NAPOLEON AS MILITARY COMMANDER. Princeton: Van Nostrand, 1967.

155. Martinien, Aristide. TABLEAUX PAR CORPS ET PAR BATAILLES DES OFFICIERS TUES ET BLESSES PENDANT LES GUERRES DE L'EMPIRE (1805-1815). Paris: Charles-Lavauzelle, 1899.

156. Marwitz, Friedrich August Ludwig von der. IENA, 1806. Berlin: n.p., 1937.

157. Masséna, André, prince d'Essling. MEMOIRES D'ANDRE MASSENA, DUC DE RIVOLI, PRINCE D'ESSLING, MARECHAL D'EMPIRE, REDIGES D'APRES LES DOCUMENTS QU'IL A LAISSES ET SUR CEUX DU DEPOT DE LA GUERRE ET DU DEPOT DES FORTIFICATIONS. Recueillis par le general Koch. Paris: J. de Bonnot, 1966-67. 7 vols. and atlas.

158. Maude, Frederic Natusch. THE JENA CAMPAIGN, 1806. London: Swan, Sonnenschein, 1909.

159. Maude, Frederic Natusch. THE ULM CAMPAIGN, 1805. London: George Allen, 1912.

160. Mikhailovich, Aleksandr, grand-duke of Russia. LES RELATIONS DE LA RUSSIE ET DE LA FRANCE D'APRES LES RAPPORTS DES AMBASSADEURS D'ALEXANDRE Ier ET DE NAPOLEON Ier. Petersburg: n.p., 1905. 6 vols.

161. Mikhailovski-Danileviski, Aleksandr Ivanovich [Alexander Michailowsky-Danilewsky]. HISTOIRE DES CAMPAGNES DE L'EMPEREUR NAPOLEON DANS LA BAVIERE ET L'AUSTRICHE EN 1805, DANS LA PRUSSE ET LA POLOGNE EN 1806 ET EN 1807, DANS LA BAVIERE ET L'AUSTRICHE EN 1809. Paris: S. Dumaine, 1843.

162. Molitor, Gabriel Jean Joseph. CAMPAGNE DE 1806 EN DALMATIE. Paris: Bourgogne et Martinet, 1840.

163. Montbe, A. von. DIE CHURSAECHSISCHEN TRUPPEN IM FELDZUG 1806. Dresden: R. Kuntze, 1866.

164. Montegut, Emile. LE MARECHAL DAVOUT: SON CARACTERS ET SON GENIE. Paris: Quantin, 1882.

165. Montesquiou-Fezensac, Raymond Aymery Philippe Joseph, duc de. JOURNAL DU CAMP DE MONTREUIL EN 1804 ET DES CAMPAGNES D'ALLEMAGNE JUSQU'EN 1807. Paris: Bénard, 1858.

166. Montesquiou-Fezensac, Raymond Aymery Philippe Joseph, duc de. SOUVENIRS MILITAIRES DE 1804 A 1814. Paris: Librairie militaire, 1863.

167. Moriggl, Alois. DER FELDZUG DES JAHRES 1805 UND SEINE FOLGEN FUER OESTERREICH UEBERHAUPT UND FUER TIROL INSBESONDERS MIT KARTEN. Innsbruck: Wagner, 1860-61. 3 vols.

168. Müffling, Friedrich Karl Ferdinand, freiherr von. OPERATIONSPLAN DER PREUSSISCH-SAECHSISCHEN ARMEE IM JAHR 1806. Weimar: Landes-Insustrie-Comptoirs, 1807.

169. Mussinam, Joseph von. GESCHICHTE DER FRANZOESISCHEN KRIEGES IN DEUTSCHLAND BEZONDERS AUF BAYERISCHEN BODEN, 1805-1806. Sulzbach: n.p., 1826.

170. Napoléon I, Emperor of the French. CORRESPONDANCE DE NAPOLEON Ier. Paris: Imprimerie impériale, 1858-69. Vols. 10-14.

171. Napoléon I, Emperor of the French. SUPPLEMENT A LA
      CORRESPONDANCE DE NAPOLEON I: L'EMPEREUR ET LA POLOGNE.
      Paris: Bureau de l'Agence Polonaise de Presse, 1908.

172. Ney, Michel Louis Félix, duc d'Elchingen, prince de la Moskowa.
      MEMOIRS OF MARSHAL NEY, PUBLISHED BY HIS FAMILY. Philadelphia:
      Carey, 1834. 2 vols.

173. Nicholas, grand duke of Russia. RELATIONS DIPLOMATIQUES DE LA
      RUSSIE ET DE LA FRANCE. Paris. n.p., n.d. 4 vols.

174. Nicolay, Fernand. NAPOLEON AT THE BOULOGNE CAMP (BASED ON
      NUMEROUS HITHERTO UNPUBLISHED DOCUMENTS). Translated by
      Georgina L. Davis. London and New York: Cassell, 1907.

175. Orloff, Nikolai Alexejevitch, comte. PRECIS DE LA CAMPAGNE DE
      NAPOLEON CONTRE LA PRUSSE EN 1806-1807. Saint Petersburg:
      n.p., 1856.

176. Oudinot, Marie Charlotte Eugénie Julienne (de Coucy), duchesse
      de Reggio. LE MARECHAL OUDINOT, DUC DE REGGIO; D'APRES LES
      SOUVENIRS INEDITS DE LA MARECHALE. Paris: Plon, 1894.

177. Paganel, Pierre. HISTOIRE DE NAPOLEON BONAPARTE, DEPUIS SES
      PREMIERES CAMPAGNES JUSQU'A SON EXIL A L'ISLE DE SAINTE-HELENE.
      Liège: C.A. Bassompierre, 1815.

178. Parquin, Denis Charles. NAPOLEON'S ARMY. Translated and
      edited by B.T. Jones. Hamden, Conn.: Archon, 1969.

179. Parquin, Denis Charles. NAPOLEON'S VICTORIES; FROM THE
      PERSONAL MEMORIS OF CAPT. C. PARQUIN, OF THE IMPERIAL GUARD,
      1803-1814. Chicago: Werner, 1893.

180. Paul, Gertrud. DIE SCHICKSALE DER STADT IENA UND IHRER
      UMGEBUNG IN DEN OKTOBERTAGEN 1806. Iena: Fischer, 1920.

181. Persat, Maurice. MEMOIRES DU COMMANDANT PERSAT, 1806 A 1844.
      Paris: Plon-Nourrit, 1910.

182. Petre, Francis Loraine. NAPOLEON'S CAMPAIGN IN POLAND,
      1806-1807, A MILITARY HISTORY OF NAPOLEON'S FIRST WAR WITH
      RUSSIA, VERIFIED FROM UNPUBLISHED OFFICIAL DOCUMENTS. New
      York: Hippocrene, 1975.

183. Petre, Francis Loraine. NAPOLEON'S CONQUEST OF PRUSSIA--1806.
      London and New York: J. Lane, 1907.

184. Peuchet, Jacques. CAMPAGNE DES ARMEES FRANCAISE EN PRUSSE, EN
      SAXE, ET EN POLOGNE. Paris: F. Buisson, 1807. 4 vols.

185. Picard, Louis Auguste. LE SIEGE DE DANTZIG EN 1807. Paris:
      Aux bureaux de la Revue, 1910.

186. Pisani, Paul. LA DALMATIE DE 1797 A 1815. Paris: Picard, 1893.

187. Plotho, Carl von. TAGEBUCH WAEHREND DES KRIEGES ZWISCHEN RUSSLAND UND PREUSSEN EINERSEITS UND FRANKREICH ANDERSEITS IN DEN JAHREN 1806 UND 1807. Berlin: Rücker, 1811.

188. Pratt, Fletcher. THE EMPIRE AND THE GLORY; NAPOLEON BONAPARTE: 1800-1806. New York: W. Sloane, 1949.

189. PRECIS DE LA CAMPAGNE DE 1805 EN ALLEMAGNE ET EN ITALIE. Brussels: Bibliothèque Internationale d'histoire militaire, 1886.

190. Rabel, André. LE MARECHAL BESSIERES, DUC D'ISTRIE. Paris: Calmann-Lévy, 1903.

191. Rabou, Charles. LA GRANDE ARMEE. Paris: Lévy, 1865. 2 vols.

192. Raisson, Horace Napoléon. HISTOIRE POPULAIRE DE NAPOLEON ET DE LA GRANDE ARMEE. Paris: J. Lefebvre, 1830. 2 vols.

193. Rapp, Jean, comte. MEMOIRES DU GENERAL RAPP, AIDE-DE-CAMP DE NAPOLEON, ECRITS PAR LUI-MEME, ET PUBLIES PAR SA FAMILLE. Paris: Bossange, 1823.

194. Rivollet, Georges. GENERAL DE BATAILLE CHARLES ANTOINE LOUIS MORAND, COMTE D'EMPIRE (1771-1835). GENERAUX FRIANT ET GUDIN DU 3e CORPS DE LA GRANDE ARMEE. Paris: J. Peyronnet, 1963.

195. Rose, John Holland, ed. SELECT DESPATCHES FROM THE BRITISH FOREIGN OFFICE, RELATING TO THE FORMATION OF THE THIRD COALITION AGAINST FRANCE, 1804-1805. London: Royal Historical Society, 1904.

196. Rousseau, François. LA CARRIERE DU MARECHAL SUCHET, DUC D'ALBUFERA. DOCUMENTS INEDITS. Paris: Firmin-Didot, 1898.

197. Rüstow, Friedrich Wilhelm. DER KRIEG VON 1805 IN DEUTSCHLAND UND ITALIEN. Frauenfeld: Verlags-Comptoir, 1853.

198. Saint-Chamans, Alfred Armand Robert, comte de. MEMOIRES DU GENERAL COMTE DE SAINT-CHAMANS, ANCIENT AIDE DE CAMP DU MARECHAL SOULT, 1803-1832. Paris: Plon, 1896.

199. [Saint-Hilaire], Emile March Hilaire, [Marco de]. HISTOIRE POPULAIRE ET ANECDOTIQUE DE NAPOLEON ET DE LA GRANDE ARMEE. SUIVIE DE L'HISTORIE DES MARECHAUX DE L'EMPIRE. Paris: Téqui, 1909.

200. Saint-Joseph. GRANDE ARMEE. CAMPAGNE DE PRUSSE EN JUIN 1807. JOURNAL D'UN OFFICIER D'ETAT-MAJOR. Paris: E. Martinet, 1863.

201. Saint-Marc, Pierre. LE MARECHAL MARMONT, DUC DE RAGUSE, 1774-1852. Paris: Fayard, 1957.

202. Savary, Anne Jean Marie René, duc de Rovigo. MEMOIRES DU DUC
     DE ROVIGO, POUR SERVIR A L'HISTOIRE DE L'EMPEREUR NAPOLEON.
     Paris: Bossange, 1828. 8 vols.

203. Schachtmeyer, Ferdinand V. DIE SCHLACHT BEI PREUSSISCH-EYLAU
     UND DAS GEFECHT BEI WALTERSDORF IM JAHRE 1807. Berlin:
     Geelaar, 1857.

204. Schlösser, Ludwig. AUS DEM KRIEGSJAHREN, 1806-1813. Berlin:
     n.p., 1913.

205. Schmölzl, Joseph. DER FELDZUG DER BAYERN VON 1806-1807 IN
     SCHLESIEN UND POLEN. Munich: Lindauer, 1856.

206. Schmölzl, Joseph. DER KLEINE KRIEG IN OBERSCHLESIEN IM JAHRE
     1807. Leipzig: F. Fleischer, 1854.

207. Schönhals, Carl Ritter von. DER KRIEG, 1805 IN DEUTSCHLAND.
     Vienna: n.p., 1821.

208. Schottmüller, Konrad. DER POLEN AUFSTAND, 1806-1807. Lissa:
     F. Ebbecke, 1907.

209. Schupp, P. THE EUROPEAN POWERS AND THE NEAR EAST QUESTION
     1806-1807. New York: Columbia University, 1931.

210. Slovak, Alves. LA BATAILLE D'AUSTERLITZ, DOCUMENTS INEDITS.
     Translated by L. Leroy. Paris: H. Daragon, 1908.

211. Sorel, Albert Emile Edouard. LOUISE DE PRUSSE. Paris: B.
     Grasset, 1937.

212. Steigler, Gaston. MEMOIRS OF MARSHAL OUDINOT, DUC DE REGGIO.
     Translated by Alexander T. de Mattos. London: H. Henry, 1896.

213. Stocklaska, Walter. DIE SCHACHT BEI AUSTERLITZ. Brunn: C.
     Winiker, 1905.

214. Strauch, H. von. DER ERSTE ZUSAMMENSTOSS IM KRIEGE VON
     1806-1807. Berlin: n.p., 1906.

215. Stutterheim, Karl, freiherr von. DIE SCHLACHT BEI AUSTERLITZ.
     Hamburg: Walthersche, 1860.

216. Suckow, Karl Freidrich Emil von. FRAGMENTS DE MA VIE; D'IENA A
     MOSCOU, PAR LE COLONEL DE SUCKOW. Translated by Commandant
     Veling. Paris: Plon-Nourrit, 1901.

217. Talleyrand-Périgord, Charles Maurice de, prince de Bénévent.
     MEMOIRS OF THE PRINCE DE TALLEYRAND. Paris: Napoleon Society,
     1895. 5 vols.

218. Tardieu, Ambroise. LA COLONNE DE LA GRANDE ARMEE D'AUSTERLITZ,
     OU DE LA VICTOIRE, MONUMENT TRIOMPHAL ELEVE A LA GLOIRE DE LA
     GRANDE ARMEE PAR NAPOLEON. 40 PLANCHES REPRESENTANT LA VUE

GENERALE, LES MEDAILLES, PIEDESTAUX, BAS-RELIEFS ET STATUE DONT SE COMPOSE CE MONUMENT, GRAVEES EN TAILLE-DOUCE. Paris: Au dépôt de l'Atlas géographique, 1822.

219. Tatishehev, Sergei Spiridonovich, ed. ALEXANDRE Ier ET NAPOLEON D'APRES LEUR CORRESPONDANCE INEDITE, 1801-1812. Paris: Perrin, 1891.

220. Thétard, Alphonse Paul. LES CAUSES D'UN DESASTRE MILITAIRE. OCTOBRE ET NOVEMBRE 1806. Paris: Charles-Lavauzelle, 1897.

221. Thibaudeau, Antoine Claire, comte. MEMOIRES DU GENERAL A.C. THIBAUDEAU. Paris: Plon-Nourrit, 1895.

222. Thiébault, Paul Charles François Adrien Henri Dieudonné, baron. MEMOIRES DU GENERAL BARON THIEBAULT. Paris: Plon-Nourrit, 1894-95. 5 vols.

223. Thienne, Friedrich. GEDENKSTAETTEN UM IENA. Iena: Vopelius, 1836.

224. Thiers, Adolphe. HISTORIE DU CONSULAT ET DE L'EMPIRE. Paris: Paulin, 1845-69. 21 vols.

225. Thiry, Jean. EYLAU, FRIEDLAND, TILSIT. Paris: Berger-Levrault, 1964.

226. Thiry, Jean. IENA. Paris: Berger-Levrault, 1964.

227. Thiry, Jean. ULM, TRAFALGAR, AUSTERLITZ. Paris: Berger-Levrault, 1962.

228. Thümmel, Alwin. KREIGSTAGE AUS SAALFELDS VERGANGENHIET. Berlin: Mittler, 1882.

229. Titeux, Eugène. "Le Maréchal Bernadotte et la manoeuvre d'Jena." REVUE NAPOLEONIENNE 4 (1903): 68-152.

230. Tranchant de La Verne, Léger Marie Philippe, comte. RELATION DES LA BATAILLE D'AUSTERLITZ, GAGNEE LE 2 DECEMBRE 1805 PAR NAPOLEON CONTRE LE RUSSES ET LES AUTRICHIENS. Paris: Dumaine, 1879.

231. Vachée, Le Commandant. ETUDE DU CARACTERE MILITAIRE DU MARECHAL DAVOUT. Paris: Berger-Levrault, 1907.

232. Vandal, Albert. NAPOLEON ET ALEXANDRE Ier. L'ALLIANCE RUSSE SOUS LE PREMIER EMPIRE. Paris: Plon-Nourrit, 1914-18. 3 vols.

233. Vandoncourt, Frédéric François Guillaume, baron de. HISTOIRE POLITIQUE ET MILITAIRE DU PRINCE EUGENE NAPOLEON, VICE-ROI D'ITALIE. Paris: Mongie, 1828. 2 vols.

234. Vigier, Henri, comte. DAVOUT, MARECHAL D'EMPIRE, DUC
     D'AUERSTAEDT,   PRINCE   D'ECKMUHL   (1770-1823).   Paris:
     Ollendorff, 1898. 2 vols.

235. Waliszewski, Kazimierz. LE REGNE D'ALEXANDRE Ier. Paris:
     Plon-Nourrit, 1923-25. 3 vols.

236. Watson, Henry Clay. THE CAMP-FIRES OF NAPOLEON: COMPRISING
     THE MOST BRILLIANT ACHIEVEMENTS OF THE EMPEROR AND HIS
     MARSHALS. Philadelphia: Porter and Coates, 1854.

237. Wencker, Friedrich. BERNADOTTE, A BIOGRAPHY. Translated by
     Kenneth Kirkness. London: Jarrolds, 1936.

238. Whitworth, Charles, earl. ENGLAND AND NAPOLEON IN 1803; BEING
     THE DESPATCHES OF LORD WHITWORTH AND OTHERS, NOW FIRST PRINTED
     FROM THE ORIGINALS IN THE RECORD OFFICE. Edited by Oscar
     Browning. London: Longman, Green, 1887.

239. Wilson, Robert Thomas. BRIEF REMARKS ON THE CHARACTER AND
     COMPOSITION OF THE RUSSIAN ARMY, AND A SKETCH OF THE CAMPAIGNS
     IN POLAND IN THE YEARS 1806 AND 1807. London: Roworth, 1810.

240. Wirth, Joseph. LE MARECHAL LEFEBVRE, DUC DE DANTZIG
     (1755-1820). Paris: Perrin, 1904.

241. Wright, Constance. LOUISE, QUEEN OF PRUSSIA: A BIOGRAPHY.
     London: F. Muller, 1969.

242. Yorck von Wartenburg, Maximilian, graf. ATLAS TO ACCOMPANY
     "NAPOLEON AS A GENERAL" BY COUNT VON WARTENBURG. Prepared by
     the Department of military art and engineering, United States
     military academy, for the course in military history, 1942.

243. Yorck von Wartenburg, Maximilian, graf. NAPOLEON AS A GENERAL.
     London: Gilbert and Rivington, 1902. 2 vols.

244. Zurlinden, Emile Auguste François Thomas. NAPOLEON ET SES
     MARECHAUX. Paris: Hachette, 1910. 2 vols.

245. Zych, Rok. 1807. Warsaw: n.p., 1957.

CHAPTER VII

ENGLAND AT WAR (1798-1815)

Gordon C. Bond, Auburn University

England joined the war against France in early 1793 and except
for the brief respite afforded by the Treaty of Amiens remained the
most steadfast of the enemies of Revolutionary-Napoleonic France.
British strategy paralleled that of its earlier conflicts with France
during the eighteenth century. Consequently, the navy was given the
primary responsibility of not only defending the British Isles, but
also of assuming an offensive role as well. Naval engagements were
significant and are discussed in Chapter VIII.

At the outset of the Napoleonic Wars the British army was poorly
prepared for the conflict. Military administration was illogical,
confusing, and complex. Cooperation between the military and naval
authorities was often difficult and cumbersome, and was frequently
complicated by political considerations. The reforms necessary to
establish a military administration capable of organizing and
conducting Britain's defense and prosecuting the war against France
were accomplished. Fortunately for the historian of Britain's
mobilization and defense, a wealth of documentation exists in
government archives although too frequently officials did not make a
clear distinction between personal and official papers; consequently
many important documents and letters must be located in private
libraries. The work of the Historical Manuscript Commission has been
instrumental in locating and publishing many of the papers of leading
figures of this period.

The navy was required to assist in the defense of the British
Isles against possible French invasion as well as transport and
support forces involved in theaters of war in Europe and elsewhere.
Amphibious operations were an important part of the overall British
strategy but the difficult nature of joint command coupled with the
uncertainties of weather and navigation made these operations
hazardous. Thus the Helder Campaign in 1799 and the Scheldt
(Walcheren) expedition in 1809 resulted in embarrassing defeat while
the two Copenhagen operations of 1801 and 1807 were dramatically more
successful. Early British historians of the war against France
tended to write in a patriotic tone and concentrated on the heroic
feats of Nelson and Wellington almost to the exclusion of these other
areas. Only in relatively recent years have serious studies of the
amphibious campaigns and the mobilization and defense of the British
Isles been undertaken. Clearly the British have dominated the field
of historical writing dealing with their war effort against
Revolutionary-Napoleonic France, but French and American scholars
have made notable contributions and have been joined in the last few
years by Dutch and Scandinavian writers.

GENERAL HISTORIES

Perhaps surprisingly, there are relatively few good general
histories of the British war effort against Revolutionary-Napoleonic
France. Still unrivaled, although now somewhat dated in light of

169

more recent studies, particularly monographs, Fortescue's HISTORY OF THE BRITISH ARMY (171) remains the standard work in the field. With his thirteen volumes of text and six atlases, the majority of which are devoted to coverage of the war of the French Revolution and Napoleon, Fortescue presents a comprehensive account of the activities of the British army. More recent sweeping studies include Barnett's military, political, and social survey of the British army between 1509 and 1970 (32) and Young's book (504) which covers the army since 1642. Individual topics are treated in Oman (352), while the more general works of Bryant (67, 68), Fremantle (176), and the contributions of Ward, Gooch and others (76, 77) are still useful in understanding the broader historical setting of the military conflict.

French historians have also produced comprehensive studies of the period, one of the earliest being the nineteen volumes of Dumas (137) and the later four-volume work by Bordeau (56) completed in 1921 with its detailed coverage and over one hundred maps and drawings. The more recent work of Dechamps (127) ends with the Treaty of Amiens. In a general context, Marianne Elliott's examination (147) of the relationship between the United Irishmen and France brings to bear modern scholarship on a significant aspect of Britain's war with France.

The naval war is treated in Chapter VIII, but some of the works helpful in studying the amphibious campaigns in Northern Europe include the nineteenth century works of Brenton (59, 60), and Mahan (312), and the later studies of Clowes (93), James (260), and more recently Marcus's THE AGE OF NELSON (315), the two volumes by Jackson (257), and the documented dramatization by Frischauer (178).

Finally, the problems of national defense and the reform of the British army and its administration during the course of the war are thoughtfully analyzed in Richard Glover's PENINSULAR PREPARATION (195). His later book (192) not only includes an excellent account of how Britain defended herself against threats of French invasion between 1803-1814, but provides a selected collection of documents to amplify his study.

BIBLIOGRAPHICAL SOURCES

Thanks to the efforts of military historians and learned societies on both sides of the Atlantic, the past twenty-five years have seen a significant outpouring of bibliographies, catalogs, and lists of importance for the study of Britain at war with Revolutionary-Napoleonic France. In 1971, Professor Robin Higham directed a team of historians and edited a most impressive GUIDE TO THE SOURCES OF BRITISH MILITARY HISTORY (235) which includes comprehensive coverage of both military and naval studies. Six years later Brown and Christie followed up the earlier work of Pargellis and Medley with their BIBLIOGRAPHY OF BRITISH HISTORY, 1789-1815 (44). These major works, along with Ballot's study (29) and bibliographical essays published in scholarly journals such as the JOURNAL OF THE SOCIETY FOR ARMY HISTORICAL RESEARCH (24, 133) serve to update some of the older works in the field including Manwaring's bibliography (314). Of tremendous value to the study of this period is Arthur S. White's BIBLIOGRAPHY OF REGIMENTAL HISTORIES OF THE

BRITISH ARMY (491). Craig's bibliography (113) is international in
scope and lists entries chronologically by publication date.
Numerous catalogs and guides to printed works and manuscripts
have appeared over the year. Of special interest are the guides and
lists of the materials in the Public Record Office in London near Kew
Gardens. For many years Guiseppi's GUIDE (223) was the standard work
but it has now been superseded by a new publication (221).
Particular guides include ALPHABETICAL GUIDE TO WAR OFFICE AND OTHER
MILITARY RECORDS PRESERVED IN THE PUBLIC RECORD OFFICE (213), lists
of Admiralty Records (214), State Papers (215), Treasury (216), War
Office (212), Foreign Office (218), and maps and plans (217).
Additional indices exist for Parliamentary Papers of the House of
Commons (208, 361), and published catalogs of other libraries and
archives include the National Maritime Museum (86, 295); the Royal
United Service Institute (224); and the Royal Artillery Institution
Library (405). Published library holdings such as Donald D.
Horward's THE FRENCH REVOLUTION AND NAPOLEON COLLECTION AT FLORIDA
STATE UNIVERSITY (250) provide excellent bibliographical assistance.
Specialized studies which have unusually extensive
bibliographies include Elliott's PARTNERS IN REVOLUTION (147) for
Franco-Irish relations and threats of invasion; Mackesy's STATESMEN
AT WAR (310) and Rodger's THE WAR OF THE SECOND COALITION (390) for
the Helder Campaign; Feldbaek's DENMARK AND THE ARMED NEUTRALITY
(157) for events in the Baltic in 1800-1801; Bond's GRAND EXPEDITION
(54) for the Scheldt campaign of 1809; Simon Schama's PATRIOTS AND
LIBERATORS (413) for Holland's involvement with Britain during the
wars; and Erin McCawley Renn's Ph.D. dissertation, "British Civil and
Military Preparations against Napoleon's Planned Invasion, 1803-1805"
(381) for works on mobilization and defense.

ARCHIVAL SOURCES

There is a wealth of manuscript sources related to Britain's
mobilization and defense as well as to the various amphibious
campaigns in Northern Europe during the wars of the Revolution and
the Empire. Not surprisingly, the British Isles hold the richest
deposits. In London, the Public Record Office houses thousands of
collections of all manner of documentation--letters, journals,
reports, statistics, army lists, maps and plans, logs, and ledgers,
under numerous classifications. Of these, the most important for the
study of Britain at war include those collections found in the papers
of the Home Office, the War Office, the Admiralty, the Auditor's
Office, the Foreign Office, the Privy Council, and numerous
manuscripts of government officials. Of these, some of the most
significant are the papers of John Pitt, the Second Earl of Chatham,
Lord Buckingham, Brownrigg, Colchester, and Cornwallis. At the
British Library (British Museum), the collection of documentation and
manuscripts is equally impressive. Here, classified under
"Additional Manuscripts" may be found the papers of the following:
Auckland, Bentinck, Bexley, Canning, Dundas, Grenville (Thomas),
Hardwicke, Huskisson, Jervis, Liverpool, Melville, Admiral Mitchell,
Mulgrave, Napier, Peel, Perceval, Rose, Southey, Wellesley, and
William Windham, to name some of the more significant ones. In
addition, many manuscripts may be found throughout the British
Isles. An important collection, including the Duke of York papers,

is deposited in the Royal Archives, Windsor Castle. The Scottish Record Office houses the Dalhousie papers and the National Library of Scotland holds the Minto papers in Edinburgh; they share the Henry Dundas papers. The National Maritime Museum holds the Keats and Owens papers among others. The National Army Museum and the Royal United Service Institution in London house numerous army memoirs and journals.

A number of important papers remain in family archives. These include the Hope papers at Luffness House, Aberlady, and the Mulgrave letters at Mulgrave Castle, Whitby. College and university libraries are also the depositories for private papers and documents. Some of the Chatham manuscripts and the Clinton papers are at John Rylands Library, Manchester; copies of the Portland papers at the University of Nottingham; the Pitt papers at Cambridge University and the University of Michigan (microfilm); and the Stowe papers at the Huntington Library, San Marino, California. Other private collections relating to the British war effort may be located through the Historical Manuscripts Commission's GUIDE (204) and the annotated bibliographies of British autobiographies and diaries compiled by William Matthews (320).

In France, the principal archival collections relative to the invasion of England (and Ireland) may be found in Paris at the Archives des Affaires Etrangères, Quai d'Orsay (Correspondance Politique, Correspondance Consulaire, Mémoires et Documents); the Archives Nationales (Pouvoir exécutif, Marine); the Service historique de l'armée, Château de Vincennes (Dossiers Personnels), and numerous cartons labeled "Expédition d'Irlande, Armée d'Angleterre, Projets de descente, etc." The archives of the Château de Vincennes also holds the most complete collection of materials relating to the French defense of the Helder in 1799 and the Scheldt estuary in 1809. Holdings include correspondence of the Armée du Nord, Armée de Brabant; papers on the Défense de Côtes; orders of Napoleon, his correspondence with various ministers and generals, and thousands of other pertinent documents. Additional sources concerning Napoleon's invasion attempt of 1803-1805 are housed at Pont de Briques along the French coast from which the Emperor hoped to launch his assault against England. These papers are gradually being printed thanks, in part, to the efforts of Fernand Beaucour (38).

The Danish archives have a wealth of documentation relative to the two Copenhagen expeditions of 1801 and 1807, with most of the holdings on the former attack. These papers which consist of diplomatic and military-naval correspondence and documents are found in Copenhagen at the Rigsarkivet [Danish State Archives], and the Marinens Bibliotek [Danish Navy Library].

PUBLISHED DOCUMENTS

Published documents on the British war effort against Revolutionary-Napoleonic France are abundant. Correspondence from various theaters of war not only appeared on the front page of the London TIMES, but frequently found their way into Parliamentary Debates, Committee Reports, and volumes of private correspondence. COBBETT'S PARLIAMENTARY HISTORY (94), his POLITICAL REGISTER (95), and his PARLIAMENTARY DEBATES (207) are all extremely useful. To

this should be added the various published journals and reports of
both houses of Parliament (205, 209-211). The evidence of secret
hearings is also contained in the PARLIAMENTARY PAPERS (206).
Published correspondence of principal governmental and military
leaders are also plentiful. These include the five volumes of the
CORRESPONDENCE OF GEORGE III (190), Canning's letters in two volumes
(27), twelve volumes of Castlereagh's correspondence (85), and four
volumes of the Spencer papers (109). Additional volumes of letters
are those of Lord Auckland (26), the three volumes of Cornwallis
(110), the CREEVEY PAPERS (114), and the correspondence of Addington
(366), Colchester (1), Charlemont (88), the Prince of Wales (21),
Granville (291), Huskisson (254), and Wellesley (365). All of these
men were influential government leaders and played a significant role
in the war effort. Additional correspondence and papers have been
collected over the years and published under the auspices of the
Historical Manuscripts Commission. Relevent volumes include the
PRIME MINISTER'S PAPERS, 1801-1902 (238), the Dartmouth papers (237),
and the Dropmore papers (239) in ten volumes.

Numerous collections of speeches exist for this period. The two
volumes of the speeches of Canning (80) and the WAR SPEECHES OF
WILLIAM PITT (111) are two of the more important collections of
published addresses. Volumes of documents, letters, journals, and
instructions are also available. The COLLECTION OF PAPERS RELATING
TO THE EXPEDITION TO THE SCHELDT (101) is useful in documenting the
campaign of 1809. ENGLISH HISTORICAL DOCUMENTS (134) and MEMOIRS OF
THE COURT AND CABINETS OF GEORGE THE THIRD (220) bring together a
wealth of material for this period.

The published correspondence of leading military and naval
figures are treated elsewhere, but some of these men do figure
prominently in the events in the Baltic and Holland. The DISPATCHES
AND LETTERS OF NELSON (340) in six volumes, the two volumes of the
KEITH PAPERS (267), and the letters of Paget (357) and St. Vincent
(426) are all important sources of information.

MEMOIRS, JOURNALS, AND EYEWITNESS ACCOUNTS

Most of the memoirs, journals, and eyewitness accounts of the
British soldiers during the Revolutionary-Napoleonic Wars are drawn
from experiences in several theaters of war with action in the
Iberian Peninsular dominating. Many of those who wrote of their
service in Portugal and Spain had also served in Holland or on the
expeditions to the Baltic. The narratives and memoirs of Henry
Bunbury (69, 70) are among the best in this category. Others of a
similar nature include Cadell (75), Cooke (104), Dyott (143), Gomm
(196), Green (219), Harris (228), Henegan (233), Kincaid (269, 270),
Mockler-Ferryman (328), Morris (333), Richardson (384), Robertson
(387), Ross-Lewin (402), Steevens (434), and Wheeler (490).
Commanding officers who served in Holland or the Baltic and left
accounts include Abercromby (141), Moore (330), Paget (358), and
Picton (369).

Journals and eyewitness accounts of individual campaigns are
also extant and some are especially valuable sources of information.
Colonel Fyers's "Journal" (182) is excellent in detailing the siege
of Flushing in 1809, especially the problems encountered by the army
under Chatham. Hargrove's ACCOUNT (227) of the British campaign in

the Scheldt estuary and St. Clair's NARRATIVE (431) are both useful in researching that expedition. Leach (283) provides an eyewitness account of the attack on Copenhagen in 1807.

SPECIALIZED WORKS

The reform of the military administration and the creation of a fighting force capable of defending the British Isles from invasion while at the same time prosecuting the war against France have been studied in detail by Glover (192, 195), Fortescue (170), Renn (381), and Ward (470). These studies examine the civil and military preparations initiated in response to the war and in particular to the threat of invasion. Books focusing on the military exertions on either side of the Channel include those by Wheeler and Broadley (488), Oman (Lenanton) (350), and from the French side--Beaucour (38, 39), Bottet (57), Desbrière (129), and Nicolay (341). Two volumes on the blockade of Brest have been edited by Leyland (294). Other specialized works dealing with British defense against Napoleon's invasion threat include Sutcliffe's MARTELLO TOWERS (443) and Vine's ROYAL MILITARY CANAL (463). The Admiralty administration has been studied by Crimmin in her dissertation (116) and Glover has provided additional insights into the army administration in his earlier study of the Duke of York as commander in chief (193).

A host of works on militia and volunteer organizations which developed during the war have appeared over the years. In addition to Fortescue's work cited above, the list includes those of Claye (91), Cruikshank (121), Evans (149), Ffoulkes (159), Sebag-Montefiore (419), Strickland (439), and the more sweeping work by Western (486). The volunteer cavalry has been the topic of studies by Freeman (175), Shenstone (421), and Stoneham and Freeman (438). Contemporary broadsides have been collected and published by Klingberg and Hustvedt (272), while patriotic songs and handbills on Napoleon's invasion threats are presented by an anonymous London bookseller (301).

Histories of some of Britain's military schools have appeared and include the records of the Royal Military Academy at Woolwich (406), Smyth's study of the royal military institutions (428), and his separate work on Sandhurst (429). Various service histories include Brown's work on the Royal Artillery (64), Fortescue's study of the Royal Army Service Corps (172), and Porter's two-volume work on the Royal Engineers (374). Hogg has studied the Royal Arsenal (243).

Turning to specific studies of the British campaigns in Northern Europe, there are two particularly significant books on the attack on Copenhagen in 1801. Dudley Pope's study (373) and the more recent volume published by Feldbaek (157) utilize both British and Danish archival sources. Other specialized works of the operations in the Baltic include Bundesen's study (71), Taylor's account of the battle (444), Feldborg's contemporary narrative (158), Laws's article on the role of the Royal Artillery (281), and the two broader treatments--Scott's study of Armed Neutrality (416) and Primon's contemporary history of the Anglo-Danish war of 1801 (376). There are a few works on the 1807 attack on Copenhagen, headed by Leach's eyewitness account (283) and the studies of Ryan (410, 411).

The Scheldt or Walcheren expedition, long neglected by historians, has been the subject of recent scholarship. Fleischman's brief study (165) appeared in 1973 and the more definitive work by Bond in 1979 (54). Creswell (115) includes an interesting chapter in his study of amphibious operations. Contemporary accounts include Rocca's LA CAMPAGNE DE WALCHEREN ET D'ANVERS (389) and an anonymous history (15) published in 1810. The "Walcheren Fever" which decimated the British Army while on the islands of the Scheldt estuary has been studied by Feibel (156) and McGuffie (307), while Crowe (120) has looked at the impact of the unfortunate campaign on bringing about reform of the Medical Board. From the French side, Fischer (163) examines Napoleon's interest in Antwerp, and Martel (314) presents a documentary history of the campaign, using the Walcheren expedition as a vehicle to criticize the work of the historian Thiers.

FUTURE RESEARCH

While Britain's struggle against Revolutionary-Napoleonic France has been and continues to be a well-worked field of historical study, there remain many opportunities for further research. Fortescue's HISTORY OF THE BRITISH ARMY (171) has held up well but it is time for a more integrated, scholarly, comprehensive study of the British Army during this period. Taking advantage of the numerous specialized studies that have appeared since his work was written early in the century, a study needs to be completed which recognizes the complexities of the relationship between the army and navy and especially the problems arising out of joint command. The development and internal administration of the various branches of the army could use a closer study. Military thought as it developed as a result of wartime experiences is a topic which still requires serious work. Individual campaigns remain to be researched with little in print on the attack against Copenhagen in 1807. While the major military and naval commanders have their biographers, secondary figures who played a significant role in military and naval affairs continue to be ignored. But one example is John Pitt, Second Earl of Chatham, whose career at the Ordnance and the Admiralty, as well as military commander of the Walcheren expedition, remains unstudied. Only when these remaining gaps in historical studies have been filled can historians approach a fuller understanding of the history of this period.

BIBLIOGRAPHY: ENGLAND

1. Abbot, Charles, lord Colchester. DIARY AND CORRESPONDENCE OF CHARLES ABBOT, LORD COLCHESTER. London: J. Murray, 1861. 2 vols.

2. Addis, John P. THE CRAWSHAY DYNASTY: A STUDY IN INDUSTRIAL ORGANIZATION AND DEVELOPMENT, 1765-1867. Cardiff: The University of Wales Press, 1957.

3. Aiken, John. ANNALS OF THE REIGN OF GEORGE THE THIRD. London: Longman, Hurst, Rees, Orme and Brown, 1816.

4. Albion, Robert Greenhalgh. FORESTS OF SEA POWER: THE TIMBER PROBLEM OF THE ROYAL NAVY, 1652-1862. Cambridge, Mass.: Harvard University Press, 1926. (Reprint, Hamden, Conn.: Archon Books, 1965.)

5. Alger, John G. ENGLISHMEN IN THE FRENCH REVOLUTION. London: Low, Marston, 1889.

6. Alger, John G. NAPOLEON'S BRITISH VISITORS AND CAPTIVES, 1801-1815. Westminster: Constable, 1904.

7. Alison, Archibald. LIVES OF LORD CASTLEREAGH AND SIR CHARLES STEWART. Edinburg: Blackwood, 1861.

8. Anderson, Charles Roger. NAVAL WARS IN THE BALTIC DURING THE SAILING EPOCH, 1522-1850. London: n.p., 1950.

9. Anderson, Major John E. A SHORT ACCOUNT OF THE MORTLAKE COMPANY. Richmond, Surrey: Printed for private circulation, 1893.

10. Anderson, Major John E. THE CUMBERLAND SHARPSHOOTERS. Richmond, Surrey: n.p., 1897.

11. Andreossy, Antoine François, comte. CAMPAGNE SUR LE MEIN ET LA REDNITZ DE L'ARMEE GALLO-BATAVE AUX ORDRES DU GENERAL AUGEREAU. Paris: Barrois, 1802.

12. THE ANNUAL REGISTER OR A VIEW OF THE HISTORY, POLITICS, AND LITERATURE FOR THE YEAR 1798-1815. London: Wilkes, 1799-1816.

13. Anonymous. FLUSHING, MIDDLEBURG, AND THE ISLAND OF WALCHEREN. Middleburg: Den Boer, 1899.

14. Anonymous. HISTORY OF THE CAMPAIGN OF 1799 IN HOLLAND. London: n.p., 1801.

15. Anonymous. A SHORT NARRATIVE OF THE LATE CAMPAIGN (IN ZEALAND) OF THE BRITISH ARMY, UNDER THE ORDER OF THE RIGHT HONOURABLE, THE EARL OF CHATHAM. London: Ridgeway, 1810.

16. Ashton, John. THE DAWN OF THE XIXth CENTURY IN ENGLAND.
    London: Fisher Unwin, 1906.

17. Ashton, John. ENGLISH CARICATURE AND SATIRE ON NAPOLEON I.
    London: Chatto and Windus, 1888. 2 vols.

18. Ashton, T.S. AN ECONOMIC HISTORY OF ENGLAND: THE 18th CENTURY.
    London: Meuthuen, 1955.

19. Ashton, T.S. AN 18th CENTURY INDUSTRIALIST: PETER STUBS OF
    WARRINGTON, 1756-1806. Manchester: Manchester University
    Press, 1939.

20. Ashton, T.S., and J. Sykes. THE COAL INDUSTRY OF THE 18th
    CENTURY. Manchester: Publications of the University of
    Manchester, Economic History Series No. 5, 1929.

21. Aspinall, Arthur. THE CORRESPONDENCE OF GEORGE, PRINCE OF
    WALES, 1770-1812. London: Cassell, 1967.

22. Aspinall, Arthur. POLITICS AND THE PRESS, ca. 1780-1850.
    London: Home and Val Thal, 1949.

23. Atkinson, C. "Foreign Regiments in the British Army,
    1793-1802." JOURNAL OF THE SOCIETY FOR ARMY HISTORICAL RESEARCH
    21, 22 (1942-1944): 2-14, 45-52, 107-115, 132-42, 187-97,
    234-50, 265-76, 313-24.

24. Atkinson, C. "Material for Military History in the Reports of
    the Historical Manuscripts Commission." JOURNAL OF THE SOCIETY
    FOR ARMY HISTORICAL RESEARCH 21 (1942): 117-34.

25. Aubrey-Fletcher, H.L. A HISTORY OF THE LOST GUARDS TO 1856.
    London: Constable, 1927.

26. Auckland, W.E. JOURNAL AND CORRESPONDENCE OF WILLIAM EDEN, 1st
    BARON AUCKLAND. London: Bentley, 1861-62. 4 vols.

27. Bagot, Josceline. GEORGE CANNING AND HIS FRIENDS, CONTAINING
    HITHERTO UNPUBLISHED LETTERS, JEUX D'ESPRIT,... London: J.
    Murray, 1909. 2 vols.

28. Balderston, Katherine C., ed. THRALIANA: THE DIARY OF MRS.
    HESTER LYNCH THRALE, 1776-1809. Oxford: Clarendon Press, 1951.

29. Ballot, H.H., et al., eds. WRITINGS ON BRITISH HISTORY,
    1901-1933. Vol. 4. THE 18th CENTURY, 1714-1815. New York:
    Royal Historical Society, 1968.

30. Bannantine, J. MEMOIRS OF EDWARD MARCUS DESPARD. London:
    Ridgway, 1899.

31. Barnes, Major Robert Money. MILITARY UNIFORMS OF BRITAIN AND
    THE EMPIRE, 1742 TO THE PRESENT TIME. London: Seeley, 1960.

32. Barnett, Correlli D. BRITAIN AND HER ARMY, 1509-1970; A MILITARY, POLTICAL AND SOCIAL SURVEY. London: Allen Lane, 1970.

33. Barrett, Charles Raymond Booth, ed. THE 85th KING'S LIGHT INFANTRY. London: Spottiswoode, 1913.

34. Barton, Dunbar Plunket. THE AMAZING CAREER OF BERNADOTTE. Boston: Houghton Mifflin, 1929.

35. Barton, Dunbar Plunket. BERNADOTTE AND NAPOLEON, 1763-1810. London: J. Murray, 1921.

36. Batty, Robert. A SKETCH OF THE LATE CAMPAIGN IN THE NETHERLANDS. London: n.p., 1815.

37. Beattie, William, ed. LIFE AND LETTERS OF THOMAS CAMPBELL. London: Hall, Virtue, 1850. 2 vols.

38. Beaucour, Fernand E. LETTRES, DECISIONS ET ACTS DE NAPOLEON A PONT DE BRIQUES ET AU CAMP DE BOULOGNE. Levallois: Chez l'auteur, 1979.

39. Beaucour, Fernand E. QUAND NAPOLEON REGNAIT A PONT DE BRIQUES. Un survol de sa vie quotidenne. Levallois: Chez l'auteur, 1978.

40. Bell, George. ROUGH NOTES OF AN OLD SOLDIER DURING FIFTY YEARS' SERVICE. London: Day, 1867. 2 vols.

41. Bennett, R. "French Prisoners of War on Parole in Britain, 1803-14." Ph.D. dissertation, University of London, 1964.

42. Beresford, John, ed. WOODEFORD: PASSAGES FROM THE FIVE VOLUMES OF THE DIARY OF A COUNTRY PARSON, 1758-1802. New York: Oxford University Press, 1935.

43. Bessborough, Earl J. GEORGIANA. EXTRACTS FROM THE CORRESPONDENCE OF GEORGIANA, DUCHESS OF DEVONSHIRE. London: J. Murray, 1955.

44. BIBLIOGRAPHY OF BRITISH HISTORY, 1789-1851. Edited by Lucy M. Brown and Ian R. Christie. Oxford: Clarendon Press, 1977.

45. Binns, John. RECOLLECTIONS OF THE LIFE OF JOHN BINNS. Philadelphia: Parry and M'Millan, 1854.

46. BIOGRAPHIE UNIVERSELLE ANCIENNE ET MODERNE. Paris: Michaud, 1811-62. 85 vols.

47. Birch, Alan. "The British Iron Industry in the Napoleonic Wars." ECONOMIC HISTORY OF THE IRON AND STEEL INDUSTRY. London: Frank Cass, 1967.

48. Blacklock, Michael. THE ROYAL SCOTS GREYS: (THE 2nd DRAGOONS). London: Leo Cooper, 1971.

49. Blackmore, Howard L. BRITISH MILITARY FIREARMS, 1650-1850.
    London: Herbert Jenkins, 1961.

50. Blanco, Richard L. WELLINGTON'S SURGEON GENERAL: SIR JAMES
    MCGRIGOR. Durham, N.C.: Duke University Press, 1974.

51. Bonaparte, Louis, king of Holland. DOCUMENTS HISTORIQUES ET
    REFLEXIONS SUR LE GOUVERNEMENT DE LA HOLLANDE. Paris: Aillaud,
    1820. Vol. 3.

52. Bonaparte, Louis, king of Holland. LOUIS BONAPARTE EN HOLLANDE
    D'APRES SES LETTRES 1806-1810. Compiled and edited by André
    Duboscq. Paris: Emile-Paul, 1911.

53. Bonaparte, Louis, king of Holland. NAPOLEON Ier ET LE ROI LOUIS
    D'APRES LES DOCUMENTS CONSERVES AUX ARCHIVES NATIONALES.
    Compiled by Félix Rocquain. Paris: Firmin-Didot, 1875.

54. Bond, Gordon C. THE GRAND EXPEDITION: THE BRITISH INVASION OF
    HOLLAND IN 1809. Athens, Ga.: University of Georgia Press,
    1979.

55. Booth, Philip. THE OXFORDSHIRE AND BUCKINGHAMSHIRE LIGHT
    INFANTRY (THE 43rd/52nd REGIMENT OF FOOT). London: Leo Cooper,
    1971.

56. Bordeau, Emile Hippolyte. CAMPAGNES MODERNES. Paris:
    Charles-Lavauzelle, 1912-21. 4 vols.

57. Bottet, M. NAPOLEON AUX CAMPS DE BOULOGNE. Paris: L'Edition
    moderne, n.d.

58. Bowman, H.M. PRELIMINARY STAGES OF THE PEACE OF AMIENS. THE
    DIPLOMATIC RELATIONS OF GREAT BRITAIN AND FRANCE FROM THE FALL
    OF THE DIRECTORY TO THE DEATH OF EMPEROR PAUL OF RUSSIA,
    NOVEMBER 1799-MARCH 1801. Toronto: University of Toronto
    Press, 1899.

59. Brenton, Edward Pelham. THE NAVAL HISTORY OF GREAT BRITAIN.
    London: Colburn, 1837. 5 vols.

60. Brenton, Edward Pelham. THE NAVAL HISTORY OF GREAT BRITAIN FROM
    THE YEAR 1783 TO 1822. London: Rice, 1825. Vol. 4.

61. Brett-James, Antony. "The Walcheren Failure." HISTORY TODAY 13
    (1963): 811-20.

62. Brodigan F., ed. HISTORICAL RECORDS OF THE TWENTY-EIGHTH NORTH
    GLOUCESTERSHIRE REGIMENT. London: Blackfriars, 1884.

63. Brougham and Vaux, Henry, lord. THE LIFE AND TIMES OF HENRY,
    LORD BROUGHAM. New York: Harper, 1871. 3 vols.

64. Brown, J.A. ENGLAND'S ARTILLERYMAN, A HISTORICAL NARRATIVE OF
    THE SERVICES OF THE ROYAL ARTILLERY, FROM THE FORMATION OF THE
    REGIMENT TO ... 1862. London: n.p., 1865.

65. Browning, B. THE LIFE AND LETTERS OF SIR JOHN MOORE. Oxford:
    Oxford University Press, 1923.

66. Bruun, Geoffrey. EUROPE AND THE FRENCH IMPERIUM, 1799-1814.
    New York: Harper, 1938.

67. Bryant, Arthur. THE YEARS OF ENDURANCE, 1793-1802. New York:
    Harper, 1942.

68. Bryant, Arthur. THE YEARS OF VICTORY, 1802-1812. New York:
    Harper, 1944.

69. Bunbury, Henry Edward. MEMOIR AND LITERARY REMAINS OF LT. GEN.
    SIR HENRY EDWARD BUNBURY, 7th BART. Edited by Charles J.F.
    BUNBURY. London: Spottiswoode, 1868.

70. Bunbury, Henry Edward. NARRATIVES OF SOME PASSAGES IN THE GREAT
    WAR WITH FRANCE (1799-1810). London: Peter Davies, 1927.

71. Bundesen, P.C. MINDESKRIFT OM SLAGET PAA REDEN DEN 2 APRIL
    1801. Copenhagen: Tryde, 1901.

72. Burne, Alfred. THE NOBLE DUKE OF YORK; THE MILITARY LIFE OF
    FREDERICK, DUKE OF YORK AND ALBANY. New York: Staples, 1949.

73. Burney, Fanny. THE JOURNAL & LETTERS OF FANNY BURNEY. Edited
    by Joyce Hemlow. Oxford: Clarendon Press, 1972. 2 vols.

74. Byrne, Miles. MEMOIRS. Edited by his widow. Dublin:
    Maunsel, 1906.

75. Cadell, Charles. NARRATIVE OF THE CAMPAIGNS OF THE
    TWENTY-EIGHTH REGIMENT, SINCE THEIR RETURN FROM EGYPT IN 1802.
    London: Whittaker, 1835.

76. CAMBRIDGE HISTORY OF BRITISH FOREIGN POLICY. Edited by A.W.
    Ward, G.P. Gooch. Cambridge: Cambridge University Press,
    1922-23. 3 vols.

77. CAMBRIDGE MODERN HISTORY. Edited by A.W. Ward, et al. New
    York: Macmillan, 1906. Vol. 9.

78. Campbell, Cdr. A.C., R.N. CUSTOMS AND TRADITIONS OF THE ROYAL
    NAVY. Aldershot: Gale & Polden, 1956.

79. Campbell, Colin, lord Clyde. THE LIFE OF COLIN CAMPBELL, LORD
    CLYDE, ILLUSTRATED BY EXTRACTS FROM HIS DIARY AND
    CORRESPONDENCE. Edited by Lieut. Gen. Lawrence Shadwell.
    London: Blackwood, 1881. 2 vols.

80. Canning, George. THE SPEECHES OF THE RIGHT HONOURABLE GEORGE CANNING. Edited by R. Therry. London: Ridgway, 1836. 2 vols.

81. Cannon, Richard, comp. HISTORICAL RECORDS OF THE BRITISH ARMY, COMPRISING THE HISTORY OF EVERY REGIMENT IN HIS MAJESTY'S SERVICE. London: (Various publishers), 1835-53. 70 vols.

82. Carew, Tim. HOW THE REGIMENTS GOT THEIR NICKNAMES. London: Leo Cooper, 1969.

83. Carman, W.Y. BRITISH MILITARY UNIFORMS FROM CONTEMPORARY PICTURES: HENRY VII TO THE PRESENT DAY. New York: Arco, 1968.

84. Carman, W.Y. THE HISTORY OF FIREARMS. London: Routledge & Kegan Paul, 195?.

85. Castlereagh, Robert Stewart, 2d marquis of Londonderry, viscount. CORRESPONDENCE, DESPATCHES, AND OTHER PAPERS OF VISCOUNT CASTLEREAGH. Edited by William W. Vane. London: Shoberl, 1851. 12 vols.

86. CATALOGUE OF THE LIBRARY OF THE NATIONAL MARITIME MUSEUM. Edited by M. Sanderson. London: H.M.S.O., 1969. 2 vols.

87. Chambers, J.D. "Enclosure and Labour Supply in the Industrial Revolution." ECONOMIC HISTORY REVIEW, Series 2, 5 (1953): 319-43.

88. CHARLEMONT MSS. THE MANUSCRIPTS AND CORRESPONDENCE OF JAMES, FIRST EARL OF CHARLEMONT, H.M.C., 12th Report. London: Eyre and Spottiswoode, 1891-94. 2 vols.

89. Charles-Edwards, Thomas, and R. Richardson. THEY SAW IT HAPPEN: AN ANTHOLOGY OF EYEWITNESS'S ACCOUNTS OF EVENTS IN BRITISH HISTORY, 1689-1897. Oxford: Basil Blackwell, 1958.

90. Chichesler, Henry Manners, and G.B. Short. RECORDS AND BADGES OF THE BRITISH ARMY. London: Muller, 1969.

91. Claye, H. Sandford. NOTES ON THE ESTABLISHMENT OF VOLUNTEERS IN MACCLESFIELD IN 1797, AND OTHER PARTICULARS. Macclesfield: n.p., 1894.

92. Cloney, Thomas. A PERSONAL NARRATIVE. Dublin: McMullen, 1832.

93. Clowes, William Laird. THE ROYAL NAVY; A HISTORY FROM THE EARLIEST TIMES TO THE PRESENT. London: Low, Marston, 1897-1903. 7 vols.

94. Cobbett, William. COBBETT'S PARLIAMENTARY HISTORY OF ENGLAND FROM THE EARLIEST PERIOD TO THE YEAR 1803. London: Hansard, 1818. 36 vols.

95. Cobbett, William. COBBETT'S POLITICAL REGISTER. London: Hansard, 1810.

96. Cochrane, Thomas, 10th earl of Dundonald. THE AUTOBIOGRAPHY OF A SERMON. London: Bentley, 1861.

97. Cocks, E.J., and B. Walters.   A HISTORY OF THE ZINC SMELTING INDUSTRY IN BRITAIN. London: Harrap, 1968.

98. Coigly, James. THE LIFE OF THE REV. JAMES COIGLY,... WRITTEN BY HIMSELF DURING HIS CONFINEMENT IN MAIDSTONE GAOL. Edited by V. Derry. London: n.p., 1798.

99. Colenbrander,   H.T.,   ed.   GEDENKSTUKKEN   DES   ALGEMEENE GESCHIEDENIS VAN NEDERLAND, 1795 TO 1840. The Hague: Nijhoff, 1905-22.

100. Coleridge, Ernest Hartley. THE LIFE OF THOMAS COUTTS, BANKER. London: J. Lane, 1920.

101. A COLLECTION OF PAPERS RELATING TO THE EXPEDITION TO THE SCHELDT PRESENTED TO PARLIAMENT IN 1810. Compiled by A. Strahan. London: A. Strahan, 1811.

102. Connelly, Owen. NAPOLEON'S SATELLITE KINGDOMS. New York: Free Press, 1965.

103. CONSTABLE'S MISCELLANY OF ORIGINAL AND SELECTED PUBLICATIONS IN THE VARIOUS DEPARTMENTS OF LITERATURE SCIENCE, AND THE ARTS. Vol. 27. "Journal of a Soldier of the 71st Regiment, from 1805-1815." MEMORIALS OF THE LATE WAR. Edinburgh: Constable, 1828.

104. Cooke, Captain John. MEMOIRS OF THE LATE WAR: COMPRISING A PERSONAL NARRATIVE OF CAPTAIN COOKE OF THE FORTY-THIRD REGIMENT OF LIGHT INFANTRY. London: Colburn & Bentley, 1831. 2 vols.

105. Cooper, Leonard. BRITISH REGULAR CAVALRY, 1644-1914. London: Chapman & Hall, 1964.

106. Cooper, Leonard. THE KING'S OWN YORKSHIRE LIGHT INFANTRY (THE 51st AND 105th REGIMENTS OF FOOT). London: Leo Cooper, 1970.

107. Cooper, W.S. A HISTORY OF THE AYRSHERI YEOMANRY CAVALRY. Edinburgh: David Douglas, 1881.

108. Coquelle, P. NAPOLEON AND ENGLAND 1803-1813.   London: G. Bell, 1904.

109. Corbett, Julian, ed. PRIVATE PAPERS OF GEORGE, SECOND EARL SPENCER, FIRST LORD OF THE ADMIRALTY, 1794-1801. London: Navy Records Society, 1914. 4 vols.

110. Cornwallis, Charles. CORRESPONDENCE OF CHARLES, 1st MARQUIS CORNWALLIS. Edited by Charles Ross. London: J. Murray, 1859. 3 vols.

111. Coupland, Reginald, ed. THE WAR SPEECHES OF WILLIAM PITT THE YOUNGER. Oxford: Clarendon Press, 1916.

112. COURT AND CITY REGISTER ... CONTAINING LISTS OF THE ARMY AND NAVY, 1742 THROUGH 1809. London: n.p., 1742-1808.

113. Craig, Hardin, comp. A BIBLIOGRAPHY OF ENCYCLOPAEDIAS AND DICTIONARIES DEALING WITH MILITARY, NAVAL AND MARITIME AFFAIRS, 1577-1971. Houston, Texas: Rice University, 1971.

114. Creevey, Thomas. THE CREEVEY PAPERS: A SELECTION FROM THE CORRESPONDENCE AND DIARIES OF THE LATE THOMAS CREEVEY, M.P. Edited by Sir Herbert Maxwell. London: J. Murray, 1904. 2 vols.

115. Creswell, John. GENERAL AND ADMIRALS: THE STORY OF AMPHIBIOUS COMMAND. Westport, Conn.: Archon Books, 1976.

116. Crimmin, Patricia K. "Admiralty Administration, 1783-1806." M. Phil. thesis, University of London, 1967.

117. Croker, John W. THE CROKER PAPERS. Edited by Louis J. Jennings. London: J. Murray, 1884. 3 vols.

118. Cross, Arthur Lynn. A HISTORY OF ENGLAND AND GREAT BRITAIN. New York: Macmillan, 1919.

119. Crouzet, François. L'ECONOMIC BRITTANIQUE ET LE BLOCUS CONTINENTAL, 1806-1813. Paris: Presses universitaires de France, 1958. 2 vols.

120. Crowe, Kate Elizabeth. "The Walcheren Expedition and the New Army Medical Board: A Reconsideration." ENGLISH HISTORICAL REVIEW 88 (1973): 770-885.

121. Cruikshank, George. A POPGUN FIRED OFF BY GEORGE CRUIKSHANK IN DEFENCE OF THE BRITISH VOLUNTEERS OF 1803, AGAINST THE UNCIVIL ATTACK UPON THAT BODY BY GENERAL W. NAPIER. London: W. Kent, 1860.

122. Czartoryski, Adam, prince. MEMOIRS OF PRINCE ADAM CZARTORYSKI. Edited by Adam Gielgud. London: Remington, 1888.

123. Daendels, Lieut. Gen. H.W. RAPPORT DES OPERATIONS DE LA DIVISION DU LIEUTENANT-GENERAL DAENDELS, DEPUIS LE 22 AOUT, JUSQU'A LA CAPITULATION DE L'ARMEE ANGLAISE ET RUSSE, LE 18 OCTOBRE 1799. The Hague: Van Cleef, 1799.

124. Daniell, David Scott. CAP OF HONOR. Gloustershire: Harrap, 1951.

125. Dawney, Major Nicolas P. THE DISTINCTION OF RANK OF REGIMENTAL OFFICERS, 1684-1855. London: Society for Army Historical Research, 1960.

126. DeBeer, Gavin. THE SCIENCES WERE NEVER AT WAR. London: Thomas Nelson, 1960.

127. Dechamps, J. LES ILES BRITANNIQUES ET LA REVOLUTION FRANCAISE, 1789-1803. Brussels: Rennaissance du livre, 1949.

128. Derrick, C. MEMOIRS OF THE RISE AND PROGRESS OF THE ROYAL NAVY. London: Cadell, 1806.

129. Desbrière, Edouard. PROJETS ET TENTATIVES DE DEBARQUEMENT AUX ILES BRITANNIQUES. Paris: Chapelot, 1902.

130. Descoubes, Emile. LA CORRESPONDANCE MILITAIRE DE NAPOLEON Ier. Paris: J. Dumaine, 1878.

131. De Selincourt, Ernest, ed. THE EARLY LETTERS OF WILLIAM AND DOROTHY WORDSWORTH, 1787-1805. Oxford: Clarendon Press, 1935.

132. Dickinson, H.W. "The Taylors of Southhampton: Their Ship's Blocks, Circular Saws and Ships' Pumps." NEWCOMEN SOCIETY TRANSACTIONS 29 (1953-55): 169-78.

133. Dobie, Marryat R., comp. "Military Manuscripts in the National Library of Scotland." JOURNAL OF THE SOCIETY FOR ARMY HISTORICAL RESEARCH 27 (1949): 118-20.

134. Douglas, D.C., gen. ed. ENGLISH HISTORICAL DOCUMENTS. Edited by A. Aspinall and E.A. Smith. Vol. 9. 1783-1832. London: Eyre & Spottiswoode, 1959.

135. Drew, Robert, ed. ROLL OF COMMISSIONED OFFICERS IN THE MEDICAL SERVICES OF THE BRITISH ARMY, 1660-1960. London: n.p., 1969.

136. Du Casse, Albert, baron, ed. LES ROIS FRERES DE NAPOLEON Ier. DOCUMENTS INEDITS RELATIFS AU PREMIER EMPIRE. Paris: Baillière, 1883.

137. Dumas, Mathieu, comte. PRECIS DES EVENEMENTS MILITAIRES; OU, ESSAIS HISTORIQUES SUR LES CAMPAGNE DE 1799-1814. Paris: Treuttel and Würtz, 1817-26. 19 vols.

138. Dunan, Marcel. NAPOLEON ET L'ALLEMAGNE; LE SYSTEME CONTINENTAL ET LES DEBUTS DU ROYAUME DE BAVIERE, 1806-1810. Paris: Plon, 1942.

139. Duncan, Francis. HISTORY OF THE ROYAL REGIMENT OF ARTILLERY. London: J. Murray, 1872. 2 vols.

140. Dundas, Colonel David. RULES AND REGULATIONS FOR THE FORMATIONS, FIELD-EXERCISES, AND MOVEMENTS OF H.M. FORCES. London: n.p., 1801.

141. Dunfermiline, James, ed. LIEUTENANT-GENERAL RALPH ABERCROMBY. Edinburgh: Edmonston and Douglas, 1861.

142. Dupin, F.P.C. VIEW OF THE HISTORY AND ACTUAL STATE OF THE MILITARY FORCE OF GREAT BRITAIN. London: J. Murray, 1822. 2 vols.

143. Dyott, William. DYOTT'S DIARY. Edited by Reginald W. Jeffrey. London: Constable, 1907. 2 vols.

144. Edmeades, J.F. SOME HISTORICAL RECORDS OF THE WEST KENT YEOMANRY, 1794-1909. London: Andrew Melrose, 1909.

145. Edwards, Major Thomas J. MILITARY CUSTOMS. 5th rev. and enlarged ed. Aldershot: Gale & Polden, 1961.

146. Edwards, Major Thomas J. REGIMENTAL BADGES. Aldershot: Gale & Polden, 1951, 1966.

147. Elliott, Marianne. PARTNERS IN REVOLUTION: THE UNITED IRISHMEN AND FRANCE. New Haven: Yale University Press, 1982.

148. Erskine, D., ed. AUGUSTUS HERVEY'S JOURNAL. London: Kimber, 1953.

149. Evans, E.T. RECORDS OF THE THIRD MIDDLESEX RIFLE VOLUNTEERS. London: Simpkin, Marshall, 1885.

150. EXTRACTS FROM THE JOURNAL OF THE LATE MARGARET WOODS FROM THE YEAR 1771 TO 1821. London: John & Arthur Arch, 1830.

151. Fane, Colonel W.K. "The Orderly Book of Captain Daniel Hebb's Company in the Loveden Volunteers (Lincolnshire), 1808-18." THE JOURNAL OF THE SOCIETY FOR ARMY HISTORICAL RESEARCH 4 (1925): 149-61.

152. Farington, Joseph, R.A. THE FARINGTON DIARY. Edited by James Greig. London: Hutchinson, 1923.

153. Farmer, John Stephen. THE REGIMENTAL RECORDS OF THE BRITISH ARMY. London: Grant Richards, 1901.

154. Fawcett, William, trans. REGULATIONS FOR THE EXERCISE OF RIFLEMEN AND LIGHT INFANTRY AND INSTRUCTIONS FOR THE CONDUCT IN THE FIELD. London: Clowes, 1852.

155. Feibel, Robert M. "Major-General Thomas Staunton St. Clair." JOURNAL OF THE SOCIETY FOR ARMY HISTORICAL RESEARCH 48 (1970): 29-34.

156. Feibel, Robert M. "What Happened at Walcheren: The Primary Sources." BULLETIN OF THE HISTORY OF MEDICINE 42 (1968): 62-79.

157. Feldbaek, Ole. DENMARK AND THE ARMED NEUTRALITY, 1800-1801. Copenhagen: University of Copenhagen Press, 1980.

158. Feldborg, A.A. A TOUR OF ZEALAND ... WITH AN HISTORICAL SKETCH
     OF THE BATTLE OF COPENHAGEN. London: C. and R. Baldwin, 1805.

159. Ffoulkes, Charles. "General Order Book of the Royal Spelthorne
     Legion, Bedfont. The 'Home Guard' of 1803." THE JOURNAL OF THE
     SOCIETY FOR ARMY HISTORICAL RESEARCH 21 (1942): 38-48.

160. Ffoulkes, Charles. THE GUN-FOUNDERS OF ENGLAND, WITH A LIST OF
     ENGLISH AND CONTINENTAL GUN-FOUNDERS FROM THE XIV TO THE XIX
     CENTURIES. Cambridge: Cambridge University Press, 1932.

161. Fiéffé, Eugène. HISTOIRE DES TROUPES ETRANGERES AU SERVICE DE
     FRANCE, DEPUIS LEUR ORIGINE JUSQU'A NOS JOURS, ET DE TOUS LES
     REGIMENTS LEVIS DANS LES PAYS CONQUIS SOUS LA PREMIER REPUBLIQUE
     ET SOUS L'EMPIRE. Paris: Librairie militaire, 1854. 2 vols.

162. Field, Cyril. BRITAINS SEA-SOLDIERS: A HISTORY OF THE ROYAL
     MARINES. Liverpool: Lyceum, 1924. 2 vols.

163. Fischer, Arthur. NAPOLEON ET ANVERS (1800-1811). Antwerp:
     Loosbergh, 1933.

164. Fitzpatrick, W.J. SECRET SERVICE UNDER PITT. London:
     Longmans, Green, 1892.

165. Fleischman, Théo. L'EXPEDITION ANGLAISE SUR LE CONTINENT EN
     1809. Brussels: La Renaissance du Livre, 1973.

166. Forbes, Arthur. A HISTORY OF THE ARMY ORDNANCE SERVICES.
     London: Medici Society, 1929. 3 vols.

167. Ford, Guy Stanton. HANOVER AND PRUSSIA, 1795-1803. A STUDY IN
     NEUTRALITY. New York: Columbia University Press, 1903.

168. Fortescue, John W. THE BRITISH ARMY, 1783-1802. London:
     Macmillan, 1905.

169. Fortescue, John W. BRITISH STATESMEN OF THE GREAT WAR. Oxford:
     Clarendon Press, 1911.

170. Fortescue, John W. THE COUNTY LIEUTENANCIES AND THE ARMY,
     1803-1814. London: Macmillan, 1909.

171. Fortescue, John W. HISTORY OF THE BRITISH ARMY. London:
     Macmillan, 1910-30. 19 vols.

172. Fortescue, John W. THE ROYAL ARMY SERVICE CORPS: A HISTORY OF
     SUPPLY AND TRANSPORT IN THE BRITISH ARMY. Cambridge: Cambridge
     University Press, 1930-31. 2 vols.

173. Fouché, Joseph, duc d'Otrante. MEMOIRS. Paris: Société des
     Bibliophiles, n.d. 2 vols.

174. Frederick, J.B.M. LINEAGE BOOK OF THE BRITISH ARMY: MOUNTED CORPS AND INFANTRY, 1660-1968. Cornwall, New York: Hope Farm Press, 1969.

175. Freeman, Benson. THE YEOMANRY OF DEVON, 1794-1927. London: St. Catherine Press, 1927.

176. Fremantle, A.F. ENGLAND IN THE NINETEENTH CENTURY. London: George Allen & Unwin, 1930. 2 vols.

177. Fremantle, Anne, ed. THE WYNNE DIARIES. London: Oxford University Press, 1952.

178. Frischauer, Paul. ENGLAND'S YEARS OF DANGER, A NEW HISTORY OF THE WORLD WAR, 1792-1815. New York: Oxford University Press, 1938.

179. Fuller, Colonel J.F.C. SIR JOHN MOORE'S SYSTEM OF TRAINING. London: Hutchinson, 1924.

180. Furber, Holden. HENRY DUNDAS, FIRST VISCOUNT MELVILLE, 1742-1811. London: Oxford University Press, 1931.

181. Furrell, G.E., and C. Goodman. "18th Century Estimates of British Sheep and Wool Production." AGRICULTURAL HISTORY 4 (1930): 131-51.

182. Fyers, Colonel William. "Journal of the Siege of Flushing, 1809." Edited by Major Evan W.H. Fyers. JOURNAL OF THE SOCIETY FOR ARMY HISTORICAL RESEARCH 13 (1934): 145-58.

183. Fyler, Colonel Arthur. THE HISTORY OF THE FIFTIETH OR THE QUEEN'S OWN REGIMENT. London: Chapman, 1895.

184. Gachot, Edouard. LES CAMPAGNES DE 1799, JOURDAN EN ALLEMAGNE ET BRUNE EN HOLLANDE. Paris: Perrin, 1906.

185. Gale, Richard. THE WORCESTERSHIRE REGIMENT (THE 29th AND 36th REGIMENTS OF FOOT). London: Leo Cooper, 1970.

186. Gardiner, Leslie. THE BRITISH ADMIRALTY. London: Blackwood, 1968.

187. Gardner, James Anthony. RECOLLECTIONS, 1775-1814. Edited by J. K. Laughton for the Navy Records Society, 1906. London: Batchworth, 1955. (Reprinted under original title, ABOVE AND UNDER HATCHES, by C. Lloyd.)

188. Gardyne, Charles Greenhill. THE LIFE OF A REGIMENT; THE HISTORY OF THE GORDON HIGHLANDERS FROM ITS FORMATION IN 1794 TO 1816. London: Medici Society, 1929.

189. Garnier, Athanase. LA COUR DE HOLLANDE SOUS LA REGNE DE LOUIS BONAPARTE. Paris: Perrin, 1823.

190. George III, king of England. THE LATER CORRESPONDENCE OF GEORGE
     III. Edited by A. Aspinall. Cambridge: Cambridge University
     Press, 1970. 5 vols.

191. Giedion, Siegfried. MECHANISATION TAKES COMMAND: A
     CONTRIBUTION TO ANONYMOUS HISTORY. New York: Oxford
     University Press, 1948.

192. Glover, Richard Gilchrist. BRITAIN AT BAY: DEFENCE AGAINST
     BONAPARTE, 1803-1814. London: George Allen & Unwin, 1973.

193. Glover, Richard Gilchrist. "Frederick, Duke of York, as
     Commander- in-chief, 1795-1809." Ph.D. dissertation, Harvard
     University, 1936.

194. Glover, Richard Gilchrist. "The French Fleet, 1807-1814:
     Britain's Problem: And Madison's Opportunity." JOURNAL OF
     MODERN HISTORY 39 (1967): 233-52.

195. Glover, Richard Gilchrist. PENINSULAR PREPARATION: THE REFORM
     OF THE BRITISH ARMY, 1795-1809. Cambridge: Cambridge
     University Press, 1963.

196. Gomm, William Maynard. LETTERS AND JOURNALS OF SIR WILLIAM
     MAYNARD GOMM. Edited by Francis Culling Carr-Gomm. London: J.
     Murray, 1881. 2 vols.

197. Goodinge, Anthony. THE SCOTS GUARDS (THE 3rd GUARDS). London:
     Leo Cooper, 1969.

198. Gordon, Anthony. A TREATISE ON THE SCIENCE OF DEFENSE FOR THE
     SWORD, BAYONET AND PIKE IN CLOSE ACTION. London: Egerton,
     1805.

199. Gordon, James. HISTORY OF THE REBELLION IN IRELAND IN THE YEAR
     1798. Dublin: Porter, 1801.

200. Gordon, Lawrence L. BRITISH BATTLES AND MEDALS: A DESCRIPTION
     OF EVERY CAMPAIGN MEDAL AND BAR AWARDED FROM THE ARMADA TO ...
     1946, TOGETHER WITH THE NAMES OF ALL THE REGIMENTS ... ENTITLED
     TO THEM. Aldershot: Gale & Polden, 1947.

201. Granville, Castalia, countess, ed. LORD GRANVILLE LEVESON-GOWER
     (FIRST LORD GRANVILLE): PRIVATE CORRESPONDENCE. London: J.
     Murray, 1917.

202. Grattan, William. ADVENTURES WITH THE CONNAUGHT RANGERS.
     London: Colburn, 1847.

203. Gray, Denis. SPENCER PERCEVAL; THE EVANGELICAL PRIME MINISTER,
     1762-1812. London: University of Manchester Press, 1963.

204. Great Britain. Historical Manuscripts Commission. A GUIDE TO
     THE REPORTS ON THE COLLECTION OF MANUSCRIPTS OF PRIVATE

FAMILIES, CORPORATIONS AND INSTITUTIONS IN GREAT BRITAIN AND IRELAND. London: H.M.S.O, 1914-38. 1906.

205. Great Britain. Parliament. House of Commons. THE JOURNALS OF THE HOUSE OF COMMONS. Vol. 65: 23 January-21 August 1810.

206. Great Britain. Parliament. House of Commons. PARLIAMENTARY PAPERS. Vols. 6-8. PAPER, PRESENTED TO THE HOUSE BY HIS MAJESTY'S COMMAND, RELATING TO THE EXPEDITION TO THE SCHELDT. London: H.M.S.O., 1810.

207. Great Britain. Parliament. COBBETT'S PARLIAMENTARY DEBATES. London: Hansard, 1803-15.

208. Great Britain. Parliament. House of Commons. GENERAL INDEX TO THE REPORTS OF SELECT COMMITTEES, PRINTED BY ORDER OF THE HOUSE OF COMMONS, 1801-1852. London: n.p., 1853. (Reprinted, H.M.S.O., 1938.)

209. Great Britian. Parliament. House of Commons. JOURNALS AND SESSIONAL PAPERS OF THE HOUSE OF COMMONS. London: H.M.S.O., 1798-1815.

210. Great Britain. Parliament. House of Commons. REPORT FROM THE COMMITTEE APPOINTED TO CONSIDER THE STATE OF H.M. LAND FORCES AND MARINES, ETC., EXTRACT FROM REPORTS OF THE COMMITTEES OF THE HOUSE OF COMMONS ... NOT INSERTED IN THE JOURNALS ... ORDERED REPRINTED BY THE HOUSE. London: H.M.S.O., 1803-1806. 16 vols.

211. Great Britain. Parliament. House of Lords. JOURNALS AND SESSIONAL PAPERS OF THE HOUSE OF LORDS. London: H.M.S.O., 1798-1815.

212. Great Britain. Public Record Office. List XXVIII. LIST OF WAR OFFICE RECORDS. Dublin: H.M.S.O, 1908.

213. Great Britain. Public Record Office. List LIII. ALPHABETICAL GUIDE TO WAR OFFICE AND OTHER MILITARY RECORDS PRESERVED IN THE PUBLIC RECORD OFFICE. London: H.M.S.O, 1931.

214. Great Britain. Public Record Office. List LVIII. LIST OF ADMIRALTY RECORDS. London: H.M.S.O., 1904.

215. Great Britain. Public Record Office. List XLIII. LIST OF STATE PAPERS, DOMESTIC 1547-1792, AND HOME OFFICE RECORDS, 1782-1837. London: H.M.S.O., 1914.

216. Great Britain. Public Record Office. List LXVI. LIST OF RECORDS OF THE TREASURY PAYMASTER - GENERAL'S OFFICE, EXCHECQUER AND AUDIT DEPARTMENT, AND BOARD OF TRADE PRIOR TO 1837. London: H.M.S.O, 1922.

217. Great Britain. Public Record Office. MAPS AND PLANS IN THE PUBLIC RECORD OFFICE. London: H.M.S.O., 1967 to present.

218. Great Britain. Public Record Office. THE RECORDS OF THE FOREIGN OFFICE, 1782-1939. London: H.M.S.O., 1969.

219. Green, John. THE VICISSITUDES OF A SOLDIER'S LIFE, OR A SERIES OF OCCURRENCES FROM 1806 TO 1815; TOGETHER WITH AN INTRODUCTORY AND A CONCLUDING CHAPTER: THE WHOLE CONTAINING, WITH SOME OTHER MATTERS, A CONCISE ACCOUNT OF THE WAR IN THE PENINSULA, FROM ITS COMMENCEMENT TO ITS FINAL CLOSE. Louth: John Green, 1827.

220. Grenville, Richard P.T., 2d duke of Buckingham and Chandos. MEMOIRS OF THE COURT AND CABINETS OF GEORGE THE THIRD FROM THE ORIGINAL FAMILY DOCUMENTS. London: Hurst & Blackett, 1855. 4 vols.

221. GUIDE TO THE CONTENTS OF THE PUBLIC RECORD OFFICE. London: H.M.S.O., 1963.

222. Guillon, Edouard. LA FRANCE ET L'IRLANDE PENDANT LA REVOLUTION. Paris: Colin, 1888.

223. Guiseppi, M.G. A GUIDE TO MANUSCRIPTS IN THE PUBLIC RECORD OFFICE. London: H.M.S.O., (Reprinted, 1963.) 2 vols.

224. Hale, Lonsdale. CALENDAR OF MILITARY MANUSCRIPTS AT THE ROYAL UNITED SERVICE INSTITUTE. London: n.p., 1914.

225. Harcourt, Leveson V., ed. THE DIARIES AND CORRESPONDENCE OF THE RIGHT HON. GEORGE ROSE: CONTAINING ORIGINAL LETTERS OF THE MOST DISTINGUISHED STATESMAN OF HIS DAY. London: Bentley, 1860.

226. Hardcastle, Mary Scarlett. LIFE OF JOHN, LORD CAMPBELL. London: J. Murray, 1881.

227. Hargrove, George, Jr. AN ACCOUNT OF THE ISLANDS OF WALCHEREN AND SOUTH BEVELAND AGAINST WHICH THE BRITISH EXPEDITION PROCEEDED IN 1809. Dublin: Gilber & Hodges, 1812.

228. Harris, John. RECOLLECTIONS OF RIFLEMAN HARRIS. Edited by Henry Curling. New York: Robert M. McBride, 1929.

229. Haswell, Chetwynd John Drake. THE FIRST RESPECTABLE SPY. By Jock Haswell. London: Hamish Hamilton, 1969.

230. Hawtrey, R.G. CURRENCY AND CREDIT. London: Longmans, Green, 1919.

231. Heaton, Herbert. "Benjamin Gott and the Industrial Revolution in Yorkshire." ECONOMIC HISTORY REVIEW 3 (1931): 45-66.

232. Hecksher, Eli Filip. THE CONTINENTAL SYSTEM: AN ECONOMIC INTERPRETATION. Edited by Harold Westergaard. Gloucester, Mass.: Peter Smith, 1964.

233. Henegan, Richard D. SEVEN YEARS' CAMPAIGNING IN THE PENINSULA AND THE NETHERLANDS, FROM 1808 TO 1815. London: Colburn, 1846. 2 vols.

234. Hervey, William. JOURNALS OF THE HON. WILLIAM HERVEY IN NORTH AMERICA AND EUROPE, 1755-1814. London: Bury St. Edmunds, Paul & Matthew, 1906.

235. Higham, Robin, ed. A GUIDE TO THE SOURCES OF BRITISH MILTIARY HISTORY. Berkeley: University of California Press, 1971.

236. Higham, Robin, ed., with Karen Cox Wing. THE CONSOLIDATED AUTHOR AND SUBJECT INDEX TO THE JOURNAL OF THE ROYAL UNITED SERVICE INSTITUTION, 1857-1963. Ann Arbor, Mich.: University Microfilms, 1964. (1965 paperback).

237. Historical Manuscripts Commission. THE MANUSCRIPTS OF THE EARL OF DARTMOUTH. Edited by William Page. London: Eyre & Spottiswoode, 1896.

238. Historical Manuscripts Commission. THE PRIME MINISTER'S PAPERS, 1801-1902. Edited by John Brooks. London: H.M.S.O., n.d.

239. Historical Manuscripts Commission. REPORT ON THE MANUSCRIPTS OF J.B. FORTESCUE, Esq., PRESERVED AT DROPMORE. Edited by William Page. London: Mackie, 1905-08. 10 vols.

240. Hittle, Colonel J.D. THE MILITARY STAFF: ITS HISTORY AND DEVELOPMENT. Harrisburg, Pa.: Stackpole, 1952.

241. Hobsbawn, E.J. INDUSTRY AND EMPIRE. London: Weidenfeld & Nicholson, 1968.

242. Hodgson, J.E. THE HISTORY OF AERONAUTICS IN GREAT BRITAIN FROM THE EARLIEST TIMES TO THE LATTER HALF OF THE 19th CENTURY. London: Humphrey Wilford, 1924.

243. Hogg, Major General Oliver F.G. THE ROYAL ARSENAL: ITS BACKGROUND, ORIGIN AND SUBSEQUENT HISTORY. London: Oxford University Press, 1963. 2 vols.

244. Holcroft, T. TRAVELS FROM HAMBURG THROUGH WESTPHALIA; HOLLAND, AND THE NETHERLANDS, TO PARIS. London: Phillips, 1804. 2 vols.

245. Holden, Matthew. THE BRITISH SOLDIER. London: Wayland, 1974.

246. Holland, Elizabeth Vassall, lady. THE JOURNAL OF ELIZABETH LADY HOLLAND, 1791-1811. Edited by Earl of Ilchester. London: Longman & Green, 1909. 2 vols.

247. Hope-Jones, Arthur. INCOME TAX IN THE NAPOLEONIC WARS. Cambridge: Cambridge University Press, 1939.

248. Horner, Leonard, ed. MEMOIRS AND CORRESPONDENCE OF FRANCIS HORNER, M.P. London: J. Murray, 1843.

249. Horrocks, Lieut. General Brian. FAMOUS REGIMENTS SERIES FROM HAMISH HAMILTON. London: n.p., 1967.

250. Horward, Donald D. THE FRENCH REVOLUTION AND NAPOLEON COLLECTION AT FLORIDA STATE UNIVERSITY. Tallahassee: Friends of Florida State University Library, 1973.

251. Hüffer, Hermann. QUELLEN ZUR GESCHICHTE DES KRIEGES VON 1799 UND 1800. Leipzig: Teubner, 1900-1907. 3 vols.

252. Hughes, Major General B.P. BRITISH SMOOTHE-BORE ARTILLERY: THE MUZZLE-LOADING ARTILLERY OF THE 18th AND 19th CENTURIES. London: Arms and Armour Press, 1969.

253. Hughes, Major General B.P. FIREPOWER, WEAPONS EFFECTIVENESS ON THE BATTLEFIELD, 1630-1850. New York: Scribner, 1974.

254. Huskisson, William. THE HUSKISSON PAPERS. Edited by L. Melville. New York: R.R. Smith, 1931.

255. INFORMATION AND INSTRUCTIONS FOR COMMANDING GENERALS AND OTHERS. London: Egerton, 1803.

256. INTERCEPTED CORRESPONDENCE BETWEEN CERTAIN PERSONS IN THIS COUNTRY AND THEIR FRIENDS IN INDIA, AS PUBLISHED BY THE FRENCH GOVERNMENT FROM THE ORIGINALS TAKEN ON BOARD THE ADMIRAL APLIN INDIAMAN. London: Badcock, 1804.

257. Jackson, George. THE DIARIES AND LETTERS OF SIR GEORGE JACKSON, K.C.H., FROM THE PEACE OF AMIENS TO THE BATTLE OF TALAVERA. Edited by Lady Jackson. London: Bentley, 1872. 2 vols.

258. Jackson, T.S. LOGS OF THE GREAT SEA FIGHTS, 1794-1805. London: Navy Records Society, 1900. Vol. 18.

259. James, John Haddy. SURGEON JAMES' JOURNAL, 1815. Edited by Jane Vansittart. London: Cassell, 1964.

260. James, William. THE NAVAL HISTORY OF GREAT BRITAIN, 1793-1827. London: Macmillan, 1902. 6 vols.

261. Jones, Major General John T. JOURNAL OF SIEGES CARRIED ON BY THE ARMY UNDER THE DUKE OF WELLINGTON IN SPAIN. London: John Weale, 1846. 3 vols.

262. Jones, William D., comp. RECORDS OF THE ROYAL MILITARY ACADEMY, 1741-1840. Woolwich: Royal Military Academy, 1851.

263. Joyce, Michael. MY FRIEND H.: JOHN CAM HOBHOUSE, BARON BROUGHTON OF BROUGHTON DE GYFFORD. London: J. Murray, 1948.

264. Kane, John. LIST OF OFFICERS OF THE ROYAL REGIMENT OF ARTILLERY, AS THEY STOOD IN 1763, WITH A CONTINUATION TO THE PRESENT TIME, 1815. London: Delahoy, 1815.

265. Kaye, John W., ed. THE LIFE AND CORRESPONDENCE OF MAJOR-GENERAL SIR JOHN MALCOLM, G.C.B. London: n.p., 1856. 2 vols.

266. Keevil, J.J.; Christopher Lloyd; and J.L.S. Coulter. MEDICINE AND THE NAVY, 1200-1900. Edinburgh: Livingstone, 1957-63. 4 vols.

267. Keith, Admiral George Keith Elphinstone, viscount. THE KEITH PAPERS. Selected and edited by Christopher Lloyd. London: Navy Records Society, 1950. 2 vols.

268. Keith, Robert Murray. MEMOIRS AND CORRESPONDENCE. Edited by Mrs. G. Smyth. London: Colburn, 1849.

269. Kincaid, Captain John. ADVENTURES IN THE RIFLE BRIGADE. London: Peter Davies, 1929.

270. Kincaid, Captain John. RANDOM SHOTS FROM A RIFLEMAN. London: Maclaren, n.d.

271. King-Hall, Stephen, and Ann Dewar, eds. HISTORY IN HANSARD, 1803-1900. London: Constable, 1968.

272. Klingberg, Frank J., and Sigurd B. Hustvedt, eds. THE WARNING DRUM: THE BRITISH HOME FRONT FACES NAPOLEON--BROADSIDES OF 1803. Los Angeles: University of California Press, 1944.

273. Krayenhoff, Lieut. General C.R., baron. GESCHIEDKUNDIGE BESCHOUWING VAN DEN OORLOG OP HET GRONDGEBIED DER BATAAFSCHE REPUBLIEK IN 1799. Nymegen: Vieweg, 1832.

274. Labarre de Raillicourt, Donimique. LOUIS BONAPARTE (1778-1846), ROI DE HOLLAND, FRERE ET PERE D'EMPEREURS. Paris: Peyronnet, 1963.

275. Laprade, William T. ENGLAND AND THE FRENCH REVOLUTION 1787-1797. Baltimore: Johns Hopkins Press, 1909.

276. Lawson, Cecil C.P. A HISTORY OF THE UNIFORMS OF THE BRITISH ARMY. London: Peter Davies, 1940-1968. 5 vols.

277. Laws, Lieut. Colonel M.E.S. BATTERY RECORDS OF THE ROYAL ARTILLERY, 1716-1859. Woolwich: Royal Artillery Institution, 1952, 1968.

278. Laws, Lieut. Colonel M.E.S. "The Dutch Immigrant Artillery." JOURNAL OF THE ROYAL ARTILLERY 73 (1946): 250-60.

279. Laws, Lieut. Colonel M.E.S. "The French Emigrant Artillery." JOURNAL OF THE ROYAL ARTILLERY 65 (1938): 356-67.

280. Laws, Lieut. Colonel M.E.S. OUTLINE HISTORY OF THE DEVELOPMENT
     AND ORGANIZATION OF THE ROYAL ARTILLERY. Woolwich: Royal
     Artillery Institute, 1950.

281. Laws, Lieut. Colonel M.E.S. "The Royal Artillery at Copenhagen
     1801." THE JOURNAL OF THE ROYAL ARTILLERY 76 (1949): 285-94.

282. Laws, Lieut. Colonel M.E.S. "The Royal Artillery Invalids."
     JOURNAL OF THE ROYAL ARTILLERY 75 (1949): 94-99.

283. Leach, Jonathan. ROUGH SKETCHES OF THE LIFE OF AN OLD SOLDIER:
     DURING A SERVICE IN THE WEST INDIES; AT THE SIEGE OF COPENHAGEN
     IN 1807.... London: Longmans, Rees, Orme, Brown, and Green,
     1831.

284. Leary, F. THE EARL OF CHESTER'S REGIMENT OF YEOMANRY CAVALRY.
     Edinburgh: privately printed, Ballantyne Press, 1898.

285. Lebon, André. L'ANGLETERRE ET L'EMIGRATION FRANCAISE DE 1794 A
     1801. Paris: Plon, 1882.

286. Lecene, Paul. LES MARINS DE LA REPUBLIQUE ET DE L'EMPIRE,
     1793-1815. Paris: Librairie Centrale des Publications
     Populaires, 1884.

287. Lecky, W.E.H. HISTORY OF ENGLAND IN THE 18th CENTURY. London:
     Longmans, 1878-1890. 8 vols.

288. LeGrand, Louis. LA REVOLUTION FRANCAISE EN HOLLANDE. Paris:
     Hachette, 1894.

289. Leslie, N.B., comp. THE SUCCESSION OF COLONELS. London: Leo
     Cooper, 1970.

290. Lever, Tresham. THE HOUSE OF PITT, A FAMILY CHRONICLE. London:
     J. Murray, 1947.

291. Leveson-Gower, lord Granville, 1st earl Granville. PRIVATE
     CORRESPONDENCE, 1781-1821. Edited by Castalia Countess
     Granville. London: J. Murray, 1916. 2 vols.

292. Lewin, Thomas Herbert, ed. THE LEWIN LETTERS, 1756-1818.
     London: Constable, n.d.

293. Lewis, M.A., ed. A NARRATIVE OF MY PROFESSIONAL ADVENTURES BY
     SIR WILLIAM DILLON. London: Navy Records Society, 1953. 2
     vols.

294. Leyland, J., ed. THE BLOCKADE OF BREST. London: Navy Records
     Society, 1899, 1902. 2 vols.

295. Lindsay-MacDougall, Katharine Francis. A GUIDE TO THE
     MANUSCRIPTS AT THE NATIONAL MARITIME MUSEUM. London: n.p.,
     1960.

296. Lloyd, Christopher. THE NATION AND THE NAVY. London: Cresset Press, 1954.

297. Lloyd, Ernest Marsh. A REVIEW OF THE HISTORY OF INFANTRY. New York: Longmans, 1908.

298. Lobanov-Rostovsky, Andrei. RUSSIA AND EUROPE, 1789-1825. Durham, N.C.: Duke University Press, 1947.

299. Löwenstern, Woldemar Hermann, freiherr. MEMOIRES DU GENERAL-MAJOR RUSSE BARON DE LOEWENSTERN 1776-1858. Edited by M.H. Weil. Paris: Fontemoing, 1903. 2 vols.

300. LONDON GAZETTE, BULLETINS OF THE CAMPAIGN OF 1799. London: n.p., 1800.

301. LOYAL AND PATRIOTIC HAND-BILLS, SONGS, ADDRESSES, etc., ON THE THREATENED INVASION OF GREAT BRITAIN BY BUONAPARTE. London: Printed for the Patriotic Booksellers of London, 1803.

302. Lukacs, John A. "Russian Armies in Western Europe, 1799, 1814, 1917." AMERICAN SLAVIC AND EAST EUROPEAN REVIEW 13 (1954): 319-33.

303. MacCarthy, M. HISTOIRE DE LA CAMPAGNE FAITE EN 1799, EN HOLLANDE. Paris: n.p., 1818.

304. MacCunn, F.J. "The Contemporary English View of Napoleon." B. Litt. thesis, Oxford University, 1913.

305. McGrigor, James. THE AUTOBIOGRAPHY AND SERVICES OF SIR JAMES MCGRIGOR BART, LATE DIRECTOR-GENERAL OF THE ARMY MEDICAL DEPARTMENT, WITH AN APPENDIX OF NOTES AND ORIGINAL CORRESPONDENCE. London: Longmans, Green, Longman, and Roberts, 1861.

306. McGuffie, Tom H. "Life in the British Army 1793-1820, in Relation to Social Conditions." M.A. thesis, University of London, 1940.

307. McGuffie, Tom H., comp. RANK AND FILE: THE COMMON SOLDIER IN PEACE AND WAR, 1642-1914. London: Hutchinson, 1964.

308. McGuffie, Tom H. "The Walcheren Expedition and Walcheren Fever." ENGLISH HISTORICAL REVIEW 62 (1947): 191-202.

309. Mackenzie, T.A., et al., eds. HISTORICAL RECORDS OF THE SEVENTY-NINTH QUEEN'S OWN CAMERON HIGHLANDERS. London: Hamilton, Adams, 1887.

310. Mackesy, Piers. STATESMEN AT WAR: THE STRATEGY OF OVERTHROW, 1798-1799. London: Longmans, 1974.

311. Mackintosh, H.B. THE GRANT, STRATHSPEY OR FIRST HIGHLAND
     FENCIBLE REGIMENT, 1793-1799. Elgin, Scotland: James D.
     Yeadon, 1934.

312. Mahan, Alfred Thayer. THE INFLUENCE OF SEA POWER UPON THE
     FRENCH REVOLUTION AND EMPIRE, 1793-1815. London: Sampson and
     Low, 1892. 2 vols.

313. Malmesbury, James Harris, 1st earl of. DIARIES AND
     CORRESPONDENCE OF JAMES HARRIS, FIRST EARL OF MALMESBURY.
     Edited by 3d earl of Malmesbury. London: Bentley, 1844. 4
     vols.

314. Manwaring, G.E. A BIBLIOGRAPHY OF BRITISH NAVAL HISTORY. A
     BIBLIOGRAPHICAL GUIDE TO PRINTED AND MANUSCRIPT SOURCES.
     London: Routledge, 1930.

315. Marcus, G.J. THE AGE OF NELSON: THE ROYAL NAVY 1793-1815. New
     York: Viking, 1971.

316. Marshall, Henry. MILITARY MISCELLANY; COMPREHENDING A HISTORY
     OF THE RECRUITING OF THE ARMY, MILITARY PUNISHMENTS, etc.
     London: J. Murray, 1846.

317. Marshall, John. ROYAL NAVAL BIOGRAPHY. London: Longmans,
     1823. 4 vols.

318. Martel, Armand Louis R., comte de. WALKEREN, D'APRES LES
     DOCUMENTS INEDITS. Paris: Dentu, 1883.

319. Matheson, Cyril. THE LIFE OF HENRY DUNDAS, FIRST VISCOUNT
     MELVILLE, 1742-1811. London: Constable, 1933.

320. Matthews, William. BRITISH AUTOBIOGRAPHIES; AN ANNOTATED
     BIBLIOGRAPHY OF BRITISH AUTOBIOGRAPHIES PUBLISHED OR WRITTEN
     BEFORE 1951. Berkeley Calif.: University of California Press,
     1955.

321. MEMOIRES HISTORIQUES SUR LA CAMPAGNE DU GENERAL EN CHEF BRUNE EN
     BATAVIE. Paris: Favre, 1801.

322. Mikhailovsky-Danilevsky, Aleksandr I. GESCHICHTE DES KRIEGES
     RUSSLANDS MIT FRANKREICH UNTER DER REGIERUNG KAISERS PAUL I ...
     1799. Translated by C. Schmitt. Munich: Lindauer, 1856-58. 5
     vols.

323. Miles, William Augustus. THE CORRESPONDENCE OF WILLIAM AUGUSTUS
     MILES ON THE FRENCH REVOLUTION, 1789-1817. Edited by Rev.
     Charles Popham Miles. London: Longmans, Green, 1890. 2 vols.

324. Millard, Midshipman W.S. "The Battle of Copenhagen."
     MACMILLAN'S MAGAZINE 72 (1895): 81-93.

325. Milne, Samuel. THE STANDARDS AND COLOURS OF THE ARMY FROM THE RESTORATION, 1661, TO THE INTRODUCTION OF THE TERRITORIAL SYSTEM, 1881. Leeds: Goodall & Suddick, 1893.

326. Minto, Countess, ed. LIFE AND LETTERS OF SIR GILBERT ELLIOT, FIRST EARL OF MINTO, FROM 1751 TO 1806. London: Longmans, Green, 1874. 3 vols.

327. Mitchell, Harvey. THE UNDERGROUND WAR AGAINST REVOLUTIONARY FRANCE, 1794-1800. Oxford: Clarendon Press, 1965.

328. Mockler-Ferryman, Augustus F. THE LIFE OF A REGIMENTAL OFFICER DURING THE GREAT WAR, 1793-1815.... Edinburgh: Blackwood, 1913.

329. Moore, James Carrick. THE LIFE OF LIEUTENANT-GENERAL SIR JOHN MOORE, K.B. BY HIS BROTHER. London: J. Murray, 1834. 2 vols.

330. Moore, John. THE DIARY OF SIR JOHN MOORE. Edited by Major General Sir J.F. Maurice. London: Arnold, 1904. 2 vols.

331. Moorsom, William S., ed. HISTORICAL RECORD OF THE FIFTY-SECOND REGIMENT ... FROM THE YEAR 1755 TO THE YEAR 1858. London: Bentley, 1860.

332. Morley, Stephen. MEMOIRS OF A SERGEANT OF THE FIFTH REGIMENT OF FOOT.... Ashford: Elliott, 1842.

333. Morris, Private T. MEMOIRS OF A SOLDIER IN THE 73rd INFANTRY REGIMENT. Edited by J. Selby. Camden, Conn: Archon Books, 1967

334. Mure, Williams, ed. SELECTIONS FROM THE FAMILY PAPERS PRESERVED AT CALDWELL. Glasgow: Maitland Club, 1854.

335. A NARRATIVE OF WHAT PASSED AT KILLALA, IN THE COUNTRY OF MAYO AND PARTS ADJACENT DURING THE FRENCH INVASION IN THE SUMMER OF 1798. By an Eye-Witness (Bishop J. Stock). Dublin: n.p., 1800.

336. THE NAVAL CHRONICLE FOR 1809: CONTAINING A GENERAL BIOGRAPHICAL HISTORY OF THE ROYAL NAVY OF THE UNITED KINGDOM. London: Joyce Gold, 1809. Vol. 22.

337. THE NAVAL MISCELLANY. Edited by John Knox Laughton. London: Naval Records Society, 1912. Vol. 2.

338. Nelson, R.R. THE HOME OFFICE, 1782-1801. Durham, N.C.: Duke University Press, 1969.

339. Newbolt, Henry. THE STORY OF THE OXFORDSHIRE AND BUCKINGHAMSHIRE LIGHT INFANTRY. London: Country Life, 1915.

340. Nicolas, Nicholas H., ed. THE DISPATCHES AND LETTERS OF VICE ADMIRAL LORD VISCOUNT NELSON. London: Colburn, 1845. 6 vols.

341. Nicolay, Fernand. NAPOLEON Ier AU CAMP DE BOULOGNE. Paris: Perrin, 1907.

342. Nicholson, John. BEACONS OF EAST YORKSHIRE. Hull: A. Brown, 1887.

343. Norie, J.W. THE NAVAL GAZETTEER. London: Norie, 1827.

344. Norman, C.B. BATTLE HONORS OF THE BRITISH ARMY, FROM TANGIERS, 1662, TO THE COMMENCEMENT OF THE REIGN OF KING EDWARD VII. London: J. Murray, 1911.

345. Oatts, Lewis B. THE HIGHLAND LIGHT INFANTRY (THE 71st H.L.I. AND 74th HIGHLANDERS). London: Leo Cooper, 1969.

346. Oatts, Lewis B. PROUD HERITAGE: THE STORY OF THE HIGHLAND LIGHT INFANTRY. London: Nelson, 1952-59. 4 vols.

347. O'Byrne, W.R. A NAVAL BIOGRAPHICAL DICTIONARY. London: J. Murray, 1849.

348. O'Donnell, H., ed. HISTORICAL RECORDS OF THE FOURTEENTH REGIMENT. Debonport: A.H. Swiss, 1893.

349. Olson, M. THE ECONOMICS OF WARTIME SHORTAGE: A HISTORY OF BRITISH FOOD SUPPLIES IN THE NAPOLEONIC WAR AND IN WORLD WAR I AND II. Durham, N.C.: Duke University Press, 1963.

350. Oman, Carola (Lenanton). NAPOLEON AT THE CHANNEL. Garden City, New York: Doubleday, Doran, 1942.

351. Oman, Carola (Lenanton). SIR JOHN MOORE. London: Hodder and Stoughton, 1953.

352. Oman, Charles W. STUDIES IN THE NAPOLEONIC WARS. New York: Scribner, 1930.

353. Omond, Lieut. Colonel John Stuart. PARLIAMENT AND THE ARMY. Cambridge: Cambridge University Press, 1933.

354. Ompteda, Christian, baron. IN THE KING'S GERMAN LEGION. London: Grevel, 1894.

355. Oprey, C. "Schemes for the Reform of Naval Recruitment, 1793-1815." M.A. thesis, University of Liverpool, 1961.

356. Otway, Robert Waller. HISTORICAL MEMOIR OF SIR ROBERT WALLER OTWAY, BT. KCB, VICE-ADMIRAL OF THE RED. London: n.p., 1840.

357. Paget, Arthur. THE PAGET PAPERS: DIPLOMATIC AND OTHER CORRESPONDENCE OF THE RIGHT HON. SIR ARTHUR PAGET, G.C.B. 1794-1807. Edited by Augustus Paget. London: Heinemann, 1896. 2 vols.

358. Paget, Henry William, 1st marquis of Anglesey. ONE LEG; THE LIFE AND LETTERS OF HENRY WILLIAM PAGET, FIRST MARQUESS OF ANGLESEY, 1768-1854. London: J. Cape, 1961.

359. Pannell, J.P.M. "The Taylors of Southampton: Pioneers in Mechanical Engineering." PROCEEDINGS OF THE INSTITUTION OF MECHANICAL ENGINEERS 46 (1955): 924-31.

360. Parker, Harry. NAVAL BATTLES. London: T. H. Parker, 1911.

361. Parrons, K.A.C. A CHECKLIST OF BRITISH PARLIAMENTARY PAPERS 1801-1950. Cambridge: Cambridge University Press, 1958.

362. Parry, Ann, ed. THE ADMIRALS FREMANTLE: A SELECTION FROM THE FREMANTLE FAMILY PAPERS (1765-1958). London: Chatto and Windus, 1971.

363. Parry, John. HISTORICAL AND DESCRIPTIVE ACCOUNT OF THE COAST OF SUSSEX. London: Longmans, 1833.

364. Peacock, Basil. THE ROYAL NORTHUMBERLAND FUSILIERS (THE 5th REGIMENT OF FOOT). London: Leo Cooper, 1970.

365. Pearce, Robert R., ed. MEMOIRS AND CORRESPONDENCE OF THE MOST NOBLE RICHARD MARQUESS WELLESLEY. London: Bentley, 1846. 3 vols.

366. Pellew, George, D.D., ed. THE LIFE AND CORRESPONDENCE OF THE RIGHT HONOURABLE HENRY ADDINGTON, FIRST VISCOUNT SIDMOUTH. London: J. Murray, 1847. 2 vols.

367. Peters, George W. THE BEDFORDSHIRE AND HERTFORDSHIRE REGIMENT (THE 16th REGIMENT OF FOOT). London: Leo Cooper, 1970.

368. Pettigrew, Thomas J., ed. MEMOIRS OF THE LIFE OF VICE-ADMIRAL LORD VISCOUNT NELSON, K.B. London: Boone, 1849. 2 vols.

369. Picton, Thomas. MEMOIRS. Edited by H.B. Robinson. London: Bentley, 1836. 2 vols.

370. Piechowiak, A.B. "The Anglo-Russian Expedition to Holland in 1799." SLAVONIC AND EAST EUROPEAN REVIEW 41 (1962-63): 182-95.

371. Pitt, William. THE SPEECHES OF THE RIGHT HONORABLE WILLIAM PITT IN THE HOUSE OF COMMONS. London: Longmans, Hurst, Rees, and Orme, 1806. 4 vols.

372. Pollock, Frederick, ed. MACREADY'S REMINISCENCES, AND SELECTIONS FROM HIS DIARIES AND LETTERS. New York: Macmillan, 1875.

373. Pope, Dudley. THE GREAT GAMBLE. London: Weidenfeld & Nicolson, 1972.

374. Porter, Whitworth. HISTORY OF THE CORPS OF ROYAL ENGINEERS.
     London: Longman & Green, 1889. 2 vols.

375. Pressnell, L.S., ed. STUDIES IN THE INDUSTRIAL REVOLUTION
     PRESENTED TO T.S. ASHTON. London: London University Press,
     1960.

376. Primon, C.F. AUTHENTISCHE GESCHICHTE DES JETZIGEN KRIEGES
     ZWISCHEN DANEMARK UND ENGLAND. Copenhagen: Schubothe, 1801.

377. Q.L. THE YEOMANRY CAVALRY OF WORCESTERSHIRE, 1794-1913.
     Deviyes, Wiltshire: Published privately, 1914.

378. Raikes, George A. THE HISTORY OF THE HONOURABLE ARTILLERY
     COMPANY. London: Bentley, 1879.

379. Ray, Cyril. THE LANCASHIRE FUSILIERS: (THE 20th REGIMENT OF
     FOOT). London: Leo Cooper, 1971.

380. Raymond, Ernest. "AN OLD PLATOON." THE BOOK OF HAMPSTEAD.
     Edited by Mavis and Ian Norrie. Hampstead: High Hill Books,
     1960.

381. Renn, Erin McCawley. "British Civil and Military Preparations
     against Napoleon's Planned Invasion, 1803-1805." Ph.D.
     dissertation, Florida State University, 1974.

382. REPORT OF THE COMMITTEE OF SECRECY OF THE HOUSE OF COMMONS.
     London: H.M.S.O, 1799.

383. Rhys-Pryce, A.R. "The French Invasions of England from the 12th
     Century to the 19th (1101-1860)." M.A. thesis, Belfast
     University, 1928.

384. Richardson, William. A MARINER OF ENGLAND: AN ACCOUNT OF THE
     CAREER OF WILLIAM RICHARDSON FROM CABIN BOY IN THE MERCHANT
     SERVICE TO WARRANT OFFICER IN THE ROYAL NAVY (1780-1819) AS TOLD
     BY HIMSELF. Edited by Colonel Spencer Childers. London:
     Conway Maritime Press, 1970.

385. Richmond, H.W. THE PRIVATE PAPERS OF GEORGE, SECOND EARL
     SPENCER. FIRST LORD OF THE ADMIRALTY, 1794-1801. London: Navy
     Records Society, 1924. Vols. 58, 59.

386. Riddick, S. "Charles Middleton, Afterwards Lord Barham, and
     Naval Administration, 1778-1805." M.A. thesis, Univeristy of
     Liverpool, 1939.

387. Robertson, D. THE JOURNAL OF SERGEANT D. ROBERTSON, LATE 92nd
     FOOT: COMPRISING THE DIFFERENT CAMPAIGNS, BETWEEN THE YEARS
     1798 AND 1818, IN EGYPT, WALCHEREN, DENMARK, SWEDEN, PORTUGAL,
     SPAIN, FRANCE, AND BELGIUM. Perth: J. Fisher, 1842.

388. Robinson, Charles Walker. WELLINGTON'S CAMPAIGNS, PENINSULA-
     WATERLOO, 1805-15.... London: Rees, 1907.

389. Rocca, Albert Jean Michel de. LA CAMPAGNE DE WALCHEREN ET D'ANVERS. Brussels: P.J. deMat, 1816.

390. Rodger, Alexander B. THE WAR OF THE SECOND COALTION, 1798-1801; A STRATEGIC COMMENTARY. Oxford: Clarendon Press, 1964.

391. Rollo, D. THE HISTORY OF THE ORKEY AND SHETLAND VOLUNTEERS AND TERRITORIALS, 1793-1958. Shetland: Shetland Times, 1958.

392. Rolt, L.T.C. THOMAS TELFORD. London: Longmans, Green, 1958.

393. Romilly, Samuel. MEMOIRS OF THE LIFE OF SIR SAMUEL ROMILLY, WRITTEN BY HIMSELF. London: J. Murray, 1840.

394. Rose, George. THE DIARIES AND CORRESPONDENCE OF THE RIGHT HONOURABLE GEORGE ROSE. Edited by Leveson V. Harcourt. London: Bentley, 1860. 2 vols.

395. Rose, John Holland. "The Contest with Napoleon, 1802-1812." Chapter 3. THE CAMBRIDGE HISTORY OF BRITISH FOREIGN POLICY 1783-1919. Edited by Sir A.W. Ward and G.P. Gooch. Cambridge: Cambridge University Press, 1922.

396. Rose, John Holland. PITT AND NAPOLEON: ESSAYS AND LETTERS. London: G. Bell, 1912.

397. Rose, John Holland, and A.M. Broadley. DUMOURIEZ AND THE DEFENSE OF ENGLAND AGAINST NAPOLEON. London: J. Lane, 1909.

398. Rosebery, Archibald Philip Primrose, 5th earl of, ed. THE WINDHAM PAPERS. London: Herbert Jenkins, 1913.

399. Ross, Steven T. "The Military Strategy of the Directory: The Campaigns of 1799." FRENCH HISTORICAL STUDIES 5 (1967): 170-87.

400. Ross, Steven T. QUEST FOR VICTORY: FRENCH MILITARY STRATEGY, 1792-1799. New York: A.S. Barnes, 1973.

401. Ross, Steven T. "The War of the Second Coalition." Ph.D. dissertation, Princeton University, 1963.

402. Ross-Lewin, Harry. WITH "THE THIRTY-SECOND" IN THE PENINSULAR AND OTHER CAMPAIGNS. Edited by John Wardell. London: Simpkin & Marshall, 1904.

403. Rothenberg, Gunther E. THE ART OF WARFARE IN THE AGE OF NAPOLEON. Bloomington, Indiana: Indiana University Press, 1978.

404. Royal Artillery. LIST OF OFFICERS OF THE ROYAL REGIMENT OF ARTILLERY AS THEY STOOD IN ... 1763, WITH A CONTINUATION TO THE PRESENT TIME (incl. military medical department of the ordnance). Compiled by John Cave. Greenwich, 1815. (4th rev. ed., London: n.p,, 1900).

405. The Royal Artillery Institution. CATALOGUE OF THE ROYAL
ARTILLERY INSTITUTION LIBRARY (MILITARY SECTION). Woolwich:
The Royal Artillery Institution, 1913.

406. Royal Military Academy. RECORDS OF THE ROYAL MILITARY ACADEMY.
Woolwich: Royal Military Academy, 1892.

407. Russell, Captain John. MOVEMENTS AND CHANGES OF POSITION OF A
BATTALION OF INFANTRY, IN STRICT CONFORMITY TO HIS MAJESTY'S
RULES AND REGULATIONS. London: n.p., 1802.

408. Russell, Lieutenant John. REMARKS ON THE INUTILITY OF THE THIRD
RANK OF FIRELOCKS, AND THE PROPRIETORY OF INCREASING THE
EFFECTIVE FORCE OF THE COUNTRY BY DRAWING UP THE MUSQUETRY TWO
DEEP, AND FORMING THE THIRD RANK OF PIKEMAN. London: n.p.,
1805.

409. Russell, John, ed. MEMORIALS AND CORRESPONDENCE OF CHARLES
JAMES FOX. London: Bentley, 1854.

410. Ryan, Anthony Nicholas. "The Copenhagen Expedition, 1807."
M.A. thesis, University of Liverpool, 1951.

411. Ryan, Anthony Nicholas. "The Navy at Copenhagen in 1807."
MARINER'S MIRROR 39 (1953): 201-10.

412. Ryan, Anthony Nicholas, ed. THE SAUMAREZ PAPERS. London:
Naval Records Society, 1968.

413. Schama, Simon. PATRIOTS AND LIBERATORS. REVOLUTION IN THE
NETHERLANDS, 1780-1813. New York: Knopf, 1977.

414. Schomberg, Isaac. THE NAVAL CHRONOLOGY, OR AN HISTORICAL
SUMMARY OF NAVAL AND MARITIME EVENTS. London: Egerton, 1802.
5 vols.

415. Scobie, I.H. Mackay. AN OLD HIGHLAND FENCIBLE CORPS.
Edinburgh: William Blackwood, 1914.

416. Scott, J.B. THE ARMED NEUTRALITIES OF 1780 AND 1800. New York:
Oxford University Press, 1918.

417. Scott, Robert Bisset. THE MILITARY LAW OF ENGLAND (WITH ALL THE
PRINCIPAL AUTHORITIES), ADAPTED TO THE GENERAL USE OF THE
ARMY ... AND THE PRACTICE OF COURTS MARTIAL. London: T.
Goddard, 1810.

418. Scott, Wilson L. "The Impact of the French Revolution in
English Science." Chapter 2. MELANGES ALEXANDRE KOYRE. Paris:
Harmann, 1964. 475-95.

419. Sebag-Montefiore, Cecil. A HISTORY OF THE VOLUNTEER FORCES FROM
THE EARLIEST TIMES TO THE YEAR 1860. London: Constable, 1908.

420. Severn, John Kenneth. A WELLESLEY AFFAIR. RICHARD MARQUESS WELLESLEY AND THE CONDUCT OF ANGLO-SPANISH DIPLOMACY, 1809-1812. Tallahassee: University Presses of Florida, 1981.

421. Shenstone, J.C., ed. "A Yeoman's Common-place Book at the Commencement of the Nineteenth Century." THE ESSEX REVIEW 16 (1907): 78-89.

422. Sherwig, John M. GUINEAS AND GUNPOWDER; BRITISH FOREIGN AID IN THE WARS WITH FRANCE 1793-1815. Cambridge, Mass.: Harvard University Press, 1969.

423. Sinclair, Donald. THE HISTORY OF THE ABERDEEN VOLUNTEERS. Aberdeen: Aberdeen Daily Journal Office, 1907.

424. Six, Georges. DICTIONNAIRE BIOGRAPHIQUE DES GENERAUX ET AMIRAUX FRANCAIS DE LA REVOLUTION ET DE L'EMPIRE (1792-1814). Paris: Saffroy, 1934. 2 vols.

425. Smirke, Robert. REVIEW OF A BATTALION OF INFANTRY, INCLUDING THE EIGHTEEN MANOEUVRES. London: Bentley, 1803.

426. Smith, D.B. THE LETTERS OF LORD ST. VINCENT, 1801-1804. London: Navy Records Society, 1922. Vol. 55.

427. Smith, Harry George W. THE AUTOBIOGRAPHY OF LT.-GENERAL SIR HARRY SMITH. Edited by G.C. Moore Smith. London: J. Murray, 1901.

428. Smyth, Brigadier General John. THE HISTORY OF THE ROYAL MILITARY ACADEMY, WOOLWICH, THE ROYAL MILITARY COLLEGE, SANDHURST, AND THE ROYAL MILITARY ACADEMY, SANDHURST, 1741-1961. London: Weidenfeld and Nicholson, 1961.

429. Smyth, Brigadier General John. SANDHURST. London: Weidenfeld and Nicholson, 1961.

430. Smythies, Raymond H. HISTORICAL RECORDS OF THE 40th (2nd SOMERSETSHIRE) REGIMENT, NOW 1st BATTALION, THE PRINCE OF WALES'S VOLUNTEERS (SOUTH LANCASHIRE REGIMENTS). Devonport: A.H. Swiss, 1894.

431. St. Clair, Lieut. Colonel Thomas Staunton. A RESIDENCE IN THE WEST INDIES AND AMERICA WITH A NARRATIVE OF THE EXPEDITION TO THE ISLAND OF WALCHEREN. London: Bentley, 1834. 2 Vols.

432. Stanhope, Philip Henry, 5th earl Stanhope. NOTES AND EXTRACTS OF LETTERS REFERRING TO MR. PITT AND WALMER CASTLE, 1801-1806. London: J. Murray, 1862.

433. Steer, D.M. "The Blockade of Brest by the Royal Navy, 1793-1805." M.A. thesis, Liverpool University 1971.

434. Steevens, Charles. REMINISCENCES OF MY MILITARY LIFE, FROM 1795-1818. Edited by Nathaniel Steevens. Winchester: Warren, 1878.

435. Stephen, J. WAR IN DISGUISE. London: Wittingham, 1805.

436. Stephen, William. HISTORY OF THE QUEEN'S CITY OF EDINBURGH RIFLE VOLUNTEER BRIGADE. Edinburgh: Blackwood, 1881.

437. Stocqueler, J.H. A PERSONAL HISTORY OF THE HORSE GUARDS, 1750-1872. London: Hurst and Blackett, 1873.

438. Stoneham, Charles, and Benson Freeman. HISTORICAL RECORDS OF THE MIDDLESEX YEOMANRY, 1797-1927. Chelsea: Regimental Committee, Duke of York's Headquarters, 1930.

439. Strickland, W.C. "The Roscommon Militia." THE JOURNAL OF THE SOCIETY FOR ARMY HISTORICAL RESEARCH 3 (1924): 145-47.

440. Stuart Jones, E.H. AN INVASION THAT FAILED. Oxford: Oxford University Press, 1950.

441. Stuart Jones, E.H. THE LAST INVASION OF BRITAIN. Cardiff: University of Wales Press, 1950.

442. Surtees, John. TWENTY-FIVE YEARS IN THE RIFLE BRIGADE. Edinburgh: n.p., 1831.

443. Sutcliffe, Sheila. MARTELLO TOWERS. London: David and Charles, 1972.

444. Taylor, A.H. "The Battle of Copenhagen, April 2, 1801." TIDSSKRIFT FOR SOVAESEN 122 (1951): 35-49.

445. Taylor, J.R. "William, Windham and the Counter-Revolution in the North and West of France, 1793-1801." M.A. thesis, Manchester University, 1967.

446. Tchitchagof, Paul. MEMOIRES DE L'AMIRAL PAUL TCHICHAGOF. Edited by C.G. Lahovary. Paris: Plon-Nourrit, 1909.

447. Teffeteller, Gordon L. THE SURPRISER, THE LIFE OF ROWLAND HILL. Newark: University of Delaware Press, 1983.

448. Terry, Charles Stanford. A CATALOGUE OF THE PUBLICATIONS OF SCOTTISH HISTORICAL AND KINDRED CLUBS AND SOCIETIES AND OF THE VOLUMES RELATIVE TO SCOTTISH HISTORY ISSUED BY HIS MAJESTY'S STATIONARY OFFICE, 1780-1908, WITH A SUBJECT INDEX. Glasgow: J. MacLehose, 1909.

449. Thiard, Auxonne Marie, comte de Bissy. SOUVENIRS DIPLOMATIQUES ET MILITAIRES DU GENERAL THIARD. Edited by Léonce Lex. Paris: Flammarion, n.d.

450. Thomas, David. AGRICULTURE IN WALES DURING THE NAPOLEONIC WARS: A STUDY IN THE GEOGRAPHICAL INTERPRETATION OF HISTORICAL SOURCES. Cardiff: University of Wales Press, 1963.

451. Thomas, Hugh. THE STORY OF SANDHURST. London: Hutchinson, 1961.

452. Thomazi, Auguste Antoine. NAPOLEON ET SES MARINS. Paris: Berger-Levrault, 1950.

453. Thomis, M.I., and P. Holt. THREATS OF REVOLUTION IN BRITAIN, 1789-1848. London: Macmillan, 1977.

454. Thursfield, H.G., and J.R. Thursfield, eds. FIVE NAVAL JOURNALS. London: Navy Records Society, 1951.

455. Trulsson, S.G. "British and Swedish Policies and Strategies in the Baltic after the Peace of Tilsit in 1807. A Study in Decision-making." BIBLIOTECA HISTORICA LUNDENSIS. Lund: Gleerup, 1976.

456. Turner, Eunice H. "The Russian Squadron with Admiral Duncan's North Sea Fleet, 1795-1800." MARINER'S MIRROR 49 (1963): 212-22.

457. Tweed, H.R. A HISTORY OF THE HOONCASTLE DETACHMENT. Horncastle: W.K. Morton, 1936.

458. Tylden, Major G. HORSES AND SADDLERY: AN ACCOUNT OF THE ANIMALS USED BY THE BRITISH AND COMMONWEALTH ARMIES FROM THE SEVENTEENTH CENTURY TO THE PRESENT DAY WITH A DESCRIPTION OF THEIR EQUIPMENT. London: Allen, 1965.

459. UNITED SERVICE JOURNAL. "Recollections of the British Army, in the Early Campaigns of the Revolutionary Wars." London: Colburn, 1836.

460. U.S. Department of the Army. THE SUBJECT AND AUTHOR INDEX TO MILITARY REVIEW. Compiled by Mark Wing and Karen Cox under the direction of Robin Higham. Fort Leavenworth, Kansas: U. S. Army Command and General Staff College and MILITARY REVIEW, 1967.

461. Vassall, Henry Richard, 3d lord Holland. FURTHER MEMOIRS OF THE WHIG PARTY, 1807-1821, WITH SOME MISCELLANEOUS REMINISCENCES. London: J. Murray, 1905.

462. Vigny, A. de. SERVITUDE ET GRANDEUR MILITAIRES. Paris: Bonnaie, 1835.

463. Vine, P.A.L. THE ROYAL MILITARY CANAL. London: David and Charles, 1972.

464. Vonk, L.C. GESCHIEDENIS DER LANDING VAN HET ENGLESCH-RUSSISCH LEGER IN NOORD-HOLLAND. Haarlem: Bohn, 1801.

465. Waite, Richard A., Jr. "Sir Home Riggs Popham, Rear Admiral of the Red Squadron." Ph.D. dissertation, Harvard University, 1942.

466. Walker, T.J. THE DEPOT FOR PRISONERS OF WAR AT NORMAN CROSS, HUNTINGDONSHIRE, 1796-1816. London: Constable, 1913.

467. Walpole, Spencer. THE LIFE OF THE RIGHT HONOURABLE SPENCER PERCEVAL. London: Hurst & Blackett, 1874. 2 vols.

468. Walsh, Edward. NARRATIVE OF THE EXPEDITION TO HOLLAND IN 1799. London: Hamilton, Falcon, and Court, 1800.

469. Walter, James. ENGLAND'S NAVAL AND MILITARY WEAKNESS: NATIONAL DANGERS: THE VOLUNTEER FORCE. London: Clowes, 1882.

470. Ward, Stephen George P. "Defence Works in Britain, 1803-1805." JOURNAL OF THE SOCIETY FOR ARMY HISTORICAL RESEARCH 27 (1949): 18-37.

471. Warner, Oliver. LORD NELSON: A GUIDE TO READING. London: Caravel Press, 1955.

472. Warner, Oliver. NELSON'S BATTLES. London: Batsford, 1965.

473. Warner, Oliver. THE SEA AND THE SWORD; THE BALTIC: 1630-1945. London: Morrow, 1965.

474. War Office. MANUAL AND PLATOON EXERCISE FOR THE LIGHT CAVALRY. London: War Office, 1812.

475. War Office. Intelligence Division. BRITISH MINOR EXPEDITIONS, 1746-1814. London: H.M.S.O,, 1884.

476. Watkins, John. A BIOGRAPHICAL MEMOIR OF FREDERICK, DUKE OF YORK. London: A. Fisher, 1827.

477. Watson, John Steven. THE REIGN OF GEORGE III, 1760-1815. Oxford: Clarendon Press, 1960.

478. Watteville, Colonel H. de. THE BRITISH SOLDIER: HIS DAILY LIFE FROM TUDOR TO MODERN TIMES. London: Dent, 1954.

479. Watts, C.N. "The Irish Rebellions of 1798 and of To-day: A Comparison." JOURNAL OF THE ROYAL UNITED SERVICE INSTITUTION 66 (1921): 117-29.

480. Weaver, Lawrence. THE STORY OF THE ROYAL SCOTS (THE LOTHIAN REGIMENT) FORMERLY THE FIRST OR THE ROYAL REGIMENT OF FOOT. London: Country Life, 1915.

481. Webster, Charles K. THE FOREIGN POLICY OF CASTLEREAGH. London: Bell, 1947-50. 2 vols.

482. Weir, Robert W. A HISTORY OF THE SCOTTISH BORDERERS MILITIA. Dumfires: Herald Office, 1877.

483. Wellesley, Henry, 1st lord Cowley. THE DIARY AND CORRESPONDENCE OF HENRY WELLESLEY, FIRST LORD COWLEY, 1790-1846. Edited by F. A. Wellesley. London: Hutchinson, 1930.

484. Wellington, Arthur Wellesley, 1st duke of. THE DISPATCHES OF FIELD MARSHALL THE DUKE OF WELLINGTON. Compiled by Lieut. Colonel Gurwood. London: J. Murray, 1838. 8 vols.

485. Werner, Jack. WE LAUGHED AT BONEY. London: W.H. Allen, 1943.

486. Western, J.R. THE ENGLISH MILITIA IN THE EIGHTEENTH CENTURY: THE STUDY OF A POLITICAL ISSUE, 1660-1802. London: Routledge & Kegan Paul, 1965.

487. Wheater, W.A. RECORD OF THE SERVICES OF THE FIFTY-FIRST, THE KING'S OWN LIGHT INFANTRY REGIMENT. London: Longmans, Green, 1870.

488. Wheeler, Harold F.B., and Alexander Meyrick Broadley. NAPOLEON AND THE INVASION OF ENGLAND. London: J. Lane, 1908. 2 vols.

489. Wheeler, Harold F.B., and Alexander Meyrick Broadley. THE WAR IN WEXFORD. London: J. Lane, 1910.

490. Wheeler, William. THE LETTERS OF PRIVATE WHEELER, 1809-1828. Edited by B.H. Liddell Hart. Boston: Houghton Mifflin, 1952.

491. White, Arthur S., comp. A BIBLIOGRAPHY OF REGIMENTAL HISTORIES OF THE BRITISH ARMY. London: Society for Army Historical Research, 1965.

492. Whyte, Frederick, and A. Hilliard Atteridge. A HISTORY OF THE QUEENS BAYS, THE SECOND DRAGOON GUARDS, 1685-1929. London: Jonathan Cape, 1930.

493. Wilberforce, Robert Isaac, and Samuel Wilbeforce. THE LIFE OF WILLIAM WILBERFORCE. London: J. Murray, 1838. 3 vols.

494. Wilde, E.T. Rodney. THE TOWER HAMLETS RIFLE VOLUNTEER BRIGADE. London: Covingham, 1892.

495. Wilkins, H.J. HISTORY OF THE LOYAL WESTBURY VOLUNTEER CORPS FROM 1803 TO 1804. Bristol: J. W. Arrowsmith, 1918.

496. Williams III, Coleman. "The Anglo-Russian Expedition to North Holland in 1799." M.A. thesis, Auburn University, 1971.

497. Wilson, Robert T. AN ENQUIRY INTO THE PRESENT STATE OF THE MILITARY FORCE OF THE BRITISH EMPIRE, WITH A VIEW TO ITS REORGANIZATION, ADDRESSED TO THE RT. HON. WILLIAM PITT. London: n.p., 1804.

498. Windham, William. SPEECHES IN PARLIAMENT OF THE RIGHT HONOURABLE WILLIAM WINDHAM. London: Longmans, Hurst, 1812. 3 vols.

499. Winstock, Lewis. SONGS AND MUSIC OF THE REDCOATS, 1642-1902.
     London: Leo Cooper, 1909.

500. Woodburne, George B.L. THE STORY OF OUR VOLUNTEERS. London:
     Newman, 1881.

501. Woods, C.J. "A Plan for a Dutch Invasion of Scotland, 1797."
     SCOTTISH HISTORICAL REVIEW 53 (1974): 108-14.

502. Yarrow, David. "A Journal of the Walcheren Expedition, 1809."
     MARINER'S MIRROR 61 (1975): 183-89.

503. Yonge, Charles D., comp. THE LIFE AND ADMINISTRATION OF ROBERT
     BANKS, SECOND EARL OF LIVERPOOL. London: Macmillian, 1868. 3
     vols.

504. Young, Brigadier Peter. THE BRITISH ARMY 1642-1970. London:
     Kimber, 1967.

ADDENDUM

505. Bruce, Anthony P.C. AN ANNOTATED BIBLIOGRAPHY OF THE BRITISH
     ARMY. New York: Garland, 1975.

506. Emeley, Clive. THE BRITISH SOCIETY AND THE FRENCH WARS, 1793-
     1815. London: Macmillan, 1979.

CHAPTER VIII

THE NAVAL WAR

Norman E. Saul, University of Kansas

The use of the plural in the term "Napoleonic Wars" is as appropriate a designation to denote the separation of the theatres of conflict into land and sea as the chronological subdivision into wars of coalitions. In many ways the land and sea wars were quite separate, but perhaps not as far removed from each other as much of the literature has indicated. The naval war has more than its share of "buffs" who find the clash of ships and men more stirring, more romantic than the long, weary marches of the foot soldiers and the bloody battles of mass armies. A ship once at sea appears more independent, less subject to bureaucratic sloth and corruption and the variety of domestic and political hassles, perhaps even freer from the diplomatic vagaries and logistical nightmares of the land campaigns. The image of a simpler, cleaner war at sea is no doubt exaggerated, one that comes to us through British eyes and largely through Romantic and Victorian prisms. Fortunately, some of the most recent research is shifting the focus from the quarterdeck and the wardroom to the gundeck and the foc'sle, from the "captains" to the men and equipment.

The naval war can be roughly divided into two phases: the active expeditionary and battle phase that resulted in British triumph by the end of 1805 and the duller, more tedious blockade phase that still had considerable economic, as well as political and military repercussions. Unsurprisingly, the literature reviewed emphasizes the former. This was the "age of Nelson," a term that suits oceanic developments as fittingly as the "age of Napoleon" does those on the continent. The figure atop the column in London's Trafalgar Square reflects perfectly the elevated status that Admiral Lord Horatio Nelson holds in historical imagination. For number of published pages on individuals of the era, Nelson must hold second place (perhaps first in English). Naturally, the period after his dramatic death in 1805 and the less heroic blockade duty that dominated the remainder of the conflict has drawn less attention from naval historians.

While the British expectedly have taken and held the lead in publication and research, they have had friendly and admiring competition from the United States, especially after America began to reach for naval supremacy in the twentieth century. The time when Britannia really ruled the seas has appealed to the fancy of a wide variety of writers of history and fiction, who found justifications for imperial rule and for seapower, bolstered by romance and nostalgia.

At heart the naval war concerned men, ships, and nature (mainly water and wind); and these are what the "pure" naval historian is concerned about. But around every battle or expedition, behind every 74-gun man-of-war, is a large fringe area that involves shipbuilding, supply, government policy, and recruitment and training. These less exciting "coastal waters" also sustain trade and merchant ships, which usually carried some armament and were indeed involved in the war, most often as victims. The most successful and lasting literature concentrates on this background or at least takes particular note of it.

GENERAL WORKS

Almost all of the overview treatments of the Napoleonic conflict refer to naval action, yet it is clear that most authors are more comfortable or feel safer on land, in the capitals where diplomatic dispatches were composed and decrees and orders drafted, or in reenacting long marches and battle scenes. From coffee table to scholar's shelf, Napoleon overshadows Nelson. The exceptions are predictably from the British side. Arthur Bryant (52), for example, devotes considerable effort to recounting the main naval action in a readable and stirringly patriotic style. On the other hand, Georges Lefebvre has much to say about Austerlitz, while barely mentioning Trafalgar.

Very few histories of naval warfare are successful in integrating all sides of the conflict and in providing a comparative framework and long-range analysis. That Alfred Thayer Mahan's work, THE INFLUENCE OF SEAPOWER UPON HISTORY (375), is still to be recommended illustrates the paucity of attention by later scholars. Perhaps Mahan's prestige and dominance has discouraged others. Following up on Mahan, R.G. Albion (2) and more recently Craig Symonds (333) have analyzed the evolution of American naval thought, which was certainly shaped by the Napoleonic experience. Raoul Castex (56), clearly influenced by Mahan, focused his attention on the eighteenth century background. A more recent, excellent study of British naval tactical thinking that led into the Napoleonic Wars is by John Creswell (69), while Guiseppe Fioravanzo (99), an Italian admiral-scholar, has published one of the best overall analyses of naval thought with emphasis on application of historical experience to the modern era.

National naval histories are more inspired and certainly more voluminous, and the British foundation is naturally strongest, beginning with Edward Pelham Brenton's (42) two-volume appraisal of the period based on first-hand experience and the classic six-volume treatment by William James (154), while William Henry Fitchett's HOW ENGLAND SAVED EUROPE (101) also emphasizes the navy. The French have produced less and the general naval histories have been written by admirals rather than scholars, for example, La Roncière (173) and Gravière (124), with considerable national bias. The most useful and up-to-date account of French naval history is, not ironically, by an English scholar, Ernest Jenkins (157).

The naval histories of the smaller powers are difficult to find and of little use in discovering insights into the Napoleonic epoch. They are better investigated through specialized studies. The two theatre histories concerning the Baltic and the Levant by R.C. Anderson (9, 10) however, provide many details and valuable linkages for the backwaters of European naval warfare.

The Napoleonic navies were the culmination of a century of professional development. In fine examples of modern scholarship, several scholars have focused their attention on the eighteenth century. Geoffrey Marcus covers the whole "Georgian era" in HEART OF OAK (220), while José Navarro's work (242) on the Spanish navy in the eighteenth century is a model for others to follow. French

scholarship has produced more narrowly defined studies that benefit
from a background of the new social history. Jacques Aman (7) has
investigated the new class of officers while the sailors of the
revolution are the subject of Georges Bordonove (38).

Those publications that concentrate on the period will naturally
be of particular value to the Napoleonic scholar. Most of them,
however, were written from the perspective of one participant. That
is true of the well-known study by Mahan, THE INFLUENCE OF SEA POWER
UPON THE FRENCH REVOLUTION AND EMPIRE (213) and even more so of the
work of Chevalier (61). A more popular but equally nationalistic and
heroic account of the French seamen is by Paul Lecène (182). British
scholarship obviously is based on firmer foundations with ample
archival resources and easier historical justifications to be made
for the many achievements. Though still tending to glorify imperial
accomplishments, the more recent literature contains much criticism.
The most reliable and readable volumes are by Geoffrey Marcus (219)
and C. Northcote Parkinson (261). Theirs are two of the most
sophisticated and scholarly general works to be found in the whole
literature of the Napoleonic naval wars. Of equal distinction and
even greater depth of scholarly endeavor is Michael Lewis's social
history of the British navy (187). It largely supplants the more
general work on British seamen of John Masefield (226), Christopher
Lloyd (191), Peter Kemp (165), and Henry Baynham (20). Important
research has also been done by Lloyd and Coulter (200), supplemented
by Eunice Turner (349), on the medical service in the British navy.
Adding to these refreshing new looks at naval affairs are the studies
of recruitment policies: an older and less reliable one by
Hutchinson (150) and articles by Emsley (94), and McCord (228).
Stephen Gradish's fine study (120) of how the navy was manned during
the Seven Years' War has much application to the Napoleonic period.
Evelyn Berckman has provided a revealing account of attendant
services from tackle stores to prostitutes in THE HIDDEN NAVY (24).

Merchant trade and economic policy obviously deserve attention
as they influenced the ways in which fleets or individual ships were
used, for example in blockading or as privateers. For an
understanding of the Continental System (or Blockade) one must begin
with François Crouzet's detailed work (74), while Frank Melvin's
older volume (230) is still a standard source in English. Soviet
historians, Tarle (335) and Zlotnikov (369), are revealing,
especially on the System's economic and political effects on Russia.
While most sources, for example, Dunan (88), emphasize the dire
results of blockade on the coastal cities (which affect the navy), a
recent study by Geoffrey Ellis (93) demonstrates how French
provincial areas could benefit from the Continental System, at least
up to 1810.

The Continental System especially affected the Scandinavian
countries, and, in fact, shifted the focus of the naval war northward
from the Mediterranean to the North Sea and Baltic littoral. The
publications of Ole Feldbaek (97), Kirsten Heils (135), and J.N.
Tonnessen (346) are especially recommended. American trade in the
Baltic has attracted a number of scholars. Alfred W. Crosby, Jr.
(72), and Aage Rasch (291) have provided the best overviews, while
A.N. Ryan (303, 307), Kustaa Hautala (132), and Norman Saul (308)
have dealt with particular aspects of Baltic naval experiences. The
work of N.N. Bolkhovitinov (28) on Russian-American relations

contains interesting insights on naval affairs, especially on the background to the War of 1812.

The Mediterranean was an even more active naval arena because of Bonaparte's dramatic campaign across it and because of the interest of almost all powers, great and small, in the region. Besides the British and the French, the naval flags of several other states could be found in the Mediterranean. Even such fledgling naval powers as the United States and Russia would find the Mediterranean the scene of considerable action. The major works, however, treat naval action only peripherally, while concentrating on diplomatic, political, or even economic history. Piers Mackesy (211) has studied the period from 1803 to 1810 thoroughly from the British perspective, while Avgusta Stanislavskaia (325) and Norman Saul (309) have looked at the Mediterranean from the Russian side. Puryear (289), Pisani (274), and Rodocanachi (296) have focused on particular portions of dispersed Mediterranean conflict. The older work of Gardner Allen (5, 6) is still reliable on American activity in the area.

Extended sailing in distant seas could not have been possible without numbers and varieties of strong, capable ships, and in the first instance that meant a good supply of high quality wood. R.G. Albion's classic FORESTS AND SEA-POWER (1) is still the basic source, while Paul Bamford (14) has provided a more particular investigation of French timber problems. Behind every warship was a fleet of merchant ships. Ralph Davis (75) and David MacGregor (205) have written excellent studies of the British shipping industry and the evolution in design of sailing ships. For research concentrating on the technology of warships, however, see James Henderson (136, 137) and C.N. Longridge (202). Brian Lavery (181) published an interesting account of the origin of the 74-gun ship, the basic Napoleonic warship, to cite only one of the many articles and notes in naval journals dealing with naval technology and armament. Visits to a good naval museum, for example, at Salem or Mystic Seaport in the U.S. or Greenwich and Portsmouth in England, and to a surviving or restored ship of the period, such as can be found at Baltimore (Constellation) and at Portsmouth, U.K. (Victory), should not be omitted.

Citations of general literature would not be complete without some mention of fiction. Perhaps the easiest way to absorb the atmosphere of naval warfare of the Napoleonic period is through the "Hornblower sagas" of C.S. Forester (104-107). And, of course, Thomas Hardy (130, 131) is a good source for the social mores of the period. Students are also fortunate to have the reflections of Parkinson (263, 264) to guide them through naval fiction.

BIBLIOGRAPHIES

Useful and convenient naval bibliographies are surprisingly sparse and inadequate. R.G. Albion's compilation of maritime history (4) is probably the best general listing of publications, but its three editions are dated and include only material published in English. Christopher Lloyd (195) has provided a good, basic list of sources on the British side in A GUIDE TO THE SOURCES OF BRITISH MILITARY HISTORY, and Oliver Warner (356) has surveyed the Nelson literature as of 1955. Ironically, the best and most complete national naval bibliography is that by Jean Polak for the French

(278). Other general bibliographies can, of course, be useful-- for example, the volume on the eighteenth century in the BIBLIOGRAPHY OF BRITISH HISTORY by Pargellis and Medley (260).

With a few exceptions bibliographies in monographs are also disappointing. Almost all include some list of references or notes but often in abbreviated and sometimes inaccurate form. The most useful are in the more "academic" publications of Marcus (219, 220) and Lewis (187). David Walder's (353) discussion of the materials on Nelson is also informative.

A very welcome addition to the few published research guides are the volumes describing the holdings of the National Maritime Museum, edited by R.J.B. Knight (168). Another useful reference is the annotated listing of British manuscript diaries of the nineteenth century, compiled by Batts (18). In most other cases researchers must consult general guides and unpublished catalogues and collection descriptions in the repositories.

ARCHIVAL SOURCES

Manuscript materials on the Napoleonic navies are especially rich, varied, and voluminous. First and foremost are the official naval records found in government archives. These consist of reports, journals, orders, proceedings, minutes, logbooks, inventories, etc., the most relevant single collection being that of the papers of the Admiralty in the Public Record Office in London. Despite the tremendous amount of research in these records, much new information is still likely to be found. Occasionally an obscure logbook can provide an essential detail or comment on an important action. Naval historians have probably been most negligent, however, in ferreting out naval materials from ancillary government documents, such as those relating to diplomacy and consular activities, commerce, finance, and ministerial or department decisions.

Because of the sense of importance attached to the events and the times, many of the participants recorded--in diaries, letters, and journals--their impressions. These are available to the researcher in a variety of places, ranging from obscure local historical societies to the British Library. Lacking a systematic overall guide, the student will have to start with the key collections such as are in the British Library and at the National Maritime Museum, and then by using previous publications as a foundation, and with imagination, locate other sources. Unfortunately, much has been lost over time and more remains buried in private hands, is uncatalogued and unnoticed, or is difficult of access as in the case of Russian records. In final analysis experienced archivists and previous researchers are the best guides.

PUBLISHED DOCUMENTS

The student of the British side of the naval war has the advantage of a large quantity of relevant documents in published form, thanks in particular to the Navy Records Society. These consist mainly of the papers--letters, dispatches, journals, diaries, etc.--of the important British naval leaders of the period and are expertly edited by scholars such as Bonner-Smith, Lloyd, Naish, Corbett, and others. A few of these collections were preceded by

pioneering work of nineteenth century compilers, such as Nicholas
Harris Nicolas, whose DISPATCHES AND LETTERS OF VICE ADMIRAL LORD
VISCOUNT NELSON (252) is still a basic source for anything relating
to that great hero. As with Napoleon, we are close to having every
surviving word written by Nelson in published form. Later editions
of Nelsoniana   are in the form of reconstructed memoirs (246),
letters to his wife (238), to Lady Hamilton (245), or in different
and augmented selections (177, 243, 244, 248).

Other important British admirals have not been neglected and are
perhaps even better served by editors, who have successfully managed
on the whole to overcome problems of readability and reliability. In
rough order of importance they are: Collingwood (250, 149), Keith
(199), St. Vincent (33), Spencer (67), Barham (178), Saumarez (306),
Fremantle (378), Sidney Smith (15), and Barrington (32). Other
document volumes contain materials such as logbooks on battles (153)
and blockades (189). Though these materials are certainly useful to
the researcher, they were edited in most cases many years ago and may
represent only a portion of what is now available in archives.

Much less can be found in convenient published form on the
French side. The great edition of Napoleon's correspondence must, of
course, be used, even though the communications with his Ministry of
Navy have been collected in one volume (68). Much of the
correspondence of Admiral Villeneuve is published as an appendix by
Gravière (124); other documents are quoted or cited in Desbrière
(79-81) and Thomazi (341-343).

Published documentation for lesser participants in naval action
varies considerably in completeness and availability. Materials on
American involvement in the Mediterranean are readily available (169,
239, 240). Publications on Russian activity in that area are also
plentiful but not as well known. For example, Admiral Ushakov's
1798-1801 campaign in the Mediterranean is covered in three volumes,
edited by R.N. Mordvinov (234), while a series of letters of a
Russian officer, written between 1806 and 1809, pertains to a later
phase of Russian naval activity (259).

Many important documents on the naval war are found in other
sources, especially those dealing with the diplomatic record. Almost
all statesmen, ministers, and even generals had to pay some attention
to the sea, and this opens up a huge quantity of published material
for the naval historian.

MEMOIRS, JOURNALS, AND EYEWITNESS ACCOUNTS

Victory at sea stimulated more retrospective accounts than
defeat. Consequently a number of British officers and seamen
recorded their views for posterity. Some of these were written many
years after the events and thus were subject to erosion from the
passage of time or influenced by other literature. Journals that
were kept more or less on a day-to-day basis could also have been
amended and amplified in process (as opposed to most letters and
reports) or upon later publication. They can, therefore, be
considered in the category of memoirs. All such "eyewitness
accounts" should be used with caution and checked with other sources.

The early publications by seaman John Nicol (251), officer
Jeffrey Raigersfeld (290), Frederick Chamier (58), Samuel Leech
(183), William Hoste (143), and Dundonald (89), whose careers spanned

much of the naval activity, are still important for the day-to-day
life in the British navy. The most important of the memoirs
appearing posthumously and that are augmented by scholarly annotation
are by James Trevenen (201), John Harvey Boteler (36), William Henry
Dillon (82), James Gardiner (118), "Landsman" Hay (133), and
Lieutenant Parsons (268). Also of interest are the memoirs of Vice
Admiral Lovell (204), Admiral Symonds (314), and Admiral James (176).
Burrows (53) edited the reflections of an anonymous naval officer,
while Thursfield (344) collected five naval journals of the period.
Two Russian memoirs that should be mentioned are by Svin'in (332) and
Bronevskii (49).

SPECIALIZED WORKS

One of the main approaches to naval history, regrettable as it
may be, has been through biography, chiefly of the one central
character of the drama on the British side--Nelson. Starting with
Robert Southey's compendium of the life of Nelson (320) the
biographical treatments maintain a popular and heroic course from
Browne (51) to Forester (109). The best among them are by Mahan
(214) and Naish (237). The first really scholarly investigation was
that by Carola Oman [Lenanton] (257), now surpassed by David Walder
(353) and Geoffrey Bennett (21), both of which are highly
recommended. On a slightly more popular level are the excellent
books by Tom Pocock (275-277), Peter Padfield (258), and Dudley Pope
(284). Nelson's romantic and other Neapolitan involvements are
natural subjects for investigation, the most colorful being that by
Jack Russell (302). Edinger and Neep (92) give a typical French
view, based unavoidably on English sources.
Next on the list of naval biographical study has been the
officers around Nelson, "the band of brothers" as they were known.
Ludovic Kennedy's book (167) by that title is probably the best
general treatment, while older works by John Knox Laughton (180),
A.M. Broadley (45, 47), and W.H. Fitchett (102) are still useful.
Tom Pocock's study of Hoste (276) is another valuable addition to the
Nelson perspectives.
The other major figures on the British side have, unfortunately,
received much less investigation and exposure. Some are best
approached through the introductions and annotations to their papers.
St. Vincent has two biographies, the one by Brenton (41) being an
early "personal" account, while Berckman's (25) is a professional and
scholarly study. John Barrow also delivered "first-hand" biographies
of Sidney Smith (15) and Lord Howe (16), and was the subject of a
more recent investigation (193), which also provides a valuable
insight into the working of the Admiralty. Several other British
admirals have had at least one biographical study: Collingwood
(355), Parker (273), Cochrane (192, 340), Hood (140), Pellow (262),
and Cornwallis (366). Little has been done on the lower ranks except
for revealing studies of surgeons with the fleet by Gray (125), Pugh
(288), and Watson (363). Shorter and sometimes inaccurate sketches
are found in the early naval biographical encyclopedias compiled by
Robert Southey (319), John Marshall (224), and for the French,
Georges Six (315). The Russians have also glorified their naval
accomplishments in biographical form, the best being the study of
Admiral Seniavin by Shapiro (313).

Another popular approach to naval history is through the study of a particular battle or event. As Nelson dominates biography, his great victories at Trafalgar and at the mouth of the Nile have virtually monopolized the battle literature. The accounts of Trafalgar, mainly from the British side, range from the detailed, technical studies by Mahan (212) and Corbett (66) to the broader and more readable surveys by Dudley Pope (281) and Oliver Warner (361). The classic French account is by Desbrière (80), which is available in an edited translation by Eastwick (91), while Thomazi (343) and Maine (216) have made briefer studies.

The Glorious First of June, 1794, or Battle of the Nile in 1798 are well served by Oliver Warner (354) and Christopher Lloyd (196). Alan Moorehead (232) and J. Christopher Herold (138) provide a broader picture of Napoleon's expedition to Egypt. There are several French accounts highlighting the expedition, the chief being those of Douin (83, 84, 86), Charles-Roux (59), and Thiry (339). The perhaps equally important battles of St. Vincent and Camperdown are covered in the general histories and more specifically by Lloyd (197).

The attempted and threatened invasions of the British Isles are the subject of several investigations. E.H.S. Jones (161, 162) deals with those of 1797. While Desbrière (81) details the preparations for the attack, Broadley and Rose (46) describe the defense of the islands. The British counterattacks at Copenhagen are expertly reviewed by Pope (283) and Ryan (305).

More distant theatres of action were of considerable importance in consolidating British naval supremacy. While the West Indies (95, 158, 329) and South America (19, 121) have received somewhat spotty coverage, C.N. Parkinson has given the Pacific the full treatment (265-267). In these and in European and Mediterranean waters, privateering and piracy were especially pronounced during the Napoleonic Wars. Douin (85) and Dearden (78) describe these activities in the Mediterranean, the latter being an especially refreshing view of the "Barbary pirates." There are several studies of privateering out of particular ports (for example, see 152, 286, 345), but probably the best general treatment is by Donald MacIntyre (207).

One other topic of importance might be considered as an "operation", and that is mutiny. The British navy was especially prone to disturbance early in the war. The most famous one began at Spithead early in 1797 and spread to other ships and bases. Conrad Gill (119) wrote the first serious study of this affair, but this should be supplemented by the modern views of Manwaring and Dobrée (217) and Patterson (269). Informative accounts of individual ship mutinies have been written by F.D. Spinney (321-323), Christopher Lloyd (194), and Dudley Pope (280).

In the final analysis, of course, navies do depend upon land-based foundations and support. Studies of these topics are rarer, perhaps because they are "unexciting" and less marketable. Interest in institutional and regional history has, nevertheless, resulted in some excellent recent investigations of British dockyards (377) and French port areas (371). T.W. Holmes (372) has also provided a brief but welcome volume concerning land-based communications.

PERIODICALS

MARINER'S MIRROR (221) is clearly the most important periodical to cover the subject of Napoleonic naval warfare. Under expert editorship for so many years this publication contains not only a large number of first-class articles, but also many interesting notes, observations, and reviews. The French LA REVUE MARITIME (172) is oriented toward more contemporary subjects but occasionally contains historical articles on the period. It too is good for reviews, and notes. The American counterpart to MARINER'S MIRROR is the AMERICAN NEPTUNE (8), but the focus is naturally on U.S. naval history. It contains a number of articles, especially dealing with the War of 1812. THE NAVAL WAR COLLEGE REVIEW (241) and UNITED STATES NAVAL INSTITUTE PROCEEDINGS, with its valuable cumulative index, (351) are both oriented toward recent naval developments but include an occasional article on retrospective events. Relevant articles may, of course, be found in a wide variety of historical journals, published throughout the world.

FUTURE RESEARCH

The main weakness in the research and publication on the naval war is that it is mostly one-dimensional. Very little effort has been made to compare the various navies, for example, in recruiting practices, victualling, training, shipbuilding, etc. The relations between the officers and men of allied fleets needs more investigation. The considerable work on the British fleet activities in the Mediterranean, with a few exceptions, ignores the existence of the Russian fleet, which was certainly not true of Nelson and other commanders at the time. Unfamiliarity or lack of language competence is a real problem in much of this literature.

Archival material is still available that can add to our knowledge of the Napoleonic period. Naval records of "smaller" participants such as the Kingdom of Naples and Sweden remain virtually untouched by researchers writing in English. There are vast manuscript collections in the naval archives of Portugal and Spain that would shed new light on the role of their naval forces. Extensive collections of correspondence of the various British squadron-commanders, rich in details of operations and personalities, are available for the future naval historian. Indications are that even Soviet materials may be accessible for certain, defined aspects of the period, but there is much more published on the Russian side than most scholars have realized. Future research can be expected along the lines of social and economic history. We need more biographies of ordinary seamen. If sources remain a problem, at least the history of an ordinary warship could be told, such as has been done for the Bellerophon (271) and Victory (365).

The surprising thing is that there is not yet a single, comprehensive history of the Napoleonic naval war. Surely, a foundation now exists in the various published documents and perspectives of participants. One would expect a British scholar such as Marcus or Lewis to tackle this admittedly difficult task of bringing together all of the national and international perspectives of the time. We might find, however, that Soviet historians, propelled by a renewed national interest in seapower, would be there first. Even more astonishing is that on the British side, where published materials abound, there is nothing to compare with C.J. Bartlett's GREAT BRITAIN AND SEA POWER, 1815-1853 (370) for this period in integrating naval activity with government and society, technological and economic change.

BIBLIOGRAPHY: THE NAVAL WAR

1. Albion, Robert Greenhalgh. FORESTS AND SEA-POWER. Cambridge, Mass.: Harvard University Press, 1926.

2. Albion, Robert Greenhalgh. THE MAKERS OF NAVAL POLICY, 1798-1947. Annapolis, Md.: Naval Institute Press, 1980.

3. Albion, Robert Greenhalgh. MARITIME ADVENTURES OF NEW YORK IN THE NAPOLEONIC ERA. Cambridge, Mass.: Harvard University Press, 1941.

4. Albion, Robert Greenhalgh. NAVAL AND MARITIME HISTORY. Mystic, Conn.: Marine Historical Association, 1955. 3d ed., rev. expanded, 1973.

5. Allen, Gardner Weld. OUR NAVAL WAR WITH FRANCE. Boston and New York: Houghton Mifflin, 1909.

6. Allen, Gardner Weld. OUR NAVY AND THE BARBARY CORSAIRS. Boston: Houghton Mifflin, 1905.

7. Aman, Jacques. LES OFFICERS BLEUS DANS LA MARINE FRANCAISE AU XVIIIe SIECLE. Geneva: Droz, 1976.

8. AMERICAN NEPTUNE. 1941 to present.

9. Anderson, R.C. NAVAL WARS IN THE BALTIC DURING THE SAILING SHIP EPOCH. London: Gilbert Wood, 1910. Reprinted as: NAVAL WARS IN THE BALTIC, 1522-1850. London: Francis Edwards, 1969.

10. Anderson, R.C. NAVAL WARS IN THE LEVANT, 1559-1853. Princeton: Princeton University Press, 1952.

11. Arkas, Z. "Deistviia Chernomorskago Flota s 1798 po 1806 g." [Activities of the Black Sea Fleet from 1798 to 1806]. ZAPISKI ODESSKAGO OBSHCHESTVA ISTORII I DREVNOSTEI 5 (1893): 846-905.

12. Auzoux, André. "Au secours de l'armée d'Egypt; Ganteaume et son escadre à Derne (1801)." LA REVUE DU XIXe SIECLE 11 (1926): 81-100.

13. Auzoux, André. "La mission de l'amiral Leisseques à Alger et à Tunis." REVUE DES ETUDES NAPOLIENIENNES 13 (1918): 65-95.

14. Bamford, Paul Walden. FORESTS AND FRENCH SEA POWER, 1660-1789. Toronto: Toronto University Press, 1956.

15. Barrow, John. LIFE AND CORRESPONDENCE OF ADMIRAL SIR WILLIAM SIDNEY SMITH. London: Bentley, 1848.

16. Barrow, John. LIFE OF RICHARD, EARL HOWE.... London: J. Murray, 1838.

17. Bartenev, Petr, ed. "Iz Putevykh Zapisok Moriaka Nikolaia Korostovtsa" [From the Travel Notes of Sailor Nikolai Korostovets]. RUSSKII ARKHIV (1905): 43-69, 201-36, 444-86.

18. Batts, John Stuart. BRITISH MANUSCRIPT DIARIES OF THE NINETEENTH CENTURY: AN ANNOTATED LISTING. Totowa, N.J.: Rowman and Littlefield, 1976.

19. Bauss, Rudy. "Rio de Janeiro, Strategic Base for Global Designs of the British Navy, 1777-1815." NEW ASPECTS OF NAVAL HISTORY. Edited by Craig L. Symonds, et al. Annapolis: Naval Institute Press, 1981.

20. Baynham, Henry. FROM THE LOWER DECK: THE OLD NAVY, 1780-1840. London: Hutchinson, 1969.

21. Bennett, Geoffrey. NELSON THE COMMANDER. London: Batsford, 1972.

22. Benoist-Michin, Jacques Gabriel Paul Michel. BONAPARTE EN EGYPTE OU LE REVE INASSOUVI (1797-1801). Paris: Perrin, 1978.

23. Berckman, Evelyn. CREATORS AND DESTROYERS OF THE ENGLISH NAVY. London: Hamilton, 1974.

24. Berckman, Evelyn. THE HIDDEN NAVY. London: Hamilton, 1973.

25. Berckman, Evelyn. NELSON'S DEAR LORD--A PORTRAIT OF ST. VINCENT. London: Macmillan, 1962.

26. Bethune, Colonel John Drinkwater. A NARRATIVE OF THE BATTLE OF ST. VINCENT. East Dulwich: Conway Maritime Press, 1969.

27. Beutlich, Frederik. NORGES SJOVAEBNING, 1750-1809. Oslo: H. Aschehoug, 1935.

28. Bolkhovitinov, Nikolai N. THE BEGINNINGS OF RUSSIAN-AMERICAN RELATIONS, 1775-1815. Cambridge, Mass.: Harvard University Press, 1975.

29. Bond, Gordon C. THE GRAND EXPEDITION: THE BRITISH INVASION OF HOLLAND IN 1809. Athens: University of Georgia Press, 1979.

30. Bonnel, Ulane. LA FRANCE, LES ETATS UNIS ET LA GUERRE DE COURSE (1797-1815). Paris: Nouvelle Editions Latines, 1961.

31. Bonner-Smith, David. "The Avenger of Nelson." MARINER'S MIRROR 22 (1936): 470-74.

32. Bonner-Smith, David, ed. THE BARRINGTON PAPERS, SELECTED FROM THE LETTERS AND PAPERS OF ADMIRAL THE HON. SAMUEL BARRINGTON. London: Navy Records Society, 1941. Vol. 81.

33. Bonner-Smith, David, ed. LETTERS OF ADMIRAL OF THE FLEET THE EARL OF ST. VINCENT, 1801-1804. London: Navy Records Society, 1921-26. Vols. 55, 61.

34. Bonner-Smith, David. "Midshipman W.G. Anderson." MARINER'S MIRROR 15 (1929): 238-50.

35. Bonner-Smith, David. "The Naval Mutinies of 1797." MARINER'S MIRROR 21 (1935): 428-29; 22 (1936): 65-86.

36. Bonner-Smith, David, ed. RECOLLECTIONS OF MY SEA LIFE FROM 1808 TO 1830, BY CAPTAIN JOHN HARVEY BOTELER, R.N. London: Navy Records Society, 1942. Vol. 82.

37. Boppe, August. L'ALBANIE ET NAPOLEON, 1797-1814. Paris: Hachette, 1914.

38. Bordonove, Georges. LES MARINS DE L'AN II. Paris: Robert Lafont, 1974.

39. Bosanquet, Captain H.T.A. "Lord Nelson and the Loss of His Arm." MARINER'S MIRROR 38 (1952): 184-94.

40. Breihan, John R. "The Addington Party and the Navy in British Politics, 1801-1806." NEW ASPECTS OF NAVAL HISTORY. Edited by Craig L. Lymonds, et al. Annapolis: Naval Institute Press, 1981.

41. Brenton, Edward Pelham. A LIFE OF LORD ST. VINCENT. London: Colburn, 1838.

42. Brenton, Edward Pelham. THE NAVAL HISTORY OF GREAT BRITAIN, FROM THE YEAR 1782 TO 1822. London: Colburn, 1837 (new edition). 2 vols.

43. Brindley, H.H. "French Junior Naval Officers of the Great Wars." MARINER'S MIRROR 18 (1932): 125-37.

44. Britton, C.J. NEW CHRONICLES OF THE LIFE OF LORD NELSON. Birmingham, Eng.: Cornish, 1946.

45. Broadley, Alexander Meyrick. THREE DORSET CAPTAINS AT TRAFALGAR. London: J. Murray, 1908.

46. Broadley, Alexander Meyrick, and J. Holland Rose. DUMOURIEZ AND THE DEFENSE OF ENGLAND AGAISNT NAPOLEON. New York: J. Lane, 1909.

47. Broadley, Alexander Meyrick, and R.G. Bartelot. NELSON'S HARDY; HIS LIFE, LETTERS AND FRIENDS. London: J. Murray, 1909.

48. Brock, P.W. "Lord Cochrane's Secret Plans." MARINER'S MIRROR, 16 (1930): 157-67.

49. Bronevskii, Vladimir. PIS'MA MORSKAGO OFITSERA [Letters of a Naval Officer]. Moscow: Semen Selevanovskii, 1825. 4 vols.

50. Brown, Lucy M., and Ian R. Christie. BIBLIOGRAPHY OF BRITISH HISTORY, 1798-1851. Oxford: Clarendon Press, 1977.

51. Browne, E. Lathom. NELSON, HIS PUBLIC AND PRIVATE LIFE. London: J. and Fisher Unwin, 1891.

52. Bryant, Arthur. YEARS OF VICTORY, 1802-1812. London: Collins, 1944.

53. Burrows, Harold, ed. PERILOUS ADVENTURES AND VICISSITUDES OF A NAVAL OFFICER, 1801-1812. Edinburgh and London: Blackwood, 1927.

54. Capes, Renalt. POSEIDON: A PERSONAL STUDY OF ADMIRAL NELSON. London: Sidgwick of Jackson, 1947.

55. Carlan, J.M. NAVIOS EN SECUESTRO: LA ESCUADRA ESPANOLA DEL OCEANO EN BREST, 1799-1802. Madrid: Instituto Historico de Marina, 1951.

56. Castex, Raoul Victor Patrice. LES IDEES MILITAIRES DE LA MARIEN DU XVIIIe SIECLE. Paris: Fournier, 1911.

57. Chamier, Frederick. BEN BRACE, THE LAST OF NELSON'S AGAMEMNONS. London: Bentley, 1836.

58. Chamier, Frederick. THE LIFE OF A SAILOR. London: Bentley, 1833. 3 vols.

59. Charles-Roux, François. LES ORIGINES DE L'EXPEDITION D'EGYPTE. Paris: Plon, 1910.

60. Charliat, Pierre Jacques. TROIS SIECLES D'ECONOMIC MARITIME FRANCAISE. Paris: Marcel Riviera, 1931.

61. Chevalier, Louis Edward. HISTOIRE DE LA MARINE FRANCAISE SOUS LE CONSULAT ET L'EMPIRE. Paris: Hachette, 1886.

62. Chichagov, Admiral P.V. MEMOIRES. Edited by C.G. Lahovary. Leipzig: A. Franck, 1862.

63. Chisholm, Henry. "Nelson at Porto Argo." MARINER'S MIRROR 5 (1979): 269-75.

64. CHRONIQUE D'HISTOIRE MARITIME. Feb. 1980 to present.

65. Coletta, Paolo E., comp. A BIBLIOGRAPHY OF AMERICAN NAVAL HISTORY. Annapolis: Naval Institute Press, 1981.

66. Corbett, Julian. THE CAMPAIGN OF TRAFALGAR. London and New York: Longmans, Green, 1919. 2 vols.

67. Corbett, Julian, and Herbert W. Richmond, eds. PRIVATE PAPERS OF GEORGE SECOND EARL SPENCER, FIRST LORD OF ADMIRAL, 1794-1801. London: Navy Records Society, 1913-1914, 1924. Vols. 46, 48, 58, 59.

68. CORRESPONDANCE DE NAPOLEON AVEC LE MINISTRE DE LA MARINE DEPUIS 1804 JUSQU'EN AVRIL 1815: EXTRAITE D'AN PORTEFEUILLE DE SAINTE-HELENE. Paris: Delloye et V. Lecou, 1837. 2 vols.

69. Creswell, John. BRITISH ADMIRALS OF THE EIGHTEENTH CENTURY: TACTICS IN BATTLE. London: George Unwin, 1972.

70. Crimmin, P.K. "Admiralty Relations with the Treasury, 1783-1806: The Preparations of Naval Estimates and the Beginnings of Treasury Control." MARINER'S MIRROR 53 (1967): 63-74.

71. Crimmin, P.K. "George Canning and the Battle of Camperdown." MARINER'S MIRROR 67 (1981): 319-25.

72. Crosby, Alfred W., Jr. AMERICA, RUSSIA, HEMP, AND NAPOLEON; AMERICA'S TRADE WITH RUSSIA AND THE BALTIC, 1783-1812. Columbus: Ohio State University Press, 1965.

73. Crosby, Alfred W., Jr. "American Trade with Mauritius in the Age of the French Revolution and Napoleon." AMERICAN NEPTUNE 25 (1965): 5-17.

74. Crouzet, François. L'ECONOMIE BRITANNIQUE ET LE BLOCUS CONTINENTAL (1806-1813). Paris: Presses Universitaires de France, 1958. 2 vols.

75. Davis, Ralph. THE RISE OF THE ENGLISH SHIPPING INDUSTRY IN THE SEVENTEENTH AND EIGHTEENTH CENTURIES. London: Macmillan, 1962.

76. Dawson, Warren R. THE NELSON COLLECTION AT LLOYD'S: A DESCRIPTION OF THE NELSON RELICS AND A TRANSCRIPT OF THE AUTOGRAPH LETTERS AND DOCUMENTS OF NELSON AND HIS CIRCLE AND OF OTHER NAVAL PAPERS OF NELSON'S PERIOD. London: Macmillan, 1932.

77. Day, Archibald. THE ADMIRALTY HYDROGRAPHIC SERVICE. London: H.M.S.O., 1967.

78. Dearden, Seton. A NEST OF CORSAIRS: THE FIGHTING KARAMANLIS OF TRIPOLI. London: J. Murray, 1976.

79. Desbrière, Edouard. LE BLOCUS DE BREST DE 1793 A 1805. Paris: Chapelot, 1902.

80. Desbrière, Edouard. LA CAMPAGNE MARITIME DE 1805: TRAFALGAR. Paris: Chapelot, 1907.

81. Desbrière, Edouard. 1793-1805: PROJETS ET TENTATIVES DE
    DEBARQUEMENT AUX ILES BRITANNIQUES. Paris: Chapelot, 1900-02.
    4 vols. in 5.

82. Dillon, William Henry. A NARRATIVE OF MY PROFESSIONAL
    ADVENTURES (1790-1839). Ed. by Michael A. Lewis. London:
    Navy Records Society, 1953, 1956. Vols. 93, 97.

83. Douin, Georges. LA CAMPAGNE DE BRUIX EN MEDITERRANEE,
    MARS-AOUT 1799. Paris: Société d'éditions géographiques,
    maritimes et coloniales, 1923.

84. Douin, Georges. LA FLOTTE DE BONAPARTE SUR LES COTES D'EGYPTE;
    LES PRODROMES D'ABOUKIR. Cairo: Institut française
    d'archéologie orientale, 1922.

85. Douin, Georges. LA MEDITERRANEE DE 1803 A 1805: PIRATES ET
    CORSAIRES AUX ILES IONIENNES. Paris: Plon, 1917.

86. Douin, Georges, and E.C. Fawtier-Jones. L'ANGLETERRE ET
    L'EGYPTE; LA POLITIQUE MAMELUKE. Cairo: Institut français
    d'archeologie orientale du Caire, 1929.

87. Dugan, James. THE GREAT MUTINY. New York: Putman, 1965.

88. Dunan, Marcel. "Napoléon et le Systeme Continental en 1810."
    REVUE D'HISTOIRE DIPLOMATIQUE 60 (1946): 71-98.

89. Dundonald, Thomas Cochran, earl. AUTOBIOGRAPHY OF A SEAMAN.
    London: Bentley, 1861.

90. Duro, Captain D. Cesareo Fernandez. LA ARMADA ESPANOLA DESDE
    LA UNION DE LOS REINOS DE CASTILLA Y DE LEON. Madrid: n.p.,
    1889-90. 9 vols.

91. Eastwick, Constance, ed. and trans. THE NAVAL CAMPAIGN OF
    1805: TRAFALGAR. Oxford: Clarendon Press, 1933.

92. Edinger, George, and E.J.C. Neep. NELSON. Paris: Payot,
    1931.

93. Ellis, Geoffrey. NAPOLEON'S CONTINENTAL BLOCKADE: THE CASE OF
    ALSACE. (Oxford Historical Monographs). New York: Clarendon
    Press of Oxford University, 1981.

94. Emsley, Clive. "The Recruitment of Petty Offenders during the
    French Wars, 1793-1815." MARINER'S MIRROR 66 (1980): 199-209.

95. D'Enguin, Ledeuil. "La Dernier Phase de l'expédition de
    Saint-Domingue." REVUE DES ETUDES NAPOLEONIENNES 12 (1917):
    287-99.

96. Farrère, Claude. HISTOIRE DE LA MARINE FRANCAISE. Paris:
    Flammarion, 1934.

97. Feldbaek, Ole. DENMARK AND THE ARMED NEUTRALITY, 1800-1801:
     SMALL POWER POLICY IN A WORLD WAR. Translated by Jean
     Lundskaer-Nielsen. (Kobenhavns Universitet Institut for
     Okonomisk Historie, number 16.) Copenhagen: Akademisk Forlag,
     1980.

98. Field, Earle. "Neutral Trade and Order in Council of 1 January
     1807." AMERICAN NEPTUNE 23 (1963): 157-73.

99. Fioravanzo, Guiseppe. A HISTORY OF NAVAL TACTICAL THOUGHT.
     Translated by Arthur W. Holst. Annapolis, Md.: U.S. Naval
     Institute, 1979. Original Italian edition, 1956.

100. Fitchett, William Henry. THE COMMANDER OF THE "HIRONDELLE".
     London: Smith, Elder, 1904.

101. Fitchett, William Henry. HOW ENGLAND SAVED EUROPE: THE STORY
     OF THE GREAT WAR, 1793-1815. New York: Scribner, 1899-1900.
     4 vols.

102. Fitchett, William Henry. NELSON AND HIS CAPTAINS. London:
     Smith, Elder, 1902.

103. Forbes, John D. "Boston Smuggling, 1807-1815." AMERICAN
     NEPTUNE 10 (1950): 144-54.

104. Forester, Cecil Scott. CAPTAIN HORNBLOWER. London: Michael
     Joseph, 1955.

105. Forester, Cecil Scott. DEATH TO THE FRENCH. London: J. Lane,
     1947.

106. Forester, Cecil Scott. FLYING COLORS. London: Michael
     Joseph, 1951.

107. Forester, Cecil Scott. THE GUN. Boston: Little, Brown, 1933.

108. Forester, Cecil Scott. THE NAVAL WAR OF 1812. London:
     Michael Joseph, 1957.

109. Forester, Cecil Scott. NELSON: A BIOGRAPHY. London: J.
     Lane, 1952.

110. Forester, Cecil Scott. SHIP OF THE LINE. Boston: Little,
     Brown, 1938.

111. Fraser, Edward. CHAMPIONS OF THE FLEET, CAPTAINS AND
     MEN-OF-WAR AND DAYS THAT HELPED TO MAKE THE EMPIRE. London and
     New York: J. Lane, 1908.

112. Fraser, Edward. THE ENEMY AT TRAFALGAR. London: Hodder and
     Stoughton, 1906.

113. Fraser, Edward. JACK CHALONER, OR WHEN EVERY MAN CAME FORWARD
     TO DO HIS DUTY TO THE COUNTRY. London: Hutchinson, 1911.

114. Fraser, Edward.   "The   Journal   of   Commander   Thomas   Colby,
     R.N.--1794-1815." MARINER'S MIRROR 13 (1927): 295-71.

115. Fraser, Edward. NAPOLEON THE GAOLER: PERSONAL EXPERIENCES AND
     ADVENTURES OF BRITISH SAILORS AND SOLDIERS DURING THE GREAT
     CAPTIVITY. London: Methuen, 1919.

116. Fraser, Edward. THE SAILORS WHOM NELSON LED: THEIR DOINGS
     DESCRIBED BY THEMSELVES. London: Methuen, 1913.

117. Fugier, André. NAPOLEON ET L'ITALIE. Paris: Janin, 1947.

118. Gardiner, James Anthony. ABOVE AND UNDER HATCHES; BEING NAVAL
     RECOLLECTIONS IN SHREDS AND PATCHES WITH STRANGE REFLECTIONS.
     Edited by C. Lloyd. n.p., 1955.

119. Gill, Conrad.   THE NAVAL MUTINIES OF 1797.   Manchester:
     University Press, 1913.

120. Gradish, Stephen F. THE MANNING OF THE BRITISH NAVY DURING THE
     SEVEN YEARS' WAR. London: The Royal Historical Society, 1980.
     Vol. 21.

121. Graham, Gerald Sandford, ed.   THE NAVY AND SOUTH AMERICA,
     1807-1923. London: Navy Records Society, 1962.

122. Graham, Gerald Sandford, ed. THE POLITICS OF NAVAL SUPREMACY:
     STUDIES IN BRITISH MARITIME ASSENDANCY. Cambridge: Cambridge
     University Press, 1965.

123. Graham, Gerald Sandford. SEA POWER AND BRITISH NORTH AMERICA,
     1783-1820: A STUDY IN BRITISH COLONIAL POLICY.   Cambridge,
     Mass.: Harvard University Press, 1941.

124. Gravière, Jean Pierre Edmond Jurien de la. GUERRE MARITIMES.
     Paris: Charpentier, 1906. 2 vols.

125. Gray, Ernest Alfred, ed. MAN MIDWIFE. THE FURTHER EXPERIENCES
     OF JOHN KNYVETOR, M.D., LATE SURGEON IN THE BRITISH FLEET
     DURING THE YEARS 1793-1809. London: Robert Hale, 1946.

126. Grenfell, Captain Russell, R.N.   HORATIO NELSON: A SHORT
     BIOGRAPHY. London: Faber and Faber, 1955.

127. Gruppe, Henry E. THE FRIGATES. Amsterdam: Time-Life Books,
     1981.

128. Gutteridge, H.C., ed.   NELSON AND THE NEAPOLITAN JACOBINS.
     London: Navy Records Society, 1903. Vol. 28.

129. Hamilton, R. Vesey, and John Knox Laughton. RECOLLECTIONS OF
     JAMES ANTHONY GARDNER COMMANDER R.N., 1775-1814. London: Navy
     Records Society, 1906. Vol. 31.

130. Hardy, Thomas. THE DYNASTS, AN EPIC-DRAMA OF THE WAR WITH NAPOLEON. New York and London: Harper, 1904. 3 vols.

131. Hardy, Thomas. THE TRUMPET-MAJOR ... AND ROBERT HIS BROTHER, FIRST MATE IN THE MERCHANT SERVICE. London: Macmillan, 1975.

132. Hautala, Kustaa. EUROPEAN AND AMERICAN TAR IN THE ENGLAND MARKET DURING THE EIGHTEENTH AND EARLY NINETEENTH CENTURIES. (Suomalainen tiedeakatemia, 130.) Helsinki: Suomalainen tiedeakatemia, 1963.

133. Hay, Robert. LANDSMAN HAY: THE MEMOIRS OF ROBERT HAY, 1789-1847. Edited by M.D. Hay. London: Hart-Davis, 1953.

134. Heath, Phoebe Anne. NAPOLEON I AND THE ORIGINS OF THE ANGLO-AMERICAN WAR OF 1812. Toulouse: Edward Prust, 1929.

135. Heils, Kirsten. LES RAPPORTS ECONOMIQUES FRANCO-DANOIS SOUS LE DIRECTOIRE, LE CONSULAT ET L'EMPIRE: CONTRIBUTION A L'ETUDE DU SYSTEME CONTINENTAL. Paris: Presses de la Cité, 1958.

136. Henderson, James. THE FRIGATES; AN ACCOUNT OF THE LESSER WARSHIPS OF THE WARS FROM 1793 TO 1815. New York: Dodd, Meade, 1971.

137. Henderson, James. SLOOPS AND BRIGS: AN ACCOUNT OF THE SMALLEST VESSELS OF THE ROYAL NAVY DURING THE GREAT WARS, 1793-1815. Annapolis: The Naval Institute Press, 1972.

138. Herold, J. Christopher. BONAPARTE IN EGYPT. New York, Evanston, and London: Harper & Row, 1962.

139. Higham, Robin D.S. "The Port of Boston and the Embargo of 1807-1809." AMERICAN NEPTUNE 16 (1956): 189-210.

140. Hood, Dorothy. THE ADMIRALS HOOD. London: Hutchinson, 1942.

141. Hornby, W.M. Phipps. "Letters Describing the Battle of Lissa, 1811." MARINER'S MIRROR 52 (1966): 193-98.

142. Horward, Donald D. "Portugal and the Anglo-Russian Naval Crisis (1808)." NAVAL WAR COLLEGE REVIEW 34 (1981): 43-73.

143. Hoste, William. MEMOIRS AND LETTERS OF CAPTAIN SIR WILLIAM HOSTE. London: Bentley, 1833.

144. Hoste, William. SERVICE AFLOAT, OR, THE NAVAL CAREER OF SIR WILLIAM HOSTE. London: W.H. Allen, 1887.

145. Howarth, David. "The Man who Lost Trafalgar." MARINER'S MIRROR 57 (1971): 361-70.

146. Howarth, David. SOVEREIGN OF THE SEAS: THE STORY OF BRITISH SEA POWER. London: Collins, 1974.

147. Howarth, David. TRAFALGAR, THE NELSON TOUCH. London: Collins, 1969; New York: Athaneum, 1969.

148. Hubback, J.H., and H.C. JANE AUSTEN'S SAILOR BROTHERS. London and New York: J. Lane, 1906.

149. Hughes, Edward, ed. THE PRIVATE CORRESPONDENCE OF ADMIRAL LORD COLLINGWOOD. London: Navy Records Society, 1957. Vol. 98.

150. Hutchinson, John Roberts. THE PRESS GANG AFLOAT AND ASHORE. London: E. Nash, 1913; New York: Dutton, 1914.

151. Il'inskii, V.P. ADMIRAL F.F. USHAKOV V SREDIZEMNOM MORE (1799-g.). St. Petersburg: Morskoi Sbornik, 1914.

152. Jackson, Melvin H. PRIVATEERS IN CHARLESTON, 1793-1796: AN ACCOUNT OF A FRENCH PALATINATE IN SOUTH CAROLINA. Washington: Smithsonian Institution Press, 1969.

153. Jackson, T. Sturges, ed. LOGS OF THE GREAT SEA FIGHTS, 1794-1805. London: Navy Records Society, 1899-1900. Vols. 16, 18.

154. James, William. NAVAL HISTORY OF GREAT BRITIAN (1793-1820). 1st edition, 1822. London: Macmillan, 1902. 6 vols.

155. James, Admiral William Milburne. THE DURABLE MONUMENT: HORATIO NELSON. London: Longmans, Green, 1948.

156. James, Admiral William Milburne. THE INFLUENCE OF SEA POWER ON THE HISTORY OF THE BRITISH PEOPLE. Cambridge: Cambridge University Press, 1948.

157. Jenkins, Ernest H. A HISTORY OF THE FRENCH NAVY: FROM ITS BEGINNINGS TO THE PRESENT DAY. London: MacDonald & Janes, 1973.

158. Jenkins, H.J.K. "The Action at Anse la Barque, Guadeloupe: 18 December 1809." MARINER'S MIRROR 61 (1975): 173-79.

159. Jenkins, H.J.K. "The Capture of H.M.S. Junon, 1809." MARINER'S MIRROR 60 (1974): 33-39.

160. Jenkins, H.J.K. "The Heyday of French Privateering from Guadeloupe, 1796-98." MARINER'S MIRROR 64 (1978): 245-56.

161. Jones, Edwyn Henry Stuart. AN INVASION THAT FAILED. Oxford: Blackwell, 1950.

162. Jones, Edwyn Henry Stuart. THE LAST INVASION OF BRITAIN. Cardiff: University of Wales Press, 1950.

163. Jouvenel, Bertrand de. NAPOLEON ET L'ECONOMIE DIRIGEE: LE BLOCUS CONTINENTAL. Brussels: Les éditions de la Toison d'or, 1942.

164. Keate, Edith Murray. NELSON'S WIFE: THE FIRST BIOGRAPHY OF
     FRANCES HERBERT VISCOUNTESS NELSON. London: Cassell, 1939.

165. Kemp, Peter. THE BRITISH SAILOR: A SOCIAL HISTORY OF THE
     LOWER DECK. London: Dent, 1970.

166. Kemp, Peter. HISTORY OF THE ROYAL NAVY. London: Barker,
     1969.

167. Kennedy, Ludovic. NELSON'S BAND OF BROTHERS. London:
     Collins, 1975.

168. Knight, R.J.B., ed. GUIDE TO THE MANUSCRIPTS IN THE NATIONAL
     MARITIME MUSEUM. Vol. 1. PERSONAL COLLECTIONS. Vol. 2. PUBLIC
     RECORDS, BUSINESS RECORDS AND ARTIFICIAL COLLECTIONS. London:
     Mansell, 1977, 1980.

169. Knox, Captain Dudley W., ed. NAVAL DOCUMENTS RELATED TO THE
     UNITED STATES WARS WITH THE BARBARY POWERS. Vol. 3. NAVAL
     OPERATIONS, SEPT. 1803-MARCH 1804. Washington: Government
     Printing Office, 1941.

170. Kristof, John J. "The Royal Navy's Defeat of the French at Sea
     in the Years 1793-1815." NAVAL WAR COLLEGE REVIEW 26 (1973):
     41-45.

171. Lacour-Gayet, G. "La Traversée de la Mediterranée en 1798."
     REVUE DES ETUDES NAPOLEONIENNES 12 (1923): 5-27.

172. LA REVUE MARITIME. 1861 to present.

173. La Roncière, Charles Germain Marie Bouel de, and A.
     Clerc-Rampal. HISTORIE DE LA MARINE FRANCAISE. Paris:
     Larouse, 1934.

174. Laughton, John Knox. THE BARKER COLLECTION; MANUSCRIPTS OF AND
     RELATING TO ADMIRAL LORD NELSON. London: Chiswick Press: C.
     Whittingham, 1913.

175. Laughton, John Knox. FROM HOWARD TO NELSON: TWELVE SAILORS.
     London: Lawrence and Bullen, 1899.

176. Laughton, John Knox, ed. JOURNAL OF REAR-ADMIRAL BARTHOLOMEW
     JAMES, 1752-1828. London: Navy Records Society, 1896. Vol.
     6.

177. Laughton, John Knox, ed. LETTERS AND DESPATCHES OF HORATIO,
     VISCOUNT NELSON, K.B., DUKE OF BRONTE, VICE-ADMIRAL OF THE
     WHITE SQUADRON. London: Longmans, Green, 1886.

178. Laughton, John Knox, ed. LETTERS AND PAPERS OF CHARLES, LORD
     BARHAM, ADMIRAL OF THE RED SQUADRON, 1758-1813. London: Navy
     Records Society, 1906, 1910, 1911. Vols. 32, 38, 39.

179. Laughton, John Knox. NELSON. New York: Macmillan, 1904.

180. Laughton, John Knox. THE NELSON MEMORIAL: NELSON AND HIS COMPANIONS IN ARMS. London: George Allen, 1896.

181. Lavery, Brian. "The Origins of the 74-Gun Ship." MARINER'S MIRROR 63 (1977): 335-50.

182. Lecène, Paul. LES MARINS DE LA REPUBLIQUE ET DE L'EMPIRE, 1793-1815. Paris: Librairie Centrale, 1885.

183. Leech, Samuel. THIRTY YEARS FROM HOME OR A VOICE FROM THE MAIN DECK. Boston: Tappan, 1843.

184. Lees, James. THE MASTING AND RIGGING OF ENGLISH SHIPS OF WAR, 1625-1860. London: Conway Maritime Press, 1979.

185. Lewis, Michael A. ENGLAND'S SEA OFFICERS: THE STORY OF THE NAVAL PROFESSION. London: Allen & Unwin, 1939.

186. Lewis, Michael A. NAPOLEON AND HIS CAPTIVES. London: Allen & Unwin, 1962.

187. Lewis, Michael A. A SOCIAL HISTORY OF THE NAVY, 1793-1815. London: Allen & Unwin, 1961.

188. Leyland, John. "The Campaign of Trafalgar." THE NAVAL ANNUAL, 1905. Edited by T.A. Brassey. Portsmouth: J. Griffin, 1905.

189. Leyland, John, ed. DISPATCHES AND LETTERS RELATING TO THE BLOCKADE OF BREST, 1803-1805. London: Navy Records Society, 1899, 1901. Vols. 14, 21.

190. Lindsay-MacDougall, K.F. "Nelson Manuscripts at the National Maritime Museum." MARINER'S MIRROR 41 (1955): 227-32.

191. Lloyd, Christopher. THE BRITISH SEAMAN 1200-1860: A SOCIAL SURVEY. London: Collins, 1968.

192. Lloyd, Christopher. LORD COCHRANE: SEAMAN, RADICAL, LIBERATOR; A LIFE OF THOMAS, LORD COCHRANE, 10th EARL OF DUNDONALD. London, New York: Longmans, Green, 1947.

193. Lloyd, Christopher. MR. BARROW OF THE ADMIRALTY: A LIFE OF SIR JOHN BARROW, 1764-1848. London: Collins, 1970.

194. Lloyd, Christopher. "The Mutiny of the Nereido." MARINER'S MIRROR 54 (1968): 245-52.

195. Lloyd, Christopher. "The Navy in the Eighteenth Century." A GUIDE TO THE SOURCES OF BRITISH MILITARY HISTORY. Edited by Robin Higham. Berkeley and Los Angeles: University of California Press, 1971.

196. Lloyd, Christopher. THE NILE CAMPAIGN: NELSON AND NAPOLEON IN EGYPT. New York: Barnes and Noble, 1973.

197. Lloyd, Christopher. ST. VINCENT AND CAMPERDOWN. London: Batsford, 1963.

198. Lloyd, Christopher, ed. THE HEALTH OF SEAMEN: SELECTIONS FROM THE WORKS OF DR. JAMES LIND, SIR GILBERT BLANE, AND DR. THOMAS TROTTER. London: Navy Records Society, 1965. Vol. 107.

199. Lloyd, Christopher, ed. THE KEITH PAPERS. London: Navy Records Society, 1950. Vol. 90.

200. Lloyd, Christopher, and J.L.S. Coulter. MEDICINE AND THE NAVY. Vol. 3. 1714-1815. Edinburgh and London: E. and S. Livingstone, 1961.

201. Lloyd, Christopher, and R.C. Anderson, eds. MEMOIR OF JAMES TREVENEN. London: Navy Records Society, 1959. Vol. 101.

202. Longridge, Charles Nepean. THE ANATOMY OF NELSON'S SHIPS. Annapolis, Md.: Naval Institute Press, 1977.

203. Lothbinière, H.A. Foly de. "Mauritius 1810." MARINER'S MIRROR 38 (1952): 195-209.

204. Lovell, Vice Admiral William Stanhope. PERSONAL NARRATIVE OF EVENTS, 1799-1815. London: W. Allen, 1879.

205. MacGregor, David R. MERCHANT SAILING SHIPS, 1775-1875: THEIR DESIGN AND CONSTRUCTION. Whatford, Herts, England: Argus Books, 1980.

206. MacIntyre, Donald. "Nelson's Tactics at Trafalgar." BRITISH HISTORY ILLUSTRATED (1974): 45-51.

207. MacIntyre, Donald. THE PRIVATEERS. London: Paul Elek, 1975.

208. Mackenzie, Colonel R.H. THE TRAFALGAR ROLL. London: G. Allen, 1913.

209. Mackesy, Piers. "Collingwood and Ganteaume: The French Offensive in the Mediterranean, January to April 1808." MARINER'S MIRROR 41 (1955): 3-14; 137-48.

210. Mackesy, Piers. "To Rescue His Holiness--The Mission of the Alceste in 1808." MARINER'S MIRROR 40 (1954): 206-11.

211. Mackesy, Piers. THE WAR IN THE MEDITERRANEAN, 1803-1810. London, New York and Toronto: Longmans, 1957.

212. Mahan, Alfred Thayer. THE BATTLE OF TRAFALGAR. Boston: Houghton, Mifflin, 1901.

213. Mahan, Alfred Thayer. THE INFLUENCE OF SEA POWER UPON THE FRENCH REVOLUTION AND EMPIRE, 1793-1812. First edition, 1892. New York, Greenwood Press, 1968.

214. Mahan, Alfred Thayer. THE LIFE OF NELSON. Boston: Little, Brown, 1907.

215. Mahan, Alfred Thayer. SEA POWER IN ITS RELATION TO THE WAR OF 1812. London: Sampson Low, 1905.

216. Maine, René. TRAFALGAR: NAPOLEON'S NAVAL WATERLOO. London: Thomas and Hudson, 1957.

217. Manwaring, G.E., and B. Dobrée. THE FLOATING REPUBLIC. New York: A.M. Kelley, 1966.

218. Manwaring, G.E. "Popham's Expedition to Ostend in 1798." MARINER'S MIRROR 7 (1921): 332-41.

219. Marcus, Geoffrey Jules. THE AGE OF NELSON: THE ROYAL NAVY, 1793-1815. New York: Viking Press, 1971.

220. Marcus, Geoffrey Jules. HEART OF OAK: A SURVEY OF BRITISH SEA POWER IN THE GEORGIAN ERA. New York: Oxford University Press, 1975.

221. MARINER'S MIRROR. 1911 to present.

222. Marliani, M. de. COMBATE DE TRAFALGAR. Madrid: Impresso de Orden Superior, 1850.

223. Marmont, Auguste Frédéric Louis Viesse, duc de Raguse. MEMOIRES DU MARECHAL MARMONT DUC DE RAGUSE DE 1792 A 1841. Paris: Halle, 1857. 6 vols.

224. Marshall, John, ed. ROYAL NAVAL BIOGRAPHY OR MEMOIRS OF THE SERVICES OF ALL FLAG-OFFICERS. London: Longman, Hurst, 1832-1835. 4 vols., each in 2 parts.

225. Martinez-Valverde, Captain Carlos. LA MARINA EN LA GUERRA DE LA INDEPENDENCIA: PATROCINADA PAR LA LIGA NAVAL ESPANOLA. Madrid: Editora Nacional, 1974.

226. Masefield, John. SEA LIFE IN NELSON'S TIME. Annapolis, Md.: Naval Institute, 1971. (Reprint of 1926 edition.)

227. Maurice, John Frederick, ed. THE DIARY OF SIR JOHN MOORE. London: Longmans, Green, 1904.

228. McCord, Norman. "The Impress Service in North-east England during the Napoleonic Wars." MARINER'S MIRROR 54 (1968): 163-80.

229. McKee, Christopher, ed. "Constitution in the Quasi-War with France: The Letters of John Roach Jr., 1798-1801." AMERICAN NEPTUNE 27 (1967): 135-49.

230. Melvin, Frank Edgar. NAPOLEON'S NAVIGATION SYSTEM: A STUDY OF
TRADE CONTROL DURING THE CONTINENTAL BLOCKADE. New York:
Appleton, 1919.

231. Mollo, John. UNIFORMS OF THE ROYAL NAVY, DURING THE NAPOLEONIC
WARS. London: Hugh Evelyn, 1965.

232. Moorehead, Alan. "Annals of Exploration: The Blue Nile." NEW
YORKER 38 (1962): 49-123.

233. Mordvinov. ARKHIV GRAFOV MORDVINOVYKH [The Mordvinov Archive].
Introduction and notes by V. A. Bil'basov. St. Petersburg:
Skorokhodov, 1902. Vols. 3, 4.

234. Mordvinov, R.N., ed. ADMIRAL USHAKOV. Moscow: Voenizdat,
1948-56. 3 vols.

235. Morriss, R.A. "Labour Relations in the Royal Dockyards,
1801-1805." MARINER'S MIRROR (1976): 337-46.

236. MORSKOI SBORNIK [Naval Journal]. St. Petersburg-Leningrad,
1848 to present.

237. Naish, George P.B. NELSON AND BRONTE: AN ILLUSTRATED GUIDE TO
HIS LIFE AND TIMES. London: H.M.S.O., 1958.

238. Naish, George P.B., ed. NELSON'S LETTERS TO HIS WIFE AND OTHER
DOCUMENTS, 1785-1831. London: Navy Records Society, 1958
Vol. 100.

239. NAVAL DOCUMENTS RELATED TO THE QUASI-WAR BETWEEN THE UNITED
STATES AND FRANCE. NAVAL OPERATIONS FROM FEBRUARY 1797 TO
OCTOBER 1798. Office of Naval Records and Library, Navy
Department. Washington: United States Government Printing
Office, 1935.

240. NAVAL DOCUMENTS RELATED TO THE UNITED STATES WARS WITH THE
BARBARY POWERS. Vol. 1. 1785-1801. Washington, 1939.

241. NAVAL WAR COLLEGE REVIEW. 1948 to present.

242. Navarro, José P. Merino. LA ARMADA ESPANOLA EN EL SIGLO XVIII.
Madrid: Fundación Universitaria Espanola, 1981.

243. Nelson, Admiral Horatio. ALCUNE LETERE DELL'AMMIRAGLIO NELSON
AI REALI DI SAVOIA (1799-1805). Rome: Rivista Maritima, 1923.

244. Nelson, Admiral Horatio. LETTERS FROM LORD NELSON. London and
New York: Staples Press, 1949.

245. Nelson, Admiral Horatio. LETTERS TO LADY HAMILTON. London:
Sisley's, 1907.

246. Nelson, Admiral Horatio. NELSON'S LAST DIARY, SEPTEMBER
13-OCTOBER 21, 1805. London: E. Mathews, 1917.

247. Nelson, Admiral Horatio, and George Lathom Browne. NELSON; THE
      PUBLIC AND PRIVATE LIFE OF HORATIO, VISCOUNT NELSON AS TOLD BY
      HIMSELF, HIS COMRADES, AND HIS FRIENDS. London: T.F. Unwin,
      1891.

248. Nelson, Admiral Horatio. THE NELSON TOUCH, BEING A LITTLE BOOK
      OF THE GREAT SEAMAN'S WISDOM; SELECTED AND ARRANGED BY WALTER
      JERROLD. London: J. Murray, 1918.

249. Newbolt, Henry. THE YEAR OF TRAFALGAR. London: J. Murray,
      1905.

250. Newnham, G.L., ed. CORRESPONDENCE OF LORD COLLINGWOOD. London:
      Ridgway, 1838.

251. Nicol, John. ADVENTURES OF JOHN NICOL, MARINER. Edinburgh:
      Blackwood, 1822.

252. Nicolas, Nicholas Harris, ed. THE DISPATCHES AND LETTERS OF
      VICE ADMIRAL LORD VISCOUNT NELSON. London: Colburn, 1844-46.

253. Norie, John William. THE NAVAL GAZATEER, BIOGRAPHER, AND
      CHRONOLOGIST, CONTAINING A HISTORY OF THE LATE WARS, 1793-1801,
      AND 1803-10. London: J.W. Norie, 1827. (New and improved
      edition, London: Wilson, 1842.)

254. Norway, Arthur H. A HISTORY OF THE POST-OFFICE PACKET SERVICE
      DURING THE YEARS 1793-1815. London: Macmillan, 1895.

255. Oman, Carola (Lenanton). BRITAIN AGAINST NAPOLEON. London:
      Faber and Faber, 1942.

256. Oman, Carola (Lenanton). NAPOLEON AT THE CHANNEL. Garden
      City, N.Y.: Doubleday, Doran, 1942.

257. Oman, Carola (Lenanton). NELSON. London: Hodder and
      Stroughton, 1954.

258. Padfield, Peter. NELSON'S WAR. London: Hart-Davis,
      MacGibbon, 1976.

259. Panafidin, P.I. PIS'MA MORSKOGO OFITSERA (1806-1809) [Letters
      of a Naval Officer (1806-1809)]. Edited by B.V. Modzalevskii.
      Petrograd: Morskoe ministerstvo, 1916.

260. Pargellis, S., and D.J. Medley. BIBLIOGRAPHY OF BRITISH
      HISTORY: THE EIGHTEENTH CENTURY. London: Oxford University
      Press, 1951.

261. Parkinson, Cyril Northcote. BRITANNIA RULES: THE CLASSIC AGE
      OF NAVAL HISTORY, 1793-1815. London: Weidenfeld and Nicolson,
      1977.

262. Parkinson, Cyril Northcote. EDWARD PELLOW, VISCOUNT EXMOUTH,
      ADMIRAL OF THE RED. London: Methuen, 1934.

263. Parkinson, Cyril Northcote. THE LIFE AND TIMES OF HORATIO HORNBLOWER. London: Michael Joseph, 1971.

264. Parkinson, Cyril Northcote. PORTSMOUTH POINT. THE NAVY IN FICTION, 1793-1815. Liverpool: University Press of Liverpool, 1948.

265. Parkinson, Cyril Northcote. TRADE IN EASTERN SEAS, 1793-1813. Cambridge: Cambridge University Press, 1937.

266. Parkinson, Cyril Northcote. THE TRADE WINDS. A STUDY OF BRITISH OVERSEAS TRADE DURING THE FRENCH WARS, 1793-1815. London: Allen & Unwin, 1948.

267. Parkinson, Cyril Northcote. WAR IN THE EASTERN SEAS, 1793-1815. London: Allen & Unwin, 1954.

268. Parsons, Lieutenant G.S. NELSONIAN REMINISCENCES. Edited by W. Long. London: Gibbings, 1905.

269. Patterson, Alfred Temple. THE NAVAL MUTINY AT SPITHEAD, 1797. Portsmouth: Portsmouth City Council, 1968.

270. Paul, Louis. "An Artist's Notes at the Battle of the Nile." MARINER'S MIRROR 4 (1914): 266-73.

271. Pengelly, Colin A. THE FIRST BELLEROPHON. London: John Baker, 1966.

272. Perkins, Bradford. PROLOGUE TO THE WAR BETWEEN ENGLAND AND THE UNITED STATES, 1805-1812. Berkeley: University of California Press, 1961.

273. Phillimore, Rear Admiral Augustus. THE LIFE OF ADMIRAL OF THE FLEET SIR WILLIAM PARKER, 1781-1866. London: Harrison, 1876-80.

274. Pisani, Paul. LA DALMATIE, 1797-1815. Paris: Picard, 1893.

275. Pocock, Tom. NELSON AND HIS WORLD. London: Thames and Hudson, 1969.

276. Pocock, Tom. REMEMBER NELSON: THE LIFE OF CAPTAIN SIR WILLIAM HOSTE. London: Collins, 1977.

277. Pocock, Tom. THE YOUNG NELSON IN THE AMERICAS. London: Collins, 1980.

278. Polak, Jean. BIBLIOGRAPHIE MARITIME FRANCAISE: DEPUIS LES TEMPS LES PLUS RECULES JUSQUA 1914. Grenoble: Editions des 4 Seigneurs, 1976.

279. Pool, Bernard. NAVY BOARD CONTRACTS, 1660-1832: ADMINISTRATION UNDER THE NAVY BOARD. Hamden, Conn.: Archon Books, 1966.

280. Pope, Dudley. THE BLACK SHIP. London: Weidenfeld and
      Nicolson, 1963.

281. Pope, Dudley. DECISION AT TRAFALGAR. Philadelphia:
      Lippincott, 1960.

282. Pope, Dudley. ENGLAND EXPECTS. London: Weidenfeld and
      Nicolson, 1959.

283. Pope, Dudley. THE GREAT GAMBLE: NELSON AT COPENHAGEN. London
      and New York: Weidenfeld and Nicolson, 1972.

284. Pope, Dudley. LIFE IN NELSON'S NAVY. Annapolis: Naval
      Institute Press, 1981.

285. Pouqueville, F.C.H.L. TRAVELS THROUGH THE MOREA, ALBANIA, AND
      SEVERAL OTHER PARTS OF THE OTTOMAN EMPIRE TO CONSTANTINOPLE
      DURING THE YEARS 1798, 1799, 1800, AND 1801. London: Richard
      Phillips, 1806.

286. Powell, J. Damer. THE BRISTOL PRIVATEERS. Bristol: Arrowsmith,
      1930.

287. Pratt, Fletcher. EMPIRE AND THE SEA. New York: Holt, 1946.

288. Pugh, Surgeon Commander Patterson David Gordon. NELSON AND HIS
      SURGEONS: NELSON CHIRURGLIQUE. Edinburgh and London:
      Livingstone, 1968.

289. Puryear, V.J. NAPOLEON AND THE DARDANELLES. Berkeley:
      University of California Press, 1951.

290. Raigersfeld, Jeffrey, baron. THE LIFE OF A SEA OFFICER.
      London: Cassell, 1829.

291. Rasch, Aage. "American Trade in the Baltic, 1783-1807." THE
      SCANDINAVIAN ECONOMIC HISTORY REVIEW 13 (1965): 31-64.

292. REVUE DES ETUDES NAPOLEONIENNES. 1912-39.

293. Richardson, W. A MARINER OF ENGLAND, 1780-1819. London: J.
      Murray, 1908.

294. Robertson, F.L. EVOLUTION OF NAVAL ARMAMENT. London: Storey,
      1968.

295. Rodger, Alexander Bankier. THE WAR OF THE SECOND COALITION,
      1798 TO 1801: A STRATEGIC COMMENTARY. Oxford: Clarendon
      Press, 1964.

296. Rodocanachi, E. LES ILES IONIENNES, 1797-1815. Paris: Alcan,
      1899.

297. Roos, Carl. PRISONEN: DANSKE OG NORSKE DRIGSFANGER I ENGLAND
      1807-1814. Copenhagen: n.p., 1953.

298. Rose, John Holland. THE INDECISIVENESS OF MODERN WAR AND OTHER ESSAYS. London: G. Bell, 1927.

299. Rose, John Holland. "The State of Nelson's Fleet before Trafalgar." MARINER'S MIRROR 8 (1922): 75-81.

300. Rose, John Holland, and Alexander Meyrick Broadley. DUMOURIEZ AND THE DEFENCE OF ENGLAND AGAINST NAPOLEON. London: J. Lane, 1909.

301. Ruppenthal, Roland. "Denmark and the Continental System." THE JOURNAL OF MODERN HISTORY 15 (1943): 7-23.

302. Russell, Jack. NELSON AND THE HAMILTONS. London: Anthony Blond, 1969.

303. Ryan, A.N. "The Defense of British Trade with the Baltic, 1808-1813." THE ENGLISH HISTORICAL REVIEW 292 (1959): 443-66.

304. Ryan, A.N. "The Melancholy Fate of the Baltic Ships in 1811." MARINER'S MIRROR 50 (1964): 123-34.

305. Ryan, A.N. "The Navy at Copenhagen in 1807." MARINER'S MIRROR 39 (1953): 201-10.

306. Ryan, A.N., ed. THE SAUMAREZ PAPERS: SELECTIONS FROM THE BALTIC CORRESPONDENCE OF VICE-ADMIRAL SIR JAMES SAUMAREZ, 1808-1812. London: Navy Records Society, 1968. Vol. 110.

307. Ryan, A.N. TRADE WITH THE ENEMY IN THE SCANDINAVIAN AND BALTIC PORTS DURING THE NAPOLEONIC WAR: FOR AND AGAINST. London: Royal Historical Society, 1962.

308. Saul, Norman E. "Jonathan Russell, President Adams, and Europe in 1810." AMERICAN NEPTUNE 30 (1970): 279-93.

309. Saul, Norman E. RUSSIA AND THE MEDITERRANEAN, 1797-1807. Chicago and London: The University of Chicago Press, 1970.

310. Savageau, David LePere. "The United States Navy and Its 'Half War' Prisoners, 1798-1801." AMERICAN NEPTUNE 31 (1971): 159-76.

311. Saxby, R.C. "The Escape of Admiral Bruix from Brest." MARINER'S MIRROR 46 (1960): 113-21.

312. Schurman, Donald M. JULIAN S. CORBETT, 1854-1922: HISTORIAN OF BRITISH MARITIME POLICY FROM DRAKE TO JELLICOE. London: Royal Historical Society, 1981.

313. Shapiro, Aleksandr L'vovich. ADMIRAL D.N. SENIAVIN. Moscow: Ministerstvo Oborony SSSR, 1958.

314. Sharp, James A., ed. MEMOIRS OF REAR ADMIRAL SIR WILLIAM
     SYMONDS. London: Longman, Brown, Green, Longmans and Roberts,
     1858.

315. Six, Georges. DICTIONNAIRE BIOGRAPHIQUE DES GENERAUX ET
     AMIRAUX FRANCAIS DE LA REVOLUTION ET DE L'EMPIRE, 1792-1814.
     Paris: G. Saffroy, 1934. 2 vols.

316. Skalovskii, R. ZHIZN' ADMIRALA FEODORA FEODOROVICHA USHAKOVA.
     St. Petersburg: n.p., 1856.

317. Smith, Admiral Sidney. MEMOIRES OF ADMIRAL SIR SIDNEY SMITH.
     London: Bentley, 1848. 2 vols.

318. Snellman, P.W. SKEPP OCH SKEPPARE I ULEABORG 1765-1815:
     ULEABORGS HANDELSFLOTTA 1765-1815. Oulu: Kirjapaine oy
     Kaleva, 1938.

319. Southey, Robert. THE BRITISH ADMIRALS. London: Longman,
     1833-48. 5 vols.

320. Southey, Robert. THE LIFE OF NELSON. New York: American
     Book, 1895.

321. Spinney, F.D. "The Albanaise Affair." MARINER'S MIRROR 43
     (1957): 194-202.

322. Spinney, F.D. "The Danae Mutiny." MARINER'S MIRROR 42 (1956):
     38-53.

323. Spinney, F.D. "The Hermione Mutiny." MARINER'S MIRROR 41
     (1955): 123-36.

324. Standing, Percy Cross. "The 'Temeraires' Captain: A Trafalgar
     Memory." CONTEMPORARY REVIEW 134 (1928): 502-3.

325. Stanislavskaia, Avgusta Mikhailovna. RUSSKO-ANGLIISKIE
     OTNOSHENIIA I PROBLEMY SREDIZEMNOMOR'IA, 1798-1807
     [Anglo-Russian Relations and the Problems of the Mediterranean,
     1798-1807]. Moscow: Akademiia Nauk, 1962.

326. Steel, Anthony. "Diana versus Caravan and Topez." MARINER'S
     MIRROR 43 (1957): 46-58.

327. Steel, David. THE ELEMENTS AND PRACTICE OF RIGGING, SEAMANSHIP
     AND NAVAL TACTICS. London: J. Norie, 1821. 6 vols. in 3.

328. Steven, Margaret. MERCHANT CAMPBELL, 1769-1846: A STUDY OF
     COLONIAL TRADE. Melburne and New York: Oxford University
     Press, 1965.

329. Stewart, James. "The Leeward Isles Command, 1795-1796."
     MARINER'S MIRROR 47 (1961): 270-80.

330. Stuart, Vivian, and George T. Eggleston. HIS MAJESTY'S SLOOP-OF-WAR 'DIAMOND ROCK'. London: Robert Hale, 1978.

331. Sullivan, F.B. "The Royal Academy at Portsmouth, 1729-1806." MARINER'S MIRROR 63 (1977): 311-26.

332. Svin'in, Pavel. VOSPOMINANIIA NA FLOT PAVLA SVIN'INA [Memoirs of the Navy of Pavel Svinin]. Saint Petersburg: V. Plavil'shchikov, 1819.

333. Symonds, Craig L. NAVALISTS AND ANTINAVALISTS: THE NAVAL POLICY DEBATE IN THE UNITED STATES, 1785-1827. Newark: University of Delaware Press, 1980.

334. Taillemite, Etienne. DICTIONNAIRE DE LA MARINE. Paris: Seghers, 1962.

335. Tarle, Eugène. LE BLOCUS CONTINENTAL AT LE ROYAUME D'ITALIE. Paris: Alcan, 1928.

336. Tarle, Eugène. TRI EKSPEDITSII RUSSKOGO FLOTA [Three Expeditions of the Russian Navy]. Moscow: Ministerstvo Oborony SSSR, 1956.

337. Taylor, Rear Admiral A.H. "The Battle of Trafalgar." MARINER'S MIRROR 36 (1950): 281-90.

338. Terrain, John. "A Question of Saddles Nelson in 1805." HISTORY TODAY (1975): 593-601.

339. Thiry, Jean, baron. BONAPARTE EN EGYPTE. Paris: Editions Berger-Levrault, 1973.

340. Thomas, Donald. COCHRANE, BRITANNIA'S LAST SEA KING. London: André Deutsch, 1978.

341. Thomazi, Auguste Antoine. MARINS BATISSEURS D'EMPIRE. Paris: Horizons de France, 1946.

342. Thomazi, Auguste Antoine. NAPOLEON ET SES MARINS. Paris: Berger-Levrault, 1950.

343. Thomazi, Auguste Antoine. TRAFALGAR. Paris: Payot, 1932.

344. Thursfield, Rear Admiral H.G., ed. FIVE NAVAL JOURNALS, 1789-1817. London: Navy Records Society, 1951. Vol. 91.

345. Timewell, H.C. "Guernsey Privateers." MARINER'S MIRROR 56 (1970): 199.

346. Tonnessen, J.N. KAPERFORT OG SKIPSFART, 1807-1814. Oslo: n.p., 1955.

347. Tregonning, K.G. "A Forgotten Naval Battle." MARINER'S MIRROR 46 (1960): 215-26.

348. Troude, Onésime Joachim. BATAILLES NAVALES DE LA FRANCE.
      Paris: Challamel, 1867-68. 4 vols.

349. Turner, Eunice H.   "Naval Medical Service; 1793-1815."
      MARINER'S MIRROR 46 (1960): 119-32.

350. Turner, Eunice H. "The Russian Squadron with Admiral Duncan's
      North Sea Fleet, 1795-1800." MARINER'S MIRROR 49 (1963):
      212-22.

351. UNITED STATES NAVAL INSTITUTE PROCEEDINGS. 1874 to present.

352. Ussher, Thomas. NAPOLEON'S LAST VOYAGE: BEING THE DIARIES OF
      SIR THOMAS USSHER AND JOHN R. GLOVER. New York: Scribner,
      1906.

353. Walder, David. NELSON. London: Hamish Hamilton, 1978.

354. Warner, Oliver.   THE GLORIOUS FIRST OF JUNE.   London:
      Batsford, 1961.

355. Warner, Oliver. THE LIFE AND LETTERS OF VICE-ADMIRAL LORD
      COLLINGWOOD. London and New York: Oxford University Press,
      1968.

356. Warner, Oliver. LORD NELSON: A GUIDE TO READING, WITH A NOTE
      ON CONTEMPORARY PORTRAITS. London: Caravel, 1955.

357. Warner, Oliver. NELSON AND THE AGE OF FIGHTING SAIL. New
      York: American Heritage, 1963.

358. Warner, Oliver. NELSON'S BATTLES. Newton Abbot, Devon: David
      and Charles, 1971.

359. Warner, Oliver, ed. NELSON'S LAST DIARY. Kent, Ohio: Kent
      State University Press, 1971.

360. Warner, Oliver. A PORTRAIT OF LORD NELSON. London: Chatto
      and Windus, 1958.

361. Warner, Oliver. TRAFALGAR. London: Batsford, 1959.

362. Warner, Oliver. VICTORY; THE LIFE OF LORD NELSON. Boston:
      Little, Brown, 1958.

363. Watson, William N.   "Thomas Robertson, Naval Surgeon,
      1793-1828." BULLETIN OF HISTORIC MEDICINE (1972).

364. Wetherell, John. THE ADVENTURE OF JOHN WETHERELL. Edited by
      C.S. Forester, Garden City, N.Y.: Doubleday, 1953.

365. Whitlock, Peter, and William Pearce.   H.M.S. VICTORY AND
      ADMIRAL LORD NELSON. Portsmouth: Royal Navy Museum, 1979.

366. Wickwire, Franklin, and Mary Wickwire. CORNWALLIS: THE IMPERIAL YEARS. Chapel Hill: University of North Carolina Press, 1980.

367. Williams, Gomer. HISTORY OF THE LIVERPOOL PRIVATEERS. London: Heinemann, 1897.

368. Zimmerman, James F. IMPRESSMENT OF AMERICAN SEAMEN. New York, 1925.

369. Zlotnikov, Mikhail Fedorovich. KONTINENTAL'NAIA BLOKADA I ROSSIIA [The Continental Blockade and Russia]. Moscow and Leningrad: Nauka, 1966.

ADDENDUM

370. Bartlett, Christopher John. GREAT BRITAIN AND SEA POWER, 1818-1853. Oxford: Oxford University Press, 1963

371. Brossard, Maurice de. DE NANTES A ST. NAZAIRE. Paris: Editions France-Empire, 1983.

372. Holmes, T.W. THE SEMAPHORE: THE STORY OF THE ADMIRALITY-TO PORTSMOUTH SHUTTER TELEGRAPH AND SEMAPHORE LINES 1797 TO 1847. Ilfracombe: Stockwell, 1983.

373. Horward, Donald D. "The Influence of British Seapower upon the Peninsular War, 1808-1814." NAVAL WAR COLLEGE REVIEW 31 (1978): 54-71.

374. James, Admiral William Melburne. OLD OAK; THE LIFE OF JOHN JERVIS, EARL OF ST. VINCENT. London: Longmans, Green, 1950.

375. Mahan, Alfred Thayer. THE INFLUENCE OF SEA POWER UPON HISTORY (1660-1783). Boston: Little, Brown, 1903.

376. Matthews, William. BRITISH DIARIES; AN ANNOTATED BIBLIOGRAPHY OF BRITISH DIARIES WRITTEN BETWEEN 1442 AND 1942. Berkeley: University of California Press, 1950.

377. Morriss, Roger B. THE ROYAL DOCKYARDS DURING THE REVOLUTIONARY AND NAPOLEONIC WARS. Leicester: Leicester University Press, 1983.

378. Parry, Ann, ed. THE ADMIRALS FREMANTLE: A SELECTION FROM THE FREMANTLE FAMILY PAPERS (1765-1958). London: Chatto and Windus, 1971.

379. Richmond, Herbert William. THE NAVY AS AN INSTRUMENT OF FOREIGN POLICY, 1558-1727. Edited by E.A. Hughes. Cambridge: Cambridge University Press, 1953.

380. Richmond, Herbert William. STATESMEN AND SEAPOWER. Oxford: Cladendon Press, 1946.

CHAPTER IX

THE PENINSULAR WAR (1807-1814)

Donald D. Horward, Florida State University

The Peninsular war had a direct and significant effect upon the
Napoleonic Empire. As many as 300,000 French soldiers were committed
at one time to this interminable struggle that sapped the strength of
the Empire. The consequences of the war were catastrophic and
ultimately played a role in the demise of Napoleon. However, despite
the extraordinary number of books devoted to the Napoleonic period,
French research in this area, contrary to the Spanish, Portuguese,
and English, has been limited. This neglect probably reflects the
disturbing nature of the conflict. Carried on by outnumbered French
armies against a bitterly hostile population, the war disintegrated
into a struggle marked by a ferocity unknown elsewhere in Western
Europe. In such a war more thought was devoted to survival than to
preserving records for posterity. Nevertheless, there are other
reasons to explain the loss of documents vital for those studying the
Peninsular war. The war zone was so far removed from Paris, both in
time and distance, that communications were exposed to untold perils
in transit. Without the special efforts of a commanding officer, his
correspondence could easily be lost, destroyed, or fall into the
hands of the enemy. In other cases, officers responsible for the
unsuccessful operations in Spain and Portugal had little interest in
preserving the evidence of their failures. Indeed, some documents
did reach the Dépôt de la Guerre only to be removed or destroyed to
protect the reputation of some high-ranking officer.

Despite this aversion for the Peninsula, many of Napoleon's
greatest marshals, including Masséna, Ney, Lannes, Soult, and Suchet,
commanded the most illustrious corps of the Grande Armée there. They
carried out complex operations facing monumental handicaps without
adequate resources. They achieved brilliant battlefield victories,
but their successes were only illusionary. Their men endured extreme
hardship heroically amid the horrors of a bitter guerrilla war, but
the final results were unalterable. Indeed, soon after the French
became involved in Spain, one perceptive young French captain, Jean
Jacques Pelet, declared in letters to Masséna and Berthier:

> Like a relentless torrent of lava, our army is quite able
> to march across Spain and devastate the countryside that
> might provide food for us. Yet we shall always find fierce
> enemies in front of us, and we leave even the worse ones
> behind. Our armies will pursue elusive armies that always
> flee and disappear toward the sea, only to reappear a few
> leagues beyond, while invisible hands destroy everyone who
> does not remain with the army.

Consequently, French writers of later generations ignored the
Peninsular war and turned enthusiastically to Napoleon's brilliant
campaigns in Italy, Germany, and Austria, or even his catastrophic
but glorious operations in Russia and Belgium. These campaigns
projected the characteristic genius of Napoleon and the brilliance of
his armies which became a significant ingredient in French

243

nationalism of the nineteenth and twentieth centuries. Hence, until the first decades of this century, few French scholars were attracted to the events in Iberia which reflected the collapse of the Empire.

On the contrary Portuguese and Spanish scholars and writers have always maintained a lively interest in the Peninsular war. The Portuguese have concentrated on specific topics although a limited number of comprehensive studies of the struggle have been published. Spanish authors, on the other hand, have written several extensive studies of the period and literally hundreds of volumes are dedicated to particular events and battles. Moreover, Spanish scholars have organized a series of international congresses on the Peninsular War and these meetings have served as catalysts for further research in the field.

While French scholars have directed their attention toward Napoleon's brilliant campaigns, British authors have concentrated on the successful allied operations during the Napoleonic period. Specifically they have focused on the Peninsular war, the naval war, and the Waterloo campaign rather than on their abortive campaigns in Holland, the Scheldt, Italy, or the Baltic. Since the Peninsula was regarded as the theater of operations most closely associated with the success of their military heroes--Wellington, Moore, Hill, Beresford, Picton, Napier, and others--hundreds of original British accounts of the struggle, and tens of thousands of dispatches and letters appeared in the nineteenth century. Without a doubt, the British have dominated the literature on this topic and two of the finest military studies in the English language, authored by Oman (459) and Fortescue (201), have been devoted to the Peninsular war.

GENERAL HISTORIES

There are a large number of general histories devoted to the Peninsular war. The earliest of these, by Sarrazin (551), Jones (323), and Southey (584), were limited in scope, unreliable, and nationalistic in nature. However, during the 1820s serious efforts were made to present relatively comprehensive accounts of the war. Charles Vane, an officer in the 10th Hussars and later Marquess of Londonderry (380), wrote an enlightening two-volume history of the war which he ended abruptly after the storming of Ciudad Rodrigo in 1812. This was soon superseded by a multivolume study of major significance by William Napier (447), colonel of the 43rd Foot, who was engaged in most of the fighting in the Peninsula. This work, the most comprehensive and complete to date, dominated Peninsular war literature throughout the 19th century and served as a catalyst for the publication of memoirs, journals, and eyewitness accounts of others who had served there. When the first comprehensive Spanish accounts of the war appeared, including the works of Toreno (614) and Principe y Vidaud (504), they were nationalistic and limited in scope but unquestionably a significant contribution to the field. However, between 1866 and 1903 a fourteen-volume study of the war by Gómez de Arteche y Moro (245) was published. This highly detailed and comprehensive work has remained one of the most significant Spanish contributions to the field. Since 1972 Colonel Juan Priego Lopez of the Servicio Histórico Militar in Madrid has been working on a general multivolume history of the war. By 1982 five volumes (502) had been published, extending the narrative through 1810. In

Portugal though there had been numerous monographs of the French invasions, no comprehensive study of the war appeared until Luz Soriano published his classic nineteen-volume study, HISTORIA DA GUERRA CIVIL (386) in the last half of the nineteenth century. A popular history of the war soon appeared by Cesar (155) while several German writers, including Baumgarten (38) and Schepeler (554), produced useful studies in their attempts to unravel the details.

Following the turn of the century two valuable works began to appear in English. In 1902 the first volume of Charles Oman's HISTORY OF THE PENINSULAR WAR (459) was published, establishing a new level of excellence in scholarship that continued through the seventh volume, ranking it among the finest military studies in the English language. Appearing simultaneously was John Fortescue's HISTORY OF THE BRITISH ARMY (201). Although the seven volumes devoted to the Peninsular war paralleled Oman's study, he introduced new details and emphasis, often reinforcing and occasionally taking issue with Oman's study. Together these works represent the most comprehensive analysis on this topic in the English language. The first extensive study of the war by a Frenchman was undertaken by Colonel Grasset (260) in 1914, but by 1930 when his third and last volume was published, less than two years of the war had been considered. The same year another French historian, Geoffroy de Grandmaison (225), completed a general three-volume study of Napoleon and the Peninsula which he had begun in 1910. Several other French scholars envisioned comprehensive multivolume studies of the Peninsular war, but this goal has yet to be achieved.

A number of valuable one or two-volume studies have recently been published including Jac Weller's (636) scholarly, but highly readable work on the Peninsula and Gabriel Lovett's (384) careful study on Spain during the period. The studies of García Rodriguez (217), Solis (523), Lucas-Dubreton (385), Goodspeed (253), Aymes (24), and Glover (236) are also helpful introductions to the topic. Recently, a number of superficial volumes, designed more for the coffee table than the serious reader, have appeared in print. All except one with exceptional visual material (472) have been eliminated from this chapter.

BIBLIOGRAPHIES

Until the twentieth century no comprehensive bibliographies existed on the Peninsular war. There were several lengthy bibliographies appended to specialized studies or included in general bibliographies of Napoleon, but the first volume listing works on Spain in the GUERRA DE LA INDEPENDENCIA was completed by Ibañez Marin (309) in 1908 to commemorate the centenary of the war. Two years later the Director of the Academia das Ciências de Lisboa, Bethencourt, published his catalogue (56) of the rich collection of books and manuscripts in the collection. The first extensive bibliography on the war was the DICIONARIO BIBLIOGRAFICO DE GUERRA PENINSULAR (25) which appeared in 1926-28 under the direction of the distinguished Portuguese military historian, Ayres de Magalhães Sepúlveda. This four-volume bibliography, certainly the most comprehensive ever attempted, included works in all languages as well as a significant section on the manuscript collections in Lisbon. In 1946 the historical division of the Estudo-mayor Central of the

Spanish army began the publication of a three-volume work, DICCIONARIO BIBLIOGRAFICO DE LA GUERRA DE LA INDEPENDENCIA ESPAÑOLA (589); this multilingual work included published works as well as manuscript sources in both the Archivo Histórico Nacional and the Servicio Histórico Militar in Madrid. Another practical aid was Sanchez Alonso's bibliography, FUENTES DE LA HISTORIA ESPAGNOLA (541), first published in 1919 and last revised in 1952. Although this work included volumes on Spain and Spanish America, there were 1235 titles listed on the Revolutionary period. Besides these specialized bibliographies, several of the more general Napoleonic bibliographies mentioned in Chapter I, especially Kircheisen, Tulard, Devois, and Horward, include a significant number of pertinent works on this topic.

Turning to bibliographies in specialized studies, among the most beneficial are those in Oman's WELLINGTON'S ARMY (460), Aranha's INVASOES FRANCEZAS (17), Fugier's NAPOLEON ET L'ESPAGNE (210), Conrad's NAPOLEON ET LA CATALOGNE (136), Connelly's GENTLE BONAPARTE (138), Vicente's FREIRE (624), Severn's WELLESLEY AFFAIR (558), Brett-James's WELLINGTON'S ARMY (80), and Lovett's NAPOLEON AND THE BIRTH OF MODERN SPAIN (384). Most of the doctoral dissertations, such as those by Barry (36), De la Fuente (163), Fryman (208), Horward (302), Teffeteller (605), and Vichness (623), have rather extensive bibliographies, listing both manuscript and published sources that should prove valuable.

The catalogues published for expositions are also helpful in locating both manuscript and published materials as exemplified by the volume produced in Lisbon by Taveira de Magalhães (603), "Biblio-iconographica," for the exposition in 1910. Several congresses have been convened during the twentieth century and valuable new information has become available as a result of their contributions. In 1964 the "Congreso Historico International de la Guerra de la Independencia y su Epoca" (137) was held and several of the papers, bibliographical in nature, have proved to be of immense value.

ARCHIVAL SOURCES

Despite significant gaps, the French archives are rich in manuscripts related to the Peninsular war. At the Service historique de l'armée, Château de Vincennes in the Paris suburbs, thirty cartons of correspondence, situations, and registers of the Army of Portugal (C7) are located along with 487 cartons of documents related to the Army of Spain (C8). Other Peninsular war documents can be found in some of the 943 cartons in the vast general collection of manuscripts labeled "Mémoires Historique" or in the 1174 cartons in the equally worthwhile collection entitled "Mémoires Réconnaissances." The service dossiers of the general officers who served in the Peninsula are also available, providing invaluable information on the activities of each officer. Without doubt the documents under the jurisdiction of the Service Historique include the most important information regarding the French war in the Peninsula. The Archives Nationales in Paris also houses important documents relative to the diplomatic, administrative, and military correspondence of many of the French officers who commanded in the Peninsula. One particularly important collection can be found in the series of documents labeled

AF IV 1604-36. At the Archives du Ministère des Affairs on the Quai d'Orsay a significant number of manuscript volumes related to Spain and Portugal are deposited while the collection of Peninsular war material at the Bibliotheque Nationale in Paris is extensive enough to require a volume (470) for its shelf list.

In England the Public Record Office, located near Kew Gardens in a London suburb, holds extremely important collections of Peninsular war materials. There are literally hundreds of boxes of documents related to the Foreign Office, the War Office, the Admiralty, the Auditor's Office, etc. Moreover, many private collections as those of Stuart de Rothesay, Torrens, and Brownrigg, are deposited there. At the British Library, formerly the British Museum, part or all of the collections of Wellington, Richard Wellesley, Wilson, Hill, Liverpool, Napier, Paget, and Bathurst are available along with papers of others who served in the Peninsula. A number of collections have been deposited at college libraries as the Vaughan papers at All Souls College, Oxford. The Hill papers are located at the county library at Shewsbury, and the valuable Wellington papers have just been moved from Stratfield Saye to the University of Southampton. Other private collections relative to the Peninsula may be located through the Historical Manuscripts Division of the Public Record Office.

The Portuguese archives include extraordinarily valuable manuscript collections regarding the Peninsular war. The Arquivo Histórico Militar has a vast collection of unused materials, including many of the papers of the Minister of War, Dom Miguel Pereira Forjaz, commander-in-chief of the Portuguese army, William Carr Beresford, and the supreme Allied commander, the Duke of Wellington, as well as the letters of various British and Portuguese officers who served in the war. There may be as many as 1,000 caixa (boxes) of documents related to the Anglo-Portuguese army and the war effort between 1807-1814. The Arquivo Nacional de Torre do Tombo, located in a wing of the Palácio da Assembleia (National Assembly) in Lisbon, has hundreds of maços (packets) related to the Council of War, the Regency Government, and foreign policy, and there are even a few maços of Peninsular war material. The Biblioteca Nacional, located at the University of Lisbon, has vast collections of material concerning the Peninsular war. Ayres de Magalhães Sepúlveda's DICIONARIO (25) lists hundreds of original documents in this collection. The documents deposited in the Biblioteca das Ciências de Lisboa include an extensive collection of Alvaras, Avisos, Circulars, Decretos, Editals, Instruções, Noticias, Ordens, Portarias, Proclamaçãos, and Relaçãos related to the Peninsular struggle. Francisco Trigoso d'Aragão Morato's COLLECAO DA ACADEMIA DAS SCIENCIAS, detailed in Ayres de Magalhães Sepúlveda and Bethencourt (56), is extremely valuable in locating original documents in this collection. The Biblioteca da Ajuda in the Palácio Nacional da Ajuda on the outskirts of Lisbon has a limited but excellent collection of documents on Junot's invasion in 1807 and the Arquivo e Museu de Arte da Universidade de Coimbra contains a collection of diocesan records relative to the third invasion of Portugal in 1810.

The Spanish archives have a wealth of manuscripts related to their so-called War of Independence. One of the most extensive collections is deposited at the Archivo Histórico Nacional in Madrid

where 84 legajos (boxes) include papers of the Supreme Junta, the
Regency Council, King José I, the Afrancesados, captured dispatches,
and other related material. The contents of each legajo is described
in an INDICES (312) as well as in the DICCIONARIO BIBLIOGRAFICO (589)
published by the Historical Service of the Spanish army. The
holdings at the Servicio Histórico Militar, also in Madrid, contain
several unique archives, including the 1008 volumes of the COLECCION
DOCUMENTAL DEL FRAILE (588). This collection, along with several
hundred newspapers of the period, was gathered by a Capuchin monk,
Joaquín de Sevilla. Information on various individuals and events
is also included in these volumes. The Biblioteca Nacional has an
extensive collection of documents concerning the war. Most of them
are included in legajos numbered in the following series: 10000,
11000, 18000, and 20000. Many provincial and municipal archives also
have vast sections of important research material. The collections
at Alicante, Barcelona, Cáceres, Gerona, Gijón, Guipúzcoa, Huesca,
Igualada, Navarra, Oviedo, San Sebastián, Tarragona, Vitoria, etc.,
house many valuable manuscripts pertinent to the Peninsular struggle.

PUBLISHED DOCUMENTS

Published documents are generally abundant for the study of the
Peninsular war. Among the letters in the published CORRESPONDANCE DE
NAPOLEON Ier and its various supplements (listed in Chapters I and
III) are literally thousands of letters relative to the war. They
are concerned with such diverse topics ranging from movements of
regiments to the reorganization of the Spanish government. The
letters in the political and military correspondence of Joseph
Bonaparte (327) as well as the laws and decrees he enacted as the
king of Spain (328) are detailed, extensive, and of inestimable
value. Similarly, the correspondence included in the papers of
Eugène de Beauharnais, Talleyrand, Foy, Masséna, Marmont, Murat,
Marat, Ney, Eblé, and others, shed important light on events in
Spain. Balagny's (31) five volumes concerning Napoleon in Spain,
with supporting documentation from the Service Historique de l'armée,
and the correspondence in Belmas's (47) multivolume work on the
sieges are equally vital for the serious scholar in the field.
Moreover, the seven volumes of the correspondence of the French
ambassador in Spain, La Forest (343), provide rare insights into
French operations in Spain.

Nevertheless, there is no French equivalent to Wellington's
(640, 642, 643) collection of dispatches, totaling 28 volumes. Such
topics as strategy, logistics, politics, and diplomacy are included
in these unique volumes. Supplemented by Wellington's GENERAL ORDERS
(641) and William Carr Beresford's ORDENS DO DIA (49) for the
Portuguese army, they form a vast reservoir of primary information
mandatory for Peninsular war research. The Spanish DEMONSTRACION
(166) in seven volumes includes proclamations and orders concerning
the Spanish army and there are collections of documents (131)
valuable in tracing its operations. Regarding the Portuguese
published documents, there are several volumes of letters and
correspondence in the works of Ayres de Magalhães Sepúlveda (26), Luz
Soriano (386), Pereira de Chaby (481-483), and the OBSERVADOR
PORTUGUEZ (456).

MEMOIRS, JOURNALS, AND EYEWITNESS ACCOUNTS

There are numerous collections of primary accounts related to the Peninsular war but three of the more significant sets are those of Beauchamp (43), Kircheisen (337), and Constable (140). Each of these collections presents a significant number of extremely important and rare eyewitness accounts of the struggle from the British, French, and German point of view. Regarding specific national groups, the accounts by British memorialists dominate the literature with well over one hundred book-length accounts of the war. Most of these volumes center around the defense of Portugal and Wellington's final drive across Spain in 1812-13. Some reflect the role of the artillery as exemplified by Dickson (169) and Frazer (206); the engineers by Burgoyne (98), Jones (324, 325), Boothby (67), and Landmann (348); the medical corps by Boutflower (72), Henry (292), McGrigor (390), and Neal (450); the quartermaster corps by Dallas (157), Henegan (291), and Schaumann (552); and the chaplains by Bradford (74) and Ormsby (462). Of the memoirs published by cavalry officers, those of Hawker (286), Vivian (628), and especially Tomkinson (611) are valuable indeed while the writings of such commanders as Cotton (134), Hay (287), Moore (432, 433), Picton (492), and Shaw Kennedy (441) are useful in understanding the interrelationship among the various line officers.

It is possible to single out only a few of the more significant memoirs and journals but clearly the works of Blakeney (59), Costello (140), Grattan (264), Harris (281), Kincaid (335, 336), Leach (359), Sherer (562), and the Napier brothers (445-448) provide valuable original material about the war. To understand the British relationship with the Portuguese army, it is necessary to utilize the works of Beresford (49-54), Bunbury (96), Wilson (150, 237, 647) and especially D'Urban (180). The works of German officers, namely Hartmann (282) and Ompteda (461), also provide worthwhile information.

French eyewitness accounts although limited in number, are significant in quality. While the British memorialists concentrate on the Portuguese campaigns and Wellington's operations, accounts by Frenchmen are diverse since they served among the various armies, often in isolated areas of Spain. Consequently, their narratives were often limited to specific campaigns. The works of Thiébault (607) and Foy (203) concentrated on Junot's first invasion of Portugal. The volumes of Illens (311), Le Noble (367), and Naylies (449) are devoted to Soult's second invasion of Portugal in 1809, and the accounts of Guingret (273), Sprünglin (592), Marcel (401), Fririon (207), Delagrave (164), and the recently published journal of Pelet (303), all extremely valuable, are concerned with Masséna's third invasion of Portugal. Similarly, the accounts of Clerc (123), Ducéré (172), Dumas (177), Lamiraux (346), Lapène (349), Pellot (478), and Régean (508) are limited to the closing years of the war in Spain. Nevertheless, since most of the French soldiers took part in several campaigns, their services in the Peninsula were often limited to a few years of a military career; consequently, the Peninsula was relegated to a chapter or two in their memoirs. This is best exemplified by the highly important but limited impressions of the Peninsular war in the works by Bigarré (57), Fantin des Odoards (190), Godart (241), Hulot (307), Lejeune (362), Lemonnier-

Delafosse (365), Levavasseur (371), Marbot (400), Noël (453), and
Thiébault (606). Similarly, segments of the memoirs or biographies
devoted to Belliard, Bessières, Colbert, Drouet, Fournier-Sarlovèze,
Hautpoul, Jourdan, Lannes, Lefebvre, Marat, Marmont, Masséna,
Mortier, Murat, Ney, Reiset, Reynier, Victor, etc., located in the
various chapters of this volume, are necessary in order to study the
war because they were given Peninsular commands at some point in
their careers.

The works of Portuguese and Spanish participants seems to have
been concentrated on specific events; therefore, their works are more
appropriately included below in specialized works.

SPECIALIZED WORKS

The sieges of Zaragoza in 1808 and 1809 have probably attracted
more Spanish interest than any other event in the Peninsular war.
Among the rare eyewitness accounts are those of Casamayor (111),
Rogniat (527), and Vaughan (620). Perhaps a hundred accounts of the
sieges, including Alcailde Ibieca's (4) detailed three-volume work,
have appeared during the last century and a half, and as recently as
1974 another account was published by Rudorff (533), demonstrating
the continual interest in the topic. The hero of Zaragoza, Palafox,
has also been a topic of considerable interest as the works of García
Mercadal (215) and Jardiel (321) clearly testify. In fact, a new
edition of the general's autobiography (466) was published in 1966.

Turning to other events in the Peninsular war, there are both
primary and secondary accounts of most of the significant campaigns
in the Peninsula. Many volumes trace the war in the various
geographical areas of Spain as illustrated by Aragon (7), Andalusia
(198, 248, 350, 535, 600, 621), Asturias (206, 216), Catalonia (61,
65, 103, 127, 136, 212, 256), Estremadura (249), Galicia (112, 213),
Murcia (543), and Santander (418, 572) while other books are limited
to specific Spanish battles. Detailed works on Astorga (537, 546),
Badajoz (48, 345, 388), Bailen (124, 352, 438, 535, 548, 559, 621),
Barcelona (197, 421), Burgos (540), Cadiz (113, 183, 314, 430, 437,
455), Ciudad Rodrigo (304, 485, 506, 542), Corunna (294), Gerona (3,
155, 220, 258, 427, 452), Lérida (260), Salamanca (402, 550, 651),
San Sebastián (347, 439, 457), Tarragona (507, 513, 555, 556),
Tortosa (512, 518, 527), Toulouse (121, 351), Valencia (153, 224,
405, 510), Vitoria (55), and Zamora (261), provide excellent
information on specific operations in the Peninsula.

The Portuguese have concentrated their interest primarily on the
three invasions of the Kingdom in 1807, 1809, and 1810. Several
general studies of the war were completed by Aranha (17), Cesar
(115), Martins Pamplona (410), Ferrão (195), Traveira de Magalhães
(603), and Martins (408). Accursio das Neves (2), Pires de Lima
(495), Dominguez (170), and OBSERVADOR PORTUGUEZ (456) are concerned
with Junot's invasion. Ibañez Marin (310), Magalhães Basto (394),
and Martins (409) concentrated on the second invasion, and Lobo (379)
and Fernandes Thomaz (193) worked on the third invasion of Portugal.
Specific battles and sieges as Almeida (304, 474, 577) and Bussaco
(117, 156, 239, 301) have been topics of special studies by both
Portuguese and foreigners, especially English and American.

Considerable attention has also been directed toward those who
commanded or played a significant role in the war. Wellington is

foremost in this category with over a hundred volumes devoted to his life and contributions to the war effort. The traditional studies of Brialmont (81), Guedalla (271), and Maxwell (416) are still useful but a number of recent works including those by Bryant (92), Weller (636), Longford (382), and Fortescue (202) probably present a more accurate picture of the Duke. Sir John Moore is also a popular topic for those interested in the Peninsula. Charles Oman's daughter, Carola Oman [Lenanton], produced a relatively comprehensive and balanced biography of Moore (366), superseding Maurice's (433) study, and more recently a number of popular biographies have appeared on Moore by Hibbert (294), Davies (160), and Parkinson (471). Other important figures who have also been the subject of significant studies over the years include Beresford (474, 625), Castaños (503), Craufurd (152), Empecinado (399), Espoz y Mina (276, 316, 429, 458), Forjaz (163), Foy (231), Freire (624), Godoy (119, 464), Graham (79, 165), Herrasti (506), Joseph Bonaparte (138, 145, 230, 235, 403, 422, 528), Jovellanos (331, 579), La Romana (254, 383, 463), Liverpool (338), Picton (444), Morillo (508, 544), Stuart (208), Suchet (529), Hill (566, 605), Smith (361), Wellesley (100, 557), and Wilson (150, 237).

There have been numerous specialized studies concerning various military units serving in the Peninsula. The King's German Legion has been carefully researched by Beamish (39), Pfannkuche (487), Schwertfeger (554), and Gray (265), while the Spanish serving with the French have been examined by Boppe (68). The French gendarmerie were the subject of works by Martin (404) and Charron (118) and both the Loyal Lusitanian Legion and the Portuguese Legion were examined by Brun (87) and Pereira de Chaby (481) respectively. Ayres de Magalhães Sepúlveda (26) and Perreira Gil (196) analyzed the Portuguese army intensively; Halliday's (277) volume is one of the few works on the early organization and operation of the Portuguese army. Santiago y Gadea (545) studied the administration of the Spanish army while the organization of the British army has been addressed by Glover (240) and Ward (633). Similarly, life within the army is carefully described in the excellent volumes of Oman (460), Brett-James (80), and Davies (161). Cope's (144) volume on the Rifle brigade, Connolly's (139) study on the sappers, and Leslie's (369) collective works on the artillery are certainly useful. The same is true of the many regimental histories that can be easily located by using the regimental bibliographies of White, Chichester, or Hanoteau (see Chapter I). Regarding the role of the navy in the Peninsular war, there are several useful studies (406, 414, 524). However, there is no comprehensive analysis of seapower and its impact during the Peninsular war, although recently the NAVAL WAR COLLEGE REVIEW has published several articles on this topic (see Chapter I).

A number of descriptive contemporary works devoted to the life, customs, and institutions of the Iberian people are extremely valuable. Laborde's five-volume study (340) is probably the most comprehensive work although the publications of Eliot (181), Graham (257), Broughton (84), Hautefort (284), and Jacob (320) also provide interesting insights into Peninsular life.

The most valuable and famous cartographic volume of Peninsular war maps was published by Wyld (651) in 1840 and it remains indispensible for research in the field although Belmas's (47) volume of maps on the sieges is equally valuable. For the names of sites and

locations in the Peninsula, the volumes on Spain and Portugal (see
Chapter I) published by the U.S. Board of Geographic Names is
obligatory despite the perplexing spelling changes that have taken
place since 1814.

PERIODICALS

In addition to the journals listed in Chapter I, there are a
number of scholarly periodicals, especially in Portuguese and
Spanish, that include a considerable number of articles relative to
the Peninsular war. The REVISTA DAS SCIENCIAS MILITARES (662), the
BOLETIM DO ARQUIVO HISTORICO MILITAR (657), the JORNAL DO EXERCITO
(660), the REVISTA MILITAR (674), the REVISTA DO EXERCITO E DA ARMADA
(671), and the BOLETIM DA ACADEMIA DAS CIENCIAS (654) are among the
most valuable journals on the Portuguese army and the Guerra
Peninsular. In Spain the editorial committees of the REVISTA TECNIA
DE INFANTERIA Y CABALLERIA (677), the REVISTA DE HISTORICO MILITAR
(670), the REVISTA DE ESTUDIOS MILITARES (667), the REVISTA
CIENTIFICO MILITAR (661), and the REVISTA MILITAR (675) published
numerous articles related to the Spanish struggle against the French.
It also should be noted that a significant number of papers have been
published on the Peninsular war in the annual PROCEEDINGS of the
Consortium on Revolutionary Europe (see Chapter I).

FUTURE RESEARCH

Although there has been a momentary decline in the number of
completed doctorates in the history of the Peninsular war as a result
of the financial exigencies faced by the teaching profession in the
United States, there has been an increase in the number of Peninsular
war publications in England.
Based on the available primary manuscript collections, literally
hundreds of untapped topics are available on various facets of the
Peninsula war. Little is known about the French operations in
Galicia, Asturias, León, Andalusia, Estremadura, and the other
Spanish provinces, or the impact of the war upon the Spanish living
in these areas. Biographies have yet to be written on such Spanish
and Portuguese commanders as Alvarez de Castro, Areizaga, Baccelar,
Ballestreros, Blake, Campoverde, Cuesta, Del Parque, D'Espana, Mahy,
Mendizabal, Merino, Moreno, and O'Donnell. Similarly, many of the
generals Napoleon sent to the Peninsula as exemplified by Bonnet,
Caffarelli, Delaborde, Duhesme, Ferey, Girard, Heudelet, Marchand,
Reille, Sebastiani, Séras, Solignac, and Souham offer fertile topics
for future research. The British commanders have been more
extensively researched, but there is still little information on
several major figures and many of the operations in which the British
took part. There is much to be done in examining the development of
guerrilla warfare and the role of the guerrillas in both Spain and
Portugal. During the past decade almost twenty doctoral studies have
been completed on Peninsular war topics, especially at Florida State
University, and these efforts continue both in Europe and the U.S.
Many gaps have yet to be filled and conflicting views must be
reexamined and reconciled in order to complete our understanding of
this complex and ambiguous period of European history. Only then
will we be able to accurately access the impact of the Peninsular
struggle and its effects upon the rest of Europe.

BIBLIOGRAPHY: PENINSULAR WAR

1. Abrantès, Laure Saint-Martin Permon Junot, duchesse d'. SOUVENIRS D'UNE AMBASSADE ET D'UN SEJOUR EN ESPAGNE ET EN PORTUGAL, DE 1808 A 1811. Paris: Ollivier, 1837. 2 vols.

2. Accursio das Neves, José. HISTORIA GERAL DA INVASAO DOS FRANCEZES EM PORTUGAL E RESTAURACAO DESTE REINO. Lisbon: Ferreira, 1810-11. 5 vols.

3. Ahumada, Fernando. GERONA LA INMORTAL (1808-1809). ESTUDIO HISTORICO. Toledo: Imprenta Sucesor de Rodríguez, [1935].

4. Alcailde Ibieca, Augustín. HISTORIA DE LOS DOS SITIOS QUE PUSIERON A ZARAGOZA EN LOS ANOS DE 1808 Y 1809 LAS TROPAS DE NAPOLEON. Madrid: Imprenta de Burgos, 1830-31. 3 vols.

5. Aldington, Richard. THE DUKE; BEING AN ACCOUNT OF THE LIFE & ACHIEVEMENTS OF ARTHUR WELLESLEY, 1ST DUKE OF WELLINGTON. New York: Viking, 1943.

6. Alexander, Don Wesley. ROD OF IRON: FRENCH COUNTERINSURGENCY POLICY IN ARAGON DURING THE PENINSULAR WAR. Wilmington, Del.: Scholarly Resources, 1985.

7. Alexander, James Edward. LIFE OF FIELD MARSHAL, HIS GRACE, THE DUKE OF WELLINGTON. EMBRACING HIS CIVIL, MILITARY, AND POLITICAL CAREER TO THE PRESENT TIME. London: Colburn, 1839-40. 2 vols.

8. Allué Salvador, Miguel. LOS SITIOS DE ZARAGOZA ANTE EL DERECHO INTERNACIONAL. Zaragoza: Tipog. de M. Sevilla, 1908.

9. Anderson, John. THE PENINSULAR WAR, MARCH 1, 1811, TO THE CLOSE OF THE WAR IN 1814. London: Rees, 1906.

10. Anderson, John. THE SPANISH CAMPAIGN OF SIR JOHN MOORE. London: Rees, 1905.

11. Anderson, Joseph Jocelyn. RECOLLECTIONS OF A PENINSULAR VETERAN. London: Arnold, 1913.

12. Andrews, John. CHARACTERISTICAL VIEWS OF THE PAST AND OF THE PRESENT STATE OF THE PEOPLE OF SPAIN AND ITALY. Addressed to an English traveller. London: Chapple, 1808.

13. Anglesey, George Charles Henry Victor Paget, marquis of. ONE-LEG; THE LIFE AND LETTERS OF HENRY WILLIAM PAGET, FIRST MARQUESS OF ANGLESEY, K.G., 1768-1854. London: Cape [1961].

14. Anton, James. RETROSPECT OF A MILITARY LIFE DURING THE MOST EVENTFUL PERIODS OF THE LAST WAR. Edinburgh: Lizars, 1841.

15. Antón de Olmet, Fernando de, marqués de Dos-Fuentes. ACLARACION HISTORICA; EL ARMA DE INFANTERIA EN EL LEVANTAMIENTO DEL DOS DE MAYO DE 1808. Madrid: Marzo, 1908.

16. Antón de Olmet, Fernando de, marqués de Dos-Fuentes. EL CUERPO DIPLOMATICO ESPANOL EN LA GUERRA DE LA INDEPENDENCIA. Madrid: [Imprenta artística española, 1912?-14]. 6 vols.

17. Aranha, Brito. INVASOES FRANCEZAS EM PORTUGAL. Lisbon: Academia Real das Sciências, 1909.

18. Arenas Gonzáles, Hillario. EL TECER MARQUES DE ALVENTOS. SU ACTUACION PATRIOTICA OFICIALMENTE DOCUMENTADA DESDE EL ANO 1808 HASTA EL ANO 1816. Seville: Edición no venal, 1956.

19. Argüelles, Agustín. EXAMEN HISTORICO DE LA REFORMA CONSTITUCIONAL QUE HICIERON LAS CORTES GENERALES Y EXTRAORDINARIAS DESDE QUE SE INSTALARON EN ... SETIEMBRE DE 1810, HASTA ... 1813. London: Wood, 1835. 2 vols.

20. Artola, Miguel. LOS AFRANCESADOS. Con un prólogo de Gregorio Marañón. Madrid: Sociedad de Estudios y Publicaciones, 1953.

21. Artola, Miguel, ed. MEMORIAS DE TIEMPOS DE FERNANDO VII. Madrid: Ediciones Atlas, 1957. 2 vols.

22. Augoyat, Antoine Marie. PRECIS DES CAMPAGNES ET DES SIEGES D'ESPAGNE ET PORTUGAL DE 1807 A 1814, D'APRES L'OUVRAGE DE M. BELMAS INTITULE: JOURNAUX DES SIEGES FAIT ET SOUTENUS PAR LES FRANCAIS DANS LA PENINSULE; LES DEPECHES DU DUC DE WELLINGTON ET AUTRES OUVRAGES. Paris: Leneveu, 1839.

23. Ayerbe y Lierta, Pedro Jordan de Urries, marqués. MEMORIAS DEL MARQUES DE AYERBE SOBRE LA ESTANCIA DE D. FERNANDO VII EN VALENCAY Y EL PRINCIPIO DE LA GUERRA DE LA INDEPENDENCIA. Zaragoza: Salas, 1893.

24. Aymes, Jean René. LA GUERRE D'INDEPENDANCE ESPAGNOLE (1808-1814). Paris, Brussels, and Montréal: Bordas, 1973.

25. Ayres de Magalhães Sepúlveda, Christovam. DICIONARIO BIBLIOGRAFICO DA GUERRA PENINSULAR. Coimbra: Imprensa da Universidade, 1924-30. 4 vols.

26. Ayres de Magalhães Sepúlveda, Christovam. HISTORIA ORGANICA E POLITICA DO EXCERCITO PORTUGUEZ. Lisbon: Imprensa Nacional, 1896-1932. 17 vols. in 21.

27. Azanza, Miguel José de. MEMOIRE DE D. MIGUEL JOSEPH DE AZANZA ET D. GONZALO O'FARRILL, ET EXPOSE DES FAITS QUI JUSTIFIENT LEUR CONDUITE POLITIQUE DEPUIS MARS 1808 JUSQU'EN AVRIL 1814. Traduit de l'espagnol par M. Alexandre Foudras. Paris: Rougeron, 1815.

28. Azcárate y Florez, Pablo de. WELLINGTON Y ESPANA. Madrid: Espansa-Calpe, 1961.

29. Bacler D'Albé, Louis Albert Guislain. SOUVENIRS HISTORIQUES DU GENERAL BACLER D'ALBE. CAMPAGNE D'ESPAGNE. Paris: Englemann, 1889-92. 2 vols.

30. Bagès, Jean François. ETUDE SUR LES GUERRES D'ESPAGNE. Paris: Charles-Lavauzelle, 1907. 2 vols.

31. Balagny, Dominique Eugène Paul. CAMPAGNE DE L'EMPEREUR NAPOLEON EN ESPAGNE (1808-1809). Paris, Nancy: Berger-Levrault, 1902-06. 5 vols.

32. Ballauff, Marie. DES KOENIGS DEUTSCHE LEGION BIS ZUR SCHLACHT BEI TALAVERA, 28 JULI 1809. Hanover: Heinrich Feesche, 1909.

33. Barkhausen, George Heinrich. TAGEBUCH EINES RHEINBUNDOFFIZIERS AUS DEM FELDZUGE GEGAN SPANIEN UND WAEHREND SPANICHER UND ENGLISCHER KRIEGSGEFANGENSCHAFT, 1808-1814. Wiesbaden: Bergmann, 1900.

34. Barral, Philippe Anne de. SOUVENIRS DE GUERRE ET DE CAPTIVITE D'UN PAGE DE NAPOLEON Ier (1812-1815). Paris: Emile-Paul, [1925].

35. Barreiros, Fernando. NOTICIA HISTORICA DO CORPO MILITAR ACADEMICO DE COIMBRA (1808-1811). Lisbon: Bertrand e Aillaud, 1918.

36. Barry, Donald H. "The Life and Career of Count Louis-Henri Loison, 1771-1816." Ph.D. dissertation, Florida State University, 1973.

37. Batty, Robert. CAMPAIGN OF THE LEFT-WING OF THE ALLIED ARMY, IN THE WESTERN PYRENEES AND SOUTH OF FRANCE, IN THE YEARS 1813-1814; UNDER FIELD-MARSHAL THE MARQUESS OF WELLINGTON. London: J. Murray, 1823.

38. Baumgarten, Hermann. GESCHICHTE SPANIENS VOM AUSBRUCH DER FRANZOESISCHEN REVOLUTION BIS AUF UNSERE TAGE. Leipzig: Hirzel, 1865-71. 3 vols.

39. Beamish, North Ludlow. HISTORY OF THE KING'S GERMAN LEGION. (1803-15). London: T. and W. Boone, 1832-37. 2 vols.

40. Beatson, Finlay C. WELLINGTON: THE BIDASSOA AND NIVELLE. London: Edward Arnold, 1931.

41. Beatson, Finlay C. WELLINGTON, THE CROSSING OF THE GAVES AND THE BATTLE OF ORTHEZ. London: Heath, Cranton, 1925.

42. Beatson, Finlay C. WITH WELLINGTON IN THE PYRENEES. London: Max Goshen, 1914.

43. Beauchamp, Alphonse de. COLLECTION DES MEMOIRES RELATIFS AUX REVOLUTIONS D'ESPAGNE. Mis en ordre et publiés par Alphonse de Beauchamp. [Memoirs of Arias, Chemineau, Vedel, Baste, Dupont, Curtwright, Pigueta, la Romana, Keats, Baretta, etc.] Paris: Michaud, 1824. 2 vols.

44. Beça, Adriano. O GENERAL SILVEIRA. Lisbon: Coelho da Cunha Brito, 1909.

45. Bécker, Jerónimo. ACCION DE LA DIPLOMACIA ESPANOLA DURANTE LA GUERRA DE LA INDEPENDENCIA, 1808-1814. Zaragoza: Tipog. de E. Casanal, 1909.

46. Bell, George. ROUGH NOTES BY AN OLD SOLDIER, DURING FIFTY YEARS SERVICE, FROM ENSIGN G.B. TO MAJOR-GENERAL C.B.... London: Day, 1867. 2 vols.

47. Belmas, Jacques Vital. JOURNAUX DE SIEGES FAITS OU SOUTENUS PAR LES FRANCAIS DANS LA PENINSULE, DE 1807 A 1814; REDIGES D'APRES LES ORDRES DU GOUVERNEMENT, SUR LES DOCUMENTS EXISTANT AUX ARCHIVES DE LA GUERRE ET AU DEPOT DES FORTIFICATIONS. Paris: Firmin-Didot, 1836-1837. 4 vols. and atlas.

48. Berdruck, Carl. DER KAMPF IM BADAJOZ IM FRUEHJAHR 1812 NACH DEZ URSPRUENGLICHEN QUELLEN UND NACH MITTHEILUNGEN VON AUGENZEUGEN. Leipzig: Dyk'sechen Buchhandlung, 1861.

49. Beresford, William Carr Beresford, viscount. COLLECCAO DAS ORDENS DO DIA DO GUILHERME CARR BERESFORD. Lisbon: por António Nunes dos Santos, 1809-[1823] Vols. 1-6, 1809-1815.

50. Beresford, William Carr, viscount. FURTHER STRICTURES ON THOSE PARTS OF COL. NAPIER'S HISTORY OF THE PENINSULAR WAR WHICH RELATE TO THE MILITARY OPINIONS AND CONDUCT OF GENERAL LORD VISCOUNT BERESFORD. London: Longman, Rees, Orme, Brown, Green and Longmans, 1832.

51. Beresford, William Carr, viscount. INSTRUCCOES PARA A FORMATURA, EXERCICIO E MOVIMENTOS DOS REGIMENTOS DE INFANTERIA. Lisbon: Impressam Regia, 1809.

52. Beresford, William Carr, viscount. INSTRUCCOES PROVISORIAS PARA A CAVALLARIA. Lisbon: Impressam Regia, 1810.

53. Beresford, William Carr, viscount. STRICTURES ON CERTAIN PASSAGES OF LIEUT. COL. NAPIER'S HISTORY OF THE PENINSULAR WAR WHICH RELATE TO THE MILITARY OPINIONS AND CONDUCT OF GENERAL LORD VISCOUNT BERESFORD. London: Longman, Rees, Orme, Brown, and Green, 1831.

54. Beresford, William Carr, viscount. SYSTEMA DE INSTRUCCAO E DISCIPLINA PARA OS MOVIMENTOS E DEVERES DOS CACADORES. Lisbon: Impressam Regia, 1810.

55. Bessa, Adriano, and João Carlos Rodrigues da Costa. COMEMORACOA
    DA BATALHA DA VITORIA GANHA PELOS EXERCITOS ALIADOS EM 21 DE
    JUNHO DE 1813. Lisbon: Universal, 1913.

56. Bethencourt, Cardozo de. CATALOGO DAS OBRAS REFERENTES A GUERRA
    DA PENINSULA. Lisbon: Academia das Sciências, 1910.

57. Bigarré, Auguste Julien, baron. MEMOIRES DU GENERAL BIGARRE,
    AIDE DE CAMP DU ROI JOSEPH, 1775-1813. Paris: Kolb [1893].

58. Billon, François Frédéric. SOUVENIRS D'UN VELITE DE LA GARDE
    SOUS NAPOLEON Ier. Extraits des manuscrits de François-Frédéric
    Billon, par son arrière-neveu A. Lombard-Dumas. Paris:
    Plon-Nourrit, 1905.

59. Blakeney, Robert. A BOY IN THE PENINSULAR WAR, THE SERVICES,
    ADVENTURES, AND EXPERIENCES OF ROBERT BLAKENEY, SUBALTERN IN THE
    28th REGIMENT. Edited by Julian Sturgis. London: J. Murray,
    1899.

60. Blakiston, John. TWELVE YEARS' MILITARY ADVENTURE IN THREE
    QUARTERS OF THE GLOBE: OR, MEMOIRS OF AN OFFICER WHO SERVED IN
    THE ARMIES OF HIS MAJESTY AND OF THE EAST INDIA COMPANY, BETWEEN
    THE YEARS 1802 AND 1814; IN WHICH ARE CONTAINED CAMPAIGNS OF THE
    DUKE OF WELLINGTON IN INDIA AND HIS LAST IN SPAIN AND THE SOUTH
    OF FRANCE. London: Colburn, 1829. 2 vols.

61. Blanch y Cortada, Adolfo. CATALUNA; HISTORIA DE LA GUERRA DE LA
    INDEPENDENCIA EN EL ANTIGUO PRINCIPADO. Barcelona: Gorchs,
    1861-62. 2 vols.

62. Blanco, Richard L. WELLINGTON'S SURGEON GENERAL: SIR JAMES
    MCGRIGOR. Durham, N.C.: Duke University Press, 1974.

63. Blayeny, Andrew Thomas. NARRATIVE OF A FORCED JOURNEY THROUGH
    SPAIN AND FRANCE, AS A PRISONER OF WAR, IN YEARS 1810 to 1814.
    London: Kerby, 1814. 2 vols.

64. Blaze, Sébastien. MEMOIRES D'UN APOTHICAIRE SUR LA GUERRE
    D'ESPAGNE, PENDANT LES ANNEES 1808 A 1814. Paris: Ladvocat,
    1828. 2 vols.

65. Bofarull y de Broca, Antonio de. HISTORIA CRITICA DE LA GUERRA
    DE LA INDEPENDENCIA EN CATALUNA. Barcelona: Nacente, 1886-87.
    2 vols.

66. Bonnal de Ganges, Edmond. WELLINGTON, GENERAL EN CHEF
    (1808-1814). Paris: Chapelot, 1912.

67. Boothby, Charles. UNDER ENGLAND'S FLAG FROM 1804 to 1809. THE
    MEMOIRS, DIARY, AND CORRESPONDENCE OF C. BOOTHBY, CAPTAIN OF
    ROYAL ENGINEERS. London: Black, 1900.

68. Boppe, Paul Louis. LES ESPAGNOLS A LA GRANDE ARMEE; LE CORPS DE
    LA ROMANA (1807-1808), LE REGIMENT JOSEPH-NAPOLEON (1809-1813).
    Paris and Nancy: Berger-Levrault, 1899.

69. Borges de Castro, José Ferreira, and J. Judice Biker. COLLECCAO
    DOS TRATADOS, CONVENCOES, CONTRACTOS E ACTOS PUBLICOS CELEBRADOS
    ENTRE A COROA DE PORTUGAL E AS MAIS POTENDIAS, DESDE 1640 ATE AO
    PRESENTE. Lisbon: Imprensa Nacional, 1856-80. 28 vols.

70. Botelho, José Justino Teixeira. HISTORIA POPULAR DA GUERRA DA
    PENINSULA. Porto: Chardron, 1915.

71. Bouillé, Louis Joseph Armour, marquis de. SOUVENIRS ET
    FRAGMENTS POUR SERVIR AUX MEMOIRES DE MA VIE ET DE MON TEMPS,
    PAR LE MARQUIS DE BOUILLE. Paris: Picard, 1906-22. 3 vols.

72. Boutflower, Charles. THE JOURNAL OF AN ARMY SURGEON DURING THE
    PENINSULAR WAR. Manchester: Refuge Printing, 1912.

73. Bradford, George Augustus. LETTERS FROM PORTUGAL, SPAIN,
    SICILY, AND MALTA IN 1812, 1813, AND 1814. London: Chiswick
    Press, 1875.

74. Bradford, William. SKETCHES OF THE COUNTRY, CHARACTER AND
    COSTUMES IN PORTUGAL AND SPAIN, MADE DURING THE CAMPAIGN AND ON
    THE ROUTE OF THE BRITISH ARMY IN 1808 AND 1809. London:
    Printed for John Booth by B.R. Houlett, 1812.

75. Bragge, William. PENINSULAR PORTRAIT, 1811-1814; THE LETTERS OF
    CAPTAIN WILLIAM BRAGGE, THIRD (KING'S OWN) DRAGOONS. Edited by
    S.A.C. Cassels. London and New York: Oxford University Press,
    1963.

76. Brandao, Paul. EL-REI JUNOT. Lisbon: Monteiro, 1912.

77. Brandt, Heinrich von. SOUVENIRS D'UN OFFICIER POLONAIS: SCENES
    DE LA VIE MILITAIRE EN ESPAGNE ET EN RUSSIE (1803-1812). Paris:
    Charpentier, 1877.

78. Brémond d'Ars, Théophile Charles. HISTORIQUE DU 21e REGIMENT DE
    CHASSEURS A CHEVAL, 1792-1814. Souvenirs militaires publiés et
    annotés par le fils de l'auteur, le comte Anatole de Brémond
    d'Ars. Paris: Champion, 1903.

79. Brett-James, Antony. GENERAL GRAHAM, LORD LYNEDOCH. New York:
    St. Martin's Press, 1959.

80. Brett-James, Antony. LIFE IN WELLINGTON'S ARMY. London: Allen
    & Unwin, 1972.

81. Brialmont, Alexis Henri. HISTORY OF THE LIFE OF ARTHUR, DUKE OF
    WELLINGTON. From the French of M. Brialmont. With emendations
    and additions, by G.R. Gleig. London: Longman, Brown, Green,
    Longmans, & Roberts, 1858-60. 4 vols.

82. Brito Aranha, Pedro Wenceslau de. NOTA ACERCA DAS INVASOES FRANCEZAS EM PORTUGAL. Lisbon: Academia Real das Sciências, 1909.

83. Broekere, Stanislaus von. MEMOIREN AUS DER FELDZUEGE IN SPANIEN (1808-14). Herausgegeben von P. von Cybulska. Posen: Heine, 1883.

84. Broughton, Samuel Daniel. LETTERS FROM PORTUGAL, SPAIN & FRANCE WRITTEN DURING THE CAMPAIGNS OF 1812, 1813, AND 1814, ADDRESSED TO A FRIEND IN ENGLAND. London: Longman, Hurst, Rees, Orme, and Brown, 1815.

85. Brownrigg, Beatrice. THE LIFE AND LETTERS OF SIR JOHN MOORE. Oxford: Blackwell, 1923.

86. Bruce, Henry Austin, ed. LIFE OF GENERAL SIR WILLIAM NAPIER. London: J. Murray, 1861. 2 vols.

87. Brun, André Francisco. SOLDADOS DE PORTUGAL. A LEGIAO PORTUGUEZA--A GUERRA PENINSULAR. Lisbon: Guimaraes, 1915.

88. Brun de Villeret, Louis. LES CAHIERS DU GENERAL BRUN, BARON DE VILLERET, PAIR DE FRANCE. 1773-1845. Publiés et présentés par Louis de Saint-Pierre. Paris: Plon, 1953.

89. Brunner, Karl. UNTER NAPOLEONS FAHNEN IN SPANIEN (1808-1809). Berlin: Gcherl, 1911.

90. Bruno, Michael D. "The Military and Administrative Career of Sir John Cradock, 1762-1814." M.A. thesis, Florida State University, 1972.

91. Bryant, Arthur. THE AGE OF ELEGANCE, 1812-1822. New York: Harper [1950].

92. Bryant, Arthur. THE GREAT DUKE; OR, THE INVINCIBLE GENERAL. London: Collins, 1971.

93. Bryant, Arthur. YEARS OF VICTORY, 1802-1812. London: Collins, 1944.

94. Bucher, August Wilhelm. TAGEBUCH DER BELAGERUNG VON GERONA IN JAHRE 1809, ALS ERLAEUTERUNG ZUM PLANE DIESER FESTUNG. Hildesheim: Gerstenberg, 1812.

95. Buckham, E.W. PERSONAL NARRATIVE OF ADVENTURES IN THE PENINSULA DURING THE WAR IN 1812-1813 BY AN OFFICER LATE IN THE STAFF CORP REGIMENT OF CAVALRY. London: J. Murray, 1827.

96. Bunbury, Henry Edward. NARRATIVES OF SOME PASSAGES IN THE GREAT WAR WITH FRANCE (1799-1810). With introduction by Sir John Fortescue. London: Peter Davies, 1927.

97. Bunbury, Thomas. REMINISCENCES OF A VETERAN, BEING PERSONAL AND
    MILITARY ADVENTURES IN PORTUGAL, SPAIN, FRANCE. London: Skeet,
    1861. 3 vols.

98. Burgoyne, John Fox. LIFE AND CORRESPONDENCE OF FIELD MARSHAL
    SUR JOHN (FOX) BURGOYNE. Edited by ... Hon. George Wrottlesley.
    London: Bentley, 1873. 2 vols.

99. Burroughs, George Frederick. A NARRATIVE OF THE RETREAT OF THE
    BRITISH ARMY FROM BURGOS. Bristol: Routh, 1814.

100. Butler, Iris. THE ELDEST BROTHER: THE MARQUESS WELLESLEY, THE
     DUKE OF WELLINGTON'S ELDEST BROTHER. London: Hodder and
     Stoughton, 1973.

101. Butler, Lewis William George. WELLINGTON'S OPERATIONS IN THE
     PENINSULA (1808-1814). London: Unwin, 1904. 2 vols.

102. Cabanes, Francisco Xavier. CAMPANA DE PORTUGAL EN 1810 y 1811.
     Traducida del Frances al Castellano, y aumentada con varias
     notas por el Brigadier Don Francisco Xavier de Cabanes. Madrid:
     Imprenta de Callado, 1815. 3 vols.

103. Cabanes, Francisco Xavier. HISTORIA DE LAS OPERACIONES DEL
     EXERCITO DE CATALUNA EN LA GUERRA DE LA USURPACION. Tarragona:
     Imprenta de la Gazeta, 1809.

104. Cadell, Charles. NARRATIVE OF THE CAMPAIGNS OF THE
     TWENTY-EIGHTH REGIMENT, SINCE THEIR RETURN FROM EGYPT IN 1802.
     London: Whittaker, 1835.

105. Calladine, George. THE DIARY OF COLOUR-SERJEANT GEORGE
     CALLADINE, 19th FOOT, 1793-1837. Edited by Major M.L. Ferrar.
     London: Fisher, 1922.

106. Camden, Theophilus. THE HISTORY OF THE PRESENT WAR IN SPAIN AND
     PORTUGAL; WITH MEMOIRS OF THE LIFE OF THE MARQUIS WELLINGTON.
     London: Stratford, 1812.

107. Canga Argüelles, José. OBSERVACIONES SOBRE LA HISTORIA DE LA
     GUERRA DE ESPANA QUE ESCRIBIERON LOS SENORES CLARKE, SOUTHEY,
     LONDONDERRY Y NAPIER. London: D.M. Calero, 1829-30. 3 vols.

108. Canovas Cervantes, Salvador. LAS CORTES DE CADIZ.
     (CONSTITUCION DE 1812.) Madrid: Editorial del Norte, 1930.

109. Cardús, Salvador. HISTORIA DE LA GUERRA NAPOLEONICA A TERRASSA.
     HEROIC SACRIFICI D'UN PATRIOTA EXAMPLAR. Terrassa: Patronato
     de la Fundación, 1962.

110. Carel, Auguste. PRECIS HISTORIQUE DE LA GUERRE D'ESPAGNE ET DE
     PORTUGAL, DE 1808 A 1814. Contenant la réfuation des ouvrages
     de M.M. Sarrazin et Alphonse de Beauchamps [sic] avec des
     détails sur la bataille de Toulouse. Paris: Jeunehomme,
     Delaunnay, Plancher, 1815.

111. Casamayor, Faustino. LOS SITIOS DE ZARAGOZA: DIARIO DE CASAMAYOR. Con prólogo y notas por José Valenzuela La Rosa. Zaragoza: Jasca, 1908.

112. Castilla, Modesto. HISTORIA DE LA JUNTA DE DEFENSA DE GALICIA. Corunna: La Papeleria de Ferrer, 1894.

113. Castro y Rossi, Adolfo de. CADIZ EN LA GUERRA DE LA INDEPENDENCIA. CUADRO HISTORICO. Cádiz: Revista medica, 1864.

114. Cavallero, Manuel. DEFENSE DE SARAGOSSE, OU RELATION DES DEUX SIEGES SOUTENUS PAR CETTE VILLE EN 1808 ET 1809; ET SIEGES DE CADIZ EN 1810, 1811 ET 1812. Traduit par M.L.V. Angliviel de la Beaumelle, Chef du Bataillon du Génie. Paris: Magimel, 1815.

115. Cesar, Vitoriano José. INVASOES FRANCESAS EN PORTUGAL. [contents: 1. pt. BREVE ESTUDO SOBRE A INVASAO FRANCO-HESPANHOLA DO 1807 EM PORTUGAL E OPERACOES REALIZADAS ATE A CONVENCAO DE CINTRA-ROLICA E VIMEIRO. 2. pt. INVASAO FRANCESA DE 1809. DE SALAMONDE A TALAVERA. 3. pt. INVASAO FRANCESA DE 1810. DE ALMEIDA AS LINHAS DE TORRES VEDRAS E DAS LINHAS DE TORRES VEDRAS A FUENTES D'ONORO, 1810-1811.] Lisbon: Cooperativa Militar, 1904-10. 3 vols.

116. Cesar da Silva, Alfredo Augusto. O MARECHAL SALDANHA; CRONICA EPISODIC DAS LUTAS LIBERAIS EM PORTUGAL. Lisbon: Romano Torres, [193?].

117. Chambers, George L. BUSSACO. With numerous original maps, and illustrations from photographs taken by the author on the spot. London: Sonnenschein, 1910.

118. Charron, Bernard. "La Participation de la gendarmerie imperiale à la guerre d'Espagne." Ph.D. dissertation, University of Bordeaux, 1972.

119. Chastenet, Jacques. GODOY, MASTER OF SPAIN, 1792-1808. Translated by J.F. Hunnington. London: Batchworth, 1953.

120. Chastenet, Jacques. WELLINGTON, 1769-1852. Paris: Fayard, 1945.

121. Choumara, Pierre Marie Théodore. CONSIDERATIONS MILITAIRES SUR LES MEMOIRES DU MARECHAL SUCHET ET SUR LA BATAILLE DE TOULOUSE. Paris: Corréard, 1840. 2 vols.

122. Christiansen, Eric. THE ORIGINS OF MILITARY POWER IN SPAIN, 1800-1854. London: Oxford University Press, 1967.

123. Clerc, Joseph Charles. CAMPAGNE DU MARECHAL SOULT DANS LES PYRENEES OCCIDENTALES EN 1813-1814. Paris: Baudoin, 1894.

124. Clerc, Joseph Charles. GUERRE D'ESPAGNE. CAPITULATION DE
     BAYLEN, CAUSES ET CONSEQUENCES. D'APRES LES ARCHIVES ESPAGNOLES
     ET LES ARCHIVES FRANCAISES DE LA GUERRE, NATIONALES ET DES
     AFFAIRES ETRANGERES. Paris: Fontemoing, 1903.

125. Clerk, Archibald. MEMOIR OF COLONEL JOHN CAMERON, FASSIEFERN
     K.T.S., LIEUT.-GENERAL OF THE GORDON HIGHLANDERS, OR 92nd
     REGIMENT OF FOOT. Glasgow: T. Murray, 1858.

126. Clinton, Herbert R. THE WAR IN THE PENINSULA, AND WELLINGTON'S
     CAMPAIGNS IN FRANCE AND BELGIUM. London: Warne, 1878.

127. Clopas Batlle, Isidro. EL INVICTO CONDE DE LLOBREGAT Y LOS
     HOMBRES DE CATALUNA EN LA GUERRA DE LA INDEPENDENCIA; LUCHAS
     CIVILES DE LA PRIMERA MITAD DEL SIGLO XIX. Barcelona: [Sección
     de Prensa de la Diputación Provincial de Barcelona] 1961.

128. Cole, Galbraith Lowry. MEMOIRS OF SIR LOWRY COLE. Edited by
     Maud Lowry Cole and Stephen Gwynn. London: Macmillan, 1934.

129. Cole, John William. MEMOIRS OF BRITISH GENERALS DISTINGUISHED
     DURING THE PENINSULAR WAR. London: Bentley, 1856. 2 vols.

130. COLECCION DE DOCUMENTOS INEDITOS DE LA GUERRA DE LA
     INDEPENDENCIA EXISTENTES EN EL ARCHIVO DE LA EXCMA. DIPUTACION
     DE VIZCAYA. Transcritos y comentados por el personal des mismo,
     dirigido por D. Carlos Gonzalez Echegaray. Bilbao: Diputación
     de Vizcaya, 1959.

131. COLECCION DE PAPELES INTERESSANTES SOBRE LAS CIRCUNSTANCIAS
     PRESENTES. Madrid: Liberias de Orea, 1808. 3 vols.

132. COLECCION DE PROCLAMAS Y DEMAS PAPELES, PUBLICADOS CON MOTIVO DE
     QUERER ... NAPOLEON BONAPARTE MUDAR LA DINASTIA DE ESPANA Y
     COLOCAR EN EL TRONO A SU HERMANO JOSEPH. Cádiz: n.p., 1808. 2
     vols.

133. COLLECTION COMPLEMENTAIRE DES MEMOIRES RELATIFS A LA REVOLUTION
     FRANCAISE. SECONDE LIVRAISON. [contents: vol. 1. MEMOIRES DE
     CEVALLOS ET D'ESCOIQUIZ. vol. 2. MEMOIRES DU BARON DE KOLLI ET
     DE LA REINE D'ETRURIE. vol. 3. MEMOIRES DE DUHESME, DE
     VAUGHAN, DE MARIA RIC ET DE CONTRERAS.] Paris: Michaud, 1823.
     3 vols.

134. Combermere, Mary W. Cotton, viscountess, and W.W. Knollys,
     MEMOIRS AND CORRESPONDENCE OF FIELD MARSHAL VISCOUNT COMBERMERE,
     G.C.B., ETC., FROM HIS FAMILY PAPERS. London: Hurst and
     Blackett, 1866. 2 vols.

135. Conard, Pierre. LA CONSTITUTION DE BAYONNE (1808). Paris:
     Cornély, 1910.

136. Conard, Pierre. NAPOLEON ET LA CATALOGNE, 1809-1814. Paris: Alcan, 1910.

137. Congreso Histórico Internacional de la Guerra de la Independencia y su Epoca. GUERRA DE LA INDEPENDENCIA: ESTUDIOS. Por J. Garcia Prado [et al. Zaragoza:] Institución Fernando el Católico (C.S.I.C.) de la Excma. Diputación Provincial de Zaragoza, 1964-67. 3 vols.

138. Connelly, Owen. THE GENTLE BONAPARTE; A BIOGRAPHY OF JOSEPH, NAPOLEON'S ELDER BROTHER. New York: Macmillan [1968].

139. Connolly, Thomas William. HISTORY OF THE ROYAL SAPPERS AND MINERS. London: Longman, Brown, Green, Longmans, and Roberts, 1857. 2 vols.

140. Constable, Archibald. CONSTABLE'S MISCELLANY ... MEMORIALS OF THE LATE WAR. Edinburgh: Constable, 1828. 2 vols.

141. Cooke, John Henry. MEMOIRS OF THE LATE WAR: COMPRISING THE PERSONAL NARRATIVE OF CAPT. COOKE, OF THE FORTY-THIRD REGIMENT LIGHT INFANTRY; THE HISTORY OF THE CAMPAIGN OF 1809 IN PORTUGAL, BY THE EARL OF MUNSTER; AND A NARRATIVE OF THE CAMPAIGN OF 1814 IN HOLLAND, BY LIEUTENANT T.W. DUNBAR MOODIE, H.P. 21st FUSILIERS. London: Colburn and Bentley, 1831. 2 vols.

142. Cooper, John Spencer. ROUGH NOTES OF SEVEN CAMPAIGNS IN PORTUGAL, SPAIN, FRANCE, AND AMERICA, 1809-15. Carlisle: Coward, 1869.

143. Cooper, Leonard. THE AGE OF WELLINGTON; THE LIFE AND TIMES OF THE DUKE OF WELLINGTON, 1769-1852. New York: Dodd, Mead, 1962.

144. Cope, William Henry. THE HISTORY OF THE RIFLE BRIGADE (THE PRINCE CONSORT'S OWN) FORMERLY THE 95th. London: Chatto and Windus, 1877.

145. Cortada, Rafael Leon. "The Government of Spain under Joseph Bonaparte, 1808-1814." Ph.D. dissertation, Fordham University, 1968.

146. Costa Cascaes, Joaquim da. IMPRESSOS E MANUSCRIPTOS RELATIVOS A HISTORIA DA GUERRA PENINSULAR E SEUS PRELIMINARES. Lisbon: Collegio Militar, 1866.

147. Costa de Serda, Paul Emile. OPERATIONS DES TROUPES ALLEMANDES AN ESPAGNE DE 1808 A 1813. Paris: Dumaine, 1874.

148. Costa Dias, Manuel da. GUERRA PENINSULAR (OPERACOES EM PORTUGAL, 1808-1811). O SERVICO DE SUBSISTENCIAS NO EXERCITO ANGLO-LUSO. Lisbon: Franco, 1913.

149. Costello, Edward. THE PENINSULAR AND WATERLOO CAMPAIGNS.
     Edited by Antony Brett-James. London: Longmans, 1967.

150. Costigan, Giovanni. SIR ROBERT WILSON: A SOLDIER OF FORTUNE IN
     THE NAPOLEONIC WARS. Madison: University of Wisconsin, 1932.

151. Cowell-Stepney, John Stepney. LEAVES FROM THE DIARY OF AN
     OFFICER OF THE GUARDS. London: Chapman and Hall [1854].

152. Craufurd, Alexander Henry. GENERAL CRAUFURD AND HIS LIGHT
     DIVISION WITH MANY ANECDOTES. London: Griffith, Farran, Okeden
     & Welsh [1891].

153. Cruz Román, Natalio. VALENCIA NAPOLEONICA. Valencia: Imprenta
     Marimontana, 1968.

154. Cúndara, Manuel. HISTORIA POLITICO-CRITICO MILITAR DE LA PLAZA
     DE GERONA EN LOS SITIOS DE 1808 Y 1809. Gerona: Instituto de
     Estudios Gerundenses, 1950-55. 2 vols.

155. Cutchet, Luis. HISTORIA DEL SITI DE GIRONA EN 1809. Barcelona:
     Estampa a cárrech d'Aleiz Sierra, 1868.

156. Dalgado, Daniel Gelanio. BUSSACO: ITS MONASTERY, BATTLE, AND
     WOODS, AND ITS USES AS A HEALTH RESORT. Lisbon: Torres, 1916.

157. Dallas, Alexander Robert Charles. FELIX ALVAREZ; OR MANNERS IN
     SPAIN: CONTAINING DESCRIPTIVE ACCOUNTS OF SOME OF THE PROMINENT
     EVENTS OF THE LATE PENINSULAR WAR. New York: Eastburn, 1818.
     2 vols.

158. Dalrymple, Hew Whitefoord. MEMOIR, WRITTEN BY SIR HEW
     DALRYMPLE, OF HIS PROCEEDINGS AS CONNECTED WITH THE AFFAIRS OF
     SPAIN, AND THE COMMENCEMENT OF THE PENINSULAR WAR. London: T.
     and W. Boone, 1830.

159. Daniel, John Edgecombe. JOURNAL OF AN OFFICER IN THE
     COMMISSARIAT DEPARTMENT OF THE ARMY: COMPRISING A NARRATIVE OF
     THE CAMPAIGNS UNDER HIS GRACE THE DUKE OF WELLINGTON IN
     PORTUGAL, SPAIN, FRANCE, AND THE NETHERLANDS, IN THE YEARS 1811,
     1812, 1813, AND 1815; AND A SHORT ACCOUNT OF THE ARMY OF
     OCCUPATION IN FRANCE, DURING THE YEARS 1816, 1817, AND 1818.
     London: Porter & King, 1820.

160. Davies, David William. SIR JOHN MOORE'S PENINSULAR CAMPAIGN,
     1808-1809. The Hague: Nijhoff, 1974.

161. Davies, Godfrey. WELLINGTON AND HIS ARMY. Oxford: Blackwell,
     1954.

162. Dehnel, Heinrich. ERINNERUNGEN DEUTSCHER OFFICIERE IN
     BRITISCHEN DIENSTEN AUS DEN KRIEGSJAHREN 1805 BIS 1816. Hanover:
     Carl Rümpler, 1864.

163. De la Fuente, Francisco A. "Dom Miguel Pereira Forjaz: His Early Career and Role in the Mobilization and Defense of Portugal during the Peninsular War--1807-1811." Ph.D. dissertation, Florida State University, 1980.

164. Delagrave, André. MEMOIRES DU COLONEL DELAGRAVE. CAMPAGNE DU PORTUGAL (1810-11). Avertissement et notes par Edouard Gachot. Paris: Delagrave, 1902.

165. Delavoye, Alexander Narin. LIFE OF THOMAS GRAHAM, LORD LYNEDOCH. London: Richardson, 1880.

166. DEMONSTRACION DE LA LEALTAD ESPANOLA. COLECCION DE PROCLAMAS, BANDOS, ORDENES, DISCURSOS, ESTADOS DEL EXERCITO Y RELACIONES DE BATALLAS, PUBLICADOS POR LAS JUNTAS DE GOBIERNO O POR ALGUNOS PARTICULARES EN LAS ACTUALES CIRCUNSTANCIAS. Cádiz: n.p., 1808-9. 7 vols.

167. Desboeufs, Marc. LES ETAPES D'UN SOLDAT DE L'EMPIRE, (1800-1815). SOUVENIRS DU CAPITAINE DESBOEUFS. Paris: Picard, 1901.

168. Díaz De Baéza, Juan. HISTORIA DE LA GUERRA DE ESPANA CONTRA EL EMPERADOR NAPOLEON. Madrid: Boix, 1843.

169. Dickson, Alexander. THE DICKSON MANUSCRIPTS. BEING DIARIES, LETTERS, MAPS, ACCOUNT BOOKS, WITH VARIOUS OTHER PAPERS ... FROM 1809 TO 1818. Edited by Major John H. Leslie. Woolwich: Royal Artillery Institution, 1908. 7 vols.

170. Dominquez, Mário. JUNOT EM PORTUGAL; EVOCACAO HISTORIA. [Lisbon:] Romano Torres, 1972.

171. Donaldson, Joseph. THE EVENTFUL LIFE OF A SOLDIER. London: Griffin, 1863.

172. Ducéré, Edouard. BAYONNE SOUS L'EMPIRE. LE BLOCUS DE 1814, D'APRES LES CONTEMPORAINS ET DES DOCUMENTS INEDITS. Bayonne: Lamaignére, 1900.

173. Ducor, Henri. AVENTURES D'UN MARIN DE LA GARDE IMPERIALE, PRISONNIER DE GUERRE SUR LES PONTONS ESPAGNOLS, DAN L'ILE DE CABRERA ET EN RUSSIE. Paris: Dupont, 1833. 2 vols.

174. Du-Fäy, Hortense G. COUP D'OEIL SUR LE MOUVEMENT EUROPEEN DE 1790 A 1814, JUSTIFIANT L'INVASION D'ESPAGNE DE 1808, OU NOTICE SUR LE MARQUIS DE SPOLETA, CONSEILLER D'ETAT DU ROI D'ESPANGE JOSEPH NAPOLEON. Paris: Janet et Magnim, 1855.

175. Dufour, Léon. SOUVENIRS D'UN SAVANT FRANCAIS. A TRAVERS UN SIECLE, 1780-1865. Paris: Rothschild, 1888.

176. Duhesme, Guillaume Philibert. MEMOIRES DE DUHESME. Paris: Michaud, 1823.

177. Dumas, Jean Baptiste. NEUF MOIS DE CAMPAGNES A LA SUITE DU
     MARECHAL SOULT. QUARTRE MANOEUVRES DE COUVERTURE EN 1813 ET
     1814: (1. PAMPELUNE; 2. SAINT-SEBASTIEN; 3. BAYONNE; 4.
     BORDEAUX, ORTHEZ, TOULOUSE). Paris: Lavauzelle, 1907.

178. Duplan, Victor Marie. VIE MILITAIRE; MEMOIRES ET CAMPAGNES.
     Moûtiers: Ducloz, 1901.

179. Dupont de l'Etang, Pierre. MEMOIRES DU GENERAL DUPONT.
     RELATION DE LA CAMPAGNE D'ANDALOUSIE. SUIVI DE DECLARATIONS
     FAITES LE 3 FEVRIER 1815 DEVANT LA HAUTE COUR SUR LA
     CAPITULATION DE BAYLEN. Paris: Michaud, 1824.

180. D'Urban, Benjamin. THE PENINSULAR JOURNAL OF MAJOR-GENERAL SIR
     BENJAMIN D'URBAN ... 1808-1817. Edited with an introduction, by
     I.J. Rousseau. London and New York: Longmans, Green, 1930.

181. Eliot, William Granville. A TREATISE ON THE DEFENSE OF
     PORTUGAL, WITH A MILITARY MAP OF THE COUNTRY; TO WHICH IS ADDED,
     A SKETCH OF THE MANNERS AND CUSTOMS OF THE INHABITANTS AND
     PRINCIPAL EVENTS OF THE CAMPAIGNS UNDER LORD WELLINGTON, IN 1808
     AND 1809. London: Egerton, 1810.

182. Elliot, George. THE LIFE OF THE MOST NOBLE ARTHUR DUKE OF
     WELLINGTON, FROM THE PERIOD OF HIS FIRST ACHIEVMENTS IN INDIA,
     DOWN TO THE BATTLE OF WATERLOO, AND HIS INVASION OF FRANCE IN
     1815. London: Sherwood, Neely and Jones, 1816.

183. Enciso Castrillón, Félix. NOTICIA EXACTA DE LO OCURRIDO EN ...
     CADIZ E ISLA DE LEON DESDE QUE EL EXERCITO ENEMIGO ECUPO ...
     SEVILLE. Cádiz: Quintana [1809? - 1811?]. 5 vols.

184. Epton, Nina Consuelo. THE SPANISH MOUSETRAP. NAPOLEON AND THE
     COURT OF SPAIN. London: Macdonald, 1973.

185. Escoiquiz, Juan de. IDEA SENCILLA DE LAS RAZONES QUE MOTIVARON
     EL VIAJE DEL REY FERNANDO VII A BAYONA EN ... 1808. Madrid:
     Imprenta Real, 1814.

186. Escoiquiz, Juan de. MEMOIRAS (1807-1808). Publicados por A.
     Paz y Mélia. Madrid: Biblioteca Museos, 1915.

187. Espinchal, Hippolyte. SOUVENIRS MILITAIRES (1792-1814). Paris:
     Ollendorff, 1901. 2 vols.

188. Espoz y Mina, Francisco. MEMORIAS DEL GENERAL DON FRANCISCO,
     ESCRITAS POR EL MISMO. Madrid: Bailly-Baillière, 1851-52. 5
     vols.

189. Esselborn, Karl. DIE HESSEN IN SPANIEN UND IN ENGLISCHER
     GEFANGENSCHAFT, 1808-1814. Darmstadt: Selbstverlag, der
     Herausgebers für den Buchhandel, H.L. Schlapp, 1912.

190. Fantin des Odoards, Louis Florimond. JOURNAL DU GENERAL FANTIN DES ODOARDS; ETAPES D'UN OFFICIER DE LA GRANDE ARMEE, 1800-1830. Paris: Plon-Nourrit, 1895.

191. Farmer, George. THE LIGHT DRAGOON. Edited by George Gleig. London: Colburn, 1844. 2 vols.

192. Fée, Antoine Laurent. SOUVENIRS DE LA GUERRE D'ESPAGNE, DITE DE L'INDEPENDANCE, 1809-1813. Paris: Berger-Levrault, 1856.

193. Fernandes Thomaz, Annibal. ESPISODIOS DA TERCEIRA INVASAO. DIARIO DO GENERAL MANUEL IGNACIO MARTINS PAMPLONA, (MAIO A SETEMBRO DE 1810). Figueira: Imprensa Lusitana, 1896.

194. Fernyhough, Thomas. MILITARY MEMOIRS OF FOUR BROTHERS. BY THE SURVIVOR. London: Sams, 1829.

195. Ferrão, Antôino. A Ia [i.e., PRIMEIRA] INVASAO FRANCESA. A INVASAO DE JUNOT VISTA ATRAVES DOS DOCUMENTES DA INTENDENCIA GERAL DA POLICIA, 1807-1808. ESTUDO POLITICO E SOCIAL. Coimbra: Imprensa da Unviersidade, 1923.

196. Ferreira Gil, José César. A INFANTARIA PORTUGUESA NA GUERRA DA PENINSULAR. Lisbon: Cooperative Militar, 1912-13. 2 vols.

197. Ferrer, Raimundo. BARCELONA CAUTIVA, O SEA DIARIO EXACTO DE LO OCURRIDO ... MIENTRAS LA OPRIMIERON LOS FRANCESES, ESTO ES, DESDE EL 13 DE FEBRERO DE 1808, HASTA EL 28 DE MAYO DE 1814. Barcelona: Brusi, 1815-19. 3 vols.

198. Férussac, André Etienne d'Audebard, baron de. EXTRAITS DU JOURNAL DE MES CAMPAGNES EN ESPAGNE, CONTENANT UN COUP D'OEIL GENERAL SUR L'ANDALOUSIE, UNE DISSERTATION SUR CADIX ET SUR SON ILE, UNE RELATION HISTORIQUE SUR LE SIEGE DE SARAGOSSE. Paris: Buisson, 1812.

199. Fitchett, William Henry. THE GREAT DUKE. London: Smith, Elder, 1911. 2 vols.

200. Fleuret, Dominique. DESCRIPTION DES PASSAGES DE DOMINIQUE FLEURET. Publiée par son petit-fils Fernand Fleuret. Paris: Firmin-Didot, 1929.

201. Fortescue, John W. A HISTORY OF THE BRITISH ARMY. London: Macmillan, 1910-30. 19 vols.

202. Fortescue, John W. WELLINGTON. London: Benn, 1960.

203. Foy, Maximilien Sébastien, comte. HISTOIRE DE LA GUERRE DE LA PENINSULE SOUS NAPOLEON. PRECEDEE D'UN TABLEAU POLITIQUE ET MILITAIRE DES PUISSANCES BELLIGERANTES. Paris: Baudouin, 1827. 4 vols.

204. François, Charles. JOURNAL DU CAPITAINE FRANCOIS (1792-1830).
     Publié d'après le manuscrit original par Charles Grolleau,
     préface de Jules Clarette. Paris: Carrington, 1903. 2 vols.

205. Fraser, Edward. THE SOLDIERS WHOM WELLINGTON LED. London:
     Methuen, 1913.

206. Frazer, Augustus Simon. LETTERS OF COLONEL SIR AUGUSTUS SIMON
     FRAZER, COMMANDING THE ROYAL HORSE ARTILLERY IN THE ARMY UNDER
     WELLINGTON. WRITTEN DURING THE PENINSULAR AND WATERLOO
     CAMPAIGNS. Edited by Edward Sabine. London: Longman, Brown,
     Green, Longmans and Roberts, 1859.

207. Fririon, François Nicolas, baron. JOURNAL HISTORIQUE DE LA
     CAMPAGNE DE PORTUGAL, ENTREPRIS PAR LES FRANCAIS, SOUS LES
     ORDERS DU MARECHAL MASSENA, PRINCE D'ESSLING. (DU 15 SEPTEMBRE
     1810 AU 12 MAI 1811). Paris: Bourgogne, 1841.

208. Fryman, Mildred Luckey. "Charles Stuart and the 'Common Cause':
     The Anglo-Portuguese Alliance, 1810-1814." Ph.D. dissertation,
     Florida State University, 1974.

209. Fugier, André. LA JUNTE SUPERIEURE DES ASTURIAS ET L'INVASION
     FRANCAISE, 1810-1811. Paris: Alcan, 1930.

210. Fugier, André. NAPOLEON ET L'ESPAGNE, 1799-1808. Paris:
     Alcan, 1930. 2 vols.

211. Funchal, Agostinho de Sousa Coutinho, marquez de. O CONDE DE
     LINHARAES, DOM RODRIGO DOMINGOS ANTONIO DE SOUSA COUTINHO.
     Lisbon: Bayard [1908].

212. Galli, Florencio. MEMOIRES SUR LA DERNIERE GUERRE DE CATALOGNE.
     Paris: Bossange, 1828.

213. García del Barrio, Manuel. SUCESOS MILITARES DE GALICIA EN 1809
     Y OPERACIONES EN LA PRESENTE GUERRA. Corunna: Martinez, 1891.

214. García Marín, Fernando. MEMORIAS PARA LA HISTORICO MILITAR DE
     LA GUERRA DE LA REVOLUCION ESPANOLA QUE TUBO PRINCIPIO EN EL ANO
     DE 1808, Y FINALIZE EN EL 1812. RESUME HISTORICO Y EXACTO DE
     LOS PRINCIPALES SUCESOS DEL IMORTAL SEGUNDO SITIO DE ZARAGOZA.
     Madrid: Miguel de Bimos, 1817.

215. García Mercadal, José. PALAFOX, DUQUE DE ZARAGOZA, 1775-1847.
     Madrid: Gran Capitan, 1948.

216. García Prado, Justiniano. HISTORIA DEL ALZAMIENTO, GUERRA Y
     REVOLUCION DE ASTURIAS, 1808-1814. Oviedo: Instituto de
     Estudios Asturianos, 1953.

217. García Rodriguez, José Maria. GUERRA DE LA INDEPENDENCIA.
     ENSAYO HISTORICO-POLITICO DE UNA EPOPEYA ESPANOLA. Barcelona:
     Caralt, 1945. 2 vols.

218. Gascón, Domingo. LA PROVINCIA DE TEREUL EN LA GUERRA DE LA INDEPENDENCIA. Madrid: Minuesa de Los Rios, 1908.

219. Gavin, William. THE DIARY OF WILLIAM GAVIN, ENSIGN AND QUARTER-MASTER, 71st HIGHLAND REGIMENT, 1806-1815. BEING HIS DAILY NOTES OF HIS CAMPAIGNS IN SOUTH AFRICA, SOUTH AMERICA, PORTUGAL, SPAIN, SOUTHERN FRANCE, AND FLANDERS, UNDER SIR DAVID BAIRD, SIR WILLIAM BERESFORD, SIR JOHN MOORE, AND THE DUKE OF WELLINGTON. n.p: Highland Light Infantry Chronicle, 1921.

220. Gebhardt, Victor. LO SITI DE GIRONA EN ... 1809. Barcelona: Tasso, 1873.

221. Geisendorf-Des Gouttes, Théophile. LES PRISONNIERS DE GUERRE SOUS LE PREMIER EMPIRE. Geneva: Editions Labor [c1932-37]. 2 vols.

222. Geissler, Carl. DENKWURDIGKEITEN AUS DEM FELDZUG IN SPANIEN IN DEN JAHREN 1810 UND 1811 MIT DEN HERZOGL. SACHS. KONTINGENT. Leipzig: Wigand, 1910.

223. GENERAL REGULATIONS AND ORDERS FOR THE ARMY. ADJUTANT GENERAL'S OFFICE, HORSE-GUARDS, 12th AUGUST 1811. London: Muller, 1970, fascimile edition.

224. Genovés Amorós, Vicente. VALENCIA CONTRA NAPOLEO. Valencia: Edicions valencianes, 1967.

225. Geoffroy de Grandmaison, Charles Alexander. L'ESPAGNE ET NAPOLEON. Paris: Plon, 1908-31. 3 vols.

226. Gille, Louis François. LES PRISONNIERS DE CABRERA; MEMOIRES D'UN CONSCRIT DE 1808. Recueillis et publiés par Philippe Gille. Paris: Havard, 1893.

227. Girard, Etienne François. LES CAHIERS DU COLONEL GIRARD, 1766-1846. Publiés d'après le manuscrit original, par Paul Desachy. Paris: Plon, 1951.

228. Girardin, Stanislas, comte de. A LA COUR DU ROI JOSEPH; SOUVENIRS DU COMTE DE GIRARDIN. Edited by Albert Savine. Paris: Michaud [1911].

229. Girod d l'Ain, Félix Jean Marie. DIX ANS DE MES SOUVENIRS MILITAIRES DE 1805 A 1815. Paris: Dumaine, 1873.

230. Girod de l'Ain, Gabriel. JOSEPH BONAPARTE; LE ROI MALGRE LUI. Paris: Perrin, 1970.

231. Girod de l'Ain, Maurice. VIE MILITAIRE DU GENERAL FOY. Paris: Plon-Nourrit, 1900.

232. Gleig, George Robert, ed. THE HUSSAR. [Norbert Landsheit]. London: Colburn, 1837. 2 vols.

233. Gleig, George Robert. THE SUBALTERN. Edinburgh and London: Blackwood, 1845.

234. Glover, Michael. BRITANNIA SICKENS; SIR ARTHUR WELLESLEY AND THE CONVENTION OF CINTRA. London: Leo Cooper, 1970.

235. Glover, Michael. LEGACY OF GLORY; THE BONAPARTE KINGDOM OF SPAIN, 1808-1813. London: Leo Cooper, 1971.

236. Glover, Michael. THE PENINSULAR WAR, 1807-1814: A CONCISE MILITARY HISTORY. London: David & Charles, 1974.

237. Glover, Michael. A VERY SLIPPERY FELLOW, THE LIFE OF SIR ROBERT WILSON, 1777-1849. Oxford and New York: Oxford University Press, 1978.

238. Glover, Michael. WELLINGTON'S ARMY IN THE PENINSULA, 1808-1814. New York: Hippocrene, 1977.

239. Glover, Michael. WELLINGTON'S PENINSULAR VICTORIES: BUSACO SALAMANCA, VICTORIA, NIVELLE. London: Batsford, 1963.

240. Glover, Richard Gilchrist. PENINSULAR PREPARATIONS; THE REFORM OF THE BRITISH ARMY, 1795-1809. Cambridge: Cambridge Univeristy Press, 1963.

241. Godart, Roch, baron. MEMOIRES DU GENERAL BARON ROCH GODART, 1792-1815. Publiés par J.B. Antoine. Paris: Flammarion, 1895.

242. Godoy Alvarez de Faría Ríos Sánchez y Zarzosa, Manuel de. CUENTA DADA DE SU VIDA POLITICA POR DON MANUEL GODOY, PRINCIPE DE LA PAZ, O SEAN MEMORIAS CRITICAS Y APOLOGETICAS PARA LA HISTORIA DEL REINADO DEL SENOR DON CARLOS IV DE BORBON. Madrid: Sancha, 1836-38. 6 vols.

243. Godoy Alvarez de Faría Ríos Sánchez y Zarzosa, Manuel de. MEMOIRAS. Madrid: Biblioteca de Autores Espanoles, 1956. 2 vols.

244. Goldstein, Morton. "Great Britain in Spain, 1807-1809." Ph.D. dissertation, University of Chicago, 1969.

245. Gómez de Arteche y Moro, José. GUERRA DE LA INDEPENDENCIA. HISTORIA MILITAR DE ESPANA DE 1808 A 1814. Madrid: Depôsitio de la Guerra, 1866-1903. 14 vols.

246. Gómez Imaz, Manuel. BIBLIOGRAFIA DE LA GUERRA DE LA INDEPENDENCIA. Madrid: Revista Tecnica de Infantria, 1908.

247. Gómez Imaz, Manuel. SEVILLA EN 1808; SERVICIOS PATRIOTICOS DE LA SUPREMA JUNTA EN 1808 Y RELACIONES ... DE LOS REGIMIENTOS CREADOS POR ELLA. Seville: Díaz, 1908.

248. Gómez Jordana, Francisco. CAMPANA DE ANDALUCIA EN 1808. Madrid: n.p., 1883.

249. Gómez Villafranca, Román. EXTREMADURA EN LA GUERRA DE LA INDEPENDENCIA ESPANOLA, MEMORIA HISTORICA Y COLECCION DIPLOMATICA. Badajoz: Uceda, 1908.

250. Gomm, William Maynard. LETTERS AND JOURNALS OF FIELD-MARSHAL SIR WILLIAM MAYNARD GOMM ... FROM 1799 TO WATERLOO, 1815. Edited by Francis Culling Carr-Gomm. London: J. Murray, 1881. 2 vols.

251. Gonneville, Aymar Olivier le Harivel de. RECOLLECTIONS OF COLONEL GONNEVILLE. Published by his daughter the Countess of Mirabeau. London: Hurst and Blackett, 1875. 2 vols.

252. González-Blanco, Edmundo. JOVELLANOS; SU VIDA Y SUS OBRAS. Madrid: Artistica espanola, 1911.

253. Goodspeed, Donald James. THE BRITISH CAMPAIGNS IN THE PENINSULA, 1808-1814. Ottawa: Directorate of Military Training, Army Headquarters, 1958.

254. Goodwin, Winslow Copley. "The Political and Military Career of Don Pedro Caro y Sureda, Marqués de la Romana." Ph.D. dissertation, Florida State University, 1973.

255. Gordon, Alexander. A CAVALRY OFFICER IN THE CORUNNA CAMPAIGN, 1808-1809: THE JOURNAL OF CAPTAIN GORDON OF THE 15th HUSSARS. Edited by Colonel H.C. Wylly. London: J. Murray, 1913.

256. Gouvion Saint-Cyr, Laurent, marquis de. JOURNAL DES OPERATIONS DE L'ARMEE DE CATALOGNE, EN 1808 ET 1809, SOUS LE COMMANDEMENT DU GENERAL GOUVION SAINT-CYR; OU MATERIAUX POUR SERVIR A L'HISTOIRE DE LA GUERRE D'ESPAGNE. Paris: Dumaine, 1865.

257. Graham, William. TRAVELS THROUGH PORTUGAL AND SPAIN, DURING THE PENINSULAR WAR. London: Printed for Richard Phillips, 1820.

258. Grahit y Papell, Emilio. EL GENERAL D. BLAS DE FOURNAS Y SU DIARIO DEL SITIO DE GERONA EN 1809. Gerona: Hospicio Provincial, 1890.

259. Grahit y Papell, Emilio. RESENA HISTORICA DE LOS SITIOS DE GERONA EN 1808 Y 1809. Gerona: [Torres, 1894]. 2 vols.

260. Grasset, Alphonse Louis. LA GUERRE D'ESPAGNE (1807-1813). Paris: Berger-Levrault, 1914-32. 3 vols.

261. Grasset, Alphonse Louis. MALAGA, PROVINCE FRANCAISE (1811-1912). Paris: Charles-Lavauzelle, 1910.

262. Gras y de Esteva, Rafael. LERIDA Y LA GUERRA DE LA INDEPENDENCIA (1808-1810). MEMORIA. Lerida: Sol y Benet, 1899.

263. Gras y de Esteva, Rafael. ZAMORA EN TIEMPO DE LA GUERRA DE LA INDEPENDENCIA (1808-1814). Madrid: n.p., 1913.

264. Grattan, William. ADVENTURES OF THE CONNAUGHT RANGERS, FROM 1808 TO 1814. London: Colburn, 1847. 2 vols.

265. Gray, Daniel Savage. "The Services of the King's German Legion in the Army of the Duke of Wellington: 1809-1815." Ph.D. dissertation, Florida State University, 1970.

266. Great Britain. BOARD OF GENERAL OFFICERS APPOINTED TO INQUIRE INTO THE ... CONVENTION, ETC. IN PORTUGAL. A COPY OF THE PROCEEDINGS UPON THE INQUIRY RELATIVE TO THE ARMISTICE AND CONVENTION ETC., MADE AND CONCLUDED IN PORTUGAL, IN AUGUST 1808, BETWEEN THE COMMANDERS OF THE BRITISH AND FRENCH ARMIES;--HELD AT THE ROYAL HOSPITAL AT CHELSEA, ON MONDAY THE 14th OF NOVEMBER; AND CONTINUED BY ADJOURNMENTS UNTIL TUESDAY THE 27th OF DECEMBER, 1808. London: House of Commons, 1809.

267. Great Britain. Foreign Office. A COLLECTION OF CORRESPONDENCE RELATIVE TO SPAIN AND PORTUGAL, PRESENTED TO PARLIAMENT IN 1810. London: Strahan, 1811.

268. Green, John. THE VICISSITUDES OF A SOLDIER'S LIFE, OR A SERIES OF OCCURRENCES FROM 1806 TO 1815. Wakefield, Eng.: E.P. Publishing, 1973, reprint.

269. Grivel, Jean Baptiste, baron. MEMOIRES DU VICE-AMIRAL BARON GRIVEL, REVOLUTION--EMPIRE. Prèface de G. Lacour-Gayet. Paris: Plon-Nourrit, 1914.

270. Grolman, Ludwig Theodor Dietrich Christian von. TAGEBUCH EINES DEUTSCHEN OFFIZIERS UEBER SEINEN FELDZUG IN SPANIEN IM JAHRE 1808. Nürenburg: Riegel und Wiessner, 1814.

271. Guedalla, Philip. WELLINGTON. New York: Literary Guild, 1931.

272. Guillon, Edouard Louis Maxime. LES GUERRES D'ESPAGNE SOUS NAPOLEON. Paris: Plon-Nourrit, 1902.

273. Guingret, Général. RELATION HISTORIQUE ET MILITAIRE DE LA CAMPAGNE DE PORTUGAL SOUS LE MARECHAL MASSENA, PRINCE D'ESSLING. Limoges: Bargeas, 1817.

274. Guiu y Marti, Estanislao. EL ANO MILITAR ESPANOL, COLECCION DE EPISODIOS, HECHOS Y GLORIAS DE LA HISTORIA MILITAR DE ESPANA. Barcelona: Montaner, 1887-92. 3 vols.

275. Guthrie, George James. COMMENTARIES ON THE SURGERY OF THE WAR, IN PORTUGAL, SPAIN. London: Renshaw, 1853.

276. Guzmán, Martín Luis. MINA EL MOZO, HEROE DE NAVARRA. Madrid: Espasa-Calpe, 1932.

277. Halliday, Andrew. OBSERVATIONS ON THE PRESENT STATE OF THE PORTUGUESE ARMY, AS ORGANISED BY LIEUTENANT-GENERAL SIR WILLIAM CARR BERESFORD, WITH AN ACCOUNT OF THE DIFFERENT MILITARY ESTABLISHMENTS AND LAWS OF PORTUGAL, AND A SKETCH OF THE CAMPAIGNS OF THE LAST AND PRESENT YEAR, DURING WHICH THE PORTUGUESE ARMY WAS BROUGHT INTO THE FIELD AGAINST THE ENEMY, FOR THE FIRST TIME AS A REGULAR FORCE. London: J. Murray, 1811.

278. Hamilton, Anthony. HAMILTON'S CAMPAIGN WITH MOORE AND WELLINGTON DURING THE PENINSULAR WAR. Troy, New York: Prescott and Wilson, 1847.

279. Hamilton, Thomas. ANNALS OF THE PENINSULAR CAMPAIGNS. A new edition revised and augmented by Frederick Hardman. Edinburgh: Blackwood, 1849.

280. Harley, John. THE VETERAN, OR FORTY YEARS IN THE BRITISH SERVICE: COMPRISING ADVENTURES IN EGYPT, SPAIN, PORTUGAL, BELGIUM, HOLLAND, AND PRUSSIA. London: Published by the author's widow, 1838. 2 vols.

281. Harris, John. RECOLLECTIONS OF RIFLEMAN HARRIS. Edited by Henry Curling, with an introduction by the Hon. Sir John Fortescue. [Portway, Bath, Eng.: Cedric Chivers, 1966].

282. Hartmann, Julius von. EINE LEBENSKIZZE MIT BESOND. BERUECKSICHTIGUNG DER VON IHM NACHGELASS. ERINHERUNGEN AUS DEN FELDZUGEN AUF DER PYRENNAISCHEN HALBINSEL U.S.W., 1808-1815. Hanover: n.p., 1858.

283. Haswell, Chetwynd John Drake. THE FIRST RESPECTABLE SPY: THE LIFE AND TIMES OF COLQUHOUN GRANT, WELLINGTON'S HEAD OF INTELLIGENCE. London: Hamilton [1969].

284. Hautefort, Charles Victor d'. COUP-D'OEIL SUR LISBONNE ET MADRID EN 1814. SUIVI D'UN MEMOIRE POLITIQUE CONCERNANT LA CONSITUTION PROMULGUEE ... A CADIX. Paris: Delaunay, 1820.

285. Hautpoul, Alphonse, marquis d'. MEMOIRES DU GENERAL MARQUIS ALPHONSE D'HAUTPOUL, PAIR DE FRANCE (1789-1856). Publiés par son arrière petit-fils Etienne Hennet de Goutel. Paris: Perrin, 1906.

286. Hawker, Peter. JOURNAL OF A REGIMENTAL OFFICER DURING THE RECENT CAMPAIGN IN PORTUGAL AND SPAIN UNDER LORD VISCOUNT WELLINGTON. London: Johnson, 1810.

287. Hay, Andrew Leith. MEMOIRS OF THE LATE LIEUTENANT-GENERAL SIR JAMES LEITH. G.C.B. WITH A PRECIS OF SOME OF THE MOST REMARKABLE EVENTS OF THE PENINSULAR WAR. By a British officer. London: Stockdale, 1821.

288. Hay, Andrew Leith. A NARRATIVE OF THE PENINSULAR WAR.
     Edinburgh: Lizars, 1831. 2 vols.

289. Hay, William. REMINISCENCES, 1808-1815, UNDER WELLINGTON.
     Edited by his daughter Mrs. S.C.I. Wood. London: Marshal,
     Hamilton, Kent, 1901.

290. Head, Charles Octavius. NAPOLEON AND WELLINGTON. London:
     Robert Hale, 1939.

291. Henegan, Richard D. SEVEN YEARS CAMPAIGNING IN THE PENINSULA
     AND THE NETHERLANDS FROM 1808-1815. London: Colburn, 1846. 2
     vols.

292. Henry, Walter. EVENTS OF A MILITARY LIFE: BEING RECOLLECTIONS
     AFTER SERVICE IN THE PENINSULAR WAR, INVASION OF FRANCE, THE
     EAST INDIES, ST. HELENA, CANADA, AND ELSEWHERE. London:
     Pickering, 1843.

293. Heusinger, Edmund, of Brunswick. ANSICHTEN, BEOBACHTUNGEN AND
     ERFAHRUNGEN, GESAMMELT WAEHREND DER FELDZUEGE IN VALENCIA UND
     CATALONIEN ... 1813 AND 1814. Braunschweig: Meyer, 1825.

294. Hibbert, Christopher. CORUNNA. London: Batsford, 1961.

295. A HISTORY OF THE CAMPAIGNS OF THE BRITISH FORCES IN SPAIN AND
     PORTUGAL, UNDERTAKEN TO RELIEVE THOSE COUNTRIES FROM THE FRENCH
     USURPATION. London: Goddard, 1812-14. 5 vols.

296. Hodenberg, Bodo, freiherr. BRIEFE DES RITTMEISTERS KARL VON
     HODENBERG DES 1. SCHWEREN DRAGONER-REGIMENTS VON DES KOENIGS
     DEUTSCHER LEGION AUS SPANIEN, 1812-1813. Hanover: Gustov
     Jacob, n.d.

297. Holland, Elizabeth (Vassall) Fox. THE SPANISH JOURNAL OF
     ELIZABETH, LADY HOLLAND. Edited by the Earl of Ilchester.
     London and New York: Longmans, Green, 1910.

298. Hook, Theodore Edward. THE LIFE OF GENERAL, THE RIGHT
     HONOURABLE SIR DAVID BAIRD, BART. London: Bentley, 1832. 2
     vols.

299. Hooper, George. WELLINGTON. London and New York: Macmillan,
     1899.

300. Hope, James. LETTERS FROM PORTUGAL, SPAIN, AND FRANCE, DURING
     THE MEMORABLE CAMPAIGNS OF 1811, 1812, AND 1813; AND FROM
     BELGIUM AND FRANCE IN THE YEAR 1815. By a British Officer
     [James Hope]. London: Underwood, 1819.

301. Horward, Donald David. THE BATTLE OF BUSSACO: MASSENA VS.
     WELLINGTON. Tallahassee: Florida State University [Press]
     1965.

302. Horward, Donald David. THE FRENCH CAMPAIGN IN PORTUGAL,
     1810-1811: AN ACCOUNT BY JEAN JACQUES PELET. Edited,
     annotated, and translated. Minneapolis: University of
     Minnesota Press; London: Oxford University Press, 1973.

303. Horward, Donald David. "The French Invasion of Portugal,
     1810-1811." Ph.D. dissertation, University of Minnesota, 1962.

304. Horward, Donald David. NAPOLEON AND IBERIA--THE TWIN SIEGES OF
     CIUDAD RODRIGO AND ALMEIDA, 1810. Tallahassee: University
     Presses of Florida, 1984. (Exma. Diputación Provincial de
     Salamanca published a Spanish edition: NAPOLEON Y PENINSULA
     IBERICA, CIUDAD RODRIGO Y ALMEIDA, DOS ASEDIOS ANALOGOS, 1810.
     Salamanca: Europa Artes Graficas, 1984.)

305. [Howell, Thomas.] A SOLDIER OF THE SEVENTY-FIRST. THE JOURNAL
     OF A SOLDIER IN THE PENINSULAR WAR. Edited with an introduction
     and notes by Christopher Hibbert. London: Leo Cooper, 1975,
     1976, reprint.

306. Hugo, Joseph Léopold, comte. MEMOIRES DU GENERAL HUGO,
     GOUVERNEUR DE PLUSIEURS PROVINCES ET AIDE-MAJOR DES ARMEES EN
     ESPAGNE. Paris: Ladvocat, 1823. 3 vols.

307. Hulot, Jacques Louis. SOUVENIRS MILITAIRES DU BARON HULOT,
     GENERAL D'ARTILLERIE, 1793-1843. Paris: Spectateur militaire,
     1886.

308. Ibañez de Ibero, Carlos, marqués de Mulhacén. EPISODIOS DE LA
     GUERRA DE LA INDEPENDENCIA. Madrid: Editora Nacional, 1963.

309. Ibañez Marin, José. BIBLIOGRAFIA DE LA GUERRA DE LA
     INDEPENDENCIA. Madrid: "Revista Técnica de Infanteria y
     Caballaria", 1908.

310. Ibañez Marin, José. EL MARISCAL SOULT EN PORTUGAL, CAMPANA DE
     1809. Madrid: "Revista Técnica de Infanteria y Caballaria",
     1909.

311. Illens, A. d'. SOUVENIRS D'UN MILITAIRE DES ARMEES FRANCAISES.
     Paris: Anselin et Pochard, 1827.

312. INDICE DE LOS PAPELES DE LA JUNTA CENTRAL SUPREMA GUBERNATIVA
     DEL REINO Y DEL CONSEJO DE REGENCIA. Publicado por el Archivo
     historico nacional. Madrid: Revista de Archivos, 1904.

313. Infantado, Pedro Alcantara de Toledo, duque del. MANIFESTO DE
     LAS OPERACIONES DEL EJERCITO DEL CENTRO DESDE EL 3 DE DICIEMBRE
     DE 1808 HASTA EL 17 DE FEBRERO DE 1809. Seville: Brusola,
     1809.

314. Iraurgui, Eugenio. DIARIO DE LAS OPERACIONES DE LA DIVISION
     EXPEDICIONARIA AL MANDO DEL MARISCAL DE CAMPO D. FRANCISCO DE
     COPONS Y NAVIA DESDE SU SALIDA DE CADIZ EN ... 1811, HASTA QUE
     REGRESO EN ... 1812. Vich: n.p., 1814.

315. Iribarren, José María. ANDRES MARTIN ABAD DE BADOSTAIN.
     HISTORIA DE LOS SUCESOS MILITAIRES DE LA DIVISION DE NAVARRA Y
     DEMAS ACONTECIMIENTOS DE ESTE REYNO DURANTE LA ULTIMA GUERRA
     CONTRA EL TIRANO NAPOLEON. Pamplona: Gómez, 1953. 2 vols.

316. Iribarren, José María. ESPOZ Y MINA: EL LIBERAL   [Madrid:]
     Aguilar [1967].

317. Jackson, Basil, and C. Rochfort Scott. THE MILITARY LIFE OF
     FIELD MARSHAL THE DUKE OF WELLINGTON. London: Longman, Orme,
     Brown, Green, and Longmans, 1840. 2 vols.

318. Jackson, George. THE BATH ARCHIVES. A FURTHER SELECTION FROM
     THE DIARIES AND LETTERS OF SIR GEORGE JACKSON FROM 1809-1816.
     London: Bentley, 1873. 2 vols.

319. Jackson, George. THE DIARIES AND LETTERS OF SIR GEORGE JACKSON,
     K.C.H., FROM THE PEACE OF AMIENS TO THE BATTLE OF TALAVERA.
     Edited by Lady Jackson. London: Bentley, 1872. 2 vols.

320. Jacob, William. TRAVELS IN THE SOUTH OF SPAIN, IN LETTERS
     WRITTEN A.D. 1809 AND 1810. London: Johnson, 1811.

321. Jardiel,   Florencio.   EL   VENERABLE   PALAFOX.   Madrid:
     Rivadineyra, 1892.

322. Jomini, Antoine Henri de, baron. GUERRE D'ESPAGNE. EXTRAIT DES
     SOUVENIRS INEDITS DU GENERAL JOMINI (1808-1814). Paris:
     Baudoin, 1892.

323. Jones, John Thomas. ACCOUNT OF THE WAR IN SPAIN, PORTUGAL, AND
     THE SOUTH OF FRANCE, FROM 1808 TO 1814 INCLUSIVE. London:
     Egerton, 1818.

324. Jones, John Thomas. JOURNALS OF SIEGES CARRIED ON BY THE ARMY
     UNDER THE DUKE OF WELLINGTON, IN SPAIN, DURING THE YEARS 1811 TO
     1814; WITH NOTES AND ADDITIONS; ALSO MEMORANDA RELATIVE TO THE
     LINES THROWN UP TO COVER LISBON IN 1810. London: Weale, 1846.
     3 vols.

325. Jones, John Thomas. MEMORANDA RELATIVE TO THE LINES THROWN UP
     TO COVER LISBON IN 1810. London: Printed for private
     circulation, 1829.

326. José de Santo Silvestre, fra. WELLINGTON AT BUSSACO: THE
     MONK'S DIARY. Translated into English by Mary Leigh de
     Havilland. London: Blackheath, 1911.

327. Joseph Bonaparte, king of Spain. MEMOIRES ET CORRESPONDANCE
     POLITIQUE ET MILITAIRE DU ROI JOSEPH. Publiés, annotés et mis
     en ordre, par baron Albert Du Casse. Paris: Perrotin, 1854-55.
     10 vols.

328. Joseph Bonaparte, king of Spain. PRONTUARIO DE LAS LEYES Y DECRETOS DEL REY NUESTRO SENOR D. JOSE NAPOLEON I, DESDE EL ANO DE 1808, CON RETRATO. Madrid: Imprenta Real, 1810-12. 3 vols.

329. Jourdan, Jean Baptiste, comte. MEMOIRES MILITAIRES DU MARECHAL JOURDAN (GUERRE D'ESPAGNE) ECRITS PAR LUI-MEME. Publiés d'après le manuscrit original par M. le vicomte de Grouchy. Paris: Flammarion [1899].

330. JOURNAL OF AN OFFICER IN THE KING'S GERMAN LEGION: COMPRISING AN ACCOUNT OF HIS CAMPAIGNS AND ADVENTURES IN ENGLAND, IRELAND, DENMARK, PORTUGAL, SPAIN, MALTA, SICILY, AND ITALY. London: Collins, 1827.

331. Jovellanos, Gaspar Melchor de. DIARIOS. Estudio preliminar de Angel de Río. Edición preparada por Julio Somoza. Oviedo: Instituto de Estudios Asturianos, 1953-56. 3 vols.

332. Jovellanos, Gaspar Melchor de. MEMOIRES POLITIQUES. Paris: Michaud, 1825.

333. Juretschke, Hans. LOS AFRANCESADOS EN LA GUERRA DE LA INDEPENDENCIA SU GENISUS DESARROLO Y CONSECUENCIAS HISTORICAS. Madrid: Rialp, 1962.

334. Juretschke, Hans. LOS AFRANCESADOS EN LA GUERRA DE LA INDEPENDENCIA.--VIDA, OBRA, Y PENSAMIENTO DE ALBERTO LISTA. Madrid: Consejo Superior de Investigaciones Cientificas Escuela de Historia Moderna, 1951.

335. Kincaid, John. ADVENTURES IN THE RIFLE BRIGADE, IN THE PENINSULA, FRANCE, AND THE NETHERLANDS FROM 1809-1815. London: T. and W. Boone, 1847.

336. Kincaid, John. RANDOM SHOTS FROM A RIFLEMAN. London: T. and W. Boone, 1835.

337. Kircheisen, Friedrich Max. MEMOIREN AUS DEM SPANISHCHEN FREIHEITSKAMPFE 1808-1811; LUDWIG VON GROLMAN--ALBERT JEAN MICHEL ROCCA--MOYLE SHERER--HEINRICH VON BRANDT--HENRI DUCOR--DON JUAN ANDRES NIETO SAMANIEGO. Hamburg: Gutenburg, 1908.

338. Knight, George D. "Lord Liverpool and the Peninsular War, 1809-1812." Ph.D. dissertation, Florida State University, 1976.

339. Knowles, Robert. THE WAR IN THE PENINSULA; SOME LETTERS OF LIEUTENANT ROBERT KNOWLES. Arranged and annotated by Sir Lees Knowles. Bolton: Tillotson, 1913.

340. Laborde, Alexander de. A VIEW OF SPAIN, COMPRISING A DESCRIPTIVE ITINERARY OF EACH PROVINCE. London: Longman, Hurst, Rees, and Orme, 1809. 5 vols.

341. Laclos, Etienne Cholderlos de. LE FILS DE LACLOS; CARNETS DE
     MARCHE DU COMMANDANT CHODERLOS DE LACLOS (AN XIV-1814). Publiés
     avec une préface et des note par Louis Chauvigny. Lausanne:
     Payot, 1912.

342. Laffaille, G. MEMOIRES SUR LA CAMPAGNE DU CORPS D'ARMEE DES
     PYRENEES ORIENTALES, COMMANDE PAR LE GENERAL DUHESME, EN 1808:
     SUIVIS D'UN PRECIS DES CAMPAGNES DE CATALOGNE DE 1810 A 1814, ET
     DE NOTES HISTORIQUES, SUR LES SIEGES DE BARCELONE ET DE GERONE;
     SUR L'EXPEDITION DES ANGLAIS CONTRE TARRAGONE, EN 1813; SUR LES
     GENERAUX DUHESME ET LACY. Paris: Anselin et Pochard, 1826.

343. La Forest, Antoine René. CORRESPONDANCE DU COMTE LA FOREST,
     AMBASSADEUR DE FRANCE EN ESPANGE, 1808-1813. Par M. Geoffroy de
     Grandmaison. Paris: Picard, 1905-12. 7 vols.

344. Lageo, Barão Luiz das. TRINTA E CINCO ANNOS DE VIDA MILITAR
     (1808-1843). Porto: Typog. Peninsular, n.d.

345. Lamare, Jean Baptiste Hippolyte. RELATION DES SIEGES ET
     DEFENSES D'OLIVENCA, DE BADAJOZ ET DE CAMPO-MAYOR, EN 1811 ET
     1812, PAR LES TROUPES FRANCAISES DE L'ARMEE DU MIDI EN ESPAGNE.
     Par le colonel L * * *. Paris: Anselin et Pochard, 1825.

346. Lamiraux, François Gustave. ETUDES DE GUERRE. LA MANOEUVRE DE
     SOULT, 1813-1814. Paris: Charles-Lavauzelle [1902].

347. Lamiraux, François Gustave. LE SIEGE DE SAINT-SEBASTIEN EN
     1813. Paris: Charles-Lavauzelle [1900].

348. Landmann, George Thomas. RECOLLECTIONS OF MY MILITARY LIFE.
     London: Hurst and Blackett, 1854. 2 vols.

349. Lapène, Edouard. CAMPAGNES DE 1813 ET 1814, SUR L'EBRE, LES
     PYRENEES ET LA GARONNE; PREDEDEES DE CONSIDERATIONS SUR LA
     DERNIERE GUERRE D'ESPAGNE. Paris: Anselin et Pouchard, 1823.

350. Lapène, Edouard. CONQUETE DE L'ANDALOUSIE, CAMPAGNE DE 1810 ET
     1811 DANS LE MIDI DE L'ESPAGNE. Paris: Ancelin et Pochard,
     1823.

351. Lapène, Edouard. EVENEMENTS MILITAIRES DEVANT TOULOUSE, EN
     1814. Paris: Ridan, 1822.

352. Larchey, Lorédan. LES SUITES D'UNE CAPITULATION. RELATIONS DES
     CAPTIFS DE BAYLEN ET DE LA GLORIEUSE RETRAITE DU 116e REGIMENT.
     Paris: Hachette, 1884.

353. Larpent, Francis Seymour. THE PRIVATE JOURNAL OF F.S. LARPENT,
     ESQ., JUDGE ADVOCATE GENERAL OF THE BRITISH FORCES IN THE
     PENINSULA. ATTACHED TO THE HEAD-QUARTERS OF LORD WELLINGTON
     DURING THE PENINSULAR WAR, FROM 1812 TO ITS CLOSE. Edited by
     Sir George Larpent. London: Bentley, 1853. 3 vols.

354. Larreguy de Civrieux, Louis Marie Sylvain. SOUVENIRS D'UN CADET, 1812-1823. Paris: Hachette, 1912.

355. Latino Coelho, José Maria. HISTORICA POLITICA E MILITAR DE PORTUGAL. Lisbon: Imprensa Nacional, 1874-91. 3 vols.

356. Lavaux, François. MEMOIRES DE FRANCOIS LAVAUX, SERGENT AU 103e DE LIGNE (1793-1814). Introduction et notes par Alfred Darimon. Paris: Dentu, 1894.

357. Lawrence, Rosamond (Napier), lady. CHARLES NAPIER, FRIEND AND FIGHTER, 1782-1853. London: J. Murray [1952].

358. Lawrence, William. MEMOIRES D'UN GRENADIER ANGLAIS (1791-1867). Traduits par Henry Gauthier-Villars. Paris: Plon, 1897.

359. Leach, Jonathon. ROUGH SKETCHES OF THE LIFE OF AN OLD SOLDIER: DURING A SERVICE IN THE WEST INDIES: AT THE SIEGE OF COPENHAGEN IN 1807: IN THE PENINSULA AND THE SOUTH OF FRANCE IN THE CAMPAIGNS FROM 1808 TO 1814, WITH THE LIGHT DIVISION: IN THE NETHERLANDS IN 1815: INCLUDING THE BATTLES OF QUATRE BRAS AND WATERLOO: WITH A SLIGHT SKETCH OF THE THREE YEARS PASSED BY THE ARMY OF OCCUPATION IN FRANCE. London: Longmans, Rees, Orme, Brown, and Green, 1831.

360. Ledesma, Santiago. LES SITIOS DE ZARAGOZA. Barcelona: Ediciones Rodegar, 1965.

361. Lehman, Joseph. REMEMBER YOU ARE AN ENGLISHMAN. A BIOGRAPHY OF SIR HARRY SMITH. London: Cape, 1977.

362. Lejeune, Louis François, baron. MEMOIRES DU GENERAL LEJEUNE. Publiés par Germaine Bapst. Paris: Firmin-Didot, 1896. 2 vols.

363. Lejeune, Louis François, baron. SIEGE DE SARAGOSSE. HISTOIRE ET PEINTURE DES EVENMENTS QUI ONT EU LIEU DANS CETTE VILLE OUVERTE PENDANT LES DEUX SIEGES QU'ELLE A SOUTENUS EN 1808 ET 1809. Paris: Firmin-Didot, 1840.

364. Lema, Salvador Bermúdez de Castro y O'Lawlor, marqués de. ANTECEDENTES POLITICOS Y DIPLOMATICOS DE LOS SUCESOS DE 1808; ESTUDIO HISTORICO-CRITICO ESCRITO CON PRESENCIA DE DOCUMENTOS INEDITOS DEL ARCHIVO RESERVADO DE FERNANDO VII, DEL HISTORICO-NACIONAL, Y OTROS. Madrid: Beltrán, 1912.

365. Lemonnier-Delafosse, Jean Baptiste. CAMPAGNES DE 1810 A 1815, OU SOUVENIRS MILITAIRES. Havre: Lemale, 1850.

366. Lenanton, Carola Mary Anima (Oman). SIR JOHN MOORE. London: Hodder and Stoughton, [1953].

367. Le Noble, Pierre Madeleine. MEMOIRES SUR LES OPERATIONS MILITAIRES DES FRANCAIS EN GALICE, EN PORTUGAL, ET DANS LA VALLEE DU TAGE. Paris: Barrois, 1821.

368. Leslie, Charles Joseph. MILITARY JOURNAL OF COLONEL LESLIE ...
     WHILST SERVING WITH THE 29th REGIMENT IN THE PENINSULA, AND THE
     60th RIFLES IN CANADA, ETC., 1807-1832. [Aberdeen:] Aberdeen
     University Press, 1887.

369. Leslie, John Henry. THE SERVICE OF THE ROYAL REGIMENT OF
     ARTILLERY IN THE PENINSULAR WAR, 1808 TO 1814. London: Rees,
     1908-12.

370. L'Estrange, George Budelt. RECOLLECTIONS OF SIR GEORGE B.
     L'ESTRANGE, LATE OF THE 31st REGIMENT, AND AFTERWARDS IN THE
     SCOTS FUSILIER GUARDS. London: S. Low, Marston, Low & Searle,
     1874.

371. Levavasseur, Octave. SOUVENIRS MILITAIRES D'OCTAVE LEVAVASSEUR,
     OFFICER D'ARTILLERIE, AIDE DE CAMP DU MARECHAL NEY. Publiés par
     le commandant Beslay. Paris: Plon-Nourrit, 1914.

372. L'Evêque, Henry. CAMPAIGNS OF THE BRITISH ARMY IN PORTUGAL
     UNDER THE COMMAND OF GENERAL THE EARL OF WELLINGTON. London:
     Colnaghi, 1812.

373. Lewin, Henry Ross. THE LIFE OF A SOLDIER: A NARRATIVE OF
     TWENTY-SEVEN YEARS' SERVICE IN VARIOUS PARTS OF THE WORLD. BY A
     FIELD OFFICER. Dublin: Hodges, Figgis, 1824. 3 vols.

374. Lignières, Marie Henry de. SOUVENIRS DE LA GRANDE ARMEE.
     Paris: Pierre Roger, 1933.

375. Lille, John Scott. A NARRATIVE OF THE CAMPAIGNS OF THE LOYAL
     LUSITANIAN LEGION, UNDER BRIGADIER GENERAL SIR ROBERT WILSON ...
     WITH SOME ACCOUNT OF THE MILITARY OPERATIONS IN SPAIN AND
     PORTUGAL DURING THE YEARS 1809, 1810 & 1811. London: Egerton,
     1812.

376. Limouzīn [Valmēcour]. SOUVENIRS DE L'ESPAGNE PENDANT LES ANNEES
     1808, 1809, 1810, 1811, 1812 ET 1813. Sainte-Menehould:
     Poignée-Darnauld, 1829.

377. Lindau, Friedrich. KRIEGSFAHRTEN VON JENA BIS BELLE-ALLIANCE:
     ERINNERUNGEN EINES SOLDATEN DER ENGLISCH-DEUTSCHEN LEGION IN
     DEUTSCHLAND, ENGLAND, PORTUGAL, SPANIEN, FRANKREICH UND DEN
     NIEDERLANDEN. Leipzig: Voigtlander, 1898.

378. Llorent, Juan Antonio. MEMOIRES POUR SERVIR A L'HISTOIRE DE LA
     REVOLUTION D'ESPAGNE. Avec des pièces justificatives, par M.
     Nellerto. Paris: Dentu, 1814-19. 3 vols.

379. Lobo, Francisco Alexandre. OBRAS. SUMMARIO HISTORICO DA
     CAMPANHA DE PORTUGAL, DESDE AGOSTO DE 1810, ATE ABRIL DE 1811.
     Lisbon: José Baptista Morando, 1848-53.

380. Londonderry, Charles William Vane, 3d marquis of. NARRATIVE OF
     THE PENINSULAR WAR, FROM 1808 TO 1813. London: Colburn, 1829.
     2 vols.

381. Long, Robert Ballard. PENINSULAR CAVALRY GENERAL, 1811-13; THE CORRESPONDENCE OF LIEUTENANT-GENERAL ROBERT BALLARD LONG. Edited with a memoir by T.H. McGuffie. London: G.G. Harrap [1951].

382. Longford, Elizabeth Harman Pakenham, countess of. WELLINGTON. [First American edition] New York: Harper & Row [1969].

383. Loucks, Judith Ann. "The Services of the Marquis de la Romana in the Spanish War for Independence." M.A. thesis, Florida State University, 1966.

384. Lovett, Gabriel H. NAPOLEON AND THE BIRTH OF MODERN SPAIN. [New York:] New York University Press, 1965. 2 vols.

385. Lucas-Dubreton, Jean. CE QU'A VU GOYA. NAPOLEON DEVANT L'ESPAGNE. Paris: Fayard, 1946.

386. Luz Soriano, Simão José da. HISTORIA DA GUERRA CIVIL E DO ESTABELECIMENTO DO GOVERNO PARLAMENTAR EM PORTUGAL, COMPREHENDENDO A HISTORIA DIPLOMATICA, MILITAR E POLITICA D'ESTE REINO DESDE 1777 ATE 1834. Lisbon: Imprensa Nacional, 1866-92. 15 vols. in 19.

387. Maag, Albert. GESCHICHTE DER SCHWEIZERTRUPPEN IM KRIEGE NAPOLEONS I IN SPANIEN UND PORTUGAL (1807-1814). Biel: Kuhn, 1892-93. 2 vols.

388. MacCarthy, J. RECOLLECTIONS OF THE STORMING OF THE CASTLE OF BADAJOZ UNDER THE COMMAND OF LIEUT. GEN. SIR THOMAS PICTON ON THE 6th OF APRIL 1812. TO WHICH ARE ADDED MEMOIRS OF THE STORMING OF FORT NAPOLEON, ALMARAZ AND THE BATTLE OF CORUNNA. London: Clowes, 1820.

389. Macedo, Jorge Borges de. O BLOQUEIO CONTINENTAL; ECONOMIA E GUERRA PENINSULAR. Lisbon: Delfos, 1962.

390. McGrigor, James. THE AUTOBIOGRAPHY AND SERVICES OF SIR JAMES MCGRIGOR, BART., LATE DIRECTOR-GENERAL OF THE ARMY MEDICAL DEPARTMENT. London: Longman, Green, Longmans and Roberts, 1861.

391. Mackinnon, Henry. A JOURNAL OF THE CAMPAIGN IN PORTUGAL AND SPAIN ... 1809 TO 1812. Bath: Privately printed, 1812.

392. Madelin, Louis. L'AFFAIRE D'ESPAGNE--1807-1809. Paris: Hachette, 1943.

393. Madureira dos Santos, H. ADITAMENTO AO CATALOGO DOS DECRETOS DO EXTINTO CONSELHO DE GUERRA (DECRETOS EXISTENTES POR COPIA NO ARQUIVO HISTORICO MILITAR). Lisbon, 1958-69. 6 vols. in 7.

394. Magahaès Basto, Artur de. 1809 [i.e. MIL OITO CENTOS E NOVE] O PORTO SOB A SEGUNDA INVASAO FRANCESA. Lisbon: Impresa literaria fluminese, [1926].

395. Maginn, William. THE MILITARY SKETCH-BOOK. REMINISCENCES OF
     SEVENTEEN YEARS IN THE SERVICE ABROAD AND AT HOME. BY AN
     OFFICER OF THE LINE. London: Colburn, 1827. 2 vols.

396. Maguire, Thomas Miller. THE BRITISH ARMY UNDER WELLINGTON,
     1813-1814; A SUMMARY. London: William Clowes, 1907.

397. Mämpel, Johan Christian. THE ADVENTURES OF A YOUNG RIFLEMAN IN
     THE FRENCH AND ENGLISH ARMIES DURING THE WAR IN SPAIN AND
     PORTUGAL FROM 1806-1816. Written by himself. London: Colburn,
     1826.

398. Manière. SOUVENIRS D'UN CANONNIER DE L'ARMEE D'ESPAGNE,
     1808-1814. Publiés par Germain Bapst. Paris: Romain, 1892.

399. Marañón, Gregorio. EL EMPECINADO. Madrid: n.p., 1932.

400. Marbot, Jean Baptiste Antoine Marcelin, baron de. THE MEMOIRS
     OF BARON DE MARBOT, LATE LIEUTENANT-GENERAL IN THE FRENCH ARMY.
     Translated from the French by Arthur John Butler. London:
     Longmans, Green, 1892. 2 vols.

401. Marcel, Nicolas. CAMPAGNES DU CAPITAINE MARCEL DU 69e DE LIGNE
     EN ESPAGNE ET EN PORTUGAL (1808-1814). Mises en ordre, anotées
     et publiées par le commandant Var. Paris: Plon-Nourrit, 1913.

402. Marindin, Arthur Henry. THE SALAMANCA CAMPAIGN. London: Rees,
     1906.

403. Martín, Claude. JOSE NAPOLEON I, "REY INTRUSO" DE ESPANA.
     Madrid: Editora Nacional, 1969.

404. Martin, Emmanuel. LA GENDARMERIE FRANCAISE EN ESPAGNE ET EN
     PORTUGAL (CAMPAGNES DE 1807 A 1814). Avec un exposé des
     opérations militaires exécutées dans les provinces du Nord de
     l'Espagne par nos armées, les troupes régulières ennemies et les
     guérillas espagnoles, d'après les archives du Ministre de la
     guerre, les Archives nationales et autres documents manuscrits
     ou imprimés. Paris: Léautey, 1898.

405. Martinez Colomer, Vicente. SUCESOS DE VALENCIA, DESDE EL DIA 23
     DE MAYO HASTA EL 28 DE JUNIO DEL ANO 1808. Valencia: Salvador
     Fauli, 1810.

406. Martínez-Valverde, Carlos. LA MARINA EN LA GUERRA DE LA
     413INDEPENDENCIA. Madrid: Editora Nacional, 1970.

407. Martins, Francisco José Rocha. A CORTES DE JUNOT EM PORTUGAL,
     1807-1808. Lisbon: Carvalho [1910].

408. Martins, Francisco José Rocha. EPISODIOS DA GUERRA PENINSULAR:
     AS TRES INVASOES FRANCESAS. Lisbon: Jornal do Comercio, 1944.
     3 vols.

409. Martins, Maria Ermelinda de Avelar Soares Fernandes. COIMBRA E A GUERRA PENINSULAR. Coimbra: Typog. da Atlantida, 1944. 2 vols.

410. Martins Pamplona Cortes Real, Manuel Ignacio. APERCU NOUVEAU SUR LES CAMPAGNES DES FRANCAIS EN PORTUGAL EN 1807, 1808, 1809, 1810 et 1811. Paris: Delaunay, 1818.

411. Massias, Nicolas, baron. LE PRISONNIER EN ESPAGNE, OU, COUP D'OEIL PHILOSOPHIQUE SUR LES PROVINCES DE CATALOGNE ET DE GRANADA. Paris: Firmin-Didot, 1831.

412. Masson, Bernard. EVASION ET ENLEVEMENT DE PRISONNIERS FRANCAIS DE L'ILE DE CABRERA. Lodève: Grillières, 1839.

413. Mateos y Sotos, Rafael. LA PROVINCIA DE ALBACETE EN LA GUERRA DE LA INDEPENDENCIA. Albacete: Lopez, 1910.

414. Matta Oliveira, Joachim da. O PODER MARTIMO NA GUERRA DE PENINSULAR. Lisbon: Cooperative Militar, 1914.

415. Maxwell, Herbert Eustace. THE LIFE OF WELLINGTON. THE RESTORATION OF THE MARTIAL POWER OF GREAT BRITAIN. London: Low, Marston [1899]. 2 vols.

416. Maxwell, William Hamilton. LIFE OF FIELD-MARSHAL HIS GRACE THE DUKE OF WELLINGTON. London: Baily, 1839-41. 3 vols.

417. Maxwell, William Hamilton, comp. PENINSULAR SKETCHES; BY ACTORS ON THE SCENE. London: Colburn, 1845. 2 vols.

418. Maza Solano, Tomás. EL REAL CONSULADO DE SANTANDER Y LA GUERRA DE LA INDEPENDENCIA; NOTICIAS Y DOCUMENTOS PARA SU HISTORIA. Santander: Centro de Estudios Montañeses, 1960.

419. MEMORIA DE LO MAS INTERESSANTE QUE HA OCURRIDO EN LA CIUDAD DE ZARAGOZA CON MOTIVO DE HABERLA AFACADO EL EXERCITO FRANCES. Madrid: Imprenta de la calle de la Greda, 1808.

420. MEMORIAS SOBRE LA RECONQUISTA ZARAGOZA, CONSERVACION DE LA PLAZA Y RENDICION DE SU CASTILLO POR LAS TROPAS ESPANOLAS EN JULIO DE 1813. Las publica un Monge Benito del monasterio de Arlanza. Madrid: Repullés, 1815.

421. Mercader Riba, Juan. BARCELONA DURANTE LA OCUPACION FRANCESA (1808-1814). Madrid: Instituto Jeronimo Zurita, 1949.

422. Mercader Riba, Juan. JOSE BONAPARTE, REY DE ESPANA, 1808-1813. HISTORIA EXTERNA DEL REINADO. Madrid: Instituto Jerônimo Zurita, 1971.

423. Merlin, María de las Mercedes Santa Cruz y Montalvo, comtesse de. SOUVENIRS ET MEMOIRES DE MADAME LA COMTESSE MERLIN. Publiés par elle-même. Paris: Charpentier, 1836. 4 vols.

424. Méry, C. de. MEMOIRES D'UN OFFICIER FRANCAIS PRISONNIER EN ESPAGNE. Paris: Boulland, 1823.

425. Milburne, H[enry]. A NARRATIVE OF CIRCUMSTANCES ATTENDING THE RETREAT OF THE BRITISH ARMY UNDER THE COMMAND OF ... LIEUT. GEN. SIR JOHN MOORE, K.B. WITH A CONCISE ACCOUNT OF THE MEMORABLE BATTLE OF CORUNNA ... AND A FEW REMARKS CONNECTED WITH THESE SUBJECTS IN A LETTER ADDRESSED TO THE RIGHT HONOURABLE LORD VISCOUNT CASTLEREAGH. London: Egerton, 1809.

426. Milford, John. PENINSULAR SKETCHES, DURING A RECENT TOUR. London: Davidson, 1816.

427. Minali, Guillermo. HISTORIA MILITAR DE GERONA, QUE COMPRENDE PARTICULARMENTE LOS DOS SITIOS DE 1808 Y 1809. Gerona: Figaró, 1840.

428. Mockler-Ferryman, Augustus Ferryman. THE LIFE OF A REGIMENTAL OFFICER DURING THE GREAT WAR, 1793-1815, COMPILED FROM THE CORRESPONDENCE OF COLONEL SAMUEL RICE, 51st LIGHT INFANTRY, AND FROM OTHER SOURCES. Edinburgh: Blackwood, 1913.

429. Moline de Saint-Yon, Alexandre Pierre. LES DEUX MINA; CHRONIQUE ESPAGNOLE DU XIXe SIECLE. Paris: Didot, 1840. 3 vols.

430. Monglave, Eugène de. SIEGE DE CADIX, PAR L'ARMEE FRANCAISE, EN 1810, 1811 ET 1812. Paris: Ponthieu, 1823.

431. Moore, James Carrick. THE LIFE OF LIEUTENANT-GENERAL SIR JOHN MOORE, K.B. By his brother. London: J. Murray, 1834. 2 vols.

432. Moore, James Carrick. A NARRATIVE OF THE CAMPAIGN OF THE BRITISH ARMY IN SPAIN. AUTHENTICATED BY OFFICIAL PAPERS AND ORIGINAL LETTERS. London: J. Johnson, 1809.

433. Moore, John. THE DIARY OF SIR JOHN MOORE. Edited by Major-General Sir J.F. Maurice. London: Arnold, 1904. 2 vols.

434. Moorsom, William Scarth, ed. HISTORICAL RECORD OF THE FIFTY-SECOND REGIMENT (OXFORDSHIRE LIGHT INFANTRY) FROM THE YEAR 1755 TO THE YEAR 1858. Compiled under direction of the committee and edited by W.S. Moorsom. London: Bentley, 1860.

435. Moraes Leito Velho, B.T. de. ESTUDO HISTORICO DAS RELACOES DIPLOMATICAS E POLITICAS ENTRE A FRANCA E PORTUGAL DESDE A CONSTITUICAO DA MONARCHIA PORTUGUEZA ATE A QUEDA DE NAPOLEAO BONAPARTE. Lisbon: Companhia nacional editora, 1895.

436. Morley, Stephen. MEMOIRS OF A SERJEANT OF THE FIFTH REGIMENT OF FOOT. Ashford [Eng.]: Elliot, 1842.

437. Moya y Jiménez, Francisco Javier de. EL EJERCITO Y LA MARINA EN LAS CORTES DE CADIZ; OBRA ESCRITA EN CONMEMORACION DEL

CENTENARIO DEL LA CONSTITUCION DE 1812, Y SITIO DE LA ISLA GADITANA. Por Francisco J. de Moya y Jiménez y Celestino Rey Joly. Cádiz: Comercial, 1914.

438. Mozas Mesa, Manuel. BAILEN; ESTUDIO POLITICO Y MILITAR DE LA GLORIOSA JORNADA. Madrid: Enciso, 1940.

439. Munárriz Urtasun, Eufrasio. 1813. SITIO Y DESTRUCCION DE SAN SEBASTIAN. Pamplona: Editorial Gómez, 1958.

440. Munster, George Augustus Frederick Fitzclarence, 1st earl of. AN ACCOUNT OF THE BRITISH CAMPAIGN IN 1809, UNDER SIR A. WELLESLEY, IN PORTUGAL AND SPAIN. By the Earl of Munster. Edited for private circulation. London: Colburn and Bentley, 1831.

441. Munster, George Augustus Frederick Fitzclarence, 1st earl of. A MANUAL OF OUT-POST DUTIES ... TO WHICH ARE ADDED: 1. LETTERS ON OUT-POST DUTIES, ADDRESSED TO HIS LORDSHIP BY SEVERAL DISTINGUISHED OFFICERS; 2. EXTRACTS FROM GENERAL ORDERS, SHOWING THE DISPOSITION OF FIELD MARSHAL THE DUKE OF WELLINGTON'S OUT-POSTS FROM 1810-1814; 3. A PRIVATE JOURNAL OF GENERAL CRAUFURD'S OUT-POST OPERATIONS ON THE COA AND AGUEDA IN 1810, BY MAJOR-GENERAL SHAW KENNEDY, C.B. London: Barker, Furnivall, and Parker, 1851.

442. Murat, Joachim Joseph André, comte. MURAT, LIEUTENANT DE L'EMPEREUR EN ESPANGE 1808, D'APRES SA CORRESPONDANCE INEDITE ET DES DOCUMENTS ORIGINAUX. Paris: Plon-Nourrit, 1897.

443. Murray, George. MEMOIR ANNEXED TO AN ATLAS CONTAINING THE PLANS OF THE PRINCIPAL BATTLES, SIEGES AND AFFAIRS ... DURING THE WAR IN THE SPANISH PENINSULA. London: James Wyld, 1841.

444. Myatt, Frederick. PENINSULAR GENERAL: SIR THOMAS PICTON 1758-1815. Newton Abbot: David and Charles, 1980.

445. Napier, George Thomas. PASSAGES IN THE EARLY MILITARY LIFE OF GENERAL SIR GEORGE T. NAPIER. Edited by W.C.E. Napier. London: J. Murray, 1884.

446. Napier, William Francis Patrick. COLONEL NAPIER'S JUSTIFICATION OF HIS THIRD VOLUME; FORMING A SEQUEL TO HIS REPLY TO VARIOUS OPPONENTS, AND CONTAINING SOME NEW AND CURIOUS FACTS RELATIVE TO THE BATTLE OF ALBUERA. London: T. and W. Boone, 1833.

447. Napier, William Francis Patrick. HISTORY OF THE WAR IN THE PENINSULA AND IN THE SOUTH OF FRANCE, FROM THE YEAR 1807 TO THE YEAR 1814. London: Barthès & Lowell, 1876. 6 vols.

448. Napier, William Francis Patrick. THE LIFE AND OPINIONS OF GENERAL SIR CHARLES JAMES NAPIER, G.C.B. London: J. Murray, 1857. 4 vols.

449. Naylies, Joseph Jacques de, vicomte. MEMOIRES SUR LA GUERRE
     D'ESPAGNE, PENDANT LES ANNEES 1808, 1809, 1810 ET 1811. Paris:
     Magimel, Anselin et Pochard, 1817.

450. Neale, Adam. LETTERS FROM PORTUGAL AND SPAIN; COMPRISING AN
     ACCOUNT OF THE OPERATIONS OF THE ARMIES UNDER THEIR EXCELLENCIES
     SIR ARTHUR WELLESLEY AND SIR JOHN MOORE, FROM THE LANDING OF THE
     TROOPS IN MODEGO BAY TO THE BATTLE AT CORUNNA. London:
     Phillips, 1809.

451. Niegolewski, Jedrzej. LES POLONAIS A SOMO-SIERRA EN ESPAGNE EN
     1808. RECTIFICATION RELATIVE A L'ATTAQUE DE SOM-SIERRA, DECRITE
     PAR DES HISTORIENS FRANCAIS. Paris: Martinet, 1855.

452. Nieto Samaniego, Juan Andrés. MEMORIAL HISTORICO DE LOS SUCESOS
     MAS NOTABLES DE ARMAS, Y ESTADO DE SALUD PUBLICA DURANTE EL
     ULTIMO SITIO DE LA PLAZA DE GERONA. Tarragona: Brusi, 1813.

453. Noël, Jean Nicolas Auguste. SOUVENIRS MILITAIRES D'UN OFFICIER
     DU PREMIER EMPIRE (1795-1832). Paris: Berger-Levrault, 1895.

454. Nunes, J. Lucio. AS BRIGADAS DA CAVALARIA PORTUGUESA NA GUERRA
     PENINSULAR. Lisbon: Edicão de Alvaro Pinto, 1954.

455. Obanos Alcalá del Olmo, Federico. LA MARINA EN EL BLOQUEO DE LA
     ISLA DE LEON (1810 A 1812). Madrid: Fortanet, 1905.

456. OBSERVADOR PORTUGUEZ, HISTORICO, E POLITICO DE LISBOA, DESDE O
     DIA 27 DE NOVEMBRO DO ANNO DE 1807, EM QUE EMBARCOU PARA O
     BRAZIL O PRINCIPE REGENT NOSSA SENHOR E TODA A REAL FAMILIA, POR
     MOTIVO DE INVASAO DOS FRANCEZES NESTE REINO, ETC. Lisbon:
     Impressão regia, 1809.

457. Oleza, José de. LA RECUPERACION DE SAN SEBASTIAN Y PAMPLONA EN
     1813. Pamplona: Gómez, 1959.

458. Olóriz, Hermilio de. NAVARRA EN LA GUERRA DE LA INDEPENDENCIA;
     BIOGRAFIA DEL GUERRILLERO DON FRANCISCO ESPOZ (ESPOZ Y MINA), Y
     NOTICIA DE LA ABOLICION Y RESTABLECIMIENTO DEL REGIMEN FORAL.
     Pamplona: Aramburu, 1910.

459. Oman, Charles William Chadwick. A HISTORY OF THE PENINSULAR
     WAR. Oxford: Clarendon Press, 1902-30. 7 vols.

460. Oman, Charles William Chadwick. WELLINGTON'S ARMY 1809-1814.
     London: Arnold, 1913.

461. Ompteda, Christian Friedrich Wilhelm, freiherr von. A
     HANOVERIAN-ENGLISH OFFICER A HUNDRED YEARS AGO. MEMOIRS OF
     BARON OMPTEDA. Translated by John Hill. London: Grevel, 1892.

462. Ormsby, James Wilmet. AN ACCOUNT OF THE OPERATIONS OF THE
     BRITISH ARMY AND OF THE STATE AND SENTIMENTS OF THE PEOPLE OF
     PORTUGAL AND SPAIN DURING THE CAMPAIGNS OF THE YEARS 1808 AND
     1809. London: Illerton and Byworth, 1809. 2 vols.

463. Osma, Joachim de. JOURNAL SOMMAIRE DES OPERATIONS DE L'ARMEE SOUS LES ORDRES DU MARQUIS DE LA ROMANA. Paris: Michaud, 1824. 2 vols.

464. Ovilo y Otero, Manuel. VIDA POLITICA DE D. MANUEL GODOY, PRINCIPE DE LA PAZ. Madrid: Lamparero, 1845.

465. Paget, Elden. LETTERS AND MEMORIALS OF GENERAL THE HONORABLE SIR EDWARD PAGET. London: Bliss, Sands, 1898.

466. Palafox y Melci, José de Rebolledo, duque de. AUTOBIOGRAFIA. Preparacion y introduccion de J. Garcia Mercadal. Madrid: Taurus, 1966.

467. [Palomar, Juan Domingo]. DIARIO DE UN PATRIOTA COMPLUTENSE EN LA GUERRA DE LA INDEPENDENCIA. Madrid: Hernandez, 1894.

468. Pano y Ruata, Mariano de. LA CONDESA DE BURETA, DA. MARIA CONSOLACION DE AZLOR Y VILLAVICENCIO Y EL REGENTE, DON PEDRO MARIA RIO Y MONTSERRAT; EPISODIOS Y DOCUMENTOS DE LOS SITIOS DE ZARAGOZA. Zaragoza: Escar, 1908.

469. Pardo de Andrade, Manuel. LOS GUERRILLEROS GALLEGOS DE 1809. Corunna: Andrés Martínez, 1892. 2 vols.

470. Paris. Bibliothèque nationale. LISTE DES OUVRAGES RELATIFS A LA GUERRE DE LA PENINSULE (1807-1814). Rédigée sous la direction de Paul Marchal, conservateur du département des imprimés, par Henri Lamaitre. Paris, 1909.

471. Parkinson, Roger. MOORE OF CORUNNA. London: Hart-Davis, MacGibbon, 1976.

472. Parkinson, Roger. THE PENINSULAR WAR. London: Hart-Davis, MacGibbon, 1973.

473. Partin, Roland. LETTERS FROM PORTUGAL AND SPAIN WRITTEN DURING THE MARCH OF THE BRITISH TROOPS UNDER SIR JOHN MOORE. London: Longman, Hurst, Rees, and Orme, 1809.

474. Passos, Carlos de. BERESFORD E O TENENTE-REI DA PRACA D'ALMEIDA; RESSURREICAO D'UMA VICTIMA DE JUGO INGLEZ DO TEMPO DA GUERRA PENINSULAR. Porto: Eduardo Tavares Martins, 1924.

475. Patterson, John. THE ADVENTURES OF CAPTAIN JOHN PATTERSON, WITH NOTICES OF THE OFFICERS, ETC. OF THE 50th, OR QUEEN'S OWN REGIMENT, FROM 1807 TO 1821. London: T. and W. Boone, 1837.

476. Paulin, Jules Antoine, comte. LES SOUVENIRS DU GENERAL BARON PAULIN (1782-1876). Publiés par le capitaine du génie Paulin-Ruelle, son petit-neveu. Paris: Plon-Nourrit, 1895.

477. Pearson, Andrew. AUTOBIOGRAPHY OF ANDREW PEARSON, A PENINSULAR VETERAN. Edinburgh: n.p., 1865.

478. Pellot, Joseph. MEMOIRE SU LA CAMPAGNE DE L'ARMEE FRANCAISE
     DITE DES PYRENEES, EN 1813 ET 1814. Bayonne: Gosse, 1818.

479. Peltier, Jean Gabriel. LA CAMPAGNE DE PORTUGAL, EN 1810 ET
     1811. Paris: Eymery, 1814.

480. Pereira, Angelo. D. JOAO VI, PRINCIPE E REI. Lisbon: Impresa
     Nacional de Publicidade, 1953. 4 vols.

481. Pereira de Chaby, Claudio Bernardo. APONTAMENTOS PARA A
     HISTORIA DA LEGIAO PORTUGUEZA AO SERVICO DE NAPOLEAO I, MANDADA
     SAHIR DE PORTUGAL EM 1808, NARRATIVA DO TENENTE THEOTONIO BANHA.
     Lisbon: Imprensa Nacional, 1863.

482. Pereira de Chaby, Claudio Bernardo. EXCEPTOS HISTORICOS E
     COLLECCAO DE DOCUMENTOS RELATIVOS A GUERRA DENOMINADA DA
     PENINSULA E AS ANTERIORES DE 1801, E DO ROUSSILLON E CATALUNA.
     Lisbon: Imprensa Nacional, 1863-82. 5 vols.

483. Pereira de Chaby, Claudio Bernardo. SYNOPSE DOS DECRETOS
     REMETTIDOS   AO   EXTINTO   CONSELHO   DE   GUERRA,   DESDE   O
     ESTABELECIMENTO D'ESTE TRIBUNAL EM 11 DE DEZEMBRO DE 1640, ATE A
     SUA EXTINCAO EM 1 DE JULHO DE 1834. Lisbon: Imprensa Nacional,
     1869-92. 8 vols.

484. Pérez de Guzmán y Gallo, Juan. EL DOS DE MAYO DO 1808 EN
     MADRID. RELACION HISTORICA DOCUMENTADA MANDADA PUBLICAR DE
     ORDEN DEL ESCMO. SENOR CONDE DE PENALVER, ALCALDE PRESIDENTE DE
     SU   EXCMO.   AYUNTAMIENTO,   Y   POR ACUERDO   DE   LA   COMISION
     ORGANIZADORA DEL PRIMER CENTENARIO DE SU GLORIOSA EFEMERIDE.
     Madrid: Establecimiento tipog., 1908.

485. Pérez de Herrasti, Andrés. RELACION HISTORICA Y CIRCUMSTANDIADA
     DE LOS SUCESOS DEL SITIO DE LA PLAZA DE CIUDAD-RODRIGO EN EL ANO
     DE 1810. Madrid: Repulles, 1814.

486. Petrie, Charles Alexander. WELLINGTON: A REASSESSMENT.
     London: Barrie, 1956.

487. Pfannkuche, Adolf. DIE KOENIGLICH DEUTSCHE LEGION, 1803-1816.
     Hanover: Helwing, 1926.

488. Pfister-Schwaighusen, Hermann von. GESCHICHTE DER THUERINGISCHEN
     TRUPPEN IN DEM FELDZUGE VON 1810-11 IN KATALONIEN. Berlin:
     Bath, 1866.

489. Phillips, George P.A. GUIDE TO MILITARY HISTORY. PENINSULAR
     WAR. London: Gale and Polden [1905-1907]. 2 vols.

490. [Picado Franco, Lino Matias]. HISTORIA DEL ORIGEN,
     ACONTECIMIENTOS Y ACCIONES DE GUERRA DE LA 6. DIVISION DEL
     SEGUNDO EXERCITO (O DE SORIA) DURANTE NUESTRA SAGRADA LUCHA AL
     MANDO DEL E.S.D. JOSE JOAQUIN DURAN Y BARAZABAL. Madrid:
     Dávila, 1817. 2 vols.

491. Picard, Louis Auguste. GUERRES D'ESPAGNE. Paris: Jouve, 1911-13. 2 vols.

492. Picton, Thomas. MEMOIRS OF LIEUTENANT-GENERAL SIR THOMAS PICTON, INCLUDING HIS CORRESPONDENCE, FROM ORIGINALS IN POSSESSION OF HIS FAMILY. Edited by Heaton Bowstead Robinson. London: Bentley, 1836. 2 vols.

493. Piétri, François. LUCIEN BONAPARTE A MADRID, 1801. Paris: Bernard Grasset [1951].

494. Pina y Ferrer, Victorio. PAGINAS DE 1808, MEMORIAS DE UN PATRIOTA, LEVANTAMIENTO DE ZARAGOZA. Zaragoza: Arino, 1889.

495. Pires de Lima, Durval Rui, ed. OS FRANCESES NO PORTO, 1807-1808; DIARIO DE UMA TESTEMUNHA PRESENCIAL, ANOTADO E PRECEDIDO DE UMA INTRODUCAO. Porto: Câmara Municipal do Porto, 1949. 2 vols.

496. Pla y Cargol, Joaquín. ALVAREZ DE CASTRO. Madrid: Gran Capitán, 1946.

497. Pla y Cargol, Joaquín. LA GUERRA DE LA INDEPENDENCIA EN GERONA Y SUS COMARCAS. Gerona: Dalmáu Carles, Pla, 1953.

498. Porter, Robert Ker. LETTERS FROM PORTUGAL AND SPAIN, WRITTEN DURING THE MARCH OF THE BRITISH TROOPS UNDER SIR JOHN MOORE. By an officer. London: Longman, Hurst, Rees, and Orme, 1809.

499. Portugal. Exercito. COLLECCAO SYSTEMATICA DAS ORDENS DO EXERCITO DESDE 1809 ATE 1858. Coordenada por Vital Prudencio Alvês Pereira. Lisbon: Sousa, 1859-61. 4 vols.

500. Pouzerewski, Général. LA CHARGE DE CAVALERIE DE SOMO-SIERRA (ESPAGNE) LE 30 NOVEMBRE 1808. Traduit du russe par Dimitry Ornobichine. Paris: Charles-Lavauzelle, 1900.

501. Pradt, Dominque Georges Frédéric de Riom de Prolhiac de Fourt de, archevêque de Mechlin. MEMOIRES HISTORIQUES SUR LA REVOLUTION D'ESPAGNE; PAR L'AUTEUR "DU CONGRES DE VIENNE." Paris: Rosa, 1816.

502. Priego López, Juan. GUERRE DE LA INDEPENDENCIA, 1804-1814. Madrid: Librería Editorial San Martin, 1972-82. 5 vols.

503. Prieto y Llovera, Patricio. EL GRANDE DE ESPANA: CAPITAN GENERAL CASTANOS, PRIMER DUQUE DE BAILEN Y PRIMER MARQUES DE PORTUGALETE, 1758-1852. Madrid: Disputación permanente y consejo de la grandeza de España, 1958.

504. Príncipe y Vidaud, Miguel Agustín. GUERRA DE LA INDEPENDENCIA. NARRACION HISTORICA. Madrid: Manini, 1844-47. 3 vols.

505. Rait, Robert Sangster. THE LIFE AND CAMPAIGNS OF HUGH, FIRST
     VISCOUNT GOUGH, FIELD MARSHAL. Westminster: Constable, 1903.
     2 vols.

506. Ramonlaca, Julio de. EL GENERAL PEREZ DE HERRASTI, HEROE DE
     CIUDAD RODRIGO. Madrid: Raycar Sa Impressores Matilde, 1967.

507. Recasens Gomes, José Maria. LA REVOLUCION Y GUERRA DE LA
     INDEPENDENCIA EN LA CIUDAD DE TARRAGONA. Tarragona: Real
     Sociedad Arqueológica Tarraconense, 1965.

508. Régean, Octave. APERCU DES CAMPAGNES DE 1813 ET 1814 SUR LES
     PYRENEES. Rouen: Bière, 1832.

509. Révesz, Andrés. MORILLO, EL TENIENTE GENERAL DON PABLO MORILLO,
     PRIMER CONDE DE CARTAGENA. Madrid: Gran Capitán, 1947.

510. Richards, Donald Sidney. THE PENINSULAR VETERANS. London:
     MacDonald and Jane's, 1975.

511. Rico, Juan. MEMORIAS HISTORICAS SOBRE LA REVOLUCION DE VALENCIA
     ... DESDE EL 23 DE MAYO DE 1808 HASTA FINES DEL MISMO ANO.
     Cádiz: Santiago de Quintana, 1811.

512. Rigel, Franz Xaver. BLOCKADE, BELAGERUNG UND EROBERUNG VON
     TORTOSA DURCH DAS DRITTE FRANZOESISCHE ARMEE CORPS IM JAHRE
     1810-1811 UND VERTHEIDIGUNG VON MONZEN. AUS DEN MEMORIEN DES
     MARSCHALLS SUCHET UBENSETZT UND MIT ANMER KUNGEN VERSEHEN.
     Mannheim: Goetz, 1847.

513. Rigel, Franz Xaver. COMBATES EM RODA DE TARRAGONA DURANTE A
     GUERRA DA RESTAURACAO DOS CATALAENS, DE 1808 A 1814. Karlsruhe,
     1824.

514. Rigel, Franz Xaver. DER SIEBENJAHRIGE KAMPF AUF DER
     PYRENAEISCHEN, HALBINSEL VOM JAHRE 1807 BIS 1814. Rastatt: Der
     Verfasser, 1819-21. 3 vols.

515. Rincón, Jesus. EL CLERO EXTREMENO EN LA GUERRA DE LA
     INDEPENDENCIA. Prólogo de Román Gómez Villafranca. Badajoz:
     Noticiero Estremeño, 1911.

516. Río Fernandez, Luciano del. PAGINAS HISTORICAS DE PONTEVEDRA.
     GUERRA DE LA INDEPENDENCIA. Pontevedra: Landin, 1918.

517. Ríos, Juan Miguel de los. CODIGO ESPANOL DEL REINADO INTRUSO DE
     JOSE BONAPARTE, O SEA COLECCION DE SUS MAS IMPORTANTES LEYES,
     DECRETOS E INSTITUCIONES. Madrid: Roix, 1845.

518. Robert, Baron. RAPPORT SUR LA DEFENSE DE LA PLACE DE TORTOSA,
     ADRESEE A S. EX. MONSEIGNEUR LE MARECHAL DUC D'ALBUFERA,
     COMMANDANT EN CHEF L'ARMEE ROYALE DU MIDI. Perpignan: Alzine,
     1814.

519. Roberts, David. THE MILITARY ADVENTURES OF JOHNNY NEWCOME, WITH AN ACCOUNT OF HIS CAMPAIGN IN THE PENINSULA AND IN PALL MALL AND NOTES, BY AN OFFICER. London: Patrick Martin, 1816.

520. Robertson, Duncan. THE JOURNAL OF SERGEANT D. ROBERTSON, LATE 92nd FOOT: COMPRISING THE DIFFERENT CAMPAIGNS, BETWEEN THE YEARS 1797 AND 1818 IN EGYPT, WALCHEREN, DENMARK, SWEDEN, PORTUGAL, SPAIN, FRANCE, AND BELGIUM. Perth: Fisher, 1842.

521. Robinson, Charles Walker. WELLINGTON'S CAMPAIGNS. PENINSULA-WATERLOO, 1808-15; ALSO MOORE'S CAMPAIGN OF CORUNNA. London: Rees, 1906-7. 3 vols.

522. Rocca, Albert Jean Michel. MEMOIRES SUR LA GUERRE DES FRANCAIS EN ESPAGNE. Geneva: Fick, 1887.

523. Rodriguez de Ledesma, Juan. HEROES Y MARTIRES GALLEGOS. LOS FRANCISCANOS DE GALICIA EN LA GUERRA DE LA INDEPENDENCIA. Santiago: El Eco. Franciscano, 1912.

524. [Rodríguez Martín, Manuel]. LA MARINA EN LA GUERRA DE LA INDEPENDENCIA. San Fernando: Capitania General, 1889.

525. Rodriguez Solis, Enrique. LOS GUERRILLEROS DE 1808, HISTORIA POPULAR DE LA GUERRA DE LA INDEPENDENCIA. Madrid: Cao y Domingo de Val, 1887. 2 vols.

526. Rogers, Hugh Cuthbert. WELLINGTON'S ARMY. London: Ian Allan, 1979.

527. Rogniat, Joseph. RELATION DES SIEGES DE SARAGOSSE ET DE TORTOSE PAR LES FRANCAIS, DANS LA DERNIERE GUERRE D'ESPAGNE. Paris: Magimel, 1814.

528. Ross, Michael. THE RELUCTANT KING: JOSEPH BONAPARTE, KING OF THE TWO SICILIES AND SPAIN. London: Sidgwick and Jackson, 1976.

529. Rousseau, François. LA CARRIERE DU MARECHAL SUCHET, DUC D'ALBUFERA. Documents inédits. Paris: Firmin-Didot, 1898.

530. Routier, Léon Michel. RECITS D'UN SOLDAT DE LA REPUBLIQUE ET DE L'EMPIRE (1792-1830). Publiés par son fils le colonel Routier. Paris: Vermot, 1899.

531. Roux, Georges. NAPOLEON ET LE GUEPIER ESPAGNOL. Paris: Flammarion, [1970].

532. Roy, Just Jean Etienne. LES FRANCAIS EN ESPAGNE; SOUVENIRS DES GUERRES DE LA PENINSULE 1808-1814. Tours: Mame, 1865.

533. Rudorff, Raymond. WAR TO THE DEATH: THE SIEGES OF SARAGOSSA, 1808-1809. London: Hamilton, 1974.

534. Saint-Chamans, Alfred Armand Robert, comte de. MEMOIRES DU
     GENERAL COMTE DE SAINT-CHAMANS, ANCIEN AIDE DE CAMP DU MARECHAL
     SOULT, 1802-1832. Paris: Plon, 1896.

535. Saint-Maurice Cabany, E. ETUDE HISTORIQUE SUR LA CAPITULATION
     DE BAYLEN, RENFERMANT DES DOCUMENTS AUTHENTIQUES ET INEDITS,
     COMPRENANT UNE NARRATION DETAILLEE DE LA CAMPAGNE DE 1808 EN
     ANDALOUSIE. Paris: Firmin-Didot, 1846.

536. Sala Valdés, Mario de la. OBELISCO HISTORICO EN HONOR DE LOS
     HEROICOS DEFENSORES DE ZARAGOZA EN SUS DOS SITIOS (1808-1809).
     Zaragoza: Salas, 1908.

537. Salcedo y Ruiz, Angel. ASTORGA EN LA GUERRA DE LA
     INDEPENDENCIA. Astorga: Lopez, 1901.

538. Salillas, Rafael. EN LAS CORTES DE CADIZ, (REVELACIONES ACERCA
     DEL ESTUDO POLITICO Y SOCIAL). Madrid: Librería de los
     sucesores de Hernando, 1910.

539. Salmón, P. Maestro. RESUMEN HISTORICO DE LA REVOLUTION DE
     ESPANA ANO DE 1808. Madrid: Imprenta Real, 1820. 6 vols.

540. Salvá, Anselmo. BURGOS EN LA GUERRA DE LA INDEPENDENCIA.
     Burgos: Marcelino Miguel, 1913.

541. Sanchez Alonso, Benito. FUENTES DE LA HISTORIA ESPANOLA E
     HISPANOAMERICANA. Madrid: Consejo Superior de Investigationes
     Científicias, 1952. 3 vols.

542. Sanchez-Arjona y de Velasco. CIUDAD RODRIGO EN LA GUERRA DE LA
     INDEPENDENCIA. Salamanca: Imprenta Nunez, 1957.

543. Sanchez Jara, Diego. INTERVENCION DE MURCIA EN LA GUERRA POR LA
     INDEPENDENCIA. Murcia: Partronato de Cultura de la Deputación
     Provincial, [1960].

544. Santiago y Gadea, Augusto C. EL GENERAL DON PABLO MORILLO;
     APUNTES HISTORICOS ACERCA DE SUS HECHO MILITARES. Madrid:
     Librería de los sucesores de Hernando, 1911.

545. Santiago y Gadea, Augusto C. 1808 [i.e. MIL OCHOCIENTOS
     OCHO]-1814: LA ADMINISTRACION MILITAR EN LA GUERRA DE LA
     INDEPENDENCIA. EL INTENDENTE DEL PRIMER SITIO DE ZARAGOZA,
     CALBO DE ROZAS, OTROS SOLDADOS Y PATRIOTAS; APUNTES HISTORICOS.
     Madrid: Hijos de Tello, 1909.

546. Santocildes, José María de. RESUMEN HISTORICO DE LOS ATAQUES,
     SITIO Y RENDICION DE ASTORGA. Madrid: Imprenta Real, 1815.

547. Sanz Cid, Carlos. LA CONSTITUCION DE BAYONA. Madrid: Reus,
     1922.

548. Sanz Martínez, Julián. RESENA HISTORICA DE LA BATALLA DE
     BAILEN. Madrid: Lopez, 1879.

549. Sanz Martínez, Julián. RESUMEN HISTORICO DE LA GUERRA DE LA INDEPENDENCIA ESPANOLA DE 1808 A 1814. Madrid: Pacheco, 1880-81.

550. Sarramon, Jean. LA BATAILLE DES ARAPILES (22 JUILLET 1812). Toulouse: Université de Toulouse-Le Mirail, 1978.

551. Sarrazin, Jean. HISTORY OF THE WAR IN SPAIN AND PORTUGAL FROM 1807 TO 1814. London: Collins, 1815.

552. Schaumann, August Ludolf Friedrich. ON THE ROAD WITH WELLINGTON; THE DIARY OF A WAR COMMISSARY IN THE PENINSULAR CAMPAIGN. Edited and translated by Anthony M. Ludovici. London: William Heinemann, 1924.

553. Schepeler, Andreas Daniel Berthold von. GESCHICHTE DER REVOLUTION SPANIENS UND PORTUGALS UND BESONDERS DES DARAUS ENTSTANDENEN KRIEGES. Berlin: Mittler, 1826-27. 2 vols.

554. Schwertfeger, Bernhard Heinrich. GESCHICHTE DER KOENIGLICH DEUTSCHEN LEGION, 1803-1816. Hanover: Hahn'sche, 1907. 2 vols.

555. Senén de Contreras, Juan. RELATION OF THE SIEGE OF TARRAGONA, AND THE STORMING AND CAPTURE OF THAT CITY BY THE FRENCH, IN JUNE, 1811. By Field Marshal Don Juan Senén de Contreras, governor of that fortress at the time of the siege. With particulars of the general's escape from the strong castle in which he was confined, his observations on the spirit of the people, and the nature, strategems, and resources of the French government, etc. London: Booth, 1813.

556. Senén de Contreras, Juan. SITIO DE TARRAGONA, LO QUE PASO ENTRE LOS FRANCESES, EL GENERAL CONTRERAS QUE LA DEFENDIO SUS OBSERVACIONES SOBRE LA FRANCIA, Y NOTICIA DEL NUEVO MODO DE DEFENDER LAS PLAZAS. Madrid: Ibarra, 1813.

557. Severn, John Kenneth. "Richard Marquess Wellesley and the Conduct of Anglo-Spanish Diplomacy, 1809-1812." Ph.D. dissertation, Florida State University, 1975.

558. Severn, John Kenneth. A WELLESLEY AFFAIR; RICHARD MARQUESS WELLESLEY AND THE CONDUCT OF ANGLO-SPANISH DIPLOMACY, 1809-1812. Tallahassee, Fla.: University Presses of Florida, 1981.

559. Séze, Romain de. BAYLEN ET LA POLITIQUE DE NAPOLEON. LE GENERAL DUPONT A BAYLON. SA DEFENSE. Lyon: Université Catholique, 1904.

560. Shand, Alexander Innes. THE WAR IN THE PENINSULA, 1808-1814. New York: Scribner, 1898.

561. Shand, Alexander Innes. WELLINGTON'S LIEUTENANTS. London: Smith, Elder, 1902.

562. Sherer, Moyle. MILITARY MEMOIRS OF FIELD MARSHAL, THE DUKE OF WELLINGTON. London: Longman, Rees, Orme, Brown, and Green, 1830. 2 vols.

563. Sherer, Moyle. RECOLLECTIONS OF THE PENINSULA. By the author of "Sketches of India." London: Longman, Hurst, Rees, Orme, and Brown, 1823.

564. Sherwig, John M. GUINEAS AND GUNPOWDER; BRITISH FOREIGN AID IN THE WARS WITH FRANCE, 1793-1815. Cambridge: Harvard University Press [1969].

565. Siddons, Joachim Heyward [J.H. Stocqueler]. THE LIFE OF FIELD MARSHAL THE DUKE OF WELLINGTON. London: Ingram, Cooke, 1852. 2 vols.

566. Sidney, Edwin. THE LIFE OF LORD HILL, G.C.B., LATE COMMANDER OF THE FORCES. London: J. Murray, 1845.

567. Silva Barreto y Almeida, Alejandro de. GUERRA DE EXTREMADURA Y SITIOS DE BADAJOZ. LEALTAD, DEFENSA DE ESTA CIUDAD Y SU DESTRUCCION. Prólogo, estudio preliminar notas y apéndices de Lino Duarte Insúa. Badajoz: Argueros, 1945.

568. Silva Mendes, João da. MEMORIA BIOGRAPHICA DO CORONEL FRANCISCO BERNARDO DA COSTA E ALMEIDA, TENENTE-REI DA PRACA DE ALMEIDA EM 1810. Porto: Silva Teixeira. 1883.

569. Silva Villar, Francisco de Paula da. O GRITO DA INDEPENDENCIA EM 1808. Coimbra: Imprensa da Universidade, 1928.

570. Silva Villar, Francisco de Paula da. A TRAVEZ DAS ORDENS DE BERESFORD DURANTE LA GUERRA PENINSULAR. Lisbon: Belenense, 1896.

571. Simmons, George. A BRITISH RIFLEMAN; THE JOURNALS AND CORRESPONDENCE OF MAJOR GEORGE SIMMONS, RIFLE BRIGADE, DURING THE PENINSULAR WAR AND THE CAMPAIGN OF WATERLOO. Edited with introduction by Lieut. Colonel Willoughby Verner. London: A.& C. Black, 1899.

572. Simon, J.N. KRIEGS-ABENTEUER UND ERLEBNISSE IN DEUTSCHLAND, DER SCHWEIZ, SPANIEN, RUSSLAND UND FRANKREICH: WAEHREND DES ZEITRAUMS VON 1805 BIS 1815. Oldenburg: Schulzesche Buchhandlung, 1849.

573. Simón Carbarga, José. SANTANDER EN LA GUERRA DE LA INDEPENDENCIA. Santander: Manufacturas Jean, 1968.

574. Smith, George Charles Moore. THE LIFE OF JOHN COLBORNE, FIELD-MARSHAL LORD SEATON. COMPILED FROM HIS LETTERS, RECORDS OF HIS CONVERSATIONS, AND OTHER SOURCES. London: J. Murray, 1903.

575. Smith, Harry George Wakelyn. THE AUTOBIOGRAPHY OF LIEUTENANT GENERAL SIR HARRY SMITH, BARONET OF ALIWAL ON THE SUTLEJ. Edited with the addition of some supplementary chapters by G.C. Moore Smith. London: J. Murray, 1901. 2 vols.

576. Soares, Carcevelos. UN BRAVODA GUERRA PENINSULAR E DAS CAMPANHAS DE LIBERDADE. Vila do Condo: Typog. do Reformatório, 1942.

577. Solís, Ramón. EL CADIZ DE LAS CORTES; LA VIDA EN LA CIUDAD EN LOS ANOS DE 1810 A 1813. Madrid: Ministituto de Estudios Politicos, 1958.

578. Solís, Ramón. LA GUERRA DE LA INDEPENDENCIA ESPANOLA. [Barcelona: Editorial Noguer, 1973].

579. Somoza de Montsoriú, Julio, comp. DOCUMENTOS PAR ESCRIBIR LA BIOGRAFIA DE JOVELLANOS. Recopilados por Julio Samoza García-Sala. Madrid: Imprenta de los hijos de Gómez Fuentenebro, 1911.

580. Sorell, Thomas Stephen. NOTES OF THE CAMPAIGN OF 1808-9 IN THE NORTH OF SPAIN. IN REFERENCE TO SOME PASSAGES IN LIEUT. COL. NAPIER'S HISTORY OF THE WAR IN THE PENINSULA AND IN SIR W. SCOTT'S LIFE OF NAPOLEON BONAPARTE. London: J. Murray, 1828.

581. Soult, Nicolas Jean de Dieu, duc de Dalmatie. CAMPAGNES DE GALICE ET DE PORTUGAL (1809). Paris: Dumaine, 1850.

582. Soult, Nicolas Jean de Dieu, duc de Dalmatie. MEMOIRES DU MARECHAL SOULT, ESPAGNE ET PORTUGAL. Texte établi et présenté par Louis et Antoinette de Saint-Pierre. Paris: Hachette, 1955.

583. Sousa Coutinho, Agostino de. O CONDE DE LINHARES, D. RODRIGO DOMINGOS ANTONIO DE SOUSA COUTINHO, PELO MARQUES DE FUNCHAL. Lisbon: Bayard, 1909.

584. Southey, Robert. HISTORY OF THE PENINSULAR WAR. London: J. Murray, 1823-32. 3 vols.

585. Spain. Cortes. ACTAS DE LAS CORTES ORDINARIAS DE 1813-1814. Cádiz, Madrid: Garcia Rico, 1813-14. 2 vols.

586. Spain. Junta Central Suprema. REALES ORDENES DE LA JUNTA CENTRAL SUPREMA ... Y REPRESENTACIONS DE LA DE SEVILLA Y DEL GENERAL CASTANOS, ACERCA DE SU SEPARACION DEL MANDO DEL EXERCITO DE OPERACIONES DEL CENTRO, CON LAS DEMAS CONTESTACIONES QUE HA PRODUCIDO ESTE ASUNTO. n.p., 1890.

587. Spain. Laws, Statutes. COLECCION DE LOS DECRETOS Y ORDENES QUE HAN EXPEDIDO LAS CORTES GENERALES Y EXTRAORDINARIAS DESDE SU INSTALACION DE 24 DE SETIEMBRE DE 1810 HASTA ... MANDADA PUBLICAR DE ORDEN DE LAS MISMAS. Madrid: Imprenta Nacional, 1820-21. 7 vols.

588. Spain. Servicio Histórico Militar. COLECCION DOCUMENTAL DEL
     FRAILE. Madrid: Ediciones Ares, 1947-50. 4 vols.

589. Spain. Servicio Histórico Militar. DICCIONARIO BIBLIOGRAFICO
     DE LA GUERRA DE LA INDEPENDENCIA ESPANOLA (1808-1814).
     Referencias y notas comentadas de obras impresas, documentos y
     manuscritos de autores nacionales y extranjeros, que tratan de
     asuntos militares, históricos, políticos, religiosos,
     económicos, etcétera, etc., relacionados con dicha guerra y su
     época. Madrid: Talleres del Servicio Geográfico del Ejército,
     1944-52. 3 vols.

590. Spain. Servicio Histórico Militar. GUERRA DE LA INDEPENDENCIA,
     1808-1814. Madrid: Libreria Editorial San Martin, 1972-82.
     (See Juan Priego López).

591. Sporschill, Johann Chrysostomus. FELDZUG DER ENGLAENDER,
     SPANIER, UND PORTUGIESSEN GEGAN DIE FRANZOESISCHEN ARMEEN DER
     PYRENAEEN UND VON ARRAGONIEN, IM JAHRE 1814. Braunschweig:
     n.p., 1842.

592. Sprünglin, D'Emmanuel Frédéric. "Souvenirs." REVUE HISPANIQUE.
     Paris: Klincksieck, 1904.

593. Staff, H. von. DER BEFREIUNGSKRIEG DER KATALONIER IN DEN JAHREN
     1808-1814. Berlin: Mitter, 1821. 2 vols.

594. Steevens, Charles. REMINISCENCES OF MY MILITARY LIFE FROM 1795
     TO 1818. Edited by Lieut. Col. Nathaniel Steevens. Winchester:
     Warren, 1878.

595. Stevenson, John. A SOLDIER IN THE TIME OF WAR, OR THE MILITARY
     LIFE OF JOHN STEVENSON, OF THE B. AND F. TEMPERANCE SOCIETY,
     WESLEYAN CLASS LEADER, 21 YEARS IN THE 3rd FOOT GUARDS,
     1793-1815. London: n.p., 1841.

596. Stothert, William. A NARRATIVE OF THE PRINCIPAL EVENTS OF THE
     CAMPAIGNS OF 1809, 1810, & 1811, IN SPAIN AND PORTUGAL;
     INTERSPERSED WITH REMARKS ON LOCAL SCENERY AND MANNERS. London:
     W. Smith, 1812.

597. Suchet, Louis Gabriel, duc d'Albufera. MEMOIRES DU MARECHAL
     SUCHET, DUC D'ALBUFERA, SUR SES CAMPAGNES EN ESPAGNE, DEPUIS
     1808 JUSQU'EN 1814. Ecrits par liu-même. Paris: Bossange,
     1828. 2 vols. and atlas.

598. Surtees, William. TWENTY-FIVE YEARS IN THE RIFLE BRIGADE.
     London: Cadell, 1833.

599. Swabey, William. DIARY OF CAMPAIGNS IN THE PENINSULA FOR THE
     YEARS 1811-12-13: BY AN OFFICER OF E TROOP (PRESENT BATTERY)
     ROYAL HORSE ARTILLERY. Edited by Col. A.W. Linyets R.H.A.
     Woolwich: Royal Artillery Institution, 1895.

600. Talandier. MEMOIRES RELATIFS AUX OPERATIONS DU DEUXIEME CORPS D'ARMEE EN ESPAGNE ET EN PORTUGAL, SOUS LES ORDRES DU MARECHAL SOULT, DUC DE DLAMATIE, DANS LES ANNEE 1808, 1809, 1810 et 1811. Verdun: Leppmann, n.d.

601. Tascher, Maurice Charles Marie de. NOTES DE CAMPAGNE ... (1806-1813). Châteauroux: Sociéte d'imprimerie d'édition et des journaux du Berry, 1932.

602. Taveira de Magalhães, Alfredo Pereira. ESTUDO HISTORICO SOBRE A CAMPANHA DO MARECHAL SOULT EM PORTUGAL, CONSIDERADO NAS SUAS RELACOES COMO A DEFENSA DO PORTO. Lisbon: Cooperativa Militar, 1898.

603. Taveira de Magalhães, Alfredo Pereira. EXPOSICAO BIBLIO-ICONOGRAPHICA COMMEMORATIVA DE 1910; CATALOGO DA ESPOSICAO. Lisbon: Tipog. Universal, 1916.

604. Taveira de Magalhães, Alfredo Pereira. SUMMARIO HISTORICO-BIBLIOGRAPHICO SOBRE A DEFEZA DE PORTUGAL. PRIMEIRA PARTE (1640 A 1815). Lisbon: Cooperativa Militar, 1906.

605. Teffeteller, Gordon. THE SURPRISER: THE LIFE OF ROWLAND LORD HILL. Newark: University of Delaware Press, 1983.

606. Thiébault, Paul Charles Francois Adrien Henri Dieudonné, baron. MEMOIRES DU GENERAL Bon. THIEBAULT. Publiés sous les auspices da sa fille Mlle. Claire Thiébault. Paris: Plon-Nourrit, 1894-95. 5 vols.

607. Thiébault, Paul Charles François Adrien Henri Dieudonné, baron. RELATION DE L'EXPEDITION DU PORTUGAL, FAITE EN 1807 ET 1808, PAR LE 1er CORPS D'OBSERVATION DE LA GIRONDE, DEVENU ARMEE DE PORTUGAL. Paris: Magimel, Anselin et Pochard, 1817.

608. Thirion, Auguste. SOUVENIRS MILITAIRES. Paris: Berger-Levrault, 1892.

609. Thiry, Jean. LA GUERRE D'ESPAGNE. Paris: Berger-Levrault, 1965.

610. Titeux, Eugène. LE GENERAL DUPONT; UNE ERREUR HISTORIQUE, D'APRES DES DOCUMENTS INEDITS AVEC DE HOMBREUSES CARTAS ET FAC-SIMILES. Puteaux-sur-Seine: Prieur et Dubois, 1903. 3 vols.

611. Tomkinson, William. THE DIARY OF A CAVALRY OFFICER IN THE PENINSULAR AND WATERLOO CAMPAIGN, 1809-1815. Edited by James Tomkinson. London: Muller, 1971.

612. Torcal, Norberto. HISTORIA POPULAR DE LOS SITIOS DE ZARAGOZA EN 1808 Y 1809. Zaragoza: Editorial, 1908.

613. Toreno, José María Queipo de Llano Ruiz de Savaría, conde de. EPISODIOS DE LA GUERRA INDEPENDENCIA. Barcelona: Casa del Libro, 1942.

614. Toreno, José María Queipo de Llano Ruiz de Saravía, conde de. HISTORIA DEL LEVANTAMIENTO, GUERRA Y REVOLUCION DE ESPANA. Paris: Baudry, 1838. 3 vols.

615. Tranie, Jean, and Juan Carlos Carmigniani. NAPOLEON'S WAR IN SPAIN: THE FRENCH PENINSULAR CAMPAIGNS. From the notes and manuscritps of Henri Lachouque. Harrisonburg, Pa.: Arms and Armour, 1982.

616. Trefcon, Toussaint Jean. CARNET DE CAMPAGNE DU COLONEL TREFCON, 1793-1815. Publié par André Lévi. Paris: Dubois, 1914.

617. Urgellés, Manuel. HOSTALRICH. MEMORIAS DE LA GUERRA DE LA INDEPENDENCIA. Barcelona: Jepus, 1888.

618. Vacani, Camilo. STORIA DELLE CAMPAGNE E DEGLI ASSEDJ DEGL'ITALIANI IN ISPAGNA DEL 1808 AL 1813. Milan: Imperiale regia atamparia, 1823. 3 vols.

619. Valicourt, Charles, comte de. LA CONQUETE DE VALENCE PAR L'ARMEE FRANCAISE D'ARAGON (1811-1812). Paris: Plon-Nourrit, 1906.

620. Vaughan, Charles Richard. NARRATIVE OF THE SIEGE OF ZARAGOZA. London: James Ridgway, 1809.

621. Vedel, Dominique Honoré. MEMOIRES MILITAIRES DU LIEUT. GENERAL COMTE DE VEDEL SUR LA CAMPAGNE D'ANDALOUSIE EN 1808. Paris: Michaud, 1824.

622. Vedel, Dominique Honoré. PRECIS DES OPERATIONS MILITAIRES EN ESPAGNE, PENDANT LES MOIS DE JUIN ET JUILLET 1808, AVANT LA CAPITULATION DU GENERAL EN CHEF DUPONT, A BAYLEN ET A ANDUJAR; SUIVI DE PIECES JUSTIFICATIVES. Paris: Gueffier, 1823.

623. Venault de Charmilly, Colonel. TO THE BRITISH NATION ... THE NARRATIVE OF HIS TRANSACTIONS IN SPAIN WITH THE RT. HON. JOHN HOOKHAM FRERE ... AND LIEUTENANT GENERAL SIR JOHN MOORE, K.B. London: D.N. Shury, 1810.

624. Vicente, Antônio Pedro. UM SOLDADO DA GUERRA PENINSULAR--BERNARDIM FREIRE DE ANDRADE E CASTRO. BOLETIM DO ARQUIVO HISTORICO MILITAR. Lisbon: Minerva, 1970.

625. Vichness, Samuel Edison. "Marshal of Portugal: The Military Career of William Carr Beresford, 1785-1814." Ph.D. dissertation, Florida State University, 1976.

626. Vidal de la Blache, Paul Marie Joseph. L'EVACUATION DE L'ESPAGNE ET L'INVASION DANS LE MIDI DE LA FRANCE (JUIN 1813-AVRIL 1814). Paris: Berger-Levrault, 1914. 2 vols.

627. Vitorino, Pedro. INVASOES FRANCESAS, 1807-1810. Porto: Pigueirinhas, 1945.

628. Vivian, Claud Hamilton. RICHARD HUSSEY VIVIAN, FIRST BARON VIVIAN. A MEMOIR. London: Isbister, 1897.

629. Vivien, Jean Stanislas. SOUVENIRS DE MA VIE MILITAIRE, 1792-1822. Paris: Hachette, 1907.

630. Wagré, Louis Joseph. LES PRISONNIERS DE CABRERA: SOUVENIRS D'UN CORPORAL DE GRENADIERS, 1808-1809. Paris: Paul, 1902.

631. Ward, Harriet. RECOLLECTIONS OF AN OLD SOLDIER; A BIOGRAPHICAL SKETCH OF THE LATE COLONEL TIDY, C.B., 24th REGIMENT, WITH ANECDOTES OF HIS CONTEMPORARIES. London: Bentley, 1849.

632. Ward, Stephen George Peregrine. WELLINGTON. London: Batsford, 1963.

633. Ward, Stephen George Peregrine. WELLINGTON'S HEADQUARTERS; A STUDY OF THE ADMINISTRATIVE PROBLEMS IN THE PENINSULA, 1809-1814. [London:] Oxford University Press, 1957.

634. Warre, William. LETTERS FROM THE PENINSULA, 1808-1812. London: J. Murray, 1909.

635. Weech, Friedrich Otto Aristides von. BADISCHE TRUPPEN IN SPANIEN, 1810-1813. Karlsruhe: n.p., 1892.

636. Weller, Jac. WELLINGTON IN THE PENINSULA, 1808-1814. London: N. Vane [1962].

637. Wellesley, Muriel. THE MAN WELLINGTON THROUGH THE EYES OF THOSE WHO KNEW HIM. By his great-grandniece, Muriel Wellesley; with illustrations and maps. London: Constable [1937].

638. Wellesley, Richard Colley, marquess. THE DISPATCHES AND CORRESPONDENCE OF THE MARQUESS WELLESLEY, K.G., DURING HIS LORDSHIP'S MISSION TO SPAIN AS AMBASSADOR EXTRAORDINARY TO THE SUPREME JUNTA IN 1809. Edited by Montgomery Martin. London: J. Murray, 1838.

639. Wellesley, Richard Colley, marquess. MEMOIRS AND CORRESPONDENCE OF ... MARQUESS WELLESLEY. Edited by Robert R. Pearce. London: Bentley, 1847. 3 vols.

640. Wellington, Arthur Wellesley, 1st duke of. THE DISPATCHES OF FIELD MARSHAL THE DUKE OF WELLINGTON DURING HIS VARIOUS CAMPAIGNS IN INDIA, DENMARK, PORTUGAL, SPAIN, THE LOW COUNTRIES, AND FRANCE, FROM 1799 TO 1818. Compiled from the official and authentic documents, by Lieut. Colonel Gurwood. London: J. Murray, 1837-39. 13 vols.

641. Wellington, Arthur Wellesley, 1st duke of. GENERAL ORDERS. London: Egerton, 1811-14. 5 vols.

642. Wellington, Arthur Wellesley, 1st duke of. SUPPLEMENTARY DESPATCHES AND MEMORANDA OF FIELD MARSHAL ARTHUR DUKE OF WELLINGTON, K.G. London: J. Murray, 1857-72. 15 vols.

643. Wellington, Arthur Wellesley, 1st duke of. WELLINGTON AT WAR, 1794-1815; A SELECTION OF HIS WARTIME LETTERS. Edited and introduced by Antony Brett-James. London: Macmillan, 1961.

644. Westmorland, John Fane, 11th earl of. MEMOIR OF THE EARLY CAMPAIGNS OF THE DUKE OF WELLINGTON, IN PORTUGAL AND SPAIN. By an officer employed in his army. London: J. Murray, 1820.

645. Wheatley, Edmund. THE WHEATLEY DIARY. A JOURNAL AND SKETCHBOOK KEPT DURING THE PENINSULAR WAR AND THE WATERLOO CAMPAIGN. Edited with an introduction and notes by Christopher Hibbert. [London:] Longmans [1964].

646. Wheeler, William. THE LETTERS OF PRIVATE WHEELER. Edited and with a foreword by B.H. Liddell Hart. London: Michael Joseph [1952].

647. Wilson, Robert Thomas. LIFE OF GENERAL SIR ROBERT WILSON ... FROM AUTOBIOGRAPHICAL MEMOIRS, JOURNALS, NARRATIVES, CORRESPONDENCE, ETC. Edited by Rev. Herbert Randolph. London: J. Murray, 1862. 2 vols.

648. Wood, George. THE SUBALTERN OFFICER, A NARRATIVE. London: Septimus Prowett, 1825.

649. Woodberry, George. JOURNAL DU LIEUTENANT WOODBERRY; CAMPAGNES DE PORTUGAL ET D'ESPAGNE, DE FRANCE, DE BELGIQUE, ET DE FRANCE (1813-1815). Translated by Georges Hélie. Paris: Plon-Nourrit, 1896.

650. Wright, George Newenham. LIFE AND CAMPAIGNS OF ARTHUR, DUKE OF WELLINGTON. London: Fisher, 1838-41. 4 vols.

651. Wyld, James, pub. MAPS AND PLANS, SHOWING THE PRINCIPAL MOVEMENTS, BATTLES & SIEGES IN WHICH THE BRITISH ARMY WAS ENGAGED DURING THE WAR FROM 1808 TO 1814, IN THE SPANISH PENINSULA AND THE SOUTH OF FRANCE. London: J. Wyld [1840]. 51 maps.

652. Young, Peter, and J.P. Lawford. WELLINGTON'S MASTERPIECE: THE BATTLE AND CAMPAIGN OF SALAMANCA. London: Allen & Unwin, 1972.

653. Zimmermann, P. ERINNERUNGEN AUS DEN FELDZUEGEN DER BERGISCHEN TRUPPEN IN SPANIEN UND RUSSLAND. Dusseldorf: n.p., 1840.

PERIODICALS

654. BOLETIM DA ACADEMIA DAS CIENCIAS DE LISBOA.

655. BOLETIM DA ACADEMIA REAL DAS SCIENCIAS DE LISBOA.

656. BOLETIM DE GEOGRAFIA DE LISBOA.

657. BOLETIM DO ARQUIVO HISTORICO MILITAR.

658. DEFESA NACIONAL.

659. ILUSTRACAO PORTUGUEZA.

660. JORNAL DO EXERCITO.

661. REVISTA CIENTIFICO MILITAR.

662. REVISTA DAS SCIENCIAS MILITARES.

663. REVISTA DE ARTILHARIA.

664. REVISTA DE CAVALLARIA.

665. REVISTA DE ENGENHARIA MILITAR.

666. REVISTA DE ESTUDOS HISTORICOS.

667. REVISTA DE ESTUDIOS MILITARES.

668. REVISTA DE INFANTRIA.

669. REVISTA DE HISTORIA.

670. REVISTA DE HISTORICO MILITAR.

671. REVISTA DO EXERCITO E DA ARMADA.

672. REVISTA HISTORIA DE PORTUGAL.

673. REVISTA ILLUSTRADA.

674. REVISTA MILITAR (Lisbon).

675. REVISTA MILITAR (Madrid).

676. REVISTA PORTUGUESA DE HISTORIA.

677. REVISTA TECNIA DE INFANTERIA Y CABALLERIA.

678. REVISTA UNIVERSAL LISBONENSE.

679. REVISTA HISPANIQUE.

680. REVUE HISPANIQUE.

CHAPTER X

AUSTRIA IN THE WARS OF THE REVOLUTIONARY PERIOD (1805-1815)

Gunther E. Rothenberg, Purdue University
Donald D. Horward, Florida State University

During the French Revolutionary and Napoleonic Wars, Austria, a
name used here for the Habsburg Empire, consistently fielded the
largest land force of all the continental powers. Its armies
sustained the War of the First Coalition, fought almost alone during
the Second Coalition, provided the bulk of the forces during the
Third Coalition, and, with little of the expected support
forthcoming, engaged Napoleon again in 1809. After a short-lived
alliance with Napoleon in 1812, Austria mobilized its last reserves
in 1813, providing the largest allied contingent as well as the
supreme commander. Its performance during the last campaign in 1814
in France was creditable, and the next year, when Napoleon returned,
its forces engaged the French in Italy.

Throughout this entire period the army struggled to overcome
monumental obstacles. The Habsburg monarchy never managed to employ
its entire resources. Hungary obstinately clung to its special
prerogatives in military affairs, while the dynasty always hesitated
to rouse popular passions. At the same time, the Austrian
leadership, even that of Archduke Charles, was never equal to that of
the French. The Austrian staff, command, and control system, though
improving, was antiquated and slow. Even so, the kaiserlich-
königliche österreichische Armee constituted the major obstacle to
French domination of the continent, and in the process it preserved
the dynasty and Austria.

Despite this impressive record, the literature on the Austrian
army during this period is curiously limited. Even a hasty survey
reveals two outstanding features. The first is the almost total
neglect of the topic by English-speaking historians. To be sure,
there exist a number of diplomatic accounts, especially ones dealing
with Chancellor Metternich, but they provide very little or nothing
of military interest. Only two books deal specifically with the army
and its direct predecessor, the army of Maria Theresa and Joseph II
(95, 317). In addition, there are a few articles, but nothing more.
The second fact is that most of the considerable body of studies in
German was compiled not by university-trained scholars or practicing
academics, but by active duty officers of the Austro-Hungarian
general staff working from the records in the Vienna Kriegsarchiv.
The exception to the second point is that in the last two decades of
the nineteenth century the descendants of Archduke Charles, Archdukes
Albrecht and Wilhelm, decided to sponsor a series on the life of
their great ancestor and to this end commissioned a number of
civilian historians, including Franz X. Malcher, the family
archivist, and Professors Zeissberg (418) and Zwiedeneck-Südenhorst.
Malcher, aided by Major Angeli of the general staff, did, in fact,
edit five volumes of the archduke's military writings (70), but the
great popular three-volume biography was ultimately completed by
Major Criste (82), an officer working with the historical section of
the army general staff. Thus, these volumes too may be considered
official histories and publications.

The reasons for the sudden surge in publicizing the history of Austria's role in the wars from 1792-1815 were diverse. Work began in the 1870s, that is, at a time when there was a strong wish to mute the continuing debate over the lost wars of 1859 and 1866 by accounts of the more glorious campaigns against the French Revolution and Napoleon. Then after a lull in publication, a new spate of books appeared at the turn of the century, their publication motivated at least in part by the desire of the Emperor Franz Josef and his military advisors not to allow Austria's military heritage to be eclipsed by the active publishing program of the German general staff, a program then moving into high gear in anticipation of the centennial of the Wars of Liberation.

The result, in addition to another five-volume life of Archduke Charles by Angeli (9), was an important series of campaign histories published by the historical section (19, 21, 22, 24). Although the limitations of such official history are obvious, especially the concern with preserving and fostering versions favorable to the dynasty and the monarchy, these various sets nonetheless constitute the single most valuable printed sources for the study of the Austrian army during this period. For the most part they are objective and provide basic material on administrative and operational history. Their gravest shortcoming is that they tend to underplay weaknesses of the high command as well as the problems of the diverse national loyalties within the empire. Perhaps their most serious weakness, however, is a concentration on the more successful campaigns. Nothing was published on the ill-fated War of the Second Coalition or the disastrous War of 1805. The official history of the War of 1809 has a separate volume on Aspern (164), but nothing on Wagram. The contention that such volumes either were contemplated or in various stages of preparation by 1914 cannot be substantiated. It is, however, true that a popular series edited by Woinovich and Veltzé, both serving officers and active in the official program, does include a volume on WAGRAM (167). At the same time, the above-mentioned biography of Charles by Criste (82) also contains a detailed account on this controversial battle.

In any case, the 1914-18 War did, of course, interrupt the historical program of the general staff and, in fact, terminated this agency. Although writing on military history during the First Austrian Republic, 1918-1938, remained dominated by kaisertreu officers of the so-called Generalstabsring, little was done on the Napoleonic period. The German occupation in 1938 did little to change this state of affairs, except for some rather mediocre efforts to recast the Austrian dynastic struggle against Napoleon into a pan-German mythology, including the work by Bibl (45) and Rössler (312), the latter much the better work though flawed by its ideological orientation.

After 1955, the reestablishment of the Second Republic and its efforts to create a consensus on armed neutrality led to the appearance of a number of somewhat uncritical works (3, 150, 182, 244, 265, 300). Gradually, however, there emerged a new Austrian school of military history that, though still primarily based on official institutions, the Kriegsarchiv, now under the Ministry of Culture and Education and the Institute for Military History, a branch of the Heeresgeschichtlichen Museum in Vienna, and supported by the Ministry of Defence, is much more objective and at times even critical of former trends (98, 180, 211, 212, 267, 297, 295, 296). With the emergence of new scholars, especially Peball (267) and Rauchensteiner (294-298), Austrian military history has truly come of age, though lack of resources has prevented the compilation of massive multivolume works to replace the earlier series. A very useful bibliography of writings on Austrian military history, not restricted to Austria since 1945, has been published by the Institute (8) and is in the process of being upgraded. Another valuable tool, including a bibliography of works completed in the archive, has been the INVENTAR DES KRIEGSARCHIVS WIEN (18), a volume that needs updating because of the recataloguing of some of the holdings.

Since works relative to France's struggle against Austria prior to 1809 are discussed in Chapters IV, VI, XII, XIII, and XIV, emphasis will be directed to the period from the beginning of the Fifth Coalition in 1809 through the collapse of the Empire. Curiously, this period, although one of triumph for the French armies, has attracted much less attention than Napoleon's earlier campaigns. Indeed, general histories of Napoleon's campaigns consider the period but there are no comprehensive, detailed studies of the 1809 or Saxon campaign of 1813. Consequently, to gain an understanding of the events that occurred between 1809 and 1814, it is necessary to read a mass of memoirs, journals, correspondence, and the biographies of major actors who took part in the conflicts.

GENERAL WORKS

A single authoritative survey of Austrian military history does not exist. The most recent survey, UNSER HEER (185), is uneven and marred by a determined attempt to accentuate the positive. Still, the relevant chapters may serve as an introduction to the overall topic. Among the older works Meynert's (235) is by far the best, followed in steeply descending order by Müller (241) and Purschka (286). For purely organizational history the reader does well to consult Wrede's five volumes, GESCHICHTE DER K.U.K. WEHRMACHT (415), an account of major developments within the various branches of the army as well as a listing of regiments, their proprietors, commanders, honors, etc. This account is far superior to the short listing given by Pivka (279). Dealing exclusively with the highest administrative body is Regele's somewhat uneven account of the Hofkriegsrat (299). The two-volume set by Ottenfeld and Teuber, DIE OESTERREICHISCHE ARMEE VON 1700 BIS 1867 (256), has a misleading title and is mainly useful for its splendid illustrations.

For the immediate background of the army just before the revolutionary wars, we have the excellent volume by Duffy, THE ARMY OF MARIA THERESA (95); Rothenberg has surveyed the army during the entire period in his NAPOLEON'S GREAT ADVERSARIES: THE ARCHDUKE CHARLES AND THE AUSTRIAN ARMY, 1792-1814 (317). Peball's essay (267) makes interesting, suggestive reading and provides informative historiography.

Turning to the history of wars, battles, and encounters, some famous and others forgotten, we find the official summary OESTERREICHS KRIEGE SEIT 1495 (313), a compilation of data regarding losses, numbers, etc., which may be supplemented by Bodart's MILITAER-HISTORISCHES KRIEGS-LEXIKON (52). Horsetzky's A SHORT HISTORY OF THE CHIEF CAMPAIGNS IN EUROPE (176, 177) provides brief strategic analyses with special attention given to the Austrians. Topographical data can be located for the Austrian campaigns in the official KRIEGS-CHRONIK (23) and more generally in Chandler's GUIDE TO THE BATTLEFIELDS OF EUROPE (68).

Finally, there are some useful sources for biographies of major commanders and for some less well known. Wurzbach's LEXIKON (416) has long been a standard reference; more specialized, if tending toward hagiography, is the official BIOGRAPHIEN K.K. HEERFUEHRER UND GENERAELE (20). The statistical data provided by Preradovich (284) must, however, be treated with caution.

ARCHIVAL SOURCES

The most important repository of manuscripts relating to Austrian participation in the wars against the French Revolution and Napoleon is the Kriegsarchiv in Vienna. The archive houses more than 200,000 fascicles, 44,000 record books, and 370,000 charts and maps. In addition, its library, with well over 400,000 volumes, has the most important single collection of books in military subjects anywhere. Established in 1711 by Emperor Joseph I, the archive became an active research agency in the first decade of the nineteenth century when Archduke Charles assigned it the task of compiling campaign accounts for the instruction and guidance of commanders in future wars.

The holdings and organization of the archive have been described in its INVENTAR (18), which, though now partially outdated by recent reorganization of the holdings, is still the best guide to the administrative organization of the Austrian military establishment. Other descriptions include the essays by Bancalari (28) and the extensive description and analysis by Egger (100).

Except for some collections of private papers and individual memoranda formerly held in the section "Memoires" but currently being reclassified and shifted to the "Nachlässe," records in the Kriegsarchiv are preserved in the same way they were filed by the originating or receiving agency. Of these agency records, those of the Hofkriegsrat, held in the section Archive der Zentralstellen des Heeres, are perhaps the most important. It must, however, be noted that because of frequent reorganization, especially during 1801-1809, the records are difficult to use. The best tools for access are the annual protocol books, the expedit volumes for incoming and the registratura for outgoing papers. For the 1801-1809 period, the remaining Kriegsministerialakten should be consulted. Attached to the archives of the Hofkriegsrat is a special series of documents from various court commissions and delegations. Of these, the papers of the Hofkommission Nostitz Rieneck are especially important for information on the army during the early years of the French Wars.

Regarding documents originated by major field formations, corps, and armies, there are the Aeltere Feldakten and the Armeeakten. These are reasonably complete records of operations, and, in addition, they also contain information on such diplomatic matters as were frequently entrusted to field commanders. It should be noted that some are also held in the famous Haus- Hof- und Staatarchiv. Holdings relating to military subjects in this archive have been described by Heydendorff (160).

Returning to the Kriegsarchiv, the researcher should not neglect the operational studies in the Manuskripte section. Although selective, these contain interesting operational details. Altogether, the Kriegsarchiv, with its wealth and diversity of materials, its knowledgeable staff, and its easy accessibility, represents an indispensable agency for the study of the Austrian army.

By comparison, the other archives and manuscript collections are of lesser importance. The Hungarian State Archives in Budapest have some holdings on the Archduke Charles. However, much of this collection was damaged during the Russian intervention in 1956, and the remainder is difficult to use because of the ever changing access policies of the authorities. In contrast, the well known Public Record Office in London is accessible, but its holdings on the Austrian army are limited to the papers found in one file of the Foreign Office, which do, however, include reports from British military observers.

Concentrating on documents relative to the organization, operation, and administration of the Austrian army, vast collections of material related to the First Coalition (Fasc. 363-626), the Second Coalition (Fasc. 627-744), the Third Coalition (Fasc. 776-800), the Fifth Coalition (Fasc. 808-890), the Russian Campaign (Fasc. 894-902), and the final wars against France (Fasc. 903-1045), as well as the isolated period of peace (Fasc. 775, 801-808, 891-893) are located in the Aeltere Feldakten at the Kriegsarchiv at Vienna. Included in the Armeeakten at the Kriegsarchiv are numerous collections related to the First and Second Coalitions (Fasc. 363-626, 260-372, 380-381), the Third and Fifth Coalitions (Fasc. 348-386a, 387-402), the wars with Russia and France (Fasc. 403-416, 417-707) and finally the periods of peace (Fasc. 373, 382-383, 801-807, 891-893). There are also records of the central army administration at the Hofkriegsrat (Akten 1792-1815), the Kriegsministerialakten (1801-1814), and the Hofkommission Nostitz-Rieneck (1791-1798). Personal records and memorandum of the Kaiser Franz I (B-473), Lindenau (B-619), Mack (B-573), Mayer (B-857), Radetzky (A-1), and Zach (B-857) are useful for the interested scholar. Also available at the Kriegsarchiv are a number of unpublished histories including three of the campaigns of 1796 (Ms. 1802/3, Ms. 1836, Ms. 1804/5) by Kasper Danzer, Johann Schels, and Josef Stutterheim respectively; two of the 1809 campaign (Ms. 1808/9, Ms. 1809) by Johann von Mayer and Friedrich von Spanoghe respectively, and one on Marengo (Ms. 1823) by Karl Mras. At the Magyar Orszāgos Levéltār (Hungarian State Archives) in Budapest, a number of Archduke Charles's papers are retained (P. 300 Kāroly Föherceg 1780-1843). Finally, at the Public Record Office in London, the Foreign Office papers include one carton of documents relative to Anglo-Austrian relations (F-7).

In the French archives the most valuable collections pertaining to the wars between France and Austria are under the jurisdiction of the Service historique de l'armée at the Château de Vincennes. The "Correspondance, Registres, et Situations" of the Grande Armée, the Armée du Rhin, and the Armée d'Allemagne can be found in 738 cartons (C2). Reports related to the French occupation of Germany and Austria can be found in 88 cartons (C13) while the correspondence of Napoleon and his état-major can be located in 286 cartons of documents (C17) at Vincennes. Within these archives, the collections entitled "Mémoires Historique" and "Mémoires Réconnaissances" contain an extraordinary amount of original material related to the Franco-Austrian struggle during the Revolutionary period. Manuscripts related to the early campaigns (608, 610-612, 730-747), the operations in Germany and Austria (661-672, 682-716), and innumerable cartons (386, 425, 800, 901, 910, 939-40, 1161, 1562-1563, 1586-1599) on related topics provide additional documentation on the hostilities and pacific relations between the two powers. There is also pertinent material among the collections scattered among other French archives. For example, the valuable papers of Ney and the Daru collection are located in the Archives Nationales, where an aggressive program is carried on by Conservateur Chantal de Tourtier-Bonazzi to acquire additional Napoleonic materials. It would be wise for every scholar working in the field to consult her articles that appear annually in the REVUE of the Institut Napoléon.

SPECIALIZED WORKS: EARLY WARS OF THE REVOLUTION, 1792-1805

There is much useful information on the relations between the Emperor Francis and his brother, the Archduke Charles, between 1792 and 1805 in Wolfsgruber's biography (413). This, however, must be supplemented by the materials found in Angeli (9), Zeissberg (418), and Criste (82). New interpretations and a new critical approach are evident in Rauchensteiner's excellent study, KAISER FRANZ UND ERZHERZOG CARL (295). A detailed description of the Austrian army at the outset of the wars is provided by Angeli's lengthy essay (10), written as a preliminary study to the definitive two-volume study on the War of the First Coalition published by the Kriegsarchiv (22). In addition to the biographies of Charles mentioned above, the archduke also provides a detailed and critical account of the 1796 campaign in his selected writings edited by Malcher (70). Additional internal criticism of the Austrian conduct of these wars can be found in the memorandum by Zach (417) and in the recollections of Radetzky (290). Ellrich (102) and Rauch (293) offer a rare insight into the enlisted ranks. There are observations on the Austrian army by Wickham (404) and a detailed account of the abortive attempt to raise popular forces during the crisis of 1796-97 by Lorenz (214).

Many of the sources are also useful for the War of the Second Coalition. We have Wertheimer's long essay (400) discussing the conflict between Charles and the imperial ministers and Rodger's book, THE WAR OF THE SECOND COALITION (311), essentially a study in grand strategy and interallied relations. Shadwell's monograph on mountain warfare (342) deals primarily with the French but has some useful information on Austrian generalship, whereas the slowly changing methods of organization, supply, and tactics are briefly mentioned by Gallina (126).

From 1801 until 1804, Archduke Charles attempted to reform the Austrian military system, an effort opposed by many soldiers and civilian officials. His attempts to influence state policy toward an accomodation with France were also resented, and, in the end, his influence waned and he was shunted aside in favor of the "unfortunate Mack" who promised much but failed to carry out his promises. The result was the Ulm campaign of 1805, the occupation of Vienna, and the final reckoning at Austerlitz.

Sources for this period are adequate. Beyond the biographical material already mentioned, we have the documents published by Walter (393) as well as the classic study of the intrigues against Charles by Fournier, GENTZ UND COBENZL (116). An anonymous article, "Zur Charakteristik des Erzherzogs Carl und der österreichishen Armee in den Jahren 1801-1804," describes the limited military reforms (69). In addition, an essay by Regele (302) sheds some new light on these issues, though Regele, a former general staff officer, provides a far too favorable interpretation of the military. Paget, the English ambassador in Vienna, was a horrified onlooker to the unfolding events as he reports in his dispatches (259).

The operations in Germany are detailed by Angeli (11), Krauss (198), Maude (229), and with much personal detail by Schönhals (334), who participated in these operations as a very junior officer. Additional personal reminiscences are in Major Mahler's diary (221). The fine study by Duffy, AUSTERLITZ (96), is the latest account of the war in Germany, the retreat and the climactic battle, and one of the minor combats of the war, as well as the feelings in Vienna; the still mysterious affair of the Tabor bridge is covered by Egger (99). Stutterheim, another participant, offers an account of the battle of Austerlitz (357), and Rüstow, a former Prussian officer who became a free-lance military critic after 1848, writes a useful analysis, DER KRIEG VON 1805 IN DEUTSCHLAND UND ITALIEN (321).

SPECIALIZED WORKS: REFORM AND THE WAR OF 1809

In 1806, Archduke Charles returned to the task of reforming the Austrian military system. In addition to the information provided in the biographical literature, above all in Criste (81, 82), there is an extensive and remarkably critical discussion in the first volume of the 1809 set issued by the Kriegsarchiv, Mayerhoffer's REGENSBURG (231). A lengthy article, again a preparatory study, compares the results of the reforms by reviewing the state of the French and the Austrian armies in 1809 (14). The heart of the reforms were the regulations and the instructions for the generalcy, the EXERCIER-REGLEMENT (71) and the GRUNDSAETZE DER HOEHEREN KRIEGSKUNST (72) issued by Charles. Discussions of these ideas and practices can be found in Criste's ERZHERZOG CARL UND DIE ARMEE (81), Gallina's REGLEMENTS UND INSTRUCTIONEN (126), and Wagner's VON AUSTERLITZ BIS KOENIGGRAETZ (391). The much overrated Landwehr is duly praised by Strobl von Ravelsberg in DIE LANDWEHR ANNO NEUN (355), but Litschel's SCHWERT UND HELM (211) provides a useful corrective. Paret draws some comparisons between the Prussian and Austrian reforms (261); these reforms are also the theme of Hahlweg's short piece (152).

The diplomatic prelude to the war is discussed by Beer (39), Vann (377), Langsam (201), and Rössler (312), while the strategic planning, especially the shift in the main line of operations, is evaluated by Binder von Krieglstein (47), whose opinion, however, must be compared with those of other writers, including Mayerhoffer (231) and Rauchensteiner (295). Besides Mayerhoffer, many authors have discussed the initial phase of operations, the Ratisbon campaign. These include Bremen (58), Cavaciocchi (67), Heller von Hellwald (157), Petre (274), and Stutterheim (356). The retreat of the detached corps on the south bank of the Danube is discussed in the official volume by Hoen et al., NEUMARKT-EBELSBERG-WIEN (169), Litschel's DAS GEFECHT BEI EBELSBERG (212), and Rauchensteiner's studies on Hiller (294, 298). Also included in these volumes are details of the surrender of Vienna. Additional information on Vienna in 1809 can be located in Hummelberger and Peball (180) and Wertheimer (402).

The climactic events in the career of the Archduke Charles, of course, were the battles of Aspern-Essling and Wagram; here there exists an extensive literature. For Aspern, the official history is a volume by Hoen and Kerchnawe (168) with some additional sidelights provided by Hoen's semi-official work ASPERN (164). In both works Charles is pictured as a great battle captain, the equal of Napoleon. This view is challenged by Prussian historians, above all Delbrück (87) and Menge (233). Rauchensteiner's short study DIE SCHLACHT VON ASPERN AM 21. UND 22. MAI 1809 (297) provides a balanced treatment.

Wagram, Charles's second great battle, in many ways has been even more controversial than Aspern-Essling. As told, the official history does not deal with this battle, but there are semi-official accounts by Hoen (167) and Angeli (12). There are a number of unpublished dissertations, including Holtzheimer (173) and Hertenberger (159). Petre (274) provides a balanced account, and for that matter Criste's biography is not uncritical. The most recent scholarly study is again by Rauchensteiner (296). Of course, most of the works cited for the entire war do have accounts of Aspern-Essling and Wagram.

Much of the blame for the lost battle has been assigned to the tardy arrival of Archduke John on the second day of the fighting. His overall conduct in 1809 has been favorably evaluated by Zwiedineck-Südenhorst (419), though Simon (344) comes to different conclusions shared inter alia by Hertenberg and Rauchensteiner. Baron Hormayr provides a partisan account of John's operations in Italy, the Tyrol, and Hungary (174); Veltzé's semi-official volume describes the archduke's retreat into Styria and Hungary (382). John's own story (188) must be used with caution. Zwiedineck-Südenhorst provides documents (420) and the Saxon view is by Gschliesser (149).

The most detailed French account of the 1809 campaign is still Saski's three-volume CAMPAGNE DE 1809 (324) although the last volume only reaches the end of May, that is five months before the war ended. The text is supplemented by copious notes and hundreds of unpublished documents from the Archives de la guerre. Gachot's work (123) on the campaign, emphasizing Masséna's role in the operations, is valuable, while the study by Renemont (304) is less reliable. There are specialized studies on the campaigns concerning Landshut (54), Styria (215), and Wagram (64, 364), and the various biographies of Masséna (37, 139, 225, 362, 368, 374), Davout (125, 178, 303, 386), Lannes (203, 366, 405), Berthier (90), Bessières (25, 43), Drouot (6, 136, 246, 341), Marmont (75), Eugène de Beauharnais (17, 115), Lasalle (179, 226), and Maret (103) are also useful in piecing together the various details of the campaign. Of the primary materials, the four volumes of memoirs by Pelet (268) are invaluable but heavy reading. After serving as Masséna's aide de camp in the campaign, he spent several years in the Dépôt de la guerre, forerunner of the Archives de la guerre, transcribing the journal he had kept during the campaign on the Danube. Supplemented by the archival documents, his account is one of the most valuable we have of French operations of the 1809 campaign. Volume six of Masséna's MEMOIRES (227), based on the private archives of the Masséna family, is also vital although sympathetic toward Masséna. The memoirs, correspondence, journals, and biographies of the senior commanders--Davout (49, 50, 85), Marmont (224), Grouchy (145), Casanova (93), Macdonald (219, 220), Eugène de Beauharnais (36), Lannes (202), Bernadotte (40), Savary (325), Lasalle (309)--supplemented by the eyewitness accounts of Marbot (222), Bausset (35), Chlapowski (74), Castellane (65), Cadet de Gassincourt (63), Bonneval (55), Dellard (89), Claparède (76), Caulaincourt (66), Parquin (262), Dumas (97), Lejeune (208), Boulart (56), Larrey (204), Pelleport (271), Friant (120), Espinchal (105), and others give us different views of the complex operations that are still open to debate.

John's operations in Italy were partly designed to support the Tyrolian uprising. Hochenegg compiles a bibliography of this revolt (162), and Allmayer-Beck places the revolt within the overall war perspective (4), as does Paulin (265). Bartsch's semi-official account, DER VOLKSKRIEG IN TIROL (34), may be supplemented by Schemfil's account of the detached Austrian corps (329). Minor engagements are described by Bischoff (48); details about the Tyrolean levies and sharpshooters can be found in Stolz (354).

Tyrol, of course, was but a secondary theatre as were Poland and Croatia-Dalmatia. The fighting here is described by Veltzé's semi-official account (382) and by Woinovich's volume (411) in the same series; Veltzé also recounts the heroic defense of the alpine blockhouse, OESTERREICHS THERMOPYLEN (383). Finally, a civilian historian, Just, contributes an account of the Treaty of Schönbrunn to the series (189).

SPECIALIZED WORKS: THE CAMPAIGNS OF 1812, 1813, and 1814

After Wagram, Archduke Charles was forced to resign, the Austrian army was limited in size by the Treaty of Schönbrunn, and the Austrian state found itself bankrupt. In political affairs Metternich assumed the direction of affairs, trying to maneuver on a cautious course between Russsia and France while simultaneously attempting to maintain contacts and credit in England. His military policy is described by Veltzé (384) and Gentz (133), his efforts to maintain relations with England analyzed by Buckland (62). In military affairs, Radetzky now came to the fore. The standard biography is Regele's FELDMARSCHALL REDETZKY (300). The marshal's autobiography (290) is instructive reading. The works by Molden (239) and Schmahl (332) suffer from lack of archival research and too much pan-German ideology. Radetzky's own view of the state of the army in 1809 was published in a lengthy memorandum (289).

Prince Schwarzenberg, Metternich's favorite commander, leader of the Austrian auxiliary corps in Russia and later allied commander in chief, can be studied in a lengthy biography written by a descendant (337); he is also intimately revealed in the letters to his beloved wife (336). His role in Russia is appraised by Fischer (113); his troubles and tribulations as supreme commander shared by his chief of staff, Radetzky, are pictured by Vitzthum von Eckstädt (388) and by

Wagner (390). Overall problems of coalition are illuminated by Craig (80), as well as by Kerchnawe and Veltzé (192).

The operational side of the 1813-14 campaigns has been very well covered. The Kriegsarchiv issued two different sets of volumes. The more scholarly account, ten volumes, can be found in the series, 1813-1815: OESTERREICH IN DEN BEFREIUNGSKRIEGEN (24); a more popular set, lacking documentation but compiled by the same group of authors, has but five volumes, possibly because the outbreak of war terminated the project, collectively entitled BEFREIUNGSKRIEG 1813 UND 1814 (19). Thus the initial phase of mobilization in Bohemia followed by the advance into Saxony is covered in the scholarly set by Glaise von Horstenau (138) and Woinovich (412) and in the popular series by Wlaschütz (408) and Hoen (166). The observations of a British officer, the famous General Wilson (406), are especially interesting for this phase. Langenau's brief account (200) illustrates his rivalry with Radetzky. Petre describes Napoleon's last campaign in Germany (275), and Maude contributes a well-written account of the Leipzig campaign (228). A complete survey of the literature was compiled by Loh (213) on the occasion of the 150th anniversary of the Battle of Leipzig. The secondary battle at Kulm is described by Ehnl (101), and the Prussian viewpoint, sometimes strikingly different from the Austrian, is represented by Friedrich's three-volume GESCHICHTE DES HERBSTFELDZUGES 1813 (121).

Secondary theatres of operation in 1813, the Tyrol, Italy, and Croatia, are discussed in Glaise von Horstenau's DIE HEIMKEHR TYROLS (137), Holtz's DIE INNEROESTERREICHISCHE ARMEE 1813 UND 1814 (172), and the well-documented, if rare, account by Sporschil (347). The problems of interallied diplomacy arising in acute form after Leipzig have already been mentioned; the next major operational issue was the campaign in France in 1814. Here the major works are by Hoen (165) and Woinovich (410), both part of the scholarly series. General Janson's volumes provide the Prussian counterpoint (181). Of course, the works relating to Schwarzenberg and Radetzky also are applicable to this phase.

Most of the French works pertinent to the campaign of 1809 will also prove useful for the study of the Saxon campaign. Of particular value are Norvin's PORTEFEUILLE (249), Fain's MANUSCRIT (109), and Pelet's CAMPAGNES DE 1813 (269). Among the primary accounts, those by Macdonald (219), Marmont (224), Savary (325), Caulaincourt (66), Teste (359), Barrès (30), Coignet (78), Rochechouart (310), Bertin (42), Peyrusse (277), Marbot (222), Paulin (264), Grabowski (140), Pastoret (263), Odenleben (250, 251), and Boutourlin (57) provide valuable insights into operations in 1813.

There are a number of studies devoted to specific operations of the Saxon campaign. Thiry's LEIPZIG (363) is an excellent study of operations in Saxony. The works of Foucart (114), Clément (77), and Grouard (144), on the autumn campaign, provide innumerable details and Ussel's study (373) on the Austrian intervention presents valuable background material. The memoirs, correspondence and biographies of Ney (15, 129, 216, 247, 398), Masséna (37, 139, 225, 227, 362, 368, 374), Oudinot (248, 257, 258, 353), Arrighi de Casanova (93), Davout (125, 178, 303, 386), Fabvier (86), Drouot (6, 136, 246, 341), Berthier (90), Maret (103), Friant (120), Bernadotte (32, 33, 40, 135, 163, 190, 243, 338, 399), and others personalize details of the various campaigns. For the French operations in

1813-14 see Chapter XIII and for the Campaign of France in 1814, Chapter XIV.

Austria did not undertake any major operations in 1815. The military considerations at the Congress of Vienna are discussed in Criste's DER WIENER KONGRESS (84), another in the Kriegsarchiv series; Möller's DIE HUNDERT TAGE (238), another volume in the same series, describes Austrian reaction to Napoleon's sudden return. Veltzé also discusses in some detail the Austrian operations against Naples in 1815 (381).

SPECIALIZED WORKS: ARMY ORGANIZATION

The availability of printed sources varies on special topics. One of the best explored subjects, with an extraordinary revival of interest since 1955, is the Military Border institution, valued as a reservoir of relatively inexpensive and reliable manpower. Among the available materials are volumes by Rothenberg (316, 318), Amstadt (8), and an extensive specialized bibliography by Wessely and Zivkovič (403). The old standby, Vanicek (376), is now outdated, but it is of use for the Napoleonic period because of its many details. The revised Border code of 1807 (148) should be utilized for any socio-economic study.

Tactics and weapons become of greater interest recently, at least in part because of the newly developed sophistication of historical war gamers. The studies by Gallina (126, 127) provide much information on tactical detail as does the work by Wagner (391). For Austrian armament we have the studies by Dolleczek. His GESCHICHTE DER OESTERREICHISCHEN ARTILLERIE (91) must, however, be supplemented by Semek's major essay on artillery in the war of 1809 (340) and by Unterberger's instructional manual (371, 372). On small arms Dolleczek's richly illustrated monograph (92) is outstanding but can be supplemented by Gabriel's introduction to a recent exhibition of weapons by the Heeresgeschichtliches Museum in Vienna (154).

The exact functioning of the Austrian high command are more difficult to ascertain from printed sources. There are references to this matter in the biographical materials on Archduke Charles, Schwarzenberg, and Radetzky, as well as in some specific works dealing with the allied supreme command in 1813-14 (80, 192, 388, 390). Regele's piece on the HOFKRIEGSRAT (299) remains unsatisfactory as does his short book on chiefs of staff (301). Angeli's essay (13), however, does provide some useful insights, and Gallina's monograph (127) should not be overlooked. The influence of the emperor's military entourage is discussed, if perhaps inadequately, by Neuhauser (245). Still, an investigation of the command structure remains a basically unexplored field.

FUTURE RESEARCH

Although much has been published on the Austrian army, there still exist large lacunae for further research. We still lack an adequate history of the War of the Second Coalition, especially regarding events in Germany leading up to the Battle of Hohenlinden. We still need a good study of the Archduke John, particularly of his performance as a field commander in 1805 and 1809 and of his relations with Charles. In fact, biographies of a number of field

commanders   such   as   Wurmser,   Clerfayt,   Alvinczy,   Klenau,
Liechtenstein, Kolowrat, and many others are unavailable. Although
there exist some special studies on tactics, historians would profit
from an overall analysis of Austrian strategy and from further
examination of tactics, especially skirmishing and open order
fighting, on the model of Paret's work (261).
      Next to nothing exists on military administration, supply, and
armament production. Specialized logistical studies here would
contribute much. Also overdue is new work on the exact structure of
civil-military relations during this period, including the blatant
failure of the civil authorities to rally resistance in 1797, 1805,
and 1809. In this connection, a reexamination of the Landwehr might
well be in order. Studies of the various branches of the Habsburg
army from the sappers, engineers, light troops, and cavalry to the
medical corps and pontoniers would be useful indeed. In short, the
field of Austrian military history during the Revolutionary period
remains one of wide open fields for research. The materials are
available and wait to be exploited.
      Histories of the French conflicts with Austria are sporadic.
The campaigns of 1796-97 and 1799-1800 in Italy are well researched
with some gaps in the operations in southern Italy.   The
Ulm-Austerlitz campaign has been well treated by French historians as
Chapter VI indicates, but there is no modern comprehensive study of
the campaign of 1809--from Ratisbonne to Znäim. Similarly, there are
numerous topics related to the French armies in Saxony in the fall of
1813 that need exploration. The strategy of Napoleon and his generals
in the fall campaign, the defections of the German forces in the
Grande Armée, and the French retreat across Germany should be
examined in relation to Schwarzenberg's overall goals. A number of
French officers who served against Austria, as well as in other
operations, warrant biographies. For example, studies of divisional
generals as Baudet and Molitor, corps commanders as Reynier and
Montbrun, and marshals as Victor and Macdonald would be welcome
additions to the literature of the period. In fact, in some ways,
less research has been carried out by those interested in analyzing
French operations than those who have examined the Austrian side of
the wars. Clearly, there are innumerable topics available for
historians interested in the Franco-Austrian campaigns after
Austerlitz.

BIBLIOGRAPHY: AUSTRIA

1. ABRISS VON DER SCHLACHT BEI ESLING UND GROSS-ASPERN AM 21. UND 22. MAY 1809: NACH DEN NEUESTEN UND SICHERSTEN QUELLEN BEARBEITET-APPERCU DE LA BATAILLE D'ESLING ET DE GROSS-ASPERN, LE 21. ET 22. MAI 1809. Weimar: Im Verlage des Geographischen Instituts, 1810.

2. Alfödi, Laszlo M. THE ARMIES OF AUSTRIA-HUNGARY AND GERMANY 1740-1914. U.S. Army Military History Research Collection, Special Bibliographic Series No. 12. Carlisle Barracks, Pa., 1975.

3. Allmayer-Beck, Johann C. "Erzherzog Carl (1771-1847)." GROSSE OESTERREICHER 14 (1960): 27-41.

4. Allmayer-Beck, Johann C. "Der Tiroler Volksaufstand im Kriegsgeschehen 1809." DER DONAURAUM 5 (1960): 1-11.

5. Allmayer-Beck, Johann C., and F. Fritz. "Verzeichnis der zwischen 1945 und 1966 erschienenen Arbeiten zur österreischen Heeres and Kriegsgeschichte von deren Anfängenbis 1938." MITTEILUNGEN DES HEERESGESCHICHTLICHEN MUSEUMS IN WIEN 3 (1967): 190-265.

6. Ambert, Joachim Marie Jean Jacques Alexandre Jules. LE GENERAL DROUOT. Tours: Mame, 1879.

7. Amic, Auguste. HISTOIRE DE MASSENA. Paris: Dentu, 1864.

8. Amstadt, Jakob. DIE K.K. MILITAERGRENZE 1522-1881 (MIT EINER GESAMTBIBLIOGRAPHIE). Würzburg: the author, 1969. 2 vols.

9. Angeli, Moriz von. ERZHERZOG CARL ALS FELDHERR UND HEERESORGANISATOR. Vienna and Leipzig: Braumüller, 1896-98. 5 vols.

10. Angeli, Moriz von. "Die Heere des Kaisers und der französichen Revolution im Beginn des Jahres 1792." MITTEILUNGEN DES K.U.K. KRIEGSARCHIVS, New Series 4 (1889): 1-112.

11. Angeli, Moriz von. "Ulm and Austerlitz." MITTEILUNGEN DES K. K. KRIEGSARCHIVS 3 (1878): 283-394.

12. Angeli, Moriz von. "Wagram. Novelle zur Geschichte des Krieges von 1908." MITTEILUNGEN DES K.K. KRIEGSARCHIVS 5 (1881): 41-105.

13. Angeli, Moriz von. ZUR GESCHICHTE DES K.K. GENERALSTABES. Vienna: Seidel, 1876.

14. "Die Armee Napoleon I. im Jahre 1809 mit vergleichenden Rückblicken auf dad österreichische Heer, nach dem Urteilen von Zeitgenossen." MITTEILUNGEN DES K.K. KRIEGSARCHIVS 5 (1881): 371-408.

15. Atteridge, Andrew Hilliard. THE BRAVEST OF THE BRAVE, MICHEL
    NEY, MARSHAL OF FRANCE, DUKE OF ELCHINGEN, PRINCE OF THE
    MOSKOWA, 1769-1815. London: Methuen, 1912.

16. Atteridge, Andrew Hilliard. MARSHAL MURAT, MARSHALL OF FRANCE
    AND KING OF NAPLES. London, Edinburgh, and New York: Thomas
    Nelson, n.d.

17. Aubriet, M. HISTOIRE POLITQUE ET MILITAIRE DE LA VIE DU PRINCE
    EUGENE. Spire, 1826.

18. Austria. Direktion des Kriegsarchiv Wien. INVENTAR DES
    KRIEGSARCHIVS WIEN. Vol. 3. INVENTARE OESTERREICHISCHER
    ARCHIVE. Vienna: Staatsarchiv, 1953. 2 vols in 1.

19. Austria-Hungary. Kriegsarchiv. BEFREIUNGSKRIEG 1813 UND 1814.
    EINZELDARSTELLUNG DER ENTSCHEIDENEN KRIEGSEREIGNISSE. Vienna:
    Seidel, 1913. 5 vols.

20. Austria-Hungary. Kriegsarchiv. BIOGRAPHIEN K.K. HEERFUEHRER
    UND GENERAELE. Vienna: K.K. Kriegsarchiv, 1888. 2 vols.

21. Austria-Hungary. Kriegsarchiv. KRIEG 1809. KRIEGE UNTER DER
    REGIERUNG DES KAISER FRANZ. Vienna: Seidel, 1907-10. 4 vols.

22. Austria-Hungary. Kriegsarchiv. KRIEGE GEGEN DIE FRANZOESISCHE
    REVOLUTION 1792-1797. KRIEGE UNTER DER REGIERUNG DES KAISER
    FRANZ. Vienna: Seidel, 1905. 2 vols.

23. Austria-Hungary. Kriegsarchiv. KRIEGS-CHRONIK OESTERREICH-
    UNGARNS. MILITAERISCHER FUEHRER AUF DEN KRIEGSCHAUPLAETZEN DER
    MONARCHIE. Vienna: K.K. Generalstab, 1885-91. 3 vols.

24. Austria-Hungary. Kriegsarchiv. 1813-1815. OESTERREICH IN DEN
    BEFREIUNGSKRIEGEN. Edited by Emil v. Woinovich und Alois
    Veltze. Vienna: Seidel, 1911-14. 10 vols.

25. Babel, André. LE MARECHAL BESSIERES, DUC D'ISTRIE. Paris:
    Calmann-Lévy, 1903.

26. Baden, Wilhelm Ludwig August Reichsgraf von Hochberg.
    DENKWUERDIGKEITEN DES MARKGRAFEN WILHELM VON BADEN AUS DEN
    FELDZUEGEN VON 1809 BIS 1815. Karlsruhe: Bielefeld, 1864.

27. Baggi, Francesco. MEMOIRE DI F. BAGGI. Edited by Corrado
    Ricci. Bologna: Zanichelli, 1898. 2 vols.

28. Bancalari, Gustav. QUELLEN DER OESTERREICHISCHEN KRIEGS- UND
    ORGANISATIONS GESCHICHTE. Vol. 2 of Austria Hungary,
    Generalstab, BEITRAEGE ZUR GESCHICHTE DES OESTERREICHISCHEN
    HEERWESENS. Vienna: Seigel, 1872.

29. Bancalari, Gustav. FELDMARSCHALL RADETZKY ALS KRIEGSHELD UND HEERFUEHRER. MIT BESONDERER BERUECKSICHTIGUNG SEINER WIRKSAMKEIT IN DEN BEFREIUNGSKRIEGEN 1813-1815. Vienna: Seidel, 1982.

30. Barrès, Jean Baptiste Auguste. SOUVENIRS D'UN OFFICIER DE LA GRANDE ARMEE. Paris: Plon, 1923.

31. Bartholdy, Jacob L. Salomon. DER KRIEG DER TYROLER LANDLEUTE IM JAHRE 1809. Berlin: Hitzig, 1814.

32. Barton, Dunbar Plunket, bart. THE AMAZING CAREER OF BERNADOTTE, 1763-1844. Boston: Houghton, 1930.

33. Barton, Dunbar Plunket, bart. BERNADOTTE AND NAPOLEON, 1763-1810. London: J. Murray, 1921.

34. Bartsch, Rudolf. DER VOLSKRIEG IN TIROL. Edited by Emil v. Woinovich and Alois Veltzé. Vol. 2. DAS KRIEGSJAHR 1809 IN EINZELDARSTELLUNGEN. Vienna: C.W. Stern, 1905.

35. Bausset, Louis François Joseph de. MEMOIRES ANECDOTIQUES SUR L'INTERIEUR DU PALAIS ET SUR QUELQUES EVENEMENS DE L'EMPIRE DEPUIS 1805 JUSQU'AU Ier MAI 1814 POUR SERVIR A L'HISTOIRE DE NAPOLEON. Paris: Baudouin, 1827.

36. Beauharnais, Eugène de, prince d'Eichstätt. MEMOIRES ET CORRESPONDANCE POLITIQUE ET MILITAIRE DU PRINCE EUGENE. Publiés, annotés et mis en ordre par baron Albert Du Casse. Paris: Lévy, 1858-60. 10 vols.

37. Beauregard, Louis Charles Octave Durand de, comte. LE MARECHAL MASSENA, DUC DE RIVOLI, PRINCE D'ESSLING, ENFANT DE NICE.Résumé de sa vie. Nice: Gauthier, 1902.

38. Béchu, Marcel Ernest [Marcel Dupont]. MURAT; CAVALIER, MARCHAL DE FRANCE, PRINCE ET ROI. Paris: Hachette, 1934.

39. Beer, Adolf. ZEHN JAHRE OESTERREICHISCHER POLITIK, 1801-1810. Leipzig: Brockhaus, 1877.

40. Bernadotte, Jean Baptiste. CORRESPONDANCE AVEC NAPOLEON, DEPUIS 1810-1814. Paris: Lhuillier, 1819.

41. Bertaut, Jules. LE MANAGE MURAT. Paris: Le Livre contemporain, 1958.

42. Bertin, Georges, ed. LA CAMPAGNE DE 1814, D'APRES DES TEMOIN SOCULAIRES. Paris: Flammarion, 1896.

43. Bessières, Jean Baptiste. VIE DU MARECHAL BESSIERES, DUC D'ISTRIE. Lille and Paris: de Brouwer, 1903.

44. Bianchi, Friedrich, freiherr von. F. FRHR. VON BIANCHI, DUCA DI CASALANZA, K.K. OESTERREICHISCHER FELDMARSCHALLEUTNANT. Vienna: Sommer, 1857.

45. Bibl, Viktor. ERZHERZOG KARL. DER BEHARRLICHE KAEMPFER FUER DEUTSCHLANDS EHRE. Vienna: Günther, 1942.

46. Bigelow, Poultney. HISTORY OF THE GERMAN STRUGGLE FOR LIBERTY. London: Osgood, 1896.

47. Binder von Krieglstein, Karl. DER KRIEG NAPOLEONS GEGEN OESTERREICH 1809. Berlin: Mittler, 1902-06. 2 vols.

48. Bischoff, Helmuth. "Das Gefecht in der Enge vor Mittenwald 1809." DIE GEBIRGSTRUPPE 9 (1960): 54-63.

49. Blocqueville, Louise Adelaide d'Eckmühl, marquise de. LE MARECHAL DAVOUT, PRINCE D'ECKMUEHL, CORRESPONDANCE INEDITE, 1790-1815. Paris: Perrin, 1887.

50. Blocqueville, L.A. d'Eckmühl. LE MARECHAL DAVOUT, PRINCE D'ECKMUEHL, RACONTE PAR LES SIENS ET PAR LUI-MEME. Paris: 1879-80. 4 vols.

51. Blücher, Gebhard Lebercht von. BLUECHER IN BRIEFEN AUS DEN FELDZUEGEN 1813-1815. Edited by E. von Colomb. Stuttgart: Cotta, 1876.

52. Bodart, Gaston. MILITAER-HISTORISCHES KRIEGS-LEXIKON. Vienna and Leipzig: Stern, 1980.

53. Bogdanowitsch, Modest. GESCHICHTE DES KRIEGS IM JAHR 1813 FUER DEUTSCHLAND UNABHAENGIGKEIT AUS DEM RUSSISCHEN. St. Petersburg: Hoenniger, 1863-68. 2 vols.

54. Bonnal, Henri. LA MANOEUVRE DE LANDSHUT. Paris: Chapelot, 1905.

55. Bonneval, Armand Alexandre de. MEMOIRES, ANECDOTIQUES DU GENERAL MARQUIS DE BONNEVAL. Paris: Plon, 1900.

56. Boulart, Jean François. MEMOIRES MILITAIRES DU GENERAL BARON BOULART SUR LES GUERRES DE LA REPUBLIQUE ET DE L'EMPIRE. Paris: Librairie illustrée ,1892.

57. Boutourlin, Demitri, comte. TABLEAU DE LA CAMPAGNE D'AUTOMNE DE 1813, DEPUIS LA RUPTURE DE L'ARMISTICE, JUSQU'AU PASSAGE DU RHIN PAR L'ARMEE FRANCAISE. Paris: Bertrand, 1817.

58. Bremen, Walter v. DIE TAGE VON REGENSBURG 10. BIS 23. APRIL 1809. Berlin: Mittler, 1907.

59. Broglie, Achille Charles Leonce Victor, duc de. SOUVENIRS (1785-1870) PUBL. PAR SON PETIT-FILS A. DUC DE BROGLIE. Paris: Lévy, 1886. 4 vols.

60. Brunschvigg, Léon. CAMBRONNE. SA VIE CIVILE, POLITIQUE ET MILITAIRE ECRITE D'APRES LES DOCUMENTS INEDITS DES ARCHIVES NATIONALES ET DES ARCHIVES DU MINISTERE DE LA GUERRE. Nantes: Schwob, 1894.

61. Buat, Edomon Alphonse Léon. ETUDE CRITIQUE D'HISTOIRE MILITAIRE: 1809. Paris: Chapelot, 1909.

62. Buckland, Charels S.B. METTERNICH AND THE BRITISH GOVERNMENT FROM 1809 TO 1813. London: Macmillan, 1932.

63. Cadet de Gassicourt, Charles Louis. VOYAGE EN AUTRICHE, EN MORAVIE ET EN BAVIERE FAIT A LA SUITE L'ARMEE FRANCAISE, PENDANT LA CAMPAGNE DE 1809. Paris: L'Huillier, 1818.

64. Camon, Hubert. LA MANOEUVRE DE WAGRAM. Paris: Berger-Levrault, 1926.

65. Castellane, Esprit Victor Elisabeth Bonifact, comte de. JOURNAL DU MARECHAL DE CASTELLANE 1804-1862. Paris: Plon, Nourrit, 1895-97. 5 vols.

66. Caulaincourt, Armand Augustin Louis, marquis de, duc de Vicence. MEMOIRES DU GENERAL DE CAULAINCOURT, DUC DE VIVENCE, GRAND ECUYER DE L'EMPEREUR. Introduction et notes de Jean Hanoteau. Paris: Plon, 1933. 3 vols.

67. Cavaciocchi, Alberto. 1809 RATISBONA-ESSLING-WAGRAM. Rome: Casa Editrice Italiana, 1901.

68. Chandler, David G. A GUIDE TO THE BATTLEFIELDS OF EUROPE. Vol. 2. CENTRAL AND EASTERN EUROPE. Philadelphia and New York: Chilton Books, 1965.

69. "Zur Charakteristik des Erzherzogs Carl und der österreichischen Armee in den Jahren 1801 bis 1804." MITTEILUNGEN DES K.K. KRIEGSARCHIVES 5 (1881): 106-21.

70. Charles (Carl), archduke of Austria. AUSGEWAEHLTE SCHRIFTEN. Edited by Franze X. Malcher. Vienna and Leipzig: Braumüler, 1893-94. 5 vols., 1 vol. maps.

71. Charles (Carl), archduke of Austria. EXERCIER-REGLEMENT FUER DIE KAISERLICH KOENIGLICHE INFANTERIE. Vienna: Hof-und Staatsdruckerei, 1807.

72. Charles (Carl), archduke of Austria. GRUNDSAETZE DER HOEHEREN KRIEGSKUNST FUER DIE GENERAELE DER OESTERREICHISCHEN ARMEE. Vienna: Hof-und Staatsdruckerei, 1806.

73. Chavanon, Jules Joseph, and Georges Saint-Yves. JOACHIM MURAT (1767-1815). Paris: Hachette, 1905.

74. Chlapowski, Désiré, baron. MEMOIRES SUR LES GUERRES DE NAPOLEON, 1806-1813. Paris: Plon-Nourrit, 1908.

75. Christophe, Robert. LES AMOURS ET LES GUERRES DU MARECHAL
    MARMONT, DUC DE RAGUSE. Paris: Hachette, 1955.

76. Claparède, Michel Marie, comte. MESTER: LE GENERAL CLAPAREDE.
    SA VIE MILITAIRE, SES CAMPAGNES. D'APRES DES DOCUMENTS INEDITS
    PROVENANT, POUR LA PLUPART DES ARCHIVES DES MINISTERES DE LA
    GUERRE ET DE LA MARINE ET DES ARCHIVES NATIONALES. Paris:
    Dupont, 1899.

77. Clément, G. CAMPAGNE DE 1813. Paris: Charles-Lavauzelle,
    1904.

78. Coignet, Jean Roch. LES CAHIERS DU CAPITAINE COIGNET
    (1799-1815). Auxerre: Periquet, 1851-53. 2 vols.

79. Comeau, Sebastien Joseph, baron de. SOUVENIRS DES GUERRES
    D'ALLEMAGNE PENDANT LA REVOLUTION ET L'EMPIRE. Paris:
    Plon-Nouritt, 1900.

80. Craig, Gordon A. "Problems of Coalition Warfare: The Military
    Alliance against Napoleon, 1813-1815." WAR, POLITICS, AND
    DIPLOMACY, SELECTED ESSAYS. New York: Prager, 1966.

81. Criste, Oskar. ERZHERZOG CARL UND DIE ARMEE. Edited by Emil
    v. Woinovich and Alois Veltze. DAS KRIEGSJAHR 1809 IN
    EINZELDARSTELLUNGEN. Vienna: C.W. Stern, 1906.

82. Criste, Oskar. ERZHERZOG CARL VON OESTERREICH. Vienna and
    Leipzig: Braumüller, 1912. 3 vols.

83. Criste, Oskar. OESTERREICHS BEITRITT ZUR KOALITION 1813 UND
    1814. Vol. 1. Austria-Hungary, Kriegsarchiv. BEFREIUNGSKRIEG
    1813 UND 1814. Vienna: Seidel, 1913.

84. Criste, Oskar. DER WIENER KONGRESS. Vol. 8. Austria-Hungary,
    Kriegsarchiv. 1813-1815. OESTERREICH IN DEN BEFREIUNGS-
    KRIEGEN. Vienna: Seidel, 1913.

85. Davout, Louis Nicolas, duc d'Auerstädt et prince d'Eckmühl.
    CORRESPONDANCE DUE MARECHAL DAVOUT, PRINCE D'ECKMUEHL: SES
    COMMANDEMENTS, SON MINISTERE, 1801-1815. Edited by Charles de
    Mazade. Paris: Plon, 1885. 4 vols.

86. Debidour, Antonin. LE GENERAL FABVIER. SA VIE MILITAIRE ET
    POLITIQUE. Paris: Plon, Nourrit, 1904.

87. Delbrück, Hans. "Erzherzog Carl." ERINNERUNGEN, AUFSAETZE,
    UND REDEN. Berlin: G. Stilke, 1902.

88. Delderfield, Ronald F. IMPERIAL SUNSET: THE FALL OF NAPOLEON,
    1813-14. Philadelphia: Chilton, 1968.

89. Dellard, Jean Pierre. MEMOIRES MILITAIRES SUR LES GUERRES DE
    LA REPUBLIQUE ET DE L'EMPIRE. Paris: Librairie illustrée,
    1892.

90. Derrécagaix, Victor Bernard. LE MARECHAL BERTHIER, PRINCE DE WAGRAM ET DE NEUCHATEL. Paris: Chapelot, 1904-05. 2 vols.

91. Dolleczek, Anton. GESCHICHTE DER OESTERREICHISCHEN ARTILLERIE. Vienna: the author, 1887.

92. Dolleczek, Anton. MONOGRAPHIE DER K.U.K. OESTERR.-UNGARISCHEN BLANKEN UND HANDFEUERWAFFEN. Vienna: Kriesel & Gröger, 1896.

93. Du Casse, Albert, baron. LE GENERAL ARRIGHI DE CASANOVA, DUC DE PADOUE: Paris: Perrotin, 1866. 2 vols.

94. Du Casse, Albert, baron. LE GENERAL VANDAMME ET SA CORRESPON- DANCE. Paris: Didier, 1870. 2 vols.

95. Duffy, Christopher. THE ARMY OF MARIA THERESA. New York: Hippocrene Books, 1977.

96. Duffy, Christopher. AUSTERLITZ 1805. London: Leo Cooper,1977.

97. Dumas, Guillaume Mathieu. SOUVENIRS DU LIEUTENANT GENERAL COMTE MATHIEU DUMAS, DE 1700 A 1836. Paris: Gosselin, Dupont, 1839. 3 vols.

98. Egger, Antoine. DIE TIROLER FREIHEITSKAEMPFE IM JAHRE 1809. Innsbruck: Verlag der Wagner, 1909.

99. Egger, Rainer. DAS GEFECHT BEI HOLLABRUNN UND SCHOENGRABERN 1805. Nr. 27. Heeresgeschichtliches Museeum, Militär- wissenschaftliches Institut, MILITAERHISTORISCHE SCHRIFTENREIHE. Vienna, 1974.

100. Egger, Rainer. "Das Kriegsarchiv Wien." MILITAER- GESCHICHTLICHE MITTEILUNGEN 7 (1970): 113-20; 8 (1970): 167-75; and 9 (1971): 173-81.

101. Ehnl, Max. SCHLACHT BEI KULM. Vol 4. Austria-Hungary, BEFREIUNGSKRIEG 1813 UND 1814. Vienna: Seidel, 1913.

102. Ellrich, August, ed. HUMORISTISCHE UND HISTORISCHE SKIZZEN AUS DEN JAHREN DER REVOLUTIONSKRIEGE. AUS DEN HINTERLASSENEN PAPIEREN EINES VERSTORBENEN SOLDATEN. Meissen: Goebsche Buchhandlung, 1844.

103. Ernouf, Alfred Auguste, baron. MARET, DUC DE BASSANO. Paris: Charpentier, 1878.

104. Ernstberger, Anton. BOEHMENS FREIWILLIGER KRIEGSEINSATZ GEGEN NAPOLEON. Vol. 14. VEROEFFENTLICHUNGEN DES COLLEGIUM CAROLINIUM. Munich: Robert Lerche Verlag, 1963.

105. Espinchal, Hippolyte d'. SOUVENIRS MILITAIRES, 1792-1814. Paris: Ollendorff, 1901.

106. Espitalier, Albert. NAPOLEON AND KING MURAT, A BIOGRAPHY
     COMPILED FROM HITHERTO UNKNOWN AND UNPUBLISHED DOCUMENTS.
     Translated from the French by J. Lewis May. London and New
     York: J. Lane, 1912.

107. Exner, Moritz. DIE ANTHEILNAHME DER KOENIGLICH SAECHSISCHEN
     ARMEE IN SACHSEN IN JAHRE 1809. Dresden: Baensch, 1894.

108. Fabry, Gabriel Joseph. ETUDE SUR LES OPERATIONS DE L'EMPEREUR
     DU 22 SEPTEMBRE AU 3 OCTOBRE 1813. Laval: Barneoud, 1913.

109. Fain, Agathon Jean François, baron. MANUSCRIT DE MIL HUIT CENT
     TREIZE. Paris: Delauney, 1824. 2 vols.

110. Fedorowicz, Wladyslaw von. CAMPAGNE DE POLOGNE, DEPUIS LE
     COMMENCEMENT JUSQU'A L'OCCUPATION DE VARSOVIE. Vol. I,
     documents et materiaux française. Paris: Plon-Nouritt, 1911.

111. Fedorowicz, Wladislaw, ritter von. FRANZ IV, ERZHERZOG VON
     OESTERREICH-ESTE, HERZOG VON MODENA: UND DIE POLNISCHE ADELIGE
     GESELLSCHAFT IN KRAKAU IM JAHRE 1809. Vienna:
     Kommissionsverlag von Gerold, 1912.

112. Finley, Milton Collins. "The Career of Count Jean Reynier,
     1792-1814." Ph.D. Dissertation, Florida State University,
     1972.

113. Fischer, Josef. "Feldmarschall Fürst Schwarzenbergs Verhalten
     im Feldzug des Jahres 1812 gegen Russland." Ph.D.
     Dissertation, University of Vienna, 1950.

114. Foucart, Paul Jean. UNE DIVISION DE CAVALERIE LEGER EN 1813.
     OPERATIONS SUR LES COMMUNICATIONS DE L'ARMEE. COMBAT
     D'ALTENBERG, 28 SEPTEMBRE 1813. Paris and Nancy:
     Berger-Levrault, 1891.

115. Fourmestraux. LE PRINCE EUGENE. Paris, 1867.

116. Fournier, August. GENTZ UND COBENZL. GESCHICHTE DER
     OESTERREICHISCHEN DIPLOMATIE IN DEN JAHREN 1801-1805. Vienna:
     Braumüller, 1880.

117. France. Armée. Armée d'Allemagne. COLLECTION DES ORDERS DU
     JOUR DE L'ARMEE D'ALLEMAGNE: CAMPAGNE DE 1809. Schönbrunn
     [Vienna]: Imprimerie impériale de l'armeé, 1809.

118. Frauenholz, Eugen v. DAS HEERWESEN DES XIX. JAHRHUNDERTS.
     Vol. 5. ENTWICKLUNGSGSSCHICHTE DES DEUTSCHEN HEERWESENS.
     Munich: Back'sche, 1941.

119. Freytagh-Loringhoven, Axel, freiherr von. NAPOLEONISCHE
     INITIATIVE 1809 UND 1814: EIN VORTRAG. Berlin: Mittler,
     1896.

120. Friant, Jean François, comte [son fils]. VIE MILITAIRE DU
     LIEUTENANT-GENERAL COMTE FRIANT. Paris: Dentu, 1857.

121. Friedrich, R. v. GESCHICHTE DES HERBSTFELDZUGES 1813. Berlin: Mittler, 1903-06. 3 vols.

122. Frignet Despréaux, Jules Charles Edouard. LE MARECHAL MORTIER, DUC DE TREVISE. Par son petit-nevue. Paris: Berger-Levrault, 1913-20. 3 vols.

123. Gachot, Edouard. 1809. NAPOLEON EN ALLEMAGNE. Paris: Plon-Nourrit, 1913.

124. Gaissart, B. d. L'INAUGURATION, LE 21 MAI 1967, A ASPERN (AUTRICHE) DE LA PLAQUE DEDIEE PAR LE "SOUVENIR NAPOLEONIEN" DE PICARDIE A LA MEMOIRE DES SOLDATS DE LA GRANDE-ARMEE TOMBES DANS LES COMBATS DE 1809. Amiens: Pillon, 1967.

125. Gallaher, John G. THE IRON MARSHAL; A BIOGRAPHY OF LOUIS N. DAVOUT. Carbondale: Southern Illinois University Press, 1976.

126. Gallina, Joseph v. REGLEMENTS UND INSTRUCTIONEN FUER DIE AUSBILDUNG DER TRUPPE UND IHRER FUEHRER VON DER BEENDIGUNG DES ERSTEN FELDZUGES GEGEN DAS FRANZOESISCHE KAISERREICH IM JAHRE 1805 BIS ZUM KRIEGE 1866. Vienna: Seidel, 1872.

127. Gallina, Joseph v. DER ZEITRAUM VON 1757-1814. MIT BESONDERER RUECKSICHT AUF ORGANIZATION, VERPFLEGUNG UND TAKTIK. Vol. 1. Austria-Hungary, Generalstab. BEITRAEGE ZUR GESCHICHTE DES OESTERREICHISCHEN HEERWESENS. Vienna: Seidel, 1872.

128. Garnier, Jean Paul. MURAT, ROI DE NAPLES. Paris: Le Club du Meilleurs Livres, 1959.

129. Garros, Louis. NEY, LE BRAVE DES BRAVE. Paris: Amiot-Dumont, 1955.

130. Gavenda, Anton B. GRUNDSAETZE DER HOEHEREN KRIEGSKUNST NACH DEN UNTER ERZHERZOG CARL FUER DIE GENERALE DER OESTERREICHISCHEN ARMEE HERAUSGEGEBENEN WERKE. Vienna: the author, 1871.

131. Geissau, Anton Ferdinand von. HISTORISCHES TAGEBUCH ALLER MERKWUERDIGEN BEGEBENHEITEN, WELCHE SICH VOR, WAEHREND UND NACH DER FRANZOSICHEN INVASION DER K.K. HAUPT-UND RESIDENZSTADT WIEN IN DEM JAHR 1809 ZUGETRAGEN HABEN. Vienna: auf Kosten des Verfassers, 1810.

132. Gentz, Friedrich von. MEMOIRES ET LETTRES INEDITS. Stuttgart: Schlesier, 1841.

133. Gentz, Friedrich von. OESTERREICHS THEILNAHME AN DEN BEFREIUNGSKRIEGEN. EIN BEITRAG ZUR GESCHICHTE DER JAHRE 1813-1815 NACH AUFZEICHUNGEN VON FRIEDRICH V. GENTZ. On behalf of Richard Prince Metternich-Winneburg, edited by Alfons v. Klinkström. Vienna: Gerold, 1887.

134. [Girault,   Philippe   René.]   "Campagne   d'Autriche
     (1809). Souvenirs d'un musicien d'état-major. Essling.--L'ile
     Lobau.--Wagram." REVUE RETROSPECTIVE (1889): 193-211.

135. Girod de l'Ain, Gabriel. BERNADOTTE, CHEF DE GUERRE ET CHEF
     D'ETAT. Paris: Perrin, 1968.

136. Girod de l'Ain, Maurice. LE GENERAL DROUOT (1774-1847). Nancy
     and Paris: Berger-Levrault, 1890.

137. Glaise von Horstenau, Edmund. DIE HEIMKEHR TIROLS. Vol. 10.
     Austria-Hungary, Kriegsarchiv. 1813-1815. OESTERREICH IN DEN
     BEFREIUNGSKRIEGEN. Vienna: Seidel, 1914.

138. Glaise von Horstenau, Edmund. DIE TAGE VON DRESDEN, 1813.
     Vol.   2.   Austria-Hungary,   Kriegsarchiv.   1813-1815.
     OESTERREICH IN DEN BEFREIUNGSKRIEGEN. Vienna: Seidel, 1911.

139. Godeau, Camille. MASSENA. Paris: A. Méricant, 1910.

140. Grabowski, Józef Ignacy Tadeusz, prince. MEMOIRES MILITAIRES
     DE JOSEPH GRABOWSKI, OFFICIER A L'ETAT-MAJOR IMPERIAL DE
     NAPOLEON Ier. Paris: Plon-Nourrit, 1907.

141. Granichstaedten-Czerva, Rudolf von. ANDREAS HOFERS ALTE GARDE.
     Innsbruck: Vereinsbuchhandlung und Buchdruckerie, 1932.

142. Gretzmiller, Franz von. GESCHICHTE OESTERREICHS: SECHSTE
     PERIODE. VON KARL DEN VI. BIS ZUM WIENER FRIEDEN AM 14.
     OKTOBER 1809. Vienna: n.p., 1824.

143. Grohmann, Karl Gottfried. DIE BRAUNSCHWEIGER IN ZITTAU: EIN
     HISTORISCHES GEMAEHLDE ALS BEITRAG ZUR GESCHICHTE DES
     FRANZOSISCH OESTREICHISCHEN KRIEGES IM JAHRE 1809. Zittau: G.
     Müller, 1810.

144. G[rouard], A. STRATEGIE NAPOLEONIENNE D'AUTOMME DE 1813 ET DES
     LIGNES INTERIEURES. Paris: Baudoin, 1897.

145. Grouchy, Emmanuel, marquis de. MEMOIRES DU MARECHAL DE
     GROUCHY. Paris: Dentu, 1873-74. 5 vols.

146. Grueber, Karl J.R. von, ed. LEBENSERINNERUNGEN EINES
     REITEROFFIZIERS VOR HUNDERT JAHREN. Vienna: Seidel, 1906.

147. Grueber, von. SOUS LES AIGLES AUTRICHIENNES; SOUVENIRS DE
     CHEVALIER DE GRUEBER, OFFICIER DE CAVALRIE AUTRICHIEN
     1800-1820. Paris: Perrin, 1909.

148. GRUNDGESETZ   FUER   DIE   CARLSTAEDTER-WARASDINER,   BANAL,
     SLAVONISCHE UND BANATISCHE MILITAER-GRAENZE. Vienna: k.k.
     Hof-und Staats-Druckerei, 1807.

149. Gschliesser, Oswald. "Als Soldat der sächsischen Rheinbund-Division im Jahre 1809 in Tirol." TIROLER HEIMATBLAETTER 34 (1959): 76-84

150. Gschliesser, Oswald. "Das Zeitalter der Koalitions und Befreiungskriege." Edited by Ludwig Jedlicka. UNSER HEER. 300 JAHRE OESTERREICHISCHES SOLDATENTUM IN KRIEG UND FRIEDEN. Vienna, Munich, and Zurich: Fürlinger, 1963, pp. 169-213.

151. Guerrini, Domenico. LA MANOVRE DI RIGENSBOURG 1809. Rome: Libreria dello Stato, 1924.

152. Hahlweg, Werner. "Clausewitz, Oesterreich und die preussische Heeresreform 1807-1812." OESTERREICHISCHE MILITAERISCHE ZEITSCHRIFT 2 (1962): 83-8.

153. Hansen, Donald W. NAPOLEON IN CENTAG; A HISTORICAL TERRAIN EXPLANATION. Carlisle Barracks, Pa.: U. S. Army College. 1979.

154. Heeresgeschichtliches Museum, Wien. VON DER LUNTENMUSKETE ZUM STURMGEWEHR. KATALOG ZUR SONDERSCHAU DER ENTWICKLUNG DER HAND-UND FAUSTFEUERWAFFEN IM OESTERREICHISCHEN HEER. Edited by Erich Gabriel. Vienna: Heeresgeschichtliches Museum, 1967.

155. Heilmann, Johann. "Der Feldzug von 1809 in Tirol, im Salzburgischen und an der Bayerischen Südrenze mit besonderer bezugnahme auf den Antheil der Bayerischen Truppen Bearbeitet." JAHRBUCHER FUER DIE DEUTSCHE ARMEE AND MARINE 68 (1888): 20-39, 151-68; 69 (1888): 29-48, 126-42, 243-77.

156. Heilmann, Johann. LEBEN DES GRAFEN B.E. v. DEROY, K.B. GENERALS DER INFANTERIE. Augsburg: Rieger, 1855.

157. Hellwald, Friedrich A. Heller von. DER FELDZUG DES JAHRES 1809 IN SUEDDEUTSCHLAND. Vienna: Gerold's Sohn, 1864. 2 vols.

158. Hellwald, Friedrich A. Heller von. DER K.K. OESTERREICHISCHE FELDMARSCHALL GRAF RADETZKY. Stuttgart-Augsburg: J.G. Cotta Verlag, 1858.

159. Hertenberger, Helmut. "Die Schlacht bei Wagram." Vienna, 1950.

160. Heydendorff, Walter. "Die Kriegsakten im Haus, Hof-und Staatsarchiv." MITTEILUNGEN DES OESTERREICHISCHEN STAATSARCHIVS 4 (1951): 251-56; 6 (1953): 410-15; 8 (1955): 322-28.

161. Hirn, Ferdinand. VORARLBERG VOR DEM HEIMFALLE AN OESTERREICH. Gregenz: Vorarlberger Landesmuseum, 1915.

162. Hochenegg, Hans. BIBLIOGRAPHIE ZUR GESCHICHTE DES TIROLER FREIHEITSKAMPFES VON 1809. Vol. 1. TIROLER BIBLIOGRAPHIE. Innsbruck and Vienna: Tirolia, 1960.

163. Höjer, Torwald Torwaldson. BERNADOTTE, MARECHAL DE FRANCE. Traduit du suédois par Lucien Maury. Paris: Plon, 1943.

164. Hoen, Max R. von. ASPERN. Vol 3. Edited by Emil Woinovich and Alois Veltze. DAS KRIEGSJAHR 1809 IN EINZELDARSTELLUNGEN. Vienna: C.W. Stern, 1906.

165. Hoen, Max R. von. DIE HAUPTARMEE 1814. Vol. 5. Austria-Hungary. Kriegsarchiv. 1813-1815. OESTERREICH IN DEN REFREIUNGSKRIEGEN. Vienna: Seidel, 1912.

166. Hoen, Max R. von. FELDZUG VON LEIPZIG. Vol. 5. Austria-Hungary. Kriegsarchiv. BEFREIUNGSKRIEG 1813 UND 1814. EINZELDARSTELLUNG DER ENTSCHEIDENEN KRIEGSEREIGNISSE. Vienna: Seidel, 1913.

167. Hoen, Max R. von. WAGRAM. Vol 8. Edited by Emil Woinovich and Alois Veltzé. DAS KRIEGSJAHR 1809 IN EINZELDARSTELLUNGEN. Vienna: C.W. Stern, 1909.

168. Hoen, Max R. von, and Hugo Kerchnawe. ASPERN. Vol. 4. Austria-Hungary. Kriegsarchiv. KRIEG 1809. KRIEGE UNTER DER REGIERUNG DES KAISERS FRANZ. Vienna: Seidel, 1910.

169. Hoen, Max R. von; Eberhard Mayerhoffer von Vedropolje; and Hugo Kerchnawe. NEUMARKT-EBELSBERG-WIEN. Vol. 3. Austria-Hungary. Kriegsarchiv. KRIEG 1809. KRIEGE UNTER DER REGIERUNG DES KAISERS FRANZ. Vienna: Seidel, 1909.

170. Hofer, Andreas. O LA SOLLEVAZION DEL TIROLO DEL 1809. Memorie storiche di Girolamo Andreis, roveretano, per la prima volta pubblicate dal dottor Alessandro Volpi,... Milano: Gnocchi, 1856.

171. Hofler, Edmund. DER FELDZUG VON JAHRE 1809 IN DEUTSCHLAND UND TYROL MIT BESONDERER BEZIEHUNG AUF DIE TAKTIK. Augsburg: Rieger, 1858.

172. Holtz, Georg v. DIE INNEROESTERREICHISCHE ARMEE 1813 UND 1814. Vol. 4. Austria-Hungary. Kriegsarchiv. 1813-1815. OESTERREICH IN DEN BEFREIUNGSKRIEGEN. Vienna: Seidel, 1912.

173. Holtzheimer, Hans. "Erzherzog Karl bei Wagram." Ph.D. dissertation, University of Berlin, 1904.

174. Hormayr, Joseph v. DAS HEER VON INNEROESTERREICH UNTER DEN BEFEHLEN DES ERZHERZOGS JOHANN IM KRIEGE VON 1809. IN ITALIEN, TYROL, UND UNGARN. Leipzig: F.A. Brockhaus, 1817.

175. Hormayr zu Hortenburg, Josef, freiherr von. MEMOIRS OF THE LIFE OF ANDREW HOFER; CONTAINING AN ACCOUNT OF THE TRANSACTIONS IN THE TYROL DURING THE YEAR 1809. Taken from the German by Charles Henry Hall, esquire. London: J. Murray, 1820.

176. Horsetzky, Adolf v. KRIEGSGESCHICHTLICHE UEBERSICHT DER WICHTIGSTEN FELDZUEGE IN EUROPA SEIT 1792. 7th ed. Vienna: Seidel, 1912.

177. Horsetzky, Adolf v. A SHORT HISTORY OF THE CHIEF CAMPAIGNS IN EUROPE SINCE 1792. London: J. Murray, 1909. Translation of 5th ed., Vienna, 1905.

178. Hourtoulle, Henry François Gabriel Léon. DAVOUT LE TERRIBLE. Paris: Maloine, 1975.

179. Hourtoulle, Henry François Gabriel Léon. LE GENERAL COMTE CHARLES LASALLE, 1775-1809. Paris: Aux depens de l'auteur, 1970.

180. Hummelberger, Walter, and Kurt Peball. DIE BEFESTIGUNGEN WIENS. Vienna and Hamburg: P.Z. Zsolnay, 1974.

181. Janson, General R. v. GESCHICHTE DES FELDZUGES 1814 IN FRANKREICH. Berlin: Mittler, 1903. 2 vols.

182. Jedlicka, Ludwig. "Erzherzog Carl, der Sieger von Aspern (1771-1847)." GESTALTER DE GESCHICHTE OESTERREICHS. INNSBRUCKER STUDIEN DER WIENER KATHOLISCHEN AKADEMIE 2 (1962): 313-22.

183. Jedlicka, Ludwig. "Militärische Archive und Museen in Oesterreich." WEHRWISSENSCHAFTLICHE RUNDSCHAU 10 (1960): 642-58.

184. Jedlicka, Ludwig. "Das Milizwesen in Oesterreich." WEHRWISSENSCHAFTLICHE RUNDSCHAU 9 (1959): 378-90.

185. Jedlicka, Ludwig, et al. UNSER HEER. 300 JAHRE OESTERREICHISCHES SOLDATENTUM IN KRIEG UND FRIEDEN. Vienna, Munich, and Zurich: Furlinger, 1963.

186. Joachim Murat, king of Naples. LETTRES ET DOCUMENTS POUR SERVIR A L'HISTOIRE DE JOACHIM MURAT, 1767-1815. Avec une introduction et des notes par Paul Le Brethon. Paris: Plon-Nourrit, 1908-14. 8 vols.

187. Johann, Archduke. FELDZUGSERZAEHLUNGEN. Edited by Alois Veltzé. Suppl. vol. to MITTEILUNGEN DES K.U.K. KRIEGSARCHIVS. Vienna, 1909.

188. John, Wilhelm. ERZHERZOG CARL DER FELDHERR UND SEINE ARMEE. Vienna: Hof-und Staatsdruckei, 1913.

189. Just, Gustav. DER FRIEDE VON SCHOENBRUNN. Vol. 9. Edited by Emil Woinovich and Alois Veltzé. DAS KRIEGSJAHR 1809 IN EINZELDARSTELLUNGEN. Vienna: C.W. Stern, 1909.

190. [Karl XIV, Johan, king of Sweden and Norway]. RECUEIL DES ORDRES DE MOUVEMENT, PROCLAMATIONS ET BULLETINS DE S.A.R. LE PRINCE ROYAL DE SUEDE, COMMANDANT EN CHEF DE L'ARMEE COMBINEE

DU NORD DE L'ALLEMAGNE EN 1813 ET 1814. Stockholm: Eckstein, 1838.

191. Keidel, Georg. GEORG KEIDELS KRIEGSFAHRTEN IN DEUTSCHLAND, TYROL, SPAINIEN, PORTUGAL UND FRANKREICH. Meiningen: n.p., 1845.

192. Kerchnawe, Hugo, and Alois Veltzé. FELDMARSCHALL KARL FUERST ZU SCHWAGRZENBERG. DER FUEHRER DER VERBUENDETEN IN DEN BEFREIUNGSKRIEGEN. Vienna: Gerlach, 1913.

193. DER K.K. OESTERREICHISCHE FELDMARSCHALL GRAF RADETZKY. EINE BIOGRAPHISCHE DARSTELLUNG NACH EIGENEN DICTATEN UND DER KORRESPONDENZ DES FELDMARSCHALLS VON EINEM OESTERREICHISCHEN VETERANEN. 2d ed. Stuttgart and Augsburg: Gotha'sche Buchh, 1858.

194. Kletke, Hermann. DEUTSCHLANDS KRIEGES-UND SIEGESJAHRE, 1809-1815, IM LIEDE DEUTSCHER DICHTER. Berlin: J. Springer, 1859.

195. Klippel, Georg Heinrich. DAS LEBEN DES GENERALS VON SCHARNHORST. NACH GROESSTENTEILS BISHER UNBENUTZEN QUELLEN DARGESTELLT. Leipzig: Brockhaus, 1869-71. 3 vols.

196. Knesebeck, E. von dem. LEBEN DES FRHRN. H. VON HALKETT. Stuttgart: Hallberger, 1865.

197. Knittel, Josef. ERNBERG IM JAHRE 1809 UND ZUR ZEIT DER NAPOLEONISCHEN KRIEGE 1789-1816: BEITRAGE ZUR HEIMATKUNDE DES POLIT. BEZIRKES REUTTE. Innsbruck: Druck and Verlag der Vereinsbuchdruckerei, 1909.

198. Krauss, Alfred. DER FELDZUG VON ULM. Vienna: Seidel, 1912.

199. Lamon, Siméon, "Souvenirs d'un chasseur de vielle garde." SOLDAT SUISSES AU SERVICE ETRANGER. Geneva, 1916. Vol. 7.

200. Langenau, Friedrich C.G. DER KRIEG DES JAHRES 1813 HISTORISCH BELEUCHTET. Vienna: Rehm, 1813.

201. Langsam, Walter Consuelo. "Count Stadion and Archduke Charles." JOURNAL OF CENTRAL-EUROPEAN AFFAIRS 6 (1946): 147-51.

202. Langsam, Walter Consuelo. THE NAPOLEONIC WARS AND GERMAN NATIONALISM IN AUSTRIA. New York: Columbia University Press, 1930.

203. Lannes, Charles Louis Maurice, duc de Montebello. LE MARCHAL LANNES, DUC DE MONTEBELLO, PRINCE, SOUVERAIN DE SIEVERS, EN POLOGNE. RESUME DE SA VIE. Par son petit-fils. Tours: A. Mame, 1900.

204. Larrey, Jean Dominique, MEMORIES DE MEDECINE ET DE CHIRURGIE MILITAIRE. Paris: Smith, 1812-17. 4 vols.

205. Lasalle, A[ntoine Charles Louis]. CORRESPONDANCE RECUEILLIE PAR [GABRIEL ADRIEN] ROBINET DE CLERY. Paris: Berger-Levrault, 1891.

206. Le Bègue de Germiny, Marc, comte. "La Bataille de Dresden, d'après des documents inédits." REVUE DES QUESTIONES HISTORIQUE 70 (1901): 47-91.

207. Lefebvre de Behaine, Edouard Alphonse, comte, ed. L'ALLEMAGNE EN 1809 ET L'ALLIANCE DE TILSIT. Paris: Amyot, 1869.

208. Lejeune, Louis François, baron. MEMOIRES; PUBL, PAR G. BAPST. Paris: Didot, 1895. 2 vols.

209. Leppa, Konrad J.F. "FML Heinrich Schmitt. Ein Soldatenleben." Ph.D. dissertation, University of Vienna, 1926.

210. Lesky, Erna. "Die österreichische Pestfront an der k.k. Militärgrenze." SAECULM 8 (1957): 82-106.

211. Litschel, Rudolf W. LANZE, SCHWERT UND HELM. BEITRAEGE ZUR OBEROESTERREICHISCHEN WEHRGESCHICHTE. Linz: R. Trauner Verlag, 1968.

212. Litschel, Rudolf W. DAS GEFECHT BEI EBELSBERG AM 3 MAI 1809. Vol. 9. Heeresgeschichtliches Museum, Militärwissenschaftliches Institut, MILITAERHISTORISCHE SCHRIFTENREIHE. Vienna, 1968.

213. Loh, Gerhard, ed. DIE VOELKERSCHLACHT BEI LEIPZIG. EINE BIBLIOGRAPHISCHE UEBERSICHT. Leipzig: Universitäts Bibliothek und Deutsche Bücherei, 1963.

214. Lorenz, Reinhold. VOLKSBEWAFFNUNG UND STAATSIDEE IN OESTERREICH (1792-1797). Vol. 4. Edited by Alfons Dopsch. DEUTSCHE KULTUR. HISTORISCHE REIHE. Vienna: Bundesverlag für Unterricht, Wissenschaft und Kunst, 1926.

215. Loy, L. LA CAMPAGNE EN STYRIE EN 1809. Paris: Chapelot, 1908.

216. Lucas-Dubreton, Jean. LE MARECHAL NEY, 1769-1815. Paris: Fayard, 1941.

217. Lucas-Dubreton, Jean. MURAT. Paris: Fayard, 1944.

218. Luckwald, Friedrich. OESTERREICH UND DIE ANFAENGE DES BEFREIUNGSKRIEG VON 1813. Berlin: Ebering, 1898.

219. Macdonald, Jacques Etienne Joseph Alexandre, duc de Tarente. RECOLLECTIONS OF MARSHAL MACDONALD, DUKE OF TARENTUM. Edited

by Camille Rousset. Translated by Stephen Louis Simeon.
London: Bentley, 1892. 2 vols.

220. Macdonald, Jacques Etienne Joseph Alexandre, duc de Tarente.
SOUVENIRS; AVEC UNE INTRODUCTION PAR C. ROUSSEL. Paris: Plon,
1892.

221. Mahler, Major. "Tagebuchblätter aus dem Jahre 1805."
MITTEILUNGEN DES K.K. KRIEGSARCHIVS 5 (1881): 499-523.

222. Marbot, Jean Baptiste Antoine Marcelin, baron de. MEMOIRES DU
GENERAL BARON DE MARBOT. Paris: Plon, 1891. 3 vols.

223. Maringon, Louis Joseph Vionnet de. CAMPAGNES DE RUSSIE ET DE
SAXE, 1812-1813. SOUVENIRS D'UN EX-COMMANDANT DE
GRENADIERS.... Paris: Dubois, 1899.

224. Marmont, Auguste Frédéric Louis Viesse de, duc de Raguse.
MEMOIRES DU MARECHAL MARMONT, DUC DE RAGUSE, DE 1792 A 1841,
IMPRIMES SUR LE MANUSCRIT ORIGINAL DE L'AUTEUR. Paris:
Perrotin, 1857. 9 vols.

225. Marshall-Cornwall, James Handyside. MARSHAL MASSENA. London
and New York: Oxford University Press, 1965.

226. Martel, Tancrède. UN GALANT CHEVALIER, LE GENERAL LASALLE
(1775-1809). Paris: A. Lamerre, 1929.

227. Masséna, André, duc de Rivoli, prince d'Essling. MEMOIRES;
REDIGES D'APRES LES DOCUMENTS QU'IL A LAISSE ET SUR CEUX DU
DEPOT DE LA GUERRE ET DU DEPOT DES FORTIFICATIONS, PAR LE
GENERAL KOCH. Paris: Paulin, 1849-50. 7 vols. and atlas.

228. Maude, Frederic Natusch. THE LEIPZIG CAMPAIGN 1813. London:
Swan-Sonnenschein, 1908.

229. Maude, Frederic Natusch. THE ULM CAMPAIGN 1805. London:
George Allen, 1912.

230. Mayer von Rosenau, D.S. UNBEKANNT GEBLIEBENE KRIEGS-EREIGNISSE
AUS DEN JAHREN 1805 UND 1809: DIE SUEDLICHE UMGEBUNG WIENS
WAEHREND DER FRANZOESISCHEN INVASION VON 1809: ZUR 90.
WIEDERKEHR DER GEDENKTAGE DER SCHLACHT VON ASPERN, NACH EINEM
BIS JETZT NOCH NICHT VEROEFFENTLICHTEN HANDSCHRIFTLICHEN.
NACHLASSE DES JOH. N. SCHRAIL. Vienna: D. Mayer von Rosenau,
1899.

231. Mayhoffer von Vedropolje, Eberhard. REGENSBURG. Vol. 1
Austria-Hungary. Kreigsarchiv. KRIEG 1809. KRIEGE UNTER DER
REGIERUNG DES KAISERS FRANZ. Vienna: Seidel, 1907.

232. Mayr, Johann Georg. DER MANN VON RINN (JOSEPH SPECKBACHER) UND
KRIEGSEREIGNISSE IN TIROL 1809. Innsbruck: Rieger, 1851.

233. Menge, August. DIE SCHLACHT VON ASPERN AM 21. UND 22. MAI 1809. EINE ERLAEUTERUND DER KRIEGSFUEHRUNG NAPOLEON I. UND ERZHERZOG CARLS VON OESTERREICH. Berlin: Georg Stilke, 1900.

234. Meynert, Hermann. KAISER FRANZ I. ZUR GESCHICHTE SEINER REGIERUNG UND SEINER ZEIT. Vienna: Holder, 1872. 2 vols.

235. Meynert, Hermann. GESCHICHTE DER K.K. OESTERREICHISCHEN ARMEE. Vienna: the author, 1852-54. 4 vols.

236. Michailowsky-Danilewsky, Alexandre. DENKWUERDIGKEITEN AUS DEM FELDZUGE VOM JAHRE 1813. Leipzig: Magazin fur Industrie, 1837.

237. MILITAER-SCHEMATISMUS DES OESTERREICHISCHEN KAISERTHUMES. Vienna: Hof-und Staats Druckerei, 1805.

238. Möller, Karl v. DIE HUNDERT TAGE 1815. Vol. 7. Austria-Hungary. Kriegsarchiv. 1813-1815. OESTERREICH IN DEN BEFREIUNGSKRIEGEN. Vienna: Seidel, 1913.

239. Molden, Ernst, ed. RADETZKY-SEIN LEBEN UND WIRKEN. Leipzig: Insel Verlag, 1916.

240. Mortemart de Boisse, François Leonard de. HISTOIRE, VOYAGES ET SCENES INTIMES. Paris: Vimont, 1834.

241. Müller, Franz. DIE KAISERL. KOENIGL. OESTERREICHISCHE ARMEE SEIT DER ERRICHTUNG DER STEHENDEN KRIEGSHEERE BIS AUF DIE NEUESTE ZEIT. Prague: Haase, 1845.

242. Müller, Wilhelm. RELATION OF THE OPERATIONS AND BATTLES OF THE AUSTRIAN AND FRENCH ARMIES, IN THE YEAR 1809. London: Printed for T. Goddard, Military Library, no. 1, by R. Wilks, 1810.

243. Nabonne, Bernard. BERNADOTTE. Paris: A. Michel, 1964.

244. Nemetz, Walther. "Erzherzog Karl." Edited by Werner Hahlweg. KLASSIKER DER KRIEGSKUNST (1960): 285-303.

245. Neuhauser, Herta. "FZM Johann Nepomuk Freiherr von Kutschera, Generaladjutant Franz I." Ph.D. dissertation, University of Vienna, 1937.

246. Nollet-Fabert, Jules. BIOGRAPHIE DU GENERAL DROUOT. Nancy: Raybois, 1850.

247. Nollet-Fabert, Jules. ELOGE HISTORIQUE DE MARECHAL NEY, DUC D'ELCHINGEN, PRINCE DE LA MOSKOWA, SUIVI DE PIECES JUTIFICATIVES. Paris: Dumaine, 1852.

248. Nollet-Fabert, Jules. HISTOIRE DE NICOLAS-CHARLES OUDINOT, MARECHAL DE L'EMPIRE ET DUC DE REGGIO. Paris: Dumaine, 1850.

249. Norvins, Jacques Marquet, baron de Montbrenton. PORTEFEUILLE
     DE MIL HUIT CENT TREIZE. Paris: Mongie, 1825. Vol. 2.

250. Odenleben, Ernst Otto Innocenz, freiherr von. CAMPAGNE DE
     FRANCAIS EN SAXE EN 1813. Traduit de l'allemand par Aubert de
     Vitry. Paris: n.p., 1817. 2 vols.

251. Odenleben, Ernst Otto Innocenz, freiherr von. NAPOLEON FELDZUG
     IN SACHSEN IN JAHR 1813. Dresden: Arnold, 1816.

252. OFFIZIELLE BERICHTE VON DER SCHLACHT BEI ENZERSDOFT UND
     DEUTSCH-WAGRAM AM 5. UND 6. JULIUS 1809: NEBST NACHTRAGEN
     EINES AUGENZEUGEN UND EINER KURZEN UEBERSICHT DER BEGEBENHEITEN
     BIS ZUM FRIEDEN VON WIEN DEN 14. OKTOBER 1809 - RAPPORTS
     OFFICIELS DE LA BATAILLE D'ENZERSDORF ET DE DEUTSCH-WAGRAM LE
     5. ET 6. JULLET 1809. Weimar: Im Verlag des Geographischen
     Instituts, 1810.

253. Ommen, Heinrich. DIE KRIEGSFUEHRUNG DES ERZHERZOGS CARL. No.
     16. HISTORISCHE STUDIEN. Berlin: Ebering, 1900.

254. Oncken, Wilhelm. OESTERREICH UND PREUSSEN IM BEFREIUNGSKRIEGE.
     Berlin: Grote, 1876-79. 2 vols.

255. ORGAN DER MILITAERWISSENSCHAFLICHEN VEREINE. BD. 1-73;
     1870-1906. Vienna: Militärwissenschaftlicher Verein. 73
     vols.

256. Ottenfeld, Rudolph O. v. (illustrator), and Oskar Teuber. DIE
     OESTERREICHISCHE ARMEE VON 1700 BIS 1867. Vienna: E. Berthie,
     and S. Cszeiger, 1895-98. 2 vols.

257. Oudinot, Marie Charlotte Eugénie Julienne (de Coucy), duchesse
     de Reggio. LE MARECHAL OUDINOT, DUC DE REGGIO; D'APRES LES
     SOUVENIRS INEDITS DE LA MARECHALE. Par Gaston Stiegler.
     Paris: Plon, 1894.

258. Oudinot, Marie Charlotte Eugénie Julienne (de Coucy), duchesse
     de Reggio. MEMOIRS OF MARCHAL OUDINOT, DUC DE REGGIO; COMPILED
     FROM THE HITHERTO UNPUBLISHED SOUVENIRS OF THE DUCHESSE DE
     REGGIO. Edited by Gaston Stiegler. Translated from the French
     by Alexander Teixeira de Mattos. New York: Appleton, 1897.

259. Paget, August B., and J.R. Green, eds. THE PAGET PAPERS.
     DIPLOMATIC AND OTHER CORRESPONDENCE OF THE RIGHT HON. SIR
     PAGET, G.C.B. 1794-1807. New York: Longman, Green, 1896. 2
     vols.

260. Pajol, Charles Pierre Victor, comte. PAJOL, GENERAL EN CHEF;
     PAR LE GENERAL DE DIVISION COMTE PAJOL, SON FILS AINE,
     (1772-1844). Paris: Dumaine, 1873. 3 vols.

261. Paret, Peter. YORCK AND THE ERA OF PRUSSIAN REFORM.
     Princeton: Princeton University Press, 1966.

262. Parquin, Dennis Charles. SOUVENIRS ET CAMPAGNES D'UN VIEUX
     SOLDAT DE L'EMPIRE. Paris: Berger-Levrault, 1892.

263. Pastoret, Amendée David de. "Souvenirs de Pastoret. Campagne
     de 1813." CARNET DE LA SABRETACHE. Series 2, 1 (1903): 37-47,
     106-14, 153-64.

264. Paulin, Jules Antoine. LES SOUVENIRS DU GENERAL BARON PAULIN
     (1782-1876). Publiés par le capitaine du génie Paulin-Ruelle.
     Paris: Plon-Nourrit, 1895.

265. Paulin, Karl. "Das Tiroler Freijeitsjahr 1809 in seinem
     geschichtlichen Verlauf." TIROLER HEIMAT 23 (1959): 27-44.

266. Paulus, G. BAYERISCHE KRIEGSVORBEREITUNGEN, MOBILMACHUNG UND
     EINLEITUNG ZUM FELDZUGE 1809. Munich: n.p., 1893.

267. Peball, Kurt. "Zum Kriegsbild der österreichischen Armee und
     seiner geschichtlichen Bedeutung in den Kriegen gegen
     die französische Revolution and Napoleon I. in den Jahren von
     1792 bit 1815." Edited by Wolfgang v. Groote and Klaus-Jürgen
     Müller. NAPOLEON I. UND DAS MILITAERWESEN SEINER ZEIT (1968):
     129-82.

268. Pelet, Jean Jacques Germain, baron. MEMOIRES SUR LA GUERRE DE
     1809, EN ALLEMAGNE, AVEC LES OPERATIONS PARTICULIERES DES CORPS
     D'ITALIE, DE POLOGNE, DE SAXE, DE NAPLES ET DE WALCHEREN; PAR
     LE GENERAL PELET, D'APRES SON JOURNAL FORT DETAILLE DE LA
     CAMPAGNE D'ALLEMAGNE; SES RECONNAISSANCES ET SES DIVERS
     TRAVAUX; LA CORRESPONDANCE DE NAPOLEON AVEC LE MAJOR-GENERAL,
     LES MARECHAUX, LES COMMANDANS EN CHEF, ETC; ACCOMPAGNES DE
     PIECES JUSTIFICATIVES ET INEDITES.... Paris: Roret, 1824-26.
     4 vols.

269. Pelet, Jean Jacques Germain, baron. DES PRINCIPLES OPERATIONS
     DE LA CAMPAGNE DE 1813. Paris: Spectateur Militaire, 1827.

270. Pelet, Jean Jacques Germain, baron, ed. HISTOIRE DES CAMPAGNES
     DE L'EMPEREUR NAPOLEON DANS LA BAVIERE ET L'AUTRICHE EN 1805,
     DANS LA PRUSSSE ET LA POLOGNE EN 1806 ET 1807, DANS LA BAVIERE
     ET L'AUTRICHE EN 1809. Paris: Picquet, 1843.

271. Pelleport, Pierre, vicomte de. SOUVENIRS MILITAIRES ET
     INTIMES, 1793-1853, PUBL. PAR SON FILES.... Paris: Didier,
     1857. 2 vols.

272. Percy, Pierre François, baron. JOURNAL DES CAMPAGNES DU BARON
     PERCY, CHIRURGIEN EN CHEF DE LA CHEF DE LA GRANDE ARMEE
     (1754-1825). Publié d'après les manuscrits inédits. Paris:
     Plon-Nourrit, 1904.

273. Pertz, Georg Heinrich. DAS LEBEN DES FELDMARSCHALL GRAFEN
     NEITHARDT VON GNEISENAU. Berlin: Reimer, 1864-81. 5 vols.

274. Petre, Francis Loraine. NAPOLEON AND THE ARCHDUKE CHARLES.
      London: J. Lane, 1909.

275. Petre, Francis Loraine. NAPOLEON'S LAST CAMPAIGN IN GERMANY
      1813. London: J. Lane, 1912.

276. Peyrusse, Guillaume, baron. 1809-15. MEMORIAL ET ARCHIVES.
      VIENNE--MOSCOU--ILE D'ELBE. Carcassonne: Labau, 1869.

277. Peyrusse, Guillaume, baron. LETTRES INEDITES, ECRITES A SON
      FRERE ANDRE PENDANT LES CAMPAGNES DE L'EMPIRE, DE 1809-1814.
      Paris: Perrin, 1894.

278. Pierron, Edouard. NAPOLEON DE DRESDE A LEIPZIG. ETUDE
      STRATIGIQUE. Paris: Baudoin, 1891.

279. Pivka, Otto von. "The Austrian Empire 1792-1815." ARMIES OF
      THE NAPOLEONIC ERA. New York: Taplinger Publishing Co., 1979.

280. Ph. Ch. Clair. ANDRE HOFER ET L'INSURRECTION DU TYROL EN 1809.
      Paris: Albanel, 1873.

281. Planat de La Faye, Nicolas Louis. VIE DE PLANAT DE LA FAYE,
      AIDE DE CAMP DES GENERAUX LARIBOSIERE ET DROUOT, OFFICIER
      D'ORDONNANCE DE NAPOLEON Ier. SOUVENIRS, LETTRES ET DICTEES
      RECUEILLIS ET ANNOTES PAR SA VEUVE. Paris: Ollendorff, 1895.

282. Plotho, Carl von. DER KRIEG IN DEUTSCHLAND UND FRANKREICH IN
      DEN JAHREN 1813 UND 1814. Berlin: Amelang, 1817-18. 4 vols.

283. Poinsot, Edmond Antoine. LE MARECHAL NEY D'APRES LES DOCUMENTS
      AUTHENTIQUES. Par Georges d'Heylli. Paris: Le Chevalier,
      1869.

284. Preradovich, Nikolaus v. DIE FUEHRUNGSSCHICHTEN IN OESTERREICH
      UND PREUSSEN 1804-1918. Wiesbaden: F. Steiner, 1955.

285. Prybila, Paul. ANTHEIL SALZBURGES AN DER VOLKSERHEBUNG IM
      JAHRE 1809. Salzburg: im Verlage des k.k. Staats-Gymnasiums,
      1894.

286. Purschka, Ferdinand R. v. RUECKBLICKE AUF DIE ENTWICKLUNG DES
      K.U.K. OESTERREICHISCHEN HEERES. Lemberg: Carl Budweiser,
      1892.

287. Rabel, Andrè. LE MARECHAL BESSIERES, DUC D'ISTRIE. Paris:
      Calmann-Lèvy, 1903.

288. Radetzky, Josef Wenzel, graf. DENKSCHRIFTEN MILITAER-
      POLITISCHEN INHALTS AUD DEM HANDSCHRIFTLICHEN NACHLASS DES K.K.
      OESTERREICHISCHEN-FELDMARSCHALLS GRAFEN RADETZKY. Stuttgart:
      J.G. Cotta, 1859.

289. Radetzky, Josef Wenzel, graf. "Eine Memoire Radetzkys das
      Heerwesen Oesterreichs beleuchtend aus dem Jahre 1809."
      MITTEILUNGEN DES K.K. KRIEGSARCHIVS 8 (1884): 361-70.

290. Radetzky, Josef Wenzel, graf. "Erinnerungen aus dem Leben des Feldmarschalls Grafen Radetzky. Eine Selbstbiographie." MITTEILUNGEN DES K.K. KRIEGSARCHIVS, New Series 1 (1887): 3-82.

291. Rambaud, Alfred Nicolas. L'ALLEMAGNE SOUS NAPOLEON Ier (1804-1811). Paris: Didier, 1874.

292. Rapp, Jean, comte. MEMOIRES DU GENERAL RAPP, AIDE-DE-CAMP DE NAPOLEON, ECRITS PAR LUI-MEME, ET PUBLIES PAR SA FAMILLE. Paris: Bossage, 1823.

293. Rauch, Josef. ERINNERUNGER EINES OFFIZIERS AUS ALTOESTERREICH. Edited by A. Weber. Vol. 21. G. Gugitz, DENKWUERDIGKEITEN AUS ALTESTERREICH. Munich: George Müller, 1918.

294. Rauchensteiner, Manfried. FELDZEUGMEISTER JOHANN FREIHERR VON HILLER. (DISSERTATIONEN DER UNIVERSITAT WIEN NR. 80). Vienna: Notring der Universität Wien, 1972.

295. Rauchensteiner, Manfried. KAISER FRANZ UND ERZHERZOG CARL. DYNASTIE UND HEERWESEN IN OESTERREICH 1796-1809. Munich: R. Oldenbourg, 1972.

296. Rauchensteiner, Manfried. DIE SCHLACHT BEI DEUTSCH-WAGRAM AM 5. UND 6. JULI 1809. Heeresgeschichtliches Museum, Militärwissenschaftliches Institut, MILITAERHISTORISCHE SCHRIFTENREIHE 36 (1979).

297. Rauchensteiner, Manfried. DIE SCHLACHT VON ASPERN AM 21. UND 22. MAI 1809. Heeresgeschichtliches Museum, Militärwissenschaftliches Institut, MILITAERHISTORISCHE SCHRIFTENREIHE 11 (1969).

298. Rauchensteiner, Manfried. "Das sechste österreichische Armeekorps im Kriege 1809. Nach den Aufzeichnungen des FZM Johann Freiherr v. Hiller." MITTEILUNGEN DES OESTERREICHISCHEN STAATSARCHIVS 17-18 (1965): 147-208.

299. Regele, Oskar. DER OESTERREICHISCHE HOFKRIEGSRAT 1556-1848. Suppl. MITTEILUNGEN DES OESTERREICHISCHEN STAATSARCHIVS 1 (1949).

300. Regele, Oskar. FELDMARSCHALL RADETZKY. LEBEN, LEITUNG, ERBE. Vienna and Munich: Herold, 1957.

301. Regele, Oskar. GENERALSTABSCHEFS AUS VIER JAHRHUNDERTEN. Vienna and Munich: Herold, 1966.

302. Regele, Oskar. "Karl Freiherr von Mack and Johann Ludwig Graf Cobenzl. Ihre Rolle im Kriegsjahr 1805." MITTEILUNGEN DES OESTERREICHISCHEN STAATSARCHIVS 21 (1969): 142-64.

303. Reichel, Daniel. DAVOUT ET L'ART DE LA GUERRE. Neuchâtel: Delachaux et Niestlé, 1975.

304. Renemont, C. de. CAMPAGNE DE 1809. ETUDE MILITAIRE,.... Paris: Charles-Lavauzelle. 1903.

305. Riv-Alpon, Giedeon Maretich von. DIE ZWEITE UND DRITTE BERG ISEL-SCHLACHT. (GEFECHTE IN DER UMGEBUNG VON INNSBRUCK AM 25 UND 29 MAI 1809). Innsbruck: Wagner, 1895.

306. Riv-Alpon, Giedeon Maretich von. JOSEPH STRUBER UND DIE KAMPFE IN DER UMGEBUNG DES PASSES LUEG IN JAHRE 1809.... Vienna: Braumüller, 1897.

307. Riv-Alpon, Giedeon Maretich, von. DIE VIERTE BERG ISEL-SCHLACHT AM 13 AUGUST 1809. (GEFECHTE IN DER UMGEBUNG VON INNSBRUCK AM 11., 13., UND 14. AUGUST, SOWIE IM UNTER-INNTHALE BIS 17. AUGUST 1809.) Innsbruck: Wagner, 1899.

308. Rivollet, Georges. GENERAL DE BATAILLE CHARLES ANTOINE LOUIS MORAND, COMTE D'EMPIRE (1771-1835). GENERAUX FRIANT ET GUDIN DU 3e CORPS DE LA GRANDE ARMEE. Paris: Peyronnet, 1963.

309. Robinet de Cléry, Gabriel Adrien. D'ESSLING A WAGRAM: LASALLE. CORRESPONDANCE. Paris: Berger-Levrault, 1891.

310. Rochechouart, Louis Victor Léon, comte de. SOUVENIRS SUR LA REVOLUTION, L'EMPIRE ET LA RESTAURATION. Paris: Plon, 1933.

311. Rodger, A.B. THE WAR OF THE SECOND COALITION, 1798-1801: A STRATEGIC COMMENTARY. Edited by Christopher Duffy. London: Oxford University Press, 1964.

312. Rössler, Helmuth. OESTERREICHS KAMPF UM DIE DEUTSCHE BEFREIUNG, DIE DEUTSCHE POLITIK DER NATIONALEN FUEHRER OESTERREICHS 1805-1815. Hamburg: Hanseatische Verlagsgesellschaft, 1940. 2 vols.

313. Rothauscher, Karl. OESTERREICHS KRIEGE SEIT 1495. CHRONOLOGISCHE ZUSAMMENSTELLUNG DER SCHLACHTEN, GEFECHTE, BELAGERUNGEN. Vienna: Seidel, 1878.

314. Rothenberg, Gunther E. THE ART OF WARFARE IN THE AGE OF NAPOLEON. London: Batsford, 1977; Bloomington: Indiana University Press, 1978.

315. Rothenberg, Gunther E. "The Habsburg Army in the Napoleonic Wars." MILITARY AFFAIRS 38 (1973): 1-5.

316. Rothenberg, Gunther E. THE MILITARY BORDER IN CROATIA 1740-1881. Chicago: University of Chicago Press, 1966.

317. Rothenberg, Gunther E. NAPOLEON'S GREAT ADVERSARIES: ARCHDUKE CHARLES AND THE AUSTRIAN ARMY 1792-1814. London: Batsford, 1982.

318. Rothenberg, Gunther E. DIE OESTERREICHISCHE MILIIAERGRENZE IN KROATIEN. 1522 BIS 1881. Vienna and Munich: Herold, 1970.

319. Rothenberg, Freidrick R. von. DIE SCHLACHT BEI LEIPZIG IN JAHRE 1813. Leipzig: Rein, 1842.

320. Rouget, François, comte. MEMOIRES MILITAIRES DU LIEUTENANT GENERAL COMTE ROUGET (FRANCOIS). Paris: Dumaine, 1862-65. 4 vols.

321. Rüstow, Wilhelm. DER KRIEG VON 1805 IN DEUTSCHLAND UND ITALIEN. Frauenfeld: A. Reimann, 1853.

322. Saint-Marc, Pierre. LE MARECHAL MARMONT, DUC DE RAGUSE, 1774-1852. Paris: Fayard, 1957.

323. Sallinger, Richard. GRAZ IM JAHRE 1809: FESTSCHRIFT AUS ANLASS DER ENTHUELLUNG DES HACKHER-DENKMALES AUF DEM SCHLOSSBERGE ZU GRAZ. Graz: U. Moser's Buchhandlung (J. Meyerhoff), 1909.

324. Saski, Charles G.L. CAMPAGNE DE 1809 EN ALLEMAGNE ET EN AUTRICHE. Paris and Nancy: Berger-Levrault, 1899-1902. 3 vols.

325. Savary, Anne Jean Marie René, duc de Rovigo. MEMOIRES DU DUC DE ROVIGO, POUR SERVIR A L'HISTOIRE DE L'EMPEREUR NAPOLEON. Paris: Bossange, 1828. 8 vols.

326. Schallhammer, Anton, ritter von. KRIEGERISCHE EREIGNISSE IM HERZOGTHUME SALZBURG IN DEN JAHREN 1800, 1805 UND 1809. Salzburg: Mayr, 1853.

327. Scheer, Johann. BLUECHER. SEINE ZEIT UND SEIN LEBEN. Leipzig: Wigand, 1862-63. 8 vols.

328. Schels, Johan Baptist. KRIEGSSZENEN, ALS BEISPIELE DES FELDDIENSTES. Pesth: C.A. Hartleben, 1843.

329. Schemfil, Viktor. "Das k.k. Tiroler Korps in Kriege 1809." TIROLER HEIMAT 23 (1959): 45-99.

330. Schilder, Otto. LAND AN MARCH UND DONAU. Druck: Ferdinand Berger, 1975.

331. Schimmer, Karl August. DIE FRANZOESISCHEN INVASIONEN IN OESTERREICH: UND DIE FRANZOSEN IN WIEN IN DEN JAHREN 1805 UND 1809. Vienna: J. Dirnbock, 1846.

332. Schmahl, E. RADETZKY. OESTERREICHS RUHM-DEUTSCHLANDS EHRE. Berlin: Vier Falken, 1938.

333. Schneidawind, Franz Joseph. DER KRIEG OESTERREICH'S GEGEN FRANKREICH, DESSEN ALLIIERTE UND DEN RHEINBUND IM JAHRE 1809. Schaffhausen: Hurter, 1842-43. 4 vols.

334. Schönhals, Carl R. v. DER KRIEG 1805 IN DEUTSCHLAND. Vienna:
     Selbstverlag Der Oesterreichischen Militärischen Zeitschrift,
     1873.

335. Schrafel, Joseph. DES NUERNBERGER FELDWEBELS JOSEPH SCHRAFEL
     MERKWUERDIGE SCHICKSALE: IM KRIEGE GEGEN TIROL 1809, IM
     FELDZUGE GEGEN RUSSLAND 1812, UND IN DER GEFANGENSCHAFT
     1812-1814 / VON IHM SELBST BESCHREIBEN. Nuremberg: Verlag der
     Korn'schen Buchhandlung, 1913.

336. Schwarzenberg, Karl P., prince.   BRIEFE DES FELDMARSCHALLS
     FUERSTEN SCHWARZENBERG AN SEINE FRAU 1799-1816.   Edited by
     Johann F. Novak. Vienna: Gerlach & Wiedling, 1913.

337. Schwarzenberg,   Karl   P.,   prince. FELDMARSCHALL   FUERST
     SCHWARZENBERG. DER SIEGER VON LEIPZIG. Vienna and Munich:
     Herold, 1964.

338. Scott, Franklin Daniel. BERNADOTTE AND THE FALL OF NAPOLEON.
     Cambridge: Harvard University Press, 1935.

339. Segur, Paul Philippe, comte de. HISTOIRE ET MEMOIRES. Paris:
     Didot, 1873. 7 vols.

340. Semek, Anton. "Die Artillerie im Jahre 1809." MITTEILUNGEN
     DES K.U.K. KRIEGSARCHIVS. Series 3, 3 (1904): 51-160.

341. Serieyx, William. DROUOT ET NAPOLEON; VIE HEROIQUE ET SUBLIME
     DU GENERAL DROUOT. Paris: Tallandier, 1929.

342. Shadwell, L. MOUNTAIN WARFARE: ILLUSTRATED BY THE CAMPAIGN OF
     1799 IN SWITZERLAND. London: H.S. King, 1875.

343. Shoberl, Frederic, comp. and trans.   NARRATIVE OF THE MOST
     REMARKABLE EVENTS WHICH OCURRED IN AND NEAR LEIPZIG....
     London: Ackermann, 1814.

344. Simon, Kurt. "Die Verspätigung des Erzherzogs Johann bei
     Wagram." MS thesis, University of Berlin, 1899.

345. Soltyk, Roman, comte. RELATION DES OPERATIONS DE L'ARMEE AUX
     ORDERS DU PRINCE JOSEPH PONIATOWSKI PENDANT LA CAMPAGNE DE 1809
     EN POLOGNE CONTRE LES AUTRICHIENS; PRECEDEE D'UNE NOTICE SUR LA
     VIE DU PRINCE. Paris: Gaultier-Laguionie, 1814.

346. Soubiran, André. LE BARON LARREY, CHIRURGIEN DE NAPOLEON.
     Paris: Fayard, 1966.

347. Sporschil, Johann. FELDZUG DER OESTERREICHER IN ILLYRIEN UND
     ITALIEN IN DEN JAHREN 1813 UND 1814. Brunswick: George
     Westermann, 1844.

348. Springer, Anton. GESCHICHTE OESTERREICHS SEIT DEM WIENER
     FRIEDEN 1809. Leipzig: S. Hirzek, 1863. 2 vols.

349. Stadion,   Johann   Philipp,   graf.   NAPOLEONS   DEUTSCHER
      GEGENSPIELER. Vienna and Munich: Herold, 1966. 2 vols.

350. Staps, Freidrich Gottlob. FRIEDRICH STAPS, ERSCHOSSEN ZU
      SCHOENBRUNN, BEI WIEN, AUF NAPOLEONS BEFEHL IM OCTOBER 1809:
      EINE BIOGRAPHIE AUS DEN HINTERLASSENEN PAPIEREN SEINES VATERS
      M. FR. GOTTL. STAPS, PREDIGER ZU ST. OTHMAR VOR NAUMBURG, NEBST
      DEN ZEUGNISSEN DER ZEITGENOSSEN, CARL JOHANN FRIEDRICH SCHULZ,
      KAMMERER ZU KYRITZ, ERSCHOSSEN DASELBST AM 8. SEPTEMBER 1807,
      AUF BEFEHL DES FRANZOESISCHEN GOUVERNEMENTS. Berlin: Berliner
      Lesecabinet, 1843.

351. Stark, Nicolaus, Sr. ERINNERUNGS-BLAETTER AN DIE SCHLACHTTAGE
      BEI ABENSBERG AM 19. U. 20. APRIL 1809. Abensberg: n.p.,
      1908. [E. Senn (J. Spirk)].

352. Steiner, Gustav. NAPOLEONS I. POLITIK UND DIPLOMATIE IN DER
      SCHWEIZ WAEHREND DER GESANDTSCHAFTSZEIT DES GRAFEN AUGUSTE DE
      TALLEYRAND. Zurich: Schulthess, 1907.

353. Stiegler, Gaston. RECITS DE GUERRE ET DE FOYER. LE MARECHAL
      OUDINOT, DUC DE REGGIO, D'APRES LES SOUVENIRS INEDITS DE LA
      MARECHALE. Paris: Plon, 1894.

354. Stolz, Otto. WEHRVERFASSUNG UND SCHUETZENWESEN IN TIROL VON
      DEREN ANFAENGEN BIS 1918. Vienna and Munich: Tyrolia, 1960.

355. Strobl von Ravelsberg, Ferdinand. DIE LANDWEHR ANNO NEUN.
      Vol. 10. Edited by Emil v. Woinovich and Alois Veltzé. DAS
      KRIEGSJAHR 1809 IN EINZELDARSTELLUNGEN. Vienna: C.W. Stern,
      1909.

356. Stutterheim, General Karl, freiherr von. DER KRIEG VON 1809
      ZWISCHEN OESTERREICH UND FRANKREICH. Vienna: A. Strauss,
      1811.

357. Stutterheim, General Karl, freiherr von. DIE SCHLACHT BEI
      AUSTERLITZ. Hamburg: Walthersche Hofbuchhandlung, 1806.

358. Tarle, A. de. MURAT. Paris: Chapelot, 1914.

359. Teste, François Antione. "Souvenirs du général baron Teste."
      CARNET DE LA SABRETACHE. Series 2, 4 (1906): 659-70; Series 2,
      5 (1908): 253; Series 2, 10 (1911): 593-623; Series 2, 11
      (1912): 7-33, 97-113, 161-68, 241-49, 289-305, 371-78.

360. Thiébault, Paul Charles François Adrien Heri Dieudonné, baron.
      MEMOIRES DU GENERAL BARON THIEBAULT. Paris: Plon-Nourrit,
      1894-95. 5 vols.

361. Thielen, Max R. v. ERINNERUNGEN AUS DEM KRIEGSERLEBEN EINES 82
      JAEHRIGEN VETERANEN DER OESTERREICHISCHEN ARMEE. Vienna: W.
      Braumüller, 1963.

362. Thierry, Augustin. MASSENA, L'ENFANT GATE DE LA VICTOIRE. Paris: A. Michel, 1947.

363. Thiry, Jean, baron. LEIPZIG. Paris: Berger-Levrault, 1972.

364. Thiry, Jean, baron. WAGRAM. Paris: Berger-Levrault, 1966.

365. Thoumas, Charles Antoine. LES GRANDS CAVALIERS DU PREMIER EMPIRE; NOTICES BIOGRAPHIQUES. (Ier series: Lasalle, Kellermann, Montbrun, Les trois Colbert, Murat). (2e series: Nansouty, Pajol, Milhaud, Curely, Fournier-Sarloveze, Chamorin, Sainte-Croix, Exelmans, Marulaz, Franceschi-Delonne). Paris: Berger-Levrault, 1890.

366. Thoumas, Charles Antoine. LE MARECHAL EXELMANS. Paris: Berger-Levrault, 1891.

367. Thoumas, Charles Antoine. LE MARECHAL LANNES. Paris: Lévy, 1891.

368. Toselli, Jean Baptiste. NOTICE BIOGRAPHIQUE SUR MASSENA. Nice: Gauthier, 1869.

369. Treuenfest, Gustav v. GESCHICHTE DES K.K. INFANTRIE REGIMENTS "HOCH UND DEUTSCHMEISTER" NO. 4, 1969-1879. Vienna: The regiment, 1879.

370. Uhlirz, Karl, and Mathilde Uhlirz. HANDBUCH DER GESCHICHTE OESTERREICHS UND SEINER NEBENLAENDER BOEHMEN UND UNGARN. Graz: Bohlau, 1937-44. 4 vols. in 5.

371. Unterberger, Leopold v. NOETHIGE KENNTNISSE VON DEM GESCHUETZE UND DESSEN GEBRAUCH. Vienna: Wappler und Beck, 1807.

372. Unterberger, Leopold v. OESTERREICHISCHE ARTILLERIE: NOETIGE KENNTNISSE VON DEM GESCHUETZ UND DESSEN GEBRAUCH. Zurich: Intersico Press, 1977.

373. Ussel, Jean d', vicomte. ETUDES SUR L'ANNEE 1813: L'INTERVENTION DE L'AUTRICHE (DECEMBRE 1812-MAI 1813). Paris: Plon-Nourrit, 1912.

374. Valentin, René. LE MARECHAL MASSENA (1758-1817). Paris: Charles-Lavauzelle, 1960.

375. Valentini, General Ritter Heinrich, freiherr von. VERSUCH EINER GESCHICHTE DES FELDZUGS VON 1809 AN DER DONAU. Berlin: Nicolai, 1812.

376. Vanicek, Franz. SPECIALGESCHICHTE DER MILITAERGRENZE AUS ORIGINALQUELLEN UND QUELLENWERKEN GESCHOEPFT. Vienna: k.k. Hof-und staatsdruckerei, 1875. 4 vols.

377. Vann, James A. "Habsburg Policy and the Austrian War of 1809." CENTRAL EUROPEAN HISTORY (1974): 291-310.

378. Varges, Willi. "Die Teilnahme des Kurfürsten Wilhelm I. Von Hessen an Oesterreichischen Kriege von 1809--die Kurhessiche Legion im Jahre 1809." ZEITSCHRIFT DES VEREINS FUER HESSISCHE GESCHICHTE 26, 31 (1891, 1896): 315-343, 86-183.

379. Varnhagen von Ense, Karl August Ludwig Philipp. DIE SCHLACHT VON DEUTSCH-WAGRAM AM 5. UND 6. JULI 1809. Vienna: Verlag des Kriegerdenkmal-Ausschusses für den Buchhandel, K.u.k. Hof-Buchdruckerei und Hof-Verlags-Buchhandlung Carl Fromme, 1909.

380. Varnhagen von Ense, Karl August Ludwig Philipp. DIE SCHLACHT VON DEUTSCH-WAGRAM AM 5ten UND 6ten JULI 1809: AUS PERSOENLICHEN DENKWUERDIGKEITEN. Leipzig: F.A. Brockhaus, 1836.

381. Veltzé, Alois. KRIEG GEGEN NEAPEL 1815. Vol. 9. Austria-Hungary. Kriegsarchiv. 1813-1815. OESTERREICH IN DEN BEFREIUNGSKRIEGEN. Vienna: Seidel, 1914.

382. Veltzé, Alois. KRIEGSBILDER AUD POLEN, STEIERMARK, UND UNGARN. Vol. 11. Edited by Emil v. Woinovich, and Alois Veltzé. DAS KRIEGSJAHR 1809 in EINZELDARSTELLUNGEN. Vienna: C.W. Stern, 1901.

383. Veltzé, Alois. OESTERREICHS THERMOPYLEN. Vol. 1. Edited by Emil v. Woinovich and Alois Veltzé. DAS KRIEGSJAHR 1809 IN EINZELDARSTELLUNGEN. Vienna: C.W. Stern, 1905.

384. Veltzé, Alois. DIE POLITIK METTERNICHS. Vol. 1. Austria-Hungary, Kriegsarchiv. 1813-1815. OESTERREICH IN DEN BEFREIUNGSKRIEGEN. Vienna: Seidel, 1914.

385. DIE VERTHEIDIGUNG DER BLOCKHAEUSER MALBORGHET UND PREDIL IM JAHRE 1809: ZWEI RUHMESBLATTER OESTERREICHISCHER KRIEGSGESCHICHTE. Vienna: Redaction der "Mittheilungen", in Commission bei L.W. Seidel, 1901.

386. Vigier, Henri, comte. DAVOUT, MARECHAL D'EMPIRE, DUC D'AUERSTAEDT, PRINCE D'ECHMUEHL (1770-1823). Par son arrière-petit-fils le comte Vigier. Paris: Ollendorff, 1898. 2 vols.

387. Vignolle, Général Martin, comte de. "Historique de la Campagne de 1809 (Armée d'Italie)." [Publiée par C.] REVUE MILITAIRE 2, 4, 3, 4 (1900-01): 465-509, 769-814, 59-106, 366-98.

388. Vitzthum von Eckstädt, Karl Friedrich, graf. DIE HAUPT-QUARTIERE IM HERBSTFELDZUGE 1813 AUF DEN DEUTSCHEN KRIEGS-SCHAUPLAETZEN. Berlin: Mittler, 1910.

389. Vordermayr, Peter. KITZBUEHEL ANNO 1809 [i.e. ACHTZEHN-HUNDERTNEUN] MIT UEBERBLICK UBER DIE KRIEGS-EREIGNISSE IN TIROL VON 1796 BIS 1809: ANLASSLICH DER ERRICHTUNG EINES DENKMALES FUER DIE FREIHEITS-KAEMPFER VON KITZBUEHEL FUER DAS JUBELJAHR 1909. Kitzbuehel: M. Ritzer, 1909.

390. Wagner, Anton. "Radetzky als Chef des Generalstabes der Heere
      der Verbündeten im Herbstfeldzug 1813." OESTERREICHISCHE
      MILITAERISCHE ZEITSCHRIFT 3 (1963): 352-58.

391. Wagner, Walter. VON AUSTERLITZ BIS KOENIGGRAETZ:
      OESTERREICHISCHE KAMPFTAKTIK IM SPIEGEL DES REGLEMENTS
      1805-1864. Osnabrück: Biblio Verlag, 1978.

392. Waldstätten, Baron v., ed. and comment. ERZHERZOG KARL.
      AUSGEWAEHLTE MILITAERISCHE SCHRIFTEN. Berlin: Richard
      Wilhelmi, 1882.

393. Walter, Friedrich. DIE ZEIT FRANZ II. (I.) Vol. 5. DIE
      OESTERREICHISCHE ZENTRALVERWALTUNG. Series 2. VON DER
      VEREINGIGUNG DER OESTERREICHISCHEN UND BOEHMISHEN HOFKANZLEI
      BIS ZUR EINRICHTUNG DER MINISTERIALVERFASSUNG. Vienna:
      Veröffentlichungen der Kommission für neuere Geschichte
      Oesterreichs Nos. 42-43, 1956.

394. Walter, Jakob. A GERMAN CONSCRIPT WITH NAPOLEON: JAKOB
      WALTER'S RECOLLECTIONS OF THE CAMPAIGNS OF 1806-07, 1809, AND
      1812-1813. Edited and translated from the German by Otto
      Springer, with collaboration of Frank E. Nelvin. Lawrence:
      University of Kansas, Department of Journalism press, 1838.

395. Weber, Beda. DAS THAL PASSEIER UND SEINE BEWOHNER. MIT
      BESONDERER RUCKSICHT AUF ANDREAS HOFER UND DAS JAHR 1809.
      Innsbruck: Wagner, 1852, [1851].

396. Weigl, J.B. LEBEN UND KRIEGSLEIDEN DES KAMINKEHRERS MATTHIAS
      WEIGL IN DEN TAGEN DES TIROLER AUFSTANDES VON 1809: GESCHILDERT
      NACH AUTHENTISCHEN QUELLEN. Munich: C.A. Sayfried, 1909.

397. Welden, Ludwig, freiherr von. DER KRIEG VON 1809 ZWISCHEN
      OESTERREICH UND FRANKREICH, VON ANFANG MAI BIS ZUM
      FRIEDENSSCHLUSSE. Vienna: C. Gerold, 1872.

398. Welschinger, Henri. LE MARECHAL NEY, 1815. Paris:
      Plon-Nourrit, 1893.

399. Wencker, Friedrich. BERNADOTTE, A BIOGRAPHY. Translated from
      the German by Kenneth Kirkness. London: Jarrolds, 1936.

400. Wertheimer, Eduard. "Erzherzog Carl und die zweite Coalition
      bis zum Frieden von Luneville 1798-1801." ARCHIV FUER
      OESTERREICHISCHE GESCHICHTE 67 (1882): 193-252.

401. Wertheimer, Eduard. GESCHICHTE OESTERREICHS UND UNGARNS IM
      ERSTEN JAHRZEHNT DES 19. JAHRHUNDERTS. Leipzig: Duncker &
      Humboldt, 1884-90. 2 vols.

402. Wertheimer, Eduard. "Zur Geschichte Wiens im Jahre 1809."
      ARCHIV FUER OESTERREICHISCHE GESCHICHTE 74 (1889): 159-95.

403. Wessely, Kurt, and Georg Zivković. "Bibliographie zur Geschichte der k.k. Militärgrenze." SCHRIFTEN DES HEERESGESCHICHTLICHEN MUSEUMS IN WIEN 7 (1973): 291-324.

404. Wickham, William, ed. THE CORRESPONDENCE OF THE RIGHT HONORABLE WILLIAM WICKHAM FROM THE YEAR 1794. London: Richard Bentley, 1870. 2 vols.

405. Willette, Luc. LE MARECHAL LANNES. Paris: Perrin, 1979.

406. Wilson, Robert. PRIVATE DIARY OF TRAVELS, PERSONAL SERVICES AND PUBLIC EVENTS DURING MISSIONS AND EMPLOYMENT WITH THE EUROPEAN ARMIES IN THE CAMPAIGNS OF 1812, 1813, 1814. Edited by Herbert Randolph. London: John Murray, 1861. 2 vols.

407. Wirth, Joseph. LE MARECHAL LEFEBVRE, DUC DE DANTZIG (1775-1820). Paris: Perrin, 1904.

408. Wlaschütz, Wilhelm. OESTERREICHS ENTSCHEIDENDES MACHTAUFGEBOT. Vol. 2. Austria-Hungary. Kriegsarchiv. BEFREIUNGSKRIEG 1813 UND 1814. Vienna: Seidel, 1913.

409. Wohlfeil, Rainer. VOM STEHENDEN HEER DES ABSOLUTISMUS ZUR ALLGEMEINEN WEHRPLICHT (1789-1814). Vol. 2. HANDBUCH ZUR DEUTSCHEN MILITAERGESCHICHTE. Frankfurt: Bernard & Graefe, 1964.

410. Woinovich, Emil v. KAEMPFE IM SUEDEN FRANKREICHS 1814. Vol. 6. Austria-Hungary. Kriegsarchiv. 1813-1815. OESTERREICH IN DEN BEFREIUNGSKRIEGEN. Vienna: Seidel, 1913.

411. Woinovich, Emil von. KAEMPFE IN DER LIKA, IN KROATIEN UND DALMATIEN. Vol. 6. Edited by Emil v. Woinovich and Alois Veltzé. DAS KRIEGSJAHR 1809 IN EINZELDARSTELLUNGEN. Vienna: C.W. Stern, 1906.

412. Woinovich, Emil von. KULM, HANAU, LEIPZIG, 1813. Vol. 3. Austria-Hungary. Kriegsarchiv. 1813-1815. OESTERREICH IN DEN BEFREIUNGSKRIEGEN. Vienna: Seidel, 1911.

413. Wolfsgruber, Cölestin. FRANZ I. KAISER VON OESTERREICH. Vienna: W. Braumüller, 1899. 2 vols.

414. Worndle von Adelsfried, Heinrich. KRIEGSEREIGNISE IN KIRCHDORF UND UMGEBUNG AUS DEN TAGEN DER TIROLER FREIHEITSKAMPFE: DENKSCHRIFT ZUR ENTHUELLUNGSFEIER DES "WINTERSTELLER-DENKMALES" IN KIRCHDORF (TIROL) MIT BENUETZUNG EIG ENHANDIE ER AUFZEICHNUNGEN DES KIRCHDORFER VIERTELSCHREIBERS LEONHARD MILLINGER; IM AUFTRAGE DES DENKMAL-COMITE'S BEARBEITET UND HERAUSGEGEBEN VON HEINRICH V. WORNDLE. Innsbruck: Selbstverlag des Wintersteller-Denkmal-Comite's, Druck Vereinsbuchdruckerei, 1901.

415. Wrede, Alphons, von. GESCHICHTE DER K.U.K. WEHRMACHT. DIE REGIMENTER, CORPS, BRANCHEN UND ANSTALTEN VON 1618 BIS ENDE DES XIX. JAHRHUNDERTS. Vienna: Seidel, 1898-1905. 5 vols.

416. Wurzbach, Constantin von.   BIOGRAPHISCHES LEXIKON DES
      KAISERTHUMS OESTERREICH.   Vienna: k.k.   Hof-und
      Staatsdruckerei, 1856-91. 60 vols.

417. Zach, Anton von. "Eine Denkschrift Zachs aus dem Jahre 1798."
      MITTEILUNGEN DES K.U.K. KRIEGSARCHIVS, Series 3, 2 (9103):
      165-95.

418. Zeissberg, Heinrich von.   ERZHERZOG CARL VON OESTERREICH.
      Vienna and Leipzig: W. Braumüller, 1895. 2 vols.

419. Zwiedineck-Südenhorst, Hans von.   ERZHERZOG JOHANN VON
      OESTERREICH IM FELDZUG VON 1809. Graz: Styria, 1892.

420. Zwiedineck-Südenhorst, Hans von. ZUR GESCHICHTE DES KRIEGES
      VON 1809 IN STEIERMARK. REGESTEN UND ACTENSTUECKE AUS DEM
      NACHLASSE DES ERZHERZOGS JOHANN. Graz: the author, 1892.

CHAPTER XI

FRANCE ON THE HOME FRONT (1800-1815)

Robert Holtman, Louisiana State University

The term "home front" is here interpreted as not being limited to France. Rather, this section deals with any area which was incorporated into France before or during the Napoleonic period, for such time as it was part of the French state. The reader will therefore find works on the Netherlands, Belgium, the Rhineland, and Italy--but not on satellite areas. There is no attempt in this essay to cite all the works in the bibliographical listing.

Napoleon was far too astute a military commander not to realize the importance of the home front. Indeed, in a switch from the usual perspective, one may look upon him primarily as the statesman and secondarily as the soldier. The question is, what aspects of the home front are significant for military success? Among them are a stable government, an economic foundation, public-opinion support, education, ability of the government to finance its military activities, and the maintenance of order. One could argue that all these activities are designed merely to mold public opinion; but it is advisable to treat them as separate areas.

GENERAL HISTORIES

As a significant era often referred to by the term "watershed," the Napoleonic period is the subject of numerous over-all studies. Napoleon is furthermore the subject of multitudinous biographies, some of which are general histories parading under the guise of biographies. The problem, therefore, is one of selection. The criteria used for inclusion here are intrinsic merit, long-standing recognition, or a challenging interpretation.

Tulard (556) illustrates the last criterion, with the theme that Napoleon was a kind of savior. Prod'homme (461) includes significant source materials. Lucas-Dubreton (370) is good on institutions and cultural life. Lanfrey, in his unfinished history, is bitterly critical of Napoleon, whose legend he sought to destroy (307). For years, despite the kind of sources he used and his pro-English bias, Thompson (549) had the best biography of Napoleon in English. Andreas (6) presents a German view, and Manfred (378) a Russian one, in the Russian language. Villat (571) is useful especially for its guidance to further reading and study. Godechot (237) is the work of a man who probably knows more about Napoleon than any other person living in 1983. Becker (29) raises the question of Napoleon's impact, but Geyl (228) is far more provocative and insightful.

Older histories, even though they may be in new editions, often require several volumes. Madelin (374) sings Napoleon's praises to an even greater extent than does Thiers (542). The two works associated with the name of the Lavisse series (321, 322) are by experts who try to be objective. Also objective is Thibaudeau (537, 538), a one-time prefect. Aulard's (16) bias in favor of democracy does not defile his work. Sussel (532) excels in depicting the economic side of the period, including the introduction of new

agricultural products. Jaurès (290) naturally presents the socialist
interpretation of the Consulate and Empire.
Works of lesser dimensions have their special attributes.
Godechot et al. (238) is especially good on the Consulate and
pacification. Godechot (235) is remarkably fine. Friedrich (207)
offers a stimulating reconsideration of the basic ideas of Napoleon's
policy. Bruun (79) lives up to the high standards of the "Rise of
Modern Europe" series. Soboul (522, 523) is best in dealing with
institutions. He also arranged a colloquium (479) which proved to be
extremely valuable on economic, social, demographic, and
institutional aspects of the period. Mistler (401) has edited a very
fine two-volume work. Latreille (315) goes beyond France to consider
the development of the western world in this period. Hampson (260)
has a similar approach, whereas Bergeron (34) confines himself to
internal affairs. Andreas (7) lies in-between these two approaches.

BIBLIOGRAPHIES

In addition to the general bibliographical works cited in the
first chapter, Besterman (43) is useful. All the other bibliographies are less general, dealing almost entirely with France. Ever
since 1811 the French government has published weekly or biweekly a
BIBLIOGRAPHIE DE LA FRANCE (206), which theoretically includes all
the books published in France. Dollinger (158) lists works on the
history of French cities, and Stewart (529) works on France from 1715
to 1815 to be found in Cleveland.
All the other bibliographies are limited to an aspect of the
Napoleonic period. Tulard (555) has a critical bibliography of the
memoirs of the time, Monglond (404) has nine volumes on revolutionary
and Napoleonic France. Davois (143) limits himself to French works
published by 1908, and Boissonnade (54) to economic history of the
Revolution and Consulate. Zaghi (586) lists the books published from
1945 to 1965 on Napoleon and Italy.
Numerous histories of the time, or one aspect of it, have
outstanding bibliographies. General histories already listed which
contain such bibliographies are by Bruun (79), Godechot (235),
Lavisse (321)--whose Volume 4 has a good bibliography on the Hundred
Days--Madelin (375), and Villat (571). Four cited specialized works
with good bibliographies in their fields are by Anchel (4), Godechot
(236), Holtman (280), and Kobler (299). Works not previously cited
which include valuable bibliographies are the CAMBRIDGE MODERN
HISTORY (87), Gottschalk (243), and the even better Gershoy (227).
A more limited uncited study with a bibliography helpful for our
topic is by Fisher (199).

ARCHIVAL SOURCES

For a discussion of archives in general, see Chapter I. The
information in Godechot's L'EUROPE ET L'AMERIQUE A L'EPOQUE
NAPOLEONIENNE (235) and Villat (571) is so useful that the reader-
scholar is referred to them instead of being presented here with a
long list of archival citations. Both works tell what the various
archival series contain. Godechot also points out that the
statistics of various departments have been printed, as that was a
responsibility of each prefect. For the early part of the period,

series L31 10 and L31 14 in the Bibliothèque Nationale contain the responses of the prefects to inquests ordered by Lucien and Chaptal as ministers of the interior. The catalog of the library reveals that the most useful series are La36 on the dynasty, La37 on Napoleon's reign, and Lb43, 44, and 46 on the Consulate, Empire, and Hundred Days respectively. Gandilhon (215) has a helpful article in the REVUE HISTORIQUE on series M of the departmental archives dealing with general administration. One might also wish to consult the archives of the Legion of Honor.

The Archives Nationales contain several series of material helpful for Napoleon's home front. Series F deals with administration in general; especially valuable is F7, which contains the papers of the Ministry of Police. The procès-verbaux of the Tribunate are in series C, those of the Legislative Body and the Senate in CC. But the most important series is AF IV, the Secretariat of State. It contains ministerial reports, minutes of decrees--in fact, all the most important administrative matters.

PUBLISHED DOCUMENTS

High on the list of primary sources is the correspondence of Napoleon. In addition to the editions cited in Chapter I, we should note Vox's selection of six hundred work letters (574), Napoleon's correspondence with the minister of the interior during the Hundred Days (415), his letters found in the Daru archives (419), the correspondence of Joseph Fiévée (197) with Napoleon, and the letters of Cambacérès to Napoleon (86).

Palluel's volume (425) shows what Napoleon said on various topics in his correspondence, and Dansette (422) has put together Napoleon's political and social ideas, especially useful with reference to his thoughts on empire. Tulard (423) has performed a similar function for Napoleon's proclamations, orders of the day, and Grand Army bulletins, all of them designed to mold public opinion. Especially valuable is Volume 3 of this five-volume work (421) dealing with Napoleon as a reformer and in the Council of State. Barral (420) has compiled his political messages and speeches.

The MONITEUR (223) was not only the official newspaper of the Napoleonic period, but one which Napoleon closely supervised and for much of whose content he took the initiative. The appropriate volumes of the ARCHIVES PARLEMENTAIRES (9) reveal the government's point of view in the debates on a wide variety of issues. Three volumes by Buchez and Roux (80) likewise include legislative debates. We have official versions of the various codes (112-116), as well as various general collections (81, 167, 183, 184, 362) of the laws enacted under Napoleon, and one (470) on the tariff.

The daily police bulletins sent to Napoleon (271, 272) under Fouché have been published by d'Hauterive. We also have the procès-verbaux of the Tribunate (460), Legislative Body (459), and the Council of State (364). Napoleon's participation in the deliberations of the Council of State (277, 433) have been re-edited more recently in two complementary volumes (65, 380).

The instructions and circulars of the ministries of justice (471) and the interior (469) have been officially collected. The letters of Tournon (552), prefect of Rome, reveal how the governmental organization was utilized. Potiquet (452) has compiled the regulations dealing with bridges and roads.

MEMOIRS, JOURNALS AND EYEWITNESS ACCOUNTS

The Napoleonic period inspired people to write their memoirs--mainly, of course, to bask in the reflection of Napoleon or to play up their relationship with him. Not all of these by any means dealt with the home front, but many did; some of them have already been mentioned in connection with the topics on which they contributed.

Count Beugnot (44) served as a prefect and councillor of state. The most valuable portion of the memoirs of Lucien Bonaparte (55, 288) deals with his term as minister of the interior. Chaptal (101) likewise served as minister of the interior. For reflections on the police we may turn to Dubois (165) as prefect of police and to the Duke of Rovigo (Savary), for a time minister of police (508). Baron Fain (191) served as Napoleon's personal secretary, as did Méneval (396). Gaudin (221) and Mollien (403) offer a first-hand view of finances. Miot de Melito (399), as a member of the Council of State, interested himself especially in the general police. Molé (402) at various times was a councillor of state, a prefect, and minister of justice. Pontécoulant (447) served as both a prefect and a senator. Réal (468) reveals how a prefect of police controlled the departmental press, and Roederer's journal and memoirs (492, 493) contain valuable information on his work as Director of Public Instruction. The memoirs of Count Thibaudeau (539) add to our knowledge of administration, and also of the legislature during the Hundred Days.

SPECIALIZED WORKS: GOVERNMENTAL ORGANIZATION

Napoleon intended the home front--which he strove to keep quiet and stable--to serve his military purposes. To achieve his intent, he utilized every possible organ of government, and created new governmental bodies as well.

Godechot (236) has by far the best general account of Napoleonic institutions; it covers all institutions, not merely the political, as had the work of Poullet (453) sixty years earlier and Blanc (50). A work encompassing a much longer period but limited to political institutions is that of Chevallier (110). Ellul (188) covers both a broad range and a long period. Bourdon (64) presents new documents and original ideas on the constitution of the Year VIII, and Radiguet (464) discusses the Additional Act. Aulard (20) indicates the topics to which the Provisional Consulate turned its attention. Volume 1 of Deslandres (155) is the most complete treatment of French constitutional history of the Napoleonic period. Edmond-Blanc (187) is critical of Napoleon's administrative institutions, as is Ponteil (448). Koechlin (300) discusses administrative and judicial competence.

The "Legislature" and Napoleon's legislative activity have both received attention. Collins (119) and Durand (172) discuss the parliaments and legislative procedure in general. Piétri (440) comes to much the same conclusion as Collins on the independence of the chambers--that it was greater than is generally assumed. Dutruch (182) studies the Tribunate and Thiry (548) the Senate. Rais (465) shows how conservative the chambers were in personnel. Massin (383) goes well beyond the legislative field in presenting the almanac of the period, while Brotonne (76) gives some background on the senators.

Although Sagnac said his book (501) dealt with civil legislation, it really is on the civil code, about which he has another two-volume work (499). Arnaud (11) traces the doctrinal origins of the code in the ideas of the authors. Two works show, respectively, the influence of Bourjon (381) and of Bonaparte (289) on the code, which Napoleon considered his most significant contribution. Arnaud (10), Brisset (74), and Ray (467) take up different aspects of the code. Brissaud (73) has written a history of French public law, and Viard (565) an excellent one on private law. Garaud's history of private law (216), stopping in 1804, shows that social inequalities still legally remained.

Two general works (181, 292) discuss the magistrature of France, and a useful older work (279) is a critical history of French judicial institutions. Bourdon's study of the judicial reform of the Year VIII (66) is an eminently important work. Festy (196) treats rural crimes, and Esmein (189) provides a history of criminal procedure. The criminal court at Reims is the object of Aron's scrutiny (12), and Morillot (407) deals with the Court of Cassation. Two works (360, 400) discuss the Court of Accounts, which Napoleon established. Closely related to the judiciary are the police (156, 270) and the question of individual liberty (370).

Durand has three studies on the Council of State (171, 173, 174)--the first is a fundamental work on the topic, and the last discusses its role during the Hundred Days. He also worked on the Council's auditors (170). Chaptal (98) analyzes the procès-verbaux of the departmental general councils. Departmental administration may also be studied by way of the prefects (473, 507) and their administration (176). Aulard (15) discusses the role of the prefects in the centralization of government.

Napoleon was naturally concerned with having a well-run army (63), with ample manpower and financial support. The first volume of Morvan's study of the soldiers (408) may be supplemented with studies on conscription (137, 561, 562). Carrot (92) treats the legal and regulatory history of the national guard. Costaz (124) considers many aspects of the French economy. Petot (438) treats the administration of roads and bridges, and Locré (363) the legislation on the mines.

Of all the individuals who helped Napoleon formulate and establish his government, Second Consul (later Archchancellor) Cambacérès has probably received the most extensive treatment (163, 428, 543, 563)--including his work on the civil code. The best work on Carnot is the second volume of Reinhard's biography (474). Napoleon's policemen--Desmarest (304) and especially Fouché (118, 372, 373)--have attracted special attention. So have several prefects: Frochot (431), with special reference to prefectural administration; Beugnot (144); Jean de Bry (442); and Tournon (409), who was also an auditor at the Council of State. Azuni, Italian by birth but French by nationality, became both a judge and a legislator (37). The treasurer Gaudin is also the topic of a study (312).

SPECIALIZED WORKS: LOCAL HISTORY

Although there is ample room--and perhaps a crying need--for
studies of localities (as a later section will mention in more
detail), considerable work has been done in this field. Monnet (405)
discusses communal and departmental administrations throughout the
country. Among the specific localities within France which have
received historical treatment are Alsace (136, 351--the latter
stressing the economic side--357), the Bouches-du-Rhône for the
evolution of Napoleon's administrative system (503), Brittany (31,
330-332), Corsica (458--which shows the significant part Napoleon
played in Frenchifying it), the Côtes-du-Nord (180) and the Côte-d'Or
(564) for their administrations, a statistical study of the Escaut
(151), and Franche-Comté (72) for its nobility. Still others were
the general council of Haute-Vienne (348), a good study of the
Meurthe (546), the Saône-et-Loire (356)--the general council of it
and its administrators (519)--the first prefect of the Var (3) and
the Hundred Days there (2), and peasant conditions in Vienne (36).
Areas incorporated into France after 1789 which have received study
include Belgium (150, 308) with special works devoted to Antwerp
(198) and Wallonia (138); the Hanseatic towns (515) and the Rhineland
(502); Holland as governed by Lebrun (305); and the political changes
and economic development of Italy (90), supporting the thesis that
French control promoted capitalism there, as evidenced in the textile
industry and the sale of national property (208, 570). Genoa (58)
and Rome (376, 521) have received separate treatment. Courvoisier's
study (126) on Neuchâtel shows the exploitation of it for monetary
gain by Napoleon. Paris naturally has come in for special treatment
as the center of French life. For its institutions and
administration see 154, 231, 558; more general approaches include
Guerrini, Lanzac de Laborie, and Poisson (251, 309, 445), the last on
its transformation.

SPECIALIZED WORKS: THE HUNDRED DAYS

The Hundred Days was the kind of dramatic episode which attracts
the attention of historians as well as other types of writers. Some
books attempt to give a complete picture of the period from March to
June of 1815. Houssaye (281), very pro-Napoleon, has written the
classic account. Other works covering all aspects of the time
include Capefigue (89), Thiry (544), Sieburg (517), Saunders (506),
and Hubert (282). Le Gallo (337) deals with internal affairs and is
therefore very valuable, and Cubberly (130) is concerned with the
role of Fouché. One of the more interesting features of the time is
Napoleon's calling for help from the liberal Benjamin Constant (23),
who has written memoirs in the form of letters (123) on the Hundred
Days. An outstanding recent work is that of Bluche (52) on the
plebiscite of 1815.

SPECIALIZED WORKS: ECONOMIC DEVELOPMENT

The second volume of Sée's economic history of France (512)
includes the Napoleonic period, as does the third volume of Braudel
and Labrousse's economic and social history of France (71), which
stresses the arrival of the industrial age, social stability, and

economic revival. Roques (494) considers only Nice and limits his
study to the Napoleonic period.

At the base of any advanced economy lies the matter of money and
credit. Marion (379) and Priouret (457) provide a general history of
French finances, and Menais (395) discusses Napoleon's monetary
policy. The best study, a bit hostile, of the financial
reorganization under the Consulate is provided by Stourm (531).
Gaudin (221) treats the history of French finances in the period from
a personal point of view. The very important question of the
cadastre (land survey) and the land tax is the topic of a study by
Dreux (162). Cottez (125) discusses the octroi (town toll) at Lyon,
and Trescaze (553) shows what the direct taxes brought in. One of
Napoleon's lasting reforms was establishment of a much-needed Bank of
France (45, 142, 466); Szramkiewicz (533) shows the backgrounds of
its directors and inspectors. A rather unscrupulous financier--and
war profiteer--of the time was Ouvrard (432, 584), alternately in and
out of favor with Napoleon.

Always the pragmatist, Napoleon forsook some of his earlier
tenets in order to wage economic warfare against the British. The
Continental System helped spur French industry (384, 491), but it
also had other, less favorable, effects (42). Heckscher (273),
Jouvenel (295), and Crouzet (129) have all written general accounts
of the Continental System, though with different emphases, and Melvin
has studied Napoleon's system of controlling commerce during the
years of the System (394).

A general history of French commerce may be found in Levasseur
(353). Bonnet (56) stresses the growing importance of commerce in
French life starting then. Trade in silks at Lyon (301) suffered
under Napoleon. His most important innovation both to promote and to
regulate commerce was the establishment of chambers of commerce in
leading cities. Pariset (429) discusses that of Lyon, and Fournier
that of Marseilles (205). Chabert (95) shows that prices kept rising
because of general prosperity, and Rémond (476) examines the price of
merchant transport.

The industry stimulated by the Napoleonic regime, which aimed to
supply its allies as well as France, began to rely on machines (25).
Napoleon's policy toward this new industry is discussed by
Darmstädter (135). Herrenschmidt (275) and Gille (229) take up the
General Council of Manufactures, which Napoleon established in 1810.
Viennet (568) deals with Napoleon's industrial policy in the
depression of that year and the next. Banking, though less important
than later in promoting industry, played a significant role, as
Cameron (88) and Bergeron (33) show. Truly, France was developing
large-scale industry. Contemporaries such as Chaptal (99) recognized
that fact. Fohlen (201) speaks of the birth of an industrial
civilization, and Léon (344) of big industry in Dauphiné. Ternaux
received credit for the first industrial integration in France (366).
Other important industrialists of the time included Dufaud (550), who
proposed substituting coal for charcoal--coal was discovered and used
in the Gard (498) and the Pas-de-Calais (575)-- and Bauwens (333).
With the growth of mechanization, technical training and proficiency
received more attention from contemporaries (100, 518).

Levasseur (352), Louis (368), and Bruhat (77) each has a history
of the French working class or classes. Napoleon did not achieve his

goal of their staying in one locality, and the prefects had to report
on their migrations (387).

Basically it was agriculture rather than industry which led to
Napoleon's confidence that he would be victorious in economic warfare
with Britain. Festy (195) gives us the best-rounded picture of that
agriculture under the Consulate. Napoleon's rural code was designed
to promote agriculture (388) and the propertied classes. Vigier
(569) considers the reallocation of land in the Alpine region. But
there was nonetheless a famine in 1812 (320) and a depression in
1805, whose social results in the Meurthe are discussed by Lacoste
(303). There were also attempts to develop and regulate forestry
(244, 367).

SPECIALIZED WORKS: SOCIAL HISTORY

Napoleon had two great interests in the social realm: to
maintain stability, and to win support by aiding various classes and
groups. The former is demonstrated by Hanotaux (262) and Stenger
(528)--each of whose volumes considers a limited number of topics.
Lepointe (346) presents a more general history of social
developments. Napoleon won public support, after an initial setback,
when he established the Legion of Honor--see Bonneville (57),
Delarbre (148), and Soulajon (526)--and a new nobility of ability for
the Empire. Tulard (558) has the outstanding work on the latter.

The study of Napoleon's social work with the most inclusive
title was sponsored by the Legion of Honor (168), with Dunan as the
major contributor. But the most inclusive work from the standpoint
of substance is that of Ponteil (449). In 1813 Napoleon ventured a
step towards what has been called "social security" and this is noted
by Troclet (554). Contemporary accounts of aspects of his social
work are those by Husson (285, 286). Imbert (287) in the mid-1950s
discussed hospitals, and Roques (495) public health at Nice. Woloch
(585) shows what Napoleon did for veterans, which historians had
tended to overlook.

SPECIALIZED WORKS: RELIGION

Napoleon had to deal with four major religious groupings: Roman
Catholics, by far the largest; Protestants; the followers of a
Revolutionary cult, in all probability Theophilanthropy; and the
Jews. Although it is not a religion, the Masonic order may
conveniently be considered part of a religious grouping.

Napoleon's most noteworthy contribution was the Concordat of
1801. The best general approach to it is Walsh (576), but Boulay de
la Meurthe (59, 60) has done the most extensive work on it. Séché
(511) deals with its origins, as do Sevestre (516), Mathieu (385),
and Joly (294). Baissac (24) includes in his study the Organic
Articles, a direct outgrowth of the Concordat. For a similar
concordat for the Cisalpine Republic, see Theiner (536). Gabriele
(210) tends to slight the gains of the Papacy by the Concordat. We
have the writings of Portalis (451), who played a very active role in
the negotiation for France, and a study of the papal secretary of
state by Crétineau-Joly (127). For studies on the application of the
Concordat in various localities, one may turn to Douarec (160), Mouly
(410)--whose work is based on excellent research--Mège (390),

Lévy-Schneider (354), and Leflon (335). Ledré's studies of the
archbishop of Rouen (327, 328) contribute significantly to an
understanding of the clergy under the Concordat. Napoleon realized
from the start that there would be opposition to the Concordat;
Chauvigny (108) treats the resistance based on general grounds, and
Latreille (318) that based on religion.

For a Catholic country, the Free Masons played a large role,
understandable only in light of the history of France in the
eighteenth century. The topic has elicited a number of recent books.
Bernardin (38), Ligou (359), and Palou (427) treat the over-all
organization in France. Dotzauer (159) and Bouton (69) study it in
specific localities. Napoleon's efforts to control the Free Masons
are the main concern of Fleischmann (200).

The Napoleonic era is part of the time-period dealt with by
Poland (446) and Lods (365), and a major part of the three volumes by
Robert (486-488), who discusses the time from 1800 to 1830 with
respect to French Protestantism. The Consulate and Empire saw a
considerable Protestant renewal, or reawakening, which Léonard (345),
Maury (389), and a book of essays (278) deal with. Durand (175)
limits himself more to the period, and Lucius (371) looks at
Bonaparte's relationship to the Protestant churches in France.

Historians differ widely on whether Napoleon was a benefactor
of, or was detrimental to, the Jews. Anchel (5) was at first very
critical of Napoleon's policy, but later (4) he moderated his views.
Blumenkranz and Soboul organized a colloquium on the Jews (525) and
one on the Great Sanhedrin (53), with the two reaching rather
contrary conclusions. More general is the history of Dubnov (164).
Piétri (441) favors the assimilation effected by Napoleon. Kobler
(299), Lémann (341), and Lemoine (342) all limit themselves to
Napoleon's relations with the Jews, as does the perspicacious article
(500) by Sagnac. Of two older works, one by Halphen (258) provides
documentation, and the other, by Fauchille (192), is based on
documents which had not previously been published.

Surprisingly, Theophilanthropy has elicited only one rather old
volume by Mathiez (386). Unsurprisingly, one aspect or another of
the Catholic religion has inspired about half of all the writings on
religion under Napoleon. Among the more general works are those of
Daniel-Rops (133)--who is interested in defending the church--
Dansette (134), Latreille (314), Latreille et al. (317) which has
some good chapters on the Napoleonic period, Leflon (334), and
Mourret (411). Constant (122) has written a useful synthesis just
for the Napoleonic period, as have Sloane (520), Chamard (97), Jette
(293), La Gorce (306), and Thiry (545). Grente (249) stops with the
Concordat, as does Pressensé (455). Several works, such as Leflon
(336), Delacroix (145, 146), and Boulay de la Meurthe (61) treat the
reorganization of the church after the Concordat. Rabaut-Dupuis
(463) has documents on and deals with Napoleon's attempt to unite all
the Christian denominations. Plongeron (444) deals in fine fashion
with the relationship of politics and theology during half a century,
and Perrod-Le Moyne (437) discusses Napoleon's attitude toward
religion. The most extensive treatment is the five-volume work of
Haussonville (264), each volume of which has "justifying pieces."

Several works treat specialized topics. Ricard (481) is
concerned with the national council of 1811. The religious orders

come in for treatment by Deries (152), Aulard (21), and Geoffroy de
Grandmaison (225) who also discusses Napoleon and the black cardinals
(226). The church in a localized area is the subject of work by
Latreille (319), Grégoire (248), Godel (239), Genevray (224),
Boussoulade (68), and Consalvi (121) for French Italy. Of these, the
most significant is Godel's work on the church in Grenoble.
     A combination of locality and individual activity is found in
the work of Plongeron (443); Michel (398) for Montpellier; Ledré
(329); and Le Coz (325, 326). Dousset (161) discusses Abbé de Pradt
as Napoleon's grand almoner.
     Several works concentrate on the relationship between Napoleon
and the Pope. Hales (256) is very biased in favor of the Papacy;
Melchior-Bonnet (393) and Welschinger (581) are more judicious in
approach. Latreille (316) deals with the embassy of Napoleon's
uncle, Cardinal Fesch, to Rome. Abbé Feret's memoirs (194) afford a
first-hand account of some of the relations. Bindel (48) shows the
importance Napoleon attached to support by the church. The same
author (47) used archival materials for his book on Napoleon's
bishops, and Grabinski (245) deals with the lower clergy. Gambasin
(214) shows how Napoleon modified the parish, and Latreille (313)
discusses the catechism.

SPECIALIZED WORKS: EDUCATION

     Since Napoleon wanted uniformity of instruction, it is only
natural that Grimaud (250) discovered a lack of freedom of teaching.
Napoleon's goals for education were to furnish the civilian officials
necessary for a smooth running of the government, and to provide the
army with officers. For this latter purpose he founded a short-lived
military school at Fontainebleau (483) and its successor at Saint-Cyr
(551).
     Aulard presents the best discussion of Napoleon's education
policy in general (17). Placed in charge of Napoleon's University,
the most important innovation in education, was Fontanes, whose
speeches have been published (203). We also have his correspondence
with Joubert (534)--who as a councillor was another important
educator connected with the University (535)--and a valuable study on
Fontanes by Wilson (583), which shows the extent to which he undercut
Napoleon's plans for the University. Rendu deals with the University
code (477) and the plan (478) for the University, while Schmidt
treats the 1811 reform of the University (509).
     Napoleon of course took steps with respect to education well
before the time of the University, most importantly with the law of
the Year X (102). The education yearbook (8) gives a valuable
insight into conditions at approximately that time, as does the work
of Uzureau (560) for Maine-et-Loire. More general accounts are those
by Guizot (255) and by Delfau (149), who concentrates on Napoleon's
personal role.
     The University directed all facets of education, but for study
purposes various historians have concentrated on more limited
aspects. Gréard (247) has edited the regulations on primary
education, which is also the concern of Gontard (240). Fontaine de
Resbecq discusses Catholic primary education (202) and Rigault (484)
the role of the Brothers of the Christian Schools. Chabot (96) and
Weill (578) are histories of secondary education. Limited to the

central schools in one locality or to one central school are the
works of Coirault (117), Spekkens (527), and Palmer (426). Beauchamp
has compiled the regulations on higher education (28), whose history
Liard (358) has written.

Specialized education was offered in a number of schools.
Napoleon was greatly interested in the normal schools (169, 241,
462), establishing the Higher Normal School at Paris. Technical
education also drew his attention. Neufchateau (424) thought
agriculture should be taught in the public schools. General accounts
of technical education are those of Artz (13) and Léon (343).
Prévost (456) discusses medical schools, and Euvrard (190) the School
of Arts and Crafts at Châlons-sur-Marne. At the summit of technical
education stood the Ecole polytechnique (84, 186), only five years
old when Napoleon came to power and therefore capable of development
and change. Napoleon's attitude to science, and its status under
him, is the topic of Barral (27). Cuvier presented a report to
Napoleon on the sciences (132) and later wrote a history of them
(131). On more limited topics, Herivel's work (274) includes a
discussion of the Academy of Sciences, and Crosland in his study of
the Society of Arcueil (128) reveals much about science education.

SPECIALIZED STUDIES: PUBLIC OPINION

Napoleon was unique in his day, and a forerunner of some later
rulers, in his attention to the role of morale on the home front.
Although there was rigid censorship, in the theater (257) and in
general (579), Napoleon did not content himself with trying merely to
keep civilians at home ignorant of new items--or such items as
historical allusions--he did not want them to know. Rather, his
major contribution in this area was the utilization of all the
resources at his command to bolster morale positively through the
press, the theater, the church, festivals, and music (Holtman, 280).

Among the artists, Napoleon especially favored the work of
Jacques Louis David (267) for propaganda purposes; Guizot (254) tells
us what was painted to glorify Napoleon. But Napoleon patronized the
arts in general (70). Two individuals who significantly helped
promote the arts were La Rochefoucault at the School of Arts and
Crafts (310) and Denon, the Director-General of Fine Arts (339, 340),
who was likewise responsible for the Louvre and the additions
Napoleon made to its collections (106). Three works treat generally
art and artists under Napoleon (32, 265, 311).

Charpentier (103) shows us how much Napoleon concerned himself
with the literary figures of his day, and Storost (530) includes his
attitude toward classical literature as well. Merlet (397) gives us
the most extensive account of French literature of the time, and
Jeanroy-Félix (291) is also comprehensive. Two works, Delalain (147)
and Chauvet (107), examine printing and bookselling under Napoleon.

The theater was very useful to Napoleon. It was a popular mode
of entertainment, and it could be used to influence the bulk of the
population which was illiterate. Especially popular were the
boulevard theaters, and Albert's study of them (1) is indispensable
for a study of the theater under Napoleon. Muret (413) offers a
general history of the theater. Lecomte (323) goes further by
listing the plays which were staged and showing how successful they
were. His other work (324), even more valuable, discusses Napoleon's

relations with the theater, as does Rosen (496), treating Napoleon as a theater-goer, patron, and critic. Despite the title of his work, Grant (246) deals mainly with the theater and the press.

It was the press that drew the major portion of Napoleon's attention in this area as it was by all odds the best medium for getting across his message and for building up morale and popular support for the army. Barère's memoirs (26) offer first-hand information on the press. Salmon (504) is a good starting point for considering the press under a dictator. Hatin (263), van Schoor (510), Avenel (22), and Cabanis (83) offer general histories of the newspapers of the time. Regaldo (472) extensively analyzes LA DECADE PHILOSOPHIQUE, and Capra (91) examines the themes treated in the Italian papers. Locré (361) offers the discussions of the Council of State on freedom of the press, and Le Poittevin (347) discusses that topic in general during the period. Ebbinghaus (185) treats Napoleon's early anti-British press campaign, and Périvier (434) exhaustively examines Napoleon's personal role in conducting press propaganda.

For the effect Napoleon achieved, there is no better source than the documents published by Aulard (18, 19) on public opinion in Paris. Rochechouart's memoirs (490) deal both with falsification and public opinion, and Pasquier's (430) are good on the effect of the propaganda. Poullet (454) writes on public opinion in Belgium when it was a part of France.

SPECIALIZED STUDIES: OPPOSITION

Despite his efforts to gratify the French and to shape public opinion, Napoleon was considerably less fortunate than the American dictator who said nothing ever happened in his realm that he did not want to happen. Numerous conspiracies were formed against him, the most famous being that of Cadoudal (39, 94, 392, 581). Ranking second in this regard was the work of General Malet (218, 259, 391). The earliest attempt on Napoleon's life, the attack as he was on the way to the opera, is discussed by Thiry (547) and Darrah (139). Others who plotted against Napoleon (219) included Moreau (217, 439), military men (252, 253), some of the police (283, 541), and royalists (41), who had secret agents of the Bourbons at Paris (475).

These last illustrate persistent opposition to Napoleon. Gaffarel discusses the literary, military, and republican opposition (211-213). Godechot (234) goes into the counter-revolution, and Hauterive the royalist counter-police in 1800 (268). Higgs traces ultraroyalism in Toulouse (276), and Gobineau's memoirs (233) reveal much about the royalist movement near the end of the Napoleonic period. An interesting facet is that Napoleon encouraged the counterrevolutionary outlook of two Paris newspapers (82). But he suppressed LA DECADE for its support of the ideologues (297). On this same issue of ideology, Destutt de Tracy split with Napoleon (296), and there was extensive liberal intellectual opposition (572). Other aspects include popular protests (111) and opposition in the assemblies (232).

The most violent large-scale opposition was found in the guerrilla warfare, the chouannerie, of the West, especially the Vendée. It included even the kidnapping of a senator (269). The chouannerie had begun long before Brumaire brought Bonaparte to power, and continued against him as the embodiment of the hated Revolution. For the early part of the Napoleonic period, we have the work of Roussel (497) and Chassin (104) on the pacification Napoleon was able to achieve. Dubreuil (166) and Chassin (105) cover the entire period, as do Gabory (209) and Montagnon (406). Muret's old work (412) is the most comprehensive, or at least most voluminous. Daudet (141) discusses the activity of the police with respect to the Chouans, Gosselin (242) takes on Norman chouannerie in the first five years of the Empire, and Lewis (355) treats the ups-and-downs of the counterrevolution in the Gard. Some of his opponents Napoleon punished with deportation (157).

FUTURE RESEARCH

Unfortunately, but understandably, the output of Napoleonic scholars has fallen even as their numbers have declined. That is not to say, however--even though the home front has received attention over a long span of time--that everything which merits study has already been done. What follows is, however, intended to be suggestive rather than complete, and not to include items which have not been treated mainly because they are of mountainous difficulty. Grateful acknowledgement is made of the assistance of Godechot's INSTITUTIONS (236).

As has already been made evident, there are numerous studies of localities; but while departments have fared reasonably well, there are not many studies of arrondissement or communal administration. These localities are so varied that, before a valid synthesis can be developed on many topics, far more local studies need to be undertaken. And the work of synthesis should then be forthcoming. Although Blanchard (51) discusses the roads in the western Alps, Napoleon's general attitude toward transportation remains a major topic not satisfactorily dealt with. There has not been any ensemble work on Napoleon's institutions--or even a general study of the chambers of commerce. Conscription in some localities has been studied, but still lacking is a general account of it.

Although Napoleon's administrative courts are the most neglected part of the judicial structure, the functioning of all the kinds of courts merits study. Closely allied with the courts is the question of whether Napoleon succeeded in reducing criminality. The application of the civil code has been neglected in many respects. The Legislative Body has been completely overlooked, and the Tribunate and Senate still need further inquiry. Finally on the governmental side, the various ministries should be looked into.

Many aspects of finance still require study: the general administration of them, taxes in the department framework, all the banks other than the Bank of France, and the sinking fund. The organization of economic activity is a wide-open field, starting with what Napoleon had in mind. How did the Council of Prud'hommes, as well as other councils--e.g., of Factories and Manufactures--operate? or the commercial courts? Utilizing some of the new methods of social history, one might well look at the social origins of local officials and member of local councils, or at the wealth of the Imperial nobility. Bougez-vous! There is work to do.

BIBLIOGRAPHY: THE HOME FRONT

1. Albert, Maurice. LES THEATRES DES BOULEVARDS, 1789-1848. Paris: Société française d'imprimerie et de librairie, 1902.

2. Alleaume, Charles. LES CENT JOURS DANS LE VAR. Draguignan: Raybaud et Grange, 1938.

3. Alleaume, Charles. JOSEPH FAUCHET, PREMIER PREFET DU VAR (1761-1834). Draguignan: Raybaud et Grange, 1940.

4. Anchel, Robert. LES JUIFS DE FRANCE. Paris: J.B. Janin, 1947.

5. Anchel, Robert. NAPOLEON ET LES JUIFS. Paris: Presses universitaires de France, 1928.

6. Andreas, Willy. NAPOLEON: ENTWICKLUNG, UMWELT, WIRKUNG. Constance: J. Thorbecke, 1962.

7. Andreas, Willy. DAS ZEITALTER NAPOLEONS UND DIE ERHEBUNG DER VOLKER. Heidelberg: Quelle & Meyer, 1955.

8. ANNUAIRE DE L'INSTRUCTION PUBLIQUE. Paris: n.p., ans X and XI. 2 vols.

9. ARCHIVES PARLEMENTAIRES. Edited by J. Mavidel and E. Laurent. Paris: Librairie administrative de P. Dupont, 1862-68. 2d series. Volumes 1-12 (an VIII-1814).

10. Arnaud, André Jean. ESSAI D'ANALYSE STRUCTURALE DU CODE CIVIL FRANCAIS, LE REGLE DU JEU DANS LA PAIX BOURGEOISE. Paris: Librairie générale de droit et de jurisprudence, 1973.

11. Arnaud, André Jean. LES ORIGINES DOCTRINALES DU CODE CIVIL FRANCAIS. Paris: Librairie générale de droit et de jurisprudence, 1969.

12. Aron, G. LE TRIBUNAL CORRECTIONEL DE REIMS SOUS LA REVOLUTION ET L'EMPIRE (1791-1811). Lille, 1910.

13. Artz, Frederick B. THE DEVELOPMENT OF TECHNICAL EDUCATION IN FRANCE, 1500-1815. Cleveland: Society for the History of Technology, 1967.

14. Aucoc, Léon. LE CONSEIL D'ETAT AVANT ET DEPUIS 1789. Paris: Imprimerie nationale, 1876.

15. Aulard, F.V.A. "La Centralisation napoléonienne, Les Préfets." ETUDES ET LECONS SUR LA REVOLUTION FRANCAISE. Paris: F. Alcan, 1913. Vol. 7, pp. 113-95.

16. Aulard, F.V.A. HISTOIRE POLITIQUE DE LA REVOLUTION FRANCAISE, 1789-1804. Paris: A. Colin, 1901.

17. Aulard, F.V.A. NAPOLEON Ier ET LE MONOPOLE UNIVERSITAIRE. Paris: A. Colin, 1911.

18. Aulard, F.V.A. PARIS SOUS LE CONSULAT: RECUEIL DE DOCUMENTS POUR L'HISTOIRE DE L'ESPRIT PUBLIC A PARIS. Paris: Cerf, 1903-9. 4 vols.

19. Aulard, F.V.A. PARIS SOUS LE PREMIER EMPIRE: RECUEIL DE DOCUMENTS POUR L'HISTOIRE DE L'ESPRIT PUBLIC A PARIS. Paris: Cerf, 1912-23. 3 vols.

20. Aulard, F.V.A. REGISTRE DES DELIBERATIONS DU CONSULAT PROVISOIRE. Paris: Société de l'histoire de la Révolution française, 1894.

21. Aulard, F.V.A. LA REVOLUTION FRANCAISE ET LES CONGREGATIONS. Paris: E. Cornély, 1903.

22. Avenel, Henri. HISTOIRE DE LA PRESSE FRANCAISE DEPUIS 1789 JUSQU'A NOS JOURS. Paris: Flammarion, 1900.

23. Baelen, Jean. BENJAMIN CONSTANT ET NAPOLEON. Paris: J. Peyronnet, 1965.

24. Baissac, Jules. LE CONCORDAT DE 1801 ET LES ARTICLES ORGANIQUES. Paris: Sandoz & Fischbacher, 1879.

25. Ballot, Charles. L'INTRODUCTION DU MACHINISME DANS L'INDUSTRIE FRANCAISE. Paris: F. Rieder, 1923.

26. Barère, Bertrand. MEMOIRS OF BERTRAND BARERE. Vols. 1 and 3. London: H.S. Nichols, 1896. 4 vols.

27. Barral, Georges. HISTOIRE DES SCIENCES SOUS NAPOLEON I. Paris: A. Savine, 1889.

28. Beauchamp, Alfred de, ed. RECUEIL DES LOIS ET REGLEMENTS SUR L'ENSEIGNEMENT SUPERIEUR. Paris: Imprimerie nationale, 1880. Vol. 1.

29. Becker, Beatrice. NAPOLEON BUONAPARTE, BUILDER OR WRECKER. Paris: Presse du Palais royal, 1967.

30. Bellanger, O.; J. Godechot; P. Guiral; and F. Terrou. HISTOIRE GENERALE DE LA PRESSE FRANCAISE. Vol. 1. DES ORIGINES A 1814. Paris: Presses universitaire de France, 1969.

31. Benaerts, Louis P. LE REGIME CONSULAIRE EN BRETAGNE. Paris: E. Champion, 1914.

32. Benoit, François. L'ART FRANCAIS SOUS LA REVOLUTION ET L'EMPIRE. Paris: L.H. May, 1897.

33. Bergeron, Louis. BANQUIERS, NEGOCIANTS, ET MANUFACTURIERS PARISIENS DU DIRECTOIRE A L'EMPIRE. Lille: Réproduction des thèses, Université Lille III, 1975. 2 vols.

34. Bergeron, Louis. L'EPISODE NAPOLEONIEN. Vol. 1. ASPECTS INTERIEURS, 1799-1815. Paris: Editions du Seuil, 1972.

35. Bergeron, Louis, and Guy Chaussinand-Nogaret. LES MASSES DE GRANIT: CENT MILLE NOTABLES DU PREMIER EMPIRE. Paris: Ecole des hautes études en sciences sociales, 1979.

36. Berland, Roger. LES CULTURES ET LA VIE PAYSANNE DANS LA VIENNE A L'EPOQUE NAPOLEONIENNE. Paris: P. Hartmann, 1937.

37. Berlinguer, Luigi. DOMENICO ALBERTO AZUNI, GIURISTA E POLITICO (1749-1827). Milan: Giuffrè, 1966.

38. Bernardin, Charles. NOTES POUR SERVIR A L'HISTOIRE DE LA FRANC-MACONNERIE A NANCY JUSQU'EN 1805, PRECEDEES D'UN PRECIS HISTORIQUE. Nancy: Bertrand, 1909.

39. Bertaud, Jean Paul. BONAPARTE ET LE DUC D'ENGHIEN, LE DUEL DES DEUX FRANCE. Paris: R. Laffont, 1972.

40. Bertaud, Jean Paul, comp. LE PREMIER EMPIRE, LEGS DE LA REVOLUTION. Paris: Presses universitaires de France, 1973.

41. Bertier de Sauvigny, Guillaume de. LE COMTE FERDINAND DE BERTIER (1782-1864) ET L'ENIGME DE LA CONGREGATION. Paris: Presses continentales, 1949.

42. Bertin, Fernand. LE BLOCUS CONTINENTAL, SES ORIGINES, SES EFFETS. Paris: L. Boyer, 1901.

43. Besterman, Theodore. A WORLD BIBLIOGRAPHY OF BIBLIOGRAPHIES. 4th ed. Lausanne: Societas Bibliographica, 1965-66. 5 vols.

44. Beugnot, Jacques Claude, comte. MEMOIRES DU COMTE BEUGNOT, ANCIEN MINISTRE (1783-1815). Paris: E. Dentu, 1886. 2 vols.

45. Bigo, Robert. LA CAISSE D'ESCOMPTE ET LES DEBUTS DE LA BANQUE DE FRANCE. Paris: Presses universitaires de France, 1927.

46. Bigo, Robert. LES BASES HISTORIQUES DE LA FINANCE MODERNE. Paris: A. Colin, 1933.

47. Bindel, Victor. LES EVEQUES DE BONAPARTE. Paris: Jouve, 1940.

48. Bindel, Victor. LE VATICAN A PARIS (1809-1814). Paris: Editions "Alsatia," 1942.

49. Biver, Marie Louise, comtesse. LE PARIS DE NAPOLEON. Paris: Plon, 1963.

50. Blanc, E. NAPOLEON, SES INSTITUTIONS, CIVILES ET ADMINISTRATIVES. Paris: 1880.

51. Blanchard, Marcel. LES ROUTES DES ALPES OCCIDENTALES A L'EPOQUE NAPOLEONIENNE. Grenoble: Allier, 1920.

52. Bluche, Frédéric. LE PLEBISCITE DES CENT JOURS (AVRIL-MAI 1815). Geneva: Droz, 1974.

53. Blumenkranz, Bernhard, and Albert Soboul, eds. LE GRAND SANHEDRIN DE NAPOLEON. Toulouse: E. Privat, 1979.

54. Boissonnade, Prosper. LES ETUDES RELATIVES A L'HISTOIRE ECONOMIQUE DE LA REVOLUTION FRANCAISE. Paris: Cerf, 1906.

55. Bonaparte, Lucien. MEMOIRS. London: Saunders and Otley, 1836.

56. Bonnet, Pierre. LE COMMERCIALISATION DE LA VIE FRANCAISE DU PREMIER EMPIRE A NOS JOURS. Paris: Plon, 1929.

57. Bonneville de Marsangy, Louis. LA LEGION D'HONNEUR, 1802-1900. 2d ed. Paris: H. Laurens, 1907.

58. Borel, Jean. GENES SOUS NAPOLEON. Paris: V. Attinger, 1929.

59. Boulay de la Meurthe, Alfred, comte. DOCUMENTS SUR LA NEGOCIATION DU CONCORDAT ET SUR LES AUTRES RAPPORTS DE LA FRANCE AVEC LE SAINT-SIEGE. Paris: E. Leroux, 1891-95. 6 vols.

60. Boulay de la Meurthe, Alfred, comte. HISTOIRE DE LA NEGOCIATION DU CONCORDAT DE 1801. Tours: A. Mame, 1920.

61. Boulay de la Meurthe, Alfred, comte. HISTOIRE DU RETABLISSEMENT DU CULTE EN FRANCE, 1802-1805. Tours: A. Mame, 1925.

62. Bouloiseau, Marc. ETUDE DE L'EMIGRATION ET DE LA VENTE DES BIENS DES EMIGRES (1792-1830). Paris: Imprimerie nationale, 1963.

63. Bourdon, Jean. L'ADMINISTRATION MILITAIRE DE NAPOLEON I. Paris, 1917.

64. Bourdon, Jean. LA CONSTITUTION DE L'AN VIII. Rodez: Carrère, 1941.

65. Bourdon, Jean. NAPOLEON AU CONSEIL D'ETAT. NOTES ET PROCES-VERBAUX INEDITS DE JEAN-GUILLAUME LOCRE, SECRETAIRE-GENERAL DU CONSEIL D'ETAT. Paris: Berger-Levrault, 1963.

66. Bourdon, Jean. LA REFORME JUDICIAIRE DE L'AN VIII. Rodez: Carrère, 1941. 2 vols.

67. Bourguignon, Jean. NAPOLEON BONAPARTE. Paris: Les Editions nationales, 1936. 2 vols.

68. Boussoulade, Jean, abbé. L'EGLISE DE PARIS DU 9 THERMIDOR AU CONCORDAT. Paris: Procure générale du clergé, [1950].

69. Bouton, André. LES FRANC-MACONS MANCEAUX ET LA REVOLUTION FRANCAISE, 1741-1815. Le Mans: Monnoyer, 1958.

70. Boyer, Ferdinand. LE MONDE DES ARTS EN ITALIE ET LA FRANCE DE LA REVOLUTION ET DE L'EMPIRE. Turin: Società editrice internazionale, 1970.

71. Braudel, Fernand, and E. Labrousse. HISTOIRE ECONOMIQUE ET SOCIALE DE LA FRANCE. Paris: Presses universitaires de France, 1977-80. 4 vols.

72. Brelot, Claude. LA NOBLESSE EN FRANCHE-COMTE DE 1789 A 1808. Paris: Belles Lettres, 1972.

73. Brissaud, Jean B. A HISTORY OF FRENCH PUBLIC LAW. Boston: Little, Brown, 1915.

74. Brisset, Jacqueline. L'ADOPTION DE LA COMMUNAUTE COMME REGIME LEGAL DANS LE CODE CIVIL. Paris: Presses universitaires de France, 1967.

75. Broc, Hervé de. LA VIE EN FRANCE SOUS LE PREMIER EMPIRE. Paris: Plon-Nourrit, 1895.

76. Brotonne, Léonce de. LES SENATEURS DU CONSULAT ET DE L'EMPIRE. Paris: H. Champion, 1895.

77. Bruhat, Jean. HISTOIRE DU MOUVEMENT OUVRIER FRANCAIS. Vol. 1. DES ORIGINES A LA REVOLTE DES CANUTS. Paris: Editions sociales, 1952.

78. Brunot, Ferdinand. HISTOIRE DE LA LANGUE FRANCAIS DES ORIGINES A 1900. Vol. 9. LA REVOLUTION ET L'EMPIRE. Paris: A. Colin, 1927.

79. Bruun, Geoffrey. EUROPE AND THE FRENCH IMPERIUM, 1799-1814. Revised ed. New York: Harper, 1957.

80. Buchez, Philippe J.B., and Pierre C. Roux. HISTOIRE PARLEMENTAIRE DE LA REVOLUTION FRANCAISE, OU JOURNAL DES ASSEMBLEES NATIONALES DEPUIS 1789 JUSQU'EN 1815. Paris: Paulin, 1834-38. Vols. 38-40.

81. BULLETIN DES LOIS. 3d series (an VIII-an XII), 9 vols. and supplement; 4th series (an XII-1814), 20 vols. Paris: Imprimerie nationale, 1816.

82. Cabanis, André. "Le Courant Contre-révolutionnaire sous le Consulat et l'Empire (dans LE JOURNAL DES DEBATS et LE MERCURE

DE FRANCE)." REVUE DES SCIENCES POLITIQUES (de Toulouse) 24 (1971): 5-87.

83. Cabanis, André. LA PRESSE SOUS LE CONSULAT ET L'EMPIRE (1799-1814). Paris: Société des études robespierristes, 1975.

84. Callot, Jean Pierre. HISTOIRE DE L'ECOLE POLYTECHNIQUE, SES LEGENDES, SA TRADITION, SA GLOIRE. Paris: Les Presses modernes, 1958.

85. Calonne d'Avesne, Albéric, baron. HISTOIRE DE LA VILLE D'AMIENS: AMIENS AU XIXe SIECLE. Amiens: Piteux, 1906.

86. Cambacérès, Jean Jacques. LETTRES INEDITES A NAPOLEON. Paris: Klincksieck, 1973. 2 vols.

87. THE CAMBRIDGE MODERN HISTORY. Vol. 9. NAPOLEON. Cambridge: The University Press, 1906.

88. Cameron, Rondo, et al. BANKING IN THE EARLY STAGES OF INDUSTRIALIZATION. New York: Oxford University Press, 1966.

89. Capefigue, Jean B. LES CENT JOURS. Paris: Langlois et Leclercq, 1841.

90. Capra, Carlo. L'ETA RIVOLUZIONARIA E NAPOLEONICA IN ITALIA, 1796-1815. Turin: Loescher, 1978.

91. Capra, Carlo. IL GIORNALISMO NELL'ETA RIVOLUZIONARIA E NAPOLEONICA. Bari: Laterza, 1976.

92. Carrot, Georges. LA GARDE NATIONALE, 1789-1871. Paris: G. Carrot, 1979.

93. Castelot, André. HISTOIRE DE NAPOLEON BONAPARTE. Paris: Edition du bi-centenaire, 1969. 10 vols.

94. Castries, René de La Croix, duc de. LA CONSPIRATION DE CADOUDAL. Paris: Del Duca, 1963.

95. Chabert, Alexandre. ESSAI SUR LES MOUVEMENTS DES PRIX ET DES REVENUS EN FRANCE DE 1798 A 1820. Paris: Librairie de Médicis, 1945-49. 2 vols.

96. Chabot, Charles, and S. Charlety. HISTOIRE DE L'ENSEIGNEMENT SECONDAIRE DANS LE RHONE (1789-1900). Paris: A. Picard, 1901.

97. Chamard, Dom F. LA REVOLUTION, LE CONCORDAT, ET LA LIBERTE RELIGIEUSE. Paris: Letouzey et Ainé, 1891.

98. Chaptal de Chanteloup, Jean A.C., comte. ANALYSE DES PROCES-VERBAUX DES CONSEILS GENERAUX DE DEPARTEMENT. Paris, 1801-2. 2 vols.

99. Chaptal de Chanteloup, Jean A.C., comte. DE L'INDUSTRIE FRANCAISE. Paris: A.A. Renouard, 1819. 2 vols.

100. Chaptal de Chanteloup, Jean A.C., comte. ESSAI SUR LE PERFECTIONNEMENT DES ARTS CHIMIQUES EN FRANCE. Paris: Deterville, 1800.

101. Chaptal de Chanteloup, Jean A.C., comte. MES SOUVENIRS SUR NAPOLEON. Paris: Plon-Nourrit, 1893.

102. Chaptal de Chanteloup, Jean A.C., comte. RAPPORT ET PROJET DE LOI SUR L'INSTRUCTION PUBLIQUE. Paris: Crapelet, Chez Deterville, an IX.

103. Charpentier, John. NAPOLEON ET LES HOMMES DE LETTRES DE SON TEMPS. Paris: Mercure de France, 1935.

104. Chassin, Charles L. ETUDES DOCUMENTAIRES SUR LA REVOLUTION FRANCAISE. LES PACIFICATIONS DE L'OUEST 1794-1801. Paris: Dupont, 1896-99. Vol. 3.

105. Chassin, Charles L. ETUDES DOCUMENTAIRES SUR LA VENDEE ET LA CHOUANNERIE. Paris: Dupont, 1900.

106. Chatelain, Jean. DOMINIQUE VIVANT DENON ET LE LOUVRE DE NAPOLEON. Paris: Perrin, 1973.

107. Chauvet, Paul. LES OUVRIERS DU LIVRE EN FRANCE, DE 1789 A LA CONSTITUTION DE LA FEDERATION DU LIVRE. Paris: Librairie M. Rivière, 1956.

108. Chauvigny, René de. LA RESISTANCE AU CONCORDAT DE 1801. Paris: Plon-Nourrit, 1921.

109. Chavanon, Jules, and G. Saint-Ives. LE PAS-DE-CALAIS DE 1800 A 1810. Paris: A. Picard, 1907.

110. Chevallier, Jean J. HISTOIRE DES INSTITUTIONS POLITIQUES DE 1789 A NOS JOURS. Paris: Dalloz, 1952.

111. Cobb, Richard. THE POLICE AND THE PEOPLE: FRENCH POPULAR PROTEST, 1789-1820. Oxford: Clarendon Press, 1970.

112. CODE CIVIL DES FRANCAIS. Paris: Imprimerie nationale, 1804.

113. CODE DE COMMERCE. Paris: Imprimerie impériale, 1807.

114. CODE D'INSTRUCTION CRIMINELLE. Paris: Imprimerie nationale, 1810.

115. CODE DE PROCEDURE CIVIL. Paris: Imprimerie impériale, 1806.

116. CODE PENAL. Paris: Imprimerie impériale, 1810.

117. Coirault, Gaston. LES ECOLES CENTRALES DANS LE CENTRE-OUEST, C'EST-A-DIRE DANS LE RESSORT DE L'ACADEMIE DE POITIERS, AN IV A AN XII. Tours: Arrault, 1940.

118. Cole, Hubert. FOUCHE, THE UNPRINCIPLED PATRIOT. London: Eyre & Spottiswoode, 1971.

119. Collins, Irene. NAPOLEON AND HIS PARLIAMENTS, 1800-1815. New York: St. Martin, 1979.

120. Connelly, Owen. THE EPOCH OF NAPOLEON. Huntington, N.Y.: Holt, Rinehart & Winston, 1978.

121. Consalvi, Ercole, cardinal. MEMOIRES. Edited. by J. Crêtineau-Joly. Paris: Plon, 1864. 2 vols.

122. Constant, Gustave L. L'EGLISE DE FRANCE SOUS LE CONSULAT ET L'EMPIRE, 1800-1814. Paris: Gabalda, 1928.

123. Constant de Rebecque, Henri Benjamin. MEMOIRES SUR LES CENT JOURS EN FORME DE LETTRES. Paris: Béchet, 1820.

124. Costaz, Claude A. HISTOIRE DE L'ADMINISTRATION, EN FRANCE, DE L'AGRICULTURE, DES ARTS UTILES, DU COMMERCE, DES MANUFACTURES, DES SUBSISTANCES, DES MINES ET DES USINES. Paris: Mme. Huzard, 1832. 2 vols.

125. Cottez, André. UN FERMIER GENERAL SOUS LA REVOLUTION ET L'EMPIRE: L'OCTROI DE LYON (AN VIII-1807). Paris: Recueil Sirey, 1938.

126. Courvoisier, Jean. LE MARECHAL BERTHIER ET SA PRINCIPAUTE DE NEUCHATEL, 1806-1814. Neuchâtel: Baconnière, 1959.

127. Crêtineau-Joly, Jacques. BONAPARTE, LE CONCORDAT DE 1801, ET LE CARDINAL CONSALVI. Paris: Plon, 1869.

128. Crosland, Maurice. THE SOCIETY OF ARCUEIL: A VIEW OF FRENCH SCIENCE AT THE TIME OF NAPOLEON I. London: Heinemann, 1967.

129. Crouzet, François. L'EMPIRE BRITANNIQUE ET LE BLOCUS CONTINENTAL (1806-1813). Paris: Presses universitaires de France, 1958. 2 vols.

130. Cubberly, Ray E. THE ROLE OF FOUCHE DURING THE HUNDRED DAYS. Madison: State Historical Society of Wisconsin, 1969.

131. Cuvier, Georges L., baron. HISTOIRE DES PROGRES DES SCIENCES NATURELLES, DEPUIS 1789 JUSQU'A CE JOUR. Paris: Baudoin, 1826-28. 4 vols.

132. Cuvier, Georges L., baron. RAPPORT HISTORIQUE SUR LES PROGRES DES SCIENCES NATURELLES DEPUIS 1789, ET SUR LEUR ETAT ACTUEL, PRESENTE A SA MAJESTE L'EMPEREUR. Paris: Imprimerie impériale, 1810.

133. Daniel-Rops, Henry. HISTOIRE DE L'EGLISE DU CHRIST. Vol. 6.
      L'ELGISE DES REVOLUTIONS. Paris: A. Fayard, 1960.

134. Dansette, Adrien.   HISTOIRE   RELIGIEUSE   DE   LA   FRANCE
      CONTEMPORAINE. Vol. 1. DE LA REVOLUTION A LA IIIe REPUBLIQUE.
      Paris: Flammarion, 1948.

135. Darmstädter, Paul. "Studien zur Napoleonischen Wirtschafts-
      politik." VIERTELJAHRSCHRIFT FUER SOCIAL-UND WIRTSCHAFTS-
      GESCHICHTE 2 (1904): 559-615; 3 (1905): 112-41.

136. Darmstädter, Paul. "Die Verwaltung des Unter-Elsass [Basrhin]
      unter Napoleon I." ZEITSCHRIFT FUER DIE GESCHICHTE DES
      OBERRHEINS   18 (1903): 283-330, 538-63; 19 (1904): 122-47,
      384-409, 631-72.

137. Darquenne, Roger. LA CONSCRIPTION DANS LE DEPARTEMENT DE
      JEMAPPES (1798-1813). Mons: Cercle archéologique de Mons,
      1970.

138. Darquenne, Roger. LES REVOLUTIONS ET L'EMPIRE EN WALLONIE
      (1780-1815). Brussels: Commission historique de la Fondation
      Charles Plisnier, 1974.

139. Darrah, David. CONSPIRACY IN PARIS; THE STRANGE CAREER OF
      JOSEPH PICOT DE LIMOELAN ... AND THE GUNPOWDER PLOT AGAINST
      NAPOLEON ON 3 NIVOSE, YEAR IX (DECEMBER 24, 1800). New York:
      Exposition Press, 1953.

140. Daudet, Ernest. HISTOIRE DE L'EMIGRATION. Paris: Librairie
      illustrée, 1866-1905. 3 vols.

141. Daudet, Ernest. LA POLICE ET LES CHOUANS SOUS LE CONSULAT ET
      L'EMPIRE, 1800-1815. 2d ed. Paris: Plon-Nourrit, 1895.

142. Dauphin-Meunier, Achille.   LA BANQUE DE FRANCE.   Paris:
      Gallimard, 1936.

143. Davois, Gustav. BIBLIOGRAPHIE NAPOLEONIENNE FRANCAISE JUSQU'EN
      1908. Paris: Edition bibliographique, 1909-11. 3 vols.

144. Dejean, Etienne. UN PREFET DU CONSULAT: JEAN-CLAUDE BEUGNOT.
      Paris: Plon-Nourrit, 1907.

145. Delacroix, Simon. DOCUMENTS SUR LA REORGANISATION DE L'EGLISE
      DE FRANCE APRES LA REVOLUTION (1801-1809). Paris: Faculté
      des lettres, 1957.

146. Delacroix, Simon. LA REORGANISATION DE L'EGLISE DE FRANCE
      (1801-1809). Paris: Vitrail, 1962.

147. Delalain, Paul A. L'IMPRIMERIE ET LA LIBRAIRIE A PARIS DE 1789
      A 1813. Paris: Delalain, 1900.

148. Delarbre, Jules. LA LEGION D'HONNEUR. Paris: Baudoin, 1887.

149. Delfau, Albert. NAPOLEON Ier ET L'INSTRUCTION PUBLIQUE. Paris: Fontemoing, 1902.

150. Delplace, Louis. LA BELGIQUE SOUS LA DOMINATION FRANCAISE. Louvain: J.B. Istas, 1896. 2 vols.

151. Deprez, Paul. MEMOIRE STATISTIQUE DU DEPARTEMENT DE L'ESCAUT PAR M. FAIPOULT, PREFET DE CE DEPARTEMENT. Ghent: Oostvlaams verbond van de kiringen voor geschiedenis, 1960.

152. Deries, Léon. LES CONGREGATIONS RELIGIEUSES AU TEMPS DE NAPOLEON Ier. Paris: Alcan, 1929.

153. Descadeillas, René. RENNES ET SES DERNIERS SEIGNEURS, 1730-1820. Toulouse: Privat, 1964.

154. Des Cilleuls, Alfred. HISTOIRE DE L'ADMINISTRATION PARISIENNE. Paris: Champion, 1900. Vol. 1.

155. Deslandres, Maurice Ch. HISTOIRE CONSTITUTIONELLE DE LA FRANCE DE 1789 A 1870. Paris: A. Colin, 1932. Vol. 1.

156. Desmarest, Pierre M. QUINZE ANS DE HAUTE POLICE SOUS LE CONSULAT ET L'EMPIRE. Paris: Garnier, 1900.

157. Destrem, Jean. LES DEPORTATIONS DU CONSULAT ET DE L'EMPIRE. Paris: Jeanmaire, 1885.

158. Dollinger, Philippe, and P. Wolff. BIBLIOGRAPHIE D'HISTOIRE DES VILLES DE FRANCE. Paris: Klincksieck, 1967.

159. Dotzauer, Winfried. FREIMAURER GESELLSCHAFTEN AUF DEM LINKEN RHEINUFER, VOM AUSGANG DES ANCIEN REGIME BIS ZUM ENDE DER NAPOLEONISCHEN HERRSCHAFT. Wiesbaden: Franz Steiner Verlag, 1977.

160. Douarec, F. Le. LE CONCORDAT DANS UN DIOCESE DE L'OUEST. MGR. CAFARELLI ET LE PREFET BOULLE. Paris: Editions Alsatia, 1958.

161. Dousset, Emile. L'ABBE DE PRADT, GRAND AUMONIER DE NAPOLEON. Paris: Nouvelles Editions latines, 1959.

162. Dreux, Th. LE CADASTRE ET L'IMPOT FONCIER. Paris: Librairie de l'enseignement technique, 1933.

163. Dubédat, Jean B. CAMBACERES ET LA PART PRISE PAR LE SECOND CONSUL AUX TRAVAUX PREPARATOIRES DU CODE NAPOLEON. Toulouse, 1858.

164. Dubnov, Semen M. HISTOIRE MODERNE DU PEUPLE JUIF. Paris: Payot, 1933. Vol. 1.

165. Dubois, Paul F. SOUVENIRS. Paris, 1902.

166. Dubreuil, Léon. HISTOIRE DES INSURRECTIONS DE L'OUEST. Paris:
      Bieder, 1930. Vol. 2.

167. Duguit, Léon, and H. Monnier. LES CONSTITUTIONS ET LES
      PRINCIPALES LOIS POLITIQUES DE LA FRANCE DEPUIS 1789. 6th ed.
      Paris: Librairie générale de droit et de jurisprudence, 1943.

168. Dunan, Marcel, et al. L'OEUVRE SOCIALE ET HUMAINE DE NAPLEON.
      Brussels: Editions Brepols, 1958.

169. Dupuy, Paul M. L'ECOLE NORMALE (1810-1883). Paris: Cerf,
      1884.

170. Durand, Charles. LES AUDITEURS DU CONSEIL D'ETAT DE 1803 A
      1815. Aix-en-Provence: La Pensée universitaire, 1958.

171. Durand, Charles. ETUDES SUR LE CONSEIL D'ETAT NAPOLEONIEN.
      Paris: Presses universitaires de France, 1949.

172. Durand, Charles. L'EXERCICE DE LA FONCTION LEGISLATIVE DE 1800
      A 1814. Aix-en-Provence: Imprimerie des Croix provençales,
      1955.

173. Durand, Charles. LA FIN DU CONSEIL D'ETAT NAPOLEONIEN.
      Aix-en-Provence, 1959.

174. Durand, Charles. LE FONCTIONNEMENT DU CONSEIL D'ETAT
      NAPOLEONIEN. Gap: Imprimerie Louis-Jean, 1954.

175. Durand, Charles. HISTOIRE DU PROTESTANTISME FRANCAIS PENDANT
      LA REVOLUTION ET L'EMPIRE. Paris: Fischbacher, 1902.

176. Durand, Charles. QUELQUES ASPECTS DE L'ADMINISTRATION
      PREFECTORALE SOUS LE CONSULAT ET L'EMPIRE, 1800-1815.
      Aix-en-Provence, 1962.

177. Durand, Charles. LES RAPPORTS ENTRE LA LOI ET LE REGLEMENT
      GOUVERNEMENTAL, DE L'AN IV A 1814. Aix-en-Provence: Presses
      universitaires d'Aix-Marseille, 1977.

178. Durand, Charles. LE REGIME DE L'ACTIVITE GOUVERNEMENTALE
      PENDANT LES CAMPAGNES DE NAPOLEON. Aix-en-Provence: La Pensée
      universitaire, 1957. [Extract from No. 49 of ANNALES DE LA
      FACULTE DE DROIT D'AIX-EN-PROVENCE.]

179. Durand, Charles. LE REGIME DE L'ACTIVITE GOUVERNEMENTALE
      PENDANT LES CAMPAGNES DE NAPOLEON. Aix-en-Provence: La Pensée
      universitaire, 1955 and 1957. 2 vols.

180. Durand, René. LE DEPARTEMENT DES COTES-DU-NORD SOUS LE
      CONSULAT ET L'EMPIRE. Paris: Alcan, 1926. 2 vols.

181. Durand, V. DE LA DISCIPLINE DE LA MAGISTRATURE. Paris, 1894.

182. Dutruch, Roger. LE TRIBUNAT SOUS LE CONSULAT ET L'EMPIRE. Paris: Rousseau, 1921.

183. Duvergier, Jean B, ed. COLLECTION COMPLETE DES LOIS, DECRETS D'INTERET GENERAL, TRAITES INTERNATIONAUX, ARRETES, CIRCULAIRES, INSTRUCTIONS. Paris: Recueil Sirey, 1834-19--.

184. Duvergier, Jean B. COLLECTION COMPLETE DES LOIS, DECRETS, REGLEMENTS, ET AVIS DU CONSEIL D'ETAT (1788-1830). Paris: Bousquet, 1834-38. 30 vols.

185. Ebbinghaus, Therese. NAPOLEON, ENGLAND UND DIE PRESSE, 1800-1803. Munich: R. Oldenburg, 1914.

186. ECOLE POLYTECHNIQUE, DU LIVRE CENTENAIRE, 1794-1894. Paris: Gauthier-Villars, 1895-97. 3 vols.

187. Edmond-Blanc, Amédée A. NAPOLEON Ier, SES INSTITUTIONS CIVILES ET ADMINISTRATIVES. Paris: Plon, 1880.

188. Ellul, Jacques. HISTOIRE DES INSTITUTIONS. Paris: Presses universitaires de France, 1956. 2 vols.

189. Esmein, Adhémar. HISTOIRE DE LA PROCEDURE CRIMINELLE EN FRANCE. Paris: L. Larose et Forcel, 1882.

190. Euvrard, F. HISTORIQUE DE L'ECOLE NATIONALE D'ARTS ET METIERS DE CHALONS-SUR-MARNE. Paris: Union républicaine, 1895.

191. Fain, Agathon J.R., baron. MEMOIRES. Paris: Plon-Nourrit, 1909.

192. Fauchille, Paul. LA QUESTION JUIVE EN FRANCE SOUS LE PREMIER EMPIRE, D'APRES DES DOCUMENTS INEDITS. Paris: Rousseau, 1884.

193. Faure-Soulet, Jean F. LES PREMIERS PREFETS DES HAUTES-PYRENEES, 1800-1814. Paris: Société des études robespierristes, 1965.

194. Feret, Pierre, abbé. HISTOIRE DIPLOMATIQUE, LA FRANCE ET LE SAINT-SIEGE SOUS LE PREMIER EMPIRE, LA RESTAURATION ET LA MONARCHIE DE JUILLET. Paris: A. Savaëte, 1911.

195. Festy, Octave. L'AGRICULTURE FRANCAISE SOUS LE CONSULAT. Paris: Académie Napoléon, 1952.

196. Festy, Octave. LES DELITS RURAUX ET LEUR REPRESSION SOUS LA REVOLUTION ET LE CONSULAT. Paris: M. Riviére, 1956.

197. Fiévée, Joseph. CORRESPONDANCE ET RELATIONS DE J. FIEVEE AVEC BONAPARTE, PREMIER CONSUL ET EMPEREUR, PENDANT ONZE ANNEES. Paris: A. Desrez, 1836. 3 vols.

198. Fischer, Arthur. NAPOLEON ET ANVERS. Antwerp: Loosbergh, 1933.

199. Fisher, Herbert A.L. STUDIES IN NAPOLEONIC STATESMANSHIP: GERMANY. Oxford: Clarendon Press, 1903.

200. Fleischmann, Hector. NAPOLEON ET LA FRANC-MACONNERIE. Paris, 1908.

201. Fohlen, Claude. NAISSANCE D'UNE CIVILISATION INDUSTRIELLE. Paris, 1961.

202. Fontaine de Resbecq, Eugène H. L'ENSEIGNEMENT PRIMAIRE CATHOLIQUE. Paris: C. Poussielgue, 1901.

203. Fontanes, Louis J.P., marquis de. COLLECTION COMPLETE DES DISCOURS DE M. DE FONTANES. Paris: Domère, 1821.

204. Forneron, Henri. HISTOIRE GENERALE DES EMIGRES PENDANT LA REVOLUTION FRANCAISE. Vol. 3. LES EMIGRES ET LA SOCIETE FRANCAISE SOUS NAPOLEON Ier. Paris: Plon-Nourrit, 1890. 3 vols.

205. Fournier, Joseph. LA CHAMBRE DE COMMERCE DE MARSEILLE. Marseilles: Typog. et Lithographie Barlatier, 1910.

206. France. BIBLIOGRAPHIE DE LA FRANCE, OU JOURNAL GENERAL DE L'IMPRIMERIE ET DE LA LIBRAIRIE,... Nendeln, Liechtenstein: Kraus, 1970. (1811-1845. 45 vols.)

207. Friedrich, Hans E. NAPOLEON I, IDEE UND STAAT. Berlin: G. Grote, 1936.

208. Fugier, André. NAPOLEON ET L'ITALIE. Paris: Janin, 1947.

209. Gabory, Emile. NAPOLEON ET LA VENDEE. Paris: Perrin, 1914.

210. Gabriele, Mariano. PER UNA STORIA DEL CONCORDATO DEL 1801 TRA NAPOLEONE E PIO VII. Milan: Giuffrè, 1958.

211. Gaffarel, Paul. "L'Opposition littéraire sous le Consulat." LA REVOLUTION FRANCAISE 16 (1889): 307-26, 397-432.

212. Gaffarel, Paul. "L'Opposition militaire sous le Consulat." LA REVOLUTION FRANCAISE 12 (1887): 982-97, 1096-1111.

213. Gaffarel, Paul. "L'Opposition républicaine sous le Consulat." LA REVOLUTION FRANCAISE 13 (1887): 530-50; 14 (1888): 609-39.

214. Gambasin, Angelo. RELIGIONE E SOCIETA DALLE REFORME NAPOLEONICHE A L'ETA LIBERALE. Padua: Liviana, 1974.

215. Gandilhon, René. "La Série M (Administration générale) des archives départementales." REVUE HISTORIQUE 241 (1969): 147-62.

216. Garaud, Marcel. HISTOIRE GENERALE DU DROIT PRIVE FRANCAIS DE 1799 A 1804. Paris: Recueil Sirey, 1953-59. 2 vols.

217. Garcot, Maurice. LE DUEL MOREAU-NAPOLEON. Paris: Nouvelles Editions latines, 1951.

218. Garros, Louis. LE GENERAL MALET, CONSPIRATEUR. Paris: Plon, 1936.

219. Gaubert, Henri. CONSPIRATEURS AU TEMPS DE NAPOLEON Ier. Paris: Flammarion, 1962.

220. Gaudin, Martin M.C. MEMOIRES, SOUVENIRS, OPINIONS ET ECRITS. Paris: A. Colin, 1826-34; new ed., 1926. 3 vols.

221. Gaudin, Martin M.C. NOTICE HISTORIQUE SUR LES FINANCES DE FRANCE, 1800-1814. Paris: A. Clo, 1818.

222. Gautier, Théodore. LA PERIODE REVOLUTIONNAIRE, LE CONSULAT, L'EMPIRE, LA RESTAURATION DANS LES HAUTES-ALPES (1790-1830). Gap: Guillaume, 1895.

223. GAZETTE NATIONAL, OU MONITEUR UNIVERSEL.

224. Genevray, Pierre. L'ADMINISTRATION ET LA VIE ECCLESIASTIQUE DANS LE GRAND DIOCESE DE TOULOUSE ... PENDANT LES DERNIERES ANNEES DE L'EMPIRE ET SOUS LA RESTAURATION. Paris: Didier, 1940.

225. Geoffroy de Grandmaison, Charles A. LA CONGREGATION, 1801-1830. Paris: Plon, 1889.

226. Geoffroy de Grandmaison, Charles A. NAPOLEON ET LES CARDINAUX NOIRS, 1810-1814. Paris: Perrin, 1895.

227. Gershoy, Leo. THE FRENCH REVOLUTION AND NAPOLEON. Englewood Cliffs, N.J.: Appleton-Century-Crofts, 1964.

228. Geyl, Pieter. NAPOLEON--FOR AND AGAINST. New Haven, Conn.: Yale University Press, 1949.

229. Gille, Bertrand. LE CONSEIL GENERAL DES MANUFACTURES (INVENTAIRE ANALYTIQUE DES PROCES-VERBAUX, 1810-1829). Paris: S.E.V.P.E.N., 1961.

230. Gille, Bertrand. LES SOURCES STATISTIQUES DE L'HISTOIRE DE FRANCE, DES ENQUETES DU XVIIe SIECLE A 1870. Geneva and Paris: Droz, 1964.

231. Gilleuls, A. des. HISTOIRE DE L'ADMINISTRATION PARISIENNE AU XIXe SIECLE. Vol. 1. 1800-1815. Paris, 1900.

232. Gobert, Adrienne. L'OPPOSITION DES ASSEMBLEES PENDANT LE CONSULAT, 1800-1804. Paris: E. Sagot, 1925.

233. Gobineau, Louis de, comte. [LES] MEMOIRES [DU COMTE LOUIS DE GOBINEAU.] Brussels: Editions Erasme, 1955.

234. Godechot, Jacques. LA CONTRE-REVOLUTION. DOCTRINE ET ACTION, 1789-1804. Paris: Presses universitaires de France, 1961.

235. Godechot, Jacques. L'EUROPE ET L'AMERIQUE A L'EPOQUE NAPOLEONIENNE (1800-1815). Paris: Presses universitaires de France, 1967.

236. Godechot, Jacques. LES INSTITUTIONS DE LA FRANCE SOUS LA REVOLUTION ET L'EMPIRE. 2d ed. Paris: Presses universitaires de France, 1968.

237. Godechot, Jacques. NAPOLEON. Paris: A. Michel, 1969.

238. Godechot, Jacques; Beatrice F. Hyslop; and David L. Dowd. THE NAPOLEONIC ERA IN EUROPE. New York: Holt, Rinehart and Winston, 1971.

239. Godel, Jean. LA RECONSTRUCTION CONCORDATAIRE DANS LE DIOCESE DE GRENOBLE APRES LA REVOLUTION (1802-1809). Grenoble: Rondeau-Montfleury, 1968.

240. Gontard, Maurice. L'ENSEIGNEMENT PRIMAIRE EN FRANCE, DE LA REVOLUTION A LA LOI GUIZOT (1789-1833). Paris: Belles Lettres, 1959.

241. Gontard, Maurice. LA QUESTION DES ECOLES NORMALES PRIMAIRES; DE LA REVOLUTION DE 1789 A LA LOI DE 1879. Toulouse: Institut pédagogique national, 1962.

242. Gosselin, Louis Léon T. [Georges Lenôtre]. LA CHOUANNERIE NORMANDE AU TEMPS DE L'EMPIRE. TOURNEBUT, 1804-1809. Paris: Perrin, 1901.

243. Gottschalk, Louis R. THE ERA OF THE FRENCH REVOLUTION (1715-1815). Boston: Houghton Mifflin, 1929.

244. Goujon, Louis. MEMORIAL FORESTIER, OU RECUEIL COMPLET ET SUIVI DES LOIS, ARRETES ET INSTRUCTIONS RELATIFS A L'ADMINISTRATION FORESTIERE (1789-1807). Paris: Goujon, 1810. 6 vols.

245. Grabinski, Joseph, comte. LES PRETRES ROMAINS ET LE PREMIER EMPIRE. Lyon: E. Vitte, 1897.

246. Grant, Hamil. NAPOLEON AND THE ARTISTS. London: G. Richards, 1917.

247. Gréard, Octave, ed. LA LEGISLATION DE L'INSTRUCTION PRIMAIRE EN FRANCE DEPUIS 1789 A NOS JOURS. 2d ed. Vol. 1. 1789-1833. Paris: Delalain, 1890-1902. 7 vols.

248. Grégoire, Pierre M. LE RETABLISSEMENT DU CULTE DANS LE DIOCESE DE NANTES, APRES LA REVOLUTION. Nantes: Vincent Forest & Emile Grimaud, 1885.

249. Grente, Joseph. LE CULTE CATHOLIQUE A PARIS DE LA TERREUR AU
      CONCORDAT. Paris: P. Lethielleux, 1903.

250. Grimaud, Louis. HISTOIRE DE LA LIBERTE D'ENSEIGNEMENT EN
      FRANCE DEPUIS LA CHUTE DE L'ANCIEN REGIME JUSQU'A NOS JOURS.
      Grenoble: Allier, 1898.

251. Guerrini, Maurice. NAPOLEON AND PARIS. Translated, abridged,
      and edited by Margery Weiner. New York: Walker, 1970.

252. Guillon, Edouard L.M. LES COMPLOTS MILITAIRES SOUS LE CONSULAT
      ET L'EMPIRE. Paris: Plon-Nourrit, 1894.

253. Guillon, Edouard L.M. NOS ECRIVIANS MILITAIRES, ETUDES DE
      LITTERATURE ET D'HISTOIRE MILITAIRE. Paris: Plon-Nourrit,
      1898.

254. Guizot, François P.G. DE L'ETAT DES BEAUX-ARTS EN FRANCE ET DU
      SALON DE 1810. Paris: Maradan, 1811.

255. Guizot, François P.G. ESSAI SUR L'HISTOIRE ET L'ETAT ACTUEL DE
      L'INSTRUCTION PUBLIQUE. Paris: Maradan, 1816.

256. Hales, Edward E.Y. NAPOLEON AND THE POPE. London: Eyre &
      Spottiswoode, 1962.

257. Hallays-Dabot, Victor. HISTOIRE DE LA CENSURE THEATRALE EN
      FRANCE. Paris: E. Dentu, 1862.

258. Halphen, Achille E., comp. RECUEIL DES LOIS, DECRETS ...
      CONCERNANT LES ISRAELITES DEPUIS LA REVOLUTION DE 1789. 2d ed.
      Paris: Aux bureaux des archives israélites, 1887.

259. Hamel, Louis Ernest. HISTOIRE DES DEUX CONSPIRATIONS DU
      GENERAL MALET. New ed. Paris: Société des gens de lettres,
      1873.

260. Hampson, Norman. THE FIRST EUROPEAN REVOLUTION, 1776-1815.
      London: Thames & Hudson, 1969.

261. Hanotaux, Gabriel. "Comment se fit l'Empire." REVUE DES DEUX
      MONDES, Series 7, 26 (1925): 944-77, 575-609, 774-807.

262. Hanotaux, Gabriel. "La Transformation sociale a l'époque
      napoléonienne." REVUE DES DEUX MONDES 33 (1926): 89-123,
      562-97.

263. Hatin, Louis E. HISTOIRE POLITIQUE ET LITTERAIRE DE LA PRESSE
      EN FRANCE. Vol. 7. Paris: Poslet-Malassis et De Broise,
      1859-61. 8 vols.

264. Haussonville, Joseph, comte d'. L'EGLISE ROMAINE ET LE PREMIER
      EMPIRE, 1800-1814. 3d ed. Paris: Michel Lévy, 1868-70. 5
      vols.

265. Hautecoeur, Louis. L'ART SOUS LA REVOLUTION ET L'EMPIRE.
      Paris: G. LePrat, 1953.

266. Hautecoeur, Louis. HISTOIRE DE L'ARCHITECTURE CLASSIQUE EN
      FRANCE. Paris: A. Picard, 1943-57. 7 vols.

267. Hautecoeur, Louis. LOUIS DAVID. Paris: La Table ronde, 1954.

268. Hauterive, Ernest d'. LA CONTRE-POLICE ROYALISTE EN 1800.
      Paris: Perrin, 1931.

269. Hauterive, Ernest d'. L'ENLEVEMENT DU SENATEUR CLEMENT DE RIS.
      Paris: Perrin, 1925.

270. Hauterive, Ernest d'. NAPOLEON ET SA POLICE. Paris:
      Flammarion, 1943.

271. Hauterive, Ernest d'. LA POLICE SECRETE DU PREMIER EMPIRE:
      BULLETINS QUOTIDIENS ADRESSES PAR FOUCHE A L'EMPEREUR, 1804-7.
      Paris: Perrin, 1908-13. 3 vols.

272. Hauterive, Ernest d'. LA POLICE SECRETE DU PREMIER EMPIRE:
      BULLETINS QUOTIDIENS ADRESSES PAR FOUCHE A L'EMPEREUR. New
      series, 1808-9 and 1809-10. Paris: Perrin, 1963-64. 2 vols.

273. Heckscher, Eli F. THE CONTINENTAL SYSTEM. Oxford: Clarendon
      Press, 1922.

274. Herivel, John. JOSEPH FOURIER, THE MAN AND THE PHYSICIST.
      Oxford: Clarendon Press, 1975.

275. Herrenschmidt, C. LA POLITIQUE INDUSTRIELLE DE NAPOLEON Ier ET
      LE CONSEIL DES FABRIQUES ET MANUFACTURES. Paris, 1943.

276. Higgs, David. ULTRAROYALISM IN TOULOUSE; FROM ITS ORIGINS TO
      THE REVOLUTION OF 1830. Baltimore: Johns Hopkins University
      Press, 1972.

277. Hilaire, Emile Marc [Marco de Saint-Hilaire]. NAPOLEON AU
      CONSEIL D'ETAT. Paris: V. Magen, 1843. 2 vols.

278. HISTOIRE DES PROTESTANTS EN FRANCE [Robert Mandrou et al.]
      Toulouse: Privat, 1977.

279. Hiver de Beauvoir, Alfred. HISTOIRE CRITIQUE DES INSTITUTIONS
      JUDICIAIRES DE LA FRANCE DE 1789 A 1848. Paris: A. Durand,
      1848.

280. Holtman, Robert B. NAPOLEONIC PROPAGANDA. Baton Rouge:
      Louisiana State University Press, 1950.

281. Houssaye, Henry. 1815. Paris: Perrin, 1895-1905. 3 vols.

282. Hubert, Emmanuelle. LES CENT-JOURS. Paris: Julliard, 1966.

283. Hue, Gustave. UN COMPLOT DE POLICE SOUS LE CONSULAT: LA
     CONSPIRATION DE CERACCHI ET D'ARENA. Paris: Hachette, 1909.

284. Hugues, Adolphe. LE DEPARTEMENT DE SEINE-ET-MARNE ... D'APRES
     LES DELIBERATIONS DU CONSEIL GENERAL. Melun: Imprimerie
     administrative, 1895.

285. Husson, Henri M. RAPPORT SUR LES VACCINATIONS PRATIQUEES EN
     FRANCE EN 1806 ET 1807. Paris: n.p., 1809.

286. Husson, Henri M. RECUEIL DES MEMOIRES SUR L'ETABLISSEMENTS
     D'HUMANITE. Paris: n.p., ans VIII-IX.

287. Imbert, Jean. LE DROIT HOSPITALIER DE LA REVOLUTION ET DE
     L'EMPIRE. Paris: Recueil Sirey, 1954.

288. Iung, Théodore. LUCIEN BONAPARTE ET SES MEMOIRES (1775-1840)
     D'APRES ... DOCUMENTS INEDITS. Paris: G. Charpentier,
     1882-83. 3 vols.

289. Jac, Ernest. BONAPARTE ET LE CODE CIVIL. DE L'INFLUENCE
     PERSONELLE EXERCEE PAR LE PREMIER CONSUL SUR NOTRE LEGISLATION
     CIVILE. Paris: Rousseau, 1898.

290. Jaurès, Jean, ed. HISTOIRE SOCIALISTE (1789-1900). Vol. 6.
     CONSULAT ET EMPIRE. Paris: J. Rouff, 1905. 13 vols.

291. Jeanroy-Félix, Victor. NOUVELLE HISTOIRE DE LA LITTERATURE
     FRANCAISE PENDANT LA REVOLUTION ET LE PREMIER EMPIRE. Paris:
     Bloud, 1886.

292. Jeanvrot, Victor. LA MAGISTRATURE. 4th ed. Paris: n.p.,
     1882-83. 2 vols.

293. Jette, Marie Henry. FRANCE RELIGIEUSE SOUS LA REVOLUTION ET
     L'EMPIRE, PRISES DE VUE. New ed. Paris: Casterman, 1958.

294. Joly, Abbé. ETUDE HISTORIQUE ET JURIDIQUE SUR LE CONCORDAT DE
     1801: SES ORIGINES, SON HISTOIRE. Paris: Imprimerie-libraire
     de l'Oeuvre de Saint-Paul, 1881.

295. Jouvenel, Bertrand de. NAPOLEON ET L'ECONOMIE DIRIGEE. LE
     BLOCUS CONTINENTAL. Paris: Les Editions de la Toison d'or,
     1943.

296. Kennedy, Emmet. A PHILOSOPHE IN THE AGE OF REVOLUTION: DESTUTT
     DE TRACY AND THE ORIGINS OF "IDEOLOGY". Philadelphia:
     American Philosophical Society, 1978.

297. Kitchin, Joanna. UN JOURNAL "PHILOSOPHIQUE": LA DECADE
     (1794-1807). Paris: Minard, 1965.

298. Knapton, Ernest J. REVOLUTIONARY AND IMPERIAL FRANCE,
     1750-1815. New York: Scribner, 1972.

299. Kobler, Franz. NAPOLEON AND THE JEWS. New York: Schocken Books, 1976.

300. Koechlin, H. François. COMPETENCE ADMINISTRATIVE ET JUDICIAIRE DE 1800 A 1830. Paris: Rousseau, 1951.

301. Labasse, Jean. LE COMMERCE DES SOIES A LYON SOUS NAPOLEON ET LA CRISE DE 1811. Paris: A. Colin, 1957.

302. Lachouque, Henry. BONAPARTE ET LA COUR CONSULAIRE. Paris: Bloud & Gay, 1958.

303. Lacoste, Maurice. LA CRISE ECONOMIQUE DE 1805 DANS LE DEPARTEMENT DE LA MEURTHE. Paris, 1951. (Dactylographiée).

304. Lafère, P. DESMAREST, POLICIER DE L'EMPEREUR. Paris, 1943.

305. La Force, Auguste de Caumont, duc de. L'ARCHITRESORIER LEBRUN, GOUVERNEUR DE LA HOLLANDE. Paris: Plon, 1907.

306. La Gorce, Pierre F.G. de. HISTOIRE RELIGIEUSE DE LA REVOLUTION FRANCAISE. Paris: Plon-Nourrit, 1923. Vol. 5.

307. Lanfrey, Pierre. THE HISTORY OF NAPOLEON THE FIRST. 2d ed. New York: AMS Press, 1973. 4 vols.

308. Lanzac de Laborie, Léon de. LA DOMINATION FRANCAISE EN BELGIQUE. DIRECTOIRE-CONSULAT-EMPIRE (1795-1814). Paris: Plon, Nourrit, 1895. 2 vols.

309. Lanzac de Laborie, Léon de. PARIS SOUS NAPOLEON. Paris: Plon-Nourrit, 1905-8. 4 vols.

310. La Rochefoucault, J-d de la; C. Wolikow; and G. Ikni. LE DUC DE LA ROCHEFOUCAULT-LIANCOURT, 1747-1827. DE LOUIS XV A CHARLES X, UN GRAND SEIGNEUR PATRIOTE ET LE MOUVEMENT POPULAIRE. Paris, Perrin, 1980.

311. La Sizeranne, Robert de; Louis Reau; and Charles Saunier. L'ART ET LES ARTISTES SOUS NAPOLEON. Paris: Art et Artistes, 1921.

312. Latour, François. LE GRAND ARGENTIER DE NAPOLEON, GAUDIN, DUC DE GAETE. Paris: Editions du Scorpion, 1962.

313. Latreille, André. LE CATECHISME IMPERIALE DE 1806. ETUDES ET DOCUMENTS POUR SERVIR A L'HISTOIRE DES RAPPORTS DE NAPOLEON ET DU CLERGE CONCORDATAIRE. Paris: Belles Lettres, 1935.

314. Latreille, André. L'EGLISE CATHOLIQUE ET LA REVOLUTION FRANCAISE. Vol. 2. L'ERE NAPOLEONIENNE ET LA CRISE EUROPEENNE, 1800-1815. Paris: Hachette, 1950.

315. Latreille, André. L'ERE NAPOLEONIENNE. Paris: A. Colin, 1974.

316. Latreille, André. NAPOLEON ET LE SAINT-SIEGE (1801-1808); L'AMBASSADE DU CARDINAL FESCH A ROME. Paris: F. Alcan, 1935.

317. Latreille, André; J.R. Palanque; E. Delaruelle; and R. Rémond. HISTOIRE DU CATHOLICISME EN FRANCE. Vol. 3. LA PERIODE CONTEMPORAINE (1750-1958). Paris: Editions Spes, 1962.

318. Latreille, Camille. L'OPPOSITION RELIGIEUSE AU CONCORDAT DE 1792 A 1803. Paris: Hachette, 1910.

319. Latreille, Camille. LA PETITE EGLISE DE LYON. Mâcon: Protat, 1911.

320. Lavalley, Gaston. NAPOLEON ET LA DISETTE DE 1812. Paris: A. Picard, 1896.

321. Lavisse, Ernest, ed. HISTOIRE DE LA FRANCE CONTEMPORAINE. Vol. 3. LE CONSULAT ET L'EMPIRE. Paris: Hachette, 1921. 10 vols.

322. Lavisse, Ernest, and A. Rambaud, eds. HISTOIRE GENERALE DU 4ème SIECLE A NOS JOURS. Vol. 9. NAPOLEON. 3d rev. ed. Paris: Hachette, 1925. 12 vols.

323. Lecomte, Louis H. HISTOIRE DES THEATRES DE PARIS, 1402-1904. Paris: Daragon, 1905-10. Vols. 1, 6, 7, 9.

324. Lecomte, Louis H. NAPOLEON ET LE MONDE DRAMATIQUE. Paris: H. Daragon, 1912.

325. Le Coz, Claude. CORRESPONDANCE DE LECOZ, EVEQUE CONSTITUTIONNEL D'ILLE-ET-VILAINE ET ARCHEVEQUE DE BESANCON. Paris: A. Picard, 1900-3. 2 vols.

326. Le Coz, Claude. MEMOIRES HISTORIQUES POUR SERVIR A L'HISTOIRE ECCLESIASTIQUE DE FRANCE PENDANT LES PREMIERES ANNEES DU XIXe SIECLE. Paris, 1819-24. 3 vols.

327. Ledré, Charles. LE CARDINAL CAMBACERES, ARCHEVEQUE DE ROUEN (1802-1812). Paris: Plon, 1943.

328. Ledré, Charles. LE CARDINAL CAMBACERES, 1812-1818. Paris: Plon, 1943.

329. Ledré, Charles. UNE CONTROVERSE SUR LA CONSTITUTION CIVILE DU CLERGE. CHARRIER DE LA ROCHE, METROPOLITAIN DES COTES DE LA MANCHE, ET LE CHANOINE BASTON. Lyon: E. Vitte, 1943.

330. Lefebvre, Théodore. LES EVENEMENTS HISTORIQUES ET LE FINISTERE DE 1800 A 1805. Morlaix, 1901.

331. Lefebvre, Théodore. LES EVENEMENTS HISTORIQUES ET LES BRETONS DU FINISTERE DE 1805 A 1813. Morlaix: Chevalier, 1902.

332. Lefebvre, Théodore. NOTES HISTORIQUES SUR LA BRETAGNE (FINISTERE) DE 1801 A 1813. Gaillac: Dugourc, 1902.

333. Lefleux, Fernand. A L'AUBE DU CAPITALISME ET DE LA REVOLUTION INDUSTRIELLE, LIEVIN BAUWENS, INDUSTRIEL GANTOIS. Paris: S.E.V.P.E.N., 1969.

334. Leflon, Jean. LA CRISE REVOLUTIONNAIRE, 1789-1846. Paris: Bloud & Gay, 1949.

335. Leflon, Jean. ETIENNE ALEXANDRE BERNIER, EVEQUE D'ORLEANS, ET L'APPLICATION DU CONCORDAT. Paris: Plon, 1938. 2 vols.

336. Leflon, Jean. MONSIEUR EMERY. Vol. 2. L'EGLISE CONCORDATAIRE ET IMPERIALE. Paris: Bonne Presse, 1947. 2 vols.

337. Le Gallo, Emile. LES CENT-JOURS. Paris: F. Alcan, 1924.

338. Leiner, Wilhelm. "L'Administration de l'arrondissement de Sarrebruck (1798-1814)." Thesis, University of Toulouse, 1949.

339. Lelièvre, Pierre. VIVANT DENON. Angers: Editions de l'Ouest, 1942.

340. Lelièvre, Pierre. VIVANT DENON, DIRECTEUR DES BEAUX-ARTS DE NAPOLEON: ESSAI SUR LA POLITIQUE ARTISTIQUE DU PREMIER EMPIRE. Angers: Editions de l'Ouest, 1942.

341. Lémann, Joseph, abbé. NAPOLEON Ier ET LES ISRAELITES. LA PREPONDERANCE JUIVE: DEUXIEME PARTIE--SON ORGANISATION. Paris: V. Lecoffre, 1894.

342. Lemoine, Albert. NAPOLEON Ier ET LES JUIFS. Paris: Fayard, 1900.

343. Léon, Antoine. LA REVOLUTION FRANCAISE ET L'EDUCATION TECHNIQUE. Paris: Société des études robespierristes, 1968.

344. Léon, Pierre. LA NAISSANCE DE LA GRANDE INDUSTRIE EN DAUPHINE. Paris: Presses universitaires de France, 1954.

345. Léonard, Emile G. HISTOIRE GENERALE DU PROTESTANTISME. Paris: Presses universitaires de France, 1964. Vol. 3.

346. Lepointe, Gabriel. HISTOIRE DES INSTITUTIONS ET DES FAITS SOCIAUX. Paris: Editions Montchrestien, 1956.

347. Le Poittevin, Gustave. LA LIBERTE DE LA PRESSE DEPUIS LA REVOLUTION, 1789-1815. Paris: Rousseau, 1900.

348. Leroux, Alfred. ANALYSE DES DELIBERATIONS MANUSCRITES DU CONSEIL DE LA HAUTE-VIENNE. Limoges, 1890.

349. Leroy, Maxime. L'ESPRIT DE LA LEGISLATION NAPOLEONIENNE. Nancy: A. Crépin-Leblond, 1898.

350. Le Sciellour, J. LA LIBERTE INDIVIDUELLE SOUS LE CONSULAT ET L'EMPIRE. Paris: Rousseau, 1911.

351. Leuilliot, Paul. L'ALSACE AU DEBUT DE XIXe SIECLE: ESSAIS D'HISTOIRE POLITIQUE, ECONOMIQUE, ET RELIGIEUSE, 1815-1830. Vol. 2. LES TRANSFORMATIONS ECONOMIQUES. Paris: S.E.V.P.E.N., 1959.

352. Levasseur, Emile. HISTOIRE DES CLASSES OUVRIERES ET DE L'INDUSTRIE EN FRANCE, 1789 A 1870. 2d ed. Paris: Rousseau, 1903-04. Vol. 1.

353. Levasseur, Emile. HISTOIRE DU COMMERCE DE LA FRANCE. Paris: Rousseau, 1912. Vol. 2.

354. Lévy-Schneider, Léon. L'APPLICATION DU CONCORDAT PAR UN PRELAT D'ANCIEN REGIME, MONSEIGNEUR CHAMPION DE CICE, ARCHEVEQUE D'AIX ET ARLES, 1802-1810. Paris: F. Rieder, 1921.

355. Lewis, Gwynne. THE SECOND VENDEE: THE CONTINUITY OF COUNTER-REVOLUTION IN THE DEPARTMENT OF THE GARD: 1789-1815. Oxford: Clarendon Press, 1978.

356. Lex, Léonce, and P.M. Siraud. LE CONSEIL GENERAL ET LES CONSEILLERS GENERAUX DE SAONE-ET-LOIRE, 1789-1889. Mâcon: Belhomme, 1888.

357. L'Huillier, Fernand. RECHERCHES SUR L'ALSACE NAPOLEONIENNE. Strasbourg: Imprimerie Strasbourgeoise, 1947.

358. Liard, Louis. L'ENSEIGNEMENT SUPERIEUR EN FRANCE. Paris: A. Colin, 1888-94. 2 vols.

359. Ligou, Daniel. LA FRANC-MACONNERIE. Paris: Presses universitaires françaises, 1977.

360. LIVRE DU CENTENAIRE DE LA COUR DES COMPTES, 1807-1907. Paris: Imprimerie nationale, 1907.

361. Locré, Jean Guillaume de Roissy, baron de. DISCUSSIONS SUR LA LIBERTE DE LA PRESSE: LA CENSURE, LA PROPRIETE LITTERAIRE, L'IMPRIMERIE ET LA LIBRAIRIE, QUI ONT EU LIEU DANS LE CONSEIL D'ETAT, PENDANT LES ANNEES 1808, 1809, 1810, et 1811. Paris: Garnery, 1819.

362. Locré, Jean Guillaume de Roissy, baron de. LEGISLATION CIVILE, COMMERCIALE ET CRIMINELLE DE LA FRANCE. Paris: Treuttel et Würtz, 1826-32. 31 vols.

363. Locré, Jean Guillaume de Roissy, baron de. LEGISLATION SUR LES MINES ET SUR LES EXPROPRIATIONS POUR CAUSE D'UTILITE PUBLIQUE. Paris: Treuttel et Würtz, 1828.

364. Locré, Jean Guillaume de Roissy, baron de. PROCES-VERBAUX DU
     CONSEIL D'ETAT, CONTENANT LA DISCUSSION DU PROJET DE CODE
     CIVIL. Paris: Imprimerie de la République, 1803-4. 5 vols.

365. Lods, Armand, ed. LA LEGISLATION DES CULTES PROTESTANTS.
     Paris: Grassart, 1887.

366. Lomüller, Louis M. GUILLAUME TERNAUX, 1763-1833, CREATEUR DE
     LA PREMIERE INTEGRATION INDUSTRIELLE FRANCAISE. Paris:
     Editions de la Cabro d'or, 1978.

367. Lorentz, Bernard. UN MANUEL FORESTIER DE L'AN X. Paris:
     Berger-Levrault, 1933.

368. Louis, Paul. HISTOIRE DE LA CLASSE OUVRIERE EN FRANCE, DE LA
     REVOLUTION A NOS JOURS. Paris: Rivière, 1927.

369. Lucas-Dubreton, Jean. LA FRANCE DE NAPOLEON. Paris:
     Hachette, 1947.

370. Lucas-Dubreton, Jean. NAPOLEON. Paris: Larousse, 1969.

371. Lucius, P.E. BONAPARTE UND DIE PROTESTANTISCHEN KIRCHEN
     FRANKREICHS. Tübingen: J.C.B. Mohr, 1903.

372. Madelin, Louis. FOUCHE, 1759-1820. Paris: Plon-Nourrit,
     1901. 2 vols.

373. Madelin, Louis. FOUCHE, 1759-1820. New ed. Paris: Plon,
     1955.

374. Madelin, Louis. LA FRANCE A l'APOGEE DE L'EMPIRE. Paris:
     Hachette, 1970.

375. Madelin, Louis. HISTOIRE DU CONSULAT ET DE L'EMPIRE. Paris:
     Hachette, 1937-54. 16 vols.

376. Madelin, Louis. LA ROME DE NAPOLEON: LA DOMINATION FRANCAISE A
     ROME DE 1809 A 1814. 3d ed. Paris: Plon-Nourrit, 1906.

377. Madelin, Sebastian A. LE PREMIER CONSUL LEGISLATEUR. ETUDE
     SUR LA PART QUE PRIT NAPOLEON AUX TRAVAUX PREPARATOIRES DU
     CODE. Paris: A. Durand, 1865.

378. Manfred, Albert. NAPOLEON BONAPARTE. [In Russian] Moscow:
     Mysl', 1971.

379. Marion, Marcel. HISTOIRE FINANCIERE DE LA FRANCE DEPUIS 1715.
     Paris: Rousseau, 1914-31. Vol. 4.

380. Marquiset, Alfred. NAPOLEON, STENOGRAPHIE AU CONSEIL D'ETAT.
     Paris: Champion, 1913.

381. Martinage-Béranger, Renée. BOURJON ET LE CODE CIVIL. Paris:
     Klincksieck, 1971.

382. Massa-Gille, Geneviève. LES RENTES FONCIERES SOUS LE CONSULAT
      ET L'EMPIRE. Paris: Bibliothèque de l'Ecole des Chartes,
      1975.

383. Massin, Jean. ALMANACH DU PREMIER EMPIRE, DU 9 THERMIDOR A
      WATERLOO. Paris: Club français du livre, 1965.

384. Mathieu, Georges. DE QUELQUES CONSEQUENCES DU BLOCUS
      CONTINENTAL EN CORREZE, DU POINT DE VUE INDUSTRIEL. Paris:
      Hayen, 1916.

385. Mathieu, Jacques M. LE CONCORDAT DE 1801: SES ORIGINES, SON
      HISTOIRE, D'APRES DES DOCUMENTS INEDITS. Paris: Perrin,
      1903.

386. Mathiez, Albert. LE THEOPHILANTHROPIE ET LE CULTE DECADAIRE,
      1796-1801. Paris: F. Alcan, 1904.

387. Mauco, Georges. LES MIGRATIONS OUVRIERES EN FRANCE AU DEBUT DU
      XIXe SIECLE D'APRES LES RAPPORTS DES PREFETS DE L'EMPIRE DE
      1808 A 1813. Paris: A. Lesot, 1932.

388. Mauguin, M. ETUDES HISTORIQUES SUR L'ADMINISTRATION DE
      L'AGRICULTURE EN FRANCE. Paris: Bouchard-Huzard, 1876. Vol.
      2.

389. Maury, A. LE REVEIL RELIGIEUX DE L'EGLISE REFORMEE. Toulouse,
      1892.

390. Mège, Francisque B. L'EXECUTION DU CONCORDAT ET LA PETITE
      EGLISE DANS LE PUY-DE-DOME. Clermont-Ferrand, 1895.

391. Melchior-Bonnet, Bernardine. LA CONSPIRATION DU GENERAL MALET.
      Paris: Del Duca, 1963.

392. Melchior-Bonnet, Bernardine. LE DUC D'ENGHIEN. Paris:
      Amiot-Dumont, 1954.

393. Melchior-Bonnet, Bernardine. NAPOLEON ET LE PAPE. Paris:
      Livre contemporain, 1958.

394. Melvin, Frank E. NAPOLEON'S NAVIGATION SYSTEM: A STUDY OF
      TRADE CONTROL DURING THE CONTINENTAL BLOCKADE. New York:
      Appleton, 1919.

395. Menais, Georges P. NAPOLEON ET L'ARGENT. Paris: Editions de
      l'Epargne, 1969.

396. Méneval, Claude F., baron de. MEMOIRES POUR SERVIR A
      L'HISTOIRE DE NAPOLEON Ier. Paris: E. Dentu, 1894. 3 vols.

397. Merlet, Gustave. TABLEAU DE LA LITTERATURE FRANCAISE,
      1800-1815. Paris: Librairie académique Didier, Perrin,
      1878-83. 3 vols.

398. Michel, Georges. UN FAMILLE PROVENCALE DU XVIe SIECLE AU
      CONSULAT. Paris: Berger-Levrault, 1950.

399. Miot de Melito, André François, comte. MEMOIRES (1788-1815).
      2d ed. Paris: Michel Lévy, 1873-74. 3 vols.

400. Mirimonde, Albert Pomme de. LA COUR DES COMPTES: HISTORIQUE,
      ORGANISATION, APUREMENT DES COMTES, CONTENTIEUX, VOIES DE
      RECOURS, CONTROLE ADMINISTRATIF. Paris: Recueil Sirey, 1948.

401. Mistler, Jean, ed. NAPOLEON ET L'EMPIRE. Paris: Hachette,
      1968. 2 vols.

402. Molé, Louis Mathieu, comte. SOUVENIRS D'UN TEMOIN DE LA
      REVOLUTION ET DE L'EMPIRE (1791-1803). Geneva: Editions du
      Milieu du monde, 1943.

403. Mollien, François Nicolas, comte. MEMOIRES D'UN MINISTRE DE
      TRESOR PUBLIC, 1780-1815. Paris: H. Fournier, 1845. 4 vols.

404. Monglond, André. LA FRANCE REVOLUTIONNAIRE ET IMPERIALE:
      ANNALES DE BIBLIOGRAPHIE. Grenoble: Arthaud, 1929-63. 9
      vols.

405. Monnet, Emile. HISTOIRE DE L'ADMINISTRATION PROVINCIALE,
      DEPARTEMENTALE, ET COMMUNALE EN FRANCE. Paris: Rousseau,
      1885.

406. Montagnon, André. LA GUERRE DE VENDEE: UNE GUERRE SUBVERSIVE.
      Paris: La Colombe, 1959.

407. Morillot, André. LA COUR DE CASSATION, CONSEIL SUPERIEUR DE LA
      MAGISTRATURE. Paris: G. Mollat, 1910.

408. [Morvan, Jean] Capitaine M. Tixier. LE SOLDAT IMPERIAL,
      1800-1814. Paris: Plon-Nourrit, 1904. 2 vols.

409. Moulard, Jacques, abbé. LE COMTE CAMILLE DE TOURNON. Paris:
      H. Champion, 1927-32. 3 vols.

410. Mouly, Dalmas. LE CONCORDAT EN LOZERE ET ARDECHE, 1801-1805.
      Mende, 1942.

411. Mourret, Fernand. HISTOIRE GENERALE DE L'EGLISE. Paris:
      Blond et Gay, 1920-28. Vol. 7.

412. Muret, Théodore C. HISTOIRE DES GUERRES DE L'OUEST; VENDEE,
      CHOUANNERIE (1792-1815). Paris: E. Proux, 1847-48. 5 vols.

413. Muret, Théodore C. L'HISTOIRE PAR LE THEATRE, 1789-1851.
      Paris: Amyot, 1865.

414. Napoleon I, Emperor of the French. CORRESPONDANCE DE NAPOLEON
      BONAPARTE AVEC LE Cte CARNOT, MINISTRE DE L'INTERIEUR, PENDANT
      LES CENT JOURS. Paris: Plancher, 1819.

415. Napoleon I, Emperor of the French. CORRESPONDANCE DE NAPOLEON
     Ier. Paris: Imprimerie impériale, 1858-70. 32 vols.

416. Napoleon I, Emperor of the French. DERNIERES LETTRES INEDITES
     DE NAPOLEON. Edited by Léonce de Brotonne. Paris: H.
     Champion, 1903. 2 vols.

417. Napoleon I, Emperor of the French. LETTRES INEDITES DE
     NAPOLEON Ier. Edited by Léonce de Brotonne. Paris: H.
     Champion, 1898.

418. Napoleon I, Emperor of the French. LETTRES INEDITES DE
     NAPOLEON Ier, AN VIII-1815. Edited by Léon Lecestre. 2d ed.
     Paris: Plon-Nourrit, 1897. 2 vols.

419. Napoleon I, Emperor of the French. LETTRES, ORDRES, ET
     APOSTILLES DE NAPOLEON Ier, EXTRAITS DES ARCHIVES DARU. Edited
     by Suzanne d'Huart. Paris: S.E.V.P.E.N., 1965.

420. Napoleon I, Emperor of the French. MESSAGES ET DISCOURS
     POLITIQUES. Publiés pour la première fois d'après les textes
     authentiques par Georges Barral. Paris: Flammarion, 1896.

421. Napoleon I, Emperor of the French. L'OEUVRE ET L'HISTOIRE.
     Paris: Le Club français du livre, 1969-71. 5 vols.

422. Napoleon I, Emperor of the French. PENSEES POLITIQUES ET
     SOCIALES. Rassemblées et présentées par Adrien Dansette.
     Paris: Flammarion, 1969.

423. Napoleon I, Emperor of the French. PROCLAMATIONS, ORDRES DU
     JOUR, ET BULLETINS DE LA GRANDE ARMEE. Paris: Union générale
     d'éditions, 1964.

424. Neufchateau, François de. ESSAI SUR LA NECESSITE ET LES MOYENS
     DE FAIRE ENTRER DANS L'INSTRUCTION PUBLIQUE L'ENSEIGNEMENT DE
     L'AGRICULTURE. Paris: n.p., 1802.

425. Palluel, André. DICTIONNAIRE DE L'EMPEREUR. Paris: Plon,
     1967.

426. Palmer, Robert R. THE SCHOOL OF THE FRENCH REVOLUTION, A
     DOCUMENTARY HISTORY OF THE COLLEGE OF LOUIS-LE-GRAND AND ITS
     DIRECTOR, JEAN-FRANCOIS CHAMPAGNE, 1762-1814. Princeton:
     Princeton University Press, 1975.

427. Palou, Jean. LA FRANC-MACONNERIE. Paris: Payot, 1964.

428. Papillard, François. CAMBACERES. Paris: Hachette, 1961.

429. Pariset, Ernest. LA CHAMBRE DE COMMERCE DE LYON. Lyon: Plon,
     1886-89. 2 vols.

430. Pasquier, Etienne Denis, duc. A HISTORY OF MY TIME; MEMOIRS OF
     CHANCELLOR PASQUIER. New York: Scribner, 1893-94. 3 vols.

431. Passy, Louis P. FROCHOT, PREFET DE LA SEINE. Evreux: A. Hérissy, 1867.

432. Payard, Maurice. LE FINANCIER OUVRARD, 1770-1846. Reims: n.p., 1958.

433. Pelet de la Lozère, Joseph C., baron. OPINIONS DE NAPOLEON I AU CONSEIL D'ETAT. Paris: Firmin-Didot, 1833.

434. Périvier, Antonin. NAPOLEON JOURNALISTE. Paris: Plon-Nourrit, 1918.

435. Pernoud, Régine. HISTOIRE DE LA BOURGEOISIE EN FRANCE. Paris: Editions du Seuil, 1962. Vol. 2.

436. Pérouse, Honoré. NAPOLEON Ier ET LES LOIS CIVILES DU CONSULAT ET DE L'EMPIRE. Paris: A. Durand, 1866.

437. Perrod-Le Moyne, Henri. NAPOLEON DEVANT LES RELIGIONS. Paris: Le Pavillon, 1970.

438. Petot, Jean. HISTOIRE DE L'ADMINISTRATION DES PONTS ET CHAUSSEES, 1559-1815. Paris: Librairie M. Rivière, 1958.

439. Picard, Ernest. BONAPARTE ET MOREAU. Paris: Plon-Nourrit, 1905.

440. Piétri, François. NAPOLEON ET LE PARLEMENT; OU, LA DICTATURE ENCHAINEE. Paris: Fayard, 1955.

441. Piétri, François. NAPOLEON ET LES ISRAELITES. Paris: Berger-Levrault, 1965.

442. Pingaud, Léonce. JEAN DE BRY (1766-1835). Paris: Plon-Nourrit, 1909.

443. Plongeron, Bernard. DOM GRAPPIN, CORRESPONDENT DE L'ABBE GREGOIRE (1796-1830). Paris: Belles Lettres, 1969.

444. Plongeron, Bernard. THEOLOGIE ET POLITIQUE AU SIECLE DES LUMIERES (1770-1820). Geneva: Droz, 1973.

445. Poisson, Georges. NAPOLEON ET PARIS. Paris: Berger-Levrault, 1964.

446. Poland, Burdette C. FRENCH PROTESTANTISM AND THE FRENCH REVOLUTION; A STUDY IN CHURCH AND STATE, THOUGHT AND RELIGION, 1685-1815. Princeton, N.J.: Princeton University Press, 1957.

447. Pontécoulant, Louis Gustave Le Doulcet, comte de. SOUVENIRS HISTORIQUES PARLEMENTAIRES. Paris: Michel Lévy, 1861-65. 4 vols.

448. Ponteil, Félix. NAPOLEON Ier ET L'ORGANISATION AUTORITAIRE DE LA FRANCE. Paris: A. Colin, 1956.

449. Ponteil, Félix. L'OEUVRE SOCIALE ET HUMAINE DE NAPOLEON. Brussels, 1958.

450. Portal, R. LE TARN SOUS L'EMPIRE. Albi, 1912.

451. Portalis, Jean E.M. DISCOURS, RAPPORTS, ET TRAVAUX INEDITS SUR LE CONCORDAT DE 1801. Paris: Joubert, 1845.

452. Potiquet, Alfred. RECUEIL PAR ORDRE CHRONOLOGIQUE DES LOIS, DECRETS ... CONCERNANT LE SERVICE DES PONTS ET CHAUSSEES. Paris, 1868-78. 5 vols.

453. Poullet, Prosper. LES INSTITUTIONS FRANCAISES DE 1795 A 1814. Paris: Plon-Nourrit, 1907.

454. Poullet, Prosper. QUELQUES NOTES SUR L'ESPRIT PUBLIC EN BELGIQUE PENDANT LA DOMINATION FRANCAISE, 1795-1814. Ghent: Van der Haeghen, 1896.

455. Pressensé, Edmond de. L'EGLISE ET LA REVOLUTION FRANCAISE. HISTOIRE DES RELATIONS DE L'EGLISE ET DE L'ETAT DE 1789 A 1802. 3d ed. Paris: Librairie Fischbacher, 1889.

456. Prévost, A. LES ETUDES MEDICALES SOUS LE DIRECTOIRE ET LE CONSULAT. Paris, 1908.

457. Priouret, Roger A. LA CAISSE DES DEPOTS, CENT CINQUANTE ANS D'HISTOIRE FINANCIERE. Paris: Presses universitaires de France, 1966.

458. PROBLEMES D'HISTOIRE DE LA CORSE, DE L'ANCIEN REGIME A 1815. ACTES DU COLLOQUE D'AJACCIO DU 29 OCTOBRE 1969. Paris: Clavreuil, 1971.

459. PROCES-VERBAL DES SEANCES DU CORPS LEGISLATIF. Paris: Imprimerie nationale, 1800-1806. 31 vols.

460. PROCES-VERBAL DES SEANCES DU TRIBUNAT, DEPUIS 11 NIVOSE AN VIII--FLOREAL AN XI. Paris: Imprimerie nationale, 1800-1803. 75 vols.

461. Prod'homme, Jacques G. NAPOLEON. Paris: Mercure de France, 1938.

462. Quignon, G. Hector. LE CENTENAIRE DES COURS PRIMAIRES NORMAUX DANS L'OISE. Paris: Champion, 1905.

463. Rabaut-Dupuis, Pierre A. DETAILS HISTORIQUES ET RECUEIL DE PIECES SUR LES DIVERS PROJETS DE REUNION DE TOUTES LES COMMUNIONS CHRETIENNES TENTES SOUS NAPOLEON EN FRANCE. Paris: Chez l'éditeur, 1806.

464. Radiguet, Leon. L'ACTE ADDITIONEL AUX CONSTITUTIONS DE L'EMPIRE. Caen: L. Jouan, 1911.

465. Rais, Jules. LA REPRESENTATION DES ARISTOCRATIES DANS LES CHAMBRES HAUTES EN FRANCE, 1789-1815. Paris: Berger-Levrault, 1900.

466. Ramon, Gabriel G. HISTOIRE DE LA BANQUE DE FRANCE D'APRES LES SOURCES ORIGINALES. Paris: B. Grasset, 1929.

467. Ray, Jean. ESSAI SUR LA STRUCTURE LOGIQUE DU CODE CIVIL FRANCAISE. Paris: Alcan, 1926.

468. Réal, Pierre F., comte. INDISCRETIONS, 1798-1830. SOUVENIRS ANECDOTIQUES ET POLITIQUES TIRES DU PORTEFEUILLE D'UN FONCTIONNAIRE DE L'EMPIRE. Paris: Dufey, 1835. 2 vols.

469. RECUEIL DES LETTRES, CIRCULAIRES ... DU MINISTERE DE L'INTERIEUR (THERMIDOR AN V-1820). Paris: n.p., an VIII-1821. 20 vols.

470. RECUEIL GENERAL DES LOIS, DECRETS, ARRETES, ET ORDONNANCES CONCERNANT LES DOUANES DE 1789 A 1876. Paris, 1877. 4 vols.

471. RECUEIL OFFICIEL DES INSTRUCTIONS ET CIRCULAIRES DU MINISTERE DE LA JUSTICE DE 1791 A 1875. Paris: Imprimerie nationale, 1879-83. 3 vols.

472. Regaldo, Marc. UN MILIEU INTELLECTUAL: LA DECADE PHILOSOPHIQUE (1794-1807). Lille: Atelier Réproduction des thèses, University of Lille III, 1976. 3 vols.

473. Regnier, Jacques. LES PREFETS DU CONSULAT ET DE L'EMPIRE. Paris: La Nouvelle Revue, 1907.

474. Reinhard, Marcel. LE GRAND CARNOT. Vol. 2. L'ORGANISATION DE LA VICTOIRE, 1792-1823. Paris: Hachette, 1952. 2 vols.

475. Remacle, Louis, comte. BONAPARTE ET LES BOURBONS. RELATIONS SECRETES DES AGENTS DE LOUIS XVIII A PARIS SOUS LE CONSULAT (1802-1803). Paris: Plon-Nourrit, 1899.

476. Rémond, André. ETUDES SUR LA CIRCULATION MARCHANDE EN FRANCE AUX XVIIIe ET XIXe SIECLES. Vol. 1. LE PRIX DES TRANSPORTS MARCHANDS DE LA REVOLUTION AU PREMIER EMPIRE. Paris, 1856.

477. Rendu, Ambroise M.M. CODE UNIVERSITAIRE. Paris: Hachette, 1827.

478. Rendu, Ambroise M.M. SYSTEME DE L'UNIVERSITE DE FRANCE, OU PLAN D'UNE EDUCATION NATIONALE. Paris: H. Nicolle, 1816.

479. REVUE D'HISTOIRE MODERNE ET CONTEMPORAINE. LA FRANCE A L'EPOQUE NAPOLEONIENNE 17 (1976).

480. REVUE DE L'INSTITUT NAPOLEON. 1938-1940; 1948 to present.

481. Ricard, Mgr. Antoine. LE CONCILE NATIONAL DE 1811. Paris: E. Dentu, 1894.

482. Richard, Jules. HISTOIRE DU DEPARTEMENT DES DEUX-SEVRES SOUS LE CONSULAT, L'EMPIRE, LA PREMIERE RESTAURATION, ET LES CENT JOURS (1800-1815). Saint-Maixent: Reversé, 1865.

483. Richon, Albert. UNE ECOLE, UN EMPEREUR, UN CHATEAU, 1803-1808. Paris: Berger-Levrault, 1958.

484. Rigault, Georges. HISTOIRE GENERALE DE L'INSTITUT DES FRERES DES ECOLES CHRETIENNES. Paris: Plon, 1940. Vol. 3.

485. RIVISTA ITALIANA DE STUDI NAPOLEONICI. 1965 to present.

486. Robert, Daniel. LES EGLISES REFORMEES DE FRANCE (1800-1830). Paris: Presses universitaires de France, 1961.

487. Robert, Daniel. GENEVE ET LES EGLISES REFORMEES DE FRANCE DE LA "REUNION" (1798) AUX ENVIRONS DE 1830. Geneva: Droz, 1961.

488. Robert, Daniel. TEXTES ET DOCUMENTS RELATIFS A L'HISTOIRE DES EGLISES REFORMEES EN FRANCE (PERIODE 1800-1830). Paris: Minard, 1962.

489. Rocal, Georges. DU 18 BRUMAIRE A WATERLOO EN PERIGORD. Paris: Floury, 1942. 2 vols.

490. Rochechouart, Louis V.L., comte de. MEMOIRS OF THE COUNT DE ROCHECHOUART. London: J. Murray, 1920.

491. Rocke, Paul. DIE KONTINENTALSPERRE UND IHRE EINWIRKUNGEN AUF DIE FRANZOESISCHE INDUSTRIE. Naumburg: Lippert, 1894.

492. Roederer, Pierre Louis, comte. AUTOUR DE BONAPARTE. JOURNAL DU COMTE P.-L. ROEDERER, MINISTRE ET CONSEILLER D'ETAT. Paris: H. Daragon, 1909.

493. Roederer, Pierre Louis, comte. MEMOIRES SUR LA REVOLUTION, LE CONSULAT, ET L'EMPIRE. Paris: Plon, 1942.

494. Roques, F. ASPECTS DE LA VIE ECONOMIQUE NICOISE SOUS LE CONSULAT ET L'EMPIRE. Aix-en-Provence: La Pensée universitaire, 1957.

495. Roques, F. L'ORGANISATION DE LA SANTE PUBLIQUE A NICE SOUS LA REVOLUTION ET L'EMPIRE. Aix-en-Provence: Faculté de Droit, 1955.

496. Rosen, Lew. NAPOLEON'S OPERA-GLASS. London: E. Mathews, 1897.

497. Roussel, Philippe. DE CADOUDAL A FROTTE; LA CHOUANNERIE DE 1792 A 1800. Paris: Editions de la Seule France, 1962.

498. Rouvière, François. L'EXPLOITATION DES MINES NATIONALES DU
      GARD. Nîmes, 1901.

499. Sagnac, Philippe. LE CODE CIVIL, LIVRE DE CENTENAIRE. Paris:
      Rousseau, 1904. 2 vols.

500. Sagnac, Philippe. "Les Juifs et Napoléon." REVUE D'HISTOIRE
      MODERNE ET CONTEMPORAINE 2, 3 (1900-1902): 461-84, 461-92.

501. Sagnac, Philippe. LA LEGISLATION CIVILE DE LA REVOLUTION
      FRANCAISE. Paris: Hachette, 1898.

502. Sagnac, Philippe. LE RHIN FRANCAIS PENDANT LA REVOLUTION ET
      L'EMPIRE. Paris: F. Alcan, 1917.

503. Saint-Yves, Georges, and Joseph Fournier. L'EVOLUTION DU
      SYSTEME ADMINISTRATIF DE NAPOLEON Ier. LE DEPARTEMENT DES
      BOUCHES-DU-RHONE DE 1800 A 1801. Paris: Champion, 1899.

504. Salmon, Lucy M. THE NEWSPAPER AND AUTHORITY. New York: Oxford
      University Press, 1923.

505. Sarrazin, M. LES MAJORATS DANS LA LEGISLATION FRANCAISE.
      Paris: Giard et Brière, 1906.

506. Saunders, Edith. THE HUNDRED DAYS. London: Longmans, 1963.

507. Savant, Jean. LES PREFETS DE NAPOLEON. Paris: Hachette,
      1958.

508. Savary, Anne Jean Marie René, duc de Rovigo. MEMOIRES DU DUC
      DE ROVIGO, POUR SERVIR A L'HISTOIRE DE L'EMPEREUR NAPOLEON.
      New ed. Paris: Garnier, 1900-1901. 5 vols.

509. Schmidt, Charles. LA REFORME DE L'UNIVERSITE IMPERIALE EN
      1811. Paris: Société nouvelle de librairie et d'édition,
      1905.

510. Schoor, Charles van. LA PRESSE SOUS LE CONSULAT ET SOUS
      L'EMPIRE. Brussels: Bruylant-Christophe, 1899.

511. Séché, Léon. LES ORIGINES DU CONCORDAT. Vol. 2. PIE VII ET
      LE CONSULAT. Paris: C. Delagrave, 1894. 2 vols.

512. Sée, Henri. HISTOIRE ECONOMIQUE DE LA FRANCE. Vol. 2.
      1789-1815. Paris: A. Colin, 1948-51. 2 vols.

513. Seilhac, Victor, comte de. HISTOIRE POLITIQUE DU DEPARTEMENT
      DE LA CORREZE SOUS LE DIRECTOIRE, LE CONSULAT, L'EMPIRE ET LA
      RESTAURATION (1797-1830). Tulle: Crauffon, 1888.

514. Serres, Jean B. HISTOIRE DE LA REVOLUTION EN AUVERGNE. LE
      DIRECTOIRE ET LE CONSULAT. Paris: Vic et Amat, 1895-99. Vol.
      10.

515. Servières, Georges. L'ALLEMAGNE FRANCAISE SOUS NAPOLEON I. Paris: Perrin, 1904.

516. Sevestre, Emile. L'HISTOIRE, LE TEXTE ET LA DESTINEE DU CONCORDAT DE 1801. Paris: P. Lethielleux, 1905.

517. Sieburg, Friedrich. NAPOLEON: DIE HUNDERT TAGE. Stuttgart: Deutsche Verlags-Anstalt, 1956.

518. Silvestre, Augustin F., baron de. ESSAI SUR LES MOYENS DE PERFECTIONNER LES ARTS ECONOMIQUES EN FRANCE, 1800-1801. Paris: Huzard, 1801.

519. Siraud, P. LES ADMINISTRATEURS ET LES PREFETS DE SAONE-ET-LOIRE. Mâcon: Chollat, 1886.

520. Sloane, William M. THE FRENCH REVOLUTION AND RELIGIOUS REFORM. New York: C. Scribner's, 1901.

521. Smet, Monique de. LES ETABLISSEMENTS NATIONAUX BELGES ET FRANCAIS DE ROME SOUS LA REVOLUTION ET L'EMPIRE (1793-1815). Brussels: Chez l'auteur, 1976.

522. Soboul, Albert. LE DIRECTOIRE ET LE CONSULAT. Paris: Presses universitaires de France, 1967.

523. Soboul, Albert. LE PREMIER EMPIRE. Paris: Presses universitaires de France, 1973.

524. Soboul, Albert. PROBLEMES PAYSANS DE LA REVOLUTION, 1789-1848. Paris: Maspero, 1976.

525. Soboul, Albert, and Bernhard Blumenkranz, eds. LES JUIFS ET LA REVOLUTION FRANCAISE. Toulouse: Privat, 1976.

526. Soulajon, Louis. LES COHORTES DE LA LEGION D'HONNEUR (1802-1809). Paris: Baudoin, 1890.

527. Spekkens, Johannes P.L. L'ECOLE CENTRALE DU DEPARTEMENT DE LA MEUSE INFERIEURE, MAESTRICHT, 1798-1804. Maastricht: Van Aëlst, 1951.

528. Stenger, Gilbert. LA SOCIETE FRANCAISE PENDANT LE CONSULAT. Paris: Perrin, 1903-8. 6 vols.

529. Stewart, John Hall. FRANCE, 1715-1815: A GUIDE TO MATERIALS IN CLEVELAND. Cleveland: Western Reserve University Press, 1942.

530. Storost, Georg. NAPOLEONS I STELLUNG ZUR ZEITGENOESSISCHEN UND KLASSISCHEN FRANZOESISCHEN LITERATUR. Schönebeck: Wullstein, 1914.

531. Stourm, René. LES FINANCES DU CONSULAT. Paris: Guillaumin, 1904.

532. Sussel, Philippe. LA FRANCE DE NAPOLEON Ier (1799-1815). Paris: Denoël, 1970.

533. Szramkiewicz, Romuald. LES REGENTS ET CENSEURS DE LA BANQUE DE FRANCE NOMMES SOUS LE CONSULAT ET L'EMPIRE. Geneva: Droz, 1974.

534. Tessonneau, Remy. CORRESPONDANCE DE FONTANES ET DE JOUBERT (1785-1819). Paris: Plon, 1943.

535. Tessonneau, Remy. JOSEPH JOUBERT, EDUCATEUR (1754-1824). Paris: Plon, 1944.

536. Theiner, Augustin. HISTOIRE DES DEUX CONCORDATS DE LA REPUBLIQUE FRANCAISE ET DE LA REPUBLIQUE CISALPINE CONCLUS EN 1801 ET 1803 ENTRE NAPOLEON BONAPARTE ET LE SAINT SIEGE. Bar-le-Duc: L. Guérin, 1869. 2 vols.

537. Thibaudeau, Antoine C., comte. BONAPARTE AND THE CONSULATE. New York: Macmillan, 1908.

538. Thibaudeau, Antoine C., comte. LE CONSULAT ET L'EMPIRE, OU HISTOIRE DE LA FRANCE ET DE NAPOLEON BONAPARTE DE 1799 A 1815. Paris: J. Renouard, 1834-35. 10 vols.

539. Thibaudeau, Antoine C., comte. MEMOIRES, 1799-1815. Paris: Plon-Nourrit, 1913.

540. Thibault-Laurent, Gérard. LA PREMIERE INTRODUCTION DU DIVORCE EN FRANCE SOUS LA REVOLUTION ET L'EMPIRE (1792-1816). Clermont-Ferrand: Imprimerie moderne, 1938.

541. Thierry, Gilbert A. CONSPIRATEURS ET GENS DE POLICE: LE COMPLOT DES LIBELLES (1802). Paris: A. Colin, 1903.

542. Thiers, Louis Adolphe. HISTOIRE DU CONSULAT ET L'EMPIRE. New ed. Paris: Paulin, 1845-74. 21 vols.

543. Thiry, Jean. CAMBACERES, ARCHICHANCELIER DE L'EMPIRE. Paris: Berger-Levrault, 1935.

544. Thiry, Jean. LA CHUTE DE NAPOLEON Ier. Vol. 5. LES CENT JOURS. Paris: Berger-Levrault, 1938-45. 7 vols.

545. Thiry, Jean. LE CONCORDAT ET LE CONSULAT A VIE, MARS 1801-JUILLET 1802. Paris: Berger-Levrault, 1956.

546. Thiry, Jean. LE DEPARTEMENT DE LA MEURTHE SOUS LE CONSULAT. Nancy: Berger-Levrault, 1959.

547. Thiry, Jean. LA MACHINE INFERNALE. Paris: Berger-Levrault, 1952.

548. Thiry, Jean. LE SENAT DE NAPOLEON, 1800-1814. 2d ed. Paris: Berger-Levrault, 1949.

549. Thompson, James M. NAPOLEON BONAPARTE. New York: Oxford University Press, 1952.

550. Thuillier, Guy. GEORGES DUFAUD ET LES DEBUTS DU GRAND CAPITALISME DANS LA METALLURGIE EN NIVERNAIS AU XIXe SIECLE. Paris: S.E.V.P.E.N., 1959.

551. Titeux, Eugène. SAINT-CYR ET L'ECOLE SPECIALE MILITAIRE EN FRANCE. Paris: Didot, 1898.

552. Tournon, Camille de. LETTRES INEDITES DU COMTE CAMILLE DE TOURNON, PREFET DE ROME, 1809-1814. PREMIERE PARTIE: LA POLITIQUE ET L'ESPRIT PUBLIC. Paris: H. Champion, 1914.

553. Trescaze, Aimé. RECUEIL CHRONOLOGIQUE DES CONTRIBUTIONS DIRECTES DE 1789 A 1820. Poitiers: n.p., 1821. 13 vols.

554. Troclet, Léon E. LA PREMIERE EXPERIENCE DE SECURITE SOCIALE. LIEGE, DECRET DE NAPOLEON DE 1813. Brussels: Editions de la Librairie encyclopédique, 1953.

555. Tulard, Jean. BIBLIOGRAPHIE CRITIQUE DES MEMOIRES SUR LE CONSULAT ET L'EMPIRE. Paris: Droz, 1971.

556. Tulard, Jean. NAPOLEON. Paris: Fayard, 1977.

557. Tulard, Jean. NAPOLEON ET LA NOBLESSE D'EMPIRE. Paris: J. Tallandier, 1979.

558. Tulard, Jean. PARIS SOUS LE CONSULAT ET L'EMPIRE, 1800-1815. Paris: Hachette, 1970.

559. Tulard, Jean. LA VIE QUOTIDIENNE DES FRANCAIS SOUS NAPOLEON. Paris: Hachette, 1978.

560. Uzureau, François Constant, abbé. L'ENQUETE SCOLAIRE DE L'AN XI DANS LE MAINE-ET-LOIRE. Angers, 1898.

561. Vallée, Gustave. COMPTE GENERAL DE LA CONSCRIPTION DE A.A. HARGENVILLIERS. Paris: Recueil Sirey, 1937.

562. Vallée, Gustave. LA CONSCRIPTION DANS LE DEPARTEMENT DE LA CHARENTE, 1798-1807. Paris: Recueil Sirey, 1937.

563. Vialles, Pierre. L'ARCHICHANCELIER CAMBACERES. Paris: Perrin, 1908.

564. Viard, Paul. L'ADMINISTRATION PREFECTORALE DANS LE DEPARTEMENT DE LA COTE-D'OR SOUS LE CONSULAT ET LE PREMIER EMPIRE. Paris: E. Champion, 1914.

565. Viard, Pierre Paul. HISTOIRE GENERALE DU DROIT PRIVE FRANCAIS DE 1789 A 1830. Paris: Presses universitaires de France, 1931.

566. Vidalenç, Jean. LES EMIGRES FRANCAIS, 1789-1825. Caen: Association des publications de la Faculté des lettres et sciences humaines de l'université de Caen, 1963.

567. Vidalenç, Jean. TEXTES SUR L'HISTOIRE DE LA SEINE-INFERIEURE A L'EPOQUE NAPOLEONIENNE (1800-1814). Rouen: C.R.D.P., 1976.

568. Viennet, Odette. NAPOLEON ET L'INDUSTRIE FRANCAISE: LA CRISE DE 1810-1811. Paris: Plon, 1947.

569. Vigier, Philippe. ESSAI SUR LA REPARTITION DE LA PROPRIETE FONCIERE DANS LA REGION ALPINE ET SON EVOLUTION DES ORIGINES DU CADASTRE A LA FIN DU SECOND EMPIRE. Paris: S.E.V.P.E.N., 1964.

570. Villani, Pasquale. ITALIA NAPOLEONICA. Naples: Guida, 1978.

571. Villat, Louis. LA REVOLUTION ET L'EMPIRE (1789-1815). Vol. 2. NAPOLEON (1799-1815). Paris: Presses universitaires de France, 1942. 2 vols.

572. Villefosse, Louis de, and Janine Bouissounouse. L'OPPOSITION A NAPOLEON. Paris: Flammarion, 1969.

573. Vion, Albert. LA VIE CALAISIENNE SOUS LE CONSULAT ET L'EMPIRE. Paris: n.p., 1972.

574. Vox, Maximilien. CORRESPONDANCE DE NAPOLEON. 600 LETTRES DE TRAVAIL (1806-1816). Paris: Gallimard, 1943.

575. Vuillemin, Emile. LE BASSIN HOUILLER DU PAS-DE-CALAIS; HISTOIRE DE LA RECHERCHE, DE LA DECOUVERTE ET DE L'EXPLOITATION DE LA HOUILLE DANS CE NOUVEAU BASSIN. Lille: L. Daniel, 1880.

576. Walsh, Henry H. THE CONCORDAT OF 1801. New York: Columbia University Press, 1933.

577. Walter, Gérard. HISTOIRE DES PAYSANS DE FRANCE. PARIS: Flammarion, 1963.

578. Weill, Georges. HISTOIRE DE L'ENSEIGNEMENT SECONDAIRE EN FRANCE DE 1802 A 1920. Paris: Payot, 1921.

579. Welschinger, Henri. LA CENSURE SOUS LE PREMIER EMPIRE. Paris: Charavay, 1882.

580. Welschinger, Henri. LE DIVORCE DE NAPOLEON. Paris: Plon-Nourrit, 1889.

581. Welschinger, Henri. LE DUC D'ENGHIEN. 2d ed. Paris: Plon, 1913.

582. Welschinger, Henri. LE PAPE ET L'EMPEREUR, 1804-1815. Paris: Plon-Nourrit, 1905.

583. Wilson, Aileen. FONTANES. Paris: E. De Boccard, 1928.

584. Wolff, Otto. OUVRARD, SPECULATOR OF GENIUS, 1770-1846. London: Barrie and Rockliff, 1962.

585. Woloch, Isser. THE FRENCH VETERAN FROM THE REVOLUTION TO THE RESTORATION. Chapel Hill: University of North Carolina Press, 1979.

586. Zaghi, Carlo. NAPOLEONE E L'ITALIA, PROSPETTIVE E PROBLEMI. Naples: Cymba, 1965.

CHAPTER XII

THE RUSSIAN CAMPAIGN

George F. Jewsbury, Oklahoma State University

Napoleon's six-month sojourn in Russia during the fateful year of 1812 has attracted the devoted and fascinated attention of a wide variety of memorialists, novelists, ideologists, popularizers, and even composers. Scholars and editors have produced rich and full collections of printed documents, and even more spectacular deposits of documentary resources await researchers in archives in Paris and Moscow, and in provincial repositories located between the two capitals. Many of the participants have left their impressions behind and modern scholars using innovative methods are bringing the testimony of formerly unheeded witnesses to bear. However, the campaign has yet to gain the attention of a historian who can weave a synthesis to explain its causes, events, and consequences, free of nationalistic self-serving and ideological bias. That such a work has not yet appeared is amply demonstrated by the practice of many teachers who recommend Tolstoy's WAR AND PEACE to students as a good way of understanding the invasion. To paraphrase a French observer's comments on another dramatic battle in another war, "C'est magnifique, mais ce n'est pas l'histoire."

Unlike the Spanish campaigns which sapped the Empire's strength over a number of years in a variety of levels and intensities of combat, the 1812 campaign took six months and featured only one battle--Borodino--of major significance. The French took three months to arrive at the deserted former capital of Russia, Moscow; they stayed one month in the burned out city, declared victory, and suffered through a two-month retreat. In this classic Pyrrhic victory, Napoleon accomplished a great logistical and tactical feat in moving hundreds of thousands of men and animals to Moscow and, after a brief period of uncharacteristic incompetence, carried out a brilliant retreat against overwhelming odds. In the interim, however, he lost over four hundred thousand men and hastened his own fall.

The historiographical wake of the 1812 campaign has remained far longer than has been the case for other aspects of Napoleon's activities, largely because of the unique developments in Russia in the past 170 years. The expulsion of the French played a key role in the development of modern Russian nationalism, and during the fiftieth anniversary and centennial celebrations, historians throughout Russia looked back on the events of 1812 with great pride for signs of re-affirmation. Surprisingly, twenty years after the 1917 revolutions, Stalin's historians--going against orthodox Marxist views--sought support in the tsarist past for the Soviet present. For the next quarter century the Russian historians found precedents for the mobilization of the entire people and for the wartime policies of Stalin against Hitler's invasion in the events of 1812. In France, much less was made of the campaign, although even there the glorious nature of the epochal struggle would be emphasized.

Each step in the campaign posed historiographical controversies: the nature of the tactics used by Barclay de Tolly and Kutuzov, the extent of the participation of the Russian people; the forces compelling Napoleon to undertake the campaign; the state of Russian preparedness; the encounter at Smolensk; the battle of Borodino; the controversy over the burning of Moscow; the role of Kutuzov; the political intrigue surrounding Alexander I; the nature of the retreat; the role of the Russian climate in Napoleon's defeat; the French escape from the Russian forces at the Beresina; Kutuzov's policies of pursuit; and the impact of the invasion on the various social levels, nationalities, and cultural developments of the empire. This incomplete list gives an indication of the problems awaiting consideration by the "master historian" mentioned above.

The Emperor himself set the tone for many French historians to follow by pointing out the decisive role of the weather in his demise. However, French historians saw something heroic in the encounter. Typical of the immediate response of historians came from Pierre François Tissot (456) who in his work attempted to harmonize the drives of the revolution and the French nation with the genius of Napoleon. He noted that "never did Napoleon take on a war that was more just, more useful, more national, and more European [than the Russian campaign] ..., never did he merit more the gaining of a complete triumph [by] overcoming ... terrible misfortune." Tissot blamed disobedience, among other factors, for the defeat. Others, such as the historian Bignon (448), saw the hand of England in the disaster, while Thiers (455) viewed the invasion as good military work but bad politics. Even critics paid tribute to Napoleon's genius, and pointed out that he had little alternative but to insure the continuity of his policies in the face of Russian perfidy.

The Russians entered the historiographical fray almost as soon as the Emperor departed the country. Nationalism and praise for the tsar filled the pages of Russian books in the first two generations after the campaign. Objectivity remained difficult as long as most of the participants remained alive, jealously guarding the essential documents. Akhsharumov (6), Buturlin (81), and Milhailovskii-Danilevskii (269, 270) wrote substantial works in the first three decades after the invasion. The first was more or less a celebration of the expulsion while the latter two, written by military men who were also historians, received and implicitly reflected official support. Most students agree that Bogdanovich's three volumes (55, 56) constitute the first professional attempt to subject the campaign to a deep, dispassionate searching analysis.

Throughout the century after 1812 the Russians wrote extensive original works and published extracts of many foreign sources about Napoleon's invasion. Zatvornitskii's bibliography (424) gives an indication of the numerous works in Russian journals while some of the works mentioned below published in 1912 illustrate the fruitful and massive amount of work done for the centennial observance.

The flood of works emerging around 1912 came to a rather abrupt end with the outbreak of World War I, and for the next twenty years comparatively little attention was paid to the heroic efforts of Napoleon, Kutuzov, and Alexander I. After all, from a Bolshevik perspective, that was a conflict which had little to do with class struggle, international revolution, or dialectical movements. The Marxist view of the period was best expressed by M.I. Pokrovsky (317) and his students. Generally, Pokrovsky found the source of the conflict in the problems caused by the Continental System and indicated that the French really had no alternative but to fight to defend their structure of dominance. The resistance of the Russians was not of a national character--only the Spanish resistance could be seen in that light. Instead, oppressing classes from two different states met in battle, with the French winning the battle and losing the war. The hymns to national glory were little more than the "ideological veils" Marx referred to; slogans to blind the people to the real nature of their drab existence. In short, the French over-extended themselves and their own problems--aided by the weather--beat them. Above all, Kutuzov did not defeat the French, nor did the Russian army, nor did the Russian people who, in the words of one of Pokrovsky's students, "rose in defense of their chickens and geese."

Pokrovsky, his views, and his students fell under brutal attack in the 1930s. They were too faithful to abstract Marxist theory. According to his critics, Pokrovsky failed to assess properly the role of the Russians and their leaders--especially Kutuzov. Another casualty of the ideological change in course was Tarle, a sophisticated and liberal historian, until his period in exile. This first class historian changed with the times and published a biography of Napoleon in 1936 which followed many of the main lines set out by Pokrovsky. There was no national resistance against Napoleon nor did Kutuzov seem to be particularly effective as a leader. Less than two years later, Tarle changed his approach (376, 377) as he suddenly found there was indeed a national movement and discerned talents in Kutuzov that he, Tarle, had missed earlier. He changed other givens in his equation concerning 1812 to reflect the new line.

The major force behind this historical transformation was the appearance of an aggressive Nazi Germany and its leader, Adolf Hitler, who thought in grandiose terms similar to the geopolitical concepts of Napoleon. When the war went badly for the USSR, the obvious precedents of 1812 were summoned up. Stalin showed great interest in any aid he could get from the annals of "Mother Russia." The list of works on 1812 during the 1940s will be apparent to anyone going through the selected bibliography at the end of the chapter. In 1947, however, Stalin went one step beyond calling up the precedents of the past for aid. In a letter responding to one Colonel Razin in VOPROSY ISTORII (The Answer of Comrade Stalin to the Letter of Comrade Razin) (368), Stalin not only "clarified" Lenin's views on Clausewitz, he even gave his own interpretation of Kutuzov's theory of "counteroffensive." He referred to "our gifted general Kutuzov who destroyed Napoleon and his army with the help of a well-prepared counteroffensive...." Stalin made the obvious analogy to himself--one that Khrushchev would devastate in his 1956 speech, "Crimes of the Stalin Era." Soviet historians fell into line, and Tarle came under attack again. He had portrayed Kutuzov as cunningly avoiding battle. Tarle's critics called such a view "unscientific." Tarle accordingly backed down again.

Since Stalin's death in 1953, Soviet military historians have avoided such rapid ideological shifts of the type that produced the veritable intellectual whiplash effect on Tarle. Under the leadership of the most important post World War II military historians, Beskrovnyi (38-48) and Zhilin (425-430), bourgeois falsifiers still receive their "rightful" condemnation, but once into the second chapters of even the most ideologically rigid works, the western historian will find useful material. Much work of value was produced for the sesquicentennial of the war, especially parts of Beskrovnyi's OTECHESTVENNAIA VOINA 1812 GODA [The Patriotic War of 1812] (45). In addition, several works to be mentioned below have appeared lending new light on the participation of several of the nationalities, the use of the press in the war, and new treatments of some of the major participants. Unfortunately, Russian historians--both in their tsarist and Soviet modes--consistently undervalue the work contributed by foreigners on the Napoleonic wars, as well as for the Hitlerian campaigns.

GENERAL WORKS

Bulgakov (77), along with others mentioned above, began the Russian reviews of the events of 1812 the next year. In the next half-century the treatments went from those of lyrical nationalism to works praising the tsar and his associates to, finally, works of some detachment such as that of Bogdanovich.

During the same period, Napoleon came out with his assessment from St. Helena followed by a number of memoirs and multivolume studies. These range from obvious justification to accurate analysis as exemplified by Labaume (230), the lengthy studies of Beauvais de Préau (29), Dumas (128), Chambray (92), and Saint-Hilaire (348). Through the rest of the century hundreds of memoirs, popular works, and documentaries appeared, including Marqueron's four-volume work (259), but nothing before or since would compare with the studies of Fabry (140-142).

General studies on the French army can be found in earlier chapters of Fabry's volumes and general works on the Russian army include those by Andolenko (13) and Kersnovsky (215). The VOENNAIA ENTSIKLOPEDIA [Military Encylopedia] (291) is a helpful reference for background on major events and personalities in the Russian army. The most significant theoretical appreciations of the campaign are those of Clausewitz (102) and Jomini (211).

Among the useful works on the background of Russian-French relations are those of Pingaud (312), West (414), and Ignatieff (203). Other works dealing with the impact of the events on specific segments of society are Ginzburg's work on the Jews (168) and Holzhausens on the Germans (200). Kukiel (228) discusses the campaign from a Polish perspective while Leuschner describes the fate of the Bavarians with Napoleon (240), and Maag (252) deals with the activities of the Swiss. The biography of Alexander I by Schilder (361) remains the most comprehensive while many edited works of Nikolai Mikhailovich (282-286) provide elegantly printed documentaries and commentaries. The works of Tatischeff (388) and Vandal (399) are standard references.

Of the many individuals who devoted their careers to the study of the period, Popov (319-323) made significant contributions dealing with Moscow's role in the war and French military movements. Nineteenth century German historians have produced substantial studies of the campaign: Beitzke (31), Liebenstein (243), and Steger (369) provide overviews; von Burkersroda deals with the Saxons (78); Förster is concerned with Napoleon (149); Furtenbach discusses prisoners of war (155); and Obst traces the role of the participants from Hamburg (292).

The centenary of 1912 saw generally useful, though often chauvinist, works published in Russia such as those of Amfiteatrov (9), Bozherianov (70), and Bozhovskii (71). Dzhivelegov et al. (132) produced a rich collection of articles with their seven volumes. Other interesting contributions were those of the Moscow nobility (275), especially by Nive (289) and Vasyutinski et al., eds. (401). Voenskii's works on the Russian journalists and a more traditional military topic (407, 408) are informative.

Various aspects of the invasion have appeared in print during this century: Artom examined the domestic impact of the campaign in France (18), Belloc produced a grand overview of the invasion (32), and Burton developed an entertaining narrative (79). Each of these are good introductions along with the works of Jacoby (208), Cooper (108), and Cuñha (110). Delderfield emphasizes the retreat (115), and there are a number of valuable surveys by Palmer (300), Fry and Fox (153), Davis (113), Madelin (255), Jackson (207), Grunwald (188), and Lachouque (231) that make useful contributions to what the Russians call their "Patriotic War of 1812." The works by Chandler (93, 94) are good summaries, while Brett-James gives a dramatic selection of views of the campaign taken from memoirs (75). Thull's article on Napoleon's conceptions is interesting (390) and Pivka's work (314) on the strategy is perceptive.

BIBLIOGRAPHICAL AND HISTORIOGRAPHICAL WORKS

Zatvornitskii's bibliography (424) is one of the most useful guides to Russian pre-revolutionary periodicals and will complement the French bibliographical works mentioned above. Other guides of general use are to be found in the New York Public Library Slavonic Collection catalog and the yearly bibliographical guides published by the American Association for the Advancement of Slavic Studies. Also useful are the bibliographies of Mezhov (267), Ikonnikov (204), and Kircheisen (219). Pohler's BIBLIOTHECA HISTORICO-MILITARIS also lists many titles for the first three generations after the invasion.

Yaresh (420) gives a penetrating review of Soviet historiographical complexities up to the 1950s and Hollingsworth (198) does likewise from 1962. Horward's article (202) points to the most important French literature on 1812. Borozdin (61) reviews the 1912 literature and bibliographical sources can be found in such diverse sources as the documentary series edited by Narochnitskii et al. (279). The scholarly studies of Brett-James (75), and Duffy (127) provide useful and readily available bibliographies of literature in the field.

ARCHIVAL SOURCES

Michel Lesure's L'HISTOIRE DE RUSSIE AUX ARCHIVES NATIONALES (239) is an indispensable guide to research on the invasion. For the Russian archives, Patricia Kennedy Grimsted's ARCHIVES AND MANUSCRIPT REPOSITORIES IN THE USSR/MOSCOW AND LENINGRAD (183) is equally essential. For the purposes of the historian, these two guides are very helpful, and the latter is full of good advice for work in the Soviet archives. For France, the most valuable military manuscripts are located at the Archives de la guerre at Vincennes. Although tens of thousands of documents were lost by the French during the retreat

from Moscow, a number of cartons of the Grande Armée (C2 285-292)
deal with the campaign. Other documents related to various
detachments serving in Russia in 1812 are scattered throughout the
738 cartons of this series.

PUBLISHED DOCUMENTS

There are rich and varied sources of published documents
concerning the invasion. Many of them are to be found in the
journals listed below. A recent collection is that of Narochnitskii
(279). The most complete include some twenty-one volumes published
by the Russians between 1900 and 1914 (298). The most useful
collection in French came from Fabry (140-143). Those documents
edited by Goriainov (179, 180) are especially useful. More recently,
Beskrovnyi's collection of five volumes of documents on Kutuzov (41),
Borodino (39), and Chicherin (40) have brought rare documents to the
use of the scholarly community. Alt'shuller's documents on Borodino
(8) are also useful, along with the collection of documents relating
to the Cossacks (121), while those collections edited by Nikolai
Mikhailovich (283, 285) are beautifully reproduced.

Shorter, more specific collections can be found in the Pozzo di
Borgo letters edited by McErlean (253) and the documents presented by
the Joussiers (213), Lemercier-Quelquejay (238), Longinov (249),
Lyautey (251), and Vilde (405). The writings of de Maistre (256),
Derzhavin (116), and Roeder (337) also yield rich reflections on the
times.

In addition, during the tsarist period, substantial editions of
family papers, such as the forty-volume ARKHIV KNIAZIA VORONTSOVA
edited by P.I. Bartenev (447), and documents, such as the SBORNIK
ISTORICHESKIKH MATERIALOV IZVLECHENNYKH IZ ARKHIVA SOBSTVENNOI E. I.
VVA. KANTSELIARII (453), were published with extensive collections
including those edited by Dubrovin in numbers 10, 11, and 13. Also
of value is the POLNOE SOBRANIE ZAKONOV' ROSSIISKOI IMPERII (452)
which contains much important documentary evidence. Finally, major
figures living during the time, such as Counts Nesselrode and
Stroganov, left papers, published later in the century.

MEMOIRS, JOURNALS, AND EYEWITNESS ACCOUNTS

The most numerous sources listed below are memoirs and
eyewitness reports, some 120 of them, on the events of 1812. Some of
the more notable are those of Arndt (17), Bennigsen (34), Bialkowski
(49), Bourgoing (67), Brandt (73), Castellane (85), Caulaincourt
(87), Chichagov (97), Comeau de Charry (106), Czartoryski (111),
Davidov (112), Dumonceau (129), Glinka (172), Golitzyn (176),
Gourgaud (181), Hogendorp (197), de Kirckhoff (221), Langeron (233),
Lignières (244), Löwenstern (248), Montesquieu-Fezensac (274),
Narichkine (278), Porter (324), Potocka (325), Rochechouart (336),
Roos (339), Rotenhan (344), Ségur (354, 355), Szymanowski (374),
Vigel' (404), and Wilson (417). Brett-James (75) captured the
richness of the memorialists in his book. A check through the titles
will indicate the diversity of points of view and specializations of
the observers.

SPECIALIZED WORKS

The Borodino struggle and the burning of Moscow have attracted the most concentrated attention. Duffy (127) provides the most detailed English language study on Borodino. This should be supplemented with BORODINSKOE SPAZHENIE (60), Fabre (139), Garin (158), Golling (177), von Hofman (196), Koliubakin (223), Nikolaieff (287), and Predtechenskii (326). The conflagration of Moscow is discussed, most notably, in Rostopchin (343), Balitzki (24), Grunwald (187), Olivier (296), Polosin (318), van het Reve (335), Schmidt (350), Tzenoff (396), and Ysarn (422).

Soviet historians have focused on the role of the militia and the activities of the partisans during 1812, as can be seen in Babkin (21), Bychkov (82, 83), Cherviakov (96), and Pavlovski (305). The participation of the Austrians, Saxons, Wurttembergers, and émigrés, among other elements, is discussed by von Angeli (16), Cerrini (89), Exner (136), Giesse (166), and Guibal (190). Supply problems are dealt with by Chalmin (91), Carbonneaux (84), and Tulard (394). Regarding regional aspects of the invasion, Abalikhin examined the Ukraine (2), Andreev studied Smolensk (14), Butkevicius [René Martel] (80) and Dundulis (130) directed their research toward Lithuania, and Glybovskii concentrated on Vitebsk (174). Khovanski was attracted to the impact of the invasion on Saratov (218), Paskin dealt with Tver (301), and Sivitskii directed his attention to the Baltic area (362).

Major participants have received treatment ranging from the enthusiasts who praise Napoleon to those who denigrate Barclay de Tolly. During the ideologically directed 1940s Soviet historians turned out a range of short biographies concerning Kutuzov and Bagration as exemplified by Bragin (72) and Borisov (59) respectively. More substantial are some of the articles contained in the edition by Beskrovnyi (47).

PERIODICALS

In addition to the French journals listed in Chapter I, the following Russian journals and collections are extremely valuable for the historian concerned with the events of the first quarter of the nineteenth century. An indispensable guide for the use of these journals and others is UKAZATELI SODERZHANIIA RUSSKIKH ZHURNALOV I PRODOLZHAIUSHCHIKHSIA IZDANII 1755-1970 GG by Iu. I. Masanov, N.V. Nitkina, and Z.D. Titova (451). This guide to the indices of both tsarist and Soviet journals will aid the researcher in his search for titles. In addition, many of the journals listed below contain material published in western languages, especially French and German. Zatvornitskii (424) is another essential guide for access to the Russian journals.

The SBORNIK IMPERATORSKOGO RUSSKOGO ISTORICHESKOGO OBSHCHESTVA (442) is an especially rich repository of documents relating to the invasion. Volumes 21, 70, 77, 82, 83, and 88 give valuable sources on diplomatic aspects of the Russo-French relations while volumes 128, 133, and 139 offer information on Napoleon's activities. In addition, RUSSKAIA STARINA (439) and RUSSKII ARKHIV (440) contain extracts of memoirs, extensive articles, and documents relating to the period. VOENNYI SBORNIK (445) is the best source for military narrative of the period. Specialists in the area should make an

extensive review of the indices of these journals, and work through
Zatvornitskii to gain a fuller appreciation of the immense amount of
literature in Russian on the topic as listed in such works as
Masanov et al. (451).

The Brockhaus-Efron ENTSIKLOPEDICHESKII SLOVAR' (433), an
eighty-six-volume collection published between 1890-1907, is a superb
reference work, as is the incomplete twenty-five-volume RUSSKII
BIOGRAFICHESKII SLOVAR' (441), printed from 1896 to 1913.   In
addition, there are provincial historical journals which are
essential to gain the fullest appreciation of the extraordinary
attention given to this topic.

Major Soviet journals are VOPROSY ISTORII (446), ISTORIIA SSSR
(435), ISTORIK MARKSIST (436), and the ISTORICHESKII ZAPISKI (434).
An incomplete list of western journals dealing with the area includes
the SLAVONIC AND EAST EUROPEAN REVIEW (443), SLAVIC REVIEW (444), LE
MONDE SLAVE (438),· CAHIERS DU MONDE RUSSE ET SOVIETIQUE (432), and
the JAHRBUECHER FUER GESCHICHTE OSTEUROPAS (437).

FUTURE RESEARCH

In many aspects, the more recent publications have not surpassed
the studies done on the invasion in the first part of this century.
In the west during the past generation, comparatively little
attention has been paid to the invasion. In Russia, there has been,
naturally, a much greater degree of activity with important new
information being made available both through research on individual
questions and the publication of documents. The difficulty of
gaining access to the necessary archives in the Soviet Union will
make it awkward for the great synthesis to be accomplished by a
western historian. At the same time, although the ideological
crudities of the Stalinist influences have been overcome, there
remain too many obstacles within the Soviet Union for a dispassionate
discussion of the causes of the war, and analysis of the political,
social, economic, religious, and psychological impact upon the
Russian people and their leaders. Perhaps the climate for such a
large synthesis with access to the necessary data will be present by
the bicentennial of the invasion.

There is much work to be done on the role of the various
elements that served in both the Grande Armée and the armies of the
tsar. Many geographical areas that suffered from the burdens of the
French occupation have not yet been examined. Regarding tactics,
strategy, and logistics, seldom does a historian have such an
opportunity to analyse such topics on so grand a scale.

BIBLIOGRAPHY: RUSSIA

1. Abalikhin, Borys S. "Rol' Ukrainy v Obespechenii Armii v Otechestvennoi Voine 1812 Goda" [The Role of the Ukraine in the Provisioning of the Army in the Patriotic War of 1812]. VOPROSY VOENNOI ISTORII ROSSII: XVIII I PERVAIA POLOVINA XIX VEKOV [Problems in Russian Military History: 18th and the first half of the 19th Century]. Moscow: "Nauka," 1969.

2. Abalikhin, Borys S. "Ukrainskoe Opolchenie 1812 G." [The Ukrainian Militia, 1812]. ISTORICHESKIE ZAPISKI 72 (1962): 87-118.

3. Adam, Albrecht. AUS DEM LEBEN EINES SCHLACHTENMALERS. Stuttgart: Cotta, 1886.

4. Afanasiev, Georgii Emelianovich. NAPOLEON' I ALEKSANDR': PRICHINY VOINY 1812 GODA [Napoleon and Alexander: Causes of the War of 1812]. Kiev: Kievskoe Obshchestvo Iskusstva i Literatury, 1912.

5. Akhlestyshev, Dmitrii P. DVENADTSATYI GOD. ISTORICHESKIE DOKUMENTY SOBSTVENNOI KANTSELIARII GLAVNOKOMANDUIUSHCHAGO 3-IU I ZAPADNOIU ARMIEIU GENERALA-OT-KAVALERII A.P. TORMASOVA, IZVLEK IZ SEMEINOGO ARKHIVA I PRIVEL V PORIADOK D.P. AKHLESTYSHEV [1812, Historical Documents from the Office of the Commander in chief of the Third and Western Army, the Cavalry General A.P. Tormasov, selected from the family archives and put in order by D.P. Aklestyshev]. St. Petersburg: M.M. Stasiulevich, 1912.

6. Akhsharumov, Dmitrii Ivanovich. ISTORICHESKOE OPISANIE VOINY 1812go GODA [An Historical Description of the War of 1812]. St. Petersburg: Imperatorskaia tipografiia, 1813.

7. Akinfov. IZ' VOSPOMINANII AKINFOVA, V. KN. KHARKEVICH, V' 1812 GOD V' DNEVNIKAKH', ZAPISKAKH', I VOSPOMINANIAKH' SOVVREMENNIKOV' [From the Recollections of Akinfov... 1812 in diaries, notes, and the recollections of contemporaries]. Vilna: Materialy Voennogo-uchenogo arkhiva Glavnogo shtaba, 1900.

8. Al'tshuller, Rozaliia Efimovna. BORODINO: DOKUMENTY, PIS' MA, VOSPOMINANIIA [Borodino: Documents, Letters, and Recollections]. Moscow: Izd-vo Sovetskaia Rossiia, 1962.

9. Amfiteatrov, Aleksandr V. 1812 GODA: OCHERK' IZ' ISTORII RUSSKAGO PATRIOTIZMA [1812: An Essay from the History of Russian Partiotism]. St. Petersburg: Prosveshchenie, 1912.

10. Andeiev, N.I. "Iz' vospominanii" [From Reminicences]. RUSSKII ARKHIV' 3 (1879): 173-202.

11. Anderson, Matthew S. "British Public Opinion and the Russian Campaign of 1812." SLAVIC AND EAST EUROPEAN REVIEW 34 (1956): 408-25.

403

12. Andolenko, Serge. AIGLES DE NAPOLEON CONTRE DRAPEAUX DU TSAR. Paris: Flammarion, 1969.

13. Andolenko, Serge.   HISTOIRE DE L'ARMEE RUSSE.   Paris: Flammarion, 1967.

14. Andreev, Pavel G. NARODNAIA VOINA V SMOLENSKOI GUBERNIU 1812 GODU [The People's War in Smolensk Gubernia in 1812]. Smolensk: Smolenskoe obl. gos. izd-vo., 1940.

15. Andreev, Vadim L. RAZVITIIA POLCHISHCHA ILI RUSSKIE V' 1812 GODU,   SBORNIK'   KHRESTOMATIIA,   RAZSKAZY   I   VOSPOMINANIIA UCHASTNIKOV',   OCHEVIDTSEV'   I   RUSSKIKH'   PISATELEI   S' RAZM'SHCHENIEM'   STATEI   V'   POSLEDOVATEL'NOM'   KHOD' ISTORICHESKIKH' SOBYTII [The Development of the Horde, or The Russians in 1812; A Collection of Stories, and Reminiscences of Participants, Eyewitnesses, and Russian Writers with annotations of articles in the successive course of historical events]. St. Petersburg: V.I. Gubimskii, 1912.

16. Angeli, Moriz von.   DIE THEILNAHME DES OESTERREICHISCHEN AUXILIAR-KORPS UNTER SCHWARZENBERG IM FELDZUG NAPOLEONS I GEGEN RUSSLAND. Vienna: Mittheilungen des k. k. Kriegs-Archivs, 1884.

17. Arndt, Ernst M. ERINNERUNGEN AUS DEM AUSSEREN LEBEN. Leipzig: Reclam, 1892.

18. Artom, Guido. NAPOLEON EST MORT EN RUSSIE. Paris: R. Laffont, 1969.

19. Askenazy, Szymon.   "Przyczyny Wielkiej Wojny 1812 Roku" [The Causes of the Great 1812 War]. BIBLIOTEKA WARSZAWSKA 3 (1899): 413-46.

20. Audiat, Pierre.   "Napoléon en Russie." LA REVUE DE PARIS 1 (1961): 148-61.

21. Babkin, Vasilii I.   "Novye materialy o klassovoi Bor'be Krest'ian V 1812 G." [New Material on the Class Struggle of the Peasants in 1812].   VOPROSY VOENNOI ISTORII ROSSII: XVIII I PERVAIA POLOVINA XIX VEKOV [Problems in Russian Military History: 18th and the First Half of the 19th Century]. Moscow: "Nauka," 1969.

22. Babkin, Vasilii I. "Organizatsiia i voennye deistviia Narodnogo Opolcheniia v Otechestvennoi Voine 1812 G." [The organization and military actions of the Peoples' Militia in the Patriotic War of 1812]. Edited by L.G. Beskrovnyi and others. 1812 GOD. K 150-LETTIIU OTECHESTVENNOI VOINY [1815: On the 150th Anniversary of the Patriotic War]. Moscow: Akademii nauk, 1962.

23. Bakunina, V.I. "Dvenadtsaty God' V' Zapiskakh' V.I. Bakuninoi" [1812 in the Notes of V.I. Bakunina]. RUSSKAIA STARINA 47 (1885): 391-410.

24. Balitzki, G., ed. POZHAR' MOSKVY, PO VOSPOMINANIIAM' I
PEREPISKI SOVREMENNIKOV' [The Burning of Moscow according to the
Recollections and Correspondence of Contemporaries]. Moscow:
Obrazovanie, 1911.

25. Barklai-de-Tolli, Mikhail B. IZOBRAZHENIE VOENNYKH DEISTVII
1812-GODA. KROME TOGO, RESKRIPTY, PIS'MA I DRUGIE DOKUMENTY,
OTNOSIASHCHIESIA DO 1812 G., A TAKZHE VYPISKA IZ PIS'MA KUPTSA
CHILIKINA O PREBYVANII FRANTSUZOV V MOSKVE [Portrayals of the
Military Actions of 1812. In addition, the Rescripts, Letters
and other Documents relating to 1812, and also extracts from the
Letter of the Merchant Chilikin on the Arrival of the French in
Moscow]. St. Petersburg: N. Gastfreind, 1912.

26. "Barklai-de-Tolli   i   Otechestvennaia   voina   1812   goda"
[Barclay-de-Tolly and the 1812 Patriotic War]. RUSSKAIA STARINA
8, 9, 10, 12 (1912): 172-207; 301-331; 108-135; 631-652.

27. Bastard, Antoine d'. "Aperçu sur la campagne de Russie en
1812." LA SCIENCE HISTORIQUE 3, 4 (1957): 116-22.

28. Bausset, Louis François. MEMOIRES ANECDOTIQUES SUR L'INTERIEUR
DU PALAIS ET SUR QUELQUES EVENEMENTS DE L'EMPIRE DEPUIS 1805
JUSQU'AU 1er MAI 1814. Paris: Baudoin, 1827. 2 vols.

29. Beauvais de Préau, Charles Théodore, comp. VICTOIRES,
CONQUETES, DESASTRES, REVERS, ET GUERRES CIVILES DES FRANCAIS,
DE 1792 A 1815, PAR UNE SOCIETE DE MILITAIRES ET DE GENS DE
LETTRES. Paris: Panckoucke, 1818-21. 27 vols.

30. Begos, Louis. SOUVENIRS DES CAMPAGNES DE LIEUTENANT-COLONEL
LOUIS BEGOS: SOLDATS SUISSES AU SERVICE ETRANGER. Lausanne:
Delafontaine, 1859.

31. Beitzke, Heinrich L. GESCHICHTE DES RUSSISCHEN KRIEGES IM JAHRE
1812. Berlin: Duncker and Humblot, 1856.

32. Belloc, Hillaire. NAPOLEON'S CAMPAIGN OF 1812 AND RETREAT FROM
MOSCOW. New York: Harper, 1926.

33. Bellot de Kergorre, Alexandre. UN COMMISSAIRE DES GUERRES
PENDANT LE PREMIER EMPIRE. Paris: E. Paul, 1899.

34. Benningsen, Levin August Gottlieb von. MEMOIRES DU GENERAL
BENNIGSEN. Paris: Charles-Lavauzelle, 1907. 3 vols.

35. Berg, Gregor M. von. LEBEN VON GREGOR VON BERG. Dresden: E.
Blochmann, 1872.

36. Bernhardi, Theodor von. DENKWUERDIGKEITEN AUS DEM LEBEN DES
KAISERL. RUSS. GENERALS VON DER INFANTERIE CARL FRIEDERICH
GRAFEN VON TOLL. Leipzig: Wigand, 1865. 4 parts.

37. Bertin, Georges. LA CAMPAGNE DE 1812, D'APRES DES TEMOINS
OCULAIRES. Paris: Flammarion, 1895.

38. Beskrovnyi, Liubomir G. "Bor'ba Rossii s Frantsiei v Kontse XVIII-nachale XIX V Otechestvennaia Voina 1812 Goda" [The Struggle of Russia with France at the end of the 18th, beginning of the 19th Century in the Patriotic War of 1812]. STRANITSY BOEVOGO PROSHLOGO, OCHERKI VOENNOI ISTORII ROSSII [Pages from the Fighting Past; Essays in the Military History of Russia]. Moscow: Nauka, 1968.

39. Beskrovnyi, Liubomir G. "Borodinskoe Srazhenie (K 150 Letnei Godovschine) [The Battle of Borodino (on the 150th Anniversary)]. ISTORIIA SSSR 6 (1962): 3-18.

40. Beskrovnyi, Liubomir G., ed. DNEVNIK ALEKSANDRA CHICHERINA 1812-1813 [The Diary of Alexander Chicherin 1812-1813]. Moscow: "Nauka," 1966.

41. Beskrovnyi, Liubomir G., ed. M.I. KUTUZOV, SBORNIK DOKUMENTOV [M.I. Kutuzov, A Collection of Documents]. Moscow: Voen. izd-vo., 1950-56. 5 vols.

42. Beskrovnyi, Liubomir G., ed. NARODNOE OPOLCHENIE V OTECHESTVENNOI VOINE 1812 GODA: SBORNIK DOKUMENTOV [The People's Volunteer Corps in the Patriotic War of 1812: A Collection of Documents]. Moscow: Akademii nauk SSSR, 1962.

43. Beskrovnyi, Liubomir G. "Nekotorye Voprosy Istorii otot Otechestvennoi Voiny 1812 Goda" [Several Issues in the History of the Patriotic War of 1812]. VOPROSY ISTORII 10 (1962): 50-60.

44. Beskrovnyi, Liubomir G. OCHERKI PO ISTOCHNIKOVEDENIIA VOENNOI ISTORII ROSSII [Essay on the Sources of Russian Military History]. Moscow: Izd-vo Akad. nauk SSSR, 1957.

45. Beskrovnyi, Liubomir G. OTECHESTVENNAIA VOINA 1812 GODA [The Patriotic War of 1812]. Moscow: Izd-vo. Sotsial'no-ekon-Lit, 1962.

46. Beskrovnyi, Liubomir G. OTECHESTVENNAIA VOINA 1812 GODA I KONTRNASTUPLENIE KUTUZOVA [The Patriotic War of 1812 and the Counterattack of Kutuzov]. Moscow: Akademii nauk SSSR, 1951.

47. Beskrovnyi, Liubomir G., ed. POLKOVODETS KUTUZOV, SBORNIK STATEI [The Army Leader Kutuzov, A Collection of Articles]. Moscow: Gos. izd-vo. polit. lit-ry., 1955.

48. Beskrovnyi, Liubomir G., and G.P. Meshcheriakov, eds. BORODINO 1812-1962: DOKUMENTY, PIS'MA, VOSPOMINANIIA [Borodino 1812-1962: Documents, Letters, Memoirs]. Moscow: Sovetskaia Rossiia, 1962.

49. Bialkowski, Antoni. PAMIETNIKI STAREGO ZOLNIERZA 1806-1814 [Memoirs of an Old Soldier, 1806-1814]. Warsaw: Gebethner i Wolff, 1903.

50. Bigarré, Auguste. MEMOIRES DU GENERAL BIGARRE, AIDE-DE-CAMP DU ROI JOSEPH 1775-1813. Paris: Kolb, 1893.

51. Billion. "Lettres de Russia." BULLETIN SOCIETE BELGE D'ETUDES NAPOLEONIENNES 88 (1974): 16-19.

52. Biornberg, Adolph. GRAND RECITATION ON THE RUSSIAN WAR IN 1812 WITH THE FRENCH ARMY. Lawrence, Mass.: Wadsworth, 1870.

53. Biot, Hubert François. CAMPAGNES ET GARNISONS, SOUVENIRS ANECDOTIQUES ET MILITAIRES DU COLONEL BIOT. Paris: Vivien, 1901.

54. Black, J.L. "N.M. Karamzin, Napoleon and the Notion of Defensive War in Russian History." CANADIAN SLAVONIC PAPERS 12 (1970): 30-46.

55. Bogdanovich, Modest I. GESCHICHTE DES FELDZUGES IM JAHRE 1812. Translated by G. Baumgarten. Leipzig: B. Schlicke, 1861-63. 3 vols.

56. Bogdanovich, Modest I. ISTORIIA OTECHESTVENNOI VOINY 1812 GODA. [The History of the Patriotic War of 1812]. St. Petersburg: S. Strugovitskii, 1859-60. 3 vols.

57. Bomsdorf, Wilhelm Karl. MITTEILUNGEN AUS DEM FELDZUGES IM JAHRE 1812. Leipzig: Engelmann, 1816-18. 2 vols.

58. Borcke, Johann Friedrich von. KRIEGERLEBEN DES JOHANN VON BORCKE. Berlin: Mittler, 1888.

59. Borisov, S.B. BAGRATION. Moscow: Voen. izd-vo., 1943.

60. BORODINSKOE SRAZHENIE [The Battle of Borodino]. Moscow: Izdanie Imperatorskogo Obshchestva Istorii i Drevnostei Rossisskikh'pri Moskovskom Universitete, 1872.

61. Borozdin, J. "Jubilaumsliteratur über das Jahr 1812." ZEITSCHRIFT FUER OESTEUROPAISCHE GESCHICHTE 3 (1913): 414-28.

62. Boulart, Jean François. MEMOIRES MILITAIRES. Paris: Librarie illustrée, 1892.

63. Bouloiseau, Marc. "Les Archives Voronzov." REVUE HISTORIQUE 230 (1963): 121-130.

64. Bourgeois, René. TABLEAU DE LA CAMPAGNE DE MOSCOU EN 1812. Paris: Dentu, 1814.

65. Bourgogne, Adrien Jean. MEMOIRES DE SERGENT BOURGOGNE, 1812-1813. Paris: Hachette, 1910.

66. Bourgogne, Adrien Jean. SES MEMOIRES. Paris: Editions de Saint-Clair, 1967.

67. Bourgoing, Paul de. SOUVENIRS MILITAIRES DU BARON DE BOURGOING. Paris: Plon-Nourrit, 1897.

68. Boyen, Leopold Hermann von. ERINNERUNGEN AUS DEM LEBEN DES GENERAL-FELD-MARSCHALLS HERMANN VON BOYEN. Leipzig: Hirzel, 1889-90. 2 vols.

69. Bozherianov, Ivan N. NASHESTVIE NAPOLEONA. [The Invasion of Napoleon]. St. Petersburg: S.M. Prokudin'-Gorskii, 1911-12.

70. Bozherianov, Ivan N. VOINA RUSSKAGO NARODA S' NAPOLEONOM' 1812 G. [The War of the Russian People with Napoleon, 1812]. St. Petersburg: A.F. Marks, 1911.

71. Bozhovskii, V. VYSTAVKA 1812 GODA [The Exposition of 1812]. Moscow: A.A. Levenson, 1913.

72. Bragin, Mikhail. FIELDMARSHAL KUTUZOV.   Moscow: Foreign Languages Publications House, 1944.

73. Brandt, Heinrich von. SOUVENIRS D'UN OFFICIER POLONAIS, SCENES DE LA VIE MILITAIRE EN ESPAGNE ET EN RUSSIE, 1808-1812. Paris: Charpentier, 1877.

74. Breaut des Marlots, Jean. LETTRE D'UN CAPITAINE CUIRASSIERS SUR LA CAMPAGNE DE RUSSIE. Paris: Chez tous les libraires, 1885.

75. Brett-James, Antony, ed., trans., and comp. 1812; EYEWITNESS ACCOUNTS OF NAPOLEON'S DEFEAT IN RUSSIA. New York: St. Martin, 1966.

76. Brodskii, Nikolai L., et al., comp.   ROSSIIA I NAPOLEON', OTECHESTENNAIA   VOINA   V   MEMUARAKH',   DOKUMENTAKH',   I KHUDOZHESTVENNYKH' PROIZVEDENIIAKH. [Russia and Napoleon--The Patriotic War in Memoirs, Documents, and Works of Art]. Moscow: Zadruga, 1912.

77. Bulgakov, Alensandr Y. RUSSKIE I NAPOLOEON' BONAPARTE, ILI RAZSMOTRENIIE POVEDENIIA NYNESHNIAGO OBLADATELIA FRANTSII S' TIL'ZITSKAGO MIRA PO IZGNANIE EGO IZ' DREVNEI ROSSIISKOI STOLITSY [The Russians and Napoleon Bonaparte, or an Examination of the Conduct of the Present Master of France from the Peace of Tilsit until his Explusion from the Ancient Russian Capital]. Moscow: S. Selivanovskii, 1813.

78. Burkersroda, Major von. DIE SACHSEN IN RUSSLAND. EIN BEITRAG ZUR GESCHICHTE DES RUSSISCHEN FELZUGES IM JAHRE 1812, BESONDERS IM   BEZUG   AUF   DAS   SCHICKSAL   DER   KGL: SACHSISCHEN TRUPPEN-ABTEILUNG   BEI   DER   GROSSEN   FRANZOESISCHEN   ARMEE. Naumburg: Weber, 1846.

79. Burton, Reginald George.   NAPOLEON'S   INVASION   OF   RUSSIA. London: George Allen, 1914.

80. Butkevicius [René Martel]. "Napoleon en Lithuanie 1812, (d'après des documents inédits)." LA REVUE DE PARIS 39 (1932): 897-912.

81. Buturlin, Dimitrii P. ISTORIIA NASHESTVIIA IMPERATORA NAPOLEONA NA ROSSIIU V 1812-M GODU. S'OFITSIAL'NYKH' DOKUMENTOV'I DRUGIKH' DOSTOVERNYK' BUMAG' ROSSISSKOGO I FRANTSUZSKOGO GENERAL-SHTABOV [The History of the Emperor Napoleon's Invasion of Russia in 1812, based on official documents and other authentic papers of the French and Russian General Staffs]. St. Petersburg: Voennaia tipografiia, 1837-38. 2 vols.

82. Bychkov, Lev Nikolaevich. KREST'IANSKOE PARTIZANSKOE DVIZHENIE V OTECHESTVENNOI VOINE 1812 GODA [The Peasant Partisan Movement in the 1812 Patriotic War]. Moscow: Gospolitizdat, 1954.

83. Bychkov, Lev Nikolaevich. PARTIZANSKOE DVIZHENIE V OTECHESTVENNOI VOINE 1812 GODA [The Partisan Movement in the 1812 Patriotic War]. Moscow: Ogiz, Gospolitizdat, 1941.

84. Carbonneaux, Colonel J. "Le Train des équipages militaires en Russie, une épreuve, un espoir." REVUE HISTORIQUE DES ARMEES 3 (1978): 21-38.

85. Castellane, Esprit Victor, comte de. JOURNAL DU MARECHAL CASTELLANE. Paris: Plon-Nourrit, 1895-97. 5 vols.

86. Cathcart, George. COMMENTARIES ON THE WAR IN RUSSIA AND GERMANY, 1812 AND 1813. London: J. Murray, 1850.

87. Caulaincourt, Armand Augustin, marquis de, duc de Vicence. MEMOIRES DU GENERAL DE CAULAINCOURT, DUC DE VICENCE, GRAND ECUYER DE L'EMPEREUR. Paris: Plon-Nourrit, 1933. 3 vols.

88. Cazalas, Jean Jules, ed. and trans. LA GUERRE NATIONALE DE 1812, PUBLICATION DU COMITE SCIENTIFIQUE DU GRAND ETAT-MAJOR RUSSE. Paris: Charles-Lavauzelle, 1903-07. 8 vols.

89. Cerrini, Clemens Franz. DIE FELDZUGE DER SACHSEN IN DEN JAHREN 1812 UND 1813. Dresden: Arnold, 1821.

90. Chair, Somerset de. NAPOLEON'S MEMOIRS. London: Faber and Faber, 1948.

91. Chalmin, Pierre. "Le Train des équipages pendant la campagne de Russie." REVUE DU TRAIN 16 (1953): 32-43.

92. Chambray, Georges de. HISTOIRE DE L'EXPEDITION EN RUSSIE. Paris: Pillet, 1823. 2 vols.

93. Chandler, David G. THE CAMPAIGNS OF NAPOLEON. New York: Macmillan, 1966.

94. Chandler, David G. "The Russian Army at War, 1807 and 1812." HISTORY TODAY 12 (1970): 867-74.

95. Chelminski, Jan V. L'ARMEE DU DUCHE DE VARSOVIE. Paris: Leroy, 1913.

96. Cherviakov, D.E. PARTIZANSKOE DVIZHENIE V PERIOD PODGOTOVKI I PROVEDENIIA KUTUZOVYM KONTR-NASTUPLENIIA V 1812 GODU [The Partisian Movement in the Period of the Preparations and the Execution of the Kutuzov Counter-attack in 1812]. Moscow: Znanie, 1953.

97. Chichagov, Pavel V. MEMOIRES DE L'AMIRAL PAUL TCHITCHAGOFF, COMMANDANT EN CHEF DE L'ARMEE DU DANUBE, GOUVERNEUR DES PRINCIPAUTES DE MOLDAVIE ET DE VALACHIE EN 1812. Paris: Plon-Nourrit, 1909.

98. Chlapowski, Dezydery. MEMOIRES SUR LES GUERRES DE NAPOLEON 1806-1813. Paris: Plon-Nourrit, 1908.

99. Choiseul-Gouffier, Sophie de Tisenhaus, comtesse de. MEMOIRES HISTORIQUES SUR L'EMPEREUR ALEXANDRE ET LA COUR DE RUSSIE. Paris: Leroux, 1829.

100. Christian, Reginald F. TOLSTOY'S "WAR AND PEACE." Oxford: Clarendon Press, 1962.

101. Chulkevich, Piotr A. RAZSUZHDENIIA O VOINE 1812 GODA [A Discourse on the 1812 War]. St. Petersburg: Senatskaia Tipografiia, 1813.

102. Clausewitz, Karl von. DER FELDZUG VON 1812 IN RUSSLAND UND DIE BEFREIUNGSKRIEGE VON 1813-1815. Berlin: Ferd. Dummlers, 1906.

103. Coignet, Jeran Roch. LES CAHIERS DU CAPITAINE COIGNET 1799-1815. Paris: Hachette, 1883.

104. Collis, A. "Some Survivors of the Russian Campaign of 1812." HISTORY TODAY 11 (1971): 796-802.

105. Combe, Michel. MEMOIRES SUR LES CAMPAGNES DE RUSSIE, 1812, DE SAXE, 1813, DE FRANCE, 1814 ET 1815. Paris: Blot, 1853.

106. Comeau de Charry, Sebastien Joseph, baron de. SOUVENIRS DES GUERRES D'ALLEMAGNE PENDANT LA REVOLUTION ET L'EMPIRE. Paris: Plon-Nourrit, 1900.

107. Compans, Jean Dominique. LE GENERAL COMPANS (1769-1845). Paris: Plon-Nourrit, 1912.

108. Cooper, Leonard. MANY ROADS TO MOSCOW: THREE HISTORIC INVASIONS. London: H. Hamilton, 1968.

109. Cosse-Brissac, Charles de. "Le maréchal Mortier pendant la campagne de Russie en 1812." LA COHORTE (1974): 19.

110. Cuñha, Ascendino da. A CAMPANHA DA RUSSIA. Rio de Janeiro: Jornal do Commercio, 1946.

111. Czartoryski, Adam. MEMOIRES DU PRINCE ADAM CZARTROYSKI ET SA CORRESPONDANCE AVEC L'EMPEREUR ALEXANDRE Ier. Paris: Plon-Nourrit, 1887. 2 vols.

112. Davidov, Denis. VOENNYE ZAPISKI [Military Recollections]. Moscow: Izd-vo. "Khudozhestvennaia Literatura," 1940.

113. Davis, Frank. "1812 Campaign: Napoleon in Russia." STRATEGY AND TACTICS 35 (1972): 21-35.

114. Dedem van de Gelder, Anton Boudewijn, graaf van. MEMOIRES DU GENERAL BARON DE DEDEM DE GELDER, 1774-1825. Paris: Plon-Nourrit, 1900.

115. Delderfield, Ronald F. THE RETREAT FROM MOSCOW. London: Hodder and Stoughton, 1967.

116. Derzhavin, Gavriil R. SOCHINENIIA [Works]. St. Petersburg: A. Smirdin, 1851. 2 vols.

117. Dinfreville, Jacques. "Les Silences d'un grognard." ECRITS DE PARIS 378 (1978): 60-66.

118. Ditfurth, Maximilian, freiherr von. DIE SCHLACHT BEI BORODINO AM 7 SEPTEMBER 1812, MIT BESONDERER RUECKSICHT AUF DIE THEIL NAHME DER DEUTSCHER REITER-KONTINGENTE. Marburg: Elwert, 1887.

119. Dodge, Theordore A. NAPOLEON. Boston and New York: Houghton Mifflin, 1904. 4 vols.

120. DONSKIE KAZAKI V 1812 GODU, SBORNIK DOKUMENTOV OB UCHASTII DONSKOGO KAZACHESTVA V OTECHESTVENNOI VOINE 1812 GODA [The Don Cossacks in 1812, A Collection of Documents on the Participation of the Don Cossacks in the 1812 Patriotic War]. Rostov-na-Don, 1954.

121. DONSKOE KAZACHESTVO V OTECHESTVENNOI VOINE 1812 G. [The Don Cossacks in the 1812 Patriotic War]. Moscow: Ogiz Gospolitizdat, 1942.

122. Dragomirov, Mikhail I. GUERRE ET PAIX DE TOLSTOI AU POINT DE VUE MILITAIRE. Paris: Baudoin, 1896.

123. Druzhinin, Nikolai F. "Osvoboditel'naia Voina 1813 G. I Russkoe Obshchestvo" [The Liberation War of 1813 and Russian Society]. VOPROSY ISTORII 11 (1963): 34-46.

124. Dubrovin, Nikolai F., ed. OTECHESTVENNAIA VOINA V PIS'MAKH SOVREMENNIKOV (1812-1815) [The Patriotic War in the Letters of Contemporaries]. St. Petersburg: Zapiski imperatorskogo Akademii nauk, 1882. Vol. 43.

125. Du Casse, Albert, baron. MEMOIRES POUR SERVIR A L'HISTOIRE DE
     LA CAMPAGNE DE 1812 EN RUSSIE, SUIVIS DES LETTRES DE NAPOLEON AU
     ROI DE WESTPHALIE PENDANT LA CAMPAGNE DE 1813. Paris: Au
     bureau de Spectateur militaire, 1852.

126. Duchinski, N., ed. 1812-I GOD' V' PROIZVEDENIIAKH' RUSSKIKH'
     PISATELEI I POETOV' [1812 in the Works of the Russian Writers
     and Poets]. Moscow: I.D. Sitina, 1912.

127. Duffy, Christopher. BORODINO AND THE WAR OF 1812. New York:
     Scribner, 1973.

128. Dumas, Mathieu. PRECIS DES EVENEMENTS MILITAIRES, OU ESSAI
     HISTORIQUE SUR LES CAMPAGNES DE 1799 A 1814. Paris: Treuttel,
     1816-21. 16 vols.

129. Dumonceau, François. MEMOIRES. MEMOIRES DU GENERAL COMTE
     FRANCOIS DUMONCEAU. Brussels: Brepols, 1958-63. 3 vols.

130. Dundulis, Bronius. NAPOLEON ET LA LITUANIE EN 1812. Paris:
     Presses universitaires de France, 1940.

131. Dupuy, Victor. SOUVENIRS MILITAIRES DE VICTOR DUPUY CHEF
     D'ESCADRONS DE HUSSARDS, 1794-1816. Paris: Calmann-Lévy, 1892.

132. Dzhivelegov, Alexsei K., et al., eds. OTECHESTVENNAIA VOINA I
     RUSSKOE OBSHCHESTVO [The Patriotic War and Russian Society].
     Moscow: Obshchestvo...znanii, 1912. 7 vols.

133. Eniden, Fritz. ERINNERUNGEN EINES OESTERREICHISCHEN
     ORDONNANZOFFIZIERS AUS DEM FELDZUGE 1812. Vienna: Seidl, 1898.

134. Ermolov, Aleksei P. MATERIAY DLIA ISTORII VOINY 1812 G.
     [Material for the History of the 1812 War]. Moscow: Got'e, 1863.

135. Esposito, Vincent J., and John R. Elting. A MILITARY HISTORY
     AND ATLAS OF THE NAPOLEONIC WARS. New York: Praeger, 1964.

136. Exner, Moritz. DER ANTHEIL DER KONIGL. SACHSISCHEN ARMEE EN
     FELDZUGE GEGEN RUSSLAND, 1812. Leipzig: Duncker, 1896.

137. Faber, Theodore von. BICH' FRANTSII [The French Scourge]. St.
     Petersburg: Senatskaia tipografiia, 1813.

138. Faber du Faur, Christian W. von. CAMPAGNE DE RUSSIE, 1812.
     Paris: Flammarion, 1895.

139. Fabre, Marc André. "De Borodino à Moscou, 8-14, septembre
     1812." REVUE HISTORIQUE DE L'ARMEE 16 (1960): 67-70.

140. Fabry, Gabriel J. CAMPAGNE DE 1812, DOCUMENTS RELATIFS A L'AILE
     DROIT 20 AOUT-4 DECEMBRE. Paris: Chapelot, 1914.

141. Fabry, Gabriel J. CAMPAGNE DE 1812, DOCUMENTS RELATIFS A L'AILE
     GAUCHE 20 AOUT-4 DECEMBRE. Paris: Chapelot, 1912.

142. Fabry, Gabriel J. CAMPAGNE DE RUSSIE, 1812. Paris: Lucien Gougy, 1900-03. 5 vols.

143. Fabry, Gabriel J., ed. CORRESPONDENCE INEDITE DE L'EMPEREUR ALEXANDRE ET BERNADOTTE. Paris: Chapelot, 1909.

144. Fadeev, Anatolii V. 1812 GOD: K STOPIATIDESIATILETIIU OTECHESTVENNOI VOINY: SBORNIK STATEI [1812: On the 150th Anniversary of the Patriotic War. A Collection of Articles]. Moscow: Akademii nauk SSSR, 1962.

145. Fain, Agathon Jean François, baron. MANUSCRIT DE 1812, CONTENANT LE PRECIS DES EVENEMENTS DE CETTE ANNEE. Paris: Delaunay, 1827. 2 vols.

146. Fain, Agathon Jean François, baron. MEMOIRES DU BARON FAIN, PREMIERE SECRETAIRE DE CABINET DE L'EMPEREUR. Paris: Plon-Nourrit, 1908.

147. Fantin des Odoards, Louis Florimond. JOURNAL DU GENERAL FANTIN DES ODOARDS, ETAPES D'UN OFFICIER DE LA GRANDE ARMEE, 1800-1830. Paris: Plon-Nourrit, 1895.

148. Faré, Charles-Armand. LETTRES D'UN JEUNE OFFICIER A SA MERE, 1803 A 1814. Paris: Delagrave, 1889.

149. Förster, Friedrich. NAPOLEONS I RUSSISCHER FELDZUG 1812. Berlin: G. Hempel, 1856.

150. France. Archives du Ministère des Affaires Etrangères à Paris. MEMOIRES ET DOCUMENTS--FONDS DIVERS. (Russie)

151. France. LES BULLETINS FRANCOIS CONCERNANT LA GUERRE EN RUSSIE, PENDANT L'ANNEE 1812. London: L. de Conchy, 1813.

152. François, Charles. JOURNAL DU CAPITAINE FRANCOIS... 1793-1830. Paris: Carrington, 1903-04. 2 vols.

153. Fry, M.G., and J.P. Fox. "The Grand Army and the Invasion of Russia." HISTORY TODAY 10 (1960): 255-69.

154. Funck, W.F. ERRINERUNGEN AUS DEM FELDZUGE DES SACHSISCHEN CORPS UNTER DEM G. REYNIER IM JAHRE 1812 AUS DEN PAPIEREN DES VESTORBENEN. Dresden and Leipzig: Arnold, 1829.

155. Furtenbach, Friedrich von. KRIEG GEGEN RUSSLAND UND RUSSISCHE GEFANGENSCHAFT. Nurnberg: U.E. Sebald, 1912.

156. Fusil, Louise. SOUVENIRS D'UNE ACTRICE. Paris: Dumont, 1841-46. 3 vols.

157. Gariainov, Afanasil V. SOVREMENNOE PREDSTAVLENIE [Contemporary Presentations]. St. Petersburg: Korolev, 1854.

158. Garin, Fabin A. "Borodinskoe Srazhenie" [The Battle of Borodino]. POLKOVODETS KUTUZOV [Army Leader Kutuzov]. Edited by L.G. Beskrovnyi. Moscow: Gos. izd-vo. polit. lit-ry, 1955.

159. Garin, Fabin A. IZGNANIE NAPOLEONA IZ MOSKVY [The Expulsion of Napoleon from Moscow]. Moscow: Moskovskii rabochii, 1948.

160. Garnich, Nikolai. 1812 GOD [1812]. Moscow: Goskul't-prosvetizdat, 1956.

161. Garnier, Jacques. "Récit du lieutenant Bressolles de la campagne de 1813 et sa captivité en Russie." REVUE DE L'INSTITUT NAPOLEON 135 (1979): 57-65.

162. Gendry, Général. "Essay sur la campagne de Russie (1812) par le général Trezel." REVUE DE LA SOCIETE DES AMIS DU MUSEE DE L'ARMEE 66 (1962): 30-38.

163. George, Hereford Brooke. NAPOLEON'S INVASION OF RUSSIA. London: Unwin, 1899.

164. Gerhardt, Oskar. DIE WUERTTEMBERGER IN RUSSLAND 1812: IHR LEIDENSWEG UND TRAGISCHES ENDE. Stuttgart: Steinkopf, 1937.

165. Gerua, A.V. BORODINO. St. Petersburg, 1912.

166. Giesse, Friedrich. KASSEL-MOSKAU-KUSTRIN 1812-1813: TAGEBUCH WAHREND DES RUSSISCHEN FELDZUGES GEFUHRT VON F. GIESSE. Leipzig: Dyk, 1912.

167. Giller, I.L., comp. BESSMERTNYI PODVIG NARODA OTECHESTVENNAIA VOINA 1812 GODA [The Immortal Exploit of the People in the 1812 Patriotic War]. Moscow, 1963.

168. Ginsburg, Saul M. OTECHESTVENNAIA VOINA 1812 GODA I RUSSKIE EVREI [The Patriotic 1812 War and Russian Jews]. St. Petersburg: Knigoizdat "Razum'", 1912.

169. Girod de l'Ain, Maurice. DIX ANS DE MES SOUVENIRS MILITAIRES DE 1805 A 1815. Paris: Dumaine, 1873.

170. Glinka, Sergei Nikolaevich. PRIBAVLENIE K' RUSSKOI ISTORII SERGEIA GLINKI [Additions to Russian History of Sergei Glinka]. Moscow: Universitetskaia tipografiia, 1818-1819. 2 vols.

171. Glinka, Sergei Nikolaevich. RUSSKOE CHTENIE [Russian Readings]. St. Petersburg: Shtabotdielnavo korpusa vnutrennei strazhei, 1845. 2 vols.

172. Glinka, Sergei Nikolaevich. ZAPISKI O 1812 GODE SERGEIA GLINKI [Notes on 1812 of Sergei Glinka]. St. Petersburg: Imperatorskaia Rossiskaia Akademiia, 1836.

173. Glinka, Sergei Nikolaevich. ZAPISKI O MOSKVE I O ZAGRANITSHNYKH' PROISSCHESTVIIACH' OT IZKHODA 1812 DO POLOVINY

1815 GODA [Notes on Moscow and on the Foreign Incidents from the End of 1812 through the First Half of 1815]. St. Petersburg: Imperatorskaia Rossiskaia Akademiia, 1837.

174. Glybovski, V.I. 1812-YI GOD' V VITEBSKOI GUBERNII [1812 in Vitebsk Gubernia]. Vitebsk': Vitebskoi uchenoi arkhivnoi komissii, 1910.

175. Goethe, Theodor. EIN VERWANDTER GOETHES IM RUSSISCHEN FELDZUGE 1812. Berlin: Morawe & Scheffelt, 1912.

176. Golitsyn, Nikolai Borisovich. SOUVENIRS ET IMPRESSIONS D'UN OFFICIER RUSSE PENDANT LES CAMPAGNES DE 1812, 1813, ET 1814. St. Petersburg: Imprimerie française, 1849.

177. Golling, Ernst. "Die Schlacht bei Borodino." WEHRWISSEN-SCHAFTLICHE RUNDSCHAU 12 (1962): 501-17.

178. Golubov, Sergei Nikolaevich, and S.N. Kuznetzov. BAGRATION. Moscow: Voennoe izd-vo., 1960.

179. Goriainov, Sergei Mikhailovich. 1812: DOKUMENTY GOSUDARSTVENNOGO I S. PETERBURGSKOGO GLAVNOGO ARKHIVOV [1812: Documents from the State and St. Petersburg Main Archives]. St. Petersburg: Izd. Ministerstva inostrannykh del', 1912.

180. Goriainov, Sergei Mikhailovich. LETTRES INTERCEPTEES PAR LES RUSSES DURANT LA CAMPAGNE DE 1812. Paris: La Sabretache, 1913.

181. Gourgaud, Gaspard, baron. NAPOLEON ET LA GRANDE-ARMEE EN RUSSIE, OU EXAMEN CRITIQUE DE L'OUVRAGE DE M. LE COMTE PH. DE SEGUR. Paris: Bossange, 1825. 2 vols.

182. Grabowski, Józef Ignacy. MEMOIRES MILITAIRES DE JOSEPH GRABOWSKI. Paris: Plon-Nourrit, 1907.

183. Grimsted, Patricia Kennedy. ARCHIVES AND MANUSCRIPT REPOSITORIES IN THE USSR. Princeton, N.J.: Princeton University Press, 1972.

184. Grimsted, Patricia Kennedy. THE FOREIGN MINISTERS OF ALEXANDER I. Berkeley: University of California Press, 1969.

185. Griois, Charles Pierre Lubin. MEMOIRES MILITAIRES DU GENERAL GRIOIS, 1792-1822. Paris: Plon-Nourrit, 1909. 2 vols.

186. Gronskii, Pavel P. "L'Administration civiles des gouvernements Russes ocupée par armée française en 1812." REVUE D'HISTOIRE MODERNE 3 (1928): 401-12.

187. Grunwald, Constantin de. "L'Incendie de Moscou, mystère de la campagne de Russie." MIROIR DE L'HISTOIRE 68 (1955): 287-95.

188. Grunwald, Constantin de. LA CAMPAGNE DE RUSSIE.   Paris:
     Julliard, 1963.

189. Guesdon, Alexandre Fursy. HISTOIRE DE LA GUERRE DE RUSSIE EN
     1812. Paris: Dupont, 1828. 2 vols.

190. Guibal, M. "Les Emigrés pouvaient-ils sauver la Grande armée
     (pendant la campagne de Russie)." REVUE DE DEUX MONDES 8, 9
     (1979): 345-53, 583-93.

191. Guins, G.K. "La Russie avant et après la guerre de 1812 d'après
     les historiens sovietiques." PROBLEMES SOVIETIQUES 6 (1963):
     127-40.

192. Haythornthwaite, Philip. UNIFORMS OF THE RETREAT FROM MOSCOW,
     1812. New York: Hippocrene Books, 1976.

193. Henckens, Lieutenant J.L. MEMOIRES SE RAPPORTANT A SON SERVICE
     MILITAIRE AU 6eme REGIMENTS DE CHASSEURS A CHEVAL FRANCAIS DE
     FEVRIER 1803 A AOUT 1816. The Hague: Nijhoff, 1910.

194. Herzen, Alexandre. ERRINERUNGEN VON ALEXANDER HERZEN.   Berlin:
     Wiegandt und Grieben, 1907. 2 vols.

195. Hess, Peter von. ILLIUSTRIROVANNAIA OTECHESTVENNAIA VOINA 1812
     GODA [The Illustrated Patriotic War of 1812].   St. Petersburg:
     F.S. Sushchinskii, 1887.

196. Hofman, von. DIE SCHLACHT BEI BORODINO, MIT EINTER UEBERSICH
     DES FELDZUGES VON 1812. Coblenz: Badeker, 1846.

197. Hogendorp, Dirk, graaf van. MEMOIRES DU GENERAL DIRK VAN
     HOGENDORP. The Hague: Nijhoff, 1887.

198. Hollinsworth, Barry. "The Napoleonic Invasion of Russia and
     Recent Soviet Historical Writing."   THE JOURNAL OF MODERN
     HISTORY 38 (1966): 38-52.

199. Holmes, Edward Richard. BORODINO. London: Knight, 1971.

200. Holzhausen, Paul. DIE DEUTSCHEN IN RUSSLAND, 1812. Berlin:
     Morawe and Scheffelt, 1912. 2 vols.

201. Hortense, queen consort of Louis, king of Holland. MEMOIRES DE
     LA REINE HORTENSE. Paris: Plon, 1927. 3 vols.

202. Horward, Donald D. "Napoleon in Review: A Bibliographical
     Essay." MILITARY AFFAIRS 43 (1974): 144-50.

203. Ignatieff, Leonide. "French Emigrés in Russia 1789-1825; The
     Interaction of Cultures in Times of Stress."   Ph.D.
     dissertation, University of Michigan, 1963.

204. Ikonnikov, Vladimir Stepanovich. OPYT RUSSKOI ISTORIOGRAFII
     [Essay in Russian Historiography]. Kiev: Tipografiia Imp. un.
     Sv. Vladimira, 1891-1908. 2 vols.

205. IM KAMPF UM FREIHEIT UND VATERLAND 1806-1815. Leipzig, 1912.

206. IZVESTIIA O VOENNIKH' DEISTVIIAKH' ROSSISSKOI ARMII PROTIV'
     FRANTSUZOV' 1812 GODA [News on the Military Activities of the
     Russian Army against the French in 1812]. St. Petersburg:
     Meditsinskaia tipografiia, 1813-14. 3 vols.

207. Jackson, William Godfrey F. SEVEN ROADS TO MOSCOW. New York:
     Philosophical Library, 1958.

208. Jacoby, Jean. NAPOLEON EN RUSSIE. Paris: Les Libertés
     français, 1938.

209. Jessup, John E. "Soviet Military History: Efforts and Results."
     MILITARY REVIEW 53 (1973): 13-26.

210. Jomini, Antoine Henri, baron de. LIFE OF NAPOLEON. Kansas
     City, Missouri: Hudson-Kimberley, 1897.

211. Jomini, Antoine Henri, baron de. PRECIS POLITIQUE ET MILITAIRE
     DES CAMPAGNES DE 1812 A 1814 EXTRAIT DES SOUVENIRS INEDITS DU
     GENERAL JOMINI AVEC UNE NOTICE BIOGRAPHIQUE. Lausanne: Benda,
     1886. 2 vols.

212. Josselson, M., and D. Josselson. THE COMMANDER: A LIFE OF
     BARCLAY DE TOLLY. Oxford: Oxford University Press, 1980.

213. Joussier, Pierre, and Irene Joussier. "Quelques lettres in-
     édites sur la campagne de Russie écrites par polycarpe Gouré."
     BULLETIN DE LA SOCIETE DES SCIENCES HISTORIQUES ET NATURELLES DE
     L'YONNE 103 (1969-70): 265-82.

214. Kallash, Vladimir Vladimirovich. DVENADTSATYI GOD' V'
     VOSPOMINANIIAKH' I PEREPISKE SOVREMENNIKOV' [1812 in the
     Recollections and Correspondence of Contemporaries]. Moscow:
     I.D. Sytin, 1912.

215. Kersnovsky, A.A. ISTORIIA RUSSKOI ARMII [The History of the
     Russian Army]. Belgrade: Izd-vo. tsarskago vestnika, 1933-38.

216. Kharkevich, Vladimir Ivanovich. 1812 GOD' V DNEVNIKAKH',
     ZAPISKAKH', I VOSPOMINANIIAKH' SOVREMENNIKOV' [1812 in Diaries,
     Notes, and Recollections of Contemporaries]. Vilna:
     Tipografiia shtaba vilenskogo voennago okruga, 1900-04. 3 vols.

217. Kholodkovski, V.M. "Napoleon li podzheg Moskva?" [Did Napoleon
     Set Fire to Moscow?]. VOPROSY ISTORII 4 (1966): 31-43.

218. Khovanski, Nikolai Feodorovich. UCHASTIE SARATOVSKOI GUVERNII
     V' OTECHESTVENNOI VOINE 1812 G [The Participation of Saratou

Gubernia in the 1812 Patriotic War]. Saratov: Tipografiia
soiuza pechatnago dela, 1912.

219. Kircheisen, Friederich Max. BIBLIOGRAPHIE NAPOLEONIENNE.
Berlin: Mittler, 1902.

220. Kircheisen, Friedrich Max, ed. WIDER NAPOLEON! EIN DEUTSCHES
REITERLEBEN 1806-1815. Stuttgart: Lutz, 1911. 2 vols.

221. Kirckhoff, Josephine Romaine Louis de. OBSERVATIONS MEDICALES,
FAITES PENDANT LES CAMPAGNES DE RUSSIE EN 1812 ET D'ALLEMAGNE EN
1813. Maestricht: Nypels, 1814.

222. Kochetkov, Andrei Nikolaevich. BARKLAI DE TOLLI [M.B. Barclay
de Tolly]. Moscow: Moskovskii Rabochii, 1970.

223. Koliubakin, B.M. 1812 GOD. BORODINSKOE SRAZHENIE 26 AVGUSTA
[1812. The Battle of Borodino, 26 August]. St. Petersburg,
1912.

224. Korbeletzki, Feodor I. ODA V CHEST' POBEDONOSNAGO ROSSIISKAGO
VOINSTVA, PO POLUCHENII IZVESTIIA O BEGSTVE IZ' MOSKVY
NAPOLEONA, I O SOVERSHENNOM' EGO PORAZHENII [Ode in Honor of the
Victorious Russian Army, on the Reception of the News of
Napoleon's Flight from Moscow, and on the Completion of His
Defeat]. St. Petersburg: Tipografiia departamenta vneshnei
torgovlii, 1813.

225. Kornilov, Aleksandr Aleksandrovich. "Epokha otechestvennoi
voiny i eia Znachenie v' Noveishei Istorii." RUSSKAIA MYSL' L 1
(1911): 104-55.

226. Korobkov, A. "Voennoe Iskusstvo Kutuzova" [Kutuzov's Military
Art]. VOPROSY ISTORII 3-4 (1945): 3-33.

227. Kugelgen, Wilhelm von. JUGENDERINNERUNGEN EINES ALTES MANNES.
Berlin: Hertz, 1883.

228. Kukiel, Marian. WOJNA 1812 ROKU [The War of 1812]. Krakow:
Gebethner i Wolff, 1937.

229. Kurz, Hauptmann von. DER FELDZUG VON 1812, DENKWUERDIGKEITEN
EINES WUERTTEMBERGISCHEN OFFIZIERS. Leipzig: n.p., n.d.

230. Labaume, Eugène. RELATION CIRCONSTANCIEE DE LA CAMPAGNE DE
RUSSIE. Paris: Panckoucke, 1814.

231. Lachouque, Henry. NAPOLEON'S BATTLES: A HISTORY OF HIS
CAMPAIGNS. Translated by Ray Monkcom. New York: Dutton, 1967.

232. Lagneau, Louis Vivant. JOURNAL D'UN CHIRUGIEN DE LA GRANDE
ARMEE. Paris: Emile-Paul, 1913.

233. Langeron, General Louis Alexandre Andrault de. MEMOIRES ... DE
CAMPAGNES DE 1812, 1813, 1814. Paris: Picard, 1902.

234. Larrey, Dominique Jean. MEMOIRES DE CHIRUGIE MILITAIRE, ET CAMPAGNES DU BARON D.J. LARREY. Paris: J. Smith, 1812-17. 4 vols.

235. Laugier, Cesare de. LE GRANDE ARMEE. Paris: Fayard, 1910.

236. Laveau, Georges Lecointe de. MOSCOU AVANT ET APRES L'INCENDIE OU NOTICE CONTENANT UNE DESCRIPTION DE CETTE CAPITALE, DES MOEURS DE SES HABITANTS, DES EVENEMENTS QUI SE PASSERENT PENDANT L'INCENDIE, ET DES MALHEURS QUI ACCABLERENT L'ARMEE FRANCAISE PENDANT LA RETRAITE DE 1812. Paris: Gide, 1814.

237. Lejeune, Louis François. MEMOIRES DU GENERAL LEJEUNE. Paris: Firmin-Didot, 1895-96. 2 vols.

238. Lemercier-Quelquejay, Chantal. "Un Document inédit sur la campagne de 1812." CAHIERS DU MONDE RUSSE ET SOVIETIQUE 3 (1963): 258-63.

239. Lesure, Michel. L'HISTOIRE DE RUSSIE AUX ARCHIVES NATIONALES. Paris and The Hague: Mouton, 1970.

240. Leuschner, Peter. NUR WENIGE KAMEN ZURUCK 3000 BAYERN MIT NAPOLEON IN RUSSLAND. Pfaffenhofen: Ludwig, 1980.

241. Levitski, Nikolai Arsen'evich. POLKOVODICHESKOE ISKUSSTVO NAPOLEONA [Napoleon's Art of Leadership]. Moscow: Gos. voennoe izd-vo., 1938.

242. Levitski, Nikolai Arsen'evich. VOINA 1812 GODA [The War of 1812]. Moscow: partizdat TsKVKP(b), 1938.

243. Liebenstein, Louis August Friedrich, freiherr von. DER KRIEG NAPOLEONS GEGEN RUSSLAND IN DEN JAHREN 1812 UND 1813. Frankfurt a.M.: Hermannsche Buchhandlung, 1819.

244. Lignières, Marie Henri, comte de. SOUVENIRS DE LA GRANDE ARMEE ET DE LA VIELLE GARDE IMPERIALE. Paris: Pierre Roger, 1933.

245. Liprandi, Ivan Petrovich. NE GOLOD' I NE MOROZ' BYLI PRICHINOIU GIBELI NAPOLEONOVYKH' POLCHISHCH' [Neither Hunger nor Frost Were the Causes of the Destruction of the Napoleonic Hordes]. St. Petersburg: Tip. Imp. Akad. nauk, 1855.

246. Liprandi, Ivan Petrovich. "Opyt' kataloga vsem' otdel'nym' sochineniiam' po 1872 god' ob' otechestvennoi voine 1812 goda" [Essay on the Catalog of All Assorted Works up to 1872 on the Patriotic War of 1812]. OBSHCHESTVO ISTORII I DREVNOSTEI ROSSISKIKH', CHTENIIA 3, 4 (1874-75): 1-49, 50-116.

247. Löwenstern, Edouard von. MIT GRAF PHALENS REITEREI GEGEN NAPOLEON. Berlin: Mittler, 1910.

248. Löwenstern, Woldemar Hermann, freiherr von. MEMOIRES DU GENERAL
     MAJOR RUSSE BARON DE LOEWENSTERN. Paris: Fontemoing, 1903. 2
     vols.

249. Longinov, Mikhail Nikolaevich. "1812-I God', Iz' Pisem' N.V.
     Longinov' K' Grafu S.R. Vorontsovu." [1812: From the Letters of
     N.V. Longinov to Graf S.R. Vorontsov]. RUSSKII ARKHIV' 1, 2
     (1912): 481-547, 30-86, 161-205, 338-416.

250. Lossberg, Friedrich Wilhelm von. BRIEFE DES WESTFALISCHEN
     STABS-OFFIZIERS FRIEDRICH WILHELM VON-LOSSBERG VOM RUSSISCHEN
     FELDZUG DES JAHRES 1812. Berlin: Christian Meyer, 1910.

251. Lyautey, Hubert. "Lettres d'un lieutenant de la Grande Armée
     (sur la campagne de Russie)." REVUE DES DEUX MONDES 24 (1962):
     485-500.

252. Maag, Albert. DIE SCHICHSALE DER SCHWEIZER REGIMENTER IN
     NAPOLEONS I, FELDZUG NACH RUSSLAND 1812. Biel: Kuhn, 1900.

253. McErlean, John, ed. "Autour de la guerre de 1812: Lettres
     inédites ... (de) 1811-1813." CANADIAN AMERICAN SLAVIC STUDIES
     9 (1975): 542-89.

254. McQueen, James. POPULATION, SOIL, AND CLIMATE OF THE RUSSIAN
     EMPIRE, DESCRIPTION OF MOSCOW, STRENGTH AND LOSSES OF THE FRENCH
     ARMIES IN RUSSIA AND SPAIN DURING 1812. Glasgow: W. Lang,
     1813.

255. Madelin, Louis. LA CATASTROPHE DE RUSSIE. Paris: Hachette,
     1949.

256. Maistre, Joseph Marie, comte de. CORRESPONDANCE DIPLOMATIQUE DE
     JOSEPH DE MAISTRE. Paris: Michel-Lévy, 1860. 2 vols.

257. Maksheyev, F.A. "Otechestvennaia voina v'Intendentskom'
     Otnoshenii" [The Patriotic War in Commissary Memoranda].
     INTENDANTSKII ZHURNAL' 7-12 (1912): 1-17; 1-17; 1-25; 1-28;
     1-22; 1-17; 1 (1913): 1-20.

258. Marbot, Jean Baptiste Antoine, baron. MEMOIRES DU GENERAL BARON
     DE MARBOT. Paris: Plon-Nourrit, 1891. 3 vols.

259. Marqueron, Louis. CAMPAGNE DE RUSSIE. Paris: Charles-
     Lavauzelle, 1897-1906. 4 vols.

260. Martens, Carl von. DENKWUERDIGKEITEN AUS DEM LEBEN EINES ALTEN
     OFFIZIERS. Dresden: Arnold, 1848.

261. Martens, Christian von. VOR FUENFZIG JAHREN, TAGEBUCH MEINES
     FELDZUGES IN RUSSLAND, 1812. Stuttgart and Oehringen: Schaber,
     1862. 2 vols.

262. Martens, Fedor Fedorovich, ed. SOBRANIE TRAKTOV I KONVENTSII
     ZAKLIUCHENNYKH ROSSIEI S INOSTRANNYMI [A Collection of Treaties

and Conventions Concluded by Russia with Foreign Powers]. St.
Petersburg: Böhnke, 1874-1909. 15 vols.

263. Meerheimb, Franz Ludwig August von. ERLEBNISSE EINES VETERANEN
DER GROSSEN ARMEE WAHREND DES FELDZUGES IN RUSSLANDS, 1812.
Dresden: Arnold, 1860.

264. Mejbaum, Maclaw. "Galicya po Klesce Napoleona W R. 1812"
[Galicia after the Defeat of Napoleon in 1812]. BIBLIOTEKA
WARSZAWSKA 4 (1913): 105-127.

265. Melnikova, M.A. "Materialy dlia Istorii Otechestennoi Voiny
1812 Goda, Izvlechennye iz' Vitebskago Gubernskago Arkhiva"
[Materials for the History of the Patriotic War of 1812,
Selected from the Vitebsk Gubernia Archive]. POLOTSKO-VITEBSKAIA
STARINA 1 (1911): 1-64.

266. Merkel, Garlieb Helwig. EIN BEWOHNER MOSKWA'S AN SEINE
LANDSLEUTE, IM OCTOBER 1812. St. Petersburg: Drechsler, 1812.

267. Mezhov, Vladimir Izmailovich. RUSSKAIA ISTORICHESKAIA
BIBLIOGRAFIIA ZA 1800-1864 [Russian Historical Bibliography for
1800-1864] St. Petersburg: I.M. Sibiriakov, 1892-93. 3 vols.

268. Mezhov, Vladimir Izmailovich. RUSSKAIA ISTORICHESKAIA
BIBLIOGRAFIIA ZA 1865-1876 [Russian Historical Bibliography for
1865-1876]. St. Petersburg: Tip. Imp. Akad. nauk, 1882-90. 8
vols.

269. Mikhailovskii-Danilevskii, Aleksandr Ivanovich. IMPERATOR'
ALEKSANDR' I' I EGO SPODVISHNIKI V 1812, 1813, 1814, 1815,
GODAKH' [Emperor Alexander I and His Associates, 1812, 1813,
1814, 1815]. St. Petersburg: Tipografiia Karla Kraiia,
1845-1849.

270. Mikhailovskii-Danilevskii, Aleksandr Ivanovich. OPISANIE
OTECHESTVENNOI VOINY V 1812 GODU [Description of the 1812
Patriotic War]. St. Petersburg: Tipografiia shtaba otdel'nago
korpusa vnutrennei strazhi, 1843. 4 vols.

271. Mikhnevich, Nikolai Petrovich. "Otechestvennaia voina 1812
Goda" [The Patriotic War of 1812]. ISTORIIA RUSSKOI ARMII I
FLOTA [History of the Russian Army and Navy] 3, 4 (1911):
84-167; 5-68.

272. Miller, M. von. DARSTELLUNG DES FELDZUGS DER FRANZOESISCH
VERBUNDETEN ARMEE GEGEN DIE RUSSEN IM JAHRE 1812 MIT BESONDERER
RUECKSICHT AUF DIE TEILNAHME DER KOENIGL. WUERTTEMBERGISCHEN
TRUPPEN. Stuttgart: Cotta, 1823.

273. Montesquieu-Fezensac, Raymond Aymery Philippe, duc de. THE
RUSSIAN CAMPAIGN, 1812. Translated by Lee Kennett. Athens:
University of Georgia Press, 1970.

274. Montesquieu-Fezensac, Raymond Aymery Philippe, duc de.
SOUVENIRS MILITAIRES DE 1804 A 1814. Paris: Dumaine, 1863.

275. MOSKOVSKOE DVORIANSTVO V 1812 GODU [The Moscow Nobility in
1812]. Moscow: Izd-vo. Moskovskago dvorianstva, 1912.

276. Nagengast, William E. "Napoleon's Retreat in 1812." RUSSIAN
REVIEW 8 (1949): 302-15.

277. Napoleon I, Emperor of France. IZBRANNYE PROIZVEDENIIA
[Selected Works]. Moscow: Voen Izd-vo., 1956.

278. Narichkine [Naryshkina], Nataliia [née Comtesse Rostopchine.]
1812: LE COMTE ROSTOPCHINE ET SON TEMPS. St. Petersburg: R.
Golicke et A. Willborg, 1912.

279. Narochnitskii, Aleksei Leont'evich, et al., eds. VNESHNAIA
POLITIKA ROSSII XIX I NACHALA XX VEKA [The Foreign Policy of
Russia in the 19th and Beginning of the 20th Century]. Seria
Pervaia, Vol. 6. 1811-1812. Moscow: Gos. izd-vo. polit. lit.,
1962.

280. Nechkina, Militsa Visil'evna, et al. 1812 GOD [1812]. Moscow:
Akademiia nauk, 1962.

281. Nersisian, Mkrtych Gegamovich. OTECHESTVENNAIA VOINA 1812 GODA
I NARODY KAVKAZA [The Patriotic War of 1812 and the Peoples of
the Caucausus]. Erevan: Izd-vo. Akad. nauk Armianskoi SSR,
1965.

282. Nikolai Mikhailovich, grand duke of Russia. IMPERATOR'
ALEKSANDR' I [Emperor Alexander I]. St. Petersburg: Eksp.
zagot. gos. bumag', 1912.

283. Nikolai Mikhailovich, grand duke of Russia. LES RELATIONS
DIPLOMATIQUES DE LA RUSSIE ET DE LA FRANCE D'APRES LES RAPPORTS
DES AMBASSADEURS D'ALEXANDRE Ier ET DE NAPOLEON 1808-1812. St.
Petersburg: Eksp. zagot. gos. bumag', 1905.

284. Nikolai Mikhailovich, grand duke of Russia. LE TSAR ALEXANDRE
Ier. Translated by Baron Wrangel. Paris: Payot, 1931.

285. Nikolai Mikhailovich, grand duke of Russia, ed.
DIPLOMATICHESKIE SNOSHENIIA ROSSII I FRANTSII PO DONESENIIAM
POSLOV IMPERATOROV ALEKSANDRA I NAPOLEONA, 1808-1812 [Diplomatic
Relations of Russia and France according to the Reports of the
Ambassadors of Emperors' Alexander and Napoleon]. St.
Petersburg: Eksp. zagot. gos. bumag', 1905-14. 7 vols.

286. Nikolai Mikhailovich, grand duke of Russia, ed. VOENNAIA
GALLEREIA 1812 GODA [The Military Gallery of 1812]. St.
Petersburg: Eksp. zagot. gos. bumag', 1912.

287. Nikolaieff, Alexander M. "BORODINO--1812." ARMY QUARTERLY
83 (1962): 229-41.

288. Nikolaieff, Alexander M. "Napoleon and 'General Winter' in the Russian Campaign." ARMY QUARTERLY 90 (1965): 205-6.

289. Nive, Petr Andreivich. OTECHESTVENNAIA VOINA [The Patriotic War]. St. Petersburg: V.K. Il'inchik, 1911-12. 5 vols.

290. Noël, Jean Nicolas Auguste. SOUVENIRS MILITIARES D'UN OFFICER DU PREMIER EMPIRE 1795-1832. Paris: Berger-Levrault, 1895.

291. Novitskii, Vasilii Fedorovich, ed. VOENNAIA ENTSIKLOPEDIIA [Military Encylopedia]. St. Petersburg: I.D. Sytin, 1911. 18 vols.

292. Obst, Arthur. DIE HAMBURGER 1812 IM RUSSISCHEN FELDZUGE. Hamburg: Hermes, 1912.

293. Oginski, Michal. MEMOIRES DE MICHEL OGINSKI SUR LA POLOGNE ET LES POLONAIS, DEPUIS 1788 JUSQU'A LA FIN DE 1815. Paris: Ponthieu, 1826-27. 4 vols.

294. Okunev, Nikolai Aleksandrovich. CONSIDERATIONS SUR LES GRANDS OPERATIONS DE LA CAMPAGNE DE 1812. Brussels: Petit, 1841.

295. Olieievich, D. "Voina 1812 G., I eia Prichiny" [The War of 1812 and Its Causes]. VESTNIK' ZNANIIA 8 (1912): 675-87.

296. Olivier, Daria. THE BURNING OF MOSCOW, 1812. Translated by M. Heron. London: Allen & Unwin, 1966.

297. OTECHESTVENNAIA VOINA 1812 GODA [The Patriotic War of 1812]. Materialy voennogo-uchenogo arkhiva Glavnogo shtaba. St. Petersburg, 1900-14. 21 vols.

298. OTECHESTVENNAIA VOINA 1812 G [The Patriotic War of 1812]. Sbornik dokumentov i materialov sost. A.V. Predtechenskii, et al. Leningrad and Moscow, 1941.

299. Oudinot, Marie Charlotte, duchesse de Reggio. LE MARECHAL OUDINOT, DUC DE REGGIO D'APRES LES SOUVENIRS INEDITS DE LA MARECHAL. Paris: Plon-Nourrit, 1894.

300. Palmer, Alan W. NAPOLEON IN RUSSIA: THE 1812 CAMPAIGN. New York: Simon and Schuster: 1967.

301. Paskin, Aleksandr Stepanovich, ed. MATERIALY DLIA ISTORII DVORIAN' TVERSKOI GUBERNII (1812) [Material for the History of the Nobility of Tver Gubernia]. Tver': Izd-vo. Tverskogo dvorianstva, 1912.

302. Pastoret, Amédée de. "De Witebsk à la Beresina." LA REVUE DE PARIS 9 (1902): 465-97.

303. Pavlov. "Ob Artilleriiskom Reserve M.I. Kutuzova Borodinskom Srazhenii" [On the Artillery Reserve of M.I. Kutuzov in the

Battle of Borodino]. VOENNO-ISTORICHESKI ZHURNAL 3 (1966): 111-14.

304. Pavlova, Karolina Karlova. "Vospominanii" [Recollections]. RUSSKII ARKHIV' 3 (1875): 222-40.

305. Pavlovski, Ivan Frantsevich. "Malorossiiskoe Kozach'e opolchenie V' 1812 Godu...." [The Little Russian Cossack Militia in 1812]. KIEVSKAIA STARINE 92, 94 (1906): 1-20; 137-154.

306. Perjes, Geza. "Die Frage der Verpflerund in Feldzuge Napoleons gegen Russland." MILITARGESCHICHTLICHE MITTEILUNGEN 4 (1968): 35-64.

307. Peszke, S.B.T. "Moj Pobyt v Niewoli Rosyjskiej" [My Stay in Russian Captivity]. BIBLIOTEKA WARSZAWSKA 4, 5: 23-58; 287-317.

308. Peyrusse, Guillaume Joseph, baron. LETTRES INEDITES DU BARON GUILLAUME PEYRUSSE, ECRITES A SON FRERE ANDRE PENDANT LES CAMPAGNES DE L'EMPIRE DE 1809 A 1814. Paris: Perrin, 1894.

309. Pfuel, Ernst von. DER RUCKZUG DER FRANZOESEN AUS RUSSLAND. Berlin: Hampel, 1867.

310. Philippart, John. NORTHERN CAMPAIGNS FROM THE COMMENCEMENT OF WAR 1812, TO THE ARMISTICE, JUNE 4, 1813. London, 1814. 2 vols.

311. Pils, François. JOURNAL DE MARCHE DU GRENADIER PILS (1804-1814). Paris: Ollendorff, 1895.

312. Pinguad, Léonce. LES FRANCAIS EN RUSSIE ET LES RUSSES EN FRANCE, L'ANCIEN REGIME; L'EMIGRATION, LES INVASIONS. Paris: Perrin, 1885.

313. Pisarev, Aleksandr. VOENNAIA PIS'MA [Military Letters]. Moscow: I. Subbotin and S. Selivanov, 1817. 2 vols.

314. Pivka, Otto von. ARMIES OF 1812. Cambridge: Stephens, 1977.

315. Planat de la Faye, Nicolas Louis. VIE DE PLANAT DE LA FAYE, AIDE-DE-CAMP DES GENERAUX LARIBOISIERE ET DROUOT. Paris: Ollendorff, 1895.

316. Pobedonostsev, Petr Vasil'evich. "Iz' Dnevnika 1812-1813 Godov'" [From the Diary of 1812-1813]. RUSSKII ARKHIV' 1 (1895): 213-24.

317. Pokrovsky, Mikhail Nikolaevich. DIPLOMATIIA I VOINY TSARSKOI ROSSII XIX STOLETIIA [Diplomacy and the Wars of Tsarist Russia in the Nineteenth Century]. Moscow: Krasnaia nov', 1923.

318. Polosin, Ivan Ivanovich. "Kutuzov i pozhar Moskvy 1812 G." [Kutuzov and the Burning of Moscow 1812]. ISTORICHESKIE ZAPISKI 34 (1950): 122-65.

319. Popov, Aleksandr Nikolaevich. "Baron Shtein v Rossii vo 1812 Godu" [Baron Stein in Russia in 1812]. RUSSKAIA STARINA 77 (1892): 383-404.

320. Popov, Aleksandr Nikolaevich. "Dvizhenie Russkikh Voisk ot Moskvy do Krasnoi Pakhry" [The Movement of the Russian Forces from Moscow to Krasnaia Pakhra]. RUSSKAIA STARINA 90 (1897): 513-33; 91 (1897): 109-24, 357-373; 92 (1897): 189-200; 96 (1898): 151-67, 397-419.

321. Popov, Aleksandr Nikolaevich. FRANTSUZY V MOSKVE V 1812 GODU [The French in Moscow in 1812]. Moscow: Gracheva i komp., 1876.

322. Popov, Aleksandr Nikolaevich. MOSKVA V 1812 GODU [Moscow in 1812]. Moscow, 1876.

323. Popov, Aleksandr Nikolaevich. OTECHESTVENNAIA VOINA 1812 OT' MALOIAROSLAVTSA DO BEREZINY [The Patriotic War of 1812 from Maloiaroslavets to the Berecina]. Moscow and St. Petersburg: Tip. V.S. Balashev, 1877.

324. Porter, Robert Ker. NARRATIVE OF THE CAMPAIGN IN RUSSIA DURING THE YEAR 1812. Hartford: Sheldon, 1814.

325. Potocka, Anna. MEMOIRES DE LA COMTESSE POTOCKA, 1794-1820. Paris: Plon-Nourrit, 1897.

326. Predtechenskii, Anatolii Vasil'evich. "Borodinskii boi Russkoe Obshchestvennoe mnenie" [The Battle of Borodino and Russian Public Opinion]. UCHENYE ZPAISKI LENINGRADSKOGO GOSUDARSTVENNOGO UNIVERSITETA 19 (1938): 101-10.

327. (Prussia). [Deutsche Demokratische Republik]. Deutsches Zentralarchiv. SAINT-PETERSBOURG DEPECHES.

328. Puibuisque, Louis Guillaume. LETTRES SUR LA GUERRE DE RUSSIE EN 1812. Paris: Anselin et Pochard, 1817.

329. Pypin, Aleksandr Nikolaevich. OBSHCHESTVENNOE DVIZHENIE V ROSSII PRI ALEKSANDR I [The Public Movement in Russia under Alexander I]. St. Petersburg: Izd-vo. Vestnik Evropy, 1871.

330. Quennerat, Jean Claude. "Albrecht Adam et Faber du Faur, 'Reporters' de la campagne de Russie." SOUVENIR NAPOLEONIENNES 262: 14-18.

331. Rambaud, Alfred N. "La Grande Armée à Moscou. Récits de Temoins Oculaires Russes." REVUE DES DEUX MONDES 106 (1873): 194-228.

332. Rambuteau, Claude Philibert Barthelot. MEMOIRES DU COMTE DE RAMBUTEAU. Paris: Lévy, 1905.

333. Rapp, Jean. MEMOIRES DU GENERAL RAPP, AIDE-DE-CAMP DE NAPOLEON. Paris: Bossange, 1823.

334. Rehtwisch, Theodor. MIT MANN UND ROSS UND WAGEN HAT SIE DER
     HERR GESCHLAGEN; BILDER AUS DEM JAHRE 1812 VON THEODOR
     REHTWISCH. Leipzig: Turm-Verlag, 1923.

335. Reve, Karel van het. "The Moscow Fire of 1812 in Soviet
     Historiography." ANALECTA SLAVICA (1955): 167-75.

336. Rochechouart, Louis Victor Léon, comte de. SOUVENIRS SUR LA
     REVOLUTION, L'EMPIRE, ET LA RESTAURATION. Paris: Plon-
     Nourrit, 1889.

337. Roeder, Franz. THE ORDEAL OF CAPTAIN ROEDER; FROM THE DIARY OF
     AN OFFICER IN THE FIRST BATTALION OF HESSIAN LIFEGUARDS DURING
     THE MOSCOW CAMPAIGN OF 1812-1813. Translated by Helen Roeder.
     London: Methuen, 1960.

338. Roguet, François, comte. MEMOIRES MILITAIRES DU LIEUTENANT-
     GENERAL COMTE ROGUET. Paris: Dumaine, 1862-65. 4 vols.

339. Roos, Henrich Ulrich von. SOUVENIRS D'UN MEDECIN DE LA GRANDE
     ARMEE. Paris: Perrin, 1913.

340. Rosselet, Abraham. SOUVENIRS DE ABRAHAM ROSSELET. Neuchâtel:
     Attinger, 1857.

341. Rossetti, M.J. "Journal du général Rossetti, la campagne de
     Russie." LA REVUE DE FRANCE (1932-33).

342. Rostopchin, Feodor, comte. MATERIAUX EN GRANDE PARTIE INEDITS
     POUR LA BIOGRAPHIE DU COMTE THEODORE ROSTOPTCHINE, RASSEMBLE PAR
     SON FILS. Brussels: M.J. Poot, 1864.

343. Rostopchin, Feodor, comte. VERITE SUR L'INCENDIE DE MOSCOU.
     Paris: Ponthieu, 1823.

344. Rotenhan. DENKWUERDIGKEITEN EINES WUERTTEMBERGISCHEN OFFIZIERS
     AUS DEM FELDZUGE IM JAHRE 1812. Munich: Finsterlin, 1900.

345. Rozhkov, Nikolai Aleksandrovich. "Dvenadtsatii God' V ego
     Vliiania na Sovremennoe emu Russkoe Obshchestvo" [1812 and Its
     Influence on Contemporaries in Russian Society]. SOVREMENNII
     MIR' 2 (1912): 202-33.

346. Rueppel, Edouard. KRIEGSGEFANGEN IM HERZEN RUSSLANDS,
     1812-1814. Berlin: Paetel, 1912.

347. Saint-Chamans, Alfred Armand Robert. MEMOIRES DU GENERAL COMTE
     DE SAINT-CHAMANS, ANCIEN AIDE-DE-CAMP DU MARECHAL SOULT. Paris:
     Plon-Nourrit, 1896.

348. Saint-Hilaire, Emile Marc Hilaire. HISTOIRE DE LA CAMPAGNE DE
     RUSSIE PENDANT L'ANNEE 1812 ET DE LA CAPTIVITE DES PRISONNIERS
     FRANCAIS EN SIBERIE ET DANS LES AUTRES PROVINCES DE L'EMPIRE.
     Paris: Penaud, 1846-48.

349. Schehl, Carl. VOM RHEIN ZUR MOSKWA 1812. Krefeld: Oberman, 1957.

350. Schmidt, Hans Gustav. DIE URHEBER DES BRANDES VON MOSKAU. Riga: Kymmel, 1912.

351. Schmitt, Hans A. "1812, Stein and Alexander in the Crusade against Napoleon." JOURNAL OF MODERN HISTORY 31 (1959): 325-28.

352. Schnitzler, Johann Heinrich. LA RUSSIE EN 1812, ROSTOPCHINE ET KOUTOUSOF. Paris: Didier, 1863.

353. Schreckenstein, Roth, freiherr von. DIE KAVALLERIE IN DER SCHLACHT AN DER MOSKWA AM 7. SEPTEMBER 1812. Munster: Schendorff, 1858.

354. Ségur, Philippe Paul, comte de. LA CAMPAGNE DE RUSSIE. Paris: Hachette, 1960. 2 vols.

355. Ségur, Philippe Paul, comte de. NAPOLEON'S RUSSIAN CAMPAIGN. Translated by J. David Townsend. Westport, Connecticut: Greenwood Press, 1959.

356. Sérignan, Arthur Maximillien, comte de Lort de. LE GENERAL MALET. Paris: Payot, 1925.

357. Séruzier, Théodore Jean, baron. MEMOIRES MILITAIRES DU BARON SERUZIER. Paris: Baudoin, 1894.

358. Seydlitz, Anton Florian Friedrich von. TAGEBUCH DES KOENIGL. PREUSSISCHEN ARMEE CORPS UNTER BEFEHL DES GENERALLIEUTENANTS VON YORK IM JAHRE 1812. Berlin and Posen: Mittler, 1823.

359. Shcherbachev, Iuri N., ed. "Otryvochnyia Zametki I Pis'ma, Kasaiushchiiasia Otechestvennoi Voiny" [Fragmentary Remarks and Letters regarding the Patriotic War]. OBSHCHESTVO ISTORII I DREVNOSTEI ROSSISKIKH', CHTENIIA 4 (1912): 1-25.

360. Shchukin, Petr Ivanovich. BUMAGI OTNOSIASHCHIIASIA DO OTECHESTVENNOI VOINY 1812 GODA [Papers Relating to the Patriotic War of 1812]. Moscow: A.I. Mamontov, 1897-1908. 10 vols.

361. Shilder, Nikolai Karlovich. IMPERATOR' ALEKSANDR' PERVYI, EGO ZHIZN' I TSARSTVO-VANIE [Emperor Alexander I: His Life and Reign]. St. Petersburg: A.S. Suvorin, 1897-98. 4 vols.

362. Sivitskii, S.N. OTECHESTVENNAIA VOINA V PRIBALTIISKOM' KRAE, 1812-1912 G [The Patriotic War in the Baltic Region]. Riga: Izd-vo. Rizhkogo pedagog. ob-va., 1912.

363. Skalon, Dmitri Antonovich, ed. STOLETIE VOENNAGO MINISTERSTVA, 1802-1902 [A Century of the Military Ministry]. St. Petersburg: Pantelev, 1902-14. 13 vols.

364. Slezsinski, A.N. "Narodnaia Voina V' Smolenskoi Gubernii V' 1812 Godu" [The Peoples War in Smolensk Gubernia in 1812]. RUSSKII ARKHIV' 2 (1901): 5-26.

365. Smittein, R., comp. AVEC NAPOLEON EN LITUANIE. Kaunas: Pribacio Leidinys, 1937.

366. Soltyk, Roman. NAPOLEON EN 1812, MEMOIRES HISTORIQUES ET MILITAIRES SUR LA CAMPAGNE DE RUSSIE. Paris: Bertrand, 1836.

367. Staël-Holstein, Anne Louise Germaine (Necker), baronne de. OEUVRES COMPLETES DE MADAME LA BARONNE DE STAEL. Paris: Treuttel et Würtz, 1821. Vol. 15.

368. Stalin, Joseph. "Otvet Tov. Stalina na Pismo Tov. Razina" [The Answer of Comrade Stalin to the Letter of Comrade Razin]. VOPROSY ISTORII 3 (1947): 5-7.

369. Steger, Friedrich. DER FELDZUG VON 1812. Braunschweig: Oehme & Muller, 1845.

370. Strokov, Aleksandr Aleksandrovich, ed. ISTORIIA VOENNOGO ISKUSSTVA [History of the Art of War]. Moscow: Voenn. izd-vo., 1965.

371. Suckow, Karl Friedrich Emil von. AUS MEINEM SOLDATENLEBEN. Leipzig: Wigand, 1910.

372. Surugue, Adrien, abbé. MOSCOU PENDANT L'INCENDIE. Paris: De Soye, 1891.

373. Svavich, Isak Semenovich. "Metternikh I Otechestvennaia voina 1812 Goda" [Metternich and the Patriotic War of 1812]. ISTORICHESKIE ZAPISKI 16 (1945): 100-125.

374. Szymanowski, Józef. MEMOIRES, 1806-1814. Translated by Bohdane Ockinczye. Paris: Lavauzelle, 1900.

375. Tarle, Evgenii Voktorovich. "M.I. Kutuzov. Polkovodets I Diplomat" [M.I. Kutuzov. General and Diplomat]. VOPROSY ISTORII 8 (1952): 34-82.

376. Tarle, Evgenii Viktorovich. NAPOLEON. Translated by Charles Steber. Paris: Payot, 1937.

377. Tarle, Evgenii Viktorovich. NASHESTVIE NAPOLEONA NA ROSSIIU 1812 GOD [Napoleon's Invasion of Russia in 1812]. Moscow: OGIZ gos. sots. ekon. izd-vo., 1938.

378. Tarle, Evgenii Voktorovich. "Otechestvennaia Voina 1812 GODA" [The Patriotic War of 1812]. BOLSHAIA SOVETSKAIA ENTSIKLOPEDIIA. 1st. ed., vol. 43, col. 556.

379. Tarle, Evgenii Viktorovich. OTECHESTVENNAIA VOINA 1812 GODA I RAZGROM IMPERII NAPOLEONA [The Patriotic War of 1812 and the

Destruction of the Empire of Napoleon]. Moscow: OGIZ, Gospolitizdat, 1941.

380. Tarle, Evgenii Viktorovich. ed. PARTIZANSKAIA BOR'BA [The Partisan Struggle]. Moscow: Ogiz gos. izd-vo. pol. lit., 1942.

381. Tarle, Evgenii Voktorovich. SOCHINENIIA [Works]. Moscow: Akad. nauk, 1957-62. 12 vols.

382. Tarle, Evgenii Voktorovich. TALEIRAN [Talleyrand]. Moscow: Izd-vo. Akad. nauk SSSR, 1948.

383. Tarle, Evgenii Viktorovich. ZAPAD' I ROSSIIA. STAT'I I DOKUMENTY IZ' ISTORIIA XVIII-XX V.V. [The West and Russia: Articles and Documents from the History of the 18th-20th Centuries]. Petrograd: Byloe, 1918.

384. Tarle, Evgenii Voktorovich. 1812 GOD [1812]. Moscow: Akademiia nauk SSSR, 1959.

385. Tartakovskii, Andrei G. VOENNAIA PUBLITSISTIKA 1812 GODA [Military Pamphleteering in 1812]. Moscow: Mysl', 1967.

386. Tartakovskii, Andrei G. "Zametki o Voennoi Propagande 1812 G." [Remarks on Military Propaganda in 1812]. VOPROSY VOENNOI ISTORII ROSSII. Moscow: Nauka, 1969.

387. Tartakovskii, Andrei G. "Iz Istorii Odnoi Zabytoi Polemiki (Ob Antikrepostnicheskikh 'Diversiiakh' Napoleona V 1812 Godu)" [From the History of One Forgotten Polemic (On the anti-serf diversion of Napoleon in 1812)]. ISTORIIA SSSR 2 (1968): 25-43.

388. Tatischeff, Sergei. ALEXANDRE Ier ET NAPOLEON. Paris: Perrin, 1891.

389. Thiry, Jean. NAPOLEON BONAPARTE, LA CAMPAGNE DE RUSSIE. Paris: Berger-Levrault, 1969.

390. Thull, Manfred. "Russland in den Augen Napoleons I." JAHR-BUECHER FUER GESCHICHTE OESTEUROPAS 21 (1973): 531-59.

391. Tikhonov, Ia. PORAZHENIE FRANTSUZOV NA SEVERE, ILI VOENNAIA ISTORIIA ZNAMENITYKH PODVIGOV ROSSISKIKH POLKOVODTSEV I VOINOV PROTIV FRANTSUZOV V 1812 GODU [The Defeat of the French in the North, or the Military History of the Celebrated Exploits of the Russian Army Leaders and Warriors against the French in 1812]. Moscow, 1814.

392. Toll. DENKWUERDIGKEITEN DES RUSSISCHEN GENERALS VON DER TOLL. Leipzig, 1856. 2 vols.

393. Tolstoi, Lev Nikolaevich. WAR AND PEACE. (Innumerable editions).

394. Tulard, Jean. "Le 'Dépôt de la guerre' et la préparation de la campagne de Russie." REVUE HISTORIQUE DE L'ARMEE 3 (1968): 104-9.

395. Tulard, Jean. "Murat, commandant en chef de l'armée de Russie" CAVALIER ET ROI 7 (1971): 41-44.

396. Tzenoff, Gancho. WER HAT MOSKAU IM JAHRE 1812 IN BRAND GESTECKT? Berlin: Ebering, 1900.

397. Ullman, J. STUDIE UEBER DE AUSRUESTUNG UND VERPFLEGS UND NACHSCHUBWESEN IN FELDZUGE NAPOLEONS I GEGEN RUSSLAND IM JAHRE 1812. Vienna: Seidel, 1891.

398. Ushakov, S.I. DEIANIIA ROSSIISKIKH' POLKOVODTSEV' I GENERALOV' OZNAMENOVAVSHIKH' SEBIA V' DOSTOPAMIATNUIU VOINU S' FRANTSIEIU V' 1812, 1813, 1814, I 1815 GODAKH' [The Deeds of the Russian Army Leaders and Generals Distinguishing Themselves in the Memorable War with France in 1812]. St. Petersburg: Tipografiia K. Kraiia, 1822. 4 vols.

399. Vandal, Albert. NAPOLEON ET ALEXANDRE Ier, L'ALLIANCE RUSSE SOUS LE PREMIER EMPIRE. Paris: E. Plon-Nourrit, 1911. 3 vols.

400. Vanel, Jean. "Murat et la campagne de Russie." CAVALIER ET ROI 7 (1975): 9-16.

401. Vasyutinski, A.M.; A.K. Dzhivelegov; S.P. Melgunov, eds. FRANTSUZY V' ROSSII [The French in Russia]. Moscow: Zadruga: 1912.

402. Vaudoncourt, Frédéric François Guillaume, baron de. MEMOIRES POUR SERVIR A L'HISTOIRE DE LA GUERRE ENTRE LA FRANCE ET LA RUSSIE EN 1812 PAR UN OFFICIER DE L'ETAT-MAJOR. London: Deboffe, 1815. 2 vols.

403. Venzky, Gabriele. DIE RUSSISCH-DEUTSCHE LEGION IN DEN JAHREN 1811-1815. Wiesbaden: Harrassowitz, 1966.

404. Vigel', Filipp Filippovich. ZAPISKI [Memoirs]. Moscow: Krug, 1928 (Reprint, Cambridge: Oriental Research Partners, 1974).

405. Vilde, Jean Marie Pierre Aubry de. "Lettres d'un officier pendant le campagne de Russie." REVUE DES ETUDES HISTORIQUES 48 (1922): 525-40.

406. Voenskii, Konstantin Adamovich, ed. AKTY, DOKUMENTY, I MATERIALY DLIA POLITICHESKOI I BYTOVOI ISTORII 1812 GODA [Acts, Documents, and Materials for the Political and Domestic History of 1812]. St. Petersburg: A.F. Shtoltzenburg, 1909-12. (Vols. 128, 133, 139, SBORNIK RUSSKOE ISTORICHESKOE OBSHCHESTVO). 3 vols.

407. Voenskii, Konstantin Adamovich. OTECHESTVENNAIA VOINA V'
RUSSKOI ZHURNALISTIKE [The Patriotic War in Russian Journalism].
St. Petersburg: "Berezhlivost'", 1906.

408. Voenskii, Konstantin Adamovich. "Svidaniia Frantsuzskikh'
Generalov' s' Russkikh' vo Vtoruiu Polovinu Kampanii 1812 Goda"
[Meetings of the French Generals with the Russians in the Second
Half of the 1812 Campaign]. VOENNYI SBORNIK 10 (1907): 19-38.

409. Voenskii, Konstantin Adamovich, et al. AKTY, DOKUMENTY I
MATERIALY DLIA ISTORII TYSIACHA VOSEM'SOT DVENADTSATAGO GODA
[Acts, Documents, and Materials for the History of 1812]. St.
Petersburg: Shtol'tsenburg, 1909-12. 3 vols.

410. Vossler, Heinrich August. WITH NAPOLEON IN RUSSIA 1812.
Translated by W. Wallich. London: Folio Society, 1969.

411. Wachsmuth, J. GESCHICHTE MEINER KRIEGSGEFANGENSCHAFT IN
RUSSLAND IN DEN JAHREN 1812 UND 1813. Magdeburg: Creutz, 1910.

412. Wedel, Karl Anton, graf von. GESCHICHTE EINES OFFIZIERS IM
KRIEGE GEGEN RUSSLAND 1812. Berlin: Asher, 1897.

413. Welden, Franz Ludwig, freiherr von. DER FELDZUG DER
OESTERREICHER GEGEN RUSSLAND IM JAHRE 1812. Vienna: Gerold,
1870.

414. West, Dalton A. "La Question français en Russie, 1806-1812."
Ph.D. dissertation, McGill University, 1972.

415. Whishaw, Frederick James. MOSCOW: A STORY OF THE FRENCH
INVASION OF 1812. New York: Longmans, Green, 1905.

416. Wilhelm, margrave of Baden. La CAMPAGNE DE 1812. MEMOIRES DU
MAGRAVE DE BADE. Traduction, introduction et notes par Arthur
Chuquet. Paris: Fontemoing, 1912.

417. Wilson, Robert. NARRATIVE OF EVENTS DURING THE INVASION OF
RUSSIA BY NAPOLEON BONAPARTE AND THE RETREAT OF THE FRENCH ARMY,
1812. London: J. Murray, 1860.

418. Wolowski, S. "Zima W 1812 R." BIBLIOTEKA WARSZAWSKA 3 (1913):
570-580.

419. Württemberg. ERRINERUNGEN AUS DEM FELDZUGE DES JAHRES 1812 IN
RUSSLAND VON DEM HERZOG EUGEN VON WURTTEMBERG. Breslau: Grass
und Barth, 1846.

420. Yaresh, Leo. "The Campaign of 1812." REWRITING RUSSIAN
HISTORY. Edited by C.E. Black. New York: Praeger, 1956.

421. Yorck von Wartenburg, Maximilien, graf. NAPOLEON AS A GENERAL.
London: Gilbert and Rivington, 1902. 2 vols.

422. Ysarn, François Joseph d'. RELATION DU SEJOUR DES FRANCAIS A
     MOSCOU ET DE l'INCENDIE DE CETTE VILLE EN 1812, PAR UN HABITANT
     DE MOSCOU. Edited by A. Gadáruel. Brussels: Gadáruel, 1871.

423. Zarin, Andrei Efimovich. 1812 G. ISTORICHESKII OCHERK'
     OTECHESTVENNOI VOINY [Historical Essay on the Patriotic War].
     St. Petersburg: V.I. Gubinskii, 1912.

424. Zatvornitskii, Nikolai Mitrofanovich. NAPOLEONOVSKAIA EPOKHA,
     BIBLIOGRAFICHESKII   UKAZATEL'   [The   Napoleonic   Epic,   A
     Bibliographic Guide]. Petrograd: Gr. Skachkov, 1915.

425. Zhilin, Pavel Andreevich. GIBEL' NAPOLEONOVSKOI ARMII V ROSSII
     [The Destruction of Napoleon's Army in Russia]. Moscow:
     Izd-vo. nauka, 1968.

426. Zhilin, Pavel Andreevich. KONTRNASTUPLENIE KUTUZOVA V 1812 G
     [Kutuzov's Counterattack in 1812]. Moscow: Voenn. izd-vo.,
     1950.

427. Zhilin, Pavel Andreevich. KONTRNASTUPLENIE RUSSKOI ARMII V 1812
     GODU [The Russian Army's Counterattack in 1812]. Moscow:
     Voenn. izd-vo., 1952.

428. Zhilin, Pavel Andreevich. "Nekotorye Voprosy Izucheniia Istorii
     Otechestvennoi Voiny 1812 GODA" [Several Problems in the Study
     of the Patriotic War of 1812]. VOPROSY ISTORII 6 (1962): 54-75.

429. Zhilin, Pavel Andreevich. VELIKII RUSSKII POLKOVODETS M.I.
     KUTUZOV [The Great Russian Army Leader, M.I. Kutuzov]. Moscow:
     Znanie, 1952.

430. Zhilin, Pavel Andreevich, and A. Iaroslavtsev. BORODINSKOE
     SRAZHENIE [The Battle of Borodino]. Moscow: Voenn. izd-vo.,
     1952.

431. Zych, Gabriel. ARMIA KSIESTWA WARSZAWSKIEGO, 1807-1812 [The
     Army of the Duchy of Warsaw, 1807-1812]. Warszawa: Wydawn.
     Ministerstwa Obrony Narodowej, 1961.

PERIODICALS AND ENCYCLOPEDIAS

432. CAHIERS DU MONDE RUSSE ET SOVIETIQUE.

433. ENTSIKLOPEDICHESKII SLOVAR' [Encyclopedia]. 1890-1907.

434. ISTORICHESKII ZAPISKI [Historical Notes].

435. ISTORIIA SSSR [History of the USSR].

436. ISTORIK MARKSIST [Marxist Historian].

437. JAHRBUECHER FUER GESCHICHTE OSTEUROPAS.

438. LE MONDE SLAV.

439. RUSSKAIA STARINA [Russian Antiquity]. 1870-1917.

440. RUSSKII ARKHIV [Russian Archives]. 1863-1917.

441. RUSSKII   BIOGRAFICHESKII   SLOVAR   [Russian   Biographical
     Dictionary]. 1896-1913.

442. SBORNIK IMPERATORSKOGO RUSSKOGO ISTORICHESKOGO OBSHCHESTVA
     [Collection of the Imperial Russian Historical Society].

443. SLAVONIC AND EAST EUROPEAN REVIEW.

444. SLAVIC REVIEW.

445. VOENNYI SBORNIK [Military Collection]. 1858-1817.

446. VOPROSY ISTORII [Problems of History].

                             ADDENDUM

447. ARKHIV KNIAZIA VORONTSOVA [The Vorontsov Archives].

448. Bignon, Louis Pierre Edouard, baron. HISTOIRE DE FRANCE, DEPUIS
     LE 18 BRUMAIRE (NOVEMBRE 1799), JUSQU'A LA PAIX DE TILSITT
     (JUILLET 1807).   Paris: Béchet, Firmin-Didot, 1829-50.   14
     vols.

449. Liprandi, Ivan Petrovich. MATERIALY OTECHESTVENNE VOINY 1812
     GODA [Materials on the Patriotic War of 1812]. St. Petersburg:
     Tip. E. Arigul'd, 1867.

450. LISTOVKI OTECHESTVENNOI VOZNY 1812 GODA: SBORNIK DOKUMENTOV
     [Document Collection of the Patriotic War of 1812].   Moscow,
     1962.

451. Masanov, Iu. I.; N.V. Nitkina; and Z.D. Titova, eds. UKAZATELI
     SODERZHANIIA RUSSKIKH ZHURNALOV I PRODOLZHAIUSHCKIKHSIA IZDANII
     1755-1970 GG [Indices of the Contents of Russian Journals and
     Continuing Publications].   Newtonville, Mass.:   Oriential
     Research Partners, 1979.

452. POLNOE SOBRANIE ZAKONOV' ROSSIISKOI IMPERII [The Complete
     Collection of the Laws of the Russian Empire].

453. SBORNIK ISTORICHESKIKH MATERIALOV IZVLECHENNYKH IZ ARKHIVA
     SOBSTVENNOI E. I. VVA. KANTSELIARII [A Collection of Historical
     Materials from the Archives of His Imperial Majesty's Own
     Chancellery].

454. Seaton, Albert. THE RUSSIAN ARMY OF THE NAPOLEONIC WARS. New
     York: Hippocrene, 1973.

455. Thiers, Adolphe. HISTOIRE DU CONSULAT ET DE L'EMPIRE. Paris:
     Paulin, 1845-69. 21 vols.

456. Tissot, Pierre François.   PRECIS, OU, HISTOIRE ABREGEE DES
     GUERRES DE LA REVOLUTION FRANCAISE; DEPUIS 1792-1815.   Paris:
     Raymond, 1821.   2 vols.

CHAPTER XIII

THE RISE OF GERMAN NATIONALISM AND THE WARS OF LIBERATION (1803-1814)

Marion W. Gray, Kansas State University

Germany's responses to Napoleonic domination constitute one of the most significant formative periods in recent German history. Napoleon and his armies thrust the French Revolution upon German-speaking Europe, but not in its original form. Modern German nationalism found its first concrete expressions in the Napoleonic era. During that time, the populations between the Rhine and the Vistula confronted the middle-class ideas of liberty and equality, and these were expressed in a language shaped by Napoleonic influence. The decade of French domination vastly accelerated social, political, economic, and military changes that had been underway for generations in German territories.

This bibliography stresses the growth of German nationalism and the military encounters which have come to be known as the Wars of Liberation. However, it would oversimplify and distort these phenomena to present them in isolation from the broader social context. For this reason, the bibliography includes sources which treat political reform, social change, and economic transformation, as well as topics expressly described by the title.

Because the Napoleonic experience was so pivotal in shaping the last two centuries of German history, scholars have produced a vast literature dealing with the interlude between the dissolution of the Holy Roman Empire and the Congress of Vienna. Researchers approaching the topic for the first time may need guidelines for assessing the relative value of the historical writings. Probably the best key is the chronology of German historiography itself.

History written before the middle of the nineteenth century generally lacked pretenses to objectivity or modern scholarly standards. Prior to the work of Leopold von Ranke, historians viewed their craft as a legitimate means of reinforcing particular political orientations, moral beliefs, or personal philosophies. Those who did not write to defend an idea, often carried on their work in order to glorify a particular individual or event. The establishment of a modern scholarly research methodology fostered by Ranke greatly impacted the nature of historical writing. Some of the fruits of Ranke's "Critical Method" (260, 261) treat Prussian history in the Napoleonic period, and they are of historiographical interest as well as of importance due to their content.

Subsequent scholarship continued, of course, to betray the biases of its origins. A nationalistic, pro-Prussian political orientation is evident in much of the writing of the Second Empire (1871-1918). There were, however, scholars who strongly dissented from this tradition, such as early socialist historians as well as southern German and Austrian writers. But the majority of material published during the reigns of William I and William II represent the events of 1803-1814 as a glorious struggle and a prelude to the successful establishment of a unified German state. Their involvement in the establishment of a nation-state led historians of the late nineteenth century to view early nationalism as both natural and progressive. Their language is revealing. Those who continued to romanticize the German response to Napoleon used the phrase "Wars of Freedom" (Freiheitskriege), while more critical scholars adopted the term, "Wars of Liberation" (Befreiungskriege).

Friedrich Meinecke's scholarship marks a turning point in German historical scholarship. In the decades preceding the First World War, Meinecke produced several important works on the Napoleonic era (213-217). His conceptualization of the interrelationship between intellectual and political developments in history has influenced many generations of historians right up to the present. However, Meinecke did not undermine the tendency to romanticize the history of Germany's defeat by Napoleon and its later victory over the French. Most historians of the Weimar era (1918-1933) were also unable to free themselves from these tendencies. Historical research under the rule of Nazism, subject to strict censorship, discarded all pretenses of objectivity.

After World War II, German historiography, like other facets of intellectual, political and social life, took two divergent paths. Historians of the German Democratic Republic succeeded earlier than those of the Federal Republic in breaking with the traditions of the past. East Germany has produced both rigid, doctrinaire scholarship and highly creative interpretations. Whereas the East German historical writing of the 1950s and early 1960s appears almost painfully forced into an ideological mold, that of more recent decades employs Marxist methodology with less self-consciousness. East German research on the Wars of Liberation (143, 332) has produced very probing analyses. West German historians, during the first decades after the war, continued to work in the idioms formulated earlier in the century. The New Social History of the 1960s and 1970s, however, has established new patterns, shedding the antiquated nationalist bias and practicing fresh, integrated approaches to the events of the Napoleonic era (90). Military history, written primarily at the Militärgeschichtliches Forschungsamt at Freiburg, is a welcome change from the older German Kriegsgeschichte (history of war) and Wehrgeschichte. The earlier traditions focused narrowly on war and strategy in order to draw conclusions on improving future military operations. Many practitioners of these specializations believed all history to be subordinated to the history of the military. Modern Militär-geschichte, however, emphasizes the primacy of politics and views armed forces as institutions of society.

It is unfortunate that East German and West German historians have seemed to learn so little from one another. Those in the Democratic Republic have attempted to systematically refute every word printed by their colleagues in the West, while those of the Federal Republic have aggressively ignored historical publications from the East.

It would be wrong to judge any historical work solely by its chronological or ideological origin. Research scholars will find much very useful material among the romanticized histories of the early nineteenth century, if for no other reason than their closeness to the events. One dare not dismiss nationalistic histories of the Second Empire, Marxist historiography from the GDR, or even the National Socialist writing produced prior to and during World War II, merely on account of political bias. Historians are products of their times, and each generation will remain indebted to its predecessors. Because of archival losses during World War II, secondary sources, whatever their ideological orientation, will retain a special importance in Germany.

GENERAL WORKS

A collection of essays edited by Sieburg (323), a study of Napoleon's satellite kingdoms by Connelly (51), and a volume issued by the Commission Internationale pour l'enseignement de l'histoire (231) all share the value of placing Napoleonic Germany in a European-wide context. The publications growing out of a recent conference on Napoleonic Germany and Italy (266) are more specialized, but they have the attribute of being comparative analyses, and they represent some of the newest Napoleonic scholarship. Chandler's work (46) focuses on the military campaigns of the period.

General histories of Germany are important for putting the Napoleonic era in perspective. The work by Raumer (264) in the well-known HANDBUCH DER DEUTSCHEN GESCHICHTE founded by Leo Just, as well as that by Braubach (36) in Gebhardt's HANDBUCH, are standard interpretations used widely by scholars and students in the West. They should be read in comparison with Streisand's handbook (334) written from an East German perspective. The works by Meinecke (216, 217), Droz (73), Denis (61), and Rambaud (259) can still be used profitably as introductions to the period if one is careful to keep them in historiographical context. The same is true of Fisher's introduction to the diplomacy of Napoleonic Germany (94) and Valjavec's analysis of the origins of modern political parties and ideologies in Germany (359). The essays by Sieburg (322) and Scheel (292) attempt to establish new general perspectives on Napoleonic Germany and should be consulted to supplement older works.

There are a number of important German military histories which treat the Napoleonic experience in enough depth to be useful as general introductions. Predictably, most focus on Prussian institutions. The handiest for English-speaking readers is Craig's POLITICS OF THE PRUSSIAN ARMY (56). The military histories by Jany (157) and Freytag-Loringhoven (100) are widely consulted in spite of their official tone. The essay by Kessel (163) is a more objective, but less detailed, critique. Ritter's four-volume analysis of Germany's "problem of militarism" (274) has attracted wide attention, and it contains significant material on the Napoleonic period. Ritter defends Prussian tradition against claims that it was responsible for the "German Problem." The work of Helmert and Usczeck (134) provides an alternative view to the standard West German and American military histories. A delightful volume of illustrations compiled by the Napoleonic specialist Kircheisen (164), while not scholarly in nature, can add significantly to one's appreciation of the period.

BIBLIOGRAPHIES

The standard, indispensable bibliography for German history is the QUELLENKUNDE DER DEUTSCHEN GESCHICHTE (58), generally called "Dahlmann-Waitz" after the two nineteenth-century historians who founded it. After having been revised eight times, it is now being completely rewritten with a new conceptualization and organization. A team of West German scholars under the direction of Hermann Heimpel and Herbert Geuss is collecting and publishing the new bibliographical material in serial form. When section 354 dealing with Napoleonic domination and the Wars of Liberation appears, it will surpass all other bibliographies of the period. Until then one should consult the ninth edition of Dahlmann-Waitz (58). A complement to this is Körner's BIBLIOGRAPHISCHES HANDBUCH (179) which is oriented more toward literary works than scholarly publications, so it is useful for literature connected with the Wars of Liberation. Wermke (374) is an extensive bibliography devoted exclusively to the provinces of East and West Prussia. Fout (98) is very helpful in locating periodical literature, though it contains omissions. Hubatsch's bibliography of the Stein-Hardenberg reforms (150) contains sources relevant to the military and political history of Prussia in the Napoleonic decade.

Military researchers now have available a splendid bibliographical volume on Germany edited by Showalter (397). It will be indispensible. In addition, many of the books cited in the present essay contain specialized bibliographies, and researchers should always be alert to these resources. Raumer (264) and Braubach (36) are almost standard bibliographies themselves. Paret's monograph on Yorck (244) includes essential bibliographical material on military history. Spies (326) and Langsam (190) provide orientation to literature relevant to the rise of nationalism.

The Wars of Liberation have been intensely researched by scholars of the German Democratic Republic. There are several published guides to the GDR scholarship on this topic: Dorpalen (68), Heydermann (138), Schäfer (290), and Heitzer (131). The assessments by these American, West German, and East German scholars vary widely depending on their perspectives.

The foremost biographical lexicon for German history is the well-known ALLGEMEINE DEUTSCHE BIOGRAPHIE (2). It will remain indispensable even after the NEUE DEUTSCHE BIOGRAPHIE (234) is completed. Scholars will welcome the new, massive compilation of biographical data contained in the DEUTSCHES BIOGRAPHISCHE ARCHIV (391), which will simplify research concerning historical personalities. These general works can be supplemented by specialized biographies such as Krollmann's Prussian biographies (188) and Hormayr's collection of material on participants in the Wars of Liberation (148). Priesdorff's ten-volume lexicon on military leaders (253), reflecting the era of its origin, is uncritical scholarship. However, it will continue to be an important reference source, in part because the World War II destruction of military archives makes it the latest source of information on many officers. Poten's handbook of military science (251), although published a century ago, is an important reference tool for the military history of the Napoleonic era.

Scholars researching nineteenth-century Germany have always found two directories of published books indispensable: Kayser's BUECHER-LEXIKON (162) and Heinsius's ALLGEMEINES BUECHER-LEXIKON (130). Both are now rendered almost obsolete by a bibliographic compilation project of major proportions--the two-series GESAMT-VERZEICHNIS (GV) (392, 393). The task of identifying the authors of works which appeared either anonymously or under pseudonyms--common practice on the patriotic literature associated with the Wars of Liberation--will be greatly facilitated by two reference works by Holzmann and Bohatta (146, 147). Welsch (372) and Haase (120) will guide scholars unfamiliar with the landscape of German research libraries to the best depositories on their respective topics. Gebhardt's guide (106) contains information on specialized library collections in West Germany.

ARCHIVAL SOURCES

Archival research in German-speaking lands is complicated by the lack of any systematic organization due in large part to political decentralization. This problem is aggravated by the vast destruction and dislocation suffered in World War II. Poll (250) and Enders (80) describe the disarray and discontinuity of German military archives due to wars. Rath (263) has surveyed the fate of Austrian archives in the Second World War. Fortunately there are several reliable published general guides to archives. The most thorough is the Minerva handbook (4). Welsch's guide (372) is less extensive, yet handy to use. Some of the information in it is dated. Both of these may be supplemented by Haase's reference work (120) which describes German archives and research institutions as well as German-language archival collections in non-German lands. Topics in military and diplomatic history require, of course, the use of archives in many national settings. For example, the Archives Nationales du Ministère des Affaires Etrangères in Paris and the Public Record Office in London contain correspondence relevant to the German experience in the Napoleonic era. Researchers should consult the appropriate chapters of this volume for detailed information and literature. They will also find Thomas's NEW GUIDE TO THE DIPLOMATIC ARCHIVES OF EUROPE (348) an important orientation tool.

The major state archive of West Germany is the Bundesarchiv, Koblenz (88). However, military documents are housed in a separate branch, Bundesarchiv-Militärarchiv in Freiburg im Breisgau. For military historians, Freiburg will be an important location because of the Militärgeschichtliches Forschungsamt located there. Unfortunately only scattered remnants of valuable material from the former Heeresarchiv Potsdam are extant in the Freiburg military history collection. Most were destroyed by Allied bombings in 1945. Another depository of importance for the Napoleonic era is the Geheimes Staatsarchiv in Berlin-Dahlem (West) (35). Holdings from the former East Prussian provincial archive of Königsberg (96), until recently located in Göttingen, are now also in Dahlem as well, under the auspices of the Stiftung Preussischer Kulturbesitz.

Other, more extensive, Prussian sources are deposited in the Deutsches Zentralarchiv, Abteilung II, Merseburg (GDR). Like several German archives, this one never made it back to its original location, Berlin, after being moved to a protective locality during World War II (226). Scholars interested in the events of 1813-1814 should consult the article by Thieme et al. (343). Dräger's essay (69) is derived from documents in Merseburg and can also serve as an orientation to the sources there. Endler (81) catalogues the holdings of individuals' papers in Merseburg, including several important personalities from the Napoleonic era. Gold (112) reports on sources related to the Wars of Liberation located in the

Brandenburg archives in Potsdam and Schmidt (303) on those in Dresden (Saxony).

The primary depository of Austrian archival material is the well-known Haus-, Hof-, und Staatsarchiv in Vienna. The five-volume inventory (26) is updated by Neck (233). Brown (38) has collected information on French-related sources in Vienna which will guide researchers to Napoleonic material.

Despite the importance of Berlin, Freiburg, Merseburg, and Vienna, research on Germany in the Napoleonic period may require that scholars visit any of dozens of regional archives scattered throughout the Federal Republic, the Democratic Republic, and Austria. Documentary material from former political entities such as Bavaria, Saxony, Hanover, Hesse, Baden, Württemberg, or Tyrol may be essential, depending on one's topic. Researchers should consult the articles by Epstein on Germany (83) and by May and Brown on Austria (211) as well as the general reference book on archives of the German Democratic Republic (338). The reference volumes by Mommsen (224) and Denecke (390) listing the collections of individuals' papers in West Germany are very thorough. The Minerva guide (4) is the most indispensable single directory of archives in German-speaking Europe.

PUBLISHED DOCUMENTS

A number of documentary collections, especially from Prussian sources, facilitate research on Napoleonic Germany. The Prussian reform movement following the Peace of Tilsit has occupied the attention of scholars since the early nineteenth century. Because the reforms are directly related to both military and diplomatic history, military historians should be familiar with the published sources. Collections from the Prussian State Archives relevant to the Napoleonic era have been edited by Winter (377), Hassel (126), Granier (115), and Vaupel (363). All are compiled with high scholarly standards, and dependable textual accuracy. Vaupel's collection deals especially with military reforms. Unfortunately, only one of several planned volumes appeared. Two collections by Rühl (285, 286) mirror the response of key Prussian officials to the French victory and occupation. The correspondence and official writings of Baron Karl vom Stein have been carefully edited by Botzenhart and are now available in a revised, expanded edition (31). Scheel's superb three-volume edition of documents from the Stein Ministry (293) is a resource welcomed by scholars. It draws upon the collection in the Deutsches Zentralarchiv II in Merseburg.

Supplementary to these are a number of more specialized documentary collections, including many in journals. Schoeps's edition of the Gerlach papers (311) is important for the perspective it gives on the conservative nobility. Stern's materials from the Public Record Office in London (329) are not only useful in themselves, but should also suggest to researchers the possibilities of using British sources for work on Napoleonic Germany. Individually published documents such as the memoranda and letters by Seydlitz (213), Clausewitz (283), Gneisenau (111), Scharnhorst (346), Lucadou (310), and Schleiermacher (257) are less handy to use but still advantageous when compared to the cost and uncertainties of archival research. The correspondence and official documents of French officials are essential to understanding French policies and

German responses. Especially important in this regard are the four volumes of Davout's correspondence (212). For other French officials, one should consult the appropriate chapters of this bibliography.

While other territories have enjoyed less historiographical attention than Prussia, there are scattered useful collections. Chroust's edition of diplomatic dispatches from Bavaria (48) includes documents relevant to the period of the Wars of Liberation and subsequent decades. Schmidt's compilation of materials from Saxon noble family archives (304) contains material that is at best difficult to locate in original form today.

Some collections relating specifically to military affairs should be noted, especially Hahlweg's documents stemming from several Prussian military reformers (124). A reproduction of the first field newspaper of the Prussian army from 1813 and 1814 (137, 170) has particular relevance to the study of the Wars of Liberation. Contemporarily published sources such as the 1812 EXERZIER-REGLEMENTS from the Prussian Cavalry (86) and Infantry (87) can also be very valuable.

The Wars of Liberation themselves have been the subject of intense study, and this accounts, perhaps, for the large number of published document collections pertaining to them.   Klessmann's edition of eyewitness reports (171), although not intended for research scholars, can be used to advantage. The same is true of a similar collection by Riedweg issued during World War II (271). Demelitsch's document collection dealing with the coalition of 1814 (59) is researched from an Austrian perspective.   Schoenach's compilation published in article form (309) contains military documents relating to the eve of the Wars of Liberation. Spies's recently published work (327) includes many documents illustrating official German responses to Napoleon and the problems brought about by defeat and occupation. These sources are especially important for the study of the growth of German nationalism.

MEMOIRS, JOURNALS, AND EYEWITNESS ACCOUNTS

Soon after the Restoration, German political and military leaders began to look back upon their experiences in the Napoleonic era with romanticized perspectives. For the participants, there was something heroic about having first endured defeat and having then helped throw off the French "yoke." This mentality may explain the myriad of published memoirs, journals, and correspondence collections which began to appear shortly after the Congress of Vienna. Some were edited by the participants themselves, others by proud family members, and yet a third group by academics interested in bringing primary sources to light. Modern research scholars will be frustrated by the bias and the incompleteness of these accounts. They remain, however, an important body of research material.

Writings of military officers are plentiful, but disarranged. Linnebach's volume of Scharnhorst's letters (205) is well edited but is only a portion of what was originally planned. The same editor's collection of letters and journals of Carl and Maria von Clausewitz (204), published during World War I, contains material relating to the personal as well as the professional life of the famous general. The most extensive edition of published Clausewitz papers is the

ten-volume edition issued in the 1830s (49). Rothfels's collection
of Clausewitz material (282) supplements earlier ones. Documents on
Clausewitz in Hahlweg's collection (124) were selected and edited
with scholarly precision. Boyen's three-volume memoirs (235) were
published by Nippold in the late nineteenth century. It is
instructive to compare this with Boyen's essay on Scharnhorst (32)
published two decades after the Wars of Liberation. Blücher's
correspondence is not systematically published. Schulze's "selected
letters" (316) is an introductory source, and it is supplemented by
two publications in article form (27, 114). The writings of a number
of other military figures are available in published form, including
Gneisenau (111, 249), Brandt (33), Schmidt (302), Natzmer (232),
Hogendorp (144), Tiedemann (200), Hiller von Gaertringen (354), Wedel
(349), Dorow (67), and Müffling (227). Müffling also published
eyewitness accounts under pseudonyms (367, 368). Kircheisen's WIDER
NAPOLEON (165) provides insight into Landwehr activities from the
view of a squadron commander. One should see as well the memoirs of
the French officer, Macdonald (209). Another perspective is provided
by the papers of Schubert (313), a German officer in Russian
service.

Civilian political leaders have also had their share of writings
and memoirs published, with varying degrees of reliability. An
example is the multivolume edition of the Schön papers (307, 308).
While these contain valuable historical material, they also embody
highly distorted autobiographical writing, and they are edited in
such a way as to flatter Schön. In comparison, Rühl's collection of
sources from the Stägemann papers (285, 286) is compiled with high
scholarly standards. Ranke's edition of Hardenberg's memoirs (261)
is of both historical and historiographical interest. Branig's
edition of Hardenberg-Wittgenstein correspondence (34) is carefully
compiled. Bassewitz's description of the fate of his home province,
Brandenburg, under the French experience (13) is a valuable source of
first-hand information. The Beguelin papers (14) contain important
material on Prussian affairs under Napoleon. The same can be said
for the writings of Niebuhr which were edited by Gerhard and Norvin
(109) and the five-volume set of correspondence from Scheffner
published by Warda (371), both products of the Weimar era. Heere's
selected documents from the Brünneck papers (128) focus on the
anti-French struggle. Viewpoints of conservative aristocratic
families are revealed in the papers of the Gerlach brothers (311) and
Marwitz (219). Gagern (103), a Hessian politician, stressed his own
role in the nationalistic campaigns, but a value of his three-volume
memoirs is its non-Prussian perspective. For similar reasons, one
should not overlook the papers of the Bavarian Minister Montgelas
(225) and of Metternich (218).

Correspondence collections and memoirs from persons whose work
was literary rather than political complement the accounts already
mentioned. Military historians will find the writings of Berenhorst
(41) especially important. The letters of Johannes von Müller (29),
a Swiss journalist who wrote for the Prussian cause, are a good
chronicle of the times. The writings of Gentz, who was influential
among the political leaders of his era, are basic to an understanding
of the Napoleonic experience. Several editions of his memoirs and
letters (254, 297, 378) contain overlapping, but not identical,

material. Fichte's correspondence (92) falls more into the category
of eyewitness accounts than into that of literature.

SPECIALIZED WORKS: CONTEMPORARY LITERATURE
AND POLEMICAL WRITINGS

The sheer volume of literature that was written directly in
response to the French reordering of German-speaking Europe is
overwhelming. During the last half of the eighteenth century the
numbers of books, pamphlets, and periodicals published annually had
been increasing dramatically, but the French wars accelerated this
trend.

The best known examples of this genre stem from the pens of
authors who are famous in their own right for literary,
philosophical, or political writing. This bibliography includes,
where possible, recent and comprehensive editions of their works.
However, researchers will often find scores of other editions. One
should use the most handy sources available. The philosophers,
Fichte (93) and Kant (160), may be the most famous in this class.
Also well-known are the philosopher-statesman W. von Humboldt (153)
and the theologian Schleiermacher (295). Poets and playwrights
enjoyed a heyday during the Napoleonic period, despite censorship
laws. The writings of Eichendorff (77), Kotzebue (185), Kleist
(169), Schlegel (294), Collin (50), Arndt (7), and Fouqué (97) reveal
not only the powerful romantic sentiment of Germany's years under
Napoleon, but also very marked regional variation. Their work
reflects the values of the increasingly important educated middle
classes.

The writings of many whose names will never be known because
they published anonymously, as well as those whose names have long
since been forgotten, also reflect these bourgeois attitudes. Every
town and province had its poet, journalist, or pastor who penned
passionate responses to Germany's plight. No systematic reference
sources exist which will guide the scholar to these important
nationalistic writings. The best starting place is with the scholars
who have studied such publications: Spies (327), Czygan (57),
Tschirch (350), and Arnold (8). Approximately a dozen such works are
included in this bibliography. They are intended only as a sample.
Their titles reveal their emotion-filled contents: SUENDENREGISTER
DER FRANZOSEN IN TEUTSCHLAND (6); DEUTSCHLAND IN SIENER TIEFEN
ERNIEDRIGUNG (62); DEUTSCHLANDS HOFFNUNGEN (178); DEUTSCHLANDS
WIEDERGEBURT (70); DEUTSCHLANDS ERWARTUNGEN VOM RHEINISCHEN BUNDE
(76); ERNSTE WORTE DER VATERLANDSLIEBE (369). The following works
are of the same style: Schmid (298), Schuderoff (314), Schutz (317),
Richter (270), and Offelsmeyer (239). Johannes von Müller (30, 229)
is not to be confused with Adam Müller (228). While the one patriot
sought to oust Napoleon and restore the order of the feudal past, the
other hoped French defeat would bring social and political change.

Journals and newspapers sprang up like mushrooms in response to
the extraordinary conditions of censorship and new freedoms. The
following list is a sample representative of the wide variety of
publications which devoted their writings to the strong expression of
political and cultural viewpoints: BERLINER ABENDBLAETTER (18),
ERHEBUNGEN (84), EUROPAEISCHE ANNALEN (85), GERMANIA (110), IRENE
(155), KOENIGLICHES BAYERISCHES REGIERUNGSBLATT (177), MINERVA (221),

DER RHEINISCHE BUND (268), RHEINISCHER MERKUR (269), and RUSSISCH-DEUTSCHES VOLKS-BLATT (287).

A few well-edited anthologies will prove helpful to scholars interested in the patriotic literature. These include Spies's recent volume (327) and an older but still sound edition by Czygan (57). Arnold and Wagner (8, 9) have also compiled valuable collections of patriotic literature.

SPECIALIZED WORKS: BATTLES AND OPERATIONS

Every generation of scholars has reinterpreted the Wars of Liberation from the perspective of its own times. Some of the most challenging recent scholarship on this subject has been produced in the German Democratic Republic. Two volumes of essays on this topic are excellent examples: Hoffmann (143) and Straube (332). Together they contain essays devoted to a wide range of issues such as historiography, tactical military history, nationalism, the relations between military activities and domestic reform, and archival sources. GDR historians enjoy the advantage of easy access to Prussian archival materials which is often difficult for western scholars to obtain.

On the diplomatic background of the Wars of Liberation, there are a number of article-length studies one should consult, especially Stern's essay on Gneisenau in London (330), Rohr's on Scharnhorst in Vienna (279), and Lehmann's on Gneisenau in Sweden (193). Seyffarth's study of Hardenberg's diplomacy (318), as well as works on Austria by Luckhardt (207), Oncken (241), and Kraehe (186) all contain valuable diplomatic material. The pre-World War I works published by Beitzke (15), Friedrich (102), Zimmerman (387), and the Military History Division of the Prussian General Staff (342) are still of value to modern scholars. A ten-volume collection (381), antiquated in its scholarship, should nevertheless not be overlooked. It is important on account of its Austrian perspective. Wertheimer's article (375), based on Austrian sources, is valuable for the same reason. Many of the centennial anniversary publications on the Wars of Liberation can be dismissed as romantic, nationalistic history. Still worth consulting are the works by Bezold (24), Müsebeck (230), and Pflugk-Harttung (248).

The history of the Convention of Tauroggen between the Prussian forces under Yorck and the Russian under Diebitsch has been the subject of heated historical debate. Many historians, influenced by the historiography of the Prussian-nationalist school, have maintained that Yorck acted with the approval of King Frederick William III (344, 345, 347). Others, however, have not been able to discover Yorck's motivation. This includes Yorck's biographer, Droysen (72). There is also a well established legend that Stein was responsible for facilitating the Russian-Prussian alliance. Schmitt presents a more objective view (305). Stein's colleague in the reform ministry of 1808, Schön, contributed to the legendary accounts of the Convention, and the historian, Max Lehmann, devoted many pages to a refutation of Schön's version (194, 195, 198, 199). New analyses of the problem have been made by the East German scholars Röder (277) and Straube (333). Holleben and Caemmerer's analysis of the Spring Campaign of 1813 (145) is surpassed by that of Straube

(331). For the Fall Campaign one should consult the work of Usczeck (355).

On the Landwehr, Showalter's (320) article is based on sound scholarship. It is instructive to read it in comparison with the analyses of Schmidt (301) and Franz (99). A thorough evaluation requires a reading of the older literature as well: Meinecke (214), Friccius (101), and Ulmann (351). The General Staff's material on the Prussian participation in the Campaign of 1812 (342) is one of the few accounts of this topic. The Freikorps in Hessen have been studied by Bader (11) and those of Krockow by Brinkmann (37). The Landwehr and Landsturm of Baden are the object of study by Haering (122).

SPECIALIZED WORKS: BIOGRAPHICAL STUDIES

The best biography of Yorck is Paret's (244). Droysen's work (72) should still be consulted because it contains material included nowhere else. The most recent work on Scharnhorst is Usczeck (356) which is ahistorical in some of its conclusions. Lehmann's several studies (196-198) are based on archival research and are superior to the three-volume work by Klippel (173). Höhn's writing on Scharnhorst (139) is disappointing as a new interpretation. Several recent journal articles bring the Scharnhorst literature up to date: Gembruch (107), Teske (340), Zwengel (388), and Wollstein (382).

Paret's study of Clausewitz, with emphasis on the military leader's thought and writing (243), is a welcome update of Rothfels's Clausewitz biography of 1920 (281). Journal literature supplements Paret's perspectives on Clausewitz: Hahlweg (123), Schmidt (299), Gembruch (108), Beyerhaus (23), and Aron (10). There is no modern biography of Gneisenau. The life-and-letters style study began by Pertz and completed by Delbrück (245) is surpassed by Delbrück's own two-volume interpretation which went through four editions between 1880 and 1920. One must rely heavily on scholarly journal literature for information about Gneisenau. The interpretations offered by Teske (339) and Will (376) are especially important. Both have a military emphasis. Usinger's article (357) though old, is still provocative. Bethcke (20) is antiquated. Secondary literature on Gneisenau must be sought in scattered works with divergent themes. Readers will recognize many works in this bibliography as relating to Gneisenau's career, although his name does not appear in the titles. The same is true about Boyen, a central figure in the Prussian reforms and in the creation of the Landwehr. One is still dependent upon Meinecke's two-volume biography (215), but obviously the literature dealing with the Landwehr is the place to find the most recent work on Boyen. The outdated biography of Blücher by Unger (353) is supplemented by an article appearing in the first volume of the ZEITSCHRIFT FUER MILITAERGESCHICHTE (71).

As for biographically oriented studies of other military leaders, researchers will find two works on Ferdinand Schill important, despite their heroic conceptualization (25, 166). Like the latter, a book-length interpretation of the important patriotic Hessian General Dörnberg (66) is a product of the National Socialist era. There is a semi-official three-volume study of Grolman published by General von Conrady in the 1890s (53) and an even older

work on Krauseneck (91) which, despite their age, contain important
biographical material.

Political figures who played leading parts in the rise of
nationalism have fared no better than military personnel in
biographical treatment. Stein's biography has been written more
often than that of others. Lehmann's three-volume work on Stein
(192) is reliable and contains a wealth of information. The same is
true of Ritter's scholarly, yet popular biography first published in
1931 but still in print in a revised postwar edition (275). On
Stein's controversial role in 1813, one should consult an article by
Hubatsch (149) and a volume published by the Freiherr-vom-Stein-
Gesellschaft (156). Thielen's biography of Hardenberg (341) is a
welcome update of Ranke's study of nearly a century earlier (260).
An American scholar, Paul Sweet, has written modern biographies of
Wilhelm von Humboldt (337) and Friedrich von Gentz (336). Gebhardt's
older work on Humboldt (105) is still very useful. Wohlfeil's
analysis of the relations of Dalberg and Napoleon (380) is supplemented by Leroux who wrote on Dalberg's thought (201). Finally, one
should not overlook Weniger's book length essay on Goethe and the
generals in the "Wars of Freedom" (373).

SPECIALIZED WORKS: SOCIETY, POLITICS,
DIPLOMACY, AND REFORM

In recent years historians have produced several innovative and
challenging studies of socio-political changes in German-speaking
lands resulting from the Napoleonic experience. Berding's research
on the Kingdom of Westphalia (17) and Fehrenbach's on the Confederation of the Rhine (89) are excellent examples. Heitzer's work on
these areas (132, 133), as well as that of Wohlfeil (380) and Bader
(11), complement the above with emphasis on the interrelationship
between internal developments and foreign affairs. Other useful
studies of western Germany under Napoleonic influence include Elbing
on Hessen (78), Dufraisse on the notables of the Left Bank of the
Rhine (74), Bernath on the foreign policy of Nassau (19), Courvoisier
on Neuchâtel (55), Vidalenç on the notables of the Hanseatic
Department (365), Schnepel on Bremen (306), and Hölzle on Württemberg
(140, 142). Two recently published article-collections, edited by
Berding (389) and Weis (399), contain quality research and up to date
bibliographies.

Work on the larger states is, of course, more extensive and
more diverse. For domestic reforms in Prussia one should see Simon
(324), Gray (118, 394), Obermann (237), Hüffer (152), Raack (256),
Vogel (398), and Ibbeken (154). The latter source is useful for the
appended documents. The volume edited by Vogel (366) provides an
excellent introduction to the newest scholarship on this topic.
The published results of a recent symposium (396) focus on several
significant interpretive issues raised in the 1980s by historians in
the German Democratic Republic. Five articles from this collection
relating to military matters are reprinted in MILITAERGESCHICHTE,
1983. For Prussian military affairs and reforms, Shanahan (319)
provides a handy English language introduction. Showalter (320) and
Nitschke (395) are more reliable because of their contemporary
scholarship. Lehmann (199), Ford (95), Huber (151), and a supplementary volume of the MILITAERWOCHENBLATT of 1862 (267) are all older

sources which incorporate essential material on military reforms. Hahlweg's essay on the Prussian military reforms (125), Kraus's on the General Staff (187), and Händel's on conscription (121) are all good examples of postwar West German Militärgeschichte. An essay by Dönhoff on the war economy (65) and a book by Haussherr dealing with the diplomatic background (127) are both important to an understanding of the military history. A recent Polish study of the diplomacy regarding Danzig (384) is a instructive case study.

The work of Klang (167, 168) on Bavaria emphasizes that principality's role in the larger Franco-German struggle. It supplants the earlier work of M. Doeberl (64) and L. Doeberl (63). The perspective of the French historian Dunan (75) is still profitable, even though the work is several decades old. Kraehe's monograph on Metternich's foreign policy (186) and Langsam's study of the Napoleonic Wars and nationalism (190) together provide an introduction to Austrian affairs in the Napoleonic era.

SPECIALIZED WORKS: THE RISE OF NATIONALISM

One of the most prolific writers on German nationalism, and one who has focused much attention on the Napoleonic era, is Hans Kohn (181, 183, 184). He, like others of his and earlier generations, such as Oncken (240), Rothfels (284), Simon (325), Mitscherlich (222, 223), Jolles (159), and Brunschwig (40), worked in the tradition fostered by Friedrich Meinecke (216) who stressed the role of ideas in shaping historical events. In the 1970s Berdahl published a critique of this approach to explaining the origins of German nationalism (16). He stressed that ideas alone could not explain nationalism. One must look as well at politics, military activity, and economics.

A number of monographic studies will be of essence to researchers interested in nationalism during the Napoleonic era. Heger (129) analyzed religious sources, especially sermons, as expressions of nationalist sentiment. Jeismann (158) wrote on nationalism in education. Many researchers have focused on particular geographic areas or political entities. On Prussian nationalist activity one should consult Anderson (3), Raack (255), Brunschwig (39), Chareton (47), and Lionnet (206). Austrian nationalism is the subject of studies by Langsam (190), Robert (276), and Rössler (278). Other regional studies include Groote on Northwest Germany (119), Granier on Silesia (116, 117), and a very old work by Lynker on Westphalia (208). German nationalism was influenced by the insurrections of the Iberian peninsula, and essays by Rassow (262) and Wohlfeil (379) help explain this relationship.

Several historians have analyzed Germany's early nationalism in the publications or public activities of single individuals. A good example of such a study is Abelein's analysis of Heinrich Steffen's political writings (1). Bahr's descriptive essay on Friedrich Buchholz (12) is also a useful source. Engelbrecht's monograph on Fichte (82) emphasizes the nationalist thought in the philosopher's writings. Father Jahn's nationalism is the subject of works by Hermann (135), Körner (180), and Kohn (182). Two historians, Meyer (220) and Raumer (265), have analyzed Kant's position regarding nation and state. Laban's analysis of Collin's writings (189) is an essay on Austrian nationalism. Sauzin's work on Müller (288) provides information on that writer's nationalist sentiment.

One cannot discuss nationalism fully without including the topic of book publication and periodical literature, both of which expanded dramatically in the Napoleonic era. Lindemann's history of the press (203) places the Napoleonic epoch in historical context. Tschirch's two volumes on public opinion in Prussia (350) also provide excellent historical background. Czygan's specialized account of periodical literature during the "Wars of Freedom" (57) is indispensable. Other important studies include Busch on censorship (44), Zimmer on "war lyrics" (386), and Wagner on Austrian pamphlet literature (370). Paisley (242) and Spies (326) have both written specialized studies on individual periodicals of the era of the Wars of Liberation.

PERIODICALS

The most prestigious journal of German history is the HISTORISCHE ZEITSCHRIFT which will keep scholars informed of research on the Napoleonic period. Those who wish to stay in touch with the latest developments in historical research in the Federal Republic should read the newer GESCHICHTE UND GESELLSCHAFT. The ZEITSCHRIFT FUER GESCHICHTSWISSENSCHAFT is the GDR's respected, general historical journal. Two English-language journals devoted to history and scholarship on Germany are GERMAN STUDIES REVIEW and CENTRAL EUROPEAN HISTORY.

There are several specialized journals on military history. They include MILITAERGESCHICHTE, published by the Militär-geschichtiches Institut der Deutschen Demokratischen Republik, and MILITAERGESCHICHTILICHE MITTEILUNGEN, published by the Federal Republic's Militärgeschichtliches Forschungsamt in Freiburg. Researchers should be aware of the 1983 merger of the two journals of military affairs, resulting in the new EUROPAEISCHE WEHRKUNDE: WEHR-WEISSENSCHAFTLICHE RUNDSCHAU. The editors promise to publish material which will satisfy the readership of both former journals, and the one whose name is now the subtitle generally included articles based on historical research. The ZEITSCHRIFT FUER HEERESKUNDE also has a historical orientation.

FUTURE RESEARCH

It is obvious from this bibliographical essay that numerous monographic studies, employing contemporary research methods, could fill in gaps in our knowledge and understanding of the German responses to Napoleon. Modern biographies of several military and political leaders have yet to be written. These include such famous personalities as Gneisenau, Scharnhorst, and Boyen. Since the Second World War, military history of the 1803-1814 period, both on the tactical and the strategic level, has been neglected. Scholars' most fruitful endeavors, however, may be in studies which explore the relationship of military events to the larger social context and examine military institutions as sources of understanding non-military issues. A model study is that of Büsch (43) which, however, does not strictly fall within the chronological period of this bibliography. Showalter's thesis concerning the interrelationship between economic development and military reform (320) is also a pattern that should be applied to related topics.

Volumes have been written on German nationalism during the years leading to the Wars of Liberation. But few have followed Berdahl's suggestion that the roots of nationalism be explored in politics, society, and economics (16). Moreover, the relationship of nationalism to military developments is a topic calling for a fresh analysis. Hopefully scholars will soon begin to synthesize the whole nexus of socio-economic change, domestic political reform, military innovation, and growing nationalist sentiment. These are subjects which historians have largely treated as separate issues. They are but facets of the constellation of experiences which constitute Germany's responses to Napoleon.

Fehrenbach emphasizes correctly that the historiography of Germany during the Napoleonic period is one-sided in favor of Prussia (90). This is true of military history as well as other specializations. Researchers must search out and emphasize patterns of western and southern German responses to the Napoleonic challenge. The work of Scheel (291, 292) provides suggestive research models. Only when this has been done can scholars legitimately draw conclusions about "German nationalism" and the Wars of "German" Liberation.

BIBLIOGRAPHY: GERMANY

1. Abelein, Werner. HENRIK STEFFENS' POLITISCHE SCHRIFTEN: ZUM POLITISCHEN DENKEN IN DEUTSCHLAND IN DEN JAHREN UM DIE BEFREIUNGSKRIEGE. Studien zur deutschen Literatur, vol. 3. Tübingen: Niemeyer, 1977.

2. ALLGEMEINE DEUTSCHE BIOGRAPHIE. Edited by Historische Kommission bei der Königlichen Akademie der Wissenschaften (Bayern). Leipzig: Duncker & Humblot, 1875-1912. 56 vols. (Reprint, Berlin: Duncker & Humblot, 1967-1971.)

3. Anderson, Eugene N. NATIONALISM AND THE CULTURAL CRISIS IN PRUSSIA, 1806-1815. New York: Farrar & Rinehart, 1939.

4. ARCHIVE IM DEUTSCHSPRACHIGEN RAUM. Minerva Handbücher: Archive. 2d ed. Berlin and New York: de Gruyter, 1974. 2 vols.

5. Aris, Reinhold. HISTORY OF POLITICAL THOUGHT IN GERMANY FROM 1789 TO 1815. London: Allen & Unwin, 1936. (Reprint, New York: Russell & Russell, 1965.)

6. [Armbruster, Johann Michael]. SUEDENREGISTER DER FRANZOSEN IN TEUTSCHLAND: EIN SEITENSTUECK ZU DER SCHRIFT: TEUTSCHLAND IN SEINER TIEFEN ERNIEDRIGUNG. [Amsterdam: n.p., 1814].

7. Arndt, Ernst Mortiz. SAEMTLICHE WERKE. Magdeburg: Magdeburger Verlags-Anstalt, 1892-1909. 14 vols.

8. Arnold, Robert Franz, ed. FREMDHERRSCHAFT UND BEFREIUNG, 1795-1815. Leipzig: Reclam, 1932. (Reprinted in the series, DEUTSCHE LITERATUR, Reihe Politische Dichtung, vol. 2. Darmstadt: Wissenschaftliche Buchgesellschaft, 1973.)

9. Arnold, Robert Franz, and Karl Wagner. ACHTZEHNHUNDERTNEUN: DIE POLITISCHE LYRIK DES KRIEGSJAHRES. Schriften des literarischen Vereins in Wien, vol. 11. Vienna: Fromme, 1909.

10. Aron, Raymond. "Clausewitz--Stratege und Patriot." HISTORISCHE ZEITSCHRIFT 234 (1982): 295-316.

11. Bader, Karl. "Zur Geschichte des grossherzoglich-hessischen freiwilligen Jägercorps 1813-1814." ARCHIV FUER HESSISCHE GESCHICHTE UND ALTERTHUMSKUNDE (Neue Folge) 2 (1895-99): 483-520.

12. Bahrs, Kurt. FRIEDRICH BUCHHOLZ: EIN PREUSSISCHER PUBLIZIST 1768-1843. Historische Studien, 57. Berlin: Ebering, 1907. (Reprint, Vaduz: Kraus, 1965.)

13. [Bassewitz, M.F. von]. DIE KURMARK BRANDENBURG IN ZUSAMMENHANG MIT DEN SCHICKSALEN DES GESAMMTSTAATS PREUSSEN WAEHREND DER ZEIT VOM 22. OKTOBER 1806 BIS ZU ENDE DES JAHRES 1808.

Leipzig: Brockhaus, 1851-60. 3 vols. (Reprint, Hildesheim: Georg Olms, in progress.)

14. Beguelin, Heinrich, and Amalie von. DENKWUERDIGKEITEN AUS DEN JAHREN 1807-1813, NEBST BRIEFEN VON GNEISENAU UND HARDENBERG. Edited by Adolf Ernst. Berlin: Springer, 1892.

15. Beitzke, Heinrich. GESCHICHTE DER DEUTSCHEN FREIHEITSKRIEGE IN DEN JAHREN 1813 UND 1814. 2d ed. Berlin: Duncker & Humblot, 1860. 3 vols.

16. Berdahl, Robert M. "New Thoughts on German Nationalism." AMERICAN HISTORICAL REVIEW 77 (1972): 65-80.

17. Berding, Helmut. NAPOLEONISCHE HERRSCHAFTS- UND GESELLSCHAFTSPOLITIK IM KOENIGREICH WESTFALEN 1807-1813. Kritische Studien zur Geschichtswissenschaft, vol. 7. Göttingen: Vandenhoeck & Ruprecht, 1973.

18. BERLINER ABENDBLAETTER (1810-1811), republished in facsimile under the title HEINRICH VON KLEIST'S BERLINER ABENDBLAETTER, Edited by Georg Minde-Pouet. Leipzig: Klinkhardt & Biermann, 1925.

19. Bernath, Mathias. "Die auswärtige Politik Nassaus 1805-1812: Ein Beitrag zur Geschichte des Rheinbundes und der politischen Ideen am Mittelrhein zur Zeit Napoleons." NASSAUISCHE ANNALEN, 63 (1952): 106-91.

20. Bethcke. "Gneisenau." GELBE HEFTE: HISTORISCHE UND POLITISCHE ZEITSCHRIFT FUER DAS KATHOLISCHE DEUTSCHLAND 12 (1935-36): 606-30.

21. Bethcke. "Yorck." GELBE HEFTE: HISTORISCHE UND POLITISCHE ZEITSCHRIFT FUER DAS KATHOLISCHE DEUTSCHLAND 11 (1934-35): 476-93.

22. Beyerhaus, Gisbert. DAS NAPOLEONISCHE EUROPA. Breslau: Korn, 1941.

23. Beyerhaus, Gisbert. "Der ursprüngliche Clausewitz." WEHRWISSENSCHAFTLICHE RUNDSCHAU 3 (1953): 102-10.

24. Bezold, Friedrich von. DER GEIST VON 1813. Bonn: Cohen, 1913.

25. Binder von Krieglstein, Carl. FERDINAND VON SCHILL: EIN LEBENSBILD: ZUGLEICH EIN BEITRAG ZUR GESCHICHTE DER PREUSSISCHEN ARMEE. Rev. ed. Berlin: Voss, 1909.

26. Bittner, Ludwig. DAS GESAMTINVENTAR DES WIENER HAUS-, HOF-, UND STAATSARCHIVS. Vienna: Holzhausen, 1936-40. 5 vols.

27. Blasendorff, C., ed. "Fünfzig Briefe Blücher's." HISTORISCHE ZEITSCHRIFT 54 (1885): 193-224.

28. Bodelschwingh, Ernst von. LEBEN DES OBER-PRAESIDENTEN
    FREIHERRN VON VINCKE. Part 1, 1774-1816. Berlin: Reimer,
    1853.

29. Bonjour, Edgar, ed. JOHANNES VON MUELLER: BRIEFE IN AUSWAHL.
    2d ed. Basel: Schwabe, 1954.

30. Bonjour, Edgar, ed. JOHANNES VON MUELLER: SCHRIFTEN IN
    AUSWAHL. 2d ed. Basel: Schwabe, 1955.

31. Botzenhart, Erich; Walther Hubatsch; and Peter G. Thielen eds.
    FREIHERR VOM STEIN: BRIEFE UND AMTLICHE SCHRIFTEN. Stuttgart:
    Kohlhammer, 1957-74. 10 vols.

32. Boyen, Hermann von. BEITRAEGE ZUR KENNTNIS DES GENERALS VON
    SCHARNHORST UND SEINER AMTLICHEN THAETIGKEIT IN DEN JAHREN
    1808-1813. Berlin: Dümmler, 1833.

33. Brandt, Heinrich von, ed. AUS DEM LEBEN DES GENERALS DER
    INFANTERIE Z.D. DR. HEINRICH VON BRANDT. 2d ed. Berlin:
    Mittler, 1870. 2 vols.

34. Branig, Hans, ed. BRIEFWECHSEL DES FUERSTEN KARL AUGUST VON
    HARDENBERG MIT DEM FUERSTEN WILHELM LUDWIG ZU
    SAYN-WITTGENSTEIN, 1806-1822. Veröffentlichungen aus den
    Archiven Preussischer Kulturbesitz, vol. 9. Berlin: Grote,
    1972.

35. Branig, Hans; Ruth Bliss; and Winfried Bliss. UEBERSICHT UEBER
    DIE BESTAENDE DES GEHEIMEN STAATSARCHIVS IN BERLIN-DAHLEM.
    Mitteilungen der Preussischen Archivverwaltung. Berlin:
    Grote, 1966-67. 2 vols.

36. Braubach, Max. "Von der Französischen Revoltuion bis zum
    Wiener Kongress." Bruno Gebhardt, HANDBUCH DER DEUTSCHEN
    GESCHICHTE, vol. 3. Edited by Herbert Grundmann. 9th ed.
    Stuttgart: Union, 1970.

37. Brinkmann, Karl. "Das Krockowsche Freikorps." FORSCHUNGEN ZUR
    BRANDENBURGISCHEN UND PREUSSISCHEN GESCHICHTE 31 (1919):
    410-15.

38. Brown, Marvin L., Jr. "France in the Haus-, Hof-, und
    Staatsarchiv." FRENCH HISTORICAL STUDIES 3 (1963): 272-77.

39. Brunschwig, Henri. "Propos sur le Prussianisme." ANNALES
    ECONOMIES, SOCIETES, CIVILISATIONS 3 (1948): 16-20.

40. Brunschwig, Henri. "Propos sur les nationalismes Allemands."
    ANNALES ECONOMIES, SOCIETES, CIVILISATIONS 5 (1950): 9-14.

41. Bülow, Eduard von, ed. AUS DEM NACHLASSE VON GEORG HEINRICH
    VON BERENHORST. Dessau: Aue, 1845-47. 2 vols.

42. Bülow, Eduard [von], and Wilhelm Rüstow, eds. MILITAERISCHE UND VERMISCHTE SCHRIFTEN VON HEINRICH DIETRICH VON BUELOW. Leipzig: Brockhaus, 1853.

43. Büsch, Otto. MILITAERSYSTEM UND SOZIALLEBEN IM ALTEN PREUSSEN 1713-1807: DIE ANFAENGE DER SOZIALEN MILITARISIERUNG DER PREUSSISCH-DEUTSCHEN GESELLSCHAFT. Veröffentlichungen der Berliner Historischen Kommission beim Friedrich-Meinecke-Institut der Freien Universität Berlin, vol. 7. Berlin: Walter de Gruyter, 1962.

44. Busch, Rüdiger. DIE AUFSICHT UEBER DAS BUECHER- UND PRESSEWESEN IN DEN RHEINBUNDSTAATEN BERG, WESTFALEN UND FRANKFURT: EIN BEITRAG ZUR GESCHICHTE DES BUCH- UND PRESSEZENSUR. Studien und Quellen zur Geschichte des Deutschen Verfassungsrechts, Series A, 7. Karlsruhe: Müller, 1970.

45. Cavaignac, Godefroy. LA FORMATION DE LA PRUSSE CONTEMPORAINE. 2d ed. Paris: Hachette, 1897.

46. Chandler, David G. THE CAMPAIGNS OF NAPOLEON. New York: Macmillan, 1966.

47. Chareton, Jean Veye de. COMMENT LA PRUSSE A PREPARE SA REVANCHE 1806-1813: LA REFORME MILITAIRE LES LEVEES DE 1813 ET LA LEGENDE DES VOLONTAIRES PRUSSIENS, LA POLITIQUE PRUSSIENNE ET L'UNITE ALLEMANDE 1806-1813. Paris: Charles-Lavauzelle, 1903.

48. Chroust, Anton, ed. GESANDSCHAFTSBERICHTE AUS MUENCHEN, 1814-1848. Schriftenreihe zur bayerischen Landesgeschichte 18-19, 21-24, 36-44. Munich: Beck-Biederstein, 1935-51. 15 vols.

49. Clausewitz, Karl von. HINTERLASSENE WERKE DES GENERALS CARL VON CLAUSEWITZ UEBER KRIEG UND KRIEGFUEHRUNG. Berlin: Dümmler, 1832-38. 10 vols.

50. Collin, Heinrich Joseph von. SAEMMTLICHE WERKE. Edited by Matthew von Collin. Vienna: Schaumburg, 1812-14. 6 vols.

51. Connelly, Owen. NAPOLEON'S SATELLITE KINGDOMS. New York: Free Press, 1965.

52. Conrady, E. von. GESCHICHTE DES KOENIGLICH PREUSSISCHEN SECHSTEN INFANTERIE-REGIMENTS VON SEINER STIFTUNG IM JAHR 1773 BIS ZU ENDE DES JAHRES 1856. Golgau: Flemming, 1857.

53. Conrady, Emil von. LEBEN UND WIRKEN DES GENERALS DER INFANTRIE UND KOMMANDIRENDEN GENERALS DES V. ARMEEKORPS CARL VON GROLMAN. Berlin: Mittler, 1894-96. 3 vols.

54. Courbière, R. de l'Homme de. GESCHICHTE DER BRANDENBURGISCH-PREUSSISCHEN HEERES-VERFASSUNG. Berlin: Decker, 1852.

55. Courvoisier, Jean. LE MARECHAL BERTHIER ET SA PRINCIPAUTE DE NEUCHATEL, 1806-1814. Neuchâtel: Attlinger, 1959.

56. Craig, Gordon. THE POLITICS OF THE PRUSSIAN ARMY, 1640-1945. London: Oxford, 1955.

57. Czygan, Paul. ZUR GESCHICHTE DER TAGESLITERATUR WAEHREND DER FREIHEITSKRIGE. Publikation des Vereins für die Geschichte von Ost- und Westpreussen. Leipzig: Duncker & Humblot, 1909-11. 2 vols. in 3.

58. DAHLMANN-WAITZ: QUELLENKUNDE DER DEUTSCHEN GESCHICHTE. Edited by Hermann Haering. 9th ed. Leipzig: Koehler, 1931. (Tenth ed., edited by Hermann Heimpel and Herbert Geuss, in progress. Stuttgart: Hiersemann, 1960-.)

59. Demelitsch, Fedor von, ed. AKTENSTUECKE ZUR GESCHICHTE DER KOALITION VOM JAHRE 1814. Fontes rerum Austriacarum, Abteilung 2, vol. 49/2. Vienna: C. Gerold's Sohn, 1899.

60. Demeter, Karl. DAS DEUTSCHE OFFIZIERKORPS IN GESELLSCHAFT UND STAAT, 1650-1945. 2d ed. Frankfurt a.M: Bernard & Graefe, 1962.

61. Denis, Ernest. L'ALLEMAGNE DE 1789 A 1810: FIN DE L'ANCIENNE ALLEMAGNE. Paris: Quantin, 1896.

62. DEUTSCHLAND IN SEINER TIEFEN ERNIEDRIGUNG. Nürnberg: n.p., 1804.

63. Doeberl, Ludwig. MAXIMILIAN VON MONTGELAS UND DAS PRINZIP DER STAATSSOUVERAENITAET. Munich: Schmidt, 1925.

64. Doeberl, M. BAYERN UND DIE DEUTSCHE ERHEBUNG WIDER NAPOLEON I. Munich: Franz, 1907.

65. Dönhoff, Fritz. "Wilhelm Krüger und die preussische Kriegswirtschaft, 1806-1813." FORSCHUNGEN ZUR BRANDEN-BURGISCHEN UND PREUSSISCHEN GESCHICHTE 48 (1936): 48-70.

66. Dörnberg-Hausen, Hugo von. WILHELM VON DOERNBERG: EIN KAEMPFER FUER DEUTSCHLANDS FREIHEIT. Marburg: Elwert, 1936.

67. Dorow, Wilhelm. ERLEBTES AUS DEN JAHREN 1790-1827. Leipzig: Hinrichs, 1843-45. 4 vols.

68. Dorpalen, Andreas. "The German Struggle against Napoleon: The East German View." JOURNAL OF MODERN HISTORY 41 (1969): 485-516.

69. Dräger, Udo. "Die nationale Befreiungsbewegung des deutschen Volkes 1813, dargestellt an einigen Quellen des Deutschen Zentralarchivs Abteilung Merseberg." DER BEFREIUNGSKRIEG 1813. Edited by Peter Hoffmann et al. Berlin: Akademie, 1967.

GERMANY   455

70. Dräseke, Johann Heinrich Bernhard. DEUTSCHLANDS WIEDERGEBURT, VERKUNDET UND GEFEIERT DURCH EINE REIHE EVANGELISCHER REDEN IM LAUFE DES UNVERGESSLICHEN JAHRES 1813. Lübeck: Michelsen, 1814.

71. Dreetz, Dieter. "Zur Rolle des Feldmarschalls Gebhardt Lebrecht von Blücher bei der Organisierung des Militärischen Widerstandskampfes gegen die Napoleonische Fremdherrschaft in den Jahren 1807-08." ZEITSCHRIFT FUER MILITAERGESCHICHTE 1 (1962): 236-44.

72. Droysen, Johann Gustav. DAS LEBEN DES FELDMARSCHALLS GRAFEN YORK VON WARTENBURG. Berlin: Viet, 1851-52. 3 vols.

73. Droz, Jacques. L'ALLEMAGNE ET LA REVOLUTION FRANCAISE. Paris: Presses Universitaires de France, 1949.

74. Dufraisse, Roger. "Les Notables de la rive gauche de Rhin a l'époque napoléonienne." REVUE D'HISTOIRE MODERNE ET COMTEMPORAINE 17 (1970): 758-76.

75. Dunan, Marcel. NAPOLEON ET L'ALLEMAGNE: LE SYSTEME CONTINENTAL ET LES DEBUTS DU ROYAUME DE BAVIERE, 1806-1810. Rev. ed. Paris: Plon, 1948.

76. Eggers, Christian Ulrich Detlev, freiherr von. DEUTSCHLANDS ERWARTUNGEN VOM RHEINISCHEN BUNDE. Braunschweig: Vieweg, 1808.

77. Eichendorff, Joseph von. WERKE UND SCHRIFTEN. Edited by Gerhard Baumann. Stuttgart: Cott, 1957-58. 4 vols.

78. Elbing, Hanswerner. "Die hessische Politik in der Rheinbundzeit, 1806-1813." ARCHIV FUER HESSISCHE GESCHICHTE UND ALTERTUMSKUNDE, NF (New Series) 24 (1952-53): 195-261.

79. Elze, Walter. DER STREIT UM TAUROGGEN. Breslau: Hirt, 1926.

80. Enders, Gerhart. "Die ehemaligen deutschen Militärarchive und das Schichsal der deutschen Militärakten nach 1945." ZEITSCHRIFT FUER MILITAERGESCHICHTE 8 (1969): 599-608.

81. Endler, Renate. "Nachlässe in der Historischen Abteilung II des deutschen Zentralarchivs." ZEITSCHRIFT FUER GESCHICHTS-WISSENSCHAFT 20 (1972): 1160-65.

82. Engelbrecht, H.C. JOHANN GOTTLIEB FICHTE: A STUDY OF HIS POLITICAL WRITINGS WITH SPECIAL REFERENCE TO HIS NATIONALISM. New York: Columbia University Press, 1933.

83. Epstein, Fritz T. "Germany." THE NEW GUIDE TO THE DIPLOMATIC ARCHIVES OF WESTERN EUROPE. Edited by Daniel H. Thomas and Lynn M. Case. Philadelphia: University of Pennsylvania Press, 1975.

84. ERHEBUNGEN: EINE ZEITSCHRIFT FUER DAS VATERLAND. Lübeck:
    n.p., 1809. Vol. 1.

85. EUROPAEISCHE ANNALEN. Edited by Ernst Ludwig Posselt.
    Tübingen: n.p., 1803-15.

86. EXERZIER-REGLEMENT FUER DIE CAVALLERIE DER KOENIGLICHEN
    PREUSSISCHEN ARMEE. Berlin: Decker, 1812.

87. EXERZIER-REGLEMENT FUER DIE INFANTERIE DER KOENIGLICHEN
    PREUSSISCHEN ARMEE. Berlin: Decker, 1812.

88. Facius, Friedrich, Hans Booms, and Heinz Boberach, eds. DAS
    BUNDESARCHIV UND SEINE BESTAENDE. Schriften des Bundesarchivs,
    vol. 10. 3d ed. Boppard-am-Rhein: Boldt, 1977.

89. Fehrenbach, Elisabeth. TRADITIONALE GESELLSCHAFT UND
    REVOLTIONAERES RECHT: DIE EINFUEHRUNG DES CODE NAPOLEON IN DEN
    RHEINBUNDSTAATEN. Kritische Studien zur Geschichts-
    wissenschaft, vol. 13. 2d ed. Göttingen: Vandenhoeck &
    Ruprecht, 1978.

90. Fehrenbach, Elisabeth. "Verfassungs- und sozialpolitische
    Reformen und Reformprojekte in Deutschland unter dem Einfluss
    des Napoleonischen Frankreich." HISTORISCHE ZEITSCHRIFT 228
    (1979): 286-316.

91. [Felgermann, K.F. von]. GENERAL W.J. VON KRAUSENECK. Berlin:
    Reimer, 1851.

92. Fichte, Johann Gottlieb. BRIEFWECHSEL: KRITISCHE
    GESAMMTAUSGABE. Edited by Hans Schulz. Leipzig: Haessel,
    1925. 2 vols.

93. Fichte, Johann Gottlieb. WERKE. Edited by I.H. Fichte.
    Berlin: Veit, 1845-1846. 11 vols. (Rev. ed., Berlin: de
    Gruyter, 1971.)

94. Fisher, Herbert A.L. STUDIES IN NAPOLEONIC STATESMANSHIP;
    GERMANY. Oxford: Clarendon Press, 1903.

95. Ford, Guy S. "Boyen's Military Law." AMERICAN HISTORICAL
    REVIEW 20 (1915): 528-38.

96. Forstreuter, Kurt. DAS PREUSSISCHE STAATSARCHIV IN
    KOENIGSBERG: EIN GESCHICHTLICHER UEBERBLICK MIT EINER
    UEBERSICHT UEBER SEINE BESTAENDE. Veröffentlichungen der
    niedersächischen Archivverwaltung, vol. 3. Göttingen:
    Vandenhoeck & Ruprecht, 1955.

97. Fouqué, Friedrich de la Mott. GEDICHTE VOR UND WAEHREND DES
    FELDZUGES 1813. Berlin: Dümmler, 1814.

98. Fout, John C. GERMAN HISTORY AND CIVILIZATION 1806-1914: A BIBLIOGRAPHY OF SCHOLARLY PERIODICAL LITERATURE. Metuchen, N.J.: Scarecrow Press, 1974.

99. Franz, Werner. "Zu einigen Fragen des Entstehens und des Charakters der preussischen Landwehr im Frühjahr 1813." ZEITSCHRIFT FUER MILITAERGESCHICHTE 3 (1964): 477-82.

100. Freytag-Loringhoven, H. von. KRIEG UND POLITIK IN DER NEUZEIT. Berlin: Mittler, 1911.

101. Friccius, Karl. GESCHICHTE DES KRIEGES IN DEN JAHREN 1813 UND 1814: MIT BESONDERER RUECKSICHT AUF OSTPREUSSEN UND DAS KOENIGSBERGSCHE LANDWEHRBATALLION. Altenburg: Pierer, 1843.

102. Friedrich, Rudolph, et al. GESCHICHTE DER BEFREIUNGSKRIEGE 1813-1815. Berlin: Mittler, 1903-9. 4 works in 9 vols.

103. [Gagern, Hans C. von]. MEIN ANTHEIL AN DER POLITIK. Stuttgart: Cotta, 1832-30. 3 vols.

104. Gebhardt, Bruno. "Wilhelm von Humboldt als Gesandter in Wien, 1810-1813." DEUTSCHE ZEITSCHRIFT FUER GESCHICHTSWISSENSCHAFT 12 (1894-95): 77-152.

105. Gebhardt, Bruno. WILHELM VON HUMBOLDT ALS STAATSMANN. Stuttgart: Cotta, 1896-99. 2 vols.

106. Gebhardt, Walther. SPEZIALBESTAENDE IN DEUTSCHEN BIBLIOTHEKEN: BUNDESREPUBLIK DEUTSCHLAND EINSCHL. BERLIN (WEST). Berlin, New York: de Gruyter, 1977.

107. Gembruch, Werner. "Das Reformwerk Scharnhorsts." WEHRWISSENSCHAFTLICHE RUNDSCHAU 8 (1958): 627-42.

108. Gembruch, Werner. "Zu Clausewitz' Gedanken über das Verhältnis von Krieg und Politik." WEHRWISSENSCHAFTLICHE RUNDSCHAU 9 (1959): 619-33.

109. Gerhard, Dietrich, and William Norvin, eds. DIE BRIEFE BARTHOLD GEORG NIEBUHRS. Veröffentlichungen der Literatur-Archiv-Gesellschaft in Berlin, vols. 1, 2. Berlin: de Gruyter, 1926-29.

110. GERMANIA: EINE ZEITSCHRIFT FUER DEUTSCHLANDS GEMEINWOHL. Oldenburg, 1814-15. 9 issues in 3 vols.

111. Gneisenau, August Neidhardt von. 1813: BRIEFE AUGUST NEIDHARDTS VON GNEISENAU. Leipzig: Koehler & Amelang, 1963.

112. Gold, Hans Sigismund. "Zur nationalen Befreiungsbewegung von 1813-14: Quellen im Brandenburgischen Landeshauptachiv Potsdam." DER BEFREIUNGSKRIEG 1813. Edited by·Peter Hoffmann et al. Berlin: Akademie, 1967.

113. Goltz, Colmar, freiherr von der. VON ROSSBACH BIS JENA UND
     AUERSTEDT: EIN BEITRAG ZUR GESCHICHTE DES PREUSSISCHEN HEERES.
     2d ed. Berlin: Mittler, 1906.

114. Granier, Hermann, ed.   "Aus   Blüchers   Korrespondez."
     FORSCHUNGEN ZUR BRANDENBURGISCHEN UND PREUSSISCHEN GESCHICHTE
     26 (1913): 149-85.

115. Granier, Hermann, ed. BERICHTE AUS DER BERLINER FRANZOSENZEIT,
     1807-1809. Publikationen aus den Königlichen Preussischen
     Staatsarchiven, vol. 88. Leipzig: Hirzel, 1913.

116. Granier, Hermann. "Noch einmal der Breslauer Horndrechsler
     Johann Konrad Seeling." ZEITSCHRIFT DES VEREINS FUER DIE
     GESCHICHTE SCHLESIENS 41 (1907): 353-68.

117. Granier, Hermann. "Partiotische Schlesier in der Franzosenzeit
     von 1806-1807." ZEITSCHRIFT DES VEREINS FUR DIE GESCHICHTE
     SCHLESIENS 40 (1906): 217-46.

118. Gray, Marion. "Der ostpreussische Landtag des Jahres 1808 und
     das Reformministerium Stein: Eine Fallstudie politischer
     Modernisation." JAHRBUCH FUER DIE GESCHICHTE MITTEL- UND
     OSTDEUTSCHLANDS 26 (1977): 129-45.

119. Groote, Wolfgang von. DIE ENTSTEHUNG DES NATIONALBEWUSSTSEINS
     IN NORDWESTDEUTSCHLANDS 1790-1830. Göttinger Bausteine zur
     Geschichtswissenschaft, 22. Göttingen: Musterschmidt, 1955.

120. Haase, Carl. THE RECORDS OF GERMAN HISTORY IN GERMAN AND
     CERTAIN OTHER RECORD OFFICES WITH SHORT NOTICES ON LIBRARIES
     AND OTHER COLLECTIONS. Boppard am Rhein: Boldt, 1975.

121. Händel, Heribert. DER GEDANKE DER ALLGEMEINEN WEHRPFLICHT IN
     DER WEHRVERFASSUNG DES KOENIGREICHS PREUSSEN BIS 1819:
     INSBESONDERE EIN BEITRAG ZUR FRAGE DES EINFLUSSES DER
     FRANZOESICHEN   REVOLUTION   AUF   DIE   SCHARNHORST-BOYENSCHE
     REFORMGESETZGEBUNG. WEHRWISSENSCHAFTLICHE RUNDSCHAU, Beiheft
     19. Berlin: Mittler, 1962.

122. Haering, Hermann. "Die Organisierung von Landwehr und
     Landsturm in Baden in den Jahren 1813 und 1814." ZEITSCHRIFT
     FUER DIE GESCHICHTE DES OBERRHEINS 68 (1914): 266-303, 464-516.

123. Hahlweg, Werner. "Clausewitz und die preussische
     Heeresreform." ZEITSCHRIFT FUER HEERES- UND UNIFORMKUNDE 23
     (1959): 27-33.

124. Hahlweg, Werner, ed. CLAUSEWITZ: SCHRIFTEN; AUFSAETZE;
     STUDIEN; BRIEFE: DOKUMENTE AUS DEM CLAUSEWITZ-, SCHARNHORST-,
     UND GNEISENAU-NACHLASS SOWIE AUS OEFFENTLICHEN UND PRIVATEN
     SAMMLUNGEN. Deutsche Geschichtsquellen des 19. und 20.
     Jahrhunderts, vol. 45. Göttingen: Vandenhoeck & Ruprecht,
     1966.

125. Hahlweg, Werner. PREUSSISCHE REFORMZEIT UND REVOLUTIONAERER KRIEG. WEHRWISSENSCHAFTLICHE RUNDSCHAU, Beiheft 18 (September 1962).

126. Hassel, Paul, ed. GESCHICHTE DER PREUSSISCHEN POLITIK 1807-1815. Part I: 1807-1808 (only volume published). Publikationen aus den Königlichen Preussischen Staatsarchiven, vol. 6. Leipzig: Hirzel, 1881.

127. Haussherr, Hans. ERFUELLUNG UND BEFREIUNG: DER KAMPF UM DIE DURCHFUEHRUNG DES TILSITER FRIEDENS 1807-08. Hamburg: Hanseatische Verlagsanstalt, 1935.

128. Heere, Paul, ed. VON PREUSSENS BEFREIUNGS- UND VERFASSUNGSKAMPF: AUS DEN PAPIEREN DES OBERBURGGRAFEN MAGNUS VON BRUENNECK. Berlin: Mittler, 1914.

129. Heger, Adolf. EVANGELISCHE VERKUENDIGUNG UND DEUTSCHES NATIONALBEWUSSTSEIN: ZUR GESCHICHTE DER PREDIGT 1806-1848. Neue deutsche Forschungen, Abteilung Religions- und Kirchengeschichte, vol. 7. Berlin: Duncker & Dünnhaupt, 1939.

130. Heinsius, Wilhelm. ALLGEMEINES BUECHER-LEXIKON ODER VOLLSTAENDGES ALPHABETISCHES VERZEICHNISS DER VON 1700 BIS ENDE 1815 ERSCHIENENEN BUECHER, WELCHE IN DEUTSCHLAND UND IN DEN DURCH SPRACHE UND LITERATUR DAMIT VERWANDTEN LAENDERN GEDRUCKT WORDEN SIND. Leipzig: Gleditsch, 1812-17. 5 vols. (Reprint, Graz: Akademische Druck- und Verlagsanstalt, 1962.)

131. Heitzer, Heinz. "Arbeiten über die Geschichte der Befreiungskriege (1806-1813)." HISTORISCHE FORSCHUNG IN DER DDR. Sonderheft, ZEITSCHRIFT FUER GESCHICHTSWISSENSCHAFT 8 (1960): 188-200.

132. Heitzer, Heinz. INSURREKTIONEN ZWISCHEN WESER UND ELBE: VOLKSBEWEGUNGEN GEGEN DIE FRANZOESISCHE FREMDHERRSCHAFT IM KOENIGREICH WESTFALEN (1806-1813). Berlin: Rütten & Loening, 1959.

133. Heitzer, Heinz. "Der Rheinbund--Kern des napoleonischen Unterdrückungssystems in Deutschland." DER BEFREIUNGSKRIEG 1813. Edited by Peter Hoffmann et al. Berlin: Akademie, 1967.

134. Helmert, Heinz, and Hansjürgen Usczeck. EUROPAEISCHE BEFREIUNGSKRIEGE 1808 BIS 1814-15: MILITAERISCHER VERLAUF. Kleine Militargeschichte: Kriege. Berlin: Militarverlag der DDR, 1976.

135. Hermann, Otto. "Der Turnvater Jahn." PREUSSISCHE JAHRBUECHER, 117 (1904): 19-37.

136. Herwig, Holger. "Military Archives in Western Germany." MILITARY AFFAIRS, 36 (1972): 121-25.

137. Hesse, Kurt, ed. PREUSSENS FREIHEITSKAMPF 1813-14: EINE
     ZEITGENOESSISCHE DARSTELLUNG. ORIGINALWIEDERGABE DER ERSTEN
     FELDZEITUNG DER PREUSSISCHEN ARMEE. Potsdam: Hayn, 1940.

138. Heydermann, Guenther. "Napoleonische Fremdherrschaft,
     Befreiungskriege und Anfänge der deutschen Burschenschaft bis
     1818 im Urteil der Geschichtswissenschaft der DDR."
     DARSTELLUNGEN UND QUELLEN ZUR GESCHICHTE DER DEUTSCHEN
     EINHEITSBEWEGUNG IM 19. UND 20. JAHRHUNDERT 10 (1978): 7-104.

139. Höhn, Reinhard. SCHARNHORSTS VERMAECHTNIS. 2d ed. Frankfurt:
     Bernard & Graefe; Bad Harzburg: Verlag für Wissenschaft und
     Technik, 1972.

140. Hölzle, Erwin. DAS ALTE RECHT UND DIE REVOLUTION: EINE
     POLITISCHE GESCHICHTE WUERTTEMBERGS IN DER REVOLUTIONSZEIT,
     1789-1815. Munich: Oldenburg, 1931.

141. Hölzle, Erwin. "Das Napoleonische Staatsystem in
     Deutschland." HISTORISCHE ZEITSCHRIFT 148 (1933): 277-93.

142. Hölzle, Erwin. WUERTTEMBERG IM ZEITALTER NAPOLEONS UND DER
     DEUTSCHEN ERHEBUNG: EINE DEUTSCHE GESCHICHTE DER WENDEZEIT IM
     EINZELSTAATLICHEN RAUM. Stuttgart: Kohlhammer, 1937.

143. Hoffmann, Peter, Karl Obermann, et al., eds. DER
     BEFREIUNGSKRIEG 1813. Deutsche Akademie der Wissenschaften zu
     Berlin, Schriften der deutschen Sektion der Kommission der
     Historiker der DDR und der UdSSR, vol. 4. Berlin: Akademie,
     1967.

144. Hogendorp, Dirk, graf van. MEMOIRES DU GENERAL DIRK VAN
     HOGENDORP. Edited by D.C.A. Hogendorp. The Hague: Nijhoff,
     1887.

145. Holleben, Albert von, and R. von Caemmerer. GESCHICHTE DES
     FRUEHJAHRSFELDZUGES 1813 UND SEINER VORGESCHICHTE. Geschichte
     der Befreiungskriege 1813-1815. Berlin: Mittler, 1904-09. 2
     vols.

146. Holzmann, Michael, and Hanns Bohatta. DEUTSCHES ANONYMEN-
     LEXIKON. Weimar, 1902-28. 7 vols. (Reprint, Hildesheim:
     Olms, 1961.)

147. Holzmann, Michael, and Hanns Bohatta. DEUTSCHES PSEUDONYMEN-
     LEXIKON. Vienna and Leipzig, 1906. (Reprint, Hildesheim:
     Olms, 1961.)

148. Hormayr zu Hortenburg, Josef, freiherr von. LEBENSBILDER AUS
     DEM BEFREIUNGSKRIEGE. Jena: Frommann, 1841-45. 3 vols.

149. Hubatsch, Walther. "Stein und die deutsche Erhebung von 1813."
     W. Hubatsch, STEIN-STUDIEN: DIE PREUSSISCHEN REFORMEN DES
     REICHSFREIHERRN KARL VOM STEIN ZWISCHEN REVOLUTION UND
     RESTAURATION. Cologne and Berlin: Grote, 1975.

150. Hubatsch, Walther. DIE STEIN-HARDENBERGSCHEN REFORMEN.
     Erträge der Forschung, vol. 65. Darmstadt: Wissenschaftliche
     Buchgesellschaft, 1977.

151. Huber, Ernst Rudolf. "Volksheer und Verfassung: Ein Beitrag
     zu der Kernfrage der Scharnhorst-Boyenschen Reform." ZEIT-
     SCHRIFT FUER DIE GESAMTE STAATSWISSENSCHAFT 97 (1936-37):
     213-57.

152. Hüffer, Hermann. DIE KABINETSREGIERUNG IN PREUSSEN UND JOHANN
     WILHELM LOMBARD: EIN BEITRAG ZUR GESCHICHTE DES PREUSSISCHEN
     STAATES, VORNEHMLICH IN DEN JAHREN 1797 BIS 1810. Leipzig:
     Duncker & Humblot, 1891.

153. Humboldt, Wilhelm, freiherr von. GESAMMELTE SCHRIFTEN. Edited
     by A. Leitzmann and Bruno Gebhardt. Berlin: Behr, 1903-18.
     15 vols.

154. Ibbeken, Rudolf. PREUSSEN 1807-1813: STAAT UND VOLK ALS IDEE
     UND IN WIRKLICHKEIT: DARSTELLUNG UND DOKUMENTATION.
     Veröffentlichungen aus den Archiven Preussischer Kulturbesitz,
     vol. 5. Berlin and Cologne: Grote, 1970.

155. IRENE: EINE ZEITSCHRIFT FUER DEUTSCHLANDS TOECHTER. Berlin,
     Münster, and Oldenburg, 1801-1806. (After 1804 appeared under
     the title, NEUE IRENE.)

156. DAS JAHR 1813 UND DER FREIHERR VOM STEIN. Schriften der
     Freiherr-vom-Stein-Gesellschaft, vol. 4. Münster: Aschendorff,
     1964.

157. Jany, Curt. GESCHICHTE DER PREUSSISCHEN ARMEE VOM 15.
     JAHRHUNDERT BIS 1914. 2d ed. Edited by Eberhard Jany.
     Osnabrück: Biblio-Verlag, 1967. 4 vols.

158. Jeismann, Karl Ernst. "Nationalerziehung: Bemerkungen zum
     Verhältnis vom Politik und Pädagogik in der Zeit der
     Preussischen Reform, 1806-1815." GESCHICHTE IN WISSENSCHAFT
     UND UNTERRICHT 14 (1968): 201-18.

159. Jolles, Matthys. DAS DEUTSCHE NATIONALBEWUSSTSEIN IM ZEITALTER
     NAPOLEONS. Studien zur Geschichte des Staats- und
     Nationalgedankens, vol. 1. Frankfurt a.M.: Klostermann, 1936.

160. Kant, Immanuel. GESAMMELTE SCHRIFTEN. Berlin, 1910-56. 24
     vols. (Reprint, Berlin: de Gruyter, 1962-.)

161. Katte, Rudolf von. "Der Streifzug des Karl Friedrich von Katte
     auf Magdeburg in April 1809." GESCHICHTSBLAETTER FUER STADT
     UND LAND MAGDEBURG 70-71 (1935-36): 17-35.

162. Kayser, Christian Gottlob. BUECHER-LEXIKON 1750-1832.
     Leipzig: Schumann, 1834-35. 3 vols. (Reprint, Graz:
     Akademische Druck- und Verlagsanstalt, 1961.)

163. Kessel, Eberhard. "Die Wandlung der Kriegskunst im Zeitalter
     der französichen Revolution." HISTORISCHE ZEITSCHRIFT 148
     (1933): 248-76.

164. Kircheisen, Friedrich Max. NAPOLEON I UND DAS ZEITALTER DER
     BEFREIUNGSKRIEGE IN BILDERN. Munich: Müller, 1914.

165. Kircheisen, Friedrich Max, ed. WIDER NAPOLEON: EIN DEUTSCHES
     REITERLEBEN 1806-1815. Stuttgart: Lutz, 1911-12. 2 vols.

166. Klaje, Hermann. SCHILL. Pommern im Wandel der Zeiten, vol. 3.
     Stettin: Saunier, 1940.

167. Klang, Daniel. "Bavaria and the War of Liberation, 1813-1814."
     FRENCH HISTORICAL STUDIES 4 (1965): 22-41.

168. Klang, Daniel. "Bavaria in the Age of Napoleon". Ph.D.
     dissertation, Princeton University, 1963.

169. Kleist, Henrich von. SAEMTLICHE WERKE UND BRIEFE. Edited by
     Helmut Sembdner. Munich: Hanser, 1977. 2 vols.

170. Klemz, Bernhard. "Die Feldzeitung der Preussischen Armee im
     Freiheitskrieg 1813-1814." WEHRWISSENSCHAFTLICHE RUNDSCHAU 20
     (1970): 81-92.

171. Klessmann, Eckart, ed. DIE BEFREIUNGSKRIEGE IN AUGENZEUGEN-
     BERICHTEN. Düsseldorf: Rauch, 1966.

172. Kling, C. GESCHICHTE DER BEKLEIDUNG, BEWAFFNUNG, UND
     AUSRUESTUNG DES KOENIGLICH PREUSSISCHEN HEERES. Weimar: Putze
     & Hölzer, 1902-12. 3 vols.

173. Klippel, Georg Heinrich. DAS LEBEN DES GENERALS VON
     SCHARNHORST. Leipzig: Brockhaus, 1869-71. 3 vols.

174. Knemeyer, Franz Ludwig. REGIERUNGS- UND VERWALTUNGSREFORMEN IN
     DEUTSCHLAND ZU BEGINN DES 19. JAHRHUNDERTS. Cologne: Grote,
     1970.

175. Kneschke, Ernst Heinrich. NEUES ALLGEMEINES DEUTSCHES
     ADELS-LEXICON. Leipzig: Voigt, 1857-1870. 9 vol. (Reprint,
     Hildesheim: Olms, 1973.)

176. Knoll, Werner. "Zur Entwicklung von Offizierschulen und
     Militärakademien in Deutschland Anfang des 19. Jahrhunderts."
     MILITAERGESCHICHTE 17 (1978): 457-62.

177. KOENIGLICHES BAYERISCHES REGIERUNGSBLATT. Munich, 1806-1813.

178. [Körner, Christain Gottfried]. DEUTSCHLANDS HOFFNUNGEN.
     Leipzig: n.p., 1813.

179. Körner, Josef. BIBLIOGRAPHISCHES HANDBUCH DES DEUTSCHEN
     SCHRIFTTUMS. 4th ed. Berlin and Munich: Francke, 1966.

180. Körner, Rudolf. "Friedrich Ludwig Jahn und sein Turnwesen." FORSCHUNGEN ZUR BRANDENBURGISCHEN UND PREUSSISCHEN GESCHICHTE 41 (1928): 38-82.

181. Kohn, Hans. "The Eve of German Nationalism." JOURNAL OF THE HISTORY OF IDEAS 12 (1951): 256-84.

182. Kohn, Hans. "Father Jahn's Nationalism." REVIEW OF POLITICS 11 (1949): 419-32.

183. Kohn, Hans. PRELUDE TO NATION-STATES; THE FRENCH AND GERMAN EXPERIENCE, 1789-1815. New York: Van Nostrand, 1967.

184. Kohn, Hans. "Romanticism and the Rise of German Nationalism." REVIEW OF POLITICS 12 (1950): 443-72.

185. Kotzebue, August von. SAEMTLICHE DRAMATISCHEN WERKE. Leipzig: Kummer, 1827-29. 44 vols. (Reprint, Frankfurt a.M.: Minerva, in progress.)

186. Kraehe, Enno E. METTERNICH'S GERMAN POLICY. Vol. 1. THE CONTEST WITH NAPOLEON, 1799-1814. Princeton, N.J.: Princeton University Press, 1963.

187. Kraus, Karl. "Der preussische Generalstab und der Geist der Reformzeit." WEHRWISSENSCHAFTLICHE RUNDSCHAU 7 (1957): 203-16.

188. Krollman, Christian, Kurt Forsteuter, and Fritz Gause. ALTPREUSSISCHE BIOGRAPHIE. Königsberg: Gräfe und Unzer; Marburg a.d. Lahn: Elwert, 1941-75. 3 vols., published in serials.

189. Laban, Ferdinand. HEINRICH JOSEPH COLLIN: EIN BEITRAG ZUR GESCHICHTE DER NEUEREN DEUTSCHEN LITERATUR IN OESTERREICH. Vienna: Gerold, 1879.

190. Langsam, Walter Consuelo. THE NAPOLEONIC WARS AND GERMAN NATIONALISM IN AUSTRIA. Columbia University Studies in the Social Sciences, 324. New York: Columbia University Press, 1930. (Reprint, New York: AMS Press, 1970.)

191. La Roche-Aymon, Antoine Charles Etienne Paul de. DES TROUPES LEGERES, OU REFLEXIONS SUR L'ORGANISATION, L'INSTRUCTION ET LA TACTIQUE DE L'INFANTRIE ET DE LA CAVALERIE LEGERES. Paris: Magimel, 1817.

192. Lehmann, Max. FREIHERR VOM STEIN. Leipzig: Hirzel, 1902-5. 3 vols.

193. Lehmann, Max. "Gneisenau's Sendung Nach Schweden und England im Jahre 1812." HISTORISCHE ZEITSCHRIFT 62 (1889): 466-517.

194. Lehmann, Max. KNESEBECK UND SCHOEN: BEITRAEGE ZUR GESCHICHTE DER FREIHEITSKRIEGE. Leipzig: Hirzel, 1875.

195. Lehmann, Max. "Major von Wrangel, der angebliche Urheber der Konvention von Tauroggen." PREUSSISCHE JAHRBUECHER 131 (1908): 428-42.

196. Lehmann, Max. SCHARNHORST. Leipzig: Hirzel, 1886-87. 2 vols.

197. Lehmann, Max. "Scharnhorst's Kampf für die stehenden Heere." HISTORISCHE ZEITSCHRIFT 53 (1885): 276-99.

198. Lehmann, Max. STEIN, SCHARNHORST UND SCHOEN: EINE SCHUTZSCHRIFT. Leipzig: Hirzel, 1877.

199. Lehmann, Max. "Zur Geschichte der preussischen Heeresreform von 1808." HISTORISCHE ZEITSCHRIFT 126 (1922): 436-57.

200. Lehmann, Max, ed. "Tagebuch und Briefwechsel des Oberstleutnants von Tiedemann aus dem Jahre 1812." JAHRBUECHER FUER DIE DEUTSCHE ARMEE UND MARINE 24 (1877): 117-48.

201. Leroux, Robert. LA THEORIE DU DESPOTISME ECLAIRE CHEZ KARL THEODOR VON DALBERG. 2d ed. Paris: Société d'édition, 1932.

202. Liebert. "Dei Rüstungen Napoleons für den Feldzug 1812." MILITAER-WOCHENBLATT 9 (1888): 355-92.

203. Lindemann, Margot. DEUTSCHE PRESSE BIS 1815. GESCHICHTE DER DEUTSCHEN PRESSE. Vol. 1. ABHANDLUNGEN UND MATERIALIEN ZUR PUBLIZISTIK. Berlin: Colloquium, 1969.

204. Linnenbach, Karl, ed. KARL UND MARIE VON CLAUSEWITZ: EIN LEBENSBILD IN BRIEFEN UND TAGEBUCHBLAETTERN. Berlin: Warneck, 1916.

205. Linnebach, Karl, ed. SCHARNHORSTS BRIEFE. Munich and Leipzig: Müller, 1914. (One of several planned volumes.)

206. Lionnet, Albert. DIE ERHEBUNGSPLAENE PREUSSISCHER PATRIOTEN ENDE 1806 UND FRUEHJAHR 1807. Historische Studien, vol. 120. Berlin: Ebering, 1914.

207. Luckwaldt, Friedrich. OESTERREICH UND DIE ANFAENGE DES BEFREIUNGSKRIEGES VON 1813. Historische Studien, vol. 10. Berlin: Eberling, 1898.

208. Lynker, Karl. GESCHICHTE DER INSURRECTIONEN WIDER DAS WESTPHAELISCHE GOUVERNEMENT: BEITRAG ZUR GESCHICHTE DES DEUTSCHEN FREIHEITSKRIEGES. Cassel: Bertram, 1857.

209. Macdonald, Jacques Etienne, duc de Tarente. SOUVENIRS DU MARECHAL MACDONALD. Edited by Camille Rousset. Paris: Plon, 1892.

210. Markov, Walter. "Institutions napoléoniennes en Allemagne: les deux faces d'un progrès." REVUE D'HISTOIRE MODERNE ET CONTEMPORAINE 17 (1970): 893-96.

211. May, Arthur J., and Marvin L. Brown. "Austria." THE NEW GUIDE TO THE DIPLOMATIC ARCHIVES OF WESTERN EUROPE. Edited by Daniel H. Thomas and Lynn M. Case. Philadelphia: University of Pennsylvania Press, 1975.

212. Mazade, Charles de, ed. CORRESPONDANCE DU MARECHAL DAVOUT PRINCE D'ECKMUEHL, SES COMMANDEMENTS, SON MINISTERE, 1801-1815. Paris: Plon, 1885. 4 vols.

213. Meinecke, Friedrich, ed. "Aus den Akten der Militärreorganisations-kommission von 1808: Eine Denkschrift des Premirleutnants von Seydlitz." FORSCHUNGEN ZUR BRANDENBURGISCHEN UND PREUSSISCHEN GESCHICHTE 5 (1892): 487-95.

214. Meinecke, Friedrich. "Landwehr und Landsturm seit 1814." SCHMOLLERS JAHRBUCH FUER GESETZGEBUNG, VERWALTUNG AND VOLKSWIRTSCHAFT IM DEUTSCHEN REICHE 40 (1916): 1087-112.

215. Meinecke, Friedrich. DAS LEBEN DES GENERALFELDMARSCHALLS HERMANN VON BOYEN. Stuttgart: Cotta, 1896-99. 2 vols.

216. Meinecke, Friedrich. WELTBUERGERTUM UND NATIONALSTAAT. (First ed., 1907) Werke, vol. 5. Edited by H. Herzfeld, C. Hinrichs, and W. Hofer. Darmstadt: Wissenschaftliche Buchgesellschaft, 1969. (English edition edited by F. Gilbert and translated by R.B. Kimber, COSMOPOLITANISM AND THE NATIONAL STATE. Princeton, N.J.: Princeton University Press, 1970.)

217. Meinecke, Friedrich. DAS ZEITALTER DER DEUTSCHEN ERHEBUNG (1795-1815). (First ed., 1906) Göttingen: Vandenhoeck & Ruprecht, 1957. (English translation by Peter Paret, THE AGE OF GERMAN LIBERATION, 1795-1815. Berkeley: University of California, 1977.)

218. Metternich, Richard von, ed. AUS METTERNICH'S NACHGELASSENEN PAPIEREN. Vienna: Braunmiller, 1880-84. 8 vols. (English translation by Mrs. Alexander Napier, MEMOIRS OF PRINCE METTERNICH. New York: Scribners, 1880-82. 5 vols.)

219. Meusel, Friedrich, ed. FRIEDRICH AUGUST LUDWIG VON DER MARWITZ: EIN MAERKISCHER EDELMANN IM ZEITALTER DER BEFREIUNGSKRIEGE: Berlin: Mittler, 1908-13. 2 vols. in 3.

220. Meyer, Friedrich. "Ueber Kants Stellung zu Nation und Staat." HISTORISCHE ZEITSCHRIFT 133 (1926): 197-219.

221. MINERVA: EIN JOURNAL HISTORISCHEN UND POLITISCHEN INHALTS. Edited by Johann Wilhelm von Archenholz. Berlin (1803-1812); Leipzig (1813-1815). Vols. 45-82.

222. Mitscherlich, Waldemar. "Der Nationalismus und seine Wurzeln."
     SCHMOLLERS JAHRBUCH FUER GESETZGEBUNG, VERWALTUNG UND
     VOLKSWIRTSCHAFT IM DEUTSCHEN REICHE 36 (1912): 1285-320.

223. Mitscherlich, Waldemar. DER NATIONALISMUS WESTEUROPAS.
     Leipzig: Hirschfeld, 1920.

224. Mommsen, Wolfgang A. DIE NACHLAESSE IN DEN DEUTSCHEN ARCHIVEN.
     Verzeichnis der schriftlichen Nachlässe in deutschen Archiven
     und Bibliotheken, vol. 1. Schriften des Bundesarchivs 17.
     Boppard-Rhein: Boldt, 1971-83. 2 vols.

225. Montgelas, Maximilian Joseph von. DENKWUERDIGKEITEN DES GRAFEN
     MAXIMILIAN JOSEPH VON MONTGELAS UEBER DIE INNERE
     STAATSVERWALTUNG BAYERNS (1799-1817). Edited by G. Laubmann
     and M. Doeberl. Munich: Beck, 1908.

226. Mork, Gordon R. "The Archives of the German Democratic
     Republic." CENTRAL EUROPEAN HISTORY 2 (1969): 273-84.

227. Müffling, Friedrich Karl, freiherr von. AUS MEINEM LEBEN.
     Berlin: Mittler, 1851.

228. Müller, Adam. KRITISCHE, AESTHETISCHE UND PHILOSOPHISCHE
     SCHRIFTEN. Edited by Walter Schroeder and Werner Siebert.
     Neuwied and Berlin: Luchterhand, 1967. 2 vols.

229. Müller, Johannes von. SAEMMTLICHE WERKE. Stuttgart: Cotta,
     1831-1835. 40 vols. in 14.

230. Müsebeck, Ernst. FREIWILLIGE GABEN UND OPFER DES PREUSSISCHEN
     VOLKES IN DEN JAHREN 1813-1815. Mitteilungen der königlichen
     preussischen Archivverwaltung, vol. 23. Leipzig: Hirzel,
     1913.

231. NAPOLEON ET L'EUROPE. Edited by the Commission Internationale
     pour l'enseignement de l'histoire. Paris: Brepols, 1961.

232. Natzmer, G.E. von, ed. UNTER DEN HOHENZOLLERN:
     DENKWUERDIGKEITEN AUS DEM LEBEN DES GENERAL OLDWIG VON NATZMER.
     Gotha: Perthes, 1887-89. 4 vols.

233. Neck, Rudolf. "The Haus-, Hof-, und Staatsarchiv: Its
     History, Holdings, and Use." AUSTRIAN HISTORY YEARBOOK 6-7
     (1970-1971): 3-16.

234. NEUE DEUTSCHE BIOGRAPHIE. Edited by Historische Kommission bei
     der Bayerischen Akademie der Wissenschaften. Publication in
     progress. Berlin: Duncker & Humblot, 1953-.

235. Nippold, F., ed. ERINNERUNGEN AUS DEM LEBEN DES GENERAL-
     FELDMARSCHALLS HERMANN VON BOYEN. Leipzig: Hirzel, 1889-90.
     3 vols.

236. Nohn, Ernst August. "Clausewitz contra Bülow." WEHRWISSEN-SCHAFTLICHE RUNDSCHAU 5 (1955): 323-30.

237. Obermann, Karl. "La Situation de la presse sous l'occupation française 1807-1813." OCCUPANTS-OCCUPES, 1792-1815: COLLOQUE DE BRUXELLES, 29 ET 30 JANVIER 1968. Edited by the Centre d'Histoire Economique et Sociale, Institut de Sociologie. Brussels: Université Libre de Bruxelles, 1968.

238. Obermann, Karl. "Zur Rolle Metternichs in der Diplomatie des Jahres 1813." DER FEFREIUNGSKRIEG 1813. Edited by Peter Hoffmann et al. Berlin: Akademie, 1967.

239. Offelsmeyer, Friedrich Wilhelm. PREDIGT, IN ANWESENHEIT DER GROSSEN HAUPTQUARTIERE, ZU FRANKFURT IN DER ST. KATHARINENKIRCHE AM 28. NOVEMBER GEHALTEN. Frankfurt a.M.: Hermann, 1813.

240. Oncken, Hermann. "Deutsche geistige Einflüsse in der europäischen Nationalitätenbewegung des 19. Jahrhunderts." DEUTSCHE VIERTELJAHRESSCHRIFT FUER LITERATURWISSENSCHAFT UND GEISTESGESCHICHTE 7 (1929): 607-27.

241. Oncken, Wilhelm. OESTERREICH UND PREUSSEN IM BEFREIUNGSKRIEGE: URKUNDLICHE AUFSCHLUESSE UEBER DIE POLITISCHE GESCHICHTE DES JAHRES 1813. Berlin: Grote, 1876-79. 2 vols. (Reprint, Hildesheim: Georg Olms, in progress.)

242. Paisley, David. "An Unrecorded German Periodical from the Time of the Napoleonic Wars: Beyträge zur Geschichte des Krieges der Jahre 1812 und 1813." BRITISH LIBRARY JOURNAL 3 (1977): 129-34.

243. Paret, Peter. CLAUSEWITZ AND THE STATE. New York: Oxford, 1976.

244. Paret, Peter. YORCK AND THE ERA OF PRUSSIAN REFORM 1807-1815. Princeton, N.J.: Princeton University Press, 1966.

245. Pertz, G.H., and Hans Delbrück. DAS LEBEN DES FELDMARSCHALLS GRAFEN NEITHART VON GNEISENAU. Berlin: Reimer, 1864-80. 5 vols.

246. Petschke, G. "Die Bekleidung und Ausrüstung der preussischen Kürassiere in der Zeit von 1809-1919." ZEITSCHRIFT FUER HEERES- UND UNIFORMKUNDE 22 (1958): 5-10, 86-94; 23 (1959): 62-69, 110-14.

247. Pflugk-Harttung, Julius von. "Aus dem Bayerischen Haupt-quartier, 1814-1815." HISTORISCHES JAHRBUCH 35 (1914): 356-74.

248. Pflugk-Harttung, Julius von. "Der Oberbefehl 1813." HISTORISCHES JAHRBUCH 35 (1914): 836-47.

249. Pflugk-Harttung, Julius von, ed. BRIEFE DES GENERALS NEIDHARDT VOS GNEISENAU 1803-1815. Gotha: Perthes, 1913.

250. Poll, Bernhard. "Vom Schicksal der deutschen Heeresakten und der amtlichen Kriegsgeschichtsschreibung." DIE WELT ALS GESCHICHTE 12 (1952): 61-68.

251. Poten, B., ed. HANDWOERTERBUCH DER GESAMTEN MILITAERWISSENSCHAFTEN. Bielefeld, Leipzig: Velhagen & Klasing, 1877-80. 4 vols.

252. DAS PREUSSISCHE HEER DER BEFREIUNGSKRIEGE. Edited by Kriegsgeschichtliche Abteilung II of the General Staff. Berlin: Mittler, 1912-14. 2 vols.

253. Priesdorff, Kurt von. SOLDATISCHES FUEHRERTUM. Hamburg: Hanseatisches Verlangsanstalt, 1936-45. 10 vols.

254. Prokesch-Osten, Anton, graf von, ed. AUS DEM NACHLASS FRIEDRICHS VON GENTZ. Vienna: Gerold, 1867. 2 vols.

255. Raack, R.C. "The Course of Political Idealism in Prussia, 1800-1813. Ph.D. dissertation, Harvard University, 1957.

256. Raack, R.C. THE FALL OF STEIN. Harvard Historical Monographs, 58. Cambridge, Mass.: Harvard University Press, 1965.

257. Raack, R.C. "A New Schleiermacher Letter on the Conspiracy of 1808." ZEITSCHRIFT FUER RELIGIONS- UND GEISTESGESCHICHTE 16 (1964): 209-23.

258. Raack, R.C. "When Plans Fail: Small Group Behavior and Decision-Making in the Conspiracy of 1808 in Germany." JOURNAL OF CONFLICT RESOLUTION 14 (1970): 3-19.

259. Rambaud, Alfred. LA DOMINATION FRANCAISE EN ALLEMAGNE: L'ALLEMAGNE SOUS NAPOLEON Ier (1804-1811). Paris: Perrin, 1874.

260. Ranke, Leopold von. HARDENBERG UND DIE GESCHICHTE DES PREUSSISCHEN STAATES VON 1793-1813. Sämmliche Werke, vols. 46, 47. Leipzig: Duncker & Humblot, 1879-81.

261. Ranke, Leopold von, ed. DENKWUERDIGKEITEN DES STAATSKANZLERS FUERSTEN VON HARDENBERG. Leipzig: Duncker & Humblot, 1877. 5 vols.

262. Rassow, Peter. "Die Wirkung der Erhebung Spaniens auf die deutsche Erhebung gegen Napoleon I. HISTORISCHE ZEITSCHRIFT, 167 (1943): 310-25.

263. Rath, R. John. "The War and the Austrian Archives." JOURNAL OF CENTRAL EUROPEAN AFFAIRS 6 (1946): 392-96.

264. Raumer, Kurt von. "Deutschland um 1800: Krise und Neugestaltung, 1789-1815." HANDBUCH DER DEUTSCHEN GESCHICHTE 3, Part 1. Edited by Leo Just. Wiesbaden: A.V. Athenaion, 1980.

265. Raumer, Kurt von. DER KANTISCHE GEIST IN DER DEUTSCHEN ERHEBUNG. Königsberg: Gräfe & Unzer, 1940.

266. Reden-Dohna, Armgard von, ed. DEUTSCHLAND UND ITALIEN IM ZEITALTER NAPOLEONS: DEUTSCH-ITALIENISCHES HISTORIKERTREFFEN IN MAINZ, 29. MAI-1. JUNI 1975. Veröffentlichungen des Instituts für Europäische Geschichte, Mainz. Abteilung Universalgeschichte, Beiheft 5. Wiesbaden: Steiner, 1979.

267. DIE REORGANISATION DER PREUSSISCHEN ARMEE NACH DEM TILSITER FRIEDEN. MILITAERWOCHENBLATT; 1862, Beiheft. Berlin: Mittler, 1862.

268. DER RHEINISCHE BUND: EINE ZEITSCHRIFT HISTORISCH- POLITISCH-STATISTISCH-GEOGRAPHISCHEN INHALTS. Edited by P.A. Winkopp. Frankfurt a.M., 1806-13. 23 vols.

269. RHEINISCHER MERKUR. Edited by Josef Görres. Koblenz, 1814-1815. 2 vols.

270. Richter, Jean Paul. FRIEDENS-PREDIGT AN DEUTSCHLAND. Heidelberg: Mohr, 1808.

271. Riedweg, Franz. AUFBRUCH ZUR FREIHEIT 1813-1814-1815: AUS ZEITGENOESSISCHEN SCHRIFTEN AUSGEWAEHLT. Berlin and Leipzig: Nibelungen, 1941.

272. Ritter, Gerhard. "Die Aechtung Steins." NASSAUISCHE ANNALEN 3 (1931): 1-17.

273. Ritter, Gerhard. "Das Problem des Militarismus in Deutschland." HISTORISCHE ZEITSCHRIFT 177 (1954): 21-48.

274. Ritter, Gerhard. STAATSKUNST UND KRIEGSHANDWERK: DAS PROBLEM DES MILITARISMUS IN DEUTSCHLAND. Munich: Oldenburg, 1954-68. 4 vols. (English translation by Heinz Norden, THE SWORD AND THE SEPTER: THE PROBLEM OF MILITARISM IN GERMANY. Coral Gables, Fla.: University of Miami Press, 1969-72.)

275. Ritter, Gerhard. STEIN: EINE POLITISCHE BIOGRAPHIE. Stuttgart: Deutsche Verlagsanstalt, 1931. 2 vols. (4th ed. in one volume, 1981.)

276. Robert, André. L'IDEE NATIONALE AUTRICHIENNE ET LA GUERRES DE NAPOLEON. Paris: Alcan, 1933.

277. Röder, Reinhold. "Zur Entwicklung der deutsch-russischen Waffenbrüderschaft am Beginn des Jahres 1813." ZEITSCHRIFT FUER MILITAERGESCHICHTE 2 (1963): 94-100.

278. Rössler, Helmut. OESTERREICHS KAMPF UM DEUTSCHLANDS BEFREIUNG: DIE DEUTSCHE POLITIK DER NATIONALEN FUEHRER OESTERREICHS, 1805-1815. Schriften des Reichsinstituts für Geschichte des neuen Deutschlands. Hamburg: Hanseatische Verlags-Anstalt, 1940. 2 vols.

279. Rohr, Wilhelm. "Scharnhorsts Sendung nach Wien Ende 1811 und Metternichs Politik." FORSCHUNGEN ZUR BRANDENBURGISCHEN UND PREUSSISCHEN GESCHICHTE 43 (1930): 76-128.

280. Rose, J. Holland. "A Report of the Battles of Jena and Auerstädt and the Surrender at Prenzlau." ENGLISH HISTORICAL REVIEW 19 (1904): 550-53.

281. Rothfels, Hans. CARL VON CLAUSEWITZ: POLITIK UND KRIEG. Berlin: Dümmler, 1920.

282. Rothfels, Hans, ed. CARL VON CLAUSEWITZ: POLITISCHE SCHRIFTEN UND BRIEFE. Munich: Drei Masken-Verlag, 1922.

283. Rothfels, Hans, ed. "Eine Denkschrift Carls von Clausewitz aus den Jahren 1807-1808." PREUSSISCHE JAHRBUECHER 177 (1919): 223-45.

284. Rothfels, Hans. "Grundsätzliches zum Problem der Nationalität." HISTORISCHE ZEITSCHRIFT 174 (1952): 339-58.

285. Rühl, Franz, ed. AUS DER FRANZOSENZEIT: ERGAENZUNGEN ZU DEN BRIEFEN UND AKTENSTUECKEN ZUR GESCHICHTE PREUSSENS UNTER FRIEDRICH WILHELM III., VORZUGSWEISE AUS DEM NACHLASS VON F.A. VON STAEGEMANN. Publication des Vereins für die Geschichte von Ost- und Westpreussen. Leipzig: Duncker & Humblot, 1904.

286. Rühl, Franz, ed. BRIEFE UND AKTENSTUECKE ZUR GESCHICHTE PREUSSENS UNTER FRIEDRICH WILHELM III., VORZUGSWEISE AUS DEM NACHLASS VON F.A. VON STAEGEMANN. Publication des Vereins für die Geschichte von Ost- und Westpreussen. Leipzig: Duncker & Humblot, 1899-1902. 3 vols.

287. RUSSISCH-DEUTSCHES VOLKS-BLATT. Edited by August von Kotzebue. Berlin, 1813.

288. Sautermeister, Reinhard. DIE TAKTISCHE REFORM DER PREUSSISCHEN ARMEE NACH 1806. Tübingen: Becht, 1935.

289. Sauzin, Louis. ADAM HEINRICH MUELLER, 1779-1829: SA VIE ET SON OEUVRE. Paris: Nizet et Bastard, 1937.

290. Schäfer, Karl Heinz. "Die Freiheitskriege in der Sicht der Marxistischen Geschichtsschreibung der DDR." GESCHICHTE IN WISSENSCHAFT UND UNTERRICHT 21 (1970): 2-21.

291. Scheel, Heinrich. "Fremdherrschaft und nationaler Befreiungskampf: Zur problematik des deutschen

Befreiungskrieges von 1813." DER BEFREIUNGSKRIEG 1813. Edited by Peter Hoffmann et al. Berlin: Akademie, 1967.

292. Scheel, Heinrich. "Probleme der deutsch-französischen Beziehungen, 1789-1830." ZEITSCHRIFT FUER GESCHICHTS-WISSENSCHAFT 18 (1970): 163-71.

293. Scheel, Heinrich, and Doris Schmidt, eds. DAS REFORMMINISTERIUM STEIN: AKTEN ZUR VERFASSUNGS- UND VERWALTUNGSGESCHICHTE AUS DEN JAHREN 1807-08. Deutsche Akademie der Wissenschaften zu Berlin: Schriften des Instituts für Geschichte. Series 1, Vols. 31a, 31b, 31c. Berlin: Akademie, 1966-68. 3 vols.

294. Schlegel, Friedrich. KRITISCHE FRIEDRICH SCHLEGEL AUSGABE (WERKE). Edited by Ernst Behler et al. Paderborn, Munich, Vienna: Thomas, 1961-80. 35 vols.

295. Schleiermacher, Friedrich. KLEINE SCHRIFTEN UND PREDIGTEN. Edited by Hayo Gerdes and Emanuel Hirsch. Berlin: de Gruyter, 1969-70. 3 vols.

296. Schlesier, Gustav, ed. FRIEDRICH VON GENTZ: SCHRIFTEN. Mannheim: Hoff, 1838-40. 3 vols.

297. Schlesier, Gustav, ed. MEMOIRES ET LETTRES INEDITS DU CHEVALIER DE GENTZ. Stuttgart: Hallberger, 1841.

298. Schmid, Karl E. DEUTSCHLANDS WIEDERGEBURT: EIN POLITISCHER VERSUCH. Jena: Frommann, 1815.

299. Schmidt, Carl. "Clausewitz als politischer Denker." DER STAAT: ZEITSCHRIFT FUER STAATSLEHRE, OEFFENTLICHES RECHT, UND VERFASSUNGSGESCHICHTE 6 (1967): 479-502.

300. Schmidt, Charles. LE GRAND-DUCHE DE BERG (1806-1813): ETUDE SUR LA DOMINATION FRANCAISE EN ALLEMAGNE SOUS NAPOLEON Ier. Paris: Alcan, 1905.

301. Schmidt, Dorothea. "Streitkräfte und Volksmassen zu Beginn der bürgerlichen Umgestaltung des Militärwesens in Preussen." MILITAERGESCHICHTE 19 (1980): 547-54.

302. Schmidt, Friedrich von. ERINNERUNGEN AUS DEM LEBEN DES GENERALLEUTNANTS FRIEDRICH KARL VON SCHMIDT. Urkundliche Beiträge und Forschungen zur Geschichte des Preussischen Heeres, 11-13. Berlin: Mittler, 1909. 3 vols.

303. Schmidt, Gerhard. "Zur nationalen Befreiungsbewegung von 1813-14: Quellen im Sächischen Landeshauptarchiv Dresden." DER BEFREIUNGSKRIEG 1813. Edited by Peter Hoffmann et al. Berlin: Akademie, 1967.

304. Schmidt, Otto Eduard, ed. AUS DER ZEIT DER DEUTSCHEN FREIHEITSKRIEGE UND DES WIENER KONGRESSES: 87 UNGEDRUCKTE

BRIEFE UND URKUNDEN AUS SAECHSISCHEN ADELSARCHIVEN. Aus
Sächsens Vergangenheit, vol. 2. Leipzig: Teubner, 1914.

305. Schmitt, Hans A. "1812: Stein, Alexander I and the Crusade
     Against Napoleon." JOURNAL OF MODERN HISTORY 31 (1959):
     325-28.

306. Schnepel, Herbert. DIE REICHSTADT BREMEN UND FRANKREICH VON
     1789 BIS 1813. Bremen: Geist, 1935.

307. Schön, Theodor von. AUS DEN PAPIEREN DES MINISTERS UND
     BURGGRAFEN VON MARIENBURG THEODOR VON SCHOEN. Halle:
     Niemeyer; Leipzig: Duncker; Berlin: Simion, 1875-76. 4
     vols.

308. Schön, Theodor von. WEITERE BEITRAEGE UND NACHTRAEGE ZU DEN
     PAPIEREN DES MINISTERS UND BURGGRAFEN VON MARIENBURG THEODOR
     VON SCHOEN. Berlin: Simion, 1881.

309. Schoenach, A. v. "Zur Vorgeschichte der Befreiungskriege:
     Kriegsberichte von 1812." ALTPREUSSISCHE MONATSSCHRIFT 49
     (1912): 463-79, 573-92.

310. Schoeps, Hans Joachim. "Vom Yorkschen Korps zum Zarenhof: Aus
     den Briefen des Johann Paul Franz von Lucadou." ZEITSCHRIFT
     FUER RELIGIONS- UND GEISTESGESCHICHTE 15 (1963): 347-60.

311. Schoeps, Hans Joachim, ed. AUS DEN JAHREN PREUSSISCHER NOT UND
     ERNEUERUNG: TAGEBUECHER UND BRIEFE DER GEBRUEDER GERLACH UND
     IHRES KREISES 1805-1820. Berlin: Haude & Spener, 1963.

312. Schoeps, Hans Joachim, ed. NEUE QUELLEN ZUR GESCHICHTE
     PREUSSENS IM 19. JAHRHUNDERT. Berlin: Haude & Spener, 1968.

313. Schubert, Friedrich von. UNTER DEM DOPPELADLER: ERINNERUNGEN
     EINES DEUTSCHEN IM RUSSISCHEN OFFIZIERSDIENST 1789-1814.
     Edited by Erik Amburger. Stuttgart: Koehler, 1962.

314. Schuderoff, Jonathan. PREDIGT AM DANKESFESTE FUER DEN BEI
     LEIPZIG ERFOCHTENEN SIEG. Ronneburg: n.p., 1814.

315. Schultze, Maximilian. KOENIGSBERG UND OSTPREUSSEN ZU ANFANG
     1813: EIN TAGEBUCH VOM 1. JANUAR BIS 25. FEBRUAR 1813.
     Bausteine zur preussischen Geschichte, vol. 1, book 2. Berlin:
     Costenoble, 1901.

316. Schulze, Friedrich, ed. AUSGEWAEHLTE BRIEFE DES FELDMARSCHALLS
     LEBERECHT VON BLUECHER. Voigtländers Quellenbücher, 4.
     Leipzig: Voigtländer, 1912.

317. [Schutz, Adolf von]. ALLES IN EINER NUSS: ODER GEIST,
     UEBERSICHT UND BEURTHEILUNG DER IM BEFREIUNGSJAHRE 1813 UND IN
     DER NAECHSTFOLGENDEN ZEIT ERSCHIENENEN FLUGSCHRIFTEN.
     Madgeburg: Lausser, 1814-15. 2 vols.

318. Seyffarth, Ursula. ZUR AUSSENPOLITIK DES STAATSKANZLERS FREIHERRN VON HARDENBERG VON 1810-1812: EIN BEITRAG ZUR VORGESCHICHTE DER BEFREIUNGSKRIEGE. Würzburg: Triltsch, 1939.

319. Shanahan, William Oswald. PRUSSIAN MILITARY REFORMS: 1786-1813. Studies in History, Economics, and Public Law, 520. New York: Columbia University Press, 1945.

320. Showalter, Dennis E. "Manifestation of Reform: The Rearmament of the Prussian Infantry, 1806-1813." JOURNAL OF MODERN HISTORY 44 (1972): 364-80.

321. Showalter, Dennis E. "The Prussian 'Landwehr' and Its Critics, 1813-1819." CENTRAL EUROPEAN HISTORY 4 (1971): 3-33.

322. Sieburg, Heinz-Otto. "Napoléon et les transformations des institutions en Allegmagne." REVUE D'HISTOIRE MODERNE ET CONTEMPORAINE 17 (1970): 897-912.

323. Sieburg, Heinz Otto, ed. NAPOLEON UND EUROPA. Neue Wissenschaftliche Bibliothek, vol. 44. Cologne: Kiepenhauer & Witsch, 1971.

324. Simon, Walter M. THE FAILURE OF THE PRUSSIAN REFORM MOVEMENT, 1807-1819. Ithaca, N.Y.: Cornell University Press, 1955. (Reprint, New York: Fertig, 1971.)

325. Simon, Walter M. "Variations in Nationalism during the Great Reform Period in Prussia." AMERICAN HISTORICAL REVIEW 59 (1953-54): 305-21.

326. Spies, Hans Bernd. "'Erhebungen'--Eine patriotische Zeitschrift aus Lübeck (1809-1810)." ZEITSCHRIFT DES VEREINS FUER LUEBECKISCHE GESCHICHTE UND ALTERTUMSKUNDE 59 (1979): 83-105.

327. Spies, Hans Bernd, ed. DIE ERHEBUNG GEGEN NAPOLEON: 1806-1814/15. Quellen zum politischen Denken der Deutschen im 19. und 20. Jahrhundert, vol. 2. Darmstadt: Wissenschaftliche Buchgesellschaft, 1981.

328. Stahl, Friedrich Christian. "Die Bestände des Bundesarchiv-Militärarchivs." MILITAERGESCHICHTLICHE MITTEILUNGEN 7 (1969): 599-608. (Also published in REVUE INTERNATIONALE D'HISTOIRE MILITAIRE 27 (1968): 307-13.)

329. Stern, Alfred, ed. "Einige Aktenstücke zur Geschichte Preussens, 1809-1812: Aus dem Public Record Office zu London." FORSCHUNGEN ZUR BRANDENBURGISCHEN UND PREUSSISCHEN GESCHICHTE 13 (1900): 174-86.

330. Stern, Alfred. "Gneisenau's Reise nach London im Jahre 1809 und ihre Vorgeschichte." HISTORISCHE ZEITSCHRIFT 85 (1900): 1-44.

331. Straube, Fritz. FRUEHJAHRESFELDZUG 1813: DIE ROLLE DER
     RUSSISCHEN TRUPPEN BEI DER BEFREIUNG DEUTSCHLANDS VOM
     NAPOLEONISCHEN JOCH. Berlin: Rütten & Loening, 1967.

332. Straube, Frtiz, ed. DAS JAHR 1813: STUDIEN ZUR GESCHICHTE UND
     WIRKUNG DER BEFREIUNGSKRIEGE. Deutsche Historiker-
     Gesellschaft: Arbeitsgemeinschaft zur Geschichte von 1789 bis
     1815, Sammelband. Berlin: Akademie, 1963.

333. Straube, Fritz. "Russische Streifkorps und antinapoleonische
     Volksbewegung in Deutschland in Frühjahr 1813." DER
     BEFREIUNGSKRIEG 1813. Edited by Peter Hoffmann et al.
     Berlin: Akademie, 1967.

334. Streisand, Joachim. DEUTSCHE GESCHICHTE. Vol. 2. VON 1789 BIS
     1917. Berlin: Deutscher Verlag der Wissenschaften, 1967.

335. Stulz, Percy. FREMDHERRSCHAFT UND BEFREIUNGSKAMPF: DIE
     PREUSSISCHE KABINETTSPOLITIK UND DIE ROLLE DER VOLKSMASSEN IN
     DEN JAHREN 1811 BIS 1813. Berlin: Deutscher Verlag der
     Wissenschaften, 1960.

336. Sweet, Paul R. FRIEDRICH VON GENTZ: DEFENDER OF THE OLD
     ORDER. Madison: University of Wisconsin Press, 1941.

337. Sweet, Paul R. WILHELM VON HUMBOLDT: A BIOGRAPHY. Columbus:
     Ohio State University Press, 1978-80. 2 vols.

338. TASCHENBUCH ARCHIVWESEN DER DDR. Edited by Staatliche
     Archivverwaltung des Ministeriums des Innern der DDR. Berlin:
     Staatsverlag der Deutschen Demokratischen Republik, 1971.

339. Teske, Hermann. "Gneisenau--Staatsbürger und Mensch."
     WEHRWISSENSCHAFTLICHE RUNDSCHAU 10 (1960): 521-47.

340. Teske, Hermann. "Scharnhorst." WEHRWISSENSCHAFTLICHE RUNDSCHAU
     5 (1955): 518-27.

341. Thielen, Peter G. KARL AUGUST VON HARDENBERG 1750-1822: EINE
     BIOGRAPHIE. Cologne, Berlin: Grote, 1967.

342. DIE THIELNAHME DES PREUSSISCHEN HUELFSKORPS AN DEM FELDZUGE
     GEGEN RUSSLAND IM JAHRE 1812. Kriegsgeschichtliche
     Einzelschriften, vol. 24. Published by Abtheilung für
     Kriegsgeschichte II of the German General Staff. Berlin:
     Mittler, 1898.

343. Thieme, Horst, Wolfgang Blöss, and Autorenkollektiv. "Zur
     nationalen Befreiungbewegung 1813-14: Quellen im Deutschen
     Zentralarchiv, Abteilung Merseburg." ARCHIVMITTEILUNGEN 13
     (1963): 84-95.

344. Thimme, Friedrich. "Freiherr Ludwig von Wrangel und die
     Konvention von Tauroggen." HISTORISCHE ZEITSCHRIFT 100 (1908):
     112-29.

345. Thimme, Friedrich. "König Friedrich Wilhelm III., sein Antheil an der Konvention von Tauroggen und an der Reform von 1807-1812." FORSCHUNGEN ZUR BRANDENBURGISCHEN UND PREUSSISCHEN GESCHICHTE 18 (1905): 1-59.

346. Thimme, Friedrich. "Zu den Erhebungsplänen der preussischen Patrioten im Sommer 1808: Ungedruckte Denkschriften Gneisenaus und Scharnhorsts." HISTORISCHE ZEITSCHRIFT 86 (1901): 78-110.

347. Thimme, Friedrich. "Zur Vorgeschichte der Konvention von Tauroggen." FORSCHUNGEN ZUR BRANDENBURGISCHEN UND PREUSSISCHEN GESCHICHTE 13 (1900): 246-64.

348. Thomas, Daniel H., and Lynn M. Case, eds. THE NEW GUIDE TO THE DIPLOMATIC ARCHIVES OF WESTERN EUROPE. Philadelphia: University of Pennsylvania Press, 1975.

349. Troeger, Curt, ed. LEBENSERINNERUNGEN DES GENERALLEUTNANTS KARL VON WEDEL. Berlin: Mittler, 1911-13. 2 vols.

350. Tschirch, Otto. GESCHICHTE DER OEFFENTLICHEN MEINUNG IN PREUSSEN VOM BASELER FRIEDEN BIS ZUM ZUSAMMENBRUCH DES STAATES (1795-1806). Weimar: Böhlau, 1933-34. 2 vols.

351. Ulmann, Heinrich. "Die Detachments der freiwilligen Jäger in den Befreiungskrigen." HISTORISCHE VIERTELJAHRSSCHRIFT 10 (1907): 483-505.

352. Ulmann, Heinrich. "Heinrich Bardeleben, ein Patriot der Franzosenzeit." FORSCHUNGEN ZUR BRANDENBURGISCHEN UND PREUSSISCHEN GESCHICHTE 31 (1919): 159-80.

353. Unger, W. von. BLUECHER. Berlin: Mittler, 1907-08. 2 vols.

354. Unger, W. von, ed. DENKWUERDIGKEITEN DES GENERALS AUGUST FREIHERRN HILLER VON GAERTRINGEN. Berlin: Mittler, 1912.

355. Usczeck, Hans Jürgen. "Einige strategische Probleme des Herbstfeldzuges." DER BEFREIUNGSKRIEG 1813. Edited by Peter Hoffmann et al. Berlin: Akademie, 1967.

356. Usczeck, Hans Jürgen. SCHARNHORST, THEORETIKER-REFORMER-PATRIOT, SEIN WERK UND SEINE WIRKUNG IN SEINER UND FUER UNSERE ZEIT. 3d ed. Berlin: Militärverlag der DDR, 1979.

357. Usinger, Rudolf. "Gneisenau." HISTORISCHE ZEITSCHRIFT 14 (1865): 351-96.

358. Ussel, Jean d'. LA DEFECTION DE LA PRUSSE, DECEMBRE 1812-MARS 1813. Paris: Plon, 1907.

359. Valjavec, Fritz. DIE ENTSTEHUNG DER POLITISCHEN STROEMUNGEN IN DEUTSCHLAND 1770-1815. Munich: Oldenbourg, 1951.

360. Varnhagen von Ense, K.A.   BIOGRAPHISCHE DENKMALE.   Berlin:
      Riemer, 1845-46. 5 vols.

361. Varnhagen von Ense, K.A.   BLAETTER AUS DER PREUSSISCHEN
      GESCHICHTE. Leipzig: Brockhaus, 1868. 3 vols.

362. Varnhagen von Ense, K.A.   DENKWUERDIGKEITEN DES EIGENEN LEBENS.
      Leipzig: Brockhaus, 1843. 3 vols.

363. Vaupel, Rudolf, ed.   DIE REORGANISATION DES PREUSSISCHEN
      STAATES UNTER STEIN UND HARDENBERG.   Part 2. DAS PREUSSISCHE
      HEER VOM TILSITER FRIEDEN BIZ ZUR BEFREIUNG: 1807-1814.
      Publikationen aus den Preussischen Staatsarchiven, vol. 94.
      Leipzig: Hirzel, 1938.

364. Venzky, Gabriele.   DIE RUSSISCH-DEUTSCHE LEGION IN DEN JAHREN
      1811-1815. Veröffentlichungen des Osteuropa-Instituts München,
      vol. 30. Wiesbaden: Harrasowitz, 1966.

365. Vidalenç, Jean.   "Les Notables des départments hanséatiques."
      REVUE D'HISTOIRE MODERNE ET CONTEMPORAINE 17 (1970): 777-92.

366. Vogel, Barbara, ed.   PREUSSISCHE REFORMEN 1807-1820.   Neue
      Wissenschaftliche Bibliothek, 96: Geschichte. Königstein/Ts.:
      Verlagsgruppe Athenäum, Hain, Scriptor, Hanstein, 1980.

367. W., C. von. [Müffling].   BETRACHTUNGEN UEBER DIE GROSSEN
      OPERATIONEN UND SCHLACHTEN DER FELDZUGE VON 1813 UND 1814.
      Berlin, Posen: Mittler, 1825.

368. W., C. von. [Müffling].   DIE PREUSSISCH-RUSSISCHE CAMPAGNE IM
      JAHR 1813 BIS ZUM WAFFENSTILLSTANDE. Breslau: Kaysers, 1813.

369. Wachler, Theodor Friedrich Ludwig.   ERNSTE WORTE DER
      VATERLANDSLIEBE AN ALLE, WELCHE DEUTSCHE SIND UND BLEIBEN
      WOLLEN. Cassel: Krieger, 1814.

370. Wagner, Karl.   DIE FLUGSCHRIFTENLITERATUR DES KRIEGES VON 1809.
      Anno Neun: Bücherei des Oesterreichischen Volksschriften-
      vereins, vol. 5. Brixen: Tyrolia, 1912.

371. Warda, Arthur, and Carl Diesch, eds.   BRIEFE VON UND AN JOHANN
      GEORG SCHEFFNER. Veröffentlichungen des Vereins für die
      Geschichte von Ost- und Westpreussen.   Munich, Leipzig,
      Königsberg: Duncker & Humblot, 1918-38. 5 vols.

372. Welsch, Erwin K.   LIBRARIES AND ARCHIVES IN GERMANY.
      Pittsburgh, Pa.: The Council for European Studies, 1975.

373. Weniger, Erich.   GOETHE UND DIE GENERALE DER FREIHEITSKRIEGE:
      GEIST, BILDUNG, SOLDATENTUM.   2d ed.   Stuttgart: Metzler,
      1959.

374. Wermke, Ernst. BIBLIOGRAPHIE DER GESCHICHTE VON OST- UND WESTPREUSSEN. Königsberg: Gräfe & Unzer; Marburg a.d. Lahn: Herder Institut, 1933-78. 8 vols.

375. Wertheimer, Eduard. "Wien und das Kriegsjahr 1813: Ein Beitrag zur Geschichte der Befreiungskriege, nach ungedruckten Quellen." ARCHIV FUER OESTERREICHISCHE GESCHICHTE 79 (1893): 355-400.

376. Will, Günther. "Neithardt Graf von Gneisenau." WEHRWISSEN-SCHAFTLICHE RUNDSCHAU 12 (1962): 437-51.

377. Winter, Georg, ed. DIE REORGANISATION DES PREUSSISCHEN STAATES UNTER STEIN UND HARDENBERG. Publikationen aus den Preussischen Staatsarchiven, vol. 93. Leipzig: Hirzel, 1931.

378. Wittichen, Friedrich Carl, ed. BRIEFE VON UND AN FRIEDRICH VON GENTZ. Munich: Oldenbourg, 1910-13. 4 vols.

379. Wohlfeil, Rainer. SPANIEN UND DIE DEUTSCHE ERHEBUNG, 1808-1814. Wiesbaden: Steiner, 1965.

380. Wohlfeil, Rainer. "Untersuchungen zur Geschichte des Rheinbundes, 1806-1813: Das Verhältnis Dalbergs zu Napoleon." ZEITSCHRIFT FUER DIE GESCHICHTE DES OBERRHEINS 108 (1960): 85-108.

381. Woinowich von Belobreska, Emil von, and Alois Veltzé, eds. OESTERREICH IN DEN BEFREIUNGSKRIEGEN, 1813-1815. Vienna: Verein für vaterländische Literatur, 1911-14. 10 vols.

382. Wollstein, Günter. "Scharnhorst und die Französische Revolution." HISTORISCHE ZEITSCHRIFT 227 (1978): 325-52.

383. Woltmann, Karl von. "Ueber den Tugendbund," and "Preussische Charaktere." Edited by Franz Hadamowsky. FORSCHUNGEN ZUR BRANDENBURGISCHEN UND PREUSSISCHEN GESCHICHTE 40 (1927): 88-124.

384. Zajewski, Wladzslaw. "Gdansk--objet de la rivalité des puissances au temps de Napoléon." ACTA POLONIAE HISTORICA 26 (1972): 31-45.

385. Zedlitz, Leopold von. DIE STAATSKRAEFTE DER PREUSSISCHEN MONARCHIE UNTER FRIEDRICH WILHELM III. Berlin: Maurersche Buchhandlung, 1828-30. 3 vols.

386. Zimmer, Hasko. AUF DEM ALTAR DES VATERLANDES: RELIGION UND PATRIOTISMUS IN DER DEUTSCHEN KRIEGSLYRIK DES 19. JAHRHUNDERTS. Germanistik, vol. 3. Frankfurt a.M.: Thiesen, 1971.

387. Zimmerman, Wilhelm. DIE BEFREIUNGSKAEMPFE DER DEUTSCHEN GEGEN NAPOLEON. 3d ed. Stuttgart: Rieger, 1859.

388. Zwengel, Otto. "Scharnhorst: Soldat und Bürger." REVUE MILITAIRE GENERALE 5 (1973): 753-59.

ADDENDUM

389. Berding, Helmut, and Hans Peter Ullmann, eds. DEUTSCHLAND
     ZWISCHEN REVOLUTION UND RESTAURATION. Athenäum-Droste
     Taschenbücher Geschichte 7240. Königstein-Ts.: Athenäum,
     1981.

390. Denecke, Ludwig. DIE NACHLAESSE IN DEN BIBLIOTHEKEN DER
     BUNDESREPUBLIK DEUTSCHLAND. Verzeichnis der schriftlichen
     Nachlässe in deutschen Archiven und Bibliotheken, vol. 2.
     Boppard-Rhein: Boldt, 1981.

391. DEUTSCH BIOGRAPHISCHES ARCHIV: EIN KUMULATION AUS 254 DER
     WICHTIGSTEN BIOGRAPHISCHEN NACHSCHLAGEWERKE FUER DEN DEUTSCHEN
     BEREICH BIS ZUM AUSGANG DES NEUNZENTEN JAHRHUNDERTS. Edited by
     Bernhard Fabian under the direction of Willi Gorzny.
     Mikrofiche. Munich: Saur, 1982-.

392. GESAMTVERZEICHNIS DES DEUTSCHSPRACHIGEN SCHRIFTTUM (GV)
     1700-1910. Munich, New York, London, and Paris: Saur, 1979-.
     (124 vols through 1984).

393. GESAMTVERZEICHNIS DES DEUTSCHSPRACHIGEN SCHRIFTTUM (GV)
     1911-1965. Munich, New York, London, and Paris: Saur,
     1976-81. 150 vols.

394. Gray, Marion. PRUSSIA IN TRANSITION: SOCIETY AND POLITICS
     UNDER THE STEIN REFORM MINISTRY OF 1808. Transaction of the
     American Philosophical Society, vol. 76. Philadelphia:
     American Philosophical Society, 1986.

395. Nitschke, Heinz G. DIE PREUSSISCHEN MILITAERREFORMEN
     1807-1813: DIE TAETIGEIT DER MIOLITAERREORGANISATIONKOMMISSION
     UND IHRE AUSWIRKUNGEN AUF DIE PUEUSSISCHEN ARMEE. Kleine
     Beiträge zur Geschichte Preussens, vol. 2. Berlin: Haude und
     Spener, 1983.

396. Scheel, Henrich, ed. PREUSSISCHEN REFORMEN, WIRKUNGEN UND
     GRENZEN: AUS ANLASS DES TODESTAGES DER FREIHERRN VOM UND ZUM
     STEIN. Sitzungsber der Akademie der Wissenschaften der DDR:
     Gesellschaftswissenschaften 1982 1G. Berlin: Akademie, 1982.

397. Showalter, Dennis E. GERMAN MILITARY HISTORY 1648-1982: A
     CRITICAL BIBLIOGRAPHY. Garland History Bibliographies of
     Social Science 113. Military History Bibliographies 3. New
     York and London: Garland, 1984.

398. Vogel, Barbara. ALLGEMEINE GEWERBEFREIHEIT: DIE REFORMPOLITIK
     DES PREUSSISCHEN STAATSKANZLERS HARDENBERG (1810-1820).
     Kritische Studien zur Geschichtsweissenschaft, vol. 57.
     Göttingen: Vandenhoeck und Ruprecht, 1983.

399. Weis, Eberhard, and Elisabeth Müller-Luckner, eds. REFORMEN IM
     RHEINBUENDISCHEN DEUTSCHLAND. Schriften des Historischen
     Kollegs: Kolloquien 4. Munich: Oldenbourg, 1984.

CHAPTER XIV

THE COLLAPSE OF EMPIRE

Col. John R. Elting, U.S. Military Academy, Emertius

Historians' interest in the muddy, bloody battles of 1814 has been concentrated, and justly so, on Napoleon's personal campaign across northeastern France. It is oddly reminiscent of his first Italian campaign of 1796--a scrambling, improvised war of swift maneuver and many small battles, waged on a frayed logistical shoestring. This time the odds against him were too heavy; his lieutenants, clogged by the combat fatigue of two years of defeat, had lost their "consecrated fire."

Of the secondary campaigns that covered Napoleon's flanks and rear, Soult's struggle in southern France has been joyfully recounted by English writers of all degrees of competence. Eugène's defense of northern Italy and Maison's operations along the the Dutch frontier have received comparatively little attention, though both were largely successful. Beyond them was a war of sieges, many of them poorly recorded, from northern Spain to Dalmatia and into central Germany where bypassed French garrisons clung to communications centers deep in Allied territory.

GENERAL WORKS

As background studies of Napoleon's whole career, and of the 1814 campaign's and the Elba interlude's places in it, we are fortunate in two comparatively recent books, Vincent Cronin's NAPOLEON BONAPARTE: AN INTIMATE BIOGRAPHY (90) and Felix Markham's NAPOLEON (239). Cronin's book is especially valuable for the unsparing common sense and scholarship with which he evaluates the memoirs, actual and alleged, of Napoleon's contemporaries. Correlli Barnett's more recent BONAPARTE (18)--as its title suggests--reverts to that mid-nineteenth century British school of "Napoleonic history" in which a squat little Corsican bounder finally meets his just deserts at the immaculate hands of that true-blue English gentleman, our own Iron Duke. Similarly, a new French work, LA GRANDE ARMEE, 1804-1815 (41), by Georges Blond is lively and pretentious but riddled with errors. By contrast, Henry Lachouque's NAPOLEON ET LA GARDE IMPERIALE (200) is more than a simple history of that famous combat organization. Unabashedly partisan in its viewpoint, it manages to be bluntly factual concerning the hasty 1813-1814 reorganization of the Guard and Napoleon's brief period on Elba. (A translation by Anne S.K. Brown, THE ANATOMY OF GLORY, is both well done and magnificently illustrated.) Lachouque also has contributed VICTOIRES SANS SOLDATS: NAPOLEON EN 1814" (202).

For the actual military developments, we have several first-rate books. Lefebvre de Béhaine's NAPOLEON ET LES ALLIES SUR LE RHIN (218) shows how both sides began the campaign militarily and diplomatically, with interesting observations as to what the Allies actually considered the "natural limits" of France. The developing operations are described in his LA CAMPAGNE DE FRANCE (216). Henry Houssaye's 1814 (178) is a meticulously researched description of the actual operations. It lacks good maps, but this need is supplied by

Vincent J. Esposito and John R. Elting's A MILITARY HISTORY AND ATLAS
OF THE NAPOLEONIC WARS (123). Other sources include Félix Bouvier's
LES PREMIERS COMBATS DU 1814 (50); I. Campana's LA CAMPAGNE DE
FRANCE, 1814 (66); Félix Ponteil's LA CHUTE DE NAPOLEON ET LA CRISE
FRANCAISE DE 1814-1815 (290); Philippe de Ségur's LA CAMPAGNE DE
FRANCE, DU RHIN A FONTAINEBLEAU, 1814 (331); and Jean Thiry's LA
CAMPAGNE DE FRANCE DE 1814 (344).

Among the traditional sources Clausewitz's LA CAMPAGNE DE 1814
EN FRANCE (81) reflects his personal involvement and sense of Prussia
triumphant to a degree unusual in his normally balanced writing, yet
contains some sharp observations. Jomini's LIFE OF NAPOLEON (187) is
comparatively useless; Jomini had no real part in this campaign and
his writings derive more from ego than research. In turn, Theodore
A. Dodge's NAPOLEON (106) is largely from Jomini and filled to boot
with Dodge's typical hero worship. NAPOLEON AS A GENERAL (385) by
Yorck von Wartenburg can be useful but is heavy reading and stuffed
with mid-Victorian moralizing. F. Loraine Petre's NAPOLEON AT BAY,
1814 (281), though written with limited knowledge of the actual
armies involved, is a work of some conscience that emphasizes the
Allied operations. By contrast, Thiers's HISTORY OF THE CONSULATE
AND THE EMPIRE UNDER NAPOLEON (343) deals loosely with facts and
historical details, yet is valuable for its wide coverage of the
period and so can be used as an overall outline.

Among the useful English-language works are David Chandler's THE
CAMPAIGNS OF NAPOLEON (72); Gordon A. Craig's PROBLEMS OF COALITION
WARFARE: THE MILITARY ALLIANCE AGAINST NAPOLEON (89); and James P.
Lawford's NAPOLEON: THE LAST CAMPAIGNS (213). The operations of the
main Allied forces under Schwarzenberg and Blücher are covered by
Westmorland in MEMOIR OF THE OPERATIONS OF THE ALLIED ARMIES (376);
Maurice H. Weil's LA CAMPAGNE DE 1814 (370) makes a detailed study of
Allied cavalry operations. For the Russian viewpoint, there is Serge
Andolenko's AIGLES DE NAPOLEON CONTRA DRAPEAUX DU TSAR (9) and Modest
Bogdanovich's GESCHICHTE DER KRIEGES 1814 (42). Von
Pflugk-Harttung's 1813-1815 (283) and Theodor Rehtwisch's GESCHICHTE
DER FREIHEITSKRIEGE IN DEN JAHREN 1812-1815 (300) cover German
viewpoints. As a final caution, descriptions of the 1814 campaigns
published in France during 1814-1820-odd must be regarded with
suspicion, this being a period productive of more-or-less bogus
memoirs and officially inspired histories lauding the Christian
virtues of France's "legitimate" rulers. INSTRUCTION SUR L'HISTOIRE
DE FRANCE by one M. le Ragois (295) is a sample of how French
children were taught to appreciate the blessings of "the beneficent
yoke of a legitimate rule," once Heaven had disposed of the "insolent
conqueror." (The Bourbons ungratefully preferred to believe they had
returned in 1814 and 1815 on the wings of divine justice rather than
in the baggage wagons of the Allied armies.)

Allied diplomats and the French traitors they suborned
undoubtedly contributed as much to Napoleon's 1814 defeat as the
frequently bumbling Allied generals. Arthur Bryant's somewhat
toplofty THE AGE OF ELEGANCE, 1812-1822 (60) makes a good
introduction to their activities, to be followed by works such as
Henry Kissinger's A WORLD RESTORED (194); Enno Kraehe's METTERNICH'S
GERMAN POLICY (198); C. Dupuis's LE MINISTERE DE TALLEYRAND EN 1814
(118); Charles Webster's THE CONGRESS OF VIENNA (368) and THE FOREIGN
POLICY OF CASTLEREAGH (369); and Auguste Fournier's DER CONGRESS VON

CHATILLON (135). The results of these diplomatic intrigues and dou-
ble-dealings appear in Marcel Dupont's NAPOLEON ET LA TRAHISON DES
MARECHAUX, 1814 (27); Alexis Durand's NAPOLEON A FONTAINEBLEAU (119);
and Rivollet and Albertini's LES MARECHAUX D'EMPIRE ET LA PREMIERE
ABDICATION (304). Other results are described in Maurice Weil's
PRINCE EUGENE ET MURAT, 1813-1814 (371); Franklin B. Scott's
"Bernadotte and the Throne of France, 1814" (330); and Léonce
Pingaud's BERNADOTTE, NAPOLEON, ET LES BOURBONS (1797-1814) (287).

General coverage of English operations during the secondary
campaign along the Pyrenees is adequately provided by Oman (270, 271)
and Napier (258). For quick reference D.J. Goodspeed's THE BRITISH
CAMPAIGNS IN THE PENINSULA, 1808-1814 (155) is handy; S.P.G. Ward's
WELLINGTON'S HEADQUARTERS (365) deals with administrative problems;
Jac Weller's WELLINGTON IN THE PENINSULA, 1808-1814 (372) is frankly
hero-worshipful, but gives unusually good studies of the terrain.
French operations are covered by General Lamiraux's ETUDES DE GUERRE:
LA MANOEUVRE DE SOULT (1813-1814) (204). Unfortunately, Foy's (137)
bitter history was cut short by his sudden death, but Geoffroy de
Grandmaison's L'ESPAGNE ET NAPOLEON (146) furnishes considerable
background. There is also E. Lapene's CAMPAGNE DE 1813-14 SUR
L'EBRE, LES PYRENEES, ET LA GARONNE (207). José Gómez de Arteche y
Moro's GUERRA DE LA INDEPENDENCIA (154) is probably the best Spanish
source; Otto von Pivka's THE PORTUGUESE ARMY IN THE NAPOLEONIC WARS
(289) is likewise helpful.

Operations in northern Italy can be reviewed in R. John Rath's
THE FALL OF THE NAPOLEONIC KINGDOM OF ITALY (297) and Martin
Vignolle's PRECIS HISTORIQUE DES OPERATIONS MILITAIRES DE L'ARMEE
D'ITALIE (359). The specific aspects of Murat's coat-turning are
assessed by Albert Espitalier in NAPOLEON ET LE ROI MURAT (1808-1815)
(122); R.M. Johnston in THE NAPOLEONIC EMPIRE IN SOUTHERN ITALY
(186); and J.P. Bellaire in PRECIS DE L'INVASION DES ETATS ROMAINS
(31). The last, lingering operations in the Adriatic area have not
attracted authors. Gunther E. Rothenberg's THE MILITARY BORDER IN
CROATIA, 1740-1881 (310) and THE HABSBURG ARMY IN THE NAPOLEONIC WARS
(311) contain useful material on them, and also on the Italian
campaign. British service publications furnish a scattering of
articles, such as D.W. King's "A Note on the Operations of George D.
Robertson's Force from Lissa" (192) and "A British Officer in the
Eastern Adriatic, 1812-1815" (191).

The campaign in Holland and Belgium had two distinct
parts--Carnot's defense of the key seaport of Antwerp and Maison's
war of maneuver. Both are given considerable attention by Thiers
(343); the first is specifically treated by Henri E. Wauwermans's
NAPOLEON ET CARNOT (367); the second by J.J.R. Calmon-Maison's LE
GENERAL MAISON ET LE Ier CORPS DE LA GRANDE ARMEE (62). Incidents of
the latter also are sprinkled through Antoine F. de Brack's famous
AVANT-POSTES DE CAVALERIE LEGERE (51). G.J. Renier's GREAT BRITAIN
AND THE NETHERLANDS, 1813-1815 (302) provides background.

An excellent introduction to the many sieges of this campaign is
Viollet-le-Duc's HISTOIRE D'UN FORTRESSE (360) with its detailed, if
imaginary, description of Napoleonic siegecraft. Davout's famous
defense of Hamburg is celebrated by Auguste d'Avout in LA DEFENSE DE
HAMBOURG EN 1813-1814 (15) and by Philip P. Holzhausen's DAVOUT IN
HAMBURG: EIN BEITRAG ZUR GESCHICHTE DER JAHRE 1813-1814 (176). LE
SIEGE DE GLOGAU, 1813-1814 (16) by Commandant Bages describes another

notable defense that lasted until news of the Emperor's abdication.
LA DEFENSE DE MONZON by F. Canonge (68) recounts the forlorn stand of
an isolated garrison in northern Spain. The CARNET DE LA SABRETACHE
provides--among others--"Le Blocus de Neuf-Brisach en 1814" (80) and
"Les Généraux Le Marois et de Valazé et la glorieuse remise de
Magdebourg en 1814" (97). E. Ducere's BAYONNE SOUS L'EMPIRE: LE
BLOCUS DE 1814 (113) deals with the most bloody-minded siege in
southern France.
      Napoleon's brief reign on Elba is well covered. Lachouque (200)
already has been cited. Neil Campbell, the British commissioner,
wrote NAPOLEON AT FONTAINEBLEAU AND ELBA (67) upon which Henry D.
Wolff's THE ISLAND EMPIRE (381) is based to a considerable extent.
French sources include Paul Bartel's NAPOLEON A L'ILE DE L'ELBE (20);
Robert Christophe's NAPOLEON, EMPEREUR DE L'ILE DE ELBE (77); Paul
Gruyer's NAPOLEON ROI DE L'ILE D'ELBE (165); and Léon Gabriel
Pélissier's LE REGISTRE DE L'ILE DE ELBE (264). Pélissier also
edited the MEMOIRES DE PONS DE L'HERAULT, the manager of the Elba
mines (277). For a geographical description of Napoleon's brief
Kingdom, see Averil MacKenzie-Grieve's ASPECTS OF ELBA AND THE OTHER
ISLANDS OF THE TUSCAN ARCHIPELAGO (234).
      The effect of 1814's European developments on the United States'
concurrent war with England are expertly covered in Henry Adams's THE
WAR OF 1812 (3). THE PEACE OF CHRISTMAS EVE by Fred L. Engelman
(121) reviews the long, battered course of peace negotiations. Naval
warfare in particular is the theme of C.S. Forester's AGE OF FIGHTING
SAIL (131), which brings up Wellington's dependence on American
foodstuffs smuggled out of the United States--a fact amplified in W.
Freeman Galpin's "The American Grain Trade to the Spanish Peninsula,
1810-1814" (142).

BIBLIOGRAPHIES

      Thoroughly useful references are Laszlo M. Alfoldi's THE ARMIES
OF AUSTRIA-HUNGARY AND GERMANY, 1740-1914 (6); Friedrich M.
Kircheisen's BIBLIOGRAPHIE NAPOLEONIENNE (193); M. Lyons's THE
RUSSIAN IMPERIAL ARMY: BIBLIOGRAPHY OF REGIMENTAL HISTORIES AND
RELATED WORKS (230); and John F. Sloan's MILITARY HISTORY OF RUSSIA:
A PRELIMINARY SURVEY OF THE SOURCES (336). As might be expected, the
British army is well represented in this category--A.P.C. Bruce's AN
ANNOTATED BIBLIOGRAPHY OF THE BRITISH ARMY, 1660-1914 (58); John B.M.
Frederick's LINEAGE BOOK OF THE BRITISH ARMY (138); and Arthur
White's A BIBLIOGRAPHY OF REGIMENTAL HISTORIES OF THE BRITISH ARMY
(377). In addition to these there are the excellent bibliographies
available in Oman's works (270, 271). During at least the first
decade of this century THE CARNET DE LA SABRETACHE published an
annual bibliography of books printed during the year which might
interest its members.

ARCHIVAL SOURCES AND PUBLISHED DOCUMENTS

      As for all other campaigns the CORRESPONDANCE DE NAPOLEON Ier
(259) is the major reference for the 1814 campaign. Some documents
missing from this truly monumental work have been picked up by the
CARNET DE LA SABRETACHE (261, 263), the latter showing Napoleon's
concern while at Elba over activities of the Barbary pirates. Adam

Skalkowski's EN MARGE DE LA CORRESPONDANCE DE NAPOLEON I: DOCUMENTS
(335) covers letters annotated or written by Napoleon, dealing with
his Polish and Lithuanian troops. Both the Bibliotheque Nationale
(260) and Charles de La Roncière (262) have published Napoleon's
letters to Marie Louise. A. Martinien's TABLEAUX PAR CORPS ET PAR
BATAILLES DES OFFICIERS TUES ET BLESSES (243) provides a quick,
definitive check on unit participation in the 1814 battles and
campaigns and a rough estimation of casualties. Another specialized
reference is Jacques Belmas's JOURNAUX DES SIEGES FAITS OU SOUTENUS
PAR LES FRANCAIS DANS LA PENINSULE, DE 1807 A 1814 (33). "Compiègne
en 1814" (315) is a local official's history of that little town's
amazing stand against the Allied army. Frédéric Masson's (246)
"Notes et documents provenant des archives du général de division
comte d'Anthouard" (Eugène's senior aide-de-camp) questions Eugène's
good faith toward Napoleon.

     For the Allies, Castlereagh's MEMOIRS AND CORRESPONDENCE (226),
and SCENES OF RUSSIAN COURT LIFE: CORRESPONDENCE OF ALEXANDER I WITH
HIS SISTER CATHERINE (5) are telling self-portraits of two very
different leaders. Even more effective are the dispatches of
Wellington (373, 374).

MEMOIRS, JOURNALS, AND EYEWITNESS ACCOUNTS

     Probably no period has been so productive of this type of
literature, which appears in all degrees of scholarship and simple
honesty. As examples of the latter, the memoirs of Talleyrand (338)
and Fouché (134) reflect only their authors' polished powers of
prevarication and talent for self-preservation. Pierre Joseph
Proudhon's COMMENTAIRES SUR LES MEMOIRES DE FOUCHE (293) is an
interesting corrective. Of the more familiar sources, Marbot (238)
remained with his regiment's depot, concerned with nothing more
glamorous than remounts, restless Belgians, and Prussian irregulars;
Private Wheeler (222) spent most of 1814 in the hospital. Coignet
(208) and Parquin (275) did their duty as, respectively, imperial
wagonmaster and captain of chasseurs à cheval of the Imperial Guard;
they have interesting little tales to tell, though Parquin seems to
have somewhat scrambled his chronology. Of the marshals, Marmont
began 1814 with credit, only to be the first to turn his coat; his
MEMOIRES (240) mirror that dichotomy, combining keen professionalism
with cheap evasions and excuses for his treason. Macdonald's
SOUVENIRS (233) obviously were written to curry favor with the
Bourbons; in addition, he sought to refurbish his 1813-1814 record
which consisted largely of arriving a day late, retreating
unnecessarily, and generally ignoring his orders. Berthier left no
memoirs, but has a thorough biography by Victor B. Derrécagaix (102)
and two simpler ones by S.J. Watson (366) and Alberto Lumbroso (229).
Ney, as might be expected, has numerous biographies (44, 133, 144) as
well as the memoirs published by his family (265), but none of these
explain his erratic character. François Victor has provided a
biography of Marshal Victor (355); Frignet Despreaux one of Mortier
(104). Oudinot's so-called "memoirs" (272) are noted as "compiled
from the hitherto unpublished souvenirs" of his wife. Jean F.B.
Koch's excellent MEMOIRES DE MASSENA (196) unfortunately is of little
use for 1814 since Masséna held a territorial command in southern
France and saw no action. Suchet (337) saw only trivial rear-guard

actions in Catalonia. Lefebvre accompanied the Emperor but had no command; his limited activities can be traced in Joseph Wirth's LE MARECHAL LEFEBVRE, DUC DE DANTZIG (379). Soult's memoirs cover only his earlier years of service. Davout has John G. Gallaher's THE IRON MARSHAL (141); two older works by L.J.G. de Chenier (75) and Henri Vigier (358) are also useful. Future marshal Grouchy (164) took an expert and honorable part in Napoleon's campaign, cut short at Craonne by another of his many wounds. Books describing Napoleon's marshals as a group are common enough, but seldom of any particular value. Early versions, such as J.T. Headley's NAPOLEON AND HIS MARSHALS (170), are more enthusiastic than informative. Modern versions tend to contain as much caricaturization as characterization; none show much research.

Albert Du Casse's MEMOIRES of Eugène (111) and of Napoleon's weakling older brother Joseph (112) are essential references, containing much of their original correspondence. Caulaincourt's NO PEACE WITH NAPOLEON (71) is equally important, though it leaves unanswered questions which moved Houssaye to dub him a "sniveler." Lavalette wrote a frank, common sense record (212); by contrast, Paul C. Thiébault (who was at Hamburg with Davout) appears to have disliked everyone (342) and to have sat up late of nights inventing clever little lies about them. Agathon Fain, Napoleon's secretary (125, 126), and the veteran staff officer Mathieu Dumas (115, 116) are excellent sources, as are Napoleon's senior medical officers, Pierre F. Percy (278) and Dominique J. Larrey (210). Normally a competent minister of police, Savary was overconfident in 1814 and so had to try to explain (328) his failure to ride close herd on Talleyrand.

There are dozens of "mémoires" and "souvenirs" left by lesser figures. "Lettres du brigadier Pilloy" (340) tell of a corporal of the 13th Cuirassier Regiment (then in Spain with Suchet) who ended up helping defend Magdeburg. Commandant Vivien was a battalion commander at Bayonne at the war's end; his accounts (361) are colorful. Louis A. Gougeat (157) of the 20th Dragoon Regiment served as "cavalier d'ordonnance" to his company commander. Lauthonnye (211) was a fervent Bonapartist from a doggedly royalist family, and a roaring boy indeed; his description of French life during the Elba interlude is wry comedy of sorts. Lauthonnye's picture of the confusion and resentment caused by the Bourbon's ham-handed reorganization of the French army is expanded and deepened by Saint-Chamans (320) and Gaspard de Soultrait (325). Hubet François Biot served through 1814 as aide-de-camp to General C.P. Pajol and was in the wild affair at Montereau (139). Elzéar Blaze (39) and J.B. Barrès (19) were cheerful young officers, always alert for the interesting and the comic aspects of life.

Among the Russian commanders, Levin von Bennigsen won victories in his MEMOIRES (34) that are not recorded elsewhere. Louis Alexandre Langeron (205) left a self-satisfied account of an undistinguished career. Woldemar Löwenstern's autobiography (223) has interesting material. Michael and Diane Josselson's THE COMMANDER (188) presents the life of Barclay de Tolly, the unpopular Scots-German who gave the Russian army much of its stability in spite of Bennigsen and Alexander. Berend von Uexküll's diaries, recently published as ARMS AND THE WOMAN (350), should have been titled "Many

Women and Occasional Arms"; its editing is remarkably ignorant, but it does give a picture of the Allied occupation of France.

German sources include Johann Wesemenn's KANONIER DES KAISERS (375); Frederich Müffling's AUS MEINEN LEBEN (256); and LEBEN DES FELDMARSCHALLS N. VON GNEISENAU (280) by G.H. Pertz and Hans Delbrück. British memoirs and biographies are more than plentiful. Elizabeth Longford's WELLINGTON: THE YEARS OF THE SWORD (227) and Antony Brett-James's WELLINGTON AT WAR (53) are outstanding. In his SOLDIER'S GLORY (30) George Bell recorded the war in southern France as a junior officer saw it, as did Edmund Wheatley (171) with the somewhat unfashionable King's German Legion. David Brown of the 21st Foot (56) took part in the sideshow attack on Genoa--and later fought at Bladensburg and New Orleans. THE MEMOIRS OF PRIVATE JAMES GUNN (313) has many stories of the professional relationship between French and British soldiers. By contrast, Captain William Verner (354) of the 7th Hussars expressed lofty disapproval of an English-speaking French officer who waged effective partisan warfare behind Wellington's lines. For an Englishman's view of the Allied invasion of France, the PRIVATE DIARY (378) of that ubiquitous and adventuresome marplot, Sir Robert Wilson, remains essential. John Burgoyne--a by-blow son of John Burgoyne of Saratoga celebrity--was an engineer officer under Wellington; his LIFE AND CORRESPONDENCE (61) covers an amazing variety of experiences. As a final note, any researcher afflicted with secondhand combat fatigue after working through dozens of such memoirs should consult F.J. Huddleston's scholarly WARRIORS IN UNDRESS (181).

SPECIALIZED WORKS

The hasty rebuilding of the French army in late 1813-early 1814 is illustrated by Pierre Devaux's "Les Gardes nationaux mobilises du Cher, 1814-1815" (105); Guy d'Ambert's "Les Légions de gardes nationaux mobilises du Gers, 1813-1814" (8); and especially in Jean and Raoul Brumon's LES ECLAIREURS DE LA GARDE IMPERIALE, 1813-1814 (59), as well as Lachouque (200). J. Cochon's "Un Remplacement militaire à la fin de l'empire" (83) is a rather poignant story of draft-dodging and substitutes. Reminders that some thousands of Spaniards and Portuguese still followed Napoleon's eagles are in Ribeiro Arthur's A LEGIAO PORTUGUEZA (11), Claude Achard's "Organization militaire des prisonniers de guerre espagnols, 1808-1814" (2), and Paul Boppe's LES ESPAGNOLS A LA GRANDE-ARMEE (46). The more numerous Poles and Lithuanians are covered by Skalkowski (335) and by Zaluski's (388) and Dautancourt's (323) accounts of the Polish lancers of the Guard. Regimental histories of all armies are plentiful, if usually uninspired. One that is especially pertinent to the 1814 campaign is that of the Imperial Guard's handymen and rear guard specialists, Dr. Lomier's LA BATAILLON DES MARINS DE LA GARDE, 1803-1815 (224).

Among useful studies of various battles, Colonel McCarthy's "L'Affaire de Montereau" (232) explains the impact of Pajol's famous charge--the raw French cavalrymen's horses literally ran away with them! J. Besnus's "Considérations militaries sur la bataille de Toulouse" (37) is a dissection of Soult's sagging army. AUTOUR DE LA BATAILLE DE MONTMIRAIL (163), by Edgard Grosjean, tells of one of Napoleon's last victories. "Un Episode du passage du 5e Corps de

cavalerie de la Grande-Armée à Nancy le 14 janvier 1814" (316)
illustrates the hasty French withdrawal during the first weeks of the
campaign. A. Dry's REIMS EN 1814 PENDANT L'INVASION (109) and R.
Ferino's SOISSONS EN 1814 (129) cover operations around these two key
cities. Episodes of the battle for Paris are in Augustin Marie
Aboville's "Notes sur l'attaque de Paris" (1); "Les Polytechniciens
en 1814" (322); and A. Dubois's LES AMBULANCES VERSAILLAISES EN 1814
(110). For southern France, F.C. Beatson's WELLINGTON: THE CROSSING
OF THE GAVES AND THE BATTLE OF ORTHEZ (22) covers one of Wellington's
most able maneuvers, while G. Doublet's L'ARIEGE EN 1814 ET 1815
(107) presents the problems of a French frontier department. The
outburst of royalist feeling that followed Wellington's invasion is
described in L. de Santi's NOTES ET DOCUMENTS SUR LES INTRIGUES
ROYALISTES DANS LE MIDI DE LA FRANCE (327). Articles by McCance
(231) and Austin (14) seek to explain the failure of the British
surprise attack on Bergen-op-Zoom in Holland. Post-war squabbling
between Louis XVIII's new fancy-pants Garde Royale and the rest of
the French army did much to prepare the way for Napoleon's return
from Elba; "La Maison du roi et la ligne" (318) gives examples of
their brawling.

PERIODICALS

The most useful of the military journals is unquestionably the
CARNET DE LA SABRETACHE (392), published by the Société "La
Sabretache" since 1893. A close competitor is the JOURNAL OF THE
SOCIETY FOR ARMY HISTORICAL RESEARCH (398), from 1921 to date. The
journal of the ROYAL UNITED SERVICE INSTITUTION (397), the REVUE
HISTORIQUE DE L'ARMEE (396), and the REVUE DE LA SOCIETE DES AMIS DU
MUSEE DE L'ARMEE (394) are all useful, as is the REVUE DE PARIS
(395). LE BRIQUET (391), published in Orleans by L'Amicale des
Collectionneurs de Figurines Historiques du Centre-Loire since 1959,
is a rough-and-ready mimeographed publication which frequently
presents sound articles. Another comparatively new magazine,
UNIFORMES (400), notable for its excellent art work, contains a good
deal of incidental information. PANOPLIES (393) is a similar
publication. SOUVENIR NAPOLEONIEN (399) covers both the First and
Second Empires.

FUTURE RESEARCH

The major puzzles, to me, of this campaign are in Paris and
Lyons. Henri Clarke, Napoleon's minister of war, had been
hardworking, if obtuse. In 1814, however, he appears to have
neglected his duties--for example, he failed to provide a bridge
train until the campaign was almost over. Once it was, he cast
himself joyfully into the arms of the Bourbons. In all probability
his incompetence was as much inspired as natural. In like fashion,
Augereau refused to carry out his assigned mission of moving
northward to cut Schwarzenberg's communications. He had fought well
in 1813, but now some of his subordinates suspected him of treason.
Was it a deliberate betrayal or had he simply mutinied as some of his
colleagues were soon to do openly? Either way, "the Emperor was not
well-served."

The full story of the definitely treasonous American trade in
foodstuffs--which fed the British forces in Canada, as well as

Wellington's army--still awaits its historian. Without it, could Wellington have pushed his forces into southern France?

Work needs to be done on the logistical operations of the various armies in the campaign. Moreover, it would be useful to continue the efforts of French scholars in analyzing the impact of the invasion upon the departments and communes of Eastern France.

Oddly, a number of the marshals who had, sometimes for better, usually for worse, key roles in 1814 still lack competent biographers. Examples are Augereau, Soult, Victor, Oudinot, Marmont, and Macdonald. In the last two cases, their autobiographies may have seemed too authoritative; also, Macdonald's ancestry has made him a special pet of English writers, far beyond his deserving. Finally, Napoleon seems to have wasted Suchet's talents. Imagine the possible outcome had he been in Augereau's boots.

BIBLIOGRAPHY: THE COLLAPSE OF EMPIRE

1. Aboville, Augustin Marie, baron de. "Notes sur l'attaque de
   Paris, et sur ce qui s'est passé à Fontainebleau après
   l'occupation par les troupes étrangères." CARNET DE LA
   SABRETACHE, Series 2, 4 (1906): 123-27.

2. Achard, Claude. "Organization militarie des prisonniers de
   guerre espagnols, 1808-1814." LE BRIQUET 2 (1980): 1-8.

3. Adams, Henry. THE WAR OF 1812. Edited by H.A. DeWeerd.
   Washington: THE INFANTRY JOURNAL, 1944.

4. Aldington, Richard. THE DUKE: BEING AN ACCOUNT OF THE LIFE
   AND ACHIEVEMENTS OF ARTHUR WELLESLEY, 1st DUKE OF WELLINGTON.
   Garden City, N.Y.: Garden City Publishing Company, 1943.

5. Alexander I, czar of Russia. SCENES OF RUSSIAN COURT LIFE:
   CORRESPONDENCE OF ALEXANDER I WITH HIS SISTER CATHERINE.
   Translated by Henry Havelock. London: Jarrolds, 1915.

6. Alfoldi, Laszlo M. THE ARMIES OF AUSTRIA-HUNGARY AND GERMANY,
   1740-1914. Special Bibliography Series No. 12. Carlisle
   Barracks, Pa.: U.S. Army Military History Institute, 1975. 2
   vols.

7. Alison, Archibald, and Patrick F. Tytler. TRAVELS IN FRANCE
   DURING THE YEARS 1814-15: COMPRISING A RESIDENCE AT PARIS
   DURING THE STAY OF THE ALLIED ARMIES AND AT AIX, AT THE PERIOD
   OF THE LANDING OF BONAPARTE. 2d ed. Edinburgh: Longman,
   1816. 2 vols.

8. Ambert, Guy d'. "Les Légions de gardes nationaux mobilises du
   Gers, 1813-1814." LE BRIQUET 3 (1973): 1-5.

9. Andolenko, Serge. AIGLES DE NAPOLEON CONTRA DRAPEAUX DU TSAR,
   1799, 1805-1807, 1812-1814. Paris: Eurimprim, 1969.

10. Aronson, Theo. THE GOLDEN BEES: THE STORY OF THE BONAPARTES.
    Greenwich, Conn.: New York Graphic Society, 1964.

11. Arthur, Ribeiro. A LEGIAO PORTUGUEZA AO SERVICO DE NAPOLEON.
    Lisbon: Perin, 1901.

12. Atkinson, C.T. "A Light Dragoon in the Peninsula: Extracts
    from the Letters of Captain Lovell Badcock, 14th Light
    Dragoons, 1809-1814." JOURNAL OF THE SOCIETY FOR ARMY
    HISTORICAL RESEARCH 33 (1956): 70-79.

13. Atteridge, Andrew Hilliard. JOACHIM MURAT: MARSHAL OF FRANCE
    AND KING OF NAPLES. New York: Brentano, 1911.

14. Austin, R.E., ed. "The 33d Foot in the Antwerp Campaign and
    Assault on Bergen-op-Zoom, 1813-1814." IRON DUKE 23 (1947);
    24 (1948).

15. Avout, Auguste Richard, baron d'. LA DEFENSE DE HAMBOURG EN 1813-1814. Dijon: Darantière, 1896.

16. Bages, Commandant. LE SIEGE DE GLOGAU, 1813-1814. Paris: Charles-Lavauzelle, 1911.

17. Baldet, Marcel. LA VIE QUOTIDIENNE DANS LES ARMEES DE NAPOLEON. Paris: Hachette, 1964.

18. Barnett, Correlli. BONAPARTE. New York: Hill and Wang, 1978.

19. Barrès, Jean Baptiste. MEMOIRS OF A NAPOLEONIC OFFICER. New York: Dial Press, 1925.

20. Bartel, Paul. NAPOLEON A L'ILE DE L'ELBE. Paris: Perrin, 1947.

21. Bausset-Roquefort, Louis François, baron de. MEMOIRES ANECDOTIQUES SUR L'INTERIEUR DU PALAIS ET SUR QUELQUES EVENEMENTS DE L'EMPIRE, DEPUIS 1805 JUSQU'AU 1er MAI 1814. Paris: Levavasseur, 1829.

22. Beatson, F.C. WELLINGTON: THE CROSSING OF THE GAVES AND THE BATTLE OF ORTHEZ. London: Heath, 1925.

23. Beauchamp, Alphonse de. HISTOIRE DE LA CAMPAGNE DE 1814, ET DE LA RESTAURATION DE LA MONARCHIE FRANCAISE. AVEC DES PIECES JUSTIFICATIVES. Paris: Le Normant, 1815. 2 vols. (Published in London in 1815 and 1816 by Henry Colburn as AN AUTHENTIC NARRATIVE OF THE INVASION OF FRANCE IN 1814.)

24. Beauchamp, Alphonse de. HISTOIRE DES CAMPAGNES DE 1814 ET 1815 ... REDIGEE SUR DES MATERIAUX AUTHENTIQUES OU INEDITS. Paris: Le Normant, 1817. 2 vols.

25. Beauvais de Préau, Charles Théodore, comp. VICTOIRES, CONQUETES, DESASTRES, REVERS ET GUERRES CIVILES DES FRANCAIS, DE 1791 A 1815. Paris: Panckoucke, 1817-22. 27 vols.

26. Béchu, Marcel Ernest [Marcel Dupont]. NAPOLEON EN CAMPAGNE. Paris: Hachette, 1950-55. 3 vols.

27. Béchu, Marcel Ernest [Marcel Dupont]. NAPOLEON ET LA TRAHISON DES MARECHAUX, 1814. Paris: Hachette, 1934.

28. Béchu, Marchel Ernest [Marcel Dupont]. NAPOLEON ET SES GROGNARDS. Paris: Hachette, 1945.

29. Begis, Alfred. INVASION DE 1814: ORDRE DONNE PAR L'EMPEREUR NAPOLEON DE FAIRE SAUTER LA POUDRIEVE DE GRENELLE AVANT LA CAPITULATION DE PARIS. Besançon: Jacquin, 1902.

30. Bell, George. SOLDIER'S GLORY. London: G. Bell, 1956.

31. Bellaire, J.P. PRECIS DE L'INVASION DES ETATS ROMAINS PAR L'ARMEE NAPOLITAINE EN 1813 ET 1814. Paris: Librairie de Prince Royal, 1838.

32. Belliard, Augustin D. MEMOIRES DU COMTE BELLIARD. Paris: Berquet et Petion, 1842. 3 vols.

33. Belmas, Jacques. JOURNAUX DES SIEGES FAITS OU SOUTENUS PAR LES FRANCAIS DANS LA PENINSULE, DE 1807 A 1814. Paris: Firmin-Didot, 1836-37. 4 vols. and atlas.

34. Bennigsen, Levin A.G. von. MEMOIRES DU GENERAL BENNIGSEN. Paris: Charles-Lavauzelle, 1907-08. 3 vols.

35. Berthezene, Pierre. SOUVENIRS MILITAIRES DE LA REPUBLIQUE ET DE L'EMPIRE. Paris: J. Dumaine, 1855.

36. Bertier de Sauvigny, Guillaume de. METTERNICH ET SON TEMPS. Paris: Hachette, 1959.

37. Besnus, J. "Considérations militaires sur la bataille de Toulouse, 10 avril 1814." LE BRIQUET 4 (1964); 1 (1965): 15-18.

38. Bigarré, Auguste, baron. MEMOIRES DU GENERAL BIGARRE: AIDE DE CAMP DU ROI JOSEPH, 1775-1813. Paris: Kolb, 1893.

39. Blaze, Elzéar. LA VIE MILITAIRE SOUS LE PREMIER EMPIRE. Paris: Garnier, 1901.

40. Blaze, Sebastien. MEMOIRES D'UN AIDE-MAJOR SOUS LE PREMIER EMPIRE. Paris: Flammarion, n.d.

41. Blond, Georges. LA GRANDE ARMEE, 1804-1815. Paris: Robert Laffont, 1979.

42. Bogdanovich, Modest Ivanovich. GESCHICHTE DES KRIEGES 1814 IN FRANKREICH UND DES STURZES NAPOLEON'S I. Leipzig: Schlicte, 1863. 3 vols.

43. Bois, Maurice. UN SOLDAT DE NAPOLEON Ier. NOISOT, SOUS-ADJUTANT-MAJOR DU BATAILLON DE L'ILE D'ELBE. Paris: Sevin et Rey, 1900.

44. Bonnal, Henri. LA VIE MILITAIRE DU MARECHAL NEY. Paris: Chapelot, 1910-14. 3 vols.

45. Boppe, Auguste. LE COLONEL NICOLE PAPAS OGLON ET LE BATAILLON DE CHASSEURS D'ORIENT (1798-1815). Paris: Berger-Levrault, 1900.

46. Boppe, Paul. LES ESPAGNOLS A LA GRANDE-ARMEE. Paris: Berger-Levrault, 1899.

47. Boudriot, Jean. ARMES A FEU FRANCAISES, 1717-1836. Paris: Private printing, 1961-63.

48. Boulart, Jean François, baron. MEMOIRES MILITAIRES. Paris: Emile Colin, n.d.

49. Bourge, Antoine Romain de. QUELQUES IDEES SUR LES TROUPES A CHEVAL DE FRANCE, ET PRINCIPALEMENT SUR LA CAVALERIE LEGERE. Paris: Magimel, Anselin et Pochard, 1817.

50. Bouvier, Félix. LES PREMIERS COMBATS DE 1814. Paris: Cerf [?], 1895.

51. Brack, Antoine F. de. AVANT-POSTES DE CAVALERIE LEGERE. Breda: Broese, 1834.

52. Breton de la Martinière, Jean Baptiste, comp. CAMPAGNES DE BUONAPARTE, EN 1812, 1813 ET 1814, JUSQU'A SON ABDICATION, D'APRES LES BULLETINS OFFICIALS DES ALLIES ET DES FRANCAIS. Paris: Dentu, 1814.

53. Brett-James, Antony, ed. WELLINGTON AT WAR, 1794-1815. London: Macmillan, 1961.

54. Breville, Jacques M.O. de ("JOB"). TENUES DES TROUPES DE FRANCE. Paris: De Vaugirard, 1898.

55. Brice, Raoul. UNE CARRIERE AVENTUREUSE. LE GENERAL BRICE, CHEF FRANCAIS DE PARTISANS LORRAINS, 1783-1851. Nancy: n.p., 1923.

56. Brown, David. DIARY OF A SOLDIER, 1805-1827. Ardrossan: Herald Office, 1934.

57. Browning, Oscar. THE FALL OF NAPOLEON. London: J. Lane, 1907.

58. Bruce, A.P.C. AN ANNOTATED BIBLIOGRAPHY OF THE BRITISH ARMY, 1660-1914. New York: Garland, 1975.

59. Brunon, Jean, and Raoul Brunon. LES ECLAIREURS DE LA GARDE IMPERIALE, 1813-1814. Marseilles: Collection Raoul et Jean Brunon, 1961.

60. Bryant, Arthur. THE AGE OF ELEGANCE, 1812-1822. London: Collins, 1950.

61. Burgoyne, John. LIFE AND CORRESPONDENCE OF FIELD MARSHAL SIR JOHN BURGOYNE, BART. Edited by George Wrottesley. London: Bentley, 1873. 2 vols.

62. Calmon-Maison, Jean Joseph Robert. LE GENERAL MAISON ET LE Ier CORPS DE LA GRANDE ARMEE. Paris: Calmann-Lévy, 1914.

63. Camon, Hubert. LA BATAILLE NAPOLEONIENNE. Paris: Chapelot, 1899.

64. Camon, Hubert. LA GUERRE NAPOLEONIENNE. Paris: Chapelot, 1903-10. 5 vols.

65. CAMPAGNE DE PARIS EN 1814 PRECEEDEE D'UN COUP D'OEIL SUR CELLE DE 1813. Paris: n.p., 1914.

66. Campana, Ignace Raphaël. LA CAMPAGNE DE FRANCE, 1814. Paris: Charles-Lavauzelle, 1922.

67. Campbell, Neil. NAPOLEON AT FONTAINEBLEAU AND ELBA. London: J. Murray, 1869.

68. Canonge, F. LA DEFENSE DE MONZON (27 SEPTEMBRE 1813 AU 18 FEVRIER 1814). Paris: Le Carnet, 1903.

69. Carnot, Lazare N.M., comte. MEMOIRES SUR CARNOT PAR SON FILS. Paris: Hachette, 1893. 2 vols.

70. Cassels, S.A.C., ed. PENINSULAR PORTRAIT: THE LETTERS OF CAPTAIN WILLIAM BRAGGE, 3d (KING'S OWN) DRAGOONS, 1811-1814. London: Oxford University Press, 1963.

71. Caulaincourt, Armand A.L., marquis de, duc de Vicence. NO PEACE WITH NAPOLEON: CONCLUDING THE MEMOIRS OF GENERAL DE CAULAINCOURT, DUKE OF VICENZA. New York: Morrow, 1936.

72. Chandler, David. THE CAMPAIGNS OF NAPOLEON. New York: Macmillan, 1966.

73. Chardigny, Louis. LES MARECHAUX DE NAPOLEON. Paris: Flammarion, 1946.

74. Chateaubriand, François R.A., vicomte de. MEMOIRS. Translated and edited by Robert Baldick. New York: Knopf, 1961.

75. Chenier, L.J. Gabriel de. HISTOIRE DE LA VIE POLITIQUE, MILITAIRE ET ADMINISTRATIVE DE MARECHAL DAVOUT. Paris: Cross, Maréchal, 1866. 2 vols.

76. Chevalier, Jean Michel. SOUVENIRS DES GUERRES NAPOLEONIENNES. Edited by Jean Mistler et Hélène Michaud. Paris: Hachette, 1970.

77. Christophe, Robert. NAPOLEON, EMPEREUR DE L'ILE DE ELBE. Paris: Fayand, 1959. (Published by MacDonald in London, 1964, as NAPOLEON ON ELBA.)

78. Chuquet, Arthur. L'ALSACE EN 1814. Paris: Plon-Nourrit, 1900.

79. Chuquet, Arthur. L'ANNEE 1814. LETTRES ET MEMOIRES. Paris: Fontemoing, 1914.

80. Chuquet, Arthur. "Le Blocus de Neuf-Brisach en 1814." CARNET
     DE LA SABRETACHE 8 (1900): 13.

81. Clausewitz, Karl von. LA CAMPAGNE DE 1814 EN FRANCE.
     Translated by G. Duval de Fraville. Paris: Lavauzelle, 1900.

82. Clausewitz, Karl von. LA CAMPAGNE DE 1813 ET LA CAMPAGNE DE
     1814 EN FRANCE. Translated by Commandant Thomann. Paris:
     Chapelot, 1900.

83. Cochon, J. "Un Remplacement militaire à la fin de l'empire."
     CARNET DE LA SABRETACHE 5 (1897): 329-69.

84. Connelly, Owen. NAPOLEON'S SATELLITE KINGDOMS. New York:
     Free Press, 1965.

85. Cornwall, James M. MARSHAL MASSENA. London: Oxford
     University Press, 1965.

86. Cossé-Brissac, René Marie de. HISTORIQUE DE 7e REGIMENT DE
     DRAGONS, 1673-1909. Paris: Leroy, 1909.

87. Couderc de Saint-Chamant, Henri. NAPOLEON; LES DERNIERES
     ARMEES. Paris: Flammarion, 1902.

88. Coulet, Jacqueline. "Le Général Cambronne." LE BRIQUET 2
     (1980): 12-14.

89. Craig, Gordon Alexander. PROBLEMS OF COALITION WARFARE: THE
     MILITARY ALLIANCE AGAINST NAPOLEON, 1813-1814. Colorado
     Springs: U.S. Air Force Academy, 1965.

90. Cronin, Vincent. NAPOLEON BONAPARTE: AN INTIMATE BIOGRAPHY.
     New York: William Morrow, 1972.

91. Cruyplants, Eugène. HISTOIRE ILLUSTREE D'UN CORPS BELGE AU
     SERVICE DE LA REPUBLIQUE ET DE L'EMPIRE: LA 112e DEMI-BRIGADE.
     Brussels: Spineux, 1903.

92. Curely, Jean N. ITINERAIRE D'UN CAVALIER LEGER, 1793-1815.
     Paris: Berger-Levrault, 1887.

93. Currie, Laurence. THE BATON IN THE KNAPSACK. New York: E.P.
     Dutton, 1935.

94. Danilewsky, A.M. CAMPAGNE DE 1814. Paris: n.p., n.d.

95. Davout, Louis Nicolas, duc d'Auerstädt et prince d'Eckmühl.
     MEMOIRE DE M. LE MARECHAL DAVOUT, AU ROI. Paris: Crapelet,
     1814.

96. Dedem van de Gelder, Anton B.G., baron van. UN GENERAL
     HOLLANDAIS SOUS LE PREMIER EMPIRE. Paris: Plon, 1900.

97. Defontaine, Henry. "Les Généraux Le Marois et de Valazé et la glorieuse remise de Magdebourg en 1814." CARNET DE LA SABRETACHE, Series 3, 7 (1924): 518-65.

98. Delderfield, Ronald F. IMPERIAL SUNSET; THE FALL OF NAPOLEON, 1813-1814. Philadelphia: Chilton, 1968.

99. Departement de la Marine. HISTORIQUE DE L'ARTILLERIE DE LA MARINE. Paris: Dumoulin, 1889.

100. Depeaux, Albert. LES GARDES D'HONNEUR D'ALSACE ET DE LORRAINE A L'EPOQUE DU PREMIER EMPIRE. Paris: J. Leroy, 1913.

101. Depeaux, Albert. "Un Souvenir des chevau-légers polonais de la Garde (1814)." CARNET DE LA SABRETACHE, Series 3, 2 (1914-19): 180-83.

102. Derrêcagaix, Victor B. LE MARECHAL BERTHIER, PRINCE DE WAGRAM ET DE NEUCHATEL. Paris: Chapelot, 1904-5. 2 vols.

103. Desmarest, Pierre Marie. TEMOIGNAGES HISTORIQUES, OU, QUINZE ANS DE HAUTE POLICE SOUS LE CONSULAT ET L'EMPIRE. Paris: Levavasseur, 1833.

104. Despreaux, Frignet. LE MARECHAL MORTIER, DUC DE TREVISE. Paris: Berger-Levrault, 1913-14. 2 vols.

105. Devaux, Pierre. "Les Gardes nationaux mobilises du Cher, 1814-1815." LE BRIQUET 4 (1968): 5-8.

106. Dodge, Theodore A. NAPOLEON. Boston and New York: Houghton Mifflin, 1904. 4 vols.

107. Doublet, G. L'ARIEGE EN 1814 ET 1815. Foix: Gadrat, 1902.

108. Driault, Edouard. NAPOLEON ET L'EUROPE: CHUTE DE L'EMPIRE; LA LEGENDE DE NAPOLEON (1812-1815). Paris: F. Alcan, 1927.

109. Dry, A. REIMS EN 1814 PENDANT L'INVASION. Paris: Plon, 1902.

110. Dubois, A. LES AMBULANCES VERSAILLAISES EN 1814. APERCU DES EVACUATIONS DE LA GRANDE ARMEE. Versailles: n.p., 1914.

111. Du Casse, Albert, baron, ed. MEMOIRES DE PRINCE EUGENE. Paris: Michel Lévy, 1859. 10 vols.

112. Du Casse, Albert, baron, ed. MEMOIRES ET CORRESPONDENCE POLITIQUE ET MILITAIRE DU ROI JOSEPH. 2d ed. Paris: Perrotin, 1854-55. 10 vols.

113. Ducere, E. BAYONNE SOUS L'EMPIRE. LE BLOCUS DE 1814 D'APRES LES CONTEMPORAINS ET DES DOCUMENTS INEDITS. Bayonne: Lamaiguere, 1900.

114. Duff Cooper, Alfred, 1st viscount Norwich. TALLEYRAND. Stanford, Calif.: Stanford University Press, 1932.

115. Dumas, Mathieu, comte. MEMOIRS OF HIS OWN TIME; INCLUDING THE REVOLUTION, THE EMPIRE, AND THE RESTORATION. Philadelphia: Lea and Blanchard, 1839. 2 vols.

116. Dumas, Mathieu, comte. PRECIS DES EVENEMENTS MILITAIRES,... SUR LES CAMPAGNES DE 1799 A 1814. Paris: Treuttel et Würtz, 1817-26. 19 vols.

117. Dunn-Pattison, R.P. NAPOLEON'S MARSHALS. Boston: Little, Brown, 1909.

118. Dupuis, C. LE MINISTERE DE TALLEYRAND EN 1814. Paris: Plon-Nourrit, 1919-20. 2 vols.

119. Durand, Alexis. NAPOLEON A FONTAINEBLEAU. Versailles: A. Bourdier, 1912.

120. Dutriez, Lt. Col. "Un Maitre de la cavalerie légère: le général de division Pajol, comte de l'Empire." VIVAT HUSSAR (1976): 35-77.

121. Engelman, Fred L. THE PEACE OF CHRISTMAS EVE. London: Rupert Hart-Davis, 1962.

122. Espitalier, Albert. NAPOLEON ET LE ROI MURAT (1808-1815). Paris: Perrin, n.d.

123. Esposito, Vincent J., and John R. Elting. A MILITARY HISTORY AND ATLAS OF THE NAPOLEONIC WARS. New York: Praeger, 1964.

124. LES EVENEMENTS DE 1814. LE BATAILLE DE PARIS. Paris: Eymery, 1814.

125. Fain, Agathon J.F., baron. MEMOIRES DU BARON FAIN, PREMIER SECRETAIRE DU CABINET DE L'EMPEREUR. Paris: Plon, 1884.

126. Fain, Agathon J.F., baron. SOUVENIRS DE LA CAMPAGNE DE FRANCE. Paris: Bossange, 1824.

127. Fanet, Valere. "Le Ier Régiment des gardes d'honneur." CARNET DE LA SABRETACHE, Series 3, 2 (1914-19): 193-208, 257-88, 321-52, 417-32.

128. Fave, Ernest Honoré, abbé. LA CAMPAGNE DE 1814 DANS LA VALLEE DE LA MARNE. Châlons-sur-Marne: Martin, 1908-09. 3 vols.

129. Ferino, R. SOISSONS EN 1814. Soissons, 1912.

130. Fleury, Colonel. "Monuments commemoratifs de la campagne de 1814 à Reims." CARNET DE LA SABRETACHE, Series 3, 2 (1914-19): 55-60.

131. Forester, Cecil S. THE AGE OF FIGHTING SAIL. Garden City,
      N.Y.: Doubleday, 1956.

132. Fortescue, John W. A HISTORY OF THE BRITISH ARMY. London:
      Macmillan, 1899-1930. 19 vols.

133. Foster, John. NAPOLEON'S MARSHAL: THE LIFE OF MICHEL NEY.
      New York: Morrow, 1968.

134. Fouché, Joseph, duc d'Otrante. MEMOIRS OF FOUCHE. New York:
      Merrill & Baker, 1903. 2 vols.

135. Fournier, August. DER CONGRESS VON CHATILLON. Leipzig,
      Vienna, and Prague: F. Tempsky, 1900.

136. Fournier, August. MARIE-LOUISE ET LA CHUTE DE NAPOLEON.
      Nogent-le-Rotrou: Daupeley-Gouverneur, 1903.

137. Foy, Maximilien S., comte. HISTOIRE DE LA GUERRE DE LA
      PENINSULE SOUS NAPOLEON. Paris: Baudouin, 1827. 4 vols.

138. Frederick, John B.M. LINEAGE BOOK OF THE BRITISH ARMY:
      MOUNTED CORPS AND INFANTRY, 1660-1968. Cornwallville, N.Y.:
      Hope Farm, 1969.

139. Froberger, Georges. SOUVENIRS ANECDOTIQUES & MILITAIRES DU
      COLONEL BIOT. Paris: Henri Vivien, 1901.

140. Gain, Commandant de. "Momuments commémoratifs de la campagne
      de 1814." CARNET DE LA SABRETACHE, Series 2, 10 (1911): 120,
      448, 511.

141. Gallaher, John G. THE IRON MARSHAL: A BIOGRAPHY OF LOUIS N.
      DAVOUT. Carbondale: Southern Illinois University Press, 1976.

142. Galpin, William Freeman. "The American Grain Trade to the
      Spanish Peninsula, 1810-1814." THE AMERICAN HISTORICAL REVIEW
      28 (1922): 22-24.

143. Garrison, Fielding H. NOTES ON THE HISTORY OF MILITARY
      MEDICINE. Washington, D.C.: Association of Military Surgeons,
      1922.

144. Garros, Louis. NEY: LE BRAVE DES BRAVES. Paris:
      Amiot-Dumont, 1955.

145. Gayda, Marcel, and André Krijitsky. L'ARMEE RUSSE SOUS LE TSAR
      ALEXANDRE Ier, DE 1805 A 1815. Paris: Sabretache, 1955.

146. Geoffroy de Grandmaison, Charles Alexander. L'ESPAGNE ET
      NAPOLEON. Paris: Plon, 1931. 3 vols.

147. Girod de l'Ain, Maurice, ed. VIE MILITAIRE DU GENERAL FOY.
      Paris: Plon-Nourrit, 1900.

148. Glover, Michael. THE NAPOLEONIC WARS. New York: Hippocrene, 1979.

149. Glover, Michael. THE PENINSULAR WAR, 1807-1814: A CONCISE HISTORY. London: David & Charles, 1974.

150. Glover, Michael. WARFARE IN THE AGE OF BONAPARTE. London: Cassell, 1980.

151. Glover, Michael. WELLINGTON AS A MILITARY COMMANDER. London: Batsford, 1968.

152. Glover, Michael. WELLINGTON'S ARMY IN THE PENINSULA, 1808-1814. New York: Hippocrene Books, 1977.

153. Goerlitz, Walter. HISTORY OF THE GERMAN GENERAL STAFF, 1657 to 1945. New York: Praeger, 1952.

154. Gómez de Arteche y Moro, José. GUERRA DE LA INDEPENDENCIA. Madrid: Depósitio de la Guerre, 1866-1903.

155. Goodspeed, Donald James. THE BRITISH CAMPAIGNS IN THE PENINSULA, 1808-1814. Ottawa: Queen's Printer, 1958.

156. Gosselin, Louis Léon Théodore [Georges Lenôtre]. LE VRAI CHEVALIER DE MAISON-ROUGE. Paris: Perrin, 1920.

157. Gougeat, Louis Antoine. "Mémoires d'un cavalier d'ordonnance du 20e Dragons." CARNET DE LA SABRETACHE 9 (1901): 400-402.

158. Gourgaud, Gaspard, baron. MEMOIRES POUR SERVIR A L'HISTOIRE DE FRANCE SOUS NAPOLEON. Paris: Firmin-Didot, 1823. 2 vols.

159. Gouvion Saint-Cyr, Laurent, marquis de. MEMOIRES POUR SERVIR A LA HISTOIRE MILITAIRE SOUS LE DIRECTOIRE, LE CONSULAT ET L'EMPIRE. Paris: Anselin, 1834. 4 vols.

160. Grabowski, Józef. MEMOIRES MILITAIRES DE JOSEPH GRABOWSKI, 1812, 1813, 1814. Translated by Jan V. Chelminski and Comdt. A. Malibran. Paris: Plon-Nourrit, 1907.

161. Gribble, Francis. EMPEROR AND MYSTIC: THE LIFE OF ALEXANDER I OF RUSSIA. New York: E.P. Dutton, 1931.

162. Grolleau, Charles, ed. JOURNAL DU CAPITAINE FRANCOIS (DIT LE DROMADAIRE D'EGYPT), 1792-1830. Paris: Carrington, 1903. 2 vols.

163. Grosjean, Edgard. AUTOUR DE LE BATAILLE DE MONTMIRAIL (11 FEVRIER 1814). Châlons-sur-Marne: Martin, 1900.

164. Grouchy, Emmanuel, marquis de. MEMOIRES DU MARECHAL DE GROUCHY. Paris: Dentu, 1873-74. 5 vols.

165. Gruyer, Paul. NAPOLEON ROI DE L'ILE D'ELBE. Paris: Hachette, 1906.

166. Guesdon, Alexander F. HISTOIRE DES CAMPAGNES EN 1814 ET 1815. Paris: Mortonval (Moronval?), 1826.

167. Guillemand, Robert. ADVENTURES OF A FRENCH SERGEANT DURING HIS CAMPAIGNS IN ITALY, SPAIN, GERMANY, RUSSIA, etc., FROM 1805 TO 1823. London: Colburn, 1826.

168. Hales, Edward Elton Young. NAPOLEON AND THE POPE: THE STORY OF NAPOLEON AND PIUS VII. London: Spottiswoode, 1962.

169. Hautpoul, Amand, marquis d'. SOUVENIRS SUR LA REVOLUTION, L'EMPIRE ET LA RESTAURATION. Paris: Emile-Paul, 1904.

170. Headley, Joel Tyler. NAPOLEON AND HIS MARSHALS. New York: Baker and Scribner, 1850. 2 vols.

171. Hibbert, Christopher, ed. THE WHEATLEY DIARY. London: Longmans, Green, 1964.

172. Hohenlohe-Ingelfingen, Kraft Karl. CONVERSATIONS ON CAVALRY. London: J.J. Keliher, 1897.

173. Hollander, O. NOS DRAPEAUX ET ETENDARDS DE 1812 A 1815. Paris: Berger-Levrault, 1902.

174. Hollander, O. "L'Etendard de l'escadron Napoléon à l'Ile d'Elbe." CARNET DE LA SABRETACHE, Series 3, 1 (1913): 758-61.

175. Holtman, Robert B. NAPOLEONIC PROPAGANDA. Baton Rouge: Louisiana State University Press, 1950.

176. Holzhausen, Philip P. DAVOUT IN HAMBURG: EIN BEITRAG ZUR GESCHICHTE DER JAHRE 1813-1814. Mulheim: Max Röder, 1892.

177. Horward, Donald D., ed. "The Journal of André Colomb: Chevalier de la légion d'honneur (1809-1815)." JOURNAL OF THE SOCIETY FOR ARMY HISTORICAL RESEARCH 46 (1968): 6-27.

178. Houssaye, Henry. 1814. Paris: Librairie Academique Didier, 1899.

179. Houssaye, Henry. NAPOLEON HOMME DE GUERRE. Paris: Daragon, 1904.

180. Houssaye, Henry, ed. LA VIELLE GARDE IMPERIALE. Tours: Alfred Mame, 1929.

181. Huddleston, F.J. WARRIORS IN UNDRESS. London: John Castle, 1925.

182. Hunter, Thomas Marshal. NAPOLEON IN VICTORY AND DEFEAT.
     Ottawa: Directorate of Military Training, Army Historical
     Section; Canadian Forces Headquarters, Queen's Printer, 1964.

183. Ivry, Ogier d'. HISTOIRE DU Ier REGIMENT DE HUSSARDS, REGIMENT
     DE BERCHENY. Valence-sur-Rhône: Ceas, 1902.

184. Jackson, Louis. "One of Wellington's Staff Officers:
     Lieut.-General William Staveley, C.B." JOURNAL OF THE SOCIETY
     FOR ARMY HISTORICAL RESEARCH 14 (1935): 155-66.

185. Johnson, David. NAPOLEON'S CAVALRY AND ITS LEADERS. London:
     Batsford, 1978.

186. Johnston, Robert Matteson. THE NAPOLEONIC EMPIRE IN SOUTHERN
     ITALY. London: Macmillan, 1904.

187. Jomini, Antoine Henri de, baron. LIFE OF NAPOLEON. Kansas
     City, Mo.: Hudson-Kimberly, 1897.

188. Josselson, Michael, and Diana Josselson. THE COMMANDER: A
     LIFE OF BARCLAY DE TOLLY. Oxford: Oxford University Press,
     1980.

189. Kann, Robert A. "Metternich, a Reappraisal of His Impact on
     International Relations." JOURNAL OF MODERN HISTORY 32 (1960):
     333-39.

190. Kincaid, John. ADVENTURES IN THE RIFLE BRIGADE. London:
     Peter Davies, 1929.

191. King, D.W. "A British Officer in the Eastern Adriatic,
     1812-1815." JOURNAL OF THE SOCIETY FOR ARMY HISTORICAL
     RESEARCH 58 (1980): 27-39.

192. King, D.W. "A Note on the Operations of George Duncan
     Robertson's Force from Lissa at Trieste and in Northern Italy,
     1813-1814." JOURNAL OF THE SOCIETY FOR ARMY HISTORICAL
     RESEARCH 56 (1978): 174-77.

193. Kircheisen, Friedrich M. BIBLIOGRAPHIE NAPOLEONIENNE. Paris:
     Chapelot, 1902.

194. Kissinger, Henry A. A WORLD RESTORED: METTERNICH, CASTLEREAGH
     AND THE PROBLEMS OF THE PEACE, 1812-1822. Boston:
     Houghton-Mifflin, 1957.

195. Klessmann, Eckart. DIE BEFREIUNGSKRIEGE IN AUGENZEUGEN-
     BERICHTEN. Fribourg: Office du Livre, 1966.

196. Koch, Jean Baptiste, ed. MEMOIRES DE MASSENA. Paris: Paulin
     et Lechevalier, 1848-50. 7 vols.

197. Koch, Jean Baptiste. MEMOIRES POUR SERVIR A L'HISTOIRE DE LA
     CAMPAGNE DE 1814. Paris: Magimel, 1819. 2 vols. and atlas.

198. Kraehe, Enno E. METTERNICH'S GERMAN POLICY. Vol. 1. THE
      CONTEST WITH NAPOLEON, 1799-1814. Princeton, N.J.: Princeton
      University Press, 1963.

199. La Barre de Nanteuil, Henri. LE COMTE DARU, OU
      L'ADMINISTRATION MILITAIRE SOUS L'EMPIRE. Paris: Peyronnet,
      1966.

200. Lachouque, Henry. NAPOLEON ET LA GARDE IMPERIALE. Paris:
      Bloud et Gay, 1956. (Illustrated, abridged translation by
      Anne S.K. Brown, THE ANATOMY OF GLORY: NAPOLEON AND HIS GUARD.
      Providence, R. I.: Brown University Press, 1961.)

201. Lachouque, Henry. NAPOLEON'S BATTLES. New York: Dutton,
      1967.

202. Lachouque, Henry. VICTOIRES SANS SOLDATS. NAPOLEON EN 1814.
      Paris: Revue Historique de l'armée, n.d.

203. La Jonquière, Clément Etienne Lucien Marie de Taffanel, marquis
      de. ORGANIZATION & ROLE DE LA CAVALERIE FRANCAISE PENDANT LES
      GUERRES DE 1800 A 1815. Paris: Charles-Lavauzelle, 1886.

204. Lamiraux, Général. ETUDES DE GUERRE. LA MANOEUVRE DE SOULT
      (1813-1814). Paris: Lavauzelle, 1902.

205. Langeron, Louis Alexandre. MEMOIRES DE LANGERON, GENERAL
      D'INFANTERIE DAN L'ARMEE RUSSE. CAMPAGNES DE 1812, 1813, 1814.
      Publiés d'après le manuscrit original pour la Societe
      d'histoire contemporaire. Paris: Picard, 1903.

206. Langeron, Louis Alexandre. "Le Récit de Langeron sur la
      bataille de Paris (30 mars 1814)." CARNET DE LA SABRETACHE 6
      (1898): 193-217.

207. Lapene, E. CAMPAGNE DE 1813-14 SUR L'EBRE, LES PYRENEES, ET LA
      GARONNE. Paris: Anselin et Pouchard, 1834.

208. Larchey, Loredan, ed. LES CAHIERS DU CAPITAINE COIGNET.
      Paris: Hachette, 1896.

209. La Roche-Aymon, Antoine C.E.P. de. DES TROUPES LEGERES.
      Paris: Magimel, Anselin et Prochard, 1817.

210. Larrey, Dominique J. MEMOIRES DE CHIRURGIE MILITAIRE ET
      CAMPAGNES DU BARON D.J. LARREY. Paris: Smith, 1817. Vol. 4.
      (A heavily edited English translation--MEMOIR OF BARON LARREY,
      SURGEON-IN-CHIEF OF THE GRANDE ARMEE--was published by Henry
      Renshaw in London, 1862.)

211. Lauthonnye, Commandant de. "Ma Vie militaire." CARNET DE LA
      SABRETACHE, Series 2, 10, 11 (1910, 1911): 1-16, 193-208,
      289-303.

212. Lavalette, Antoine Marie Chamant, comte de. MEMOIRS OF COUNT
     LAVALETTE, ADJUTANT AND PRIVATE SECRETARY TO NAPOLEON AND
     POSTMASTER-GENERAL UNDER THE EMPIRE. Philadelphia: Lippin-
     cott, 1894.

213. Lawford, James P. NAPOLEON: THE LAST CAMPAIGNS. New York:
     Crown, 1977.

214. L.D. JOURNAL HISTORIQUE SUR LA CAMPAGNE DE PRINCE EUGENE, EN
     ITALIE, PENDANT LES ANNEES 1813 ET 1814. Paris: Plancher,
     1817.

215. Lefebvre, Théodore. LES EVENEMENTS HISTORIQUES ET LES BRETONS
     DU FINISTERE, DE 1805 A 1815. Morlaix: Chevalier, 1903.

216. Lefebvre de Béhaine, François Armand Edouard, comte. LA
     CAMPAGNE DE FRANCE. Paris: Perrin, 1913-35. 4 vols.

217. Lefebvre de Béhaine, François Armand Edouard, comte. LE COMTE
     D'ARTOIS SUR LA ROUTE DE PARIS, 1814. Paris: Perrin, 1921.

218. Lefebvre de Béhaine, François Armand Edouard, comte. NAPOLEON
     ET LES ALLIES SUR LE RHIN. Paris: Librairie academique, 1913.

219. Legrand-Mollerat, Antoine Vincent Judes Louis. RELATION DE LA
     SURPRISE DE BERG-OP-ZOOM, LE 8 ET 9 MARS 1814 ... NOTICE
     HISTORIQUE ET TOPOGRAPHIQUE MILITAIRE, ET D'UN PLAN-CROQUIS.
     Paris: Magimel, Anselin et Pochard, 1816.

220. Lejune, Louis François, baron. SOUVENIRS D'UN OFFICIER DE
     L'EMPIRE. Paris: Germain Bapst, n.d.

221. Lewis, Michael. NAPOLEON AND HIS BRITISH CAPTIVES. London:
     Allen & Unwin, 1902.

222. Liddell Hart, Basil H., ed. THE LETTERS OF PRIVATE WHEELER.
     Boston: Houghton Mifflin, 1952.

223. Löwenstern, Woldemar H., freiherr von. MEMOIRES DU
     GENERAL-MAJOR RUSSE BARON DE LOEWENSTERN. Edited by M.H. Weil.
     Paris: Fontemoing, 1903. 2 vols.

224. Lomier, Docteur. LA BATAILLON DES MARINS DE LA GARDE,
     1803-1815. Saint-Volery-sur-Somme: Lefebvre, 1905.

225. Londonderry, Charles W. Vane, 3d marquis of. NARRATIVE OF THE
     WAR IN GERMANY AND FRANCE, IN 1813 AND 1814. Philadelphia:
     Corey, 1931.

226. Londonderry, Robert Stewart, 2d marquis of. MEMOIRS AND
     CORRESPONDENCE OF VISCOUNT CASTLEREAGH, SECOND MARQUESS OF
     LONDONDERRY. Edited by Charles Vane. London: Colburn,
     1848-53. 12 vols.

227. Longford, Elizabeth. WELLINGTON: THE YEARS OF THE SWORD.
      London: Wiedenfeld and Nicolson, 1969.

228. Loy, L.   "L'Abdication conditionnelle du 4 avril, 1814."
      CARNET DE LA SABRETACHE, Series 3, 2 (1919): 49-54.

229. Lumbroso, Alberto, barone.   ALESSANDRO BERTHIER, PRINCIPE DE
      NEUCHATEL ET DI WAGRAM. Rome: Mendel, 1900.

230. Lyons, M., comp.   THE RUSSIAN IMPERIAL ARMY: BIBLIOGRAPHY OF
      REGIMENTAL HISTORIES AND RELATED WORKS.   Stanford, Calif.:
      Hoover Institution on War, Revolution, and Peace, 1968.

231. McCance.   "How the Colours of the 55th Foot were saved at
      Bergen-op-Zoom, in March 1814." JOURNAL OF THE SOCIETY FOR
      ARMY HISTORICAL RESEARCH 7 (1928): 201-4.

232. McCarthy, M. Dugue.   "L'Affaire de Montereau, le 18 fevrier
      1814." VIVAT HUSSAR 13 (1978): 6-11.

233. Macdonald, Jacques E.J.A., duc de Tarente.   SOUVENIRS DU
      MARECHAL MACDONALD, DUC DE TARENTE. Paris: Plon-Nourrit,
      1892.

234. Mackenzie-Grieve, Averil.   ASPECTS OF ELBA AND THE OTHER
      ISLANDS OF THE TUSCAN ARCHIPELAGO. London: J. Cape, 1964.

235. Madelin, Louis. HISTOIRE DU CONSULAT ET DE L'EMPIRE. Vol. 14.
      LA CAMPAGNE DE FRANCE. Paris: Hachette, 1937.

236. Maindreville, Général de.   "Incendie de Mery-sur-Seine (22
      fevrier 1814)."   CARNET DE LA SABRETACHE, Series 3, 2
      (1914-19): 305-11.

237. Manteyer, de. LA FIN DE L'EMPIRE DANS LES ALPES (19 MAI 1813-
      30 JUIN 1815). Gap: n.p., 1842.

238. Marbot, Jean Baptiste A.M., baron de.   MEMOIRES DU GENERAL
      BARON DE MARBOT. Paris: Plon, 1892. 3 vols. (An English
      translation in 2 volumes was published in London by Longmans,
      Green in 1892.)

239. Markham, Felix. NAPOLEON. New York: New American Library,
      1963.

240. Marmont, Auguste Frédéric Louis Viesse de, duc de Raguse.
      MEMOIRES DU MARECHAL MARMONT, DUC DE RAGUSE.   Paris:
      Perrotine, 1857. 9 vols.

241. Martin, Emmanuel.   "Les Monnaies obsidionales d'Anvers (1814)."
      CARNET DE LA SABRETACHE, Series 2, 1 (1903): 304-16.

242. Martinien, Aristide.   "Les Généraux de Grand-Duché de Varsovie,
      de 1812 à 1814." CARNET DE LA SABRETACHE, Series 2, 4 (1906):
      257-71, 415-33.

243. Martinien, Aristide. TABLEAUX PAR CORPS ET PAR BATAILLES DES OFFICIERS TUES ET BLESSES PENDANT LES GUERRES DE L'EMPIRE (1805-1815). Paris: Charles-Lavauzelle, [1899].

244. Masson, Frédéric. CAVALIERS DE NAPOLEON. Paris: Ollendorff, 1895.

245. Masson, Frédéric. NAPOLEON ET SA FAMILLE. Paris: Ollendorff, 1900-1920. 13 vols.

246. Masson, Frédéric. "Notes et documents provenant des archives du général de division comte d'Anthouard." CARNET DE LA SABRETACHE, Series 2, 4 (1906): 387-407.

247. Mauduit, Hyacinthe Hippolyte de. LES DERNIERS JOURS DE LA GRANDE ARMEE, OU SOUVENIRS, DOCUMENS ET CORRESPONDANCE INEDITE DE NAPOLEON EN 1814 ET 1815. Paris: Chez l'auteur, 1847-48. 2 vols.

248. Maxwell, Herbert. THE LIFE OF WELLINGTON. London: Sampson, Low, Marston, 1907. 2 vols.

249. Maycock, F.W.O. THE INVASION OF FRANCE, 1814. London: Allen & Unwin, 1914.

250. Melchior-Bonnet, Bernadine. DICTIONNAIRE DE LA REVOLUTION ET DE L'EMPIRE. Paris: Larousse, 1965.

251. Melish, John. DOCUMENTS RELATIVE TO THE NEGOTIATIONS FOR PEACE BETWEEN THE UNITED STATES AND GREAT BRITAIN. Philadelphia: George Palmer, 1814.

252. MEMOIRE SUR LA CREANCE DE DEUX MILLIONS RESULTANT DE L'ARTICLE IX DU TRAITE DE FONTAINBLEAU, DU 11 AVRIL 1814. Paris: Firmin-Didot, 1852.

253. Monegelia, Vincent. "Marulaz: hussard de l'empereur." VIVAT HUSSAR 14 (1979): 19-34.

254. Moodie, J.W. Dunbar. "Narration de la campagne de 1814 en Hollande." CARNET DE LA SABRETACHE, Series 2, 5-6 (1907): 729-49; (1908): 37-40.

255. [Morvan, Jean] Capitaine M. Tixier. LE SOLDAT IMPERIAL, 1800-1814. Paris: Plon-Nourrit, 1904. 2 vols.

256. Müffling, Friedrich K.F., freiherr von. AUS MEINEN LEBEN. Berlin: n.p., 1855.

257. Murat, Joachim, king of Naples. LETTRES ET DOCUMENTS POUR SERVIR A L'HISTOIRE DE JOACHIM MURAT (1767-1815). Paris: Plon-Nourrit, 1908-14. 8 vols.

258. Napier, William F.P. WAR IN THE PENINSULA AND IN THE SOUTH OF FRANCE. New York: A.C. Armstrong, 1882. 5 vols.

259. Napoleon I, Emperor of the French. CORRESPONDANCE DE NAPOLEON Ier. Paris: Plon, 1858-70. 32 vols.

260. Napoleon I, Emperor of the French. LETTRES INEDITES DE NAPOLEON Ier A MARIE LOUISE, ECRITES DE 1810 A 1814. Paris: Editions des Bibliothèques Nationales de France, 1935.

261. Napoleon I, Emperor of the French. "Lettres, ordres et décrets de Napoléon Ier, non insères dans la CORRESPONDANCE." CARNET DE LA SABRETACHE 5 (1897): 266-78.

262. Napoleon I, Emperor of the French. NAPOLEON'S LETTERS TO MARIE LOUISE. With a foreword and commentary by Charles de La Roncière. New York: Farrar & Rinehart, 1935.

263. Napoleon I, Emperor of the French. "Un Ordre inédit de Napoléon Ier." CARNET DE LA SABRETACHE, Series 2, 2 (1904): 484.

264. Napoleon I, Emperor of the French. LE REGISTRE DE L'ILE DE ELBE. Publiés par Léon Gabriel Pélissier. Paris: Fontemoing, 1897.

265. Ney, Michel L.F., duc d'Elchingen, prince de la Moskowa. MEMOIRS DU MARECHAL NEY, PUBLIES PAR SA FAMILLE. Paris: Fournes, 1833. 2 vols. (One English-language version was published in London by E. Bell in 1833, another in Philadelphia by Carey in 1834.)

266. Nollet-Fabert, Jules. HISTOIRE DE NICOLAS CHARLES OUDINOT, MARECHAL DE L'EMPIRE ET DUC DE REGGIO. Paris: Dumaine, 1850.

267. North, R.E.F.G. "The Raising and Organizing of the King's German Legion." JOURNAL OF THE SOCIETY FOR ARMY HISTORICAL RESEARCH 39 (1961): 167-84.

268. Okinczyc, Bohdane, trans., ed. MEMOIRES DE GENERAL SZYMANOWSKI (OFFICIER D'ORDONNANCE DU MARECHAL DAVOUST), 1806-1814. Paris: Lavauzelle, 1900.

269. Oman, Carola (Lenanton). NAPOLEON'S VICEROY: EUGENE DE BEAUHARNAIS. New York: Funk and Wagnalls, 1966.

270. Oman, Charles William Chadwick. A HISTORY OF THE PENINSULAR WAR. Oxford: Clarendon Press, 1902-30. 7 vols.

271. Oman, Charles William Chadwick. WELLINGTON'S ARMY, 1809-1814. London: Arnold, 1913.

272. Oudinot, Marie Charlotte Eugénie (de Coucy), duchesse de Reggio. MEMOIRS OF MARSHAL OUDINOT, DUC DE REGGIO, COMPILED FROM THE HITHERTO UNPUBLISHED SOUVENIRS OF THE DUCHESSE DE REGGIO. Edited by Gaston Stiegler and translated by Alexander Teixeira de Mattos. London: H. Henry, 1896.

273. Pardiellan, chef de bataillon de. RECITS MILITAIRES D'ALSACE DE 1814 A 1870. Paris: Michel, 1903.

274. Paret, Peter. YORCK AND THE ERA OF PRUSSIAN REFORM. Princeton, N.J.: University Press, 1966.

275. Parquin, Denis Charles. SOUVENIRS DU CAPITAINE PARQUIN, 1803-1814. Paris: Boussod, Valadon, 1892. (An English-language version, translated and edited by B.T. Jones, was published in London by Longmans-Green in 1969.)

276. Pelet, Jean Jacques Germain, baron. MEMOIRES SUR LES GUERRES DE NAPOLEON DEPUIS 1796 JUSQU'EN 1815. n.p., n.d.

277. Pélissier, Léon Gabriel, ed. NAPOLEON, SOUVERAIN DE L'ILE D'ELBE: MEMOIRES DE PONS DE L'HERAULT. Paris: Plon, 1934.

278. Percy, Pierre François, baron. JOURNAL DES CAMPAGNES DU BARON PERCY, CHIRURGIEN EN CHEF DE LA GRANDE ARMEE, 1754-1825. Paris: Plon-Nourrit, 1904.

279. Perrin, Claude Victor. EXTRAITS D'UNE HISTORIE INEDITE DES GUERRES DE LA REPUBLIQUE ET DE L'EMPIRE. Paris: Donde-Dupre, 1853.

280. Pertz, G.H., and Hans Delbrück. LEBEN DES FELDMARSCHALLS N. VON GNEISENAU. Berlin: G. Reimer, 1864-80. Vols. 2-4.

281. Petre, Francis Loraine. NAPOLEON AT BAY, 1814. London and New York: J. Lane, 1914.

282. Peyrusse, Guillaume Joseph Roux, baron. MEMORIAL ET ARCHIVES DE M. LE BARON PEYRUSSE ... VIENNE--MOSCOU--ILE D'ELBE. Carcassonne: P. Labau, 1869.

283. Pflugk-Harttung, Julius A.C. von. 1813-1815. Stuttgart: Deutsche Verlagsgesellschaft, 1913.

284. Philip, Raymond M.A. de. ETUDE SUR LE SERVICE D'ETAT-MAJOR PENDANT LES GUERRES DU PREMIER EMPIRE. Paris: Chapelot, 1900.

285. Picard, Louis Auguste. LA CAVALERIE DANS LES GUERRES DE LA REVOLUTION ET DE L'EMPIRE. Saumur: Librairie Militaire, 1895-96. 2 vols.

286. Pils, François. JOURNAL DE MARCHE DU GRENADIER PILS (1804-1814). Paris: Ollendorff, 1895.

287. Pingaud, Léonce. BERNADOTTE, NAPOLEON, ET LES BOURBONS (1797-1814). Paris: Plon-Nourrit, 1901.

288. Pion des Loches, Antoine Augustin Flavien. MES CAMPAGNES, 1792-1815; NOTES ET CORRESPONDANCE DU COLONEL D'ARTILLERIE PION DES LOCHES. Paris: Firmin-Didot, 1889.

289. Pivka, Otto von. THE PORTUGUESE ARMY IN THE NAPOLEONIC WARS.
      London: Osprey, 1977.

290. Ponteil, Félix. LA CHUTE DE NAPOLEON ET LA CRISE FRANCAISE DE
      1814-1815. Paris: Aubier, 1943.

291. Prat, Olivier.   MEDECINS   MILITAIRES   D'AUTREFOIS.   Paris:
      Leniforme, 1935.

292. PRECIS HISTORIQUE DE LA CAMPAGNE DE 1814. Paris: F.H. Arnaud,
      1814.

293. Proudhon, Pierre Joseph. COMMENTAIRES SUR LES MEMOIRES DE
      FOUCHE. Paris: Ollendorff, 1900.

294. Quennevat, Jean Claude. ATLAS DE LA GRANDE ARMEE, NAPOLEON ET
      SES CAMPAGNES, 1803-1815. Paris: Sequoia, 1966.

295. Ragois, le. INSTRUCTION SUR L'HISTOIRE DE FRANCE. Paris:
      Moronval, 18?-1829.

296. Rapp, Jean, comte. MEMOIRES DU GENERAL RAPP, AIDE-DE-CAMP DE
      NAPOLEON, ECRITS PAR LUI-MEME ET PUBLIES PAR SA FAMILLE.
      Paris: Bossange, 1823. (An English-language version was
      published in London in 1823 by Colburn.)

297. Rath, R. John. THE FALL OF THE NAPOLEONIC KINGDOM OF ITALY.
      New York: Columbia University Press, 1941.

298. Reboul, Antoine Joseph. MES SOUVENIRS DE 1814 ET 1815, PAR M.
      ***. Paris: Eymery, 1824.

299. Régnault, Jean. LES AIGLES IMPERIALES ET LE DRAPEAU TRICOLORE,
      1804-1815. Paris: Peyronnet, 1967.

300. Rehtwisch, Theodor. GESCHICHTE DER FREIHEITSKRIEGE IN DEN
      JAHREN 1812-1815. Leipzig: Wigand, 1908. 3 vols.

301. Reiffenberg, Frédéric G.E.C.M. de. LES REGIMENTS DE FER.
      Paris: Ferdinand Sartorius, 1862.

302. Renier, Gustaaf J. GREAT BRITAIN AND THE NETHERLANDS,
      1813-1815. London and The Hague: Allen & Unwin, 1930.

303. Richardson, Hubert N.B. A DICTIONARY OF NAPOLEON AND HIS
      TIMES. Detroit: Gale Research, 1977. (Reprint)

304. Rivollet, Georges, and Paul Albertini. LES MARECHAUX D'EMPIRE
      ET LA PREMIERE ABDICATION. Paris: Berger-Levrault, 1957.

305. Robinson, Charles Walker. WELLINGTON'S CAMPAIGNS:
      PENINSULA--WATERLOO, 1808-15. London: Rees, 1907. 3 vols.

306. Robiquet, Jean. DAILY LIFE IN FRANCE UNDER NAPOLEON.
      Translated by Violet M. MacDonald. New York: Macmillan, 1963.

307. Ropes, John C. THE FIRST NAPOLEON. Boston and New York: William Sloan Associates, 1886.

308. Rosebery, Archibald P. Primrose, 5th earl of. NAPOLEON, THE LAST PHASE. New York: Harper, 1901.

309. Rossignol, Auguste. LE GENERAL COMTE DONZELOT. Besançon: Jacquin, 1903.

310. Rothenberg, Gunther E. THE MILITARY BORDER IN CROATIA, 1740-1881. Urbana: University of Illinois Press, 1966.

311. Rothenberg, Gunther E. THE HABSBURG ARMY IN THE NAPOLEONIC WARS. Manhattan: Kansas State University Press, 1973.

312. Rousseau, François. LA CARRIERE DU MARECHAL SUCHET, DUC D'ALBUFERA. Paris: Firmin-Didot, 1898.

313. Roy, R.H., ed. "The Memoirs of Private James Gunn." JOURNAL OF THE SOCIETY FOR ARMY HISTORICAL RESEARCH 49 (1971): 90-120.

314. SABRETACHE, ed. "Campagnes et souvenirs militaires de Jean-August Oyon." CARNET DE LA SABRETACHE, Series 3, 2 (1914-19): 28-32, 97-113.

315. SABRETACHE, ed. "Compiègne en 1814, d'après un manuscrit du temps." (Extracts from the records of the librarian of the Chateau de Compiègne.) CARNET DE LA SABRETACHE 6 (1898): 570-76, 633-39, 820-50.

316. SABRETACHE, ed. "Un Episode du passage du 5e Corps de cavalerie de la Grande-Armée à Nancy le 14 janvier 1814." CARNET DE LA SABRETACHE 8 (1900): 160-61.

317. SABRETACHE, ed. "Lettres et notes de campagne du général Sigismond du Pouget, marquis de Nadaillac." CARNET DE LA SABRETACHE, Series 2, 9 (1911): 678-87.

318. SABRETACHE, ed. "La Maison du roi et la ligne (1814)." CARNET DE LA SABRETACHE 4 (1896): 265-72.

319. SABRETACHE, ed. "Le marquis de Belmont-Briançon, major du 3e gardes d'honneur, tue à Reims le 13 mars 1814." CARNET DE LA SABRETACHE 8 (1900): 727-30.

320. SABRETACHE, ed. "Les Mémoires du général Saint-Chamans." CARNET DE LA SABRETACHE 3 (1895): 542-68.

321. SABRETACHE, ed. "Nouvelles lettres du général Drouot." CARNET DE LA SABRETACHE 5 (1897): 453-65. (General Antoine Drouot, "The Sage of the Grande Armée.")

322. SABRETACHE, ed. "Les Polytechniciens en 1814." CARNET DE LA SABRETACHE 4 (1896): 281-87.

323. SABRETACHE, ed. "Le Ier Régiment des chevau-légers lanciers
      polonais de la garde impériale: Notes sur les campagnes de
      1813 et de 1814." (Extracts from the MEMOIRS of General
      Dautancourt.) CARNET DE LA SABRETACHE 2 (1894): 275-89.

324. SABRETACHE, ed. "Souvenirs militaires de Pierre Auvray,
      sous-lieutenant au 23e regiment de Dragons (1807-1815)."
      CARNET DE LA SABRETACHE, Series 3, 2 (1914-19): 533-77.

325. SABRETACHE, ed. "La Vie militaire sous la restauration:
      Lettres de Gaspard Richard de Soultrait." CARNET DE LA
      SABRETACHE, Series 3, 6 (1923): 406-79.

326. Saint Denis, Louis E. NAPOLEON FROM THE TUILERIES TO ST.
      HELENA. Translation by Frank H. Potter. New York: Harper,
      1922.

327. Santi, L. de. NOTES ET DOCUMENTS SUR LES INTRIGUES ROYALISTES
      DANS LE MIDI DE LA FRANCE DE 1792 A 1815. Toulouse:
      Douladoure, 1916.

328. Savary, Anne Jean Marie René, duc de Rovigo. MEMOIRES DU DUC
      DE ROVIGO. Paris: Bossange, 1828. 8 vols.

329. Schuermans, Albert. ITINERAIRE GENERAL DE NAPOLEON Ier.
      Paris: Picard, 1908.

330. Scott, Franklin B. "Bernadotte and the Throne of France,
      1814." JOURNAL OF MODERN HISTORY 5 (1933): 465-78.

331. Ségur, Philippe P., comte de. LA CAMPAGNE DE FRANCE, DU RHIN A
      FONTAINEBLEAU, 1814. Geneva: Editions de Cremille, 1969.

332. Sellar, Robert J.B. "The Glorious Amateur: The Story of
      Thomas Graham, Lord Lynedoch." SCOTS MAGAZINE (1948).

333. Sheppard, Eric W. A SHORT HISTORY OF THE BRITISH ARMY.
      London: Constable, 1950.

334. Six, Georges. LES GENERAUX DE LA REVOLUTION ET DE L'EMPIRE.
      Paris: Bordas, 1947.

335. Skalkowski, Adam. EN MARGE DE LA CORRESPONDANCE DE NAPOLEON I:
      DOCUMENTS. Warsaw: Gebethner and Wolff, 1911.

336. Sloan, John F. MILITARY HISTORY OF RUSSIA: A PRELIMINARY
      SURVEY OF THE SOURCES. Garmisch: U.S. Army Institute for
      Advanced Russian and East European Studies, 1971.

337. Suchet, Louis G., duc d'Albufera. MEMOIRES DU MARECHAL SUCHET,
      DUC D'ALBUFERA, SUR SES CAMPAGNES EN ESPAGNE. Paris:
      Bossange, 1828. 2 vols. and atlas.

338. Talleyrand-Périgord, Charles Maurice de, prince de Bénévent.
      MEMOIRES. Paris: Société des Bibliophiles, 1891. Vols. 1-3.

(Also published in 5 volumes by G.P. Putnam, New York, 1891-1892, as MEMOIRS OF THE PRINCE DE TALLEYRAND.)

339. Tartary, Madeleine. EIPISODE DE LA CAMPAGNE DE FRANCE. NOGENT-SUR-SEINE EN 1814. Paris, 1939.

340. Tattet, Eugene. "Lettres du brigadier Pilloy." CARNET DE LA SABRETACHE, Series 2, 5 (1907): 505-67.

341. Thibaudeau, Antoine Claire, comte. HISTOIRE GENERAL DE NAPOLEON BONAPARTE. Paris: Ponthieu, 1827-28. 2 vols.

342. Thiébault, Paul C., baron. THE MEMOIRS OF BARON THIEBAULT. Translated and edited by Arthur J. Butler. New York: Macmillan, 1896.

343. Thiers, Louis Adolphe. HISTORY OF THE CONSULATE AND THE EMPIRE OF FRANCE UNDER NAPOLEON. London: Colburn, 1845. 20 vols.

344. Thiry, Jean. LA CAMPAGNE DE FRANCE DE 1814. Paris: Berger-Levrault, 1946.

345. Thiry, Jean. LA CHUTE DE NAPOLEON Ier. Paris: Berger-Levrault, 1938. 2 vols.

346. Tissot, Pierre François. MEMOIRES HISTORIQUES ET MILITAIRES SUR CARNOT. Paris: Baudouin, 1824.

347. Tournes, Renel. "Le G.Q.C. (headquarters) de Napoléon Ier." LE REVUE DE PARIS (1921).

348. Tuetey, Louis. SERURIER (1742-1819). Paris: Berger-Levrault, 1899.

349. Turner, G.A. THE DIARY OF PETER BUSSELL (1806-1814). London: Peter Davis, 1931.

350. Uexküll, Berend Johann Friedrich, freiherr von, ed. ARMS AND THE WOMAN: THE DIARIES OF BARON BORIS UEXKUELL, 1812-1819. Edited by Detlev von Uexküll. London: Secker & Warburg, 1966.

351. Vallaux, Camille. LES CAMPAGNES DES ARMEES FRANCAISES, 1792-1815. Paris: Alcan, 1899.

352. Vaudoncourt, Frédéric F.G., baron de. HISTOIRE DES CAMPAGNES D'ITALIE EN 1813 ET 1814, AVEC UN ATLAS MILITAIRE. London: Egerton, 1817.

353. Vaudoncourt, Frédéric F.G., baron de. HISTOIRE DES CAMPAGNES DE 1814 ET 1815, EN FRANCE. Paris: A. de Gastel, 1826.

354. Verner, Emily. REMINISCENCES OF WILLIAM VERNER (1782-1871), 7th HUSSARS. London: Journal of the Society for Army Historical Research, Special Publication No. 8, 1965.

355. Victor, François. VICTOR, DUC DE BELLUNE: Paris: Damaine,
      1847.

356. Viennet, Jean Pons Guillaume. SOUVENIRS DE LA VIE MILITAIRE.
      Moulins: Crepin-Leblond, 1929.

357. Vietmeyer, Fred H. NAPOLEONIC ARMY ORGANIZATION, CIRCA 1812.
      Visalia, Calif.: Jack Scruby's Military Miniatures, 1965.

358. Vigier, Henri, comte. DAVOUT: MARECHAL D'EMPIRE. Paris:
      Ollendorff, 1898. 2 vols.

359. Vignolle, Martin. PRECIS HISTORIQUE DES OPERATIONS MILITAIRES
      DE L'ARMEE D'ITALIE EN 1813 ET 1814, PAR LE CHEF DE
      L'ETAT-MAJOR-GENERAL DE CETTE ARMEE. Paris: Barrios, 1817.

360. Viollet-le-Duc, Eugéne E. HISTOIRE D'UNE FORTRESSE. Paris:
      S. Hetzel, n.d. (Available in English translation, ANNALS OF A
      FORTRESS, by James R. Osgood, Boston, 1876.)

361. Vivien, Commandant. "Souvenirs de ma vie militaire." CARNET
      DE LA SABRETACHE, Series 2, 4 (1906): 5-21, 106-9.

362. Ward, Stephen George Peregrine. "General Sir George Murrray."
      JOURNAL OF ARMY HISTORICAL RESEARCH 58 (1980): 191-208.

363. Ward, Stephen George Peregrine. "The Portuguese Infantry
      Brigades, 1809-1814." JOURNAL OF THE SOCIETY FOR ARMY
      HISTORICAL RESEARCH 53 (1975): 103-8.

364. Ward, Stephen George Peregrine. "The Quartermaster-General's
      Department in the Peninsula, 1809-1814." JOURNAL OF THE
      SOCIETY FOR ARMY HISTORICAL RESEARCH 23 (1945): 133-54.

365. Ward, Stephen George Peregrine. WELLINGTON'S HEADQUARTERS: A
      STUDY OF THE ADMINISTRATIVE PROBLEMS IN THE PENINSULA,
      1809-1814. Oxford: Oxford University Press, 1957.

366. Watson, S.J. BY COMMAND OF THE EMPEROR. London: Bodley Head,
      1957.

367. Wauwermans, Henri E. NAPOLEON ET CARNOT: EPISODE DE
      L'HISTOIRE MILITAIRE D'ANVERS, 1803-1815. Brussels: Muquardt,
      1888.

368. Webster, Charles K. THE CONGRESS OF VIENNA. New York: Barnes
      & Noble, 1966.

369. Webster, Charles K. THE FOREIGN POLICY OF CASTLEREAGH,
      1812-1815. London: G. Bell, 1931-34. 2 vols.

370. Weil, Maurice H. LA CAMPAGNE DE 1814. Paris: Librairie
      Militaire, 1914. 2 vols.

371. Weil, Maurice H. PRINCE EUGENE ET MURAT, 1813-1814; OPERATIONS
      MILITAIRES, NEGOCIATIONS DIPLOMATIQUES. Paris: Fontemoing,
      1902. 5 vols.

372. Weller, Jac. WELLINGTON IN THE PENINSULA, 1808-1814. London:
      N. Vane, 1963.

373. Wellington, Arthur Wellesley, 1st duke of. THE DISPATCHES OF
      FIELD MARSHAL THE DUKE OF WELLINGTON. Edited by Lt. Col.
      Gurwood. London: J. Murray, 1838. 13 vols.

374. Wellington, Arthur Wellesley, 1st duke of. SUPPLEMENTARY
      DESPATCHES, CORRESPONDENCE, AND MEMORANDA. Edited by Arthur R.
      Wellesley. London: J. Murray, 1858-72. Vols. 8-11.

375. Wesemann, Johann H.C. KANONIER DES KAISERS: KRIEGSTAGEBUCH
      DES   HEINRICH   WESEMANN,   1808-1814.   Cologne: Verlag
      Wissenschaft und Politik, 1971.

376. Westmorland, John Fane, 11th earl of. MEMOIR OF THE OPERATIONS
      OF THE ALLIED ARMIES, UNDER PRINCE SCHWARZENBERG AND MARSHAL
      BLUCHER, DURING THE LATTER END OF 1813, AND THE YEAR 1814. 2d
      ed. London: J. Murray, 1822. 2 vols.

377. White, Arthur S. A BIBLIOGRAPHY OF REGIMENTAL HISTORIES OF THE
      BRITISH ARMY. London: Society for Army Historical Research,
      1965.

378. Wilson, Robert T. PRIVATE DIARY OF TRAVELS, PERSONAL SERVICE
      AND PUBLIC EVENTS, DURING MISSION AND EMPLOYMENT WITH THE
      EUROPEAN ARMIES IN THE CAMPAIGNS OF 1812, 1813, 1814. FROM THE
      INVASION OF RUSSIA TO THE CAPTURE OF PARIS. Edited by the Rev.
      Herbert Randolph. London: J. Murray, 1861. 2 vols.

379. Wirth, Joseph. LE MARECHAL LEFEBVRE, DUC DE DANTZIG,
      (1755-1820). Paris: Perrin, 1904.

380. Woerl, J.E. GESCHICHTE DER KRIEGE VON 1792 MIT 1815 MIT
      SCHLACHTEN ATLAS. Freiburg im Breisgau: Herber'fche
      Berlagshandlung, 1852.

381. Wolff, Henry Drummond. THE ISLAND EMPIRE; OR, SCENES OF THE
      FIRST EXILE OF THE EMPEROR NAPOLEON I. Philadelphia: Parry
      and Macmillan, 1855.

382. Woodberry, George. JOURNAL DU LIEUTENANT WOODBERRY; CAMPAGNES
      DE PORTUGAL ET D'ESPAGNE, DE FRANCE, DE BELGIQUE, ET DE FRANCE
      (1813-1815). Translated from the English by Georges Hélie.
      Paris: Plon, 1896.

383. Wyld, James, pub. MAPS AND PLANS, SHOWING THE PRINCIPAL
      MOVEMENTS, BATTLES & SIEGES IN WHICH THE BRITISH ARMY WAS
      ENGAGED DURING THE WAR FROM 1808 TO 1814, IN THE SPANISH
      PENINSULA AND THE SOUTH OF FRANCE. London: J. Wyld, 1840.

384. Yaple, R.L. "The Auxiliaries: Foreign and Miscellaneous
     Regiments in the British Army." JOURNAL OF THE SOCIETY FOR
     ARMY HISTORICAL RESEARCH 50 (1972): 10-28.

385. Yorck von Wartenburg, Maximilian, graf. NAPOLEON AS A GENERAL.
     Edited by Walter H. James. London: Gilbert and Rivington,
     1902. 2 vols.

386. Young, Peter. NAPOLEON'S MARSHALS. New York: Hippocrene
     Books, 1973.

387. Yvert, Louis. HISTORIQUE DU 13e REGIMENT DE CUIRASSIERS,
     1807-1814 A NOS JOURS. Chartres: Garnier, 1895.

388. Zaluski, General. "Les Chevau-légers polonais de la garde en
     1813 et 1814." CARNET DE LA SABRETACHE 6 (1898): 472-500.

389. Zayas, Julio R. de. "Les Hussards Cantabres, 1808-1814: Les
     Hussards espagnols dans la Guerre d'Independence." VIVAT
     HUSSAR 13 (1978): 12-20.

390. Zeller, André. SOLDATS PERDUS: Paris: Perrin, 1977.

                              PERIODICALS

391. LE BRIQUET. 1959 to present.

392. LA CARNET DE LA SABRETACHE. 1893 to present.

393. PANOPLIES.

394. REVUE DE LA SOCIETE DES AMIS DU MUSEE DE L'ARMEE. 1905 to
     present.

395. REVUE DE PARIS. 1894-1940.

396. REVUE HISTORIQUE DE L'ARMEE. 1945 to present.

397. ROYAL UNITED SERVICE INSTITUTION. 1888 to present.

398. SOCIETY FOR ARMY HISTORICAL RESEARCH. 1921 to present.

399. SOUVENIR NAPOLEONIEN. 1937 to present.

400. UNIFORMES.

401. VIVAT HUSSAR. 1966 to present.

CHAPTER XV

THE HUNDRED DAYS: A POLITICAL AND MILITARY PERSPECTIVE

Daniel P. Resnick, Carnegie-Mellon University
Guillaume de Bertier de Sauvigny, Institut Catholique, Paris

The Napoleonic inter-regnum between the First and Second Restorations has been called the "Hundred Days," a term used by the Prefect of Paris, Chabrol-Volvic, when he welcomed the returning Bourbon monarch to Paris. This epilogue to the Empire and rude hiatus in the Restoration lasted, in fact, for 110 days, from March 20 to July 8, 1815. During that period, Napoleon again occupied the Tuileries palace and controlled the government of France.

Despite its brevity, it was a period of great moment in the history of both France and Europe, marked by continuing conflict at home and a set of major battles on the northeastern frontier, culminating in the defeat of the Napoleonic forces at Waterloo. This defeat not only put an end to the rule of Bonaparte's family dynasty in Europe, and made possible the return of the Bourbons to power in France, but it also introduced a military occupation, extending at its peak to two-thirds of France.

The political history of this period is closely tied to warfare because of two developments. The first of these flows from decisions by the Bourbons; the second from steps taken by the Allied powers. Acting for the established dynasty, Louis XVIII, at Ghent in temporary exile, refused to abdicate, and gave support through his family and advisors to the internal forces resisting the Emperor's authority. At the same time, the Allied governments, still gathered at Vienna, determined to dethrone Napoleon, seen as a threat to the peace of Europe. The two acts of military confrontation that followed involved both regular forces and guerrilla groupings, extending within France through the Midi and Vendée, and beyond France to the Belgian plain.

GENERAL WORKS

Essential contributions to the history of this period have been made by recent major studies of both the Empire and the Restoration. The strongest and most recent of the synthetic works on Napoleon, with critical and extended bibliographical references, is Jean Tulard's NAPOLEON (215), which extends the important earlier work of Georges Lefebvre (132), Jacques Godechot (86), and the distinguished scholars who collaborated on the attractive illustrated volumes produced under the sponsorship of Jean Mistler (161). For the Restoration, the essential single volume is G. de Bertier de Sauvigny's LA RESTAURATION (22), with an English translation by Lynn Case (20). The most recent edition, with an updated bibliography, appeared in 1974. A number of regional histories provide a context for dealing with the inter-regnum. To be noted are H. Contamine for Metz and the Moselle (54), J. Vidalenç for the Eure (225), and P. Leuillot for Alsace (138).

A number of nineteenth-century multivolume histories of the Restoration still offer useful chapters on the Hundred Days, especially those of A. Nettement (165) and A. Vaulabelle (220), which

must be read, nonetheless, with some caution. See G. de Bertier de
Sauvigny's "Restoration Historiography" (21) for a critical
perspective. The most important contribution, with references to the
sources, is the trilogy of Henry Houssaye, LA PREMIERE RESTAURATION;
LE RETOUR DE L'ILE D'ELBE; LES CENT JOURS (108). Although it makes
an effort to give every party its due, it is overwhelmed by the
legend of Napoleon. Other important works for the political as well
as the military context of the Hundred Days, with bibliographies, are
the thesis of E. Le Gallo, LES CENT JOURS (133), the series of
volumes by J. Thiry (207-210), and R. Margerit's WATERLOO (152),
which is of more political interest than its title suggests. The
work of E. Hubert, LES CENT JOURS (110), is less significant.

A number of works on the local history of the Hundred Days have
appeared in the proceedings of provincial academies and societies,
and some have been published separately. The following are
substantial enough to be of interest: Firino's "Soissons en 1815"
(76), Alleaume's "Les Cent Jours dans le Var" (2), Cauvin's "Les
Cent-Jours dans les Basses-Alpes" (41), Richard's "Les Cent Jours à
Nancy" (189), Perroud's "Les Cent-Jours à Saint-Genix" (175),
Pingaud's LA FRANCHE COMTE EN 1815 (178), Marzin's "Morlaix pendant
les Cent Jours et la Restauration" (156), Vauthier's "Versailles et
la Seine-et-Oise pendant les Cent Jours" (221), Goulet's "La Defense
de Toulon" (89), and Leroy's "Episodes des Cent-Jours à Melun" (135).

These take their place beside a number of monographs on the
Hundred Days in the countryside. Among them, we note the following:
Breistroff's EPISODE DE 1815 DANS LE BRIANCONNAIS (31), Develay's LA
BOURGOGNE PENDANT LES CENT JOURS (70), Cornillon's LE BOURBONNAIS
PENDANT LES CENT JOURS (57), La Place's LA FLANDRE EN 1815 (122), and
Leuillot's LA PREMIERE RESTAURATION ET LES CENT JOURS EN ALSACE
(138).

ARCHIVAL SOURCES

The manuscript sources for the military history of this period
are rich and varied. At the Archives Nationales, the F1c series is
particularly important for assessments of public opinion, the F7
series for a study of the conflicts between royalists and supporters
of Bonaparte in the South and West. At the Archives de la Guerre,
the C series is especially valuable for the Hundred Days in the West.
Departmental and municipal archives contain much as yet unexploited
material. The bibliographical contributions in Jean Tulard's
NAPOLEON (215) introduce manuscript as well as published sources.

SPECIALIZED WORKS: NAPOLEON RECONQUERS PARIS

There are a number of accounts of Napoleon's return from Elba.
Claude Manceron's NAPOLEON REPREND PARIS (148) is the most lively, a
detailed exploration of the last week before he reached Paris, 14-20
March 1815. It begins with Marshal Ney's defection ("the cause of
the Bourbons is lost forever"), the hostile declaration of the Allied
powers at Vienna, and Napoleon's encounter with prefectoral
resistance in Macôn. This study is strongly hostile to the Bourbons,
from a left-revolutionary rather than a liberal perspective. It
criticizes Napoleon for his failure to champion the revolutionary
aspirations of 1793-94. Also of interest are S. and A. Troussier's

LA CHEVAUCHEE HEROIQUE (212), Jean Thiry's LE VOL DE L'AIGLE (210), and A. Chollier's LA VRAIE ROUTE NAPOLEON (48).

Various memoirs are important in describing the return and its political context. For Napoleon's designs, see the correspondence and the memoirs of Las Cases (123) and Gourgaud (90). Those accompanying Napoleon or joining him on his route north have also left their recollections: see the contributions of Marchand (151), but especially of Coignet, a demi-solde who took up arms again (51).

For royalist responses, see Vitrolles (230) and Chateaubriand (46), and for accounts by former officers of the Emperor who respected their oath to the Bourbons, the memoirs of Macdonald (145) and Marmont (154). Also of considerable interest are the accounts of officials who served or would serve both regimes: see Talleyrand (206) and Fouché (78), the latter important despite questions of its authenticity. See also the testimony of Pasquier (172), who remained loyal to Louis during the Hundred Days.

For a discussion of public responses in the first week after leaving Elba, see E. Martin's "Napoleon à Barreme" (155) and G. de Manteyer's "Le Passage à Gap" (150). The defections within the army and tensions between officers and ordinary soldiers are discussed in P. de Damassy's "Epreuves morales de l'armée" (63), as well as in studies of the Restoration trials of key military leaders. For the trial of Marshal Ney, see the work of H. Kurtz (118).

SPECIALIZED WORKS: ROYALIST STRUGGLE FOR FRANCE

Early in the morning of 20 March, the day on which Napoleon occupied the Tuilleries palace, Louis left Paris eventually to establish his court at Ghent. Louis Aragon's LA SEMAINE SAINTE (5) recreates the exodus from Paris in vivid detail. Philip Mansel's LOUIS XVIII (149), a superb recent biography, describes family and politics there, and J.P. Haebert re-examines the king's position in "Louis XVIII à Gand" (100). Essential primary material will be found in Hüe's SOUVENIRS (111), the memoirs of Marmont (154), Maine de Biran's JOURNAL (147), Semallé's SOUVENIRS (197), the memoirs of Vitrolles (230), and LE MONITEUR DE GAND. For dispatches and correspondence, see Romberg and Malet's LOUIS XVIII ET LES CENT-JOURS A GAND (194).

The duchesse d'Angoulême, daughter of the late king, was in the Midi at Bordeaux on 5 March when news of Napoleon's escape from Elba reached the city. Her husband left on the 10th for Nîmes, to take command of the Rhône Valley forces in the royalist army, while the duchess attempted to rally the army garrisons in the city to the royalist cause. Entering the barracks to ask the soldiers to honor the oath of loyalty they had taken the previous year to Louis XVIII, she earned the admiration of General Clauzel (50), whose troops were ready to take over the city on behalf of the Emperor on 1 April. For Napoleon, she was "the only man" among the Bourbons. The duchess maintained her efforts in Bordeaux until 12 April, thirteen days after Napoleon had regained Paris, and then sailed for England to avoid capture. For the struggle in and around Bordeaux, see F. Laurentie's "Souvenirs de 1815. Manuscrit inédit de la duchesse d'Angoulême" (127); Damas's LETTRE ... SUR LES EVENEMENTS (62); Beauchamp's LA DUCHESSE ... A BORDEAUX (14); and Jean Cavignac's "Les Cent-Jours à Bordeaux" (42).

The biographical literature on the duchess also remains an important source for her political and military activity during the Hundred Days. Some useful perspectives on her efforts in Bordeaux may be found in A. Nettement's VIE DE MARIE-THERESE (166) which offers an eyewitness account of one confrontation; Langeron's MADAME ROYALE (121), a warm empathetic study, and the respectful account offered by Colonel Herbillon (102). Judgments of her are almost universally favorable, even when there is antipathy to the duke, as in the study by Gros (93). Also useful on these events, despite its moralizing about appropriate sex roles, is Turquan's LA DERNIERE DAUPHINE (216). It draws heavily on the memoirs and recollections of Barante (11), de Broglie (33), the Comte de Neuilly (167), the Comte de Montgaillard (163), the Comte de Lavalette (130), and Madame de Chastenay (45). A long letter from the duchess to Louis XVIII in Ghent, sent from Bordeaux on 20 March, may be found in Docteur Véron's MEMOIRES D'UN BOURGEOIS DE PARIS (222).

Contemporary accounts of the campaign of the Duc d'Angoulême deal with the period from 10 March, when he left Bordeaux for Nîmes, to 16 April, when he embarked for Spain. During those five weeks he raised an army of about 10,000 men in the Midi. The economic dislocations to Bordeaux and other southern cities which created a favorable environment for royalist recruiting efforts are discussed in Jean Vidalenç's "La Vie économique" (226) and François Crouzet's "Le Sous-développement économique du Sud-ouest" (60). The organization of a royalist network in the area under the late empire is examined in G. de Bertier de Sauvigny's UN TYPE D'ULTRA-ROYALISTE (23) and J. Verrier's "Sur les traces de la congregation à Bordeaux" (223). As part of an unsuccessful campaign to gain control of Lyon, engagements were fought at Sisteron in the Basses-Alpes and Loriol, on the route to Valence. More than one hundred were killed and at least that number taken prisoner. Overviews of the campaign are offered by contemporaries in L. Suleau's RECIT DES OPERATIONS (205), L. Pagezy de Bourdeliac's OPERATIONS MILITAIRES (170), F. Licquet's CAMPAGNE DE S.A.R. (141), and L. Bonnardet's LA CAMPAGNE (28).

The personal courage of the Duke is underlined in Eugène de Guichen's LE DUC D'ANGOULEME (98). But after initial successes in recruiting troops, Angoulême found his ranks decimated by defections. The conduct of the only line regiment in the south that remained largely loyal to the Bourbons until early April is described in M. Marion's "Le 10e de Ligne en 1815" (153). LE MONITEUR (241), 5-8 April, offers reports of Angoulême's movements. A truce was arranged at La Palud, about twenty miles north of Avignon, after Angoulême's troops had been hemmed in by the separate forces of Generals Gilly and Grouchy. H. Houssaye's 1815 (108) offers a number of references on this subject. See, among others, O. Monge's LA CAPITULATION (162). The text of the truce can be found in the Bibliothèque Nationale (Paris) manuscript collections.

Toulouse, Marseilles, and Nîmes were all centers of royalist activity in the Midi. The prior history of social conflict in the area under revolutionary and royalist banners is reviewed in G. Lewis's THE SECOND VENDEE (139), L. Sancti's "Les intrigues royalistes" (196), and A. Vincent's HISTOIRE DES GUERRES (229). For Toulouse, the following secondary accounts are useful: Armand Praviel's "Le Massacre de Ramel" (182) and J. Loubet's "Le Gouvernement Toulousain" (144). In his HISTOIRE DE TOULOUSE (1) A.

d'Aldéguier also discusses the Hundred Days in the city, as does Comte Begouen in "Les Débuts des Cent-Jours" (17). Essential primary sources can be found in two memoirs: Charles de Rémusat's MEMOIRES DE MA VIE (186) and J. de Villèle's MEMOIRES ET CORRESPONDANCE (228). Royalist activities in Marseilles are detailed in P. Gaffarel's "Un Episode ... les massacres de Marseille" (81) and R. Joxe's "Le Comité royal provisoire de Marseille" (115). Several histories of the city are also important including L. Lautard's ESQUISSES HISTORIQUES: MARSEILLE (128) and R. Busquet's HISTOIRE DE MARSEILLE (36). An overview of developments in Nîmes may be found in P.L. Baragnon's ABREGE DE L'HISTOIRE DE NIMES (10), and James Hood (106) provides an excellent analysis of the social and religious tensions during the early revolutionary period.

Since anti-Protestant feelings were used to mobilize royalist forces, and Protestant office-holders, business elites, and artisans were the principal victims of royalist violence, all accounts of what happened in this city deal with the layers of political, socio-economic, and religious tension. See the prefect J. d'Arbaud-Joucques's TROUBLES ET AGITATIONS (6) and the Protestant perspective by P.J. Lauze de Peret (129). The cause of Protestants in Bas-Languedoc was taken up by English dissenters, who sent representatives to the scene. For their views, see Rev. C. Perrot's REPORT ON THE PERSECUTIONS (174), H. Williams's LATE PERSECUTION OF THE PROTESTANTS (236), and A. Wemyss's "L'Angleterre et la Terreur Blanche" (235). For broader historical perspectives on the Protestant communities of the south, see B. Poland's FRENCH PROTESTANTISM (180) and D. Robert's LES EGLISES REFORMEES (191).

The White Terror that spread through the Midi at the end of the Hundred Days, after Napoleon's defeat at Waterloo, is placed in its national political context in D. Resnick's THE WHITE TERROR (187). See also the earlier monograph of E. Daudet, LA TERREUR BLANCHE (66). The work by the Duc de Castries on this topic (39) is only of moderate interest.

For the Vendée, the major secondary work is Roger Grand's LA CHOUANNERIE DE 1815 (91), the preface of which offers a brief bibliographical essay. Three divisions in the Army of the Loire, stationed at Rennes, Nantes, and Tour, under the direction of General Lamarque, were ordered to contain the insurrections in the West of France. The departments involved were principally the Loire-Inférieure, the Maine-et-Loire, the Deux-Sèvres, and the Vendée. Primary sources for the civil war in this region have been provided by memoirs of the royalist leaders d'Autichamp (9) and Canuel (37), and by those of General Lamarque (120). Issues of strategy in this campaign are discussed in Bertrand Lasserre's LES CENT-JOURS EN VENDEE (124), a work based on primary sources. See also Boëssière's "La Campagne de 1815" (27) and Bouton's "Les Royalistes Sarthois" (30).

Royalist leadership came from peasant elites in the Morbihan, and small landed nobility and clergy elsewhere. Royalists mobilized perhaps 25,000 men, more than three times the number Napoleon sent against them. But artillery and ammunition was lacking, even though England delivered some supplies to the ports. And the royalists' strategy was poorly co-ordinated, despite occasional successes. For the latter, see L. Merle (158). The campaign lasted four months, and stretched over the former provinces of Maine, Anjou, Bas-Poitou,

Brittany, and Basse-Normandie. Known as the Petite Chouannerie, the combat was less murderous, more calculated, and fought with more mutual respect and restraint than the Grande Chouannerie of the revolutionary period. The temporary resolution of the Catholic issue by the Concordat contributed to the more measured conduct of this campaign. By the end of June the royalist resistance had been broken. Royalist losses included General Louis de La Rochejacquelein, General Suzannet, a dozen lower ranking leaders, and about two hundred others, in the estimate of Grand (91). The Pacification of Cholet, an agreement signed on 26 June, brought the fighting on the left bank of the Loire to an end, and was honored on the royalist side even after news of Napoleon's defeat at Waterloo reached the area. The campaign on the right bank of the Loire continued until the Prussians entered Paris on 7 July.

SPECIALIZED WORKS: THE CONGRESS OF VIENNA

Contrary to the expectations of Napoleon, the Allied powers, who had gathered at Vienna in November, 1814, remained in session, and on 25 March, declared war on the Usurper. For the direction of the alliance against Napoleon, C.K. Webster's THE FOREIGN POLICY OF CASTLEREAGH (231) and A. Sorel's L'EUROPE ET LA REVOLUTION FRANCAISE (201) are still essential. Nicolson's THE CONGRESS OF VIENNA, (168) offers a valuable study of the relationship between military developments and political action in Vienna. Klüber's AKTEN DES WIENER KONGRESSES (117) is a basic primary source. Among the memoirs and published correspondence, see Metternich's MEMOIRES (159) and Wellington's dispatches (233, 234).

SPECIALIZED WORKS: CAMPAIGN OF 1815

On 15 June, Napoleon crossed the Sambre on the route to Brussels. In three battles over four days--Ligny, Quatre Bras, and Waterloo--the French lost more than 50,000 men, and the Allies almost as many. There is more literature on this campaign than on any other of that duration in European history. The major bibliographies are C.W. Robinson's WELLINGTON'S CAMPAIGNS (193); Kircheisen's BIBLIOGRAPHIE DU TEMPS DE NAPOLEON (116), and the GUIDE BIBLIOGRAPHIQUE SOMMAIRE (160), compiled by the history section of the French Ministry of the Army, under the direction of René Couret.

On this campaign, the principal secondary works on the French side are Henry Houssaye's WATERLOO (108), Charras's CAMPAGNE DE 1815 (43), Thiry's LES DEBUTS (208), Le Gallo's LES CENT JOURS (133), Lachouque's NAPOLEON A WATERLOO (119), and Margerit's WATERLOO (152). For the British, the major secondary works are Philip Guedalla's THE HUNDRED DAYS (97), A.F. Becke's NAPOLEON AND WATERLOO (16), J.C. Ropes's CAMPAIGN OF WATERLOO (195), Weller's WELLINGTON AT WATERLOO (232), C.W. Robinson's WELLINGTON'S CAMPAIGNS (193), and John Fortescue's HISTORY OF THE BRITISH ARMY (77). The principal Prussian histories of the Waterloo campaign are those of C. von Damitz (64) and O. von Lettow-Vorbeck (136). The larger works of C. von der Goltz, KRIEGSGESCHICHTE DEUTSCHLANDS (88), and Julius von Pflugk-Harttung, ELBA UND DIE HUNDERT TAGE (176), are still useful. On the Dutch-Belgian side, see J. de T'Serclaes de Wommersom's CAMPAGNE DE 1815 (213), Colonel de Bas's PRINZ FREDERIK DER NEDERLANDEN EN ZIJN

TIJD (12), and Van Loben Sels's LA CAMPAGNE DE 1815 DANS LES PAYS-BAS (218).

Tactical issues on the French side are the focus of a number of studies. In the debate over Napoleon's judgment and decisiveness, see, in defense of Napoleon, Vaulabelle's CAMPAGNE ET BATAILLE (219). The critique of Napoleon's behavior is most effectively made by Jomini in his PRECIS POLITIQUE ET MILITAIRE (113) and taken up again by Grouard (94) and Charras (43). Grouchy defends his failure to provide timely reinforcements in FRAGMENTS HISTORIQUES (95). On the allied side, there is some dispute in the campaign histories over the respective contributions and merits of Wellington and Blücher as commanders. Some light on Wellington's tactics is shed in studies by Gleig (84), Siborne (199), Gurwood (99), and Wood (237). Napoleon's reasons for forcing a struggle for Brussels are well explored in Philip Guedalla's THE HUNDRED DAYS (97), which stresses the popularity at home of regaining control over territory which the French had held during the Revolution and Empire. For Napoleon's retrospective view of the campaign from Saint Helena, see COMMENTAIRES (164).

Military leadership was provided on the French side by the small number of marshals who had not gone over to the Bourbons or fled, and by a larger number of experienced generals. Among the marshals who served Napoleon during the Hundred Days, we have memoirs or campaign accounts by Davout (67), who was made Minister of War, Soult (203), who served as chief of staff, and Grouchy (96). Among the generals, Rapp (185), Suchet (204), Clauzel (50), and Decaen (68) have all contributed to this literature. Unfortunately, some of the accounts, like those of Soult and Suchet, do not cover the Waterloo campaign. Others, as those of Grouchy, are rich for this period. Jean Tulard's essential guide to the memoir literature (214) offers some assistance in identifying the relevant material. This was the first military campaign in history to provide a large literature of first-hand accounts by participants who were mainly in the lower grades of service. Accounts by French, British, Dutch, Prussian, and other participants have been gathered in a number of recent anthologies. See Antony Brett-James (32), D. Howarth (109), and C. Hibbert (104). Useful biographical information can be found in G. Six's DICTIONNAIRE BIOGRAPHIQUE DES GENERAUX ET AMIRAUX FRANCAIS (200), J. Gavard's GALERIES HISTORIQUES (83), and J. Valynseele's LES MARECHAUX DU PREMIER EMPIRE (217).

To illustrate the terrain, there are a number of excellent collections of maps, essential for the Waterloo campaign. Of particular interest are Esposito and Elting's A MILITARY HISTORY AND ATLAS (75), and J. Quennevat's ATLAS DE LA GRANDE ARMEE (183). Similarly, in the tradition of the images of Epinal, the historical literature on this campaign is rich in lithographs and other forms of pictorial representation. See the chapter by Colonel Lachouque in Jean Mistler's NAPOLEON ET L'EMPIRE (161), Lachouque's NAPOLEON A WATERLOO (119), and Ugo Pericoli's 1815 (173), for a splendid volume on military dress.

SPECIALIZED WORKS: NAPOLEON'S ABDICATION

The political circumstances that surrounded the abdication are reviewed in L. Madelin's FOUCHE (146); MEMOIRES DE LA REINE HORTENSE

(15), Lord Broughton's RECOLLECTIONS OF A LONG LIFE (105), James
Gallatin's A GREAT PEACE MAKER (82), Marquis de Noailles's LE COMTE
MOLE (169), and Ray Cubberly's THE ROLE OF FOUCHE (61).   For
American reaction to Waterloo, see Donald D. Horward's "L'Opinion
américaine" (107). The debates in the Chambers may be followed in
ARCHIVES PARLEMENTAIRES (7).   Leroux-Cesbron studies negotiations
between Wellington, Talleyrand, and Fouché in "La Folie--Saint-James"
(134).

SPECIALIZED STUDIES: MILITARY OCCUPATION

A military occupation by allied forces began shortly after
Waterloo and brought a million and a quarter men onto French soil.
On July 3, Marshal Davout turned over Paris to the Allies and agreed
to withdraw the main units of the French army south of the Loire
within eight days. The recognition of the occupation is marked
officially in the LE MONITEUR (241), 6 July, by Provisional Minister
of the Interior Carnot's assurance to the Prefects that the Allies
would respect persons, property, institutions, and the symbols of
sovereignty.
       Despite an agreement on 17 July, for evacuation of all the
garrisons by line regiments and national guard units, there were many
instances of resistance, and many forts were attacked. For Mézières,
see Colin (52); Casteig (38) and Bulos (35) for Huningue; Lorin (142)
and Bénard (19) for Rambouillet; and Laulan (126) for Vincennes.
Fromageot (79), and Quennevat (184) deal with Versailles, Seyssel
with l'Ecluse (198); Jacquemart with La Fère (112), and Golaz (87)
with Mont-Dauphin. Pillaging was also a problem, involving most
often troops from Prussia, Bavaria, Baden, and Württemberg. The
abundant archival documentation on this period in the Ministries of
War and Foreign Affairs is described in the excellent monograph by R.
André, L'OCCUPATION (3), which includes maps and tables. More than
sixty departments were invaded, and only south and west of a line
marked by the Loire, Allier, Arc, Ardèche, and Rhône rivers did Louis
XVIII retain full control of his territory. The lines of occupation
were regularized on 24 July, after negotiations with the new
government.
       Regional and local histories of the occupation, drawn on by
André, are those of A. Bénard (19), M. Bruchet (34), A. Chuquet (49),
E. Duminy (72), P. Gaffarel (80), A. Gras (92), G. de Hautecloque
(101), A. Joubert (114), E. Lecomte (131), F. Libaudière (140), F.
Lorin (143), L. Piccard (177), F. Pougiat (181), and L. Vignols
(227). Since the publication of André's monograph, studies have
appeared on the Ardennes, by M. Colin (53); on the Aisne, by E.
Crevaux (59) and J. Dejente (69); by R. Parent (171) on Montargis;
and by T. Catta (40) on the Maine-et-Loire. There has also been work
by F. Dutacq (73) on Lyon; J. Duvivier (74) on Bouchain; F. Blanchet
(24) on the pays de Bray; J. Auriac (8) on Provins; P. Bayaud (13) on
the Basses-Pyrénées, C. Ansart (4) on the Oise; H. Corbes (55) on the
Côtes-du-Nord; Hervé (103) on the Ille-et-Vilaine; and P. Leuillot
(138) on Alsace. The depredations of the Allies are discussed in the
memoirs of Talleyrand (206), Pasquier (172), Vitrolles (230), and
Bourrienne (29).
       The treaty of 20 November 1815, established an indemnity of
700,000 francs and authorization for occupying troops to remain in

France for five years. See J. Crétineau-Joly's TRAITES DE 1815 (58)
for the text, and A. Sorel's LE TRAITE DE PARIS (202) for a
comparison with the one signed on 30 May 1814. However, evacuation
of foreign troops began in September, 1815, and by the beginning of
1816, only 150,000 troops were left. The last units were withdrawn,
ahead of schedule, in 1817. For the withdrawal of French army units
south of the Loire and to the West in the summer of 1815, linked to
the terms of the treaty, see the articles of P. Massé (157) and J.
Ribault (188). On the general subject of military occupations, see
the work of R. Robin (192).

SPECIALIZED WORKS: PUBLIC OPINION

The regional and local studies listed above are also important
for an understanding of public attitudes toward rival political
camps, the political system, the war, and the occupation. The
plebiscite of 1815 on the Acte additionnel is the most important
single source for public attitudes toward the Bourbons and Napoleon.
See J. Godechot's LES CONSTITUTIONS DE LA FRANCE (85) for the text.
An excellent and revisionist monograph on the plebiscite by F.
Bluche, LE PLEBISCITE DES CENT-JOURS (26), compares the portion of
the adult male populations by regions and city that gave Napoleon's
constitution its approval in May with the size of the same group in
the same areas in the plebiscites of the Empire. It becomes clear,
from this analysis that, during the Hundred Days, Napoleon had lost
much of the support he enjoyed during the early Empire, and that
public opinion was divided between the Bourbons and the Emperor.

In the cities, during the plebiscite of May, only 15% of the
adult males voted yes in Lyon, 12% in Paris, 11% in Strasbourg, 3% in
Bordeaux, and 1% in Marseille. See the excellent assessment of the
meaning of this vote in Mansel's LOUIS XVIII (149). Royalist support
was strong in cities and among liberals, as well as in areas that
were rural and reactionary. The royalists were strongly identified,
thanks to the CHARTE CONSTITUTIONNELLE and the moderate policies of
the First Restoration, with liberal constitutionalism. They were
also the party of peace. The recent study by K. Tönneson, "Les
Fédéres de Paris pendant les Cent-Jours" (211) confirms the absence
of support for Napoleon in the Parisian population. For the opinion
of political elites, see the study of J. Chaumié, "Les Girondins et
les Cent Jours" (47).

PERIODICALS

The leading French journals which include material on the
Hundred Days are the ANNALES HISTORIQUES DE LA REVOLUTION FRANCAISE,
the BULLETIN D'HISTOIRE ECONOMIQUE ET SOCIALE DE LA REVOLUTION
FRANCAISE, the REVUE HISTORIQUE, the REVUE DE L'INSTITUT NAPOLEON,
the REVUE HISTORIQUE DES ARMEES, the REVUE DES ETUDES NAPOLEONIENNES,
and the CARNET DE LA SABRETACHE. Much of the history of this period
can still be pursued, profitably, through the publications of
regional academies, scholarly congresses, and local societies, which
are difficult to access. For work in this category that appeared in
the period 1880-1910, see the BIBLIOGRAPHIE ANNUELLE ... SOCIETES
SAVANTES (125) by R. Lasteyrie and A. Vidier.

FUTURE RESEARCH

There is a need for continuing research on three sets of questions. The first concerns the continuity in political elites that governed France during the Hundred Days; the second, the apathy of local publics toward the Napoleonic regime; and the third, more properly within the domain of military history, the recruitment of the Army of the North, sent into the Belgian campaign.

Nicholas Richardson's THE FRENCH PREFECTORAL CORPS (190) shows the continuity in departmental administration at the highest level over the Hundred Days, and the growth in the recruitment of nobles in these positions under Napoleon. Further studies would be useful of the mayoral corps, and the sub-prefects, to better establish the social recruitment of political elites, and the variations in administrative continuity by regions. Jean Tulard's guide to the memoir literature of the Napoleonic period (214), complemented by Bertier de Sauvigny's guide to the memoirs of the Restoration, currently in the process of preparation, should encourage some prosopographical studies of individuals in civilian and military roles with common sets of experiences.

Studies of public opinion, after the pioneering work of Bluche (26), might well focus on the sources of political apathy in this period, and the different meanings that support for Napoleon or the Bourbons had for different regions and social classes. More studies of national scope, comparing the behavior of different regions are also needed.

Although we have some understanding of the attitude of the demi-solde toward Napoleon from the work of Jean Vidalenç (224) and others, the recruitment of the Army of the North by Napoleon needs further study. Detailed studies of recruitment efforts in specific regions would help clarify public understanding of the war issue and illuminate Napoleon's strategy for molding public opinion during the Hundred Days. An analysis of various aspects of military operations following Waterloo would be useful to determine the scope and strength of resistance. The same is true of the demobilization of the army and its impact upon the officers and men.

BIBLIOGRAPHY: THE HUNDRED DAYS

1. Aldéguier, Auguste d'. HISTOIRE DE LA VILLE DE TOULOUSE. Toulouse: Chauvin, 1833-35. 4 vols.

2. Alleaume, Charles. "Les Cent Jours dans le Var." BULLETIN DE LA SOCIETE D'ETUDES SCIENTIFIQUES ET ARCHEOLOGIQUES DE DRAGUIGNAN 49 (1938-39): 5-205.

3. André, Roger. L'OCCUPATION DE LA FRANCE PAR LES ALLIES EN 1815. Paris: Boccard, 1924.

4. Ansart, Charles. "Aspects de l'occupation ennemie en 1814 et 1815 dans le department de l'Oise." ACTES DU 81e CONGRES DES SOCIETES SAVANTES, COMITE DES TRAVAUX HISTORIQUES ET SCIENTIFIQUES (1956): 535-46.

5. Aragon, Louis. LA SEMAINE SAINTE. Paris: Gallimard, 1958.

6. Arbaud-Joucques, Joseph Charles André, marquis d'. TROUBLES ET AGITATIONS DU DEPARTEMENT DU GARD EN 1815, CONTENANT LE RAPPORT DU REVEREND PERROT. Paris: Demonville, 1818.

7. ARCHIVES PARLEMENTAIRES DE 1787 A 1860, 2e série. Paris: Librairie administrative de P. Dupont, 1862-69. Vols. 13-16.

8. Auriac, J. d'. "L'Occupation ennemie à Provins en 1814 et 1815." COMITE DES TRAVAUX HISTORIQUES ET SCIENTIFIQUES; SECTION D'HISTOIRE MODERNE ET CONTEMPORAINE 11 (1925): 149-69.

9. Autichamp, Charles d'. MEMOIRES POUR SERVIR A L'HISTOIRE DE LA CAMPAGNE DE 1815 DANS LA VENDEE. Paris: Egron, 1817.

10. Baragnon, P.L. ABREGE DE L'HISTOIRE DE NIMES, DE MENARD; CONTINUE JUSQU'A NOS JOURS. Nîmes: Gaude, 1835. Vol. 4.

11. Barante, Amable Guillaume Prosper Brugière, baron de. SOUVENIRS DU BARON DE BARANTE, DE L'ACADEMIE FRANCAISE. Paris: Calmann-Lévy, 1890-91. 8 vols.

12. Bas, Colonel F. de. PRINZ FREDERIK DER NEDERLANDEN EN ZIJN TIJD. Schiedam: H.A.M. Roclants, 1887-91. 8 vols.

13. Bayaud, Pierre. "Une Invasion espagnole dans les Basses-Pyrénée en 1815." ACTES DU 87e CONGRES DES SOCIETES SAVANTES, SECTION D'HISTOIRE MODERNE ET CONTEMPORAINE (1963): 443-88.

14. Beauchamp, Alphonse de. LA DUCHESSE D'ANGOULEME A BORDEAUX SUIVI DU RAPPORT INEDIT DE M. LE COMTE LYNCH. Versailles: J. A. Lebel, 1815.

15. Beauharnais, Hortense de, queen consort of Louis, king of Holland. MEMOIRES DE LA REINE HORTENSE PUBLIES PAR LE PRINCE NAPOLEON. Avec des notes de Jean Hanoteau. Paris: Plon, 1927. 3 vols.

16. Becke, Archibald Frank. NAPOLEON AND WATERLOO; THE EMPEROR'S
    CAMPAIGN WITH THE ARMEE DU NORD, 1815; A STRATEGICAL AND
    TACTICAL STUDY. London: K. Paul, Trench Trübner, 1914.   2
    vols.

17. Begouen, Comte. "Les Débuts des Cent-Jours à Toulouse, d'après
    les souvenirs de la comtesse de Saint-Aulaire." MEMOIRES DE
    L'ACADEMIE DES SCIENCES, INSCRIPTIONS ET BELLES LETTRES DE
    TOULOUSE, Series 12, 3 (1925): 483-532.

18. Bénard, A. "Les Invasions de 1814 et de 1815 dans l'Ain,"
    ANNALES DE LA SOCIETE D'EMULATION, AGRICULTURE, LETTRES ET ARTS
    DE L'AIN 20 (1887): 140-81, 241-89.

19. Bénard, Adjudant.   JOURNAL   DU   BLOCUS   DE   VINCENNES,
    JUILLET-NOVEMBRE 1815.   Publié par A. Philippe.   Paris:
    Charavay, 1881.

20. Bertier de Sauvigny, Guillaume de. THE BOURBON RESTORATION.
    English trans. by Lynn Case. Philadelphia: University of
    Pennsylvania Press, 1967.

21. Bertier de Sauvigny, Guillaume de. "A Century of Restoration
    Historiography." FRENCH HISTORICAL STUDIES 12 (1981): 41-67.

22. Bertier de Sauvigny, Guillaume de. LA RESTAURATION. 3d ed.
    Paris: Flammarion, 1974.

23. Bertier de Sauvigny, Guillaume de. UN TYPE D'ULTRA-ROYALISTE:
    LE COMTE FERDINAND DE BERTIER (1782-1864) ET L'ENIGME DE LA
    CONGREGATION. Paris: Les Presses Continentales, 1948.

24. Blanchet, François. "L'Occupation en 1815 et 1870-71 de
    Sommery, Commune du pays de Bray." ACTES DU 81e CONGRES DES
    SOCIETES   SAVANTES,   COMITE   DES   TRAVAUX   HISTORIQUES   ET
    SCIENTIFIQUES (1956): 547-54.

25. Bluche, Frédéric. "Les Pamphlets royalistes des Cent-Jours."
    REVUE DE L'INSTITUT NAPOLEON 131 (1975): 145-56.

26. Bluche, Frédéric. LE PLEBISCITE DES CENT-JOURS (AVRIL-MAI
    1815). Geneva: Droz; Paris: Minard, 1974.

27. Boëssière, Marquis de la. "La Campagne de 1815 dans le
    Morbihan." REVUE DE BRETAGNE ET DE VENDEE, Series 31, 5 (1869):
    169-84.

28. Bonnardet, Louis. LA CAMPAGNE DU DUC D'ANGOULEME DANS LE MIDI.
    Lyon: Perrin et Martinet, 1816.

29. Bourrienne, Louis Antoine Fauvelet de. MEMOIRES DE M. DE
    BOURRIENNE SUR NAPOLEON, LE DIRECTOIRE, LE CONSULAT, L'EMPIRE,
    ET LA RESTAURATION. Paris: Ladvocat, 1829. 10 vols.

30. Bouton, André. "Les Royalistes Sarthois pendant les Cent-Jours." LA PROVINCE DU MAINE, Series 2, 39 (1959): 93-106.

31. Breistroff. EPISODE DE 1815 DANS LE BRIANCONNAIS. Grenoble: Imprimerie de Prudhomme, 1850.

32. Brett-James, Antony, ed. THE HUNDRED DAYS: NAPOLEON'S LAST CAMPAIGN FROM EYEWITNESS ACCOUNTS. New York: St. Martin's Press, 1964.

33. Broglie, Achille Charles Léonce de. SOUVENIRS (1785-1870) DU FEU DUC DE BROGLIE. Paris: Calmann-Lévy, 1886. 4 vols.

34. Bruchet, M. "L'Invasion et l'occupation du département du Nord par les Alliés (1814-1818)." REVUE DU NORD 6 (1920): 261-99; 7 (1921): 30-61.

35. Bulos, A. PRECIS DES OPERATIONS DES ARMEES DU RHIN ET DU JURA EN 1815, SUIVI DU SIEGE D'HUNINGUE ET L'INSURRECTION DE STRASBOURG. Paris: Baudoin, 1819.

36. Busquet, Raoul. HISTOIRE DE MARSEILLE. Paris: Laffont, 1945.

37. Canuel, Simon. MEMOIRES SUR LA GUERRE DE VENDEE EN 1815. Paris: Dentu, 1817.

38. Casteig, J.B. LA DEFENSE D'HUNINGUE EN 1815 ET LE GENERAL BARBANEGRE. Paris et Nancy: Berger-Levrault, 1897.

39. Castries, René de La Croix, duc de. LA TERREUR BLANCHE: L'EPURATION DE 1815. Paris: Perrin, 1981.

40. Catta, Tony. "Le Général d'Andigné et l'occupation Prussienne de 1815 en Mayenne et en Maine-et-Loire." MEMOIRES DE L'ACADEMIE DES SCIENCES ET BELLES-LETTRES D'ANGERS, Series 9, 3-4 (1969-70): 111-22.

41. Cauvin, Christian. "Le Retour de l'Ile d'Elbe et les Cent-Jours dans les Basses-Alpes." ANNALES DES BASSES-ALPES 17 (1915): 1-108; 18 (1918): 283-328; 19 (1919-20): 29-85; 21 (1926-27): 72-141; 22 (1928-29): 275-84; 23 (1930-31): 212-46, 276-317.

42. Cavignac, Jean. "Les Cent-Jours à Bordeaux, à travers la correspondance de Clauzel." REVUE HISTORIQUE DE BORDEAUX 15 (1966): 65-72.

43. Charras, Jean Baptiste Adolphe. HISTOIRE DE LA CAMPAGNE DE 1815: WATERLOO. 5th ed. Brussels: Guyot, 1857. 2 vols.

44. Chassin, C.L. LES PACIFICATIONS DE L'OUEST. Vol. 3. DU DIX-HUIT FRUCTIDOR AU CONSULAT ET A L'INVASION. Paris: Dupont, 1899.

45. Chastenay-Lanty, Victorine, comtesse de. MEMOIRES DE MADAME DE CHASTENAY (1771-1815). Publiés par Alphonse Roserot. Paris: Plon-Nourrit, 1896. 2 vols.

46. Chateaubriand, François Auguste René, vicomte de. MEMOIRES D'OUTRE-TOMBE. Edition nouvelle par Maurice Levaillant et Georges Moulinier. 3d ed. Paris: Gallimard, 1957. 2 vols.

47. Chaumié, Jacqueline. "Les Girondins et les Cent Jours. Essai d'explication de leur comportement par leurs origines géographiques et sociales et leur passé politique (1793-1815)." ANNALES HISTORIQUES DE LA REVOLUTION FRANCAISE 43 (1971): 329-65.

48. Chollier, A. LA VRAIE ROUTE NAPOLEON. Paris: Editions Alpina, 1950.

49. Chuquet, Arthur Maxime. "Les Prussiens et le musée du Louvre en 1815." REVUE DES SCIENCES POLITIQUES, Series 3, 36 (1916): 264-94.

50. Clauzel, Bertrand. EXPOSE JUSTIFICATIF DE LA CONDUITE POLITIQUE DE M. LE LIEUTENANT GENERAL COMTE CLAUZEL DEPUIS LE RETABLISSEMENT DES BOURBONS EN FRANCE, JUSQU'AU 24 JUILLET, 1815. Paris: Pillet, 1816.

51. Coignet, Jean Roch. LES CAHIERS DU CAPITAINE COIGNET (1799-1815). Publiés par Lorédan-Larchey, d'après le manuscrit original. Paris: Hachette, 1883. 4 vols.

52. Colin, Hubert. LE SIEGE DE MEZIERES PAR LES ALLIES EN 1815, PRECEDE D'UNE NOTICE HISTORIQUE SUR CETTE VILLE ET SUR LE PAYS DE CASTRICE. Vouziers: A. Lopie, 1865.

53. Colin, Maurice. "A Propos de l'occupation des Ardennes par les troupes Alliées (1815-1818). Peut-on parler d'un 'patriotisme des frontières'?" REVUE HISTORIQUE ARDENNAISE 14 (1979): 69-95.

54. Contamine, Henry. METZ ET LA MOSELLE DE 1814 A 1870, ETUDE DE LA VIE ET DE L'ADMINISTRATION AU XIXe SIECLE. Nancy: Société d'impressions typographiques, 1932.

55. Corbes, H. "Les Prussiens dans les Côtes-du-Nord, 1815." MEMOIRES DE LA SOCIETE D'EMULATION DES COTES-DU-NORD 84 (1955): 133-49.

56. Cornelius, John C. THE MILITARY FORCES OF FRANCE. SPECIAL BIBLIOGRAPHY 15. Carlisle Barracks, Penn.: U.S. Army Military History Institute, 1977.

57. Cornillon, J. LE BOURBONNAIS PENDANT LES CENT-JOURS. Moulins: Progrès de l'Allier, 1925.

58. Crétineau-Joly, Jacques Augustin Marie. HISTOIRE DES TRAITES DE 1815 ET DE LEUR EXECUTION. Paris: Colomb de Batines, 1842.

59. Crevaux, E. "L'Occupation étrangere dans le département de l'Aisne en 1814 et 1815." COMITE DES TRAVAUX HISTORIQUE SCIENTIFIQUE SECTION D'HISTOIRE MODERNE ET CONTEMPORAINE 22 (1936): 151-232.

60. Crouzet, François. "Le Sous-développement économique du Sud-ouest." ANNALES DU MIDI 71 (1959): 71-79.

61. Cubberly, Ray Ellsworth. THE ROLE OF FOUCHE DURING THE HUNDRED DAYS. Madison: State Historical Society of Wisconsin, 1969.

62. Damas, Comtesse de. LETTRE DE MME. LA COMTESSE DE DAMAS A M... SUR LES EVENEMENTS QUI SE SONT PASSES A BORDEAUX AU Ier AVRIL 1815. Bordeaux, n.d.

63. Damassy, Pierre de. "Epreuves morales de l'armée lors du débarquement de l'Ile d'Elbe. Differents exemples pris dans les unites stationées dans le département de la Manche." REVUE DU DEPARTEMENT DE LA MANCHE 2 (1960): 131-37.

64. Damitz, Carl von. HISTOIRE DE LA CAMPAGNE DE 1815, POUR FAIRE SUITE A L'HISTOIRE DES GUERRES DES TEMPS MODERNES. Paris: Corréard, 1840-41. 2 vols.

65. Daudet, Ernest. MADAME ROYALE, FILLE DE LOUIS XVI ET DE MARIE-ANTOINETTE; SA JEUNESSE ET SON MARIAGE. Paris: Hachette, 1912.

66. Daudet, Ernest. LA TERREUR BLANCHE: EPISODES ET SOUVENIRS DE LA REACTION DANS LE MIDI EN 1815. 2e éd. Paris: Hachette, 1906.

67. Davout, Louis Nicolas, duc d'Auerstädt, prince d'Eckmühl. "Après Waterloo, Paris." REVUE DE PARIS (1897): 705-43; (1898): 151-72.

68. Decaen, Charles Mathieu Isidore, comte. MEMOIRES ET JOURNAUX DU GENERAL DECAEN. Publiés avec une introduction, des notes et des cartes par E. Picard et Victor Paulier. Paris: Plon, 1910-11. 2 vols.

69. Dejente, J. LE MARLOIS. INVASION DE 1815-16 DANS LE MARLOIS ET LES ENVIRONS. Laon: Journal de l'Aisne, 1912.

70. Develay, Victor. LA BOURGOGNE PENDANT LES CENT JOURS, D'APRES LES DOCUMENTS ORIGINAUX ET LES TRADITIONS CONTEMPORAINES. Paris: Corréard, 1860.

71. "Documents inedits. Procès-verbaux des séances de la commission du gouvernement (22 juin 1815-7 juillet 1815)." LA REVOLUTION FRANCAISE 46 (1904): 336-69.

72. Duminy, E. "Notes sur le passage des Alliés dans le departement de la Nièvre." BULLETIN DE LA SOCIETE NIEVERNAISE DES LETTRES, SCIENCES ET ARTS, Series 3, 11 (1905): 249-89.

73. Dutacq, François. "L'Occupation Autrichienne à Lyon en 1815."
    REVUE DES ETUDES NAPOLEONIENNES 42 (1936): 270-91.

74. Duvivier, Jules. "Occupation d'une ville par l'ennemi après
    Waterloo; les Danois à Bouchain." ACTES DU 80e CONGRES DES
    SOCIETES SAVANTES, SECTION D'HISTOIRE MODERNE ET CONTEMPORAINE
    (1955): 301-10.

75. Esposito, Vincent J., and John R. Elting. A MILITARY HISTORY
    AND ATLAS OF THE NAPOLEONIC WARS. New York: Praeger, 1964.

76. Firino, R. "Soissons en 1815." BULLETIN DE LA SOCIETE
    ARCHEOLOGIQUE, HISTORIQUE ET SCIENTIFIQUE DE SOISSONS, Series 3,
    17 (1910): 87-227.

77. Fortescue, John W. A HISTORY OF THE BRITISH ARMY. London:
    Macmillan; New York: Macmillan, 1910-30. 19 vols.

78. Fouché, Joseph, duc d'Otrante. MEMOIRES DE JOSEPH FOUCHE, DUC
    D'OTRANTE. Paris: Le Rouge, 1824. 2 vols.

79. Fromageot, P. "Versailles en 1815. Le combat du Ier juillet,
    son origine et ses suites." REVUE DE L'HISTOIRE DE VERSAILLES
    ET DE SEINE-ET-OISE 14 (1912): 337-54.

80. Gaffarel, Paul. DIJON EN 1814 ET 1815. Dijon: Darantière,
    1897.

81. Gaffarel, Paul. "Un Episode de la Terreur blanche: Les
    massacres de Marseille en juin, 1815." LA REVOLUTION FRANCAISE
    49 (1905): 317-50.

82. Gallatin, James. A GREAT PEACE MAKER. THE DIARY OF JAMES
    GALLATIN, SECRETARY TO ALBERT GALLATIN: U.S. ENVOY TO FRANCE
    AND ENGLAND, 1813-27.... EDITED BY COUNT GALLATIN. London:
    Heinemann, 1914.

83. Gavard, James Dominique Charles. GALERIES HISTORIQUES DE
    VERSAILLES. Paris: Duverger, 1839-41. 17 vols.

84. Gleig, George Robert. STORY OF THE BATTLE OF WATERLOO. London:
    J. Murray, 1847.

85. Godechot, Jacques, ed. LES CONSTITUTIONS DE LA FRANCE DEPUIS
    1789. Paris: Garnier-Flammarion, 1970.

86. Godechot, Jacques. NAPOLEON. Paris: A. Michel, 1969.

87. Golaz, André. "Le Blocus de Mont-Dauphin en 1815." BULLETIN DE
    LA SOCIETE D'ETUDES HISTORIQUES, SCIENTIFIQUES ET LITTERAIRES
    DES HAUTES-ALPES 53 (1961): 55-70.

88. Goltz, Colmar, freiherr von der. KRIEGSGESCHICHTE DEUTSCHLANDS
    INS NEUNZEHNTEN JAHRHUNDERT. Berlin: G. Bondi, 1910.

89. Goulet, E. "La Défense de Toulon, 1815, le maréchal Brune, le marquis de Rivière." BULLETIN DE LA SOCIETE DES AMIS DU VIEUX TOULON 10 (1933): 77-165.

90. Gourgaud, Gaspard, baron. SAINTE-HELENE. JOURNAL INEDIT DE 1815 A 1818. Avec préface et notes de MM. le vicomte de Grouchy et Antoine Guillois. Paris: Flammarion, 1889. 2 vols.

91. Grand, Roger. LA CHOUANNERIE DE 1815. Paris: Perrin, 1942.

92. Gras, A. "Grenoble en 1814 et 1815." BULLETIN DE LA SOCIETE DE STATISTIQUE, DES SCIENCES NATURELLE ET DES ARTS INDUSTRIELS DU DEPARTEMENT DE L'ISERE, Series 2, 3 (1856): 1-80.

93. Gros, Jean. "Le Duc et la duchesse d'Angoulême dans le Midi." MEMOIRES DE L'ACADEMIE DES SCIENCES, INSCRIPTIONS ET BELLES-LETTRES DE TOULOUSE, Series 12, 2 (1924): 47-66.

94. Grouard, Auguste Antoine. LA CRITIQUE DE LA CAMPAGNE DE 1815. Paris: Chapelot, 1904.

95. Grouchy, Emmanuel, marquis de. FRAGMENTS HISTORIQUES RELATIFS A LA CAMPAGNE DE 1815, ET LA BATAILLE DE WATERLOO, PAR LE GENERAL GROUCHY. Paris: Firmin-Didot, 1829.

96. Grouchy, Emmanuel de, marquis de. MEMOIRES DU MARECHAL DE GROUCHY, PUBLIES PAR LE MARQUIS DE GROUCHY. Paris: Dentu, 1873-74. 5 vols.

97. Guedalla, Philip. THE HUNDRED DAYS. Manchester: Peter Davies, 1934.

98. Guichen, Eugène de. LE DUC D'ANGOULEME 1775-1884. Paris: E. Paul, 1909.

99. Gurwood, John, ed. SELECTIONS FROM THE DISPATCHES AND GENERAL ORDERS OF FIELD MARSHAL THE DUKE OF WELLINGTON. London: J. Murray, 1841.

100. Haebert, Jean Paul. "Louis XVIII à Gand en 1815." REVUE DU NORD 49 (1967): 521-33.

101. Hautecloque, G. de. "La Seconde Restauration dans le Pas-de-Calais." MEMOIRES DE L'ACADEMIE DES SCIENCES, LETTRES ET ARTS D'ARRAS, Series 2, 42 (1911): 7-208.

102. Herbillon, Colonel. UNE ANTIGONE ROYALE, LA DUCHESSE D'ANGOULEME. Paris: Tallandier, 1936.

103. Hervé, Abbé. "Les Prussiens à Monfort en 1815." BULLETIN ET MEMOIRES DE LA SOCIETE ARCHEOLOGIQUE DU DEPARTEMENT D'ILLE-ET-VILAINE 55 (1928-29): 155-98.

104. Hibbert, Christopher. WATERLOO, NAPOLEON'S LAST CAMPAIGN. New York: The New American Library, 1967.

105. Hobhouse, John Cam. RECOLLECTIONS OF A LONG LIFE. BY BARON BROUGHTON. London: J. Murray, 1909. 6 vols.

106. Hood, James. "Protestant-Catholic Relations and the Roots of the First Popular Counter-Revolutionary Movement in France." JOURNAL OF MODERN HISTORY 43 (1971): 245-75.

107. Horward, Donald D. "L'Opinion américaine et Waterloo." REVUE DE L'INSTITUT NAPOLEON 124 (1973): 97-107.

108. Houssaye, Henry. 1815. Vol. 1. LA PREMIERE RESTAURATION; LE RETOUR DE L'ILE D'ELBE; LES CENT JOURS. 10th ed. Paris: Perrin, 1893. Vol 2. WATERLOO. Paris: Perrin, 1898. Vol. 3. LA SECONDE ABDICATION: LA TERREUR BLANCHE. 7th ed. Paris: Perrin, 1905.

109. Howarth, David. WATERLOO: DAY OF BATTLE. New York: Atheneum, 1968.

110. Hubert, Emmanuelle. LES CENT JOURS. Paris: Julliard, 1966.

111. Hüe, François. SOUVENIRS DU BARON HUE (1787-1815). Publiés par le baron de Maricourt. Paris: Calmann-Lévy, 1903.

112. Jacquemart, René. "Blocus de la ville de la Fère (en 1815)." BULLETIN DE LA SOCIETE ACADEMIQUE DE CHAUNY 5 (1894-95): 33-95.

113. Jomini, Antoine Henri de, baron. PRECIS POLITIQUE ET MILITAIRE DE LA CAMPAGNE DE 1815. Paris: Anselin et Laguyonie, 1839.

114. Joubert, A. "Souvenirs de l'occupation Prussienne en Maine-et-Loire, 1815." MEMOIRES DE LA SOCIETE D'AGRICULTURE, SCIENCES ET ARTS D'ANGERS, Series 4, 5 (1891): 171-75.

115. Joxe, Roger. "Le Comité royal provisoire de Marseille (25 juin-10 juillet, 1815)." ANNALES HISTORIQUES DE LA REVOLUTION FRANCAISE 95 (1939): 385-415.

116. Kircheisen, Friedrich M. BIBLIOGRAPHIE DU TEMPS DE NAPOLEON, COMPRENANT L'HISTOIRE DES ETATS-UNIS. New York: Burt Franklin, 1968. 2 vols.

117. Klüber, J.L. AKTEN DES WIENER KONGRESSES IN DEN JAHREN 1814 UND 1815. Erlangen: Palm, 1835. 8 vols.

118. Kurtz, Harold. THE TRIAL OF MARSHAL NEY: HIS LAST YEARS AND DEATH. New York: Knopf, 1957.

119. Lachouque, Henry. NAPOLEON A WATERLOO. Paris: Peyronnet, 1965.

120. Lamarque, Jean Maximilien. MEMOIRES ET SOUVENIRS DU GENERAL MAXIMILIEN LAMARQUE, PUBLIES PAR SA FAMILLE. Paris: Fournier, 1835-36. 3 vols.

121. Langeron, Roger. MADAME ROYALE, LA FILLE DE MARIE-ANTOINETTE.
     Paris: Hachette, 1958.

122. La Place, Charles de. LA FLANDRE EN 1815. Lille: Leleux,
     1859.

123. Las Cases, Marie Joseph Emmanuel, comte de. LE MEMORIAL DE
     SAINTE-HELENE. Première édition intégrale et critique, établie
     et annotée par Marcel Dunan. Paris: Flammarion, 1951. 2 vols.

124. Lasserre, Bertrand. LES CENT-JOURS EN VENDEE. LE GENERAL
     LAMARQUE ET L'INSURRECTION ROYALISTE. D'APRES LES PAPIERS
     INEDITS DU GENERAL LAMARQUE. Paris: Plon, 1906.

125. Lasteyrie, Robert de, and Alexandre Vidier. BIBLIOGRAPHIE
     ANNUELLE DES TRAVAUX HISTORIQUES ET ARCHEOLOGIQUES PUBLIES PAR
     LES SOCIETES SAVANTES DE LA FRANCE. Paris: Imprimerie
     nationale, 1911-14.

126. Laulan, Robert. "Remarques sur un épisode douteux du blocus de
     Vincennes en 1858." 84e CONGRES DES SOCIETE SAVANTES (1960):
     561-74.

127. Laurentie, François. "Souvenirs de 1815. Manuscrit inédit de
     la duchesse d'Angoulême." LE CORRESPONDANT 216 (1913): 650-82.

128. Lautard, Laurent. ESQUISSES HISTORIQUES: MARSEILLE DEPUIS 1789
     JUSQU'EN 1815. Marseille: M. Olive, 1844. Vol. 2.

129. Lauze de Peret, P.J. CAUSES ET PRECIS DES CRIMES, DES DESORDRES
     DANS LE DEPARTEMENT DU GARD ET DANS D'AUTRES LIEUX DU MIDI DE LA
     FRANCE EN 1815 ET 1816. Paris: Poulet, 1819.

130. Lavalette, Antoine Marie Chamant, comte de. MEMOIRES ET
     SOUVENIRS DU COMTE DE LAVALETTE, PUBLIES PAR SA FAMILLE ET SUR
     SES MANUSCRITS. Paris: Fournier, 1831. 2 vols.

131. Lecomte, Elisée. LES AUTRICHIENS DANS LE DEPARTEMENT DE L'AIN
     ET DANS LE PAYS DE GEX EN 1814 ET 1815. Paris: Martinou, 1859.

132. Lefebvre, Georges. NAPOLEON. Paris: Alcan, 1935.

133. Le Gallo, Emile. LES CENT JOURS. Paris: Alcan, 1923.

134. Leroux-Cesbron, C. "La Folie--Saint-James en 1815." BULLETIN
     DE LA COMMISSION MUNICIPALE HISTORIQUE ET ARTISTIQUE DE
     NEUILLY-SUR-SEINE 16 (1923): 73-76.

135. Leroy, G. "Episodes des Cent-Jours à Melun." BULLETIN DE LA
     SOCIETE D'ARCHEOLOGIE, SCIENCES, LETTRES ET ARTS DU DEPARTEMENT
     DE SEINE-ET-MARNE 15 (1912-21): 283-98.

136. Lettow-Vorbeck, Oscar von. NAPOLEONS UNTERGANG 1815.
     GESCHICHTE DER BEFREIUNGSKRIEGE 1813-15. Berlin: Mittler,
     1904. 2 vols.

137. Leuillot, Paul. "L'Occupation Alliée à Colmar et dans le Haut
     Rhin (1815-18)." ANNUAIRE DE COLMAR (1937): 157-64.

138. Leuillot, Paul. LA PREMIERE RESTAURATION ET LES CENT JOURS EN
     ALSACE. Paris: S.E.V.P.E.N., 1858.

139. Lewis, Gwynn. THE SECOND VENDEE: THE CONTINUITY OF
     COUNTER-REVOLUTION IN THE DEPARTMENT OF THE GARD, 1789-1815.
     Oxford: Clarendon Press, 1978.

140. Libaudière, Félix. "Précis des événements qui se sont passés à
     Nantes du 11 juillet, 1815, au 4 août, 1830." ANNALES DE LA
     SOCIETE ACADEMIQUE DE NANTES, Series 8, 4 (1905): 13-83.

141. Licquet, François Isidore. CAMPAGNE DE S.A.R. MGR. LE DUC
     D'ANGOULEME DANS LE MIDI DE LA FRANCE EN 1815. Rouen: J.
     Duval, 1818.

142. Lorin, Félix. "Au Château de Rambouillet, 29 et 30 juin, 1815.
     Un récit nouveau." MEMOIRES DE LA SOCIETE ARCHEOLOGIQUE DE
     RAMBOUILLET 24 (1928): 121-34.

143. Lorin, Félix. HENRI LEVASSEUR, MAIRE ET SOUS-PREFET DE
     RAMBOUILLET. NAPOLEON Ier A RAMBOUILLET, L'INVASION. Tours:
     Deslis, 1897.

144. Loubet, Jean. "Le Gouvernement Toulousain du duc d'Angoulême
     après les Cent-Jours." LA REVOLUTION FRANCAISE 14 (1913):
     149-65, 337-66.

145. Macdonald, Jacques Etienne, duc de Tarente. SOUVENIRS DU
     MARECHAL MACDONALD, DUC DE TARENTE. Introduction par Camille
     Rousset. Paris: Plon, 1892.

146. Madelin, Louis. MEMOIRES DE FOUCHE. Introduction et notes de
     Louis Madelin. Paris: Flammarion, 1945.

147. Maine de Biran, Pierre François Marie Gonthier. JOURNAL.
     Edited by H. Gouhier. Neuchâtel: La Baconnière, 1954. 2 vols.

148. Manceron, Claude. NAPOLEON REPREND PARIS (20 mars 1815).
     Paris: Laffont, 1965.

149. Mansel, Philip. LOUIS XVIII. London: Blond and Briggs, 1981.

150. Manteyer, G. de. "Le Passage à Gap de l'Empereur Napoléon (5-6
     mars 1815)." BULLETIN DE LA SOCIETE D'ETUDES DES HAUTES-ALPES
     45(1932): 355-64.

151. Marchand, Louis Joseph, comte. MEMOIRES DE MARCHAND, PREMIER
     VALET DE CHAMBRE ET EXECUTEUR TESTAMENTAIRE DE L'EMPEREUR.
     Publiés d'après le manuscrit original par Jean Bourguignon.
     Paris: Plon, 1952-55. 2 vols.

152. Margerit, Robert. WATERLOO, 18 JUIN 1815. Paris: Gallimard, 1964.

153. Marion, M. "Le 10e de Ligne en 1815." SEANCES ET TRAVAUX DE L'ACADEMIE DES SCIENCES MORALES ET POLITIQUES 89 (1929): 415-29.

154. Marmont, Auguste Frédéric Louis Viesse de, duc de Raguse. MEMOIRES DE 1792 A 1841, IMPRIMES SUR LE MANUSCRIT ORIGINAL DE L'AUTEUR. Paris: Perrotin, 1856-57. 9 vols.

155. Martin, Etienne. "Napoleon à Barreme, le vendredi 3 mars 1815. Quelques détails inédits." MEMOIRES DE L'ACADEMIE DES SCIENCES, BELLES-LETTRES ET ARTS DE MARSEILLE 54 (1941): 301-13.

156. Marzin, Jean. "Morlaix pendant les Cent Jours et la Restauration." BULLETIN DE LA SOCIETE D'ETUDES ARTISTIQUES, LITTERAIRES ET SCIENTIFIQUES DU FINISTERE 7 (1934): 17-40.

157. Massé, Pierre. "L'Armée de la Loire dans l'arrondissement de Chatellerault (juillet-novembre 1815)." BULLETIN DE LA SOCIETE DES ANTIQUAIRES DE L'OUEST Series 4, 4 (1957): 39-61.

158. Merle, Louis. "L'Occupation de la Roche-sur-Yon par les Vendéens en 1815." LA REVUE DU BAS-POITOU 70 (1959): 495-99.

159. Metternich-Winneburg, Clemens Lothar Wenzel, fürst von. MEMOIRES, DOCUMENTS ET ECRITS DIVERS LAISSES PAR LE PRINCE DE METTERNICH, CHANCELIER DE COUR ET D'ETAT. Publiés par son fils le Prince Richard de Metternich. Classés et réunis par A. de Klinckowstroem. Paris: Plon, 1880-86. 8 vols.

160. Ministère des Armées, France, Service historique, sous la direction de René Couret. GUIDE BIBLIOGRAPHIQUE SOMMAIRE D'HISTOIRE MILITAIRE ET COLONIALE FRANCAISE. Paris: Imprimerie nationale, 1969.

161. Mistler, Jean, comp. NAPOLEON ET L'EMPIRE. Paris: Hachette, 1968. 2 vols.

162. Monge, O. LA CAPITULATION DE LAPALUD. CAMPAGNE DU DUC D'ANGOULEME DANS LE VAUCLUSE (MARS-AVRIL 1815). Avignon: Seguin, 1894.

163. Montgaillard, Jean Gabriel Maurice Rocques, comte de. SOUVENIRS DU COMTE DE MONTGAILLARD, AGENT DE LA DIPLOMATIE SECRETE PENDANT LA REVOLUTION, L'EMPIRE ET LA RESTAURATION, PAR CLEMENT DE LACROIX. Paris: Ollendorff, 1895.

164. Napoléon I, Emperor of the French. COMMENTAIRES DE NAPOLEON PREMIER. Paris: Imprimerie impériale, 1867. 6 vols.

165. Nettement, Alfred. HISTOIRE DE LA RESTAURATION. Paris: Lecoffre, 1860-72. 8 vols.

166. Nettement, Alfred. VIE DE MARIE-THERESE DE FRANCE, FILLE DE LOUIS XVI. Paris: Jeulin, 1843.

167. Neuilly, Ange Achille Charles, comte de. SOUVENIRS ET CORRESPONDANCE DU COMTE DE NEUILLY. Publiés par son neveu Maurice de Barberoy. Paris: Douniol, 1865.

168. Nicolson, Harold. THE CONGRESS OF VIENNA: A STUDY IN ALLIED UNITY, 1812-1822. New York: Harcourt, Brace, 1946.

169. Noailles, Marquis de. LE COMTE MOLE (1781-1855). SA VIE, SES MEMOIRES. Paris: Champion, 1922. 6 vols.

170. Pagezy de Bourdeliac, Louis. OPERATIONS MILITAIRES DE S.A.R. MGR. LE DUC D'ANGOULEME DANS LE MIDI DE LA FRANCE EN 1815. Paris: Anselin et Pochard, 1832.

171. Parent, Roger. "Les Cent Jours et l'invasion de 1815 à Montargis et dans ses environs." BULLETIN DE LA SOCIETE D'EMULATION DE L'ARRONDISSEMENT DE MONTARGIS 27 (1974): 22-88.

172. Pasquier, Etienne Denis, duc. HISTOIRE DE MON TEMPS. MEMOIRES DU CHANCELIER PASQUIER, PUBLIES PAR M. LE DUC D'AUDIFFRET-PASQUIER. Paris: Plon, 1893-94. 6 vols.

173. Pericoli, Ugo. 1815: THE ARMIES AT WATERLOO. New York: Scribner, 1973.

174. Perrot, Clement. REPORT ON THE PERSECUTIONS OF THE FRENCH PROTESTANTS, PRESENTED TO THE COMMITTEE OF DISSENTING MINISTERS OF THE THREE DENOMINATIONS IN AND ABOUT THE CITIES OF LONDON AND WESTMINSTER. London: Longman, Hurst, Rees, Orme, 1816.

175. Perroud, M. "Les Cent-Jours à Saint-Genix." MEMOIRES DE L'ACADEMIE DES SCIENCES BELLES-LETTRES ET ARTS DE SAVOIE, Series 3, 9 (1937): 167-79.

176. Pflugk-Harttung, Julius von. ELBA UND DIE HUNDERT TAGE IN DAS ERWACHEN DER VÖLKER. Berlin: J.M. Spaeth, 1903.

177. Piccard, L.E. "Les Autrichiens en Chablais." CONGRES DE SOCIETES SAVANTES SAVOISIENNES 8 (1896): 289-318.

178. Pingaud, Léonce. LA FRANCHE COMTE EN 1815. DOCUMENTS INEDITS. Besançon: P. Jacquin, 1896.

179. Poirier, Jules. SIEGE ET BLOCUS DE LA VILLE ET DES CHATEAUX DE SEDAN EN 1815. Sedan: Laroche, 1888.

180. Poland, Burdette C. FRENCH PROTESTANTISM AND THE FRENCH REVOLUTION. Princeton, N.J.: Princeton University Press, 1957.

181. Pougiat, F.E. L'INVASION DES ARMEES ETRANGERES DANS LE DEPARTEMENT DE L'AUBE. Troyes: Roret, 1833.

182. Praviel, Armand. "Le Massacre de Ramel." OEUVRES LIBRES 78 (1927): 269-320.

183. Quennevat, Jean Claude. ATLAS DE LA GRANDE ARMEE; NAPOLEON ET SES CAMPAGNES, 1803-1815. Paris: Editions Sequoia, 1966.

184. Quennevat, Jean Claude. "Le Dernier Coup de Sabre (Ier juillet 1815). Villacoublay, Versailles, Rocquencourt, Le Chesnay." REVUE DE L'HISTOIRE DE VERSAILLES ET DE SEINE-ET-OISE 56 (1965-67): 155-210.

185. Rapp, Jean, comte. MEMOIRES ECRITS PAR LUI-MEME ET PUBLIES PAR SA FAMILLE. Paris: Bossange, 1823.

186. Rémusat, Charles François, comte de. MEMOIRES DE MA VIE. Vol. 1. ENFANCE ET JEUNESSE; LA RESTAURATION. Edited by Charles Pouthas. Paris: Plon, 1958.

187. Resnick, Daniel P. THE WHITE TERROR AND THE POLITICAL REACTION AFTER WATERLOO. Cambridge: Harvard University Press, 1966.

188. Ribault, Jean Yves. "Le Sejour de l'armée de la Loire dans le département du Cher (été 1815)." CAHIERS D'ARCHEOLOGIE ET D'HISTOIRE DU BERRY 5 (1966): 36-40.

189. Richard, Gabriel. "Les Cent Jours à Nancy." LE PAYS LORRAIN 38 (1957): 81-96.

190. Richardson, Nicholas. THE FRENCH PREFECTORAL CORPS, 1814-1830. Cambridge and London: Cambridge University Press, 1966.

191. Robert, Daniel. LES EGLISES REFORMEES EN FRANCE (1800-1830). Paris: Presses Universitaires de France. 1961.

192. Robin, Raymond. DES OCCUPATIONS MILITAIRES EN DEHORS DES OCCUPATIONS DE GUERRE. Paris: L. Larose et L. Tenin, 1913.

193. Robinson, Charles Walker. WELLINGTON'S CAMPAIGNS: PENINSULA-WATERLOO, 1808-1815; ALSO MOORE'S CAMPAIGN OF CORUNNA. London: H. Rees, 1906-07. 3 vols.

194. Romberg, Edouard, and Albert Malet. LOUIS XVIII ET LES CENT-JOURS A GAND. RECUEIL DE DOCUMENTS INEDITS. Paris: Picard, 1898, 1902.

195. Ropes, John Codman. THE CAMPAIGN OF WATERLOO--A MILITARY HISTORY. London: Putnam, 1890.

196. Sancti, L. "Notes et documents sur les intrigues royalistes dans le Midi de la France de 1792 à 1815." MEMOIRES DE L'ACADEMIE DES SCIENCES; INSCRIPTIONS ET BELLES-LETTRES DE TOULOUSE 4 (1916): 37-114.

197. Semallé, Jean René Pierre, comte de. SOUVENIRS DU COMTE SEMALLE, PAGE DE LOUIS XVI. Paris: Picard, 1898.

198. Seyssel, Comte de. "Le Fort de l'Ecluse, suivi de journal du
     siège de 1815." CONGRES DES SOCIETES SAVANTES DE LA SAVOIE 17
     (1905): 519-31.

199. Siborne, H.T. WATERLOO LETTERS: A SELECTION FROM ORIGINAL AND
     HITHERTO UNPUBLISHED LETTERS HEARING ON THE OPERATIONS OF THE
     16th, 17th, and 18th JUNE, 1815, BY OFFICERS WHO SERVED IN THE
     CAMPAIGN. London: Cassell, 1891.

200. Six, Georges. DICTIONNAIRE BIOGRAPHIQUE DES GENERAUX ET AMIRAUX
     FRANCAIS DE LA REVOLUTION ET DE L'EMPIRE (1792-1814). Paris:
     G. Saffroy, 1934. 2 vols.

201. Sorel, Albert. L'EUROPE ET LA REVOLUTION FRANCAISE. Paris:
     Plon-Nourrit, 1885-1911. 9 vols.

202. Sorel, Albert. LE TRAITE DE PARIS DU 20 NOVEMBRE 1815. Paris:
     Baillière, 1872.

203. Soult, Nicolas Jean de Dieu, duc de Dalmatie. MEMOIRES DU
     MARECHAL SOULT. ESPAGNE ET PORTUGAL. TEXTE ETABLI ET PRESENTE
     PAR LOUIS ET ANTOINETTE DE SAINT-PIERRE. Paris: Hachette,
     1955.

204. Suchet, Louis Gabriel, duc d'Albufera. MEMOIRES DU MARECHAL
     SUCHET, DUC D'ALBUFERA, SUR SES CAMPAGNES EN ESPAGNE, DEPUIS
     1808 JUSQU'EN 1814, ECRITS PAR LUI-MEME. Paris: Bossange,
     1828. 2 vols. and atlas.

205. Suleau, Louis Ange Antoine Elysée de. RECIT DES OPERATIONS DE
     L'ARMEE ROYALE DU MIDI SOUS LES ORDRES DE MGR. LE DUC
     D'ANGOULEME DEPUIS LE 9 MARS JUSQU'AU 16 AVRIL 1815. Paris:
     Pélicier, 1816.

206. Talleyrand-Périgord, Charles Maurice de, prince de Bénévent.
     MEMOIRES DU PRINCE DE TALLEYRAND PUBLIES AVEC UNE PREFACE ET DES
     NOTES, PAR LE DUC DE BROGLIE. Paris: Calmann-Lévy, 1891-92. 5
     vols.

207. Thiry, Jean. LES CENT JOURS. Paris: Berger-Levrault, 1943.

208. Thiry, Jean. LES DEBUTS DE LA SECONDE RESTAURATION. Paris:
     Berger-Levrault, 1947.

209. Thiry, Jean. LA SECONDE ABDICATION DE NAPOLEON Ier. Paris:
     Berger-Levrault, 1945.

210. Thiry, Jean. LE VOL DE L'AIGLE: LE RETOUR DE NAPOLEON DE L'ILE
     D'ELBE AUX TUILERIES. Paris: Berger-Levrault, 1942.

211. Tönneson, K. "Les Fédérés de Paris pendant les Cent-Jours."
     ANNALES HISTORIQUES DE LA REVOLUTION FRANCAISE 54 (1982):
     393-415.

212. Troussier, S. and A. LE CHEVAUCHEE HEROIQUE DU RETOUR DE L'ILE D'ELBE. Lausanne: Editions du Grand Chêne, 1964.

213. T'Serclaes de Wommerson, Jacques, comte de. LA CAMPAGNE DE 1815 AUX PAYS-BAS, D'APRES LES RAPPORTS OFFICIELS NEERLANDAIS. Bruxelles: A. Dewit, 1908-09. 4 vols.

214. Tulard, Jean. BIBLIOGRAPHIE CRITIQUE DES MEMOIRES SUR LE CONSULAT ET L'EMPIRE. Genève: Droz, 1971.

215. Tulard, Jean. NAPOLEON OU LE MYTHE DU SAUVEUR. 2ième édition revue et complétée. Paris: Fayard, 1977.

216. Turquan, Joseph. LA DERNIERE DAUPHINE: MADAME, DUCHESSE D'ANGOULEME, 1778-1851. Paris: Emile-Paul, 1909.

217. Valynseele, Joseph. LES MARECHAUX DU PREMIER EMPIRE, LEUR FAMILLE ET LEUR DESCENDANCE. Paris: Chez l'Auteur, 1957.

218. Van Loben Sels, E. PRECIS DE LA CAMPAGNE DE 1815 DANS LES PAYS-BAS. Trans. from the Dutch. The Hague: Chez Doorman, 1849.

219. Vaulabelle, Achille de. CAMPAGNE ET BATAILLE DE WATERLOO. Paris: Perrotin, 1845.

220. Vaulabelle, Achille de. HISTOIRE DES DEUX RESTAURATIONS JUSQU'A LA CHUTE DE CHARLES X. 2d ed. Paris: Perrotin, 1847. 7 vols.

221. Vauthier, Gabriel. "Versailles et la Seine-et-Oise pendant les Cent Jours d'après les rapports de police." REVUE DE L'HISTOIRE DE VERSAILLES ET DE SEINE-ET-OISE 32 (1930): 24-37.

222. Véron, Louis Désiré. MEMOIRES D'UN BOURGEOIS DE PARIS, PAR LE DOCTEUR LOUIS VERON, COMPRENENANT LA FIN DE L'EMPIRE, LA RESTAURATION, LA MONARCHIE DE JUILLET, ET LA REPUBLIQUE JUSQU'AU RETABLISSEMENT DE L'EMPIRE. Paris: Gonet, 1853-55. 6 vols.

223. Verrier, Joseph. "Sur les traces de la congrégation, à Bordeaux sous les Cent Jours." REVUE D'HISTOIRE DE L'EGLISE DE FRANCE 41 (1955): 282-91.

224. Vidalenç, Jean. LES DEMI-SOLDE: ETUDE D'UNE CATEGORIE SOCIALE. Paris: Rivière, 1955.

225. Vidalenç, Jean. LE DEPARTEMENT DE L'EURE SOUS LA MONARCHIE CONSTITUTIONNELLE, 1814-1848. Paris: Rivière, 1952.

226. Vidalenç, Jean. "La Vie économique des départements Méditerranéens pendant l'Empire." REVUE D'HISTOIRE MODERNE ET CONTEMPORAINE 1 (1954): 165-98.

227. Vignols, Léon. LES PRUSSIENS DANS L'ILLE-ET-VILAINE EN 1815. Rennes: Plihonet et Hervé, 1893.

228. Villèle, Jean Baptiste Joseph, comte de. MEMOIRES ET CORRESPONDANCE DU COMTE DE VILLELE. Paris: Perrin, 1888-90. Vol. 1.

229. Vincent, Andéol. HISTOIRE DES GUERRES DU VIVARAIS ET AUTRES CONTREES VOISINES EN FAVEUR DE LA CAUSE ROYALE, DEPUIS LE CAMP DE JALES (1790) JUSQU'EN 1816. Privas: F. Agard, 1817.

230. Vitrolles, Eugène d'Arnault, baron de. MEMOIRES ET RELATIONS POLITIQUES DU BARON DE VITROLLES, PUBLIES PAR EUGENE FORGUES. Paris: Charpentier, 1884. 3 vols.

231. Webster, Charles Kingsley. THE FOREIGN POLICY OF CASTLEREAGH, 1812-1815. London: G. Bell, 1931.

232. Weller, Jac. WELLINGTON AT WATERLOO. New York: Crowell, 1967.

233. Wellington, Arthur Wellesley, 1st duke of. THE DISPATCHES OF FIELD MARSHALL THE DUKE OF WELLINGTON. London: J. Murray, 1934-39. 13 vols.

234. Wellington, Arthur Wellesley, 1st duke of. SUPPLEMENTARY DESPATCHES, CORRESPONDENCE, AND MEMORANDA. London: J. Murray, 1862-72.

235. Wemyss, Alice. "L'Angleterre et la Terreur blanche de 1815 dans le Midi." ANNALES DU MIDI 63 (1961): 287-311.

236. Williams, Helen Maria. ON THE LATE PERSECUTION OF THE PROTESTANTS IN THE SOUTH OF FRANCE. London: Baldwin, Craddock and Joy, 1816.

237. Wood, Evelyn. CAVALRY IN THE WATERLOO CAMPAIGN. Boston: Roberts, 1896.

ADDENDUM

238. Boulger, Demetrius. THE BELGIANS AT WATERLOO. London: Billings, 1901.

239. Chesney, Charles. WATERLOO LECTURES: A STUDY OF THE CAMPAIGNS OF 1815. London: Longmans, Green, 1869.

240. Couvreur, Hector Jean. LE DRAME BELGE DE WATERLOO. Brussels: Brepols, 1959.

241. LE MONITEUR UNIVERSEL

242. Müffling, Friedrich Karl. A SKETCH OF THE BATTLE OF WATERLOO TO WHICH ARE ADDED OFFICIAL DISPATCHES. Brussels: Gérard, 1883.

243. Parker, Harold T. THREE NAPOLEONIC BATTLES. Durham, N.C.: Duke University Press, 1983.

244. Siborne, William. HISTORY OF THE WAR IN FRANCE AND BELGIUM IN 1815.... London: T. and W. Boone, 1848.

CHAPTER XVI

ST. HELENA AND THE NAPOLEONIC LEGEND

Susan P. Conner, Tift College

As Napoleon traveled along the rain-soaked roads from Waterloo to Paris, the Napoleonic legend began. At Malmaison a group of followers gathered around him. They were prepared to accept his fate or to profit from it by publishing their memoirs of the Napoleonic era. From Malmaison, the group traveled to Rambouillet, from there to Niort and to Rochefort where they arrived on 3 July 1815. No longer could Napoleon's decision be postponed. Should he attempt to join the Army of the Loire as Lallemand suggested? Should he escape on the Danish brig as Montholon suggested, or should he consider asylum in England as Captain Maitland proposed? It was this third option that Napoleon chose, and he composed the following letter to the Prince Regent:

> Pursued by the factions which divide my country and
> by the hostility of the Powers of Europe, I have
> finished my political career, and I come like
> Themistocles, to sit at the hearth of the British
> people. I put myself under the protection of the
> laws which I claim from your Royal Highness as the
> most powerful, constant and generous of my enemies.

So it was that Napoleon carefully began to construct his image as victim. British liberals, Bonapartists, and republicans agreed with him and seconded his efforts in their writings during the first half of the century.

Throughout the negotiations concerning Napoleon's future, the British government remained cool and distant, although the British people were excited and curious about the man whom they had visualized as ogre and tyrant. At Plymouth where crowds pressed for a glimpse of him, the Emperor received word that he was to be exiled to St. Helena where he was to be addressed not as Emperor or Napoleon but as General Bonaparte. Supporters in England within the Whig party petitioned for reconsideration of Napoleon's exile charging that his deportation was a violation of the Habeas Corpus Act. To avoid legal snarls, the Bellerophon cruised the Channel instead of remaining in port while awaiting the Northumberland which would transport Napoleon and his party to his Atlantic prison.

From among those who threw their lot with the Emperor, Napoleon was allowed to select three officers to accompany him: Grand Maréchal Bertrand, Montholon, and Gourgaud. The Duc de Rovigo and Lallemand were refused permission, and Las Cases was included as a personal secretary. Bertrand and Montholon took their wives and families with them. The small entourage also included O'Meara as surgeon, members of the household staff, and personnel for the stables. Of these, eleven kept journals or left records which have since been published, the first in 1822 and the most recent in 1959.

After considering suicide, according to Gourgaud, Napoleon turned his thoughts first to escape and then to what he could accomplish in memorializing his deeds. It was, in fact, during the sea voyage that Napoleon succumbed to his ennui and began composing his memoirs aided by Las Cases. Finally after two months at sea, land was sighted, ending one ordeal and beginning another. "[St. Helena was] the ugliest and most dismal rock conceivable...," wrote a British army surgeon, "rising like an enormous black wart from the face of the deep." Here on the black wart, Napoleon lived out his days capitalizing on his martyrdom as the new Prometheus. First at "The Briars" and then at "Longwood", Napoleon made his residence, a stay marked by quarrelling among the Emperor's entourage, his own erratic and then declining health, and difficult relations with Sir Hudson Lowe, under whose charge he had been placed.

Throughout the years of the captivity, volumes of literature analyzed, glorified or challenged Napoleon's influence on European affairs. In the works which Napoleon dictated, his concern lay both in what had occurred and in what he had intended to do. According to his analysis, he had been a representative of the principles of 1789, a man whose ideas were liberal but who had become a strong governor out of necessity. He constantly desired peace and glorified the brief peaceful interludes of his reign, but he had been forced into war by the European powers. Furthermore, he supported the law of nationalities and would have continued to aid its cause if the Russian campaign had ended differently. Napoleon had become, in the words of H.A.L. Fisher, "the great captain, hero of adventures wondrous as the Arabian Nights, [who] passes over the mysterious ocean to his lonely island and emerges transfigured as in some ennobling mirage."

Napoleon's death in 1821 brought with it further additions to the legend. His treatment by the English, the climate of St. Helena, and the cause of his death became new polemics. Sir Hudson Lowe, his irascible and psychologically unstable gaoler became the agent of his death. The legend was augmented by literature, plays, hymns, and by petitions for the return of Napoleon's corpse to France. This became reality in 1840 when the Emperor's body was exhumed and plans were agreed to place his remains on the banks of the Seine in Les Invalides. The mantle of empire which Napoleon had carefully preserved for his son was passed to Louis Napoleon. In spite of the defeat, the legend of Napoleon I did not die. Rather, the demi-dieu became the grand homme, the legend became the legacy, and the myth was tempered with reality.

Napoleon as republican, as military giant, as victim of circumstance, as dissimulator, or as amoral dictator--these themes of his life and of his death are as present today as they were in 1815. Over the years, distance from the glories and the crimes has allowed them to become more balanced.

GENERAL HISTORIES

There have been a number of general histories about Napoleon's captivity on St. Helena. Over the years they have reflected the particular biases of their authors, and their documentation has been based solely on the memoir and documentary evidence available at the times when they were published. The memoirs of two of Napoleon's key personnel were not released until the 1950s, and it should be noted that not until 1969 was the last of the major journals published.

Some of the earliest histories include Debraux (101) and Abbott (2), neither of which is particularly important. Abbott's popular glorification of the Emperor proposed to take the reader back to St. Helena and "to give him a seat in an armchair" to listen to Napoleon's conversations. It was based on the memoirs of O'Meara, Las Cases, Montholon, and Antommarchi, and it began a trend of popular, unscientific accounts which dramatized the events.

The first clearly historical work blending the memoirs and the papers of leading figures was by Forsyth (140). In his monumental three-volume work, Forsyth used the unpublished Lowe papers to defend the governor as a man who observed regulations and whose gubernatorial role was made more difficult by Napoleon's erratic behavior. The book, however, is a ponderous display of various materials found in the British Museum. The same thesis and materials were later used by Seaton (364, 365) in his works on Napoleon. Seaton's writings so parallel Forsyth that they may be called a "Pocket Forsyth." The exoneration of Lowe, a theme in St. Helena studies, was further promoted by Pillans (318) who argued that Lowe was "the real martyr of St. Helena." A more temperate, although sympathetic treatment of Lowe is found in Young's two-volume work (429), which returned to the Lowe papers for additional documentation and reviewed the extant memoir sources. Recognized as a leading history of the period, it was, however, never translated into French.

Both as a history of Napoleon at St. Helena and as a part of the Napoleonic legend, Thiers's SAINTE-HELENE (388) cannot be ignored. Completed in 1862, the monumental study of the consulate and empire reflected the Napoleonic legend at its height; but in the later volumes, Thiers also recognized the faults and desire for power which obsessed the Emperor. After the fall of Napoleon III, Taine and Michelet responded to Thiers in their critical, general studies of the Napoleonic era.

During the first two decades of the twentieth century, St. Helena became a subject of scholarly inquiry again. Gonnard's study (159, 160) of the Napoleonic legend as it developed in Napoleon's St. Helena writings remains a classic today. Between 1909 and 1915, Masson published a three-volume study of the captivity (259, 260) which traced Napoleon's suffering at St. Helena nearly day-by-day. As an historical sleuth, he sought the unpublished eyewitness accounts which he knew to exist and succeeded in gaining access to Marchand's unpublished journal and Ali's memoirs. He was unable to use Bertrand's writings which were held by the family. A less scholarly but equally literary study is Rosebery's NAPOLEON (347). As a disciple of Holland (178), Rosebery's sympathetic portrayal of Napoleon used none of the Lowe papers and brought a storm of criticism from British writers.

A major source of biographical information on visitors and residents of St. Helena is Chaplin's WHO'S WHO (77), which also contains vignettes on the historical controversies surrounding Napoleon's captivity and death and reviews of major manuscript collections. Other early twentieth century studies include Runciman (351), Frémeaux (142) and Cahuet (58, 59, 60).

In 1935, Aubry's two-volume history of Napoleon's captivity and death was published. In order to provide a more balanced view than previous works, Aubry went to St. Helena to use the records at Jamestown and to view the sites. Since then a number of other important studies have appeared including Ganière (148), Korngold (209), Fisher (134), Martineau (257), Bonnel (45), and Tulard (397, 399).

Unlike earlier sympathetic views of the governor, Korngold argued that Lowe was not a martyr but that his difficulties came from his paranoid temperament, unstable character, and mediocre abilities. Lowe simply could not cope with the demands made upon him. Fisher's essay (134) on Napoleon's captivity remains a standard in the field and should be consulted along with the social history of St. Helena written by Martineau, which was the first major work to use Gorrequer's diary. More recently Bonnel and other historians of Napoleon's decline published a series of essays in honor of Marcel Dunan (45). It is particularly useful for views of the Emperor's companions in exile and for the evolution of the legend. Other general works on Napoleon's years at St. Helena include Thiry (389), Castelot (63, 64), and Thompson (391).

A topic inseparable from St. Helena is the Napoleonic legend. The history of the legend which was promoted by the Emperor himself and propagated by his followers, forms the subject of works by Gonnard (160), Dechamps (105), Driault (118), Evans (128), Lucas-Dubreton (238), Soboul (373), Tulard (396), and Geyl (154). Geyl's study, published in 1949, remains the major source to be consulted.

BIBLIOGRAPHIES

No comprehensive bibliographies exist concerning either the St. Helena captivity or the Napoleonic legend. Fortunately some substantial bibliographies have been published as parts of specific studies.

One of the most helpful bibliographies accompanies Tomiche's NAPOLEON ECRIVAIN (393). It is an annotated topical listing which provides notes on archival collections as well as major works by and about Napoleon. Other extensive bibliographies appear in Bonnel (45), Ganière (148), Gonnard (159), Korngold (209), and Young (429). Dechamps (105) includes sources on the legend which are organized by nationality, and Tulard (396) notes the major writings which comprise the légende noire.

Several general Napoleonic guides are also helpful. Howard's guide to the collection at Florida State University indexes over a hundred titles on the captivity and legend. John Hall Stewart's guide to the materials in Cleveland is much briefer in its listing but also contains a number of rare sources. The catalog of the Colonial Office Library in London provides a list of works and pamphlets which are particularly useful for the British perspective on St. Helena, and Tulard's BIBLIOGRAPHIE CRITIQUE indexes and analyzes the memoirs relative to Napoleon's captivity which were written or translated into French.

There is no adequate bibliography, however, which lists popular writings contemporary to Napoleon's death or non-historical literature which became part of the Napoleonic legend. Catalogs of the Bibliothèque Nationale and the BIBLIOGRAPHIE DE LA FRANCE still provide the best assistance.

ARCHIVAL SOURCES

Archives in Great Britain abound with significant collections of documents and accounts of Napoleon's exile and captivity. Of them, no study of Napoleon's last years would be complete without consulting the "Lowe Papers" in the British Library collection. Among the 142 volumes are 97 which relate to St. Helena and to Governor Lowe's activities there. Listed as Additions to the Manuscripts (1815-1945), they include expense accounts of the establishment (MS. 14,059), lists of properties and correspondence (MS. 15,729), papers relating to the will (MS. 24,324), and registers and documents concerning the custody of the Emperor, visitors to the island and instructions to the garrison (MSS. 20,114-20,240). Included also are reports and correspondence of Gorrequer, Reade, Malcolm, Piontkowski, Bertrand, Gourgaud, Las Cases, Stokoë, Montholon, Bingham, Baxter, Antommarchi, and others.

Other materials at the British Library concerning Napoleon may be found in the Liverpool Papers, Wellesley Papers, Melville Papers, Warren Hastings Papers, and Miscellaneous Papers (Add. MSS. 37,728 and 41,996). The Public Record Office in London contains the Bathurst Papers in which Sir Hudson Lowe's official reports to the minister and private correspondence can be found. The collection also holds letters from members of Napoleon's family to the British government. Portions of the Bathurst Papers are described in a report on the documents relating to Napoleon (338). Foreign Office and Admiralty papers in the P.R.O. include documents on Napoleon's passage on the Bellerophon and the Northumberland, and the treaties concerning Napoleon's status as prisoner; the Colonial Office papers contain pamphlets and reports, both published and unpublished, on the captivity. Lord Holland's REMINISCENCES (178) and the Holland House Papers provide a view of the British liberals' concern for the fate of Napoleon.

Another source of archival materials is the collection at Jamestown, St. Helena, which was inventoried by Kitching (206) and used particularly by Martineau and Aubry in their studies. Among the papers are plans of Longwood, accounts, orders for the garrison, and plans for the defense of the island.

A recently opened source of documents is the Gorrequer collection which was listed by the Public Record Office in 1963 after a century of litigation kept its contents secret. Gorrequer, Lowe's aide-de-camp and military secretary, kept meticulous records both for the governor and himself. These documents along with a personal diary (162) elucidate the difficult and frustrating relationship between Lowe and Napoleon. Outwardly Gorrequer agreed with his superior; however, his personal papers show that he was highly opinionated, disagreed with Lowe on certain issues, and probably warranted the name "sly dog" which was given to him at St. Helena.

Across the Channel in France, the Archives des affaires étrangères on the Quai d'Orsay contain the reports of Commissioner Montchenu and his secretary Gors (Mémoires et documents, France 1804) and various correspondence of Lowe and reports on the exhumation of the Emperor's remains (FR. 1805). In the Archives privées of the Archives Nationales are the papers of Gourgaud (314 AP) which contain records of the travels to Rochefort, the commission of 1840, and manuscripts of some of the Emperor's dictations. Also located at the

Archives Nationales in the F series are various reports of the
Emperor's alleged escape from St. Helena.

At the Bibliothèque Nationale documents relating to Sir Hudson
Lowe, Antommarchi, and the captivity have been collected in MSS.
angl. 3-24. In Fonds français n.a. 6645, a copy of Maitland's
RELATION in French can be found. Documents and papers concerning St.
Helena are also located in the Bibliothèque Thiers in Paris. In the
general collection (1242, Baroche) is a copy of the Emperor's will,
and in the Collection Frédéric Masson are letters (both originals and
copies) from Las Cases to Montholon and papers of Bertrand, Gourgaud,
Antommarchi, Las Cases, and Marchand.

At the Staatsarchive in Vienna are the papers of Commissioner
Stürmer (379, 380) which were published in 1886.

PUBLISHED DOCUMENTS

There is no major collection of published documents relating to
St. Helena, however, a number of British proclamations and acts have
been issued in English (328) and in French (333). The latter volume
is interesting for the letters and notes on the "vexations" of both
Napoleon and Lowe.

Particularly notable is the twelve-volume collection of
documents (288) including reports and memoirs of Napoleon, O'Meara,
Gourgaud, and Bertrand. Another collection (88), published in 1822,
included various papers of Las Cases and correspondence from St.
Helena. The last will and testament (289) has been published dozens
of times, most recently in 1977 (286).

For the Emperor's letters, the CORRESPONDANCE DE NAPOLEON (282)
and additional collections (283) should be consulted. The St. Helena
records which were kept and indexed by Janisch (191) were published
in condensed and edited form by his son in 1885. Other
correspondence and documents concerning Napoleon have been published
as appendices in the myriads of studies which have been issued since
1816. In some cases, care must be exercised to separate the
apocryphal from the authentic.

MEMOIRS, JOURNALS, AND EYEWITNESS ACCOUNTS

When Napoleon boarded the Northumberland beginning his voyage to
St. Helena, he was joined in captivity by twenty-seven followers. Of
those, eleven either left records or published works during their
lifetimes concerning the St. Helena experience. Their writings, the
memoirs of island residents, the accounts of government officials,
and interviews conducted by visiting dignitaries form the "flood of
memoirs, diaries, anecdotes, [and] drawing-room reminiscences" which
issued from St. Helena.

One of the earliest and most popular of the St. Helena memoirs
was written by Las Cases, a "rhetorical little man very devoted to
his master." The MEMORIAL (217), which is particularly important for
its view of daily life at Longwood and for the transcriptions of
Napoleon's conversations, must be read with a critical eye. From the
time Las Cases began the voyage to St. Helena, he intended to publish
whatever he could gather (91, 215, 216). He was also an active
conspirator smuggling messages from the island during the first year
of the captivity until his release from service in 1816.

Of substantial success also were the memoirs of O'Meara (304, 305), who had been surgeon-general on board the Bellerophon and who became Napoleon's physician. An admirer of Napoleon, he first challenged Theodore Hook's pro-English tract on Napoleon's treatment in exile (181) with his RELATION (306). He wrote copious letters to Finlaison of the Admiralty Office, quarreled with Lowe, and was recalled in 1818. After the publication of his book, Governor Lowe initiated legal proceedings against him.

In an effort to reap the profits which intimacy with the Emperor could bring, Montholon (272) published his memoirs in 1847. Viewed as both a charmer and liar, overindulgent in wine and bickering, he was one of the few close associates who remained at St. Helena throughout Napoleon's captivity. It seems clear, however, that Montholon did not keep careful notes, and the memoirs are unreliable and repetitious. His earlier collaboration (273) and letters (271) prove to be better sources. Mme. de Montholon's remembrances (270) concerning the first two years of Napoleon's exile were released by her grandson in 1901. Neither set of memoirs is significant.

In 1899 Gaspard Gourgaud's JOURNAL (164, 166) was published. It had not been intended for publication, and in it Gourgaud jotted down his feelings as well as the events of the day, recording the ennui, jealousies, and annoyances he felt during his stay at St. Helena. Extraordinary for its frankness, it became the basis for Rosebery's NAPOLEON (347) and was used subsequently both by admirers and detractors.

Since World War II, two other important sources have been released. Between 1949 and 1959, Bertrand's personal journal (37) was published and Marchand's memoirs (253) were released. Bertrand, who was Napoleon's Grand maréchal, kept his diary in a kind of shorthand and code, and scholars remain baffled by some of the passages. Its value lies in its frankness and sincerity since Bertrand was unconcerned about the literary merit of his personal notes. Marchand, who was Napoleon's first valet, recorded a wealth of conversations and anecdotes about the Emperor, yet he remained distant, almost dispassionate, in his writings. An admirer, he was chosen to be among the executors of Napoleon's will.

Of less significance, although interesting and informative, are the memoirs of St. Denis (8), Napoleon's valet de chambre who had earlier shared the Emperor's exile on Elba. Although the memoirs were written many years later and without the assistance of notes, they provide an interesting view of Napoleon through the eyes of a supporter. Another admirer was Santini (359), whose writings rival hagiography. Charged with threatening to assassinate Lowe, he was deported in 1816. He claimed authorship of AN APPEAL which included Napoleon's charges against the British for cruelty and mistreatment. Santini later became the guardian of Napoleon's tomb at Les Invalides (360).

English residents and officials at St. Helena also provided views of Napoleon's captivity. Betzy Balcombe, Napoleon's fourteen-year-old companion at "The Briars" later recorded their pleasant, colorful times in her memoirs (3) which were published in 1898. More substantial were the writings of Lady Malcolm (248) who recorded nineteen conversations between her husband and the Emperor. Other conversations were recorded by Meynell (266). Sympathetic to Napoleon, Admiral Malcolm tried to serve as a liaison with Lowe.

Of the primary characters in the St. Helena drama, only Sir
Hudson Lowe left no memoirs. The MEMORIAL (233, 235, 395) which was
published originally in 1830 is apocryphal. Lowe's papers, which
remain relatively untouched by St. Helena scholars, were used by
Forsyth (140) in a substantial work on Napoleon and by Frémeaux (142)
in a popular glance at the governor. Fortunately in 1963 Gideon
Gorrequer's papers became available through the Public Record Office.
His diary (162) was edited and published in 1969. Gorrequer, Lowe's
aide-de-camp and military secretary, diligently recorded the
governor's activities and his own opinions which were frequently
uncomplimentary. After his unexpected death, the papers were
restricted as being too political.

Each of the three commissioners sent to St. Helena left a record
of his observations on the captivity. The reports of the Austrian
commissioner Baron von Stürmer (379, 380), who left St. Helena in
1818, were published in 1886. His Russian colleague Balmain left the
island in 1820. Balmain's reports (24), which were read carefully by
the czar, are an interesting assemblage of facts, carefully written
in an entertaining and informative style. The French commissioner
Montchenu, who remained throughout the captivity, left the least
satisfactory records (82, 269). A bizarre gentleman, he has been
described as grotesque, comical, an old fool, and a chatterbox.

Memoirs on specific aspects of the captivity abound. Beker (23)
and Planat de la Faye (319, 320) chronicled the Emperor's path from
Malmaison to the Bellerophon. Maitland, who was captain of the
Bellerophon, published his own analysis of the events of Napoleon's
surrender (246, 247). His narrative, however, is a defense against
charges that his perfidy had sealed Napoleon's doom. The voyage on
the Northumberland forms the subject of the memoirs of Bingham (40,
274), Lyttleton (240, 366), Ussher and Glover (402, 403), Warden
(366, 416), Ross and Home (47, 366). Of particular note are the
writings of Sir George Cockburn (86, 87), who was captain of the
Northumberland and commander at St. Helena until Lowe's arrival. He
was more liberal in his treatment of Napoleon than his successor, and
he recognized the charisma of the Emperor.

For the later years of Napoleon's life and the controversy
concerning his death, the memoirs of Arnott (14) and Antommarchi (11)
should be consulted along with Bertrand (37) and Las Cases (217).
Antommarchi, who was a capable anatomist, apparently was not
particularly knowledgeable in medicine. This may account for the
prescriptions which exacerbated Napoleon's suffering. His memoirs
were borrowed heavily from other published sources and were not
particularly successful when they were published. The only
contemporary criticism of Antommarchi's medical practice was made by
Rutledge who was present at the autopsy (78). Napoleon was frankly
skeptical of Antommarchi's qualifications, and visitors described him
as ignorant and vulgar. Arnott, surgeon to the 20th Foot Regiment,
arrived in St. Helena in 1819 and made his first professional visit
to Napoleon in 1821. He was on generally good terms with the
Emperor, and published his account of the autopsy in 1822.

Other memoirs on the Emperor's captivity include Henry (174,
175) who was present at the autopsy; Janisch (190, 191) who fulfilled
secretarial duties for Lowe; Jackson (188) who supervised repairs and
building projects; Nicholls (296) who was orderly officer from 1818
until 1820; Darroch (96, 97) who was present when Burton made the

death mask; Piontkowski (418) who joined Napoleon's household in December 1815 and who was deported in 1816; Poppleton (324) who served as orderly officer from 1815 until 1817; Stokoë (378) who attended the Emperor as his physician and who was later court-martialed and dismissed on vague charges; Verling (410) an English physician on the island; and Wilks (423) who was governor of St. Helena from 1813 until 1816. Warden, who served as surgeon on the <u>Northumberland</u> frequently conversed with Napoleon during the early months of captivity. His writings (416, 417) which were published in 1816 elicited Napoleon's reply in LETTERS FROM THE CAPE.

Even visitors to St. Helena profited from their experience by immortalizing their customarily brief conversations with Napoleon. Ellis (125) and McLeod (244) interviewed the Emperor in July 1817; Hall (171) and Clifford (85) visited him in August. The Russells who visited separately in 1817 and 1820 (99, 352) commented particularly on the accomplishments of Lowe.

Such an historic event as the death of the Emperor certainly did not escape the pens of forgers and profit-seekers. Among the fictitious accounts are Tyder (401), Monkhouse (268), Simmonin (368) and an anonymous journal (197) containing papers allegedly taken from Napoleon's desk just after his death. The most interesting document, however, was the MANUSCRIT VENU DE SAINTE-HELENE (239, 251, 252) which was originally attributed to Napoleon. It caused a storm of speculation (264, 332) until authorship was finally ascribed to Lullin de Châteauvieux.

SPECIALIZED STUDIES

In recent years, the circumstances surrounding Napoleon's death have generated more popular interest than any other part of the St. Helena story. Weider and Hapgood's (420) MURDER OF NAPOLEON, for example, was offered as a History Book Club selection and condensed for READERS DIGEST after its publication in 1982. Although it suggested no new hypothesis and generally reiterated the Forshufvud (137, 138, 139) thesis, Weider and Hapgood's book attempted to reopen a controversy that many historians had laid to rest in the 1960s. For the most part, little response has come from the historical profession; rather the scientific community has challenged the accusation that the Emperor died from chronic arsenic poisoning. Jones and Ledington (193) noted that arsenic was a common property in wallpaper and could have imperiled the Emperor's health, and Lewin, et al. (226) challenged the entire hypothesis by their studies of hair samples.

Near the time of Forshufvud's publication in 1962, a number of other studies on Napoleon's death appeared as well: Cawadias (67), Groen (167), Godlewski (157), Magdelaine (245), Hildebrand (177), Richardson (343), some scientific notes (381), and a French medical thesis (127). Earlier studies, beginning in 1821 and continuing into the twentieth century, speculated on the questions of climate, care, and cancer: Abbatucci (1), Andrews (9), Aretz (13), Audibert (19), Barginet (25), Chaplin (76), Héreau (176) and a number of anonymous tracts (5, 43, 84, 335).

Other specialized studies have described the fifty days which Napoleon spent off the coast of England and the Emperor's voyage to St. Helena, for example the works of Chanlaine (74), Duhamel (120),

Fabry (131), Parisot (310), Pesme (315), Silvestre (367), and
Thornton (392). St. Helena and its physical setting are the subjects
of Gosse (163), Jackson (189), Lockwood (228), Melliss (265),
Pluchonneau (322), Poulleau (325), Toulouzan de Saint-Martin (394),
and several period descriptions (186, 404).

Writings specifically on "Longwood" include Godlewski (156),
Martineau (255) and several descriptive publications (303, 229); on
"The Briars," Fleuriot de Langle (136) should be consulted. For a
more comprehensive social history of the island and its inhabitants
during the captivity, Martineau (257) and Hauterive (172) are the
best sources. Other more confined studies include Broadley (54) on
the art of the captivity, Carême (61) on the Emperor's cuisine, and
Guillois (169), Advielle (6), and Healey (173) on Napoleon's library.
On the controversy which Antommarchi began over the death mask,
Veauce (408, 409, 435), Jousset (198, 199), and Watson (419) have
written clearly the leading works.

Members of the St. Helena community have also been the subject
of a number of biographies and brief studies, although there is much
room for additional research on the people who surrounded the Emperor
during his captivity. Within the existing literature are works on
O'Meara (22, 33), Las Cases (361), Antommarchi (68), Bertrand (155,
237), Piontkowski (205), Betzy Balcombe (17, 145), Ali (262),
Montholon (298), a cook (387), and various churchmen (231).

A more controversial topic--Napoleon and Christianity--has been
reviewed by Beauterne (31), Robson (344) and others (290). Plans for
escape, the Emperor's attitudes toward those plans, and the American
connection have also been topics on which opinion varies. The major
source on the Champ d'Asile remains Soulié (376), and other works
include Brice (52, 53), Driant (117), Fisher (133), Macartney (241),
and a contemporary account by Hyde de Neuville (184). The most
bizarre treatment, however, is Ebeyer's study (124) which traced an
allegedly successful substitution and escape.

To describe specialized studies on the Napoleonic legend is a
much more difficult task, because the literature is not of one
particular genre. Exposition catalogs (65, 66, 107, 254), petitions
for the Emperor's statue in the Place Vendôme (10, 295), poems,
hymns, and writings (129), describing either Napoleon's apotheosis or
his descent into hell, all form part of this legend. One of the more
substantial collections, however, deals with the return of the
Emperor's body to be buried on the banks of the Seine. Among the
primary sources are those edited by Bennett (32) and Chautard (80)
and the writings of Bertrand (36), Coquereau (90), Emmett (126), Hugo
(183), Joinville (192), Janisch (190), Las Cases (214), Jourdain de
la Passardière (196), Norvins (300), Rohan Chabot (345), Thackeray
(386), Vanel (405), and Wormeley (427). Vast numbers of funérailles
were also issued at that time, and recently the SOUVENIR NAPOLEONIEN
devoted portions of a special issue (342) to "le retour des cendres."

PERIODICALS

Articles on the exile, captivity, and Napoleonic legend have
appeared in numerous popular and scholarly periodicals and journals.
Three noteworthy special issues have also appeared since 1959.
"Sainte-Hélène et la mort de Napoléon" (356), which was issued by the
REVUE DE L'INSTITUT NAPOLEON in 1971, provides an analysis of the

state of scholarship on St. Helena and the Emperor's captivity. Among the articles are reviews of American opinion and new views of Montholon, Gorrequer, Mme. Bertrand, and Antommarchi. On a more popular level, the MIROIR DE L'HISTOIRE devoted a special issue in 1959 to "La Légende Napoléonienne" (222).

In 1960 YALE FRENCH STUDIES issued "The Myth of Napoleon" (280), which consisted of historical and literary excursions into the creation of the Napoleonic legend. Of particular interest to historians will be Sonnenfeld's "Napoleon as Sun Myth," which describes Pérès's GRAND ERRATUM (314) and Whately's HISTORICAL DOUBTS (421).

FUTURE RESEARCH

Although a wealth of general and specific studies have been devoted over the years to Napoleon's exile on St. Helena and to the Napoleonic legend, there is still ample opportunity for further analysis. Certainly subjects like Napoleon's death have been studied, challenged, reanalyzed and for all intents and purposes exhausted. On the other hand, the more than ninety volumes of Lowe's papers and the literally thousands of documents and letters in the Gorrequer cartons remain scarcely touched. Only after they have been perused and used adequately can a true portrait of the governor emerge. Was Lowe the mediocre leader whose lack of ability left him unable to cope with the demands made upon him by his famous prisoner? Was he instead an ogre who was responsible for the Emperor's premature death, or was he simply a royal official whose discipline required him to observe the regulations which he had been instructed to follow?

Research should also be conducted on contemporary opinion and the development of the Napoleonic legend outside of France and Great Britain. Although some excellent studies already exist, there are gaps in the national coverage. Many of the characters in the drama should also be studied, but they should be treated as individuals as well as creators and curators of the Napoleonic legend.

As Napoleon himself carefully fashioned the legend by becoming his own historian, he planned for his son to wear the mantle of the Empire which he had worn. This was among his greatest desires; and to assure that the Napoleonic revival would come, he could not be forgotten. He has been viewed as a victim of circumstance, a victim of his own power, a victim of greed. He has, however, never been a victim of obscurity.

BIBLIOGRAPHY: ST. HELENA AND THE LEGEND

1. Abbatucci, S., and A. de Mets. LES DERNIERS MOMENTS: LA VRAI FIGURE DU DOCTEUR ANTOMMARCHI ET L'ENIGME PATHOLOGIQUE DE SAINTE-HELENE. Antwerp: Editions St. Jacques, 1938.

2. Abbott, John Stevens Cabot. NAPOLEON AT ST. HELENA; OR, INTERESTING ANECDOTES AND REMARKABLE CONVERSATIONS OF THE EMPEROR DURING THE FIVE AND A HALF YEARS OF HIS CAPTIVITY. Collected from the memorials of Las Cases, O'Meara, Montholon, Antommarchi, and others. New York: Harper [1855].

3. Abell, Lucia Elizabeth (Balcombe). NAPOLEON A SAINTE-HELENE; SOUVENIRS DE BETZY BALCOMBE. Traduction annotée et précédée d'une introduction par Aimé de Gras. Paris: Plon-Nourrit, 1898.

4. Abrantès, Laure Adelaide Constance Permon Junot, duchesse d'. MEMOIRES SUR LA RESTAURATION, OU SOUVENIRS HISTORIQUES SUR CETTE EPOQUE, LA REVOLUTION DE JUILLET (1830) ET LES PREMIERES ANNEES DU REGNE DE LOUIS-PHILIPPE Ier. Paris: J. L'Henry, 1835-36. 6 vols.

5. ACCUSATION CONTRE LES MEURTRIERS DE NAPOLEON. Paris: L'Huillier, 1821.

6. Advielle, Victor. LA BIBLIOTHEQUE DE NAPOLEON A SAINTE-HELENE. Paris: Lechevalier, 1894.

7. Aldanov, Mark Aleksandrovich. SAINTE-HELENE, PETITE ILE. Traduit du manuscrit russe par M. Hirchwald. Paris: Povolozky, 1921.

8. Ali (Louis Etienne Saint-Denis). SOUVENIRS DU MAMELUCK ALI SUR L'EMPEREUR NAPOLEON. Introduction by G. Michaut. Paris: Payot, 1926.

9. Andrews, Edmund. "The Diseases, Death and Autopsy of Napoléon I." JOURNAL OF THE AMERICAN MEDICAL ASSOCIATION 25 (1895): 1081.

10. ANNIVERSAIRE DE LA MORT DE NAPOLEON-LE-GRAND. DETAILS INTERESSANS SUR LA STATUE DE L'EMPEREUR, QUI DOIT ETRE PLACEE SUR LA COLONNE DE LA PLACE VENDOME. Paris: Sétier, 1832.

11. Antommarchi, Francesco A. MEMOIRES DU DOCTEUR ANTOMMARCHI, OU LES DERNIERS MOMENTS DE NAPOLEON. Paris: Barrois, 1825. 2 vols.

12. L'APOTHEOSE DE L'EMPEREUR NAPOLEON. Paris: Rion, 1831.

13. Aretz, Paul. NAPOLEONS GEFANGENSCHAFT UND TOD. SANKT-HELENA ERINNUNGEN. Dresden: Reissner, 1921.

14. Arnott, Archibald. AN ACCOUNT OF THE LAST ILLNESS, DISEASE AND POST MORTEM APPEARANCE OF NAPOLEON BONAPARTE TO WHICH IS ADDED A LETTER FROM DR. ARNOTT TO LIEUTENANT-GENERAL SIR HUDSON LOWE. London: J. Murray, 1822.

15. ARRIVEE DE MME BERTRAND, SON DEBARQUEMENT AVEC TOUTE SA FAMILLE; ARTICLES DU TESTAMENT DE BONAPARTE, ET RELATION DES CIRCONSTANCES QUI ONT PRECEDE, ACCOMPAGNE ET SUIVI SA MORT. Paris: Renaudière, 1821.

16. Aubry, Octave. NAPOLEON ET SON TEMPS: SAINTE-HELENE. Paris: Flammarion, 1935. 2 vols.

17. Aubry, Octave. "La Petite Fille de Sainte-Hélène." [Betzy Balcombe.] HISTORIA 139 (1958): 597-604.

18. Aubry, Octave. ST. HELENA. Authorized translation by Arthur Livingston. Philadelphia and London: Lippincott, 1936.

19. Audibert, Victor. "Comment fut soigné Napoléon à Sainte-Hélène." PROVENCE MEDICALE (MARSEILLE) 25 (1957): 121-26.

20. Augé, Lazare. QUELQUES PENSEES APOLOGETIQUES SUR BONAPARTE. Paris: Brasseur, 1821.

21. Baelen, Jean. "A Sainte-Hélène, Hudson Lowe était-il pleinement responsable?" LA PRESSE MEDICALE 77 (1969): 691-93.

22. Baelen, Jean. "A Sainte-Hélène: La position du docteur O'Meara." LA PRESSE MEDICALE 77 (1969): 1911-12.

23. Bajert-Beker, comte de Mons. RELATION DE LA MISSION DU LIEUTENANT-GENERAL COMTE BEKER AUPRES DE L'EMPEREUR NAPOLEON, DEPUIS LA SECONDE ABDICATION JUSQU'AU PASSAGE A BORD DU BELLEROPHON. Clermont-Ferrand: Perol, 1941.

24. Balmain, Aleksandr Antonovich, graf. NAPOLEON IN CAPTIVITY. REPORTS OF COUNT BALMAIN, RUSSIAN COMMISSIONER ON THE ISLAND OF ST. HELENA, 1816-1820. Translated and edited with introduction and notes by Julian Park. New York: Century, 1927.

25. Barginet, Alexandre. DE LA REINE D'ANGLETERRE ET DE NAPOLEON, TOUS DEUX MORTS D'UN CANCER. Paris: Constant-Chantpie, 1821.

26. Barginet, Alexandre. SUR NAPOLEON, OU REPONSE AUX JOURNAUX CONTRE-REVOLUTIONNAIRES QUI S'INTITULENT QUOTIDIENNE, GAZETTE DE FRANCE, JOURNAL DES DEBATS, ET DRAPEAU BLANC. Paris: Constant-Chantpie, 1821.

27. Barnes, John. A TOUR THROUGH THE ISLAND OF ST. HELENA, etc. London: Richardson, 1817.

28. Barthe, Félix. REFUTATION DE LA RELATION DU CAPITAINE MAITLAND COMMANDANT LE BELLEROPHON, TOUCHANT L'EMBARQUEMENT DE NAPOLEON A SON BORD, REDIGEE PAR M. BARTHE... SUR LES DOCUMENTS DE M. LE COMTE DE LAS CASES; AUGMENTEE DU TESTAMENT ORIGINAL DE NAPOLEON. Paris: Dupont, 1827.

29. Bathurst, Lord. "Napoleon at St. Helena." Speech, 1817. Colonial Office Library, no. 2660.

30. Beatson, Major General A. "Tracts Relating to St. Helena." 1816. Colonial Office Library, no. 2658A.

31. Beauterne, Robert François Antoine, chevalier de. SENTIMENT DE NAPOLEON Ier SUR LE CHRISTIANISME RECUEILLI PAR BATHILD BOUNIOL. Paris: Pierre Téqui, 1912.

32. Bennett, George. "Napoleon's Burial and Exhumation." [Reminiscences of G.B. Bennett. Edited by A.H.U. Colquhoun.] CANADIAN MONTHLY 35 (1910): 387-93.

33. Bertaut, Jules. "Le Docteur O'Meara à Sainte-Hélène." HISTOIRE DE LA MEDECINE 7 (1957): 57-64.

34. Bertier de Sauvigny, Guillaume de. "Pourquoi Sainte-Hélène?" SOUVENIR NAPOLEONIEN 34 (1971): 5-9.

35. Berton, Jean Baptiste. LETTRE A M. LE BARON MOUNIER, DIRECTEUR-GENERAL DE LA POLICE AU ROYAUME, SUR LA MORT DE NAPOLEON. Paris: Dupont, 1821.

36. Bertrand, Arthur. LETTRE SUR L'EXPEDITION DE SAINTE-HELENE EN 1840. Paris: Paulin, 1841.

37. Bertrand, Henri Gratien, comte. CAHIERS DE SAINTE-HELENE. Manuscrit déchiffré et annoté par Paul Fleuriot de Langle. Paris: A. Michel [1949-59]. 3 vols.

38. BIBLIOTHEQUE HISTORIQUE, OU RECUEIL DE MATERIAUX POUR SERVIR A L'HISTOIRE DU TEMPS (1817-1820). Paris: Delaunay, Pelicier, Treuttel and Würtz, 1817-20. 14 vols.

39. Bigonnet, Jean Adrien. NAPOLEON BONAPARTE CONSIDERE SOUS LE RAPPORT DE SON INFLUENCE SUR LA REVOLUTION. Paris: Dupont, 1821.

40. Bingham, George. "Napoleon's Voyage to Saint Helena." [Excerpts from the Diary of Sir George Bingham.] BLACKWOOD'S EDINBURGH MAGAZINE 160 (1896): 540-49.

41. Boisson, Jean. LE RETOUR DES CENDRES. Paris: Etudes et Recherches historiques, 1913.

42. Bonaparte, Louis. REPONSE A SIR WALTER SCOTT SUR SON HISTOIRE DE NAPOLEON PAR LOUIS BONAPARTE, COMTE DE SAINT-LEU, ANCIEN ROI DE HOLLANDE, FRERE DE L'EMPEREUR. Paris: Trouvé, 1828.

43. BONAPARTE N'EST PAS MORT D'UN CANCER. Dédié aux mânes de Napoléon. Paris: Bataille et Bousquet, 1821.

44. Boniface, Alexander, ed. BUONAPARTE PREDIT PAR DES PROPHETES ET PEINT PAR DES HISTORIENS, DES ORATEURS ET DES POETES. Paris: Boniface, 1814.

45. Bonnel, Ulane, et al. SAINTE-HELENE, TERRE D'EXIL. Paris: Hachette, 1971.

46. Bordonove, Georges. LA VIE QUOTIDIENNE DE NAPOLEON EN ROUTE VERS SAINTE-HELENE. Paris: Hachette, 1977.

47. Borjane, Henry. NAPOLEON A BORD DU NORTHUMBERLAND. Paris: Plon, 1936.

48. Bourguignon, Jean. LE RETOUR DES CENDRES, 1840; SUIVI D'UN EPILOGUE SUR LE RETOUR DU ROI DE ROME. Paris: Plon [1941].

49. Bowerbank, John. AN EXTRACT FROM A DIARY KEPT ON BOARD H.M.S. BELLEROPHON FROM JULY 15, 1815 TO AUGUST 7, 1815. London: Whittingham and Arliss, 1815.

50. Boyer, Ferdinand. "La Place de Napoléon dans une histoire universelle." REVUE DE L'INSTITUTE NAPOLEON 80 (1961): 104-5.

51. Braun, Jean. "Napoléon en Alsace, son culte et sa légende." SAISONS D'ALSACE (STRASBOURG) 8 (1963): 7-28.

52. Brice, Médecin général Raoul. LES ESPOIRS DE NAPOLEON A SAINTE-HELENE. Paris: Payot, 1938.

53. Brice, Médecin général Raoul. LE SECRET DE NAPOLEON. Paris: Payot, 1936.

54. Broadley, Alexander Meyrick. "Napoleon's Saint Helena Portraits (1815-1821)." [Portraits by Denzil Ibbetson.] THE CENTURY 83 (1912): 824-35.

55. Burton, June. NAPOLEON AND CLIO: HISTORICAL WRITING, TEACHING, AND THINKING DURING THE FIRST EMPIRE. Durham, N.C.: Carolina Academic Press, 1979.

56. Burton, June. "Napoléon et l'histoire." REVUE DE L'INSTITUT NAPOLEON 126 (1973): 1-4.

57. Cabanès, Augustin. AU CHEVET DE L'EMPEREUR. Paris: A. Michel, 1958.

58. Cahuet, Albéric. APRES LA MORT DE L'EMPEREUR; LES DERNIERS SERVITEURS DE NAPOLEON, LA FIN D'UNE CAPTIVITE, LE MARIAGE DE MARCHAND, NOEL SANTINI ET LA SAINTE-ALLIANCE, L'"OURS D'HELVETIE," LE BIBLIOTHECAIRE DE LONGWOOD, LES PELERINS DE SAINTE-HELENE. DOCUMENTS INEDITS. Paris: Emile-Paul, 1913.

59. Cahuet, Albéric. NAPOLEON DELIVRE. DOCUMENTS ET TEMOIGNAGES INEDITS. Paris: Emile-Paul, 1914.

60. Cahuet, Albéric. RETOURS DE SAINTE-HELENE (1821-1840). Paris: Fasquelle, 1932.

61. Carême, Antoine. L'ART DE LA CUISINE FRANCAISE AU XIXe SIECLE. Paris: l'auteur, 1833-44.

62. CARNET D'UN VOYAGEUR, OU, RECUEIL DE NOTES CURIEUSES SUR LA VIE, LES OCCUPATIONS, LES HABITUDES DE BUONAPARTE A LONGWOOD; SUR LES PRINCIPAUX HABITANS DE SAINTE-HELENE, LA DESCRIPTION PITTORESQUE DE CETTE ILE, etc. PRISES SUR LES LIEUX DANS LES DERNIERS MOIS DE 1818. Paris: Pillet, 1819.

63. Castelot, André. LE DRAME DE SAINTE-HELENE. Paris: Rombaldi, 1975. 2 vols.

64. Castelot, André. LE LIVRE DE SAINTE-HELENE. Paris: Solar, 1969.

65. CATALOGUE DE L'EXPOSITION: LA LEGENDE NAPOLEONIENNE, 1769-1900, ORGANISEE A PARIS, BIBLIOTHEQUE NATIONALE, 11 JUIN-20 OCTOBRE 1969. Paris: La Bibliothèque Nationale, 1969.

66. CATALOGUE DE L'EXPOSITION LAS CASES ET LE MEMORIAL DE SAINTE-HELENE, ORGANISEE AU MUSEE GOYA. Castres: Musée Goya, 1967.

67. Cawadias, A.P. "La Maladie fatale de Napoléon le Grand." LA PRESSE MEDICALE 70 (1962): 2833-35.

68. Cazes Tombeck, Jacqueline. "Antommarchi dernier médecin de l'empereur." Thèse Méd., Paris, 1972.

69. CENTENAIRE DE NAPOLEON; 5 MAI 1821-5 MAI 1921. Paris: La Sabretache; Plon, 1921.

70. Chaboulon, Fleury de. DISCOURS SUR LA TRANSLATION DES CENDRES DE L'EMPEREUR NAPOLEON. Paris: Vinchon, 1835.

71. Chalman, P. "Les Variations de la légende napoléonienne." REVUE HISTORIQUE DE L'ARMEE 17 (1961): 40-56.

72. [Chalons d'Arge, Auguste P.] TOMBEAU DE NAPOLEON Ier ERIGE DANS LE DOME DES INVALIDES PAR M. VISCONTI. Paris: chez l'auteur, 1853.

73. Chanlaine, Pierre. LE CHEMIN DE SAINTE-HELENE. Paris: Editions des Portiques, 1934.

74. Chanlaine, Pierre. NAPOLEON VERS SAINTE-HELENE. Paris: Peyronnet, 1960.

75. Chapier, Georges. LE RETOUR DE L'EMPEREUR; 1840-1940. Préface de M. le général Koechlin-Schwartz. Paris: Livres nouveaux, 1940.

76. Chaplin, Arnold. THE ILLNESS AND DEATH OF NAPOLEON BONAPARTE (A MEDICAL CRITICISM). London: Hirschfeld, 1913.

77. Chaplin, Arnold. A ST. HELENA WHO'S WHO, OR A DIRECTORY OF THE ISLAND DURING THE CAPTIVITY OF NAPOLEON. New York: Dutton, 1919.

78. Chaplin, Arnold. THOMAS SHORTT, PRINCIPAL MEDICAL OFFICER AT ST. HELENA WITH BIOGRAPHIES OF SOME OTHER MEDICAL MEN ASSOCIATED WITH THE CASE OF NAPOLEON. London: Stanley Paul, 1914.

79. Chateaubriand, François Auguste René, vicomte de. NAPOLEON. Présentation et introd. par Christian Melchior-Connet. Paris: Egloff, 1949.

80. Chautard, Joseph. DE SAINTE-HELENE AUX INVALIDES; SOUVENIRS DE SANTINI, GARDIEN DU TOMBEAU DE L'EMPEREUR NAPOLEON Ier. Précédés d'une lettre de M. le comte Emmanuel de Las Cases; rédigés par J. Chautard. Paris: Ledoyen, 1853.

81. Chauvin, Léon. L'ANCIEN REGIME ET LA REVOLUTION, OU, REVUE HISTORIQUE, CRITIQUE ET MORAL DE L'ANCIEN REGIME. Paris: Lemarchand, 1842.

82. Choppin, Capitaine. "La Vie à Sainte-Hélène pendant la captivité de Napoléon." [Lettre du M. de Montchenu, 1817.] CARNET DE LA SABRETACHE 4 (1896): 94-101.

83. Ciana, Albert. DEFENSE DE NAPOLEON CONTRE UNE MYSTIFICATION HISTORIQUE. LA LETTRE AU PRINCE REGENT D'ANGLETERRE: MANUSCRIT DE CUBA. Paris: Janvier, 1938.

84. LE CINQ MAI OU RELATION EXACTE DES DIVERSES CIRCONSTANCES QUI ONT PRECEDE, ACCOMPAGNE ET SUIVI LA MORT DE NAPOLEON BONAPARTE A L'ILE DE SAINTE-HELENE. Traduit textuellement des gazettes anglaises. Paris: Ponthieu, Terry, Chambet et Audin, 1821.

85. Clifford, H.J. "A Visit to Longwood. Extracts from the Diary of Lieutenant H.J. Clifford." CORNHILL MAGAZINE 80 (1899): 665-75.

86. Cockburn, George. BONAPARTE'S VOYAGE TO SAINT-HELENA. Boston: Lilly, 1833.

87. Cockburn, George. "How Napoleon Impressed a Foe at St. Helena." [A letter from Sir George Cockburn to Sir Alexander Campbell.] THE CENTURY 54 (July 1897): 473-74.

88. COLLECTION NOUVELLE DE DOCUMENS HISTORIQUES SUR NAPOLEON CONTENANT NOTES SUR LES LETTRES DU CAP, RECUEILLIES DES CONVERSATIONS DU COMTE DE LAS CASES, A SON RETOUR DE

SAINTE-HELENE EN 1818, ET LETTRES, ADRESSEES AUX SOUVERAINS
ALLIES ET A L'IMPERATRICE MARIE-LOUISE. Paris: Rignoux, 1822.

89. CONSTABLE'S MISCELLANY. MEMORIALS OF THE LATE WAR. [contents:
    Vol. 1. Journal of a soldier of the 71st regiment from
    1805-1815.--The Spanish campaign of 1808, by Adam Neale
    (incomplete)--Vol. 2. Memoirs of the war of the French in Spain,
    by M. de Rocca.--Narrative of the battles of Quatre Bras, Ligny
    and Waterloo.--The Duke of Wellington's despatch from
    Waterloo.--The Death of Napoleon Bonaparte]. Edinburgh:
    Constable, 1828. 2 vols.

90. Coquereau, Félix. SOUVENIRS DU VOYAGE A SAINTE-HELENE. Paris:
    H.L. Delloye, 1841.

91. Corti, Comte. "Napoléon à Sainte-Hélène. Lettre de Las Cases à
    Lucien Bonaparte interceptée par la police de Metternich."
    REVUE DU XIXe SIECLE, NAPOLEON 26 (1926): 79.

92. LA COURONNE D'IMMORTELLES, OU NAPOLEON SUR LA CALONNE PAR J.A.P.
    Paris: Bellemain, 1833.

93. LES CRIMES SECRETS DE NAPOLEON BONAPARTE... RECEUILLIS PAR UNE
    VICTIME DE SA TYRANNIE. Brussels: Marchands de nouveautés,
    1815.

94. Dansette, Adrien. NAPOLEON: PENSEES POLITIQUES ET SOCIALES
    RASSEMBLEES ET PRESENTEES PAR ADRIEN DANSETTE. Paris:
    Flammarion, 1969.

95. Dansette, Adrien. "Napoléon, victime des historiens." PLAISIR
    FRANCE 267 (1961): 4-9.

96. Darroch, Duncan. "Letters Written by Ensign Duncan Darroch."
    Edited by Major Smythe. ANNUAL OF THE LANCASHIRE FUSILIERS,
    1904.

97. Darroch, Duncan. "Un Témoinage de Sainte-Hélène: Lettre de
    l'enseigne Duncan Darroch." BULLETIN DE LA SOCIETE BELGE
    D'ETUDES NAPOLEONIENNES 24 (1957): 39-47.

98. Darst, Diane. "Napoleon in Romantic Thought: A Study of
    Hazlitt, Stendhal and Scott." Ph.D. dissertation, Columbia
    University, 1976.

99. Davies, C.C. "A Sainte-Hélène, deux mois avant la mort de
    Napoléon." [Le journal de Sir Henry Russell.] ANNALES
    HISTORIQUES DE LA REVOLUTION FRANCAISE 28 (1956): 279-91.

100. Davin, Emmanuel. "Pourquoi Napoléon ne partit pas pour les
     Etats-Unis en 1815?" FURETEUR 17 (1958): 129-40.

101. Debraux, Emile. HISTOIRE DU PRISONNIER DE SAINTE-HELENE.
     DETAILS CURIEUX SUR SA FAMILLE, SA NAISSANCE ET SON EDUCATION.
     Paris: Lebigre, 1833.

102. Debray, André. "Moulange de la main de l'Empereur." BULLETIN DE LA SOCIETE BELGE D'ETUDES NAPOLEONIENNES 88 (1974): 5-8.

103. Décamps, Maurice. MON VOYAGE A SAINTE-HELENE ET DESTRUCTION DES TERMITES DANS LA MAISON DE L'EMPEREUR. Bordeaux: Delmas, 1937.

104. Dechamps, Jules. "Les Défenseurs de Napoléon en Grande Bretagne de 1815 à 1830." REVUE DE L'INSTITUT NAPOLEON 69 (1958): 129-40.

105. Dechamps, Jules. SUR LA LEGENDE DE NAPOLEON. Paris: Champion, 1931.

106. De Paoli, Erasmo. COME FU MANIPOLATA A SANTA ELENA LA NOTIZIA DE LA MORTE DI NAPOLEONE. Genoa: Le Opere e i Giorni, 1926.

107. LES DERNIERS JOURS DE L'EMPEREUR NAPOLEON DANS L'ILE DE SAINTE-HELENE OU RECIT DETAILLE DES SOUFFRANCES DE CE HEROS. Paris: Demonville, 1831.

108. LES DERNIERES REFLEXIONS DE NAPOLEON, ECRITES PAR LUI-MEME A L'ILE DE SAINTE-HELENE, TROUVEES EN AOUT 1836 PAR UN OFFICIER ANGLAIS, QUI VIENT SEULEMENT DE LES FAIRE CONNAITRE EN FRANCE. Lyon: Deleuze, 1837.

109. Desanti, Grégoire. "La Légende napoléonienne." LES CONFERENCES DE L'INSTITUT HISTORIQUE DE PROVENCE 47 (1969): 255-56.

110. DESCRIPTION DES FUNERAILLES DE NAPOLEON. Paris: Bouchard-Huzard, 1840.

111. DESCRIPTION DU TOMBEAU DE NAPOLEON-LE-GRAND, DEPOSE DANS LA CHAPELLE ARDENTE DE SAINTE-JEROME, A L'HOTEL ROYAL DES INVALIDES. Paris: Gauthier, 1841.

112. DETAILS ET ORDRE DE LA MARCHE DE TOUTES LES CEREMONIES QUI ONT EU LIEU A SAINTE-HELENE APRES LA MORT DE BONAPARTE. Paris: Pillet, 1821.

113. DOCUMENTS POUR SERVIR A L'HISTOIRE DE LA CAPTIVITE DE NAPOLEON BONAPARTE A SAINTE-HELENE. Paris: Pillet, 1822.

114. Dolly, Charles. ITINERAIRE DE NAPOLEON BONAPARTE. Paris: A. et G. Laguionie, 1842.

115. Doumic, R. "At St. Helena." [A review of Gourgaud.] LITTELL'S LIVING AGE 222 (1899): 45-54.

116. Dowd, David L. NAPOLEON: WAS HE THE HEIR OF THE REVOLUTION? New York: Rinehart, 1957.

117. Driant, Emile Augustin Cyprien [Capitaine Danrit] EVASION D'EMPEREUR. Paris: Flammarion, 1913.

118. Driault, Edouard. L'IMMORTELLE EPOPEE DU DRAPEAU TRICOLORE; NAPOELOPN-LE GRAND, 1769-1821. Le Chesnay: Rousseaux, 1930. 3 vols.

119. Driault, Edouard. NAPOLEON ET L'EUROPE. LA CHUTE DE L'EMPIRE, LA LEGENDE DE NAPOLEON. Paris: Alcan, 1927.

120. Duhamel, Jean. THE FIFTY DAYS: NAPOLEON IN ENGLAND. Translated [from the French] by R.A. Hall. London: Hart-Davis, 1969.

121. Duhamel, Jean. "Ruses anglaises pour sauver Napoléon." REVUE DE PARIS 69 (1962): 46-59.

122. Durand-Brager, J.B.H. SAINTE-HELENE. TRANSLATION DU CERCUEIL DE L'EMPEREUR NAPOLEON A BORD DE LA FREGATE LA BELLE-POULE. Paris: Gide, 1844.

123. Duvivier, Paul. LA DERNIERE FILLEULE DE L'EMPEREUR: JOSEPHINE-NAPOLEONE DE MONTHOLON-SEMONVILLE (1818-1819) D'APRES DES DOCUMENTS INEDITS. Liège: Imprimerie La Meuse, 1909.

124. Ebeyer, Paul Pierre. REVELATIONS CONCERNING NAPOLEON'S ESCAPE FROM ST. HELENA. New Orleans: Windmill Publishing, 1947.

125. Ellis, Henry. JOURNAL OF PROCEEDINGS OF THE LATE EMBASSY TO CHINA. London: J. Murray, 1817.

126. Emmett, Anthony. "New Records of Napoleon: Funeral at Saint Helena and Exhumation of his Body." [Extracts from the diary of Major-General A. Emmett, in charge of the funeral of the Emperor; Record of the exhumation ... by Charles C. Alexander, officer in charge.] THE CENTURY 83 (1912): 401-8.

127. Erard, Patrick. "La Maladie qui causa la mort de Napoléon," Thèse Méd., [Paris-Sud], 1976.

128. Evans, Henry Ridgely Evans. THE NAPOLEON MYTH. Chicago: The Open Court Publishing Company, 1905.

129. EXAMEN ANALYTIQUE ET RAISONNE DES PRINCIPALES BROCHURES QUI ONT PARU DEPUIS LA MORT DE NAPOLEON. Par A.G...n, ancien officier. Paris: Chanson, 1821.

130. "Extract from 'The Noble Game of Billiards.'" EASTERN PAMPHLET, 1934. Colonial Office Library, no. 345.

131. Fabry, Jean Baptiste Germain. ITINERAIRE DE BONAPARTE A L'ILE DE SAINTE-HELENE, DEPUIS SON DEPART DE L'ELYSEE-BOURBON, AVEC DES DETAILS TRES CIRCONSTANCES ET DES ANECDOTES SUR SES DIFFERENS SEJOURS A LA MALMAISON, RAMBOUILLET, TOURS, NIORD [sic], ROCHEFORT, L'ILE D'AIX, A BORD DE LA FREGATE FRANCAISE DU BELLEROPHON ET DU NORTHUMBERLAND.... Paris: Imprimerie de Laurens, 1815.

132. Faure, Elie. NAPOLEON. Paris: Crès, 1921.

133. Fisher, H.A.L. "If Napoleon Had Escaped to America." SCRIBNERS 89 (1931): 35-48.

134. Fisher, H.A.L. "St. Helena." THE CAMBRIDGE MODERN HISTORY. Vol. 9. NAPOLEON. Cambridge: Cambridge University Press, 1969.

135. Fleischman, Théo. "Ce que Napoléon disait de Waterloo à Sainte-Hélène." BULLETIN DE LA SOCIETE BELGE D'ETUDES NAPOLEONIENNES 21 (1956): 28-43.

136. Fleuriot de Langle, Paul. "Les Briars: les heures claires de Sainte-Hélène." HISTOIRES DE L'HISTOIRE 1 (1959): 64-73.

137. Forshufvud, Sten; Hamilton Smith; and Anders Warren. "Arsenic Content of Napoleon I's Hair Probably Taken Immediately after His Death." NATURE 192 (1961): 103-5.

138. Forshufvud, Sten. NAPOLEON A-T-IL ETE EMPOISONNE? UNE ENQUETE JUDICIAIRE. Traduit du suédois par Edy Manpaix. Préface du Professeur Griffon, avant-propos de Henry Lachouque. Paris: Plon, 1962.

139. Forshufvud, Sten. WHO KILLED NAPOLEON? Translated from the Swedish by Alan Houghton Broderick. London: Hutchinson, [1962].

140. Forsyth, William. HISTORY OF THE CAPTIVITY OF NAPOLEON AT ST. HELENA; FROM THE LETTERS AND JOURNALS OF THE LATE LIEUT.-GEN. SIR HUDSON LOWE, AND OFFICIAL DOCUMENTS NOT BEFORE MADE PUBLIC. London: J. Murray, 1853. 3 vols.

141. Frémeaux, Paul. NAPOLEON PRISONNIER. MEMOIRES D'UN MEDECIN [STOKOE] DE L'EMPEREUR A SAINTE HELENE. Deuxième édition. Paris: Flammarion, 1901.

142. Frémeaux, Paul. SAINTE-HELENE, LES DERNIERS JOURS DE L'EMPEREUR. Paris: Flammarion, 1908.

143. Froidcourt, Georges de. "Un Témoin de la persistance de la légende napoléonienne." BULLETIN DE LA SOCIETE BELGE D'ETUDES NAPOLEONIENNES 52 (1965): 45-47.

144. Gagneur, Maurice. NAPOLEON D'APRES LE MEMORIAL DE SAINTE-HELENE. Paris: Delagrave, 1921.

145. Gal, Mme. "Napoléon et Betsy Balcombe à Sainte-Hélène." ANNALES DE LA SOCIETE DES LETTRES, SCIENCES ET ARTS DES ALPES-MARITIMES (NICE) 51 (1960-61): 203-6.

146. Galantaris, Christian. "Sur quelques imprimés de la légende napoléonienne." BULLETIN DE LA LIBRAIRIE ANCIENNE ET MODERNE 118 (1969): 142-46.

147. Ganière, Paul. "La Mission Joinville à Sainte-Hélène."
     SOUVENIR NAPOLEONIEN 38 (1975): 7-10.

148. Ganière, Paul. NAPOLEON A SAINTE-HELENE. Paris: Amiot-Dumont,
     1957-62. 3 vols.

149. Ganière, Paul. "Pèlerinage à Sainte-Hélène." MIROIR DE
     L'HISTOIRE 8 (1957): 719-26.

150. Geer, Walter. NAPOLEON AND HIS FAMILY: THE STORY OF A CORSICAN
     CLAN. Vol. 3. MOSCOW-ST. HELENA, 1813-1821. London: Allen,
     1928-29.

151. Geoffroy, Louis. NAPOLEON APOCRYPHE: HISTOIRE DE LA CONQUETE
     DU MONDE ET DE LA MONARCHIE UNIVERSELLE, 1812-1832. Paris:
     Paulin, 1836.

152. Geoffroy de Grandmaison, Charles. NAPOLEON ET SES RECENTS
     HISTORIENS. Paris: Perrin, 1896.

153. A GEOGRAPHICAL AND HISTORICAL ACCOUNT OF THE ISLAND OF ST.
     HELENA ... TO WHICH IS SUBJOINED A BRIEF MEMOIR OF NAPOLEON
     BONAPARTE, DURING HIS SECLUSION AT ROCHEFORT, HIS SUBSEQUENT
     SURRENDER AND APPEARANCE OFF THE BRITISH SHORES, AND HIS FINAL
     TRANSFER TO THE NORTHUMBERLAND,... BOUND FOR ST. HELENA.
     London, 1815.

154. Geyl, Pieter. NAPOLEON, FOR AND AGAINST. New Haven: Yale
     University Press, 1949.

155. Girard de Vasson, Jacques. BERTRAND, LE GRAND-MARECHAL DE
     SAINTE-HELENE. Paris: Issoudon, Laboureur, 1935.

156. Godlewski, Guy. "Longwood." SOUVENIR NAPOLEONIEN 34 (1971):
     14-20.

157. Godlewski, Guy. "Napoléon est-il mort d'un cancer?" REVUE DE
     L'INSTITUT NAPOLEON 73-74 (1959-60): 145-51.

158. Goldsmith, Lewis. PROCES DE BUONAPARTE, OU ADRESSES, LETTRES,
     ECRITS, DEBATS SURVENUS, EN ANGLETERRE TOUCHANT LA DEPORTATION
     DE NAPOLEON BUONAPARTE. Brussels: Plancher, 1816.

159. Gonnard, Philippe. THE EXILE OF ST. HELENA, THE LAST PHASE IN
     FACT AND FICTION. London: Heinemann; Philadelphia:
     Lippincott, 1909.

160. Gonnard, Philippe. UN LYONNAIS A SAINTE-HELENE. Lyon: Rey,
     1903.

161. Gonnard, Philippe. LES ORIGINES DE LA LEGENDE NAPOLEONIENNE:
     L'OEUVRE HISTORIQUE DE NAPOLEON A SAINTE-HELENE. Geneva:
     Slatkine, 1976.

162. Gorrequer, Gideon. ST. HELENA DURING NAPOLEON'S EXILE:
     GORREQUER'S DIARY. With introduction, biographies, notes and
     explanations, and index of pseudonyms by James Kemble. London:
     Heinemann, 1969.

163. Gosse, Philip. ST. HELENA, 1502-1938. London: Cassell, 1938.

164. Gourgaud, Gaspard, baron. JOURNAL DE SAINTE-HELENE, 1815-1818.
     EDITION AUGMENTEE D'APRES LE TEXTE ORIGINAL. Introduction et
     notes par Octave Aubry. Paris: Flammarion, 1944. 2 vols.

165. Gourgaud, Gaspard, baron. LETTRE DE SIR WALTER SCOTT, ET
     REPONSE DU GENERAL GOURGAUD AVEC NOTES ET PIECES JUSTIFICATIVES.
     Paris: A. Dupont, 1827.

166. Gourgaud, Gaspard, baron. SAINTE-HELENE, JOURNAL INEDIT
     (1815-1818). Paris: Flammarion, 1899. 2 vols.

167. Groen, Jacques. LA DERNIERE MALADIE ET LA CAUSE DE MORT DE
     NAPOLEON. ETUDE PSYCHOLOGIQUE, HISTORIQUE ET MEDICALE. Leiden:
     Brill, 1962.

168. Guérard, Albert Léon. REFLECTIONS ON THE NAPOLEONIC LEGEND.
     New York: Scribner, 1924.

169. Guillois, Antoine. LES BIBLIOTHEQUES PARTICULIERES DE L'EMPEREUR
     NAPOLEON. Paris: Henri Leclerc, 1900.

170. Hachette, Alfred. NAPOLEON. LE DOSSIER DE LA JOURNEE DU RETOUR
     DES CENDRES. Paris: F. Michel, [185?].

171. Hall, Basil. NARRATIVE OF A VOYAGE TO JAVA ... WITH AN
     INTERVIEW WITH NAPOLEON BONAPARTE AT ST. HELENA. London: E.
     Moxon, 1840.

172. Hauterive, Ernest d'. SAINTE-HELENE AU TEMPS DE NAPOLEON ET
     AUJOURD'HUI. Paris: Calmann-Lévy, 1933.

173. Healey, F.G. "La Bibliothèque de Napoléon à Sainte-Hélène.
     Documents inédits trouvés parmi les 'Hudson Lowe Papers.'"
     REVUE DE L'INSTITUT NAPOLEON 80 (1961): 79-88.

174. Henry, Walter. EVENTS OF A MILITARY LIFE: BEING RECOLLECTIONS
     AFTER SERVING IN THE PENINSULAR WAR, INVASION OF FRANCE, THE
     EAST INDIES, ST. HELENA, CANADA, AND ELSEWHERE. London: W.
     Pickering, 1843.

175. Henry, Walter. TRIFLES FROM MY PORTFOLIO OR RECOLLECTIONS OF
     SCENES AND SMALL ADVENTURES DURING TWENTY-NINE YEARS OF MILITARY
     SERVICE BY A STAFF SURGEON. Quebec: W. Neilson, 1839.

176. Héreau, Joachim. NAPOLEON A SAINTE-HELENE, OPINION D'UN MEDECIN
     SUR LA MALADIE DE L'EMPEREUR NAPOLEON ET SUR LA CAUSE DE SA
     MORT. Paris: F. Louis, 1829.

177. Hildebrand, P. PATHOLOGIE DE NAPOLEON, SES MALADIES, LEURS CONSEQUENCES. Paris: Genève, 1970.

178. Holland, Henry Richard Vassall Fox, 3d baron. FOREIGN REMINISCENSES. Edited by Henry Edward Lord Holland. London: Longman, Brown, Green, and Longmans, 1851.

179. Holzhausen, Paul. NAPOLEONS TOD IM SPIEGEL DER ZEITGENOESSISCHEN PRESSE UND DICHTUNG. Frankfurt a.M.: M. Diesterweg, 1902.

180. Hone, William. INTERESTING PARTICULARS OF NAPOLEON'S DEPORTATION FOR LIFE TO SAINT HELENA. London: Printed for W. Hone, 1816.

181. Hook, Theodore. FACTS ILLUSTRATIVE OF THE TREATMENT OF NAPOLEON AT ST.-HELENA. London: W. Stockdale, 1819.

182. Houssaye, Henry. 1815: LA SECONDE ABDICATION; LA TERREUR BLANCHE. Paris: Perrin, 1905.

183. Hugo, Victor. LE RETOUR DE L'EMPEREUR. Paris: n.p., 1840.

184. Hyde de Neuville. MEMOIRES ET SOUVENIRS. Paris: Plon-Nourrit, 1888-92. 3 vols.

185. IL N'EST PAS MORT!!! PAR UN CITOYEN AMI DE LA PATRIE. Paris: Brasseur, 1821.

186. L'ILE DE SAINTE-HELENE, DERNIERE DEMEURE DE NAPOLEON BONAPARTE. Paris: n.p., [1820].

187. ITINERAIRE DE TOULON A SAINTE-HELENE DE LA FREGATE LA BELLE-POULE, COMMANDEE PAR M. LE PRINCE DE JOINVILLE, AVEC DES NOTES HISTORIQUES, BIOGRAPHIQUES ET TOPOGRAPHIQUES PAR M.D. Paris: Baudouin, 1840.

188. Jackson, Basil. NOTES AND REMINISCENCES OF A STAFF OFFICER, CHIEFLY RELATING TO THE WATERLOO CAMPAIGN AND TO ST. HELENA MATTERS DURING THE CAPTIVITY OF NAPOLEON. Edited by R.C. Seaton. London: J. Murray, 1903.

189. Jackson, E.L. ST. HELENA; THE HISTORIC ISLAND FROM ITS DISCOVERY TO THE PRESENT DATE. London: Melbourne, 1903.

190. Janisch, Hudson Ralph. THE EXHUMATION OF THE REMAINS OF NAPOLEON BONAPARTE. James Town, St. Helena: by the author, 1840.

191. Janisch, Hudson Ralph. EXTRACTS FROM THE ST. HELENA RECORDS FROM 1673 TO 1835. St. Helena: B. Grant, 1885.

192. Joinville, François Ferdinand Philippe Louis d'Orléans. VIEUX SOUVENIRS DE MGR. LE PRINCE DE JOINVILLE. Paris: Calmann-Lévy, 1894.

193. Jones, David E.H., and Kenneth W.D. Ledingham.   "Arsenic in Napoleon's Wallpaper." NATURE 299 (1982): 626-27.

194. Jones, R. Ben. NAPOLEON: MAN AND MYTH. London: Hodden and Stroughton, 1977.

195. Jourdain, J.A. ARRIVEE DE BONAPARTE AUX ENFERS. Paris: Mme Ve Porthmann, 1821.

196. Jourdain de la Passardière, Ollivier. "Relation de M. Jourdain de la Passardière, commandant le brick l'Epervier." NOUVELLE REVUE RETROSPECTIVE. 7e semestre (1897).

197. JOURNAL CURIEUX ET INTERESSANT TROUVE DANS LE CHAMBRE DE L'EMPEREUR NAPOLEON A SAINTE-HELENE CONTENANT SES PENSEES SUR LA FRANCE, SES CONSEILS A SON FILS ET SES ADIEUX A SON EPOUSE. Nancy: Imprimerie de Richard-Durupt, n.d.

198. Jousset, Jacques. "L'Affaire de masque de Napoléon." REVUE DE L'INSTITUT NAPOLEON 64 (1957): 100-106.

199. Jousset, Jacques. "L'Enigme des masques mortuaires de Napoléon I: Antommarchi et le masque Burghersh." SCIENCE HISTORIQUE (PARIS) 34 (1955): 100-110.

200. JUGEMENT DE L'HISTOIRE SUR NAPOLEON. Paris: Didot jeune, 1821.

201. Keith, Arthur. "An Address on the History and Nature of Certain Specimens alleged to have been obtained at the post-mortem examination of Napoleon the Great." BRITISH MEDICAL JOURNAL (1913).

202. Kelly, Christopher. A FULL AND CIRCUMSTANTIAL ACCOUNT OF THE MEMORABLE BATTLE OF WATERLOO; THE SECOND RESTORATION OF LOUIS XVIII; AND THE DEPORTATION OF NAPOLEON BUONAPARTE TO THE ISLAND OF ST. HELENA, AND EVERY RECENT PARTICULAR RELATIVE TO HIS CONDUCT AND MODE OF LIFE IN HIS EXILE: TOGETHER WITH AN INTERESTING ACCOUNT OF THE AFFAIRS OF FRANCE, AND BIOGRAPHICAL SKETCHES OF THE MOST DISTINGUISHED WATERLOO HEROES. London: T. Kelly, 1818.

203. Kemble, James. NAPOLEON IMMORTAL. London: J. Murray, 1959.

204. Kircheisen, Friedrich Max. NAPOLEON. Translated from the German by Henry St. Lawrence. London: Gerald Howe, 1931.

205. Kirkor, S. "Un Adventurier ou un missionaire de Sainte-Hélène? [Charles-Frédéric-Jules] Piontkowski." REVUE DE L'INSTITUT NAPOLEON 132 (1976): 185-93.

206. Kitching, G.C. "Records of the Island of Saint-Helena, Lat. 15°55'S. Long. 5°428'W." AMERICAN ARCHIVIST 10 (1947): 151-71.

207. Kitching, S.A. "Relics of Napoleon and St. Helena, Together with particulars regarding the British Medical Officers who

attended Napoleon professionally, and comments regarding cases
of Yellow fever in ships arriving at St. Helena in 1830, 1832,
and 1834." EASTERN PAMPHLET, 1937. Colonial Office Library,
no. 380.

208. Knowles, L. A GIFT OF NAPOLEON, BEING A SEQUEL TO LETTERS OF
     CAPT. EUG. LUTYENS, ORDERLY OFFICER AT LONGWOOD, ST. HELENA
     (1820-1823). London: J. Lane, 1921.

209. Korngold, Ralph. THE LAST YEARS OF NAPOLEON: HIS CAPTIVITY ON
     ST. HELENA. New York: Harcourt, Brace, 1959.

210. Lachouque, Henry. "Longwood 7 Mai 1821." SOUVENIR NAPOLEONIEN
     19 (1955): 2-3.

211. Lallemand, Charles Frédéric Antoine. "Napoléon refuse de passer
     en Amérique." THE FRENCH AMERICAN REVIEW (1949): 63-80.

212. Langlé, Joseph Adolphe Ferdinand. FUNERAILLES DE L'EMPEREUR
     NAPOLEON. RELATION OFFICIELLE DE LA TRANSLATION DE SES RESTES
     MORTELS DEPUIS L'ILE SAINTE-HELENE JUSQU'A PARIS, ET DESCRIPTION
     DU CONVOI FUNEBRE. Paris: L. Curmer, 1840.

213. Las Cases, Barthélemy, baron de. DERNIER MOT SUR HUDSON LOWE,
     SUR SES MEMOIRES PUBLIES PAR WILLIAM FORSYTH, ET SUR L'ANALYSE
     QUI EN A ETE FAITE PAR LOUIS DE VIEL-CASTEL DANS LA "REVUE DES
     DEUX-MONDES." Paris: W. Remquet, 1855.

214. Las Cases, Emmanuel, comte de. JOURNAL ECRIT A BORD DE LA
     FREGATE LA BELLE-POULE. Paris: H.L. Delloye, 1841.

215. Las Cases, Marie Joseph Emmanuel Dieudonné, comte de. ENTRETIEN
     DE NAPOLEON AVEC LE DOCTEUR O'MEARA, SES REFLEXIONS ET SA
     JUSTIFICATION DES ACCUSATIONS PORTEES CONTRE LUI APRES SA CHUTE.
     Trouvés dans les papiers du docteur O'Meara, médecin de Napoléon
     à Sainte-Hélène. Toulon: Bellue, 1837.

216. Las Cases, Marie Joseph Emmanuel Dieudonné, comte de. MEMOIRES
     D'EMMANUEL DIEUDONNE COMTE DE LAS CASES, ECRITES PAR LUI-MEME,
     AVEC UNE LETTRE DE LUI PENDANT SON SEJOUR A SAINTE-HELENE, A
     LUCIEN BONAPARTE, CONTENANT UN RECIT FIDELE DU VOYAGE DE
     NAPOLEON JUSQU'A CETTE ILE, SON SEJOUR, SA MANIERE DE VIVRE ET
     LE TRAITEMENT QU'IL Y EPROUVE. Brussels: A. Walhlen, 1818.

217. Las Cases, Marie Joseph Emmanuel Dieudonné, comte de. MEMORIAL
     DE SAINTE-HELENE OU JOURNAL OU SE TROUVE TOUT CE QU'A DIT ET
     FAIT NAPOLEON DURANT DIX-HUIT MOIS, DU 20 JUIN AU 25 NOVEMBRE
     1816. Paris: chez l'auteur, 1823. 8 vols.

218. Latimer, E. W. TALKS WITH NAPOLEON AT SAINT-HELENA WITH GENERAL
     GOURGAUD, TOGETHER WITH THE JOURNAL KEPT BY GOURGAUD ON THEIR
     JOURNEY FROM WATERLOO TO ST. HELENA. Chicago: McClung, 1903.

219. Latreille, André.   "Napoléon pour ou contre?" MEMOIRES DE
     L'ACADEMIE DES SCIENCES, BELLES-LETTRES ET ARTS DE LYON 30
     (1977): 19.

220. Laumann, Ernest Maurice. L'EPOPEE NAPOLEONIENNE. LE RETOUR DES
     CENDRES. Deuxième édition. Paris: Daragon, 1904.

221. Lee, Henry. THE LIFE OF THE EMPEROR NAPOLEON WITH AN APPENDIX
     CONTAINING AN EXAMINATION OF SIR WALTER SCOTT'S 'LIFE OF
     NAPOLEON' WITH A NOTICE OF PRINCIPAL ERRORS OF OTHER WRITERS
     RESPECTING HIS CHARACTER AND CONDUCT. Paris: Galignani, 1834.

222. "La Légende Napoléonienne." [Numéro spécial.]   MIROIR DE
     L'HISTOIRE 103 (1959): 26-103.

223. Legouvé, Ernest. "Napoléon Ier depuis sa mort." REVUE BLEUE 51
     (1893): 645-50.

224. Leighton, R.   "With Napoleon at St. Helena." MISCELLANEOUS
     PHAMPLETS, 1933. Colonial Office Library, no. 502.

225. LETTERS FROM THE ISLAND OF SAINT-HELENA, EXPOSING THE
     UNNECESSARY SEVERITY EXERCISED TOWARDS NAPOLEON. London:
     Ridgeway, 1818.

226. Lewin, Peter K.; Ronald G.V. Hancock; and Paul Voynovich.
     "Napoleon Bonaparte--No Evidence of Chronic Arsenic Poisoning."
     NATURE 299 (1982): 627-28.

227. Lloyd, Christopher. KEITH PAPERS. London: Navy Records
     Society, 1955, 2 vols.

228. Lockwood, Joseph. A GUIDE TO SAINT HELENA, DESCRIPTIVE AND
     HISTORICAL, WITH A VISIT TO LONGWOOD AND NAPOLEON'S TOMB. St.
     Helena: by the author, 1851.

229. LONGWOOD OLD HOUSE, RESIDENCE OF THE EMPEROR NAPOLEON,
     1815-1821, ST. HELENA. Norwich: Jarrold, n.d.

230. Lorenzi de Bradi, Michel. LES MISERES DE NAPOLEON. Paris:
     Tallandier, 1934.

231. Lorion, André. "Le Vrai Visage des Aumôniers de Sainte-Hélène."
     REVUE DE L'INSTITUT NAPOLEON 123 (1972): 75-78.

232. Lowe, Hudson. AGONIE DE NAPOLEON. [Paris: La Revue de Paris,
     1910.]

233. Lowe, Hudson. LE CONTRE-MEMORIAL DE SAINTE-HELENE. Préface,
     adaptation et notes par Maurice Bessy et Lo Duca. Paris:
     Fasquelle, 1949.

234. Lowe, Hudson. DANS LA CHAMBRE DE NAPOLEON MOURANT. JOURNAL
     INEDIT D'HUDSON LOWE PAR PAUL FREMEAUX. Paris: Mercure, 1910.

235. Lowe, Hudson. MEMORIAL DE SIR HUDSON LOWE RELATIF A LA
     CAPTIVITE DE NAPOLEON A SAINTE-HELENE. Paris: Dureuil, 1830.

236. Lows, M. de. NAPOLEON BONAPARTE ENVISAGE COMME VAINQUER DES
     NATIONS, RESTAURATEUR DES LOIS, PROTECTEUR DES LETTRES ET
     FONDATEUR DES EMPIRES. Paris: Gueffier, 1821.

237. Lubin, Georges. "Compagnon de Sainte-Hélène, le Grand Maréchal
     Bertrand." MIROIR DE L'HISTOIRE 67 (1955): 185-91.

238. Lucas-Dubreton, Jean. LE CULTE DE NAPOLEON, 1815-1848. Paris:
     Albin Michel, 1960.

239. Lullin de Châteauvieux, Jacob Frédéric. MANUSCRIT VENU DE
     SAINTE-HELENE D'UNE MANIERE INCONNUE. [Paris: Plancher, 1819?]

240. Lyttleton, W.H. SOME ACCOUNT OF NAPOLEON BONAPARTE'S COMING ON
     BOARD H.M.S. NORTHUMBERLAND, AUGUST 7, 1815, WITH NOTES OF THE
     CONVERSATION HELD WITH HIM ON THAT DAY. London: published
     privately, 1836.

241. Macartney, Clarence Edward, and Gordon Dorrance. THE BONAPARTES
     IN AMERICA. Philadelphia: Doubleday, 1939.

242. MacCarthy, Dugue. "Les Cendres de l'Empereur sont-elles aux
     Invalides?" REVUE DE LA SOCIETE DES AMIS DU MUSEE DE L'ARMEE 75
     (1975): 31-43.

243. MacIntyre, Duncan. NAPOLEON: THE LEGEND AND THE REALITY.
     Glasgow: Blackie, 1976.

244. MacLeod, John. THE VOYAGE AND SHIPWRECK OF THE "ALCESTE."
     London: J. Murray, 1817.

245. Magdelaine, M. "A Propos d'un diagnostic de cause de décès
     celui de Napoléon." LA PRESSE MEDICALE 70 (1962): 2835-36.

246. Maitland, Frederick Lewis. NAPOLEON A BORD DU "BELLEROPHON."
     SOUVENIRS DU CAPITAINE DE VAISSEAU, F.L. MAITLAND, ET GEORGE
     HOME. Traduction de Henry Borjane. Paris: Plon, 1934.

247. Maitland, Frederick Lewis. NARRATIVE OF THE SURRENDER OF
     BUONAPARTE AND OF HIS RESIDENCE ON BOARD H.M.S. BELLEROPHON;
     WITH A DETAIL OF THE PRINCIPAL EVENTS THAT OCCURRED IN THAT
     SHIP, BETWEEN THE 24TH OF MAY AND THE 8TH OF AUGUST, 1815.
     London: Colburn, 1826.

248. Malcolm, Clementina Elphinstone, lady. A DIARY OF ST. HELENA;
     THE JOURNAL OF LADY MALCOLM (1816-1817) CONTAINING THE
     CONVERSATIONS OF NAPOLEON WITH SIR PULTENEY MALCOLM. Edited by
     Sir Arthur Wilson, K.C.I.E. With an introduction by Muriel
     Kent. London: Allen & Unwin, 1929.

249. Malvardi, Aimé. "Napoléon et sa Légende." Thèse. [La Crau]
     n.d.

250. Manceron, Claude. LE DERNIER CHOIX DE NAPOLEON. Paris: Robert Laffont, 1960.

251. "Manuscript from St. Helena." 1817. Colonial Office Library, no. 2661.

252. MANUSCRIT VENU DE SAINTE-HELENE D'UNE MANIERE INCONNUE. London: J. Murray, 1817.

253. Marchand, Louis, comte. MEMOIRES DE MARCHAND, PREMIER VALET DE CHAMBRE ET EXECUTEUR TESTAMENTAIRE DE L'EMPEREUR, PUBLIES D'APRES LE MANUSCRIT ORIGINAL PAR JEAN BOURGUIGNON. Paris: Plon, 1952-55. 2 vols.

254. Marie, Alfred. "Catalogue de l'exposition Napoléon, la légende, le roi de Rome, organisée aux Invalides." REVUE DE L'INSTITUT NAPOLEON 63 (1957): 36-81.

255. Martineau, Gilbert. "Les Domains français de Sainte-Hélène." REVUE DE LA SOCIETE DES AMIS DE LA MUSEE DE L'ARMEE 61 (1958): 25-31.

256. Martineau, Gilbert. NAPOLEON SE REND AUX ANGLAIS. Paris: Hachette, 1969.

257. Martineau, Gilbert. LA VIE QUOTIDIENNE A SAINTE-HELENE AU TEMPS DE NAPOLEON. Paris: Hachette, 1966.

258. Masselin, E[ugène François]. SAINTE-HELENE. Paris: Plon, 1862.

259. Masson, Frédéric. AUTOUR DE SAINTE-HELENE. Paris: Ollendorff, 1909-15. 3 vols.

260. Masson, Frédéric. NAPOLEON AT ST. HELENA, 1815-1821. Translated by Louis B. Frewer. New York: McBride, 1950.

261. Maugham, F. "Napoleon and St. Helena--A German Calumny." [An extract from the LONDON MERCURY, January 1926.] ST. HELENA PAMPHLET. Colonial Office Library, no. 26.

262. Mauguin, Georges. "Deux Versaillais, fidèles à l'Empereur déchu, l'accompanerez à Sainte-Hélène." [Général Gourgaud and Louis-Etienne Saint-Denis.] REVUE DE L'HISTOIRE DE VERSAILLES ET DE SEINE-ET-OISE 53 (1959-60): 103-6.

263. Mauguin, Georges. LE NAPOLEON DE SAINTE-HELENE. ESSAI D'ETUDE PSYCHOLOGIQUE. Avant-propos par Ernest d'Hauterive. Vichy: Wallon, 1951.

264. Méhee de la Touche, Jean. C'EST LUI, MAIS PAS DE LUI, OU REFLEXIONS SUR LE MANUSCRIT DIT DE SAINTE-HELENE. Paris: Ponthieu, 1821.

265. Melliss, John Charles. SAINTE-HELENA, A PHYSICAL, HISTORICAL
     AND TOPOGRAPHICAL DESCRIPTION. London: n.p., 1875.

266. Meynell, Henry. CONVERSATIONS WITH NAPOLEON AT ST. HELENA.
     London: Humphreys, 1911.

267. Moggio, Anna Maria. "The Napoleonic Image in the Press of
     Toulouse, 1830-1848." Ph.D. dissertation, Fordham University,
     1974.

268. Monkhouse, John. LES SIX DERNIERES SEMAINES DE NAPOLEON
     BONAPARTE. RELATION ECRITE A SAINTE-HELENE PAR JEAN MONKHOUSE,
     OFFICIER DE LA MARINE ROYALE. Paris: Decosson, 1821.

269. Montchenu, Claude Marie Henri, marquis de. LA CAPTIVITE DE
     SAINTE-HELENE D'APRES LES RAPPORTS INEDITS DU MARQUIS DE
     MONTCHENU. Par Georges Firmin-Didot. Paris: Firmin-Didot,
     1894.

270. Montholon, Albine Hélène de Vassal, comtesse de. SOUVENIRS DE
     SAINTE-HELENE PAR LA COMTESSE DE MONTHOLON, 1815-1816. Publiés
     sous les auspices du vicomte Du Couëdic de Kergoualer, son
     petit-fils, par le comte Fleury. Paris: Emile-Paul, 1901.

271. Montholon, Charles Jean Tristan, marquis de. LETTRES DU COMTE
     ET DE LA COMTESSE DE MONTHOLON (1819-1821). Publiées avec une
     introduction et des notes par Philippe Gonnard. Paris: Picard,
     1906.

272. Montholon, Charles Jean Tristan, marquis de.   RECITS DE LA
     CAPTIVITE DE L'EMPEREUR A SAINTE-HELENE. Paris: Paulin, 1847.
     2 vols.

273. Montholon, Charles Jean Tristan, marquis de, and Gaspard
     Gourgaud, baron. MEMOIRES POUR SERVIR A L'HISTOIRE DE FRANCE,
     SOUS NAPOLEON, ECRITS A SAINTE-HELENE, PAR LES GENERAUX QUI ONT
     PARTAGE SA CAPTIVITE, ET PUBLIES SUR LES MANUSCRITS ENTIEREMENT
     CORRIGES DE LA MAIN DE NAPOLEON. Paris: Didot, 1823-26. 6
     vols.

274. "More Light on St. Helena, from the Papers of Sir G. Bingham,
     Major Harrison and Colonel Gorrequer." CORNHILL MAGAZINE 83
     (1901): 18-155.

275. Moreau, Achile, ed. EXILE ET CAPTIVITE DE NAPOLEON: EXTRAITS
     DU MEMORIAL DE SAINTE-HELENE PAR LE COMTE DE LAS CASES, ET
     MEMOIRES D'O'MEARA, MONTHOLON, SANTINI, ETC. Paris: Charles
     Noblet, n.d.

276. Moreau, Achile. NOUVEAU MEMORIAL DE SAINTE-HELENE D'APRES LES
     RELATIONS AUTHENTIQUES ANCIENNES ET RECENTES: JOURNAL COMPLET
     DE LA TRANSLATION, DE LA CAPTIVITE, ET LA MORT DE L'EMPEREUR
     NAPOLEON. Paris: Baudouin, 1841.

277. LA MORT DE L'EMPEREUR NAPOLEON, DETAILS HISTORIQUES SUR LA MORT
     DE CE HEROS, SUIVIS DE REGRETS D'UN GRAND HOMME, DE LA CENDRE DE
     NAPOLEON, DU PORTRAIT DE NAPOLEON ET DES DERNIERS MOMENS DE
     L'EMPEREUR. Paris: Dauphine, 1831.

278. Mougins-Roquefort, Joseph de. NAPOLEON PRISONNIER VU PAR LES
     ANGLAIS: AVEC DE NOMBREUX TEMOINAGES INEDITS EN FRANCAIS.
     Paris: Tallandier, 1978.

279. Moussard, P. MEMOIRE SUR LA TRANSLATION DE NAPOLEON A L'ILE DE
     SAINTE-HELENE, ADRESSE AU CONGRES DES ROIS DE L'EUROPE ET AUX
     DEPUTES DE LA NATION FRANCAISE. Paris: C.F. Patris, 1815.

280. "The Myth of Napoleon." YALE FRENCH STUDIES 26 (1960): 1-130.

281. Napoleon I, Emperor of the French. COMMENTAIRES DE NAPOLEON I.
     Paris: Imprimerie impériale, 1867. 6 vols.

282. Napoleon I, Emperor of the French. CORRESPONDANCE DE NAPOLEON
     Ier, PUBLIEE PAR ORDRE DE L'EMPEREUR NAPOLEON III. Paris:
     Imprimerie impériale, 1858-69. Vols. 29-32.

283. Napoleon I, Emperor of the French. EXTRAITS DE LETTRES ECRITES
     PENDANT LA TRAVERSEE DE SPITHEAD A SAINTE-HELENE, ET DURANT
     QUELQUES MOIS DE SEJOUR DANS CETTE ISLE. Paris: Gide, 1817.

284. Napoleon I, Emperor of the French. MAXIMES ET PENSEES DU
     PRISONNIER DE SAINTE-HELENE. MANUSCRIT TROUVE DANS LES PAPIERS
     DE LAS CASES. Traduit de l'anglais. Paris: L'Huillier, 1820.

285. Napoleon I, Emperor of the French. MEMOIRES DE NAPOLEON; ECRITS
     SOUS SA DICTEE A SAINTE-HELENE, PAR UN DE SES VALETS-DE-CHAMBRE.
     Paris: Philippe, 1829.

286. Napoleon I, Emperor of the French. NAPOLEON'S LAST WILL AND
     TESTAMENT.... Edited by Jean Pierre Babelon and Suzanne
     D'Huart. Translated by Alex de Jonge. London: Paddington,
     1977.

287. Napoleon I, Emperor of the French. PRECIS DES GUERRES DE CESAR,
     PAR NAPOLEON, ECRIT PAR M. MARCHAND, A L'ILE SAINT-HELENE, SOUS
     LA DICTEE DE L'EMPEREUR; SUIVI DE PLUSIEURS FRAGMENS INEDITS.
     Paris: Gosselin, 1836.

288. Napoleon I, Emperor of the French. RECUEIL DE PIECES
     AUTHENTIQUES SUR LE CAPTIF DE SAINTE-HELENE, DE MEMOIRES ET
     DOCUMENS ECRITS OU DICTES PAR L'EMPEREUR NAPOLEON. Paris:
     Corréard, 1821-25. 12 vols.

289. Napoleon I, Emperor of the French. TESTAMENT DE NAPOLEON.
     Paris: Dupont, 1822.

290. NAPOLEON A SAINTE-HELENE; SES SENTIMENTS RELIGIEUSES ET SA MORT.
     Toulouse: J.M. Douladoure, 1854.

291. NAPOLEON AU PANTHEON DE L'HISTOIRE, RESUME DE TOUT CE QUE CE
     GRAND HOMME A FAIT DE MERVEILLEUX. Paris: Bellemain, 1830.

292. NAPOLEON AUX INVALIDES: DEDIE A TOUS LES FRANCAIS. Paris: F.
     Knab, 1840.

293. NAPOLEON DEVANT LA POSTERITE. Par L.G., ancien administrateur
     du département de la Marne. Paris: Tastu, 1830.

294. NAPOLEON SUR LA CALONNE. Epinal: Pellerin, 1834.

295. Napoleon, Joseph Charles Paul Bonaparte, prince. NAPOLEON ET
     SES DETRACTEURS. London: W.H. Allen, 1888.

296. Nicholls, George. "Sainte-Hélène: Journal du capitaine George
     Nicholls, Officier d'ordonnance de Longwood (septembre
     1818-février 1820), traduit pour la première fois par Emile
     Brouwet." CARNET DE LA SABRETACHE, Series 3, 4 (1921): 62-81.

297. Nolan, J. Bennett. "Where Napoleon lived in Exile." MENTOR 16
     (1928): 33-37.

298. Normand, Francis. GENERAL MONTHOLON (1783-1853), COMPAGNON DE
     NAPOLEON A SAINTE-HELENE. [Paris: n.p., 1914].

299. Norvins, Jacques, baron de Montbreton. HISTOIRE DE NAPOLEON.
     Paris: Furne, 1833. 4 vols.

300. Norvins, Jacques, baron de Montbreton. TRANSLATION DES CENDRES
     DE NAPOLEON. Paris: Furne, 1840.

301. NOS SOUVENIRS, OU LES PECHES DE NAPOLEON BONAPARTE. Paris:
     Davi et Locard, 1815.

302. O'Flaherty, Kathleen. "The Genesis of Napoleonic Legend."
     STUDIES (DUBLIN) 58 (1969): 256-78.

303. "Old Longwood House." ST. HELENA PAMPHLET, 1855. Colonial
     Office Library. No. 2.

304. O'Meara, Barry Edward. DOCUMENTS HISTORIQUES SUR LA MALADIE ET
     LA MORT DE NAPOLEON BONAPARTE. Paris: Mongie, 1821.

305. O'Meara, Barry Edward. NAPOLEON EN EXIL, OU L'ECHO DE
     SAINTE-HELENE. Paris: Marchands de Nouveautés, 1822. 2 vols.

306. O'Meara, Barry Edward. RELATION DES EVENEMENTS ARRIVES A
     SAINTE-HELENE, POSTERIEUREMENT A LA NOMINATION DE SIR
     HUDSON-LOWE, AU GOUVERNEMENT DE CETTE ILE, EN REPONSE A UNE
     BROCHURE ANONYME, INTITULEE: FAITS DEMONSTRATIFS DES
     TRAITEMENTS QU'ON A FAIT EPROUVER A NAPOLEON BONAPARTE,
     CONFIRMES PAR UNE CORRESPONDANCE ET DES DOCUMENTS OFFICIELS,
     etc. Paris: Chaumerot, 1819.

307. ORAISON FUNEBRE DE NAPOLEON BONAPARTE OU L'ON TROUVE ETABLI,
     D'APRES LE MONITEUR, CE QUE LES VERTUS DU CI-DEVANT EMPEREUR ONT
     COUTE D'HOMMES ET D'ARGENT A LA FRANCE; SUIVI DU TESTAMENT DUDIT
     N. BONAPARTE. Paris: N. Pichard, 1821.

308. Pamart, Général P. "Les Lectures de Napoléon à Sainte-Hélène."
     REVUE HISTORIQUE DE L'ARMEE 25 (1969): 110-26.

309. Pardée, Marie Antoinette (Ruelle). L'ETRANGE HISTOIRE D'APRES
     DES DOCUMENTS AUTHENTIQUES DU VRAI ET UNIQUE MASQUE DE NAPOLEON
     LE GRAND EN SECRET A SAINTE-HELENE A L'AUBE DU 6 MAI 1891 PAR LE
     DOCTEUR ARCHIBALD ARNOTT. Cannes: F. Robaudy, 1933.

310. Parisot, Jacques Théodore. "Napoléon et le Bellérophon."
     [Extracted from LA FRANCE MARITIME. Paris, 1815?].

311. Patorni, F.M. L'EPEE DE NAPOLEON. LETTRE A M. LE GENERAL
     BERTRAND. Paris: Herhan, 1833.

312. Pengelly, Colin A. THE FIRST BELLEROPHON. With a preface by
     Christopher Lloyd. London: Baker, 1966.

313. PENSEE D'UN PATRIOTE SUR NAPOLEON BONAPARTE SUIVI D'UN MOT SUR
     LE CANCER HEREDITAIRE, PAR UN ETUDIANT DE MEDECIN. Paris:
     Dupont, 1821.

314. Pérès, Jean Baptiste. GRAND ERRATUM: COMME QUOI NAPOLEON N'A
     JAMAIS EXISTE. Paris: J.J. Risler, 1838.

315. Pesme, Gérard. LES DERNIERES HEURES DE NAPOLEON AVANT A'EXIL.
     Bordeaux: Delmas, 1936.

316. Picard, Charles. L'OMBRE DE NAPOLEON POUR LA FRANCE, AU MONDE
     DEMOCRATIQUE OU CONSTITUTIONNEL CONTRE LES ROIS ABSOLUS DE
     L'EUROPE, EN GUERRE, CONTRE MEHEMET-ALI. Toulouse: Legarrique,
     1840.

317. Pieri, Jean. "Napoléon et les médecins." FLOREAL AN X 16
     (1973): 12-27.

318. Pillans, T. Dundas. THE REAL MARTYR OF ST. HELENA. London: A.
     Melrose, 1913.

319. Planat de la Faye, Nicholas Louis. ROME ET SAINTE-HELENE DE
     1815 A 1821. Paris: Furne, 1862.

320. Planat de la Faye, Nicholas Louis. VIE DE PLANAT DE LA FAYE.
     SOUVENIRS, LETTRES ET DICTEES RECUEILLIS ET ANNOTES PAR SA
     VEUVE. Paris: Ollendorff, 1895.

321. Plouin, Renée. "Le Tombeau des Invalides (Oeuvre de Visconti)."
     SOUVENIR NAPOLEONIEN 38 (1975): 18-20.

322. Pluchonneau. SAINTE-HELENE EN 1840, OU, STATISTIQUE RAISONNEE ET HISTORIQUE DE CETTE ILE DEPUIS SA DECOUVERTE JUSQU'A NOS JOURS. Paris: E. Proux, 1840.

323. Poisson, Georges. "La Volière de Sainte-Hélène." REVUE DE L'INSTITUT NAPOLEON 97 (1965): 237-38.

324. Poppleton, Thomas William. "Napoleon at Saint Helena: Reminiscence." LITTELL'S LIVING AGE 206 (1895): 61-63.

325. Poulleau, Alice [Alice Guibon]. LES ILES FATALES: CORSE, ELBE, AIX, SAINTE-HELENE. Dieppe: La Floride, 1956.

326. "The Powers of the Crown in St. Helena During Napoleon's Captivity." EASTERN PAMPHLET, 1937. Colonial Office Records, no. 384.

327. "Procès-verbal d'exhumation des restes de Napoléon Ier." (Sainte-Hélène, 15 octobre 1840). LE VIEUX SAINT-MAUR (SAINT-MAUR, SEINE) 1 (1929): 25-26.

328. PROCLAMATIONS AND ACTS ISSUED IN 1815 AND 1816 RELATIVE TO THE DETENTION OF NAPOLEON BONAPARTE. 1817. British Museum, 279.b.8.

329. Pujol, Edouard. NAPOLEON DE LA VALLEE DU TOMBEAU AU DOME DES INVALIDES. Paris: H.L. Delloye, 1841.

330. Quentin-Bauchart, Maurice. LE RETOUR DES CENDRES. Paris: Monde moderne, 1897.

331. Rabbe, Alphonse. MEDITATIONS SUR LA MORT DE NAPOLEON. Paris: Mesnier et Chaumerot, 1831.

332. RAISONS DICTEES EN REPONSE A LA QUESTION SI L'OUVRAGE INTITULE 'MANUSCRIT DE SAINTE-HELENE' EST L'OUVRAGE DE NAPOLEON OU NON. London: Phillipps, 1820.

333. RECUEIL DE PIECES OFFICIELLES SUR LE PRISONNIER DE SAINTE-HELENE, AVEC LES OBSERVATIONS SUR LES DISCOURS DE LORD BATHURST DANS LA CHAMBRE DES PAIRS, LE 18 MARS 1817, ENVOYES, SCELLES, A SIR HUDSON LOWE, A L'ADRESSE DE LORD LIVERPOOL, LE 7 OCTOBER 1817. Traduction littérale de l'anglais. Paris: Plancher, 1819.

334. REFLEXIONS SUR LA LETTRE ADRESSEE AU REDACTEUR DU MONITEUR PAR M. LE COMTE DE MONTHOLON RELATIVEMENT AU TESTAMENT DE NAPOLEON. Paris: Plancher, 1822.

335. REFLEXIONS SUR LA MORT DE NAPOLEON SUIVIS DE QUELQUES CONSIDERATIONS SUR L'EMPOISONNEMENT PAR LES SUBSTANCES INTRODUITES DANS L'ESTOMAC. PAR UN CHIRURGIEN DE LA VIEILLE ARMEE. Paris: Hocquet, 1821.

336. RELATION DE CE QUI S'EST PASSE A CHERBOURG A L'OCCASION DU TRANSBORDEMENT DES RESTES MORTELS DE L'EMPEREUR NAPOLEON. Cherbourg: Noblet, 1841.

337. RELATION HISTORIQUE DE L'INSTITUTION DE LA MEDAILLE DE SAINTE-HELENE, PAR UN VIEUX SOLDAT DU PREMIER EMPIRE. Marseilles: n.p., 1861.

338. REPORT ON THE MANUSCRIPTS OF EARL BATHURST PRESERVED AT CIRENCESTER PARK. Documents sur Napoléon à Sainte-Hélène. [Historical MSS. Commission.] London: Stationery Office, 1923.

339. LA REPUBLIQUE, LE CONSULAT, L'EMPIRE, Ste-HELENE, D'APRES LES PEINTRES, LES SCULPTEURS ET LES GRAVEURS. Paris: Hachette, 1895.

340. Rétif de La Bretonne, Georges. ANGLAIS, RENDEZ-NOUS NAPOLEON. Paris: J. Martineau, 1969.

341. Rétif de La Bretonne, Jean. LA VERITE SUR LE LIT DE MORT DE NAPOLEON. [Par] le Commandant et son fils Georges Rétif de La Bretonne. Préface de M. Isorni. Monte-Carlo: Editions Regain, 1960.

342. "Le Retour des Cendres." [Numéro spécial sous la direction de Florence Poisson.] SOUVENIR NAPOLEONIEN 38 (1975): 2-20.

343. Richardson, Frank. NAPOLEON'S DEATH: AN INQUEST. London: W. Kimber, 1974.

344. Robson, Thomas. ST. HELENA MEMOIRS, AN ACCOUNT OF A REMARKABLE REVIVAL OF RELIGION THAT TOOK PLACE AT ST. HELENA DURING THE LAST YEARS OF THE EXILE OF NAPOLEON BONAPARTE. London: n.p., 1827.

345. Rohan Chabot, Ph. de. "Exhumation des restes de l'Empereur Napoléon." Procès verbal. St. Helena, 15 October 1840.

346. Rose, John Holland. "The Detention of Napoleon at Saint-Helena." TOUT AND TAIT: HISTORICAL ESSAYS (1902): 495-522.

347. Rosebery, Archibald Philip Primrose, 5th earl of. NAPOLEON, THE LAST PHASE. London: Hodder, 1922.

348. Rousseau, Hervé. "La Légende noire de Napoléon." CRITIQUE 23 (1967): 476-86.

349. Royer, Colin. COUP D'OEIL SUR LA FRANCE PENDANT, AVANT ET APRES L'EMPIRE OU NAPOLEON UN DEMI-DIEU. Toulon: Baume, 1832.

350. Royer, Colin. ENCORE UNE LARME SUR LA TOMBE DE NAPOLEON. Perpignan: Mlle Tastu, 1832.

351. Runciman, Walter Runciman, baron. THE TRAGEDY OF ST. HELENA.
     London: Unwin, 1911.

352. Russell, Constance Charlotte Elisa, lady. SWALLOWFIELD AND ITS
     OWNERS. London: Longmans, 1901.

353. Rustan, E. "Un Tarnais Compagnon de Sainte-Hélène." [Victor
     Arcambal ou Archambault.] REVUE DU TARN 5 (1957): 147-51.

354. Rusterrucci, A. [Officier du bataillon des flanquers de l'île
     d'Elbe.] UN MOT SUR LE MARTYR DE SAINTE-HELENE. Lyon: Gayné
     neveu, 1834.

355. [Saint-Edme] Edme Théodore Bourg. NAPOLEON CONSIDEREE COMME
     GENERAL, PREMIER CONSUL, EMPEREUR, PRISONNIER A L'ILE D'ELBE ET
     A SAINTE-HELENE, OU VIE IMPARTIALE DE CE GRAND CAPITAINE.
     Paris: Mme Ve Jeunehomme, 1821.

356. "Sainte-Hélène et la mort de Napoléon." [Numéro spécial du
     centcinquantenaire.] REVUE DE L'INSTITUT NAPOLEON 120 (1971):
     97-157.

357. Samic, Michaut. "Quelques échos de la légende et de l'époque
     napoléonienne dans la littérature yougoslave." REVUE DE
     LITTERATURE COMPAREE 32 (1958): 249-54.

358. Santiné [Sentini, Saintiné], Edwige. CHAGRINS DOMESTIQUES DE
     NAPOLEON BONAPARTE A L'ILE DE SAINTE-HELENE, PRECEDE DE FAITS
     HISTORIQUES DE LA PLUS HAUTE IMPORTANCE, LE TOUT DE LA MAIN DE
     NAPOLEON. Paris: Germain Mathiot, 1821.

359. Santini, Jean Noël. AN APPEAL TO THE BRITISH NATION ON THE
     TREATMENT EXPERIENCED BY NAPOLEON BONAPARTE ON THE ISLAND OF ST.
     HELENA, WITH THE AUTHENTIC COPY OF THE OFFICIAL MEMOIR, DICTATED
     BY NAPOLEON AND DELIVERED TO SIR HUDSON LOWE. London: by the
     author, 1817.

360. Santini, Jean Noël. SAINTE-HELENE, LE TOMBEAU DE L'EMPEREUR ET
     SOUVENIRS DE NOEL SANTINI. Paris: Ledoyen, 1855.

361. Sarrut, Germain, and Saint-Edme. BIOGRAPHIE DE M.A.-D.-E. LAS
     CASES. Paris: Poussielgue, 1936.

362. Schommer, P. "Culte napoléonien." REVUE DE LA SOCIETE DES AMIS
     DE LA MUSEE DE L'ARMEE 73 (1969): 5-6.

363. Scott, Walter, bart. THE LIFE OF NAPOLEON. London: Longman,
     Rees, Orme, Brown and Green, 1827. 9 vols.

364. Seaton, Robert C. NAPOLEON'S CAPTIVITY IN RELATION TO SIR
     HUDSON LOWE. London: George Bell, 1903.

365. Seaton, Robert C. SIR HUDSON LOWE AND NAPOLEON. London: D.
     Nutt, 1898.

366. Shorter, Clement King, ed. NAPOLEON AND HIS FELLOW TRAVELLERS; BEING A REPRINT OF CERTAIN NARRATIVES OF THE VOYAGES OF THE DETHRONED EMPEROR ON THE BELLEROPHON AND THE NORTHUMBERLAND TO EXILE IN ST. HELENA; THE ROMANTIC STORIES TOLD BY GEORGE HOME, CAPTAIN ROSS, LORD LYTTELTON, AND WILLIAM WARDEN. London and New York: Cassell, 1908.

367. Silvestre, Pierre Jules. DE WATERLOO A SAINTE-HELENE (20 juin-16 octobre 1815) LA MALMAISON-ROCHEFORT-SAINTE-HELENE. Paris: Alcan, 1904.

368. Simmonin, A.J.B. HISTOIRE DES TROIS DERNIERS MOIS DE LA VIE DE NAPOLEON BONAPARTE ECRITE D'APRES DES DOCUMENTS AUTHENTIQUES. Paris: n.p., 1821.

369. Simonnot, J.F. L'OMBRE DE NAPOLEON AUX FRANCAIS PAR J.F. SIMONNOT, ANCIEN AIDE-DE-CAMP. Paris: Guiraudet, 1821.

370. Simonnot, J.F. POURQUOI DONC SE FACHE-T-IL M. LE GENERAL BERTON ET VOYONS SI LA CONFESSION DE BONAPARTE LUI EN DONNE DE JUSTES MOTIFS? Paris: Guiraudet, 1821.

371. "Sir Stamford Raffles' Interview with the Emperor." ST. HELENA PAMPHLET, 1904. Colonial Office Library, no. 17.

372. Sirotkin, V.G. "L'Exil et la mort de Napoléon." (in Russian) NOVAJA I NOVEJSAJA ISTORIJA (MOSCOU) 5 (1974): 149-66.

373. Soboul, Albert. "Napoléon: le héros, la légende, et l'histoire." PENSEE 143 (1969): 37-61.

374. Sorokine, Dimitri. "Napoléon dans la littérature russe." Thesis, University of Paris, 1959.

375. Soulié, Frédéric. LE TOMBEAU DE NAPOLEON. Paris: Marchant, 1840.

376. Soulié, Maurice. AUTOUR DE "L'AIGLE ENCHAINE"; LE COMPLOT DU CHAMP D'ASILE. Paris: Marpon, 1929.

377. SOUVENIRS D'UN SEJOUR A SAINTE-HELENE, PAR UN NAVIGATEUR FRANCAIS VENANT DES INDES-OCCIDENTALES. Toulon: Pierron, n.d.

378. Stokoë, John. NAPOLEON PRISONNIER: MEMOIRES D'UN MEDECIN DE L'EMPEREUR A SAINTE-HELENE. Paris: Flammarion, 1901.

379. Stürmer, Batholomäus, freiherr von. DIE BERICHTE DAS KAIS. KOEN COMMISSAERS BARTHOLOMAEUS FRHR. VON STUERMER AUS SANKT HELENA ZUR ZEIT DER DORTINGEN INTERNIERUNG NAPOLEON BONAPARTES 1816-1818. Hrsg. von Hanns Schlitter. Vienna: In commission bei C. Gerald, 1886.

380. Stürmer, Bartholomäus, freiherr von. NAPOLEON A SAINTE-HELENE. RAPPORTS OFFICIELS DU BARON STURMER. Paris: Librairie illustrée, 1888.

381. "Sur la teneur en arsenic des cheveux de Napoléon Ier." REVUE
     GENERALE DES SCIENCES PURES ET APPLIQUES 69 (1962): 111.

382. Taillard, Constant. REVUE DES BROCHURES PUBLIEES SUR NAPOLEON.
     Paris: Doublet, 1821.

383. Tartary, Madeleine.   SUR LES TRACES DE NAPOLEON.   Paris:
     Peyronnet, 1955.

384. Tercinet, Louis.   "Quels médicaments administrés à Napoléon
     agonisant?" REVUE DE L'HISTOIRE DE LA PHARMACIE 51 (1963):
     230-31.

385. Tézenas, Claude.   FRAGMENT POLITIQUE ECRIT DES PAPIERS DE
     NAPOLEON MORT A SAINTE-HELENE.   Paris: Delaunay, Dupont et
     Mongie, 1821.

386. [Thackeray, William Makepeace.] THE SECOND FUNERAL OF NAPOLEON:
     IN THREE LETTERS TO MISS SMITH, OF LONDON. AND THE CHRONICLE OF
     THE DRUM. BY M.A. TITMARSH. London: H. Cunningham, 1841.

387. Thibaud, Walter.   "Catherine Sablon, de Limal, cuisinière de
     Napoléon à Sainte-Hélène." BRABANT 1 (1966).

388. Thiers, Adolphe. HISTOIRE DU CONSULAT ET DE L'EMPIRE. Vol. 20.
     SAINTE-HELENE. Paris: Lheureux, 1862.

389. Thiry, Jean. SAINTE-HELENE. Paris: Berger-Levrault, 1976.

390. Thomassy, M.   DE LA SENSATION QU'A FAIT EN FRANCE LA MORT DE
     BUONAPARTE, ET DES ECRITS PUBLIES A CE SUJET. Paris: G.C.
     Hubert, 1821.

391. Thompson, James Matthew. NAPOLEON BONAPARTE, HIS RISE AND
     FALL. Oxford: Blackwell, 1952.

392. Thornton, Michael John. NAPOLEON AFTER WATERLOO; ENGLAND AND
     THE ST. HELENA DECISION. Stanford, Calif.: Stanford University
     Press, 1968.

393. Tomiche, Nada. NAPOLEON ECRIVAIN. Paris: Colin, 1952.

394. Toulouzan de Saint Martin. DE L'ILE DE SAINTE-HELENE ET DE
     BONAPARTE: ESSAI CONTENANT LA DESCRIPTION ET LA STATISTIQUE DE
     L'ILE, UN PRECIS HISTORIQUE SUR LA NAVIGATION DE LA MER
     ATLANTIQUE ET DES REFLEXIONS SUR LE SORT DE NAPOLEON BONAPARTE.
     Paris: n.p., 1815.

395. T'Sas, François.   "Le 'Contre-mémorial de Sainte-Hélène' [par
     Hudson Lowe (?)]."   BULLETIN DE LA SOCIETE BELGE D'ETUDES
     NAPOLEONIENNES 61 (1967): 14-20.

396. Tulard, Jean. L'ANTI-NAPOLEON, LA LEGENDE NOIRE DE L'EMPEREUR.
     Paris: Julliard, 1964.

397. Tulard, Jean, ed. NAPOLEON A SAINTE-HELENE. Paris: F. Laffont, 1981.

398. Tulard, Jean. "Napoléon dans la littérature populaire (1870-1914)." HISTOIRE 8 (1978): 4-12.

399. Tulard, Jean. NAPOLEON OU LE MYTHE DU SAVEUR. 2d ed. revised. Paris: France-loisirs, 1979.

400. Tulard, Jean. "Sainte-Hélène et l'opinion française." SOUVENIR NAPOLEONIEN 34 (1971): 21-25.

401. Tyder, James. BONAPARTE A SAINTE-HELENE. Traduit de l'anglais. Paris: Blanchat, 1816.

402. Ussher, Thomas. NAPOLEON BANISHED: THE JOURNEYS TO ELBA AND ST. HELENA RECORDED IN THE LETTERS AND JOURNALS OF TWO BRITISH NAVAL OFFICERS: CAPTAIN THOMAS USSHER AND LIEUTENANT NELSON MILLS. London: Rodale, 1955.

403. Ussher, Thomas. NAPOLEON'S LAST VOYAGES; BEING THE DIARIES OF SIR THOMAS USSHER, R.N.,K.C.B. (ON BOARD THE "UNDAUNTED"), AND JOHN R. GLOVER, SECRETARY TO REAR ADMIRAL COCKBURN (ON BOARD THE "NORTHUMBERLAND"). Introduction and notes by J. Holland Rose. New York: Scribner, 1906.

404. LA VALLEE DE SAINTE-HELENE OU VEILLEES AU TOMBEAU D'UN HOMME CELEBRE. MEMOIRES PARTICULIERES SUR LA VIE ET LA MORT DE N. BONAPARTE, RAPPORTEES DE SAINTE-HELENE ET PUBLIEES PAR UN OFFICIER DE L'UN DES REGIMENS EN STATION DANS CETTE ILE PENDANT LA CAPTIVITE DE L'EX-EMPEREUR. Paris: Ledentu, 1821.

405. Vanel, Eugène. L'OMBRE DE NAPOLEON, OU L'ARRIVEE DE SES CENDRES, CHANT NATIONAL, SUR L'AIR DE LA MARSEILLAISE. Paris: Guyolot et Lasserrre, 1840.

406. Variot, Jean James. LES COURSIERS DE SAINTE-HELENE, SCENES DE LA VIE ROMANTIQUE. Paris: Gallimard, 1933.

407. Vaudoncourt, Frédéric François Guillaume, baron de. QUINZE ANNEES D'UN POSTSCRIPT. Paris: Duféy, 1835. 4 vols.

408. Veauce, Eugène de. L'AFFAIRE DU MASQUE DE NAPOLEON. Avec une préface de Paul Fleuriot de Langle. Lyon: Bosc, 1957.

409. Veauce, Eugène de. NAPOLEON POST MORTEM. DEUX ARTICLES SUR LE MASQUE MORTUAIRE DE L'EMPEREUR, SUIVIS D'UNE ANALYSE, PAR JACQUES JOUSSET, DE "L'AFFAIRE DU MASQUE DE NAPOLEON." Avec un postscriptum et des notes. Lyon: Bosc, 1958.

410. Verling, James Roch. "Sainte-Hélène, juillet 1818-avril 1819." Traduction par E. Brouwet. CARNET DE LA SABRETACHE, Series 3, 4 (1921): 194-221, 418-32, 477-93; Series 3, 5 (1922): 160-214.

411. Vidalenç, Jean. "L'Opinion publique en Normandie et le retour des restes de Napoléon en décembre 1840." MELANGES OFFERTS A CH. H. POUTHAS (1973): 212-24.

412. Vigny, Alfred de. SERVITUDE ET GRANDEURS MILITAIRES. Paris: E. Pelletan, 1897-98. 2 vols.

413. Villenave,   Th.   RELATION   DES   FUNERAILLES   DE   NAPOLEON, EXHUMATION, TRANSLATION, PIECES OFFICIELLES. Paris: Rigaud, 1840.

414. Voitelain, Louis. LE CONVOI DE NAPOLEON, STANCES DEDIEES AUX PATRIOTES. Paris: Prévot, 1840.

415. Wagner, J.B. ALMANACH HISTORIQUE OU UN SOUVENIR POUR NAPOLEON. Nancy: Richard Durupt, 1832.

416. Warden, William. LETTERS WRITTEN ON BOARD HIS MAJESTY'S SHIP THE NORTHUMBERLAND, AND AT ST. HELENA; IN WHICH THE CONDUCT AND CONVERSATIONS OF NAPOLEON BUONAPARTE, AND HIS SUITE, DURING THE VOYAGE, AND THE FIRST MONTHS OF HIS RESIDENCE IN THAT ISLAND, ARE FAITHFULLY DESCRIBED AND RELATED. BY WILLIAM WARDEN, SURGEON ON BOARD THE NORTHUMBERLAND. London: R. Ackermann, 1816.

417. Warden, William. NAPOLEON JUGE PAR UN ANGLAIS. CONVERSATIONS DE NAPOLEON AVEC UN CHIRURGIEN DE LA MARINE ANGLAISE. Traduit de l'anglais, publié et commenté par le docteur Cabanès. Deuxième édition. Paris: Emile-Paul, 1908.

418. Watson, George Leo de St. M. A POLISH EXILE WITH NAPOLEON; EMBODYING THE LETTERS OF CAPTAIN PIONTKOWSKI TO GENERAL SIR ROBERT WILSON AND MANY DOCUMENTS FROM THE LOWE PAPERS, THE COLONIAL OFFICE RECORDS, THE WILSON MANUSCRIPTS, THE CAPEL LOFFT CORRESPONDENCE, AND THE FRENCH AND GENEVESE ARCHIVES HITHERTO UNPUBLISHED. London and New York: Harper, 1912.

419. Watson, George Leo de St. M. THE STORY OF NAPOLEON'S DEATH-MASK, TOLD FROM THE ORIGINAL DOCUMENTS. London and New York: J. Lane, 1915.

420. Weider, Ben, and David Hapgood. THE MURDER OF NAPOLEON. New York: Congdon and Lattès, 1982.

421. Whately, Richard.   DOUTES HISTORIQUES RELATIFS A NAPOLEON BONAPARTE. Traduit de l'anglais sur la quatrième édition. Paris: Ducessois, 1833.

422. Wheeler, Thomas. WHO LIES HERE? A NEW INQUIRY INTO NAPOLEON'S LAST YEARS. New York: Putnam, 1974.

423. Wilks, Mark. COLONEL WILKS AND NAPOLEON: TWO CONVERSATIONS AT ST. HELENA IN 1816. Edited by J.S. Corbett. London: J. Murray, 1901.

424. Willaume, Juliusz. "La Version polonaise de la légende
     napoléonienne." (in Polish) ANNALES UNIVERSITATIS MARIAE
     CURIE-SKLODOWSKA. SECTIO FI NAUKI HUMANISTICZNE (LUBIN)   30
     (1975): 19-28.

425. "With Napoleon at St. Helena."   ST. HELENA PAMPHLET, 1903.
     Colonial Office Library, no. 16.

426. Wolseley, Garnet Joseph, 1st viscount. LE DECLIN ET LA CHUTE DE
     NAPOLEON. Paris: Ollendorf, 1934.

427. Wormeley, K.P.   "Napoleon's Return from Saint Helena: An
     Eyewitness account of a memorable event." PUTNAM'S MONTHLY   4
     (1908): 387-93.

428. Wyndham, Horace. "Saint-Helena; Island Prison of Bonaparte."
     NAUTICAL MAGAZINE (GLASGOW) 144 (1940): 275-77.

429. Young, Norwood. NAPOLEON IN EXILE: ST. HELENA (1815-1821).
     London: S. Paul, 1915. 2 vols.

                              ADDENDUM

430. Abeshouse, Benjamin Samuel. A MEDICAL HISTORY OF NAPOLEON
     BONAPARTE. Norwich and New York: Eaton Laboratories, 1964.

431. Horward, Donald D. "Napoleon and Sir Walter Scott, A Study in
     Propaganda." PROCEEDINGS OF THE WESTERN SOCIETY FOR FRENCH
     HISTORY 9 (1982): 133-44.

432. Horward, Donald D.   "Napoleon, His Legend, and Sir Walter
     Scott." SOUTHERN HUMANITIES REVIEW 16 (1982): 1-13.

433. Pilss, Franz.   "Die Beiden Napoleonmasken des Badner
     Rollett-Museums." UNSERE HEIMAT [Austria] 52 (1981): 200-207.

434. Sténuit, R. "Na Waterloo." SPIEGEL HISTORIAEL [Netherlands] 17
     (1981): 494-550

435. Veauce, Eugène de. LES MASQUES MORTUAIRES DE NAPOLEON: LE
     POINT DE LA QUESTION. Paris: La Pensée universelle, 1971.

CHAPTER XVII

THE SCANDINAVIAN STATES

Michael F. Metcalf, University of Minnesota

Once united in the so-called Kalmar Union (1397), the three Nordic kingdoms of Denmark, Norway, and Sweden (including Finland) realigned over the ensuing century into two competing political formations, with Denmark dominating Norway but unable to dominate Sweden. In 1523, the Union was inexorably dissolved, for the Swedes selected Gustav Vasa as their rightful monarch, thus reverting to a state of independence. Norway's status as an independent entity under the king of Denmark was nullified in 1536 by Christian III's pronouncement that Norway should in the future be treated as a mere Danish province.

In the sixteenth, seventeenth, and eighteenth centuries, the dichotomy between Denmark-Norway and Sweden (including Finland) was to continue, with the two kingdoms struggling for hegemony in the Baltic and supremacy in the North. By and large it was the Swedes who gained most from this contest during the sixteenth and seventeenth centuries, but the trans-Baltic Swedish empire established by Erik XIV, Gustav II Adolf, Axel Oxenstierna, and Karl X Gustav was reduced drastically in size during the Great Northern War (1700-1721), in which Denmark-Norway joined with Peter the Great's Russia against their common rival, Karl XII.

While the old antagonisms and rivalries between the Danish and Swedish monarchies did not disappear entirely after 1721, the foreign policy makers in both states clearly recognized that their influence in European affairs had been reduced to the level of second-rank powers, and both states strove for the most part to cut an unimposing figure in the community of European nations. Indeed, in 1756, in 1780, and again in 1800, Denmark and Sweden sought refuge and advantage in the concept of armed neutrality. The Napoleonic era, however, was to bring Scandinavia into the whirlwind of great power diplomacy and military conflict despite the best efforts of Danish and Swedish ministers.

Prior to 1807, Scandinavia's involvement in the Napoleonic wars was limited to the participation of Denmark and Sweden in the Armed Neutrality of 1800 and to Sweden's participation in the Third Coalition against Napoleon. It was Great Britain's displeasure with Denmark's active pursuit of the Armed Neutrality that first brought the war to Scandinavia; on 2 April 1801, an English fleet under Parker and Nelson defeated the Danish navy off Copenhagen and effectively put an end to Danish adherence to the Armed Neutrality. On the other hand, the participation of Gustav IV Adolf in the Third Coalition was limited to actions conducted from Swedish Pomerania between 1805 and 1807, none of which led to French retaliation against Sweden proper.

It was not until the establishment of the Continental System, the issuance of the Orders in Council, and the agreement between Napoleon and Alexander I at Tilsit in July 1807 that the vital interests of the two Scandinavian kingdoms were threatened seriously. For Sweden, Tilsit meant the removal of the keystone of Gustav IV Adolf's foreign policy; his active participation in the Third

Coalition was based on British and Russian support for his efforts in Swedish Pomerania, and the July 1807 agreements between France and Russia and between France and Prussia effectively destroyed his position. Still allied with Great Britain, Sweden was one of the powers now threatened with Franco-Russian action if Britain did not conclude an agreement with Napoleon by 1 December 1807. Denmark, Sweden, and Portugal were, in that event, to be forced to close their harbors to the British and declare war on Great Britain, but Gustav IV Adolf was determined to retain his freedom of action as long as possible.

For Denmark, the threat was even more immediate, but it came from Great Britain rather than from France and Russia. Believing that the Danes had secretly been a party to the Tilsit agreement and unwilling to allow Denmark's still respectable fleet to fall into Napoleon's hands, Canning withdrew 10,000 British troops from Swedish Pomerania and sent them against Denmark to force the Danes to relinquish their fleet to the Royal Navy. The combined British naval and military action against Copenhagen in September 1807--which, by the way, was the first exercise of total warfare against a civilian population in modern times--did force the Danes to surrender their navy, but it also forced an enraged Danish regent to turn to France. The British had acquired a few ships, but instead of depriving Napoleon of an ally they had in fact deprived themselves of one.

Britain's unwarranted devastation of Copenhagen and the Danish fleet drove Crown Prince Frederick and the kingdom of Denmark right into Napoleon's arms, and a Franco-Danish treaty of alliance was concluded in October 1807, thus marking Denmark-Norway's adherence to the Continental System and bringing a British blockade into effect along the coasts of Denmark and Norway. Whereas Denmark was not committed to immediate aid to Napoleon, the British blockade was to prove disastrous for the maintenance of Dano-Norwegian economic and political ties between 1807 and 1814. Over the course of this seven-year period, the Norwegians were effectively cut off from the central administrative, financial, and educational institutions of the realm, all of which were located at Copenhagen. Both this fact and the extreme economic hardships imposed on the Norwegians by the British blockade led to discussions in Norway about the potential advantages of a separation from Denmark, with or without a union with Sweden.

In February 1808, Alexander I seized upon the opportunity offered by his agreement with Napoleon at Tilsit and by Sweden's refusal to join the Continental System; without any declaration of war, Russian forces invaded Finland, and Denmark, bound under these circumstances by the October 1807 treaty with France, declared war on Sweden in March. While many Swedish-Finnish units fought well in the defense of Finland, and while the peasants in particular accounted for themselves very well, the key Swedish fortress at Helsinki (the famous Sveaborg) was surrendered without a fight in the face of no real threat. The Russian forces met with great success during the 1808 campaigns in Finland, and it was soon clear that they had come to stay. These Russian successes convinced everyone but Gustav IV Adolf that Finland was indeed lost to Sweden, and when the king insisted throughout the following winter upon preparing a counteroffensive for the spring of 1809, he provoked a coup d'état which removed him from his throne on 13 March 1809.

Since Alexander I refused to negotiate a peace treaty with anything but a legitimate Swedish government, the Swedes quickly drafted and adopted a new constitution and elected both a king (Gustav IV Adolf's childless uncle, Karl XIII) and a crown prince (Prince Christian August of Augustenborg). Yet, the Swedes had been unable to complete all of their constitutional business in time; Russian military units operated in Northern Sweden during the spring and summer. Negotiations with the Russians finally got under way at Fredrikshamn in Finland in August, and a treaty recognizing Russia's acquisition of Finland was signed the next month. Peace with Denmark followed in December 1809, and peace with France came in January 1810, although only on condition that Sweden join the Continental System and break off diplomatic relations with Great Britain.

The loss of Finland fired new interest in Sweden for the acquisition of Norway. For this reason, the estates of the realm elected the commander of Dano-Norwegian forces in Norway, Prince Christian August, as Sweden's new crown prince. Christian August insisted upon waiting for peace to be concluded between Denmark and Sweden before accepting his election, and then he died of a stroke just four months after his arrival in Sweden in January 1810. The goal of bringing Norway under Swedish rule through the popularity of Christian August had not been achieved, and now the Swedish estates had to elect another successor to the throne. This time, in June 1810, the choice fell upon one of Napoleon's marshals, Jean-Baptiste Bernadotte, who accepted the offer with Napoleon's blessing. While there was little hope that Napoleon would look with favor on Sweden's acquiring Norway, there was hope that he would support the return of Finland to the Swedish realm. Bernadotte, who assumed the name Karl Johan upon his acceptance of the Swedish succession, was from the beginning determined that Norway would be Swedish. It was this goal that he was to pursue over the next three and a half years, and it was this goal that he eventually achieved.

While Norway's links to Denmark had been weakened considerably by Britain's blockade--and thus Britain's interdiction of normal intercourse between Denmark and Norway--what support there was for a union with Sweden had not proven to be very significant. In the absence of a Norwegian ground swell for union with Sweden, Karl Johan and the Swedes looked first to Napoleon and then to Russia and Great Britain for support in gaining possession of Norway by force of arms. Early in April 1812, Sweden and Russia signed a treaty calling for mutual guarantees of their respective territories and Russian help in securing Norway for Sweden in return for Sweden's aid against France. A similar treaty was signed with Great Britain in March 1813, and the way was paved for Karl Johan's and Sweden's participation in the great allied offensive of 1813. At his meeting at Trachenburg with Alexander I and Frederick William III on 9-12 July 1813, the Swedish crown prince appears to have been the principal author of the plan of operation that was subsequently put into operation. Among other things, this plan put Karl Johan in command of the Northern Army of 58,000 men, which included Swedish units that the crown prince did everything he could to keep in the wings. After the successful campaigns of the summer and fall, with the French in retreat across the Rhine, Karl Johan took his remaining 60,000 men of the Northern Army northward to meet the Danes and to impose a peace requiring that the Danish monarchy cede Norway to Sweden.

Faced with an overwhelming enemy force and isolated diplomatically because of his alliance with France, Frederik VI of Denmark had little choice but to accept Karl Johan's demands. On the night of 14-15 January 1814, the Danish and Swedish negotiators signed the Treaty of Kiel, by which Frederik VI ceded Norway to Karl XIII of Sweden and his heirs in return for one million riksdaler, Swedish Pomerania, and the promise of help from Karl Johan in securing further compensation for Frederik VI in Germany at the conclusion of the war. With that, Karl Johan and the Swedes had achieved what they thought was their final goal. The problem was, however, that no one had consulted the Norwegians, and the Norwegians--having received word of the Treaty of Kiel--were by no means willing to accept what the Swedes and the Danes had planned for them.

With the active participation and leadership of the Danish viceroy in Norway, Prince Christian Frederik, the Norwegians set about preparing their response to the developments of January 1814. Meeting at Eidsvold in April and May 1814, the duly elected representatives of the Norwegian burghers, farmers, and civil servants debated the relative merits of independence and of union with Sweden. The result of their deliberations was the drafting and adoption of a constitution, as well as the election of Christian Frederik as king of Norway. Thus, the representatives had chosen independence over union with Sweden, and the stage was set for the final military confrontation in Scandinavia during the Napoleonic era--the clash in the summer of 1814 between Karl Johan's Swedish forces and the Norwegian forces under the command of Christian Frederik.

Militarily, the invasion of Norway by Sweden in the summer of 1814 was not a particularly complicated matter. The Swedish forces, which numbered between forty and fifty thousand to Norway's thirty thousand, were better equipped and under more experienced leadership, and they were able to move about quite freely. Nonetheless, Karl Johan offered to negotiate with the Norwegians almost immediately, and upon their acceptance of that offer talks were opened that were soon to lead to a peaceful settlement. In return for Christian Frederik's abdication and Karl XIII's election in his place as king of Norway, the Swedes recognized the Norwegian constitution and allowed the Norwegians to rule themselves in a personal union with Sweden. This agreement was accepted and effected, and in 1815 a formal Act of Union was drawn up between Norway and Sweden. The uncertainty and the tension had passed, and the political map of Scandinavia had been redrawn drastically.

Prior to the Napoleonic period, Scandinavia consisted of two monarchies--Denmark-Norway and Sweden (including Finland)--but in 1815 the situation was much altered. Denmark had lost control of Norway, Sweden had lost control of Finland, Norway had become a second realm under the king of Sweden, and Finland had become an autonomous grand duchy within the Russian empire. Denmark had been involved in hostilities with Great Britain in April 1801 and with Sweden from March 1808 until December 1809 and again in November and December 1813. Sweden had been involved in hostilities with France between 1805 and 1807, with Russia from 1808 to 1809, with France and Denmark in 1813, and with Norway in the summer of 1814. Although tucked away in a remote corner of Northern Europe, the Scandinavian powers had been unable to avoid the maelstrom of European politics in the age of Napoleon.

GENERAL WORKS

The best introductions to the history of the Scandinavian countries in English, French, and German for this period are the works by Derry (1), Fol (2), and Kan (4), while an article in DIE WELT ALS GESCHICHTE by Emil Schieche (8) provides an introduction to Scandinavian historiography of this era in the productive period 1939-1950. For more detailed treatments, however, it is necessary to turn to the national histories in English and eventually to those in the respective languages. The best English-language national histories for this period are, for Denmark, Stewart Oakley's SHORT HISTORY OF DENMARK (70); for Finland, Eino Jutikkala & Kauko Pirinen's HISTORY OF FINLAND (150); for Norway, Karen Larsen's HISTORY OF NORWAY (51); and, for Sweden, Franklin D. Scott's SWEDEN: THE NATION'S HISTORY (184). The best national histories covering the Napoleonic period in the respective languages of the region are, for Denmark, volume 4 in DANMARKS HISTORIE (37), volume 4 in SCHULTZ DANMARKSHISTORIE (42), and volume 10 in Politiken's DANMARKS HISTORIE (30); for Finland, volumes 3 and 4 in SUOMEN KANSAN HISTORIA (152) and volume 2 in KANSAKUNNAN HISTORIA (177); for Norway, volume 9 in NORGES HISTORIE (64); and, for Sweden, volume 2 in SVENSK HISTORIA (113) and volumes 7 and 8 in DEN SVENSKA HISTORIEN (115). Also useful as a guide to the complicated diplomatic situation facing Sweden during the period is volume 3 of DEN SVENSKA UTRIKESPOLITIKENS HISTORIA (114).

BIBLIOGRAPHIES

The historical societies of each of the four major Nordic countries publish exhaustive and very useful cumulative bibliographies, which contain special sections on military history. These bibliographies include DANSK HISTORISK BIBLIOGRAFI (29), SUOMEN HISTORIALLINEN BIBLIOGRAFIA (189), BIBLIOGRAFI TIL NORGES HISTORIE (21), and SVENSK HISTORISK BIBLIOGRAFI (191). Other useful bibliographies of book length include Samuel E. Bring's now dated BIBLIOGRAFISK HANDBOK TILL SVERIGES HISTORIA (101), Arne Odd Johnsen and Gunnar Christie Wasberg's NORSK MILITAERHISTORISK BIBLIOGRAFI (47), and Gurli Taube's SVENSK REGIMENTSHISTORISK BIBLIOGRAFI (194). In addition, there are naval history bibliographies for Denmark, Norway, and Sweden, namely Hans C. Bjerg's DANSK MARINEHISTORISK BIBLIOGRAFI 1500-1975 (23) for Denmark, Rolf Scheen's 300-work bibliography on Norwegian naval history in NORSK TIDSSKRIFT FOR SJOEVESEN (80), and Uno Willers's now rather dated SVENSK SJOEHISTORISK LITTERATUR 1800-1943 (213).

ARCHIVAL SOURCES

An overview of the archives of Scandinavia, Harald Joergensen's NORDISKE ARKIVER (3), was published in Danish in the late 1960s, but it is of limited interest to the researcher trying to pinpoint sources for Scandinavian military history during the Napoleonic era. Much the better course of action is to contact the respective

archives with specific requests for information about the holdings
one is interested in exploring. In Denmark, Finland, and Norway, the
relevant military archives are integrated into the holdings of the
national archives themselves. In Sweden, both the national archives
and the military history archives must be consulted, although the
latter hold by far the greater wealth of pertinent sources for
military history during this period. The national archives of the
four nations are Rigsarkivet (the Danish National Archives) in
Copenhagen, Valtionarkisto (the Finnish National Archives) in
Helsinki, Riksarkivet (the Norwegian National Archives) in Oslo, and
Riksarkivet (the Swedish National Archives) in Stockholm. Sweden's
Krigsarkivet (Military History Archives) is also located in
Stockholm.

PUBLISHED DOCUMENTS

The publication of documents concerning the Napoleonic period in
Scandinavia has not followed any particular plan in any of the four
countries. Instead, documents have appeared in several different
forms and with several differing grades of utility. The relevant
international treaties for Denmark-Norway have been published in
DANSKE TRACTATER EFTER 1800 (28), while the Swedish series of
published international treaties has failed to produce the volume
intended to cover this period. Above and beyond these documents,
perhaps the most useful documents have been published by the
Norwegians. These include diplomatic and political (50, 66, 73),
military (10, 13, 67), and naval history (19, 31), of which perhaps
the most useful set is Fredrik Beutlich's "Aktstykker vedroerende
Norges sjoeforsvar under krigen 1807-1814," published in NORSK
TIDSSKRIFT FOR SJOEVESEN between 1935 and 1941 (19). Then, too THE
SAUMAREZ PAPERS: SELECTIONS FROM THE BALTIC CORRESPONDENCE OF
VICE-ADMIRAL SIR JAMES SAUMAREZ, 1808-1812 (7) provide a useful
insight into the naval thinking of the British during a critical
period.

MEMOIRS, JOURNALS, AND EYEWITNESS ACCOUNTS

Much more has been published in the area of memoirs, journals,
and eyewitness accounts than in the area of contemporary military and
political documents. Among the political leadership of the
Scandinavian monarchies, the diaries of three monarchs stand out; the
diary and notations of Christian VIII of Denmark through the year
1814 have been published by Axel Linvald in the first volume of his
KONG CHRISTIAN VIII:S DAGBOEGER OG OPTEGNELSER (27), while the diary
of Gustav IV Adolf of Sweden has been edited by Erik Gamby (125), and
that of Christian Frederik of Norway (later Christian VIII of
Denmark) for the year 1814 has been translated and published by Jan
Joergen Alnaes (26). Of equal interest is the extremely insightful
political diary kept by the wife of Karl XIII of Sweden, Hedvig
Elisabeth Charlotta; volumes 7-9 of her diary, edited by Cecilia af
Klercker (129), cover the years 1800-1817.

While some accounts of Norwegian military action in 1808 (24)
and in 1814 (44, 71), of Swedish action in the Battle of the Nations
at Leipzig (160), and of Norwegian privateering (48) have been
published, by far the best represented military conflict in this

particular genre of publication is the Russo-Swedish war for the
control of Finland in 1808-1809. Notable among these publications is
the NARRATIVE OF THE CONQUEST OF FINLAND BY THE RUSSIANS IN THE YEARS
1808-9. FROM AN UNPUBLISHED WORK BY A RUSSIAN OFFICER OF RANK (168),
but most of the accounts are from the pens of Finnish and Swedish
soldiers and officers (91, 119, 120, 139, 142, 145, 180). Of the
latter, Jonas Hedberg has edited a fascinating collection of
Finnish-Swedish artillery officers' diaries in KUNGLIGA FINSKA
ARTILLERIOFFICERARES DAGBOECKER (128).

SPECIALIZED WORKS

There are many detailed and very valuable interpretations of
various aspects of the military and political history of the
Scandinavian states during the Napoleonic period. For an excellent
study of Denmark's experience as a neutral, one should read Ole
Feldbaek's DENMARK AND THE ARMED NEUTRALITY: SMALL POWER POLICY IN A
WORLD WAR (36). The final trial of that neutrality, i.e., the
British bombardment of Copenhagen in April 1807, is treated in
several of the readings (25, 32, 39, 89), but perhaps best in Villads
Christensen's "Koebenhavn under Belejringen 1807" (25). For
Denmark's military and naval history during the war years, one should
turn to the now dated treatment of the 1807-1809 period by Jacob
Thode Raeder (75) and to Carl Fredrik Wandel's SOEKRIGEN I DE
DANSK-NORSKE FARVANDE 1807-14. FRA TABET AF FLAADEN TIL FREDEN I
KIEL (90). Otherwise, Denmark's experiences in the war are dealt
with in Roland Ruppenthal's "Denmark and the Continental System"
(79), in Poul Ib Liebe's NAPOLEONS DANSKE HJAELPETROPPER.
"AUXILIAERKORPSET 1813" (55), and in Georg Noerregaard's study of
DANMARK OG WIENERKONGRESSEN 1814-1815 (67).

Much attention has been paid by Norwegian historians to the
military and naval history of their country during the 1807-1814
period. These works include studies of individual battles (9, 62)
and of the military experience of specific towns (17) and regiments
(15, 16), but most of them deal with broader aspects of the military
and naval history of the period. Perhaps the best works with which
to begin are, for military history, Rudolf Muus's DEN NORSKE HAERS
KAMPE I 1808-09 OG 1814 (63) and Odd Lindbaeck-Larsen's DEN NORSKE
HAER OG 1814 (56). For naval history one should consult, in
particular, N.A. Larsen's FRA KRIGENS TID (1807-1814). BIDRAG TIL DEN
NORSKE MARINES HISTORIE (53) and Fredrik Beutlich's NORGES
SJOEVAEBNING (volume 2) 1810-1814 (20). The common experience of
Danish and Norwegian privateering and imprisonment in British prison
ships has been treated by Kay Larsen in DANMARKS KAPERVAESEN
1807-1814 (52), by Johan Nicolay Toennessen in KAPERFART OG SKIBSFART
1807-1814 (88), and by Carl N. Roos in PRISONEN. DANSKE OG NORSKE
KRIGSFANGER I ENGLAND 1807-1814 (77).

Aside from this focus on military and naval history, Norwegian
and Danish historians have devoted a great deal of attention to
Norway's separation from Denmark in 1814 and to the dilemma that this
caused for both the Danes and the Norwegians. Included in this
literature is one volume devoted specifically to the military aspects
of this crisis, namely Carl Theodor Soerensen's two-volume KAMPEN OM
NORGE I AARENE 1813 OG 1814. ET BIDRAG TIL DE NORDISKE RIGERS
KRIGSHISTORIE (86), but more typically it is the political aspects of

the problem that have received the most attention. Georg
Noerregaard's FREDEN I KIEL 1814 (68) deals with the problem seen
from the perspective of a Danish monarch finding it necessary to
renounce his sovereignty over Norway, while Axel Linvald has
concentrated on the Norwegian perspective of the same problem in his
CHRISTIAN FREDERIK OG NORGE 1814. DE STORE BESLUTNINGER MELLEM
KIELFREDEN OG EIDSVOLDMOEDET JANUAR-FEBRUAR (58) and in other
publications (59, 60).

The Swedish-Finnish military historical literature for this
period is richer than is that of Denmark-Norway for the same period.
There are several significant regimental histories (127, 130, 138,
195), as well as a study of the attempt at introducing
conscription--Gunnar Samuelsson's LANTVAERNET 1808-09 (181)--and
several studies of individual battles and sieges. The major works
for the several military conflicts Sweden faced during the Napoleonic
period include Gustaf Bjoerlin's SVERIGES KRIG I TYSKLAND AAREN
1805-1807 (98), the nine-part official SVERIGES KRIG AAREN 1808 OCH
1809 (193), Julius Mankell's FAELTTAAGET I NORGE AAR 1814. KRITISK
BELYSNING (165), and Sture M. Waller's GEORG CARL VON DOEBELN.
STUDIER I SVERIGES MILITAERISKA OCH POLITISKA HISTORIA 1808-1813
(209). There are many works dealing with the military conflicts with
Denmark-Norway (97, 155, 166, 170), but the greatest attention has
perhaps been paid to the Russo-Swedish war for control of Finland in
1808-1809. Matti Lauerma has presented this conflict to an
international public in "La Guerre de 1808-09" in REVUE
INTERNATIONALE D'HISTOIRE MILITAIRE (159) and there is a Soviet study
of the conflict published in Russian (216), but the bulk of the
literature has appeared in Finnish and in Swedish, including
book-length studies by Johan Richard Danielsson (117), Eirik Hornborg
(141), Carl Otto Nordensvan (171), Wilhelm Odelberg (172), and Lars
Tingsten (196).

Otherwise, a great deal of attention in Swedish scholarship has
been devoted to the overthrow of Gustav IV Adolf in 1809 and to the
subsequent developments of Bernadotte's election as crown prince in
1810 and his leadership of Sweden's diplomatic and military efforts
during the remainder of the Napoleonic period. Especially useful for
the fall of Gustav IV Adolf is Sten Carlsson's GUSTAV IV ADOLFS FALL.
KRISEN I RIKSSTYRELSEN, KONSPIRATIONERNA OCH STATSVAELVNINGEN
(1807-1809) (109), while the several works by Torvald T. Hoejer on
Crown Prince Karl Johan (especially, 132, 133, 135) taken together
with Joergen Weibull's CARL JOHAN OCH NORGE 1810-1814 (212) provide
excellent coverage of Bernadotte's influence on the foreign and
military policy of his new homeland. Hoejer has also dealt with
Bernadotte's ambitions concerning his role in post-Napoleonic Europe
(136), as has Franklin D. Scott in his BERNADOTTE AND THE FALL OF
NAPOLEON (182) and in his article on "The Propaganda Activities of
Bernadotte, 1813-1814" (183). Finally, from the Finnish perspective
it is very important to read Paeivioe Tommila's LA FINLANDE DANS LA
POLITIQUE EUROPEENE 1809-1815 (201).

FUTURE RESEARCH

There are many areas for further research in the military
history of the Napoleonic era in the Scandinavian region. Not least
of all, it would be of great benefit to have integrated military

histories for Denmark-Norway and for Sweden (including Finland), respectively, covering the period 1800-1815. Many topics that have in the past been treated in isolation could in such works be brought into the perspective of the total experience, thus reshaping our present understanding of the various ways in which the Napoleonic wars affected the Scandinavian states. Much needs to be done in terms of the recruitment experiences of the two states, both in terms of officers and of men, and there remains a great deal to be done, as well, in regard to what the Scandinavian military establishments learned from observing the great powers at war. Given the fact that Scandinavian historians themselves are reluctant to work on a comparative basis as between their various countries, a very important role for a non-Scandinavian would be to publish a series of studies concerning the relative and comparative military and strategic positions of Denmark-Norway and Sweden (including Finland) under the shifting conditions of the Napoleonic wars.

BIBLIOGRAPHY: SCANDINAVIA

GENERAL WORKS

1. Derry, Thomas Kingston. A HISTORY OF SCANDINAVIA. Minneapolis: University of Minnesota Press, 1979.

2. Fol, Jean Jacques. LES PAYS NORDIQUES AUX XIXe ET XXe SIECLES. Paris: Presses universitaires de France, 1978.

3. Joergensen, Harald. NORDISKE ARKIVER. Copenhagen: Arkivforeningen, 1968.

4. Kan, Aleksandr Sergeivich. GESCHICHTE DER SKANDINAVISCHEN LAENDER. Berlin: VEB Deutscher Verlag der Wissenschaften, 1978.

5. Pugh, David C. "Norway and Sweden in 1814: The Security Issue." SCANDINAVIAN JOURNAL OF HISTORY 5 (1980): 121-36.

6. Ryan, A.N. "The Defence of British Trade with the Baltic 1808-1813." ENGLISH HISTORICAL REVIEW 74 (1959): 443-66.

7. Saumarez, James. THE SAUMAREZ PAPERS; SELECTIONS FROM THE BALTIC CORRESPONDENCE OF VICE-ADMIRAL SIR JAMES SAUMAREZ, 1808-1812. Edited by A.N. Ryan. London: Navy Records Society, 1968. Vol. 110.

8. Schieche, Emil. "Die skandinavische Geschichtsschreibung der Gegenwart und die grosse nordische Krise von 1808 bis 1814." DIE WELT ALS GESCHICHTE 10 (1950): 263-75.

DENMARK AND NORWAY

9. Aamodt, Harald. "Nytt lys over slaget ved Trangen den 25 April 1808" [New Light on the Battle of Trangen, 25 April 1808]. NORSK MILITAERT TIDSSKRIFT 121 (1962): 632-57.

10. "Aktstykker angaaende Norge, henhoerende til Perioden Juli-August 1808" [Documents Concerning Norway during the Period July-August 1808]. MEDDELELSER FRA KRIGSARKIVERNE 3 (1888): 526-34.

11. Angell, Henrik. SYV-AARS-KRIGEN FOR 17. MAJ 1807-1814 [The Seven Years' War before the Seventeenth of May, 1807-1814]. Kristiania: H. Aschehoug, 1914.

12. Arentz, Ragnvald. "Den norske defensjonseskadre i 1808" [The Norwegian Defense Squadron, 1808]. NORSK TIDSSKRIFT FOR SJOEVESEN 85 (1970): 116-28.

13. Aubert, C. "Aktstykker vedkommende krigsbegivenhederne 1814" [Documents Concerning the Military Events of 1814]. MEDDELELSER FRA DET NORSKE RIKSARKIV 3 (1933): 1-256.

14. Barfod, Joergen H. "Marinens historie" [The History of the Navy]. TIDSSKRIFT FOR SOEVAESEN 121 (1950): 257-66.

15. Barstad, Hans Jacob. BERGENHUSISKE NATIONALE SKARPSKYTTERBATALJONS HISTORIE 1810-1817, STABELLS KAMPE PAA OESTSIDEN AV GLOMMEN OG NORSKE JAEGERSKORPS'S RETRAET TIL RAKKESTAD I 1814 MED KART [The History of the Bergenhus Sharpshooter Battalion, 1810-1817, Stabell's Fight on the East Bank of Glommen, and the Retreat of the Norwegian Jaeger Corps to Rakkestad in 1814]. Kristiania: S. & Jul Soerensens Bogtrykkeri, 1914.

16. Barstad, Hans Jacob. BERGENHUSISKE REGIMENT I KRIGEN MOD SVERIGE 1813-1814 [The Bergenhus Regiment in the Wars against Sweden, 1813-1814]. Kristiania: S. & Jul Soerensens Bogtrykkeri, 1918.

17. Barstad, Hans Jacob. BERGENS FORSVAR I 1801 OG 1807-1814 [The Defense of Bergen in 1801 and in 1807-1814]. Bergen: E.B. Giertsen, 1887.

18. Bergsgaard, Arne. "Folket og krigen i 1814" [The People and the Wars in 1814]. SYN OG SEGN 47 (1941): 145-59, 207-19.

19. Beutlich, Fredrik. "Aktstykker vedroerende Norges sjoeforsvar under krigen 1807-1814" [Documents Concerning Norway's Naval Defense during the Wars of 1807-1814]. NORSK TIDSKRIFT FOR SJOEVESEN 53 (1935): 343-55; 54 (1936): 24-38, 177-83, 236-43, 363-73; 55 (1937): 24-28, 81-88, 263-74, 391-402, 495-502; 56 (1938): 130-37, 235-42, 340-45, 486-99; 57 (1939): 162-70, 303-15, 396-405; 58 (1940): 16-26, 351-61; 59 (1941): 16-28, 96-102, 158-64, 181-87.

20. Beutlich, Fredrik. NORGES SJOEVAEBNING [Norway's Naval Defense]. Vol. 2. 1810-1814. Oslo: Aschehoug, 1940.

21. BIBLIOGRAFI TIL NORGES HISTORIE [Bibliography of Norwegian History]. Oslo: Den Norske Historiske Forening, 1916 to present.

22. "Bidrag til Norges Krigshistorie fra Krigsaarene 1807, 8 og 9" [Contributions to Norway's Military History during the War Years 1807-1809]. NORSK MILITAERT TIDSSKRIFT 13 (1848-49): 76-183, 318-422.

23. Bjerg, Hans C. DANSK MARINEHISTORISK BIBLIOGRAFI 1500-1975 [Naval History Bibliography, 1500-1975]. Copenhagen: Akademisk Forlag, 1975.

24. "Breve og Rapporter fra Norge i Perioden April-Juni 1808" [Letters and Reports from Norway during the Period April to June 1808]. MEDDELELSER FRA KRIGSARKIVERNE 3 (1888): 383-416.

25. Christensen, Villads. "Koebenhavn under Belejringen 1807" [Copenhagen during the Siege of 1807]. HISTORISKE MEDDELELSER OM KOEBENHAVN AARBOK 1 (1907-08): 97-150.

26. Christian VIII, king of Denmark. CHRISTIAN FREDERIKS DAGBOK FRA 1814 [Christian Frederik's Diary from 1814]. Translated by Jan Joergen Alnaes. Oslo: Gyldendal, 1954.

27. Christian VIII, king of Denmark. KONG CHRISTIAN VIII:S DAGBOEGER OG OPTEGNELSER [King Christian VIII's Diaries and Notes]. Edited by Axel Linvald. Vol. 1. 1799-1814. Copenhagen: Det Kongelige danske selskab for faedrelandets historie, 1943.

28. DANSKE TRACTATER EFTER 1800 [Danish Treaties after 1800]. Series 1. POLITISKE TRACTATER [Political Treaties]. Vol. 1. 1800-1863. Copenhagen: J.H. Schultz, 1877. Series 2. HANDELS- OG ANDRE TRACTATER [Commercial and Other Treaties]. Vol. 1. 1800-1863. Copenhagen: J.H. Schultz, 1874.

29. DANSK HISTORISK BIBLIOGRAFI [Bibliography of Danish History]. Copenhagen: Den danske historiske Forening, 1917 to present.

30. Danstrup, Johan, and Hal Koch. DANMARKS HISTORIE [The History of Denmark]. Vol. 10. REFORM OG FALLIT 1784-1830 [Reform and Bankruptcy, 1784-1830] by Jens Vibaek. 2d ed. Copenhagen: Politikens Forlag, 1971.

31. de la Cour, C. FORSVARET AF VORE KYSTER 1810-1814. UDDRAG AF DE I RIGSARKIVET OPBEVAREDE ORIGINALE SKRIVELSER OG RAPPORTER FRA SJOEDEFENSIONENS CHEF TIL VICESTATHOLDEREN [The Defense of Our Coasts, 1810-1814. Excerpts from the Original Documents and Reports from the Chief of Naval Defense to the Vice Governor Preserved in the National Archives]. Kristiania: Norges Sjoefartstidendes trykkeri, 1895.

32. "Det engelske Overfald i 1807 eller Perioden fra August til November 1807" [The English Attack of 1807 or the Period from August to November 1807]. MEDDELELSER FRA KRIGSARKIVERNE 3 (1888): 1-41.

33. Domaas, K. "Om ordningen af vort kystforsvar under krigen 1807 til 1814" [On the Arrangements for Our Coastal Defense during the Wars from 1807 to 1814]. NORSK MILITAERT TIDSSKRIFT 54 (1891): 20-36, 77-93, 131-34, 192-213.

34. Elgvin, Johannes. "Danmark-Norges assuransepolitikk fra 1807 til sommeren 1810" [Denmark-Norway's Insurance Policy from 1807 Until the Summer of 1810]. HISTORISK TIDSSKRIFT (Norway) 47 (1968): 104-32.

35. Faye, A. "Landkrigen i Norge 1808, et lidet Bidrag til Norges nyere Historie" [The War on the Ground in Norway, 1808: A Small Contribution to Modern Norwegian History]. NORDISK UNIVERSITETS-TIDSSKRIFT 7 (1861): 62-118.

36. Feldbaek, Ole. DENMARK AND THE ARMED NEUTRALITY 1800-1801: SMALL POWER POLICY IN A WORLD WAR. Copenhagen: Akademisk Forlag, 1980.

37. Feldbaek, Ole. TIDEN 1730-1814 [The Period 1730-1814]. Vol. 4. DANMARKS HISTORIE [A History of Denmark]. Edited by Aksel E. Christensen et al. Copenhagen: Gyldendal, 1982.

38. "Felttoget i Norge eller Perioden April-Juni 1808" [The Campaign in Norway, or the Period April-June 1808]. MEDDELELSER FRA KRIGSARKIVERNE 3 (1888): 348-82.

39. Flamand, Ludvig Joseph [B.H. Faber]. KJOEBENHAVNS BOMBARDEMENT 1807 ELLER DE 3 RAEDSELNAETTER [The Bombardment of Copenhagen 1807, or the Three Nights of Terror]. Copenhagen: F.C. Meier, 1857. (2d ed. Copenhagen: J.C. Borup, 1860).

40. Flood, Constantius. FRA AGDESIDEN. SKILDRINGER OG OPTEGNELSER (1807-1814). [From the Agde Side. Descriptions and Notes, 1807-1814]. Kristiania: P.T. Mallings Boghandel, 1877.

41. Frederik VI, king of Denmark. FREDERIK DEN SJETTES FORTROLIGE BREVVEXLING MED NORGE I AARET 1809 [Frederik VI's Confidential Correspondence with Norway, 1809]. Edited by Carl Theodor Soerensen. Copenhagen: Gyldendalske Boghandel, 1889.

42. Friis, Aage; Axel Lindval; and Mogens Mackeprang. SCHULTZ DANMARKSHISTORIE [Schultz's History of Denmark]. Copenhagen: J.H. Schultz Forlag, 1942. Vol. 4.

43. "Historiske, kritiske bemerkninger til den norske soekrigs historie fra krigens udbrud 1807 indtil udgangen of aaret 1813" [Historical, Critical Comments on Norway's Naval History from the Outbreak of the War in 1807 up until the End of 1813]. NORSK TIDSSKRIFT FOR SJOEVESEN 14 (1895-96): 247-54, 263-80; 15 (1896-97): 1-15, 75-92.

44. Hjorth, Jens Edward. "Fra 1814. Av major Jens Edward Hjorts efterlatte papirer" [From 1814. Selections from the Papers of Major Jens Edward Hjort]. NORSK MILITAERT TIDSSKRIFT 105 (1946): 97-114.

45. Holm, Edvard. DANMARK-NORGES HISTORIE FRA DEN STORE NORDISKE KRIGS SLUTNING TIL RIGERNES ADSKILLELSE (1720-1814) [The History of Denmark-Norway from the End of the Great Northern War until the Divorce between the Two Realms]. Copenhagen: G.E.C. Gad, 1891-1912. 7 vols.

46. Holmboe, H.P. "Briternes Krigsforetagender langs Norges Kyster fra 1808 til 1814" [The Naval Activities of the British along the Coast of Norway from 1808 until 1814]. SAMLINGER TIL DET NORSKE FOLKS SPROG OG HISTORIE 2 (1834): 246-72.

47. Johnsen, Arne Odd, and Gunnar Christie Wasberg, eds. NORSK #1 MILITAERHISTORISK BIBLIOGRAFI [Bibliography of Norwegian Military History]. Oslo: Gyldendal, 1969. See also supplement to this work edited by Harald Sandvik (Oslo: Gyldendal, 1977).

48. Kaald, Andreas. PAA KAPERTOGT OG I PRISONEN 1808-1810. AV KAPTEIN ANDREAS KAALDS ETTERLATTE PAPIRER [At Sea as a Privateer and in Prison, 1808-1810: From the Papers of Captain Andreas Kaald]. Edited by Johan Nicolay Toennessen. Trondheim: H. Holbaek Eriksen, 1950.

49. Kiaerland, Lars. OVERSIKTSPLAN OVER DEN NORSKE HAERS ORGANISASJON 18/1 1628-30/9 1940 [Survey of the Organization of the Norwegian Army, 18 January 1628-30 September 1930]. Oslo: Forsvarsdepartementet, n.d.

50. Lange, Chr., and Carl Stoud Platou. "Bidrag til Norges Historie 1807-1809. A. 52 Rapporter fra Prinds Christian August til Frederik VI. B. To Breve fra Prinds Christian August i Anledning of Major Carl Anckarsvaerds Sendelse i Marts 1809. C. Prinds Christian Augusts Breve til General v. Krogh. D. Darres Besoeg hos General Armfelt i Juni 1808" [Contributions to the History of Norway, 1807-1814. A. 52 Reports from Prince Christian August to King Frederik VI. B. Two Letters from Prince Christian August Concerning Major Carl Anckarsvaerd's Mission in March 1809. C. Prince Christian August's Letters to General von Krogh. D. Darre's Visit to General Armfelt in June 1808]. NORSKE SAMLINGER 2 (1860): 145-273, 336-469.

51. Larsen, Karen. A HISTORY OF NORWAY. Princeton, N.J.: Princeton University Press, 1948.

52. Larsen, Kay. DANMARKS KAPERVAESEN 1807-1814 [Denmark's Privateering Activities, 1807-1814]. Copenhagen and Kristiania: Gyldendal Nordisk Forlag, 1915.

53. Larsen, N.A. FRA KRIGENS TID (1807-1814). BIDRAG TIL DEN NORSKE MARINES HISTORIE [From the Time of the Wars (1807-1814). Contributions to the History of the Norwegian Navy]. Kristiania: Den norske Forlagsforening, 1878.

54. Leiren, Terje I. "Norwegian Independence and British Opinion: January to August 1814." SCANDINAVIAN STUDIES 47 (1975): 364-82.

55. Liebe, Poul Ib. NAPOLEONS DANSKE HJAELPETROPPER. "AUXILIAERKORPSET 1813" [Napoleon's Danish Support Troops. "The Auxiliary Corps, 1813"]. Copenhagen: Zac, 1968.

56. Lindbaeck-Larsen, Odd. DEN NORSKE HAER OG 1814 [The Norwegian Army and 1814]. Oslo: Forsvarsdepartementet, 1945.

57. "Linieskibet Prinds Christian Frederiks sidste Campagne i Aarene 1807-08" [The Ship of the Line Prinds Christian Frederik's Last Campaign, 1807-08]. ARCHIV FOR SOEVAESENET 11 (1839): 241-73, 402-37; 12 (1840): 172-204.

58. Linvald, Axel. CHRISTIAN FREDERIK OG NORGE 1814. DE STORE BESLUTNINGER MELLEM KIELFREDEN OG EIDSVOLDMOEDET JANUAR-FEBRUAR [Christian Frederik and Norway, 1814: The Great Decisions between the Treaty of Kiel and the Eidsvold Meeting, January-February]. Oslo: Universitetsforlaget, 1962.

59. Linvald, Axel. KONG CHRISTIAN VIII [King Christian VIII]. Vol. 2. NORGES STATHOLDER 1813-1814 [Norway's Viceroy, 1813-1814]. Copenhagen: Gyldendal, 1952.

60. Linvald, Axel. "Omkring Kielerfreden. Bidrag til Danmarks og Norges historie i de foerste maaneder of 1814" [On the Treaty of Kiel: Contributions to the History of Denmark and Norway during the First Months of 1814]. HISTORISK TIDSSKRIFT (Denmark) Series 11, 4 (1954): 165-231.

61. Maurseth, Per. "Christian Frederiks myndighet som stattholder og planene om en regjeringskommisjon" [Christian Frederik's Authority as Viceroy and the Plans for a Governing Commission]. HISTORISK TIDSSKRIFT (Norway) 42 (1963): 1-29.

62. Munthe, C.O. "Kampen ved Trangen den 25 april 1808. En krigshistorisk-taktisk studie" [The Battle at Trangen, 25 April 1808: A Military Historical-Tactical Study]. NORSK MILITAERT TIDSSKRIFT 62 (1899): 1-27, 73-89.

63. Muus, Rudolf. DEN NORSKE HAERS KAMPE I 1808-09 OG 1814 [The Norwegian Army's Struggle, 1808-09 and 1814]. Kristiania: J. Aass' Forlag, 1905.

64. Mykland, Knut. KAMPEN OM NORGE 1784-1814 [The Struggle for Norway, 1784-1814]. Vol. 9 of NORGES HISTORIE [A History of Norway]. Edited by Knut Mykland. Oslo: J.W. Cappelens Forlag, 1978.

65. Mykland, Knut. "Medens der endnu er tid (Christian Frederik's juledagsdepesje 1813 og Kong Frederik VI's planer i januar 1814)" [While There is Still Time (Christian Frederik's Christmas Day Despatch of 1813 and King Frederik VI's Plans in January 1814)]. HISTORISK TIDSSKRIFT (Norway) 41 (1961): 1-41.

66. Nielsen, Yngvar. "Aktstykker vedkommende Konventionen i Moss 14de August 1814" [Documents Concerning the Convention of Moss, 14 August 1814]. VIDENSKAPSSELSKAPET I KRISTIANIA SKRIFTER. Series 2, 4 (1893).

67. Noerregaard, Georg. DANMARK OG WIENERKONGRESSEN 1814-1815 [Denmark and the Congress of Vienna, 1814-1815]. Copenhagen: Gyldendal, 1948.

68. Noerregaard, Georg. FREDEN I KIEL 1814 [The Treaty of Kiel, 1814]. Copenhagen: Rosenkilde og Bagger, 1954.

69. "Nogle aktstykker vedr. begivenhederne om Oerjesoe i may 1808"
    [Some Documents Concerning the Events around Oerjesoe in May
    1808]. NORSK MILITAERT TIDSSKRIFT 56 (1893): 405-22, 444-77,
    483-99.

70. Oakley, Stewart. A SHORT HISTORY OF DENMARK. New York:
    Praeger, 1972.

71. Ohme, Johan. GENERAL OHMES JOURNAL OVER FREDRIKSSTENS
    FAESTNINGS BELEIRING FRA 30. JULI TIL 16. AUGUST 1814 [General
    Ohme's Journal from the Siege of Fredrikssten Fortress, 30
    July-16 August 1814]. Bergen: Johan Anderssens Forlag, 1899.

72. Oppegaard, S. "Krigen 1814" [The Wars of 1814]. NORSK
    TIDSSKRIFT FOR SJOEVESEN 32 (1914): 231-45.

73. Platou, Carl Stoud. "25 Skrivelser fra Frederik VI til Prins
    Christian August i Aarene 1807, 1808 og 1809" [25 Despatches
    from Frederik VI to Prince Christian August, 1807-1809]. NORSKE
    SAMLINGER 1 (1852): 290-320.

74. Raeder, J. "Paa Kongsvinger i 1814" [At Kongsvinger, 1814].
    HISTORISK TIDSSKRIFT (Norway). Series 5, 3 (1916): 17-80.

75. Raeder, Jacob Thode. DANMARKS KRIGS- OG POLITISKE HISTORIE, FRA
    KRIGENS UDBRUD 1807 TIL FREDEN TIL JOENKOEPING DEN 10de DECEMBER
    1809 [The Military and Political History of Denmark from the
    Outbreak of the War in 1807 until the Peace of Joenkoeping, 10
    December 1809]. Copenhagen: C.A. Reitzel, 1845-52. 3 vols.

76. Rasmussen, P.H. "Dansk udenrigspolitik 1812-1813" [Danish
    Foreign Policy, 1812-1813]. HISTORISK TIDSSKRIFT (Denmark) 77
    (1977): 65-84.

77. Roos, Carl N. PRISONEN. DANSKE OG NORSKE KRIGSFANGER I ENGLAND
    1807-1814 [The Prison: Danish and Norwegian Prisoners of War in
    England, 1807-1814]. Copenhagen: Gyldendal, 1953.

78. Rosenkrantz, Niels. JOURNAL DU CONGRES DE VIENNE 1814-1815.
    Edited by Georg Noerregaard. Copenhagen: G.E.C. Gad, 1953.

79. Ruppenthal, Roland. "Denmark and the Continental System."
    JOURNAL OF MODERN HISTORY 15 (1943): 7-23.

80. Scheen, Rolf. "Litt om studiet av norsk sjoekrigshistorie"
    [Something about the Study of Norwegian Naval History]. NORSK
    TIDSSKRIFT FOR SJOEVESEN 50 (1932): 17-86, 214-21.

81. Schioetz, Johannes. "Haeren av 1814" [The Army of 1814]. NORSK
    MILITAERT TIDSSKRIFT 91 (1928): 58-96.

82. Schitler, Didrik. BLADE AV NORGES KRIGSHISTORIE. SKILDRINGER
    [Pages from Norway's Military History: Descriptions].
    Kristiania: H. Aschehoug, 1895.

83. Skaar, Fritz C.   NORD-NORGES LANDFORSVAR 1807-1814 [North
    Norway's Defenses, 1807-1814].   Supplement to NORSK MILITAERT
    TIDSSKRIFT 108 (1938).

84. Skeie, Jon. NORGES FORSVARS HISTORIE [The History of Norwegian
    Defense]. Oslo: O. Norli, 1953.

85. Sneedorff, Hans Christian.   KONTREADMIRAL H.C. SNEEDORFF'S
    EFTERLADTE BREVE FRA 1807-1814 [Rear Admiral H.C. Sneedorff's
    Letters from 1807-1814].   Edited by Carl Johan Anker.
    Kristiania: J.M. Stenersen & Co.s Forlag, 1899.

86. Soerensen, Carl Theodor. KAMPEN OM NORGE I AARENE 1813 OG 1814.
    ET BIDRAG TIL DE NORDISKE RIGERS KRIGSHISTORIE [The Struggle for
    Norway in 1813-1814: A Contribution to the Military History of
    the Nordic Realms]. Copenhagen: Den Gyldendalske Boghandel,
    1871. 2 vols.

87. Tangeraas, Lars. "Canning og Norge" [Canning and Norway].
    HISTORISK TIDSSKRIFT 52 (1973): 293-313.

88. Toennessen, Johan Nicolay. KAPERFART OG SKIBSFART 1807-1814
    [Privateering and Shipping, 1807-1814]. Oslo: J.W. Cappelen,
    1955.

89. Trulsson, Sven G.   "Canning, den hemliga kanalen till
    foerhandlingarna i Tilsit och invasionsfoeretaget mot Koepenhamn
    1807" [Canning, the Secret Channel to the Negotiations at
    Tilsit, and the Plans for the Invasion of Copenhagen, 1807].
    SCANDIA 29 (1963): 320-59.

90. Wandel, Carl Fredrik. SOEKRIGEN I DE DANSK-NORSKE FARVANDE
    1807-14. FRA TABET AF FLAADEN TIL FREDEN I KIEL [Naval Warfare
    in Danish-Norwegian Waters, 1807-1814: From the Loss of the
    Fleet to the Treaty of Kiel]. Copenhagen: Jacob Lund, 1915.

SWEDEN AND FINLAND

91. Aakerstein, Nils Harald Joachim. EN KRIGARES MINNEN FRAAN OFRED
    OCH FAANGENSKAP [A Soldier's Memoirs from War and Imprisonment].
    Edited by Harald Aakerstein.   Malmoe: Bokfoerlaget Scania,
    1933.

92. Barton, H. Arnold. "The Swedish Succession Crisis of 1809 and
    1810, and the Question of Scandinavian Union." SCANDINAVIAN
    STUDIES 42 (1970): 309-33.

93. Bensow, Einar. KUNGLIGA SKARABORGS REGEMENTES HISTORIA [The
    History of the Royal Skaraborg Regiment]. Vol. 3. FRAAN KARL
    XII:9S DOED TILL REGEMENTETS OMORGANISATION 1942 [From the Death
    of Karl XII to the Reorganization of the Regiment in 1942].
    Skoevde: Vaestergoetlands tryckeri, 1956.

94. Berg, Lars O. "Norra finska skaergaardsflotiljan 1808-1809" [The Northern Finnish Skerrygard Flotilla, 1808-1809]. FORUM NAVALE 23 (1967): 56-62.

95. Berg, Lars O. "Svenska flottans fartyg 1808-1809, skaergaardsfartyg. En tabellarisk framstaellning" [The Ships of the Swedish Navy, 1809-1809: The Skerrygard Ships--A Tabular Presentation]. FORUM NAVALE 24 (1968): 91-102.

96. Bjoerklund, Stefan, ed. OM REGERINGSFORMENS TILLKOMST [On the Creation of the Form of Government]. Stockholm: Wahlstroem & Widstrand, 1965.

97. Bjoerlin, Gustaf. KRIGET I NORGE 1814. EFTER SAMTIDAS VITTNESBOERD FRAMSTAELLT [The War in Norway, 1814, Presented According to the Testimony of Contemporaries]. Stockholm: P.A. Norstedt & Soener, 1893.

98. Bjoerlin, Gustaf. SVERIGES KRIG I TYSKLAND AAREN 1805-1807 [Sweden's War in Germany, 1805-1807]. Stockholm: Militaerlitteratur foereningens foerlag, 1882.

99. Bobovich, I.M. "K voprosu o prisoedinenii Finljandii k Rossii" [Concerning the Question of Finland's Unification with Russia]. SKANDINAVSKII SBORNIK 15 (1970): 247-54.

100. Bonsdorf, Carl von. "G.M. Armfelt om kriget i Finland" [G.M. Armfelt on the War in Finland]. HISTORISK TIDSKRIFT FOER FINLAND 6 (1921): 119-30.

101. Bring, Samuel E. BIBLIOGRAFISK HANDBOK TILL SVERIGES HISTORIA [Bibliographical Handbook for Sweden's History]. Stockholm: P.A. Norstedt & Soener, 1934.

102. Carlgren, Wilhelm. "Drag ur nordiskt ekonomiskt liv under napoleonkrisen" [Aspects of Nordic Economic Life during the Napoleonic Crisis]. NORDISK TIDSKRIFT 18 (1942): 275-95.

103. Carlgren, Wilhelm. "Goeteborg och vaestkusten under napoleonkrigen. En blokadkris foer snart halvtannat sekel sedan" [Gothenburg and the West Coast during the Napoleonic Wars: A Blockade Crisis Nearly 150 Years Ago]. SVERIGES FLOTTA 40 (1944): 103-6.

104. Carlgren, Wilhelm. "Nytt och gammalt i Nordens naeringsliv under napoleonkrisen" [New and Old in the Economic Life of Scandinavia during the Napoleonic Crisis]. NORDISK TIDSKRIFT 18 (1942): 391-404.

105. Carlsson, Einar. "Karl Johans utrikespolitiska program vid ankomsten till Sverige 1810" [Bernadotte's Foreign Policy Program upon His Arrival in Sweden, 1810]. HISTORISK TIDSKRIFT 68 (1948): 335-43.

106. Carlsson, Einar. "Napoleon och svenska Pommern aar 1812" [Napoleon and Swedish Pomerania, 1812]. HISTORISK TIDSKRIFT 74 (1954): 146-70.

107. Carlsson, Sten. "Aabofoerdraget och krigsrustningarna 1812" [The Treaty of Aabo and War Preparations, 1812]. SCANDIA 18 (1947): 192-201.

108. Carlsson, Sten. "Gardesregementernas degradering 1808" [The Degradation of the Guards Regiments, 1808]. HISTORISK TIDSKRIFT 63 (1943): 369-97.

109. Carlsson, Sten. GUSTAV IV ADOLFS FALL. KRISEN I RIKSSTYRELSEN, KONSPIRATIONERNA OCH STATSVAELVNINGEN (1807-1809) [The Fall of Gustav IV Adolf: The Crisis in the National Government, the Plots, and the Coup d'Etat (1807-1809)]. Lund: C. Bloms boktryckeri, 1944.

110. Carlsson, Sten. "Karl Johan i Aabo 1812" [Bernadotte at Aabo, 1812]. SCANDIA 21 (1951-52): 72-76.

111. Carlsson, Sten. "Kring 1809 aars revolution" [Concerning the Revolution of 1809]. SCANDIA 17 (1946): 108-118.

112. Carlsson, Sten. "Slaget vid Lappo. Verklighet och myt" [The Battle of Lapua in 1808: Reality and Myth]. SCANDIA 18 (1947): 184-91.

113. Carlsson, Sten. TIDEN EFTER 1718 [The Period after 1718]. Vol. 2. SVENSK HISTORIA [The History of Sweden] by Sten Carlsson and Jerker Rosén. 4th ed. Stockholm: Esselte Studium, 1980.

114. Carlsson, Sten, and Torvald T. Hoejer. 1792-1844. Vol. 3. DEN SVENSKA UTRIKESPOLITIKENS HISTORIA [The History of Swedish Foreign Policy]. Edited by Ivar Beskow. Stockholm: P.A. Norstedt & Soener, 1954.

115. Carlsson, Sten, and Jerker Rosén. DEN SVENSKA HISTORIEN [Sweden's History]. Vol. 7. GUSTAVIANSKA TIDEN 1772-1809 [The Gustavian Period, 1772-1809]; Vol. 8. KARL JOHANSTIDEN OCH DEN BORGERLIGA LIBERALISMEN 1809-1865 [The Bernadotte Period and the Era of Bourgeois Liberalism, 1809-1865]. Stockholm: Albert Bonniers Foerlag, 1968.

116. Carr, Raymond. "Gustavus IV and the British Government 1804-9." ENGLISH HISTORICAL REVIEW 60 (1945): 36-66.

117. Danielson, Johan Richard. FINSKA KRIGET OCH FINLANDS KRIGARE 1808-1809 [The Finnish War and Finland's Soldiers, 1808-1809]. Helsinki: Osa Keyhtioe Weilin & Goeoes, 1897.

118. Edstroem, Sten. "Det tyska faelttaaget och Leipzigs stormning 19 oktober 1813" [The German Campaign and the Attack on Leipzig, 19 October 1813]. KAMRATFOERENINGEN SMAALANDSARTILLERISTEN. AARSBOK 23 (1963): 69-88.

119. Feilitzen, Johan von. JOURNAL HAALLEN UNDER 1808-1809 AARS FAELTTAAG [Journal Kept during the Campaign of 1808-1809]. Stockholm: P.A. Norstedt & Soener, 1955.

120. Fieandt, Otto H. von. "Otto H. v. Fieandtin sotapaivakirja [1808]" [Otto H. von Fieandt's War Diary, 1808]. HISTORIALLINEN ARKISTO 54 (1953): 381-426.

121. Frykberg, Nils, et al., eds. KUNGLIGA HAELSINGE REGEMENTES HISTORIA. FOERBANDET OCH BYGDEN [The History of the Royal Haelsinge Regiment: The Unit and the Community]. Gaevle: Westlund & Soener, 1968.

122. Furtenbach, Boerje. "'Frontbrev' fraan 1807" ["Frontline Letters" from 1807]. AKTUELLT OCH HISTORISKT (1966): 139-61.

123. Gasslander, Olle. "The Convoy Affair of 1798." SCANDINAVIAN ECONOMIC HISTORY REVIEW 2 (1954): 22-30.

124. Girod de l'Ain, Gabriel. BERNADOTTE, CHEF DE GUERRE ET CHEF D'ETAT. Paris: Perrin, 1968.

125. Gustav IV Adolf, king of Sweden. MEMOARER [Memoirs]. Edited by Erik Gamby. Uppsala: Bokgillet, 1960.

126. "Handlingar roerande Kungliga Oesterbottens infanteriregemente foer aaren 1806, 1807, 1808 och 1809" [Documents concerning the Royal Ostrobothnia Infantry Regiment for the Years 1806-1809]. FINSK MILITAER TIDSKRIFT (1892): 227-49, 283-302, 371-94, 437-53; (1893): 25-34, 148-55, 328.

127. Hedberg, Jonas. KUNGLIGA FINSKA ARTILLERIREGIMENTET [The Royal Finnish Artillery Regiment]. Helsinki: Svenska litteratursaellskapet i Finland, 1964.

128. Hedberg, Jonas, ed. KUNGLIGA FINSKA ARTILLERIOFFICERARES DAGBOECKER (1808-1809) [Diaries Kept by Officers of the Royal Finnish Artillery, 1808-1809]. Helsinki: Svenska litteratursaellskapet i Finland, 1969.

129. Hedvig Elisabeth Charlotta. HEDVIG ELISABETH CHARLOTTAS DAGBOK [Hedvig Elisabeth Charlotta's Diary]. Edited by Cecilia af Klercker. Vols. 7-9. 1800-1817. Stockholm: P.A. Norstedt & Soener, 1936, 1939, 1942.

130. Hirn, Hans. FRAAN LANTINGSHAUSEN TILL JAEGERHORN. ETT VAERVAT REGEMENTE I FINLAND 1751-1808 [From Lantingshausen to Jaegerhorn: A Salaried Regiment in Finland, 1751-1808]. Helsinki: Svenska litteratursaellskapet i Finland, 1970.

131. Hoejer, Torvald T. "Bernadotte och Bonaparte. Ett par fullstaendiganden" [Bernadotte and Bonaparte: A Couple of Clarifications]. HISTORISK TIDSKRIFT 61 (1941): 233-40.

132. Hoejer, Torvald T. CARL XIV JOHAN. KRONPRINSTIDEN [Karl XIV Johan (Bernadotte): The Years as Crown Prince]. Stockholm: P.A. Norstedt & Soener, 1943.

133. Hoejer, Torvald T. CARL JOHAN I DEN STORA KOALITIONEN MOT NAPOLEON. SVERIGE OCH KONGRESSEN I CHATILLON [Bernadotte in the Great Coalition against Napoleon: Sweden and the Congress of Chatillon]. Uppsala, Leipzig: A.B. Lundequistska Bokhandeln, Otto Harrassowitz, 1940.

134. Hoejer, Torvald T. "Carl Johan och Bourbonerna 1813-1814" [Bernadotte and the Bourbons, 1813-1814]. KARL JOHANS FOERBUNDETS HANDLINGAR (1935-37): 1-84.

135. Hoejer, Torvald T. KARL XIV JOHAN OCH ALEXANDER I. EN VAENDPUNKT I DE SVENSK-RYSKA FOERBINDELSERNAS HISTORIA [Karl XIV Johan (Bernadotte) and Alexander I: A Turning Point in the History of Swedish-Russian Relations]. Stockholm: H. Gerber, 1945.

136. Hoejer, Torvald T. "En ny teori om 1812 aars politik" [A New Theory about the Policy of 1812]. HISTORISK TIDSKRIFT 69 (1949): 263-78.

137. Hoejer, Torvald T. "1810-1812. Naagra anmaerkningar" [1810-1812: Some Notes]. HISTORISK TIDSKRIFT 69 (1949): 263-78.

138. Holm, Torsten, ed. KUNGLIGA UPPLANDS REGEMENTES HISTORIA [The History of the Royal Uppland Regiment]. Uppsala: Lundequistska Bokhandeln, 1958.

139. Hornborg, Eirik. "Faeltpraesten Erik Johan Cumenius' anteckningar fraan krigen 1807-1809" [The Notes of Field Chaplain Erik Johan Cumenius from the Wars of 1807-1809]. HISTORISKA OCH LITTERATURHISTORISKA STUDIER 27-28 (1952): 359-81.

140. Hornborg, Eirik. FAENRIK STAALS SAEGNEN OCH VERKLIGHETEN [The Sagas of Second Lieutenant Staal and Reality]. Helsinki: Svenska litteratursaellskapet i Finland, 1954.

141. Hornborg, Eirik. NAER RIKET SPRAENGDES. FAELTTAAGEN I FINLAND OCH VAESTERBOTTEN 1808-1809 [When the Realm was Divided: The Campaigns in Finland and Vaesterbotten, 1808-1809]. Stockholm: P.A. Norstedt & Soener, 1955.

142. Hultin, Carl Magnus. EN GAMMAL KNEKTS MINNEN [1808-1814] [An Old Soldier's Memories, 1808-1814]. Edited by Nils Nilén. Lund: Gleerup, 1954.

143. Jansson, Allan. "Karl Johan och Sveriges foersvar" [Bernadotte and the Defense of Sweden]. KARL JOHANS FOERBUNDETS HANDLINGAR (1938-42): 11-31.

144. Johannesson, Bror E. OFREDENS AAR. HISTORISK SKILDRING AV KRIGET I VAESTERBOTTEN 1809 [The War Years: A Historical Portrayal of the War in Vaesterbotten 1809]. Umeaa: n.p., 1959.

145. Johansson, Maans. "En krigsskildring. Maans Johanssons anteckningar fraan finska kriget 1808-1809" [A Portrayal of War: Maans Johansson's Notes from the Finnish War, 1808-1809]. VAERENDSBYGDER (1962): 52-56.

146. Johnson, Seved. "Legend och verklighet kring Gustav IV Adolfs brytning med Napoleon" [Legend and Reality around Gustav IV Adolf's Break with Napoleon]. SVENSK TIDSKRIFT 37 (1950): 460-66.

147. Johnson, Seved. "Neutralitetsfoerbundet 1800 i sitt storpolitiska sammanhang" [The League of Neutrality of 1800 in the Context of Great Power Politics]. HISTORISK TIDSKRIFT 73 (1953): 313-27.

148. Johnson, Seved. SVERIGE OCH STORMAKTERNA 1800-1804. STUDIER I SVENSK HANDELS-OCH UTRIKESPOLITIK [Sweden and the Great Powers, 1800-1804: Studies in Swedish Commercial and Foreign Policy]. Gothenburg: Wettergren & Kerber, 1957.

149. Julku, Kyoesti. "Englannin suunnitelmat ja toimenpioteet Ruotsi-Suomen autamiseksi Suomen sodan aikana vv. 1808-1809" [England's Plans and Measures to Help Sweden-Finland during the Finnish War of 1808-1809]. TURUN HISTORIALLINEN ARKISTO 13 (1956): 102-43.

150. Jutikkala, Eino, and Kauko Pirinen. A HISTORY OF FINLAND. Revised Edition. New York: Praeger, 1974.

151. Juva, Einar W. "Uppfattningar om Finlands foersvar vid boerjan av 1800-talet" [Opinions concerning Finland's Defense at the Beginning of the Nineteenth Century]. DET FOERGYLLDA STAMTRAEDET (1964): 141-57.

152. Juva, Einar W., and Mikko Juva, eds. SUOMEN KANSAN HISTORIA [A History of the Finnish People]. Vol. 3. RUOTSIN AJAN LOPPUKAUSI [The last years of the Swedish period] by Einar W. Juva and Mikko Juva. Helsinki: Otava, 1967. Vol. 4. KANSALLINEN HERAEAEMINEN [The National Awakening] by Mikko Juva. Helsinki: Otava, 1966.

153. Kaeivaeraeinen, I.I. MEZHDUNARODNYE OTNOSHENIIA NA SEVERE EVROPY V NACHALE 19 VEKA I PRISOEDENENIE FINLANDII K ROSSII V 1809 GODU [International Relations in Northern Europe at the Beginning of the Nineteenth Century and the Incorporation of Finland with Russia in 1809]. Petrozavodsk: Petrozavodskii gosudarstvennyi universitet imeni O.V. Kuusinena, 1965.

154. Karlbom, Rolf. "Bernadottes vaeg till Sverige. Tvaa traditionsbildningar om tronfoeljarvalet 1810" [Bernadotte's Path to Sweden: Two Traditions concerning his Election as Crown Prince in 1810]. HISTORISK TIDSKRIFT 99 (1979): 166-93.

155. Kleen, Carl William. DETALJER UR FAELTTAAGET I NORGE 1814 [Details from the Campaign against Norway, 1814]. Stockholm: Militaerlitteratur-Foereningens Foerlag, 1915.

156. Kroon, Allan. "Expeditionen till Vaesterbotten 1809" [The Expedition to Vaesterbotten, 1809]. AKTUELLT OCH HISTORISKT 2 (1954): 69-107.

157. KUNGLIGA FORTIFIKATIONENS HISTORIA [The History of the Royal Fortifications Administration]. Vol. 4: 5. DET FASTA FOERSVARET 1772-1811 OCH FORTIFIKATIONSVAESENDET I FAELT UNDER DENNA TID [The Permanent Defense, 1772-1811, and Fortification Activities in the Field during the Same Period]. Stockholm: n.p., 1962.

158. Kuylenstierna, Oswald. "Sverige-Finlands sista krig 1808-1809" [Sweden-Finland's Last War, 1808-1809]. AARSBOK UTGIVEN AV RIKSFOERENINGEN FOER SVENSKHETENS BEVARANDE I UTLANDET (1931): 69-84.

159. Lauerma, Matti. "La Guerre de 1808-1809." REVUE INTERNATIONALE D'HISTOIRE MILITAIRE 23 (1961): 174-92.

160. Liljencrantz, Axel, ed. "Ett brev om slaget vid Leipzig [1813]" [A Letter about the Battle of Leipzig]. KARL JOHANS FOERBUNDETS HANDLINGAR (1953-57): 48-52.

161. Lilliehoeoek, Christer; Gustaf Berggren; and Erik Hagge. KUNGLIGA VAESTGOETADALS REGEMENTE OCH KUNGLIGA HALLANDS REGEMENTE 1624-1921. REGEMENTETS HISTORIA OCH GLIMTAR UR DESS LIV I FRED OCH KRIG, I HELG OCH SOCKEN [The Royal Vaestgoetadal Regiment and the Royal Halland Regiment, 1624-1921: The History of the Regiment and Glimpses from its Life in Peace and in War.] Stockholm: Seelig, 1964.

162. Loit, Alexander. "Sverige 1808-1809: statskupp eller borgerlig revolution?" [Sweden, 1808-1809: Coup d'Etat or Bourgeois Revolution?]. HISTORISK TIDSKRIFT 93 (1973): 536-43.

163. Lundh, Hans Lennart. KUNGLIGA GOETA ARTILLERIREGEMENTE [The Royal Goeta Artillery Regiment]. Gothenburg: Rundqvists Boktryckeri, 1954.

164. Lundh, Herbert. GUSTAF IV ADOLF OCH SVERIGES UTRIKESPOLITIK, 1801-1804; FOERHISTORIEN TILL SVERIGES DELTAGANDE I DET TREDJE KOALITIONSKRIGET MOT FRANKRIKE [Gustav IV Adolf and Sweden's Foreign Policy, 1801-1804: The Prelude to Sweden's Participation in the Third Coalition War against France]. Uppsala: Appelbergs Boktryckeri, 1926.

165. Mankell, Julius. FAELTTAAGET I NORGE AAR 1814. KRITISK BELYSNING [The Campaign in Norway, 1814: Critical Evaluation]. Stockholm: Carl Suneson, 1887.

166. Meijer, Carl Fredrik. KRIGET EMELLAN SVERIGE OCH DANMARK AAREN 1808 OG 1809 [The War between Sweden and Denmark, 1808 and 1809]. Stockholm: O.L. Lamm, 1867.

167. Moerner, Carl Otto. HUR MARSKALK BERNADOTTE BLEV SVERIGES KRONPRINS. MINNEN FRAAN KURIRFAERDEN 1810 [How Marshal Bernadotte became Crown Prince of Sweden: Memories from Courier Trips in 1810]. Edited by Erik Gamby. Uppsala: Bokgillet, 1960.

168. Monteith, William, ed. NARRATIVE OF THE CONQUEST OF FINLAND BY THE RUSSIANS IN THE YEARS 1808-9. FROM AN UNPUBLISHED WORK BY A RUSSIAN OFFICER OF RANK. London: L. Booth, 1854.

169. Morén, Fredrik Wilhelm. "Naagra problem i samband med tronfoeljdsfraagan 1809" [Some Problems in Connection with the Issue of the Succession in 1809]. HISTORISK TIDSKRIFT 58 (1938): 46-56.

170. Mosséen, Ulf. "Kriget i Norge 1814. Naagra anteckningar till 150-aarsminnet" [The War in Norway, 1814: Some Notes on the Occasion of the 150th Anniversary]. ARTILLERITIDSKRIFTEN 93 (1964): 43-60.

171. Nordensvan, Carl Otto. FINSKA KRIGET 1808-1809 [The Finnish War, 1808-1809]. Stockholm: Albert Bonniers Foerlag, 1898.

172. Odelberg, Wilhelm. SVEABORGS GAATA. EN STUDIE I DEFAITISM [The Mystery of Sveaborg: A Study of Defeatism (1809)]. Stockholm: Gebers, 1958.

173. Olsson, Henrik A. "Carl Johan, Lars von Engestroem och den norska statusfraagan 1810-1814" [Bernadotte, Lars von Engestroem, and the Question of Norway's Status, 1810-1814]. HISTORISK TIDSKRIFT 78 (1958): 377-402.

174. Olsson, Henrik A. "Till fraagan om '1813 aars politik'" [About "The Policy of 1813"]. HISTORISK TIDSKRIFT 79 (1959): 241-65.

175. Osmonsalo, Erkki K. SUOMEN VALLOITUS 1808 [The Conquest of Finland, 1808]. Helsinki: Soederstroem, 1947.

176. Petri, Gustaf, and Herman Levin. REGEMENTETS OEDEN FRAAN STORA NORDISKA KRIGETS SLUT FRAM TILL 1928 [The Fate of the Regiment from the End of the Great Northern War until 1928]. Vol. 4. KUNGLIGA FOERSTA LIVGRENADJAERREGEMENTETS HISTORIA [The History of the First Royal Life Grenadier Regiment]. Stockholm, n.p., 1962.

177. Pohjolan-Pirhonen, Helge. KANSAKUNTA ETSII ITSEAEAEN, 1772-1808 [A Nation in Search of Itself]. Vol. 2. KANSAKUNNAN HISTORIA [The Nation's History]. Edited by Helge Pohjolan-Pirhonen and Veikko Huttunen. Porvoo, Helsinki: Werner Soederstroem, 1970.

178. Reuterskioeld, Carl Axel. "Kiel-Eidvold-Moss." SCANDIA 14 (1941): 74-85.

179. Rosell, Lennart, ed. KUNGLIGA JAEMTLANDS FAELT JAEGARREGEMENTETS HISTORIA [The History of the Royal Jaemtland Jaeger Regiment]. Oestersund: Wisénska Bokhandeln, 1966.

180. Ruuth, Marttii. "Matthias Gottlundin Muistoonmerkinnaet Suomen sodan alkuvaiheista 1808" [Matthias Gottlund's Recollections from the Beginning of the War of 1808]. HISTORIALLINEN ARKISTO 56 (1958): 5-15.

181. Samuelsson, Gunnar. LANTVAERNET 1808-1809 [The Home Guard, 1808-1809]. Uppsala: Almqvist & Wiksell, 1944.

182. Scott, Franklin D. BERNADOTTE AND THE FALL OF NAPOLEON. Cambridge, Mass.: Harvard University Press, 1935.

183. Scott, Franklin D. "The Propaganda Activities of Bernadotte, 1813-1814." ESSAYS IN THE HISTORY OF MODERN EUROPE. Edited by Donald Cope McKay. New York and London: Harper, 1936.

184. Scott, Franklin D. SWEDEN: THE NATION'S HISTORY. Minneapolis: University of Minnesota Press, 1977.

185. Sjoevall, A., and Bengt Bengtsson. "Nelsons 'Victory' i Blekingeskaeren [1810-11]" [Nelson's Victory in the Blekinge Skerrygard]. FATABUREN (1961): 101-12, 237.

186. Skantze, Leif. "Striden vid Bornhoeft den 7 december 1813" [The Battle at Bornhoeft, December 7, 1813]. MEDDELANDEN FRAAN KUNGLIGA ARMEMUSEUM 25 (1964): 52-93.

187. Sparre, G.M. "Fra felttoget mot Norge 1808" [From the Campaign against Norway, 1808]. NORSK MILITAERT TIDSSKRIFT 64 (1901): 48-77, 108-33.

188. Stade, Arne. "Gustav IV Adolf och Norge 1798 och 1801. Till fraagan om den svenska utrikespolitikens karaktaer och maalsaettning 1796-1803" [Gustav IV Adolf and Norway, 1798 and 1801: On the Character and Goals of Swedish Foreign Policy, 1796-1803]. HISTORISK TIDSKRIFT 75 (1955): 353-83.

189. SUOMEN HISTORIALLINEN BIBLIOGRAFIA [Bibliography of Finnish History]. Helsinki: Suomen historiallinen seura, 1940 to present.

190. SVENSKA FLOTTANS HISTORIA. OERLOGSFLOTTAN I ORD OCH BILD FRAAN DESS GRUNDLAEGGNING UNDER GUSTAV VASA FRAM TILL VAARA DAGAR [The History of the Swedish Navy: The Fleet in Words and Pictures from its Formation under Gustav Vasa up to Our Days]. Vol. 2. 1680-1814. Malmoe: Allhems Foerlag, 1943.

191. SVENSK HISTORISK BIBLIOGRAFI [Bibliography of Swedish History].
     Stockholm: Svenska historiska foereningen, 1907 to present.

192. Svensson, Sven G. GATTJINATRAKTATEN 1799. STUDIER I GUSTAV IV
     ADOLFS UTRIKESPOLITIK 1796-1800 [The Gattjina Treaties of 1799:
     Studies in the Foreign Policy of Gustav IV Adolf, 1796-1800].
     Uppsala: Almqvist & Wiksell, 1952.

193. SVERIGES KRIG AAREN 1808 OCH 1809 [Sweden's Wars, 1808 and
     1809]. Stockholm: Generalstabens krigshistoriska avdelning,
     1890-1922. 9 parts.

194. Taube, Gurli. SVENSK REGIMENTSHISTORISK BIBLIOGRAFI
     [Bibliography of Swedish Regimental Histories]. Uppsala:
     Almqvist & Wiksell, 1949.

195. Tidander, L.G.T. "Kronobergs regementes deltagande i 1808-1809
     aars faelttaag" [The Participation of the Kronoberg Regiment in
     the Campaign of 1808-1809]. KUNGLIGA KRIGSVETENSKAPSAKADEMIENS
     HANDLINGAR OCH TIDSKRIFT (1877): 563-67, 585-98.

196. Tingsten, Lars. GUSTAF WILHELM AF TIBELL. HUVUDDRAGEN AV HANS
     LIV, HANS VERKSAMHET SAASOM GENERALADJUTANT FOER ARMEN OCH HANS
     AVSKEDANDE, TILLIKA EN STUDIE AV SVERIGES KRIGFOERING AAR 1808
     [Gustaf Wilhelm af Tibell: Main Aspects of His Life, His
     Activities as Adjutant General of the Army and His Dismissal,
     Being at the Same Time a Study of Sweden's Conduct of the War in
     1808]. Stockholm: Militaerlitteratur foereningen, 1924.

197. Tingsten, Lars. HUVUDDRAGEN AV SVERIGES KRIG OCH YTTRE POLITIK
     AUGUSTI 1813-JANUARI 1814 [Main Aspects of Sweden's War and
     Foreign Policy, August 1813-January 1814]. Stockholm: P.A.
     Norstedt & Soener, 1924.

198. Tingsten, Lars. HUVUDDRAGEN AV SVERIGES KRIG OCH YTTRE POLITIK
     FEBRUARI-AUGUSTI 1814 (FRAAN KIEL TILL MOSS) [Main Aspects of
     Sweden's War and Foreign Policy, February-August 1814 (From Kiel
     to Moss)]. Stockholm: P.A. Norstedt & Soener, 1925.

199. Tingsten, Lars. HUVUDDRAGEN AV SVERIGES YTTRE POLITIK.
     KRIGSFOERBEREDELSER M.M. FRAAN OCH MED FREDSSLUTEN 1809-1810
     TILL MITTEN AF JULI 1813 [Main Aspects of Sweden's Foreign
     Policy: Preparations for War, etc., from the Conclusion of
     Peace 1809-1810 to the Middle of July 1813]. Stockholm: P.A.
     Norstedt & Soener, 1923.

200. Tingsten, Lars. "Konung Gustaf IV Adolfs militaerpolitiska och
     militaera synpunkter aaren 1808 och 1809" [King Gustav IV
     Adolf's Security and Military Views in 1808 and 1809], KUNGLIGA
     KRIGSVETENSKAPS-AKADEMIENS HANDLINGAR OCH TIDSKRIFT (1932):
     178-86.

201. Tommila, Paeivioe. LA FINLANDE DANS LA POLITIQUE EUROPEENE
     1809-1815. Helsinki: Suomen historiallinen seura, 1962.

202. Trulsson, Sven G. BRITISH AND SWEDISH POLICIES AND STRATEGIES IN THE BALTIC AFTER THE PEACE OF TILSIT IN 1807: A STUDY OF DECISION-MAKING. Lund: Liber Laeromedel-Gleerup, 1976.

203. Varenius, Otto. CARL JOHAN OCH DANMARK 1814 [Bernadotte and Denmark, 1814]. Uppsala: Humanistiska vetenskapssamfundet, 1938.

204. Waller, Sture M. "Aabomoetet 1812. Ett foerbisett aktstycke" [The Aabo Meeting of 1812: An Overlooked Document]. SCANDIA 21 (1951-52): 61-71.

205. Waller, Sture M. AABOMOETET 1812 OCH DE SVENSKA KRIGSRUSTNINGARNAS INSTAELLANDE [The Aabo Meeting of 1812 and the Discontinuation of Sweden's Arming Herself for War]. Lund: C.W.K. Gleerup, 1951.

206. Waller, Sture M. "Bernadotte och Gustaf Lagerbjelke i augusti 1810" [Bernadotte and Gustaf Lagerbjelke, August 1810]. HISTORISK TIDSKRIFT 70 (1950): 300-308.

207. Waller, Sture M. "Ett aaterfunnet dokument om Karl Johans foerhandlingar med Napoleon vaaren 1812" [A Rediscovered Document concerning Bernadotte's Negotiations with Napoleon in the Spring of 1812]. HISTORISK TIDSKRIFT 66 (1946): 169-71.

208. Waller, Sture M. "Finska armêns retraett fraan Tavastehus till Oesterbotten vaaren 1808" [The Retreat of the Finnish Army from Tavastehus to Oesterbotten in the Spring of 1808]. SCANDIA 19 (1948-49): 63-115.

209. Waller, Sture M. GEORG CARL VON DOEBELN. STUDIER I SVERIGES MILITAERISKA OCH POLITISKA HISTORIA 1808-1813 [Georg Carl von Doebeln: Studies in Sweden's Military and Political History, 1808-1813]. Lund: P. Lindstedts Universitets Bokhandel, 1947.

210. Waller, Sture M. "Karl Johans brev till kejsar Napoleon den 20 (23) mars 1813 och dess publicering" [Bernadotte's Letter to Emperor Napoleon of 20 (23) March 1813, and its Publication]. HISTORISK TIDSKRIFT 68 (1948): 139-45.

211. Waller, Sture M. "Karl Johans yttre politik och syften 1812-1813. En oeversikt" [Bernadotte's Foreign Policy and Goals, 1812-1813: A Survey]. SCANDIA 20 (1950): 128-68.

212. Weibull, Joergen. CARL JOHAN OCH NORGE 1810-1814. UNIONSPLANERNA OCH DERAS FOERVERKLIGANDE [Bernadotte and Norway, 1810-1814: The Plans for Union and their Realization]. Lund: Gleerup, 1957.

213. Willers, Uno. SVENSK SJOEHISTORISK LITTERATUR 1800-1943. BIBLIOGRAFI [Swedish Naval History Literature, 1800-1943: Bibliography]. Stockholm: Sjoehistoriska samfundet, 1956.

214. Wolkonsky, Grégoire. "Napoleon et la Suède (1810-1813)." REVUE
     D'HISTOIRE DIPLOMATIQUE 72 (1958): 304-12.

215. Wolkonsky, Grégoire. "Ryska trupper under svenske kronprinsens
     oeverbefaell 1813" [Russian Troops under the Command of the
     Swedish Crown Prince, 1813]. KARL JOHANS FOERBUNDETS HANDLINGAR
     (1953-57): 38-47.

216. Zakharov, G. RUSSKO-SHVEDSKAIA VOINA 1808-1809 GG. [The
     Russo-Swedish War of 1808-1809]. Moscow: Voenizdat, 1940.

CHAPTER XVIII

HUNGARY

Béla K. Király, Professor Emeritus and Director,
Brooklyn College Program on Society in Change

During the era of French Revolutionary and Napoleonic Wars
Hungary had partially separate national defense establishments, no
independent diplomatic service, and only limited military policies.
In the spheres of international relations and national defense,
Hungary was an integral part of the Habsburg Empire. The
Kriegsrat, an imperial institution situated at Vienna, was
responsible directly to the emperor and king for the organization of
defense and conduct of wars. Yet Hungary exercised a non-negligible
effect on the issues of national defense with regard to finances,
supply, and recruiting, all having been within the prerogatives of
Hungary's national legislative body--the Diet. The general
political, social, and financial framework of the Hungarian armed
forces is described by Béla K. Király (41). Other major works which
place Hungarian society, national defense, and warfare--in the
Napoleonic era--into historical context are in reverse order of the
date of their publication. Zsigmond Pál Pach's (chairman of the
editorial board) MAGYARORSZAG TORTENETE [A History of Hungary] (55);
Gyula Mérei and Károly Vörös's MAGYARORSZAG TORTENETE, 1790-1848 [The
History of Hungary, 1790-1848] (54); and Bálint Hóman and Gyula
Szekfü's MAGYAR TORTENET [Hungarian History] (31). A ten-volume
study edited by Sándor Szilágyi, A MAGYAR NEMZET TORTENETE [A History
of the Hungarian Nation], includes volume eight of MAGYARORSZAG
TORTENETE III. KAROLYTOL A BECSI KONGRESSZUSIG (1711-1815) [The
History of Hungary from Charles III to the Vienna Congress
(1711-1815)] (68) which is devoted to this period.

In the entire territory of the Kingdom of Hungary (the lands of
the Crown of St. Stephen), three politico-military jurisdictions
existed in the era under consideration. In the kingdom proper (inner
Hungary), the Hungarian standing army--an integral part of the
Habsburg armed forces--functioned according to Hungarian basic laws
on national defense passed by the Diet in 1711 (55). This army was
under the direct supervision of the monarch but recruiting, finances,
and supply were under the jurisdiction of the Hungarian Diet. Only
some of these regiments were stationed in Hungary, others were
located in the hereditary provinces of the Habsburg dynasty. On the
other hand, some imperial regiments which were not part of the
Hungarian standing army were garrisoned in Hungary. The second
politico-military unit of the Kingdom of Hungary was the Grand
Principality of Transylvania. Only imperial armed forces were
garrisoned all over this province. Finally, the southern regions of
Hungary (Croatia) were segregated from the political entity of the
Kingdom and as Military Borders, were directly controlled by the
Kriegsrat. Gunther E. Rothenberg analyzed this area in THE MILITARY
BORDER IN CROATIA (62).

Hungary's contribution in men, material, and finances to the
Habsburg war effort is a subject wholly misrepresented in Western
historiography. The general, and incorrect view, is that Hungary
contributed to the war efforts much less than its size and wealth

would have warranted. The mistake originates in the fact that the dynasty collected two kinds of incomes from the Kingdom of Hungary. One was the contributio (war tax) which was under the jurisdiction of the Hungarian Diet and was precisely recorded. The other was the regaliae, an ancient privilege of the king of Hungary which allowed the monarch to collect all the revenues of mines, crown lands, tariffs, and many other sources. These funds were not under the jurisdiction of the diet and were not recorded as Hungarian contributions to the Habsburg treasury, although indeed they were. According to recent research, the unrecorded Habsburg incomes from Hungary (regaliae) amounted to a sum much above the total of the contributio. The general historiography takes into account the war taxes alone and disregards the regaliae, thereby wholly underestimating the factual contribution of Hungary to the Habsburg war finances.

During the Napoleonic wars Hungary constituted 55 percent of the Habsburg lands (Transylvania and the Military Borders included). The Kingdom (Transylvania and the Military Borders excluded) contributed 42 million Florins to the Habsburg Treasury in 1809--a ratio basically constant during the Napoleonic era--approximately one-third of the Habsburg budget, domestic and military expenses combined. But the domestic budget of the Kingdom of Hungary was secured from other sources. This disparity combined with the regaliae system made Hungary a land which contributed to the Habsburg finances much more than her real share would have been.

The utilization of Hungary's manpower was no less intensive than her financial contribution was. Not taking into account the major contribution of Transylvania and the Military Borders, inner Hungary contributed in two ways to Habsburg manpower needs. One was the enlistments for the standing army, the other was the nemesi felkelés (insurrectio or noble levy). The 10.4 million population of inner Hungary yielded 110,000 men for the standing army, one-third of the entire Habsburg force.

The traditional Hungarian national defense force as already mentioned was the noble levy. Every able-bodied adult male nobleman in Hungary had an obligation to serve under arms in case of war if the king announced and the Diet endorsed the insurrectio; that is the calling to arms of the personalis insurrectio (noble levy). During the Napoleonic era the noble population of Hungary amounted to a total of 400,000 persons of whom 197,616 were males and thus the manpower reservoir for the levy. Every noble family had to provide one mounted, armed male and pay his expenses. Poverty-stricken lesser nobles served in the infantry and their expenses were covered by the counties. The disabled had to secure a substitute and pay his expenses.

The nobility was responsible for outfitting the portalis insurrectio, another kind of military force. In this system each porta (larger landed property designed as a tax unit) had to provide six equipped infantry men and two mounted soldiers. In 1805 the estimated yield of the portalis insurrectio was 51,000 men, while the contingents of the personalis insurrectio during the Napoleonic era averaged between 34,000 and 42,000 armed men.

During this period the noble levy was called to arms four times--in 1797, 1800, 1805, and 1809. Only in 1809 did the levy see battle (10, 28, 29). In 1797 and 1800 the levy only attained battle

readiness when the war ended.   In 1805 the organizational work was
not yet completed when the war ended.   This fact and other
circumstances generated a general derogatory view of the noble levy.
However, the facts do not warrant an unquestionable condemnation of
this system.   The system, contrary to allegations, was not the
nobility's design to secure tax-exempt status on the basis of
national defense services, which they really never performed.   The
fact is that the levy was indeed an obsolete institution, but the
Hungarian nobility made repeated efforts to modernize the levy.
Plans were drafted to maintain a permanent organizational structure
with a certain number of professional officers, to prepare up-to-date
mobilization plans, to store modern weapons, and to train the noble
youth periodically (26).   This system is comparable to the current
American National Guard system.   If the dynasty had endorsed these
plans, the Hungarian noble levy would have become an efficient
auxiliary force to the professional imperial standing army.   However,
the Habsburg dynasty expected that a modernized noble levy could have
become a Hungarian national army under the jurisdiction of the
Hungarian Diet.   The emperor therefore prevented all reforms but did
not stop from blaming the Hungarian noble levy for its obsolescence,
thereby artificially creating a vicious circle.

Partly because of the political significance of the Hungarian
noble levy and partly because it was the truly national defense
force, albeit obsolete, substantial literature exists on the noble
levy.   On the other hand, because the Hungarian standing army was
nothing more than regiments manned and paid for by Hungary but
otherwise an integral part of the Habsburg imperial army, the
historiography of this part of Hungary's armed forces is poor.
However, the general historiography of the Habsburg army contains
great amounts of material on the Hungarian regiments.   Chapter 10 of
Professor Gunther E. Rothenberg's study on the Austrian Army (62)
should therefore be consulted to gain the full picture.
Consequently, the historiography of the Hungarian standing army only
contains histories of individual regiments, personalities, and a very
few more general works.

GENERAL WORKS

The most comprehensive publication on Hungarian military history
during the Napoleonic era, WAR AND SOCIETY IN EAST CENTRAL EUROPE,
was edited by Béla K. Király.   Volume 4, EAST CENTRAL EUROPEAN
SOCIETY AND WAR IN THE ERA OF REVOLUTIONS, 1775-1856 (43),
concentrates on the Napoleonic period.

Other publications include those on Hungarian mounted soldiers
(48); the Hungarian Standing Army--a part of the Habsburg Army (65);
Napoleon's effects on Hungary (1-3, 21, 42, 46, 69, 73); Hungarians
and Hungarian regiments in the Habsburg army (9, 14, 15, 17, 18, 20,
22, 30, 33, 38, 41, 47, 51, 53, 58-61, 66, 70, 72, 74); the Hungarian
noble levy (3, 7, 10, 19, 23-27, 32, 33, 44, 50); Population
statistics (57, 63); and press accounts of the French Revolutionary
and Napoleonic Wars (67).

BIBLIOGRAPHIES

A most comprehensive bibliography, by Domokos Kosáry, is
BEVEZETES MAGYARORSZAG TORTENETENEK FORRASAIBA ES IRODALMABA [An
Introduction into the Sources and Historiography of Hungary's
History] (45). Volume 1 can be utilized for bibliographies (pp.
33-131) and archives (pp. 131-772). In volume 2 (pp. 398-628) and
volume 3 (pp. 117-128) useful archival bibliographies can be found.

ARCHIVAL SOURCES

In addition to the archives in Vienna on which Professor
Rothenberg's essay above should be consulted, the main archives are
the Magyar Országos Levéltár (Hungarian National Archives) and the
Hadtörténelmi Intézet Levéltára (The Archives of the Institute of
Military History) in Budapest. There are a multitude of archives in
Hungary which contain documents of local significance. A list of
these articles can be located in Kosáry's BEVEZETES (Vol. 1, pp.
131-772) (45). This same volume also includes a useful list of
archives in the countries neighboring Hungary which contain related
material (Vol. 1, pp. 773-776).

PUBLISHED DOCUMENTS

Kálmán Benda has edited A MAGYAR JAKOBINUS MOZGALOM IRATAI [The
Papers of the Hungarian Jacobins] (5) and Sándor Domanovszky has
directed the publication of JOZSEF NADOR IRATAI [The Papers of
Palatine Joseph] (15). Károly Kecskeméti was the editor of the two-
volume study SOURCES FRANCAISES RELATIVE A L'HISTOIRE DE HONGRIE (40)
which appeared in the series "Fontes rerum historiae hungaricae in
archivis extraneis" in Brussels between 1960-1963. The first volume
is entitled TEMOIGNAGES FRANCAIS SUR LA HONGRIE A L'EPOGUE DE
NAPOLEON, 1802-1809 and the second volume includes notes and reports
on eighteenth century Hungary. Hermann Hüffer also edited several
volumes of documents under the following titles: QUELLEN ZUR
GESCHICHTE DES KRIEGES VON 1799 (35), QUELLEN ZUR GESCHICHTE DES
KRIEGES VON 1800 (36), DER KRIEG DES JAHRES 1799 UND DIE ZWEITE
KOALITION (34) which provide valuable documentation for the period.
See also Archduke Karl's work (38) and the correspondence of Ferenc
Kazinczy (39).

MEMOIRS, JOURNALS, EYEWITNESS ACCOUNTS

Memoirs are available on the French occupation of the western
parts of Hungary (4, 7), and on the military reforms needed to resist
Napoleon (37). The memoirs of Sándor Kisfaludy, the poet and
aide-de-camp of Archduke Joseph, are invaluable on the Hungarian
noble levy (19). Equally important are the memoirs of Hungary's
leading intellectual, Ferenc Kazinczy (39). A hussar officer's
diaries during the 1812 campaign (64) is also an important eyewitness
account.

SPECIALIZED WORKS

The Campaign of 1796-1797 (11, 12, 56, 66), the Campaign of
1805-1806 (13, 27), and the Campaign of 1809 (3, 19, 25, 32, 33, 42,

44) are examined in numerous studies. The Battle of Györ [Raab], June 14, 1809 (10, 28, 29), and the Campaign of 1812-1813 (8, 16, 49, 58-60, 64, 70, 71) are treated at length, but Field Marshal Hadik (51) has attracted little attention.

FUTURE RESEARCH

Hungarian historiography on the Napoleonic period is rich in detailed studies. Alas, a comprehensive monograph on Hungarian participation in the French Revolutionary and Napoleonic Wars has yet to be published. In western languages, little is available on the Hungarian contribution to the Habsburg war effort or the impact of the French intervention in Hungary. Yet, scholars with some facility in the Magyar tongue will find scores of topics awaiting exploration.

BIBLIOGRAPHY: HUNGARY

1. Balázs, Eva H. NOTES SUR L'HISTOIRE DE BONAPARTISME EN HONGARIE. "Nouvelles études hongroise." Budapest: Akadémiai Kiadó, 1970.

2. BATSANYI JANOS OSSZES MUVEI [The Collected Works of János Batsányi]. Vol. 4. DER KAMPF. Edited by Endre Zsindeley. Budapest: Akadémiai Kiadó, 1967.

3. Bay, Ferenc. NAPOLEON MAGYARORSZAGON [Napoleon in Hungary]. Budapest: Officina, 1941.

4. DIE BELAGERUNG VON PRESSBURG IM JAHRE 1809. DEN MEMORIEN EINES OFFIZIERS NACH EZAHLT. Pozsony, 1839.

5. Benda, Kálmán. A MAGYAR JAKOBINUSOK MOZGALOM IRATAI [Papers of the Hungarian Jacobins]. Budapest: Akadémiai Kiadó, 1952. 3 vols.

6. Benda, Kálmán. "Penzügyi válság és devalváció Magyarországon 1811-ben" [Financial Crisis and Devaluation in Hungary in 1811]. EMBERBARAT VAGY HAZAFI [Philanthropist or Patriot] 1 (1978): 335-47.

7. Benda, Kálmán, and Géza Erszegi. "Magyarővár és Moson megy. az 1809-es francia megszállás alatt Szöllösy Pál naplófeljegyzései" [The City of Magyarővár and Moson County during the French Occupation in 1809. The Diaries of Pál Szöllösy]. HADTORTENELMI KOZLEMENYEK [Journal of Military History] 19 (1972): 346-53.

8. Berkő, István. "Magyarok Napóleon Grande armeéjában" [Hungarians in Napoleon's Grande Armée]. MAGYAR KATONAI KOZLONY [Hungarian Military Journal] (1940).

9. Berkő, István. "A magyarság a régi hadseregben" [Hungarians in the Old Army]. Appendix to the Nos. 11-12 of the MAGYAR KATONAI KOZLONY [Hungarian Military Journal] (1926).

10. Bodnár, István. "A györi csata 1809 jun. 14-én" [The Battle of Györ on June 14]. HADTORTENELMI KOZLEMENYEK [Journal of Military History] 10 (1897): 388-433, 484-536.

11. Breit, József. A MAGYAR NEMZET HADTORTENELME [The Military History of the Hungarian Nation]. Vol. 20. A FRANCIA HABORUK IDOSZAKA, 1792-1815 [The Era of the French Wars, 1792-1815]. Budapest: Grill, 1926-42.

12. Darvas, István. "Szuvorov hadai Magyarországon" [The Armies of Suvorov in Hungary]. SZAZADOK [Centuries] 83 (1949): 282-91.

13. Domanovszky, Sándor. "Francia emisszáriusok Magyarországon, 1806-ban" [French Emissaries in Hungary in 1806]. BECSI MAGYAR INTEZET EVKONYVE 2 (1932): 220-58.

14. Domanovszky, Sándor. JOZSEF NADOR ELETE [Life of Palatine Joseph]. Budapest: Egyetemi Nyomda, 1944.

15. Domanovszky, Sándor, ed. JOZSEF NADOR IRATAI [The Papers of Palatine Joseph]. Budapest: Egyetemi Nyomda, 1925-35. 3 vols.

16. Dormándy, Géza. "Magyar csapatok az 1813. dresdai csatában" [Hungarian Troops in the Battle of Dresden in 1813]. HADTÖRTENELMI KOZLEMENYEK [Journal of Military History] 15 (1914): 76-113, 262-81, 442-57.

17. Ernst, Georg. GESCHICHTE DES K.K. NEUNTEN HUSZAREN-REGIMENT FUERST FRANZ LICHTENSTEIN. Vienna: Kaiserlich-Königliche Hof- und Staats Druckerei, 1862.

18. Fiedler, Rudolf, freiherr von. GESCHICHTE DES K. UND K. INFANTERIE REGIMENTS FREIHERR VON APPEL. Erlau: In Selbstverlage des Regimentes, 1898.

19. Gálos, Rezsö, ed. KISFALUDY SANDOR HATRAHAGYOTT MUNKAI [Papers Left Behind by Sándor Kisfaludy]. Györ: Kisfaludy Irodalmi Kör, 1931. (Contains the history of the noble levy of 1809.)

20. Gárdonyi, Albert. "Fedák Mihály ezredes a katonai Mária Terézia-rend vitéze" [Colonel Mihály Fedák the Knight of the Maria Theresa Military Order]. HADTORTENELMI KOZLEMENYEK 19 (1918): 50-58.

21. Gesmey, Borbála. LES DEBUTS DES ETUDES FRANCAISES EN HONGRIE, 1789-1830. Szeged: Etudes françaises; publiées par l'Institut français de Université de Szeged, 1938.

22. Gömöry, Gusztáv. "Ausztria hadereje az 1792-töl 1866-ig folytatott háborúkban" [The Armed Forces of Austria in the Wars Waged from 1792 to 1866]. HADTORTENELMI KOZLEMENYEK [Journal of Military History] 6 (1893): 394-411.

23. Gömöry, Gusztáv. "A magyar nemesi felkelés, 1797, és 1800-1801" [The Hungarian Noble Levy in 1797 and 1800-1801]. HADTORTENELMI KOZLEMENYEK [Journal of Military History] 1 (1888): 47-63.

24. Gömöry, Gusztáv. "Az 1809-i nagyar nemesi felkelés" [The Hungarian Noble Levy of 1809]. HADTORTENELMI KOZLEMENYEK [Journal of Military History] 2 (1889): 79-100, 223-43, 484-501.

25. Gömöry, Károly, ed. "Des Erzherzogs Palatinus K.K. Hoheit, on die Insurrections-Armee des Adels von Ungarn, Buda, 1809." HADTORTENELMI KOZLEMENYEK [Journal of Military History] 6 (1894): 110-32.

26. Gyalókai, Jenö. "A magyar nemesiinsurrectio reformtervei
    1797-töl 1809-ig" [The Reform Plans of the Hungarian Noble Levy
    from 1797 to 1809]. SZAZADOK 59 (1925): 126-59.

27. Gyalókai, Jenö. "A magyar nemesiinsurrectio 1805-ben."
    HADTORTENELMI KOZLEMENYEK [Journal of Military History] 26
    (1925): 254-310.

28. Hertelendy, K. NEMES FELKELO EZREDEK AZ 1809-IK EVI GYORI
    CSATABAN [Regiments of the Noble Levy in the Battle of Györ in
    the Year of 1809]. Veszprém, 1859.

29. Hohenegger, Lörinc. GYOR OSTROMANAK NAPLO KONYVE, 1809 JUN.
    13-24 [The Diary of the Siege of Györ, June 13-24, 1809].
    TUDOMANYOS GYUJTEMENY [Journal of the Sciences] 2 (1820):
    47-89.

30. Hold, Alexander. GESCHICHTE DES K.K. 48 LINIEN-INFANTERIE
    REGMINENTES VON SEINER ZWEITEN ERRICHTUNG IM JAHRE 1798.
    Vienna: Seidel, 1875.

31. Hóman, Bálint, and Gyula Szekfü. MAGYAR TORTENET [Hungarian
    History]. Budapest: Egyetemi Nyomda, 1941-43. 5 vols.

32. [Hormayr zu Hortenburg, Josef, freiherr von]. DAS HEER VON
    INNEROESTERREICH UNTER DEN BEFEHLEN DES ERZHERZOGS JOHANN IM
    KRIEGE VON 1809 IN ITALIEN, TIROL UND UNGARN. DURCHGEHENDS AUS
    OFFIZIELLEN QUELLEN. Leipzig: Brockhaus, 1817.

33. Horváth, István. A MAGYAR RENDES KATONASAGNAK ES FELKELO NEMES
    SEREGNEK NEHANY VITEZ ES DITSO TETTEI AZ 1809-DIKI ESZTENDEI
    HABORUBAN [Some Gallant and Glorious Deeds of the Hungarian
    Regular Military and the Noble Levy in the War of the Year
    1809]. Pest, 1812.

34. Hüffer, Hermann. DER KRIEG DES JAHRES 1799 UND DIE ZWEITE
    KOALITION. Gotha: Perthes, 1904-5. 2 vols.

35. Hüffer, Hermann, ed. QUELLEN ZUR GESCHICHTE DER KRIEGE VON
    1799. Leipzig: Teubner, 1900.

36. Hüffer, Hermann, ed. QUELLEN ZUR GESCHICHTE DES KRIEGES VON
    1800. Leipzig: Teubner, 1901.

37. [Joseph, Palatine, archduke]. FREIMUETHIGE GEDANKEN EINES
    UNGARISCHEN PATRIOTEN UEBER DIE VERBESSERUNG DES DEFENSIONS
    SYSTEMS SEINES VATERLANDES. (The Papers of Archduke Joseph
    edited by Domanovszky). Vol. 4. Document No. III, 254-321.

38. Karl, archduke of Austria. "Vortrag über die Entlassung der auf
    die Kriegsdauer zu den ungarischen Regimenten gestellten
    Mannschaften" [dated June 14, 1801]. ERZHERZOG KARL'S
    AUSGEWAHLTE SCHRIFTEN 5 (1895): 429-32.

39. Kazinczy, Ferenc. KAZINCZY FERENC LEVELEZESE [The Correspondence of Ferenc Kazinczy]. Budapest: Magyar Tudomànyos Akadēmia, 1890-1960. 23 vols.

40. Kecskemēti, Kāroly, ed. SOURCES FRANCAISES RELATIVE A L'HISTOIRE DE HONGRIE. Vol. 1. TEMOIGNAGES FRANCAIS SUR LA HONGRIE A L'EPOQUE DE NAPOLEON, 1808-09. Vol. 2. NOTES ET RAPPORTS FRANCAIS SUR LA HONGRIE AU XVIIIème SIECLE. Brussels: Institut Imre Nagy de Sciēnces Politiques, 1960-63.

41. Kirāly, Bēla K. HUNGARY IN THE LATE EIGHTEENTH CENTURY: THE DECLINE OF ENLIGHTENED DESPOTISM. New York: Columbia University Press, 1969.

42. Kirāly, Bēla K. "Napoleon's Proclamation of 1809 and its Hungarian Echo." INTELLECTUAL AND SOCIAL DEVELOPMENTS IN THE HABSBURG EMPIRE FROM MARIA THERESA TO THE FIRST WORLD WAR. Edited by Stanley B. Winters, and Joseph Held. New York: Eastern European Quarterly, distributed by Columbia University Press, 1975.

43. Kirāly, Bēla K., ed. WAR AND SOCIETY IN EAST CENTRAL EUROPE. Vol. 4. EAST CENTRAL EUROPEAN SOCIETY AND WAR IN THE ERA OF REVOLUTIONS, 1775-1856. New York: Social Science Monographs, distributed by Columbia University Press, 1983.

44. Kiss, Istvān Rugonfalvi. AZ UTOLSO NEMESI FELKELES SZAZADIK EVFORDULOJA EMLEKERE [The Last Hungarian Noble Insurrection]. Budapest: Gy. Benkö, 1909-11. 2 vols.

45. Kosāry, Domokos. BEVEZETES MAGYARORSZAG TORTENETENEK FORRASAIBA ES IRODALMABA [An Introduction into the Sources and Historiography of Hungary's History]. Budapest: Müvelt Nep, 1954-70. 3 vols.

46. Kosāry, Domokos. "Napoleōn et la Hongrie." STUDIA HISTORICA (1980): 130 ff.

47. Maendl, Maximilian. GESCHICHTE DES K. UND K. INFANTERIE-REGIMENTS NR. 51. Vol. 1. (1702-1802) Klusenburg: Verlag des Regimensts, 1897.

48. A MAGYAR LOVASKATONA EZER EVENEK TORTENETE [A History of the Hungarian Mounted Soldier's Thousand Years]. Budapest, n.d.

49. Mārki, Sāndor. "Magyarok az 1812-ki orosz Hadjaratban" [Hungarians in the Russian Campaign of the Year 1812]. HAZANK [Our Fatherland] 5 (1886): 243-54.

50. Markō, Arpād. A CS. ES KIR. 34. MAGYAR GYALOGEZRED TORTENETE, 1734-1918 [A History of the Imperial Royal Hungarian 34th Infantry Regiment, 1734-1918]. Budapest: Akadēmiai Kiadō, 1937.

51. Markó, Arpád. FIELDMARSHAL COUNT ANDREAS HADIK FUTAKI.
    Budapest: Athenaeum, 1944.

52. Markó, Arpád. "A francia forradalom és a napóleoni idök magyar
    katonája" [The Hungarian Soldier of the French Revolutionary and
    Napoleonic Era]. HADTORTENELMI KOZLEMENYEK [Journal of Military
    History] 40 (1939): 34-73.

53. Markó, Arpád. "Insurrectió és állandó hadsereg" [Noble Levy and
    the Standing Army]. Vol. 4. MAGYAR MUVELODESTORTENET [History
    of Hungarian Culture].   Edited by Sándor Domanovszky.
    Budapest: Magyar Történelmi Társulat, 1932-42.

54. Mérei, Gyula, and Károly Vörös.   MAGYARORSZAG TORTENETE,
    1790-1848 [The History of Hungary, 1790-1848].   Budapest:
    Akadémiai Kiadó, 1980. Vols. 5/1, 2.

55. Pach, Zsigmond Pál, ed.   MAGYARORSZAG TORTENETE [A History of
    Hungary].   Budapest: Akadémiai Kiadó, 1976. 10 vols.

56. Palóczi, Edgár.   "Az elsö orosz sereg hazánkban, 1799 maj.
    10-jun. 10" [The First Russian Army in Our Country from May 10
    to June 10, 1799]. PESTI HARLAP [Pest Journal] 279 (24 Nov.
    1912).

57. Pápai, Béla. MAGYARORSZAG NEPESSEGE A FEUDALIZMUS MEGEROSODESE
    ES BOMLASA IDEJEN, 1711-1867 [The Population of Hungary during
    the Stabilization and Disintegration of Feudalism, 1711-1867].
    Budapest: Akadémiai Kiadó, 1957.

58. Pilch, Jenö. "A cs. és k. 2. sz. magyar gyalogezred az 1813.
    évi drezdai csatában" [The Imperial and Royal Hungarian 2d
    Infantry Regiment in the Battle of Dresden in 1813].
    HADTORTENELMI KOZLEMENYEK [Journal of Military History] 14
    (1913): 467-69.

59. Pilch, Jenö. "A 37. Számú József föherceg nevét viselö magyar
    gyalogezred a leipzigi csatában" [The Hungarian 37th Infantry
    Regiment Bearing the Name of Archduke Joseph in the Battle of
    Leipzig].   HADTORTENELMI KOZLEMENYEK [Journal of Military
    History] 14 (1913): 286-88.

60. Pilch, Jenö.   "Magyar csapatok az 1812. évi hadjáratban"
    [Hungarian Troops in the Campaign of the Year 1812].
    HADTORTENELMI KOZLEMENYEK [Journal of Military History] 14
    (1913): 1-43, 195-233, 395-434.

61. Pizzighelli, Cajetan. GESCHICHTE DES K.U.K. HUSAREN-REGIMENTES
    FRIEDRICH LEOPOLD PRINZ VON PREUSSEN NR. 2., 1742-1905.
    Kronstadt: Selbstverlag des Regimentes, 1905.

62. Rothenberg, Gunther E.   THE MILITARY BORDER IN CROATIA,
    1740-1811. Chicago: University of Chicago Press, 1966.

63. Söllner, I. STATISTIK DES GROSSFUERSTENTHUMS SIEBENBUERGEBN. Hermannstadt (Sibiu), 1856.

64. Suhay, Imre. "Egy magyar huszártiszt feljegyzései I. Napoleon 1812 évi hadjáratáról" [The Notes of a Hungarian Hussar Officer on Napoleon I's Campaign of 1812]. HADTORTENELMI KOZLEMENYEK [Journal of Military History] 42 (1941): 103-14.

65. Szabó, Dezsö. "Az állandó hadsereg beczikkelyezésének története III. Károly korában 1708-1715" [A History of Enactment of Laws during the Reign of Charles III on the Standing Army, 1708-1715]. HADTORTENELMI KOZLEMENYEK [Journal of Military History] 11 (1910): 23-51, 349-87, 549-87.

66. Szendrei, János. A BLANKENSTEIN HUSZAROK A WURZBURGI UTKOZETBEN, 1796 SZEPTEMBER 3. [The Blankenstein Hussars in the Battle of Würzburg on 3 September 1796]. HADTORTENELMI KOZLEMENYEK [Journal of Military History] 11 (1910): 260.

67. Szendrei, János. "Egykorú hirlapi tudósitások a francia háborúk idejéböl, 1800-1801" [Account of Contemporary Journals in the Era of French Wars, 1800-1801]. HADTORTENELMI KOZLEMENYEK [Journal of Military History] 12 (1911): 585-90; 13 (1912): 104-9.

68. Szilágyi, Sándor, ed. A MAGYAR NEMZET TORTENETE [A History of the Hungarian Nation]. Vol. 8. MAGYARORSZAG TORTENETE III. KAROLYTOL A BECSI KONGRESSZUSIG (1711-1815) [The History of Hungary from Charles III to Congress of Vienna (1711-1815)]. Budapest: Athenaeum, 1895-98. 10 vols.

69. Tarnai, Andor. MAGYAR JAKOBINUSOK, BONAPARTISTAK ES NYELVUJITOK [Hungarian Jacobins, Bonapartists and Reformers of the Language]. Kossuth Kiadó, 1972.

70. Thurzo, Kálmán. "A 19. számú cs. és kir. Ferenc Ferdinánd magyar gyalogezred a lipcsei csatában" [The 19th Francis Ferdinand Hungarian Infantry Regiment in the Battle of Leipzig]. HADTORTENELMI KOZLEMENYEK [Journal of Military History] 14 (1913): 612-13.

71. Thurzó, Kálmán. "Gróf Széchenyi István szerepe a lipcsei csatában" [The Role of Count István Széchenyi in the Battle of Leipzig]. HADTORTENELMI KOZLEMENYEK [Journal of Military History] 15 (1914): 335-62.

72. Treuenfest, Gustav Ritter Amon von. GESCHICHTE DES K.K. HUSZAREN-REGIMENTES ALEXANDER FREIHERR V. KOELLER NR. 8. VON SEINER ERRICHTUNG 1696-1880. Vienna: L. Mayer, 1880.

73. Wertheimer, Ede. "I. Napoleon viszonya Magyarországhoz" [The Relationship of Napoleon I to Hungary]. BUDAPESTI SZEMLE [Budapest Review] 34 (1883): 161-79.

74. Wrede, Alphons, freiherr von. GESCHICHTE DER K. UND K. WEHRMACHT: DIE REGIMENTER, CORPS, BRANCHEN UND ANSTALTEN VON 1618 BIS ENDS DES XIX. JAHRHUNDERTS. Vienna: Seidel, 1898-1905. 5 vols in 6.

CHAPTER XIX

ILLYRIA AND DALMATIA

Norman E. Saul, University of Kansas

Of all the areas encompassed by the "Napoleonic Revolution" the one that retains the most dispute, confusion, and uncertainty is the Adriatic littoral and its Balkan hinterland. Opened to direct French military occupation by the Treaty of Campo Formio in 1797, the region, by geography and historical development, was both the site of scenic beachheads of Napoleonic rationalism and the existence of natural barricades of Old World ecclecticism. All of the usual controversies come quickly to bear upon a romantic world of dazzling scenery and rich Slavic folklore, invaded first by seaborne economic and cultural Enlightenment and then by a sporadic but at times intensive French presence.

As might be expected the literature on this subject is rich, varied, and often distorted by nationalistic bias, and, unlike most areas affected by the phenomenal upheaval of the early nineteenth century, retains at the present time many of the attributes of the early disputes. The Illyrian question is still very much alive in the search for meaning in the heritage of modern-day Yugoslavia. All of the Great Powers of Europe brought their culture and civilization, in varying degrees and mixtures, upon the area--French, British, Austrian, Russian, and Italian. The question, however, pertains not only to these nations and their economic, military, and ideological emissaries, but to the fate of a whole region, to major effects upon Italy, the Ottoman Empire, the entire Eastern Mediterranean. Add to this the religious polyglot of Orthodox, Catholic, Moslem, Jewish, Protestant, and even Freemasonry and the mixture of relatively primitive villages within walking distance (the only way to go through much of the territory) of "modern" commercial ports and you have a modern historian's dream or nightmare, depending on the perspective. The very names from Trieste to Ithaca--Split, Hvar, Herceg-Novi, Dubrovnik (or Ragusa if you prefer), Bocca di Cattaro (Kotor), Budva, Cetinje, Janina, Corfu--conjure more the impression of a Disney-like fantasyland than the real world of Napoleonic battlegrounds.

The bibliographical listing of historical literature that follows is far from exhaustive but at least attempts to be representative. One thing is apparent--that there is no really satisfactory and current synthesis of the area for this period. It would tax the powers of a Ranke, a Braudel, or a McNeil, all of whom have been interested in this general region. The historical sources are scattered and not well known; both language and geographical obstacles exist; the subject is still affected by such modern-day sensitivities as Croatian nationalism and Soviet interest in the excellent Kotor Bay harbor as a Mediterranean base; and the elusive mystery of Albania extends into the 1980s. A noteworthy development, however, is the painstaking and rewarding efforts by modern Yogoslav scholars. In particular, I wish to thank Milorad Ekmecic, a visiting Fulbright lecturer from the University of Sarajevo, for his advice and assistance. He is, of course, not responsible for any omissions or the comments contained herein. It should also be noted that a

bibliography entitled BALKAN MILITARY HISTORY, by John Jessup, will
be published by Garland Publishing Inc. in the near future.

BIBLIOGRAPHIES

The best guides to study and research are found in some of the
recent articles and monographs. Of particular relevance is the
discussion of the literature on the French in Croatia (extending
through Dalmatia) by George Prpic (90), and the source discussion
appendix in Harriet Bjelovucic's study of Dubrovnik (13). Probably
the most recent and complete listing of Yugoslav research is found in
Sime Pericic's study of the Venetian Republic (86). David R. Jones
has provided an excellent bibliography as well as a summary of the
Russian Adriatic campaign (51).

ARCHIVAL SOURCES

Searching the manuscripts for this area and period will take
time and travel. The most fruitful investigations are likely to be
in the region, which has the compensation of providing delightful
surroundings: the Yugoslav State Archives in Dubrovnik, Split, and
Zagreb; the Italian State Archives in Venice and Naples; and the old
Royal Library of Corfu, which houses the records of the Ionian
Republic. The military and diplomatic records of the great
powers--France, Britain, Austria, Russia, and the Ottoman Empire--are
also naturally important on this topic and for the first three of
relatively easy access.

PUBLISHED DOCUMENTS

Primary published materials on Illyria and Dalmatia are sparse
and generally confined to what is scattered through or appended to
the memoirs and many of the books and articles. Yugoslav historians
have provided some of their own and relevant French materials (42,
49), but no systematic collection yet exists. Searches of major
documentary sources for the period are certainly required: for
example, CORRESPONDANCE DE NAPOLEON Ier (75); the publications of the
Historical Manuscript Commission and the Navy Records Society for
Britain; and, fortunately, VNESHNIAIA POLITIKA ROSSII XIX I NACHALA
XX VEKA [Foreign Policy of Russia in the 19th and Early 20th
Centuries] (122), which includes documents in their original
language, as do the older diplomatic correspondence of the Russian
Imperial Historical Society and the family archives of the
Vorontsovs.

MEMOIRS, JOURNALS, AND EYEWITNESS ACCOUNTS

The serious student researching Illyria must start with the
extensive but uneven memoirs, beginning with the inflated multivolume
production of the French Marshal Marmont, styled the Duke of Ragusa
(69), much of which is irrelevant or to be used with caution. Still,
it contains important observations and reminiscences, as do the
complementary works of Bellaire (11), Mangourit (68), Pouqueville
(89), Stephanoupouli (113), and Vaudoncourt (119). The British
accounts of Holland (48) and Jervis (50) resemble romantic

travelogues, while the Russians (Metaks, Panafidin, and Seniavin) listed in Chapter VIII emphasize scenic and naval detail. Representative examples of local diary-memoirs are the ones by Stulli (114) and Bersa (12) on Ragusa-Dubrovnik, Gelcich (45) on Kotor, Zelic (129) on the Orthodox church and Russian influence, and Obradovic (83) on raising national consciousness in the region. The feature of many of the first-hand accounts, however, is to focus on where the action was (Dubrovnik and Corfu), and neglect the backroads and villages.

GENERAL HISTORIES

The most valuable early historical studies by authors with direct experience in the area are by Paul Pisani (87) and Lujo Vojnovic (126). An anti-British bias mars these studies as it does the works of Pauthier (84), Ermano Lunzi (60, 61) and Rodocanachi (93) on the Ionian Islands, and Paul Coquelle (28) on Bosnia and Montenegro. A pro-Russian tendency in these books may be surprising, because Russia was the chief French opponent in the area up to 1807, but fits the political climate in which they were written. This slant is more naturally the case with those studies that deal directly with the Russian occupation of the Ionian Islands and the siege of Ragusa (34, 38, 46, 130).

SPECIALIZED WORKS

In the early twentieth century historical studies became more focused on particular aspects of the Dalmatian problems, but retained a pro-French bias: Auguste Boppe on French influence in Albania (16), Emile Haumant on Ragusa (47), and Charles Schmidt on the interior (99). And after World War I the establishment of a national Yugoslav historical consciousness based on Dalmatian origins and French influences was led by Peter Serovic (100), Grga Novak (78), Maixner (67), Voinovitch (125), Poparic (88), and Antoljak (5).

A veritable explosion of publication accompanied the area's borderland status on the Cold War. Soviet historians, such as Tarle (115), Shapiro (101), Arsh (7), and Stanislavskaia (109, 110), found there historic Russian military and diplomatic successes. They were followed by historians in the West who undertook the first detailed studies of certain aspects of the subject using a wide range of available materials: a study of the war in the Mediterranean (65), the Russian presence in the Adriatic (98, 127), Ragusa under the French (13), the Ionian Republic (66), the Ottoman Empire (102), the Greek Revolution (18, 26, 128), the origins of the Serbian nationalism (69, 85), and Italian interests in the Adriatic (21, 24).

These Western scholars and those who will be studying Illyria and Dalmatia in the future are especially indebted to a number of post-war Yugoslav scholars for serious archival research and investigation in the 1950s and 1960s. Especially valuable are the studies of Bogdan Krizman (55) on the diplomatic history of Dubrovnik, Stjepan Antoljak (6) on the social unrest created by Venetian withdrawal and French arrival, and Midhat Samic (97) on the French penetration into the interior. Others have concentrated on specific cities: Luetic (58) and Stanojevic (111) on Dubrovnik, Lukovic (62, 63) on Kotor, and Novak (80) on Split. Besides using new material from local archives, several of these scholars, Samic and Stanojevic, for example, made important use of French and Venetian archives. While stressing social and economic history, they do not totally avoid a nationalistic bias. A new maturity and more sophisticated synthesis is apparent in the recent studies of Sime Pericic (86) on the eighteenth century background of the Venetian Republic and Dinko Foretic (40) on Dubrovnik.

FUTURE RESEARCH

Excellent foundations have been set for further work on Illyrian and Dalmatian history. While Western scholars have tended to neglect Yugoslav archives and historical writings, Yugoslav historians have not always been able to make full use of Western archives such as consular records. What is needed most is a new synthesis of Illyrian and Dalmatian history in the Napoleonic period in English. Several languages and a patience for bibliographic searches and a variety of working conditions will be required. Cooperative endeavors between Yugoslav and other historians would be the ideal beginning.

BIBLIOGRAPHY: ILLYRIA AND DALMATIA

1. ANALI HISTORIJSKOG INSTITUTA U DUBROVNIKU [Annals of the Historical Institute of Dubrovnik]. 1952 to present.

2. Anastassiadou, Iph. "Les Russo-Turcs à Zante en 1798." BALKAN STUDIES 14 (1973): 12-46.

3. Anderson, M.S. THE EASTERN QUESTION, 1774-1923: A STUDY IN INTERNATIONAL RELATIONS. London: Macmillan, 1966.

4. Antoljak, Stjepan. BUNE PUCANA I SELJAKA U HRVATSKOJ [Revolts of People and Peasants in Croatia]. Zagreb: Matica Hrvatska, 1956.

5. Antoljak, Stjepan. DALMACIJA I VENECIJA NA PRELIMINARIMU U LEOBENU I NA MIRU U CAMPO-FORMIJ [Dalmatia and Venetia at the Preliminaries of Leoben and at the Peace of Campo Formio]. Zagreb: Tisak Nadbiskupske tiskare, 1936.

6. Antoljak, Stjepan. PREDAJA DALMACIJA FRANCUZIMA (1806) [The Surrender of Dalmatia to the French (1806)]. Zagreb: Jugoslavenska akademija znanosti i umjetnosti, 1952.

7. Arsh, Grigorii L'vovich. ALBANIIA I EPIR V KONTSE XVIII-NACHALE XIX V [Albania and Epirus at the End of the 18th Century and the Beginning of the 19th]. Moscow: Akademiia Nauk, 1963.

8. Avakumovic, Ivan. "An Episode in the Continental System in the Illyrian Provinces." THE JOURNAL OF ECONOMIC HISTORY 14 (1954): 254-61.

9. Bagally, John W. ALI PASHA AND GREAT BRITAIN. Oxford: Blackwell, 1938.

10. Beauchamp, Alphonse de. THE LIFE OF ALI PASHA OF JANNINA, LATE VIZIER OF EPIRUS SURNAMED ASLAM, OR THE LION. London: Lupton Relfe, 1823.

11. Bellaire, J.P. PRECIS DES OPERATIONS GENERALES DE LA DIVISION FRANCAISE DU LEVANT CHARGEE, PENDANT LES ANNEES V, VI, ET VII, DE LA DEFENSE DES ILES ET POSSESSIONS EX-VENITIENNES DE LA MER IONIENNE, FORMANT AUJOURD'HUI LA REPUBLIQUE DES SEPT-ILES. Paris: Magimel, 1805.

12. Bersa, Josip. DUBROVACKE SLIKE I PRILIKE 1800-1880 [Dubrovnik Pictures and Situations, 1800-1880]. Zagreb: Matica Hrvatska, 1941.

13. Bjelovucic, Harriet. THE RAGUSAN REPUBLIC: VICTIM OF NAPOLEON AND ITS OWN CONSERVATISM. Leiden: Brill, 1970.

14. Black, Cyril. "Fouché in Illyria 1813." JOURNAL OF CENTRAL EUROPEAN AFFAIRS 2 (1943): 386-95.

15. Bona, Francesco. "Memorie riguardanti l'insurrezione seguita a Ragusa nel 1813 a 1814." Edited by J. Gelcich. ARCHIV FUER OESTERREICHISCHE GESCHICHTE 64 (1882): 537-74.

16. Boppe, Auguste. L'ALBANIE ET NAPOLEON (1797-1814). Paris: Hachette, 1914.

17. Boppe, Paul Louis Hippolyte. LA CROATIE MILITAIRE, 1809-1813. Paris: Berger-Levrault, 1900.

18. Botzaris, Notis. VISIONS BALKANIQUES DANS LA PREPARATION DE LA REVOLUTION GRECQUE (1789-1821). Geneva: Droz, 1962.

19. Breyer, Mirko. ANTUN CONTE ZANOVIC I NJEGOVI SINOVI [Count Antun Zanovic and His Sons]. Zagreb: Matica Hrvatska, 1928.

20. Bulgari, Nicolas Timoleon. LES SEPT-ILES IONIENNES ET LES TRAITES QUI LES CONCERNMENT. Leipzig: n.p., 1859.

21. Caizzi, Bruno. INDUSTRIA E COMMERCIO DELLA REPUBBLICA VENETA NEL SECOLO XVIII. Milano: Banca Commerciale Italiana, 1965.

22. Carter, Francis W. DUBROVNIK (RAGUSA): A CLASSIC CITY-STATE. London and New York: Seminar Press, 1972.

23. Cassi, Gellia. "Les Population Juliennes-Illyriennes pendant la domination Napoléonienne, 1806-1814." REVUE DES ETUDES NAPOLEONIENNES, Series 4, 31 (1930): 193-212, 257-75, 335-69.

24. Cessi, Roberto. LA REPUBLICA DI VENEZIA E IL PROBLEMA ADRIATICO. Napoli: Edizioni scientifiche italime, 1953.

25. Clogg, Richard. "The Dhildaskalia Patriki (1798): An Orthodox Reaction to French Revolutionary Propaganda." MIDDLE EASTERN STUDIES 5 (1964): 97-115.

26. Clogg, Richard, ed. THE STRUGGLE FOR GREEK INDEPENDENCE: ESSAYS TO MARK THE 150th ANNIVERSARY OF THE GREEK WAR OF INDEPENDENCE. London: Macmillan, 1973.

27. Colak, N. "Navigazione marittima fra i porti dalmato-istriani e i porti pontifici alla fine del Settecento." STUDI VENEZIANI 10 (1969): 614-20.

28. Coquelle, Paul. HISTOIRE DU MONTENEGRO ET DE LA BOSNIE DEPUIS LES ORIGINES. Paris: Leroux, 1895.

29. Dabinovic, Ante. "La Révolution française et le nationalisme croate." ANNALES DE L'INSTITUT FRANCAIS DE ZAGREB 3 (1939).

30. Damerini, Gino. LE ISOLE JONIE NEL SISTEMA ADRIATICA DEL DOMINO VENEZIANO A BONAPARTE. Milano: Instituto per gli Stui 8di Politica Internazionale, 1943.

31. Deak, Doctor. "Les Français en Croatie, 1809 à 1813." REVUE DES ETUDES NAPOLEONIENNES 20 (1923): 148-52.

32. D'Istria, Dora, countess. "Les Iles-Ioniennes sous la domination de Venise et sous le protectorat britannique." REVUE DES DEUX MONDES 16 (1858): 381-422.

33. Djordjevic, Dimitrije. REVOLUTIONS NATIONALES DES PEUPLES BALKANIQUES 1804-1914. Belgrade: Institute d'Histoire, 1965.

34. Dobranskii, S. K ISTORII SNOSHENII RAGUZSKOI RESPUBLIKI S ROSSIEI V XVIII I XIX VEKAKH [Toward a History of Relations of the Republic of Ragusa with Russia in the 18th and 19th Centuries]. Moscow: Snegirev, 1909.

35. Dostian, I.S. ROSSIIA I BALKANSKII VOPROS: IZ ISTORII RUSSKO-BALKANSKIKH POLITICHESKIKH SVIAZEI V PERVOI TRETI XIX V. [Russia and the Balkan Question: From the History of the Russo-Balkan Political Connections in the First Third of the 19th Century]. Moscow: Nauka, 1972.

36. Douin, Georges. LA MEDITERRANEE DE 1803 A 1805: PIRATES ET CORSAIRES AUX ILES IONIENNES. Paris: Plon, 1917.

37. Dragovic, Marko. "Prilozi za istoriju Crne Gore" [Supplement to the History of Montenegro]. SPOMENIK SRPSKE KRALJEVSKE ACADEMIJE 31 (1898).

38. Dragovich, Zhivko. "Chernogoriia i eia otnosheniia k Rossii v tsarstvovanie Imperatora Pavla, 1797-1801 gg." [Montenegro and its Relations to Russia in the Reign of Emperor Paul, 1794-1807]. RUSSKAIA STARINA 33, 35 (1882): 419-42, 362-73.

39. Erber, Tullio. STORIA DELLA DALMAZIA DAL 1797 AL 1814. Zara: G. Woditzka, 1886-1890. 3 vols.

40. Foretic, Dinko. POVIJEST DUBROVNIKA DO 1808 [History of Dubrovnik in 1808]. Zagreb, 1980. Vol. 2.

41. Garagnin, Giovanni Luca. RIFLESSIONI ECONOMICO-POLITICHE SOPRA LA DALMAZIA. Zadar: n.p., 1806.

42. Gavrilovic, Michael. "Ispisi iz Pariskikh Arhiva" [Excerpts from the Paris Archives]. ZBORNIK ZA ISTORIIJU, JEZIK I KNIZEVNOST SRPSKOG NARODA 1, 2 (1904).

43. Gelcich, Giuseppe. MEMORIE STORICHE SULLA BOCHE DI CATTARO. Zara: G. Woditzka, 1880.

44. Gelcich, Giuseppe. DELLA ISTITUZIONI MARITIME E SANTIARIE DELLA REPUBBLICA DI RAGUSA: informazione storice documentata. Trieste: Hermanstorfer, 1882.

45. Gelcich, Giuseppe. STORIA DOCUMENTATA DELLA MARINEZZA BOCHESE. Dubrovnik, 1889.

46. Goloviznin, Lieutenant K. "Ocherki iz istorii russkago flota: Kapitan-Komandor Sorokin v Ionicheskoi Respublike" [Excerpts from the History of the Russian Navy: Captain-Commander Sorokin in the Ionian Republic]. MORSKOI SBORNIK 192 (1882): 33-54.

47. Haumant, Emile. "Les Français à Raguse." LA REVUE DE PARIS 12 (1912): 150-74.

48. Holland, Henry. TRAVELS IN THE IONIAN ISLES, ALBANIA, THESSALY, MACEDONIA, etc., DURING THE YEARS 1812 AND 1813. London: Longmans, Hurst, Rees, Orme, and Brown, 1815.

49. Jaksic, Grgur, and Vojislav Vuckovic, eds. FRANCUSKI DOKUMENTI O PRVOM I DRUGOM USTANKU, 1804-1830 [French Documents about the First and Second Uprisings, 1804-1830]. Belgrade, 1959.

50. Jervis, Henry Jervis-White. HISTORY OF THE ISLAND OF CORFU AND THE REPUBLIC OF THE IONIAN ISLANDS. London: Colburn, 1852.

51. Jones, David R. "Adriatic Expedition, 1805-1806." Vol. 4. THE MILITARY-NAVAL ENCYCLOPEDIA OF RUSSIA AND THE SOVIET UNION. n.p., 1984.

52. Kisovec, V. "La Révolution française et le royaume de l'Illyrie." LA REVUE SLAVE 4 (1909): 253-78.

53. Kitromilides, Paschalis M. "The Enlightenment East and West: A Comparative Perspective on the Ideological Origins of the Balkan Political Traditions." CANADIAN REVIEW OF STUDIES IN NATIONALISM 10 (1983): 51-70.

54. Kovacevic, P. "Pomorstvo Herceg-Novog" [Maritime Herceg-Novi]. BOKA 1 (1969).

55. Krizman, Bogdan. DIPLOMATI I KONZULI U STAROM DUBROVNIKU [Diplomats and Consuls in Old Dubrovnik]. Zagreb: Poduzece za izdavanje, prodaju i distribuciju knjiga, 1957.

56. Kroviakov, N. RUSSKIE V KORFU [Russians in Corfu]. Moscow: Voenmorizdat, 1943.

57. Lavalle, J. VOYAGE PITTORESQUE ET HISTORIQUE DE L'ISTRIE ET DE LA DALMATIE. Paris: n.p., 1802.

58. Leutic, Josip. O POMORSTVU DUBROVACKE REPUBLIKE U XVIII STOLJECU [About the Naval Life of the Regusian Republic in the 18th Century]. Dubrovnik: Yugoslav Academy of Arts and Sciences, 1955.

59. Leutic, Josip. POMORAC I DIPLOMAT IVAN KAZNACIC [Sailor and Diplomat, Ivan Kuznacic]. Zagreb: Jugoslavenska Akademija Znanosti i Umjetnosti u Zagrebu, 1954.

60. Lunzi, Ermano. DELLA REPUBBLICA SETTINSULARE. Bologna: Fava e Garagnani, 1863.

61. Lunzi, Ermano. STORIA DELLA ISOLE JONIE SOTTO IL REGGIMENTO DEI REPUBLICANI FRANCESI. Venice: Tipographia del Commercia, 1860.

62. Lukovic, Niko. BOKA KOTORSKA: KULTURNO-ISTORICKI VOCH [Kotor: Cultural-History]. Cetine: Narodna Knjiga, 1951.

63. Lukovic, Niko. "Privreda Boke Kotorske krajem XVIII i pocetkom XIX vijeka u vezi s pomorstvom" [The Economy of the Bay of Kotor at the End of the 18th Century and Beginning of the 19th Century in Connection with the Sea]. GODISNJAK POMORSKOG MUZEJA U KOTORU 3 (1955).

64. Macesich, Susana S. "The French Revolution, Napoleon and the Balkan Enlightenment." EAST EUROPEAN QUARTERLY 9 (1975): 455-70.

65. Mackesy, Piers. THE WAR IN THE MEDITERRANEAN, 1803-1810. London: Longmans, Green, 1957.

66. McKnight, James L. "Admiral Ushakov and the Ionian Republic: The Genesis of Russia's First Balkan Satellite." Ph.D. dissertation, University of Wisconsin, 1965.

67. Maixner, R. "Marmont et l'organization de la Croatie militaire." ANNALES DE L'INSTITUTE FRANCAISE DE ZAGREB 5 (1941).

68. Mangourit, Michael Ange. DEFENSE D'ANCONE AUX ANNEES VII ET VIII. Paris: n.p., an X (1802). 2 vols.

69. Marmont, Augusta Frédéric Louis Viesse de, duc de Raguse. MEMOIRES DU MARECHAL MARMONT, DUC DE RAGUSE, DE 1792 A 1841. 2d ed. Paris: Perrotin, 1857. 9 vols.

70. Meriage, Lawrence P. "The First Serbian Uprising (1804- 1813): National Revival or a Search for Regional Security." CANADIAN REVIEW OF STUDIES IN NATIONALISM 4 (1977): 187-205.

71. Milosevic, Milos. "Neki aspekti pomorske privrede Boke kotorske u doba mletacke vladavine" [Certain Aspects of the Maritime Economy of Kotor at the Time of the Venetian Rule]. POMORSKI ZORNIK 2 (1968): 1801-18.

72. Mourvaieff, Boris. L'ALLIANCE RUSSO-TURQUE AU MILIEU DES GUERRES NAPOLEONIENNES. Neuchâtel: Baconnière, 1954.

73. Naff, Thomas. "Ottoman Diplomacy and the Great European Powers, 1797-1802." Ph.D. dissertation, University of London, 1960.

74. Nakicenovic, S. "Boka" [Kotor]. SRPSKI ETNOGRAFSKI ZBORNIK 20 (1913).

75. Napoleon I, Emperor of the French. CORRESPONDANCE DE NAPOLEON Ier, PUBLIEE PAR ORDRE DE L'NAPOLEON III. Paris: Imprimerie impériale, 1858-69. 32 vols.

76. Nokakovic, St. "Francuske Sluzbene Beleske o Zapadno Balkanskim Zemljama iz 1806-1813" [French Official Notes about the Western Balkan Territories from 1806-1813]. SPOMENIK SRPSKE KRALJEVSKE AKADEMIJE 31 (1898).

77. Nolhac, Stanislas de. LA DALMATIE, LES ILES IONIENNES, ATHENES ET LE MONT ATHOS. Paris: Plon, 1882.

78. Novak, Grga. "Pokret za sjedinjenje Dalmacije s Hrvatskom (1797-1814)" [The Movement for the Unification of Dalmatia with Croatia (1797-1814)]. RAD JAZU (1940).

79. Novak, Grga. "Poljoprivreda Dalmaciji u drugoj polovini XVIII stoljeca" [Agriculture of Dalmatia in the Second Half of the 18th Century]. STARINE 50 (1960).

80. Novak, Grga. POVIJEST SPLITA [History of Split]. Split: Matica Hrvatska, 1957-65. 3 vols.

81. Novak, Grga. PROSLOST DALMACIJE [The Dalmatian Past]. Zagreb, 1944. Vol. 2.

82. Novak, Grga. "Trgovina i pomorstvo Dalmacije u drugoj polovini XVIII stoljeca" [Trade and Maritime Commerce of Dalmatia in the Second Half of the 18th Century]. STARINE 53 (1966).

83. Noyes, George Rapall, ed. and trans. THE LIFE AND ADVENTURES OF DIMITRIJE OBRADOVIC. Berkeley: University of California Press, 1953.

84. Pauthier, Jean Pierre Guillaume. LES ILES IONIENNES PENDANT L'OCCUPATION FRANCAISE ET LE PROTECTORAT ANGLAIS. Paris: Duprat, 1863.

85. Paxton, Roger V. "Nationalism and Revolution: A Re-examination of the First Serbian Insurrection, 1804-1807." EAST EUROPEAN QUARTERLY 6 (1971): 337-62.

86. Pericic, Sime. DALMACIJA UOCI PADA MLETACKE REPUBLIKE [Dalmatia on the Eve of the Fall of the Venetian Republic]. Zagreb: Sveuciliste u Zagrebu, 1980.

87. Pisani, Paul. LA DALMATIE DE 1797 A 1815: EPISODE DES CONQUETES NAPOLEONIENNES. Paris: Picard, 1893.

88. Poparic, Bara. PREGLED POVIJESTI POMORSTVA [A Survey of Naval History]. Zagreb: Izdanje Matice Hrvatske, 1932-33. 2 vols.

89. Pouqueville, F.C.H.L. TRAVELS THROUGH THE MOREA, ALBANIA, AND SEVERAL OTHER PARTS OF THE OTTOMAN EMPIRE TO CONSTANTINOPLE DURING THE YEARS 1798, 1799, 1800, AND 1801. London: Richard Phillips, 1806.

90. Prpic, George J. "French Rule in Croatia, 1806-1813." BALKAN STUDIES 5 (1964): 221-76.

91. Puryear, Vernon J. NAPOLEON AND THE DARDANELLES. Berkeley and Los Angeles: University of California Press, 1951.

92. Robert, Christophe. LES AMOURS ET LES GUERRES DU MERECHAL MARMONT, DUC DE RAGUSE. Paris: Hachette, 1955.

93. Rodocanachi, Emmanuel. BONAPARTE ET LES ILES IONIENNES: UN EPISODE DES CONQUETES DE LA REPUBLIQUE ET DU PREMIER EMPIRE (1797-1 816). Paris: Alcan, 1899.

94. Romano, Ruggiero. IL COMMERCE DU ROYAUME DE NAPLES AVEC LA FRANCE ET LES PAYS DE L'ADRIATIQUE AU XVIII SIECLE. Paris: Colin, 1951.

95. Rusko, Ivo. "Stanjo Dubrovacke Trgovacke Mornarice pred samo Propast Dubrovacke Republike Pocetkom XIX Stoljeca" [The State of the Ragusan Merchant Marine on the Eve of the Fall of the Republic in the Early 19th Century]. DUBROVACKO PO MORSTVO. Dubrovnik: Odbor za proslavu sto godina Nouticke skole u Dubrovniku, 1952.

96. Samardzic, Dj. "Motivi formiranja Ilirskih provincija i polozaj Marmonta kao generalnog guvernera" [The Motives for the Formation of the Illyrian Provinces and the Position of Marmont as Governor-General]. GODISNJAK PRAVNOG FAKULTET A U SARAJEVU 5 (1957): 341-50.

97. Samic, Midhat. LES VOYAGEURS FRANCAIS BOSNIE A LA FIN DU XVIIIe SIECLE ET AU DEBUT DU XIXe ET LES PAYS TEL QU'ILS L'ON VU. Paris: Didier, 1960.

98. Saul, Norman E. RUSSIA AND THE MEDITERRANEAN, 1797-1807. Chicago and London: University of Chicago Press, 1970.

99. Schmidt, Charles. "Napoléon et les routes Balkaniques." REVUE DE PARIS 19 (1912): 335-52.

100. Serovic, Petar. O POMORSTVU BOKE KOTORSKE [On the Maritime Commerce of Kotor]. Belgrade, 1924.

101. Shapiro, Aleksandr L'vovich. ADMIRAL D.N. SENIAVIN. Moscow Ministerstvo Oborony SSSR, 1958.

102. Shaw, Stanford J. BETWEEN THE OLD AND THE NEW: THE OTTOMAN EMPIRE UNDER SELIM III 1789-1807. Cambridge: Cambridge University Press, 1971.

103. Shupp, Paul F. THE EUROPEAN POWERS AND THE NEAR EASTERN QUESTION, 1806-1807. New York: Columbia University Press, 1931.

104. Sisic, Ferdo. "Neke stranice iz novije nase historije: 1797-1814" [Some Pages from Our Modern History, 1797-1814]. HRVATSKO KOLO 5 (1909): 192-245.

105. Sisic, Ferdo. "Pad mletacke republike i ulaz Austrijanaca u Dalmaciju" [The Fall of the Venetian Republic and the Entry of the Austrians into Dalmatia]. PROSVJETA 2 (1894).

106. Sisic, Ferdo. PREGLED POVIJESTI HRVATSKOGA NARODA [A Survey of the History of the Croatian People]. Zagreb: Matica Hrvatska, 1962.

107. Skok, Petar. "Dalmacija" [Dalmatia]. HRVATSKA ENCIKLOPEDIJA 4 (1942): 439-95.

108. Sorgo, Antonia, comte de. FRAGMENTS SUR L'HISTOIRE DE RAGUSE. Paris, 1839.

109. Stanislavskaia, Avgusta Mikhailovna. ROSSIIA I GRETSIIA V KONTSE XVIII-NACHALE XIX VEKA: POLITIKA ROSSII V IONICHESKOI RESPUBLIKE, 1798-1807 GG. [Russia and Greece at the End of the 18th and the Beginning of the 19th Centuries: Russian Policies in the Ionian Republic, 1798-1807]. Moscow: Nauka, 1976.

110. Stanislavskaia, Avgusta Mikhailovna. RUSSKO-ANGLIISKIE OTNOSHENIIA I PROBLMY SREDIZEMNOMOR'IA, 1798-1807 [Anglo-Russian Relations and the Problems of the Mediterranean, 1798-1807]. Moscow: Akademiia nauk, 1962.

111. Stanojevic, Gligor. "Venecija i austrijsko-crnogorski odnosi krajem 18. vijeka" [Venice and Austro-Montenegrin Relations at the End of the 18th Century]. ISTORIJSKI ZAPISI 11 (1955).

112. Stavrianos, L.S. "Antecedents to the Balkan Revolutions of the Nineteenth Century." JOURNAL OF MODERN HISTORY 29 (1957): 335-48.

113. Stephanopouli, Dino, and Nicolo Stephanopouli. VOYAGE DE DINO ET NICOLO STEPHANOPOULI EN GRECE, PENDANT LES ANNEES 1797 ET 1798 D'APRES DEUX MISSIONS, DONT L'UNE DU GOVERNEMENT FRANCAIS, ET L'AUTRE DU GENERAL EN CHEF BUONAPARTE. Paris: Guilleminet, 1800. 2 vols.

114. Stulli, Biaggio. "Notizie Storiche dal Diario di Biaggio Stulli di Ragusa." L'EPIDAURITANO (1898).

115. Tarle, Evgenii Viktorovich. TRI EKSPEDITSII RUSSKOGO FLOTA [Three Expeditions of the Russian Navy]. Moscow: Ministerstvo Oborony SSSR, 1956.

116. Tripkovic, M. CRTICE O BOKI KOTORSKOJ [Sketches of Bocca di Cuttaro]. Hercegnovi: n.p., 1912.

117. Urlic, S. "Bartuo Benincasa urednik Kraljskoga Dalmatina" NASTAVNI VJESNIK 25 (1917).

118. Valentinelli, Giuseppi. BIBLIOGRAFIA DELLA DALMAZIA E DEL MONTENEGRO; SAGGIO. Zagreb: L. Gaj, 1855.

119. Vaudoncourt, Frédéric François, baron de. MEMOIRS OF THE IONIAN ISLANDS ... INCLUDING THE LIFE AND CHARACTER OF ALI PACHA. Translated by William Walton. London: Baldwin, Cradock, and Jay, 1816.

120. Vekaric, Stjepan. PELJESKI JEDRENACI [Peljesac Sailors]. Split: Izdanje Mornickog Glasnika, 1960.

121. Vekaric, Stjepan. "Podaci o Dubrovackim brodomina za vrijeme i nakon francuzke okupacije" [Details about Dubrovnik Shipping at the Height and after the French Occupation]. ANALI HISTORIJSKOG INSTITUTA JUGOSLAVENSKE AKADEMIJE ZNANOSTI I UMJETNOSTI U DUBROVNIKU 2 (1953): 359-68.

122. VNESHNIAIA POLITIKA ROSSII XIX I NACHALA XX VEKA [Foreign Policy of Russia in the 19th and Early 20th Centuries]. Moscow, 1960-62. Vols. 1-6.

123. Villari, Luigi. THE REPUBLIC OF RAGUSA, AN EPISODE OF THE TURKISH CONQUEST. London: Dent, 1904.

124. Viskovic, F. SOTIA DI PERASTO. Trieste, 1898.

125. Voinovitch. HISTOIRE DE DALMATIE. Vol. 2. DES GRIFFES DU LION AILE A LA LIBERATION (1409-1918). 2d ed. Paris: Hachette, 1934.

126. Vojnovic, Lujo Knez. PAD DUBROVNIKA [The Fall of Dubrovnik]. Vol. 1. 1797-1806. Vol. 2. 1807-1815. Zagreb: Tisak Dionicke, 1908.

127. White, D. Fedotoff. "The Russian Navy in Trieste during the Wars of the Revolution and the Empire." AMERICAN SLAVIC AND EAST EUROPEAN REVIEW 6 (1947): 25-52.

128. Woodhouse, C.M. CAPODISTRIA: THE FOUNDER OF GREEK INDEPENDENCE. London and New York: Oxford University Press, 1973.

129. Zelic, Gerasim. ZITIJE GERAIMA ZELICA [The Life of Gerasim Zelic]. Belgrade, 1897-1900. 3 vols.

130. Zhmakin, V. "Rossiia i Chernogoriia v nachale XIX veka" [Russia and Montenegro at the Beginning of the 19th Century]. DREVNAAIA I NOVAIA ROSSIIA 19 (1881): 407-54.

131. Zwitter, K. "Les Provinces Illyriennes de Napoléon." QUESTIONS
      ACTUELLES DU SOCIALISME (1956): 101-19.

CHAPTER XX

THE DUCHY OF WARSAW

John Stanley, Ministry of Citizenship and
Culture, Ontario

Despite the disappearance of the Polish state and army in 1795, military history has long played a large role in Polish historiography. The military reforms begun during the reign of Stanislas Augustus (1764-1795) could not save the Polish Commonwealth but soon after the disappearance of the Polish state, Polish armed units reappeared under French revolutionary banners, then under Napoleon, and finally in the newly created military of the Duchy of Warsaw (1807-1813). The role which the Duchy's army played in the formation of a modern, national spirit has never been denied. Consequently, it has received the attention of some of Poland's finest historians in this century: Szymon Askenzy, Marian Kukiel, Jan Pachoński, and Adam Skalkowski.

Unfortunately, little of the material is available in English and only a few works are in western European languages. Even for those knowing Polish, there are difficulties in doing research in the United States in the military history of this period. Due to the disregard of Polish history in the North American university curriculum until after World War II, library collections only began to be developed systematically after 1945. As a result, much of the material listed in the bibliography is available only in Europe. Indeed, even those works present in North America are sometimes located only in the New York City Public Library which does not permit borrowing through inter-library loan. In Western Europe, the most extensive collections are located in the various archives of Paris but they are also lacking in basic research tools.

GENERAL WORKS

The finest single-volume history of the Polish military is the work of an emigré historian, Marian Kukiel (40), but there are a number of valuable multivolume histories of the Polish army (28, 94, 96). Tadeusz Korzon, one of the finest historians of his day, made a contribution (28), and ZARYS DZIEJOW WOJSKOWOSCI POLSKIEJ DO ROKU 1864 [Outline of the History of the Polish Military until 1864] (94) serves as a useful update to Korzon. ZOLNIERZ POLSKI [The Polish Soldier] (96) is a more popular work, despite its length.

In examining works concerned only with the Napoleonic period, one quickly discovers the importance of Marian Kukiel. His works (36-39) represent a firm foundation for any exploration of this period. A later work, also dealing with the Napoleonic period, DZIEJE OREZA POLSKIEGO 1794-1838 [A History of Polish Arms 1794-1838] is a part of a much larger project (30).

ARCHIVAL SOURCES

In Warsaw, the most valuable archives for the study of the period are the Archiwum Glôwne Akt Dawnych (Main Archives of Ancient Documents), the Biblioteka Narodowa (National Library), the Biblioteka Uniwersytecka (University Library, University of Warsaw), and the Muzeum Wojska Polskiego w Warzawie (Museum of the Polish Army in Warsaw). At Cracow, the Biblioteka Czartorskich (Library of the Czartoryski's), Biblioteka Jagiellońska (Jagiellonian Library, Jagiellonian University), the Biblioteka PAN (Library of the Polish Academy of Sciences), and the Zaklad Dokumentacji Institutu Historii PAN (Documentation Institute of the Polish Academy of Sciences) house important collections of manuscript material. Other pertinent material can be found at the Biblioteka Zakladu Narodowego im. Ossolińskich (Library of the National Institute of the Ossoliński's) in Wroclaw.

In Paris, documents can be found in the correspondance of the Grande Armée, as well as the collections entitled "Mémoires Historiques" and "Mémoires Réconnaissances" at the Service historique de l'armée at the Château de Vincennes. The Polish Library in Paris, Biblioteka Polska w Paryzu, and the Muzeum im. Adama Mickiewicza w Paryu (the Adam Mickiewicz Museum) also hold valuable material. The Archives Nationales also prove useful.

MEMOIRS, JOURNALS, AND EYEWITNESS ACCOUNTS

Few periods in Polish military history have provided such dashing figures as those who served in the Duchy of Warsaw's army. Three military figures are dominant: Henryk Dabrowski, the founder of the Polish Legions, Prince Józef Poniatowski, the minister of war, and Józef Zajaczek, veteran of numerous Napoleonic military campaigns. There have long been historiographical debates between the proponents of Dabrowski and Poniatowski. The historians' dispute has its origin in the quarrel between the two men themselves. Despite Dabrowski's long service to Napoleon and the French cause, the Emperor chose Poniatowski as leader of the Polish forces in 1806 and supported the prince's candidacy as minister of war in the new Duchy. Poniatowski had retreated into a hedonistic social whirl after the Commonwealth's fall while Dabrowski had chosen to live in exile, from where he organized the Polish Legions and devoted his life to creating a Polish armed force despite the destruction of the Polish state. Dabrowski's biography has been written by Klemens Kolaczkowski (27) and, most recently, by Jan Pachoński (50). Two fine historians, Waclaw Tokarz and Marian Kukiel (83), devoted a monograph to Dabrowski's organizational talents as well.

Despite Dabrowski's devotion to the national cause, no figure from this period can rival the flair of Prince Józef Poniatowski. "Prince Józef" as he is known even today, had an aristocratic sophistication and a sense of honour which were incorporated into the Polish military tradition after his heroic death at Leipzig in 1813. Skalkowski's edition of Poniatowski's correspondence is an extremely important source for the history of the period (59) and Askenazy's biography of Poniatowski is considered a classic of Polish historiography (2). Skalkowski's earlier treatment may be considered an antidote to Askenazy's admiring portrait (63). In contrast, the third member of the Duchy's military triumvirate, Józef Zajaczek, has had only a single biography devoted to his activities (46). Zajaczek, like Dabrowski, was offended by Poniatowski's advancement and jealous of his successes. Fortunately, Jadwiga Nadzieja's work reveals Zajaczek's importance in the military history of the period.

Although Dabrowski, Poniatowski, and Zajaczek are the most important military figures in the Duchy's history, the large role played by the military during this period has produced numerous biographies of lesser figures. Furthermore, there are numerous volumes of memoirs, diaries, and correspondence which create the backdrop for the most important figures. While the biographies of the generals, such as Henryk Dembiński (9), Amilkar Kosiński (88), and Józef Szymanowski (82) are informative, the memoirs of lower ranks are also quite useful. Both Kajetan Koźmian (31) and Franciszek Gajewski (16) were officers whose memoirs provide fascinating insights into the military life of the period. The most famous Jewish officer in the Duchy's army, Berek Joselewicz, has received much attention. Dawid Kandel's article, although published in 1909, is still among the most useful works devoted to this man who became a symbol for those Jews who saw themselves as Poles of the Mosaic faith (25). The comic playwright, Aleksander Fredro, left memoirs of this period, which are a classic in their genre (15). Another interesting set of memoirs is GAWEDY ZOLNIERSKIE [Soldiers Tales] (17) which brings together recollections of this time. Finally, Stanislas Kirkor has studied the donations of Polish lands which Napoleon gave to both Frenchmen and Poles (26). These estates represented not only a reward for many Polish military men but also their principal livelihood.

SPECIALIZED STUDIES

From his first entrance onto Polish soil shortly after the occupation of Berlin in 1806, Napoleon used the Polish Question to strengthen his own hand and create the army for the Duchy of Warsaw. The promise of their own state encouraged the Poles to give much materiel and many men to the Napoleonic cause. Even before the Duchy's formal establishment, the Polish provisional government, the Governing Commission (Komisya Rzadzaca) had as its major goal the supply of men and provisions to the French, as is abundantly shown in MATERYALY DO DZIEJOW KOMISYI RZADZACEJ Z R. 1807 [Materials for the History of the Governing Commission from 1807] (45). All the major collections of Napoleon's correspondence contain letters concerning the Poles and the uses to which they were put. The small selection of correspondence collected by Adam Skalkowski concerning Poland itself, however, gives a good indication of how much Napoleon valued the Poles (47). After the establishment of the Duchy of Warsaw by the Treaty of Tilsit, the French residents in Warsaw had numerous military functions to fulfill--spying, pressuring the Duchy's government to supply men, supervising the construction of a system of fortresses--which is obvious from a perusal of the collection of documents assembled by Marceli Handelsman (22).

There are four works which treat with the full history of the Duchy's army (6, 18, 57, 99). Unfortunately, the sole English-language source, NAPOLEON'S POLISH TROOPS, (57), published in 1974, is rather superficial. Much better are the French-language L'ARMEE DU DUCHE DE VARSOVIE (6) of 1913 and the Polish work WOJSKO POLSKIE: KSIESTWO WARSZAWSKIE 1807-1814 [The Polish Army: The Duchy of Warsaw 1807-1814] (18). The usefulness of both these works is limited by their age, however. Fortunately, a solid contemporary work is available: Gabriel Zych's excellent ARMIA KSIESTWA

WARSZAWSKIEGO 1807-1812 [Army of the Duchy of Warsaw 1807-1812] (99).
Of related interest is the history of the Polish troops in the free
city of Gdańsk (WOLNE MIASTO GDANSK, FREISTADT DANZIG). Janusz
Staszewski, who wrote much on the presence of Polish troops in
Pomerania and Silesia in the Napoleonic era, has also contributed an
interesting article on the history of the Polish garrison in Gdansk
(78).
    Napoleon chiefly prized the Poles for their cavalry. Two
Polish-language works specifically deal with the Polish cavalry of
this period. Jerzy Grobicki's article (20) is a basic survey while
Janusz Albrecht's short monograph concentrates on the cavalry's
administration (1).
    The administration of the Napoleonic army required an
organization quite different from that known to the Polish
Commonwealth. The Duchy's army was modeled on the French example and
its administration was patterned on the French model. The adoption
of French reforms was one of the most important methods of mod-
ernization in the Duchy's life, not least in its military. Henryk
Eile has devoted two small monographs to the problem of the military
administration in the Duchy (12, 13) and Józef Stojanowski has
written an article devoted to the Ministry of War itself (80). An
attempt to reform the ministry in 1810 is brought to light in an
article in PRZESZLOSC [The Past] (87). A constant problem for the
Duchy's government was the provisioning of the army. The Duchy had
few available funds and depended chiefly on a group of Warsaw
merchants to supply Polish troops. Jan Kosim has discussed the
method of supply and payment in his article in ROCZNIK WARSZAWSKI
[Warsaw Annual] (29). Henryk Eile also looks at the method of
provisioning the army (14) as does a more recent article by Leslaw
Dudek (10).
    Education, both secular and military, received much attention
from the ducal government. There were military academies (Szkół)
kadetów) in both Kalisz and Chelm. A general history of these
schools (79) is supplemented by Zieliński's article on the Kalisz
academy (95) and Alfons Mankowski's series of articles on the Chelm
school (44). Military health services are discussed in Eugeniusz
Grzelak's article "Chirurgia Polowa w okresie Ksiestwa Warszawskiego
i Królestwa Polskiego" [Field Surgery in the period of the Duchy of
Warsaw and the Kingdom of Poland] (21). As in France, the Duchy's
army was supplemented by a National Guard (Gwardja Narodowa). It was
much less successful in the Duchy than in France, however. Janusz
Staszewski provides an overview (73).
    Having a wider range than the individual biographies and
memoirs, regimental histories offer a more selective view of the
Duchy's military life. Stanislaw Ostrowski discussed the history of
an infantry division (49), but it is the cavalry which generates the
most interest among military historians. One Uhlan has left memoirs
concerning the first division of the Vistula Legion (Legia
Nadwiślańska) in its various campaigns (91) and there is Józef
Zaluski's memoirs about the Polish light cavalry division of
Napoleon's Guard (92). There is also a later compilation of
documents for the history of this same unit (97).
    Although the Duchy's army dates from the creation of the state
in 1807, its military history is inseparable from that of the Polish
Legions, founded in 1794 in Italy by Henryk Dabrowski. In the

Legions, the Polish volunteers received training in the modern, French style of warfare; the army was turned into a tool of patriotic consciousness. Jan Pachoński has finally concluded his massive work, the four-volume LEGIONY POLSKIE 1794-1807 [The Polish Legions 1794-1807] (51), now the standard reference for the topic. However, for further information on Polish involvement outside the boundaries of Europe, the reader may look to the works of Adam Skalkowski on the Polish involvement in Egypt (67) and San Domingo (66).

Józef Sulkowski died before the foundation of the new Polish state, but his imprint was placed upon the national consciousness through his cooperation with the French in Italy and Egypt. The memoirs of this military genius have been published (81) and there are two useful biographies. Karol Kozmiński's work (32) was written before the Second World War; Jan Reychman, an Orientalist, has written the most recent biography of Sulkowski (61) in 1951. Szymon Askenazy began an ambitious history of the relations between Napoleon and the Poles which he never finished. Even in its incomplete state, it reached three volumes which cover the period up to the establishment of the Duchy of Warsaw (3). Naturally, much of it deals with the Poles' military involvement with Napoleon.

During the campaigns from 1807 to 1813, the Polish lands were engulfed by war on three occasions. The first campaign resulted from the Franco-Prussian War of 1806 and led to the establishment of the Duchy of Warsaw by the Treaty of Tilsit. Oscar Lettow-Vorbeck's history of the military campaigns of 1806-7 is still the most detailed contribution (43). There is a useful English-language contribution by Loraine Petre as well (55). Finally, there is the excellent overview in Polish by Gabriel Zych (100). Of particular interest to the Poles is the uprising which accompanied the entry of French troops onto Polish soil. Jan Wasicki has written the best survey of this phenomenon (86) and there are two German sources as well (54, 58). For a local view of these levées en masse (Pospolite Ruszenia), there are studies available for the Kalisz region (74) and Pomerania (85). After World War I, Polish historians were eager to show the participation of Polish troops in Pomerania and Silesia; these areas had once been Polish and were partially returned to Warsaw's rule after 1918. After 1945 this historical trend became even more pronounced. Janusz Staszewski was among those historians most active between the wars, seeking to demonstrate the historic continuity of the Polish presence in these territories. He devoted two important works to the Polish participation in the fighting in Pomerania (76, 98) and another to the Polish military presence in Silesia during the Napoleonic period (77). Marian Pawlak has discussed the Poles fighting in Warmia and Mazuria (East Prussia) (52). The siege of Kolobrzeg (Kolberg) has occupied an important place in Prussian military history but Hieronim Kroczyński has partially deflated the myth in his work (33). The siege of Gdańsk (Danzig) has received much attention as well. Jules Bourelly's volume represents a useful discussion of the military activity around Gdańsk not only in 1807 but throughout this period (5).

In the Spanish campaign of 1808 Polish troops served under direct French command with support from the Duchy of Warsaw. The Polish participation in the Spanish campaign represents one of the most important chapters of the Napoleonic legend. An old but useful overview of the Poles in Spain is provided by Walery Przyborowski

(60). Somosierra is the battle in the Spanish campaign for which the Poles are most famous. An early treatment of this battle was written by Andrzej Niegolewski (48) and Adam Skalkowski has collected contemporaries' reactions (62). Other Polish battles in Spain are discussed by Marian Kujawski, an emigré historian (34).

In 1809, after only two years of existence, the Duchy found itself invaded by the Austrian Empire. West European historians view this campaign as merely auxiliary to the main war between France and Austria. Therefore, they have given the Galician campaign little attention. However, it demonstrated that the military reforms carried out under Poniatowski's leadership had been absorbed, while his brilliant tactics in the Galician campaign forced the Austrians to retreat from Warsaw and added luster to his name. The fullest treatment of the Polish-Austrian conflict was written by Bronislaw Pawlowski (53). There are also two other histories of the war worth examining (7, 24). The diary and field correspondence of General Sokolnicki has been published for 1809 (70) and the siege of the fortress at Zamość has also received attention (56). Once again, a levée en masse was called and the result in the Poznań region has been described by Janusz Staszewski (75).

Napoleon's greatest demands upon the Poles were made during the campaign of 1812 or what he called the Second Polish War. Ultimately 100,000 Poles fought in the campaign but they were divided among numerous armies. Their presence therefore did not have the expected impact in the Lithuanian, Belorussian, and Ukrainian lands. The finest and most comprehensive Polish work concerning the Russian campaign is Marian Kukiel's magisterial WOJNA 1812 ROKU [The War of 1812] (38). Provisioning during the campaign is discussed by Wladyslaw Kwiatkowski (41) and the health services within the Duchy's armed forces were described by Juliusz Willaume (90) who also discusses the the Duchy of Warsaw itself during 1812 (89). The experiences of Aleksander Fredro during the 1812 campaign once again give the military events a human touch (42). The participation of troops from Gdańsk in the Russian campaign is described by Staszewski in two articles (11, 72). Although the Duchy itself had no seacoast, Marian Kukiel has discussed the Baltic situation in an article which fortunately is available in English translation (35).

When the Russian campaign led to disaster, the remnants of the Duchy's army were reorganized by Poniatowski. Forced to withdraw from Warsaw as a result of the Austrian retreat, the army moved first to Cracow and then through Bohemia and Moravia to join the French forces in Dresden. During the Russian occupation between 1813 and 1815, the Poles were disappointed by Napoleon's refusal to proclaim a reconstituted Polish Kingdom, but they continued in their loyalty to the Emperor. Józef Tyszkiewicz wrote the history of the 17th Polish cavalry regiment as it served Napoleon from 1812 through 1815 (84). The memoirs of Charles Turno, a Polish officer in the final years of Napoleon's rule, shows the change in Poles' perception of the Emperor and his goals (71).

Szymon Askenazy has discussed the Polish army in 1813 (4) and Milan Smerda, a Czech historian, has published articles concerning the Polish passage through the Habsburg Empire in the same year (69). There is also a short German article discussing the retreat from Cracow through the Czech lands to Zittau (Zitawa) in Saxony during the late spring of 1813 (23). Even after Poniatowski's death at

Leipzig, in the Battle of Nations, and the Emperor's retreat across the Rhine, Polish units continued to fight for Napoleon. By 1814 it was well known to most Poles that Napoleon was quite willing to sacrifice the Duchy to gain peace with the Allies. Nevertheless, many soldiers believed their oaths of loyalty to the Emperor remained valid and continued to serve. Andrzej Zaremba has discussed the First and Second Polish cavalry regiments during the French campaign of 1814 (93); Adam Skalkowski described the activities of the Polish Honor Guard in the same year (68). Even after Napoleon's return from Elba, Poles flocked to join him; Skalkowski lists the Polish officers who served during the Hundred Days (65).

Although there is little doubt that Napoleon used the Polish cause for his own imperial ends, the Poles regarded themselves as junior partners in the Emperor's cause. The Poles looked upon the Duchy of Warsaw as the promise of a future Polish kingdom within the boundaries of 1772. Eager to prove their loyalty and usefulness to the Emperor, they fought for him in 1807, 1809, and 1812, indeed continuing to fight with Napoleon until the end. The suicidal courage of Koziutulski at Somosierra, the aristocratic sense of honor and glory demonstrated by Poniatowski, and the democratic and nationalist doctrines of the Polish Legions were the legacy bequeathed by the Napoleonic period to the Polish military.

FUTURE RESEARCH

The bibliography below merely touches the surface of material available to the military historian of the Napoleonic era in Poland. Unfortunately, the language of these publications has placed them beyond the reach of most historians in North America and Western Europe. The Poles' contribution to the French cause was significant. Certainly, their loyalty surpassed that of any other ally of Napoleon. If actions speak louder than words, Poland played a large role in the Napoleonic enterprise. The military historians of the Napoleonic era therefore ignore the contribution of Polish historians at their own risk. Those venturing into the field, however, will find an unlimited number of unexplored topics. Studies in the western languages concerning the Polish commanders, their campaigns and operations, the role of the Polish forces in the Grande Armée, and the impact of the French in Poland exemplify some of the topics that need investigation.

BIBLIOGRAPHY: POLAND

1. Albrecht, Janusz. Z DZ IEJOW JAZDY KSIESTWAW WARSZAWSKIEGO. PRZYCZYNEK HISTORYCZNO-ADMINISTRACYNY DO LAT 1806-1808 [From the History of the Cavalry of the Duchy of Warsaw. An Historical-Administrative Contribution for the Years 1806-1808]. Warsaw: Wojskowy Instytut Naukowo-Wydawniczy, 1922.

2. Askenazy, Szymon. KSIA ZE JOZEF PONIATOWSKI 1763-1813 [Prince Józef Poniatowski 1763-1813]. 5th edition. Warsaw: Panstwowy Instytut Wydawniczy, 1974.

3. Askenazy, Szymon. NAPOLEON A POLSKA [Napoleon and Poland]. Warsaw and Cracow: Towarzystwo Wydawnicze, 1918-19. 3 vols.

4. Askenazy, Szymon. "Napoleon a wojsko polskie w 1813 r." [Napoleon and the Polish Army in 1813]. KWARTALNIK HISTORYCZNY [Historical Quarterly] 13 (1899): 73-76.

5. Bourelly, Jules. LES SIEGES DE DANTZIG ET L'OCCUPATION FRANCAISE (1807-1813). Paris: Chapelot, 1904.

6. Chelminski, Jan, and A. Malibran. L'ARMEE DU DUCHE DE VARSOVIE. Paris: Leroy, 1913.

7. Cichowicz, Augustyn. ROK 1809 [The Year 1809]. Poznan: Rzepecki, 1925.

8. Davout, Louis Nicolas, duc d'Auerstädt et prince d'Eckmühl. CORRESPONDANCE DU MARECHAL DAVOUT PRINCE D'ECKMUEHL. Paris: Plon-Nourrit, 1885. 4 vols.

9. Dembiński, Henryk. PAMIETNIK HENRYKA DEMBINSKIEGO JENERAA WOJSK POLSKICH [The Memoir of Henryk Dembinski, General of the Polish Armies]. Poznan: L. Mierzbach, 1860. 2d ed. Warsaw: Biblioteka Dziél Wyborowych, 1911).

10. Dudek, Leslaw. "System zaopatrywania wojska Ksiestwa Warszawskiego." cz. 1-2. [The System of Supplying the Army of the Duchy of Warsaw]. PRZEGLAD KWATERMISTRZOWSKI (Quartermaster's Review) 21 (1970): 111-19, 170-77.

11. "Dziennik dzialan wojennych 7 dywizji (gdanskiej) w 1812 r." [Diary of the Military Activities of the 7th Division (Gdansk) in 1812]. Edited by Janusz Staszewski. ROCZNIK GDANSKI [Gdansk Yearbook] 11 (1937): 337-55.

12. Eile, Henryk. ADMINISTRACJA W WOJSKU KSIESTWA WARSZAWSKIEGO. [Administration in the Army of the Duchy of Warsaw]. PRZEGLAD INTENDENKCI [Intendant Review] 1 (1926): 3.

13. Eile, Henryk. DZIEJE ADMINISTRACJI WOJSKU KSIESTWA
    WARSZAWSKIEGO. KSIAZE JOZEF JAKO ADMINISTRATOR [The History of
    the Administration of the Army of the Duchy of Warsaw. Prince
    Jozef as Administrator]. Warsaw: Towarzystwo Wiedzy
    Wojskowy, 1928.

14. Eile, Henryk. "Zaopatrzenie wojska w dobie Ksiestwa
    Warszawskiego" [Provisioning the Army in the Period of the
    Duchy of Warsaw]. PRZEGLAD INTENDENCKI [Intendant Review] 2
    (1927): 53-94.

15. Fredro, Aleksander. TRZY PO TRZY, PAMIETNIKI Z EPOKI
    NAPOLEONSKIEJ [Three By Three. Memoirs from the Napoleonic
    Era]. Warsaw: Gebethner i Wolff, 1917.

16. Gajewski, Franciszek. PAMIETNIKI FRANCISZKA GAJEWSKIEGO
    PULKOWNIKA WOJSK POLSKICH (1802-1831) [The Memoirs of
    Franciszek Gajewski, Colonel in the Polish Armies]. Poznan:
    Zdzislaw Rzepecki i s-ka, 1913. 2 vols.

17. GAWEDY ZOLNIERSKIE. POKLOSIE SPUSCIZNY PAMIETNIKARSKIEJ
    NAPOLEONCZYKOW [Soldiers Tales. Gleanings from the Heritage of
    Napoleonic Memoirs]. Edited by Waclaw Gasiorowski. Warsaw:
    J. Przeworski, 1938.

18. Gembarzewski, Bronislaw. WOJSKO POLSKIE. KSIESTWO
    WARSZAWSKIE 1807-1814 [The Polish Army. The Duchy of Warsaw
    1807-1814]. Warsaw: Gebethner i Wolff, 1912.

19. Grobicki, Jerzy. "Kawalerzysci polscy w sluzbie u obcych
    mocarstw w dobie napoleonskiej (1779-1815)" [Polish Cavalrymen
    in the Service of Foreign Powers in the Napoleonic Period].
    PRZEGLAD KAWALERYJSKI [Cavalry Review] 7 (1930): 205-20,
    285-305.

20. Grobicki, Jerzy. "Rozwój i dzieje kawalerji Ksiestwa
    Warszawskiego" [The Development and History of the Cavalry of
    the Duchy of Warsaw]. PRZEGLAD KAWALERYJSKI [Cavalry Review] 11
    (1934): 387-421, 519-60.

21. Grzelak, Eugeniusz. "Chirurgia polowa w okresie Ksiestwa
    Warszawskiego i Królestwa Polskiego" [Field Surgery in the
    Period of the Duchy of Warsaw and the Kingdom of Poland].
    STUDIA I MATERIALY DO HISTORII WOJSKOWOSCI [Studies and
    Materials for the History of Military Affairs] 16 (1970):
    125-231.

22. INSTRUKCYE I DEPESZE REZYDENTOW FRANCUSKICH W WARSZAWIE,
    1807-1813 [The Instructions and Dispatches of the French
    Residents in Warsaw, 1807-1813]. Edited by Marceli
    Handelsman. Cracow: Akademia Umiejetności, 1914. 2 vols.

23. Jäkel, M. "Der Marsch der Polen von Krakau nach Zittau in Mai
    u. Juni 1813; Die polnische Besatzung in Zittau während des
    Waffenstillstandes Juni bis August 1813". [The March of the

Poles from Cracow to Zittau in May and June 1813; The Polish
Occupation in Zittau during the Armistice from June to August
1813]. OBERLAUSITZE HEIMAT [Upper Lusatian Homeland] 1938:
169, 206.

24. Just, Gustav. POLITIK ODER STRATEGIE. KRITISCHE STUDIEN UEBER
    DEN WARSCHAUER FELDZUG OESTERREICHS UND DIE HALTUNG RUSSLANDS
    1809 [Policy or Strategy. Critical Studies on Austria's Warsaw
    Campaign and Russia's Attitude in 1809]. Vienna: Seidel,
    1909.

25. Kandel, Dawid. "Berek Joselowicz." PRZEGLAD HISTORYCZNY
    [Historical Review] 9 (1909): 290-98.

26. Kirkor, Stanislas. "Les donataires polonais de Napoléon."
    ANTEMURAL 16 (1972): 15-39. (A more extensive treatment is
    available in Polish: Stanislas Kirkor, POLSCY DONATARIUSZE
    NAPOLEONA. London: Poets' and Painters' Press, 1974.)

27. Kolaczkowski, Klemens. HENRYK DABROWSKI, TWORCA LEGIONOW
    POLSKICH WE WLOSZECH 1755-1818. WSPOMNIENIE HISTORYCZNE
    [Henryk Dabrowski, Creator of the Polish Legions in Italy
    1755-1818. Historical Memoirs]. Cracow: Spólka Wydawnicze,
    1901.

28. Korzon, Tadeusz. DZIEJE WOJEN I WOJSKOWOSCI W POLSCE [The
    History of Wars and Military Affairs in Poland]. Cracow:
    Akademia Umiejetności, 1912. 3 vols.

29. Kosim, Jan. "Warszawscy liweranci wojskowi w latach 1807-1830"
    [Warsaw Provisioners to the Army in the Years   1807-1830].
    ROCZNIK WARSZAWSKI [Warsaw Annual] 10 (1971): 81-111.

30. Kozlowski, Eligiusz, and Mieczyslaw Wrzosek. DZIEJE OREZA
    POLSKIEGO 1794-1938 [History of Polish Arms 1794-1938].
    Warsaw, 1973. (This work is volume 2 of DZIEJE OREZA POLSKIEGO
    963-1945. Edited by Marian Anusiewicz. Warsaw:
    Wydawnictwo Ministerstwa Obrony Narodowej, 1968-74. 3 vols.)

31. Koźmian, Kajetan. PAMIETNIKI KAJETANA KOZMIANA OBEJMUJACE
    WSPOMNIENIA OD ROKU 1780-1815 [The Memoirs of Kajetan Koźmian
    Including the Reminiscences from 1780 to 1815]. Poznań:
    Nakl. J.K. Zupanskiego, 1858-65. 3 vols. (Wroclaw:
    Ossolineum, 1972. 3 vols.)

32. Kozmiński, Karol. JOZEF SULKOWSKI. Warsaw: Glówna Ksiegarnia
    Wojskowa, 1935.

33. Kroczyński, Hieronim. POLACY W WALCE O KOLOBRZEG 1807 [The
    Poles in the Battle for Kolobrzeg 1807]. Warsaw: Wydawnictwo
    Ministerstwa Obrony Narodowej, 1974. (Also see the author's
    article "Rola Kolobrzegu w kampanii 1807 roku--mit a prawda
    historyczna" [The Role of Kolobrzeg in the Campaign of
    1807--Myth and Historical Truth]. KOSZALINSKIE ZESZYTY
    MUZEALNY [Koszalin Museum Fascicles] 2 (1972): 83-103.)

34. Kujawski, Marian. Z BOJOW POLSKICH W WOJNACH NAPOLEONSKICH. MAIDA--SAMOSIERRA--FUENGIROLA--ALBUERA [From the Polish Battles in the Napoleonic Wars]. London: Nakl. Polskiej Fundacji Kulturalnej, 1967.

35. Kukiel, Marian. "Baltic Problems of the War of 1812." BALTIC AND SCANDINAVIAN COUNTRIES 4 (1938): 10-16. (This is an English translation of "Zagadnienia baltyckie wojny 1812 roku" JANTAR 2 (1938): 1-8.)

36. Kukiel, Marian. DZIEJE OREZA POLSKIEGO W EPOCE NAPOLEONSKIEJ 1795-1815 [The History of Polish Arms in the Napoleonic Era]. Poznan: Rzepecki, 1912.

37. Kukiel, Marian. DZIEJE WOJSKA POLSKIEGO W DOBIE NAPOLEONSKIEJ, 1795-1815 [The History of the Polish Army in the Napoleonic Period, 1795-1815]. Warsaw: Wende, 1920. 2 vols.

38. Kukiel, Marian. WOJNA 1812 ROKU [The War of 1812]. Cracow: Polska Akademie Umiejetności, 1937. 2 vols.

39. Kukiel, Marian. WOJNY NAPOLEONSKIE [The Napoleonic Wars]. Warsaw: Kurs Historji Wojenny, 1927.

40. Kukiel, Marian. ZARYS HISTORII WOJSKOWOSCI W POLSCE [An Outline of the History of Military Affairs in Poland]. 5th ed. London: Orbis, 1949.

41. Kwiatkowski, Wladyslaw. "Zaopatrzenie w roku 1812" [Provisionment in 1812]. PRZEGLAD INTENDENCKI [Intendant Review] 5 (1930): 67-101; 6 (1931): 40-66.

42. Leśnia, Wladyslaw. "Aleksander Fredro w kampanii 1812 roku" [Aleksander Fredro in the 1812 Campaign]. Breslau. Uniwersytet. PRACE LITERACKI [Literary Works] 16 (1974): 111-38.

43. Lettow-Vorbeck, Oscar. DER KRIEG VON 1806 UND 1807 [The War of 1806 and 1807]. Berlin: Mittler, 1891-96. 4 vols.

44. Mankowski, Alfons. "Szkola kadetów chelmińskich w dobie Ksiestwa Warszawskiego" [The School of Chelm Cadets in the Period of the Duchy of Warsaw]. DZIENNIK POZNANSKI [Poznań Daily] 59 (1917): no. 288, p. 3, no. 289, p. 3, no. 290, p. 3, no. 291, p. 3.

45. MATERYALY DO DZIEJOW KOMISYI RZADZACEJ Z R. 1807. I. DZIENNIK CZYNNOSCI KOMISYI RZADZACEJ [Materials for a History of the Governing Commission from 1807. Vol. 1. Diary of the Governing Commission's Activities]. Edited by Michal Rostworowski. Cracow: Akademia Umiejetności, 1918. (Only the first volume ever appeared.)

46. Nadzieja, Jadwiga. GENERAL JOZEF ZAJACZEK 1752-1826. Warsaw: Wydawnictwo Ministerstwa Obrony Narodowej, 1975.

47. Napoleon I, Emperor of the French. SUPPLEMENT A LA
    CORRESPONDANCE DE NAPOLEON I. L'EMPEREUR ET LA POLOGNE.
    Edited by Adam Skalkowski. Paris: Bureau de l'Agence
    Polonaise de Presse, 1908.

48. Niegolewski, Andrzej. SOMO-SIERRA. Poznan: Kamieński, 1854.

49. Ostrowski, Stanislaw. Z DZIEJOW PULKU. PULK DWUNASTY PIECHOTY
    KSIESTWA WARSZAWSKIEGO [From the History of the Regiment. The
    20th Infantry Regiment of the Duchy of Warsaw]. Warsaw:
    Gebethner i Wolff, 1910.

50. Pachoński, Jan. GENERAL JAN HENRYK DABROWSKI 1755-1818.
    Warsaw: Wydawnictwo Ministerstwa Obrony Narodowej, 1981.

51. Pachoński, Jan. LEGIONY POLSKIE 1794-1807. PRAWDA I LEGENDA
    [The Polish Legions 1794-1807. The Truth and the Legend].
    Warsaw: Wydawnictwo Ministerstwa Obrony Narodowej, 1969-79. 4
    vols.

52. Pawlak, Marian. "Dzialania bojowe dywizji poznańskiej na Warmii
    i Mazurach w 1807 roku" [Battle Action of the Poznan Division
    in Warmia and Mazuria in 1807]. KOMUNIKATY MAZURSKO-WARMSKIE
    [Mazurian-Warmian Communications] 6 (1962): 569-80.

53. Pawlowski, Bronislaw. HISTORIA WOJNY POLSKO-AUSTRIACKIEJ 1809
    ROKU [The History of the Polish-Austrian War of 1809].
    Warsaw: Glówna Ksiegarnia Wojskowa, 1935.

54. Perdelwitz, Richard. "Der preussische Polenaufstand 1806-7.
    Ein Beitrag zur Geschichte der französisch-polnischen
    Beziehungen" [The Prussian Polish Uprising 1806-7. A
    Contribution to the History of French-Polish Relations].
    GRENZMAERKISCHE HEIMATBLATT [Grenzmärk Home Bulletin] 15
    (1939): 203-49.

55. Petre, Francis Loraine. NAPOLEON'S CAMPAIGN IN POLAND 1806-7;
    A MILITARY HISTORY OF NAPOLEON'S FIRST WAR WITH RUSSIA.
    London: Sampson-Low, Marston, 1901. (Reprinted, London:
    Arms and Armour, 1976.)

56. Pieszko, Michal. ZAMOSC W ROKU 1809. SZKICE HISTORYCZNY
    [Zamość in 1809. Historical Sketches]. Zamość: Salve Alma
    Materna Polonia, 1931.

57. Pivka, Otto von. NAPOLEON'S POLISH TROOPS. Reading: Osprey
    Publishing, 1974.

58. DER POLENAUFSTAND 1806-7. URKUNDEN UND AKTENSTUECKE AUS DER
    ZEIT ZWISCHEN JENA UND TILSIT [The Polish Uprising, 1806-7.
    Sources and Documents from the Period between Jena and Tilsit].
    Edited by Kurt Schottmuller. Lissa: Ebbeckes, 1907.

59. Poniatowski, Józef, prince. KORRESPONDENCYA KSIECIA JOZEFA
    PONIATOWSKIEGO Z FRANCYA [The Correspondence of Prince

Poniatowski with France]. Edited by Adam Skalkowski. Poznan: Poznańskie Towarzystwo Przyjaciól, 1921-29. 5 vols.

60. Przyborowski, Walery [Zygmunt Lucyan Sulima]. POLACY W HISZPANII 1808-1812 [The Poles in Spain 1808-1812]. Warsaw: Gebethner i Wolff, 1888.

61. Reychman, Jan. JOZEF SULKOWSKI, 1773-1798. Warsaw: Wydawnictwo Ministerstwa Obrony Narodowej, 1952.

62. Skalkowski, Adam Mieczyslaw. "Echa Somo-Sierry" [Echoes of Somo-Sierra]. KWARTALNIK HISTORYCZNY [Historical Quarterly] 38 (1924): 91-103.

63. Skalkowski, Adam Mieczyslaw. KSIAZE JOZEF [Prince Józef]. Bytom: Katolik, 1913.

64. Skalkowski, Adam Mieczyslaw. O CZESC IMIENIA POLSKIEGO. OPOWIADANIA I MATERYALY HISTORYCZNE [In Honor of the Polish Name. Historical Tales and Materials]. Lwów: Towarzystwo Wydawnictwo, 1908.

65. Skalkowski, Adam Mieczyslaw. "Oficerowie polscy stu dni" [Polish Officers of the Hundred Days]. KWARTALNIK HISTORYCZNY [Historical Quarterly] 29 (1915): 105-76.

66. Skalkowski, Adam Mieczyslaw. POLACY NA SAN DOMINGO 1802-1809 [The Poles in San Domingo 1802-1809]. Poznan: Gebethner i Wolff, 1921.

67. Skalkowski, Adam Mieczyslaw. LES POLONAIS EN EGYPTE 1798-1801. Cracow: G. Gebethner, 1910.

68. Skalkowski, Adam Mieczyslaw. "Polskie gwardye honorowe 1814 r." [The Polish Guard of Honor in 1814]. KSIEGA PAMIATKOWA KU CZCI OSWALDA BALZERA [Commemorative Book in Honor of Oswald Balzer] 2 (1925): 479-87.

69. Smerda, Milan. "Tazení polského vojska pres ceske zeme v r. 1813" [The Expedition of the Polish Army through the Czech Lands in 1813]. HISTORIE A VOJENSTVI [History and Military Affairs] (1967): 405-36. (See also the author's article "Polské vojsko v ceskych zemich w roce 1813" [The Polish Armies in the Czech Lands in 1813]. SLEZSKY SBORNIK 70 (1972): 248-64.)

70. Sokolnicki, Michal. DZIENNIK HISTORYCZNY I KORESPONDENCJA POLOWA GENERALA MICHALA SOKOLNICKIEGO 1809 R. [Historical Diary and Field Correspondence of General Michal Sokolnicki from 1809]. Edited by Bronislaw Pawlowski. Cracow: Polska Akademia Umiejetności, 1932.

71. "Souvenirs d'un officier polonais. Général Charles Turno (1811-1814)." Edited by Adam Skalkowski. REVUE DES ETUDES NAPOLEONIENNES 33 (1931): 99-116, 129-45.

72. Staszewski, Janusz. "Dywizja gdańska w walkach nad Dźwina i w
     obronie Gdańska (1812-13)" [The Gdansk Division in the Battle
     of the Dvina and in the Defense of Gdansk (1812-13)]. ROCZNIK
     GDANSKI [Gdansk Annual] 11 (1937): 210-25.

73. Staszewski, Janusz. "Gwardje narodowe w czasach Ksiestwa
     Warszawskiego" [The National Guard in the Duchy of Warsaw].
     PRZEGLAD HISTORYCZNO-WOJSKOWE [Historical-Military Review] 1
     (1929): 99-116.

74. Staszewski, Janusz. KALISKI WYSILEK ZBROJNY 1806-1813 [The
     Kalisz   Armed   Effort   1806-1813].   Kalisz: Towarzystwo
     Przyjaciól Ksiazki, 1931.

75. Staszewski, Janusz. "Powstanie poznańskie 1809 r." [The Poznań
     Uprising of 1809]. KRONIKA MIASTA POZNANIA [Chronicle of the
     City of Poznań] 8 (1930): 1-16, 160-80, 264-77.

76. Staszewski, Janusz. WOJSKO POLSKIE NA POMORZU W ROKU 1807 [The
     Polish Army in Pomerania in 1807]. Gdańsk: Gdańskie
     Towarzystwo Naukowe, 1958.

77. Staszewski, Janusz. WOJSKO POLSKIE NA SLASKIE W DOBIE
     NAPOLEONSKIEJ [The Polish Army in Silesia in the Napoleonic
     Period]. Katowice: Kasa J. Mianowskiego, Instytut Popierania
     Nauki, 1935.

78. Staszewski, Janusz. "Z dziejów garnizonu polskiego w Gdańsku w
     latach 1808-1812" [From the History of the Polish Garrison in
     Gdansk in the Years 1808-1812]. ROCZNIK GDANSKI [Gdansk
     Annual] 7/ 8 (1933-34): 222-72.

79. Stojanowski, Józef. KORPUSY KADETOW W KSIESTWIE WARSZAWSKIM
     [Cadet Corps in the Duchy of Warsaw]. Warsaw: Drukarnia
     Literacka, 1924.

80. Stojanowski, Józef. "Ministerjum wojny w Ksiestwa Warszawskim.
     (Zarys organizacji)" [The Ministry of War in the Duchy of
     Warsaw.   An   Outline   of   the   Organization].   PRZEGLAD
     HISTORYCZNO-WOJSKOWE [Historical-Military Review] 1 (1929):
     207-42.

81. Sulkowski, Józef. MEMOIRES HISTORIQUES, POLITIQUES ET
     MILITAIRES, SUR LES REVOLUTIONS DE POLOGNE 1792, 1794, LA
     CAMPAGNE D'ITALIE 1796, 1797, L'EXPEDITION DU TYROL, ET LES
     CAMPAGNES D'EGYPTE 1798-1799. Paris: Mesnier, 1832.

82. Szymanowski, Józef. MEMOIRES DU GENERAL SZYMANOWSKI
     (1806-1814). Paris: Charles-Lavauzelle, 1900.

83. Tokarz, Waclaw, and Marian Kukiel. DABROWSKI JAKO
     ORGANIZATOR I WODZ. [Dabrowski as an Organizer and Leader].
     Warsaw: Ksiegarnia Wojskowa, 1919.

84. Tyszkiewicz, Joseph. HISTOIRE DU 17ème REGIMENT DE CAVALERIE POLONAISE (LANCIERS DE COMTE MICHEL TYSZKIEWICZ) 1812-1815. Cracow: Anczyc, 1904.

85. "Udzial pospolitego ruszenia w walkach na Pomorzu i pod Gdańskiem w 1807 r." [The Participation of the Levée en masse in the Battles in Pomerania and at Gdansk]. Edited by Janusz Staszewski. ROCZNIK GDANSKI [Gdansk Annual] 9, 10 (1935-36): 486-510.

86. Wasicki, Jan. POWSTANIE 1806 ROKU W WIELKOPOLSCE [The 1806 Uprising in Wielkopolska]. Poznań: Wydnawnictwo Poznanskie, 1958.

87. Wielhorski, Józef. "Projekt reformy ministerstwa wojny Ksiestwa Warszawskiego w 1810 r." [The Project for the Reform of the Ministry of War of the Duchy of Warsaw in 1810]. PRZESZLOSC [The Past] 7 (1935): 13-16, 27-30, 61-64, 87-94.

88. Willaume, Juliusz. AMILKAR KOSINSKI 1769-1823. Poznan: Ostoja, 1930.

89. Willaume, Juliusz. "Obrona Ksiestwa Warszawskiego w 1812 r." [The Defense of the Duchy of Warsaw in 1812]. PRZEGLĄD HISTORYCZNO-WOJSKOWE [Historical-Military Review] 2 (1930): 145-80.

90. Willaume, Juliusz. "Sluzba zdrowia armii Ksiestwa Warszawskiego w przededniu kampanji 1812 r" [The Health Service of the Army of the Duchy of Warsaw on the Eve of the 1812 Campaign]. LEKARZ WOJSKOWE [The Military Doctor] 6 (1925): 1002-11.

91. "Wspomnienia ulana pulku pierwszego legii nadwiślańskiej o kampaniach lat 1807-1814" [Memoirs of an Uhlan of the 1st Regiment of the Vistula Legion about the Campaign from 1807 to 1814]. BIBLIOTEKA WARSZAWSKA [The Warsaw Library] 68 (1908): 314-53.

92. Zaluski, Józef. WSPOMNIENIA O PULKU LEKKO-KONNYM POLSKIM GWARDYI NAPOLEONA I, PRZEZ CALY CZAS OD ROZWIAZANIA PULKU W R. 1807 AZ DO KONCA W ROKU 1814 PRZEZ JOZEFA ZALUSKIEGO BYLEGO JENERALA BRYGADY W GLOWNYM SZTABIE WOJSKA POLSKIEGO, NIEGDYS OFICERA I SZEFA SZWADRONU RZECZONEJ GWARDYI CESARZA FRANCUZOW [Memoirs about the Polish Light Cavalry Regiment of Napoleon's Guard, from the Formation of the Regiment in 1807 until its End in 1814]. Cracow: K.J. Turowski, 1862. (Reprinted, Cracow: Wydawnictwo Literackie, 1976.)

93. Zaremba, Andrzej. "1 i 2 Pulk Ulanów polskich w kampanii francuskiej 1814 r." [The First and Second Regiments of Polish Uhlans in the French Campaign of 1814]. STUDIA DO DZIEJOW DAWNEGO UZBROJENIA I UBIORU WOJSK [Studies in the History of Ancient Military Arms and Uniforms] 6 (1974): 31-53.

94. ZARYS DZIEJOW WOJSKOWOSCI POLSKIEJ DO ROKU 1864 [Outline of the
    History of Polish Military Affairs until 1864]. Edited by
    Janusz Sikorski. Warsaw: Wydawnictwo Ministerstwa Obrony
    Narodowej, 1966. Vol. 2.

95. Zieliński, Kazimierz. "Dzieje Korpusu Kadetów w Kaliszu
    (1807-1832)" [History of the Cadet Corps in Kalisz
    (1807-1832)]. ROCZNIK KALISKI [Kalisz Annual] 7 (1974):
    79-112.

96. ZOLNIERZ POLSKI: UBIOR, UZBROJENIE I OPORZADZENIE OD WIEKU XI
    DO ROKU 1960 [The Polish Soldier: Uniforms, Arms and Equipment
    from the 11th Century to 1960]. Edited by Zofia Stefańska.
    Warsaw: Wydawnictwo Ministerstwa Obrony Narodowej, 1960-66.
    5 vols.

97. ZRODLA DO HISTORYI PULKU POLSKIEGO LEKKOKONNEGO GWARDYI
    NAPOLEONA I. [Sources for the History of the Polish First
    Cavalry Regiment of Napoleon's Guard]. Warsaw: Bib. Ord.
    Krasińskich, Muz. K. Swidzińskiego, 1899.

98. ZRODLA WOJSKOWE DO DZIEJOW POMORZA W CZASACH KSIESTWA
    WARSZAWSKIEGO. Cz. 1 ZAJECIE POMORZA 1806-07 [Military Sources
    for the History of Pomerania during the Duchy of Warsaw. Part
    1. The Occupation of Pomerania 1806-07]. Edited by Janusz
    Staszewski. Toruń: Towarzystwo Naukowe w Toruniu, 1933.

99. Zych, Gabriel. ARMIA KSIESTWA WARSZAWSKIEGO 1807-1812 [The
    Army of the Duchy of Warsaw 1807-1812]. Warsaw: Wydawnictwo
    Ministerstwa Obrony Narodowej, 1961.

100. Zych, Gabriel. ROK 1807 [The Year 1807]. Warsaw: Wydawnictwo
     Ministerstwa Obrony Narodowej, 1957.

ADDENDUM

101. BIBLIOGRAFIA HISTORII POLSKIEJ [Bibliography of Polish
     History]. Wroclaw: Zaklad Narodowej im. Ossolinskich,
     annually since 1944/47.

102. Daszkiewicz, Kazimierz, and Janina Gasiorowski. POLSKA
     BIBLIOGRAFIA WOJSKOWA [Polish Military Bibliography]. Cz. 1,
     t. 1. NAUKI WOJSKOWE DO R. 1904. Warsaw: Wydawnictwo
     Centralnej Biblioteki Wojskowej, 1921.

103. "Historia wojska polskiego, wojeń i sztuki wojenny" [The
     History of the Polish Army, of Wars and of the Military
     Arts]. KOMUNIKAT BIBLIOGRAFICZNY [Bibliographic
     Communications] 20 (1956): 20-38; 21 (1957): 30-65; 22 (1958):
     88-110. No further updates published.

104. Kirkor, Stanislaw. LEGIA NADWISLANSKA, 1808-1814 [The Vistula
     Legion]. London: Oficyna Poetów i Malarzy, 1981.

105. Kirkor, Stanislaw. POD SZTANDARAMI NAPOLEONA [Under Napoleon's Standards]. London: Oficyna Poetów i Malarzy, 1982.

106. Kukiel, Marian. "Polish Military Effort in the Napoleonic Wars." CAMBRIDGE HISTORY OF POLAND 2 (1941): 220-35.

107. Lakoma, Balbina. "Materialy do Bibliografii wojskowo-historycznej za lata 1952-1953" [Materials for a Military-Historical Bibliography for the Years 1952-1953]. STUDIA I MATERIALY DO HISTORII SZTUKI WOJENNEJ 1 (1954).

108. Pachoński, Jan. "Les Formations militaires polonaises de 1794 à 1807. Organisations, effectifs, faits d'armes." REVUE INTERNATIONAL D'HISTOIRE MILITAIRE 28 (1969): 468-81.

109. "Przeglad literatury historyczno-wojskowy" [Review of the Historical-Military Literature]. PRZEGLAD HISTORYCZNO-WOJSKOWY [Historical-Military Review] 1-10 (1929-38).

110. Rutkowski, Andrzej. "Materialy do bibliografii wojskowo-historycznej za r. 1954" [Materials for a Military-Historical Bibliography for the Year 1954]. STUDIA I MATERIALY DO HISTORII SZTUKI WOJENNEJ 3 (1956); 4 (1958). (No further updates published).

CHAPTER XXI

THE LOW COUNTRIES: BELGIUM

Gerlof D. Homan, Illinois State University

During much of the Middle Ages and the early modern period
Belgium and the Netherlands shared a common political and cultural
heritage under the Burgundian and Hapsburg monarchs. They became
separated during the time of the Reformation when the seven northern
provinces successfully revolted against Spain and formed the Republic
of the Seven United Provinces. The ten southern provinces remained
under Spanish rule and in 1714, by the Treaty of Utrecht, became part
of the Hapsburg territories. They became a battleground between
French and Austrian armies during the War of the First Coalition and
were annexed by France in 1795. In 1814 the southern Netherlands was
merged with the former Dutch Republic to form the Kingdom of the
Netherlands. Belgium formally gained its independence in 1839 after
a short war and prolonged negotiations.

The era of French domination was an important period in modern
Belgian history. The French introduced many lasting reforms and
centralized the administration. Napoleon's regime enjoyed a special
measure of popularity because it brought economic prosperity and
religious peace by the Concordat of 1801. The most important
grievance against the Emperor was conscription. About 130,000
Belgians were conscripted during the period of the Empire. Most of
these recruits were dispersed among various units, but some, such as
the 122th Régiment de Ligne and the 27th Corps Chasseurs à Cheval,
retained a Belgian character. Belgian soldiers fought in all the
major battles and campaigns during the period of French domination,
and some attained the rank of general. Among them were Jean-Baptiste
Dumonceau and Louis Joseph Lahure. It was the latter who captured
with a small number of men some 14 Dutch battleships frozen in the
ice near Texel in January 1795.

Although most Belgians were unhappy over the allied decision to
merge their country with the Netherlands many joined the newly-formed
army of the Kingdom in 1815 and some 6000 men fought bravely at
Quatre Bras and Waterloo. Belgian historians have been chagrined
over British criticism that Belgian and Dutch forces did not perform
well in those two battles. All evidence seems to bear out that they
fought well. After Napoleon's demise in 1814 many Belgian soldiers
and officers remained loyal to France and fought with the Emperor at
Waterloo against their own countrymen. Even after the debacle of
1815 many Belgians remained in French service.

While many Belgians fought for France and Napoleon, others
offered their services to the Hapsburg monarchy. Thus, the so-called
Latour Regiment participated in various campaigns against France and
one small unit, the Gardes Wallones fought against Napoleon in Spain.

Belgians have recognized the importance of French denomination
as is reflected in the abundance of historial literature on this era.
Military history has been given much attention as is shown by the
selection of some of the works and articles cited below.

BIBLIOGRAPHICAL SOURCES

The most important bibliographical sources on Belgian military history during the Napoleonic era include Paul Gérin's BIBLIOGRAPHIE DE L'HISTOIRE DE BELGIQUE 1789-21 JUILLET, 1831 (22) and the bibliographical section in the REVUE BELGE DE PHILOLOGIE ET D'HISTOIRE.

ARCHIVAL SOURCES

Much material can be found in local Belgian archives and many of the works and articles cited below are based on such holdings. Some materials are in the archives of the Museum van het Koninklijke Leger (Museum of the Royal Army). However, the largest amount is in the Archives Nationales in Paris and the archives of the Service historique de l'armée at the Château de Vincennes. For specific holdings see especially M.J. Tits-Dieuaide, "Les Archives nationales à Paris et l'histoire de nôtre pays sous le régime français" (29) and A. Duchesne, LES ARCHIVES DE LA GUERRE ET DE LA MARINE A PARIS ET L'HISTOIRE DE BELGIQUE (18).

PUBLISHED DOCUMENTS

Anatole France commented once that soldiers' letters were among the "chef d'oeuvre inconnu." If he is correct, and I believe he is, Belgian historians have repaired the gap by publishing many such letters which give us much information on such problems as conscription, battles, and the suffering and grief of the soldier. Among these publications are the LETTRES DE GROGNARDS (21) which consists of 1183 letters by Napoleonic veterans of the Ourthe Department compiled by Emile Fairon and Henri Heuse. The volume by J. van Bakel and P.C. Rolf entitled VLAAMSE SOLDATENBRIEVEN UIT DE NAPOLEONTISCHE TIJD [Flemish Soldiers' Letters during the Napoleonic Period] (3) is based upon 317 soldiers' letters found in the State Archives in Bruges; and François Decker's LETTRES DE SOLDATS LUXEMBOURGEOIS AU SERVICE DE LA FRANCE 1789-1814 (16) provides valuable insights into service in the French armies. Unfortunately space does not permit the citing of many letters published by J. de Smet in the periodical BIEKORF from 1930 to 1939.

GENERAL WORKS

There are no general works on Belgian military history during the Napoleonic era. However, some information can be obtained from Léon de Lanzac de Laborie's LA DOMINATION FRANCAISE EN BELGIQUE (25), which is based both on materials in the National Archives in Paris and on those at Vincennes, especially volumes 1 and 2. Also useful is volume five of Verhaegen's LA BELGIQUE SOUS LA DOMINATION FRANCAISE 1792-1814 (30).

MEMOIRS, JOURNALS, AND EYEWITNESS ACCOUNTS

There are a number of memoirs and personal recollections by Belgian officers among which are François Dumonceau's MEMOIRES (20), the SOUVENIRS of L.J. Lahure (24), C. Terlinden's COLONEL SCHELTENS:

SOUVENIRS D'UN GROGNARD BELGE (28), Pierre Martin Pirquet's JOURNAL (26) which relates his activities as an officer in Austrian service, and G.P. Baert's "Het dagboek van Carolus Blomme (1813-1814). Een gezondheids officier van Napoleon" [The Diary of Carolus Blomme, a Medical Officer under Napoleon] (2).

SPECIALIZED WORKS

The amount of secondary literature is rather voluminous, much more so than Dutch historical literature on the same subject. Important biographical data on Belgian officers in Napoleon's armies is given by F. Bernaert in FASTES MILITAIRES DES BELGES (5) and by W. Aerts in "Au sujet des généraux belges" (1). There are few good biographical studies of Belgians who served in the imperial armies. We do have A. Duchesne's UN GENERAL BELGE DE NAPOLEON: J.B. VAN MERLEN (19) and Henri F. Dejardin's "Le lieutenant-général baron Michel de Tiecken de Terhove" (17), but there is very little else.

Belgian military participation is discussed by Hector Jean Couvreur in LES WALLONS DANS LA GRANDE ARMEE (10) which also gives some important statistical data. E. Cruyplants discusses the history of the 112th Regiment (13) and the Belgian cavalry (12), and A. Bikar details the history of the hussars (7). C. Schaak has made a study of the Luxemburg soldiers in French military service and volume 2 deals with the Napoleonic era (27). Roger Darquenne has made two good studies of French conscription in Belgium (14, 15) which show inter alia that in 1806 the percentage of draftees in all Belgian departments was less than that for all of France. Naval history is discussed by L.J.B. Keraval in CHRONIQUES MARITIMES (23), a work that includes many documents pertaining to the navy as well as the defense of Walcheren in 1809.

No military events occurred on Belgian soil during the Napoleonic era, except for the events of 1809, until 1814. H. Carnot discusses his father's role in the siege of Antwerp in 1814 and includes many letters (8). Belgian participation in the Battles of Quatre Bras and Waterloo is discussed by A. Bikar (6), Hector Jean Couvreur (9), Eugène Cruyplants (11), and most thoroughly by François de Bas and J. de T'Serclaes de Wommersom in their LA CAMPAGNE DE 1815 AUX PAYS BAS (4).

FUTURE RESEARCH

While many local studies have been made on such problems as conscription and the participation of various local soldiers in different campaigns and battles, more could and should be done to explore local archives. Also the rich resources of the Archives Nationales and the archives of the Service historique de l'armée at Vincennes must be tapped. A synthetic work on the entire Belgian military experience during the Napoleonic era would be most welcome.

BIBLIOGRAPHY: BELGIUM

1. Aerts, W. "Au Sujet des généraux belges de la République et de l'Empire (1792-1815)." CARNET DE LA FOURRAGERE, Series 9, 4 (1950): 247-53.

2. Baert, G.P. "Het dagboek van Carolus Blomme (1813-1814). Een gezondheidsofficier van Napoleon" [The Diary of Carolus Bloome, A Medical Officer under Napoleon]. BIJDRAGEN TOT DE GESCHIEDENIS DER STAD DEINZE EN HET LAND VAN LEIE EN SCHELDE 25 (1958): 7-100.

3. Bakel, J. van, and P.C. Rolf. VLAAMSE SOLDATENBRIEVEN UIT DE NAPOLEONTISCHE TIJD. Bruges: Orion; Nimwegen: Dekker and Van de Vegt, 1977.

4. Bas, François de, and J. de T'Serclaes de Wommersom. LA CAMPAGNE DE 1815 AUX PAYS BAS. Brussels: Dewit, 1908-09. 3 vols.

5. Bernaert, F. FASTES MILITAIRE DES BELGES AU SERVICE DE LA FRANCE (1789-1815). Brussels: Lamartin, 1898.

6. Bikar, A. "Les Belges à Waterloo." REVUE INTERNATIONALE D'HISTOIRE MILITAIRE 24 (1965): 365-92.

7. Bikar, A. "Hussards belges de Napoléon." REVUE BELGE D'HISTOIRE MILITAIRE 16 (1966): 422-36; 17 (1967): 118-27, 259-67; 18 (1968): 110-20, 272-94, 408-20, 576-87.

8. Carnot, H. "Le Siège d'Anvers en 1814." REVUE DE PARIS 35 (1857): 481-517.

9. Couvreur, Hector Jean. LE DRAME BELGE DE WATERLOO. Bussels: Brepols, 1959.

10. Couvreur, Hector Jean. LES WALLONS DANS LA GRANDE ARMEE. Gembloux: Duculot, 1971.

11. Cruyplants, Eugène. "Les Combattants belges à Waterloo." BULLETIN DE LA SOCIETE D'ETUDES NAPOLEONIENNES 16 (1966): 5-8.

12. Cruyplants, Eugène. HISTOIRE DE LA CAVALRIE BELGE AU SERVICE D'AUSTRICHE, DE FRANCE, DES PAYS BAS ET PENDANT LES PREMIERES ANNEES DE NOTRE NATIONALITE. 2d ed. Brussels: Spineux, 1883.

13. Cruyplants, Eugène. HISTOIRE ILLUSTREE D'UN CORPS BELGE AU SERVICE DE LA REPUBLIQUE ET DE L'EMPIRE. LA 112e DEMI-BRIGADE. Brussels: Spineux, 1902.

14. Darquenne, Roger. "La Conscription dans le département de Jemappes (1789-1813). Bilan démographique et médico-social." ANNALES DU CERCLE ARCHEOLOGIQUE DE MONS 67 (1970): 1-425.

15. Darquenne, Roger. "La Situation conscriptionnelle en 1806 dans six départements belges." REVUE BELGE DE PHILOLOGIE ET D'HISTOIRE 48 (1969): 488-501.

16. Decker, François. LETTRES DE SOLDATS LUXEMBOURGEOIS AU SERVICE DE LA FRANCE 1789-1814. CONSERVEES AUX ARCHIVES DE L'ETAT. Luxemburg: Editions François Mersch, 1971.

17. Dejardin, Henri F. "Le Lieutenant-général baron Michel de Tiecken de Terhove (1777-1848)." BULLETIN DE LA SOCIETE BELGE DES ETUDES NAPOLEONIENNES 17 (1955): 10-15.

18. Duchesne, A. LES ARCHIVES DE LA GUERRE ET DE LA MARINE A PARIS ET L'HISTOIRE DE BELGIQUE. Brussels: Palais des Académies, 1962.

19. Duchesne, A. UN GENERAL BELGE DE NAPOLEON: J.B. VAN MERLEN. Brussels: l'Avenir, 1949.

20. Dumonceau, François, comte. MEMOIRES DU GENERAL COMTE FRANCOIS DUMONCEAU 1790-1811. Brussels: Brepols, 1958-63. 3 vols.

21. Fairon, Emile, and Henri Heuse. LETTRES DE GROGNARDS. Liège: Bénard; Paris: Courville, 1936.

22. Gérin, Paul, ed. BIBLIOGRAPHIE DE L'HISTOIRE DE BELGIQUE 1789-21 JUILLET 1831. Louvain: Editions Nauwelaerts, 1960.

23. Keraval, L.J.B. CHRONIQUES MARITIMES D'ANVERS DE 1804 A 1814. HISTOIRE D'UN FLOTTE DU TEMPS PASSE. Paris: Baudoin, 1890.

24. Lahure, Louis Joseph, baron. SOUVENIRS DE LA VIE MILITAIRE DU LIEUTENANT-GENERAL BARON L.J. LAHURE 1787-1815. Publiés par le baron P. Lahure. Paris: Lahure, 1895.

25. Lanzac de Laborie, Léon de. LA DOMINATION FRANCAISE EN BELGIQUE. Paris: Librairie Plon, 1895. 2 vols.

26. Pirquet, Pierre Martin. JOURNAL DE CAMPAGNE DE PIERRE-MARTIN PIRQUET 1781-1811. OFFICIER AU SERVICE D'AUSTRICHE. Liège: Soc. des bibliophiles liégeois, 1970. 2 vols.

27. Schaak, Charles. LES LUXEMBOURGEOIS, SOLDATS DE LA FRANCE. Diekirch: Schroell, 1904-1910. 2 vols.

28. Terlinden, C. COLONEL SCHELTENS: SOUVENIRS D'UN GROGNARD BELGE. 2d ed. Brussels: Dessart, 1941.

29. Tits-Dieuaide, M.J. "Les Archives Nationales à Paris et l'histoire de notre pays sous le régime français (1789-1815)." BULLETIN DE LA COMMISSION ROYALE D'HISTOIRE 126 (1960): 123-96.

30. Verhaegen, P. LA BELGIQUE SOUS LA DOMINATION FRANCAISE 1789-1814. Brussels: Goemaere, 1929. 5 vols.

Domination] (15).   The life of Carel Hendrik Ver Huell, the most important admiral during the period and one who remained loyal to Napoleon after 1814, is discussed by Q.M.R. Ver Huell in HET LEVEN EN KARAKTER VAN CAREL HENDRIK, GRAAF VER HUELL [Life and Character of Count Carel Hendrik Ver Huell] (26) and by H. Hardenberg in "Admiraal Ver Huell" (14).

One of the most important military episodes on Dutch soil was the British invasion of Walcheren in 1809.   No Dutch study of this episode has been made except J.A. van Hamel's "De Engelse landing op Zeeland en haar achtergronden" [The English Landing in Zeeland and Its Background] (13).   Other studies are Antony Brett-James's "The Walcheren Failure" (4) and T.H. McGuffie's "The Walcheren Expedition" (23).

Though military conscription was widely resented and dreaded, no public opposition occurred until the spring of 1813 in one of the western departments.   The establishment of the so-called garde d'honneur in 1813 brought resistance among the well-to-do.   This episode is discussed by W.F. Lichtenauer in DE NEDERLANDERS IN NAPOLEONS GARDE D'HONNEUR (22).   The revolt against the defeated and retreating imperial armies is treated in great detail in the edited work of G.J.W. Koolemans Beijnen, HISTORISCH GEDENKBOEK DER HERSTELLING VAN NEERLANDS ONAFHANKELIJKHEID [Historical Memorial of the Restoration of the Netherlands Independence] (19).   Dutch participation in the Battles of Quatre Bras and Waterloo is thoroughly discussed by F. de Bas and J. de T'Serclaes de Wommersom in LA CAMPAGNE DE 1815 AUX PAYS BAS [The Campaign of 1815 in the Low Countries] (1).

FUTURE RESEARCH

Almost every aspect of Dutch military experience during the Napoleonic era needs a thorough study.   Various Belgian works and studies could serve as a model.   A search of the local archives might lead to the publication of soldiers' letters.   An exploration of the archival materials in Vincennes could produce some badly needed studies on conscription and an up-to-date account of the Dutch participation in the Russian campaign of 1812.   Studies on Dutch support for the French war effort, Napoleon's naval policies, and an analysis of the impact of the French occupation upon the various regions of the Netherlands would prove useful.

BIBLIOGRAPHY: THE NETHERLANDS

1. Bas, François de, and J. de T'Serclaes de Wommersom. LA CAMPAGNE DE 1815 AUX PAYS-BAS. Brussels: Dewit, 1908-09. 3 vols.

2. Benthien, G.D. "Doorlopend verhaal van de dienstverrichting der Nederlandsche pontonniers onder den majoor G.D. Benthien, 1797-1825" [Continuous Account of the Service Activities of the Dutch Pontoniers under Major G.D. Benthien]. BIJDRAGEN EN MEDEDEELINGEN VAN HET HISTORISCH GENOOTSCHAP 32 (1911): 100-77.

3. Bonaparte, Louis, king of Holland. DOCUMENS HISTORIQUES ET REFLEXIONS SUR LE GOUVERNEMENT DE LA HOLLANDE. Paris: Aillaud, 1820. 3 vols.

4. Brett-James, Antony. "The Walcheren Failure." HISTORY TODAY 13 (1963): 811-20; 14 (1964): 60-68.

5. Buck, Hendrick de, ed. BIBLIOGRAPHIE DER GESCHIEDENIS VAN NEDERLAND [Bibliography of the History of the Netherlands]. Leiden: Brill, 1968.

6. Colenbrander, H.T., ed. GEDENKSTUKKEN DER ALGEMEENE GESCHIEDENIS DER NEDERLANDEN VAN 1795 TOT 1840 [Documents on General History of the Netherlands from 1795 to 1815]. The Hague: Nijhoff, 1905-22. 10 vols.

7. Colenbrander, H.T. INLIJVING EN OPSTAND [Annexation and Revolt] Amsterdam: Meulenhoff, 1913.

8. Dedem van de Gelder, Anton B.G., baron van. MEMOIRES DU GENERAL BARON DE DEDEM DE GELDER. Paris: Plon-Nourrit, 1900.

9. Eerens, D.J. de. "Napoleons Russische veldtocht" [Napoleon's Russian Campaign]. HAAGSCH MAANDBLAD 15 (1938): 272-92.

10. Es, N.J.A.P. van. DE RIJDENDE ARTILLERIE BIJ DEN VELDTOCHT IN RUSLAND IN 1812 [The Mobile Artillery during the Campaign in Russia in 1812]. Arnhem: Coers en Roest, n.d.

11. Fehrmann, C.N. ONZE VLOOT IN DE FRANSE TIJD. DE ADMIRALEN DE WINTER EN VER HUELL [Our Fleet in the French Period. Admirals De Winter and Ver Huell]. The Hague: Kruseman, 1969.

12. Gijsberti-Hodenpijl, C.F. "Mededeelingen over het 2e regiment Hollandsche lansiers der Keizerlijke garde in 1812" [Information concerning the 2d Regiment of Dutch Lancers of the Imperial Guard in 1812]. NEDERLAND. VERZAMELING VAN OORSPRONKELIJKE BIJDRAGEN DOOR NEDERLANDSCHE LETTERKUNDIGEN 1 (1899): 449-62.

13. Hamel, J.A. van. "De Engelse landing op Zeeland en haar achtergronden" [The English Landing in Zeeland and Its Background]. PUBLICATIES VAN HET GENOOTSCHAP VOOR NAPOLEONTISCHE STUDIEN 7 (1955): 7-25.

14. Hardenberg, H. "Admiraal Ver Huell." PUBLICATIES VAN HET GENOOTSCHAP VOOR NAPOLEONTISCHE STUDIEN 7 (1955): 129-47.

15. Herman, H. GESCHIEDENIS ONZER ZEEMACHT TIJDENS DE FRANSCHE OVERHEERSCHING, 1810 TOT 1814 [History of Our Naval Power during the French Domination, 1810-1814]. n.p.: Vereeniging "Het Nederlandsch Zeewezen," 1923.

16. Hogendorp, Dirk, graaf van. MEMOIRES. The Hague: Nijhoff, 1887.

17. Homan, Gerlof D. NEDERLAND IN DE NAPOLEONTISCHE TIJD, 1795-1815 [The Netherlands in the Napoleonic Era]. Haarlem: Fibula-Dishoeck, 1978.

18. Kool, A. DE RUSSISCHE VELDTOCHT VAN 1812 [The Russian Campaign of 1812]. Rotterdam: Nijgh en Van Ditmar, 1912.

19. Koolemans Beijnen, G.J.W., ed. HISTORISCH GEDENKBOEK DER HERSTELLING VAN NEERLANDS ONAFHANKELIJKHEID IN 1813 [Historical Memorial of the Restoration of the Netherlands Independence in 1813]. Haarlem: Bohn, 1912-13. 4 vols.

20. Krayenhoff, C.R.T., baron. BIJDRAGEN TOT DE VADERLANDSCHE GESCHIEDENIS VAN DE BELANGRIJKE JAREN 1809 EN 1810 [Contributions to National History of the Important Years of 1809 and 1810]. Nimwegen: Vieweg, 1831.

21. Krayenhoff, C.R.T., baron. LEVENSBIJZONDERHEDEN [Autobiography]. Nimwegen: Vieweg, 1844.

22. Lichtenauer, W.F. DE NEDERLANDERS IN NAPOLEONS GARDE D'HONNEUR [Netherlanders in Napoleon's Guard of Honor]. Rotterdam and The Hague: Nijgh en Van Ditmar, 1971.

23. McGuffie, Tom H. "The Walcheren Expedition and the Walcheren Fever." ENGLISH HISTORICAL REVIEW 62 (1947): 191-202.

24. Naber, J.W.A. OVERHEERSCHING EN VRIJWORDING [Domination and Liberation]. 3d ed. Haarlem: Tjeenk Willink, 1913.

25. Sabron, F.H.A. GESCHIEDENIS VAN HET 124ste REGIMENT INFANTERIE VAN LINIE ONDER KEIZER NAPOLEON I. [History of the 124th Infantry Line Regiment under Emperor Napoleon I]. 2d ed. Breda: Koninklijke Militaire Academie, 1910.

26. Ver Huell, Q.M.R. HET LEVEN EN KARAKTER VAN CAREL HENDRIK GRAAF VER HUELL [Life and Character of Count Carel Hendrik Ver Huell]. Amsterdam: Beijerinck, 1847. 2 vols.

27. Vlijmen, Bernard R.F. van. LES HOLLANDAIS DANS LA GRANDE ARMEE. n.p.: n.p., 1907.

CHAPTER XXII

SWITZERLAND

Colonel EMG Daniel Reichel
Captain Dominic Pedrazzini

As a result of its central position in the heart of Europe, Switzerland has been a privileged observer for the wars of the Revolutionary Period, and more specifically, the campaigns of Napoleon. Indeed, Napoleon reconnoitered the Swiss cantons in 1797 and the next year, before the word "blitzkreig" had been coined, the French swept into Switzerland in a lightning campaign. In 1800 Switzerland was again the scene of classic operations, culminating in the battle of Marengo.

During the Consulat and the Empire, Switzerland paid a very heavy price in men. Almost 80,000 men, about ten percent of the active population, died on the battlefields of Europe. Swiss regiments served in Spain, Germany, Austria, and Russia. A Swiss regiment covered the bridge over the Berezina in 1812 and helped save the remains of the Grande Armée but it lost 1,000 of its complement of 1,300 men. Swiss soldiers have been involved in almost every campaign of the Napoleonic wars. Consequently, Swiss history during the Revolutionary period offers lucrative possibilities for students interested in this field.

GENERAL WORKS

There are a number of broad studies devoted to Switzerland and Napoleon. A general eight-volume study of Swiss troops in foreign service (103) includes a series of monographs concerning the officers who served in Napoleon's armies; Vallière's HONNEUR ET FIDELITE (114) is a more general study of the same topic. The volumes by Maag (71-73) concentrate on the Swiss regiments serving in Spain, Russia, and France, while Schaller's HISTOIRE DES TROUPES SUISSES (100) is a more superficial study of the Napoleonic period. Works by Lecomte (64), Wieland (118), and the Historical Service of the Swiss Army (51) are also useful in assessing the role of the Swiss regiments. Cerenville's SYSTEME CONTINENTAL (22) and Guillon's NAPOLEON ET LA SUISSE (45) provide useful information on the Swiss cantons during the period.

BIBLIOGRAPHIES

The most important bibliography for Switzerland and the Swiss troops in the French army can be found in the three-volume work by Barth (6). A source book on Swiss history, QUELLEN ZUR SCHWEIZER GESCHICHTE (89), is a useful guide to library collections and the DICTIONNAIRE HISTORIQUE (32) provides detailed information on Swiss biographies and topography.

ARCHIVES

Swiss archives contain a number of valuable collections for this period. Troop situations, registers, acts, memoirs, and correspondence can be found in the Federal Archives at Berne or in the various cantonal archives. The Departmental Archives of Leman in Geneva contain manuscripts related to the health of the conscripts. At Lausanne there are numerous manuscripts of Jomini. Berne and Basel have several university libraries with collections of the Napoleonic period. Manuscripts relative to Masséna's campaign of 1799 can be found in the National Swiss Museum and the Zentralbiblioteka in Zurich. At Neuchâtel there are documents related to Berthier. The archives at Sion, the capital of the Valais and later of the department of Simplon, house documents on the Swiss troops in Spain. There is also a valuable collection of material at the Musée des Suisses de l'étrangère at the Château de Penthes near Geneva as well as in the private archives scattered across Switzerland. Scholars interested in such archival work should contact the Service Historique de l'armée Suisse at the Bibliothèque militaire federal, in the Palais fédéral, Berne (CH 3003), where they will find a most cooperative staff.

PUBLISHED DOCUMENTS

Documents concerning the Swiss cantons in the Napoleonic period can be found in the eleven-volume ACTENSAMMLUNG AUS DER ZEIT DER HELVETISCHEN REPUBLIK (1) and the REPERTORIUM DER ABSCHIEDE DER EIDGENOESSISCHEN TAGSATZUNGEN (92).

MEMOIRS, JOURNALS, AND EYEWITNESS ACCOUNTS

Primary accounts of Swiss soldiers who served in Spain during the Peninsular War include the works of Benziger (8), Bruckner (16), Donnet (33), Engelhard (35), Geisendorf (42), Muralt (80), Roverea (97), and Sprünglin (106). Sprünglin's SOUVENIRS, published in 1904 by the REVUE HISPANIQUE, are particularly rich in details of the 6th Corps in Spain, since he served as Marshal Ney's aide-de-camp. Works of those who served in Russia include DAS TAGEBUCH EINER LUZERNERIN AUS DEM FELDZUGE NACH RUSSLAND 1812 by Bucher (17), "Mort d'un officier vaudois à la Beresina [1812]" by Burnand (19), and BERESINA. SOUVENIRS DE RUSSIE DE 1812 by Muralt and Legler (80). MÉMOIRES DU LANDAMAN MONOD POUR SERVIR A L'HISTOIRE DE LA SUISSE EN 1815 (77) details the campaign of 1814 and 1815 in France and Belgium.

SPECIALIZED WORKS: JOMINI

One of the most important Swiss collections of both primary and secondary material is concerned with General Antoine Henri Jomini who served in the Grande Armée until 1812 when he joined the Allied cause. Firsthand, he observed the operations of the great protagonists--Napoleon, Archduke Charles, and Alexander I--so his works occupy a central position in the history of the Napoleonic Wars. A comprehensive introduction to Jomini's works can be found in John Alger's BIBLIOGRAPHICAL SURVEY (2). Additional information can be located in the bibliography of de Courville's biography (26) and in Olivier Pavillon's "Bibliographie" in LE GENERAL ANTIONE HENRI JOMINI, published by the Bibliographie historique Vaudoise (86). Among Jomini's own works, the fifteen-volume HISTOIRE CRITIQUE ET MILITAIRE DES GUERRES DE LA REVOLUTION (57), his four-volume study of Napoleon (58), and his study on the war in Spain, edited by Lecomte (56), present valuable insights and details.

OTHER SPECIALIZED WORKS

Most of the research on the Swiss cantons and the Swiss regiments during the Napoleonic period has been concentrated in the same general areas as the eyewitness accounts. The campaign of 1799 was of monumental significance for the history of the Second Coalition; therefore, numerous works have been devoted to operations in Switzerland. Among the most useful works are those of Gachot (40), Hennequin (50), Reding-Biberegg (90), Michailowski-Danilewski (78), Hüffer (52-54), Shadwell (102), Boillot (14), Becker (7), Hartmann (48), Trumeau (112), Dedon (28), Ross (95), Orloff (84), and Suvoroff-Rimniksky (110). In addition to the biographies and memoirs of Masséna listed in Chapter X, the memoirs of Soult (104), Lecourbe (65), Thiébault (111), and Dellard (29) are invaluable in understanding French operations. Volumes devoted to the Russian generalissimo, Alexandre Suvorov, include those by La Verne (62), Longworth (70), Boguslavskii (13), Jacoby (55), Valka (113), Blease (12), Osipov (85), Vassiluef (116), and Polevoi (88). For the studies of the Russian campaign of 1812 the volumes of Hellmueller (49), Kummer (61), Kuepfer (60), Legler (66), and Vallotton (115) should be consulted. The campaign of 1796-97 is analyzed by Rüstow (98), and operations in 1805-08 are considered by Steiger (107).

There are regimental studies by Castella de Delley (21), Dick (31), Erismann (37), and Guye (46), as well as "Napoleon's Schweizertruppen in Spainen und Russland," published in the NEUJAHRSBLAETTER DER FEUERWERKERGESELLSCHAFT (82). Works concerning Berthier and Neuchâtel(27), the Swiss official Monteggio (11), General Rivaz (43), the Caprez family (117), and Karl Ziegler (119) are also significant for the study of Helvetian history.

JOURNALS

There are a number of Swiss newspapers and periodicals that should prove valuable for scholars working in the Revolutionary period. Among those available are the HELVETISCHE MILITAER-ZEITSCHRIFT (121), the REVUE MILITAIRE SUISSE (123), as well as the contemporary GAZETTE DE LAUSANNE (120) and the NEUE ZUERICHER ZEITUNG (122).

FUTURE RESEARCH

There are several research projects now in progress and there are many more available for the interested scholar. The staff of the Historical Service for the Swiss Army is currently preparing the unpublished memoires of Jomini for print and a new edition of Jomini's HISTOIRE ... DES GUERRES DE LA REVOLUTION. Pedrazzini is hard at work compiling a dictionary of Swiss generals in foreign service and a number of theses are currently in preparation at various Swiss universities. Nevertheless, there are numerous Swiss topics yet to be explored. What was the impact of French domination upon the specific Swiss cantons militarily, politically, economically, socially, etc.? Which Swiss generals in foreign service deserve a biography--Hotze, Reynier? Several military operations in Switzerland are yet to be scrutinized and even aspects of Masséna's famous campaign of 1799 remain to be considered and evaluated.

1. ACHTENSAMMLUNG AUS DER ZEIT DER HELVETISCHEN REPUBLIK (1798-1803). Berne: Stämpfil, 1886-1911. 11 vols.

2. Alger, John. ANTOINE HENRI JOMINI: A BIBLIOGRAPHICAL SURVEY. West Point, N.Y.: United States Military Academy, 1975.

3. Andolenko, Serge. AIGLES DE NAPOLEON CONTRE DRAPEAUX DU TSAR: 1799, 1805-1807, 1812-1814: DRAPEAUX RUSSES CONQUIS PAR LES FRANCAIS, EMBLEMES FRANCAIS PAR LES RUSSES. Paris: Eurimprim, 1969.

4. Anthing, Johann Friedrich. HISTORY OF THE CAMPAIGNS OF COUNT ALEXANDER SUWOROW RYMNIKSKI, FIELD-MARSHAL-GENERAL IN THE SERVICE OF HIS IMPERIAL MAJESTY, THE EMPEROR OF ALL THE RUSSIAS: WITH A PRELIMINARY SKETCH OF HIS PRIVATE LIFE AND CHARACTER. Translated from the German. London: Wright, 1799. 2 vols.

5. Bagration, Peter Ivanovitch, prince. JOURNAL OF THE CAMPAIGN OF 1799. [Suvorof Museum, Petrograd].

6. Barth, Hans. BIBLIOGRAPHIE DER SCHWEIZER GESCHICHTE. Basel: Geering, 1914-15. 3 vols.

7. Becker, F[riedrich?]. DIE ERSTE SCHLACHT BEI ZUERICH DEN 4. JUNI 1799. Zurich: Schulthess, 1899.

8. Benziger, C. "Die Schweizer in spanischen kriegsdienstes." VATERLAND 4 (1924).

9. Beretta, G. "I militari Ticinesi nei Reggimenti Svizzeri al Servizio di Napoleone I." BOLL. STORIA DELLA SVIZZERA ITALIANA (1910).

10. Beretta, G. I TICINESI NELLA CAMPAGNA DI RUSSIA (1812). Bellinzona: Istituto Editoriale Ticinese, 1937.

11. Beretta, G. "Un ufficiale ticinese decorato della medaglia di Sant'Elena: Michel Angiolo De Ambrosi di Monteggio 1775-1859." BOLL. STORIA DELLA SVIZZERA ITALIANA 1 (1911).

12. Blease, W. Lyon. SUVOROF. London: Constable, 1920.

13. Boguslavskii, G.A., comp. A.V. SUVOROV: DOKUMENTY. Moscow: Iskusstvo, 1949-53.

14. Boillot, Jean[?]. LA CAMPAGNE DE 1799 EN SUISSE. Neuchâtel: Libraire militaire, 1890.

15. Borel, F.G. NEUCHATEL SOUS LE PRINCE BERTHIER. LE BLOCUS CONTINENTAL ET LE BATAILLON DES CANARIS 1806-1814. Neuchâtel: Chez l'auteur, 1898.

16. Bruckner, A. DIE KAPITULATION VON LERIDA, 14 MAI 1810.
    Frauenfeld, 1938.

17. Bucher, J.F. DAS TAGEBUCH EINER LUZERNERIN [Katharina Peyer]
    AUS DEM FELDZUGE NACH RUSSLAND 1812. Lucerene: Bucher, 1901.

18. Burgener, L. "Napoléon et la Suisse: Méthodes et décisions."
    [D'après la correspondance de Napoléon I]. L'INFORMATION
    HISTORIQUE 4 (1971): 150-60.

19. Burnand, A. "Mort d'un officier vaudois à la Beresina [1812]."
    REVUE HISTORIQUE VAUDOISE (1908).

20. Burturlin, Dimitrii Petrovich, graf. RELATION HISTORIQUE ET
    CRITIQUE DE LA CAMPAGE DE 1799 DES AUSTRO-RUSSES EN ITALIE.
    Par ***. Saint Petersburg: Pluchart, 1812.

21. Castella de Delley, Rodolphe de. 2e REGIMENT SUISSE,
    1806-1814. Wallenried FR: Chez l'auteur, 1966.

22. Cerenville, B. de. LE SYSTEME CONTINENTAL ET LA SUISSE,
    1803-1813. Lausanne: Payot, 1906.

23. Clausewitz, Karl von. LA CAMPAGNE DE 1799 EN ITALIE ET EN
    SUISSE. Paris: Champ Libre, 1979.

24. CORRESPONDANCE DE FREDERIC-CESAR DE LA HARPE ET ALEXANDRE Ier.
    Publiée par Jean-Charles Biaudet et Françoise Nicod.
    Neuchâtel: Baconnière, 1978-80. 3 vols.

25. CORRESPONDENZ DES ... FUERSTEN ITALIJSKY GRAFEN ALEXANDER
    WALLILJEWITSCH SUWOROFF-RIMNIKSKY UEBER DIE RUSSISCH-
    OESTREICHISCHE KAMPAGNE IM JAHRE 1799. Glogau and Leipzig:
    Heymann, 1835. 2 vols.

26. Courville, Xavier de. JOMINI OU LE DEVIN DE NAPOLOEN.
    Lausanne: Centre d'Histoire reprints, 1981.

27. Courvoisier, Jean. LE MARECHAL BERTHIER ET SA PRINCIPAUTE DE
    NEUCHATEL (1806-1814). Neuchâtel: Baconnière, 1959.

28. Dedon, General François Louis. RELATION DETALILLEE DU PASSAGE
    DE LA LIMMAT, EFFECTUE LE 3 VENDEMIAIRE, AN VIII; SUIVIE DE
    CELLE DU PASSAGE DU RHIN DU 11 FLOREAL SUIVANT. Paris: Didot,
    1801.

29. Dellard, Jean Pierre, baron. MEMORIES MILITAIRES DU GENERAL
    DELLARD SUR LES GUERRES DE LA REPUBLIQUE ET L'EMPIRE. Paris:
    Librairie illustrée 1892.

30. Despreaux, Frignet. LE MARECHAL MORTIER, DUC DE TREVISE.
    Paris: Berger-Levrault, 1914. 3 vols.

31. Dick, F. "Das 3. schw. Regiment, 1806-1812 und seine Solothurner Offiziere im Dienste Naploeons I." JAHRBUCH FUER SOLOTHURNISCHE GESCHICHTE 17. BD (1944): 108-18.

32. DICTIONNAIRE HISTORIQUE ET BIOGRAPHIQUE DE LA SUISSE. Neuchâtel: Attinger, 1921-34. 8 vols.

33. Donnet, A. MEMORIES DE LOUIS ROBATEL (1788-1877) OFFICER VALAISAN AU SERVICE D'ESPAGNE, PUIS DE FRANCE. Martigny: Biblioteca Vallesiana, 1966.

34. Engel-Egli, R. FRAU OBERST ENGEL, VON CAIRO BIS NEW YORK, VON ELBA BIS WATERLOO. MEMOIREN EINER AMAZONE AUS NAPOLEONISCHER ZEIT. Munich: Artemis Verlag, 1977.

35. Engelhard, J.F.L. ERINNERUGEN AUS MEINEN FELDZUGEN IN SPANIEN EN DEN JAHREN 1808-1810. 1856.

36. ERINNERUGEN DES HERRN OBERST BERNHARD ISLER VON WOHLEN. i. A.: Weiland Lt in napoleonischen Diensten 1805-1815. Aarau, 1895.

37. Erismann, O. "Organisation und innerer Haushalt der Schweizerregimenter in Frankreich." SCHW. MONATSCHRIFT FUER OFFIZIERE ALLER WAFFEN (1915).

38. Fuchs, Egor. HISTORY OF THE CAMPAIGN OF 1799. Petrograd, 1825.

39. Fuchs, G. CORRESPONDENZ DES KAIS. RUSS. GENERALISMUS, FUERSTEN ITALIISKY GRAFEN A.W. SUWOROFF-RIMNIKSKY UEBER DIE RUSSISCH-OESTREICHISCHE KAMPAGNE IM JAHRE 1799. Golgau and Leipzig: 1835. 2 vols.

40. Gachot, Edouard. LA CAMPAGNE D'HELVETIE (1799). Paris: Perrin, 1904.

41. Gachot, Edouard. SOUVAROW EN ITALIE. Paris: Perrin, 1903.

42. Geisendorf-Des Gouttes, Théophile. LES PRISONNIERS DE GUERRE SOUS LE PREMIER EMPIRE. Geneva: Editions Labor, 1932-37. 2 vols.

43. Gonard, A. UN VALAISAN AU SERVICE DE FRANCE; VIE DU GENERAL DE RIVAZ, 1745-1833. Neuchâtel: Messseiller, 1943.

44. Grellet, Pierre. AVEC BONAPARTE DE GENEVE A BALE. Lausanne: Rouge, 1946.

45. Guillon, Edouard Louis Maxime. NAPOLEON ET LA SUISSE, 1803-1815; D'APRES LES DOCUMENTS INEDITS DES AFFAIRS ETRANGERES. Paris: Plon, 1910.

46. Guye, A. LE BATAILLON DE NEUCHATEL DIT DES CANARIS AU SERVICE DE NAPOLEON, 1807-1814. Neuchâtel: La Baconnière, 1964.

47. Haller, Karl Ludwig von. GESCHICHTE DER WIRKUNGEN UND FOLGEN
     DES OESTERREICHEN FELDZUGS IN DER SCHWIEIZ. Weimar: Gädicke,
     1801. 2 vols.

48. Hartmann, Otto. DER ANTHEIL DER RUSSEN AM FELDZUG VON 1799 IN
     DER SCHWEIZ. Zurich: Munk, 1892.

49. Hellmueller, C.T. DIE ROTEN SCHWEIZER, 1812. ZUM HUNDERT-
     JAEHRIGEN GEDAECHTNIS AN DIE KAEMPFE DER ROTEN SCHWEIZER
     NAPOLEON I. AN DER DUENA UND BERESINA. Berne: Francke, 1912.

50. Hennequin, Louis. ZURICH. MASSENA EN SUISSE, MESSIDOR AN
     VILL-BRUMAIRE AN VIII (JUILLET-OCTOBRE 1799). Paris and Nancy:
     Berger-Levrault, 1911.

51. HISTOIRE MILITAIRE DE LAS SUISSE, 8e ET 9e CAHIERS. Berne:
     CCG, 1921.

52. Hüffer, Hermann. "La Campagne de 1799. L'armée russe en
     Suisse." REVUE HISTORIQUE 72 (1900).

53. Hüffer, Hermann. DER KRIEG DES JAHRES 1799 UND DIE ZWEITE
     KOALITION. Gotha: Perthes, 1904-5. 2 vols.

54. Hüffer, Hermann. QUELLEN ZUR GESCHICHTE DER KRIEGE VON 1799
     UND 1800. Leipzig: Teubner, 1900-1901.

55. Jacoby, H. SOUVAROV, 1730-1800. Paris: Payot, 1935.

56. Jomini, Antoine Henri de, baron. GUERRE D'ESPAGNE. EXTRAIT
     DES SOUVENIRS INEDITS DU GENERAL JOMINI, 1808-1814, par
     Ferdinand Lecomte. Paris: Buadoin, 1892.

57. Jomini, Antoine Henri de, baron. HISTOIRE CRITIQUE ET
     MILITAIRE DES GUERRES DE LA REVOLUTION. Paris: Anselin et
     Pochard, 1819-24. 15 vols. and 4 altases.

58. Jomini, Antoine Henri de, baron. VIE POLITIQUE ET MILITAIRE DE
     NAPOLEON. Paris: Anselin, 1827. 4 vols. and atlas.

59. Karl, archduke of Austria. CAMPAGNE DE 1799 EN ALLEMAGNE ET EN
     SUISSE. Ouvrage traduit de l'allemand par un officier
     autrichien. Vienna: Strauss; Paris: Bertrand, 1820. 2 vols.

60. Kuepfer, E. LES SUISSES A POLOTZK ET A LA BERESINA. Lausanne:
     Payot, 1912.

61. Kummer, E. MUEHSALE DER SCHW. REGIMENTER AUF NAPOLEONS FELDZUG
     NACH RUSSLAND IM JAHRE 1812. Thun: Selborverlag 1972.

62. La Verne, Léger Marie Philippe Tranchant, comte de. HISTOIRE
     DU FELD-MARECHAL SOUVAROF, LIEE A CELLE DE SON TEMPS; AVEC DES
     CONSIDERATIONS SUR LES PRINCIPAUX EVENEMENS POLITIQUES ET
     MILITAIRES AUXQUELS LA RUSSIE A PRIS PART PENDANT LE XVIIIe
     SIECLE. Paris: Egron, 1809.

63. Lecomte, Ferdinand. ETUDES D'HISTOIRE MILITAIRE. Vol. 3. Frederic--Washington--Napoléon. Lausanne: Rouge, 1900.

64. Lecomte, Ferdinand. LES SUISSES AU SERVICE DE NAPOLEON Ier ET LES MEMOIRES DU GENERAL BARON DE MARBOT. Paris: Baudoin, 1892.

65. Lecourbe, Charles Jacques. LE GENERAL LECOURBE, D'APRES SES ARCHIVES, SA CORRESPONDANCE, ET AUTRES DOCUMENTS. Edited by J. Henri Philebert. Paris: Charles-Lavauzelle, 1895.

66. Legler, Th. DENKWUERDIGKEITEN AUS DEM RUSSISCHEN FELDZUGE VOM JAHR 1812.

67. Leplus, Henri. LA CAMPAGNE DE 1800 A L'ARMEE DE GRISONS. Paris: Chapelot, 1980.

68. LETTERS AND PAPERS OF SUVOROF. Petrograd, 1900.

69. Löwenstern, Woldemar Hermann, freiherr. MEMORIES DU GENERAL-MAJOR RUSSE BARON DE LOEWENSTERN (1776-1858). Publiés d'après manuscrit original et annotés par M.H. Weil. Paris: Fontemoing, 1903. 2 vols.

70. Longworth, Philip. THE ART OF VICTORY; THE LIFE AND ACHIEVEMENTS OF FIELD-MARSHAL SUVOROV, 1729-1800. London: Constable, 1965.

71. Maag, Albert. GESCHICHTE DER SCHWEIZER TRUPPEN IM KRIEGE NAPOLEONS I. IN SPANIEN UND PORTUGAL (1807-1814). Biel: Kuhn, 1892-93. 2 vols.

72. Maag, Albert. GESCHICHTE DER SCHWEIZER TRUPPEN IN FRANZOESISCHEN DIENSTEN (1813-1815). Biel: Kuhn, 1894.

73. Maag, Albert. DIE SCHICKSALE DER SCHWEIZER REGIMENTER IN NAPOLEONS I. FELDZUG NACH RUSSLAND, 1812. Biel: Kuhn, 1890.

74. Macready, Edward Nevil. A SKETCH OF SUWAROW, AND HIS LAST CAMPAIGN. WITH OBSERVATIONS ON MR. ALISON'S OPINIONS OF THE ARCHDUKE CHARLES AS A MILITARY CRITIC, AND A FEW OBJECTIONS TO CERTAIN MILITARY STATEMENTS IN MR. ALISON'S "HISTORY OF EUROPE." London: Smith, Elder, 1851.

75. Marès, Louis. PAPIERS DE MARE. PRECIS DE LA GUERRE EN SUISSE (1799). Edited by Edouard Gachot. Lausanne: Payot, 1910.

76. Masséna, André, prince d'Essling. MEMOIRES D'ANDRE MASSENA, DUC DE RIVILI, PRINCE D'ESSLING, MARECHAL D'EMPiRE, REDIGES D'APRES LES DOCUMENTS QU'IL A LAISSES ET SUR CEUX DE DEPOT DE LA GUERRE ET DU DEPOT DES FORTIFICATIONS. Recueillis par le général Koch. Paris: Paulin et Lechevalier, 1848-50. 7 vols. and atlas.

77. MEMOIRES DU LANDAMMAN MONOD POUR SERVIR A L'HISTOIRE DE LA
    SUISSE EN 1815. Publiés par J.C. Biaudet et M.C. Jequire.
    Berne: AGGS, 1975. 3 vols.

78. Michailowski-Danilewski, Alexander Iwanowitsch, and Dmitry
    Alexiewitsch von Miliutin. GESCHICHTE DES KRIEGES RUSSLAND MIT
    FRANKREICH UNTER DER REGIERUNG KAISEER PAUL'S I. IM JAHRE 1799.
    Translated by Christian Schmitt. Munich: Lindauer, 1856-58.
    5 vols.

79. Milyutin. HISTORY OF THE WAR OF 1799. Petrograd, 1852, 1857.

80. Muralt, Albrecht von, and Thomas Legler. BERESINA. SOUVENIRS
    DE LA CAMPAGNE DE RUSSIE DE 1812. Traduit de l'allemand par
    Claude van Muyden. Neuchâtel and Paris: Delachaux et
    Niestlé, 1942.

81. Muret, H., and B. de Cérenville. LA SUISSE EN 1815. LE SECOND
    PASSAGE DES ALLIES ET L'EXPEDITION DE FRANCHE-COMTE. Lausanne:
    Revue militaire Suisse, 1913.

82. "Napoleon's Schweitzertruppen in Spanien under Russland."
    NEUJAHRSBLAETTER DER FEUERWERKERGESELLSCHAFT 4 (1871-74).

83. Ney, Michel Louis Félix, duc d'Elchingen, prince de la Moskowa.
    MEMOIRES DU MARECHAL NEY. Edited by Antoine Bulos. Brussels:
    Hauman, 1833. 2 vols.

84. Orloff, Nikolai Alexejevitch, comte. LA CAMPAGNE DE SOUVOROV
    EN 1799 D'APRES LES MEMOIRES DE GRJAZEV. Saint Petersburg:
    Beresovsky, 1898.

85. Osipov, K. ALEXANDER SUVOROV. Translated by Edith Bone.
    London, New York, and Melbourne: Hutchinson, 1941.

86. Pavillon, Olivier. "Bibliographie," LE GENERAL ANTOINE-HENRI
    JOMINI (1779-1869). Lausanne: Imprimeries Réunies, 1969.

87. Phipps, Ramsey Weston. THE ARMIES OF THE FIRST FRENCH REPUBLIC
    AND THE RISE OF THE MARSHALS OF NAPOLEON I. London: Oxford
    University Press, 1926-39. 5 vols.

88. Polevoi, Nilolai Aleksieevich. GESCHICHTE DES FUERSTEN
    ITALIISKI GRAFEN SUWOROFF-RIMNIKSKI, GENERALISSIMUS DER
    RUSSISCHEN ARMEEN. In frier deutscher Uebertragung
    herausgegeben von J. de la Crox. Mitau: Reyher, 1851.

89. QUELLEN ZUR SCHWEIZER GESCHICHTE. Basel: A. Geering, 1908.

90. Reding-Biberegg, R. von. DER ZUG SUWOROFF'S DURCH DIE SCHWEIZ
    24. HERBST BIS 10. WEINMONAT 1799. Zurich: Schultess, 1896.

91. Reichel, Daniel. LE MARECHAL DAVOUT, DUC D'AUERSTAEDT, PRINCE
    D'ECKMUEHL (1770-1823). Neuchâtel: Delachaux et Niestlé,
    1975.

92. REPERTORIUM DER ABSCHIEDE DER EIDGENOESSISCHEN TAGSATZUGEN AUS DEN JAHREN 1803 BIS 1848. Berne: Wyss, 1874-86. 2 vols.

93. Rochette, Désiré Raoul. HISTOIRE DE LA REVOLUTION HELVETIQUE DE 1797 A 1803. Paris: Nepveu, 1823.

94. Rodger, Alexander Bankier. THE WAR OF THE SECOND COALITION, 1789 TO 1801, A STRATEGIC COMMENTARY. Oxford: Clarendon Press, 1964.

95. Ross, Steven T. QUEST FOR VICTORY, FRENCH MILITARY STRATEGY, 1792-1799. South Brunswick and New York: Barnes; London: Yoseloff, 1973.

96. Rott, Edouard. PERROCHEL ET MASSENA, L'OCCUPATION FRANCAISE EN HELVETIE, 1798-1799. Neuchâtel: Attinger, 1899.

97. Roverea, Ferdinand de. MEMOIRES. Berne: Stämpfli, 1848. 4 vols.

98. Rüstow, Wilhelm. DIE ERSTEN FELDZUEGE NAPOLEON BONAPARTE'S IN ITALIEN UND DEUTSCHLAND, 1796 UND 1797. Zurich: Schultness, 1867.

99. Schafroth, M.F. "Die kirchlichen Register der Schweizertruppen in fremden Diensten, 1671-1859." JAHRBUCH SCHW. GESELLSCHAFT FUER FAMILIENFORSCHUNG (1976): 119-25.

100. Schaller, Henri de. HISTOIRE DES TROUPES SUISSES AU SERVICE DE FRANCE SOUS LE REGNE DE NAPOLEON Ier. Fribourg: Henseler, 1882.

101. [Schaller, Jean François Joseph Pierre Damien de.] SOUVENIRS D'UN OFFICIER FRIBOURGEOIS, 1798-1848. Edited by Henri de Schaller. Fribourg: Henseler, 1890.

102. Shadwell, Lawrence. MOUNTAIN WARFARE ILLUSTRATED BY THE CAMPAIGN OF 1799 IN SWITERZLAND. BEING A TRANSLATION OF SWISS NARRATIVE, COMPILED FROM THE WORKS OF THE ARCHDUKE CHARLES, JOMINI, AND OTHERS. London: King, 1875.

103. SOLDATES SUISSES AU SERVICE ETRANGER. Geneva: Jullien, 1908-19. 8 vols.

104. Soult, Nicolas Jean de Dieu, duc de Dalmatie. MEMOIRES DU MARECHAL-GENERAL SOULT. Paris: Amyot, 1854. 3 vols.

105. "Souvenirs d'un officier valaisan au service de France. La Capitaine Hyacinthe Clemenso, 1781-1862." ANNALES VALAISANNES 1 (1957): 1-110.

106. Sprünglin, Emmanuel Frédéric. SOUVENIRS. [In "Revue Hispanique"]. Paris: Klincksieck, 1904.

107. Steiger, R. von. EIN SCHWEIZERBATAILLION IN FRANZOESISCHEN
     KRIEGSDIENSTE UND DESSEN KAEMPFE GEGEN DIE NEAPOLITANISCHEN
     BRIGANTEN, 1805-1808.

108. Steiger, R. von. SOUVENIRS DE ABRAHAM ROSSELET. Neuchâtel,1857.

109. Steiner, Gustav. NAPOLEONS I. POLITIK UND DIPLOMATIE IN DER
     SCHWEIZ WAEHREND DER GESANDTSCHAFTZEIT DES GRAFEN AUGSUTE DE
     TALLEYRAND. MIT BENUETZUNG SCHWEIZERISCHER UND FRANZOESISCHER
     ARCHIVE. Zurich: Schulthess, 1907.

110. Suvorov, Alexksandr Vasil'evich, knaiz' Italiiskii.
     CORRESPONDENZ DES KAIS. RUSS. GENERALISSIMUS, FUERSTEN
     ITALIISKY GRAFEN ALEXANDER VASILIEVITSCH SUVOROFF-RIMNIKSKY
     UEBER DIE RUSSISCH-OESTREICHISCHE KAMPAGNE IM JAHRE 1799.
     Glogau: Hehmann, 1835. 2 vols.

111. Thiébault, Paul Charles François Adrien, baron. MEMORIES DU
     GENERAL BARON THIEBAULT. Paris: Plon-Nourrit, 1894-95. 5 vols.

112. Trumeau, E. "Marche du corps d'armée du maréchal Souverov du
     11 septembre au 5 octobre 1799." ANNUAIRE DU CLUB ALPIN
     FRANCAIS 22 (1895): 505-51.

113. Valka, S.N. OPISANIYE SOBRANIYA RUKOPISNYKH MATERIALOV A.V.
     SUVOROVA. Leningrad, 1955.

114. Vallière, Paul Emanuel de. HONNEUR ET FIDELITE. Lausanne:
     Les Editions d'art suisse ancien, 1940.

115. Vallotton, Georges. LES SUISSES A LA BERESINA. Neuchâtel:
     Baconnière, 1942.

116. Vassiluef. SUVOROF. Vilna, 1899.

117. Vincenz, Major. "Offiziere der Familie Caprez; Truns im
     französischen Fremdendienste." BUENDNER MONATSBLATT (1936).

118. Wieland, C. DIE VIER SCHWEIZER REGIMENTER IM DIESTE NAPOLEONS
     I, 1803-1814. n.p., 1879.

119. Zimmermann, J. "Soldat des Kaisers. Erlebnisse eines
     Schaffhausers in französischen Diensten. Briefe des David-Karl
     von Ziegler aus den Jahren 1804-1807." SCHAFFHAUSEN BEITRAEGE
     ZUR GESCHICHTE 50 (1973): 185-233.

PERIODICALS

120. GAZETTE DE LAUSANNE, 1798.

121. HELVETISCHE MILITAER-ZEITSCHRIFT, 1834.

122. NEUE ZUERICHER ZEITUNG, 1779.

123. REVUE MILITAIRE SUISSE, 1856.

CHAPTER XXIII

THE WEST INDIES

Thomas Ott, University of North Alabama

Even before the last shattered remnants of the Leclerc expedition departed Saint-Domingue in 1802, French apologists rushed with their pens to mend the damaged military reputation of France. Those leading the charge were military officials who wrote field reports to the First Consul. An anonymous manuscript entitled, "Mémoire historique. Saint-Domingue, 1791-1803" reflects this attitude. The writer had a low regard for black ability and laid stress on yellow fever and the lack of reinforcements as causes of French defeat. Another anonymous reporter expressed similar views in the Rochambeau Papers, as did Hector Duare, quartermaster-general of the ill-fated expedition, whose "Comte rendu de l'administration général de St. Domingue" can be located at the Archives Nationales.

These apologists were the leading edge of a group of nineteenth-century French historians, best described as the Imperial School. In his LA VIE DE TOUSSAINT LOUVERTURE, Louis du Broca (19) attemped to lend his scholarship in support of the French invasion of Saint-Domingue. He condemned Toussaint as an anti-Republican cannibal who bit the generous hand of Napoleon. Toussaint, he added, could not even speak good French. Those historians who followed tended to concentrate more on military history and less upon the direct attacks on Toussaint's character. A.P.M. Laujon (35), A. Dalmas (16), A. Métral (49), and A. Poyen (66) were prominent among these writers. In his HISTOIRE DE LA REVOLUTION DE SAINT-DOMINGUE, Poyen polished the French argument on the finer points of the Leclerc expedition. He argued that the First Consul never intended to restore slavery and that the blacks incorrectly read his intentions.

In the twentieth century the French Imperial School has yielded to better scholarship. One effort was Gabriel Debien's historiographical article "Les Travaux d'histoire sur Saint-Domingue" (17). Debien reviewed the main issues of the Leclerc expedition, especially reasons for Napoleon's initiation of the scheme. He laid blame on those refugees from Saint-Domingue who ill-advised the First Consul.

In nineteenth-century Haiti, mulatto historians interpreted the Leclerc expedition from the point of view of their caste interests. Essentially the mulatto interpretation was that the real hero of the struggle against Leclerc was Pétion, not Toussaint. They asserted that Toussaint courted the French too much, misled the black masses, and hated mulattoes--the true liberators of Haiti from France. The wrath of these historians became even more intense when they considered Jean Jacques Dessalines. They saw him as a brutal ignoramus who misunderstood and mistreated mulattoes. Grudgingly they did concede his capable generalship. Among these historians are Joseph Saint-Rémy (73) and Alexis Beaubrun Ardouin (4).

The best history of the Leclerc expedition by a nineteenth-century Haitian historian is in volume three of Thomas Madiou's HISTOIRE D'HAITI (46). Though he was a mulatto, Madiou did not promote the interests of his caste. He emphasized instead the essential roles of Toussaint, Christophe, and Dessalines in defeating the French.

675

In twentieth-century Haiti, H. Pauléus Sannon, Auguste Nemours, and Jacques Stéphen Alexis have written the best accounts. These historians belong to a nationalistic school of writers who sought to exault the Haitian past and thus condemn U.S. occupation of their small country. Sannon (74) produced a highly detailed and favorable biography of Toussaint. Nemours (55, 56) mainly confined his attention to matters of military maneuvers in his works on the Leclerc expedition. In 1949 Alexis unveiled yet another study of Toussaint's life (3). He especially emphasized that Toussaint lost the support of his generals and suffered the treachery of Napoleon.

West Indian writers outside of Haiti have also taken an interest in the Leclerc expedition. Aimé Césaire, Martiniquen political activist and poet, authored TOUSSAINT LOUVERTURE (11) in 1960. He maintained that Toussaint and not Dessalines was the real architect of Haitian independence. Césaire did criticize Toussaint for failing to make his political goal clear to his followers. By not doing so Napoleon cleverly convinced them that he and not Toussaint protected their liberty. In agreement with Césaire on this point, C.L.R. James of Trinidad-Tobago viewed the Leclerc expedition from a Marxist position in his BLACK JACOBINS (28). Napoleon was a counterrevolutionary and Leclerc served as his instrument against the black proletariat.

Anglo-American authors exhibited immediate interest in the Haitian struggle for independence. In the nineteenth century they romanticized Toussaint and condemned Napoleon. One panegyric was by J.R. Beard (6) who read his own Protestant values into the struggle between Toussaint and Napoleon. Toussaint represented "good" and Napoleon "evil." In the twentieth century the quality of Anglo-American scholarship has improved. In 1914 T. Lothrop Stoddard published his FRENCH REVOLUTION IN SAN DOMINGO (76). Although he researched his work well, Stoddard exhibited a strong pro-French bias. For him, the mosquito and not the black soldier defeated the French. Ralph Korngold (31) and Wenda Parkinson (61) have authored the best biographies on Toussaint in English. Korngold claimed that Toussaint only pretended to surrender to save lives and let yellow fever substitute for the force of arms against the French. Parkinson believed that Toussaint lost to Leclerc because of the treachery of his own lieutenants. Hubert Cole presented a different view in CHRISTOPHE, KING OF HAITI (15). Christophe never deserted Toussaint; instead Toussaint lost because he judged his situation as hopeless. In 1973 Thomas Ott emphasized black military achievements and explored reasons for Toussaint's surrender in his HAITIAN REVOLUTION, 1789-1804 (60). Toussaint may have capitulated to the French in the sincere belief that this was the only way to guarantee black freedom from slavery.

Motives for Napoleon's invasion of Saint-Domingue may always remain opaque. Georges Lefebvre, author of a two-volume biography of Napoleon (36), contended that economic necessity and planter influence persuaded the First Consul to subdue Toussaint. Shelby McCloy (45) maintained that Toussaint's high-handed acts of imprisoning the First Consul's special agent, Philippe Roume, and of writing a constitution convinced Napoleon that the black leader intended to separate Saint-Domingue from France. In THE AGE OF NAPOLEON (25), J. Christopher Herold saw the collapse of Napoleon's Egyptian campaign, planter complaints, and the need to conduct his

imperial designs forcefully as strong influences in the First
Consul's decision to attack Saint-Domingue. That Napoleon must have
been suspicious of Toussaint's clever diplomacy with the enemies of
France gained treatment in the writings of Carl L. Lokke (39, 40),
Henry Adams (1, 2), and H.B.L. Hughes (27). The best comprehensive
study of Toussaint's diplomacy is Auguste Nemours's HISTOIRE DES
RELATIONS INTERNATIONALES DE TOUSSAINT LOUVERTURE (55).

ARCHIVAL SOURCES

Archival materials are scattered in various depositories in
Europe and North America. At the Archives Nationales in Paris can be
found the "Déclaration que fait François Beaumont," "Compte rendu de
l'administration générale de St. Domingue par le Hector Duare, ex-
préfect de cet colonie et ordonnateur en chef de l'armée
expéditionnaire," and Ménard's "Le chef de l'Etat-Major général de
l'armée au Ministère de la guerre (CC9A 41, CC9A 31, and CC7A 57
respectively). Among the documents at the Ministère des affaires
étrangères is the "Correspondance politique, Etats-Unis" (Vol. 53)
which is also located in the U.S. Library of Congress. The valuable
"Mémoire historique, Saint-Domingue, 1791-1803," can be found at the
Service historique de l'armée at the Château de Vincennes in Paris as
well as in the U.S. Library of Congress. At Vincennes there are
also 28 cartons (B7) of "Correspondance, Registres, et Situations" of
the Armée de Saint-Domingue. In addition, the collections labeled
"Mémories Historique" and "Mémories Réconnaissance" contain a
significant number of cartons concerning Saint-Domingue (399,
592-602, 783-84, 1102, 1107-8, 1524, 1669, 1839, 1842).
In the Public Record Office in London, the Jamaican
Correspondence can be located among the Colonial Office Papers
(137/50). These documents can also be seen at the U.S. Library of
Congress in Washington D.C. Other manuscripts located in the United
States include the State Department Consular Dispatches, Cap-Haitien,
(Vols. 1-4) at the National Archives; the Philippe Roume papers at
the Library of Congress; Lieutenant Howard's "Journal of the Army of
Occupation in Haiti..." at the Boston Public Library; the Rufus King
papers at the Huntington Library, Stanford University; the Leclerc
and Rochambeau papers at the University of Florida Research Library
in Gainesville; and the papers of Sir George Nugent at the Institute
of Jamaica in Kingston.

MEMOIRS, JOURNALS, AND EYEWITNESS ACCOUNTS

The most significant primary sources reveal clues to Napoleon's
motives for attacking Saint-Domingue. In the MEMOIRES SUR LE
CONSULAT, 1799 A 1804, PAR UN ANCIEN CONSEILLER D'ETAT (77), Antoine
Thibaudeau claimed that Napoleon viewed the blacks as barbarians who
needed to be put in their proper place. Gaspard Gourgaud (23), who
shared Napoleon's St. Helena exile, maintained that Martinique-born
Josephine must bear much blame for influencing Napoleon's decision.
Josephine (30) claimed in her memoirs that the charge was false and
that she had advised against the expedition. Las Cases (34), another
of Napoleon's companions in exile, found that the former Emperor had
been persuaded by colonial refugees, economics, and a grand political
design to undertake his war against Toussaint. Even though Toussaint

swore no disloyalty to France in his memoirs (43), many records reveal the First Consul's growing distrust of the black leader. Especially enlightening are the "Jamaica Correspondence," the dispatches of the U.S. consul, Edward Stevens, and the papers of Roume, Rufus King, and George Nugent--all archival sources. The thirty-two-volume collection of the CORRESPONDANCE DE NAPOLEON Ier (53) might yield further clues to a historian's detective-like search.

There are numerous primary accounts of the actual operations of the French army in Saint-Domingue. Those French soldiers who fought against the Haitians gave them praise for their combat tenacity. Among the best accounts are those of Lemmonier-Delafosse (37), Michel Descourtilz (18), an anonymous officer (59), François Joseph Lacroix (33), and François Beaumont's "Déclaration," found at the Archives Nationales in Paris. Toussaint's disciplined control over his generals and troops especially caught the attention of Lacroix. Even more important, according to Lacroix, Toussaint equated the battlefield with freedom from bondage in the minds of his followers. Thus the blacks fought like fanatics. The papers of General Charles Victor Leclerc and General Donatien Rochambeau further attest to the combat ability of the black soldier. But one must guard against accepting the low French casualty figures in these collections, because both Leclerc and Rochambeau found combat losses to blacks embarrassing.

Two Haitian accounts give a favorable view of Haitian soldiers. Edmund Bonnet (7) served with General Alexandre Pétion in southern Haiti and found the rebel army there well organized and capable of resisting the French. General Brisrond Tonnère (79), one of Dessalines's lieutenants, was equally enthusiastic about the black soldiers under the command of his fierce chief.

The "Journal" of Lieutenant Howard, as well as the accounts of Mary Hassall (24), Peter Chazotte (14), and Samuel Perkins (64) have left the best eyewitness accounts in English of black fighting qualities. The most reliable of these reports is the one by Howard. He had been a member of a British expedition which Toussaint's army defeated. In his judgment, the blacks were formidable opponents.

Newspapers contain another fine source of information about the black soldier. Often a visiting ship captain in Saint-Domingue would return to his home port and publish a long epistle about the struggle between Toussaint and Leclerc. Letters from exiles and the participants of the conflict would also find their way into newspapers. The most useful newspapers were the following: Providence GAZETTE AND COUNTRY JOURNAL (67), THE TIMES (London) (78), New York EVENING POST (58), Newport MERCURY (57), MONITEUR DE LA LOUISIANE (New Orleans) (51), MIRROR OF THE TIMES AND GENERAL ADVERTISER (Wilmington, Del.) (50), Boston INDEPENDENT CHRONICLE (9), Charleston CITY GAZETTE (12), Charleston TIMES (13), Boston GAZETTE (8), and Baltimore FEDERAL GAZETTE (5).

SPECIALIZED WORKS

The restoration of slavery, angry blacks led by Dessalines, and the breakdown of the Peace of Amiens did more than yellow fever to bring French defeat. But thousands of French soldiers did die from this pestilence; thus was the French military position weakened. The volume of Tonnère (79), and the manuscripts of Leclerc, Rochambeau, and Duare have left the most graphic accounts about the impact of this disease upon the French army. Paul Navarranne (54) has written the best monograph on this subject.

The question of why Toussaint surrendered to Leclerc has remained a mystery. There is no known source which historians may use to explore this question with any degree of accuracy. Toussaint's own statements that his loyalty to France prompted his surrender is unreliable (43). The black leader was a complex person, and his statements usually masked his intentions. Historians may find uneasy footing even on the assumption that Toussaint's main consideration was to protect his people from re-enslavement. David Geggus's article (22) about Toussaint's initial commitment to this cause revealed a leader as much self-serving as altruistic.

The minor military expedition to Guadeloupe, commanded by General Antoine Richepanse, departed France on 2 April 1802, with orders to crush Magkoire Pélage's rebel army and re-enslave the blacks. Although Napoleon succeeded in Guadeloupe where he failed in Haiti, the two expeditions have interesting parallels. Yellow fever plagued both ventures, both commanders died, and French plans of pacification in its two Carribbean colonies collapsed when blacks learned of Napoleon's intention to restore slavery in the French West Indies.

The Guadeloupe venture has not gained much scholarly attention. Scattered references may be found in secondary works already cited. The best description in English is McCloy's NEGRO IN THE FRENCH WEST INDIES (45). The most satisfactory account in French is a general history of Martinique and Guadeloupe by Alfred Martineau and Louis May (47). J. Saintoyant's LA COLONISATION FRANCAISE PENDANT LA PERIODE NAPOLEONIENNE, 1799-1815 (71) and J.L. Franco y Ferrán's REVOLUCIONES Y CONFLICTOS INTERNATIONALES EN EL CARIBE, 1789-1854 (20) contain some useful information about the Richepanse expedition. Primary sources for the French invasion of Guadeloupe do not abound. The aforementioned newspapers do contain several eyewitness accounts of the struggle. General Ménard, a member of Richepanse's staff, wrote a report of the conflict which is still in manuscript form. His account along with other records of the Guadeloupe venture can be found in the colonial section of the Archives Nationales in Paris.

PERIODICALS

THE JOURNAL OF CARRIBEAN STUDIES (83), published by the University of Puerto Rico, and THE JOURNAL OF CARRIBBEAN HISTORY (82), published by the University of the West Indies, are the only two periodicals which specialize in Antillean history.

FUTURE RESEARCH

There are a number of polemical questions concerning Napoleon's West Indian expeditions which continue to haunt historians. Did Napoleon only plan to restore the colonial order in Haiti or did he plan to use Haiti as a base of operations against the Spanish Empire? How persuasive were French planters in convincing Napoleon to undertake his Caribbean expeditions? Was yellow fever more important than black resistance in defeating the French? Did

Leclerc know <u>before</u> the landing of his expedition that Napoleon planned to restore slavery in the French West Indies? Why did Toussaint surrender his forces to Leclerc when he apparently had the French expeditionary force on the verge of defeat?

BIBLIOGRAPHY: WEST INDIES

1. Adams, Henry. HISTORY OF THE UNITED STATES OF AMERICA DURING THE ADMINISTRATION OF THOMAS JEFFERSON. New York: A. and C. Boni, 1930. 2 vols.

2. Adams, Henry. "Napoleon I and San Domingo." HISTORICAL ESSAYS. New York: Scribner, 1891.

3. Alexis, Jacques Stéphen. BLACK LIBERATOR: THE LIFE OF TOUSSAINT LOUVERTURE. New York: Macmillan, 1949.

4. Ardouin, Alexis Beaubrun. ETUDES SUR L'HISTOIRE D'HAITI SURVIES DE LA VIE DU GENERAL J.M. BORGELLA. Port-au-Prince: Dalencour, 1958. 11 vols. (Originally published in 1853-60.)

5. Baltimore FEDERAL GAZETTE, 1800-1804.

6. Beard, J.R. THE LIFE OF TOUSSAINT L'OUVERTURE. London: Ingram, Cooke, 1853.

7. Bonnet, Edmund. SOUVENIRS HISTORIQUES DU GENERAL BONNET. Paris: Durand, 1864.

8. Boston GAZETTE, 1800-1802.

9. Boston INDEPENDENT CHRONICLE, 1800-1804.

10. Cancelalada, Juan Lopez. LA VIDA DE J.J. DESSALINES. Mexico City: Ontiveros, 1809.

11. Césaire, Aimé. TOUSSAINT LOUVERTURE: LA REVOLUTION FRANCAISE ET LE PROBLEME COLONIAL. Paris: Le club français du Livre, 1960.

12. Charleston CITY GAZETTE, 1800-1804.

13. Charleston TIMES, 1800-1804.

14. Chazotte, Peter S. HISTORICAL SKETCHES OF THE REVOLUTION AND THE FOREIGN AND CIVIL WAR IN THE ISLAND OF ST. DOMINGO, WITH A NARRATIVE OF THE ENTIRE MASSACRE OF THE WHITE POPULATION OF THE ISLAND: EYEWITNESS REPORT. New York: Applegate, 1840.

15. Cole, Hubert. CHRISTOPHE, KING OF HAITI. New York: Viking, 1967.

16. Dalmas, A. HISTOIRE DE LA REVOLUTION DE SAINT-DOMINGUE. Paris: Mame, 1814. 2 vols.

17. Debien, Gabriel. "Les Travaux d'histoire sur Saint-Domingue." REVUE DE L'HISTOIRE DES COLONIES FRANCAISES 36-37 (1949-50): 282-330.

18. Descourtilz, Michel E.   VOYAGES D'UN NATURALISTE ET SES OBSERVATIONS. Paris: Dufort, 1809. 3 vols.

19. Du Broca, Louis. LA VIE DE TOUSSAINT LOUVERTURE. Paris: Du Broca, 1802.

20. Franco y Ferrán, J.L. REVOLUCIONES Y CONFLICTOS INTERNACIONALES EN EL CARIBE, 1789-1854. Havana: Oficina del Historiador de la Ciudad de la Habana, 1954.

21. GAZETTE NATIONALE, OU LE MONITEUR UNIVERSEL (Paris), 1800-1804.

22. Geggus, David F. "From His Most Catholic Majesty to the godless Republique: The 'volte-face' of Toussaint Louverture and the ending of slavery in Saint-Domingue." REVUE FRANCAISE D'HISTOIRE D'OUTRE-MER 65 (1978): 481-99.

23. Gourgaud, Gaspard. SAINTE HELENE: JOURNAL INEDIT DE 1815 A 1818. Paris: Flammarion: n.d., 2 vols.

24. Hassall, Mary. SECRET HISTORY; OR THE HORRORS OF ST. DOMINGO, IN A SERIES OF LETTERS, WRITTEN BY A LADY AT CAPE FRANCOIS TO COLONEL BURR, LATE VICE-PRESIDENT OF THE UNITED STATES, PRINCIPALLY DURING THE COMMAND OF GENERAL ROCHAMBEAU. Philadelphia: Bradford and Inskeep, 1808.

25. Herold, J. Christopher. THE AGE OF NAPOLEON. New York: American Heritage, 1963.

26. Howard, John E., ed. LETTERS AND DOCUMENTS OF NAPOLEON. New York: Oxford University Press, 1961. 1 vol.

27. Hughes, H.B.L. "British Policy Towards Haiti, 1801-1805." CANADIAN HISTORICAL REVIEW 25 (1944): 80-98.

28. James, C.L.R. THE BLACK JACOBINS. New York: Dial, 1938.

29. Jenkins, H.J.K. "Guadeloupe, savagery, and emancipation: British comment, 1794-1796." REVUE FRANCAISE D'HISTORIE D'OUTRE-MER 65 (1978): 325-31.

30. Josephine, empress consort of Napoleon I. MEMOIRS OF THE EMPRESS JOSEPHINE. New York: Merrill and Baker, 1903. 2 vols.

31. Korngold, Ralph. CITIZEN TOUSSAINT: A BIOGRAPHY. New York: Hill and Wang, 1944.

32. LaCoste, G. TOUSSAINT L'OUVERTURE. Paris: n.p., 1877.

33. Lacroix, François Joseph. MEMOIRES POUR SERVIR A L'HISTOIRIQUE DE LA REVOLUTION DE SAINT-DOMINGUE. Paris: Pillet, 1820. 2 vols.

34. Las Cases, Marie Joseph Emmanuel Auguste, comte de. MEMORIAL DE SAINTE-HELENE. JOURNAL DE LA VIE PRIVEE ET DES CONVERSATIONS DE L'EMPEREUR NAPOLEON A SAINTE-HELENE. London: Colburn, 1823. 4 vols.

35. Laujon, A.P.M. PRECIS HISTORIQUE DE LA DERNIERE REVOLUTION DE SAINT-DOMINQUE. Paris: Laujon, 1803.

36. Lefebvre, Georges. NAPOLEON. New York: Columbia University Press, 1969. 2 vols.

37. Lemmonier-Delafosse, Jean Baptiste. SECONDE CAMPAGNE DE SAINT-DOMINGUE. Havre: n. p., 1846.

38. "Letters of Toussaint L'Ouverture and of Edward Stevens, 1798-1800." AMERICAN HISTORICAL REVIEW 16 (1910): 64-101.

39. Lokke, Carl L. FRANCE AND THE COLONIAL QUESTION; 1793-1801. New York: Columbia University Press, 1932.

40. Lokke, Carl L. "Jefferson and the Leclerc Expedition." AMERICAN HISTORICAL REVIEW 33 (1928): 322-28.

41. Lokke, Carl L. "The Leclerc Instructions." JOURNAL OF NEGRO HISTORY 10 (1925): 80-98.

42. Lokke, Carl L. "A Plot to Abduct Toussaint Louverture's Children." JOURNAL OF NEGRO HISTORY 21 (1936): 47-51.

43. Louverture, Toussaint. MEMOIRES DU GENERAL TOUSSAINT LOUVERTURE. Paris: Pagnerre, 1853.

44. Lyon, E. Wilson. BONAPARTE'S PROPOSED LOUISIANA EXPEDITION. Chicago: University of Chicago Press, 1932.

45. McCloy, Shelby T. THE NEGRO IN THE FRENCH WEST INDIES. Lexington: University of Kentucky Press, 1966.

46. Madiou, Thomas. HISTOIRE D'HAITI. Port-au-Prince: Madiou, 1847-48. 3 vols.

47. Martineau, Alfred, and Louis Philippe May. TROIS SIECLES D'HISTOIRE ANTILLAISE, MARTINIQUE ET GUADELOUPE 1635 A NOS JOURS. Paris: Société de l'histoire des colonies française et Librairie Leroux, 1935.

48. Maurel, Blanche. LE VENT DU LARGE; OU, LE DESTIN TOURMENTE DE JEAN-BAPTISTE GERARD, COLON DE SAINT-DOMINGUE. Paris: La Nef de Paris, 1952.

49. Métral, Antoine. HISTOIRE DE L'EXPEDITION DES FRANCAIS A SAINT-DOMINGUE, SOUS LE CONSULAT DE NAPOLEON BONAPARTE. Paris: Fanjat, 1825.

50. MIRROR OF THE TIMES AND GENERAL ADVERTISER (Wilmington, Del.), 1800-1804.

51. MONITEUR DE LA LOUISIANE (New Orleans), 1800-1804.

52. Monti, Laura V., ed. A CALENDAR OF THE ROCHAMBEAU PAPERS AT THE UNIVERSITY OF FLORIDA RESEARCH LIBRARIES. Gainesville: University of Florida Libraries, 1972.

53. Napoleon I, Emperor of the French. CORRESPONDANCE DE NAPOLEON Ier; PUBLIEE PAR ORDRE DE L'EMPEREUR NAPOLEON III. Paris: Plon, 1858-80. 32 vols.

54. Navarranne, Paul. UNE EXPEDITION COLONIALE AVANT TOURNE A LA CATASTROPHE EPIDEMIOLOGIQUE: SAINT-DOMINGUE. Marseilles: n.p., 1943.

55. Nemours, Auguste. HISTOIRE DES RELATIONS INTERNATIONALES DE TOUSSAINT LOUVERTURE. Port-au-Prince: Imprimerie du Collège Vertières, 1945.

56. Nemours, Auguste. HISTOIRE MILITAIRE DE LA GUERRE DE L'INDEPENDANCE DE SAINT-DOMINGUE. Paris: Berger-Levrault, 1925, 1928. 2 vols.

57. Newport MERCURY, 1800-1804.

58. New York EVENING POST, 1801-1804.

59. NOTICE HISTORIQUE SUR LES DESASTRES DE SAINT-DOMINGUE, PAR UN OFFICER FRANCAIS DETENU PAR DESSALINES. Paris: n.p., n.d.

60. Ott, Thomas O. THE HAITIAN REVOLUTION, 1789-1804. Knoxville: University of Tennessee Press, 1973.

61. Parkinson, Wenda. THIS GILDED AFRICAN: TOUSSAINT L'OUVERTURE. London: Quartet Books, 1980.

62. Perin, René. L'INCENDIE DU CAP; OU LE REGNE DE TOUSSAINT LOUVERTURE. Paris: Marchand, 1802.

63. Perkins, Bradford. THE FIRST RAPPROCHEMENT. Berkeley: University of California Press, 1967.

64. Perkins, Samuel G. REMINISCENCES OF THE INSURRECTION IN ST. DOMINGO. Cambridge, Mass.: Harvard University Press, 1886.

65. Placide, Justine. HISTOIRE POLITIQUE ET STATISTIQUE DE L'ILE DE HAYTI. Paris: Placide, 1826.

66. Poyen, A. de. HISTOIRE MILITAIRE DE LA REVOLUTION DE SAINT-DOMINGUE. Paris: Imprimerie nationale, 1899.

67. Providence GAZETTE AND COUNTRY JOURNAL, 1800-1804.

68. Rainsford, Marcus. AN HISTORICAL ACCOUNT OF THE BLACK EMPIRE OF HAYTI. London: J. Cundee, 1805.

69. Roussier, Michel. "L'Education des enfants de Toussaint L'Ouverture et l'institution nationale des colonies." REVUE FRANCAISE D'HISTOIRE D'OUTRE-MER 64 (1977): 308-49.

70. Roussier, Paul, ed. LETTRES DU GENERAL LECLERC. Paris: Société de l'histoire des colonies françaises, 1937.

71. Saintoyant, J. LA COLONISATION FRANCAISE PENDANT LA PERIODE NAPOLEONIENNE, 1799-1815. Paris: La Renaissance du livre, 1931.

72. Saint-Rémy, Joseph. PETION ET HAITI. Paris: Chez l'auteur, 1853-1857. 5 vols.

73. Saint-Rémy, Joseph. LA VIE DE TOUSSAINT L'OUVERTURE. Paris: Moquet, 1850.

74. Sannon, H. Pauléus. HISTOIRE DE TOUSSAINT LOUVERTURE. Port-au-Prince: Heraux, 1920-33. 3 vols.

75. Schoelcher, Victor. LA VIE DE TOUSSAINT L'OUVERTURE. Paris: Ollendorff, 1889.

76. Stoddard, T. Lothrop. THE FRENCH REVOLUTION IN SAN DOMINGO. Boston: Houghton Mifflin, 1914.

77. Thibaudeau, Antoine Claire. MEMOIRES SUR LE CONSULAT, 1799 A 1804, PAR UN ANCIEN CONSEILLER D'ETAT. Paris: Ponthieu, 1827.

78. THE TIMES (London), 1800-1804.

79. Tonnère, Boisrond. MEMOIRES POUR SERVIR A L'HISTOIRE D'HAITI. Port-au-Prince: Fardin, 1981. (Originally published in 1804.)

80. Tyson, George F., ed. TOUSSAINT L'OUVERTURE. Englewood Cliffs, N. J.: Prentice-Hall, 1973.

81. Vastey, Pompée de. ESSAI SUR LES CAUSES DE LA REVOLUTION ET DES GUERRES CIVILES D'HAYTI. Sans Souci, Haiti: Imprimerie royale, 1819.

PERIODICALS

82. JOURNAL OF CARIBBEAN HISTORY. 1970 to present.

83. JOURNAL OF CARIBBEAN STUDIES. 1961 to present.

CHAPTER XXIV

THE OTTOMAN EMPIRE

George F. Jewsbury, Oklahoma State University

The vigor and force of the French Revolutionary and Napoleonic epoch were felt directly in the Ottoman Empire. The Balkan peoples began their national re-birth on the one hand while on the other the Sultan's advisers became aware of the need to modernize the armed forces. French influences would play a major role in each development. In addition, Napoleon's invasion of Egypt and the subsequent diplomatic and military results took a great toll. Finally, the traditionally difficult relations between the Russians and the Porte were made even more tortuous as a result of the growth of French influence in the region. The works listed below will introduce those scholars unfamiliar with the area to the complexities of the Eastern Question, and give indications of paths of research to follow.

For a good introduction of the dilemmas faced by the Turks as they entered the nineteenth century see Lewis (14), Stavrianos (30), Shaw (26), Anderson (2), and Ancel (1). A discussion of the nature of military changes going on at the time can be found in any of the following sources: Shaw (24, 25), Bey (3), and Morier (20).

Several extensive works have traced the French diplomatic activities and have been analyzed by a number of first rate scholars: Driault (7), Sorel (28), Marcère (17), Ciragan (6), and Boppe (4). The Russians' relations with the Porte at this time are covered by Bradisteanu (5), Jewsbury (11), Naff (21), and Shupp (27). Lengthy descriptions of the Russo-Turkish war are by Mikhailovskii-Danilevskii (18) and Petrov (22).

General references are the ENCYCLOPEDIA OF ISLAM (8) and Gibb and Bowen (9). Spillmann's work (29) approaches the French role in the area from a unique vantage point.

One book, Vernon J. Puryear's NAPOLEON AND THE DARDANELLES (23), remains one of the truly masterful works in the area. Beautifully written, the book's bibliographical essay gives the reader excellent advice regarding research on the problem in the French archives.

BIBLIOGRAPHY: THE OTTOMAN EMPIRE

1. Ancel, J. MANUEL HISTORIQUE DE LA QUESTION D'ORIENT, 1792-1923. Paris: Delagrave, 1923.

2. Anderson, Matthew Smith. THE EASTERN QUESTION, 1774-1923. New York: St. Martin, 1966.

3. Bey, Ahmed D [Ahmad Jawad]. ETAT MILITAIRE OTTOMAN DEPUIS LA FOUNDATION DE L'EMPIRE JUSQU'A NOS JOURS. Constantinople: Imprimerie du journal "La Turquie," 1882.

4. Boppe, Auguste. "La France et le 'Militaire Turc' au XVIIIe siècle." FEUILLES D'HISTOIRE (1912): 386-402, 490-501.

5. Bradisteanu, Stancu. DIE BEZIEHUNGEN RUSSLANDS UND FRANKREICHS ZUR TURKEI IN DEN JAHREN 1806-1807. Berlin: Ebering, 1912.

6. Ciragan, Ertugrul Oguz. LA POLITIQUE OTTOMANE PENDANT LES GUERRES DE NAPOLEON. Paris: Aurillac, 1954.

7. Driault, Edouard. LA POLITIQUE ORIENTALE DE NAPOLEON 1806-1808. Paris: Alcan, 1904.

8. ENCYCLOPEDIA OF ISLAM. Leiden: Brill, 1954-.

9. Gibb, H.A.R., and H. Bowen. ISLAMIC SOCIETY AND THE WEST. London: Oxford University Press, 1950, 1957. 2 vols.

10. Hammer-Purgstall, J. von. GESCHICHTE DES OSMANISCHEN REICHES. Pest: Hartleben, 1827-1835. 10 vols.

11. Jewsbury, George F. THE RUSSIAN ANNEXATION OF BESSARABIA, 1774-1828. Boulder and New York: East European Quarterly, distributed by Columbia University Press, 1976.

12. Jucherau de Saint-Denys, Antoine de, baron. HISTOIRE DE L'EMPIRE OTTOMAN DEPUIS 1792 JUSQU'EN 1844. Paris: Au Comptoir des imprimeurs-unis, 1844. 4 vols.

13. Jucherau de Saint-Denys, Antoine de, baron. REVOLUTIONS DE CONSTANTINOPLE EN 1807 ET 1808. Paris: Brissot-Thivars, 1819. 2 vols.

14. Lewis, Bernard. THE EMERGENCE OF MODERN TURKEY. Oxford: Oxford University Press, 1968.

15. Lewis, Bernard. "The Impact of the French Revolution on Turkey." JOURNAL OF WORLD HISTORY 1 (1953): 105-25.

16. McGarity, J.M. "Foreign Influence on the Ottoman Turkish Army, 1800-1918." Ph.D. dissertation, American University, 1968.

688

17. Marcère, Edouard de. UNE AMBASSADE A CONSTANTINOPLE; LA POLITIQUE ORIENTALE DE LA REVOLUTION FRANCAISE. Paris: Alcan, 1927. 2 vols.

18. Mikhailovskii-Danilevskii, Aleksandr Ivanovich. OPISANIE TURETSKOI VOINY V'TSARSTVOVANIE IMPERATORA ALEKSANDRA S' 1806 DO 1812 G. St. Petersburg: Voenn. izd-vo., 1843. 2 vols.

19. Miller, A.F. MUSTAFA PASHA BAIRAKTAR. Moscow and Leningrad: Akademiia nauk, 1947.

20. Morier, James Philip. MEMOIR OF A CAMPAIGN WITH THE OTTOMAN ARMY IN EGYPT. London: Debrett, 1801.

21. Naff, T. "Reform and the Conduct of Ottoman Diplomacy in the Reigh of Selim III, 1789-1807." JOURNAL OF THE AMERICAN ORIENTAL SOCIETY 83 (1965): 295-315.

22. Petrov, A.N. VOINA ROSSII S' TURTSIEI 1806-1812 GG. St. Petersburg, 1885-87. 3 vols.

23. Puryear, Vernon J. NAPOLEON AND THE DARDANELLES. Berkeley: University of California Press, 1951.

24. Shaw, Stanford J. "The Established Ottoman Army Corps Under Sultan Selim III (1789-1807)." DER ISLAM 40 (1965): 142-185.

25. Shaw, Stanford J. "The Origins of Ottoman Military Reform: The Nizami Cedid Army of Sultan Selim III." THE JOURNAL OF MODERN HISTORY 37 (1965): 219-306.

26. Shaw, Stanford J., and K. Ezel. HISTORY OF THE OTTOMAN EMPIRE AND MODERN TURKEY. Cambridge: Cambridge University Press, 1977. 2 vols.

27. Shupp, Paul Frederick. THE EUROPEAN POWERS AND THE NEAR EASTERN QUESTION, 1806-1807. New York: Columbia University Press, 1931.

28. Sorel, Albert. LA QUESTION D'ORIENT AU XVIIIe-SIECLE. Paris: Plon-Nourrit, 1902.

29. Spillmann, Georges. NAPOLEON ET L'ISLAM. Paris: Perrin, 1969.

30. Stavrianos, Leften Stavros. THE BALKANS SINCE 1453. New York: Holt, Rinehart, Winston, 1961.

31. Wittman, W. TRAVELS IN TURKEY, ASIA MINOR.... London: R. Phillips, 1803.